10TH CANADIAN EDITION

ESSENTIALS OF
BUSINESS
COMMUNICATION

Essentials of Business Communication, Tenth Canadian Edition
Dr. Mary Ellen Guffey, Dr. Dana Loewy, Dr. Richard Almonte

Senior Director, Product: Jackie Wood

Senior Portfolio Manager: Lenore Taylor-Atkins

Product Marketing Manager: Sydney Pope

Director, Content and Production: Toula Dileo

Content Development Manager: Catherine Gillespie-Lopes

Senior Content Production Manager: Jennifer Hare

IP Analyst: Christine Myaskovsky

Production Service: MPS Limited

Copy Editor: Dawn Hunter

Compositor: MPS Limited

Text Designer: Sharon Lucas

Cover Designer: John Montgomery

For product information and technology assistance, contact us at **Canada Support, canadasupport.cengage.com.**

For permission to use material from this text or product, submit all requests online at **www.cengage.com/permissions.**

Library and Archives Canada Cataloguing in Publication:

Title: Essentials of business communication / Dr. Mary Ellen Guffey, Emerita Professor of Business, Los Angeles Pierce College, Dr. Dana Loewy, Emerita Lecturer, Business Communication, California State University, Fullerton, Dr. Richard Almonte, Centre for Business, George Brown College.

Other titles: Business communication

Names: Guffey, Mary Ellen, author. | Loewy, Dana, author. | Almonte, Richard, author.

Description: 10th Canadian edition. | Includes bibliographical references and index.

Identifiers: Canadiana (print) 20200347357 | Canadiana (ebook) 20200347438 | ISBN 9780176909659 (softcover) | ISBN 9780176909765 (PDF)

Subjects: LCSH: Business writing—Textbooks. | LCSH: English language—Business English—Textbooks. | LCSH: Business communication—Textbooks. | LCGFT: Textbooks.

Classification: LCC HF5718.3 .G84 2021 | DDC 808.06/665—dc23

ISBN-13: 978-0-17-690965-9
ISBN-10: 0-17-690965-6

Cengage Canada
333 Bay Street, Suite 2400
Toronto, ON M5H 2T6
Canada

Cengage is a leading provider of customized learning solutions with employees residing in nearly 40 different countries and sales in more than 125 countries around the world. Find your local representative at **www.cengage.com.**

To learn more about Cengage platforms and services, register or access your online learning solution, or purchase materials for your course, visit **www.cengage.ca.**

Printed in Canada
Print Number: 02   Print Year: 2022

10TH CANADIAN EDITION

ESSENTIALS OF BUSINESS COMMUNICATION

DR. MARY ELLEN GUFFEY
Emerita Professor of Business
Los Angeles Pierce College

DR. DANA LOEWY
Emerita Lecturer, Business Communication
California State University, Fullerton

DR. RICHARD ALMONTE
Centre for Business
George Brown College

Australia • Brazil • Canada • Mexico • Singapore • United Kingdom • United States

Learning with Guffey

From the emphasis on writing in an increasingly digital workplace to updated model documents, Guffey, Loewy, and Almonte have updated tools and created new ways to keep you interested and engaged with these features, which will help you succeed in today's technologically enhanced workplace.

BUSINESS COMMUNICATION RESEARCH UPDATE

Emails From the Boss—Curse or Blessing? Relations Between Communication Channels, Leader Evaluation, and Employees' Attitudes

Stephan Braun, Alina Hernandez Bark, Alexander Kirchner, Sebastian Stegmann, and Rolf Van Dick. International Journal of Business Communication 2019, Vol. 56(1) 50–81
© The Author(s) 2015.

Abstract: The present research investigates if and how a more digitally centered communication between supervisors and employees satisfies employees' needs regarding the communication with their supervisors and influences employees' attitudes toward the supervisor and the job. In a cross-sectional online study, 261 employees rated their supervisors' actual and ideal use of different communication channels (i.e., telephone, face-to-face, email) regarding quality and quantity. Employees' job satisfaction and their perceptions of their supervisors' effectiveness and team identification were measured as dependent variables. Employees perceived face-to-face communication to be of higher quality than telephone and email communication, and they indicated a prefer-

This ongoing development toward electronic communication also changes the face of leadership in modern organizations. Indeed, a wide range of scholars agree that "e-leadership" will be the regular state instead of the exception in the future (Avolio, Sosik, Kahai, & Baker, 2014; Zaccaro & Baider, 2003). One reason for this trend could be that leadership proves to be especially important in virtual work contexts. For example, Purvanova and Bono (2009) compared the impact of transformational leadership between face-to-face and virtual teams. They found that transformational leadership had a stronger positive effect on team performance in virtual teams than in face-to-face settings. A possible reason for this need for leadership in virtual teams

◀ BUSINESS COMMUNICATION RESEARCH UPDATE

Units open with selections from peer-reviewed articles by researchers studying business communication in today's technology-driven workplace. Insights from these articles make excellent starting points for classroom discussion, research, and communication practice

BIZ COMM BYTE ▶

In computer systems, a byte is a unit of data or digital information. In this edition, you will find an essential piece of information or "byte" called out at the start of each chapter.

BIZ COMM BYTE

In a recent survey of "547 businesspeople . . . 81% of them agree that poorly written material wastes a lot of their time. A majority say that what they read is frequently ineffective because it's too long, poorly organized, unclear, filled with jargon, and imprecise."

Source: Bernoff, J. (2016, September 6). Bad writing is destroying your company's productivity. *Harvard Business Review*. https://hbr.org/2016/09/bad-writing-is-destroying-your-companys-productivity

◀ WORDS OF WISDOM FROM CANADIAN BUSINESS

Words of Wisdom features some topical and sage advice from Canadian business professionals.

WORDS OF WISDOM FROM CANADIAN BUSINESS

❝What Canada can do better than anywhere . . . is diversity and inclusivity in communications. It's part of Canada's DNA,

BEFORE-AND-AFTER MODEL ▶ DOCUMENTS

Before-and-after sample documents and descriptive callouts create a road map to the writing process, demonstrating the effective use of the skills being taught, as well as the significance of the revision process.

◢ **FIGURE 7.9** / Negative Employee Announcement

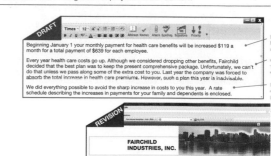

◀ WORKPLACE IN FOCUS

Real-world Canadian applications highlight business communication concepts in each chapter. Each feature concludes with a critical thinking question to encourage discussion and research.

WRITING PLANS ▶

Ample step-by-step writing plans help you get started quickly on organizing and formatting messages.

◀ CHAPTER REVIEW AND CRITICAL THINKING EXERCISES

End-of-chapter questions reinforce concepts covered in each chapter.

ACTIVITIES AND CASES ▶

Chapter concepts are translated into action as you try out your skills in activities designed to mirror real-world experiences.

Cengage
___
MINDTAP

◀ MINDTAP RESOURCES

To find interactive tools that support concepts discussed in the text, visit specific sections of MindTap for interactive learning resources.

Brief Contents

Contents

Unit 4: Business Reports and Proposals 193

Unit 5: Professionalism and Speaking Skills 269

Unit 6: Communicating for Employment 333

Chapter 13: Interviews and Follow-Up 372

Appendixes 401

Grammar/Mechanics Handbook 430

Preface

The Tenth Canadian Edition of *Essentials of Business Communication* maintains the streamlined approach that has equipped past learners with the communication skills needed to be successful at work. It is most helpful for postsecondary and adult learners preparing for new careers, planning a change in their current careers, or upgrading their writing and speaking skills. The aim of this edition is to incorporate more of the suggestions provided by adopters and reviewers over the past few years, along with cutting-edge research in business communication (e.g., in Unit-opening articles, in Biz Comm Bytes, and in the Workplace in Focus feature). For those new to the book, some of the most popular features include the following:

- **Text/Workbook Format.** The convenient text/workbook format presents an all-in-one teaching–learning package that includes concepts; workbook application exercises; writing, speaking, and interpersonal challenges; and a combination handbook/reference manual.
- **Comprehensive but Concise Coverage.** An important reason for the success of *Essentials of Business Communication* is that it practises what it preaches. The Tenth Canadian Edition follows the same strategy, concentrating on essential concepts presented without wasted words.
- **Writing Plans and Writing Improvement Exercises.** An increased number of step-by-step writing plans structure the writing experience so that novice writers get started quickly—without struggling to provide unknown details to unfamiliar, hypothetical cases. Many revision exercises build confidence and skills.
- **Coverage of Communication Technology.** All relevant chapters include discussions of and practice involving email, messaging, texting, social media, infographics, and so on. The Tenth Canadian Edition stays on top of the use of mediated communication and artificial intelligence within organizations, including the use of social media sites like Twitter for both business and marketing communication.
- **Challenging Cases.** The reality of the work world is that communication situations won't always easily fit the models provided in a business communication textbook. As a result, we've threaded ambiguity and complexity into the tasks so that students have a chance to use their critical thinking skills, as well as their business communication skills, regularly.
- **Workplace in Focus.** Each chapter contains a Workplace in Focus feature that connects chapter concepts to real-world Canadian examples. These features make ideal starting points for in-class discussion and research.
- **Situational Focus.** The reality of business communication is that people need to be able to respond effectively and professionally in a variety of workplace situations. This is different from memorizing a number of genres or formats. For this reason, we include a rich introductory chapter covering a multitude of daily forms of communication (e.g., text, email, Web conference, social media) and expand on this generic way of thinking by considering important, realistic, and recurring business situations divided into three categories: daily, persuasive, and negative.
- **Plagiarism.** An unfortunate reality of the digital age is the challenges students have in understanding the need for proper citation and documentation and the seriousness of plagiarism and its repercussions. We address the issue of plagiarism by offering concrete examples of the real-world ramifications of this behaviour.

◤ Revision Highlights

The following features were updated for the Tenth Canadian Edition:

- **New and Revised End-of-Chapter Exercises and Activities.** This edition features a significant revision of the end-of-chapter exercises, activities, and cases. As with the last edition, these new cases recognize the pedagogical usefulness of scripting, role-play, and performance as effective means of practising business communication skills.
- **Business Communication Research Update Feature.** Units open with selections from peer-reviewed articles by researchers studying business communication in today's technology-driven workplace. Insights from these articles make excellent starting points for classroom discussion, research, and communication practice.
- **New Workplace in Focus Boxes.** These boxes have been refreshed to reflect current trends in communication in the workplace.
- **Biz Comm Byte Boxes.** In computer systems, a byte is defined is a unit of data or digital information. In this edition, each chapter begins with a key piece of information or *byte*.
- **Words of Wisdom from Canadian Business.** This new feature offers some topical and sage advice from Canadian business professionals.
- **MindTap Callouts.** To find tools that support concepts discussed in the text, visit specific sections of MindTap for interactive learning resources.

◤ Other Features That Enhance Teaching and Learning

Although the Tenth Canadian Edition of *Essentials of Business Communication* packs considerable information into a small space, it covers all of the critical topics necessary in a comprehensive business communication course; it also features many pedagogical "shortcuts" to facilitate instruction, application, and retention:

- **Focus on writing skills but also listening, speaking, and interpersonal skills.** Most students need significant instruction and practice in developing professional writing strength, particularly in view of today's increased volume on communication. *Essentials* includes specific business writing plans to help students achieve this strength. At the same time, employers seek well-rounded individuals who can interact with fellow employees as well as represent the organization effectively. *Essentials* provides tips for managing nonverbal cues, overcoming listening barriers, developing speaking skills, planning and participating in meetings, and making productive telephone calls.
- **Realistic emphasis.** *Essentials* devotes a chapter to the writing of email, texts, and instant messages, plus other daily forms of communication, recognizing that the business world no longer operates via letter or memo except in certain specialized situations (e.g., direct-mail sales letter, collection letters, cover letters for job applications).
- **Models comparing effective and ineffective documents.** To facilitate speedy recognition of good and bad writing techniques and strategies, *Essentials* presents many before-and-after documents. Marginal notes spotlight targeted strategies and effective writing. We hope that instructors turn this before-and-after technique into effective pedagogy whereby all their students' written assignments undergo the scrutiny of an editing and revising process before being handed in as final products.
- **Variety in end-of-chapter activities.** A wide array of review questions, critical-thinking questions, activities, and realistic case problems holds students' attention and helps them apply chapter concepts meaningfully.

- **Grammar/Mechanics handbook.** A comprehensive Grammar/Mechanics Handbook supplies a thorough review of English grammar, punctuation, capitalization style, and number usage. Its self-teaching exercises may be used for classroom instruction or for supplementary assignments. The handbook also serves as a convenient reference throughout the course and afterwards.

◥ Student Resources

MindTap

Modern students require modern solutions. MindTap is a flexible all-in-one teaching and learning platform that includes the full ebook, a customizable learning path, and various course-specific activities that drive student engagement and critical thinking.

Download the Cengage Mobile App

Get access to a full, interactive ebook, readable online or off; study tools that empower anytime, anywhere learning; and 24/7 course access. The Cengage Mobile app keeps students focused and ready to study whenever it is convenient for them.

◥ Instructor Resources

The following instructor resources have been created for *Essentials of Business Communication*, Tenth Canadian Edition. Access these ultimate tools for customizing lectures and presentations at login.cengage.com.

Test Bank

This resource was written by Karen McLaren, Cambrian College. It includes over 325 multiple-choice questions written according to guidelines for effective construction and development of higher-order questions. Also included are over 195 true/false questions and over 130 fill-in-the-blank questions.

The Test Bank is available on a cloud-based platform. **Testing Powered by Cognero®** is a secure online testing system that allows instructors to author, edit, and manage test bank content from anywhere Internet access is available. No special installations or downloads are needed, and the desktop-inspired interface, with its drop-down menus and familiar, intuitive tools, allows instructors to create and manage tests with ease. Multiple test versions can be created in an instant, and content can be imported or exported into other systems. Tests can be delivered from a learning management system, the classroom, or wherever an instructor chooses. Testing Powered by Cognero for *Essentials of Business Communication*, Tenth Canadian Edition, can be accessed through login.cengage.com.

PowerPoint

Microsoft® PowerPoint® lecture slides were revised and updated by Lisa Jamieson, Red River College. There is an average of 30 slides per chapter, many featuring key figures, tables, and photographs from *Essentials of Business Communication*, Tenth Canadian Edition. Instructor notes include additional activities and ideas for discussion, making it simple for instructors to customize the deck for their courses.

Image Library

This resource consists of digital copies of figures, short tables, and photographs used in the book. Instructors may use these JPEGs to customize the PowerPoint slides or create their own PowerPoint presentations. The Image Library Key describes the images and lists the codes under which the JPEGs are saved.

Instructor Guide

This resource was updated and revised by by Karen McLaren, Cambrian College. It is organized according to the textbook chapters, and contains sample lesson plans, learning objectives, and suggested classroom activities to give instructors the support they need to engage their students within the classroom.

Instructor's Solutions Manual

This manual, prepared by Karen McLaren of Cambrian College, contains complete solutions to Critical Thinking Questions, Chapter Review Questions, and Activities and Cases.

Media Guide

The Media Guide includes teaching materials for all video cases selected to accompany *Essentials of Business Communication*, Tenth Canadian Edition.

MindTap

Cengage

MINDTAP

MindTap is the digital learning solution that powers students from memorization to mastery. It gives instructors complete control of their course—to provide engaging content, challenge every individual, and build student confidence. Instructors can customize interactive syllabi to emphasize priority topics as well as add their own material or notes to the ebook as desired. This outcome-driven application gives instructors the tools needed to empower students and boost both understanding and performance.

Acknowledgments

The Tenth Canadian Edition of *Essentials of Business Communication* includes many of the constructive suggestions and advice provided by educators and students who use the book across Canada. These dedicated reviewers include the following:

Chelsa Budd, Saskatchewan Polytechnic
Nili Berner, University of Saskatchewan, Edwards School of Business
Janet Charron, Red River College
Susan Hesemeier, MacEwan University
Paisley Mann, Langara College
Jody Merritt, St. Clair College
Judy Puritt, Algonquin College, School of Business

Special thanks go to Alexis Hood, Lenore Taylor-Atkins, Jacquelyn Busby, Catherine Gillespie-Lopes, Sydney Pope, and Jennifer Hare. We would also like to thank Neha Chawla and the team at MPS. Thanks also go to the copy editor, Dawn Hunter.

Richard Almonte
Mary Ellen Guffey
Dana Loewy

LDprod/Shuttterstock

BUSINESS COMMUNICATION TODAY

BUSINESS COMMUNICATION RESEARCH UPDATE

Using Active Empathetic Listening to Build Relationships With Major-Gift Donors

Tanya Drollinger. (2018). Journal of Nonprofit & Public Sector Marketing, 30(1), 37–51.

Building a relationship with a major gift donor is an important form of fundraising for nonprofits. Fundraisers become relationship managers tasked with building trust and developing mutual goals with the donor through effective communication. The importance of effective listening on the fundraisers part is explored in this paper by overlaying Active Empathetic Listening (AEL) on the Major Donor Model. AEL is discussed as a method that if used by fundraisers will help them in their efforts to connect in a meaningful way with major donors by enabling the fundraiser to work with more accurate information regarding the donor's motivations, interest and desires as well as instill a sense of trust and genuineness between both parties.

Keywords: Major donor; listening; relationship

Case studies reveal that major donors have profound reasons for giving to nonprofit organizations (Breeze, 2011; Burnett, 2002; Schervish, 2005). It has been found that their donations reflect their interests and values in a way in which they can be cocreators with a nonprofit to benefit society. On the other side, it is important for fundraisers to build relationships with major donors because the financial gift is large enough to make a considerable impact on the nonprofit's mission. Furthermore, there is evidence that working with major donors is a more effective use of solicitation dollars and can create efficiencies on the nonprofit's part rather than campaigning for short-term, low-dollar-amount contributions (Burnett, 2002; Schervish, 2005). Fundraisers are tasked with developing healthy relationships with major donors as they seek to fulfill the mission of the organization. A key to a good relationship is effective communication between both parties so that trust and ultimately commitment can be obtained (Burnett, 2002; MacMillan et al., 2005; Sargeant, Ford, & West, 2006).

Over the past decade the idea of "relationship fundraising" has been gaining popularity as it emphasizes the importance of building and then continually nurturing the relationship between major donors and nonprofits (Burnett, 2002; Schervish, 2005). Much like previous research on developing relationships with major donors (Breeze, 2011; Burnett, 2002; Schervish, 2005), Knowles and Gomes (2009) have developed a model that is meant to facilitate the relationship-building process between the fundraiser and major donor. However, the authors are very explicit with regard to the order of steps and outcomes that should take place in the relationship-building process. The major-donor model employs a strategic approach that has a long-term focus on building relationships founded on good communication. . . .

BACKGROUND

Listening is generally conceived of as a multidimensional process (Bodie, 2011; Comer & Drollinger, 1999). It consists of three dimensions: sensing, processing, and responding. Sensing refers to the receiving of messages; processing refers to events that take place in the mind of the listener such as organizing and assessing the significance of information; and responding involves recognizing receipt of messages. These dimensions occur almost simultaneously but are successive in that one dimension must take place before the next can occur. A message must be sensed before it is processed and must be processed before it can be responded to. . . .

Listening can happen on several levels. The distinction between the various levels of listening depends on the listener's ability to be cognizant of verbal and nonverbal language and the feeling behind the speaker's words (Comer & Drollinger, 1999). On the lowest level, the listener pays little attention to the words and doesn't take in information from nonverbal cues or feeling behind the words. On the highest level, the listener senses, processes, and responds to the verbal and nonverbal message and the feeling behind the message. Listening has been described as marginal, evaluative, and active, and as active empathetic listening (AEL) in the literature (Bodie, 2011; Comer & Drollinger, 1999; Pryor, Malshe, & Paradise, 2013). . . .

AEL AND THE MAJOR GIFT MODEL

Knowles and Gomes (2009) view the fundraiser as a consultant that identifies key information regarding the donor's interest in various aspects of the nonprofit's mission, motivations for donation, goals, and expectations of the exchange. Past research on major donors has pointed to the importance of fully understanding the motivations and goals of the donor as they are inclined to be active in their role as a donor (Breeze, 2011; Burnett, 2002; Schervish, 2005). Secondly, the authors maintain that their model can help serve fundraisers in their actions as they go from one step to the next and become more effective in their job. The purposes of each of the steps are additive and should increase the fundraiser's understanding of the potential donor's motivations and expectations and build commitment to invest in the mission of the nonprofit. In the following discussion, the six steps of the major gift model (awareness, interest and involvement, desire to help, trial gift, information on giving, and major-gift action) will be discussed along with the role of AEL on the fundraisers' part. . . .

MANAGERIAL IMPLICATIONS AND CONCLUSION

Presently, fundraisers are well trained in the mission and goals of their nonprofit organizations and how to present it well to potential donors; however, effective listening tends to be assumed as an innate ability as opposed to a valuable skill. Evidence in for-profit marketing has demonstrated a strong relationship between the use of AEL among salespeople and buyers' trust, relationship satisfaction, excellent communication, and intention to purchase in the future (Drollinger & Comer, 1999; Pryor et al., 2013). Managers can use the AEL scale in two ways, first, by initially assessing a fundraiser's level of AEL. The scale published by Drollinger, Comer, and Warrington (2005) is a useful tool that can be easily adapted for fundraisers. Managers who are aware of fundraisers' AEL levels will have a baseline to assess which of the three dimensions fundraisers excel in and which they might need to improve. Further, more emphasis during training can be placed on the importance of listening to donors to build healthier relationships. Effective listening and being more empathetic can be taught and are not considered to be simply innate abilities. Secondly, the AEL scale may also be used as a selection tool when hiring fundraisers. Training for fundraisers should go beyond

knowledge of the mission of the nonprofit and types of gifts and should include AEL, assessing the communication style of donors, rapport-building skills, need discovery, asking meaningful questions, expectations from the exchange, and appropriate follow-up after the donation has been made (Burnett, 2002; Sargeant & Jay, 2004; Schervish, 2005).

Understanding communication styles is a straightforward process through which the fundraiser gains awareness of his or her own style and then is informed on the possible communication styles of potential donors and how to adapt their own communication style to better suit that of the donor. Common communication styles assessments are available through Merrill and Reid (1981) and Bolton and Bolton (2009). When assessing a communication style it is important to pick up on subtle cues, and using AEL should enhance the fundraiser's ability to do so. . . .

Although rapport building seems like an instinctive skill it also requires some training to ensure that the fundraiser is competent. Listening should play a key role in rapport building as it largely consists of picking up on nonverbal and verbal cues (e.g., hobbies and family) about the donor through casual conversation. It is important to develop a rapport with the potential donor as it creates feelings of comfort and trust in the relationship (Nickels, Everett, & Klien, 1983). Rapport building can be enhanced when the fundraiser uses AEL to get to know the donor as they are highly adept at listening and not just presenting (Comer & Drollinger, 1999). . . .

Major donors have profound reasons for giving to nonprofit organizations and their gifts reflect their unique interests and values and may even be given in such a way that they become cocreators with a nonprofit (Breeze, 2011; Burnett, 2002; Schervish, 2005). The fundraiser has the important job of building a good relationship so that trust and ultimately commitment can be secured (MacMillan et al., 2005; Sargeant et al., 2006). The relationship-building process outlined by Knowles and Gomes (2009) requires that the fundraiser understand the donor's motivations for investing in the nonprofit while building trust and evaluating levels of commitment. Through the use of AEL, the fundraiser is positioned to better understand the donor's motivations as the fundraiser listens not only to the literal message but also attends to nonverbal cues and the emotion behind the words. The parties are equipped to build a healthy relationship based on understanding and trust. Furthermore, the relationship is much different from that of persistence and determination on the fundraiser's part. It is a softer form of persuasion. It is proposed that AEL will enhance the process of the major-gift decision model if it is employed throughout all of the process stages.

REFERENCES

Bodie, G. (2011). The Active-Empathetic Listening Scale (AELS): Conceptualization and evidence of validity within the interpersonal domain. *Communication Quarterly, 59*(3), 277–295. https://doi.org/10.1080/01463373.2011.583495

Bolton, R., & Bolton, D. G. (2009). *People styles at work and beyond* (2nd ed.). New York, NY: AMACOM.

Breeze, B. (2011). *The million pound donors report, 2011*. Kent, England: Coutts & Co.

Burnett, K. (2002). *Relationship fundraising* (2nd ed.). London, England: White Lion Press/Jossey Bass.

Comer, L. B., & Drollinger, T. (1999). Active empathetic listening and selling success: A conceptual framework. *Journal of Personal Selling and Sales Management, 19*(1), 15–29.

Drollinger, T., Comer, L. B., & Warrington, P. T. (2005). Development and validation of the active empathetic listening scale. *Psychology and Marketing, 23*(2), 161–180. https://doi.org/10.1002/mar.20105

Knowles, P., & Gomes, R. (2009). Building relationships with major-gift donors: A major-gift decision-making, relationship building model. *Journal of Nonprofit and Public Sector Marketing, 21*, 384–406. https://doi.org/10.1080/10495140802662580

MacMillan, K., Money, K., Money, A., & Downing, S. (2005). Relationship marketing in the not-for-profit sector: An extension and application of the commitment-trust theory. *Journal of Business Research, 58*(6), 806–818.

Merrill, D. W., & Reid, R. H. (1981). *Personal styles and effective performance*. Radnor, PA: Chilton Books.

Nickels, W. G., Everett, R. F., & Klein, R. (1983). Rapport building for salespeople: A neuro-linguistic approach. *Journal of Personal Selling and Sales Management, 3*(2), 1–8.

Pryor, S., Malshe, A., & Paradise, K. (2013). Salesperson listening in the extended sales relationship and exploration of cognitive, affective and temporal dimensions. *Journal of Personal Selling and Sales Management, 33*(2), 185–196. https://doi.org/10.2753/PSS0885-3134330203

Sargeant, A., Ford, J. B., & West, D. (2006). Perceptual determinants of nonprofit giving behavior. *Journal of Business Research, 59*, 155–165. https://doi.org/10.1016/j.jbusres.2005.04.006

Sargeant, A., & Jay, E. (2004). *Building donor loyalty: The fundraiser's guide to increasing lifetime value*. San Francisco, CA: Jossey Bass.

Schervish, P. G. (2005). Major donors, major motives: The people and purposes behind major gifts. *New Directions for Philanthropic Fundraising, 47*, 59–87. https://doi.org/10.1002/pf.95

QUESTIONS

1. How does what you've learned from this research article change your perception of what business communication is or is not?

2. How might what you've learned in this article be useful in changing your own school or workplace communication?

3. Come up with pro and con arguments for the following debate/discussion topic: In the digital age, employees should focus less on writing and speaking and more on listening skills. How does Drollinger's research help you support your point?

Yuri_Arcurs/istock by Getty Images

COMMUNICATING IN TODAY'S WORKPLACE

BIZ COMM BYTE

According to Canadian job site Workopolis (workopolis.com), the top three skills recruiters look for in job seekers are good communication, good writing, and good customer relations.

Source: Kohut, T. (2015, August 26). New study reveals top 10 skills Canadian employers are looking for. *Global News.* https://globalnews.ca/news/2187705/new-study-reveals-top-10-skills-canadian-employers-are-looking-for/

OBJECTIVES

1.1 Describe how solid communication skills will improve your career prospects.

1.2 Confront barriers to effective listening.

1.3 Explain the importance of nonverbal communication.

1.4 Understand five common dimensions of culture and how they affect communication.

1.5 Use intercultural communication strategies to prevent miscommunication.

1.1 The Relationship Between Solid Communication Skills and Workplace Success

When you graduate, you will enter a fast-moving, competitive, and information-driven digital work environment. Communication technology provides unmatched mobility and connects individuals anytime and anywhere in the world. Today's communicators interact using mobile electronic devices and access information stored on remote servers in the cloud. This mobility and instant access explain why increasing numbers of workers must be available practically around the clock and must respond quickly.

1.1a Solid Communication Skills: Your Path to Success

Your ability to communicate is a powerful career sifter.[1] When jobs are few and competition is fierce, superior communication skills will give you an edge over other job applicants. Recruiters rank communication high on their wish lists.[2]

In a poll, 1,000 executives cited writing, critical-thinking, and problem-solving skills, along with self-motivation and team skills, as their top choices in new hires. Effective writing skills can be a stepping stone to great job opportunities; poorly developed writing skills, on the other hand, will derail a career. Given the increasing emphasis on communication, Canadian corporations are paying millions of dollars to communication coaches and trainers to teach employees the very skills that you are learning in this course. For example, Toronto-based Livewire, a leading provider of business communication services, and the winner of a 2018 International Association of Business Communicators Award of Excellence, lists among its clients well-known Canadian companies like BMO, Four Seasons, McCain Foods, and Telus.[3]

1.1b The Digital Revolution: Why Writing Skills Matter More Than Ever

People in today's workforce communicate more, not less, since information technology and the Internet have transformed the world of work. Messages travel instantly to distant locations, reaching potentially huge audiences with a minimum of expense and effort. Team members collaborate even when they are physically apart. And social media plays an increasingly prominent role in business. In such a hyperconnected world, writing matters more than ever.

For example, leading Canadian recruitment firm Robert Half surveyed 270 Canadian financial services CEOs in 2016 and found that the firms "give equal billing to soft skills and to technical expertise when filling staff-level positions." Drilling down more deeply, the survey found that communication skills, including writing, are in the top five of the most requested soft skills by these employers.[4] In addition, as you will learn in later chapters, recruiters will closely examine your social media presence to learn about your communication skills and professionalism. Naturally, they will not hire candidates who write poorly or post inappropriate content online.[5]

TECHIES WRITE TOO. Even in technical fields such as accounting and information technology, you will need strong communication skills. An Accountemps poll of 1,400 chief financial officers revealed that 75 percent said that verbal, written, and interpersonal skills are more important today than they were in the past.[6] Technical experts must be able to communicate with others, tell stories with data, and explain their work clearly, says an analytics specialist.[7] Another survey conducted by the Society for Information Management revealed that network professionals ranked written and oral communication skills among the top five most desired skills for new hires.[8]

BUSINESSES GENERATE A WIDE RANGE OF MESSAGES. Be prepared to use a variety of media. In addition to occasional traditional letters and memos, expect to communicate with the public and within the company by email, instant messaging and texting, company blogs, collaboration software such as wikis, and social media sites such as Facebook, Twitter, Instagram, and YouTube. You will learn more about workplace communication technology in Chapter 5.

WRITING IS IN YOUR FUTURE. Regardless of career choice, you will probably be sending many digital messages, such as the email shown in Figure 1.1. Because email and other digital media have become important channels of communication in today's workplace, all digital business messages must be clear, concise, and professional. Notice that the message in Figure 1.1 is more professional than the kind of informal email or text you might send socially. Learning to write professional digital messages will be an important part of this course.

FIGURE 1.1 / Professional Email

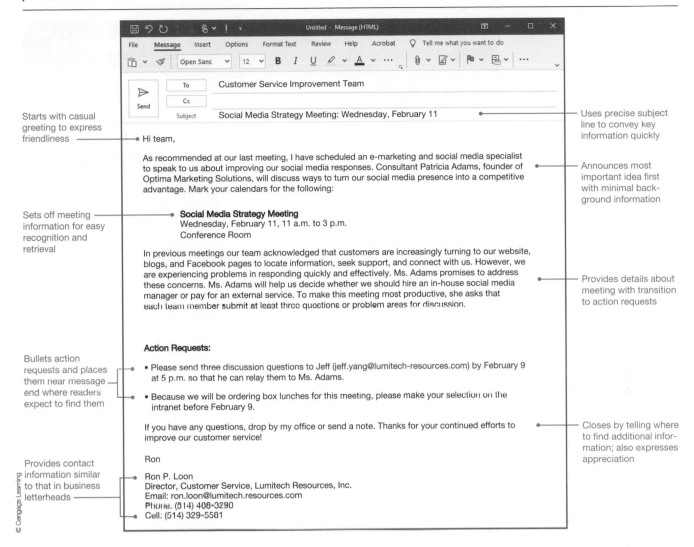

Starts with casual greeting to express friendliness

Sets off meeting information for easy recognition and retrieval

Bullets action requests and places them near message end where readers expect to find them

Provides contact information similar to that in business letterheads

Uses precise subject line to convey key information quickly

Announces most important idea first with minimal background information

Provides details about meeting with transition to action requests

Closes by telling where to find additional information; also expresses appreciation

[Email content:]

To: Customer Service Improvement Team

Subject: Social Media Strategy Meeting: Wednesday, February 11

Hi team,

As recommended at our last meeting, I have scheduled an e-marketing and social media specialist to speak to us about improving our social media responses. Consultant Patricia Adams, founder of Optima Marketing Solutions, will discuss ways to turn our social media presence into a competitive advantage. Mark your calendars for the following:

Social Media Strategy Meeting
Wednesday, February 11, 11 a.m. to 3 p.m.
Conference Room

In previous meetings our team acknowledged that customers are increasingly turning to our website, blogs, and Facebook pages to locate information, seek support, and connect with us. However, we are experiencing problems in responding quickly and effectively. Ms. Adams promises to address these concerns. Ms. Adams will help us decide whether we should hire an in-house social media manager or pay for an external service. To make this meeting most productive, she asks that each team member submit at least three questions or problem areas for discussion.

Action Requests:
• Please send three discussion questions to Jeff (jeff.yang@lumitech-resources.com) by February 9 at 5 p.m. so that he can relay them to Ms. Adams.

• Because we will be ordering box lunches for this meeting, please make your selection on the intranet before February 9.

If you have any questions, drop by my office or send a note. Thanks for your continued efforts to improve our customer service!

Ron

Ron P. Loon
Director, Customer Service, Lumitech Resources, Inc.
Email: ron.loon@lumitech.resources.com
Phone: (514) 408-3290
Cell: (514) 329-5581

© Cengage Learning

1.1c What Employers Want: Professionalism

Your employer will expect you to show professionalism and possess what are often referred to as "soft skills" in addition to your technical knowledge. Soft skills are essential career attributes that include the ability to communicate, work well with others, solve problems, make ethical decisions, and appreciate diversity.[9] Sometimes called *employability skills* or *key competencies*, these soft skills are desirable in all business sectors and job positions.[10]

Projecting and maintaining a professional image can make a real difference in helping you obtain the job of your dreams. Figure 1.2 reviews areas you will want to check to be sure you are projecting professionalism. You will learn more about soft skills and professionalism in Chapter 10.

1.1d How Your Education Drives Your Income

The effort and money you invest in earning your degree or diploma will most likely pay off. Graduates earn more, suffer less unemployment, and can choose from a wider variety of career options than workers without a postsecondary education. And graduates have access to the highest-paying and fastest-growing careers, many of which require a degree.[11] As Figure 1.3 shows, graduates with college diplomas and bachelor's degrees earn significantly higher salaries than high school diploma earners and are much less likely to be unemployed.[12]

WORDS OF WISDOM FROM CANADIAN BUSINESS

"Communication, emotional intelligence, critical thinking, analysis: young Canadians will need these skills in an age of rapid change. They will need to work well with an increasingly diverse range of other people—business partners from around the world, plus co-workers of all ages, genders, languages and cultures—and to complement technology, which will become ever more pervasive."

—Royal Bank of Canada, *Humans Wanted: How Canadian Youth Can Thrive in the Age of Disruption*, 2018, https://www.rbc.com /dms/enterprise/futurelaunch/_assets -custom/pdf/RBC-Future-Skills-Report -FINAL-Singles.pdf

Unprofessional		Professional
✘		✔
Speaking in uptalk, a speech pattern that has a rising inflection making sentences sound like questions; using like to fill in mindless chatter; substituting go for said; relying on slang; or letting profanity slip into your conversation.	**Speech habits** (*$&#$)	Recognize that your credibility can be seriously damaged by sounding uneducated, crude, or adolescent.
Writing emails with incomplete sentences, misspelled words, exclamation points, texting slang, and senseless chatting. Sloppy, careless messages send a nonverbal message that you don't care or don't know what is correct.	**Email**	Employers like to see subjects, verbs, and punctuation marks. They may not recognize abbreviations and they value conciseness and correct spelling, even in brief emails.
Using your personal social media at work.	**Social Media**	Workplace communication should be related to work. Use lunch and break times only to check and post on social media.
Using an outgoing message with strident background music, weird sounds, or a joke message.	**Voice mail**	Use an outgoing message that states your name or phone number and provides instructions for leaving a message.
Playing soap operas, thunderous music, or a hockey game loudly in the background when you answer the phone.	**Telephone**	Have a quiet background when you answer the phone, especially if you are expecting a prospective employer's call.
Taking or placings calls or sending texts during business meetings or during conversations with fellow employees; raising your voice (cell yell) or engaging in cell calls that others must reluctantly overhear; obviously using your phone during meetings.	**Cellphones**	Turn off phone and message notification, both audible and vibrating, during meetings; use your cell only when conversations can be private.

© Cengage Learning

Writing is one aspect of education that is particularly well rewarded. Numerous surveys of employers confirm that soft skills such as solid communication can tip the scale in favour of one job applicant over another, especially as your career progresses. Your ticket to winning in a tight job market and launching a successful career is having good communication skills.

EDUCATION	EARNINGS*	UNEMPLOYMENT RATE (2018)**
High school diploma	Women: $43, 254 Men: $55,774	6.8%
College diploma	Women: $48,599 Men: $67,965	5.6%
Bachelor's degree	Women: $68,342 Men: $82,082	4.6%

* Statistics Canada. (2017). Census of population, 2016. https://www12.statcan.gc.ca/census-recensement/2016/as-sa/98-200-x/2016024/98-200-x2016024-eng.cfm

** Statistics Canada. (2018). Table 14-10-0020-01: Unemployment rate, participation rate and employment rate by educational attainment, annual. https://www150.statcan.gc.ca/t1/tbl1/en/tv.action?pid=1410002001

1.1e Meeting the Challenges of Today's Workplace

Today's workplace is changing rapidly. As a business communicator, you will be affected by many trends, including new communication tools such as social media, the "anytime, anywhere" office, and team-based projects. Other trends are flattened management hierarchies, global competition, and a renewed emphasis on ethics. The following overview reveals how communication skills are closely tied to your success in a constantly evolving workplace.

- **Rapidly changing communication technologies.** New communication technology is dramatically affecting the way workers interact. In our always-connected world, businesses exchange information by email, instant messaging, and text messaging using tablets, laptops and desktops, and cell phones. Satellite communications, wireless networking, teleconferencing, and videoconferencing help workers conduct meetings with associates around the world. Social media sites such as Facebook, Twitter, Instagram, and YouTube, as well as blogs, wikis, forums, and peer-to-peer tools, help businesspeople collect information, serve customers, and sell products and services. Figure 1.4 illustrates many new technologies you will encounter in today's workplace.
- **"Anytime, anywhere," coworking, and nonterritorial offices.** High-speed and wireless Internet access have led to flexible working arrangements that allow us to work at home, on the road, or in shared coworking spaces. Meet the "work shifter," a teleworker who largely remains outside the territorial office. The "anytime, anywhere" office requires only a mobile electronic device and a wireless connection.[13] Teleworkers now represent almost 20 percent of the working adult population.[14] To save on office real estate, some industries provide *nonterritorial* workspaces, or *hot desks*. At the same time, 24/7 availability has blurred the line between work and leisure, so some workers are always on duty.
- **Self-directed workgroups and virtual teams.** Many companies have created cross-functional teams to empower employees and boost their involvement in decision making. You can expect to collaborate with a team in gathering information, finding and sharing solutions, implementing decisions, and managing conflict. You may even become part of a virtual team whose members are in remote locations. Increasingly, organizations are also forming ad hoc teams to solve particular problems. Such project-based teams disband once they have accomplished their objectives. Moreover, parts of our economy already rely on free agents who will be hired on a project or "gig" basis, which is very different from the full-time and relatively steady jobs of the past.

- **Flattened management hierarchies.** To better compete and to reduce expenses, businesses have for years been trimming layers of management. As a front-line employee, you will have fewer managers. You will be making decisions and communicating them to customers, to fellow employees, and to executives.
- **Heightened global competition.** Because many Canadian companies continue to move beyond domestic markets, you may be interacting with people from many cultures. To be a successful business communicator, you'll need to learn about other cultures. You'll also need to develop intercultural skills, including sensitivity, flexibility, patience, and tolerance.
- **Renewed emphasis on ethics.** Ethics is once again a hot topic in business. On the heels of the banking crisis and the collapse of the real estate market, a calamitous recession followed, caused largely, some say, by greed and ethical lapses. The government now requires greater accountability. As a result, businesses are eager to regain public trust by building ethical environments. Many publicize their ethical mission statements, install hotlines, and appoint compliance officers to ensure strict adherence to their high standards and the law.

These trends mean that your communication skills are constantly on display. If you can write clear and concise messages, you'll contribute to efficient operations and be rewarded.

◣ 1.2 Developing Listening Skills

In a time when many of us are glued to our phone screens, effective listening has become a value-added skill. We saw this in the unit-opening research article by Dr. Drollinger of Lethbridge University in Alberta, which shows that finely honed listening skills are necessary for success in one specific type of business: fundraising and donor relations. However, by all accounts most of us are not very good listeners. Do you ever pretend to be listening when you are not? Do you know how to look attentive in class when your mind wanders? How about tuning out people when their ideas are boring or complex? Do you find it hard to focus on ideas when a speaker's clothing or mannerisms are unusual?

You probably answered *yes* to one or more of these questions. In fact, some researchers suggest that we listen at only 25 to 50 percent efficiency. Such poor listening habits are costly in business, and they affect professional relationships. Messages must be rewritten, shipments reshipped, appointments rescheduled, contracts renegotiated, and directions restated.

To develop better listening skills, you must first recognize barriers that prevent effective listening. Then you can focus on specific techniques for improving listening skills.

1.2a Overcoming Barriers to Effective Listening

Bad habits and distractions can interfere with effective listening. Have any of the following barriers and distractions prevented you from hearing what has been said?

- **Physical barriers.** You can't listen if you can't hear what's being said. Physical impediments include hearing disabilities, poor acoustics, and noisy surroundings. It is also difficult to listen if you're wearing earbuds or earphones, or are ill, tired, or uncomfortable.
- **Psychological barriers.** Everyone brings a unique set of cultural, ethical, and personal values to communication. Each of us has an idea of what is right and what is important. If other ideas run counter to our preconceived thoughts, we tend to tune out speakers and thus fail to receive their messages.
- **Language problems.** Using unfamiliar words or speaking with an accent can make the communication process more challenging because the receiver must decode your message. In addition, emotion-laden, or charged, words can adversely affect listening. If the mention of words or phrases such as *bankruptcy* or *real*

estate meltdown has an intense emotional impact, a listener may be unable to focus on the information that follows.

- **Nonverbal distractions.** Many of us find it hard to listen if a speaker is different from what we view as normal. Unusual clothing or speech mannerisms, body twitches, or a radical hairstyle can cause enough distraction to prevent us from hearing what the speaker has to say.
- **Thought speed.** Because we can process thoughts at least three times faster than speakers can say them, we can become bored and allow our minds to wander.
- **Faking attention.** Most of us have learned to look as if we are listening even when we are not. Such behaviour was perhaps necessary as part of our socialization. Faked attention, however, seriously threatens effective listening because it encourages the mind to engage in flights of unchecked fancy. Those who fake attention often find it hard to concentrate even when they want to.
- **Grandstanding.** Because our own experiences and thoughts are most important to us, we tend to grab the attention in conversations. We sometimes fail to listen carefully because we are just waiting politely for the next pause so that we can have our turn to speak.

1.2b Building Powerful Listening Skills

You can reverse the harmful effects of poor listening habits by making a conscious effort to become an active listener. The following tips will help you become an active listener:

- **Stop talking.** The first step to becoming a good listener is to stop talking. Let others explain their views. Learn to concentrate on what the speaker is saying, not on what your next comment will be.
- **Control your surroundings.** Whenever possible, remove competing sounds. Close windows or doors, turn off TVs and smartphones, and move away from loud people, noisy appliances, or engines. Take off your earbuds or earphones. Choose a quiet time and place for listening.
- **Establish a receptive mindset.** Expect to learn something by listening. Strive for a positive and receptive frame of mind. If the message is complex, think of it as mental gymnastics. It is hard work but good exercise to stretch and expand the limits of your mind.
- **Keep an open mind.** We all sift through and filter information based on our own biases and values. For improved listening, discipline yourself to listen objectively. Be fair to the speaker. Hear what is really being said, not what you want to hear.
- **Listen for main points.** Heighten your concentration and satisfaction by looking for the speaker's central themes. Congratulate yourself when you find them!
- **Capitalize on lag time.** Make use of the quickness of your mind by reviewing the speaker's points. Anticipate what is coming next. Evaluate evidence the speaker has presented. Don't allow yourself to daydream. Try to guess what the speaker's next point will be.
- **Listen between the lines.** Focus on both what is spoken and what is unspoken. Listen for feelings as well as for facts.
- **Judge ideas, not appearances.** Concentrate on the content of the message, not on its delivery. Avoid being distracted by the speaker's looks, voice, or mannerisms.
- **Hold your fire.** Force yourself to listen to the speaker's entire argument or message before responding. Such restraint may enable you to understand the speaker's reasons and logic before you jump to false conclusions.
- **Take selective notes.** In some situations thoughtful note taking may be necessary to record important facts that must be recalled later. Select only the most important points so that the note-taking process does not interfere with your concentration on the speaker's total message.
- **Provide feedback.** Let the speaker know that you are listening. Nod your head and maintain eye contact. Ask relevant questions at appropriate times. Getting involved improves the communication process for both the speaker and the listener.

◣ 1.3 Learning Nonverbal Communication Skills

Communicating often involves more than listening to spoken words. Nonverbal cues can speak louder than words. These cues include eye contact, facial expression, body movements, time, space, territory, and appearance. All these nonverbal cues affect how a message is interpreted, or decoded, by your receiver.

Nonverbal communication includes all unwritten and unspoken messages, whether intended or not. These silent signals have a strong effect on receivers. However, understanding them is not simple. Does a downward glance indicate modesty? Fatigue? Does a constant stare reflect coldness? Dullness? Aggression? Do crossed arms mean a person is defensive or withdrawn, or just that the person is shivering?

Messages are even harder to decipher when the verbal and nonverbal cues do not agree. What will you think if Scott says he is not angry, but he slams the door when he leaves? What if Alicia assures the host that the meal is excellent, but she eats very little? The nonverbal messages in these situations speak louder than the words. In fact, researchers believe that the bulk of any message we receive is nonverbal.

1.3a Your Body Sends Silent Messages

Psychologist and philosopher Paul Watzlawick claimed that we cannot not communicate.[15] In other words, it's impossible to not communicate. This means that our every behaviour is sending a message even if we don't use words. The eyes, face, and body can convey meaning without a single syllable being spoken.

EYE CONTACT. The eyes are often the best predictor of a speaker's true feelings. Most of us cannot look another person straight in the eye and lie. As a result, in Canadian culture we tend to believe people who look directly at us. Sustained eye contact suggests trust and admiration; brief eye contact signals fear or stress. Good eye contact enables the message sender to see whether a receiver is paying attention, showing respect, responding favourably, or feeling distress. From the receiver's viewpoint, good eye contact reveals the speaker's sincerity, confidence, and truthfulness.

FACIAL EXPRESSION. The expression on a person's face can be almost as revealing of emotion as the eyes. Recent research shows that facial expressions are ways of communicating what we want out of a social interaction. If I purse my lips during a sales meeting, it may not be that I'm angry; it may be that I think the person I'm communicating with should stop the behaviour he's displaying.[16] While facial expressions can be strategic in this way, they can often be not-strategic. Raising or lowering the eyebrows, squinting the eyes, swallowing nervously, clenching the jaw, smiling broadly—these voluntary and involuntary facial expressions can add to or entirely replace verbal messages.

POSTURE AND GESTURES. A person's posture can convey anything from high status and self-confidence to shyness and submissiveness. Leaning toward a speaker suggests attentiveness and interest; pulling away or shrinking back denotes fear, distrust, anxiety, or disgust. Similarly, gestures can communicate entire thoughts via simple movements. However, the meanings of some of these movements differ across cultures. Unless you know local customs, such differences can get you into trouble. In Canada and the United States, for example, forming the thumb and forefinger in a circle means everything is OK. But in parts of South America, the OK sign is obscene.

1.3b Time, Space, and Territory Send Silent Messages

In addition to nonverbal messages transmitted by your body, three external elements convey information in the communication process: time, space, and territory.

TIME. How we structure and use time tells observers about our personalities and attitudes. For example, when Prem Watsa, famous Canadian investor and philanthropist, gives a visitor a prolonged interview, he signals his respect for, interest in, and approval of the visitor or the topic to be discussed.

SPACE. How we order the space around us tells something about ourselves and our objectives. Whether the space is a bedroom, a dorm room, or an office, people reveal themselves in the design and grouping of their furniture. Generally, the more formal the arrangement, the more formal and closed the communication style. An executive who seats visitors in a row of chairs across from her desk sends a message about hierarchy. A team leader who arranges chairs informally in a circle rather than in straight rows conveys his desire for a more open exchange of ideas.

TERRITORY. Each of us has a certain area that we feel is our own territory. Your father may have a favourite chair in which he is most comfortable, a cook might not tolerate intruders in the kitchen, and veteran employees may feel that certain work areas and tools belong to them. We all maintain zones of privacy in which we feel comfortable. Figure 1.5 categorizes the four zones of social interaction among North

▼ FIGURE 1.5 / Four Space Zones for Social Interaction

ZONE	DISTANCE	USES	
Intimate	0 to 45 cm (1.5 feet)	Reserved for members of the family and other loved ones.	Intimate Zone (1 to 1½ feet)
Personal	45 cm to 1.25 m (1.5 to 4 feet)	For talking with friends privately. The outer limit enables you to keep someone at arm's length.	Personal Zone (1½ to 4 feet)
Social	1.25 to 3.5 m (4 to 12 feet)	For acquaintances, coworkers, and strangers. Close enough for eye contact yet far enough for comfort. 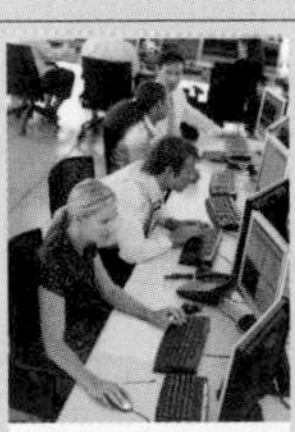	Social Zone (4 to 12 feet)
Public	3.5 m and over (12 feet and over)	For use in the classroom and for speeches before groups. Nonverbal cues become important as aids to communication. 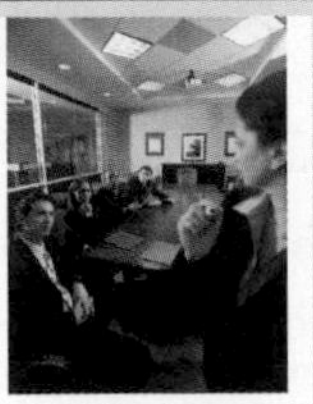	Public Zone (12 or more feet)

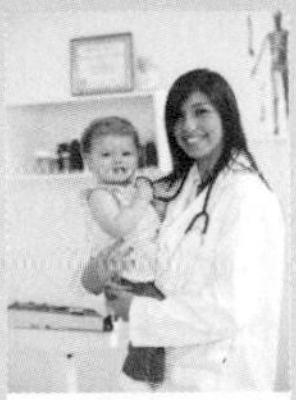

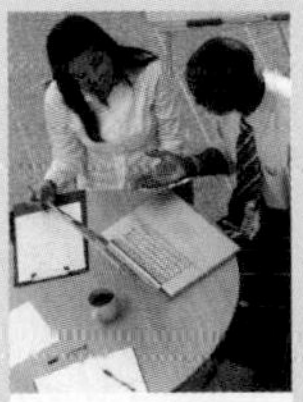

WORKPLACE IN FOCUS

Americans, as formulated by anthropologist Edward T. Hall.[17] Notice that they are a bit standoffish; only intimate friends and family may stand closer than about 45 centimetres. If someone violates that territory, North Americans feel uncomfortable and may step back to reestablish their space.

1.3c Appearance Sends Silent Messages

Much like the personal appearance of an individual, the physical appearance of a business document transmits immediate and important nonverbal messages. Ideally, documents should be pleasing to the eye.

"EYE APPEAL" OF BUSINESS DOCUMENTS. The way an email, a letter, or a report looks can have either a positive or a negative effect on the receiver. Sloppy emails send a nonverbal message that you are in a hurry or that you do not value the receiver. Letters and reports can look neat, professional, well organized, and attractive—or just the opposite. In succeeding chapters you will learn how to create business documents that send positive nonverbal messages through their appearance, format, organization, readability, and correctness.

PERSONAL APPEARANCE. The way you look—your clothing, grooming, and posture—sends an instant nonverbal message about you. Based on what they see, viewers make quick judgments about your status, credibility, personality, and potential. Even though some workplaces today are informal, it's best (especially early in your time there) to dress professionally—which means more formally than choosing the relaxed clothing you wear at home, for going out, or to the gym.

1.3d Building Strong Nonverbal Skills

Nonverbal communication can influence how others perceive us even more than words do. You can harness the power of silent messages by reviewing the following tips for improving nonverbal communication:

- **Establish and maintain eye contact.** Remember that in Canada appropriate, regular eye contact shows interest, attentiveness, strength, and credibility.

- **Use posture to show interest.** Encourage interaction by leaning forward, sitting or standing tall, and looking alert.
- **Reduce or eliminate physical barriers.** Move out from behind your desk; arrange meeting chairs in a circle.
- **Improve your decoding skills.** Watch facial expressions and body language to understand the complete verbal and nonverbal messages being communicated.
- **Probe for more information.** When you perceive nonverbal cues that contradict verbal meanings, politely seek additional cues (*I'm not sure I understand*, *Please tell me more about . . .* , or *Do you mean that . . .*).
- **Interpret nonverbal meanings in context.** Make nonverbal assessments only when you understand a situation or a culture.
- **Associate with people from diverse cultures.** Learn about other cultures to widen your knowledge and tolerance of intercultural nonverbal messages.
- **Use the power of appearance.** Keep in mind that the appearance of your business documents, your business space, and you sends immediate positive or negative messages to receivers.
- **Observe yourself on video.** Ensure that your verbal and nonverbal messages are in sync by recording and evaluating yourself making a presentation.

◤ 1.4 Recognizing How Culture Affects Communication

Global business, new communication technologies, the Internet, and social media span the world, shrinking distances. However, cultural differences still exist and can cause significant misunderstandings. Comprehending the verbal and nonverbal meanings of a message can be difficult even when communicators are from the same culture. When they come from different cultures, special sensitivity and skills are necessary.

For our purposes, *culture* may be defined as "the complex system of values, traits, morals, and customs shared by a society, region, or country." Culture is a powerful operating force that moulds the way we think, behave, and communicate.

We will describe five key dimensions of culture: context, individualism, time orientation, power distance, and communication style. The section closes with a look at the interaction between culture and social media.

1.4a Context

Context is probably the most important cultural dimension and also the most difficult to define. In a model developed by cultural anthropologist Edward T. Hall, cultures are arranged on a continuum, shown in Figure 1.6, from low to high in relation to context.

Communicators in low-context cultures (such as those in North America, Scandinavia, and Germany) depend little on the context of a situation to convey their meaning. They assume that messages must be explicit, and listeners rely exclusively on the written or spoken word. Low-context cultures tend to be logical, analytical, and action oriented. Business communicators stress clearly articulated messages that they consider to be objective, professional, and efficient. Words are taken literally.

Communicators in high-context cultures (such as those in China, Japan, and Arab countries) assume that the listener does not need much background information.[18] Communicators in high-context cultures are more likely to be intuitive and contemplative. They may not take words literally. Instead, the meaning of a message may be implied from the social or physical setting, the relationship of the communicators, or nonverbal cues. For example, a Japanese communicator might say *yes* when he really means *no*. From the context of the situation, his Japanese conversation partner would conclude whether *yes* really meant *yes* or whether it meant *no*. The context, tone, time taken to answer, facial expression, and body cues would convey the meaning of *yes*.[19] Communication cues are transmitted by posture, voice inflection, gestures, and facial expression.

Culture has a powerful effect on business communicators. The following observations point out selected differences. However, these are simplifications and practices within a given culture vary considerably. Moreover, as globalization expands, low- and high-context cultures are experiencing change and differences may be less pronounced.

Higher Context

Lower Context

Asian

Arabian

South European

African

South American

Central European

Canadian

American

Northern European

German

Swiss

- Tend to prefer direct verbal interaction
- Tend to understand meaning at only one sociocultural level.
- Are generally less proficient in reading nonverbal cues
- Value individualism
- Rely more on logic
- Say *no* directly
- Communicate in highly structured, detailed messages with literal meanings
- Give authority to written information

- Tend to prefer indirect verbal interaction
- Tend to understand meanings embedded at many sociocultural levels
- Are generally more proficient in reading nonverbal cues
- Value group membership
- Rely more on context and feeling
- Talk around point, avoid saying *no*
- Communicate in sometimes simple, sometimes ambiguous messages
- Understand visual messages readily

© Cengage Learning

1.4b Individualism

An attitude of independence and freedom from control characterizes individualism. Members of low-context cultures, particularly North Americans, tend to value individualism. They believe that initiative and self-assertion result in personal achievement.

Members of high-context cultures are more collectivist. They emphasize membership in organizations, groups, and teams; they encourage acceptance of group values, duties, and decisions. In group-oriented cultures such as those in many Asian societies, for example, self-assertion and individual decision making are discouraged. "The nail that sticks up gets pounded down" is a common Japanese saying.

Many cultures, of course, are quite complex and cannot be characterized as totally individualistic or group oriented.

1.4c Time Orientation

Canadians consider time a precious commodity. They correlate time with productivity, efficiency, and money. Keeping people waiting for business appointments is considered a waste of time and rude.

In other cultures time may be perceived as an unlimited resource to be enjoyed. A Canadian businessperson, for example, was kept waiting two hours past a scheduled appointment time in South America. She wasn't offended, though, because she was familiar with South Americans' more relaxed concept of time.

People in one culture may look at time as formal and task oriented. In another culture time may be seen as an opportunity to develop interpersonal relationships.

1.4d Power Distance

One important element of culture is power distance, a concept first introduced by social psychologist Geert Hofstede. The power distance index measures how people in different societies cope with inequality, in other words, how they relate to more powerful individuals. In high power distance countries, subordinates expect formal hierarchies and embrace relatively authoritarian, paternalistic power relationships. In low power distance cultures, however, subordinates consider themselves as equals of their supervisors. They confidently voice opinions and participate in decision making.[20]

As you probably guessed, in Western cultures people are more relaxed about social status and the appearance of power. Deference is not generally paid to individuals merely because of their wealth, position, seniority, or age. In many Asian cultures, however, these characteristics are important and must be respected.

1.4e Communication Style

People in low- and high-context cultures tend to communicate differently with words. To Canadians words are very important, especially in contracts and negotiations. People in high-context cultures, on the other hand, place more emphasis on the surrounding context than on the words describing a negotiation. For example, the Japanese may treat contracts as statements of intention and assume that changes will be made as projects develop. A traditional Arab business person may be insulted by mentioning a contract; a person's word is more binding in that culture.

In communication style Canadians value straightforwardness, are suspicious of evasiveness, and distrust people who might have a hidden agenda or who "play their cards too close to the chest." We also tend to be uncomfortable with silence and impatient with delays. Some Asian businesspeople have learned that the longer they drag out negotiations, the more concessions impatient Canadians are likely to make.

1.4f Intercultural Communication, Social Media, and Communication Technology

Much has been made of the connectedness that social media and communication technology provide today. With minimal resources, communicators can reach out to larger and more varied audiences than ever before.

SOCIAL NETWORKING: BRIDGING CULTURAL DIVIDES? "Digital media is an amplifier. It tends to make extroverts more extroverted and introverts more introverted," says Clay Shirky, a social media expert.[21] At the same time, the online environment may deepen feelings of isolation; it can make interpersonal contact more difficult because all contact is mediated electronically.[22]

In real life, as online, we instinctively tend to gravitate toward people who seem similar to us, believes Gaurav Mishra, a social media strategist: "Human beings have a strong tendency to prefer the familiar, so we pay attention to people with a shared context and treat the rich Twitter public stream as background noise."[23] Twitter and other social media can boost intercultural communication; however, we must be willing to reach out across the boundaries that separate us. The benefits of embracing diversity can be seen in the results of a recent study done by the Boston Consulting Group, summarized in Figure 1.7.

SOCIAL NETWORKING: ERASING CULTURAL DIFFERENCES? Despite the equalizing influence of globalization, regional and cultural differences persist, as those who design media for markets in other countries know. Asian users may prefer muted pastel colours and anime-style graphics that North Americans would find unusual. Conversely, Korean and Japanese employees may baulk at being compelled

▼ FIGURE 1.7 / Positive Relationship Between Diversity and Innovation

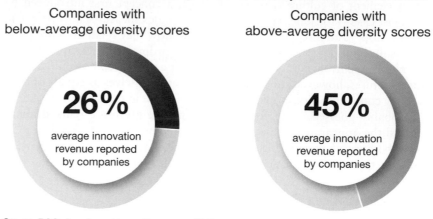

Boston Consulting Group's Diversity and Innovation study (2017) shows a positive relationship between increased organizational diversity and innovation revenue.

Companies with below-average diversity scores

26% average innovation revenue reported by companies

Companies with above-average diversity scores

45% average innovation revenue reported by companies

Source: BCG diversity and innovation survey, 2017

to post photos of themselves on company intranet pages. They opt for avatars or pictures of pets instead, possibly as an expression of personal modesty or because of expectations of privacy, whereas North Americans believe photos promote cohesion and make them seem accessible.

It remains to be seen whether social networking will slowly erase many of the cultural differences present today or whether distinct national, even local, networks will emerge.

◣ 1.5 Building Intercultural Workplace Skills

Being aware of your own culture and how it contrasts with others is a first step in learning intercultural skills. Another important step involves recognizing barriers to intercultural accommodation and striving to overcome them. The digital-age economy needs workers who can thrive on diverse teams and interact effectively with customers and clients at home and abroad.

1.5a Curbing Ethnocentrism and Stereotyping

Two barriers often hamper the process of successfully understanding and interacting with people from other cultures: ethnocentrism and stereotyping. These barriers can be overcome by developing tolerance, a powerful and effective aid to communication.

ETHNOCENTRISM. The belief in the superiority of one's own culture is known as *ethnocentrism*. This natural attitude is found in all cultures. Ethnocentrism causes us to judge others by our own values. If you were raised in Canada, values such as punctuality and directness described previously probably seem "right" to you, and you may wonder why the rest of the world doesn't function in the same sensible fashion.

STEREOTYPES. Our perceptions of other cultures sometimes cause us to form stereotypes about groups of people. A *stereotype* is an oversimplified perception of a behavioural pattern or characteristic applied to entire groups. For example, the Swiss are hardworking, efficient, and neat; Germans are formal, reserved, and blunt; Americans are loud, friendly, and impatient; Canadians are polite, trusting, and tolerant; Asians are gracious, humble, and inscrutable. These attitudes may or may not accurately describe cultural norms. Look beneath surface stereotypes and labels to discover individual personal qualities.

TOLERANCE. As global markets expand and as our society becomes increasingly multiethnic, tolerance is critical. *Tolerance* here means learning about and appreciating beliefs and practices different from our own. It means being open-minded and receptive to new experiences. One of the best ways to develop tolerance is to practise *empathy*, defined as trying to see the world through another's eyes. It means being less judgmental and more eager to seek common ground. A concrete example of tolerance in the Canadian business context has been the widespread adoption in the past five years of land rights acknowledgments. Sometimes the acknowledgement is written, in an email signature. Sometimes it is spoken, as for example in a theatre performance.

1.5b Successful Spoken Communication With Intercultural Audiences

When you have a conversation with someone from another culture, you can reduce misunderstandings by following these tips:

- **Use simple English.** Speak in short sentences using familiar, short words. Eliminate puns, sports and cultural references, slang, and jargon. Be especially alert to idiomatic expressions that can't be translated, such as *burn the midnight oil* and *throw a curve ball*.
- **Speak slowly and enunciate clearly.** Avoid fast speech, but don't raise your voice. Overpunctuate with pauses and full stops.
- **Encourage accurate feedback.** Ask probing questions, and encourage the listener to paraphrase what you say. Don't assume that a *yes*, a nod, or a smile indicates comprehension or assent.
- **Check frequently for comprehension.** Avoid waiting until the end of a long explanation to request feedback. Instead, make one point at a time, pausing to check for comprehension. Don't proceed to B until A has been grasped.
- **Observe eye messages.** Be alert to a glazed expression or wandering eyes. These tell you the listener is lost.
- **Accept blame.** If a misunderstanding results, graciously accept the responsibility for not making your meaning clear.
- **Listen without interrupting.** Curb your desire to finish sentences or to fill out ideas for the speaker. Keep in mind that North Americans abroad are often accused of listening too little and talking too much.
- **Smile when appropriate.** The smile is often considered the single most understood and most useful form of communication. In some cultures, however, excessive smiling may seem insincere.[24]
- **Follow up in writing.** After conversations or oral negotiations, confirm the results and agreements with written messages—if necessary, in the local language.

1.5c Successful Written Communication With Intercultural Audiences

When you write to someone from a different culture, you can improve your chances of being understood by following these suggestions:
- **Consider local styles and conventions.** Learn how documents are formatted in the intended reader's country. Decide whether to use your organization's preferred format or adjust to local styles. Observe titles and rank. Be polite.
- **Hire a translator.** Engage a professional translator if (a) your document is important, (b) your document will be distributed to many readers, or (c) you must be persuasive. Otherwise consider using free software like Google Translate—which is not without its problems—for informal, "off the record," intercultural messaging.

- **Use short sentences and short paragraphs.** Sentences with fewer than 20 words and paragraphs with fewer than eight lines are most readable.
- **Avoid ambiguous wording.** Include relative pronouns (*that, which, who*) for clarity in introducing clauses. Stay away from contractions (especially ones such as *here's the problem*). Avoid idioms (*once in a blue moon*), slang (*my presentation really bombed*), acronyms (*ASAP* for *as soon as possible*), abbreviations (*DBA* for *doing business as*), jargon (*ROI, bottom line*), and sports references (*play ball, slam dunk*). Use action-specific verbs (*buy a printer* rather than *get a printer*).
- **Cite numbers carefully.** In international trade learn and use the metric system. In citing numbers, use figures (*15*) instead of spelling them out (*fifteen*). Always convert dollar figures into local currency. Spell out the month when writing dates. In North America, for example, *March 5, 2018*, might be written as *3/5/18*, whereas in Europe the same date might appear as *5.3.18*.

1.5d Globalization and Workplace Diversity

While Canadian companies like Shopify are expanding global operations and adapting to a variety of emerging markets, the domestic workforce is also becoming more diverse. This diversity has many dimensions—race, ethnicity, age, religion, gender, national origin, physical ability, and sexual orientation.

An article in the *National Post* stated that "in 2011, the percentage of visible minorities was 19.1 percent, according to Statistics Canada. By 2031, that number is expected to grow to 30.6 percent, with South Asian and Chinese immigrants driving much of that growth. Vancouver and Toronto are expected to become 'majority-minority' cities with three out of five people—60 percent—belonging to a visible minority group by then."*[25] Additionally, the proportion of women in the workforce will grow significantly as will the number of workers ages 55 and older.

What do all these changes mean for you? Simply put, your job will require you to interact with colleagues and customers with backgrounds from around the world. You will need to cooperate with individuals and teams. What's more, your coworkers may differ from you in race, ethnicity, gender, age, and other ways.

1.5e Benefits of a Diverse Workforce

As society and the workforce become more diverse, successful communication among various groups brings distinct advantages. We saw this earlier in Figure 1.7's proof that diversity equals more innovation. Customers want to deal with companies that respect their values. They are more likely to say, "If you are a company whose ads do not include me, or whose workforce does not include me, I will not buy from you."

A diverse staff is better able to respond to and exploit the increasingly diverse customer base in local and world markets. For example, one recent Canadian report finds that "for every 1 percent increase in ethnocultural diversity, on average companies saw a 2.4 percent bump in revenue."[26]

Most important, though, is the growing realization among organizations that diversity is a critical bottom-line business strategy to improve employee relationships and to increase productivity. Developing a diverse staff that can work together cooperatively is one of the biggest challenges facing business organizations today.

1.5f Tips for Communicating With Diverse Audiences on the Job

Harmony and acceptance do not happen automatically when people who are dissimilar work together. Harnessed effectively, diversity can enhance productivity and

---

*From National Post, June 27 © 2014 Postmedia. All rights reserved. Material republished with the express permission of: National Post, a division of Postmedia Network Inc.

propel a company to success. Mismanaged, it can become a drain on a company's time and resources. The following suggestions can help you find ways to improve communication and interaction:

- **Seek training.** Look upon diversity as an opportunity, not a threat. Intercultural communication, team building, and conflict resolution are skills that can be learned in diversity training programs.

- **Understand the value of differences.** Diversity makes an organization innovative and creative. Sameness can foster an absence of critical thinking called *groupthink*. Real-world examples like the recent airline and train crashes, the meltdown of the financial services industry in the late 2000s, and others suggest that groupthink may prevent alternatives from being considered. Even smart people working collectively can make foolish decisions if they do not see different perspectives.[27]

- **Learn about your cultural self.** Begin to think of yourself as a product of your culture, and understand that your culture is just one among many. Try to look at yourself from the outside. Do you see any reflex reactions and automatic thought patterns that are a result of your upbringing? These may be invisible to you until challenged by people who are different from you. Be sure to keep what works and yet be ready to adapt as your environment changes.

- **Make fewer assumptions.** Be careful of seemingly insignificant, innocent workplace assumptions. For example, don't assume that everyone wants to observe the holidays with a Christmas party and a decorated tree. Moreover, in workplace discussions don't assume anything about others' sexual orientations or attitudes toward marriage. For invitations, avoid phrases such as *managers and their wives*. Using *spouses* or *partners* is more inclusive. Valuing diversity means making fewer assumptions that everyone is like you or wants to be like you.

- **Build on similarities.** Look for areas in which you and others not like you can agree or at least share opinions. Be prepared to consider issues from many perspectives, all of which may be valid. Although you can always find differences, it is much harder to find similarities. Look for common ground in shared experiences, mutual goals, and similar values. Concentrate on your objective even when you may disagree on how to reach it.

Cengage

MINDTAP

In MindTap go to the Study Tools for Chapter 1 and complete the Practice Test.

◤ LEARNING SUMMARY

1.1 Describe how solid communication skills will improve your career prospects.

- Employers hire and promote job candidates who have excellent communication skills; writing skills make or break careers.

- Because workers interact more than ever using communication technology, even technical fields require communication skills.

- New hires and other employees must project a professional image and possess soft skills.

- Job challenges in the information age include changing communication technologies, mobile 24/7 offices, flatter management, an emphasis on teams, and global competition.

1.2 Confront barriers to effective listening.

- Most of us are poor listeners; we can learn active listening by removing physical and psychological barriers, overlooking language problems, and eliminating distractions.

- A fast processing speed allows us to let our minds wander; we fake attention and prefer to talk than to listen.

- Poor listening can be overcome as long as we stop talking, focus fully on others, control distractions, keep an open mind, and listen for the speaker's main ideas.

- Capitalizing on lag time, listening between the lines, judging ideas instead of appearances, taking good notes, and providing feedback are other methods for building listening skills.

1.3 Explain the importance of nonverbal communication.

- Be aware of nonverbal cues such as eye contact, facial expression, and posture that send silent, highly believable messages.

- Understand that how you use time, space, and territory is interpreted by the receiver, who also "reads" the eye appeal of your business documents and your personal appearance.

- Build solid nonverbal skills by keeping eye contact, maintaining good posture, reducing physical barriers, improving your decoding skills, and probing for more information.

- Interpret nonverbal meanings in context, learn about other cultures, and understand the impact of appearance—of documents, your office space, and you.

1.4 Understand five common dimensions of culture and how they affect communication.

- Culture is a complex system of values, traits, and customs shared by a society; culture moulds the way we think, behave, and communicate both offline and online.

- Culture can be described using key dimensions such as context, individualism, time orientation, power distance, and communication style.

- Today's communicators need to be aware of low- and high-context cultures, individualistic versus collectivist societies, differing attitudes toward time, clashing perceptions of power, and varying reliance on the written word.

- Whether social media and technology can bridge cultural divides and erase differences will depend on the users as much as it would among strangers who meet at a dinner party.

1.5 Use intercultural communication strategies to prevent miscommunication.

- Beware of ethnocentrism and stereotyping; instead, embrace tolerance and keep an open mind.

- When communicating orally, use simple English, speak slowly, check for comprehension, observe eye messages, accept blame, don't interrupt, smile, and follow up in writing.

- When writing, consider local styles, hire a translator, use short sentences, avoid ambiguous wording, and cite numbers carefully.

- As the domestic workforce becomes more diverse, appreciate diversity as a critical business strategy.

- To communicate well with diverse audiences, seek training, understand the value of diversity, learn about your own culture, make fewer assumptions, and look for similarities.

◤ CHAPTER REVIEW

1. Based on what you have learned in this chapter, describe the kind of work environment you can expect to enter when you graduate. (Obj. 1)

2. Why are writing skills more important in today's workplace than ever before? (Obj. 1)

3. List six trends in the digital-age workplace that affect business communicators. Be prepared to discuss how they might affect you in your future career. (Obj. 1)

4. List bad habits and distractions that can act as barriers to effective listening. (Obj. 2)

5. List 11 techniques for improving your listening skills. Be prepared to discuss each. (Obj. 2)

6. What is nonverbal communication and are nonverbal cues easy to read? (Obj. 3)

7. How do we send messages to others without speaking? (Obj. 3)

8. What is culture, and what are five key dimensions that can be used to describe it? (Obj. 4)

9. List seven or more suggestions for enhancing comprehension when you are talking with non-native speakers of English. Be prepared to discuss each. (Obj. 5)

◤ CRITICAL THINKING

1. Do you consider your daily texting, Instagram updates, tweets, emails, and other informal writing to be "real writing"? How might such writing differ from the writing done in business? (Obj. 1)

2. Why do executives and managers spend more time listening than do workers? (Obj. 2)

3. What arguments could you give for or against the idea that body language is a science with principles that can be interpreted accurately by specialists? (Obj. 3)

4. Consider potential culture clashes in typical business situations. Imagine that businesspeople from a

high-context culture, say, China, meet their counterparts from a low-context culture, Canada, for the first time to negotiate and sign a manufacturing contract. What could go wrong? How about conflicting perceptions of time? (Obj. 4)

5. A stereotype is an oversimplified perception of a behavioural pattern or characteristic applied to entire groups. For example, Germans are formal, reserved, and blunt; Americans are loud, friendly, and impatient; Asians are gracious, humble, and inscrutable. In what way are such stereotypes harmless or harmful? (Obj. 5)

◤ ACTIVITIES AND CASES

1.1 MAKING JOB DESCRIPTIONS MORE SPECIFIC AROUND COMMUNICATION (OBJ. 1)

You know from reading this chapter that solid communication skills are among the top two skills Canadian employers are looking for. However, job descriptions don't usually go into more detail than that—they assume everyone knows what "excellent communication" means.

Your Task. Working individually or in teams, compile a database of people you know who work in a supervisory/managerial role—it doesn't matter at what type of organization. Develop a brief questionnaire (perhaps using Surveymonkey.com) in which you ask these people to be more specific about what "excellent communication" means. For example, a question could be, "In your organization, what specific types of writing does an entry-level employee need to know how to do? What specific types of speaking? How do you know when an entry-level employee is not showing effective writing skills? Speaking skills?" After you receive your answers, analyze them and look for similarities and differences. Share your analysis with your instructor or your class in a brief report or presentation.

1.2 INTRODUCE YOURSELF (OBJ. 1)

Your instructor wants to know more about you, your motivation for taking this course, your career goals, and your writing skills.

Your Task. Send a professional email of introduction to your instructor. See Chapter 5 for formats and tips on drafting emails. In your message include the following:

a. Your reasons for taking this class

b. Your career goals (both short term and long term)

c. A brief description of your employment and your favourite activities

d. An evaluation and discussion of your communication skills, including your strengths and weaknesses

For online classes, write a message of introduction about yourself with the preceding information. Post your message to your discussion board. Read and comment on the posts of other students. Think about how people in virtual teams must learn about each other through online messages.

Alternatively, your instructor may assign this task as a concise individual voice mail message to establish your telephone etiquette and speaking skills.

1.3 SMALL-GROUP PRESENTATION: INTRODUCE EACH OTHER (OBJS. 1, 2)

Many organizations today use teams to accomplish their goals. To help you develop speaking, listening, and teamwork skills, your instructor may assign team projects. One of the first jobs in any team is selecting members and becoming acquainted.

Your Task. Your instructor will divide your class into small groups or teams. At your instructor's direction, either (a) interview another group member and introduce that person to the group or (b) introduce yourself to the group. Think of this as an informal interview for a team assignment or for a job. You will want to make notes from which to speak. Your introduction should include information such as the answers to following:

a. Where did you grow up?

b. What work and extracurricular activities have you engaged in?

c. What are your interests and talents? What are you good at doing?

d. What have you achieved?

e. How familiar are you with various computer technologies?

f. What are your professional and personal goals? Where do you expect to be five years from now?

To develop listening skills, practise the listening techniques discussed in this chapter and take notes when other students are presenting. In addition to mentioning details about each speaker, be prepared to discuss three important facts about each speaker.

1.4 REMEMBERING A TIME WHEN SOMEONE DIDN'T LISTEN TO YOU (OBJ. 2)

Think of a time when you felt that someone didn't listen to you—for example, on the job, at home, at the doctor's office, or at a store where you shop. Your instructor will split the class into pairs of speakers and listeners. The speakers will share their stories. The listeners must try to recognize two things: (a) what the poor listener in the story did that demonstrated non-listening and (b) what impact this had on the speaker's feelings. The speakers and listeners then reverse roles. After this second round, the class compares notes to debrief. All ideas are collected to identify patterns of nonlistening behaviour and its negative impact on the speakers.

Your Task. In pairs or individually, identify behaviour that would reverse what happened in the stories told in class. Based on your insights, write an email or a short report that describes several principles of good listening illustrated with brief examples. You could end by concisely explaining an encounter that shows ideal active listening.

1.5 LISTENING: AN IN-PERSON OR VIRTUAL SOCIAL MEDIA INTERVIEW (OBJ. 2)

How much and to whom do businesspeople listen?

Your Task. Interview a businessperson about his or her workplace listening. Connect with a worker in your circle of friends, family, and acquaintances; in your campus network; at a prior or current job; or via LinkedIn or Facebook. Come up with questions to ask about listening, such as the following:

a. How much active listening do you practise daily?

b. To whom do you listen on the job?

c. How do you know that others are or are not listening to you?

d. Can you share anecdotes of poor listening that led to negative outcomes?

e. Do you have tips for better listening?

Summarize the findings from your interview in a professional email, brief report, or brief presentation.

1.6 LISTENING AND NONVERBAL CUES: SKILLS REQUIRED IN VARIOUS CAREERS (OBJS. 2, 3)

Do the listening skills and behaviours of individuals differ depending on their careers?

Your Task. Your instructor will divide you into teams and give each team a role to discuss, such as business executive, teacher, physician, police officer, lawyer, accountant, administrative assistant, customer service representative, or team leader. Create a list of verbal and nonverbal cues that a member of this profession would display to indicate that he or she is listening. Be prepared to act out these cues in front of your class to see if they can figure out what you're "saying."

1.7 BODY LANGUAGE (OBJ. 3)

Can body language be accurately interpreted?

Your Task. What attitudes do the following body movements suggest to you? Do these movements always mean the same thing? What part does context play in your interpretations? Be prepared to act out one or more of these movements in front of your class. Does the class get the same meanings as you did just from reading the behaviour?

a. Whistling, wringing hands

b. Bowed posture, twiddling thumbs

c. Steepled hands, sprawling sitting position

d. Rubbing hand through hair

e. Open hands, unbuttoned coat

f. Wringing hands, tugging ears

1.8 NONVERBAL COMMUNICATION: UNIVERSAL SIGN FOR "I GOOFED" (OBJ. 3)

To promote safe highway driving and reduce road rage, motorists submitted the following suggestions. The suggestions were sent to a newspaper writer who asked for a universal nonverbal signal admitting that a driver had goofed.

Your Task. In small groups consider the pros and cons of each of the following gestures intended as an apology when a driver makes a mistake. Why would some fail?

a. Lower your head slightly and bonk yourself on the forehead with the side of your closed fist. The message is clear: *I'm stupid. I shouldn't have done that.*

b. Make a temple with your hands, as if you were praying.

c. Move the index finger of your right hand back and forth across your neck—as if you were cutting your throat.

d. Flash the well-known peace sign. Hold up the index and middle fingers of one hand, making a V, as in *victory.*

e. Place the flat of your hands against your cheeks, as children do when they have made a mistake.

f. Clasp your hand over your mouth, raise your brows, and shrug your shoulders.

g. Use your knuckles to knock on the side of your head. Translation: *Oops! Engage brain.*

h. Place your right hand high on your chest and pat a few times, like a basketball player who drops a pass or a football player who makes a bad throw. This says, *I'll take the blame.*

i. Place your right fist over the middle of your chest and move it in a circular motion. This is universal sign language for *I'm sorry.*

j. Open your window and tap the top of your car roof with your hand.

k. Smile and raise both arms, palms outward, which is a universal gesture for surrender or forgiveness.

l. Use the military salute, which is simple and shows respect.

m. Flash your biggest smile, point at yourself with your right thumb, and move your head from left to right, as if to say, *I can't believe I did that.*

1.9 NONVERBAL COMMUNICATION: SIGNALS SENT BY CASUAL ATTIRE (OBJ. 3)

Although many employers allow casual attire, not all employers and customers are happy with the results. To learn more about the implementation, acceptance, and effects of casual-dress programs, select one of the following activities, all of which involve some form of interviewing.

Your Task.

a. In teams, gather information from human resources employees to determine which companies allow casual or dress-down days, how often, and under what specific conditions. The information may be collected by personal interviews, email, telephone, instant messaging, or on the Web.

b. In teams, conduct interviews in your communities. Ask individuals in the community how they react to casual dress in the workplace. Develop a set of standard interview questions.

c. In teams, visit local businesses on both casual days and traditional business-dress days. Compare and contrast the effects of business-dress standards on such factors as the projected image of the company, the nature of the interactions with customers and with coworkers, employee morale, and employee productivity. What generalizations can you draw from your findings?

d. Using library databases, learn about dress code rules and laws and policies in your province or territory and municipality.

1.10 NONVERBAL COMMUNICATION AROUND THE WORLD (OBJS. 3, 4)

Gestures play an important role when people communicate. Because culture shapes the meaning of gestures, miscommunication and misunderstanding can easily result in international situations.

Your Task. Use the Internet to research the meanings of selected gestures. Make a list of ten gestures (other than those discussed in the text) that have different meanings in different countries. Consider the fingertip kiss, nose thumb, eyelid pull, nose tap, head shake, and other gestures. How are the meanings different in other countries?

1.11 MAKING SENSE OF IDIOMS (OBJ. 4)

Many languages have idiomatic expressions that do not always make sense to outsiders.

Your Task. Explain in simple English what the following idiomatic expressions mean. Assume that you are explaining them to non-native speakers of English.

a. Have an axe to grind

b. Under wraps

c. Come out of left field

d. Hell on wheels

e. Drop the ball

f. Get your act together

g. Stay the course

h. In the limelight

1.12 EXAMINING CULTURAL STEREOTYPES (OBJS. 4, 5)

Generalizations are necessary as we acquire and categorize new knowledge. Almost all of us are at some point in our lives subject to stereotyping by others, whether we are immigrants, minorities, women, members of certain professions, or Canadians working abroad. Generally speaking, negative stereotypes sting. However, even positive stereotypes can offend or embarrass because they fail to acknowledge the differences among individuals.

Your Task. Think about a nation or culture about which you have only a hazy idea. Jot down a few key traits that come to mind. For example, you may not know much about the Netherlands and the Dutch. You may think of gouda cheese, wooden clogs, Heineken beer, tulips, and windmills. Anything else? Then consider a culture with which you are very familiar, whether it's yours or that of a country you have visited or studied. For each culture, in one column, write down a few stereotypical perceptions that are positive. Then, in another column, record negative stereotypes you associate with that culture. Share your notes with your team or the whole class, as your instructor directs. How do you respond to others' descriptions of your culture? Which stereotypes irk you and why? For a quick fact check and overview at the end of this exercise, google the *CIA World Factbook* or *BBC News Country Profiles*.

1.13 EXAMINING DIVERSITY IN JOB INTERVIEWS (OBJS. 4, 5)

Today's workforce benefits from diversity, and most businesses have embraced explicit non-discrimination policies. Governments have passed legislation that makes it illegal to discriminate based on race, colour, creed, ethnicity, national origin, disability, sex, age, and other factors such as sexual orientation and gender identity.

Your Task. Consider how such differences could affect the communication, for instance, between an interviewer and a job candidate. If negatively, how could the differences and barriers be overcome? Role-play or discuss a potential job interview conversation between the following individuals. After a while summarize your findings, either orally or in writing:

a. A female executive is interviewing a prospective assistant, who is male.

b. A candidate with a strong but not disruptive foreign accent is being interviewed by a native-born human resources manager.

c. A manager who doesn't wear a head a covering is interviewing a person wearing a turban.

d. A person over 50 is being interviewed by a hiring manager in his early 30s.

e. A recruiter who doesn't use a wheelchair is interviewing a job seeker who uses a wheelchair.

◤ GRAMMAR/MECHANICS CHALLENGE 1

NOUNS

Review Sections 1.02–1.06 in the Grammar/Mechanics Handbook. Then study each of the following statements. Underline any inappropriate form. In the space provided, write the correct form (or *C* if correct) and the number of the G/M principle illustrated. When you finish, compare your responses with those provided near the end of the book. If your responses differ, study carefully the principles in parentheses.

<u>sexes (1.05b)</u> **Example**   The tennis match turned out to be a battle of the <u>sex's</u>.

_____ 1. Canadian marketing efforts are increasing in all Pacific Rim <u>countrys</u>.

_____ 2. None of the CEO's used their smartphones during the meeting.

_____ 3. We were surprised that the companies' two highly respected employee's disagreed on the best strategy.

_____ 4. That restaurant is open on Sunday's but not on Monday's.

_____ 5. Many <u>turkies</u> had to be destroyed after the virus outbreak.

_____ 6. Only the Samsons and the Alvarez's brought their entire families.

_____ 7. Parliament established the Nunavut territory in the 1990's.

_____ 8. My grandfather had four <u>brother-in-laws</u> serving in World War 2.

_____ 9. I have never seen so many klutz's on one dance floor.

_____ 10. The OSFI conducted several <u>inquirys</u> regarding new banking fees.

_____ 11. The instructor was surprised to have three <u>Anthonies</u> in one class.

_____ 12. All the mountains and valleys were visible on Google Earth.

_____ 13. CRA required copies of all documents showing the company's assets and <u>liabilitys</u>.

_____ 14. My tablet monitor makes it difficult to distinguish between i's and l's.

_____ 15. McClung was one of the best-known woman to fight for human rights.

◤ EDITING CHALLENGE 1

To fine-tune your grammar and mechanics skills, in every chapter you will be editing a message. These are the skills that employers frequently find lacking in employees. It's during the revising process that you will put these skills to work. That's why we provide a complete message with errors in proofreading, grammar, spelling, punctuation, capitalization, word use, and number form. Your job is to find and correct all errors. This first Editing Challenge focuses on nouns, but other writing faults also need revision.

Your Task. Edit the following message by correcting its errors (a) in your textbook or (b) on a photocopy using standard proofreading marks from Appendix B.

To: Amanda Stapleton <a.stapleton@dobbsmfg.com>
From: Kevin Williams <k.williams@dobbsmfg.com>
Subject: Tip for Working From Home
Cc:
Bcc:

Hi Amanda,

Because you will be working from home during the next 6 months, we have some tips on how to do it efficiently while stay in touch with the office

- **Set boundarys for your work.** Establish a starting and ending time, and when its quitting time, wrap every thing up and shut down.
- **Check your email regularly.** Such as 3 times a day. Answer all message promply, and send copys of relevant messages to the appropriate office staff.
- **Transmit all work order to Andrea.** She will analyze each weeks activitys and update all sales assignments and inventorys.
- **Provide a end of week report.** Send a summary of your weeks work to me indicating the major accounts you serviced.

If your not a big email user get acquainted with it right away and don't be afraid to use it. Please shoot emails to any staff member. When you need clarification on a project or if you just want to keep us updated.

We will continue to hold once a week staff meeting on Friday's at 10 a.m. in the morning. Do you think it would be possible for you to attend 1 or 2 of these meeting. The next one is Friday, May 5th.

I know you will enjoy working at home Amanda. Following these basic guideline should help you complete your work, and provide the office with adequate contact with you.
Kevin Williams
[Full contact Information]

Chris Schmidt/istockphoto

UNIT
02

THE BUSINESS
WRITING
PROCESS

BUSINESS COMMUNICATION RESEARCH UPDATE

Writing in the Workplace: Constructing Documents Using Multiple Digital Sources

Mariëlle Leijten, Luuk van Waes, Karen Schriver & John R. Hayes, 2014, Journal of Writing Research, *5(3), 285–337.*

Abstract: In today's workplaces professional communication often involves constructing documents from multiple digital sources—integrating one's own texts/graphics with ideas based on others' text/graphics. This article presents a case study of a professional communication designer as he constructs a proposal over several days. Drawing on keystroke and interview data, we map the professional's overall process, plot the time course of his writing/design, illustrate how he searches for content and switches among optional digital sources, and show how he modifies and reuses others' content. The case study reveals not only that the professional (1) searches extensively through multiple sources for content and ideas but that he also (2) constructs visual content (charts, graphs, photographs) as well as verbal content, and (3) manages his attention and motivation over this extended task. Since these three activities are not represented in current models of writing, we propose their addition not just to models of communication design, but also to models of writing in general.

1. INTRODUCTION

Professional writing seldom starts from a blank screen. Like most writing today—whether at school or in the workplace—professional writing takes place in a digital context in which professionals have easy access to a wide variety of sources that are only a mouse click away. In fact, professional writing processes are now more than ever characterized by features of the digital workplace. Professional communication involves intense collaborations with others (both face-to-face and electronic). Professional communication is also characterized by dynamic interactions among evolving texts and graphics, previously produced documents, and a plethora of additional digital sources (both internal and external to the organization). These interactions involve constructing and reconstructing one's own and other's texts—refashioning and reusing content from multiple sources.

Professional communicators need to juggle both what tools to employ and what digital sources to access. These demands result in continuous decision making about their own texts and other people's texts as they work toward a document's completion. In other words, professionals do not rely solely on their own long-term memories to create new content, but instead, constantly search for available information that serves their communication needs and facilitates their writing process (McCarthy et al., 2011). Document reuse and adaptation now pervade the practice of professional communication (Swarts, 2010).

We contend that writing from and searching for information in multiple digital sources has fundamentally changed the way in which professionals approach communication design. Moreover, digital composing allows for multimodal collaboration, enabling writers to continuously interact with their colleagues and other experts. To account for these phenomena and the pragmatic realities of workplace communication, we examine the existing literature to identify important features of professional communication in digital environments. Next, we present a case study in which we observed a professional as he produced a lengthy proposal. We captured the professional's process with keystroke logging, onsite observations, and retrospective interviews. In the course of consolidating the process data, we offer novel visualizations for aggregating fine-grained logging data and for representing complexity in a comprehensible way. Finally, we suggest some ways that existing writing models might be modified to better reflect key features revealed by professional writing, such as those characteristic of writing from (digital) sources. . . .

2. WRITING FROM SOURCES

Previous researchers have focused mainly on understanding writing from sources as a discourse synthesis task. For example, Spivey and King (2011) studied writing from sources as junior high-school students worked on various writing assignments. They found that writing from sources called on students to select, connect, and organize content from source texts as they composed their own new texts. Studies of college-level students writing from sources have emphasized the idea that students' goal in writing from sources is to first produce a text akin to a summary, which then positions them to extend that summary, making a unique argument or contribution to the ideas under discussion. In contrast, workplace research has not focused on the writer's personal transformation and growth as they write from sources. Instead, research on professional communication tends to examine how writers transform others' content as they draw on various paper or digital sources and on how doing so requires sensitivity to the rhetorical situation. . . .

The communicator's goal is to use the resulting "bricolage" (Turkle, 1997) as a starting point for generating "new" text or graphics. As Slattery (2007)—who studied writers working for a technical documentation service—observed, texts were "not so much written as assembled—a pastiche of contributions from multiple individuals over the duration of a project" (p. 315). We suspect that when professionals employ digital resources, they do so not with an eye toward summary, though summarizing could be part of what they do (Solé et al., 2013). Rather, professionals writing from sources tend to focus on analyzing what others have done textually and visually, distilling best practices for the genre and gleaning ideas for invention. As professionals do so, they may engage in paraphrasing source documents and sampling other professionals' visual or verbal content. Professionals may also compare their proposed strategies for solving a communication problem with the strategies and tactics of other organizations. . . .

4. ETHNOGRAPHIC CASE STUDY

To better understand the nature of writing in the workplace, we sought out a company to study that took information design and interdisciplinary collaboration seriously. To show both the possibilities and complexity of information design, we also wanted to study a company that paid considerable attention to the visual aspects of their products. These criteria lead us to the Design Consulting Agency we will call Nova, located in Brussels (Belgium). Nova is a midsized Design Consulting Agency founded in 1987. Its main goal is to help organizations create products, services, or tools based on principles of user-centered design. Nova's core expertise in Human–Computer Interaction (HCI) was augmented by expertise in engineering disciplines, cognitive ergonomics, visual design, and the social sciences. This mix of skills helped Nova understand and solve problems for a variety of complex business domains.

As Schriver (2012) noted, professional communicators typically write and design as their primary work or as part of their work in another field, for example, engineering, law, or computer science. The participant in the present case study was a professional who was not trained in technical or professional communication, but he was quite experienced in writing on the job. We will call him Aiden. He was a 45-year-old project manager and proposal writer who had worked at Nova for 15 years. Aiden had studied economics and management, but found he also had skill in creating winning proposals. . . .

4.6 RESULTS

This section reports on how Aiden constructed his document over the five sessions. . . .

Aiden regularly chose to leave his text in search of suitable information elsewhere. Based on the data in the general logging file from Inputlog, we identified all of the sources Aiden accessed (called focus events in the general logging file). Inputlog identified about 280 unique focus events. We grouped these focus events into 31 categories, which were further recoded into nine main categories based on software or program types. For instance, various programs for email (Outlook, Webmail, etc.) were grouped into the main category "mail". . . .

6. CONCLUSIONS

In this article, we proposed an adaptation of Hayes' (2012) model to better account for the activities we observed in the current case study of a skilled communication designer. In particular, we added three new features to that model. First, we added (and modeled) a process by which writers search for external information or content. Second, we allowed for (but did not model) processes for constructing graphics; we consider visual design processes on par with the writing processes already included in the Hayes model. Finally, we included a motivation management function to take into account the observation that in an extended design task—like the one we presented in the case study—designers may elect to take breaks from their task (downtime).

This article presented a case study of an experienced professional as he worked for more than eight and a half hours on a visual and verbal design project. The most striking observations in this case study concerned the way the writer distributed his time. He spent less than a third of his time (30%) in the proposal document itself. Most of his time (61%) was spent searching in a wide variety of external sources. He used about 280 different sources and made 305 switches per hour, or no less than 5 switches per minute. Clearly there was an intensive and continuous interaction between the text-and-graphics-created-so-far and the available sources. The remainder of the designer's time (9%) was devoted to downtime, both voluntary and involuntary. As we suggested earlier, we believe that the voluntary downtime reflects the designer's ability to manage his own motivation. . . .

REFERENCES

Hayes, J. R. (2012). Modeling and remodeling writing. *Written Communication*, 29(3), 369–388. doi: 10.1177/0741088312451260

McCarthy, J. E., Grabill, J. T., Hart-Davidson, W., & McLeod, M. (2011). Content management in the workplace: Community, context, and a new way to organize writing. *Journal of Business and Technical Communication*, 25(4), 367–395. doi: 10.1177/1050651911410943

Schriver, K. A. (2012). What we know about expertise in professional communication. In V. W. Berninger (Ed.), *Past, present, and future contributions of cognitive writing research to cognitive psychology* (pp. 275–312). New York, NY: Psychology Press.

Slattery, S. (2007). Undistributing work through writing: How technical writers manage texts in complex information environments. *Technical Communication Quarterly*, 16(3), 311–325. doi: 10.1080/10572250701291046

Solé, I., Miras, M., Castells, N., Espino, S., & Minguela, M. (2013). Integrating information: An analysis of the processes involved and the products generated in a written synthesis task. *Written Communication*, 30(1), 63–90. doi: 10.1177/0741088312466532

Spivey, N. N., & King, J. R. (1989). Readers as writers composing from sources. *Reading Research Quarterly*, 24(1), 7–26.

Swarts, J. (2010). Recycled writing: Assembling actor networks from reusable content. *Journal of Business and Technical Communication*, 24(2), 127–163.

Turkle, S. (1997). *Life on the screen: Identity in the age of the Internet.* New York, NY: Simon & Schuster. 15–29.

QUESTIONS

1. How does what you've learned in this research article change your perception of what business communication is or is not?

2. How might what you've learned in this article be useful in changing your own school or workplace communication?

3. Come up with pro and con arguments for the following debate/discussion topic: In the digital age of communication, the writing process is less about starting from scratch and more about mashing-up various existing documents into a new message. How does Leijten et al.'s research help you support your point?

vm/istock by Getty Images

PLANNING YOUR MESSAGE

BIZ COMM BYTE

According to Carleton University Professor Linda Duxbury, people now spend one third of their time at the office—and half of the time they work at home—reading and answering emails.

Source: Dubé, D.-E. (2017, April 21). This is how much time you spend on work emails every day, according to a Canadian survey. *Global News.* https://globalnews.ca/news/3395457/this-is-how-much-time-you-spend-on-work-emails-every-day-according-to-a-canadian-survey/

OBJECTIVES

2.1 Explain the steps in the communication process.

2.2 Recognize the goals and process of business writing.

2.3 Know the purpose of a message, anticipate its audience, and select the best communication channel for it.

2.4 Incorporate audience adaptation techniques.

2.5 Use additional expert writing techniques.

2.1 Understanding the Communication Process

The digital revolution has profoundly changed the way we live our lives, do business, and communicate, as the Biz Comm Byte box shows. People are sending more and more messages, and they are using new media as the world becomes increasingly interconnected. However, even as we become accustomed to new channels, the nature of communication remains largely unchanged. No matter how we create or send our messages, the communication process remains a human process of interaction, in which an idea is shared and reacted to.

In its simplest form, *communication* can be defined as "the transmission of information and meaning from a sender to a receiver." The crucial element in this definition is *meaning*. The process is successful once the receiver understands an idea as the sender intended it. The process is shown as a diagram in Figure 2.1, but keep in mind that what the diagram doesn't show is that at each stage of the process, *noise* such as distraction, boredom, or frustration can get in the way and cause miscommunication.

The Communication Process

1 Sender has idea	**2** Sender encodes message	**3** Sender selects channel, transmits message	**4** Receiver decodes message	**5** Feedback returns to sender

To communicate effectively:

Sender should	**Sender should**	**Sender should**	**Receiver should**	**Receiver should**
• Clarify idea	• Consider receiver's background, communication skills, experience, culture, context	• Consider importance of message, feedback required, interactivity	• Avoid prejudging message	• Craft clear and complete response that reveals comprehension of message meaning
• Decide on purpose of message	• Choose concrete words and appropriate symbols	• Choose a channel that the receiver prefers	• Strive to understand both verbal and nonverbal cues	• Begin the cycle again when the receiver becomes the sender with the same concerns
• Analyze idea and how it can best be presented	• Encourage feedback	• Think of ways to reduce channel noise and distractions	• Ignore distractions	
• Anticipate effect on receiver		• Be aware of competing messages	• Create receptive environment	
			• Expect to learn	

© Cengage Learning

2.1a Sender Has Idea

The communication process begins when a sender has an idea, like a request or something to share. The form of the idea may be influenced by complex factors surrounding the sender. These factors may include mood, frame of reference, background, culture, and physical makeup, as well as the context of the situation and many other factors.

2.1b Sender Encodes Idea

The next step in the process is *encoding*, which means converting the idea into words or gestures to convey meaning. Mostly this is done through words, though sometimes it's done through images, gestures, and body language. Recognizing how easy it is to be misunderstood, skilled communicators choose familiar, concrete words. In choosing the right words and symbols, senders must be alert to the receiver's communication skills, attitudes, background, experiences, and culture. Including a smiley face in an email to shareholders may turn them off.

2.1c Sender Selects Channel and Transmits Message

The medium over which the message travels is the *channel*. Messages may be delivered by email, text, smartphone, letter, memo, report, announcement, image, conversation, fax, Web page, or some other channel. Today's messages are increasingly carried over digital networks. Receivers may be overloaded with incoming messages or unable to receive messages clearly on their devices. Anything that interrupts the transmission of a message in the communication process is called *noise*. Channel noise ranges from a weak Wi-Fi signal to sloppy formatting and typos in emails. Noise may even include the annoyance a receiver feels when the sender chooses an improper channel for transmission or when the receiver is overloaded with messages and information.

2.1d Receiver Decodes Message

The individual for whom the sender's message is intended is the *receiver*. Decoding takes place when the receiver reads or listens to—that is, internalizes—the sender's message. Only when the receiver understands the meaning intended by the sender—that is, successfully decodes the message—does communication take place. Such success is often difficult to achieve because of a number of barriers that block the process.

2.1e Feedback Returns to Sender

The receiver usually creates *feedback*, a vital part of the communication process. Sometimes lack of feedback—that is, ignoring a message—is its own type of feedback (though not a productive type). Feedback helps the sender know that the message was received and understood. Senders can encourage feedback by asking questions such as *Am I making myself clear?* and *Is there anything you don't understand?* Senders can further improve feedback by timing the delivery appropriately and by providing only as much information as the receiver can handle. Receivers improve the communication process by providing clear and complete feedback. In the business world, one of the best ways to advance understanding is to paraphrase the sender's message with comments such as *Just to confirm what you're requesting* . . . .

The communication process theorized here is sometimes known as the "transmission model."[1] While the transmission model does a good job explaining communication, it also has shortcomings as described by later communication theorists like Marshall McLuhan.

McLuhan claims that meaning isn't transmitted only in a linear way, as the earlier model would have it, but is instead transmitted in a "field" in which multiple inputs, such as the channel itself, or nonverbal gestures help create meaning.[2] For example, the instantaneous speed of texting could be seen as eliminating the decoding step—receivers tend to respond to texts instantly.

◤ 2.2 Using the 3-×-3 Writing Process as a Guide

Today's technologies enable you to choose from many communication channels to create, transmit, and respond to messages. Nearly all business communication, however, involves thinking and writing.

Many of your workplace messages will be digital. A *digital message* is "one that is generated, stored, processed, and transmitted electronically by computers using strings of positive and nonpositive binary code." That definition encompasses many forms, including email, Facebook posts, tweets, and other messages. We will focus primarily on messages exchanged on the job. Because writing is central to all business communication, this chapter presents a systematic plan for preparing written business messages.

2.2a Defining Business Writing Goals

A recent Canadian Management Centre/Ipsos Reid study conducted among Canadian employees indicates that "only 42 percent of Canadian employees . . . agree that change is communicated well in their workplace." The study concludes by stating that managers must recognize "building an engaged workforce relies heavily on leadership behaviour and communication."[3] Behind the study's findings lies a sometimes-unacknowledged reality about communication: it's not just *what* you want to say that's important; it's also *how* your audience will react upon seeing, reading, or hearing your communication. In other words, all workplace communicators need to think about their audience.

One thing you should immediately recognize about business writing is that it differs from other writing. Business writing is different from high-school writing; it also differs from personal texts you may exchange with your friends and family. These messages enable you to stay connected and express your feelings. In the workplace, however, you will want your writing to have the following characteristics:

- **Purposeful.** Write only to solve problems and convey information.
- **Economical.** Present ideas clearly but concisely; length is not rewarded.
- **Audience oriented.** Solve problems and convey information with the receiver's perspective—not your own—in mind.

Keeping these characteristics top of mind makes your work life easier. Whether you are presenting your message in an email, in a report, or in a podcast, conciseness, clarity, and the audience are what count in business.

The ability to prepare purposeful, concise, and audience-centred messages doesn't come naturally. Very few people, especially beginners, can sit down and compose an effective email, letter, or report without training. However, following a systematic process, studying model messages, and practising the craft can make you a successful business writer or speaker.

2.2b Introducing the 3-×-3 Writing Process

Regardless of what you write, the process will be easier if you follow a systematic plan. The 3-×-3 writing process breaks the entire task into three phases: *prewriting*, *drafting*, and *revising*, as shown in Figure 2.2.

To illustrate the writing process, let's say that you own a successful local Tim Hortons franchise. At rush times, you face a problem. Customers complain about the chaotic multiple waiting lines to approach the service counter. You once saw two customers nearly get into a fight over cutting into a line. What's more, customers often are looking for ways to improve their positions in line and fail to examine the menu. Then they are undecided when their turn arrives. You've also taken note of McDonald's move into self-ordering via touch screen. You want to convince other franchise owners that a single-line system with touch screens would work better. To present a serious argument that they will remember and be willing to act on when they gather for their next district meeting, you decide to send a persuasive email.

PREWRITING. The first phase of the writing process involves analyzing the audience and your purpose for writing. The audience for your message will be other franchise owners. Your purpose in writing is to convince them that a change in policy would improve customer service. You think that a single-line system, such as that used in banks, would reduce chaos and make customers happier because they would not have to worry about where they are in line.

Prewriting also involves *anticipating* how your audience will react to your message. You're sure that some of the other owners will agree with you, but others might fear that customers seeing a long single line might go elsewhere. In *adapting* your message to the audience, you try to think of the right words and tone that will win over the skeptics.

DRAFTING. The second phase of writing involves researching, organizing, and then drafting the message. In *researching* information for this message, you would probably investigate other kinds of businesses that use single lines for customers. You can research how successful your competitors have been with their touch-screen ordering. You can call to see whether other franchise owners are concerned about chaotic lines. Before writing to the entire group, you can brainstorm with a few owners to see what ideas they have for solving the problem.

1 Prewriting

Analyze

- What is your purpose?
- What do you want the receiver to do or believe?
- What channel should you choose: face-to-face conversation, group meeting, email, memo, letter, report, blog, wiki, tweet, etc.

Anticipate

- Profile the audience.
- What does the receiver already know?
- Will the receiver's response be neutral, positive, or negative? How will this affect your organizational strategy?

Adapt

- What techniques can you use to adapt your message to its audience?
- How can you promote feedback?
- Strive to use positive, conversational, and courteous language.

2 Drafting

Research

- Gather data to provide facts.
- Search company files, previous correspondence, and the Internet.
- What do you need to know to write this message?
- How much does the audience already know?

Organize

- Organize direct messages with the big idea first, followed by an explanation in the body and an action request in the closing.
- For persuasive or negative messages, use an indirect, problem-solving strategy.

Draft

- Prepare a first draft, usually quickly.
- Focus on short, clear sentences using the active voice.
- Build paragraph coherence by repeating key ideas, using pronouns, and incorporating appropriate transitional expressions.

3 Revising

Edit

- Edit your message to be sure it is clear, concise, conversational, readable.
- Revise to eliminate wordy fillers, long lead-ins, redundancies, and trite business phrases.
- Develop parallelism.
- Consider using headings and numbered and bulleted lists for quick reading.

Proofread

- Take the time to read every message carefully.
- Look for errors in spelling, grammar, punctuation, names, and numbers.
- Check to be sure the format is consistent.

Evaluate

- Will this message achieve your purpose?
- Does the tone sound pleasant and friendly rather than curt?
- Have you thought enough about the audience to be sure this message is appealing?
- Did you encourage feedback?

After you've collected enough information, focus on *organizing* your message. As Leijten et al. show in the unit-opening article, in today's workplace, complex messages like proposals and reports often begin as pieces of earlier-produced messages or as models of such documents found online that are then organized into a new, audience-appropriate document. The final step in this phase of the writing process would be actually drafting the document to fellow Tim Hortons franchisees. Should it be an email or an email with an attachment? Is the attachment a report or proposal? Or is it an infographic? At this point many writers draft quickly, realizing that they will polish their document in the next phase, when they revise.

REVISING. The third phase of the process involves editing, proofreading, and evaluating your message. After writing the first draft, you should spend time *editing* the message for clarity, conciseness, tone, and readability. Could parts of it be rearranged to make your point more effectively? This is when you look for ways to improve the organization and tone of your message. Next you should spend time *proofreading* to ensure correct spelling, grammar, punctuation, and format. The final step is *evaluating* to decide whether the message accomplishes your goal. Will your fellow franchisees see things the way you want them to? Only now should you press Send!

2.3 Analyzing and Anticipating the Audience

If you analyze your purpose *before* you begin to write, you can avoid backtracking and starting over. The remainder of this chapter covers Phase 1 of the writing process: knowing the purpose for writing, anticipating how the audience will react, and adapting the message to the audience.

2.3a Know Your Purpose

As you plan a workplace message, ask yourself two important questions: (a) Why am I sending this message? and (b) What do I hope to achieve? Your responses will determine how you organize and present your information.

Your message may have primary and secondary purposes. The primary purposes for sending business messages are typically to inform, request, and persuade. A secondary purpose is to promote goodwill.

Many business messages simply *inform*. They explain procedures, announce meetings, answer questions, and transmit findings. Other business messages are meant to *persuade*. These messages sell products, convince managers, motivate employees, and win over customers. Still other messages are requests: for information, help, or a donation.

2.3b Anticipate and Profile the Audience

A good writer anticipates the audience for a message: What is the reader or listener like? How will that person react to the message? Although we can't always know exactly who the receiver is, it is possible to imagine some of that person's characteristics. For example, a copywriter at Hudson's Bay Company may picture his sister-in-law whenever he writes product descriptions for the website. The questions in Figure 2.3 will help you to profile your audience.

How much time you devote to answering these questions depends on your message and its context. A report that you write for management or an oral presentation that you deliver to a big group will demand considerable audience anticipation. An email to a coworker or a text to a familiar supplier might require only a few moments of planning. That said, both types of message, after they've been published, attract the same type of risk: that something insensitive, belligerent, misleading, or

> **FIGURE 2.3 /** Asking the Right Questions to Profile Your Audience

Primary Audience	**Secondary Audience**
• Who is my primary reader or listener?	• Who might see or hear this message in addition to the primary audience?
• What are my personal and professional relationships with this person?	• How do these people differ from the primary audience?
• What position does this person hold in the organization?	• Do I need to include more background information?
• How much does this person know about the subject?	• How must I reshape my message to make it understandable and acceptable to others to whom it might be forwarded?
• What do I know about this person's education, beliefs, culture, and attitudes?	• What risk is involved in saying what I'm about to say?
• Should I expect a neutral, positive, or negative response to my message?	

politically incorrect might become known by the outside world and perhaps embarrass or cost your company.

No matter how routine or seemingly inconsequential your message, spend some time thinking about the audience so that you can tailor your words to your readers. Remember that they will be thinking *What's in it for me (WIIFM)?* One of the most important writing tips you can take away from this book is to recognize that every message you write should begin with the notion that your audience is thinking WIIFM. Another important tip is to realize that the audience for anything you write, because of the Forward and Copy (cc) functions available with digital messages, is potentially much larger than you think (and perhaps less forgiving than your coworkers)—keep all audiences in mind, not just internal ones, when you write.

2.3c Make Choices Based on Your Audience Profile

Profiling your audience helps you make decisions about shaping the message. You'll figure out what language is appropriate, whether you can use specialized technical terms, and whether you should explain the background. Profiling the audience helps you decide whether your tone should be formal or informal and whether the receiver will feel neutral, positive, or negative about your message.

Another advantage of profiling your audience is the possibility of a secondary audience. Let's say you start to write an email to your supervisor, Sheila, describing a problem you are having. Halfway through the message you realize that Sheila will probably forward this message to her boss, the vice president. Sheila will not want to summarize what you said; instead she will take the easy route and forward your email.

When you realize that the vice president may see this message, you decide to use a more formal tone, remove your inquiry about Sheila's family, reduce your complaints, and tone down your language about why things went wrong. Instead, you provide more background information, and are more specific in explaining issues with which the vice president is unfamiliar.

2.3d Select the Best Channel

After identifying the purpose of your message, you'll want to select the most appropriate communication channel. In the digital age, the number of channels continues to expand, as shown in Figure 2.4. Whether to send an email, schedule a videoconference, or have a face-to-face conversation or group meeting depends on some of the following factors:

- Importance of the message
- Amount and speed of feedback and interactivity required
- Necessity of a permanent record
- Cost of the channel
- Degree of formality desired
- Confidentiality and sensitivity of the message
- Receiver's preference and level of technical expertise.

You'll also want to consider how *rich* the channel is. The *richness* of a channel involves the extent to which it conveys all the information available in the original message. A richer channel, such as a face-to-face conversation, permits more interactivity and feedback. A leaner channel, such as a letter or an email, presents a flat, one-dimensional message. Richer channels enable the sender to provide more verbal and visual cues (e.g., facial gestures), whereas lean messages use substitutes such as emoji to help fill this gap.

Choosing the wrong medium can result in the message being less effective or even misunderstood. A marketing manager must motivate her sales force to increase sales in the fourth quarter and is unlikely to achieve her goal if she merely posts an announcement on the office bulletin board, writes a memo, or sends an email. She could be more persuasive with a richer channel, such as individual

Cengage

MINDTAP

In MindTap, go to the Chapter 2 reading, section 2.3c, and watch the video of industry expert Mike Stiers discussing the importance of planning your business messages.

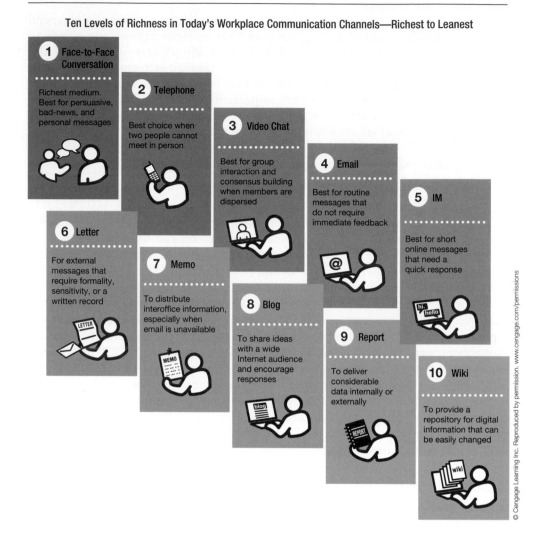

Ten Levels of Richness in Today's Workplace Communication Channels—Richest to Leanest

1 Face-to-Face Conversation

Richest medium. Best for persuasive, bad-news, and personal messages

2 Telephone

Best choice when two people cannot meet in person

3 Video Chat

Best for group interaction and consensus building when members are dispersed

4 Email

Best for routine messages that do not require immediate feedback

5 IM

Best for short online messages that need a quick response

6 Letter

For external messages that require formality, sensitivity, or a written record

7 Memo

To distribute interoffice information, especially when email is unavailable

8 Blog

To share ideas with a wide Internet audience and encourage responses

9 Report

To deliver considerable data internally or externally

10 Wiki

To provide a repository for digital information that can be easily changed

© Cengage Learning Inc. Reproduced by permission. www.cengage.com/permissions

face-to-face conversations or a group video meeting to stimulate sales. Keep in mind the following tips for choosing a communication channel:

- Use the richest channel available.
- Employ richer channels for more persuasive or personal communications.

◤ 2.4 Adapt to Your Audience With Expert Writing Techniques

As part of the Prewriting process, after you've analyzed the purpose and anticipated the audience, you'll begin to think about how to adapt your message to the task and the audience. Adaptation is the process of creating messages that suit and motivate the audience. You'll sometimes hear the process called *framing*. Expert writers employ a number of adaptation or framing techniques such as spotlighting audience benefits, cultivating a "you" view, and sounding conversational but professional.

2.4a Spotlight Audience Benefits

Adapting your messages to the receiver's needs means putting yourself in that person's shoes. It's a skill known as *empathy*. Empathic senders think about how a

WORKPLACE IN FOCUS

A lot has been said about the need to market differently to the Millennial generation—young people born near to or just after the year 2000. Apparently, old-fashioned advertising on billboards, in flyers, and on TV and radio doesn't quite cut it with this generation. In fact, as Jenny Cahill-Jones shows, numerous Canadian companies are embracing what's known as "omnichannel" or "multiple touchpoint marketing." As you may have guessed, this new type of marketing is about meeting the consumer (i.e., adapting to the audience) in numerous places and ways and many times to lead to more frequent purchases and higher profitability. A good example is well-known Montréal-based retailer David's Teas. Besides in its small number of traditional retail locations, the brand meets its customers online, on social media channels, through subscriber emails, and with promotions— importantly, all to drive traffic back to the retail locations (e.g., by ensuring that online promotions must be redeemed in person, in-store). In addition, David's Teas holds contests and shares its Teas of the Week across its social media channels, once again driving customers back to its stores. *Why might organizations use multiple communication channels to send messages to customers? As a customer, how do you like to be engaged by brands, retailers, and other organizations? Is there something about omnichannel marketing that you would critique?*

Source: Cahill Jones, J. (2018, March 8). True North: 3 Omnichannel Success Stories in Canada. Sweet IQ. Retrieved from https://sweetiq.com/blog/omnichannel-retail-strategy/

receiver will decode a message. They always try to give something to the receiver, solve the receiver's problems, save the receiver time or money, or just understand the feelings and position of that person. Such communicators are experts because they realize that by writing in this way (i.e., thinking about the receiver), they are more likely to have that person on their side in future, which is invaluable in business.

Which version of each of the following messages is more appealing to the audience as a result of focusing on audience benefits?

DON'T Sender Focus	DO✓ Audience Focus
✗ All employees are instructed herewith to fill out the enclosed questionnaire so that we can allocate our training funds to employees.	✓ By filling out the enclosed questionnaire, you can be one of the first employees to sign up for our training funds.
✗ Our warranty becomes effective only when we receive an owner's registration.	✓ Your warranty begins working for you as soon as you return your owner's registration.

2.4b Use the "You" View

By concentrating on audience benefits, skilled communicators naturally develop a habit known as the "you" view. They emphasize second-person pronouns (*you, your*) instead of first-person pronouns (*I, we, us, our*). Whether the goal is to inform, request, persuade, or promote goodwill, the catchiest words you can use are *you* and *your*, because they signal that you have your receiver's needs uppermost in your mind.

Compare the following examples:

DON'T "I/We" View	DO "You" View
✗ We are requiring all employees to respond to the attached survey about health benefits.	✓ Because your ideas count, please complete the attached survey about health benefits.
✗ I need your account number before I can do anything.	✓ Please send me your account number so that I can locate your records and help you solve this problem.

Focusing on the reader or listener is important, but don't overuse or misuse the second-person pronoun *you*. The authors of some sales messages, for example, are guilty of overkill when they include *you* dozens of times in a direct-mail promotion. What's more, the word can sometimes create the wrong impression. Consider this statement: *You cannot return merchandise until you receive manager approval.* The word *you* appears twice, but the reader may feel singled out for criticism. In the improved version, the message is less personal and more positive: *Customers can return merchandise with management approval.*

Another difficulty in emphasizing the "you" view and de-emphasizing *we/I* is that it may result in overuse of the passive voice. For example, to avoid writing *We will give you* (active voice), you might write *You will be given* (passive voice). The active voice is generally preferred because it identifies who is doing the acting. You'll learn more about active and passive voice in Chapter 3.

While recognizing the value of the "you" view, don't sterilize your writing and totally avoid any first-person pronouns or words that show your feelings. Don't be afraid of phrases such as *I'm happy* or *We're delighted* if you truly are. When speaking face to face, you can show sincerity and warmth with nonverbal cues such as a smile and a pleasant tone. In letters, emails, and texts, however, only expressive words (e.g., *amazing*) and phrases (e.g., *Great work!*) can show your feelings. These phrases suggest hidden messages that say, *You are important, I hear you*, and *I'm honestly trying to please you*.

2.4c Sound Conversational but Professional

Business messages are most effective when they convey an informal, conversational tone instead of a formal, stuffy tone. Just how informal you can be depends greatly on the workplace. At Google, casual seems to be preferred. In a short message to users describing changes in its privacy policies, Google recently wrote, "We believe this stuff matters."[4]

In more traditional organizations, that message probably would have been more formal. The dilemma, then, is in knowing how casual to be in your writing. We suggest that you strive to be conversational but professional, especially until you learn what your organization prefers.

Email, texting, Twitter, and other short messaging channels enable you and your coworkers to have spontaneous conversations. Don't, however, let your messages become sloppy, unprofessional, or even dangerous.

To project a professional image, you want to sound educated and mature. Overuse of expressions such as *totally awesome, you know, and like*, as well as a

Unprofessional (Low-level diction)	Conversational (Middle-level diction)	Formal (High-level diction)
badmouth	criticize	denigrate
guts	nerve	courage
pecking order	line of command	dominance hierarchy
ticked off	upset	provoked
rat on	inform	betray
rip off	steal	expropriate
If we just hang in there, we'll snag the contract.	If we don't get discouraged, we'll win the contract.	If the principals persevere, they will secure the contract.

© Cengage Learning

reliance on unnecessary abbreviations (BTW for *by the way*), make a businessperson sound like a teenager. Professional messages do not include texting abbreviations, slang, sentence fragments, and chit-chat. Strive for a warm, conversational tone that avoids low-level diction. Levels of diction, as shown in Figure 2.5, range from unprofessional to formal:

DON'T Unprofessional	DO✓ Professional
✗ Hey, boss, Gr8 news! Firewall now installed!! BTW, check with me b4 announcing it.	✓ Mr. Smith, our new firewall software is now installed. Please check with me before announcing it.
✗ Look, dude, this report is totally bogus. And the figures don't look kosher. Show me some real stats. Got sources?	✓ Because the figures in this report seem inaccurate, please submit the source statistics.

DON'T Overly Formal	DO✓ Conversational
✗ All employees are herewith instructed to return the appropriately designated contracts to the undersigned.	✓ Please return your contracts to me.
✗ Pertaining to your order, we must verify the sizes that your organization requires prior to consignment of your order to our shipper.	✓ We will send your order as soon as we confirm the sizes you need.

◤ 2.5 Adapt to Your Audience With Additional Expert Writing Techniques

As you improve your business writing skills, you can start integrating expert techniques that improve the clarity, tone, and effectiveness (i.e., motivational ability) of a message. These adaptation and framing techniques include using a positive and courteous tone, bias-free language, simple expression, and precise words. Look at Figure 2.6 to see how a writer can improve an email by applying numerous expert writing techniques.

DRAFT

Untitled - Message (HTML)

Insert   Options   Format Text   Review   Help   Acrobat   ⓠ Tell me what you want to do

en Sans   ⌄   12   ⌄   **B**   *I*   U̲   ✎ ⌄   A̲   ⌄   ⋯   ⁐ ⌄   ✉ ⌄   🏳 ⌄   🖳 ⌄   ⋯

To   All BioTech Team Members

Cc

Subject   Company Needs to Reduce Employee Driving Trips to Office ●————— Negative-sounding subject line

Focuses on sender rather than presenting ideas with audience benefits ●———→ Our company faces harsh governmental penalties if we fail to comply with the Air Quality Management District's program to reduce the number of automobile trips made by employees.

The aforementioned program stipulates that we offer incentives to entice employees to discontinue driving their vehicles as a means of transportation to and from this place of employment. ●————— Uses unfamiliar words (*aforementioned, stipulates, entice*)

Presents ideas negatively (*penalty, must not drive, will not be limited, will not be forced*) and assumes driver will be male ●———→ First, we are prepared to offer a full day off without penalty. However, the employee must not drive to work and must maintain a 75 percent vanpool participation rate for six months. Second, we offer a vanpool subsidy of $100 a month, and the vanpool driver will not be limited in the personal use he makes of the vehicle on his own time. Third, employees in the vanpool will not be forced to park in outlying lots.

Doesn't use plain English or conversational tone (*pertaining to, herewith, facilitating, above-referenced*)

Pertaining to our need to have you leave your cars at home, all employees are herewith instructed to communicate with Saul Salazar, who will be facilitating the above-referenced program. ●

REVISION

Untitled - Message (HTML)

Insert   Options   Format Text   Review   Help   Acrobat   ⓠ Tell me what you want to do

en Sans   ⌄   12   ⌄   **B**   *I*   U̲   ✎ ⌄   A̲   ⌄   ⋯   ⁐ ⌄   ✉ ⌄   🏳 ⌄   🖳 ⌄   ⋯

To   All BioTech Team Members

Cc

Subject   Great Perks for Driving Less

Positive-sounding subject line ●

Hi, Team,

Opens with "you" view and audience benefits ●———→ Want to earn a full day off with pay, reduce the stress of your commute, and pay a lot less for gas? You can enjoy these and other perks if you make fewer driving trips to the office.

As part of the Air Quality Management District's Trip Reduction Plan, you can enjoy the following benefits by reducing the number of trips you make to work:

Phrases option in bulleted list with "you" view highlighting benefits (*day off, less driving stress, lower gas bill*) ●———→ **Full Day Off.** If you maintain a 75 percent participation rate in our ride-share program for a six-month period, you will receive one day off with pay.

Vanpool Subsidy. By joining a vanpool, you will receive assistance in obtaining a van along with a monthly $100 subsidy. Even better, if you become a vanpool driver, you will also have unlimited personal use of the vehicle off company time.

●———→ **Preferential Parking.** By coming to work in vanpools, you can park close to the building in reserved spaces.

Repeats audience benefits with conversational tone and familiar words ●———→ Why not help the environment, reduce your gas bill, and enjoy other perks by joining this program? For more information and to sign up, please contact Saul Salazar at ssctlazar@biotech.com before February 1.

Chris

Christina Watkins
Senior Coordinator, Human Resources
cwatkins@biotech.ca
(902) 349-5871

2.5a Be Positive Rather Than Negative

One of the best ways to improve the tone of a message is to use positive rather than negative language. Positive language conveys more information than negative language does. And positive messages are uplifting and pleasant to read. Positive wording tells what *is* and what *can be done* rather than what *isn't* and what *can't be done*. For example, *Your order cannot be shipped by January 10* is not nearly as informative as *Your order will be shipped January 15*. An office supply store adjacent to an ice cream parlour posted a sign on its door that reads: *Please enjoy your ice cream before you enjoy our store*. That sounds much more positive and inviting than *No food allowed!*[5]

Some words appear to blame or accuse your audience. For example, opening a letter to a customer with *You claim that* suggests that you don't believe the customer. Other loaded words that can get you in trouble are *complaint, criticism, defective, failed, mistake,* and *neglected*. Also avoid phrases such as *you are apparently unaware of* or *you did not provide* or *you misunderstood* or *you don't understand*. You may be unaware of the effect of these words. Notice in the following examples how you can revise the negative tone to create a more positive impression.

DON'T Negative	DO✓ Positive
✗ This plan definitely cannot succeed if we don't obtain management approval.	✓ This plan definitely can succeed if we obtain management approval.
✗ You failed to include your credit card number, so we can't mail your order.	✓ We look forward to completing your order as soon as we receive your credit card number.

2.5b Express Courtesy

A courteous tone involves avoiding rudeness, as well as any language that sounds demanding or preachy. Expressions such as *you should, you must,* and *you have to* cause people to instinctively react with *Oh, yeah?*

Even if you feel justified in displaying anger, remember that losing your temper or being sarcastic seldom accomplishes your goals as a business communicator: to inform, request, persuade, and create goodwill. When you're irritated, frustrated, or infuriated, keep cool and try to defuse the situation. In telephone conversations with customers, use polite phrases such as *I would be happy to assist you with that, Thank you for being so patient,* and *It was a pleasure speaking with you.*

DON'T Less Courteous	DO✓ More Courteous and Helpful
✗ Can't you people get anything right? This is the second time I've written!	✓ Please credit my account for $340. My latest statement shows that the error noted in my letter of May 15 has not yet been corrected.
✗ Sohil, you must complete all performance reviews by Friday.	✓ Stewart, will you please complete all performance reviews by Friday?

2.5c Employ Bias-Free Language

In adapting a message to its audience, be sure your language is sensitive and bias-free. Sometimes we say things that we didn't know could be hurtful. The problem is that we don't always think about the words that stereotype groups of people, such as *the boys in the mailroom* or *the girls in the front office*. Be cautious about expressions that might be biased in terms of gender, race, ethnicity, age, sexuality, and disability.

Generally, you can avoid gender-biased language by choosing alternative language for words involving *man* or *woman*, by using plural nouns and pronouns, or by changing to a gender-free word (*person* or *representative*). Avoid the *his or her* option whenever possible. It's wordy and conspicuous.

Specify age only if it is relevant, and to avoid disability bias, don't refer to an individual's disability unless it is relevant. The following examples give you a quick look at a few problem expressions and possible replacements. The real key to bias-free communication, though, lies in your awareness and commitment. Be on the lookout to be sure that your messages do not exclude, stereotype, or offend people.

DON'T Gender Biased	DO Bias Free
✘ female doctor, woman attorney, cleaning woman	✔ doctor, attorney, cleaner
✘ waiter/waitress, authoress, stewardess	✔ server, author, flight attendant
✘ mankind, man-hour, man-made	✔ humanity, working hours, artificial
✘ office girls	✔ office workers
✘ the doctor . . . he	✔ doctors . . . they
✘ the teacher . . . she	✔ teachers . . . they
✘ executives and their wives	✔ executives and their spouses [or partners]
✘ foreman, flagman, workman, craftsman	✔ lead worker, flagger, worker, artisan
✘ businessman, salesman	✔ businessperson, sales representative

DON'T Racially or Ethnically Biased	DO Bias Free
✘ An Indian accountant was hired.	✔ An accountant was hired.
✘ Jim Nolan, an African Canadian, applied.	✔ Jim Nolan applied.

DON'T Age Biased	DO Bias Free
✘ The law applied to old people.	✔ The law applied to people over 65.
✘ Sally Kay, 55, was transferred.	✔ Sally Kay was transferred.
✘ a sprightly old gentleman	✔ a man
✘ a little old lady	✔ a woman

DON'T	Disability Biased	DO✓	Bias Free
✗	afflicted with arthritis, crippled by arthritis	✓	has arthritis
✗	confined to a wheelchair	✓	uses a wheelchair

2.5d Choose Plain Language and Familiar Words

In adapting your message to your audience, use plain language and familiar words that audience members will recognize. Don't, however, avoid a big word that conveys your idea efficiently and is appropriate for the audience. Your goal is to shun pompous and pretentious language. If you mean *begin*, don't say *commence* or *initiate*. If you mean *pay*, don't write *compensate*. By substituting everyday, familiar words for unfamiliar ones, as shown here, you help your audience comprehend your ideas quickly.

DON'T	Unfamiliar	DO✓	Familiar
✗	commensurate	✓	equal
✗	interrogate	✓	question
✗	materialize	✓	appear
✗	obfuscate	✓	confuse
✗	remuneration	✓	pay, salary
✗	terminate	✓	end

At the same time, be selective in your use of jargon. *Jargon* is a technical or specialized term within a field. These terms enable insiders to communicate complex ideas briefly, but to outsiders they mean nothing. Human resources professionals, for example, know precisely what's meant by *cafeteria plan* (a benefits option program), but most of us would be thinking about lunch. Marketers refer to *gated content*, and managers talk about *gaining traction*. These terms mean little to most of us. Use specialized language only when the audience will understand it. In addition, don't forget to consider secondary audiences: Will those potential receivers understand any technical terms used?

2.5e Use Precise, Vigorous Words

Strong verbs and concrete nouns give receivers more information and keep them interested. Don't overlook the thesaurus for expanding your word choices and vocabulary. Whenever possible, use precise, specific words, as shown here:

DON'T	Imprecise, Dull	DO✓	More Precise
✗	a change in profits	✓	a 25 percent hike in profits a 10 percent plunge in profits
✗	to say	✓	to promise, confess, understand to allege, assert, assume, judge
✗	to think about	✓	to identify, diagnose, analyze to probe, examine, inspect

Cengage

MINDTAP

In MindTap go to the Study Tools for Chapter 2 and complete the Practice Test.

LEARNING SUMMARY

2.1 Explain the steps in the communication process.

- A sender encodes (selects) words or symbols to express an idea in a message.
- The message travels over a channel (such as email, website, tweet, letter, or smartphone call).
- *Noise* (loud sounds, misspelled words, other distractions) may interfere with the transmission.
- The receiver decodes (interprets) the message and responds with feedback.

2.2 Recognize the goals and process of business writing.

- Business writing should be purposeful, economical, and audience oriented.
- The 3-×-3 writing process helps writers create efficient and effective messages.
- Phase 1 (prewriting): analyze the message, anticipate the audience, and consider how to adapt the message to the audience.
- Phase 2 (drafting): research the topic, organize the material, and draft the message.
- Phase 3 (revising): edit, proofread, and evaluate the message.

2.3 Know the purpose of a message, anticipate its audience, and select the best communication channel for it.

- Before composing, decide what you hope to achieve.
- Select the appropriate channel to inform, persuade, or convey goodwill.
- After identifying the purpose, visualize both the primary and the secondary audiences.

- Remember that receivers will usually be thinking, *What's in it for me (WIIFM)?*
- Select the best channel by considering (a) the importance of the message, (b) the amount and speed of feedback required, (c) the necessity of a permanent record, (d) the cost of the channel, (e) the degree of formality desired, (f) the confidentiality and sensitivity of the message, and (g) the receiver's preference and level of technical expertise.

2.4 Incorporate audience adaptation techniques.

- Look for ways to shape the message from the receiver's view rather than the sender's.
- Apply the "you" view without attempting to manipulate.
- Use conversational but professional language.

2.5 Use additional expert writing techniques.

- Use positive language that tells what can be done rather than what can't be done (The project will be successful with your support rather than The project won't be successful without your support).
- Be courteous rather than rude, preachy, or demanding.
- Provide reasons for a request to soften the tone of a message.
- Avoid biased language that excludes, stereotypes, or offends people (*lady lawyer, spry old gentleman, confined to a wheelchair*).
- Strive for plain language (*equal* instead of *commensurate*), familiar terms (*end* instead of *terminate*), and precise words (*analyze* instead of *think about*).

CHAPTER REVIEW

1. Define *communication*. When is it successful? (Obj. 1)
2. List the five steps in the communication process. (Obj. 1)
3. In what ways is business writing different from high-school writing and private messages? (Obj. 2)
4. Describe the components in each stage of the 3-×-3 writing process. (Obj. 2)
5. What does *WIIFM* mean? Why is it important to business writers? (Obj. 3)
6. What seven factors should writers consider in selecting an appropriate channel to deliver a message? (Obj. 3)
7. What is the "you" view? When can the use of the pronoun *you* backfire? (Obj. 4)
8. How can a business writer sound conversational but also be professional? (Obj. 4)
9. Why is positive wording more effective in business messages than negative wording? (Obj. 5)
10. What are three ways to avoid biased language? Give an original example of each. (Obj. 5)

CRITICAL THINKING

1. Have digital channels changed the nature of communication? (Obj. 1)

2. Why do you think employers prefer messages that are not written like high-school writing? (Obj. 2)

3. Why should business writers strive to use short, familiar, simple words? Does this oversimplify business messages? (Obj. 5)

4. A wise observer once said that bad writing makes smart people look less intelligent. Do you agree or disagree, and why? (Objs. 1–5)

5. In a letter to the editor, a teacher criticized a newspaper article on autism because it used the term *autistic child* rather than *child with autism*. She championed *people-first* terminology, which avoids defining individuals by their ability or disability.[6] For example, instead of identifying someone as a *disabled person*, one would say, *she has a disability*. What does *people-first language* mean? How can language change perceptions? (Obj. 5)

ACTIVITIES AND CASES

2.1 ADAPTING MESSAGES TO YOUR AUDIENCE (OBJS. 4, 5)

You work in the marketing department at ATB Financial in Edmonton, Alberta. Your manager has asked you to start sketching out some ideas for how to redesign the company's personal banking pages on its main website (www.atb.com). Specifically, your manager has asked that the new design work effectively to target a number of important customer groups and experiences: Millennials/new professionals; retirees/senior citizens; recent immigrants; graduation; new family; retirement—without simply including images of people who are members of these groups or who are experiencing these situations.

Your Task. Research targeted marketing to various groups and experiences using Internet search engines and your library's research databases. Summarize your findings and recommendations (with potential design ideas) in a short PowerPoint presentation or infographic. Make sure you highlight *how* communication and messaging will be different in this new version of ATB's personal banking Web pages.

2.2 CHANNEL SELECTION: BUSINESS SCENARIOS (OBJ. 3)

Your Task. Using Figure 2.4, suggest the best communication channels for the following messages. Assume that all channels shown are available, ranging from face-to-face conversations to texts, blogs, wikis, and podcasts. Be prepared to justify your choices based on the richness of each channel.

a. As part of a task force to investigate cell phone marketing, you need to establish a central location where each team member can see general information about the task as well as add comments for others to see. Task force members are located throughout the country.

b. You're sitting on the couch in the evening watching TV when you suddenly remember that you were supposed to send Jeremy some information about a shared project. Should you text him right away before you forget?

c. As an event planner, you have been engaged to research sites for a celebrity golf tournament. What is the best channel for conveying your findings to your boss or planning committee?

d. You want to persuade your manager to change your work schedule.

e. As a sales manager, you want to know which of your sales reps in the field is available immediately for a quick teleconference meeting.

f. You need to know whether Amanda in Reprographics can produce a rush job for you in two days.

g. Your firm must respond to a notice from the Canada Revenue Agency announcing that the company owes a penalty because it underreported its income in the previous fiscal year.

2.3 RESEARCH AND REPORT: GENERATIONAL COMMUNICATION (OBJ. 4)

In the past five years or so, a discussion has arisen about how different generations behave differently in the workplace, based mostly on the varying expectations younger and older people have of their jobs and the workplace. For example, it is generally agreed that Millennials (people born in the 1990s) communicate differently from GenXers (people born in the 1970s).

Your Task. Using your college or university library's research databases, find two to three reputable articles (i.e., from well-known newspapers or magazines) on the topic of generational communication differences in the workplace. Summarize your findings in a brief email to your instructor. In your email offer some "adaptive" suggestions for how workers from different generations can communicate effectively with each other (and their clients or customers) in the workplace.

2.4 TURNING NEGATIVES INTO POSITIVES (OBJ. 5)

There has been a lot of bad business news in the past couple of years. Between the lingering recession and the catastrophic train derailment and explosion in Lac-Mégantic, Québec, the world has witnessed large corporations going bankrupt or having to be bailed out by taxpayers, CEOs losing their jobs because of mismanagement of corporate disasters, and national governments negotiating bailouts (e.g., Ireland, Greece). From the point of view of one of the bailed-out companies or governments or corporations suffering from bad media publicity, how do you move the focus away from the negative news and toward a more positive perspective?

Your Task. In your school's library databases or on the Internet, using a search term such as *bad publicity*, see if you can find a source that gives good advice on how companies or governments can turn negatives into positives. Then, imagine that your college or university has just experienced a horrible health or environmental disaster or some large-scale scandal that has been reported in the media. Create some business communications for various stakeholders (e.g., students, parents, media, government, corporate partners) that turn negatives into positives. Present your communications to your instructor or to the class.

2.5 SCRIPT AND ROLE-PLAY (OBJ. 5)

Imagine the following situation: A customer enters her RBC bank branch in Brandon, Manitoba, to transfer money from her accounts in Canada to her accounts in Florida, where she spends the winter. The customer service representative is not helpful, makes it sound as if this is a problematic request, and needs to call over his manager to help him deal with the request.

Your Task. Expand the scenario by developing a script with three characters: friendly customer, unhelpful service representative, manager. Try to include at least five examples when the customer service rep or manager uses negative language (i.e., what can't be done) instead of positive language (what can be done). Role-play your script in front of your class, asking audience members to raise their hand each time they encounter negative language. Ask the audience to offer a positive solution each time before moving on with the rest of your role-play.

2.6 SCRIPT AND ROLE-PLAY (OBJ. 5)

Imagine the following situation, similar to that in 2.5: A new customer enters his local TD bank branch in Sydney, Nova Scotia, to open a new savings account, but he has not brought ID, a cheque, or any cash. As the customer service representative works to onboard this new customer, the customer becomes increasingly demanding and rude.

Your Task. Expand the scenario by developing a script with three characters: rude customer, helpful service representative, manager. Try to include at least five examples when the customer is rude or demanding. Role-play your script in front of your class, asking audience members to raise their hand each time they encounter rude or demanding language or gestures. Ask the audience to offer a positive solution each time before moving on with the rest of your role-play.

◢ WRITING IMPROVEMENT EXERCISES

AUDIENCE BENEFITS AND THE "YOU" VIEW (OBJ. 4)

Your Task. Revise the following sentences to emphasize the perspective of the audience and the "you" view.

1. We have prepared the enclosed form that may be used by victims to report identity theft to creditors.

2. To help us process your order with our new database software, we need you to go to our website and fill out the customer information required.

3. We are now offering RapidAssist, a software program we have developed to provide immediate technical support through our website to your employees and customers.

4. We find it necessary to restrict parking in the new company lot to those employee vehicles with "A" permits.

5. To avoid suffering the kinds of customer monetary losses experienced in the past, our credit union now prohibits the cashing of double-endorsed cheques presented by our customers.

6. Our warranty goes into effect only when we have received the product's registration card from the purchaser.

7. Unfortunately, you will not be able to use our computer and telephone systems on Thursday afternoon because of upgrades to both systems.

8. As part of our company effort to be friendly to the environment, we are asking all employees to reduce paper consumption by communicating by email and avoiding printing.

CONVERSATIONAL BUT PROFESSIONAL (OBJ. 4)

Your Task. Revise the following to make the tone conversational yet professional.

1. Per your recent email, the undersigned takes pride in informing you that we are pleased to be able to participate in the Toys for Tots drive.

2. Pursuant to your message of the 15th, please be advised that your shipment was sent August 14.

3. Yo, Jeff! Look, dude, I need you to sweet talk Ramona so we can drop this budget thingy in her lap.

4. BTW, Danika was totally ticked off when the manager accused her of ripping off office supplies. She may split.

5. He didn't have the guts to badmouth her 2 her face.

6. The undersigned respectfully reminds affected individuals that employees desirous of changing their health plans must do so before November 1.

POSITIVE AND COURTEOUS EXPRESSION (OBJ. 5)

Your Task. Revise the following statements to make them more positive.

1. Employees are not allowed to use instant messaging until a company policy is established.

2. We must withhold authorizing payment of your consultant's fees because our CPA claims that your work is incomplete.

3. Plans for the new health centre cannot move forward without full community support.

4. This is the last time I'm writing to try to get you to record my October 3 payment of $359.50 to my account! Anyone who can read can see from the attached documents that I've tried to explain this to you before.

5. Although you apparently failed to read the operator's manual, we are sending you a replacement blade for your food processor. Next time read page 18 carefully so that you will know how to attach this blade.

6. Everyone in this department must begin using new passwords as of midnight, June 15. Because of flagrant password misuse, we find it necessary to impose this new rule so that we can protect your personal information and company records.

BIAS-FREE LANGUAGE (OBJ. 5)

Your Task. Revise the following sentences to reduce gender, racial, ethnic, age, and disability bias.

1. Every employee must wear his photo identification on the job.
2. The conference will offer special excursions for the wives of executives.
3. Does each salesman have his own smartphone loaded with his special sales information?
4. A little old lady returned this item.
5. Serving on the panel are a lady veterinarian, an Indian CPA, two businessmen, and a female doctor.
6. Each nurse is responsible for her patient's medications.

PLAIN LANGUAGE AND FAMILIAR WORDS (OBJ. 5)

Your Task. Revise the following sentences to use plain language and familiar words.

1. The salary we are offering is commensurate with remuneration for other managers.
2. To expedite ratification of this agreement, we urge you to vote in the affirmative.
3. In a dialogue with the manager, I learned that you plan to terminate our contract.
4. Did your e-bike's braking problem materialize subsequent to our recall effort?
5. Pursuant to your invitation, we will interrogate our agent.

PRECISE, VIGOROUS WORDS (OBJ. 5)

Your Task. From the choices in parentheses, select the most precise, vigorous words.

1. Government economists (*say, hypothesize, predict*) that employment will (*stabilize, stay the same, even out*) next year.
2. The growing number of (*people, consumers, buyers*) with (*devices, gadgets, smartphones*) provides (*an idea, an indicator, a picture*) of economic growth.
3. Although international trade can (*get, offer, generate*) new profits and (*affect, lower*) costs, it also introduces a (*different, higher, new*) level of risk and complexity.
4. The World Bank sees international trade as a (*good, fine, vital*) tool for (*decreasing, changing, addressing*) poverty.

◣ GRAMMAR/MECHANICS CHALLENGE 2

PRONOUNS

Review Sections 1.07–1.09 the Grammar/Mechanics Handbook. Then study each of the following statements. In the space provided, write the word that completes the statement correctly and the number of the G/M principle illustrated. When you finish, compare your responses with those provided near the end of the book. If your responses differ, study carefully the principles in parentheses.

<u>its (1.09d)</u>	**Example**	The employee development committee will make (*its, their*) recommendation soon.

_____ 1. The manager said that Elena would call. Was it (*she, her*) who left the message?

_____ 2. Every member of the men's soccer team must have (*his, their*) medical exam completed by Monday.

_____ 3. Even instant messages sent between the CEO and (*he, him*) were revealed in the court case.

_____ 4. (*Who, Whom*) have you hired to create cutting-edge ads for us?

_____ 5. It looks as if (*yours, your's*) is the only report that cites electronic sources correctly.

_____ 6. Mark asked Kadesha and (*I, me, myself*) to help him complete his research.

_____ 7. My friend and (*I, me, myself*) were interviewed for the same job.

8. To park the bus, turn (*it's, its*) wheels to the left.

_____

9. Give the budget figures to (*whoever, whomever*) asked for them.

_____

10. Everyone except the interviewer and (*I, me, myself*) heard the alarm.

_____

11. No one knows that case better than (*he, him, himself*).

_____

12. A proposed budget was sent to (*we, us*) owners before the vote.

_____

13. One of the female travellers left (*their, her*) smartphone on the seat.

_____

14. Neither the glamour nor the excitement of the job had lost (*its, it's, their*) appeal.

_____

15. If neither Cory nor I receive confirmation of our itinerary, (*him and me, him and I, he and I*) cannot make the trip.

◤ EDITING CHALLENGE 2

The following email is a short report about beverage sweeteners from a researcher to his boss. The message has faults in proofreading, spelling, grammar, punctuation, and other errors. Study the guidelines in the Grammar/Mechanics Handbook, as well as the lists of Confusing Words and Frequently Misspelled Words at the end of the book, to sharpen your skills.

Your Task. Edit the following message by correcting its errors (a) in your textbook or (b) on a photocopy using proofreading marks from Appendix B.

To: Vicky Miranda <v.miranda@dino.ca>
From: Aliriza Kasra <a.kasra@dino.ca>
Subject: Sending Information on Beverage Sweeteners
Cc:
Bcc:

Vicky,

Per your request, herewith is a short report of the investigation you assigned to Oliver Orenstein and I pertaining to sweeteners. As you probaly already know, Coca-Cola co. and PepsiCo inc. market many drinks using sweeteners that are new to the market. Totally awesome!

Coca-Cola brought out Sprite Green, a reduced calorie soft drink that contains Truvia. Which it considers a natural sweetener because it is derived from an herb. The initial launch focused on locations and events oriented to teenagers and young adults. According to inside information obtained by Ollie and I, this product was tested on the shelfs of grocerys, mass merchants, and conveience stores in 5 citys in Florida. PepsiCo has it's own version of the herbal sweetener, however it was developed in collaboration with Green earth sweetener co. Its called Pure Via. The first products that contained the sweetener were 3 flavors of zero-calorie SoBe Lifewater. It may also be used in a orange-juice drink with half the calorys and sugar of orange juice. Another new sweetener is Nectresse, marketed by Splenda. It comes from the monk fruit. Which has been cultivated for centurys, and only recently rediscovered as a source of natural sweetness.

BTW, approval by the Canadian food inspection Agency did not materialize automatically for these new sweeteners. CFIA approval was an issue because studys conducted in the early 1990s suggested that their was possible adverse health effects from the use of stevia-based products. However the herb has been aproved for use in 12 countrys.

Both companys eventually received CFIA approval and there products are all ready on the market. We cannot submit our full report until October 15.

Al
Aliriza Kasra
a.kasra@dino.com
Research and Development
Office: (647) 443-9920

CHAPTER

3

OBJECTIVES

3.1 Research to collect background information for messages.

3.2 Organize information into strategic relationships.

3.3 Compose a first draft using a variety of sentence types.

3.4 Improve your message by using style effectively.

3.5 Organize paragraphs effectively.

ORGANIZING AND DRAFTING YOUR MESSAGE

BIZ COMM BYTE

In a recent survey of "547 businesspeople . . . 81% of them agree that poorly written material wastes a lot of their time. A majority say that what they read is frequently ineffective because it's too long, poorly organized, unclear, filled with jargon, and imprecise."

Source: Bernoff, J. (2016, September 6). Bad writing is destroying your company's productivity. *Harvard Business Review.* https://hbr.org/2016/09 /bad-writing-is-destroying-your-companys-productivity

3.1 Drafting Workplace Messages

With today's advances in technology, many people believe they will never be required to write on the job. The truth is that professionals in the digital age are exchanging more messages than ever before. The faster you can put your ideas down and the more succinctly and clearly you can explain to your receiver what needs to be said (as noted in the Biz Comm Byte box), the more successful you will be in your career.

3.1a Researching Background Information

No experienced professional would begin drafting a message before doing research. For our purposes *research* simply means "collecting information about a certain topic." This is an important step in the writing process outlined in Chapter 2 (see Figure 3.1 for a reminder) because information helps you shape

1 Prewriting

Analyze: Decide on the message purpose. What do you want the receiver to do or believe?

Anticipate: What does the audience already know? How will it receive this message?

Adapt: Think about techniques to present this message most effectively. Consider how to elicit feedback.

2 Drafting

Research: Gather background data by searching files and the Internet.

Organize: Arrange direct messages with the big idea first. For persuasive or negative messages, use an indirect, problem-solving strategy.

Draft: Prepare the first draft, using active-voice sentences, coherent paragraphs, and appropriate transitional expressions.

3 Revising

Edit: Eliminate wordy fillers, long lead-ins, redundancies, and trite business phrases. Strive for parallelism, clarity, conciseness, and readability.

Proofread: Check carefully for errors in spelling, grammar, punctuation, and format.

Evaluate: Will this message achieve your purpose? Is the tone pleasant? Did you encourage feedback?

© Cengage Learning

your message and build credibility. Business writers collect information to answer several questions:

- What does the receiver need to know?
- What is the receiver to do?
- How is the receiver to do it?
- When must the receiver do it?
- What will happen if the receiver doesn't do it?

Whenever your message requires more information than you have in your head or at your fingertips, you must conduct research. This research may be informal or formal.

3.1b Informal Research Methods

Many routine messages—such as emails, letters, informational reports, and oral presentations—require information that you can collect informally. The following informal research techniques are useful at work.

- **Search your company's files.** If you're responding to an inquiry or drafting a routine message, you often can find background information such as previous messages in your own files or those of your coworkers. You might consult the company wiki or other digital and manual files.
- **Talk with your manager.** Get information from the individual to whom you report. Your superior will probably know something about the topic and the slant you should take. Your manager can also point you to other sources.
- **Interview the target audience.** Consider talking with the message receiver(s). They can provide clarifying information that tells you what they want to know and how you should shape your remarks. Suggestions for conducting interviews are presented in Chapter 9.
- **Conduct an informal survey.** Gather helpful information through questionnaires, telephone surveys, or online surveys. In preparing a report predicting the success of a proposed company fitness centre, for example, circulate a questionnaire asking for employee reactions.
- **Brainstorm for ideas.** Alone or with others, discuss ideas for the writing task at hand, and record at least a dozen ideas without judging them. Small groups are especially fruitful in brainstorming because people spin ideas off one another.
- **Do a quick Google search.** Sometimes the information to persuade your receiver will be found online. When using Google, make sure you're visiting reputable

Cengage

MINDTAP

In MindTap go to the Whiteboard Animation for Chapter 3 and watch it now.

WORKPLACE IN FOCUS

At workplace-giving software company Benevity's world headquarters in Calgary, brainstorming and informal research is built right into the office architecture. In a recent head-office move, Benevity decided to listen to its employees, and over its three floors has created a series of spaces "where people [can] do their best work . . . an open concept, light-filled office with colourful furniture, large murals, and a collaborative atmosphere."[1] Encouraging employees to seek out information in this way, instead of sitting in a cubicle or an office all day, has a double impact: it encourages the type of research gathering necessary in an ideas-based economy, and it suits the preferences of younger workers who appreciate collaboration and informality in the workplace. *What type of collaborations have you participated in at work? Were they spontaneous or more formalized?*

Photograph by Alana Willerton, from article in Avenue Magazine (Calgary).

sites: well-known magazines and newspapers (e.g., *The Globe and Mail*) and government sites (e.g., Statistics Canada) that have verified facts before publishing information on the Internet.

3.1c Research Methods

Complex business problems lead to longer reports and generally require formal research methods. Let's say you are part of the management team for an international retailer such as Roots, and you have been asked to help launch a new store in Japan. Or let's assume you're writing an end-of-term essay for a college or university class. Both tasks require more data than you have in your head or at your fingertips. To conduct formal research, consider the following research options:

- **Access electronic sources.** University, college, and public libraries provide digital catalogues and research databases offering access to a wide array of high-quality books, journals, magazines, newspapers, and other materials. An alternative is Google Scholar's free database of articles published in peer-reviewed journals. Library research tends to take longer but leads to guaranteed high-quality sources, whereas Internet research is very fast but doesn't always lead to high-quality sources.
- **Investigate primary sources.** To develop firsthand, primary information for a project, go directly to the source. In helping to launch a new Roots location in Tokyo, you might travel to possible sites and check them out. If you need information about how many shoppers pass by a location or visit a shopping centre, you might conduct a traffic count. If you need information about consumers, you could search blogs, Twitter, wikis, and Facebook fan pages. To learn more about specific shoppers, you could use questionnaires, interviews, or focus groups. Formal research includes scientific sampling methods that enable investigators to make accurate judgments and valid predictions.
- **Conduct scientific experiments.** Instead of merely asking for the target audience's opinion, scientific researchers present choices with controlled variables. Imagine, for example, that the management team at Roots wants to know at what price and under what circumstances consumers would purchase

Cengage

MINDTAP

In MindTap, go to the Chapter 3 reading, section 3.1c, and watch the video of industry expert Mike Stiers discussing the importance of research in your business messages.

sweatpants from Roots instead of from H&M. Or let's say that management wants to study the time of year and type of weather conditions that motivate consumers to begin purchasing sweaters, jackets, and cold-weather gear. The results of such experimentation would provide valuable data for managerial decision making.

◤ 3.2 Organizing Information to Show Relationships

After you've collected data, you need to organize it. Organizing includes two processes: grouping and strategizing. Well-organized messages group similar items together, and ideas follow a sequence that helps the reader understand relationships and accept the writer's views. Unorganized messages jump from one thought to another. Such messages fail to emphasize important points. Puzzled readers can't see how the pieces fit together, and they become frustrated and irritated. Many communication experts regard poor organization as the greatest failing of business writers. Two simple techniques can help you organize data: the quick list and the outline.

Some writers draft a quick list of the topics they'd like to cover in a message. They then write the message directly from the list. Most writers, though, need to organize their ideas—especially if the project is complex—into a hierarchy such as an outline. The beauty of preparing an outline is that it gives you a chance to organize your thinking before you are bogged down in word choice and sentence structure. Figure 3.2 shows an outline format.

DIRECT ORGANIZATION FOR RECEPTIVE AUDIENCES. After preparing a list or an outline, think about how the audience will respond to your ideas. When you expect the receiver (reading or listening) to be pleased, mildly interested, or, at worst, neutral—use the direct strategy. That is, put your main point—the purpose of your message—in the first or second sentence.

◤ FIGURE 3.2 / Format for an Outline

Title: Major Idea or Purpose

I. First major component
   A. First subpoint
      1. Detail, illustration, evidence
      2. Detail, illustration, evidence
      3. Detail, illustration, evidence
   B. Second subpoint
      1.
      2.
II. Second major component
   A. First subpoint
      1.
      2.
   B. Second subpoint
      1.
      2.
      3.

Tips for Writing Outlines
- Define the main topic in the title.
- Divide the main topic into major components or classifications (preferably three to five).
- Break the components into subpoints.
- Don't put a single item under a major component; if you have only one subpoint, integrate it with the main item above it or reorganize.
- Strive to make each component exclusive (no overlapping).
- Use details, illustrations, and evidence to support subpoints.

© Cengage Learning

Compare the direct and indirect strategies in the following email openings. Notice how long it takes to get to the main idea in the indirect opening.

DON'T Indirect Opening	DO✓ Direct Opening
✗ Bombardier is seeking to improve the process undertaken in producing its annual company awards ceremony. To this end, the Marketing Department, which is in charge of the event, has been refining last year's plan, especially as regards the issue of rental costs and food and beverage costs.	✓ The Marketing Department at Bombardier suggests cutting costs for the annual awards ceremony by adjusting the way we order food and the way we handle rentals.

The direct method shown here, also called *frontloading*, has at least three advantages:

- **Saves the reader's time.** Many businesspeople can devote only a few moments to each message.
- **Sets a proper frame of mind.** Without a clear opening, the reader may be thinking, *Why am I being told this?*
- **Reduces frustration.** Readers forced to struggle through wordy language before reaching the main idea can become frustrated and begin to resent the writer.

Typical business messages that follow the direct strategy include routine requests and responses, orders and acknowledgments, non-sensitive emails, informational reports, and informational oral presentations. All these tasks have one element in common: none has a sensitive subject that will upset the reader.

INDIRECT ORGANIZATION FOR UNRECEPTIVE AUDIENCES. When you expect the audience to be uninterested, unwilling, displeased, or perhaps even hostile, the indirect strategy is more appropriate. In this strategy you reveal the main idea only after you have offered an explanation and evidence. This approach works well with three kinds of messages: (a) bad news, (b) ideas that require persuasion, and (c) sensitive news, especially when being transmitted to superiors. The indirect strategy shown in the example has these benefits:

- **Respects the feelings of the audience.** Bad news is difficult, and preparing the receiver for it can lessen the pain.
- **Facilitates a fair hearing**. Messages that may upset the reader are more likely to be read when the main idea is delayed.
- **Minimizes a negative reaction.** A reader's reaction to a negative message is generally improved if the news is delivered gently.

Typical messages that are organized indirectly include request refusals, claim denials, and credit disapprovals. Persuasive requests, sales letters, sensitive messages, and some reports and oral presentations may also benefit from the indirect strategy.

In summary, business messages may be organized directly (with the main idea first) or indirectly. How you expect the audience to respond determines which strategy to use, as illustrated in Figure 3.3. Although these two methods cover many communication problems, they shouldn't be considered universal. Some messages are mixed: part good news, part bad; part goodwill, part persuasion. In upcoming chapters you'll practise applying the direct and indirect organization in many typical workplace situations.

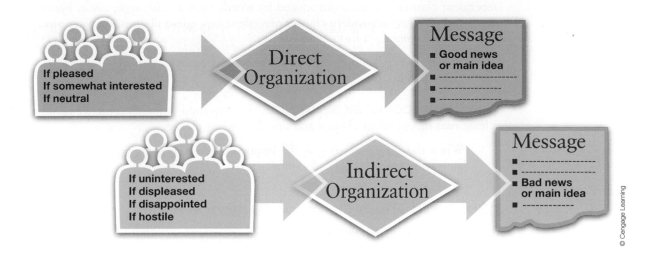

© Cengage Learning

3.3 Drafting With Effective Sentences

After you've researched your topic, organized the data, and selected an organization method, you're ready to begin drafting. Many writers have trouble getting started, especially if they haven't completed the preparatory work. Organizing your ideas and working from an outline are very helpful in overcoming writer's block. Writing is also easier if you have a quiet environment in which to concentrate, if you set aside time to concentrate, and if you limit interruptions.

As you begin writing, think about what style fits you best. Some experts suggest that you write quickly (*freewriting*). Get your thoughts down now and refine them in later versions. As you begin each idea, imagine that you are talking to the reader. If you can't think of the right word, insert a substitute or type *find perfect word later*. Freewriting works well for some writers, but others prefer to move more slowly and think through their ideas more deliberately. Whether you are a speedy or a deliberate writer, keep in mind that you're writing the first draft. You'll have time later to revise and polish your sentences.

3.3a Achieve Variety With Four Sentence Types

Messages that repeat the same sentence pattern soon become boring (e.g., We need to keep growing market share. We also need to increase shareholder satisfaction. Finally, we need to nurture ethical responses . . .). To avoid monotony and add spark to your writing, use a variety of sentence types.

SIMPLE SENTENCE. A simple sentence contains one complete thought (an independent clause) with a subject and predicate verb:

The <u>entrepreneur</u> saw an opportunity.

COMPOUND SENTENCE. A compound sentence contains two complete but related thoughts. May be joined by (a) a conjunction such as *and, but,* or *or*; (b) a semicolon; or (c) a conjunctive adverb such as *however, consequently,* or *therefore*:

The <u>entrepreneur</u> <u>saw</u> an opportunity, and <u>she</u> <u>responded</u> immediately.

The <u>entrepreneur</u> <u>saw</u> an opportunity; <u>she</u> <u>responded</u> immediately.

The <u>entrepreneur</u> <u>saw</u> an opportunity; consequently, <u>she</u> <u>responded</u> immediately.

COMPLEX SENTENCE. A complex sentence contains an independent clause (a complete thought) and a dependent clause (a thought that cannot stand by itself). Dependent clauses are often introduced by words such as *although*, *since*, *because*, *when*, and *if*. When dependent clauses precede independent clauses, they are always followed by a comma:

> When the <u>entrepreneur</u> <u>saw</u> the opportunity, <u>she</u> <u>responded</u> immediately.

COMPOUND-COMPLEX SENTENCE. A compound-complex sentence contains at least two independent clauses and one dependent clause:

> When the <u>entrepreneur</u> <u>saw</u> the opportunity, <u>she</u> <u>responded</u> immediately; however, <u>she</u> <u>needed</u> capital.

3.3b Avoid Three Common Sentence Faults

As you craft your sentences, beware of three common traps that reduce your credibility: fragments, run-on (fused) sentences, and comma-splice sentences.

One serious error a writer can make is punctuating a fragment as if it were a complete sentence. A *fragment* is usually a broken-off part of a complex sentence. Fragments can often be identified by the words that introduce them—words such as *although*, *as*, *because*, *even*, *except*, *for example*, *if*, *instead of*, *since*, *such as*, *that*, *which*, and *when*. These words introduce dependent clauses, as italicized in the following fragment examples. They should not be punctuated as sentences. Make sure such clauses always connect to independent clauses, as shown in the revisions.

DON'T	Fragment	DO ✓	Revision
✗	*Because most transactions require a permanent record.* Good writing skills are critical.	✓	Because most transactions require a permanent record, good writing skills are critical.
✗	The recruiter requested a writing sample. *Even though the candidate seemed to communicate well.*	✓	The recruiter requested a writing sample even though the candidate seemed to communicate well.

A second serious writing fault is the *run-on (fused) sentence*. A sentence with two independent clauses must be joined by a coordinating conjunction (*and*, *or*, *nor*, *but*) or by a semicolon (;) or separated into two sentences. Without a conjunction or a semicolon, a run-on sentence results.

DON'T	Run-on Sentence	DO ✓	Revision
✗	Many job seekers prepare traditional résumés some also use websites as electronic portfolios.	✓	Many job seekers prepare traditional résumés. Some also use websites as electronic portfolios.
✗	One candidate sent an email résumé another sent a link to her Web portfolio.	✓	One candidate sent an email résumé; another sent a link to her Web portfolio.

A third sentence fault is a *comma splice*, which happens when a writer joins (splices together) two independent clauses with a comma. Independent clauses may be joined with a coordinating conjunction (*and, or, nor, but*) or a conjunctive adverb (*however, consequently, therefore,* and others). Notice that clauses joined by coordinating conjunctions require only a comma. Clauses joined by a conjunctive adverb require a semicolon and a comma. To fix a comma splice, try one of the possible revisions shown here:

DON'T Common Splice	DO✓ Revision
✗ Jeremy prefers his laptop, Nadia prefers her tablet.	✓ Jeremy prefers his laptop, but Nadia prefers her tablet. ✓ Jeremy prefers his laptop; however, Nadia prefers her tablet. ✓ Jeremy prefers his laptop; Nadia prefers her tablet.

3.3c Use Short Sentences Wisely

Instead of stringing together multiple clauses with and, but, and however (e.g., We need to move into new markets, and the best way to do that is to follow our competitor's lead, but at the same time we need to be careful not to repeat their mistakes.) break some of those complex sentences into separate segments (e.g., We need to move into new markets; the best way to do that is to follow our competitor's lead. That said, let's be careful not to repeat their mistakes.). Business readers want to grasp ideas immediately. They can do that easily when thoughts are separated into short sentences. On the other hand, too many monotonous short sentences (e.g. Let's follow their lead. They raised their profit by 300 percent. But they made mistakes too. Let's not make the same mistakes.) will sound unintelligent and may bore or even annoy the reader. Strive for a balance between longer sentences and shorter ones.

◢ 3.4 Developing Stylish Sentences

Business writers can significantly improve their messages by working on a few sentence style techniques like emphasis and voice.

3.4a Show Emphasis

When you're talking with someone, you emphasize your main ideas by saying them loudly or by repeating them slowly. You might pound the table if you want to show real emphasis! Another way you signal the relative importance of an idea is by raising your eyebrows, by shaking your head, or by whispering in a low voice. But when you write, you need to rely on other ways of telling your readers which ideas are more important than others. Emphasis in writing can be achieved mechanically or stylistically.

EMPHASIS THROUGH MECHANICS. To emphasize an idea in writing, use any of the following devices:

Underlining	<u>Underlining</u> draws the eye to a word.
Italics and boldface	Using *italics* or **boldface** conveys special meaning.
Font changes	Selecting a large, small, or different font draws interest.
All caps	Printing words in ALL CAPS is like shouting them.
Dashes	Dashes—used sparingly—can be effective.

Listing	Listing items vertically makes them stand out:	
	1. First item	
	2. Second item	
	3. Third item	
Emoji	☺ Softens what might otherwise come across as angry or sarcastic. Use them only if you know the receiver well enough.	

Other ways of achieving mechanical emphasis include the arrangement of space, colour, lines, boxes, columns, titles, headings, and subheadings. Today's software and colour printers provide an array of capabilities for highlighting ideas.

EMPHASIS THROUGH STYLE. Although mechanical devices are occasionally appropriate, more often a writer achieves emphasis stylistically, by choosing words carefully and constructing sentences skillfully to emphasize main ideas and de-emphasize minor or negative ideas. Here are four suggestions for emphasizing ideas stylistically:

Use vivid, not general, words. Vivid words are emphatic because the reader can picture ideas clearly.

DON'T General	DO✓ Vivid
✘ The way we seek jobs has changed.	✓ The Internet has dramatically changed how job hunters search for positions.
✘ Someone will contact you as soon as possible.	✓ Ms. Rivera will call you before 5 p.m. tomorrow, May 3.

Label the main idea. If an idea is significant, tell the reader.

DON'T Unlabelled	DO✓ Labelled
✘ Consider looking for a job online, but also focus on networking.	✓ Consider looking for a job online; but, *most important*, focus on networking.
✘ We shop here because of the customer service and low prices.	✓ We like the customer service, but the *primary reason* for shopping here is the low prices.

Place the important idea first or last. Ideas have less competition from surrounding words when they appear first or last in a sentence. Notice how the concept of productivity can be emphasized by its position in the sentence:

DON'T Main Idea Lost	DO✓ Main Idea Emphasized
✘ Profit-sharing plans are more effective in increasing *productivity* when they are linked to individual performance rather than to group performance.	✓ *Productivity* is more likely to be increased when profit-sharing plans are linked to individual performance rather than to group performance.

Give the important idea the spotlight. Don't dilute the effect of the main idea by making it share the stage with other words and clauses. Instead, put it in a simple sentence or in an independent clause.

DON'T **Main Idea Lost**	DO✓ **Main Idea Clear**
✗ Although you are the first trainee we have hired for this program, we had many candidates and expect to expand the program in the future. (The main idea is lost in a dependent clause.)	✓ You are the first trainee we have hired for this program. (Simple sentence)

DE-EMPHASIZE WHEN NECESSARY. To de-emphasize an idea, such as bad news, try one of the following stylistic devices:

Use abstract, not specific, words and phrases.

DON'T **Emphasizes Harsh Statement**	DO✓ **De-emphasizes Harsh Statement**
✗ Our records indicate that you were recently fired.	✓ Our records indicate that your employment status has recently changed.

Place the bad news in a dependent clause connected to an independent clause that contains something positive. In sentences with dependent clauses, the main emphasis is always on the independent clause.

DON'T **Emphasizes Bad News**	DO✓ **De-emphasizes Bad News**
✗ We cannot issue you credit at this time, but we have a special plan that will allow you to fill your immediate needs on a cash basis.	✓ Although credit cannot be issued at this time, you can fill your immediate needs on a cash basis with our special plan.

3.4b Use the Active and Passive Voice Effectively

In active-voice sentences, the subject performs the action. In passive-voice sentences, the subject receives the action. Active-voice sentences are more direct because they reveal the performer immediately. They are easier to understand and usually shorter. Most business writing should be in the active voice. However, passive voice is useful to (a) emphasize an action rather than a person, (b) de-emphasize negative news, and (c) conceal the doer of an action.

Active Voice	Passive Voice
Actor → Action Justin must submit a tax return.	Receiver ← Action The tax return was submitted [by Justin].
Actor → Action Officials reviewed all tax returns	Receiver ← Action All tax returns were reviewed [by officials]
Actor → Action We cannot make cash refunds	Receiver ← Action Cash refunds cannot be made
Actor → Action Our accountant made a big error in the budget.	Receiver ← Action A big error was made in the budget.

3.4c Integrate Parallelism

Parallelism is a technique that creates balanced writing. Sentences written so that their parts are balanced, or parallel, are easy to read and understand. To achieve parallelism, use similar structures to express similar ideas. For example, the words *computing*, *coding*, *recording*, and *storing* are parallel because the words all end in *-ing*. To express the list as *computing*, *coding*, *recording*, and *storage* is unbalanced because the last item is not what the reader expects. Try to match nouns with nouns, verbs with verbs, and clauses with clauses. Avoid mixing active-voice verbs with passive-voice verbs.

DON'T **Lacks Parallelism**	DO✓ **Illustrates Parallelism**
✗ The wedding planner will arrange for the venue, the flowers, and *a person to take videos.*	✓ The wedding planner will arrange for the venue, the flowers, and a videographer. (Matches nouns.)
✗ Our primary goals are to increase productivity, reduce costs, and *the improvement of product quality.*	✓ Our primary goals are to increase productivity, reduce costs, and *improve product quality.* (Matches verbs.)
✗ We are scheduled to meet in Atlanta on January 5, *we are meeting in Montréal on the 15th of March,* and in Vancouver on June 3.	✓ We are scheduled to meet in Atlanta on January 5, *in Montréal on March 15,* and in Vancouver on June 3. (Matches phrases.)
✗ Shelby audits all accounts lettered A through L; accounts lettered M through Z are audited by Andrew.	✓ Shelby audits all accounts lettered A through L; Andrew audits accounts lettered M through Z. (Matches clauses.)
✗ Our Stanley Cup ads have three objectives: 1. We want to increase product use. 2. Introduce complementary products. 3. Our corporate image will be enhanced.	✓ Our Stanley Cup ads have three objectives: 1. Increase product use 2. Introduce complementary products 3. Enhance our corporate image (Matches verbs in listed items.)

3.4d Replace Dangling and Misplaced Modifiers

A modifier dangles when the word or phrase it's supposed to describe is missing from the sentence—for example: *After working overtime, the report was finally finished.* This sentence is saying that the report was working overtime! Revised, the sentence contains a logical subject: *After working overtime, we finally finished the report.*

A modifier is misplaced when the word or phrase it describes is not close enough to be clear—for example: *Firefighters rescued a dog from a burning car that had a broken leg.* Obviously, the car did not have a broken leg. The solution is to position the modifier closer to the word(s) it describes or limits: *Firefighters rescued a dog with a broken leg from a burning car.*

DON'T Dangling or Misplaced Modifier	DO Clear Modification
✗ Working together as a team, the project was finally completed.	✓ Working together as a team, we finally completed the project.
✗ To meet the deadline, your Excel figures must be sent by May 1.	✓ To meet the deadline, you must send your Excel figures by May 1.
✗ The recruiter interviewed candidates who had excellent computer skills in the morning.	✓ This morning the recruiter interviewed candidates with excellent computer skills.
✗ As an important customer to us, we invite you to our spring open house.	✓ As you are an important customer to us, we invite you to our spring open house. *OR:* ✓ As an important customer to us, you are invited to our spring open house.

▶ 3.5 Drafting Well-Organized, Effective Paragraphs

Skilled business writers develop well-organized paragraphs by focusing on a single main idea. In addition, the sentences in their paragraphs cohere, or stick together, through the use of transitional expressions.

3.5a Craft a Topic Sentence

A paragraph is unified when it develops a single main idea, usually expressed in a topic sentence. Business writers generally place the topic sentence at the beginning of the paragraph. This sentence tells readers what to expect and helps them understand the paragraph's central thought immediately (e.g., *This report investigates consumer confidence changes in Canada in the past 10 years.*).

3.5b Develop Support Sentences

Support sentences illustrate, explain, or strengthen the topic sentence. One of the hardest things for beginning writers to remember is that all support sentences in the paragraph must relate to the topic sentence. Any other topics should be treated separately. The following example starts with a topic sentence about flexible work scheduling and is followed by three support sentences that explain how flexible scheduling could function. Transitional expressions are italicized:

> **Topic sentence:** Flexible work scheduling could immediately increase productivity and enhance employee satisfaction in our organization.

> **Support sentences:** Managers would maintain their regular hours. For many other employees, *however*, flexible scheduling provides extra time to manage family responsibilities. Feeling less stress, employees are able to focus their attention better at work; *therefore*, they become more relaxed and more productive.

3.5c Build Paragraph Coherence

Paragraphs are coherent when ideas are linked—that is, when one idea leads logically to the next. Well-written paragraphs (and effective presentations) take the

To Add or Strengthen	To Show Time or Order	To Clarify	To Show Cause and Effect	To Contradict	To Contrast
additionally	after	for example	accordingly	actually	as opposed to
accordingly	before	for instance	as a result	but	at the same time
again	earlier	I mean	consequently	however	by contrast
also	finally	in other words	for this reason	in fact	conversely
beside	first	put another way	hence	instead	on the contrary
indeed	meanwhile	that is	so	rather	on the other hand
likewise	next	this means	therefore	still	previously
moreover	now	thus	thus	yet	similarly

© Cengage Learning

Cengage

MINDTAP

In MindTap go to the Study Tools for Chapter 3 and complete the Practice Test.

reader through a number of steps. When the writer skips from Step 1 to Step 3 and forgets Step 2, the reader is lost. Several techniques allow the reader to follow the writer's ideas:

- **Repeat key ideas by using the same expression or a similar one:** Employees treat guests as VIPs. <u>These VIPs</u> are never told what they can or cannot do.
- **Use pronouns to refer to previous nouns:** All new employees receive a two-week orientation. <u>They</u> learn that every team member has a vital role.
- **Show connections with transitional expressions:** *Hospitality is our business;* <u>*as a result*</u>, *training is critical to achieve success.* For a list of transitional expressions, see Figure 3.4.

3.5d Control Paragraph Length

In a world of slides and infographics, business audiences have naturally begun to prefer short paragraphs. In documents like emails, proposals, and reports, paragraphs with five to eight printed lines look inviting and readable. But longer chunks of text will be skipped over. If a topic can't be covered in eight or fewer printed lines (not sentences), consider breaking it into smaller segments.

▰ LEARNING SUMMARY

3.1 Research to collect background information for messages.

- Shape messages and increase credibility by collecting information. Collect information by answering questions about what the receiver needs to know and what the receiver is to do.

- Conduct informal research for routine messages by looking in the company's digital and other files, talking with the supervisor, interviewing the target audience, organizing informal surveys, and brainstorming for ideas.

- Conduct formal research for long reports and complex problems by searching electronically or manually, investigating primary sources, and organizing scientific experiments.

3.2 Organize information into strategic relationships.

- For simple messages, make a quick scratch list of topics; for more complex messages, create an outline.

- To prepare an outline, divide the main topic into three to five major components.

- Break the components into subpoints consisting of details, illustrations, and evidence.
- Organize the information using *direct organization* (with the main idea first) when audiences will be pleased, mildly interested, or neutral.
- Organize information using *indirect organization* (with explanations preceding the main idea) for audiences that will be unwilling, displeased, or hostile.

3.3 Compose a first draft using a variety of sentence types.

- Decide whether to compose quickly (*freewriting*) or to write more deliberately—but remember that you are writing a first draft.
- Employ a variety of sentence types including simple (one independent clause), complex (one independent and one dependent clause), compound (two independent clauses), and compound-complex (at least two independent clauses and one dependent clause).
- Avoid fragments (broken-off parts of sentences), run-on sentences (two clauses fused improperly), and comma splices (two clauses joined improperly with a comma).
- Remember that sentences are most effective when they are short (20 or fewer words).

3.4 Improve your message by using style effectively.

- Emphasize an idea mechanically by using underlining, italics, boldface, font changes, all caps, dashes, tabulation, and other devices.

- Emphasize an idea stylistically by using vivid words, labelling it, making it the sentence subject, placing it first or last, and removing competing ideas.
- For most business writing, use the active voice by making the subject the doer of the action (*the company hired the student*).
- Use the passive voice (*the student was hired*) to de-emphasize negative news, to emphasize an action rather than the doer, or to conceal the doer of an action.
- Employ parallelism for balanced construction (*jogging, hiking, and biking* rather than *jogging, hiking, and to bike*).
- Avoid dangling modifiers (sitting at my computer, the words would not come) and misplaced modifiers (I have the report you wrote in my office).

3.5 Organize paragraphs effectively.

- Build well-organized, unified paragraphs by focusing on a single idea.
- Always include a topic sentence that states the main idea of the paragraph.
- Develop support sentences to illustrate, explain, or strengthen the topic sentence.
- Build coherence by repeating a key idea, using pronouns to refer to previous nouns, and showing connections with transitional expressions (*however, therefore, consequently*).
- Control paragraph length by striving for eight or fewer lines.

◤ CHAPTER REVIEW

1. What is *research*, and how do informal and formal research methods differ? (Obj. 1)
2. Before drafting a message, what questions should writers ask as they collect information? (Obj. 1)
3. Why do writers need to outline complex projects before beginning? (Obj. 2)
4. What business messages are better organized directly, and which are better organized indirectly? (Obj. 2)
5. What are the four sentence types? Provide an original example of each. (Obj. 3)
6. What is the relationship between sentence length and comprehension? (Obj. 3)
7. What is the difference between active-voice and passive-voice sentences? Give an original example of each. When should business writers use each? (Obj. 4)
8. How are topic sentences different from support sentences? (Obj. 5)
9. Name three techniques for building paragraph coherence. (Obj. 5)

◤ CRITICAL THINKING

1. To what degree are trends in business and developments in technology forcing workers to write more than ever before? What evidence supports this trend? (Obj. 1)
2. Molly, a twenty-three-year-old college graduate with a 3.5 GPA, was hired as an administrative assistant. She was a fast learner on all the software, but her supervisor had to help her with punctuation. On the ninth day of her job, she resigned, saying: "I just don't think this job is a good fit. Commas, semicolons, spelling, typos—those kinds of things just aren't all that important to me. They just don't matter." What do you think of Molly's reasoning? Why? (Objs. 1–5)

3. Why is audience analysis so important in the selection of the direct or indirect organization strategy for a business message? (Obj. 2)
4. How are speakers different from writers in the way they emphasize ideas? (Obj. 4)
5. Now that you have studied the active and passive voice, what do you think when someone in government or business says, "Mistakes were made"? Is it unethical to use the passive voice to avoid specifics? (Obj. 4)

ACTIVITIES AND CASES

3.1 RESEARCHING BEFORE DRAFTING (OBJ. 1)

Manitoba-based Richardson International (richardson.ca) is one of Canada's leading and most diversified agricultural companies. One of its lines of business, Richardson Milling, is the largest miller of oats in North America. Recently, VP Business Development Cory Bohatenko has been asked to submit strategic proposals to senior management for growing the current business. Your manager, Cory Bohatenko, has asked you to join the team that's creating new growth proposals for senior management, because you've already done some research about the size and growth potential of the food processing industry in Canada.

Your Task. Using some of the informal and formal research methods mentioned in this chapter (e.g., questionnaires, Internet research) make the case to Cory—in a short informational report or email—that Richardson Milling should create a new division, Richardson Food Processing, to take Richardson Milling's milled oats and produce products (e.g., granola bars) to sell directly to retailers.

3.2 OUTLINING BEFORE DRAFTING (OBJ. 2)

As part of the Richardson Milling research project discussed in Case 3.1, create an outline before you draft your report or email to Cory. Cory has just mentioned that he'd like you to present your ideas at a departmental meeting at the end of the week, so you also need to create a PowerPoint slide deck.

Your Task. Using the outlining method mentioned in this chapter (i.e.., break a concept into its major components, with subpoints for each component, and supporting details for each subpoint), create a written outline of your research. Then, translate the outline into five straightforward PowerPoint slides that could be used at your upcoming meeting.

3.3 ORGANIZING BEFORE DRAFTING (OBJ. 2)

The Case 3.1 and 3.2 discuss your participation, so far, in the strategic business development process at Richardson Milling, one of Canada's largest agricultural companies. You researched the reasons that moving into food processing makes sense for Richardson Milling. You outlined your findings in a traditional outline format. You also presented your findings in a recent departmental meeting and received good feedback from your manager, Cory Bohatenko. He agrees with your recommendation, but he would like to see it framed more flexibly before he shows it to senior management.

Your Task. Review the information in the chapter on organizing information directly and indirectly. Use your top three reasons that Richardson should move into food processing to create a set of PowerPoint slides in which the reasons are presented in a direct way, and a set of slides in which the reasons are presented in an indirect way. Do an informal survey of 10 to 15 friends, coworkers, or family members and ask them which set of slides they find more useful or persuasive. Report the results of your survey back to your instructor and class.

WRITING IMPROVEMENT EXERCISES

SENTENCE TYPE (OBJ. 3)

Your Task. For each of the following sentences, select the letter that identifies its type:

a. Simple sentence

b. Compound sentence

c. Complex

d. Compound-complex

1. Many companies are now doing business in international circles.
2. If you travel abroad on business, you may bring gifts for business partners.
3. In Latin America a knife is not a proper gift; it signifies cutting off a relationship.
4. When Arabs, Middle Easterners, and Latin Americans talk, they often stand close to each other.

5. Unless they are old friends, Europeans do not address each other by first names; consequently, businesspeople should not expect to do so.

6. In the Philippines men wear a long embroidered shirt called a *barong*, and women wear a dress called a *terno*.

SENTENCE FAULTS (OBJ. 3)

Your Task. In each of the following sentences, identify the sentence fault (fragment, run-on, comma splice). Then revise the sentence to remedy the fault.

1. Because 90 percent of all business transactions involve written messages. Good writing skills are critical.

2. Darcy agreed to change her password. Even though she thought her old one was just fine.

3. Major soft-drink companies considered a new pricing strategy, they tested vending machines that raise prices in hot weather.

4. Thirsty consumers may think that variable pricing is unfair they may also refuse to use the machine.

5. About 95 percent of Pizza Pizza's 750 outlets make deliveries, the others concentrate on walk-in customers.

6. McDonald's sold its chain of Chipotle Mexican Grill restaurants the chain's share price doubled on the next day of trading.

EMPHASIS (OBJ. 4)

Your Task. For each of the following sentences, choose (a) or (b). Be prepared to justify your choice.

1. Which is more emphatic?
   a. Our dress code is fine.
   b. Our dress code reflects common sense and good taste.

2. Which is more emphatic?
   a. A budget increase would certainly improve hiring.
   b. A budget increase of $70,000 would enable us to hire two new people.

3. Which is more emphatic?
   a. The committee was powerless to act.
   b. The committee was unable to take action.

4. Which de-emphasizes the refusal?
   a. Although our resources are committed to other projects this year, we hope to be able to contribute to your worthy cause next year.
   b. We can't contribute to your charity this year.

5. Which sentence places more emphasis on the date?
   a. The deadline is November 30 for health benefit changes.
   b. November 30 is the deadline for health benefit changes.

6. Which is *less* emphatic?
   a. One division's profits decreased last quarter.
   b. Profits in beauty care products dropped 15 percent last quarter.

7. Which sentence *de-emphasizes* the credit refusal?
   a. We are unable to grant you credit at this time, but we welcome your cash business and encourage you to reapply in the future.
   b. Although credit cannot be granted at this time, we welcome your cash business and encourage you to reapply in the future.

8. Which sentence gives more emphasis to *leadership*?
   a. Jason has many admirable qualities, but most important is his leadership skill.
   b. Jason has many admirable qualities, including leadership skill, good judgment, and patience.

9. Which is more emphatic?

    a. We notified three departments: (1) Marketing, (2) Accounting, and (3) Distribution.

    b. We notified three departments:

        1. Marketing

        2. Accounting

        3. Distribution

ACTIVE VOICE (OBJ. 4)

Your Task. Business writing is more forceful when it uses active-voice verbs. Revise the following sentences so that verbs are in the active voice. Put the emphasis on the doer of the action.

Passive: Antivirus software was installed by Ching on his computer.

Active: Ching installed antivirus software on his computer.

1. Employees were given their cheques at 4 p.m. every Friday by the manager.
2. New spices and cooking techniques were tried by Ali Baba's to improve its falafels.
3. Our new company logo was designed by my boss.
4. The managers with the most productive departments were commended by the CEO.

PASSIVE VOICE (OBJ. 4)

Your Task. Revise the following sentences so that they are in the passive voice.
1. The auditor discovered a computational error in the company's tax figures.
2. We discovered the error too late to correct the balance sheet.
3. Stacy did not submit the accounting statement on time.
4. Competition Bureau Canada targeted deceptive diet advertisements by weight-loss marketers.

PARALLELISM (OBJ. 4)

Your Task. Revise the following sentences so that their parts are balanced.
1. (**Hint:** Match adjectives.) To be hired, an applicant must be reliable, creative, and show enthusiasm.
2. (**Hint:** Match active voice.) If you have decided to cancel our service, please cut your credit card in half and the pieces should be returned to us.
3. (**Hint:** Match verbs.) Guidelines for improving security at food facilities include inspecting incoming and outgoing vehicles, restriction of access to laboratories, preventing workers from bringing personal items into food-handling areas, and inspection of packaging for signs of tampering.
4. (**Hint:** Match adjective-noun expressions.) The committee will continue to monitor merchandise design, product quality, and check the feedback of customers.
5. (**Hint:** Match verb clauses.) To use the fax copier, insert your meter, the paper trays must be loaded, indicate the number of copies needed, and your original sheet should be inserted through the feeder.
6. (**Hint:** Match -*ing* verbs.) Sending an email establishes a more permanent record than to make a telephone call.

DANGLING AND MISPLACED MODIFIERS (OBJ. 4)

Your Task. Revise the following sentences to avoid dangling and misplaced modifiers.
1. After leaving the midtown meeting, Angela's car would not start.
2. Walking up the driveway, the Hummer parked in the garage was immediately spotted by the detectives.
3. To complete the project on time, a new deadline was established by the team.

4. Acting as manager, several new employees were hired by Mr. Singh.

5. Michelle Mitchell presented a talk about workplace drug problems in our boardroom.

ORGANIZING PARAGRAPH SENTENCES (OBJ. 5)

Your Task. In a memo to the college president, the athletic director argues for a new stadium scoreboard. One paragraph will describe the old scoreboard and why it needs to be replaced. Study the following list of ideas for that paragraph.

1. The old scoreboard is a tired warhorse that was originally constructed in the 1970s.

2. It is now hard to find replacement parts when something breaks.

3. The old scoreboard is not energy efficient.

4. Pizza Nova has offered to buy a new sports scoreboard in return for exclusive rights to sell pizza on campus.

5. The old scoreboard should be replaced for many reasons.

6. It shows only scores for football games.

7. When we have soccer games or track meets, we are without a functioning scoreboard.

   1. Which sentence should be the topic sentence?

   2. Which sentence(s) should be developed in a separate paragraph?

   3. Which sentences should become support sentences?

BUILDING COHERENT PARAGRAPHS (OBJ. 5)

1. **Your Task.** Use the information in the following sentences to write a coherent paragraph about replacing the sports scoreboard. Strive to use three devices to build coherence: (a) repetition of key words, (b) pronouns that clearly refer to previous nouns, and (c) transitional expressions. **Note:** Many possible revisions may be appropriate for all of the following sentences.

   - The old scoreboard is a tired warhorse that was originally constructed in the 1970s.
   - It is now hard to find replacement parts when something breaks.
   - The old scoreboard is not energy efficient.
   - Pizza Nova has offered to buy a new sports scoreboard in return for exclusive rights to sell pizza on campus.
   - The old scoreboard should be replaced for many reasons.
   - It shows only scores for football games.
   - When we have soccer games or track meets, we are without a functioning scoreboard.

2. **Your Task.** Revise the following paragraph. Add a topic sentence and improve the organization. Correct problems with pronouns, parallelism, wordiness, and misplaced or dangling modifiers. Add transitional expressions if appropriate.

   > You may be interested in applying for a new position within the company. The Human Resources Department has a number of jobs available immediately. The positions are at a high level. Current employees may apply immediately for open positions in production, for some in marketing, and jobs in administrative support are also available. To make application, these positions require immediate action. Come to the Human Resources Department. We have a list showing the open positions, what the qualifications are, and job descriptions are shown. Many of the jobs are now open. That's why we are sending this now. To be hired, an interview must be scheduled within the next two weeks.

3. **Your Task.** Revise the following paragraph. Add a topic sentence and improve the organization. Correct problems with pronouns, parallelism, wordiness, and misplaced or dangling modifiers.

   > As you probably already know, this company (Lasertronics) will be installing new computer software shortly. There will be a demonstration April 18, which is a Tuesday. You are invited. We felt this was necessary because this new software is so different from our previous software. It will be from 9 to 12 a.m. in the morning. This will show employees how the software programs

work. They will learn about the operating system, and this should be helpful to nearly everyone. There will be information about the new word processing program, which should be helpful to administrative assistants and product managers. For all you people who work with payroll, there will be information about the new database program. We can't show everything the software will do at this one demo, but for these three areas there will be some help at the Tuesday demo. Presenting the software, the demo will feature Paula Roddy. She is the representative from Quantum Software.

4. **Your Task.** From the following information, develop a coherent paragraph with a topic and support sentences. Strive for conciseness and coherence.

- Car dealers and lenders offer a variety of loan terms.
- To get the best deal, shop around when buying a new or used car.
- You have two payment options: you may pay in full or finance over time.
- You should compare offers and be willing to negotiate the best deal.
- If you are a first-time buyer—or if your credit isn't great—be cautious about special financing offers.
- Buying a new or used car can be challenging.
- Financing increases the total cost of the car because you are also paying for the cost of credit.
- If you agree to financing that carries a high interest rate, you may be taking a big risk. If you decide to sell the car before the loan expires, the amount you get from the sale may be far less than the amount you need to pay off the loan.
- If money is tight, you might consider paying cash for a less expensive car than you originally had in mind.

◣ GRAMMAR/MECHANICS CHALLENGE 3

VERBS

Review Sections 1.10–1.15 of the Grammar/Mechanics Handbook. Then study each of the following statements. Underline any verbs that are used incorrectly. In the space provided, write the correct form (or *C* if correct) and the number of the G/M principle illustrated. When you finish, compare your responses with those provided near the end of the book. If your responses differ, study carefully the principles in parentheses.

has (1.10c)   **Example**   Every one of the top-ranking executives <u>have</u> been insured.

_____   1. Are you convinced that Google's database of customers' messages and private information are secure?

_____   2. Google's data team have been carefully studying how to shield users from unwarranted government intrusion.

_____   3. BMO, along with most other large national banks, offer a variety of savings plans.

_____   4. In the next building is the administrative staff and our marketing people.

_____   5. The city council have unanimously approved the parking fee hike.

_____   6. If you was in my position, you might agree with my decision.

_____   7. Everyone except the temporary workers employed during the past year has become eligible for health benefits.

_____   8. All employees should have went to the emergency procedures demonstration.

_____   9. The reports have laid on his desk for 11 days and are now overdue.

_____   10. Either of the flight times are fine with me.

_____   11. Some of the jury members believes that the Crown's evidence is not relevant.

In the space provided, write the letter of the sentence that illustrates consistency in subject, voice, tense, and mood.

_____   12. a. By carefully following the instructions, much time can be saved.

_____   b. By carefully following the instructions, you can save much time.

_____ 13. a. All employees must fill out application forms; only then will you be insured.

_____ b. All employees must fill out application forms; only then will they be insured.

_____ 14. a. First, advertise the position; then, evaluate applications.

_____ b. First, advertise the position; then, applications must be evaluated.

_____ 15. a. Our manager was a computer whiz who was always ready to help.

_____ b. Our manager was a computer whiz who is always ready to help.

◤ EDITING CHALLENGE 3

This message is from a financial planner answering an inquiry about eBay profits. The message has proofreading, spelling, grammar, punctuation, wordiness, and other writing faults that require correction. Study the guidelines in the Grammar/Mechanics Handbook, as well as the lists of Confusing Words and Frequently Misspelled Words at the end of the book, to sharpen your skills.

Your Task. Edit the following message by correcting its errors (a) in your textbook or (b) on a photocopy using proofreading marks from Appendix B.

CAPITAL FINANCIAL PLANNERS
Certified Financial Planners
1001-128 Sparks St.
Ottawa, ON K1A 2B7
613 205-5000
c.chagnon@capitalplanners.ca

September 12, 2020
Ms. Stephanie Papineau
2509 Hunt Club Rd.
Ottawa, ON K7B 5R3

Dear Stephany:

I just wanted to let you know that, as your Financial Planner, I'm happy to respond to your request for more information and clarification on the Tax status of eBay profits.

As you in all probability are all ready aware of, you can use eBay to clean out your closets or eBay can be used to run a small business. Your smart to enquire about your tax liability. Although there is no clear line that separates fun from profit or a hobby from a business. One thing is certin, the CRA taxes all income.

There are a number of factors that help determine whether or not your hobby should or should not be considered a business. To use eBay safely, the following questions should be considered:

1. Do you run the operation in a businesslike manner? Do you keep records, is your profit and loss tracked, and how about keeping a seperate checking account?

2. Do you devote a lot of time and effort to eBay? If you spend eighteen hours a day selling on eBay the CRA would tend to think your in a business.

3. Some people depend on the income from their eBay activitys for their livelihood.

Are you selling items for more then they cost you? If you spend five dollars for a Garage Sale vase and sell it for fifty dollars the CRA would probably consider this a business transaction.

All profits is taxable. Even for eBay sellers who are just playing around. If you wish to discuss this farther please call me at 613-205-5000.

Sincerely,
Charles Chagnon
Certified Financial Planner

Monkey Business Images/Shutterstock.com

REVISING YOUR MESSAGE

BIZ COMM BYTE

A recent study on patient information brochures contained in inhalers prescribed to Canadians with chronic pulmonary disease (e.g., emphysema, asthma) found that "consumer information intended to educate patients on medications . . . provides adequate instructions for use; however, the main messages contained in the documents were negative, severe, and sometimes inappropriate. In addition, improvements in the readability of the patient information sections are possible since none of them were rated at the appropriate reading level. Previous calls to improve the design of educational materials have not been acted upon."

Source: Fullmann, K., Blackburn, D. F., Fenton, M. E., & Mansell, H. (2017). Readability and suitability of COPD consumer information. *Canadian Respiratory Journal*, Article 2945282. https://doi.org/10.1155/2017/2945282

4.1 Taking Time to Revise

In this digital age of emailing, texting, and tweeting, the idea of stopping to revise a message before clicking "send" seems almost alien to productivity. However, sending quick but sloppy business messages (especially over time) not only fails to enhance productivity but produces the opposite result. And in cases like the Biz Comm Byte above, in which the quality of a message *can directly affect a person's well-being*, there are clearly even more severe consequences than lost productivity.

In businesses from pharmaceuticals to construction to banking, rushed messages can be confusing and frustrating and take away from your credibility. They often set into motion a frustrating series of back-and-forth messages seeking clarification.

To avoid messages that waste time, create confusion, and reduce credibility, take time to slow down and revise—even for short messages.

The final phase of the 3-x-3 writing process focuses on editing, proofreading, and evaluating. Editing means improving the content and sentence structure of your message. Proofreading is correcting its grammar, spelling, punctuation, format, and mechanics. Evaluating involves analyzing whether your message achieves its purpose.

The revision phase is your chance to make sure your message says what you mean, makes you look good, and achieves its audience-centred purpose.

Whether you revise immediately or after a break, you'll want to examine your message critically. You should be especially concerned with ways to improve its conciseness, clarity, and readability.

Cengage

MINDTAP

In MindTap go to the Whiteboard Animation for Chapter 4 and watch it now.

4.1a Tighten Messages by Revising for Conciseness

In business, time is money. Translated into writing, this means that concise messages save reading time and, thus, money. In addition, messages that are written directly and efficiently are easier to read and comprehend. In the revision process, look for more efficient ways to say what you mean. Could the thought be conveyed in fewer words? Your writing will be more concise if you eliminate flabby expressions, drop unnecessary introductory words, get rid of redundancies, and purge empty words.

ELIMINATE FLABBY EXPRESSIONS. As you revise, focus on eliminating flabby expressions. This takes conscious effort. For example, notice the flabbiness in this sentence: *Due to the fact that sales are booming, profits are strong.* It could be said more concisely: *Because sales are booming, profits are strong.* Many flabby expressions can be shortened to one concise word as illustrated in the table below and in Figure 4.1.

DON'T Flabby	DO✓ Concise
✗ as a general rule	✓ generally
✗ at a later date	✓ later
✗ at this point in time	✓ now, presently
✗ despite the fact that	✓ although
✗ due to the fact that, inasmuch as, in view of the fact that	✓ because
✗ feel free to	✓ please
✗ for the period of, for the purpose of	✓ for
✗ in addition to the above	✓ also
✗ in all probability	✓ probably
✗ in the event that	✓ if
✗ in the near future	✓ soon
✗ in very few cases	✓ seldom, rarely
✗ until such time as	✓ until

LIMIT LONG LEAD-INS. Another way to create concise sentences is to delete unnecessary introductory words. Consider this sentence: *I am sending you this email*

Revising Digital Documents Using Microsoft Word's Track Changes

~~This is a short note to let you know that, as~~ **As** you requested, I ~~made an investigation of~~ investigated several of our competitors' websites. Attached ~~hereto~~ is a summary of my findings. ~~of my investigation.~~ I was ~~really~~ most interested in ~~making a comparison of the employment of strategies for~~ comparing marketing **strategies** as well as ~~the use of~~ navigational graphics ~~used~~ to guide visitors through the sites. ~~In view of the fact that~~ Because we will be revising our own website ~~in the near future~~ soon, I was ~~extremely~~ intrigued by the organization, ~~kind of~~ marketing tactics, and navigation at each ~~and every~~ site I visited.

When revising Word documents, you can use Word's easy Track Changes feature which strikes out (in red) what you'd like to delete, and adds in (also in red) what you'd like to add. Track Changes can be enabled by going to the "Review" tab at the top of any Word document and clicking on "Track Changes."

Revising Printed Documents Using a Pencil or Pen and Proofreading Symbols
When revising printed documents, use proofreading symbols to manually show your revisions.

~~This is a short note to let you know that,~~ as you requested, I ~~made an~~ investigat~~ion of~~^ed several of our competitors' websites. Attached ~~hereto~~ is a summary of my findings. ~~of my investigation.~~ I was ~~really~~ most interested in ~~making a comparison of the employ~~^comparing ~~ment of~~ strategies ~~for marketing~~^marketing as well as ~~the use of~~ navigational graphics ~~used~~ to guide visitors through the sites. ~~In view of the fact that~~^Because we will be revising our own website ~~in the near future,~~^soon I was ~~extremely~~ intrigued by the organization, ~~kind of~~ marketing tactics, and navigation at each ~~and every~~ site I visited.

Popular Proofreading Symbols

Delete	℘
Capitalize	≡
Insert	∧
Insert comma	⋀
Insert period	⊙
Start paragraph	¶

to announce that a new manager has been hired. A more concise and more direct sentence deletes the long lead-in: *A new manager has been hired.* The meat of the sentence often follows the long lead-in.

DON'T	Wordy	DO ✓	Concise
✗	We are sending this announcement to let everyone know that we expect to change Internet service providers within six weeks.	✓	We expect to change Internet service providers within six weeks.
✗	This is to inform you that you may find lower airfares at our website.	✓	You may find lower airfares at our website.
✗	I am writing this letter because Professor Brian Wilson suggested that your organization was hiring trainees.	✓	Professor Brian Wilson suggested that your organization was hiring trainees.

DROP UNNECESSARY THERE IS/ARE AND IT IS/WAS FILLERS. In many sentences the expressions *there is/are* and *it is/was* function as unnecessary fillers. In addition to taking up space, these fillers delay getting to the point of the sentence. Eliminate them by tweaking the sentence. Many—but not all—sentences can be revised so that fillers are unnecessary.

DON'T Wordy	DO✓ Concise
✗ *There are* more women than men enrolled in college today.	✓ More women than men are enrolled in college today.
✗ *There is* an aggregator that collects and organizes blogs.	✓ An aggregator collects and organizes blogs.
✗ *It was* the *Globe and Mail* that first reported the story.	✓ The *Globe and Mail* first reported the story.

REJECT REDUNDANCIES. Expressions that repeat the same idea or include unnecessary words are redundant. Saying *unexpected surprise* is like saying *surprise surprise* because *unexpected* carries the same meaning as *surprise*. Excessive adjectives, adverbs, and phrases often create redundancies and wordiness. Redundancies do not add emphasis, as some people think. Instead, they identify a writer as inexperienced. As you revise, look for redundant expressions such as the following:

DON'T Redundant	DO✓ Concise
✗ absolutely essential	✓ essential
✗ adequate enough	✓ adequate
✗ basic fundamentals	✓ fundamentals *or* basics
✗ big in size	✓ big
✗ combined together	✓ combined
✗ exactly identical	✓ identical
✗ each and every	✓ each *or* every
✗ necessary prerequisite	✓ prerequisite
✗ new beginning	✓ beginning
✗ refer back	✓ refer
✗ repeat again	✓ repeat
✗ true facts	✓ facts

DELETE EMPTY WORDS. Familiar phrases roll off the tongue easily, but many contain unnecessary parts. Be alert to these empty words and phrases: *case, degree,* *the fact that*, *factor*, *instance*, *nature*, and *quality*. Notice how much better the following sentences sound when we remove all the empty words:

> ~~In the case of~~ GO Transit, ~~they~~ improved customer satisfaction by adding more trips between Kitchener-Waterloo and Toronto.

> Because of ~~the degree of~~ support from upper management, the plan worked.

> We are aware ~~of the fact~~ that sales of new products soar when pushed on social media.

> Except for ~~the instance of~~ Toyota, Japanese imports sagged.

> She chose a career in a field that was analytical ~~in nature~~. [OR: She chose a career in an analytical field.]

> Student writing in that class is excellent ~~in quality~~.

Also avoid saying the obvious. In the following examples, notice how many unnecessary words can be omitted through revision:

> ~~When it arrived,~~ I deposited your e-transfer immediately. (Announcing the e-transfer's arrival is unnecessary. That fact is assumed in "deposited.")

> As consumers learn more about ingredients ~~and as they become more knowledgeable~~, they are demanding fresher foods. (Avoid repeating information.)

Look carefully at clauses beginning with *that*, *which*, and *who*. They can often be shortened without loss of clarity. Search for phrases such as *it appears that*. These phrases often can be reduced to a single adjective or adverb such as *apparently*.

> Changing the name of a ^successful^ company ~~that is successful~~ is always risky.

> All employees ~~who are among those~~ completing the course will be reimbursed.

> Our ^final^ proposal, ~~which was~~ slightly altered ~~in its final form~~, was approved.

> We plan to schedule ^weekly^ meetings ~~on a weekly basis~~.

4.1b Write Concisely When Microblogging and Posting on Social Media

Concise expression is especially important in microblogging. As its name suggests, *microblogging* consists of short messages exchanged on social media such as Twitter and Facebook. Many businesses are eagerly joining these microblogging networks to hear what's being said about them and their products. When they hear complaints, they can respond immediately and often solve customer problems. Companies are also using microblogging to make marketing announcements, improve their image, and sell their products.

Microblogging may be public or private. Twitter and similar social networks are predominantly public channels with messages broadcast externally to the world. Twitter limits each post ("tweet") to 140 characters, including spaces, punctuation, and links. Recognizing the usefulness of microblogging, some Canadian companies like Edmonton's DevFacto Technologies (devfacto.com) have adopted services like Slack or Yammer exclusively for internal communication among employees.[1]

In this type of digital communication, your messages must be short—without straying too far from conventional spelling, grammar, and punctuation. Sound difficult? It is, but it can be done, as shown in the following 140-character examples of workplace tweets:

Henry's Camera Response to Customer Issue
@complainer The manual can be confusing about that problem. Call me at 800-123-4567 or see http://bit.ly/xx for easy fix. Thanks, Henry's

Frank + Oak CEO Announces Meeting
Livestreaming the Frank + Oak Family quarterly all hands meeting 4-6 PM EST today! Tune in: http://on.fb.me/allhandslive

Air Canada Explains
Air Canada responds to loss of pressurization event on flight from YYC to YHZ [with a link to an Air Canada statement about the event]

Starbucks Thanks Customers
Throughout April, you contributed 231,000+ hours of community service in 34 countries across five continents. Thank You! #monthofservice

When microblogging, (a) include only main ideas, (b) choose descriptive but short words, (c) personalize your message if possible, and (d) be prepared to write several versions striving for conciseness, clarity, and, yes, even correctness.

4.2 Making Your Message Clear

A major revision task is assessing the clarity of your message. A clear message is one that's immediately understood. Employees, customers, and investors increasingly want to be addressed in a clear and genuine way. Fuzzy, long-winded, and unclear writing prevents comprehension. Readers understand better when information is presented clearly and concisely, as illustrated in a financial services example in Figure 4.2. Three techniques can improve the clarity of your writing: applying the KISS formula (Keep It Short and Simple), dumping trite business phrases, and avoiding clichés and slang.

4.2a Keep It Short and Simple (KISS)

To achieve clarity, resist the urge to show off or be fancy. As a business writer, your goal is to *express*, not *impress*. One way to achieve clear writing is to apply the KISS formula: active-voice sentences that avoid indirect, pompous language.

▌ FIGURE 4.2 / Conciseness Aids Clarity in Understanding Banking Facts

Consumers understand banking better when information is presented concisely and clearly, as in the bulleted list from this banking website.

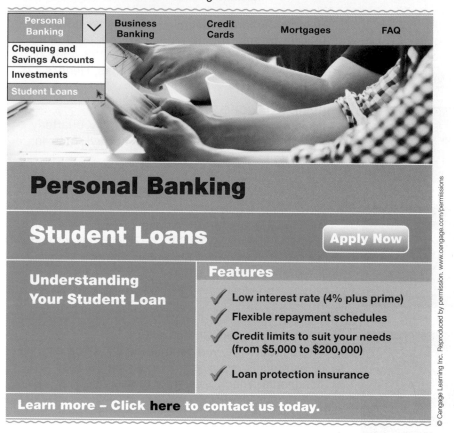

4.2b Dump Stale Business Phrases

To sound "businesslike," some business writers repeat the same stale expressions that others have used over the years. Your writing will sound fresher and more vigorous if you eliminate these phrases or find simpler or more original ways to convey the ideas.

DON'T Wordy and Unclear	DO✓ Short and Simple
✗ Employees have not been made sufficiently aware of the potentially adverse consequences regarding the use of these perilous chemicals.	✓ Warn your employees about these dangerous chemicals.
✗ In regard to the matter of obtaining optimal results, it is essential that employees be given the implements that are necessary for jobs to be completed satisfactorily.	✓ To get the best results, give employees the tools they need to do the job.

	Stale Phrase		Improvement
✗	as per your request	✓	as you request/asked
✗	pursuant to your request	✓	at your request
✗	enclosed please find	✓	enclosed is
✗	every effort will be made	✓	we'll try
✗	in accordance with your wishes	✓	as you requested
✗	in receipt of	✓	have received
✗	please do not hesitate to	✓	please
✗	respond forthwith	✓	respond immediately
✗	thank you in advance	✓	thank you
✗	under separate cover	✓	separately
✗	with reference to	✓	about

4.2c Drop Clichés

Clichés are expressions that have become exhausted by overuse. Many cannot be explained, especially to those who are new to our culture. Clichés lack not only freshness but also clarity. Instead of repeating clichés such as the following, try to find another way to say what you mean.

at the end of the day	last but not least
better than new	make a bundle
beyond a shadow of a doubt	pass with flying colours
easier said than done	quick as a flash
exception to the rule	shoot from the hip
fill the bill	step up to the plate
first and foremost	think outside the box
good to go	true to form

4.2d Avoid Slang and Buzzwords

Slang is informal words with arbitrary and changing meanings. Slang words quickly go out of fashion because they are no longer appealing when everyone begins to understand them. If you want to sound professional, avoid slangy expressions such as *stoked*, *blow the budget*, *the bomb*, and *getting burned*.

Buzzwords are technical expressions that have become fashionable and often are meant to impress rather than express. Business buzzwords include empty terms such as *optimize*, *incentivize*, *innovative*, *leveraging*, *scale*, and *paradigm shift*. Countless businesses today use vague rhetoric in the form of phrases such as *blue-sky*, *positioned to perform*, *solutions-oriented*, *ramping up*, and *value-add*.

WORDS OF WISDOM FROM CANADIAN BUSINESS

"Jargon provides familiarity and comfort; however, it can create a false sense of leadership security. Spitting out clichés and overworn vernacular may give you the feeling as though you're effectively leading, but in reality it brands leaders as shallow and lacking true leadership depth."

—Telus executive and author Dan Pontefract quoted in *The Globe and Mail.*

Source: Eichler, L. (2013, November 29). Let's move the needle on corporate jargon. *The Globe and Mail.* https://www. theglobeandmail.com/report-on-business/ careers/career-advice/life-at-work/lets-move-the-needle-on-corporate-jargon/ article15678358/

Consider the following statement by a government official who had been asked why he was dropping a proposal to license offshore oil drilling: *The Ministry has an awful lot of other things in the pipeline, and this has more wiggle room, so we just moved it down the totem pole.* He added, however, that the proposal might be offered again since *there is no pulling back because of hot-potato factors.* What exactly does this mean? And why use the culturally insensitive phrase "down the totem pole"? The official could simply have said: "We won't be licensing offshore drilling at this time, though we may consider doing so in future."

4.2e Rescue Hidden Verbs

Hidden verbs have been needlessly converted to wordy noun expressions. Verbs such as *acquire*, *establish*, and *develop* are made into nouns such as *acquisition*, *establishment*, and *development*. Such nouns often end in *-tion*, *-ment*, and *-ance*. Sometimes called *zombie nouns* because they cannibalize and suck the life out of active verbs,[2] these nouns increase sentence length, slow the reader, and muddy the thought. You can make your writing cleaner and more forceful by avoiding buried verbs and zombie nouns:

DON'T ✗ Hidden Verbs	DO ✓ Clear Verbs
✗ conduct a discussion of	✓ discuss
✗ create a reduction in	✓ reduce
✗ engage in the preparation of	✓ prepare
✗ give consideration to	✓ consider
✗ make an assumption of	✓ assume
✗ make a discovery of	✓ discover
✗ perform an analysis of	✓ analyze
✗ reach a conclusion that	✓ conclude
✗ take action on	✓ act

4.2f Control Exuberance

Occasionally, we show our exuberance with words such as *very*, *definitely*, *quite*, *completely*, *extremely*, *really*, *actually*, and *totally*. These intensifiers can emphasize and strengthen your meaning. Overuse, however, makes your writing sound unbusinesslike. Control your enthusiasm and guard against excessive use.

DON'T ✗ Excessive Exuberance	DO ✓ Businesslike
✗ The manufacturer was *extremely* upset to learn that its smartphones were *definitely* being counterfeited.	✓ The manufacturer was upset to learn that its smartphones were being counterfeited.
✗ We *totally* agree that we *actually* did not give his proposal a *very* fair trial.	✓ We agree that we did not give his proposal a fair trial.

4.2g Choose Clear, Precise Words

As you revise, make sure your words are precise so that the audience knows exactly what you mean. Clear writing creates meaningful images in the mind of the reader. Such writing includes specific verbs, concrete nouns, and vivid adjectives. Unclear messages contain sloppy references that may require additional inquiries to clarify their meaning.

DON'T Less Precise	DO✓ More Precise
✘ She requested that everyone help out.	✓ Our manager asked each team member to volunteer.
✘ They will consider the problem soon.	✓ Our steering committee will consider the recruitment problem on May 15.
✘ We received many responses.	✓ The Sales Division received 28 job applications.
✘ Someone called about the meeting.	✓ Russell Vitello called about the June 12 sales meeting.

◤ 4.3 Enhancing Readability Through Document Design

Well-designed messages are important in two ways. First, they enhance readability and comprehension. Second, they make readers think you are a well-organized and intelligent person. In the revision process, you have a chance to adjust formatting and make other changes so that readers grasp your main points quickly. Design techniques to improve readability include appropriate use of white space, margins, typefaces, fonts, numbered and bulleted lists, and headings for visual impact.

4.3a Use White Space

Empty space on a page is called *white space*. A page or screen crammed full of text or graphics appears busy, cluttered, and unreadable. To increase white space, use headings, bulleted or numbered lists, and effective margins. Remember that short sentences and short paragraphs improve readability and comprehension. As you revise, think about shortening long sentences. Consider breaking long paragraphs into shorter chunks.

4.3b Understand Margins and Text Alignment

Margins determine the white space on the left, right, top, and bottom of a block of type. They define the reading area and provide important visual relief. Business documents usually have side margins of 2.5 to 3.5 centimetres (1 to 1.5 inches).

Your writing software (e.g., Microsoft Word) probably offers four forms of margin alignment: (a) lines align only at the left, (b) lines align only at the right, (c) lines align at both left and right (*justified*), and (d) lines are centred. Nearly all text in Western cultures is aligned at the left and reads from left to right. The right margin may be either *justified* or *ragged right*. The text in books and other long works is usually justified on the left and right for a formal appearance.

On the other hand, as you type your own work, you'll notice that while it is left-justified, it is ragged on the right. This makes sense for academic assignments or for drafts of documents that might later be published (e.g., reports, websites). Finally, centred text is appropriate only for headings and short invitations, not for complete messages.

FIGURE 4.3 / Fonts with Different Personalities for Different Purposes

Serif	Sans Serif	Happy, Creative Script/Funny	Assertive, Bold Modern Display	Plain Monospaced
Century	Arial	*Brush Script*	**Britannic Bold**	Courier
Garamond	Calibri	Comic Sans	**Broadway**	Letter Gothic
Georgia	Helvetica	*Gigi*	**Elephant**	Monaco
Goudy	Tahoma	*Jokerman*	**Impact**	Prestige Elite
Palatino	Univers	Lucinda	Bauhaus 93	
Times New Roman	Verdana	Kristen	**SHOWCARD**	

© Cengage Learning

4.3c Choose Appropriate Fonts

Business writers can choose from a number of fonts (or typefaces) in their writing software. A font defines the shape of text characters. A wide range of fonts, as shown in Figure 4.3, is available for various purposes. Some are decorative and useful for special purposes. For most business messages, however, you should choose from *serif* or *sans serif* categories.

Serif typefaces have small features at the ends of strokes. The most common serif typeface is Times New Roman. Serif typefaces suggest tradition, maturity, and formality. They are frequently used for business and academic messages and longer documents. Because books, newspapers, and magazines favour serif typefaces, readers are familiar with them.

Sans serif typefaces include Arial, Calibri, Gothic, Tahoma, Helvetica, and Univers. These fonts are widely used for headings, signs, and material that does not require continuous reading. Web designers often prefer sans serif typefaces for simple, pure pages. For longer documents, however, sans serif typefaces may seem colder and less appealing than familiar serif typefaces.

For less formal messages or special decorative effects, you might choose one of the "happy" fonts such as Comic Sans or a bold typeface such as Impact. You can simulate handwriting with a script typeface. Despite the possibilities available in your software, don't get carried away with fancy typefaces (there has been a backlash against the use of Comic Sans for some time now, for example). Traditional serif fonts are most appropriate for your business messages, unless you're using PowerPoint in which case sans serif fonts are also useful. Generally, use no more than two typefaces within one document.

4.3d Choose an Appropriate Font Style

Font refers to a specific typeface family. Within that typeface, there are also a variety of styles you can use when creating messages. Below are examples of different font styles within the Verdana font/typeface:

CAPITALIZATION	underline
SMALL CAPS	Outline
bold	Shadow
italics	Emboss

Font styles are a mechanical way of adding emphasis to your words. ALL CAPS, SMALL CAPS, and **bold** are useful for headings, subheadings, and single words or short phrases in the text. ALL CAPS, HOWEVER, SHOULD NEVER BE USED FOR LONG STRETCHES OF TEXT BECAUSE ALL THE LETTERS ARE THE SAME HEIGHT. This makes it difficult for readers to differentiate words. In addition, excessive use of all caps feels like shouting and irritates readers.

Bold, *italics*, and <u>underlining</u> are effective for calling attention to important points and terms. Be cautious, however, that your use of fancy font styles is not excessive. Don't use them if they will confuse, annoy, or delay readers.

As you revise, think about type size. Readers are generally most comfortable with 12-point type for body text. Smaller type enables you to fit more words into a space. Tiny type, however, makes text look dense and unappealing. Slightly larger type makes material more readable. Overly large type (14 points or more) looks amateurish and out of place for body text in business messages. Larger type, however, is appropriate for headings.

4.3e Number and Bullet Lists for Quick Comprehension

One of the best ways to ensure rapid comprehension of ideas is to use numbered or bulleted lists. Lists provide high "skim value": readers can browse quickly and grasp main ideas. By breaking up complex information into smaller chunks, lists improve readability, understanding, and retention. They also force the writer to organize ideas and write efficiently.

When revising, look for ideas that could be converted to lists, and follow these techniques to make your lists look professional:

- **Numbered lists.** Use for items that represent a time-sequence or reflect a numbering system.
- **Bulleted lists.** Use to highlight items that don't necessarily show a chronology.
- **Capitalization.** Capitalize the initial word of each line.
- **Punctuation.** Add end punctuation only if the listed items are complete sentences.
- **Parallelism.** Make all the lines in the list consistent; for example, start each with a verb.

In the following examples, notice that the list on the left presents a sequence of steps with numbers. The bulleted list on the right does not show a sequence of ideas; therefore, bullets are appropriate. Also notice the parallelism in each example. In the numbered list, each item begins with a verb. In the bulleted list, each item follows an adjective/noun sequence. Business readers appreciate lists because they focus attention and save time.

Numbered List	Bulleted List
Follow these steps when hiring applicants: 1. Examine the application. 2. Interview the applicant. 3. Check the applicant's references.	To attract upscale customers, we feature the following: • Quality fashions • Personalized service • Generous return policy

4.3f Add Headings for Visual Impact

Headings help the reader separate major ideas from supporting details. They also provide a quick preview or review. Headings appear most often in reports, which you will study in Chapters 9 and 10. However, headings can also improve readability in emails, memos, and letters (see Figure 4.4). In the following example, notice how a *category heading* highlights each listing:

FIGURE 4.4 / Document Design Improves Readability

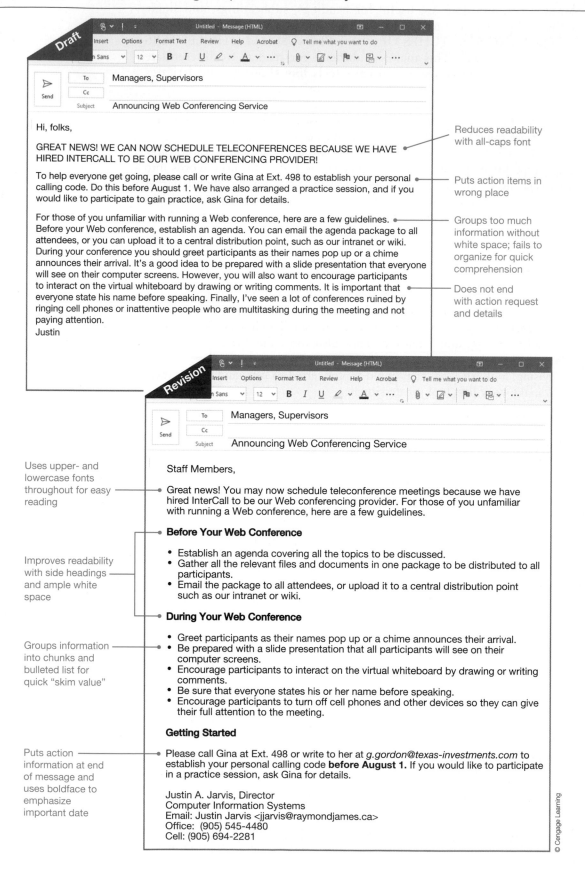

Draft

Untitled – Message (HTML)

Insert   Options   Format Text   Review   Help   Acrobat   Tell me what you want to do

Sans   12   **B** *I* U ...

To: Managers, Supervisors
Cc:
Subject: Announcing Web Conferencing Service

Hi, folks,

GREAT NEWS! WE CAN NOW SCHEDULE TELECONFERENCES BECAUSE WE HAVE HIRED INTERCALL TO BE OUR WEB CONFERENCING PROVIDER! ● — Reduces readability with all-caps font

To help everyone get going, please call or write Gina at Ext. 498 to establish your personal calling code. Do this before August 1. We have also arranged a practice session, and if you would like to participate to gain practice, ask Gina for details. ● — Puts action items in wrong place

For those of you unfamiliar with running a Web conference, here are a few guidelines. ● — Groups too much information without white space; fails to organize for quick comprehension
Before your Web conference, establish an agenda. You can email the agenda package to all attendees, or you can upload it to a central distribution point, such as our intranet or wiki. During your conference you should greet participants as their names pop up or a chime announces their arrival. It's a good idea to be prepared with a slide presentation that everyone will see on their computer screens. However, you will also want to encourage participants to interact on the virtual whiteboard by drawing or writing comments. It is important that ● — Does not end with action request and details
everyone state his name before speaking. Finally, I've seen a lot of conferences ruined by ringing cell phones or inattentive people who are multitasking during the meeting and not paying attention.
Justin

Revision

Untitled – Message (HTML)

Insert   Options   Format Text   Review   Help   Acrobat   Tell me what you want to do

Sans   12   **B** *I* U ...

To: Managers, Supervisors
Cc:
Subject: Announcing Web Conferencing Service

Uses upper- and lowercase fonts throughout for easy reading —

Staff Members,

Great news! You may now schedule teleconference meetings because we have hired InterCall to be our Web conferencing provider. For those of you unfamiliar with running a Web conference, here are a few guidelines.

Before Your Web Conference

Improves readability with side headings and ample white space —

- Establish an agenda covering all the topics to be discussed.
- Gather all the relevant files and documents in one package to be distributed to all participants.
- Email the package to all attendees, or upload it to a central distribution point such as our intranet or wiki.

During Your Web Conference

Groups information into chunks and bulleted list for quick "skim value" —

- Greet participants as their names pop up or a chime announces their arrival.
- Be prepared with a slide presentation that all participants will see on their computer screens.
- Encourage participants to interact on the virtual whiteboard by drawing or writing comments.
- Be sure that everyone states his or her name before speaking.
- Encourage participants to turn off cell phones and other devices so they can give their full attention to the meeting.

Getting Started

Puts action information at end of message and uses boldface to emphasize important date —

Please call Gina at Ext. 498 or write to her at *g.gordon@texas-investments.com* to establish your personal calling code **before August 1.** If you would like to participate in a practice session, ask Gina for details.

Justin A. Jarvis, Director
Computer Information Systems
Email: Justin Jarvis <jjarvis@raymondjames.ca>
Office: (905) 545-4480
Cell: (905) 694-2281

© Cengage Learning

WORKPLACE IN FOCUS

The need for readability in the workplace has recently led to the creation of a new type of business document: the infographic. A typical infographic, like the Statistics Canada infographic shown here, usually includes a number of iconic symbols (with 20 icons, this infographic has a higher number than is usual) representing in one page what a written report would need many pages to achieve, that is, highlight important findings on a useful topic for a general readership. Infographics leverage a number of the strategies outlined in this chapter: keep it short and simple, avoid slang, choose appropriate fonts, use lists for comprehension, and so on. However, some issues are present in the use of infographics. Most notable is that the need for simplicity in these documents can lead to important information being left out. For example, a reader can't tell from the government's infographic that significant unclean, unsafe, and unsustainable industrial practices exist in Canadian business. For example, according to Pulp and Paper Canada, in 2018 New Brunswick-based energy company Irving was charged for "several incidents that occurred between June 2014 and August 2016, when improperly treated and deleterious effluent was released from one of three outfall structures, all of which deposit into the Saint John River." The company paid one of the largest-ever environment violation-related fines in Canadian history as a result. *When a business infographic is attractive and easy to understand readable, how might it also be unethical? How can businesses be transparent about the good and the bad that takes place in their operations?*

Source: Statistics Canada, Environment, Energy and Transportation Statistics Division, Biennial Drinking Water Plants Survey. 2019. Published by authority of the Minister responsible for Statistics Canada, © Her Majesty the Queen in Right of Canada as represented by the Minister of Industry, 2019. All rights reserved. Use of this publication is governed by the Statistics Canada Open Licence Agreement. Catalogue no. 11-627-M.

Our company focuses on the following areas in the employment process:

- **Attracting applicants.** We advertise for qualified applicants, and we also encourage current employees to recommend good people.

- **Interviewing applicants.** Our specialized interviews include simulated customer encounters, as well as scrutiny by supervisors.

- **Checking references.** We investigate every applicant thoroughly. We contact former employers and all listed references.

In Figure 4.4 the writer converts a dense, unappealing email into an easier-to-read version by applying professional document design. Notice that the all-caps font shown earlier makes its meaning difficult to decipher. Lack of white space further reduces readability. In the revised version, the writer changes the unfriendly all-caps font to traditional upper- and lowercase. One of the best document design techniques in this message is the use of headings and bullets and white space to help the reader see chunks of information in similar groups. All of these improvements are made in the revision process.

◣ 4.4 Proofreading to Find Errors

Even the best writers make mistakes. The problem is not making the mistakes; the real problem is not finding and correcting them. Documents with errors affect your credibility and the success of your organization, as illustrated by the infographic in Figure 4.5.

After your message is in its final form, it's time to proofread. Don't proofread earlier because you may waste time checking items that eventually will be changed or omitted. Important messages—such as those you send to management or to customers—deserve careful revision and proofreading. When you finish a first draft of an important document, try to put the document aside and return to it after a suitable break. Proofreading our own work is especially difficult because most of us read what we *thought* we wrote. That's why it's important to look for specific problem areas.

▼ **FIGURE 4.5** / Why Proofread?

WHY PROOFREAD? IN BUSINESS, ACCURACY MATTERS

A survey of business professionals revealed the following:

100% said that writing errors influenced their opinions about a business.

57% will stop considering a company if its print brochure has one writing error.

77% have eliminated a prospective company from consideration in part because of writing errors.

75% thought misspelled words were inexcusable.

30% of Web visitors will leave if a website contains writing errors.

© Cengage Learning; Goodluz/Shutterstock.com

4.4a What to Watch for in Proofreading

Professional proofreaders check for problems in the following areas:

- **Spelling.** Now is the time to consult the dictionary. Is *recommend* spelled with one or two *c*'s? Do you mean *affect* or *effect*? Use your computer spell-checker, but don't rely only on it.
- **Grammar.** Locate sentence subjects; do their verbs agree with them? Do pronouns agree with their antecedents? Review the principles in the Grammar/Mechanics Handbook if necessary. Use your computer's grammar-checker, but don't rely on it.
- **Punctuation.** Make sure that introductory clauses are followed by commas. In compound sentences put commas before coordinating conjunctions (*and, or, but, nor*). Double-check your use of semicolons and colons.
- **Names and numbers and facts.** Compare all names and numbers and facts with their sources because inaccuracies are not always visible. Verify the spelling of the names of individuals receiving the message. Most of us immediately dislike someone who misspells our name.
- **Format.** Be sure that your document looks balanced on the page. Compare it with the standard documents (email, memo, letter) shown in Appendix A. If you indent paragraphs, be certain that all are indented and that their spacing is consistent.

4.4b How to Proofread Documents

Most routine documents require a light proofreading. If you read on screen, use the down arrow to reveal one line at a time. This focuses your attention at the bottom of the screen. A safer proofreading method, however, is reading from a printed copy. Regardless of which method you use, look for typos and misspellings. Search for easily confused words, such as *to* for *too* and *then* for *than*. Read for missing words and inconsistencies.

For printed messages, use standard proofreading marks, shown briefly in Figure 4.1 and completely in Appendix B. For digital documents and collaborative projects, use your software's **Comment** and **Track Changes** functions.

For longer, complex, or important documents proofread extra-carefully. Apply the previous suggestions but also add these techniques:

- Print a copy, preferably double-spaced, and set it aside for some time. You will proofread more effectively after a break.
- Allow enough time to proofread carefully. A common excuse for sloppy proofreading is lack of time.
- One student confessed, "I can find other people's errors, but I can't seem to locate my own." Psychologically, we don't expect to find errors, and we don't want to find them. You can overcome this obstacle by anticipating errors and congratulating, not criticizing, yourself each time you find one.
- Read the message at least twice—once for word meanings and once for grammar and mechanics. For very long documents, read a third time to verify consistency in formatting.
- Reduce your reading speed. Concentrate on individual words rather than ideas.
- For documents that must be perfect, enlist a proofreading buddy. Have someone read the message aloud, spelling names and difficult words, noting capitalization, and reading punctuation.
- Use the standard proofreading marks shown in Appendix B to indicate changes.

Many of us struggle with proofreading our own writing because we tend to see what we expect to see as our eyes race over the words without looking at each one carefully. We tend to know what is coming next and glide over it. To change the appearance of what you are reading, you might print it on a different coloured paper or change the font. If you are proofing on screen, enlarge the page view or change the background colour of the screen.

◤ 4.5 Evaluating the Effectiveness of Your Message

Remember that everything you write, after it's sent out, represents you and the organization you work for. If you were meeting in person, you'd be certain to dress appropriately and professionally. The same standard should apply to your writing.

- The best way to judge the success of your communications is through feedback. You should encourage the receiver, if appropriate, to respond to your message. His or her feedback will tell you how to modify future efforts to improve your communication technique.

- In school, your instructor will also evaluate your writing. Remember, this is constructive criticism, so don't be defensive. Look at these comments as valuable advice tailored to your specific writing weaknesses and strengths. Many businesses today spend significantly to hire communication consultants to improve employees' writing skills. You are getting the same training in this course.

- You, of course, are the best judge of the quality of your writing. In Chapter 2, this book provided you with three guiding questions to keep in mind *each time you communicate in business*: Is my message **Purposeful**? **Economical**? **Audience oriented**? Only when you can say *yes* each time you judge your draft message against these three criteria have you written an effective message.

- Finally, keep in mind the "professionalism" characteristics of business communicators discussed in Chapter 1. Employers and customers want their problems solved, not worsened. Therefore, a final way of evaluating your message before sending it is to ask yourself, "In this message, do I solve my audience's or receiver's problem, or do I add to the problem or make it worse?" *Only* if your message solves a problem should you hit "send"—if it doesn't, then rewrite the message until it does.

Cengage

MINDTAP

In MindTap go to the Study Tools for Chapter 4 and complete the Practice Test.

◤ LEARNING SUMMARY

4.1 Revise business messages for conciseness.

- Revise for conciseness by eliminating flabby expressions (*as a general rule, at a later date, at this point in time*).

- Exclude opening fillers (*there is, there are*), redundancies (*basic essentials*), and empty words (*in the case of, the fact that*).

- In microblogging messages, include only main ideas, choose descriptive but short words, personalize your message if possible, and be prepared to write several versions striving for conciseness, clarity, and correctness.

4.2 Improve clarity in business messages.

- To be sure your messages are clear, apply the KISS formula: Keep It Short and Simple.

- Avoid foggy, indirect, and pompous language.

- Do not include stale business phrases (*as per your request, enclosed please find, pursuant to your request*), clichés (*better than new, beyond a shadow of a doubt, easier said than done*), slang (*snarky, lousy, bombed*), and buzzwords (*optimize, paradigm shift, incentivize*).

- Avoid hiding verbs (*to conduct an investigation* rather than *to investigate, to perform an analysis* rather than *to analyze*).

- Don't overuse intensifiers that show exuberance (*totally, actually, very, definitely*) but sound unbusinesslike.

- Choose precise words (*the report was well-organized* rather than *the report was great*).

4.3 Enhance readability through effective document design.

- Enhance readability and comprehension by using ample white space, appropriate side margins, and ragged-right (not justified) margins.

- Use serif typefaces (fonts with small features at the ends of strokes, such as Times New Roman, Century, and Palatino) for body text; use sans serif typefaces (clean fonts without small features, such as Arial, Helvetica, and Tahoma) for headings and signs.

- Choose appropriate font styles and sizes for business messages.

- Provide high "skim value" with numbered and bulleted lists.

- Include headings to add visual impact and aid readability in business messages and reports.

4.4 Proofread to find mistakes in routine and complex documents.

- In proofreading be especially alert to spelling, grammar, punctuation, names, numbers, and document format.

- Proofread routine documents immediately after completion by reading line by line on the computer screen or, better yet, from a printed draft.

- Proofread more complex documents after a breather.

- Allow adequate time, reduce your reading speed, and read the document at least three times—for word meanings, for grammar and mechanics, and for formatting.

4.5 Evaluate messages to judge overall effectiveness.

- Encourage feedback from the receiver so that you can determine whether your communication achieved its goal.

- Welcome any advice from your instructor on how to improve your writing skills.

- Use principles outlined in Chapter 2—purpose, length, and audience—to judge all messages before they're sent

- Use professionalism competencies outlined in Chapter 1—namely, that problem solving is what employers and customers want today—to ensure your messages solve, not worsen, problems

CHAPTER REVIEW

1. What's involved in the revision process? Is revision still necessary in a digital age when workplace messages fly back and forth in split seconds? (Obj. 1)

2. What's wrong with a message that begins, *I am writing this announcement to let everyone know that . . .* ? (Obj. 1)

3. What is microblogging, and why is conciseness especially important in microblogging messages and social media posts? (Obj. 1)

4. What's wrong with familiar business phrases such as *as per your request* and *enclosed please find*? (Obj. 2)

5. Why should writers avoid expressions such as *first and foremost* and *think outside the box*? (Obj. 2)

6. What are buried verbs and zombie nouns? Give an original example of each. Why should writers avoid them? (Obj. 2)

7. How do bulleted and numbered lists improve readability? (Obj. 3)

8. In proofreading, why is it difficult for writers to find their own errors? How could they overcome this barrier? (Obj. 4)

9. What are five items to check in proofreading? Be ready to discuss methods you find useful in spotting these errors. (Obj. 4)

10. How can you overcome defensiveness when your writing is criticized constructively? (Obj. 5)

CRITICAL THINKING

1. In this digital age of rapid communication, how can you justify the time it takes to stop and revise a message? (Objs. 1–5)

2. Assume you have started a new job in which you respond to customers by using boilerplate (previously constructed) paragraphs. Some of them contain clichés such as *pursuant to your request* and *in accordance with your wishes*. Other paragraphs are wordy and violate the principle of using concise and clear writing that you have learned. What should you do? (Obj. 2)

3. Because business writing should have high "skim value," why not write everything in bulleted lists? (Obj. 3)

4. Conciseness is valued in business. However, can messages be too short? (Obj. 1)

5. What advice would you give in this ethical dilemma? Brittany is serving as interim editor of the company newsletter. She receives an article written by the company president describing, in abstract and pompous language, the company's goals for the coming year. Brittany thinks the article will need considerable revising to make it readable. Attached to the president's article are complimentary comments by two of the company vice presidents. What action should Brittany take and why? (Obj. 5)

ACTIVITIES AND CASES

4.1 CORPORATE ANNUAL REPORTS AND READABILITY (OBJ. 5)

One important channel a publicly traded corporation uses each year to get its message across is its corporate annual report. This document is important because it provides both shareholders and the general public with information about the organization's financial performance and any important activities it has undertaken that year. Most large Canadian corporations post their annual corporate reports on their websites. For example, Sobeys, the supermarket chain, includes its annual reports on its corporate website under "Our Company" and "Financial Information."

Your Task. Choose three well-known Canadian publicly traded companies in three different sectors (e.g., food, telecommunications, natural resources, manufacturing). Go to the companies' websites and download copies of their most recent corporate annual report. Spend 15 minutes scanning each report, making notes on ways in which the designer of the report has created readability. Based on your research, summarize what you find into three top strategies and then create a PowerPoint presentation or informational report on best practices in readability in Canadian corporate annual reports that you can with your class.

4.2 CORPORATE WEBSITES AND CONCISENESS (OBJ. 1)

Another very important communication channel is an organization's website. In fact, so important is this channel that for over 20 years, the International Academy of Digital Arts and Sciences has been handing out The Webby Awards to the best websites in a number of categories. Several Canadian individuals and organizations have won or been nominated for Webby Awards, as you can discover by visiting https://www.cbc.ca/news/entertainment/webby-2019-winners-1.5107088.

Your Task. Go to the Webby Awards site (https://www.webbyawards.com) and click on "Winners." Then, choose the most recent awards year. Next, choose three business-related websites from the list of winners and examine them closely. Spend about 15 minutes on each website, making notes on how the designers have achieved conciseness, especially in the written text on these sites. Based on your research, summarize what you find into the three top strategies and then create a PowerPoint presentation or informational report on best practices in conciseness in award-winning websites that you can share with your class. (Another way of completing this activity is to choose three well-known Canadian corporations and compare their websites for conciseness strategies.)

4.3 CORPORATE TWEETING AND CLARITY (OBJ. 2)

A number of recent high-profile cases demonstrate that the way a company or organization uses (or misuses) Twitter during a crisis can make or break its reputation. For example, during the Lac-Mégantic train derailment disaster in Québec in 2013, many members of the public used Twitter to find out what was going on in the small Québec town, because it was the only detailed information available. The train company involved in the disaster chose not to participate in social media and was roundly criticized as a result.

Your Task. Using the Google Scholar database, type in the keywords *tweeting and corporate crises*. Choose three recent peer-reviewed articles to scan or read. From your research, develop an instruction manual for your own organization or a different Canadian organization on how Twitter communications can be effectively written (as well as ineffectively written) during crises. Ensure that your manual (which can be written or given as a presentation) includes not just suggestions but also actual examples of good and bad tweets from previous organizational crises. How do effective tweeters create clarity in stressful situations?

WRITING IMPROVEMENT EXERCISES

FLABBY EXPRESSIONS (OBJ. 1)

Your Task. Revise the following sentences to eliminate flabby expressions.

1. We are sending a revised proposal at this point in time due to the fact that building costs have jumped at a considerable rate.

2. In the normal course of events, we would seek additional funding; however, in view of the fact that rates have increased, we cannot.

3. In very few cases has it been advisable for us to borrow money for a period of 90 or fewer days.

4. Inasmuch as our Web advertising income is increasing in a gradual manner, we might seek a loan in the amount of $50,000.

5. Despite the fact that we have had no response to our bid, we are still available in the event that you wish to proceed with your building project.

LONG LEAD-INS (OBJ. 1)

Your Task. Revise the following to eliminate long lead-ins.

1. This is an announcement to tell you that all computer passwords must be changed every six months for security purposes.

2. We are sending this memo to notify everyone that anyone who wants to apply for telecommuting may submit an application immediately.

3. I am writing this letter to inform you that your new account executive is Edward Ho.

4. This is to warn you that cyber criminals use sophisticated tools to decipher passwords rapidly.

5. This message is to let you know that social media services can position your company at the forefront of online marketing opportunities.

THERE IS/ARE AND IT IS/WAS FILLERS (OBJ. 1)

Your Task. Revise the following to avoid unnecessary *there is/are* and *it is/was* fillers.

1. There is a password-checker that is now available that can automatically evaluate the strength of your password.

2. It is careless or uninformed individuals who are the most vulnerable to computer hackers.

3. There are computers in Internet cafes, at conferences, and in airport lounges that should be considered unsafe for any personal use.

4. A computer specialist told us that there are keystroke-logging devices that gather information typed on a computer, including passwords.

5. If there are any questions that you have about computer safety, please call us.

REDUNDANCIES (OBJ. 1)

Your Task. Revise the following to avoid redundancies.

1. Because his laptop was small in size, he could carry it everywhere.

2. A basic fundamental of computer safety is to avoid storing your password on a file in your computer because criminals will look there first.

3. The manager repeated again his warning that we must use strong passwords.

4. Although the two files seem exactly identical, we should proofread each and every page.

5. The presenter combined together a PowerPoint presentation and a handout.

EMPTY WORDS (OBJ. 1)

Your Task. Revise the following to eliminate empty words.

1. Are you aware of the fact that social media can drive brand awareness and customer loyalty?
2. Except for the instance of MySpace, social networking sites are booming.
3. If you seek to build an online community that will support your customers, social media services can help.
4. With such a degree of active participation on Facebook and Twitter, it's easy to understand why businesses are flocking to social media sites.
5. We plan to schedule online meetings on a monthly basis.

STALE BUSINESS PHRASES (OBJ. 2)

Your Task. Revise the following sentences to eliminate stale business phrases.

1. Pursuant to your request, I will submit your repair request immediately.
2. Enclosed please find the list of customers to be used in our promotion.
3. As per your request, we are sending the contract under separate cover.
4. Every effort will be made to proceed in accordance with your wishes.
5. If we may help in any way, please do not hesitate to call.

CLICHÉS, SLANG, BUZZWORDS, AND WORDINESS (OBJ. 2)

Your Task. Revise the following sentences to avoid confusing clichés, slang, buzzwords, and wordiness.

1. Our manager insists that we must think outside the box in promoting our new kitchen tool.
2. I think we should be careful with budgets on a go-forward basis.
3. HR is going to have to pivot away from engagement surveys towards a more helpful metric
4. If you refer back to our five-year plan, you will see that we highlight ten divisional core competencies
5. BTW, did we get Marketing's buy-in yet or are they still blue-skying over there?

HIDDEN VERBS (OBJ. 2)

Your Task. Revise the following sentences to recover hidden verbs.

1. After doing an investigation, the fire department reached the conclusion that the blaze was set intentionally.
2. Our committee made a promise to give consideration to your proposal at its next meeting.
3. When used properly, zero-based budgeting can bring about a reduction in overall costs.
4. Did our department put in an application for increased budget support?
5. The budget committee has not taken action on any projects yet.
6. Homeowners must make a determination of the total value of their furnishings.

LISTS, BULLETS, AND HEADINGS (OBJ. 3)

1. **Your Task.** Revise the following poorly written sentences and paragraphs. Use lists, bullets, and category headings, if appropriate. Improve parallel construction and reduce wordiness.

Three Best Twitter Practices. There are three simple ways you can build an online following, drive your reputation, and develop customers' trust by using these uncomplicated and simple Twitter practices. First off, share some of your photos and information about your business from behind the scenes. Sharing is so important! Next, listen. That is, you should regularly monitor the comments about your company, what's being said about your brand, and any chatter about your products. And, of course, you should respond. In real time it is necessary to respond to statements that are compliments and just general feedback.

2. **Your Task.** Revise the following by incorporating a numbered list. Eliminate all the wordiness.

Computer passwords are a way of life at this point in time. In the creation of a strong password, you should remember a few things. First, you should come up with an eight-word phrase that is easy to remember, such as this: *my goal is a degree in 4 years*. Then take each of those words and the first letter should be selected, such as this: *mgiadi4y*. The last step for creating a really strong password is to exchange—that is, swap out—some of those letters for characters and capital letters: *Mgia$in4Y*.

3. **Your Task.** Revise the following paragraph by incorporating a bulleted list with category headings. Eliminate all the wordiness.

In response to your inquiry with questions about how credit scores are made, this is to let you know that there are four important factors that make up your credit score. Because you say you are interested in improving your score so that it reaches the highest level, you will be interested in this. One of the most important items lenders consider before approving anyone for a loan is your payment history. It is important that you have a long history of making payments on time. Almost as important is the amount of available credit that you have. If you are close to maxing out your accounts, you are a higher risk and will have a lower score. How long you have had accounts is also important. Accounts that have been open for ten years will help your credit score. Finally, if you are opening lots of new accounts, you can lower your credit score.

◤ GRAMMAR/MECHANICS CHALLENGE 4

ADJECTIVES AND ADVERBS

Review Sections 1.16 and 1.17 of the Grammar/Mechanics Handbook. Then study each of the following statements. Underline any adjectives and adverbs verbs that are used incorrectly. In the space provided, write the correct form (or *C* if correct) and the number of the G/M principle illustrated. You may need to consult your dictionary for current practice regarding some compound adjectives. When you finish, compare your responses with those provided near the end of the book. If your responses differ, carefully study the principles in parentheses.

cost-effective (1.17e)   **Example** We need a <u>cost effective</u> solution for this continuing problem.

_____   1. The newly opened restaurant offered many tried and true menu items.

_____   2. Amazingly, most of the ten year old equipment is still working.

_____   3. Although purchased ten years ago, the equipment still looked brightly.

_____   4. Global messages today are exchanged so quick that international business moves more rapidly than ever.

_____   5. The Senate's rewrite of the tax legislation couldn't have sent a more clearer message.

_____   6. You may submit only work related expenses to be reimbursed.

_____   7. Amanda and Max said that they're planning to open there own business next year.

_____   8. Haven't you ever made a spur of the moment decision?

_____   9. Not all decisions that are made on the spur of the moment turn out badly.

_____   10. The committee offered a well thought out plan to revamp online registration.

_____   11. You must complete a change of address form when you move.

_____   12. Each decision will be made on a case by case basis.

_____   13. I could be more efficient if my printer were more nearer my computer.

_____   14. If you reject his offer to help, Kurt will feel badly.

_____   15. The truck's engine is running smooth after its tune-up.

This message transmits a suggestion from an employee to her boss. The message has proofreading, spelling, grammar, punctuation, wordiness, and other writing faults that require correction. Study the guidelines in the Grammar/Mechanics Handbook, as well as the lists of Confusing Words and Frequently Misspelled Words at the end of the book, to sharpen your skills.

Your Task. Edit the following message by correcting its errors (a) in your textbook or (b) on a photocopy using proofreading marks from Appendix B.

To: Daniel R. Kesling <daniel.kesling@cibc.com>
From: Holly McKenney <holly.mckenney@cibc.com>
Subject: My Idea
Cc:
Bcc:

Mr. Kesling,

Due to the fact that you recently asked for ideas on how to improve customer relations I am submitting my idea. This message is to let you know that I think we can improve customer satisfaction easy by making a change in our counters.

Last June glass barriers were installed at our branch. There are tellers on one side and customers on the other. The barriers, however, do have air vents to be able to allow we tellers to carry on communication with our customers. Management thought that these bullet proof barriers would prevent and stop thiefs from jumping over the counter.

I observed that there were customers who were surprised by these large glass partitions. Communication through them is really extremely difficult and hard. Both the customer and the teller have to raise there voices to be heard. Its even more of a inconvenience when you are dealing with an elderly person or someone who happens to be from another country. Beyond a shadow of a doubt, these new barriers make customers feel that they are being treated impersonal.

I made an effort to research the matter of these barriers and made the discovery that we are the only bank in town with them. There are many other banks that are trying casual kiosks and open counters to make customers feel more at home.

Although it may be easier said than done, I suggest that we actually give serious consideration to the removal of these barriers as a beginning and initial step toward improving customer relations.
Holly McKenney
E-mail: misty.mckenney@cibc.com
Support Services
(514) 448-3910

Rawpixel.com/Shutterstock.com

UNIT
03

WRITING AT WORK

BUSINESS COMMUNICATION RESEARCH UPDATE

Emails From the Boss—Curse or Blessing? Relations Between Communication Channels, Leader Evaluation, and Employees' Attitudes

Stephan Braun, Alina Hernandez Bark, Alexander Kirchner, Sebastian Stegmann, and Rolf Van Dick. International Journal of Business Communication 2019, Vol. 56(1) 50 –81
© *The Author(s) 2015,*

Abstract: The present research investigates if and how a more digitally centered communication between supervisors and employees satisfies employees' needs regarding the communication with their supervisors and influences employees' attitudes toward the supervisor and the job. In a cross-sectional online study, 261 employees rated their supervisors' actual and ideal use of different communication channels (i.e., telephone, face-to-face, email) regarding quality and quantity. Employees' job satisfaction and their perceptions of their supervisors' effectiveness and team identification were measured as dependent variables. Employees perceived face-to-face communication to be of higher quality than telephone and email communication, and they indicated a preference for more face-to-face communication with their supervisors than they actually had. Moreover, the perceived quality of communication, especially via face-to- face, was strongly and positively related to the dependent variables. These results provide insights into potential problems of increasing e-leadership in organizations. We conclude with recommendations to reduce these problems.

INTRODUCTION

Leaders' communication behavior is essential for the success of organizations. As communication is a key component in coordinating and leading team members toward a common goal, leaders use roughly 80% of their working time for interactions with coworkers and employees (Neuberger, 2002; Riggio, Riggio, Salinas, & Cole, 2003). Leaders use communication to convey visions, assign tasks, establish relationships with employees, and to explain how tasks can be accomplished (Awamleh & Gardner, 1999; Den Hartog & Verburg, 1997; Riggio et al., 2003). One crucial aspect of such communication is the transfer and reception of all relevant information. To achieve this, leaders can utilize a variety of communication channels. . . .

This ongoing development toward electronic communication also changes the face of leadership in modern organizations. Indeed, a wide range of scholars agree that "e-leadership" will be the regular state instead of the exception in the future (Avolio, Sosik, Kahai, & Baker, 2014; Zaccaro & Baider, 2003). One reason for this trend could be that leadership proves to be especially important in virtual work contexts. For example, Purvanova and Bono (2009) compared the impact of transformational leadership between face-to-face and virtual teams. They found that transformational leadership had a stronger positive effect on team performance in virtual teams than in face-to-face settings. A possible reason for this need for leadership in virtual teams could be that the effects of various detrimental group processes are enhanced in such settings. For example, perceived social loafing of fellow team members is shown to affect team cohesion and work satisfaction more negatively in virtual settings than in face-to-face interactions (Monzani, Ripoll, Peiró, & van Dick, 2014). Effective e-leadership could counterbalance these heightened risks of virtual teamwork. Therefore, as computer-mediated communication and advanced communication technologies will likely gain in importance, e-leadership will gain in importance as well. . . .

THEORIES OF COMMUNICATION CHANNEL QUALITY

It has already been shown that the appropriate use of channels in communication at work is related to managerial effectiveness (Alexander, Penley, & Jernigan, 1991; Daft, Lengel, & Trevino, 1987). While face-to-face communication usually represents the most preferred communication channel, this preference varies strongly depending on the type of task (Reder & Conklin, 1987). Considering the trend toward more computer-mediated communication at work in general, it is important to examine whether the trend to more computer-mediated leadership reflects employees' needs. As comparisons of face-to-face communication, we chose the two considerably most common electronic communication channels used at work, that is, telephone and email. Vor dem Esche and Hennig-Thurau (2013), for instance, have shown that in 2012, over 75% of communication in the work context, besides face-to-face communication, was transmitted via email or telephone. . . .

Hypothesis 1: Employees prefer most of their communication with their leaders to be face-to-face. . . .

Hypothesis 2: Employees perceive a discrepancy between the actual and the ideal amount of (a) face-to-face, (b) email communication, and (c) telephone communication. Employees desire (a) more face-to-face communication, (b) less email communication, and (c) less telephone communication with their leader than they actually have. . . .

Hypothesis 3: The amount of face-to-face communication between leader and employee relates more positively to (a) job satisfaction and (b) the perceived effectiveness and team identification of the leader compared with the amount of the other communication channels (telephone and email). . . .

Hypothesis 4: Employee perceptions of (Hypothesis 4a) clarity, (Hypothesis 4b) leadership behavior, and (Hypothesis 4c) reliability in face-to-face communication will be more positive than in telephone and email communication.

METHOD

Sample and Procedure

Altogether, 328 participants took part in an online survey. As in previous research, participants were recruited by distributing the link to the online questionnaire through various mailing lists and social networks (see Escartin, Ullrich, Zapf, Schlüter, & van Dick, 2013). As an incentive for participation, two Amazon vouchers with a value of 50 Euros each were randomly raffled among the participants. After excluding participants with missing values on the core variables, the final sample consisted of 265 participants. . . .

RESULTS

Preference for Different Communication Channels and Comparison of Actual and Ideal Channel Amounts

In line with Hypothesis 1, participants showed a clear preference for face-to-face communication.

They reported that they wished to have almost two thirds (60%) of the communication with their leader to be face-to-face, followed by 26% of communication by email and only 13% to be communication by phone (see Table 4). Furthermore, the results of a paired t test showed that participants reported significant differences between the actual and ideal amount of communication channel use (see Table 4). These results confirmed Hypothesis 2: Participants reported that they ideally wanted more face-to-face communication than they actually have and less phone and email communication than they actually have. Additionally, repeated measurement analyses of covariance (ANCOVAs) with part- versus full-time working as control and the actual and ideal amount of each channel use revealed similar results. . . .

DISCUSSION

The results of our study regarding the quantity of communication channel use show that employees want to communicate mostly via face-to-face with their leaders, and even though leaders use face-to-face communication most often, employees still express a desire for an even more frequent use of this channel. The opposite patterns emerged for email communication and telephone communication. Although email only constitutes one-third and telephone around 14% in the actual communication, employees indicated the desire to communicate even less through these channels. Therefore, the general trend of greater electronic communication was not perceived positively as the communication of choice between leader and employee.

This is an important finding since we also find that the quantity of which the communication channels are used is related to employees' perceptions of the leader. The more face-to-face communication a leader uses, the more employees perceive him or her to be effective and identified. On the other hand, the more email communication is used, the less the leader appears identified to employees, and the more telephone communication is used, the less effective the leader seems to his or her employees.

In contrast, electronic communication is likely to produce a lack of social information and therefore feels "impersonal" as the qualitative data show (see also Kiesler, Siegel, & McGuire, 1984; Sproull & Kiesler, 1986). Thus, the excessive use of email conversation could lead to an emerging impression of the leader as not being interested in spending time with her or his employees (comparable to the effect of email as evidence that a communicator wants to avoid personal contact shown by Markus, 1994b).

This might result in a low perceived identification of the leader with the team or the organization. In this respect, out of the three communication channels in our study, face-to-face communication allows the strongest focus on social aspects. Because this focus on social aspects addresses the social side of employees' work life better than telephone conversations and much better than email communication, participants might show greater liking for face-to-face contact. . . .

CONCLUSIONS

The present study provides four important insights into employees' perceptions of the trend toward e-leadership and of how the use of different communication channels shape the impression they have of their leader. First, employees generally want to have more face-to-face communication with their leaders than they actually have—only in specific situations where email is better suited to the communication requirements than face-to-face, it is favored as communication channel. Second, out of the three communication channels, the frequency of face-to-face communication shows the strongest positive relationships with employee job satisfaction, and employees' perceptions of their leaders' effectiveness and team identification. Third, employees perceive face-to-face communication to be of better quality than communication via other channels. Fourth, the perceived communication quality of communication, especially via face-to-face, has a particular positive relationship with outcome variables like job satisfaction and is an important factor in the leader-employee interaction. In summary, our study provides evidence for employees' need for more personal interaction with their leader via face-to-face communication and less communication via telephone or email. We established that both the frequency of certain communication channels usage and the quality of communication are important for employees' evaluation of their leader and their own job satisfaction.

REFERENCES

Alexander, E. R., III, Penley, L. E., & Jernigan, I. E. (1991). The effect of individual differences on managerial media choice. *Management Communication Quarterly, 5*, 155–173.

Avolio, B. J., Sosik, J. J., Kahai, S. S., & Baker, B. (2014). E-leadership: Re-examining transformations in leadership source and transmission. *Leadership Quarterly, 25*, 105–131. doi:10.1016/j.leaqua.2013.11.003

Awamleh, R., & Gardner, W. L. (1999). Perceptions of leader charisma and effectiveness: The effects of vision content, delivery, and organizational performance. *Leadership Quarterly, 10*, 345–373.

Daft, R. L., Lengel, R. H., & Trevino, L. K. (1987). Message equivocality, channels selection, and manager performance: Implications for information systems. *MIS Quarterly, 11*, 355–366.

Den Hartog, D. N., & Verburg, R. M. (1997). Charisma and rhetoric: Communicative techniques of international business leaders. *Leadership Quarterly, 8*, 355–391.

Escartin, J., Ullrich, J., Zapf, D., Schlüter, E., & van Dick, R. (2013). Individual- and group-level effects of social identification on workplace bullying. *European Journal of Work and Organizational Psychology, 22*, 182–193. doi:10.1080/135 9432X.2011.647407

Kiesler, S., Siegel, J., & McGuire, T. W. (1984). Social psychological aspects of computer mediated communication. *American Psychologist, 39*, 1123–1134. Markus, M. L. (1994b). Finding a happy medium: Explaining the negative effects of electronic communication on social life at work. *ACM Transactions on Information Systems, 12*, 119–149.

Monzani, L., Ripoll, P., Peiró, J. M., & van Dick, R. (2014). Loafing in the digital age: The role of computer mediated communication in the relation between perceived loafing and group affective outcomes. *Computers in Human Behavior, 33*, 279–285. doi:10.1016/j. chb.2014.01.013

Neuberger, O. (2002). Führen und führen lassen. Ansätze, Ergebnisse und Kritik der Führungsforschung (6th ed.). [To lead and to allow leadership. Approaches, results, and criticism of leadership research]. Stuttgart, Germany: Lucius & Lucius.

Purvanova, R. K., & Bono, J. E. (2009). Transformational leadership in context: Face-to-face and virtual teams. *Leadership Quarterly, 20*, 343–357.

Reder, S., & Conklin, N. F. (1987, May). Selection and effects of channels in distributed communication and decision-making tasks: A theoretical review and a proposed research paradigm. Paper presented at the 37th Annual Conference of the International Communication Association, Montreal, Quebec, Canada.

Riggio, R. E., Riggio, H. R., Salinas, C., & Cole, E. J. (2003). The role of social and emotional communication skills in leader emergence and effectiveness. *Group Dynamics: Theory, Research, and Practice, 7*, 83–103.

Sproull, L., & Kiesler, S. (1986). Reducing social context cues: Electronic mail in organizational communication. *Management Science, 32*, 1492–1512.

Vor dem Esche, J., & Hennig-Thurau, T. (2013). German social media consumer report 2012/2013. Retrieved from http://www.rolandberger.de/media/pdf/Roland_Berger_Social_Media_Consumer_Report_20130219.pdf

Zaccaro, S. J., & Baider, P. (2003). E-leadership and the challenges of leading e-teams: Minimizing the bad and maximizing the good. *Organizational Dynamics, 31*, 377–387.

QUESTIONS

1. How does what you've learned in this article change your perception of what business communication is or is not?

2. How might what you've learned in this article be useful in changing your own school or workplace communication?

3. Come up with pro and con arguments for the following debate/discussion topic: "Managers need to put down their phones and take time away from their inbox to engage with employees face to face for the good of organizations." Make sure to reference Braun et al.'s findings in your arguments.

Fotos593.com/Shutterstock.com

WRITING DAILY MESSAGES

OBJECTIVES

5.1 Write daily messages using major workplace writing channels.

5.2 Format daily messages based on the sender's intentions.

5.3 Use instant messages and text messages professionally.

5.4 Create professional blog postings.

5.5 Create professional social media postings.

> ### BIZ COMM BYTE
>
> The most recent statistics on texting usage by Canadians show that 89 percent of Canadians text daily, and 30 percent text with coworkers and their favourite brands. If asked, 75 percent would give their consent to text with a trusted brand.
>
> Source: TTAG Systems. (2018, January 9). Canadian text messaging usage preferences: What marketers need to know. http://www.ttagsystems.com/sms-marketing-blog/canadian-sms-usage-preferences-what-marketers-need-to-know-infographic/

◤ 5.1 Daily Writing at Work

Writing today is a dynamic, interactive activity. This is quite different from writing before the Internet, which was a more static exchange between sender and receiver, following the model of communication we looked at in Chapter 2. Writers today are empowered by their devices to be active participants who correspond (often in real time) with colleagues and outsiders.

Virtual private networks (VPNs) offer secure access to company information from any location in the world that provides an Internet connection. In addition, in many businesses, desktop computers are fast becoming obsolete with the adoption of ever-smaller laptops, smartphones, and tablets. As a result, mobile and cloud computing are the two most important technological trends impacting business communication today.

Businesspeople today are connected—and writing—at all times. Many of them are expected to respond to messages on their smartphones wherever they are, even

Cengage

MINDTAP

In MindTap go to the Whiteboard Animation for Chapter 5 and watch it now.

on weekends or while on vacation. As a result, some argue that the communications technology revolution of the past 20 years has resulted in amazing productivity gains, whereas others point out that technological advances have perhaps created more (unnecessary) work.

You're already sharing pictures and music and messages digitally with your friends and family. Even though "personal" technology has entered the workplace, *this does not mean your workplace messages should look and sound the same as your personal messages.* The main difference is more structure and formality should be apparent at work than at home. Maintaining this difference is probably the most important lesson in business communication today.

5.1a Some Challenges and Advantages of Email

Email is by far the most frequently used daily writing channel in the majority of workplaces. For this reason, you should expect to use email extensively to communicate at work with colleagues, managers, and clients, and it's important to learn how to do it expertly.

Although email is recognized as the main channel for business communication, in a recent study of 1,800 workers, 40 percent stated that "they had received emails that made no sense whatsoever."[1] Adding to the complaints, Chris Carlson, former recruiting officer at the consulting firm of Booz Allen Hamilton Inc., says that new MBA graduates exchange more than 200 emails a day, and some look like text messages. "They're not [even] in complete sentences," he says.[2]

OVERLOAD. In addition to complaints about confusing and poorly written emails, many workers are overwhelmed by too many messages. The average employee receives 11,680 emails per year.[3] The unfortunate use of "Reply All" irritates those who have to plow through dozens of messages that barely relate to them. Others blame email for eliminating the distinction between work life and home life. They feel an urgency to be available 24/7 and respond immediately.

EVERLASTING EVIDENCE. After deletion, email files still leave trails on servers within and outside organizations. Messages are also backed up on other servers, making them traceable and recoverable by forensic experts. Your best bet is to put nothing in an email that you wouldn't post on your office door. Also, be sure that you know your organization's email policy before sending personal messages.

Email is, however, incredibly useful for all those short daily messages that offer and request information and respond to inquiries. It's especially effective for messages to multiple receivers and messages that need to be saved. Emails are also used as cover documents when sending longer attachments like proposals and reports and slide decks.

Finally, email isn't a substitute for face-to-face conversations or phone calls. These channels are much more successful if your goal is to convey enthusiasm or warmth, explain a complex situation, present a persuasive argument, or smooth over disagreements. One expert gives this wise advice: "Sometimes it's better to get off the computer and make a phone call. If emails are . . . just not getting the job done, call or walk over to that colleague."[4] Managers and employees echo this advice, as revealed in recent research. They believe in using face-to-face contact for critical work situations such as human resources annual reviews, discipline, and promotions.[5]

5.1b Drafting Professional Emails

Professional emails are different from messages you send to friends and family. Instead of a casual vocabulary and tone, professional emails are organized messages with a slightly formal tone that communicate non-sensitive information unlikely to upset readers. Therefore, they should be organized directly and contain the five elements described in the writing plan below (and shown in Figure 5.1).

Cengage

MINDTAP

In MindTap, go to the Chapter 5 reading, section 5.1a, and watch the video of industry expert Taylor Roberts discussing the importance of effective emails in the workplace.

FIGURE 5.1 / Professional Business Email

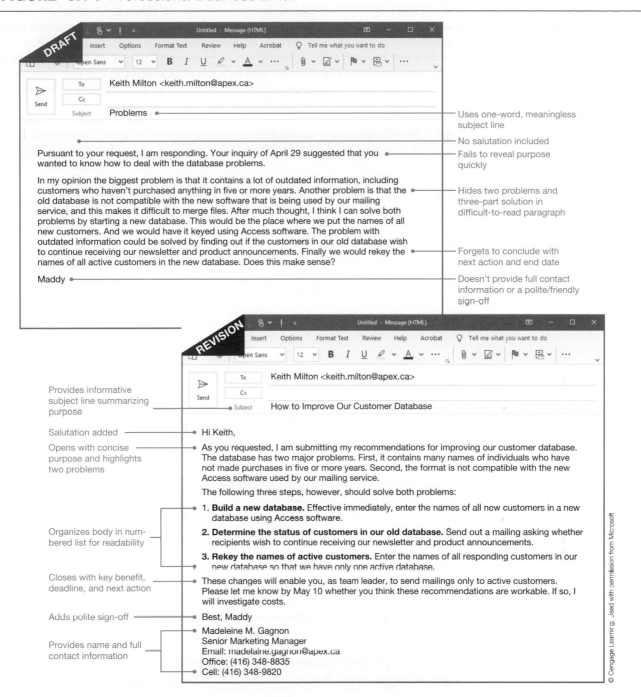

The following three steps, however, should solve both problems:

1. **Build a new database.** Effective immediately, enter the names of all new customers in a new database using Access software.

2. **Determine the status of customers in our old database.** Send out a mailing asking whether recipients wish to continue receiving our newsletter and product announcements.

3. **Rekey the names of active customers.** Enter the names of all responding customers in our new database so that we have only one active database.

Annotations (draft):
- Uses one-word, meaningless subject line
- No salutation included
- Fails to reveal purpose quickly
- Hides two problems and three-part solution in difficult-to-read paragraph
- Forgets to conclude with next action and end date
- Doesn't provide full contact information or a polite/friendly sign-off

Annotations (revision):
- Provides informative subject line summarizing purpose
- Salutation added
- Opens with concise purpose and highlights two problems
- Organizes body in numbered list for readability
- Closes with key benefit, deadline, and next action
- Adds polite sign-off
- Provides name and full contact information

© Cengage Learning; Used with permission from Microsoft

WRITING PLAN FOR PROFESSIONAL EMAILS

- **Subject line:** Summarize the main information or request.
- **Greetings:** Say hello and goodbye politely.
- **Opening:** Reveal the reason for writing in a more expanded form than in the subject line.
- **Body:** Explain the reason using headings, bulleted lists, and other high-skim techniques when appropriate.
- **Closing:** Include action information, dates, or deadlines; a summary of the message; and/or a closing thought.

COMPELLING SUBJECT LINE. The most important part of an email is its subject line. Avoid meaningless statements such as *Help*, *Important*, or *Meeting*. Summarize the purpose of the message clearly and make the receiver want to open the message. Try to include a verb (*Attending Mississauga Trade Show*). Remember that in some instances the subject line can be the entire message (*Meeting Changed from May 3 to May 10*). Also be sure to adjust the subject line if the topic changes after repeated replies. Subject lines should appear as a combination of uppercase and lowercase letters—never in all upper- or lowercase letters.

DON'T Poor Subject Lines	DO ✓ Improved Subject Lines
✗ Trade Show	✓ Need You to Showcase Two Items at Our Next Trade Show
✗ Staff Meeting	✓ Staff Meeting Rescheduled for May 12

GREETING AND SIGNOFF. To help receivers see the beginning and end of your message and to help them recognize whether they are the primary or secondary receiver, include greetings and a signoff. The greeting sets the tone for the message and reflects your audience analysis. For friends and colleagues, try friendly greetings (*Hi Julie; Good morning, Julie*). For messages to outsiders, begin more formally (e.g., *Dear Ms. Stevens*). At the end of your message, again depending on your audience analysis, sign off with *Cheers*, *Best*, *Regards*, or *Sincerely*, plus your name and signature block.

THE OPENING. Open emails by revealing your main idea immediately (e.g., information, instruction, request, concern, question). Even though the purpose of the email is summarized in the subject line, that purpose should be restated in more detail in the first sentence. Busy readers want to know immediately why they are reading a message. As you learned in Chapter 3, most messages should begin directly. Notice how the following indirect opening can be improved by becoming direct.

Indirect Opening	Direct Opening
For the past six months, the Human Resources Department has been considering changes in our employee benefit plan.	Please review the attached draft changes to employee benefits and let me know by May 20 if you approve these changes.

THE BODY. After your opening sentence that reveals your main reason for writing, add another short paragraph in which you go into a bit more detail about the reason for writing. In this brief explanation section, use headings, numbering, bulleting, and spacing to make your explanation easy for the reader to skim, as in the examples below.

Hard-to-Read Email Body	Easy-to-Read Email Body
Here are the instructions for operating the copy machine. First, you insert your copy card in the slot. Then you load paper in the upper tray. Last, originals are fed through the feed tray.	Follow these steps to use the copy machine: 1. Insert your copy card in the slot. 2. Load paper in the upper tray. 3. Feed originals through the feed tray

Hard-to-Read Email Body	Easy-to-Read Email Body		
On May 16 we will be in Regina, and Dr. Susan Dillon is the speaker. On June 20, we will be in Saskatoon, and Dr. Diane Minger is the speaker	**Date**	**City**	**Speaker**
	May 16	Regina	Dr. Susan Dillon
	June 20	Saskatoon	Dr. Diane Minger

Hard-to-Read Email Body	Easy-to-Read Email Body
To keep exercising, you should make a written commitment to yourself, set realistic goals for each day's workout, and enlist the support of a friend.	To keep exercising, you should (a) make a written commitment to yourself, (b) set realistic goals for each day's workout, and (c) enlist the support of a friend.

THE CLOSING. End business emails with action information or questions, dates, or deadlines. For certain emails it may be appropriate to close with a summary of the message or a closing thought. The closing is where readers look for deadlines and action language. An effective email closing might be *Please send me the PowerPoint deck by June 15 so that we can have your data before our July planning session.*

In some messages a summary of the main points may be the right closing. If no action request is made and a closing summary is unnecessary (this is most often the case), you can end with a simple concluding thought (*I'm glad to answer any questions* or *This sounds like a useful project*). You don't need to close messages to coworkers with goodwill statements such as those found in letters to customers or clients. However, a closing thought is often necessary—especially if the email exchange is being sent in a tense or stressful time—to prevent a feeling of abruptness.

Closings can show gratitude or encourage feedback with remarks such as *I sincerely appreciate your help* or *What are your ideas on this proposal?* Other closings look forward to what's next, such as *How would you like to proceed?* Avoid closing with overused expressions such as *Please let me know if I may be of further assistance.* This ending sounds mechanical and insincere. Figure 5.1 shows an employee's revision of a problematic email draft into a highly professional email.

5.1c Drafting Professional Memos and Letters

Long before email, interoffice memos (along with phone calls and face-to-face discussions) were the primary daily communication channel for delivering information inside organizations. Memos are still useful for certain specific internal messages that require a permanent record or formality. For example, organizations use memos to explain and enforce changes in procedures and for new official instructions.

MEMO FEATURES. Some organizations have their own memo templates. In addition to the name of the organization, these templates include the basic elements of *Date, To, From,* and *Subject.* Large organizations may include other identifying headings, such as *File Number, Floor, Extension, Location,* and *Distribution.*

If your company or organization doesn't have its own template for memos, Word offers a number of memo templates you can use. Simply open a new Word document, go to Templates (usually in the File menu), and search for memos. Start writing in the template, using the writing plan below. A typical business memo draft and revision are shown in Figure 5.2.

Notice the following important elements: there are spaces between the title and the guide words, and spaces among the guide words—this increases readability. Next, notice that memos follow the writing pattern discussed earlier for emails: specific subject line, opening with the main idea, body that explains the main idea, and closing. Finally, notice that a memo is the only type of business correspondence form that does not include an opening or a closing salutation (i.e., *Hi* or *Dear* or *Sincerely* or *Cheers*). This is because memos were developed to save time and to be impersonal. See Appendix A for more details on memo and fax (a form of memo) formatting.

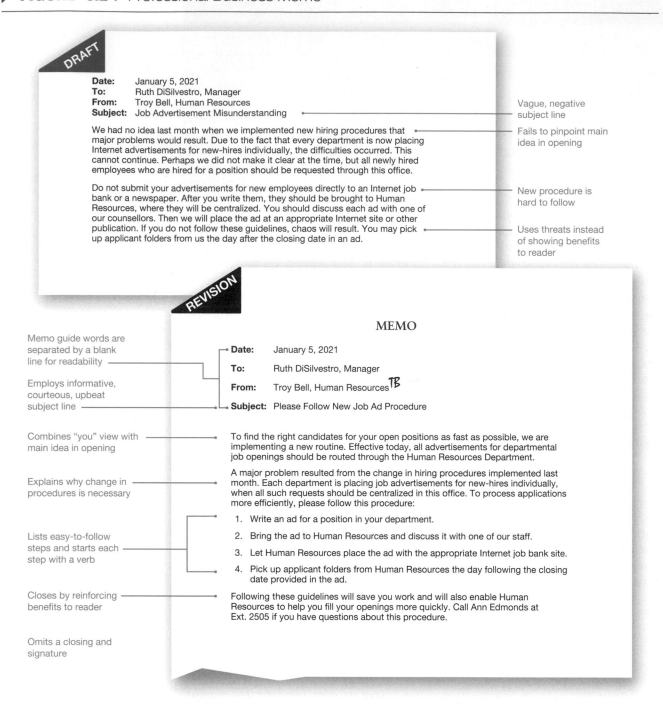

DRAFT

Date:	January 5, 2021
To:	Ruth DiSilvestro, Manager
From:	Troy Bell, Human Resources
Subject:	Job Advertisement Misunderstanding

We had no idea last month when we implemented new hiring procedures that major problems would result. Due to the fact that every department is now placing Internet advertisements for new-hires individually, the difficulties occurred. This cannot continue. Perhaps we did not make it clear at the time, but all newly hired employees who are hired for a position should be requested through this office.

Do not submit your advertisements for new employees directly to an Internet job bank or a newspaper. After you write them, they should be brought to Human Resources, where they will be centralized. You should discuss each ad with one of our counsellors. Then we will place the ad at an appropriate Internet site or other publication. If you do not follow these guidelines, chaos will result. You may pick up applicant folders from us the day after the closing date in an ad.

- Vague, negative subject line
- Fails to pinpoint main idea in opening
- New procedure is hard to follow
- Uses threats instead of showing benefits to reader

REVISION

MEMO

Date:	January 5, 2021
To:	Ruth DiSilvestro, Manager
From:	Troy Bell, Human Resources ᵀᴮ
Subject:	Please Follow New Job Ad Procedure

To find the right candidates for your open positions as fast as possible, we are implementing a new routine. Effective today, all advertisements for departmental job openings should be routed through the Human Resources Department.

A major problem resulted from the change in hiring procedures implemented last month. Each department is placing job advertisements for new-hires individually, when all such requests should be centralized in this office. To process applications more efficiently, please follow this procedure:

1. Write an ad for a position in your department.
2. Bring the ad to Human Resources and discuss it with one of our staff.
3. Let Human Resources place the ad with the appropriate Internet job bank site.
4. Pick up applicant folders from Human Resources the day following the closing date provided in the ad.

Following these guidelines will save you work and will also enable Human Resources to help you fill your openings more quickly. Call Ann Edmonds at Ext. 2505 if you have questions about this procedure.

- Memo guide words are separated by a blank line for readability
- Employs informative, courteous, upbeat subject line
- Combines "you" view with main idea in opening
- Explains why change in procedures is necessary
- Lists easy-to-follow steps and starts each step with a verb
- Closes by reinforcing benefits to reader
- Omits a closing and signature

WRITING PLAN FOR PROFESSIONAL MEMOS

- **Subject line:** Summarize the content of the memo.
- **Opening:** Expand the subject line by stating the main idea concisely in a full sentence.
- **Body:** Explain the main idea. Consider using lists, bullets, or headings to improve readability. In describing a procedure or giving instructions, use command language (*do this, don't do that*).
- **Closing:** Request a specific action, summarize the message, and/or present a closing thought. If appropriate, include a deadline and a reason.

LETTER FEATURES. Before memos and email, businesses used letters for centuries. Despite the widespread use of email and other digital channels, in certain situations letters are still the preferred channel for communicating *outside* an organization. Such letters go to suppliers, government agencies, other businesses, and most important, customers. Letters to customers receive a high priority because they are seen as important by receivers, encourage product feedback, project a favourable image of the organization, and promote future business.

A letter remains a powerful and effective channel for businesspeople to get their message across. Business letters are particularly necessary when (a) a permanent record is required; (b) confidentiality is paramount; (c) formality and sensitivity are essential; and (d) a persuasive, well-considered presentation is important.

Many organizations have their own letter templates that include their logo and company name and address. Unless instructed not to, always use your company's letter template when drafting a letter.

If your company or organization doesn't have its own template for letters, Word offers a number of letter templates you can use. Simply open a new Word document, go to Templates (usually in the File menu), and search for letters. Choose one that looks professional and formal, not informal or too busy. Start writing in the template, using the writing plan shown in the box. A typical business letter is shown in Figure 5.3.

Notice the following important elements: the letter begins with your company's letterhead—the company name and any logo associated with the company, plus your address. The date of the letter goes a few line spaces underneath the letterhead. A few line spaces farther down are the name and address of the person to whom you're writing. Then, there is an opening salutation (like in an email), which usually begins with *Dear*. The letter opens after the salutation. It has a body that explains the main point of the letter. The letter closes politely and ends with a closing salutation (usually *Sincerely*) and a signature and title. See Appendix A for more details about letter formatting.

WRITING PLAN FOR PROFESSIONAL LETTERS

- **Letterhead:** Your company name, logo, and address
- **Date and address:** The date of the letter followed by the name and address to which it is being sent
- **Body:** Three sections: an opening, a body that explains your main reason for writing, and a polite closing
- **Closing salutation and signature:** A polite "goodbye" with your signature and title

---

SENDING MEMOS AND LETTERS AS ATTACHMENTS. Because email is inappropriate for writing overly long documents, with such messages, writers can draft a memo or a letter and send it as an attachment with a cover email.

When attaching a memo or letter to an email, be sure to include identifying information in the attachment name (e.g., Letter to Manulife Clients re: Flood Insurance). This is because the cover email may become separated from the attachment, and the receiver won't know who sent the attachment. If your email attachment is a memo, there shouldn't be any problems, as memos identify the date, sender, receiver, and subject.

◣ 5.2 Using Communication Intention to Format Daily Messages

You now know about the three main daily business writing channels: email, memos, and letters; you also know what professional versions of messages sent via these channels should look and sound like. We'll now look at how communication channels like email, memos, and letters intersect with communication intentions.

FIGURE 5.3 / Professional Business Letter

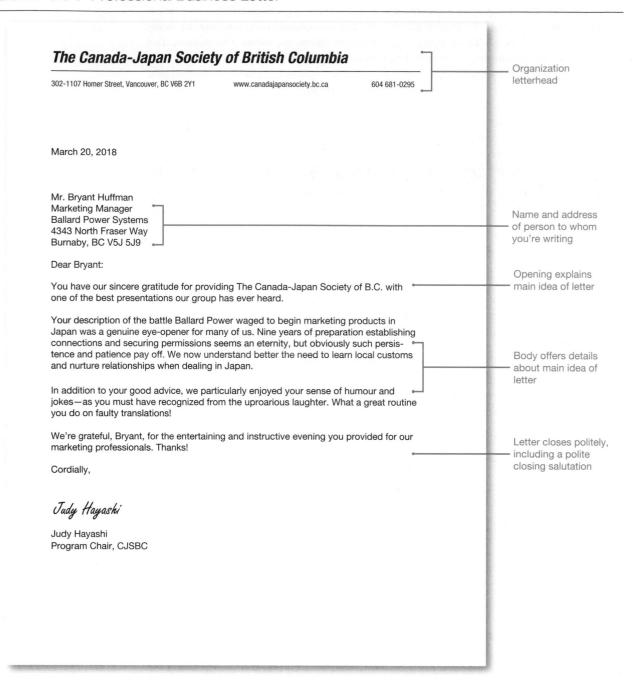

The Canada-Japan Society of British Columbia

302-1107 Homer Street, Vancouver, BC V6B 2Y1   www.canadajapansociety.bc.ca   604 681-0295

> Organization letterhead

March 20, 2018

Mr. Bryant Huffman
Marketing Manager
Ballard Power Systems
4343 North Fraser Way
Burnaby, BC V5J 5J9

> Name and address of person to whom you're writing

Dear Bryant:

You have our sincere gratitude for providing The Canada-Japan Society of B.C. with one of the best presentations our group has ever heard.

> Opening explains main idea of letter

Your description of the battle Ballard Power waged to begin marketing products in Japan was a genuine eye-opener for many of us. Nine years of preparation establishing connections and securing permissions seems an eternity, but obviously such persistence and patience pay off. We now understand better the need to learn local customs and nurture relationships when dealing in Japan.

In addition to your good advice, we particularly enjoyed your sense of humour and jokes—as you must have recognized from the uproarious laughter. What a great routine you do on faulty translations!

> Body offers details about main idea of letter

We're grateful, Bryant, for the entertaining and instructive evening you provided for our marketing professionals. Thanks!

Cordially,

Judy Hayashi

Judy Hayashi
Program Chair, CJSBC

> Letter closes politely, including a polite closing salutation

5.2a Communication Intentions in Business

A *communication intention* is a straightforward concept: it's a synonym for your "reason" for communicating. Even though we've called this chapter the "Daily" business writing chapter, clearly no manager or employee would ever say to a colleague, "Give me a minute, I'm just writing Heather a daily message." "Daily" is a way of classifying the frequency of messages, not the reason for them.

Instead, that person might say, "I'm emailing Heather to get the fourth-quarter sales report," or "I'm just responding to Raj—he had a question about cross-border logistics." In other words, communication intentions are *the functional or strategic reasons why we communicate.*[6] They were briefly introduced in Chapter 2, and we'll expand on them now (they're also summarized in the table below).

The major functional or strategic intentions for communicating at work include informing, instructing, requesting, replying, and expressing goodwill. There are other intentions, but they can be nested under one of these five main types (e.g., a complaint or criticism is a subtype of information message or perhaps a subtype of request message if the intention is to receive something based on the complaint or criticism . . .).

All these intentions, when combined with the communication channels discussed earlier—and later—in this chapter (i.e., email, memo, letter, text, blog, social media) create very specific types of communication (e.g., a request letter, a response text message, an instruction memo, a social media shout-out). You'll see examples of these specific types of communication next and in Chapters 6 and 7.

Communication Intention	Appropriate Channels and Sample Message Content
To inform	**Email, memo, letter, text, blog post, social media post, phone call, in-person meeting** For example, a corporate blog post lets customers know that the company will no longer be manufacturing a type of dresser because of safety issues.
To instruct	**Email, memo, PowerPoint presentation** For example, an email from the IT Department offers step-by-step instructions for employees on how to migrate their inbox to an updated email program.
To request	**Email, text, IM, letter, phone call, social media post, in-person meeting** For example, your dentist's office assistant leaves a voice mail and asks you to call back to confirm your upcoming appointment.
To reply	**Email, text, IM, social media post, phone call** For example, you phone your dentist's office to confirm your upcoming appointment.
To express goodwill	**Email, text, IM, letter, social media post, phone call, in-person meeting** For example, an event manager sends a text or posts an Instagram shout-out to her beverage supplier to thank him for providing outstanding service at a big wedding she managed last weekend.

To see how the five communication intentions could play out in a typical organizational setting, let's use the example of a crisis communication situation that took place in Canada in May 2019. CTV News reported that South Shore Furniture (www.southshorefurniture.com), a Québec-based manufacturer of furniture since 1940, was recalling its Libra dresser because it could "tip over if not securely anchored to the wall."[7] The dresser had been responsible for the death of a two-year-old child in the United States.

The communication situation might play out as follows. Tipped off by social media traffic about the child's death, a reporter from a Montréal TV station contacts South Shore Furniture via email with a **request** for comment about the child's death and what the company is going to do as a result. After the company's president is made aware of the request and the company has been in touch with its legal team, it asks a member of the legal team to **respond** to the reporter via phone call with a comment.

At the same time, the company president instructs South Shore's VP of Marketing and Communication to draft two messages. The first is an **informational** press release and blog posting aimed at the media, company partners (e.g., furniture retailers), and the general public stating that the Libra dresser is being recalled and that free pickup of the Libra dresser or free in-person installation of wall anchors will be available to any customer by calling a 1-800 number. The second is an **instructional** email for the company's employees, with clear three-step instructions for how to deal with any requests for comment made by members of the public or the media. Finally, two weeks after the story hits the media and the recall is issued, the VP of Marketing and Communication sends a short text message to the freelance crisis communication consultant he hired when the crisis began, **expressing his thanks and goodwill.**

Figure 5.4 offers writing plans for the five main daily communication intentions. These plans are *not* channel sensitive: they apply to any written channel, including email, memo, letter, text, blog posting, and so on.

▶ **FIGURE 5.4 /** Writing Plans and Samples for Daily Business Writing Intentions

This figure shows you how to write messages across channels based on the top five daily business writing intentions. Each writing plan includes a sample showing how the plan was put into practice.

WRITING PLAN TO INFORM

- **Subject line:** Says specifically what the information is (e.g., *Change in photocopying procedures*) (Exceptions: not required in letters)
- **Greeting and signoff:** Opens and closes politely based on audience analysis (e.g., *Hi . . . , Dear . . . , Cheers, Sincerely*) (Exceptions: only signoff required in memos)
- **Opening:** Says in one expanded sentence what the information is (e.g., *Please note the following change in photocopying procedures effective June 5, 2021:*)
- **Body:** Explains with a bulleted or numbered list the details about the information in the opening (e.g., * *Your staff card becomes your photocopy card.* * *Your staff card can be used at any photocopier at any location.* * *Your photocopies are billed directly to your department.*)
- **Closing:** Summarizes, offers a parting thought, motivates action, or offers a contact method for those who have questions (e.g., *If you have any questions, please contact me via email or at Ext. 6695.*)

MEMO

Date: January 7, 2021

To: All Employees

From: Corey Macdonald, Operations Manager

Subject: Change in photocopying procedures

Please note the following change in photocopying procedures effective June 5, 2021:

- Your staff card becomes your photocopy card.
- Your staff card can be used at any photocopier at any location.
- Your photocopies are billed directly to your department.

If you have any questions, please contact me via email or at Ext. 6695.

WRITING PLAN TO INSTRUCT

- **Subject line:** Says specifically what the instructions are for (e.g., *Instructions for accessing Microsoft Teams*)
- **Greeting and signoff:** Opens and closes politely based on audience analysis (e.g., *Hi . . . , Dear . . . , Cheers, Sincerely*) (Exceptions: only signoff required in memos)
- **Opening:** Says in one expanded sentence what the instructions are about (e.g., *To access Microsoft Teams, please follow these instructions:*)
- **Body:** Provides a numbered list of instructions mentioned in the opening (e.g., *1. Click the "Teams" icon on your company desktop or phone. 2. Enter your employee email address and employee number as your login credentials. 3. Choose the Project to be worked on from the menu on the left.*)
- **Closing:** Summarizes, offers a parting thought, motivates action, or offers a contact method for those who have questions (e.g., *If you have any questions, click microsoftteams.lynda.com and watch the tutorial or send me an email.*)

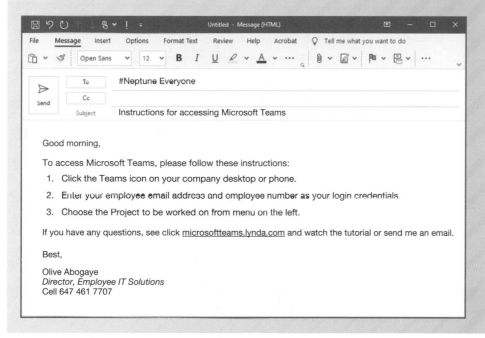

WRITING PLAN TO REQUEST

- **Subject line:** Says specifically what the request is about (e.g., *Request to procure organic fruits in season*)
- **Greeting and signoff:** Opens and closes politely based on audience analysis (e.g., *Hi . . . , Dear . . . , Cheers, Sincerely*) (Exceptions: only signoff required in memos)
- **Opening:** Says in one expanded sentence what the request is (e.g., *Green Life supermarkets would like to enter into an agreement to procure organic fruits from growers in the London, Ontario, area.*)
- **Body:** Explains details of the request (e.g., *We are interested in purchasing bulk quantities of organic strawberries, blueberries, peaches, and apples for the Spring-Summer 2021 season . . . .*)

(Continued)

- **Closing:** Summarizes, offers a parting thought, motivates action, or offers a method of contact for those who have questions (e.g., *Please contact me at this address, email me at cwadlow@greenlife.ca, or call me at 613-835-9511, Ext. 32 at your earliest convenience to schedule a time to discuss this partnership opportunity.*)

Green Life Foods
1427 Simpson Road, 2nd Floor
Ottawa, ON K1J 6M3
Toll Free: 1-855-743-1001
Greenlife.ca

February 5, 2021

London Area Organic Growers
c/o Ellen Laing
45415 Fruit Ridge Line
St. Thomas, ON N5P 3S9

Dear Ms. Laing,

Subject: Request to procure organic fruits in season

Green Life supermarkets would like to enter into an agreement to procure organic fruits from growers in the London, Ontario, area.

We are interested in purchasing bulk quantities of organic strawberries, blueberries, peaches, and apples for the Spring–Summer 2021 season.

Please contact me at this address, email me at cwadlow@greenlife.ca, or call me at 613-835-9511, Ext. 32, at your earliest convenience to schedule a time to discuss this partnership opportunity.

Sincerely,

Claire Wadlow
VP Produce Procurement

WRITING PLAN TO REPLY

- **Subject line:** Refers back to original request (e.g., *Your interest in procuring organic fruits from LAOG*)
- **Greeting and signoff:** Opens and closes politely based on audience analysis (e.g., *Hi . . . , Dear . . . , Cheers, Sincerely*) (Exceptions: only signoff required in memos)
- **Opening:** Offers a reply in one expanded sentence (e.g., *Member growers at LAOG would be very interested in discussing a procurement partnership with Green Life Foods.*)
- **Body:** Explains any conditions to the reply (e.g., *I'm available for a phone call any Monday or Wednesday between 9 and 10 a.m. After our conversation I'll need to get member approval for any agreement we might sign.*)
- **Closing:** Summarizes, offers a parting thought, motivates action, or offers a method of contact for those who have questions (e.g., *Send me your preferred date and then give me a call at 519-653-2084. I look forward to the discussion!*)

(Continued)

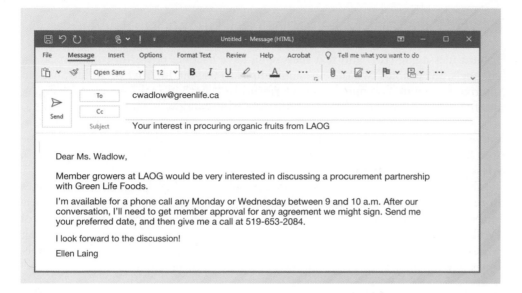

Dear Ms. Wadlow,

Member growers at LAOG would be very interested in discussing a procurement partnership with Green Life Foods.

I'm available for a phone call any Monday or Wednesday between 9 and 10 a.m. After our conversation, I'll need to get member approval for any agreement we might sign. Send me your preferred date, and then give me a call at 519-653-2084.

I look forward to the discussion!

Ellen Laing

WRITING PLAN TO SHOW GOODWILL

- **Subject line:** States the occasion for the message (e.g., *Recommendation for Brian Ye*)
- **Greeting and signoff:** Opens and closes politely based on audience analysis (e.g. *Hi . . . , Dear . . . , Cheers, Sincerely*) (Exceptions: only signoff required in memos)
- **Opening:** Says in one expanded sentence what the goodwill is for (e.g., *I'm happy to provide a very positive informal recommendation for Brian Ye, who worked for me until December 2019.*)
- **Body:** Explains clearly and quickly why the goodwill is being offered (e.g., *In the five years he worked here in logistics at Lululemon, Brian distinguished himself as a detail-oriented problem solver, who demonstrated excellent soft skills in all client, partner, and colleague interactions.*)
- **Closing:** Offers a specific, thoughtful parting message that shows the message is authentic and not written for personal gain (e.g., *If you'd like any more details about Brian's successful time at our organization, and why I'm recommending him so positively to you, please contact me at this address or at 604-327-4848, Ext. 2140.*)

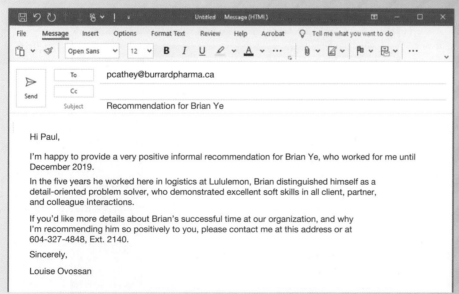

Hi Paul,

I'm happy to provide a very positive informal recommendation for Brian Ye, who worked for me until December 2019.

In the five years he worked here in logistics at Lululemon, Brian distinguished himself as a detail-oriented problem solver, who demonstrated excellent soft skills in all client, partner, and colleague interactions.

If you'd like more details about Brian's successful time at our organization, and why I'm recommending him so positively to you, please contact me at this address or at 604-327-4848, Ext. 2140.

Sincerely,

Louise Ovossan

5.3 Instant Messaging and Texting at Work

Instant messaging (IM) and text messaging have become powerful communication channels. IM enables two or more individuals to use the Internet or an intranet (an internal corporate communication platform) to "chat" in real time by exchanging brief text-based messages. One such intranet chat window is shown in Figure 5.5.

Many companies now provide live online chats with customer service representatives, in addition to the usual contact options, such as telephone and email. The free IM apps most popular among mobile device users include Skype, Facebook Messenger, and WhatsApp.

Text messaging, or texting, is another popular way of exchanging brief messages in real time. Usually delivered by smartphone, texting requires a short message service (SMS) supplied by a cell phone service provider or a voice over Internet protocol (VoIP) service. Some common apps for unlimited mobile text messaging are Facebook Messenger, WhatsApp, and WeChat. Texting requires a smartphone, and users sometimes pay for the service as part of their cell phone carriers' monthly package.

5.3a Some Challenges and Advantages of IM and Texting

Texting and IM are convenient alternatives to the telephone and are replacing email for short internal communication. French IT giant Atos switched its in-house communication entirely from email to a Facebook-style interface and instant messaging.[8] More than 2.7 billion IM accounts worldwide[9] attest to IM's popularity. Sixty-four percent of business professionals use IM.[10]

BENEFITS OF IM AND TEXTING. The major attraction of instant messaging is real-time communication with colleagues anywhere in the world. Because IM allows people to share information immediately and make decisions quickly, its impact on business communication has been dramatic. Group online chat capabilities allow

FIGURE 5.5 / Instant Messaging for Brief, Fast Communication

Brief IMs or texts can provide quick answers to coworkers who need responses immediately. For security reasons, large companies use proprietary messaging systems behind firewalls. These platforms—for example, Adobe's Unicom—combine functions such as IM, email, voice mail, phone directory, video chat, and presence technology.

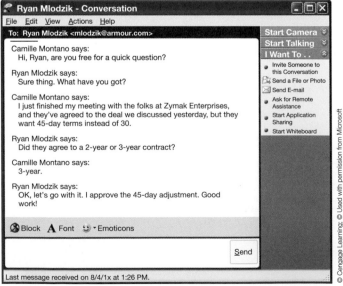

coworkers on far-flung project teams to communicate instantly. Many people consider instant messaging and texting productivity boosters because they enable users to get answers quickly and allow for multitasking.[11]

LOW COST, SPEED, AND UNOBTRUSIVENESS. Both IM and texting can be low-cost substitutes for voice calls, delivering messages between private mobile phone users quietly and discreetly. Organizations around the world provide news alerts, financial information, and promotions to customers via text. Credit card accounts can be set up to notify account holders by text or email of approaching payment deadlines. Wireless providers send automated texts helping customers track their data usage. A sample of corporate text alerts is shown in Figure 5.6.

IMMEDIACY AND EFFICIENCY. The immediacy of instant and text messaging has created many fans. A user knows right away whether a message was delivered. Messaging avoids phone tag and eliminates the downtime associated with phone and email conversations. Another benefit includes *presence functionality*. Coworkers can locate each other online, thus avoiding wasting time trying to reach someone who is out of the office.

RISKS OF IM AND TEXTING. Some organizations forbid employees from using instant and text messaging for several reasons. Employers consider instant messaging yet another distraction in addition to the phone, email, and the Internet. Some organizations also fear that employees using free instant messaging systems will reveal privileged information and company records. One UK study found that 72 percent of businesses have banned IM, although 74 percent of the respondents believe that IM could boost collaboration in their organizations. IT directors worry about security risks posed by free consumer IM services, with loss of sensitive business data a primary concern.[12]

◤ FIGURE 5.6 / Business Use of Texting for Marketing and Promotions

SIGN UP FOR MOBILE ALERTS TODAY!

Get EXCLUSIVE OFFERS and SNEAK PEEKS at new arrivals

☐ TEXT 3090 TO 653-689 TO SIGN UP*

OLD NAVY

Old Navy Deal Alerts: Reply Y to agree to 1 automated msg/wk with deals to this number. Not required for purchase. Msg&data rates apply www.oldnavy.com/text

Old Navy Deal Alerts: Thanks, your $5 off $35 offer will be sent to you tomorrow! 1 msg/week. Reply STOP to quit Reply HELP for help. Msg&data rates may apply.

Jacek Lasa/Alamy Stock Photo; Source: Tatango

LIABILITY BURDEN. A worker's improper use of mobile devices while on company business can expose the organization to legal liability. A jury awarded $18 million to a victim struck by a transportation company's transport truck because the driver had been checking text messages. Another case resulted in a $21 million verdict to a woman injured by a trucker who had used a cell phone while driving a company truck.[13]

SECURITY AND COMPLIANCE. Companies also worry about *phishing* (fraudulent schemes), viruses, *malware* (malicious software programs), and *spim* (IM spam). Like email, instant and text messages, as well as all other electronic records, can be used as evidence in lawsuits. Businesses must track and store messaging conversations to comply with legal requirements. Finally, IM and texting have been implicated in inappropriate uses such as bullying and sexting.

5.3b Drafting Professional Instant Messages and Texts

If your organization allows IM or texting, you can use it professionally by following these best practices and the advice in Figure 5.7:

- Especially for initial IMs and texts, use the basics from older channels, that is, start with a polite greeting (e.g., *Hi*), explain your idea, and end with a polite signoff (e.g., *Thanks*).
- Don't disclose sensitive financial, company, customer, employee, or executive data.

▼ **FIGURE 5.7 /** Texting Etiquette

Timing
- Don't text when calling would be inappropriate or rude; for example, at a performance, a restaurant, in a meeting, or a movie theater.
- Don't text or answer your phone during a face-to-face conversation. If others use their cell phones while talking to you, you may excuse yourself until they stop.

Addressing
- Check that you are texting to the correct phone number to avoid embarrassment. If you receive a message by mistake, alert the sender. No need to respond to the message itself.
- Avoid sending confidential, private, or potentially embarrassing texts. Someone might see your text at the recipient's end or the message might be sent to an unintended recipient.

Responding
Don't expect an instant reply. As with email, we don't know when the recipient will read the message.

Introducing
Identify yourself when texting a new contact who doesn't have your phone number: "Hi—it's Erica (Office World). Your desk has arrived. Please call 877-322-8989."

Expressing
Don't use text messages to notify others of sad news, sensitive business matters, or urgent meetings, unless you wish to set up a phone call about that subject.

© Cengage Learning

- Don't forward or link to inappropriate photos, videos, and art.
- Don't text or IM while driving; pull over if you must read or send a message.
- Separate business contacts from family and friends.
- Avoid unnecessary chit-chat and know when to say goodbye.
- Keep your presence status up-to-date, and make yourself unavailable when you need to meet a deadline.
- Use standard grammar and spelling; don't use jargon, slang, and abbreviations, which can be confusing and appear unprofessional.

5.4 Blogging for Business

In the digital age, individuals wield enormous influence because they can potentially reach huge audiences. Today's Internet users have the power to create Web content; interact with businesses and each other; review products, self-publish, or blog; contribute to wikis; or tag and share images and other files. Until recently, businesses feared the wrath of disgruntled employees and customers. Today, they are being proactive by hiring social media managers to expand their digital footprint and by partnering with digital influencers.

Like other digital media, an organization's blogs—websites that are organized like a journal with dated entries—help create virtual communities, build brands, and develop relationships. In other words, blogs are part of a marketing or brand communication strategy to create engagement, which results in customers' and stakeholders' goodwill and brand loyalty. Organizations use blogs for public relations, customer relations, crisis communication, market research, viral marketing, internal communication, and recruitment. Figure 5.8 shows a good example from the Ontario Nonprofit Network's blog.

PUBLIC RELATIONS, CUSTOMER RELATIONS, AND CRISIS COMMUNICATION. One prominent use of blogs is providing up-to-date company information to the media and the public. Blogs can be written by junior employees

▼ FIGURE 5.8 / An Organization's Blog: ONN

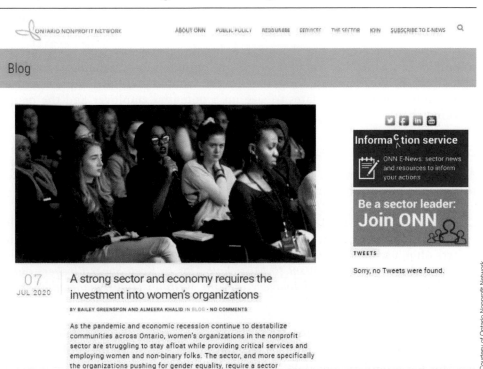

or by top managers. Under the heading Best Buy Influencer Network, the electronics retailer operates several niche blogs that target various constituencies and actively solicits customer input.[14]

Social media experts believe that brands should embrace negative blog posts and turn them into opportunities to reach out to the customer and strengthen the relationship.[15] Whether businesses choose to respond angrily or surprise and delight customers, "the world is watching."[16]

An organization's blog is a natural forum for late-breaking news, especially when disaster strikes. Although a blog cannot replace other communication channels in an emergency, it should be part of the overall effort to soothe the public's emotional reaction with a human voice of reason. In the aftermath of the devastating fires in Fort McMurray, Alberta, in 2016, various corporate blogs like Allstate's "Good Hands" blog, chronicled recovery and rebuilding efforts, offering vital information to the public.[17]

MARKET RESEARCH AND VIRAL MARKETING. Because most blogs invite feedback, they can be invaluable sources of ideas from customers and industry experts. Mountain Equipment Co-op understands blogging. The outdoor retailer's *MEC Blog* (www.mec.ca/en/blog) contains sections where MEC's community members offer skills and tips, personal stories, and information on community events. The blog is curated by a mix of employees, co-op members, and other people who interact with MEC. Many companies now have employees who scrutinize the blogosphere for buzz and positive and negative postings about their organizations and products.

The term *viral marketing* refers to the rapid spread of messages online, much like infectious diseases that pass from person to person. Marketers realize the potential of getting the word out about their products and services in the blogosphere where their messages are often picked up by well-connected bloggers, the so-called *influencers*, who boast large audiences. Viral messages must be authentic and elicit an emotional response, but for that very reason they are difficult to orchestrate. People resent being co-opted by companies using overt hard-sell tactics.

INTERNAL COMMUNICATION AND RECRUITMENT. Blogs can be used to keep virtual teams on track and share updates on the road. Members in remote locations can stay in touch by smartphone and other devices, exchanging text, images, sound, and video clips. In some companies, blogs have replaced hard-copy publications for sharing late-breaking news or tidbits of interest to employees. Blogs can create a sense of community and stimulate employee participation. Furthermore, blogs mirror the company culture and present an opportunity for job candidates to size up a potential employer and the people working there.

5.4a Blog Best Practices: Seven Tips

As with any public writing, your blog posts will be scrutinized; therefore, you want to make the best impression possible.

CRAFT A CATCHY BUT CONCISE TITLE. The headline is what draws online readers to open your post. It can be an intriguing question or a promise. Online writers often use numbers to structure their posts. Here are some examples of blog titles: *Six Apps You Don't Want to Miss; Five Tips to Keep Spear Phishers out of Your Inbox; Create Powerful Imagery in Your Writing; How Financially Sexy Is Your Household?*

ACE THE OPENING PARAGRAPH. The lead paragraph must deliver on the promise of the headline. Identify a need and propose to solve the problem. Ask a relevant question. Say something startling. Tell an anecdote or use an analogy to

WORKPLACE IN FOCUS

In recent years, blogging has become an increasingly important communication channel for businesses and other organizations looking to capture the attention of busy potential customers. This is even more important in the nonprofit sector (e.g., charities, arts organizations, educational organizations), where budgets for marketing are not as generous as in the for-profit sector. As Nick Morpus demonstrates in his recent blog posting "3 Reasons a Blog Is Crucial to Your Nonprofit," nonprofits need to be blogging to build awareness of their brand in an inexpensive way that isn't time-consuming, to drive traffic to their main website for sales, and to take control of their own story. A couple of Manitoba-based examples of nonprofit sector blogging are the University of Manitoba Press's blog (uofmpress.ca/blog) and the Royal Winnipeg Ballet's blog (rwb.org/news/blog/). Both blogs include posts that allow the organization to frame its story the way it wants to, as well as posts about organization events and announcements. Compared to the (also nonprofit) ONN blog shown in Figure 5.8, these two blogs

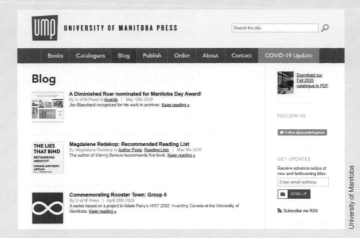

Source: Morpus, N. (2017, August 4). 3 Reasons a blog is crucial to your nonprofit. https://blog.capterra.com/3-reasons-a-blog-is-crucial-to-your-nonprofit/

are more basic in terms of design, but they still get the job done. *To what degree is blogging a writing channel versus a design channel? Can a blog be successful if its design is basic? Can a fantastically designed blog be successful if its writing is basic?*

connect with the reader. The author of "How Many Lives Does a Brand Have?" opened with this:

> It's said that cats have nine lives, but how many lives does a brand have? The answer, it seems, is definitely more than one. Recently, in Shanghai, a friend took me to one of the city's most sophisticated luxury malls . . . .[18]

PROVIDE DETAILS IN THE BODY. Remember your reader's *So what?* and *What's in it for me?* questions. Use vivid examples, quotations and testimonials, or statistics. Structure the body with numbers, bullets, and subheadings. Use expressive action verbs (*buy* for *get*; *own* for *have*; *travel* or *jet* for *go*). Use conversational language to sound warm and authentic. Use contractions (*can't* for *cannot*; *doesn't* for *does not*; *isn't* for *is not*).

CONSIDER VISUALS. Add visual interest with relevant images and diagrams. Keep paragraphs short and use plenty of white space around them. Aim to make the look simple and easy to scan.

INCLUDE CALLS TO ACTION. Call on readers (in the title or lead paragraph) to do something, or else provide a takeaway and gentle nudge at the end. Ask open-ended questions or tell the reader what to do: *So be sure to ask about 360-degree security tactics that aim to stop inbound attacks, but also to block outbound data theft attempts.*

EDIT AND PROOFREAD. Follow the revision tips in Chapter 4 of this book. Cut unneeded words, sentences, and irrelevant ideas. Fix awkward, wordy, and repetitive sentences. Edit and proofread: your reputation might depend on it. The best blogs are error free.

RESPOND TO POSTS RESPECTFULLY. Build a positive image by posting compelling comments on other bloggers' posts. Politely and promptly reply to comments on your site. When a customer asked a question about WestJet's blog posting about why it doesn't overbook seats, WestJet responded. The company reply begins by making a positive observation about the post and adds a valuable insight from the company's point of view.

Don't ramble. If you disagree with a post, do so respectfully. Remember, your comments may remain online practically forever and could come back to haunt you long after posting.

◣ 5.5 Social Media for Business

Popular social media sites such as Facebook, Instagram, and Twitter are used by businesses for similar reasons and in much the same way as podcasts and blogs: to market services and products, to create and solidify brand image, and to reach out to customers with news and with problem resolutions, as can be seen in the Twitter feed in Figure 5.9. Social media enables businesses to connect with customers and employees, share company news, and exchange ideas.

▶ FIGURE 5.9 / Corporate Twitter Feed: Airline Industry

True North Airlines
Welcome to the Twitter page of True North Airlines. Our Twitter feed is active between 8:00 am and 4:00 pm EST seven days a week!
Vancouver, BC Joined 2009

Tweets	Photos/Videos	Following	Followers	
65K	817	9.5K	257K	**Follow**

Tweets

True North @TrueNorth Oct 4
Check out TN's Movember charity pics at <u>truenorthair.ca/movember</u>!

True North @TrueNorth Oct 4
Pre-Xmas sale – flights and vacations – just announced:
check details <u>here</u>!

Retweeted by True North @gilbran Oct 3
Hey @ TrueNorth – found <u>this stuffed animal</u> at Calgary departure level – in lost and found now…

True North @TrueNorth Oct 4
Our new route to Dallas has just been announced: find details and specials <u>here</u>.

True North @TrueNorth Oct 4
Thank you True North Twitter followers – signing off now.
Find us 24/7 at <u>truenorthair.ca</u>.

5.5a Using Social Media at Work

Businesses are increasingly using a customer experience (CX) approach to manage their engagement with their customers, clients, and partners. The CX approach starts with the premise that customers (and others) experience a brand, a company, or an organization in two main ways: through perceptions and through interactions.[19] These can be passive (e.g., seeing a company's billboard on a bus) or active (e.g., interacting with a teller at a bank). Because an increasing number of customer perception and interaction "touchpoints" happen on social media, the argument goes that investing sufficiently in a company's social media presence is a necessity.

Therefore, over the past five years or so, many large and some medium-size organizations have created positions such as social media writer, social media content specialist, and social media coordinator. The people who hold these jobs spend their days "writing, editing and publishing engaging content for various social networks, including Facebook, Twitter and Instagram" and "respond[ing] to questions and comments on . . . social media pages in a timely and accurate manner,"[20] among many other tasks.

This kind of writing is slightly different from the writing we looked at earlier in the chapter—email, memos, and letter writing—which are increasingly coming to be seen, along with journalism, books, and academic writing, as "long-form" writing as opposed to social media's "short-form" writing. For example, according to tech blogger Amanda Zantal-Wiener,[21] social media writing best practices include the following:

- For Facebook writing, keeping your posts under 80 characters. Short posts receive 66 percent higher engagement than longer messages. Include an image: Facebook posts with images have 2.3 times the engagement that posts without have. Finally, Facebook is great for pointing people in other directions, but with your links, make sure include a brief explanation of where they are sending the reader.
- For Twitter writing, keeping your post around 120 to 130 characters. Posts like that have the highest click-through rate. Use at least two hashtags to summarize or explain your tweet: tweets with hashtags receive twice the engagement as those without.

Similar advice holds for other social media sites like LinkedIn, Instagram, and Snapchat: the common thread in social media writing to keep things short, link or hashtag to other posts or sites that underscore the point you're making (known as a call to action), and include an image.

CROWDSOURCING CUSTOMERS. Besides using social media as a promotion and engagement vehicle, companies also invite customer input at the product design stage. On its IdeaStorm site, Dell has solicited over 26,000 new product ideas and suggested improvements, including a USB port that also acts as a charger (see Figure 5.10).[22] Canadian fast-food restaurant A&W has used Facebook to let followers know about the quality of its ingredients. According to a testimonial at Facebook Business, this campaign led to a 23 percent increase in burger sales.[23]

Cengage

MINDTAP

In MindTap go to the Study Tools for Chapter 5 and complete the Practice Test.

▌ **FIGURE 5.10** / Business Crowdsourcing on Social Media

USB Port

Jul 10, 2017
Posted By parshys
Status: Acknowledged

1 VOTE

How about having a USB port on the Power Adaptor of DELL E5470 laptop which would act as a charger for the USB devices as well. It can be made into a Power Bank as well by implementing a long battery into it.

1 Votes | *1 Comment*

Categories: Accessories (Keyboards, etc.), Desktops and Laptops, IdeaStorm,

LEARNING SUMMARY

5.1 Write daily messages using major workplace writing channels.

- Although sometimes annoying, email will likely remain a mainstream communication channel.

- Email is especially effective for informal messages to multiple receivers and as a cover document for attachments.

- Business emails should feature a compelling subject line, include a greeting, be organized for readability, and close effectively.

- Memos, which include a subject line, a dateline, and the names of senders and receivers, are sometimes used for internal messages that are too long for email, require a lasting record, demand formality, or inform workers who don't have email.

- Letters, which include letterhead, the date, an inside address, an opening salutation, the message opening, the body and close, and a closing salutation, are used when a permanent record and confidentiality are required, when formality and sensitivity are essential, and when a persuasive presentation is important.

5.2 Format daily messages based on the sender's intentions.

- Business communications can be analyzed not only by channel (e.g. email, letter), but also by the sender's intention.

- Common workplace communication intentions are to inform, to instruct, to make requests, to reply to requests or information shares, and to spread goodwill with thanks, employee recommendations, sympathy, and other messages.

5.3 Use instant messages and text messages professionally.

- Individuals use the Internet or corporate intranets to exchange brief text-based messages, which require a cellular connection or a VoIP service.

- The benefits of messaging are the low cost, high speed, unobtrusiveness, immediacy, and efficiency.

- The risks of messaging include legal liability, security breaches, and compliance issues.

- Best practices for messaging include minding policies, protecting sensitive data, not driving while messaging, separating personal and work contacts, and using correct language.

5.4 Create professional blog postings.

- External or internal corporate blogs help create virtual communities, build brands, and develop relationships.

- Companies use blogs for public relations, customer relations, crisis communication, market research, viral marketing, the building of online communities, internal communication, and recruitment.

- Best practices include crafting a catchy title and intriguing opening, providing details in the body, using visuals, calling for action, editing carefully, and commenting respectfully.

5.5 Create professional social media postings.

- Social networking sites enable businesses to connect with customers and employees, share news, exchange ideas, and boost their brand image.

- In addition to Facebook, Twitter, and other very public social media, many businesses also run private social networks behind corporate firewalls.

- The risks of social media use in business include productivity losses, leaked trade secrets, angry Internet audiences, security breaches, and damaging employee posts.

CHAPTER REVIEW

1. Why do some businesspeople criticize email? (Obj. 1)

2. When is email appropriate? (Obj. 1)

3. Describe the writing plan for business emails. (Obj. 1)

4. What are communication intentions? Provide at least three examples of main intentions. (Obj. 2)

5. What are the risks of instant messaging and texting? (Obj. 3)

6. List five best practices for using IM and texting that you consider most important. (Obj. 3)

7. How do companies use blogs? (Obj. 4)

8. What tips would you give to a beginning blogger? (Obj. 4)

9. Name some potential risks of social media for businesses. (Obj. 5)

CRITICAL THINKING

1. Some people are concerned that privacy is increasingly rare in our hyperconnected world as our online presence leaves a lasting footprint. To what degree do you fear that disclosing personal matters online will hamper your job search? Why? (Objs. 1–5)

2. Experts have argued that social media fool us into thinking that we are connected when in reality they do not help us develop true friendships. To what degree do you agree that technology diminishes personal relationships rather than bringing us closer together? Why? (Objs. 1–5)

3. Are texting abbreviations such as *lol* and *imho* and other all-lowercase writing acceptable in texting or instant messaging for business? Why or why not? (Obj. 3)

4. Traditional media act as *gatekeepers* that decide what kind of content is published or broadcast. However, social media networks have changed the game. Now anyone with an Internet connection can potentially publish or broadcast anything and reach vast audiences. What are the benefits and dangers of this unprecedented access? (Obj. 5)

5. Some marketers employ machines to inflate the number of likes and fans online. So-called Facebook bot networks (*botnets*) operate large numbers of fake accounts around the world. For example, a big-city rental agency went from two fans to almost 15,000 within a few days. How do you feel about companies and their brands pretending they have actual traffic on their sites and buying *likes*? (Obj. 5)

ACTIVITIES AND CASES

5.1 EMAIL THAT INFORMS AND REQUESTS: DRESS CODE CONTROVERSY (OBJ. 1)

As the Montréal-based director of Human Resources at Sensational, you have not had a good week. The national media recently reported the fact that Sensational—a leading women's fashion chain—has been taken before the Nova Scotia Human Rights Commission to defend against a claim by a young woman. The woman recently applied for a job at a Halifax Sensational location and was told in a pre-interview with a manager that "she'd never be hired if she wore her headdress to work." Citing the Commission's website claim that it's against the law to discriminate in workplaces based on religion, the young woman lodged a complaint.[24] Head office in Vancouver has been in damage-control mode ever since.

Your Task. Draft an email to all employees. The purpose of the email is to reaffirm that Sensational abides by and supports all Canadian human rights legislation and, at the same time, advise that employees should not talk to any media that may ask them for comments. You realize that these two messages are somewhat contradictory (one positive, one negative), but you feel time is of the essence.

Related website: Nova Scotia Human Rights Commission (www.humanrights.novascotia.ca).

5.2 MEMO THAT INFORMS: CHANGE IN INSURANCE PREMIUMS (OBJ. 1)

You are the benefits manager for a national furniture retail chain, The Home Centre, headquartered in Richmond, British Columbia. Most of the full-time employees who work for the chain pay into an employee benefits plan. This plan includes dental and vision care, prescription drug coverage, and other benefits. One of the most expensive benefits employees pay for is long-term disability (LTD) insurance. Recently, your insurance provider, Cansafe, has informed you that because of the high number of recent LTD claims, premiums for LTD insurance will rise by 15 percent. For the average employee, this means an increase of more than $20 per month.

Your Task. Write a well-organized memo informing The Home Centre employees about the impending increase. From past experience, you know that employees who are closer to retirement are big supporters of LTD insurance, whereas younger employees tend to be frustrated by the high premiums.

Related website: Manulife's site has a useful description of LTD insurance. Google *Manulife LTD* to find the page.

5.3 LETTER THAT REQUESTS: DONATION FOR ANNUAL AUCTION (OBJ. 1)

A common business-to-business writing situation is the donation letter. Nonprofit organizations, for example, often hold high-profile fundraising events for which they need to solicit prizes, donations, and other gifts-in-kind.

Your Task. Casey House, a health services provider for people living with HIV/AIDS, has been holding a successful fundraiser for over 20 years, lately in conjunction with TD Canada Trust. The fundraiser, called Art With Heart, supports the activities of Casey House and is structured as an art auction. For the event to be successful each year, staff at Casey House and TD Canada Trust must secure roughly 100 art donations from commercial galleries and artists around Canada. As a staff member at one of these organizations, write a letter to dc3 Art Projects, a commercial gallery in Edmonton, asking for a donation of a work by Travis McEwen, one of the gallery's artists.

Related websites: www.dc3artprojects.com, artwithheart.ca

5.4 SAME REQUEST, DIFFERENT CHANNEL (OBJ. 2)

Daily workplace messages that inform, instruct, request, reply, and show goodwill can be written using various channels. But tweaks must be made when moving across channels.

Scenario: You're a pharmaceutical sales rep for Ovativa, a drug maker that has developed a promising new treatment, Brovinoxen, for certain aggressive brain tumours. You recently met a brain cancer physician, Dr. Kamla Atal from New Dehli, at an out-of-town conference, and promised to follow up when you both got home about her using the new treatment in her clinic. Dr. Atal responds to your request a day after it's sent.

Scenario: You're a sales rep for a Muse (muse.ca), a TV production company from Montréal that makes a very popular reality show, *Moving Up*, about young married couples moving out of condos and into houses after they have their first child. You met a network broadcast executive from Serbia, Zivko Jovanovic, at a recent out-of-town conference and promised to follow up when you both got home about him purchasing your show for Serbian TV. Jovanovic replies to your request two days after it's sent.

Scenario: You're the internal communications specialist at AGT Foods (www.agt-foods.com) in Regina, Saskatchewan. Your clients include various senior executives at the company. Currently you're working for Barb Sihota, VP Human Resources. Her annual employee engagement survey had only a 59 percent response rate last year, and she's asked you to create messaging for employees to help raise the response rate this year.

Your Task. For the three scenarios, write the messages using at least two channels (e.g., a text, an email, a letter, an IM). When writing an email or a text, create it in a Word document and make it look as much as possible like one of these channels.

5.5 SENDING INSTRUCTIONS (OBJ. 2)

If you've had a part-time or full-time job, you've likely gotten good at giving instructions. New colleagues don't understand procedures, new team members haven't used your collaboration software before, inexperienced colleagues haven't been on a high-profile sales call or to a sales conference before, and so on. We all give instructions verbally, but sometimes you need to write them down.

Your Task. Choose two of the following scenarios to create an instruction email or memo to fellow employees: (a) tips for meeting new customers for the first time, (b) tips for using PowerPoint effectively, (c) tips for dealing with unhappy customers, or (d) tips for using Google Docs for someone who's never done so before. Then, write a set of clear, brief, useful instructions using two communication channels: memo and email. For each scenario you choose, also choose an intended audience to receive the instructions.

5.6 GOODWILL MESSAGES FOR VARIOUS OCCASIONS (OBJ. 2)

People tend to criticize coworkers much more easily than they thank them. In fact, numerous studies have shown the benefits of displaying gratitude, including improved productivity, mental health, and confidence. After completing this activity, you'll be equipped to help your workplace achieve a balance of constructive criticism and goodwill messages.

Your Task. Choose two of the following scenarios, decide what type of daily message this is, pick the most appropriate channel for your response, and then write an appropriate goodwill message for the situation.

Scenario: Your colleague Dave spent 15 minutes to show you how to use the software Camtasia so that your presentations will look even more professional than they already do.

Scenario: The five employees that report to you volunteered to work over lunch three times last week, helping out at the company-wide fundraising event for Heart and Stroke Month.

Scenario: Marie, a college accounting graduate who has worked at your small accounting firm for three years, has asked if you'd be a reference for her as she applies for jobs at larger firms starting later this month. You will need to make up some of Marie's workplace strengths.

Scenario: The wife of an important ex-client of yours recently died. You heard about her death through a colleague you have in common, but you haven't been in touch with him for over two years. You'd like to get back in contact with him and extend your condolences.

5.7 INSTANT MESSAGING MESS AT AUTO DEALERSHIP (OBJ. 3)
Read the following log of a live IM chat between a customer service representative and a visitor to an Ottawa car dealership's website.

Your Task. In class discuss how Mark could have made this interaction with a customer more effective. Is his IM chat with Young Jae Kim professional, polite, and respectful? Rewrite five of Mark's responses to Young Jae's queries to show professional messaging style.

Dealer rep:	Hey, I'm Mark. How's it goin? Welcome to Fields BMW South Ottawa!
Customer:	??
Dealer rep:	Im supposed to provid live assistance. What can I do for you?
Customer:	I want to buy a car.
Dealer rep:	Can I get your name fist?
Customer:	Young Jae Kim.
Dealer rep:	Interesting name . . . Okay. What model? New inventory or preowned?
Customer:	BMW 2021 model.
Dealer rep:	Right, but what model? Where are you from?
Customer:	Do you have this model in green?
Dealer rep:	Which BMW model are you looking for???
Customer:	Sorry: i3.
Dealer rep:	I wouldn't recommend buying a hybrid car . . .
Customer:	Excuse me?
Dealer rep:	They're not dependable like our numbered or X series. Might be easier if I can get your number and give you a call . . .
Customer:	Please send email about i3 stock to yjkim@t-tech.net. Thanks.

5.8 BLOGGING: LEARNING FROM THE BEST (OBJ. 4)

Use Google to search for high-quality blogs in an area of business that interests you: fashion, design, or real estate are just a few choices. When searching, make sure to look for diverse blogs: blogs by women, men, and nonbinary people; blogs written by members of racial minorities; blogs by people with disabilities. After you've located three to four blogs you like, examine what clever strategies and ways of doing things you can adopt and make work for you.

Your Task. Write a blog entry detailing your analysis of the professional blogs you have examined, and post it using free blog software like WordPress. Apply the same best practices for professional business blogs outlined in this chapter. Remember to offer a catchy title on a popular topic that will attract readers, in this case, your peers in class and your instructor. Share helpful advice in easy-to-read numbered items and, if applicable, provide links to other relevant articles. Include one or more images that help illustrate your post. To motivate readers to respond, ask questions at the end of your blog entry.

5.9 COMPOSING A PERSONAL BLOG ENTRY (OBJ. 4)

Review the guidelines for professional blogging in this chapter. Find a recent social media–related study or survey, and target an audience of business professionals who may want to know more about social networking. Search for studies conducted by respected organizations and businesses, such as the Conference Board of Canada, Pew Internet, Robert Half International, Burson-Marsteller, ePolicy Institute, and Canadian government agencies. As you plan and outline your post, follow the advice provided in this chapter. Although the goal is usually to offer advice, you could also give your opinion regarding a controversy. For example, do you agree with companies that forbid employees from using company computers for social networking? Do you agree that Millennials are losing social skills because of excessive online connectivity?

Your Task. Compose and design a one-page blog entry in MS Word and submit it in hard copy. Alternatively, post it to the discussion board on the class course management platform, email it to your instructor, or post it on WordPress as in Activity 5.8, as appropriate. Because you will be using outside sources, be careful to paraphrase correctly.

5.10 REVIEWING CORPORATE BLOGS (OBJ. 4)

As we have seen, many organizations today are blogging, and researchers note an increase in corporations with active blogs. The companies and their CEOs who do blog can impart valuable lessons.

Your Task. Search online for *CEO blogs*, *index of corporate blogs, index of CEO blogs*, and similar keywords. You will likely end up at ChiefExecutive.net, on SlideShare, and at other sites that may list the top ten or so most popular corporate blogs, perhaps even one penned by a CEO. Select a corporate or CEO blog you find interesting, browse the posts, and read some of the content. Note how many aspects of the blog match the guidelines in this book. If your instructor directs, write a brief informational memo or email summarizing your observations about the business blog, its style, the subjects covered, and so forth.

5.11 MONITORING TWITTER CHATTER AND FACEBOOK POSTS (OBJ. 5)

Many large companies monitor Twitter chatter and Facebook posts. They have discovered social media is a tool for averting public relations disasters. Rogers, Telus, Bell, WestJet, and others are quick to apologize to irate customers and to correct problems that they discover via Twitter or other social media networking sites.

Your Task. You are a social media intern working at the head office of a major telecommunications company such as Rogers, Shaw, Telus or Videotron. Your job is to search through tweets and Facebook posts to find those that are both positive about and critical of your company and to inform your manager about any that could potentially end up hurting the company's image. Deciding which post could cause trouble is difficult, given that even with tracking software, you may need to scan hundreds of posts every day. You know that if many users retweet, or redistribute, the news, the problem may get out of hand. Create a Twitter account and search for posts about your company. Make a list of three positive and three negative tweets. Recommend or draft responses to them. If you identify a trend, make a note of it and report it either in class or in writing as directed by your instructor.

5.12 WRITING COPY FOR SOCIAL MEDIA (OBJ. 5)

We've all heard about times when a celebrity or an influencer posts about a particular product, that product quickly sells out, and the company that makes it gains wide publicity that positively affects its sales and profits for months to come. Suppose you are the paid influencer hired by various brands to write copy and upload images of their products to create the kind of frenzy that leads to sold-out situations.

Your Task. Using the following scenarios, and the advice provided in this chapter, write social media copy for two social media channels.

Scenario: Vancouver-based knapsack maker Herschel Supply (herschel.ca) is about to blow up (yet again!) because it's just signed a deal with the Canadian Olympic Committee (olympic.ca) to design hip cross-body knapsacks for Canadian athletes to wear as they enter the Olympic stadium in Paris, France, in 2024. Leverage (and manage) this opportunity for Herschel on two social media channels.

Scenario: Car manufacturer Nissan Canada (www.nissan.ca) is adding a fourth manufacturing facility in Moncton, New Brunswick, to the list of its facilities that manufacture the Leaf, its best-selling fully electric vehicle. The news hasn't hit the mainstream press yet. Leverage this opportunity for Nissan Canada on two social media channels.

Scenario: Canadian beauty bar chain The Ten Spot (www.thetenspot.com) is moving its Halifax location from downtown South Street to the new Westfield Halifax shopping centre in the far north suburbs of the city. Some long-time customers may not be happy about this move. Leverage this news for The Ten Spot on two social media channels.

5.13 WRITING CRISIS AND CALL-TO-ACTION COPY FOR SOCIAL MEDIA (OBJ. 5)

In social-media writing, two of the most common reasons for writing copy are to deal with a crisis and to create calls-to-action. A crisis is any emergency situation that has a negative impact on the organization. (You can find more information here: https://blog.pocketstop.com/5-crisis-communications-message-templates.) A call to action is a request by the organization that readers take some sort of action. (You can find more information here: www.crazyegg.com/blog/glossary/call-to-action/.)

Your Task. Using the following scenarios, and the advice provided in this chapter, write crisis and call-to-action social media copy for two social media channels.

Scenario: An oil pipeline that crosses pristine ranch lands in central Alberta has burst, spewing oil into a nearby river. Manage the crisis on behalf of the municipality and the oil company in two social media posts.

Scenario: An armed person has entered the biggest shopping mall in your area. Shots have been reported by bystanders. Manage the crisis on behalf of mall management and the local police in two social media posts.

Scenario: Your company has just created a paraben-free sunscreen that also acts as a moisturizer without being too heavy or greasy. Create a call-to-action for the new product in two social media posts.

Scenario: Your company has just created a line of stevia-sweetened milk chocolate bars that deliver all the sweetness and creaminess of chocolate without any of the negative effects of sugar. Create a call-to-action for the new products in two social media posts.

WRITING IMPROVEMENT EXERCISES

MESSAGE OPENERS AND SUBJECT LINES (OBJ. 1)

Your Task. Compare the following sets of message openers. Choose the letter of the opener that illustrates a direct opening. Write an appropriate subject line for each opening paragraph.

1. An email requesting information about creating online surveys:

   a. Our company needs to conduct occasional consumer surveys regarding new products. We used to invest in focus groups, but now we would like to try online research, about which we have heard good things. We hope this will save much time and money. We need information on how to do it, and your program called MySurvey might be just what we need. We are especially interested in how incentives such as reward points might work.

   b. Please send information about your program MySurvey so that our company can learn about online surveys.

2. An email announcing a low-cost daycare program:

   a. Employees interested in enrolling their children in our new low-cost daycare program are invited to attend an HR orientation on January 18.

   b. For several years we have studied the possibility of offering a daycare option for those employees who are parents. Until recently, our management team was unable to agree on the exact parameters of this benefit, but now some of you will be able to take advantage of this option.

3. A memo announcing an upcoming employee satisfaction survey:

   a. We have noticed recently increased turnover among our marketing staff. We are concerned about this troubling development and would like to study its causes. We have hired an outside consulting firm to gauge the satisfaction level and attitudes of our marketing staff in confidential qualitative interviews. You may be asked to participate in this important survey in which you can recommend strategies to avoid the situation.

   b. You may be asked to participate in qualitative interviews to explore the satisfaction level among our marketing staff and recommend strategies to stem the tide of recent departures.

4. A memo announcing a new policy:

   a. It has come to our attention that some staff members write blogs, sometimes publicly addressing sensitive company information. Although we respect the desire of employees to express themselves and would like to continue allowing the practice, we have decided to adopt a new policy providing binding rules to ensure the company's and the bloggers' safety.

   b. The following new policy for blog authors will help staff members create posts that maintain the integrity of the company's sensitive information and keep writers safe.

BULLETED AND NUMBERED LISTS (OBJ. 1)

Emails and memos frequently contain numbered (for items in a sequence) or bulleted lists. Study how the following wordy paragraph was revised into a more readable format with a list:

Before Revision:

Our office could implement better environmental practices such as improving energy efficiency and reducing our carbon footprint. Here are three simple things we can do to make our daily work practices greener. For one thing, we can power down. At night we should turn off monitors, not just log off our computers. In addition, we could "light right." This means installing energy-efficient lighting throughout the office. A final suggestion has to do with recycling. We could be recycling instantly if we placed small recycling bins at all workstations and common use areas.

After Revision:

Our office could use energy more efficiently and reduce our carbon footprint in three simple ways:

- **Power down:** Turn off monitors rather than just logging off our computers.
- **Light right:** Install energy-efficient lighting throughout the office.
- **Recycle instantly:** Place small recycling bins at all workstations and common use areas to encourage recycling.

Your Task. Revise the following wordy, unorganized paragraphs. Include an introductory statement followed by a bulleted or numbered list. Look for ways to eliminate unnecessary wording.

1. If you are a job candidate interviewing for a job, you should follow a few guidelines that most people consider basic. You will be more successful if you do these things. One of the first things to do is get ready. Before the interview, successful candidates research the target company. That is, they find out about it. If you really want to be successful, you will prepare success stories. Wise candidates also clean up any digital dirt that may be floating around the Internet. Those are a few of the things to do before the interview. During the interview, the best candidates try to sound enthusiastic. They answer questions clearly but with short, concise responses. They also are prepared to ask their own questions. After the interview, when you can relax a bit, you should remember to send a thank-you note to the interviewer. Another thing to do after the interview is contact references. One last thing to do, if you don't hear from the interviewer within five days, is follow up with an inquiry.

2. Winning the lottery can bring a colossal chunk of income. What would you do if you had won the lottery and come home with mega millions? Smart winners can save their sanity and their cash, as well as live well for years into the future if they take precautionary steps. Step No. 1 is staying anonymous. Don't broadcast your good news because long-lost friends and relatives become vultures, all seeking handouts. A second step involves seeking out a tax pro immediately. You may think you have a huge chunk of money to spend, but the government may be taking a hefty hunk. You need a tax expert to help minimize the tax burden. Experts also warn against making immediate and major changes in your lifestyle within six months after winning. Examples: quitting your job, buying yachts, or purchasing European castles.

◣ GRAMMAR/MECHANICS CHALLENGE 5

PREPOSITIONS AND CONJUNCTIONS

Review Sections 1.18 and 1.19 of the Grammar/Mechanics Handbook. Then study each of the following statements. In the space provided, write *a* or *b* to indicate the sentence in which the idea is expressed more effectively. Also record the number of the G/M principle illustrated. When you finish, compare your responses with those provided near the end of the book. If your answers differ, study carefully the principles in parentheses.

<u>b (1.18a)</u>   **Example**

       a. When did you graduate high school?

       b. When did you graduate from high school?

_____   1. a. Your iPad was more expensive than mine.

       b. Your iPad was more expensive then mine.

_____   2. a. Don't you hate when your inbox is filled with spam?

       b. Don't you hate it when your inbox is filled with spam?

_____   3. a. If the company called you, than it must be looking at your résumé.

       b. If the company called you, then it must be looking at your résumé.

_____   4. a. Ethnocentrism is when you believe your culture is best.

       b. Ethnocentrism involves the belief that your culture is best.

	5.	a.	Business messages should be clear, correct, and written with conciseness.
		b.	Business messages should be clear, correct, and concise.
_____	6.	a.	What type of computer monitor do you prefer?
		b.	What type computer monitor do you prefer?
_____	7.	a.	Do you know where the meeting is at?
		b.	Do you know where the meeting is?
_____	8.	a.	Did you send an application to the headquarters in Winnipeg or to the branch in Brandon?
		b.	Did you apply to the Winnipeg headquarters or the Brandon branch?
_____	9.	a.	Shelby hopes to graduate college next year.
		b.	Shelby hopes to graduate from college next year.
_____	10.	a.	She had a great interest, as well as a profound respect for, historical homes.
		b.	She had a great interest in, as well as a profound respect for, historical homes.
_____	11.	a.	Volunteers should wear long pants, bring gloves, and sunscreen should be applied.
		b.	Volunteers should wear long pants, bring gloves, and apply sunscreen.
_____	12.	a.	His PowerPoint presentation was short, as we hoped it would be.
		b.	His PowerPoint presentation was short, like we hoped it would be.
_____	13.	a.	An ethics code is where a set of rules spells out appropriate behaviour standards.
		b.	An ethics code is a set of rules spelling out appropriate behaviour standards.
_____	14.	a.	Please keep the paper near the printer.
		b.	Please keep the paper near to the printer.
_____	15.	a.	A behavioural interview question is when the recruiter says, "Tell me about a time . . . ."
		b.	A behavioural interview question is one in which the recruiter says, "Tell me about a time . . . ."

◣ EDITING CHALLENGE 5

This message explains a task being assigned to Antonella Doolittle by her boss Jared Nguyen. The message has proofreading, spelling, grammar, punctuation, wordiness, and other writing faults that require correction. Study the guidelines in the Grammar/Mechanics Handbook, as well as the lists of Confusing Words and Frequently Misspelled Words at the end of the book to sharpen your skills.

Your Task. Edit the following message by correcting its errors (a) in your textbook or (b) on a photocopy using proofreading marks from Appendix B.

To: Antonella Doolittle <antonella.doolittle@circa.com>
From: Jared Nguyen <jared.nguyen@circa.com>
Subject: Big Job for You
Cc:
Bcc:

Antonella,

Due to the fact that you have done excellent work on various projects here at Circa the vice president and the undersigned has picked you to work on a special project conducting research for next years annual report. In all likelihood, you should plan to visit each and every department head personal to collect department information individually from them.

Staff members of the Corporate Communications division which oversee the production of the annual report is of the opinion that you should concentrate on the following items:

- specific accomplishments—not just activitys—for the past year
- You should also out about goals of each department for the coming year
- in each department get names of interesting employees who have made a contribution to the department or ones who have contributed to the community.
- Be sure to ask about special events featuring outstanding employees and corporate officers

Because of the fact that this is an assignment that is big in size, Mary Mansfield has been given the assignment of offering assistance to you. We made the decision that it was better to assign an assistant rather then have you be overwhelmed with this task.

Oh, one more thing. As you do your interviewing, try to collect digital photos that are in colour and that illustrate employees and special events.

Inasmuch as the annual report must be completed by August first you must submit this material to Julie Armstrong or I by June 5th. We are greatful for your expertise and have that you will do a job.

Warm regards,
Jared
Jared Nguyen, Director
Corporate Communications
Circa Industries, Inc.
jared.nguyen@circa.com
Cell: 250-430-9018

OBJECTIVES

6.1 Explain digital-age persuasion and the AIRA persuasive technique.

6.2 Write persuasive help request messages.

6.3 Write persuasive claim or complaint messages.

6.4 Write persuasive employee buy-in messages.

6.5 Write persuasive direct-mail, email, and social media sales messages.

PeopleImages/istock by Getty Images

WRITING TO PERSUADE

▶ BIZ COMM BYTE

According to the latest census, the number of Canadian farmers selling directly to consumers (instead of relying on others to do their selling for them) is growing, with British Columbia leading the way at 33 percent. Overall, three out of five (60 percent) of poultry/egg farmers; three out of five (60 percent) of beekeeping farms; and four out of five (80 percent) of fruit/vegetable farmers are marketing directly to consumers through one or more channels.

Source: Statistics Canada. (2017, June 21). Direct marketing in Canada. https://www150.statcan.gc.ca/n1/pub/11-627-m/11-627-m2017015-eng.htm

◢ 6.1 Persuasion in the Digital Age

Getting others to do or think what we want—a straightforward definition of *persuasion*—isn't easy. For example, a peach farmer in the Niagara or Okanagan region can't just assume that people in Toronto or Vancouver will regularly get in their cars and drive for two hours to buy peaches fresh from the farm—persuasion in some form will be needed to make this happen. Persuasion is necessary whenever we're making more than routine requests of others, which can result in skeptical, busy, distracted, or hostile audiences.

Experts say that the average adult sees between 4,000 and 10,000 ads and other persuasive appeals a day.[1] As citizens and consumers, we need to be alert to persuasive practices and how they influence behaviour. Being informed is our best defence. On the other hand, social media networks have put power into the hands of many. Persuasion guru B. J. Fogg points out that social media enable individuals or groups to reach virtually limitless audiences and practise "mass interpersonal persuasion."[2]

In Chapter 5 you studied plans for daily request messages that require minimal persuasion (e.g., *Please join us at next week's brainstorming session—time and place to come*). This chapter focuses on requests that require significant persuasion. It also addresses selling, both offline and online. Perhaps the most persuasive writing situation of all—the cover letter—is dealt with separately in Chapter 12.

Cengage

MINDTAP

In MindTap go to the Whiteboard Animation for Chapter 6 and watch it now.

6.1a Persuasion in the Digital Age

The preoccupation with persuasion isn't new. From the days of Aristotle in ancient Greece and Machiavelli in Renaissance Italy, philosophers, politicians, and businesspeople have tried to understand the art of influencing others. However, persuasion in the 21st century is different from persuasion in historic periods in distinct ways.[3]

PERSUASIVE MESSAGES HAVE EXPLODED IN VOLUME AND REACH. The Internet, mobile phones, and TV blast huge volumes of messages around the world. This can be positive, as occurs when popular culture trends in fashion, music, or art spread over Instagram from somewhere like Japan or China to Canada; or it can be negative, as occurs when incitements to terrorism are coordinated via social media and spread quickly around the world.

PERSUASIVE MESSAGES SPREAD AT WARP SPEED. Citizen reporters can deliver instant updates from disaster areas on Twitter and other social media, and people can instantly persuade each other to do positive things (support Go Fund me campaigns, for example), as well as negative things (incite others to bully someone on social media or actually harm people who've said something against their favourite celebrity, for example).

EVERYONE IS IN THE PERSUASION BUSINESS. Companies, ad agencies, PR firms, social activists, lobbyists, individuals, marketers, and more are now routinely sending persuasive messages. Although outspent by corporations that can sink millions into image campaigns, activists and individuals use social networks to rally their followers and create their brands.

PERSUASIVE TECHNIQUES ARE SUBTLER AND MORE MISLEADING. Instead of a blunt, pushy hard-sell approach, persuaders today play on emotions by using flattery, empathy, nonverbal cues, and likability appeals. They sell images (e.g., on Pinterest and Instagram) and lifestyles, not just products.[4] Social media is increasingly infiltrated by partisan interests, and these interests spread messages (e.g., *clickbait*) that masquerade as news.

PERSUASION IS INVISIBLE YET EVERYWHERE. Powerful social media artificial intelligence programs gather information on each click we make, becoming able to predict the sorts of things we are interested in and respond to. Then, these same social media sites sell information about our clicking to organizations who market (i.e., persuade) back to us in posts that look like they've come from people in our network on that social media site but are actually paid ads. This is less of a problem when our interest is in something harmless like sneakers, but it's potentially quite harmful when our interest is in something like overthrowing the government.

6.1b A Proven Persuasion Strategy

Despite these sometimes dramatic and problematic changes to persuasion, for people in business a traditional indirect persuasion strategy is still necessary in day-to-day relations with busy coworkers, managers, people in outside organizations, and the general public. This occurs because as part of persuading others, you'll meet resistance. This resistance is natural because in persuading, you're asking people for something valuable: money (e.g., in a sales presentation, in a charity solicitation), time (e.g., in a negotiation over increased vacation time), or goods (e.g., in a situation when a donation is requested). And they don't automatically want to say *yes* or *sure*.

Knowing you're going to encounter resistance, it makes sense that you should reduce or counter the resistance of the person you're trying to persuade before actually asking for what you want. For example, if after eight years of working for a furniture manufacturing company as a territory sales manager, with six straight years of growth in your sales but no growth to speak of in your vacation time, you may decide to ask your manager for more time off. Knowing that your company overall has had a slow sales period (not in your territory, however), you know you can't simply make a direct request to your boss: "Ken, I've been thinking it's time I received an increase in my vacation time."

Instead, you'll need an *indirect* persuasion strategy that begins with countering resistance: "Ken, I've got some ideas the other territory managers can use to emulate my reps' success in growing business in these tough times. Can we talk about the ideas over lunch this week? When we meet, I'd also like to make a formal request for two extra days of vacation time going forward. After eight years with the company and a lot of success in my job, I feel this is an appropriate time for me to see a small bump in my vacation time. Let me know a time that works for you."

The indirect strategy requires more practice and experience than the direct strategy used in daily writing situations covered in Chapter 5. For this reason, pay close attention to the writing plans in this chapter as they show you how to perform the "persuasive moves" necessary to make things happen in the world of work.

6.1c The AIRA Technique

The indirect strategy used by the territory sales manager in the example above contains separate strategies, but to be successful all four should appear together as a unified whole. This unified strategy for persuasive writing is called AIRA, which stands for *attention, interest, resistance,* and *action*. These are the four crucial elements of any persuasive message. The order of the four elements isn't set in stone; for example, not every persuasive situation will require you to build interest before you reduce resistance. However, most persuasive messages do begin by gaining attention and end by motivating action.

A: GAIN ATTENTION. In the brief opening of the message, gain the reader's attention by describing a problem, making an unexpected statement, mentioning a reader benefit, paying the reader a compliment, or posing a stimulating question. For example, in a persuasive voice mail message left by a local theatre company to its current subscribers, the speaker might begin by mentioning a listener benefit: *All of our returning subscribers will be able to take advantage of special access to our subscribers' lounge and attend after-show talks by members of the cast and creative team!*

I: BUILD INTEREST. The message's body is intended to keep the reader's attention and persuade him or her that the request is reasonable. This section is often the longest part of the message, as it includes facts and statistics, expert opinion, direct benefits to the receiver, examples, and specific details, as well as indirect benefits to the receiver. Together, these facts create desire, which is especially important when your persuasive message is a sales message. In the theatre subscription example, the person leaving the voice mail may build interest by stating, *We rely on our subscribers to join us year after year because your subscription helps generate the largest part of our revenue. Government grants and donations currently make up only 30 percent of our revenue. This is why we need subscribers to keep coming back.*

R: REDUCE RESISTANCE. A crucial step in creating a persuasive message, yet one that's often left out by novice communicators, is to put yourself in the receiver's shoes and ask, *What kinds of problems might the receiver have with my request?*

For example, the employee selling theatre subscriptions may learn through experience that numerous people will say they have other important uses for their time and money. The employee therefore begins planning to reduce this specific resistance by anticipating and naming it in her voice mail and then countering it with a benefit: *While we understand you have competing priorities for your hard-earned money, we also know that supporting the arts is good for our city and good for our health. An evening at the theatre is a sure-fire way to leave the pressures and worries of everyday life behind for a few hours.*

A: MOTIVATE ACTION. Finally, no persuasive message is complete without the sender closing by telling the receiver exactly what he or she wants and when he or she wants it. The goal is to sound confident but not pushy, and to motivate the reader to say yes. In essence, a persuasive message should end with a specific request that is confident but not demanding. In the theatre subscription example, the voice mail might end: *I'm sorry I missed you tonight, but I'll try you again tomorrow after dinnertime. In the meantime, feel free to call me at (416) 922-0018 or go to our website to re-subscribe immediately. I can offer you special access to the subscribers' lounge and after-show talks until March 15.*

◣ 6.2 Persuasive Intention: Help Requests

You learned in the previous chapter that communication can be analyzed in terms of its *intentions*: the reasons why we write or speak to someone. At some point we all need to ask for help. Small help requests, such as asking a coworker to lock up the office for you on Friday, are straightforward and direct. Little resistance is expected. Larger requests, though, require careful planning and an indirect strategy. A busy executive is asked to serve on a committee to help at-risk children; a florist is asked to donate table arrangements for a charity fundraiser; a well-known author is asked to speak before a local library group—why should they agree to do so? In each instance, persuasion is necessary to overcome the recipient's natural resistance.

Fortunately, most of us are willing to grant requests for time, money, information, cooperation, and special privileges. We grant these favours for a variety of reasons. We're either interested in your project or may see goodwill potential in it for ourselves. Often, we comply because we see that others will benefit from the request. Professionals decide to contribute their time or expertise to give back to the community.

Figure 6.1 shows a persuasive help request. Michelle Moreno's research firm needs to persuade other companies to complete a questionnaire on salary data. For most organizations, salary information is strictly confidential. What can Michelle do to convince strangers to share such private information?

The quickly written draft version of Michelle's request has many faults. It doesn't attract the interest of the reader in the opening. It also provides an easy excuse for Mr. Mansker to refuse (*filling out surveys can be tedious*). In the body Mr. Mansker doesn't receive any incentives or reasons to accept the request. The writing is self-serving and offers few specifics. In addition, the draft doesn't reduce resistance by anticipating his objections and suggesting counterarguments. Finally, the closing doesn't motivate action by providing a deadline or a final benefit.

In the revised version, Michelle **gains attention** by beginning her persuasive request with two short questions that spotlight the need for salary information. To **build interest** and credibility, she mentions that Moreno Renaud has been collecting business data for a quarter century and has received awards from the Canadian Marketing Association. Making a reasonable request tied to benefits is also important. Michelle does this by emphasizing the need for current salary information.

To **reduce resistance**, Michelle promises confidentiality and explains that the questionnaire takes only a few moments to complete. She offers free salary data

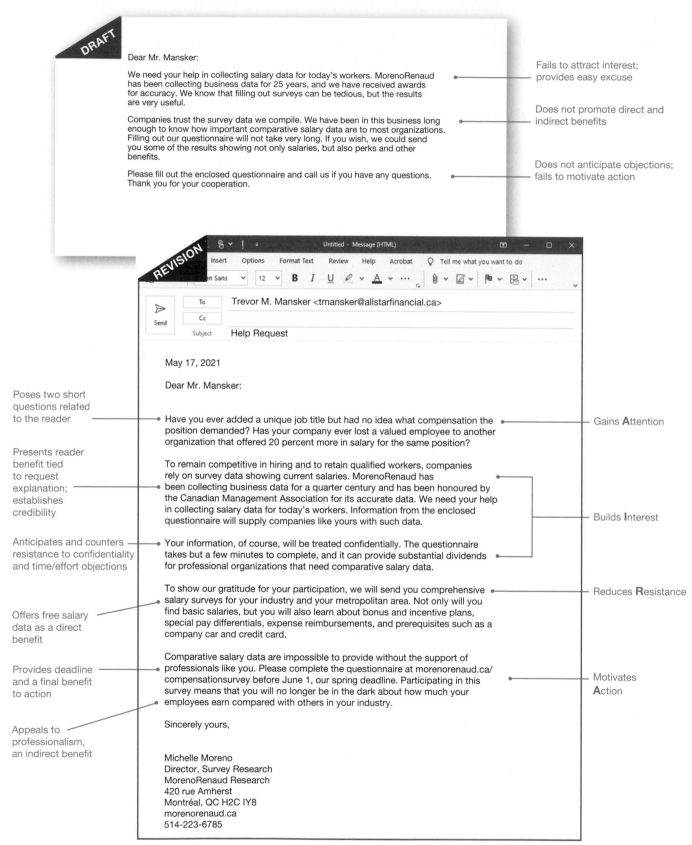

DRAFT

Dear Mr. Mansker:

We need your help in collecting salary data for today's workers. MorenoRenaud has been collecting business data for 25 years, and we have received awards for accuracy. We know that filling out surveys can be tedious, but the results are very useful.

Fails to attract interest; provides easy excuse

Companies trust the survey data we compile. We have been in this business long enough to know how important comparative salary data are to most organizations. Filling out our questionnaire will not take very long. If you wish, we could send you some of the results showing not only salaries, but also perks and other benefits.

Does not promote direct and indirect benefits

Please fill out the enclosed questionnaire and call us if you have any questions. Thank you for your cooperation.

Does not anticipate objections; fails to motivate action

REVISION

Untitled - Message (HTML)

Insert Options Format Text Review Help Acrobat Tell me what you want to do

en Sans   12   **B** *I* U ✏ A

To   Trevor M. Mansker <tmansker@allstarfinancial.ca>

Cc

Subject   Help Request

May 17, 2021

Dear Mr. Mansker:

Poses two short questions related to the reader

Have you ever added a unique job title but had no idea what compensation the position demanded? Has your company ever lost a valued employee to another organization that offered 20 percent more in salary for the same position?

*Gains **A**ttention*

Presents reader benefit tied to request explanation; establishes credibility

To remain competitive in hiring and to retain qualified workers, companies rely on survey data showing current salaries. MorenoRenaud has been collecting business data for a quarter century and has been honoured by the Canadian Management Association for its accurate data. We need your help in collecting salary data for today's workers. Information from the enclosed questionnaire will supply companies like yours with such data.

*Builds **I**nterest*

Anticipates and counters resistance to confidentiality and time/effort objections

Your information, of course, will be treated confidentially. The questionnaire takes but a few minutes to complete, and it can provide substantial dividends for professional organizations that need comparative salary data.

Offers free salary data as a direct benefit

To show our gratitude for your participation, we will send you comprehensive salary surveys for your industry and your metropolitan area. Not only will you find basic salaries, but you will also learn about bonus and incentive plans, special pay differentials, expense reimbursements, and prerequisites such as a company car and credit card.

*Reduces **R**esistance*

Provides deadline and a final benefit to action

Comparative salary data are impossible to provide without the support of professionals like you. Please complete the questionnaire at morenorenaud.ca/compensationsurvey before June 1, our spring deadline. Participating in this survey means that you will no longer be in the dark about how much your employees earn compared with others in your industry.

*Motivates **A**ction*

Appeals to professionalism, an indirect benefit

Sincerely yours,

Michelle Moreno
Director, Survey Research
MorenoRenaud Research
420 rue Amherst
Montréal, QC H2C IY8
morenorenaud.ca
514-223-6785

How could Michelle's email be even more effective with graphic highlighting techniques like bolding, listing, numbering, and so on, from Chapter 4?

as a direct benefit. This data may help the receiver learn how his company's salary scale compares with others in its industry. But Michelle doesn't count on this offer as the only motivator. As an indirect benefit, she appeals to the professionalism of the receiver. She's hoping that the receiver will recognize the value to the entire profession of providing salary data. To **motivate action**, Michelle closes with a deadline and reminds Mr. Mansker that his company doesn't need to be in the dark about comparative salaries within the industry.

This help request incorporates many of the techniques that are effective in persuasion: establishing credibility, making a reasonable and precise request, tying requests to reader benefits, and overcoming resistance. These techniques are summarized in the writing plan.

WRITING PLAN FOR A PERSUASIVE REQUEST

- **Opening:** Gain attention in the opening.
- **Body:** Build interest in the body with facts and benefits.
- **Body:** Reduce resistance in the body by acknowledging potential objections, and with more benefits.
- **Closing:** Motivate action in the closing.

6.3 Persuasive Intention: Claims and Complaints

Let's say you're the manager of Canadian furniture retailer Structube's recently opened Kingston, Ontario, location. Your store isn't large enough to warehouse bulky items like sofas and mattresses, so you've been leasing warehouse space in another part of the city for the past two months. Five times this past month, you've had angry customers call you because they've received a delivery from Structube (shipped from your leased warehouse) and the furniture and packaging it was delivered in are damaged, sometimes quite seriously. It's definitely time to persuade the manager of the warehouse location to pay for the replacement cost of these items and ask him to stop being negligent with Structube property. A persuasive claim and complaint like this one—which you know will probably be resisted—is most effective when structured indirectly, using the AIRA technique.

First, decide what action you want taken to satisfy the claim. Then, decide how you can prove the worth of your claim. Carefully plan the reasoning you will follow in convincing the reader to take the action you request. If the claim is addressed to a business, the most effective appeals are generally to the organization's pride in its products and its services. Refer to its reputation for integrity and your confidence in it. Show why your claim is valid and why the company will be doing the right thing in granting it. Most organizations are sincere in their efforts to showcase quality products and services that gain consumer respect.

Although claim messages often contain an aspect of complaint, try not to be angry. Hostility and emotional threats toward an organization do little to achieve the goal of a claim message. Claims are usually referred to a customer service department. The representative answering the claim probably had nothing to do with the design, production, delivery, or servicing of the product or service. An abusive message may serve only to offend, making it hard for the representative to evaluate the claim rationally.

A writing plan for an indirect persuasive claim or complaint follows the steps shown in the box.

Notice how the claim email shown in Figure 6.2 uses the suggestions above. When Arte International Furnishings in Concord, Ontario, purchased two VoIP

WRITING PLAN FOR A PERSUASIVE CLAIM OR COMPLAINT

- **Opening:** Gain attention in the opening by paying the receiver a compliment.
- **Body:** Build interest in the body by explaining and justifying the claim or complaint with convincing reasons and without anger.
- **Body:** Reduce resistance in the body by subtly suggesting the responsibility of the receiver. Appeal to the receiver's sense of fairness or desire for customer satisfaction.
- **Closing:** Motivate action in the closing by explaining exactly what action you want taken and when.

▚ FIGURE 6.2 / Claim

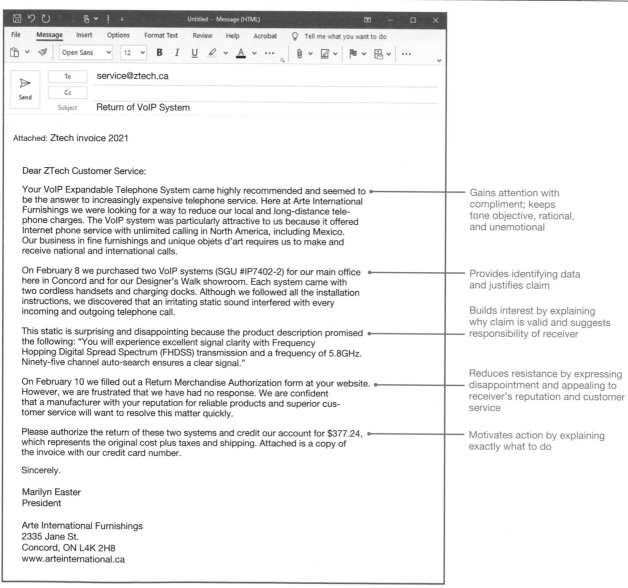

How could Marilyn's email be even more effective with graphic highlighting techniques like bolding, listing, numbering, and so on, from Chapter 4?

systems, it discovered that they would not work without producing an annoying static sound. The company's attempt to return the systems online has been ignored by the retailer. Despite these difficulties, notice the writer's positive opening, her well-documented claims, and her specific request for action.

6.4 Persuasive Intention: Coworker and Manager Buy-In

When it comes to persuasion, where you sit on the hierarchy at work determines how you write—with some equals or people lower on the hierarchy than you, it's OK to ask for things directly, whereas with other equals and people higher on the hierarchy than you, an indirect approach to requests is necessary. Other things to consider include what type and amount of evidence to include and whether to adopt a formal or informal tone. Remember the audience analysis techniques from earlier in this book as you make these decisions.

6.4a Persuading Fellow Employees

Instructions or directives moving downward from employees to other employees whom they manage (i.e., direct reports) usually require little persuasion. Employees expect to be directed on how to perform their jobs. These messages (such as information about procedures, equipment, or customer service) follow the direct pattern, with the purpose immediately stated. However, employees are sometimes asked to perform in a capacity outside their work roles or to accept changes that are not in their best interests (such as pay cuts, job transfers, or reduced benefits). Occasionally, superiors need to address sensitive workplace issues such as bullying or diversity programs. Similarly, supervisors may want to create buy-in when introducing a healthier cafeteria menu or mandatory volunteering effort. In these instances, a persuasive message using the indirect pattern may be most effective.

The goal is not to manipulate employees or to deceive them with trickery. Instead, present a strong but honest argument, emphasizing points that are important to the receiver or the organization. In business, honesty is not just the best policy—it is the only policy. People see right through puffery and misrepresentation. For this reason, the indirect pattern is effective only when supported by accurate, honest evidence.

6.4b Persuading Managers

Convincing management to adopt a procedure or invest in a product or new equipment generally requires skillful communication. Managers are just as resistant to change as others are. Knowing precisely what they're asking for and providing evidence of why the request is necessary are critical factors when employees submit recommendations to their manager. It's also important to be realistic in your requests, recognizing that your manager has other employees whose needs may be different from your own. Equally important when asking something of your manager is to focus on the manager's needs. How can you make your suggestion sound like something your manager also wants or needs?

Obviously, when you set out to persuade someone at work who is above you in the company hierarchy, do so carefully. Use words like *suggest* and *recommend*, and write sentences using conditional verb tenses such as: *It might be a good idea if . . .* ; *We might think about doing . . . .* The conditional tense lets you offer suggestions without threatening the person's authority.

In Figure 6.3 you can see a persuasive memo (attached to an email) written by Marketing Assistant Monica Cho, who wants her manager to authorize the

FIGURE 6.3 / Suggestion to Manager

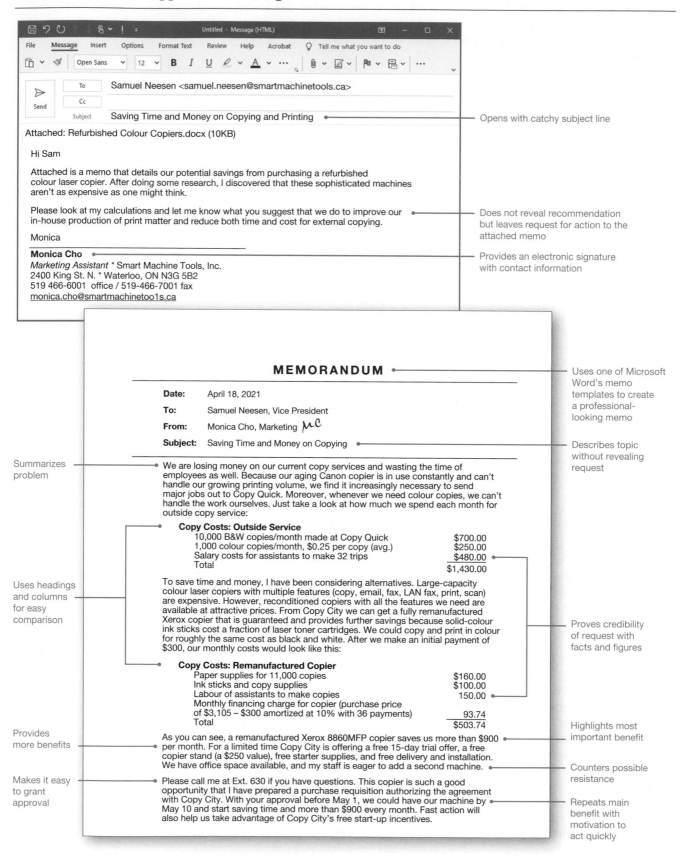

Opens with catchy subject line

Does not reveal recommendation but leaves request for action to the attached memo

Provides an electronic signature with contact information

Uses one of Microsoft Word's memo templates to create a professional-looking memo

Describes topic without revealing request

Summarizes problem

Uses headings and columns for easy comparison

Proves credibility of request with facts and figures

Provides more benefits

Highlights most important benefit

Makes it easy to grant approval

Counters possible resistance

Repeats main benefit with motivation to act quickly

purchase of a multifunction colour laser copier. She has researched the prices, features, and maintenance costs of the machines. They often serve as copiers, faxes, scanners, and printers and can cost several thousand dollars.

Monica has found an outstanding deal offered by a local office supplier. Because Monica knows that her boss, Samuel Neesen, favours cold, hard facts, she lists current monthly costs for copying at Copy Quick to increase her chances of gaining approval. Finally, she calculates the amortization of the purchase price and monthly costs of running the new colour copier.

Notice that Monica's memo isn't short. An indirect persuasive request will typically take more space than a direct request because proving a case requires evidence. In the end Monica chose to send her memo as an email attachment accompanied by a polite, short note because she wanted to keep the document format in Microsoft Word intact.

She also felt that the message was too long to paste into an email. Monica's persuasive memo and her cover email include a subject line that announces the purpose of the message without disclosing the actual request. By delaying the request until she has had a chance to describe the problem and discuss a solution, Monica prevents the reader's premature rejection.

The strength of this persuasive message, though, is in the clear presentation of comparison figures showing how much money the company can save by purchasing a remanufactured copier. Buying a copier that uses low-cost solid ink instead of expensive laser cartridges is another argument in this machine's favour.

Although the organization pattern is not obvious, the memo follows most of the Writing Plan for a Persuasive Request from earlier in this chapter, by beginning with an attention-getter (a frank description of the problem), building interest (with easy-to-read facts and figures), providing benefits, and reducing resistance. Notice that the conclusion suggests what action to take, makes it easy to respond, and repeats the main benefit to motivate action.

◣ 6.5 Persuasive Intention: Selling and Promoting

Sales messages use persuasion to sell specific products and services. The focus in this part of the chapter is on direct-mail sales letters, but this communication strategy can be applied to all forms of sales and promotions, including print, online, and social and digital media, as well as traditional copywriting for radio and TV advertisements. Smart companies strive to develop an omnichannel approach to their overall marketing strategy, including both traditional direct mail and social/digital marketing and other approaches.

6.5a Sales Messages

Sales letters are part of a package that may contain a brochure, price list, illustrations, testimonials, and other persuasive appeals. Professionals who specialize in traditional direct-mail have made a science of analyzing a market, developing an effective mailing list, studying the product, preparing a sophisticated campaign aimed at a target audience, and motivating the reader to act. You have probably received many direct-mail packages, often called "junk mail."

Because sales letters are usually written by marketing communications specialists, you may never write one on the job. Why, then, learn how to write a sales letter? In many ways, every message we draft is a type of sales letter. We sell our ideas, our organizations, and ourselves. When we apply for a job, we're both the seller and the product. Learning the techniques of sales writing helps you be more successful in any communication that requires persuasion and promotion.

Your primary goal in writing a sales message is to get someone to devote a few moments of attention to it, and the best way to do so is to use the persuasive request writing plan from earlier in the chapter (the AIRA technique), but with a few extras added in to reflect that this is a sales message.[5]

WORKPLACE IN FOCUS

One of the most important groups to market to is the Millennials—that group of 10 million Canadians born around the year 2000 that makes upwards of 35 percent of online purchases, according to research conducted for Canada Post.[6] This research further finds that direct-mail pieces (like the letters you're learning to write in this section) have higher-than-average impact with this group because while Millennials' email inboxes are constantly full, their old-fashioned mailbox is often empty. In addition, the research finds that sending something that's personalized, tactile, and entertaining makes the biggest impression. When Halifax-based grocery giant Sobeys decided it wanted a way to influence its most regular clients in its IGA chain of stores, it created a piece of direct mail called the "Best Clients" campaign and sent it out during the holiday season. The personalized, nice-looking, memorable piece of mail—which won the 2017 Canadian Print Award

Andriy Blokhin/Shutterstock

for top direct-mail campaign—uses all the suggestions mentioned in this section to great effect. *As a young person, do you agree with Canada Post research that finds that direct mail that looks good, is personalized, and is useful or entertaining, tends to be kept?*

WRITING PLAN FOR A SALES MESSAGE

Professional marketers and salespeople follow the AIRA pattern (attention, interest, desire, and action) when persuading consumers.

- **Opening:** Gain *attention*. Offer something valuable; promise a benefit to the reader; ask a question; or provide a quotation, fact, product feature, testimonial, startling statement, or personalized action setting.
- **Body:** Build *interest and desire;* reduce *resistance*. Describe central selling points and make rational and emotional appeals. Elicit desire in the reader and reduce resistance. Use testimonials, money-back guarantees, free samples, performance tests, or other techniques.
- **Closing:** Motivate *action*. Offer a gift, promise an incentive, limit the offer, set a deadline, or guarantee satisfaction.

ATTENTION. A critical element in sales letters is the opening paragraph, the attention-getter. This opener should be short (one to five lines), honest, relevant, and stimulating. Marketing pros have found that eye-catching typographical arrangements or provocative messages, such as the following, can hook a reader's attention:

- **Offer.** A free trip to Hawaii is just the beginning!
- **Benefit.** Now you can raise your sales income by 50 percent or even more with the proven techniques found in . . . .
- **Open-ended suggestive question.** Do you want your family to be safe?
- **Quotation or proverb.** Necessity is the mother of invention.
- **Compliment.** Life is full of milestones. You have reached one. You deserve . . . .
- **Fact.** A recent Environics poll says that three quarters of Canadians are not happy with the quality of financial advice they're receiving.

- **Product feature.** Electronic stability control, ABS, and other active and passive safety features explain why the ultra-compact Smart Fortwo has achieved a four-star crash rating in Québec.
- **Testimonial.** The most recent J.D. Power survey of "initial quality" shows that BMW ranks at the top of brands with the fewest defects and malfunctions, ahead of Chrysler, Hyundai, Lexus, Porsche, and Toyota.
- **Startling statement.** Let the poor and hungry feed themselves! For just $100 they can.
- **Personalized action setting.** It's 6:30 p.m. and you're working overtime to meet a pressing deadline. Suddenly your copier breaks down. The production of your colour-laser brochures screeches to a halt. How you wish you had purchased the Worry-Free-Anytime service contract from Canon.

Other openings calculated to capture attention might include a solution to a problem, an anecdote, a personalized statement using the receiver's name, or a relevant current event.

BUILD INTEREST AND DESIRE. In this phase of your message, you should clearly describe the product or service to build interest and desire. Think of this part as a promise that the product or service will satisfy the audience's needs. In simple language emphasize the central selling points that you identified during your prewriting analysis. Those selling points can be developed using rational or emotional appeals.

Rational appeals speak to reason and intellect. They can include references to making or saving money, increasing efficiency, or making the best use of resources. In general, rational appeals are appropriate when a product is expensive, long lasting, or important to health, security, and financial success. Emotional appeals, on the other hand, speak to status, ego, concerns or worries we have, and sensual feelings. Appealing to the emotions is sometimes effective when a product is inexpensive, short-lived, or nonessential. Many clever sales messages, however, combine emotional and rational strategies for a dual appeal. Consider these examples:

Rational Appeal
Cheery Maids is a one-stop solution: for one low monthly charge, you will receive biweekly visits from a team of our professional, fully bonded cleaning staff who will clean your house from top to bottom. Enjoy both peace of mind and your time away from work without having to do your own cleaning.

Emotional Appeal
Tired of 9 to 5? Tired of commutes that seem to stretch longer and longer each day? Tired of getting home only to find you need to cook and clean the house because it's such a mess? Let Cheery Maids take part of the "tired" out of your life by providing you with cheerful, competitively priced home-cleaning services.

Dual Appeal
By signing up today with Cheery Maids, you'll receive two free cleanings in the next calendar year. Not only will you be able to leave the "dirty work" to our trained professionals, you'll have money left over to enjoy a couple of relaxing nights out at dinner and a movie with the family—on us!

An appealing description of your product is not enough, however. Experienced communicators know that no matter how well you know your product or service, no one is persuaded by facts alone. In the end, people buy products and services because of their benefits. Your job is to translate those facts into warm feelings and reader benefits.

Let's say a sales message promotes a hand cream made with Vitamin A and aloe and cocoa butter extracts. Those facts, translated, might become *Nature's hand helpers—including soothing aloe and cocoa extracts, and firming Vitamin A— form invisible gloves that protect your sensitive skin against the hardships of work, harsh detergents, and constant environmental assaults.*

REDUCE RESISTANCE. The goal at this stage in the sales message is to overcome resistance. You also try to make the audience want the product or service and to anticipate objections, focusing strongly on reader benefits. Communication pros use a number of techniques to overcome resistance.

- **Testimonials.** I always receive friendly and on-time service when I take my car to a Canadian Tire mechanic for servicing. I just wouldn't go anywhere else!—Vince McRae, Edmundston, NB. (Testimonial overcome the resistance that this is just a marketing campaign with no truth behind it.)

- **Names of satisfied users (with permission, of course).** See the bottom of this message to learn about some of the IT professionals who are already taking advantage of our conference webinar subscription service and are 100 percent satisfied with the experience. (This overcomes the resistance that the service or product isn't guaranteed to be successful.)

- **Money-back guarantee or warranty.** Not only do we offer free shipping on all online orders over $25, we guarantee everything we sell. If you're not happy, simply use the enclosed postage coupon to return your purchase to us free of charge and receive a full refund. (Guarantees overcome the resistance that the product or service is expensive.)

- **Free trial or sample.** Welcome to the Wine Store. Would you care for a sample of a wonderful new white wine? Go ahead and enjoy a piece of cheddar and a cracker—they pair nicely with the mineral quality of this Riesling. I have a coupon for $1 off per bottle if you'd like to take some home. (Samples overcome the resistance that you've never tried this product or service.)

- **Performance tests, polls, or awards.** At Luce this week, Chef Ferretti, who has just returned from Washington, DC, where he won the prestigious North American Chef Competition for best innovative dish, is offering a three-course tasting menu including one-course wine pairing for $89. (Awards overcome the resistance that you'd rather stick with what you know.)

- **Turn objections into selling points.** Tax season can be a stressful time, and you want to make sure you can trust the person who prepares your income tax returns. For this reason we offer a free 30-minute consultation with one of our tax preparation specialists who will walk you through your return and explain how we arrived at our calculations. (This overcomes the resistance that professional tax preparation is expensive.)

When price is an obstacle, consider these suggestions:

- Delay mentioning price until after you have created a desire for the product.
- Show the price in small units, such as the price per month or per ten downloads of a magazine subscription service.
- Demonstrate how the reader saves money by, for instance, subscribing for two or three years.

- Compare your prices with those of a competitor.
- If applicable, offer advantageous financing terms.

MOTIVATE ACTION. All the effort put into a sales message is wasted if the reader fails to respond. To make it easy for readers to act, you can provide a reply card, a stamped and addressed envelope, a toll-free telephone number, an Internet link, or a promise of a follow-up call. Because readers often need an extra push, consider including additional motivators, such as the following:

- **Offer a gift.** You will receive a free Apple Watch Series 4 with the purchase of any new car.
- **Promise an incentive.** With every new, paid subscription, we will plant a tree in one of Canada's pollution-busting boreal forests.
- **Limit the offer.** Only the first 100 customers receive free delivery.
- **Set a deadline.** You must act before June 1 to get these low prices.
- **Guarantee satisfaction.** We will return your full payment if you are not entirely satisfied—no questions asked.

The final paragraph of the sales letter carries the call to action. This is where you tell readers what you want done and give them reasons for doing it. Most sales letters also include postscripts because they make for irresistible reading. Even readers who might skim over or bypass paragraphs are drawn to a P.S. Therefore, use a postscript to reveal your strongest motivator, to add a special inducement for a quick response, or to reemphasize a central selling point.

PUTTING IT ALL TOGETHER. Direct-mail sales letters are the number two preferred marketing medium, right behind email, because they can be personalized, directed to target audiences, and filled with a more complete message than other advertising media.[7] However, direct mail is expensive. That is why the total sales message is crafted so painstakingly.

Figure 6.4 shows a sales letter addressed to a target group of existing bank customers. To sell the new Groceries Plus MasterCard, the letter incorporates all four AIRA components. Notice that the personalized action-setting opener places the reader in a familiar situation (walking into a supermarket) and draws an analogy between choosing which aisle to go down first and choosing between many credit cards.

The writer develops a rational central selling point (a credit card that earns you free groceries is one you'll use happily) and repeats this selling point in all the components of the letter. Notice, too, how a testimonial from a satisfied customer lends support to the sales message and how the closing pushes for action. Also, see how call-outs (bolded, indented attention-grabbing messages) appear within the body of the letter.

Because the price of the credit card (a $100 yearly fee) is not a selling feature, it is mentioned only on the reply card. This sales letter repeats its strongest motivator—$25 in free groceries for signing up—in the high-impact P.S. line.

Although you want to be persuasive in sales letters, never overstep legal and ethical boundaries.

6.5b Promotional Messages

To make the best use of limited advertising dollars while reaching large numbers of potential customers, many businesses are turning to the Internet and to digital marketing campaigns in particular. Much like traditional direct mail, digital marketing can attract new customers, help keep existing ones, encourage future sales, cross-sell, and cut costs. As consumers become more comfortable and secure with online purchases, they will receive more email sales messages.

Email has in fact become the primary channel that consumers use to interact with brands. It is the most used channel for written, personal communication (45 percent), and 77 percent of consumers prefer permission-based marketing through email.[8]

FoodCo. Financial *Life.Easier.*

April 2, 2021

Mr. Tony Stronge
1501 Whitechurch Way
Dartmouth, NS
B3E 48V

Dear Mr. Stronge,

You've probably experienced this situation recently: it's the end of a busy weekend and you still have to • — Places reader in a recognizable situational context
do the groceries. When you arrive at the store, it's crowded, people are in a rush, and you're confused —
where should I begin? The produce aisle? The frozen aisle? The meat and dairy? Choices can be
daunting as well as frustrating, which is why we're here to make your life easier. • — Gains attention

The new FoodCo Groceries Plus Mastercard takes making the choice of which credit card to use simple. • — Implies analogy with opening situation
Which other credit card offers you instantaneous free groceries? Only ours. Watch your free groceries
pile up each time you use your card. Don't be frustrated by all the choice that's out there. Pick the card
you know you'll find useful — the only one that earns you instant free groceries with each purchase. • — Builds interest

> **Already convinced? Go to www.foodco.ca/groceriesplus to apply immediately. Just for** • — Inserts call-out with offer and to re-ignite attention
> **filling out the online application, you'll receive $25 in free groceries!**

If you're wondering why you should switch to the Groceries Plus Mastercard, just listen to what one • — Creates desire (and reduces resistance) via rational credibility of testimonial
satisfied customer has to say:

> *You might take trips once a year, and it takes you 30 years to pay off a mortgage, so why tie your*
> *credit card to one of these rare occurences? I buy groceries each week (and sometimes more than*
> *once a week), which is why I think my Groceries Plus Mastercard makes a lot of sense. Each time*
> *I use it, I'm earning money off my next grocery purchase. It makes a lot of sense. – Barb Lyons,*
> *Windsor, NS*

There are plenty of reasons to switch cards. It's easy and quick to do so online and you can start • — Repeats sales pitch in final sentence
earning free groceries today.

Sincerely,

Tom Ramanauskas
Director, Consumer Cards

P.S. Apply right now at www.foodco.ca/groceriesplus and receive $25 off your next grocery purchase! • — Motivates action by spotlighting free offer in post-script to prompt reply

---

One recent estimate suggests that email-only marketing campaigns perform 95 times better than direct mail in terms of return on investment.[9]

In the future customers will be more likely to receive ads for products and services they actually use and like, and they can always opt out of receiving such marketing emails. An Econsultancy study of 1,400 US consumers found that 42 percent prefer to receive ads by email compared to 3 percent who favoured social networking sites and only 1 percent who preferred Twitter.[10]

EMAIL PROMOTION MESSAGES. If your organization requires an online sales message, try using the following techniques gleaned from the best-performing emails.

Communicate only with those who have given permission! By sending messages only to people who opt in, you greatly increase your "open rate"—those email messages that will be opened. Email users detest spam. However, receivers are surprisingly receptive to offers tailored specifically for them. Remember that today's customer is somebody—not anybody. Marketers must make it easy for the recipient to unsubscribe.

The principles you've learned in crafting traditional sales messages also work with electronic promotional tools. However, online promotions are often shorter than direct mail, not structured as letters, feature colourful graphics, and occasionally even have sound or video clips. They offer a richer experience to readers, who can click hyperlinks to access content that interests them.

Here are a few guidelines that will help you create effective online sales messages, like the one from The Soothing Spa in Vancouver, BC, which is shown in Figure 6.5:

- **Craft a catchy subject line.** Offer discounts or premiums: *Spring Sale: Buy now and save 20 percent!* Promise solutions to everyday work-related problems. Highlight hot new industry topics. Invite readers to scan a top-ten list of items such as issues, trends, or people.
- **Keep the main information "above the fold."** Email messages should be top heavy. Primary points should appear early in the message so that they capture the reader's attention.
- **Provide more than one link.** Emailed promotion messages should include links to your organization's website or social media presence to help you keep your audience.
- **Make the message short, conversational, and focused.** Because on-screen text is taxing to read, be brief. Focus on one or two central selling points only.

▼ FIGURE 6.5 / Emailed Promotion Message to Opt-In Customer

Notice how The Soothing Sauna's Father's Day email promotion uses the tips mentioned above: catchy subject line, links, urgency, easy unsubscribe option, and so on.

- **Convey urgency.** Top-performing sales emails state an offer deadline or demonstrate why the state of the industry demands action on the reader's part. Good messages also tie the product to relevant current events.
- **Sprinkle testimonials throughout the copy.** Consumers' own words are the best sales copy. These comments can serve as call-outs or be integrated into the copy.
- **Provide a means for opting out.** It is polite and a good business tactic (and in many places, a law) to include a statement that tells receivers how to be removed from the sender's mailing database.

SOCIAL MEDIA PROMOTION MESSAGES. Besides email as a promotions channel, businesses are increasingly looking to social media and blogs to send out persuasive promotional messages to partner firms and customers. As we've seen, social media are not primarily suited for overt selling; however, tweets and other posts can be used to influence others and to project a professional, positive online presence. These new tools can also be useful internally when communicating with employees.

- **Facebook.** Facebook is the Internet's dominant social network. Nike's three-minute commercial "Write the Future" was first launched on the company's Facebook site. The video went viral, and over one weekend, the number of Nike's Facebook fans doubled from 1.6 million to 3.1 million. Soft-drink giant Coca-Cola maintains by far the largest presence on Facebook with more than 12 million fans. Coca-Cola has made Facebook a central focus of its marketing plans.

◢ FIGURE 6.6 / Promotional Tweets

- **Blogs.** In the right hands, blogs can be powerful marketing tools. Information technology giant Hewlett-Packard (HP) invites guest bloggers to contribute to its site as advisors to small businesses, for example. Executives, HP employees, and outside experts discuss a wide range of technology- and company-related topics. Although not overtly pushing a marketing message, ultimately HP wants to generate goodwill; hence, the blogs serve as a public relations tool.[11] Many companies now use blogs to subtly market their products and develop a brand image.
- **Twitter.** Twitter has become a big part of marketing today. As Dominique Jackson, author of the blog post "The Complete Guide to Twitter Marketing," puts it: "Growing a real following on Twitter takes more than sending out Tweets whenever your company has a product being released or an upcoming event. It's about engaging with your target audience and interacting with them. . . . If you can become a pro with this fast-paced social networking site, you'll unlock new opportunities to grow your business online."[12]

Note that the compact format of a tweet requires extreme conciseness and efficiency. Don't expect the full AIRA technique to be deployed in a 140-character Tweet. Instead, you may see only the "gain attention" and "motivate action" part of the persuasion, both of which must be catchy and intriguing. Regardless, many of the principles of persuasion discussed in this chapter apply even to micromessages.

Cengage

MINDTAP

In MindTap go to the Study Tools for Chapter 6 and complete the Practice Test.

◤ LEARNING SUMMARY

6.1 Explain digital-age persuasion and the AIRA persuasive technique.

- Business communicators need to use persuasion when making more than routine demands and facing a skeptical audience.

- Digital-age persuasion techniques are different from those used in earlier periods because persuasive messages have exploded in volume and reach; messages now travel at warp speed; all kinds of organizations are persuaders; persuasion is subtler and more misleading; and it has become more complex and impersonal.

- Effective persuasion involves establishing credibility; making specific, reasonable requests; linking facts to benefits; recognizing the power of loss; overcoming resistance; and sharing solutions and compromising.

6.2 Write persuasive help request messages.

- Convincing a reluctant person requires planning and skill and sometimes a little luck.

- The AIRA writing plan for persuasive requests consists of an opening that captures the reader's attention; a body that establishes credibility, builds interest by using specific details, and reduces resistance; and a closing that motivates action while showing courtesy.

6.3 Write persuasive claim or complaint messages.

- Complaints and some persuasive claims deliver bad news; some vent anger, yet persuasion is necessary to effect change.

- Persuasive claims and complaints may involve damaged products, billing errors, wrong shipments, warranty problems, limited return policies, or insurance snafus.

- Employing a moderate tone, claim or complaint messages need to be logical and open with praise, a statement of fact or agreement, and a quick review of what was done to resolve the problem.

- In the body, writers highlight what happened and why the claim or complaint is legitimate; they enclose supporting documents such as invoices, shipping orders, warranties, and payments.

- The closing specifies what is to be done (e.g., a refund, replacement, or credit).

6.4 Write persuasive employee buy-in messages.

- Today's executives try to achieve buy-in from subordinates instead of forcing them to do things such as volunteer for projects or join programs that require lifestyle changes.

- Messages flowing downward require attention to tone and rely on honest, accurate evidence.

- Messages to management should provide facts, figures, and evidence and make strong dollars-and-cents cases for proposed ideas using a warm, professional tone.

6.5 Write persuasive direct-mail, email, and social media sales messages.

- Whether the messages are delivered by postal mail or by email, marketers design sales messages to encourage consumers to read and act on the message.

- Sales letters are still an important part of multichannel marketing campaigns that can make sales, generate leads, boost retail traffic, solicit donations, and direct consumers to websites.

- Skilled e-marketers create catchy subject lines, start with the most important points, make the message conversational and focused, use testimonials, and allow readers to opt out.

- Short persuasive posts and tweets concisely pitch offers, prompt responses, and draw attention to events and media links. Principles of persuasion apply even to micromessages.

CHAPTER REVIEW

1. List the characteristics of persuasion in the digital age. (Obj. 1)
2. List effective persuasion techniques. (Obj. 1)
3. How is asking for help at work a persuasive situation? (Obj. 2)
4. What do claim or complaint messages typically involve, and how should they be crafted? (Obj. 3)
5. How can you ensure that your claim or complaint message is developed logically? (Obj. 3)
6. How have shifts in authority in digital-age organizations affected the strategies for creating goodwill and the tone of workplace persuasive messages? (Obj. 4)
7. When might persuasion be necessary in messages flowing upward? (Obj. 4)
8. What is the four-part AIRA writing plan for sales messages, and what does the acronym stand for? (Objs. 1, 5)
9. What distinguishes rational, emotional, and dual appeals in persuasion? (Obj. 5)
10. Name the best practices for e-marketers hoping to write effective email and online sales messages. (Obj. 5)
11. Describe the purpose and characteristics of persuasive tweets and other online posts. (Obj. 5)

CRITICAL THINKING

1. Recline in your first-class seat and snooze, or sip a freshly stirred drink while listening to 12 channels of superb audio. Of what type of persuasive appeal is this an example? How does it compare to the following: Take one of four daily direct flights to Europe on our modern Airbus aircraft, and enjoy the most leg room of any airline. If we are ever late, you will receive coupons for free trips. (Obj. 5)
2. The word persuasion turns some people off. What negative connotations can it have and why? (Objs. 1, 5)
3. What motivating impulse may prompt individuals to agree to requests that do not directly benefit them or their organizations? (Obj. 2)
4. If many direct-mail messages are thrown in the garbage, and if email sales messages are often deleted before they're opened, why should we learn how to write them effectively? (Obj. 5)
5. Two students at Cambridge University in England raised more than $40,000 toward their university tuition by wearing business logos painted on their faces for a day.[13] To what degree is it ethical for advertisers to resort to such promotions dubbed "skinvertising"? To what degree do you find such messages effective? Would you participate—why or why not? (Objs. 1, 5)

ACTIVITIES AND CASES

6.1 HELP REQUEST: INVITING A SPEAKER (OBJ. 2)

Your Task. Analyze the following poorly written invitation. List its weaknesses and outline a writing strategy. If your instructor directs, revise it.

Dear Dr. Schulz:

Because you're a local Nanaimo author, we thought it might not be too much trouble for you to speak at our Canadian Association of Independent Management banquet May 5. Some of us business students here at Glenbow Valley College admired your book *Beyond Race and Gender,* which appeared last spring and became such a hit across the country. One of our instructors said you were now the country's management guru. What exactly did you mean when you said that Canada is the "Mulligan stew" of the Americas?

Because we have no funds for honoraria, we have to rely on local speakers. Dr. Lester Pierfont and Deputy Mayor Shirley Slye were speakers in the past. Our banquets usually begin at 6:30 with a social hour, followed by dinner at 7:30, and the speaker from 8:30 until 9:00 or 9:15. We can arrange transportation for you and your wife if you need it.

We realize that you must be very busy, but we hope you'll agree. Please let our adviser, Duncan Rankin, have the favour of an early response.

1. List at least five weaknesses.
2. Outline a writing plan for a favour request.

   Opening:

   Body:

   Closing:

6.2 HELP REQUEST: ASKING FOR TUITION REIMBURSEMENT (OBJ. 2)

Your Task. Analyze the poorly written email in Figure 6.7. List its weaknesses. If your instructor directs, revise it.

1. List at least five weaknesses in this email.
2. Outline a writing plan for this email.

   Opening:

   Body:

   Closing:

▼ **FIGURE 6.7 /** Tuition Help Request

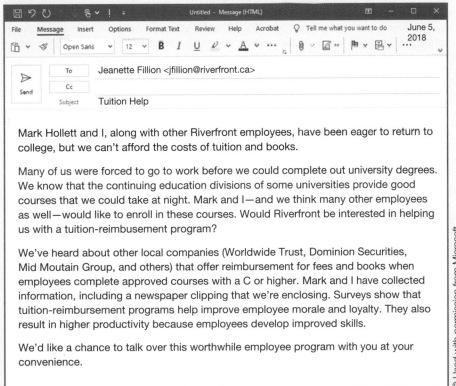

Mark Hollett and I, along with other Riverfront employees, have been eager to return to college, but we can't afford the costs of tuition and books.

Many of us were forced to go to work before we could complete out university degrees. We know that the continuing education divisions of some universities provide good courses that we could take at night. Mark and I—and we think many other employees as well—would like to enroll in these courses. Would Riverfront be interested in helping us with a tuition-reimbusement program?

We've heard about other local companies (Worldwide Trust, Dominion Securities, Mid Moutain Group, and others) that offer reimbursement for fees and books when employees complete approved courses with a C or higher. Mark and I have collected information, including a newspaper clipping that we're enclosing. Surveys show that tuition-reimbursement programs help improve employee morale and loyalty. They also result in higher productivity because employees develop improved skills.

We'd like a chance to talk over this worthwhile employee program with you at your convenience.

6.3 SALES LETTER: ANALYZING THE PITCH (OBJ. 5)

Read the following sales letter and analyze its effectiveness by answering the questions listed after the letter.

Dear Friend of the University of Prince Edward Island,

You are part of a special group of alumni—doctors, lawyers, bankers, managers, professors—who have a wide variety of credit cards available to them. For this reason I am inviting you to choose the superior benefits of the UPEI *Platinum Preferred* Visa credit card.

The UPEI Alumni Association has planned, in association with Atlantic Bank, a superior credit card with excellent benefits, personalized customer care, and best of all, no annual fee.

Each purchase made with your UPEI *Platinum Preferred* Visa card leads directly to a contribution to the UPEI Alumni Association. This extra benefit costs nothing, but allows the Association to continue its vital work on campus and in the community.

Yours sincerely,

Margaret Simpson
Director of Alumni Relations
UPEI Alumni Association

1. What technique captures the reader's attention in the opening? Is it effective?
2. What are the central selling points?
3. Does the letter use rational, emotional, or a combination of appeals? Explain.
4. What technique builds interest in the product? Are benefits obvious?
5. How is price handled?
6. Does the letter anticipate reader resistance and offer counterarguments?
7. What action is the reader to take? How is the action made easy?

Your Task. Revise the above letter, adding any improvements you think necessary based on your answers to the above questions.

6.4 CLAIM: PRICEY HOTEL BREAKFAST (OBJ. 3)

As regional manager for an auto parts manufacturer, you and two other employees attended a conference in Windsor, Ontario. You stayed at the Country Inn & Suites because your company recommends that employees use this hotel chain. Generally, your employees have liked their accommodations, and the rates have been within your company's budget.

Now, however, you are unhappy with the charges you see on your company's credit statement from Country Inn & Suites. When your department's administrative assistant made the reservations, she was assured that you would receive the weekend rates and that a hot breakfast—in the hotel restaurant, the Atrium—would be included in the rate. So you and the other two employees went to the restaurant and ordered a hot meal from the menu.

When you received the credit statement, though, you saw a charge for $132 for three champagne buffet breakfasts in the Atrium. You hit the ceiling! For one thing, you didn't have a buffet breakfast and certainly no champagne. The three of you got there so early that no buffet had been set up. You ordered pancakes and sausage, and for this you were billed $40 each. What's worse, your company may charge you personally for exceeding the maximum per diem rates.

In looking back at this event, you remember that other guests on your floor were having a continental breakfast in a lounge on your floor. Perhaps that's where the hotel expected all guests on the weekend rate to eat. However, your administrative assistant had specifically asked about this matter when she made the reservations, and she was told that you could order breakfast from the menu at the hotel's restaurant.

Your Task. You want to straighten out this problem, and you can't do it by telephone because you suspect that you will need a written record of this entire mess. Online you have tried in vain to find an email address for guest relations at the Windsor location. Write a persuasive claim to Customer Service, Country Inn & Suites, 1310 Darby Drive, Toronto, Ontario M2K 3B8. Should you include a copy of the credit card statement showing the charge?

6.5 CLAIM: EXCESSIVE LEGAL FEES (OBJ. 3)

You are the business manager for McConnell's, a producer of gourmet ice cream. McConnell's has 12 ice-cream shops in the Toronto area and a reputation for excellent ice cream. Your firm was approached by an independent ice-cream vendor who wanted to use McConnell's name and recipes for ice cream to be distributed through grocery stores and drugstores. As the business manager you worked with a law firm, Peretine, Valcon, and Associates, to draw up contracts regarding the use of McConnell's name and quality standards for the product.

When you received the bill from Louis Peretine, you couldn't believe it. The bill itemized 38 hours of legal preparation, at $300 per hour, and 55 hours of paralegal assistance, at $75 per hour. The bill also showed $415 for telephone calls, which might be accurate because Mr. Peretine had to speak with McConnell's owners, who were living in Ireland at the time. However, you doubt that an experienced lawyer would require 38 hours to draw up the contracts in question.

Perhaps some error was made in calculating the total hours. Moreover, you have checked with other businesses and found that excellent legal advice can be obtained for $200 per hour. McConnell's would like to continue using the services of Peretine, Valcon, and Associates for future legal business. Such future business is unlikely if an adjustment is not made on this bill.

Your Task. Write a persuasive request letter or email to Louis Peretine, legal counsel, Peretine, Valcon, and Associates, 2690 Whyte Avenue, Toronto, Ontario M2N 2E6, lperetine@pva.ca.

6.6 EMPLOYEE BUY-IN MESSAGE FLOWING UPWARD: TRAINING TELECOMMUTERS (OBJ. 4)

Jared Johnson woke up in his New Brunswick home and looked outside to see a heavy snowstorm creating a fairyland of white. However, he felt none of the giddiness that usually accompanies a potential snow day. Such days were a gift from heaven when schools closed, businesses shut down, and the world ground to a halt. As an on-and-off telecommuter for many years, he knew that snow days were a thing of the past. These days, work for Jared Johnson and 20 percent of other workers around the globe is no farther than their home offices.[14]

More and more employees are becoming telecommuters, the well-publicized ban on telecommuting at Yahoo notwithstanding. They want to work at home, where they feel they can be more productive and avoid the hassle of driving to work. Some need to telecommute only temporarily while they take care of family obligations, births, illnesses, or personal problems. Others are highly skilled individuals who can do their work at home as easily as in the office. Businesses definitely see advantages to telecommuting. They don't have to supply office space for workers. What's more, as businesses continue to flatten management structures, bosses no longer have time to micromanage employees. Increasingly, they are leaving workers to their own devices.

However, the results have not been totally satisfactory. For one thing, in-house workers resent those who work at home. More important are problems of structure and feedback. Telecommuters don't always have the best work habits, and lack of communication is a major issue. Unless the telecommuter is expert at coordinating projects and leaving instructions, productivity can fizzle. Appreciating the freedom but recognizing that they need guidance, employees are saying, "Push me, but don't leave me out there all alone!"

As the human resources manager at your company, you already have 83 employees who are either full- or part-time telecommuters. With increasing numbers asking to work in remote locations, you decide that workers and their managers must receive training on how to do it effectively. You are considering hiring a consultant to train your prospective telecommuters and their managers. Another possibility is developing an in-house training program.

Your Task. As human resources manager, you must convince Chris Crittenden, vice president, that your company needs a training program for all workers who are currently telecommuting or who plan to do so. Their managers should also receive training. You decide to ask your staff of four to help you gather information. Using the Web, you and your team read several articles on what such training should include. Now you must decide what action you want the vice president to take. Meet with you to discuss a training program? Commit to a budget item for future training? Hire a consultant or agency to come in and conduct training programs? Individually or as a team, write a convincing email that describes the problem, suggests what the training should include, and asks for action by a specific date. Add any reasonable details necessary to build your case.

6.7 EMPLOYEE BUY-IN MESSAGE FLOWING DOWNWARD: SAVING CASH ON SHIPPING (OBJ. 4)

As office manager of a Victoria software company, write a memo persuading your technicians, engineers, programmers, and other employees to reduce the number of overnight or second-day mail shipments. Your FedEx and other shipping bills have been sky high, and you feel that staff members are overusing these services.

You think employees should send messages by email. Sending a zipped file or PDF file as an email attachment costs nothing. Compare this with $20 or $30 for FedEx service! Whenever possible, staff members should obtain the FedEx account number of the recipient and use it for charging the shipment. If staff members plan ahead and allow enough time, they can use UPS or FedEx ground service, which takes three to five days and is much cheaper. You wonder whether staff members consider whether the recipient is really going to use the message as soon as it arrives. Does it justify an overnight shipment? You would like to reduce overnight delivery services voluntarily by 50 percent over the next two months. Unless a sizable reduction occurs, the CEO threatens severe restrictions in the future.

Your Task. Address your memo to all staff members. What other ways could employees reduce shipping costs?

6.8 HELP REQUEST: INVITING AN ALUMNA TO SPEAK (OBJ. 2)

As public relations director for the Business and Accounting Association on your campus, you have been asked to find a keynote speaker for the first meeting of the school year. The owner of a successful local firm, TempHelp4You, is an alumna of your university. You think not only that many students would enjoy learning about how she started her business but also that some might like to sign up with her temporary help agency. She would need to prepare a 30-minute speech and take questions after the talk. The event will be held from noon until 1:30 p.m. on a date of your choosing in Branford Hall. You can offer her lunch at the event and provide her with a parking permit that she can pick up at the information kiosk at the main entrance to your campus. You need to have her response by a deadline you set.

Your Task. Write a direct approach email to Marion Minter in which you ask her to speak at your club's meeting. Send it to *mminter@temphelp4you.com*.

6.9 EMPLOYEE BUY-IN MESSAGE FLOWING DOWNWARD: BECOME AN URBAN FARMING VOLUNTEER (OBJ. 4)

As employee relations manager of Paychex in Halifax, one of your tasks is to promote Urban Farming, a global organization that has established almost 60,000 gardens in nearly 40 cities. Originating in the Detroit area, Urban Farming is a combined effort of major corporations. You must recruit 12 coworkers who will volunteer to plant gardens and teach community families about healthy eating.

Your task is to find volunteers in your company to start a community garden and in turn recruit other Paychex volunteers. Halifax offers more than 1,000 vacant lots to choose from, and the city already manages 40 gardens. Paychex volunteers will be expected to attend training sessions and then to supervise and instruct participating members of the community. In return, employees will receive two hours of release time per week to work on their Urban Farming projects. The program has been very successful thus far, and the interest in community gardens is growing.

Your Task. Learn more about Urban Farming by searching the Web. Then write a persuasive memo or email with convincing appeals that will bring you 12 volunteers to work with Urban Farming.

6.10 SALES LETTER: FITNESS AT THE LOCAL BREWERY (OBJ. 5)

Health research shows that 33 percent of Canadians between the ages of 20 and 64 are overweight.[15] Long-term health risks could be reduced if overweight employees shed their excess weight.

As a sales representative for Fitness Associates (FA), you think your fitness equipment and programs could be instrumental in helping people lose weight. With regular exercise at an on-site fitness centre, employees lose weight and improve overall health. As employee health improves, absenteeism is reduced and overall productivity increases. And employees love working out before or after work. They make the routine part of their workday, and they often have work buddies who share their fitness regimen.

Though many companies resist spending money to save money, fitness centres need not be large or expensive to be effective. Studies show that moderately sized centres coupled with motivational and training programs yield the greatest success. For just $30,000, Fitness Associates will provide exercise equipment including stationary bikes, weight machines, and treadmills. Their fitness experts will design a fitness room, set up the fitness equipment, and design appropriate programs. Best of all, the one-time cost is usually offset by cost savings within one year of centre installation. For additional fees, FA can also provide fitness consultants for employee fitness assessments. FA specialists will also train employees on proper use of the equipment, and they will clean and manage the facility—for an extra charge, of course.

Your Task. Write a sales letter to Ms. Kathleen Stewart, human resources VP, Good Times Brewing Company, 3939 Brewery Row, Moose Jaw, Saskatchewan S6H 0V9, kstewart@gtbc.ca. Assume you are writing on company letterhead. Ask for an appointment to meet with her. Send her a brochure detailing the products and services that Fitness Associates provides. As an incentive, offer a free fitness assessment for all employees if Good Times Brewing installs a fitness facility by December 1.

6.11 SALES LETTER: GETTING AN OLD FRIEND TO SWITCH TO ACCURACY PLUS (OBJ. 5)

You are the owner of Software Solutions, a software consultancy based in Prince George, BC. Recently, at a major industry trade show in Chicago, you were introduced to a new accounting software package, ACCuracy Plus. Quickly realizing its merits, you signed a deal with the American manufacturer to become the exclusive sales agent for the software in Canada, west of Ontario. Now that you own the right to sell the software, you have to make some sales. One day, while brainstorming possible clients, you remember your old friend from college, Tim Thom. While reading the newspaper last year you found out that Tim Thom has been promoted to VP operations for Health & Co., a Victoria-based national retail chain selling vitamins, supplements, and natural foods. Even though you haven't seen or spoken to Tim in over eight years, you used to be good friends, and you believe a persuasive sales letter about your new software will not go unanswered. The question is, should you make a strong pitch for a sale, or should you just pitch for a get-together over lunch?

Your Task. Write a persuasive sales letter to Tim Thom (tthom@healthco.ca), where you try to interest him in switching from his current accounting software to ACCuracy Plus.

Related websites: To build interest in ACCuracy Plus, browse the Internet for the features of its competitors such as Sage (sage.com) and Dynamics GP (dynamics.microsoft.com/en-ca/gp-overview). Be careful not to plagiarize when you write your letter.

6.12 ONLINE ALUMNI CAMPAIGN (OBJ. 5)

Your college or university has traditionally been very conservative in contacting its alumni about donations. For example, a paper-based alumni magazine is mailed out three times a year to all alumni. Also, a paper-based letter mailer goes out once a year to alumni asking them to donate to the scholarship and building funds. Recognizing that social media, blogs, and other new media are revolutionizing the way people get their information, entertain themselves, and plan their lives, the new alumni director at your institution decides that something has to change.

Your Task. As the new alumni coordinator, examine the alumni websites of various postsecondary institutions, but not your own, looking for evidence of new media presence/use. Then, create a persuasive online sales campaign (which may include a traditional Web page, a social media page or account, a series of email promotion messages or a combination of the three) whose goal is to persuade recent alumni (those who have graduated in the past five years) to stay connected with your institution and to make a regular donation. What can you offer these people in return for their time and money?

Related website: Visit www.alumnifutures.com/2011/03/chiclets.html for a critique of the omnipresent links to social media on alumni websites.

6.13 PROMOTIONAL TWEETS AND POSTS (OBJS. 1, 5)

Being able to compose effective and concise micromessages and posts will positively contribute to your professional online persona.

Your Task. Brainstorm to identify a special skill you have, an event you want others to attend, a charitable cause dear to your heart, or a product you like. Applying what you have learned about short persuasive messages online, write your own 140-character persuasive tweet or post. Use Figure 6.6 as a starting point and model.

6.14 USING AIRA TO ANALYZE ONLINE PROMOTIONS (OBJ. 1)

As you learned in this chapter, most of us encounter thousands of persuasive appeal messages per day: on bus shelters, in stores and restaurants, at school and at work, on television, on the radio, and most importantly, on the Internet and social media. But we don't often slow down to analyze these messages and see how effectively they're doing their persuasive job.

Your Task. Go through your inbox or your social media account feeds and identify three to five recent examples of promotional messages sent to you by brands, companies, charities, and other organizations. Download or create a screen capture of the messages, and create a Word document. Create a table in your Word document with three columns and as many rows as you have promotional messages. Paste each promotional message into a row under the first column, and label that column Promotional Message. Label the second column AIRA Techniques Used and the third column AIRA Techniques Missing. For each promotional message, fill out the table: which AIRA techniques are used in this promotion (and how?), and which are not used? Present your results to your instructor or classmates as assigned.

◤ WRITING IMPROVEMENT EXERCISES

STRATEGIES

Your Task. For each of the following situations, say whether the direct strategy (DS) or indirect strategy (IS) is most appropriate.

Direct Strategy	Indirect Strategy	
_____	_____	1. A request from one company to another to verify the previous employment record of a job applicant
_____	_____	2. An announcement that must convince employees to stop smoking, start exercising, and opt for a healthy diet to lower health care expenses and reduce absenteeism
_____	_____	3. An email message to employees telling them that the company parking lot will be closed for one week while it is being resurfaced
_____	_____	4. A letter to a cleaning service demanding a refund for sealing a dirty tiled floor and damaging a fresh paint job
_____	_____	5. A request for information about a wireless office network
_____	_____	6. A letter to a grocery store requesting permission to display posters advertising a college fundraising carwash
_____	_____	7. A request for a refund of the cost of a computer program that does not perform the functions it was expected to perform
_____	_____	8. A request for correction of a routine billing error on your company credit card
_____	_____	9. A letter to the local school board from a nearby convenience store owner expressing disapproval of a proposal allowing Coca-Cola to install vending machines on the school campus
_____	_____	10. A memo to employees describing the schedule and menu selections of a new mobile catering service

---

◤ GRAMMAR/MECHANICS CHALLENGE 6

COMMAS 1 AND 2

Review Sections 2.01–2.09 of the Grammar/Mechanics Handbook. Then study each of the following statements and decide where to insert necessary commas. In the space provided, write the number of commas that you add; write *0* if no commas are needed. Also record the number of the G/M principle illustrated. When you finish, compare your responses with those provided near the end of the book. If your responses differ, study carefully the principles shown in parentheses.

1 (2.06a) Example When preparing for a job interview, you should conduct considerable research into the target company.

_____ 1. If candidates appear overly eager or desperate they may blow the opportunity.

_____ 2. Some job seekers are becoming more aggressive and they often end up hurting their chances.

_____ 3. You can be best prepared if you look up information about the hiring company and if you know more than just the basics about the company's leadership and core businesses.

_____ 4. Deborah Wang the founder of an executive search firm says that the most successful candidates offer examples of past accomplishments.

_____ 5. Most firms are looking for reliable hardworking candidates who can explain how they will contribute to the organization.

_____ 6. During the last 16 months the number of qualified candidates has doubled.

_____ 7. The position of marketing manager which has been open for the past six months is difficult to fill.

_____ 8. Recruiters look for candidates who are a strong fit for a particular position and who have exactly the skills required.

_____ 9. When interviewing a recent candidate the recruiter said that the applicant clearly and effectively explained how he could cut costs and increase sales.

_____ 10. The candidates who had the best qualifications were screened by means of telephone interviews before being offered in-person interviews.

REVIEW OF COMMAS 1 AND 2

Review Sections 2.01–2.09 of the Grammar/Mechanics Handbook. Then study each of the following statements and decide where to insert necessary commas. In the space provided, write the number of commas that you add; write *0* if no commas are needed. Also record the number of the G/M principle illustrated. When you finish, compare your responses with those provided near the end of the book. If your answers differ, study carefully the principles shown in parentheses.

_____ 11. To learn about your target company read recent company press releases annual reports media coverage and industry blogs.

_____ 12. After he was hired Joseph was told to report for work on Monday May 15 in Toronto.

_____ 13. Regarding the subject of pay which may come up early in an interview it's better to hold off the discussion until you have been extended a job offer.

_____ 14. As a matter of fact the salary you request may affect the organization's decision to hire you.

_____ 15. Although she wasn't excited about the opportunity Julie scheduled an interview for Tuesday February 3 at 2 p.m.

◣ EDITING CHALLENGE 6

The following persuasive internal memo has proofreading, spelling, grammar, punctuation, wordiness, number form, negative words, and other writing faults that require correction. Study the guidelines in the Grammar/Mechanics Handbook, as well as the lists of Confusing Words and Frequently Misspelled Words at the end of the book, to sharpen your skills.

Your Task. Edit the following message by correcting its errors (a) in your textbook or (b) on a photocopy using the standard proofreading marks from Appendix B. When you finish making corrections, your instructor can show you the revised version of this memo.

Beverage Inc.

To: Sara W. Morrisseau, Vice President
From: Jackson Pardell, Market Research
CC:

Date: August 5, 2017

Re: ANALYSIS OF GULPIT XL

Here is a summery of the research of Clemence Willis' and myself. Regarding the reduced sugar sports drink being introduced by our No. 1 compititor, GulpIT.

In just under a years time GulpIT developed this new drink, it combines together a mixture of 50 percent sugar and 50 percent artificial sweetener. Apparently GulpIT plans to spend over $8 million to introduce the drink, and to assess consumers reactions to it. It will be tested on the shelfs of convience stores grocerys and other mass merchants in five citys in the Atlantic provinces.

The companys spokesperson said, "The 'X' stands for excelent taste, and the 'L' stands for less sugar." Aimed at young adult's who don't like the taste of sweetener but who want to control calories. The new sports drink is a hybrid sugar and diet drink. Our studys show that simular drinks tryed in this country in the 1990's were unsuccessful. On the other hand a 50 calorie low sugar sports drink introduced in Europe two year ago was well received, similarly in Japan a 40 calorie soda is now marketed sucessfully by a cola manufactuerer.

However our research in regard to trends and our analysis of GulpIT XL fails to indicate that this countrys consumers will be interested in a midcalorie sports drink. Yet the Toronto Stock Exchanges response to GulpITs announcement of it's new drink was not unfavourable.

In view of the foregoing the writer and his colleague are of the opinion that we should take a wait and see attitude. Toward the introduction of our own low sugar sports drink.

WRITING TO GIVE BAD NEWS

mediaphotos/istock by Getty Images

OBJECTIVES

7.1 Explain the goals of business communicators when conveying negative information.

7.2 Compare the direct and indirect strategies for communicating negative information.

7.3 Describe the components of effective indirect negative messages, including opening with a buffer, apologizing, showing empathy, presenting the reasons, cushioning the bad news, and closing pleasantly.

7.4 Write negative messages for external situations: refusals (e.g., denying requests or claims) and situations when customers and the public are disappointed (e.g., collections, crises).

7.5 Write negative messages for internal situations (e.g., employee bad news).

BIZ COMM BYTE

Recent peer-reviewed research into the effectiveness of apologies when business conflicts arise shows that six linguistic elements (i.e., phrases, words) need to be included for a business apology to be effective: an expression of regret, an explanation of what went wrong, an acknowledgment of responsibility, a declaration of repentance, an offer to repair, and a request for forgiveness.

Source: Morin, A. (2016, April 14). Study reveals the 6 key components of an effective apology. *Forbes.* https://www.forbes.com/sites/amymorin/2016/04/14/study-reveals-the-6-key-components-of-an-effective-apology/#4f3040265be4

◤ 7.1 Why We Communicate Negative Information

Even the best-run businesses sometimes make mistakes. Goods arrive late or are not delivered at all, products fail, service disappoints, billing is mishandled, or customers are misunderstood. You may have to write messages ending business relationships, declining proposals, announcing price increases, refusing requests for donations, terminating employees, turning down invitations, or responding to unhappy customers. You might also have to apologize for mistakes in orders, the rudeness of employees, overlooked appointments, pricing errors, faulty accounting, defective products, or jumbled instructions. As a company representative, you could also be responding to complaints voiced about your organization on Twitter or Facebook.

Cengage

MINDTAP

In MindTap go to the Whiteboard Animation for Chapter 7 and watch it now.

Cengage

MINDTAP

In MindTap, go to the Chapter 7 reading, section 7.1a, and watch the video of industry expert Karen Richardson discussing best practices when communicating negative messages over the phone.

It's precisely because bad news disappoints, irritates, and sometimes angers the receiver that your main goal in such messages is to be thoughtful. The bad feelings associated with disappointing news can generally be reduced if the receiver knows the reasons for the rejection, feels that the news was revealed sensitively, and believes that the matter was treated seriously and fairly.

In this chapter you'll learn when to use the direct strategy and when to use the indirect strategy to deliver negative information. You'll also learn the goals of business communicators when writing negative messages and learn techniques for achieving those goals in several typical situations.

7.1a Five Goals in Communicating Negative Information

Delivering bad news isn't the easiest writing (or speaking) task, but it can be gratifying if done effectively. As a business communicator dealing with a negative situation, the following are your goals:

- **Explain clearly and completely.** Your message should be so clear that the receiver understands and accepts the bad news. The receiver shouldn't have to call or write back again to clarify the message.
- **Project a professional image.** Your message should project a professional and positive image of you and your organization. Even when irate customers use a threatening tone or overstate their claims, you must use polite language, control your emotions, and respond with clear explanations of why a negative message was necessary.
- **Convey empathy and sensitivity.** Negative news is more easily accepted if it is delivered sensitively. Use language that respects the receiver and attempts to reduce bad feelings. Accepting blame, when appropriate, and apologizing goes far in smoothing over negative messages. But avoid creating legal liability or responsibility for you or your organization (e.g., by making promises you can't keep).
- **Be fair.** Show that the situation or decision was fair, impartial, and rational. Receivers are far more likely to accept negative news if they feel they were treated fairly.
- **Maintain the relationship.** Include future-looking statements that show your desire to continue the relationship with the receiver. A consistent goal of any business message is to maintain the confidence of your receiver.

These goals are ambitious, and you may not always be successful in achieving them all. With experience, however, you'll be able to vary these strategies and adapt them to your organization's specific communication needs.

7.1b Timely Responses in Negative Situations

Because of the speed of communication in today's workplace (i.e., most employees have smartphones, are on social media, etc.), negative information—which has always travelled fast—now travels even faster and sometimes gets broadcast outside the company to people and organizations that shouldn't be seeing it. For this reason, timeliness is extremely important when communicating in negative situations.

Whenever possible, negative situations such as firings, restructurings, and company-related crises should be dealt with immediately and personally. As one crisis communications expert argues, "The timeliness of communication is paramount in a crisis,"[1] and existing communication approval systems may need to be stepped around to deliver the message quickly. That said, timeliness is not so vital that you should switch to informal and inappropriate communication channels. For example, texting a termination notice (as some employers have begun to do) is a risky communication choice because it indicates that the terminated employee is so unimportant that an informal channel (texting) was deemed the appropriate way to fire him or her.[2]

7.2 Direct and Indirect Negative Writing Strategies

In any negative situation, you have a choice between two strategies for delivering negative information: direct and indirect—negative information upfront or somewhat delayed. Which approach is best suited for your message? To answer this question, you'll need to analyze how your receiver will react to this information, as well as the degree of negativity included in the message.

7.2a When to Use the Direct Strategy

Not all negative situations at work are crises or involve personal misfortune. In these cases, as a business communicator, you should feel free to use a direct-strategy negative message. The direct strategy, shown in the writing plan, which has the bad news appearing first followed by the reasons and a pleasant closing, is effective in situations such as the following:

- **When the information isn't damaging.** If the bad news is insignificant (such as a small increase in cost) and doesn't personally affect the receiver, then the direct strategy makes sense.
- **When the receiver may overlook the information.** Rate increases, changes in service, new policy requirements—these critical messages may require directness to ensure attention.
- **When organizations prefer directness.** Some companies expect all internal messages and announcements—even negative information—to be straightforward and presented without frills.
- **When the receiver prefers directness.** If you suspect that the reader prefers that the facts be presented immediately, use the direct pattern.
- **When firmness is necessary.** Messages that demonstrate determination and strength shouldn't use delaying techniques. For example, the last in a series of collection letters seeking payment of overdue accounts requires a direct opener.

WRITING PLAN FOR A DIRECT-STRATEGY NEGATIVE MESSAGE

- Negative information in the **opening**
- Reason(s) for negative information in the **body**
- Pleasant **closing**

Figure 7.1 is an example of a typical direct-strategy negative message that follows the writing plan above. In this case, a routine notice arrives in your mailbox (or inbox) announcing a price increase in your electricity bill. Notice that the bad news is communicated in the opening sentence of the message. The reason comes after. Also notice how much shorter this message is than the indirect-style negative messages we will examine later in the chapter.

7.2b When to Use the Indirect Strategy

On the other hand, the indirect strategy, shown in the next writing plan, doesn't reveal the negative information immediately. At least theoretically, the indirect strategy enables you to keep the reader's attention until you've been able to explain the reasons for the bad news. Some writing experts suggest that the indirect strategy doesn't suit "today's skeptical, impatient, even cynical audience."[3] Clearly, in social media, bluntness seems to dominate public debate. Directness is equated with honesty; indirectness, with deceit. Regardless, many communicators prefer to use

FIGURE 7.1 / Negative Message—Direct Strategy

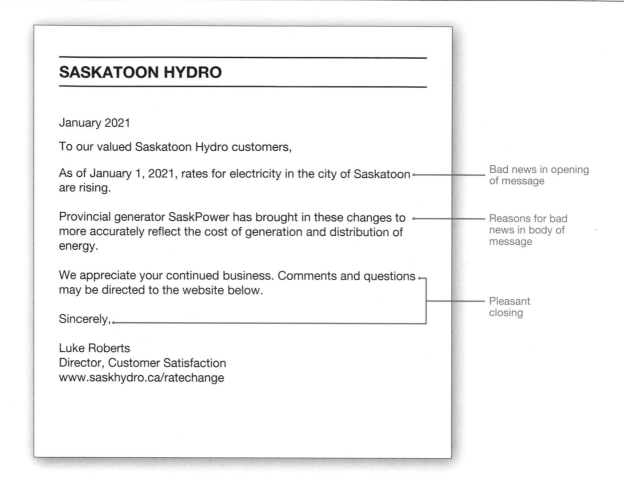

SASKATOON HYDRO

January 2021

To our valued Saskatoon Hydro customers,

As of January 1, 2021, rates for electricity in the city of Saskatoon are rising. — Bad news in opening of message

Provincial generator SaskPower has brought in these changes to more accurately reflect the cost of generation and distribution of energy. — Reasons for bad news in body of message

We appreciate your continued business. Comments and questions may be directed to the website below.

Sincerely,

Luke Roberts
Director, Customer Satisfaction
www.saskhydro.ca/ratechange

— Pleasant closing

the indirect strategy to soften negative news. Whereas good news can be revealed quickly, bad news may be easier to accept when broken gradually. Here are typical instances when the indirect strategy works well:

- **When the information is personally upsetting.** If the negative information involves the receiver personally, such as a layoff notice, the indirect strategy makes sense. Telling an employee that he or she no longer has a job is probably best done in person and by starting indirectly and giving reasons first. When a company has made a mistake that inconveniences or disadvantages a customer, the indirect strategy also makes sense.
- **When the information will provoke a hostile reaction.** When your message will irritate or infuriate the recipient, the indirect method may be best. It begins with a buffer and reasons, thus encouraging the reader to finish reading or hearing the message. A blunt announcement may make the receiver stop reading.
- **When the information threatens the customer relationship.** If the negative message may damage a customer relationship, the indirect strategy may help salvage the customer bond. Beginning slowly and presenting reasons that explain what happened can be more helpful than directly announcing negative information or failing to adequately explain the reasons.
- **When the information is unexpected.** Readers who are totally surprised by bad news tend to have a more negative reaction than those who expected it. If a company suddenly closes an office or a plant and employees had no inkling of the closure, that news would be better received if it were revealed cautiously with reasons first.

The indirect strategy doesn't guarantee that recipients will be pleased; however, many communicators prefer to use it.

WRITING PLAN FOR AN INDIRECT-STRATEGY NEGATIVE MESSAGE

- **Buffer**: Delay the negative information in the opening.
- **Reason(s)**: Offer reasons for or causes of the negative information in the body.
- **Negative information**: Embed the negative message among the reasons in the body.
- **Pleasant closing**: Attempt to maintain the relationship in the closing.

◣ 7.3 The Four-Part Strategy for Indirect Negative Messages

Although you probably won't make receivers happy when delivering negative information, you can reduce resentment by structuring your message sensitively. To do so, indirect negative messages should contain these components: buffer, reasons, bad news, and closing. Details about each component are discussed below.

7.3a Buffer the Opening

A buffer is a device that reduces shock or pain. Although it avoids revealing the bad news immediately, the buffer shouldn't convey a false impression that good news follows. It should provide a natural transition to the explanation. The individual situation will help determine what you should put in the buffer. Here are some possibilities:

- **Best news first.** Start with the part of the message that represents the best news. For example, in a website announcement and in-branch signage that discloses reduced operating hours but increased staffing, you might say, *Beginning July 1, we're adding extra staff in our branch locations, and we'll be open to serve you between 9:30 a.m. and 4:30 p.m.*
- **Compliment.** Praise the receiver's accomplishments, organization, or efforts, but do so with honesty and sincerity. For instance, in a letter declining an invitation to speak, you could write, *I admire the Canadian Red Cross for its disaster response efforts in Canada and overseas. I am honoured that you asked me to speak Friday, November 5.*
- **Appreciation.** Convey thanks to the reader for doing business, for sending something, for a service or job well done, for showing confidence in your organization, for expressing feelings, or for simply providing feedback. In a letter terminating an employee's contract, you might say, *Thank you for your work on the past two seasons of* Riley's Cove. *Your efforts contributed to a wonderful television program enjoyed across Canada.* Avoid thanking the reader, however, for something you are about to refuse.
- **Agreement.** Say something that both sender and receiver can agree on. A letter that rejects an application for a credit card might be phrased, *Having access to a credit card is an important part of your financial well-being. While we thank you for your recent application for a GoldPlus Visa Card, your application did not meet our criteria for approval. However, we're happy to offer you a Classic Visa Card.*
- **Facts.** Provide objective information that introduces the bad news. For example, in a memo announcing cutbacks in the hours of the employees' cafeteria, you might say, *During the past five years the number of employees eating breakfast in our cafeteria has dropped from 32 percent to 12 percent.*

- **Understanding.** Show that you care about the reader. In announcing a product defect, the writer can still manage to express concern for the customer: *We know you expect superior performance from all the products you purchase from OfficeCity. That's why we're writing personally about the Excell printer cartridges you recently ordered.*

APOLOGIZE IN THE BUFFER. You learned about apologies earlier in the book. We expand that discussion here because apologies are often part of negative situations. The truth is that sincere apologies work, as seen in the Biz Comm Byte that started this chapter. An apology can be defined as a statement that admits blame and regret because of an undesirable event. Apologies to customers are especially important if you or your company made a mistake. They cost nothing, and they go a long way in soothing hard feelings. Here are some tips on how to apologize effectively in business messages:

- **Apologize sincerely.** People dislike hollow apologies (We regret that you were inconvenienced or We regret that you are disturbed). Focusing on your regret does not convey sincerity. Instead say We apologize for the recent inconvenience you experienced.
- **Accept responsibility.** One CEO was criticized for the following weak apology: I want our customers to know how much I personally regret any difficulties you may experience as a result of the unauthorized intrusion into our computer systems. The apology was criticized because it didn't acknowledge responsibility.
- **Use good judgment.** Don't admit blame if it might prompt a lawsuit.

Consider these poor and improved apologies:

Poor Apology	Improved Apology
We regret that you are unhappy with the price of frozen yogurt purchased at one of our self-serve scoop shops.	We are genuinely sorry that you were disappointed in the price of frozen yogurt recently purchased at one of our self-serve scoop shops. Your opinion is important to us, and we appreciate your giving us the opportunity to look into the problem you describe.
We apologize if anyone was affected.	I apologize for the frustration our delay caused you. As soon as I received your message, I began looking into the cause of the delay and realized that our delivery tracking system must be improved.

"Dear Valued Customer: We're sorry, but company policy forbids apologies. Sincerely yours."

SHOW EMPATHY IN THE BUFFER. One of the hardest things to do in apologies is to convey sympathy and empathy. As discussed in Chapter 2, *empathy* is the ability to understand and enter into the feelings of another. When ice storms trapped JetBlue Airways passengers on hot planes for hours, then-CEO David Neeleman wrote a letter of apology that sounded as if it came from his heart. He said, "Dear JetBlue Customers: We are sorry and embarrassed. But most of all, we are deeply sorry." Later in his letter he said, "Words cannot express how truly sorry we are for the anxiety, frustration, and inconvenience that you, your family, friends, and colleagues experienced."[4] Neeleman put himself into the shoes of his customers and tried to experience their pain.

You can express empathy in various business situations:

- **Writing to an unhappy customer.** We did not intentionally delay the shipment, and we sincerely regret the disappointment and frustration you must have suffered.
- **Terminating employees.** It is with great regret that we must take this step. Rest assured that I will be more than happy to write letters of recommendation for anyone who asks.
- **Responding to a complaint.** I am deeply saddened that our service failure disrupted your sale, and we will do everything in our power to . . . .
- **Showing genuine feelings after a negative incident.** You have every right to be disappointed. I am truly sorry that . . . .

7.3b Present the Reasons for the Negative Information

The most important part of an indirect negative message is the reasons that explain the negative information. Without sound reasons for denying a request or refusing a claim, for example, a message will fail, no matter how cleverly it is organized or written. Providing reasons reduces feelings of ill will and improves the chances that the reader or listener will accept the bad news. Here are some tips for writing the reasons section of your negative message:

- **Explain clearly and cautiously.** If the reasons are not confidential or legally questionable, you can be specific: *Growers supplied us with a limited number of patio roses, and our demand this year was twice that of last year.* In responding to a billing error, explain what happened: *After you informed us of an error on your January bill, we investigated the matter and admit the mistake was ours. Until our new automated system is fully online, we are still subject to human error. Rest assured that your account has been credited, as you will see on your next bill.* In refusing a favour request, explain why the request can't be fulfilled: *On January 17 we have a board of directors meeting that I must attend.* However, in an effort to be the good person, don't make dangerous or unrealistic promises: *Although we can't contribute now, we expect increased revenues next year and promise a generous gift then.*
- **Mention believable reader benefits.** Readers are more open to negative information if in some way, even indirectly, it may help them. In refusing a customer's request for free clothes hemming, a clothing retailer wrote: *We tested our ability to hem skirts a few years ago. This process proved to be very time-consuming. We have decided not to offer this service because the additional cost would have increased the selling price of our skirts substantially, and we did not want to impose that cost on all our customers.* Readers also accept bad news more readily if they recognize that someone or something else benefits, such as other workers or the environment: *Although we would like to consider your application, we prefer to fill managerial positions from within.* Avoid trying to show reader benefits, though, if they appear insincere: *To improve our service to you, we're increasing our brokerage fees.*
- **Explain company policy.** Readers don't like blanket policy statements prohibiting something: Company policy prevents us from making cash refunds or Proposals will be accepted from local companies only or Company policy requires us to promote from within. Instead of hiding behind company policy, gently explain why the policy makes sense: We prefer to promote from within because it rewards the loyalty of our employees. In addition, we've found that people familiar with our organization make the quickest contribution to our team effort. By offering explanations, you demonstrate that you care about your readers and are treating them as important individuals.
- **Choose positive words.** Because the words you use can affect a reader's response, choose carefully. Remember that the objective of the indirect pattern is to hold the reader's attention until you've had a chance to explain the reasons justifying the bad news. To keep the reader in a receptive mood, avoid expressions that might cause the reader to tune out. Be sensitive to negative words such as *claim,*

WORKPLACE IN FOCUS

La Maison Simon's, or Simon's for short, is one of Canada's oldest retailers, dating back to 1840. The Québec City-based department store now has locations across the country, and is known for its inexpensive yet fashionable men's and women's clothing. Recently, the president of the company, Peter Simons, issued an apology letter to the public for a marketing campaign gone wrong. The chain decided to market a line of bras using the names of famous Canadian women, both historical and current. At least one of those women, former chief justice of the Supreme Court Beverley McLachlin wasn't impressed and complained. In his letter, Simons wrote, "This initiative was in poor taste, and I offer my heartfelt and sincerest apologies for this inappropriate use of Ms. McLachlin's name as well as that of the other women." But instead of just apologizing, he went further (and, as you've learned to do in this chapter), described the action he'd taken, and made a pitch to "resell" his company's image: "Since 1840, five generations of my family have aspired to build an

organization that never wavers from our values of respect, empathy and responsibility to the communities we live in. . . . Realizing my error, I have discontinued and destroyed all material related to this campaign. Our organization will be meeting to ensure that we learn from this incident." *What about Simons's negative message seems authentic to you? If anything seems inauthentic, how would you change it?*

Source: CBC News. (September 17, 2018) Simon's Sorry for Campaign Selling Bras Named after Famous Canadian Women. https://www.cbc.ca/news/business/simons-underwear-advertising-1.4827053

---

error, failure, fault, impossible, mistaken, misunderstand, never, regret, unwilling, unfortunately, and *violate.*

- **Show fairness and seriousness.** In explaining reasons, demonstrate to the reader that you take the matter seriously, have investigated carefully, and are making an unbiased decision. Customers are more accepting of disappointing news when they feel that their requests have been heard and that they have been treated fairly. Avoid deflecting responsibility, known as "passing the buck," or blaming others within your organization. Such unprofessional behaviour makes the reader lose faith in you and your company.

7.3c Cushion the Negative Information

Although you can't prevent the disappointment that bad news brings, you can reduce the pain somewhat by presenting it sensitively. Be especially considerate when the reader will suffer personally from the negative information. A number of thoughtful techniques can lessen the impact.

- **Position the information strategically.** Instead of spotlighting it, enclose the negative information between other sentences, perhaps among your reasons. Try not to let the refusal begin or end a paragraph—the reader's eye will linger on these high-visibility spots. Another technique that reduces shock is putting a painful idea in a subordinate clause: *Although the board did not award you a bonus this year, we are thankful for your enthusiasm and loyalty and highly encourage you to apply once again next year.* Subordinate clauses often begin with words such as *although, as, because, if,* and *since.*
- **Use the passive voice.** Passive-voice verbs enable you to describe an action without connecting the action to a specific person. Where the active voice focuses

attention on a person (*We don't accept unsolicited proposals*), the passive voice highlights the action (*Unsolicited proposals are not accepted because . . .*). Use the passive voice for the negative information. In some instances you can combine passive-voice verbs and a subordinate clause: *Although unsolicited proposals are not currently being accepted, we encourage you to try again beginning March 30, after which time our policy may have changed.*

- **Highlight the positive.** As you learned earlier, messages are far more effective when you describe what you can do instead of what you can't do. Rather than *We will no longer accept requests for product changes after June 1*, try a more positive appeal: *We are accepting requests for product changes until June 1.*
- **Imply the refusal.** It's sometimes possible to avoid a direct refusal statement. In this refusal to contribute to a charity, for example, the writer never actually says no: *Because we'll soon be relocating to new offices, all our funds are earmarked for moving costs and furnishings. We hope that next year we'll be able to support your worthwhile charity.* This implied refusal is effective even though the negative information is not explicitly stated. The danger of an implied refusal, of course, is that it can be so subtle that the reader misses it. Be certain that you make the negative information clear, thus preventing the need for further correspondence.
- **Suggest a compromise or an alternative.** A refusal is not so harsh—for the sender or the receiver—if a suitable compromise, substitute, or alternative is available. In denying permission to a class to visit a research facility, for instance, this writer softens the bad news by proposing an alternative: *Although class tours of the entire research facility are not given for safety and security reasons, we do offer tours of parts of the facility during our open house in the fall.* You can further reduce the impact of the negative information by refusing to dwell on it. Present it briefly (or imply it), and move on to your closing.

7.3d Close Pleasantly

After explaining the negative news sensitively, close the message with a pleasant statement that promotes goodwill and maintains the relationship. The closing should be personalized and may include an alternative, good wishes, special offers, resale information, or a future-looking thought.

- **Alternative follow-up.** If an alternative exists, end your letter with follow-through advice. For example, in a letter rejecting a customer's demand for replacement of landscaping plants, you might say, *We'll be happy to give you a free inspection and consultation. Please call 746-8112 to arrange a date for a visit.* In a message to a prospective homebuyer, you could say, *Although the lot you saw last week is now sold, we do have two other excellent lots available at a slightly higher price.* In reacting to a typo on a website, something else could be offered: *Please note that our website contained an unfortunate misprint offering $850-per-night Banff luxury chalets at $85. Although we cannot honour that rate, we are offering a special half-price rate of $425 to those who responded.*
- **Special offers.** When customers complain—primarily about food products or small consumer items—companies often send coupons, samples, or gifts to restore confidence and to promote future business. In response to a customer's complaint about a frozen dinner, you could write, *Thank you for your loyalty and for sharing in our efforts to make Green Valley frozen entrées the best they can be. We appreciate your input so much that we'd like to buy you dinner. We've enclosed a coupon to cover the cost of your next entrée.*
- **Good wishes.** A conversation in which someone is fired or downsized might read: We want you to know your contribution here has been highly valued, and we wish you all the best as you look for rewarding work in a different setting. Please be in touch with your manager about securing a reference.
- **Resale or sales promotion.** When the bad news isn't devastating or personal, references to resale information or promotion may be appropriate: *The tablets you ordered are unusually popular because they have more plug-ins for peripheral*

FIGURE 7.2 / Negative Message—Indirect Strategy

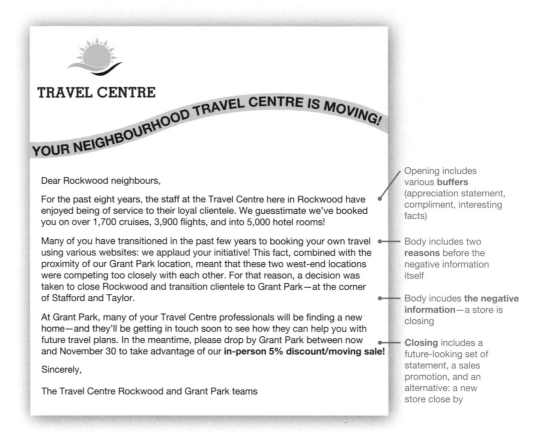

devices than any others in their price range. To help you locate additional acces-sories for these computers, we invite you to visit our website at . . . , where we provide a huge selection of peripheral devices such as speakers, printers, external hard drives, etc.

- **Future look.** Anticipate a future business relationship with the receiver. A letter that refuses a contract proposal might read: *Thank you for your bid. We look forward to working with your talented staff when future projects demand your special expertise.*

Try not to end negative messages in a superficial, insincere, or self-serving way, and at the same time, don't invite unnecessary further correspondence (*If you have any questions, do not hesitate . . .*), and definitely don't refer again to the negative information. The message in Figure 7.2 is a typical indirect negative message, show-casing all four components discussed.

7.4 Writing Negative Messages for External Situations

You've learned the components that are included in direct and indirect negative workplace messages. Now it's time to apply your knowledge. When a negative situation comes up at work that's external-facing, that is, it concerns someone or a group *outside* of the company (clients, partners, the public, etc.), you'll need to decide between the two strategies and then draft your message. Typical external-facing negative writing situations include refusing requests, dealing with disappointed clients, responding to negative reviews or to a crisis, denying claims, and collecting unpaid bills.

7.4a Request Refusals

Requests for favours, money, information, time, and action can come from friends, charities, or business partners, including clients. Many are from people representing commendable causes, and you may wish you could comply. However, resources are usually limited. In refusing requests (and claims, and when dealing with criticism) your goal is always to resolve the situation in a prompt, fair, and tactful manner. Use the indirect strategy and the following writing plan that was discussed earlier in the chapter:

WRITING PLAN FOR REFUSING REQUESTS OR CLAIMS AND FOR DEALING WITH DISAPPOINTMENT, CRITICISM, OR CRISES

- **Buffer:** Start with a neutral statement that both reader and writer can agree on, such as a compliment, an appreciative comment, a quick review of the facts, or an apology. Add a key idea or word that acts as a transition to the reasons.
- **Reasons:** Present valid reasons for the refusal or refutation, avoiding words that create a negative tone. Include resale or sales promotion material if appropriate.
- **Bad news:** Soften the blow by de-emphasizing the bad news, using the passive voice, accentuating the positive, or implying a refusal. Suggest a compromise, alternative, or substitute if possible. The alternative can be part of the bad news or part of the closing.
- **Closing:** Renew good feelings with a positive statement. Avoid referring to the bad news. Include resale or promotion information, if appropriate. Look forward to the continued business or relationship.

Two versions of a request refusal are shown in Figure 7.3. A magazine writer requested salary information for an article, but this information couldn't be released. The ineffective refusal begins with needless information that could be implied. The second paragraph creates a harsh tone with such negative words as *sorry*, *must refuse*, *violate*, and *liable*. Since the refusal precedes the explanation, the reader probably won't be in a receptive frame of mind to accept the reasons for refusing. Notice, too, that the negative information is emphasized by being placed in a short sentence right at the beginning of a paragraph! It stands out and adds more weight to the rejection already felt by the reader.

The refusal explanation is also overly graphic, containing references to possible litigation. The tone at this point is threatening and unduly harsh. Then, suddenly, the author throws in a self-serving comment about the high salary and commissions of his salespeople. Instead of offering constructive alternatives, the ineffective version reveals only tiny bits of the desired data. Finally, the closing sounds insincere and doesn't build goodwill.

In the improved version, the opening reflects the writer's genuine interest in the request. But it doesn't indicate compliance. The second sentence acts as a transition by introducing the words *salespeople* and *salaries*, repeated in the following paragraph. Reasons for refusing this request are objectively presented in an explanation that precedes the refusal. Notice that the refusal (*Although specific salaries and commission rates cannot be released*) is "hidden" in a subordinate clause in a long sentence in the middle of a paragraph. To further soften the blow, the letter offers an alternative. The polite closing refers to an alternative, avoids mention of the refusal, and looks to the future.

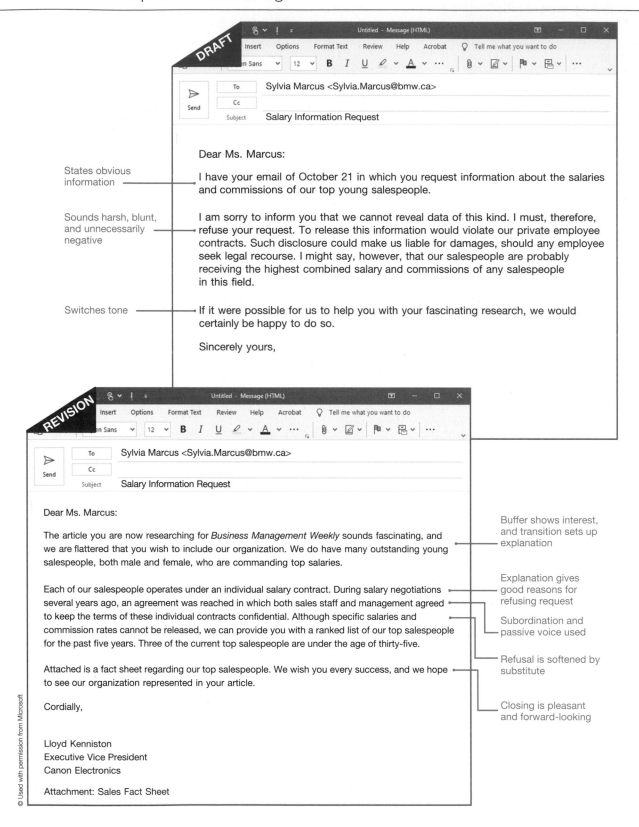

States obvious information

Sounds harsh, blunt, and unnecessarily negative

Switches tone

DRAFT

To: Sylvia Marcus <Sylvia.Marcus@bmw.ca>
Cc:
Subject: Salary Information Request

Dear Ms. Marcus:

I have your email of October 21 in which you request information about the salaries and commissions of our top young salespeople.

I am sorry to inform you that we cannot reveal data of this kind. I must, therefore, refuse your request. To release this information would violate our private employee contracts. Such disclosure could make us liable for damages, should any employee seek legal recourse. I might say, however, that our salespeople are probably receiving the highest combined salary and commissions of any salespeople in this field.

If it were possible for us to help you with your fascinating research, we would certainly be happy to do so.

Sincerely yours,

REVISION

To: Sylvia Marcus <Sylvia.Marcus@bmw.ca>
Cc:
Subject: Salary Information Request

Dear Ms. Marcus:

The article you are now researching for *Business Management Weekly* sounds fascinating, and we are flattered that you wish to include our organization. We do have many outstanding young salespeople, both male and female, who are commanding top salaries.

Each of our salespeople operates under an individual salary contract. During salary negotiations several years ago, an agreement was reached in which both sales staff and management agreed to keep the terms of these individual contracts confidential. Although specific salaries and commission rates cannot be released, we can provide you with a ranked list of our top salespeople for the past five years. Three of the current top salespeople are under the age of thirty-five.

Attached is a fact sheet regarding our top salespeople. We wish you every success, and we hope to see our organization represented in your article.

Cordially,

Lloyd Kenniston
Executive Vice President
Canon Electronics

Attachment: Sales Fact Sheet

Buffer shows interest, and transition sets up explanation

Explanation gives good reasons for refusing request

Subordination and passive voice used

Refusal is softened by substitute

Closing is pleasant and forward-looking

7.4b Claim Refusals

Customers occasionally want something they aren't entitled to or something you can't grant. They may misunderstand warranties or make unreasonable demands. Because these customers are often unhappy with a product or service, they are emotionally involved. Writing or saying *no* to emotionally involved receivers will probably be your most challenging communication task.

Fortunately, the indirect reasons-before-refusal writing plan (shown earlier) helps you be empathetic and subtle in breaking bad news. Obviously, in a claim refusal message you'll need to adopt the proper tone. Don't blame customers, even if they are at fault. Avoid "you" statements that sound preachy (*You would have known that refunds after 30 days are impossible if you had read your contract*). Use neutral, objective language to explain why the claim must be refused. Consider offering resale information to rebuild the customer's confidence in your products or organization.

Messages responding to claims that can't be approved because the customer is mistaken, misinformed, unreasonable, or possibly even dishonest are essentially delivering negative news. As you've learned, the indirect strategy communicates negative news with the least pain. It also allows the sender to explain why the claim must be refused before the reader realizes the bad news and begins resisting.

In the email shown in Figure 7.4, the writer refuses a customer's claim for the difference between the price the customer paid for speakers and the price she saw advertised locally (which would have resulted in a cash refund of $151). While Premier Sound Sales does match any advertised lower price, the price-matching policy applies only to exact models. This claim must be refused because the ad the customer submitted shows a different, older speaker model.

The email to Stephen Dominique opens with a buffer that agrees with a statement in the customer's letter. It repeats the key idea of product confidence as a

▼ FIGURE 7.4 / Claim Refusal Message

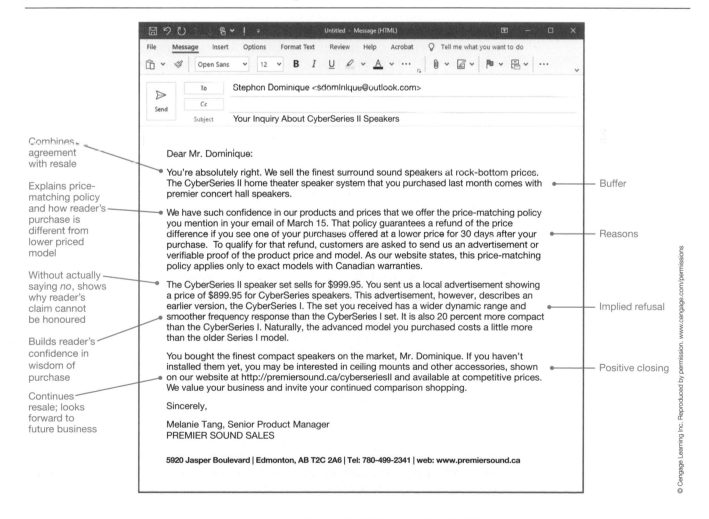

Combines agreement with resale

Explains price-matching policy and how reader's purchase is different from lower priced model

Without actually saying no, shows why reader's claim cannot be honoured

Builds reader's confidence in wisdom of purchase

Continues resale; looks forward to future business

To Stephen Dominique <sdominique@outlook.com>
Cc
Subject Your Inquiry About CyberSeries II Speakers

Dear Mr. Dominique:

You're absolutely right. We sell the finest surround sound speakers at rock-bottom prices. The CyberSeries II home theater speaker system that you purchased last month comes with premier concert hall speakers. — Buffer

We have such confidence in our products and prices that we offer the price-matching policy you mention in your email of March 15. That policy guarantees a refund of the price difference if you see one of your purchases offered at a lower price for 30 days after your purchase. To qualify for that refund, customers are asked to send us an advertisement or verifiable proof of the product price and model. As our website states, this price-matching policy applies only to exact models with Canadian warranties. — Reasons

The CyberSeries II speaker set sells for $999.95. You sent us a local advertisement showing a price of $899.95 for CyberSeries speakers. This advertisement, however, describes an earlier version, the CyberSeries I. The set you received has a wider dynamic range and smoother frequency response than the CyberSeries I set. It is also 20 percent more compact than the CyberSeries I. Naturally, the advanced model you purchased costs a little more than the older Series I model. — Implied refusal

You bought the finest compact speakers on the market, Mr. Dominique. If you haven't installed them yet, you may be interested in ceiling mounts and other accessories, shown on our website at http://premiersound.ca/cyberseriesII and available at competitive prices. We value your business and invite your continued comparison shopping. — Positive closing

Sincerely,

Melanie Tang, Senior Product Manager
PREMIER SOUND SALES

5920 Jasper Boulevard | Edmonton, AB T2C 2A6 | Tel: 780-499-2341 | web: www.premiersound.ca

transition to the second paragraph. Next comes an explanation of the price-matching policy. The writer doesn't assume that the customer is trying to trick the store. Nor does the writer suggest that the customer is unintelligent and didn't read or understand the price-matching policy.

The safest path is a neutral explanation of the policy along with precise distinctions between the customer's speakers and the older ones. The writer also gets a chance to resell the customer's speakers and demonstrate what a quality product they are. By the end of the third paragraph, it's evident to the reader that his claim is unjustified.

Notice how most of the components in an effective claim refusal are woven together in this letter: buffer, transition, explanation, and pleasant closing. The only missing part is an alternative, which was impossible in this situation.

7.4c Disappointment Acknowledgments

Businesses need to regularly acknowledge and respond to disappointed customers, especially in the digital age of instant social media postings. Whenever possible, these disappointed customers should be dealt with immediately and personally. Most businesses strive to control the damage and resolve such problems in the following manner:

- Write, call, or message the individual on social media immediately.
- Describe the problem and apologize.
- Explain why the problem occurred, what you're doing to resolve it, and how you'll prevent it from happening again.
- If appropriate, promote goodwill by following up phone and social media messages with a letter that documents the call or social media exchange.

Consultant Jane Moffatt found herself in the embarrassing position of explaining why she had given out the name of her client to a salesperson. The client, Premier Resources International, had hired her firm, Azad Consulting Associates, to help secure payroll outsourcing functions. Jane mistakenly mentioned to a potential vendor (QuickPay Services, Inc.) that her client was considering hiring an outside service to handle its payroll. An overly eager salesperson from QuickPay Services immediately called Premier, thus angering the client.

Jane first called her client to acknowledge his complaint, explain, and apologize. She was careful to control her voice and rate of speaking. She also followed up the same day with the letter shown in Figure 7.5 (which she attached to an email). The letter not only confirms the phone call but also adds the right touch of formality. It sends the nonverbal message that the writer takes the matter seriously and that it's important enough to warrant a hard-copy letter.

Today, many consumer disappointment acknowledgments are handled directly via email and social media messages.

7.4d Online and Social Media Complaint Acknowledgments

Today's impatient, hyperconnected consumers embrace the idea of delivering their complaints on social media and other sector-specific online communities. Such negative posts are common on Twitter, Facebook, Yelp, Cruise Critic, and other sites.

Besides having an at-the-ready communications team in-house, including a social media specialist (not always possible for many medium and small businesses), how can the communicator-in-charge at an organization respond to negative posts and reviews online? Experts suggest the following pointers:

- **Verify the situation.** Investigate to learn what happened. If the complaint is legitimate and your organization fouled up, it's best to admit it with a quick indirect-strategy message like the Twitter message in Figure 7.6: brief buffer, brief reasons

FIGURE **7.5** / Disappointment Acknowledgment Message

AZAD CONSULTING ASSOCIATES

7200 Keele St.
Toronto, ON M7A 2B8

Voice: (416) 259-0971
Web: www.azadassociates.com

May 7, 2021

Mr. Carl Bahadur
Director, Administrative Operations
Premier Resources International
538 North Service Road, Suite 2010
Oakville, ON L35 2B7

Dear Mr. Bahadur:

Opens with **buffer:** agreement and apology

You have every right to expect complete confidentiality in your transactions with an independent consultant. As I explained in yesterday's telephone call, I am very distressed that you were called by a salesperson from QuickPay Services, Inc. This should not have happened, and I apologize to you again for inadvertently mentioning your company's name in a conversation with a potential vendor, QuickPay Services, Inc.

Takes responsibility and promises to prevent recurrence

All clients of Azad Consulting are assured that their dealings with our firm are held in the strictest confidence. Because your company's payroll needs are so individual and because you have so many contract workers, I was forced to explain how your employees differed from those of other companies. Revealing your company name was my error, and I take full responsibility for the lapse. I can assure you that it will not happen again. I have informed QuickPay Services that it had no authorization to call you directly, and its actions have forced me to reconsider using its services for my future clients.

Explains **reasons** for disappointment and how it was resolved

Closes with forward look

A number of other payroll services offer outstanding programs. I'm sure we can find the perfect partner to enable you to outsource your payroll responsibilities, thus allowing your company to focus its financial and human resources on its core business. I look forward to our next appointment when you may choose from a number of excellent payroll outsourcing firms.

Sincerely,

Jane Moffatt

Jane Moffatt
Partner

Tips for Resolving Problems and Following Up
- Whenever possible, call or see the individual involved.
- Describe the problem and apologize.
- Explain why the problem occurred.
- Take responsibility, if appropriate.
- Explain what you are doing to resolve it.
- Explain what you are doing to prevent recurrence.
- Follow up with a message that documents the personal contact.
- Look forward to positive future relations.

plus admitting to and regretting of negative event, and brief future-looking closing. Use the same channel as the person who made the complaint—and try to remedy it.

- **Respond quickly and constructively.** Offer to follow up offline; send your contact information. Be polite and helpful.
- **Consider freebies.** Suggest a refund or a discount on future services. Dissatisfied customers often write a second more positive review if they have received a refund.
- **Learn how to improve.** Look at online and social media comments as opportunities for growth and improvement. See complaining customers as real-time focus groups that can provide valuable insights.
- **Accept the inevitable.** Recognize that nearly every business will experience some negativity. Do what you can to respond constructively, and then move on.

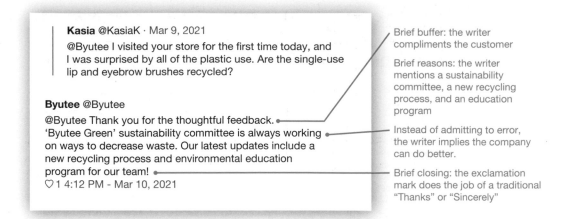

Kasia @KasiaK · Mar 9, 2021

@Byutee I visited your store for the first time today, and I was surprised by all of the plastic use. Are the single-use lip and eyebrow brushes recycled?

Byutee @Byutee

@Byutee Thank you for the thoughtful feedback. 'Byutee Green' sustainability committee is always working on ways to decrease waste. Our latest updates include a new recycling process and environmental education program for our team!
♡ 1 4:12 PM - Mar 10, 2021

Brief buffer: the writer compliments the customer

Brief reasons: the writer mentions a sustainability committee, a new recycling process, and an education program

Instead of admitting to error, the writer implies the company can do better.

Brief closing: the exclamation mark does the job of a traditional "Thanks" or "Sincerely"

7.4e Crisis Communication Messages

In the past ten years or so, roughly in parallel with the widespread use of social media by organizations, a new sub-branch of business communication has appeared: crisis communication. If you go to Indeed or Workopolis, you can search for jobs in *crisis communication* or *crisis management.*

Essentially, when a situation is more serious than a complaint about a good or service, usually because a terrible accident has taken place or unfortunate language has been used by a senior executive or some other event that falls under the category of *disaster* or *crisis*, a company has to do more than send out acknowledgment messages.

In crisis situations, a *crisis communication strategy or plan* needs to be deployed, often by the in-house corporate communications team, but if there isn't such a team, then often by a freelance communication expert. You can google *crisis communication plan* to find best-practice examples from industry.

This plan usually consists of a number of messages, such as a *key message and support map*. For example, if a company has a chemical leak that's affecting local drinking water, the first key message is that the company is providing clean drinking water to everyone affected. Support for this key message is that X thousand litres were delivered this morning. Another part of the crisis communication plan will be a press release or series of releases that goes out to all local media. For example, a release about what's happened, a release communicating the organization's feelings of empathy or regret, a release about injuries sustained or fatalities, and a release that moves toward reputation recovery (e.g., industry safety statistics).

Although crisis communication is a highly specialized form of business communication, it does adhere to the principles of negative messaging discussed in this chapter, with a heavier reliance on direct over indirect messaging. When something serious or disastrous has happened, a buffer can look thoughtless. It's better to be direct.

7.4f Collection Messages

Collection is the process companies use to ensure that their unpaid invoices are paid. The first phase in the collection process is usually the sending of a short reminder letter or email that lets clients or customers know their invoice is outstanding. Best practices stipulate that a copy of the outstanding invoice should be attached to this short reminder message, in case the client has misplaced the original.

Understanding how to write a negative message becomes useful in the second step of the collection process. If the client or customer with the outstanding invoice

FRASER, AHMET, AND GRANDPRE

3017–66 Avenue Northwest, Suite 222
Edmonton, AB T6H 1Y2

August 14, 2021

Tom Przybylski
Unity Ltd.
9 Givins Dr., Unit 5
Edmonton, AB T2A 4X3

Dear Mr. Przybylski:

Re: Invoice No. 443-2010

Outstanding Amount Due: $19,567.87

You are indebted to the firm of Fraser, Ahmet, and Grandpre in the amount of $19,567.87, for services rendered and for which you were invoiced on March 30, 2021. A copy of the outstanding invoice is enclosed for your reference, as is a copy of a reminder letter sent to you on July 2, 2021.
Negative information up front

Unless we receive a certified cheque or money order, payable to Fraser, Ahmet, and Grandpre, in the amount of $19,567.87, or unless satisfactory payment arrangements are made within seven (7) business days, we are left no choice but to pursue collection of the amount owing. We are not prepared to continue carrying your accounts receivable and we will take all necessary steps for the recovery of this amount from you.
Reasons for negative information explained in body

We do not wish to proceed in this fashion and would appreciate your cooperation instead. We look forward to hearing from you on or before August 21, 2021.
Closes pleasantly and firmly with motivating deadline

Yours sincerely,

Pat McAfee

Pat McAfee
Office Manager/Collections Clerk

doesn't reply in a timely manner to the short reminder message described above, it's time to write a direct bad-news message demanding payment. Figure 7.7 shows a typical example of such a message, using the direct strategy discussed earlier in the chapter: put the negative information up front, give reasons, then close pleasantly.

The objective of a collection letter is not only to receive payment, but also to make sure that the goodwill of the client or customer is retained. According to Credit Guru Inc., a company that offers advice on the collection process, the main features of a well-written collection letter are a reminder of the dates of the invoice, a reminder of the total amount outstanding, a request for immediate payment or payment by a specified date, a request for the payment to be sent by the quickest means (e.g., courier, e-transfer), and finally, a sense of urgency coupled with an unapologetic and nonthreatening tone.[5]

7.5 Negative Messages for Internal Situations

A polite tone and reasons-first approach help preserve friendly relations with customers. These techniques are also useful when delivering negative information within organizations. This might involve telling the boss that something went wrong or confronting an employee about poor performance. Organizational bad news might involve declining profits, lost contracts, harmful lawsuits, public relations controversies, and changes in policy. Generally, negative information is better received when reasons are given first.

7.5a Workplace Request Refusals

Occasionally, managers must refuse requests from employees. In Figure 7.8 you see the first draft and revision of a message responding to a request from employee Melvin Arroyo. He wants permission to attend a conference. However, he can't attend the conference because the timing is bad; he must be present at budget planning meetings scheduled for the same two weeks. Normally, this matter would be discussed in person. However, Melvin has been travelling among branch offices, and he hasn't been in the office recently.

The vice president's first inclination was to send a quick email, as shown in the Figure 7.8 draft, and "tell it like it is." However, the vice president realizes that

FIGURE 7.8 / Internal Request Refusal

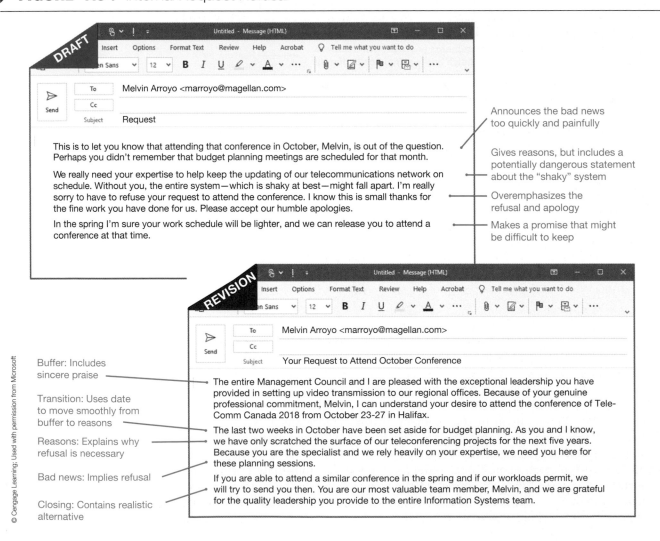

this message will hurt and that it has possible danger areas. Moreover, the message misses a chance to give Melvin positive feedback. An improved version of the email starts with a buffer that delivers honest praise (*pleased with the exceptional leadership you have provided and your genuine professional commitment*). By the way, don't be stingy with compliments; they cost you nothing. The buffer also includes the date of the meeting, used strategically to connect the reasons that follow.

The middle paragraph provides reasons for the refusal. Notice that they focus on positive elements: Melvin is the specialist; the company relies on his expertise; and everyone will benefit if he passes up the conference. In this section it becomes obvious that the request will be refused. The writer is not forced to say *No, you may not attend*. Although the refusal is implied, the reader understands the refusal.

The closing suggests a qualified alternative (*if our workloads permit, we will try to send you then*). It also ends positively with gratitude for Melvin's contributions to the organization and with another compliment (*you're a valuable team player*). The improved version focuses on explanations and praise rather than on refusals and apologies. The success of this message depends on sincerity and attention to the entire writing process, not just on using a buffer or scattering a few compliments throughout.

7.5b Negative Employee Announcements

In the age of social media, damaging information can rarely be contained for long. Executives can almost count on it to be leaked. Employees who fail to communicate effectively and proactively may end up on the defensive, facing an uphill battle to limit the damage. Many of the techniques used to communicate bad news in person are useful when organizations face a crisis or must deliver negative news to their workers and other groups.

KEEP COMMUNICATION OPEN AND HONEST. Smart organizations in crisis prefer to communicate the news openly to employees and other stakeholders. A crisis might involve serious performance problems, a major relocation, massive layoffs, a management shakeup, or public controversy. Instead of letting rumours distort the truth, managers ought to explain the organization's side of the story honestly and promptly.

> **WRITING PLAN FOR ANNOUNCING NEGATIVE NEWS TO EMPLOYEES**
>
> - **Buffer:** Start with a neutral or positive statement that transitions to the reasons for the bad news. Consider opening with the best news, a compliment, appreciation, agreement, or solid facts. Show understanding.
> - **Reasons:** Explain the logic behind the bad news. Provide a rational explanation using positive words and displaying empathy. If possible, mention reader benefits.
> - **Bad news:** Position the bad news so that it does not stand out. Be positive, but don't sugar-coat the bad news. Use objective language.
> - **Closing:** Provide information about an alternative, if one exists. If appropriate, describe what will happen next. Look forward positively.

CHOOSE THE BEST COMMUNICATION CHANNEL. Morale can be destroyed when employees learn of major events affecting their jobs through the grapevine or from news accounts—rather than from management. When bad news must be delivered to individual employees, management may want to deliver the news personally. With large groups, however, this is generally impossible. Instead, organizations deliver bad news through multiple channels, ranging from hardcopy memos to digital media. Such messages can take the form of intranet posts, emails, videos, webcasts, internal as well as external blogs, and voice mail.

DRAFT A NEGATIVE NEWS INTRANET POST. The draft of the intranet blog post shown in Figure 7.9 announces a substantial increase in the cost of employee health care benefits. However, the message suffers from many problems. It announces jolting news bluntly in the first sentence. Worse, it offers little or no explanation for the steep increase in costs. It also sounds insincere (*We did everything possible . . .*) and arbitrary. In a final miscue, the writer fails to give credit to the company for absorbing previous health cost increases.

The revision of this negative news message uses the indirect strategy and improves the tone considerably. Notice that it opens with a relevant, upbeat buffer

▼ FIGURE 7.9 / Negative Employee Announcement

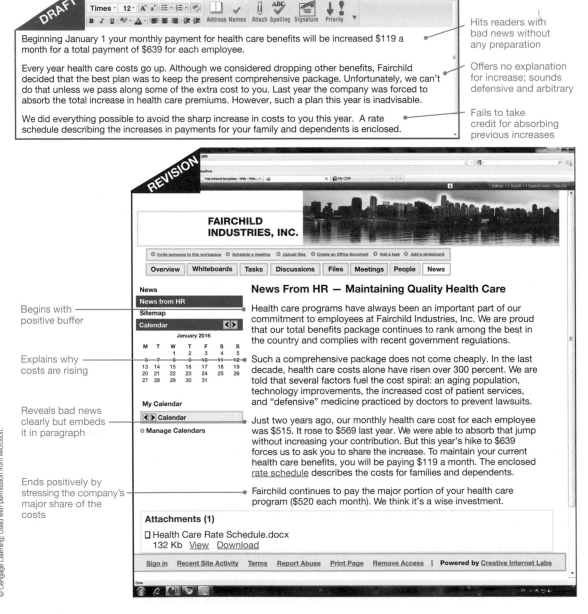

Beginning January 1 your monthly payment for health care benefits will be increased $119 a month for a total payment of $639 for each employee.

Hits readers with bad news without any preparation

Every year health care costs go up. Although we considered dropping other benefits, Fairchild decided that the best plan was to keep the present comprehensive package. Unfortunately, we can't do that unless we pass along some of the extra cost to you. Last year the company was forced to absorb the total increase in health care premiums. However, such a plan this year is inadvisable.

Offers no explanation for increase; sounds defensive and arbitrary

We did everything possible to avoid the sharp increase in costs to you this year. A rate schedule describing the increases in payments for your family and dependents is enclosed.

Fails to take credit for absorbing previous increases

FAIRCHILD INDUSTRIES, INC.

Overview | Whiteboards | Tasks | Discussions | Files | Meetings | People | News

News
News from HR
Sitemap
Calendar
January 2016

M	T	W	T	F	S	S
				1	2	3
4	5	6	7	8	9	10
13	14	15	16	17	18	19
20	21	22	23	24	25	26
27	28	29	30	31		

My Calendar
◄ ► Calendar
○ Manage Calendars

News From HR — Maintaining Quality Health Care

Health care programs have always been an important part of our commitment to employees at Fairchild Industries, Inc. We are proud that our total benefits package continues to rank among the best in the country and complies with recent government regulations.

Begins with positive buffer

Such a comprehensive package does not come cheaply. In the last decade, health care costs alone have risen over 300 percent. We are told that several factors fuel the cost spiral: an aging population, technology improvements, the increased cost of patient services, and "defensive" medicine practiced by doctors to prevent lawsuits.

Explains why costs are rising

Just two years ago, our monthly health care cost for each employee was $515. It rose to $569 last year. We were able to absorb that jump without increasing your contribution. But this year's hike to $639 forces us to ask you to share the increase. To maintain your current health care benefits, you will be paying $119 a month. The enclosed rate schedule describes the costs for families and dependents.

Reveals bad news clearly but embeds it in paragraph

Fairchild continues to pay the major portion of your health care program ($520 each month). We think it's a wise investment.

Ends positively by stressing the company's major share of the costs

Attachments (1)
☐ Health Care Rate Schedule.docx
132 Kb View Download

Sign in Recent Site Activity Terms Report Abuse Print Page Remove Access | Powered by Creative Internet Labs regarding health care—but says nothing about increasing costs. For a smooth transition, the second paragraph begins with a key idea from the opening (*comprehensive package*). The reasons section discusses rising costs with explanations and figures. The bad news (*you will be paying $119 a month*) is clearly presented but embedded within the paragraph. Throughout, the writer strives to show the fairness of the company's position. The ending, which does not refer to the bad news, emphasizes how much the company is paying and what a wise investment it is.

The entire message demonstrates a kinder, gentler approach than that shown in the first draft. Of prime importance in breaking bad news to employees is providing clear, convincing reasons that explain the decision. Parallel to this internal blog post, the message was also sent by email. In smaller companies in which some workers do not have company email, a hardcopy memo would be posted prominently on bulletin boards and in the lunchroom.

7.5c Keeping the Indirect Strategy Ethical

You may worry that the indirect strategy is unethical or manipulative or contains a lie because the writer deliberately delays the main idea. But consider the alternative. Breaking bad news bluntly can cause pain and hard feelings. By delaying bad news, you soften the blow somewhat, as well as ensure that your reasoning will be read while the receiver is still receptive. Your motives are not to deceive the reader or to hide the news. Rather, your goal is to be a compassionate, yet effective, communicator.

The key to ethical communication lies in the motives of the sender. Unethical communicators intend to deceive. Although the indirect strategy requires you to delay announcing bad news, it shouldn't be used to avoid or misrepresent the truth.

Cengage

MINDTAP

In MindTap go to the Study Tools for Chapter 7 and complete the Practice Test.

▲ LEARNING SUMMARY

7.1 Explain the goals of business communicators when conveying negative information.

- Explain clearly and completely while projecting a professional image.
- Convey empathy, sensitivity, and fairness.
- Maintain friendly relations, especially with customers.

7.2 Compare the direct and indirect strategies for communicating negative information.

- Use the direct strategy, with the bad news first, when the news is not damaging, when the receiver may overlook it, when the organization or receiver prefers directness, or when firmness is necessary.
- Use the indirect strategy, with a buffer and explanation preceding the bad news, when the bad news is personally upsetting, when it may provoke a hostile reaction, when it threatens the customer relationship, and when the news is unexpected.
- To avoid being unethical, never use the indirect method to deceive or manipulate the truth.

7.3 Describe the components of effective indirect negative messages, including opening with a buffer, apologizing, showing empathy, presenting the reasons, cushioning the bad news, and closing pleasantly.

- To soften bad news, start with a buffer such as the best news, a compliment, appreciation, agreement, facts, understanding, or an apology.

- If you apologize, do it promptly and sincerely. Accept responsibility but don't admit blame without consulting a superior or company counsel. Strive to project empathy.
- In presenting the reasons for the bad news, explain clearly, cite reader or other benefits if plausible, explain company policy if necessary, choose positive words, and strive to show fairness and serious intent.
- In breaking the bad news, position it and word it strategically by (a) sandwiching it between other sentences, (b) presenting it in a subordinate clause, (c) using passive-voice verbs to depersonalize an action, (d) highlighting whatever is positive, (e) implying the refusal instead of stating it directly, and (f) suggesting a compromise or an alternative.
- To close pleasantly, you could (a) suggest a means of following through on an alternative, (b) offer freebies, (c) extend good wishes, (d) anticipate future business, or (e) offer resale information or a sales promotion.

7.4 Write negative messages for external situations: refusals (e.g., denying requests or claims) and situations when customers and the public are disappointed (e.g., collections, crises).

- In rejecting requests for favours, money, information, and action, follow the bad-news strategy: (a) begin with a buffer, (b) present valid reasons, (c) explain the bad news and possibly an alternative, and (d) close with good feelings and a positive statement.

- To deal with disappointed customers in print, (a) call or email the individual immediately; (b) describe the problem and apologize; (c) explain why the problem occurred, what you are doing to resolve it, and how you will prevent it from happening again; and (d) promote goodwill with a follow-up message.

- To handle negative posts and reviews online, (a) verify the situation, (b) respond quickly and constructively, (c) consider giving freebies such as refunds or discounts, (d) learn to improve by considering people who made negative comments as real-time focus groups, and (e) be prepared to accept the inevitable and move on.

- To deny claims, (a) use the reasons-before-refusal plan, (b) don't blame customers (even if they are at fault),

(c) use neutral objective language to explain why the claim must be refused, and (d) consider offering resale information to rebuild the customer's confidence in your products or organization.

7.5 Write negative messages for internal situations (e.g., employee bad news).

- In announcing bad news to employees, strive to keep the communication open and honest, choose the best communication channel, and consider applying the indirect strategy.

- Be positive, but don't sugar-coat the bad news; use objective language.

- Recognize that the indirect strategy, while it does soften the truth, must, to stay ethical, never deny the truth.

► CHAPTER REVIEW

1. When denying a claim from an irate customer who is threatening and overstates the claim, why do you want to remain professional and fair? (Obj. 1)

2. What is the primary difference between the direct and the indirect strategies? (Obj. 2)

3. When would you be more inclined to use the direct strategy in delivering negative news? (Obj. 2)

4. What is a buffer? Name five or more techniques to buffer the opening of a negative-news message. (Obj. 3)

5. Why should you apologize to customers if you or your company erred? What is the best way to do it? (Obj. 3)

6. In delivering negative news, what five techniques can be used to soften that news? (Obj. 3)

7. What is a process used by many business professionals in resolving problems with disappointed customers? (Obj. 4)

8. How can negative online comments be turned into positive growth for an organization? (Obj. 4)

9. How can a subordinate tactfully, professionally, and safely deliver upsetting news personally to a superior? (Obj. 5)

10. What are some channels that large organizations may use to deliver bad news to employees? (Obj. 5)

11. How is the indirect negative news strategy an ethical strategy? (Obj. 5)

► CRITICAL THINKING

1. One communication expert likens delivering bad news to removing a Band-Aid—you can do it slowly or quickly. She thinks that doing so quickly is better, particularly when companies must give bad news to employees. Do you agree or disagree? Why? (Objs. 1, 2)

2. In a survey of business professionals, most respondents reported that every effort should be made to resolve business problems in person. Why is this logical? Why is this problematic? (Objs. 1, 2)

3. To what degree should organizations fear websites on which consumers post negative messages about products and services? What actions can companies take in response to this disruptive influence? (Objs. 3, 4)

4. Does bad news travel faster and farther than good news? Why? What implications would this have for companies responding to unhappy customers? (Obj. 4)

5. Why might it be a bad idea to be blunt toward people with a low income when denying them credit? (Objs. 1, 2)

6. Why is the "reasons" section of a negative news message so important? (Objs. 4, 5)

7. Radio Shack infamously fired 400 of its employees by email a number of years ago. More recently, the CEO of electric-car manufacturer Tesla, Elon Musk, used his blog to announce layoffs. Why would most business communication and management experts frown upon such behaviour? Do you agree or disagree with these experts? (Objs. 1, 4, 5)

◣ ACTIVITIES AND CASES

7.1 REQUEST REFUSAL: PINK DRAGONS SINK APPLICATION (OBJS. 1–4)

Shopify, the Ottawa-based ecommerce company, prides itself on its commitment to employees who receive generous benefits and enjoy a supportive corporate culture. This core value may have contributed to the company's ranking as the top place to work in Canada.[6] The software giant is also known for its community involvement and corporate social responsibility efforts. This is why, like most large companies, Shopify receives many requests for sponsorships of charity events and community projects. True to its innovative spirit, the software company has streamlined the application process by providing an online sponsorship request form at its website.

You work in Corporate Affairs/Community Relations at Shopify and periodically help decide which nonprofits will obtain support. Just yesterday you received an email from the Pink Dragons of Ottawa-Hull, a dragon boat racing team of breast cancer survivors. The ancient Chinese sport has spread around the globe with competitions held not only in Asia but also in many Western countries. Dragon boat racing has gained popularity in North America among breast cancer patients who bond with fellow survivors, engage in healthy competition, and exercise regularly on the water. Synchronicity and technique are more important than brute strength, which is the main reason even recreational paddlers enjoy this fast-growing water sport.

The newly formed survivor team would like Shopify to sponsor a dragon boat festival in Toronto in less than a month, an event potentially drawing at least 20 survivor teams that would compete against one another. Your company is already funding several cancer charities and has a policy of sponsoring many causes. Naturally, no corporate giving program has infinite funds, nor can it say yes to every request. Shopify steers clear of religious, political, and sexually explicit events. The team judging the sponsorship entries wants to ensure that each proposal reaches audiences affiliated with Shopify. Most important, applicants must submit their requests at least six weeks before the event.

Your Task. As a junior staff member in Corporate Affairs/Community Relations, write an email to Pink Dragon captain Josephine Rosa (jrosa@pinkdragons.ca) refusing her initial request and explaining the Shopify sponsorship philosophy and submission rules.

7.2 CLAIM DENIAL: LOST IN FLIGHT (OBJS. 1–4)

Air Transat has an unhappy customer. Genna Frymoyer-Morris flew from Montreal to Lisbon. The flight stopped briefly at the Ponta Delgada International Airport in the Azores, where she got off the plane for half an hour. When she returned to her seat, her $500 prescription reading glasses were gone. She asked the flight attendant where the glasses were, and the attendant said they probably were thrown away since the cleaning crew had come in with big bags and tossed everything left on the plane in them.

Ms. Frymoyer-Morris tried to locate the glasses through the airline's lost-and-found service, but she failed. Then she wrote a strong letter to the airline demanding reimbursement for the loss. She felt that it was obvious that she was returning to her seat. The airline, however, knows that a large number of passengers arriving at hubs switch planes for their connecting flights. The airline does not know who is returning. What's more, flight attendants usually announce that the plane is continuing to another city and that passengers who are returning should take their belongings. Cabin cleaning crews speed through planes removing newspapers, magazines, leftover foods, and trash. Airlines feel no responsibility for personal items left in cabins.

Your Task. As a staff member of the customer relations department of Air Transat, deny the customer's claim but retain her goodwill using techniques learned in this chapter. The airline never refunds cash, but it might consider travel vouchers for the value of the glasses. Remember that apologies cost nothing. Write a claim denial to Ms. Genna Frymoyer-Morris, 1805 Rue du Chemin, Mont Tremblant, QC J8E 0A3.

7.3 CUSTOMER NEGATIVE NEWS: COSTLY SUV UPGRADE (OBJ. 4)

Steven Chan, a consultant from Regina, Saskatchewan, was surprised when he picked up his rental car from Budget at the Calgary airport over Easter weekend. He had reserved a full-size car, but the rental agent told him he could upgrade to a Ford Expedition for an additional $25 a day. "She told me it was easy to drive," Mr. Chan reported. "But when I saw it, I realized it was huge—like a tank. You could fit a full-size bed inside."

On his trip Mr. Chan managed to scratch the paint and damage the rear-door step. He didn't worry, though. He thought the damage would be covered because he had charged the rental on his American Express card. He knew that the company offered backup car rental insurance coverage. To his dismay, he discovered that its car rental coverage excluded large SUVs. "I just assumed they'd cover it," he confessed. He wrote to Budget to complain about not being warned that certain credit cards may not cover damage to large SUVs or luxury cars.

Budget agents always encourage renters to sign up for Budget's own "risk product." They don't feel that it is their responsibility to study the policies of customers' insurance carriers and explain what may or may not be covered. Moreover, they try to move customers into their rental cars as quickly as possible and avoid lengthy discussions of insurance coverage. Customers who do not purchase insurance are at risk. Mr. Chan does not make any claim against Budget, but he is upset about being "pitched" to upgrade to the larger SUV, which he didn't really want.

Your Task. As a member of the customer care staff at Budget, respond to Mr. Chan's complaint. Budget obviously is not going to pay for the SUV repairs, but it does want to salvage his goodwill and future business. Offer him a coupon worth two days' free rental of any full-size sedan. Write to Steven Chan, 201-548 Hillsdale Street, Regina, SK S32 0A2.

7.4 INTERNAL REFUSAL: WANT TO TELECOMMUTE? LEARN TO COMMUNICATE (OBJ. 5)

Pamela Gershon, a young software developer from Edmonton, Alberta, is thrilled at the prospect of working from home where she would be able to take care of her two small children, three dogs, and a cat. Like many forward-looking employers, Northrop Grumman Corporation, a leading aerospace and defence technology company, is encouraging workers to consider telecommuting. The company has created a formal program with specific policies explaining eligibility and requirements. Currently, only positions in technical sales, information technology, Web and graphic design, and software development qualify for telecommuting. In addition, workers must be dependable, self-motivated, and organized. Because telecommuting is a sought-after privilege, employees with proven high performance, seniority, minimal absenteeism, and superb communication skills receive priority consideration. Telecommuters need to follow company policies determining work hours, break times, and work schedules, even off site. Moreover, they must visit the main office located on CFB Cold Lake at least once every two weeks to report to their supervisors in person.

Northrop Grumman promotes telecommuting because it benefits the company and its workers. In addition to flexibility, telecommuters usually experience gains in productivity and efficiency. The employer lowers overhead costs and is able to retain valuable workers who may not be able or willing to commute to remote corporate offices.

Pamela has been a diligent worker, but after only a year and a half at Northrop Grumman, she doesn't have the seniority needed for a successful application. Her performance has been satisfactory but not outstanding. It seems as if she still needs time to prove herself. In addition, her major weakness is average communication skills, something her supervisor has already discussed with Pamela.

Your Task. Draft an email addressed to Pamela Gershon for Human Resources Director Gabrielle Anicker turning down Pamela's telecommuting application. Be gentle but honest in revealing your reasons for the *no*, but don't close the door on a future application once Pamela meets certain conditions.

7.5 REQUEST REFUSAL: THE END OF FREE CREDIT REPORTS (OBJ. 4)

You're part of the customer service team at Experian, the largest supplier of consumer and business credit information in the world. Experian took over TRW Information Systems & Services back in 1996. Experian currently employs more than 11,000 people in North America, the United Kingdom, Continental Europe, Africa, and Asia Pacific. As a service to consumers, Experian at one time provided complimentary credit reports. However, it now offers them only in certain locations and to certain groups of people.

Experian's website explains its new policy in its FAQ (frequently asked questions) section. Your supervisor says to you, "I guess not everyone is able to learn about our new policy by going to our website, because we still receive a lot of phone requests for free reports. I'm unhappy with a letter we've been using to respond to these requests. I want you to compose a draft of a new form letter that we can send to people who inquire. You should look at our website to see who gets free reports and in what locations."

Because you're fairly new to Experian, you ask your boss what prompted the change in policy. She explains, "It was a good idea, but it got out of hand. So-called credit repair companies would refer their clients to us for free credit reports, and then they advised their clients to dispute every item on the report. We had to change our policy. But you can read more about it on our website."

Your Task. You resolve to study the Experian website closely. Your task is to write a letter refusing the requests of people who want free credit reports. But you must also explain the reasons for the change in policy, as well as its exceptions. Decide whether you should tell consumers how to order a copy and how to pay for it. Although your letter will be used repeatedly for such requests, address your draft to Ms. Cherise Benoit, 250 Rue Bruce, Montréal, QC H2X 1E1. Sign it with your boss's name, Elisabeth Bourke.

7.6 CUSTOMER NEGATIVE NEWS: THESE FUNDS ARE WORTH HOLDING ON TO (OBJ. 4)

You are a financial planner in Hamilton, Ontario, with over 200 clients. Since you began your practice as a financial planner, you have been a strong believer in BMC's mutual funds, which are heavily invested in the financial services sector. Over the past few years, though, these funds have been underperforming dismally.

For example, in 2019 when the S&P/TSX Index was 10.5 percent, BMC funds were averaging 2.2 percent; in 2020 when the index was at 11.9 percent, BMC funds averaged 2.5 percent; and in 2021 when the Index is at 10.9 percent, BMC funds are averaging –0.1 percent. BMC funds have been criticized in major newspapers of late, and for the past few months you have had at least five clients per week calling to sell their funds.

You believe BMC funds are still a good value because the financial services sector will rebound soon. Also, with Canadian demographic trends pointing to a large retired population in the next decade, you believe BMC funds are a smart investment.

Your Task. Write a letter to your clients in which you discuss the recent bad news about BMC funds, but at the same time, in which you attempt to put this bad news into a broader context. Related website: For general information on Canadian mutual fund performance, go to www.morningstar.ca.

7.7 CREDIT REFUSAL: UNDERWATER CAMERAS FOR RUDY'S CAMERA SHOP (OBJ. 4)

As a Uniworld Electronics sales manager, you are delighted to land a sizable order for your new Nikon Coolpix UW200 cameras. This hot new camera features a sleek, lightweight design, brilliant optical quality, guaranteed waterproof design, vibrant images, and outstanding image capture in low-light conditions.

The purchase order comes from Rudy's Camera Shop, a retail distributor in Victoria, British Columbia. You send the order on to Pamela Kahn, your credit manager, for approval of the credit application attached. To your disappointment, Ms. Kahn tells you that Rudy's Camera doesn't qualify for credit. Experian, the credit-reporting service, reports that extending credit to Rudy's would be risky for Uniworld. But Experian did offer to discuss your client's report with him.

Because you think you can be more effective in writing than on the telephone, you decide to write to Rudy's Camera with the bad news and offer an alternative. Suggest that Rudy's order a smaller number of the Nikon cameras. If it pays cash, it can receive a 2 percent discount. After Rudy's has sold these fast-moving cameras, it can place another cash order through your toll-free order number. With your next-day delivery fulfillment, its inventory will never be depleted. Rudy's can get the cameras it wants now and can replace its inventory almost overnight. Credit Manager Kahn tells you that your company generally reveals to credit applicants the name of the credit-reporting service it used and encourages them to investigate their credit record.

Your Task. Write an email credit refusal to Ron Kasbekar, Rudy's Camera Shop, 316 Lucas Drive, Victoria, BC V8N 1H6, rkaskebar@rudys.ca. Add any information needed.

7.8 REFUSING A CLAIM: EVICTING A NOISY NEIGHBOUR (OBJ. 4)

As Robert Hsu, you must deny the request of Arman Aryai, one of the tenants in your three-storey office building. Mr. Aryai, a chartered accountant, demands that you immediately evict a neighbouring tenant who plays loud music throughout the day, interfering with Mr. Aryai's concentration and his conversations with clients. The noisy tenant, Bryant Haperot, seems to operate an entertainment booking agency and spends long hours in his office.

You know you can't evict Mr. Haperot immediately because of his lease. Moreover, you hesitate to do anything drastic because paying tenants are hard to find. You called your lawyer, and he said that the first thing you should do is talk to the noisy tenant or write him a letter asking him to tone it down. If this doesn't work within 30 days, you could begin the eviction process.

Your Task. Decide on a course of action. Because Mr. Aryai doesn't seem to answer his telephone, you must write to him. You need a permanent record of this decision anyway. Write to Arman Aryai, CA, Suite 203, Pico Building, 1405 Bower Boulevard, Vancouver, BC V6L 1Y3 or aryai@aplusaccountants.ca. Deny his request, but tell him how you plan to resolve the problem.

7.9 CUSTOMER BAD NEWS: SORRY—SMOKERS MUST PAY (OBJ. 4)

Recently, the Century Park Hotel embarked on a two-year plan to provide enhanced value and improved product quality to its guests. It always strives to exceed guest expectations. As part of this effort, Century Park has been refurbishing many rooms with updated finishes. The new carpet, paint, upholstery, and draperies, however, absorb the heavy odour of cigarette smoke. To protect the hotel's investment, Century Park enforces a strict non-smoking policy for selected rooms.

Century Park makes sure that guests know about its policy regarding smoking in non-smoking rooms. It posts a notice in each designated room, and it gives guests a handout from the manager detailing its policy and the consequences for smoking. The handout clearly says, "Should a guest opt to disregard our non-smoking policy, we will process a fee of $150 to the guest's account." For those guests who prefer to smoke, a smoking accommodation can be provided.

On May 10 Wilson M. Weber was a guest in the hotel. He stayed in a room clearly marked "non-smoking." After he left, the room cleaners reported that the room smelled of smoke. According to hotel policy, a charge of $150 was processed to Mr. Weber's credit card. Mr. Weber has written to demand that the $150 charge be removed. He doesn't deny that he smoked in the room. He just thinks that he should not have to pay.

Your Task. As hotel manager, deny Mr. Weber's claim. You would certainly like to see Mr. Weber return as a Century Park guest, but you cannot budge on your non-smoking policy. Address your response to Mr. Wilson M. Weber, 634 Wetmore Avenue, Saskatoon, SK M5A 3G8.

7.10 CREDIT REFUSAL: CASH ONLY AT GOODLIFE FITNESS CLUBS (OBJ. 4)

As manager of the Moncton GoodLife Fitness Club, you must refuse the application of Monique Cooper for an Extended Membership. This is strictly a business decision. You liked Ms. Cooper very much when she applied, and she seems genuinely interested in fitness and a healthful lifestyle. However, your Extended Membership plan qualifies the member for all your testing, exercise, recreation, yoga, and aerobics programs. This multi service program is expensive for the club to maintain because of the huge staff required. Applicants must have a solid credit rating to join. To your disappointment, you learned that Ms. Cooper's credit rating is decidedly negative. Her credit report indicates that she is delinquent in payments to four businesses, including Pros Athletic Club, your principal competitor.

You do have other programs, including your Drop In and Work Out plan, which offers the use of available facilities on a cash basis. This plan enables a member to reserve space on the racquetball and handball courts. The member can also sign up for yoga and exercise classes, space permitting. Because Ms. Cooper is far in debt, you would feel guilty allowing her to plunge in any more deeply.

Your Task. Refuse Monique Cooper's credit application, but encourage her cash business. Suggest that she make an inquiry to the credit-reporting company Experian to learn about her credit report. She is eligible to receive a $10 credit report if she mentions this application.

Write to Monique Cooper, 303 Magnetic Boulevard, Moncton, NB E1A 4B8 or mcooper@mymail.ca.

7.11 CUSTOMER CRITICISM: SOCIAL MEDIA FORCES CHOCOLATE SHOP TO CHANGE SUPPLIERS (OBJS. 1–4)

For over 50 years, Lisson's has been one of Canada's most trusted retail brands. Lisson's sells chocolates and ice cream, as well as other sweets, in over 75 mall and other retail locations across the country.

Besides the regular marketing presence of in-store signage and design, Lisson's has had a social media presence for almost ten years, including a Twitter feed, a Facebook page, a YouTube channel, and an Instagram account. Kelly Ann Kallender is the social media manager at Lisson's headquarters in Halifax, Nova Scotia. From head office, she not only uploads material onto the various Lisson's social media accounts, but also monitors what's being said, written, and photographed about Lisson's on other social media accounts.

One morning Ms. Kallender arrives at her office and listens to a frustrated voice mail from the company's CEO, Rich Klein. Mr. Klein asks Ms. Kallender whether she's heard about the Facebook page "Lisson's Loves Palm Oil." Apparently the page has over 250,000 likes, and a local TV station has called Mr. Klein and asked him to comment on-camera about the page. Like earlier protests against food industry giants like Nestlé and Unilever, the new anti-Lisson's Facebook page claims that the company is buying palm oil for its products from producers who are damaging the environment and animal life. Mr. Klein tells Ms. Kallender that it's true that a small amount of the palm oil (about 15,000 litres out of 100,000 total litres) bought by Lisson's is coming from an "untrustworthy" supply chain, but the majority is from regulated, sustainability-approved sources.

Your Task. On behalf of Lisson's, craft a social media and media relations strategy—that is, what will you say on social media and to television and newspaper outlets—about the palm oil controversy. CEO Klein says it will take a while to get out of the untrustworthy palm oil contract.

7.12 EMPLOYEE BAD NEWS: STRIKEOUT FOR EXPANDED OFFICE TEAMS (OBJ. 5)

Assume you are Walter Cervello, vice president of operations at Copiers Plus, 508 West Inverary Road, Kingston, ON K2G 1V8. Recently several of your employees requested that their spouses or friends be allowed to participate in Copiers Plus's intramural sports teams. Although the teams play only once a week during the season, these employees claim that they can't afford more time away from friends and family. Over 100 employees currently participate in the eight coed volleyball and softball teams, which are open to company employees only. The teams were designed to improve employee friendships and to give employees a regular occasion to have fun together.

If non-employees were to participate, you're afraid that employee interaction would be limited. And while some team members might have fun if spouses or friends were included, you're not so sure all employees would enjoy it. You're not interested in turning intramural sports into date night. Furthermore, the company would have to create additional teams if many non-employees joined, and you don't want the administrative or equipment costs of more teams. Adding teams would also require changes to team rosters and game schedules, which could be a problem for some employees. You do understand the need for social time with friends and families, but guests are welcome as spectators at all intramural games. Besides, the company already sponsors a family holiday party and an annual company picnic.

Your Task. Write an email or hard-copy memo to the staff denying the request of several employees to include non-employees on Copiers Plus's intramural sports teams.

7.13 EMPLOYEE BAD NEWS: REFUSING HOLIDAY SEASON EVENT (OBJ. 5)

In the past your office has always sponsored a holiday season party at a nice restaurant. As your company has undergone considerable downsizing and budget cuts during the past year, you know that no money is available for holiday entertaining.

Your Task. As executive vice president, send an email to Dina Gillian, office manager. Ms. Gillian asked permission to make restaurant reservations for this year's holiday party. Refuse Ms. Gillian, but offer some alternatives. How about a potluck dinner?

7.14 CUSTOMER BAD NEWS: IMAGE CONSULTANT PLAYS BAD GUY (OBJ. 4)

As the owner of Polished Pro Image Consultants, you hate the part of your job that requires you every so often to write collection letters. Your work is all about making people look good, so when they don't pay their bills, it's difficult for you to get in touch with them—it's as if nothing you taught them has sunk in. Still, as a small business owner, you cannot afford a collections clerk, and you dread the cost of hiring a third-party collection agency to take care of your outstanding accounts. Recently, you provided extensive consulting services to David M. Fryer, a local businessperson who will be running in the next election to be the local Member of Parliament. You billed Mr. Fryer for 18 hours at $100 per hour for in-person consulting, plus another 10 hours at $50 per hour for telephone consulting. In total your invoice dated May 14, 2014, amounted to $2,300 plus HST. A reminder email you sent to Mr. Fryer on June 30 went unanswered, and you've decided now that August has arrived, it's time to act. The only thing holding you back is that Mr. Fryer is prominent in your community, and while you definitely want your invoice paid, you're not sure you want to get on his bad side.

Your Task. Write a collection letter to Mr. David M. Fryer, President, Hexago Plastics, 230 Queen St., Saint John, NB E3K 4N6.

7.15 EMPLOYEE BAD NEWS: THE WORST PUBLICITY EVER (OBJ. 5)

Sometimes relaying negative news using new communications technology can turn into a public relations disaster. A case in the United States demonstrates just how bad things can become.

Your Task. Do two sets of secondary research: first, type the phrase *email termination radio shack* into an Internet search engine such as Google. How many articles about the infamous Radio Shack "firing by email" situation can you find? Next, type the same phrase into an online research database in your college or university library. How many articles can you find now? Develop a three-slide PowerPoint presentation in which you offer (a) a short explanation of what happened, (b) a short explanation of the difference in tone between the articles you found via the Internet and those you found via the research database, and (c) a suggestion to Radio Shack and other employers about a better channel and message they can use when delivering negative messages such as the one in this case.

7.16 ANNOUNCING BAD NEWS TO CUSTOMERS (OBJS. 3, 4)

You are the owner of Miss Twinkle's Treats, a small bakery in London, Ontario. The delicious cakes, squares, cookies, and breads that Miss Twinkle's is known for are made from scratch daily at your location on the outskirts of the city. Although you operate a small storefront, most of your business comes from supplying local restaurants and coffee shops with your tantalizing treats. You own a small truck that is used to deliver orders to your customers throughout the London area. Although Miss Twinkle's is financially successful, rising costs have severely undercut your profits over the past few months. You know that you are not the only business owner dealing with rising prices—many of your suppliers have raised their prices over the last year. Specifically, the higher price of wheat and sugar has resulted in a drastic increase in your production costs. Previously, you did not charge for deliveries made to your wholesale clients. However, you now feel that you have no choice but to add a delivery charge to each order to cover your increased costs and the rising price of gas.

Your Task. As the owner of Miss Twinkle's Treats, write a letter to your clients in which you announce a $20 charge per delivery. See if you can come up with an offer or special to placate your customers. Use the indirect writing strategy and explain your reasons for introducing the charge.

7.17 EMPLOYEE BAD NEWS: REFUSING THE USE OF GOOGLE DOCS ON THE JOB (OBJ. 5)

As the vice president of the Green Group, an environmental firm, you've had a request from team leader Emily Tsonga. She wants to know whether her team can use Google Docs on the job. Ms. Tsonga is working on the plans for an environmentally friendly shopping centre, Westbury Mall. Her team project is moving ahead on schedule, and you have had excellent feedback from the shopping centre developers.

Ms. Tsonga's team is probably already using Google Docs through public systems, and this worries you. You are concerned about security, viruses, and wasted time. However, the company has been considering a secured enterprise-level collaboration software. The principal drawbacks are that such a system is expensive, requires administration, and limits use to organizational contacts only. You are not sure your company will ever adopt such a system.

You will have to refuse Ms. Tsonga's request, but you want her to know how much you value her excellent work on developing sustainability and green building techniques for the Westbury Mall project. You know you cannot get by with a quick refusal. You must give her solid reasons for rejecting her request.

Your Task. Send an email to Emily Tsonga at etsonga@greengroup.ca refusing her request. To help your message sound authoritative, do some research using the search term *collaboration software risk* to find out what issues exist with the use of this type of software.

7.18 COMPANY CRISIS: RESULTING COMMUNICATIONS (OBJS. 3, 4)

Companies regularly face various crises. These are dramatic situations in which business doesn't run as usual, in fact, it takes a complete turn for the worst. As a result, a crisis communication strategy has to be set in motion, with various messages sent to various stakeholders. These messages can include emails, social media posts, blog posts, traditional letters and memos, as well as press releases and articles for news media. Messages will also include oral communication: interviews with media, podcasts, and phone calls.

Your Task. Imagine you work on the corporate communications team at Headwaters Insurance. This large national company, with offices in London, Ontario, as well as Winnipeg and Halifax, has recently weathered a number of crises (explained next). For each crisis detail what the crisis communication plan should look like and produce at least one written message per crisis, using an indirect strategy.

a. *Financial crisis*: Headwaters experiences five consecutive quarters in a row in which it doesn't meet its financial targets, its stock price tumbles, and its debt level rises.

b. *Technology crisis*: Headwaters experiences a tornado-induced power outage at its London, Ontario, headquarters resulting in no Internet, no email, no social media, etc. for 48 hours. Thousands of insurance claims across the country go unprocessed.

c. *Natural crisis*: The tornado that hits the London, Ontario, Headwaters headquarters causes flooding, fire, and at least $45 million in damage. Work for its 1,500 head-office employees is disrupted for at least three weeks.

d. *Labour crisis*: The 375 customer service representatives at Headwaters' call centre bases in Manila, Philippines, go on strike. The strike has lasted over seven days and clients find the "chat" function on the Headwaters website is overwhelmed. There's no way for clients to reach Headwaters.

◤ WRITING IMPROVEMENT EXERCISES

USE PASSIVE-VOICE VERBS (OBJ. 3)

Passive-voice verbs may be preferable in breaking bad news because they enable you to emphasize actions rather than personalities. Compare these two refusals:

Active voice: I cannot authorize you to take three weeks of vacation in July.

Passive voice: Three weeks of vacation in July can't be authorized.

Your Task. Revise the following refusals so they use passive-voice instead of active-voice verbs.

1. We do not allow used merchandise to be returned or exchanged.

2. Managers may not advertise any job openings until those positions have first been posted internally.

3. Your car rental insurance does not cover large SUVs.

4. We cannot meet the sales income projected for the fourth quarter.

5. Titan Insurance Company will not process any claim not accompanied by documented proof showing that a physician treated the injuries.

SUBORDINATE NEGATIVE NEWS (OBJ. 3)

Your Task. Revise the following sentences to position the bad news in a subordinate clause. (Hint: Subordinate clauses often begin with *Although*.) Use passive-voice verbs for the bad news.

1. A shipping strike makes it impossible for us to ship your complete order at this time. However, we are able to send two corner workstations now, and you should receive them within five days.

2. We were forced to stop taking orders for flowers the week before Mother's Day. To make up for this disappointment, we apologize and ask you to try again with free shipping for the next week.

3. We now offer all of our catalogue choices at our website, which is always current. We are sorry that we no longer mail print catalogues. Our sustainability goals made it impossible for us to continue doing that.

4. We appreciate your interest in our organization, but we're unable to make an employment offer to you at this time.

5. The shipment of your last order was late for a reason. We had some really large orders that had to be filled ahead of yours that tied up our facilities. After that tie-up, we realized we had to improve our shipping process. Your next order will arrive within a week. That's a promise.

IMPLY THE NEGATIVE NEWS (OBJ. 3)

Your Task. Revise the following statements to *imply* the negative news. If possible, use passive-voice verbs and subordinate clauses to further de-emphasize the news.

Direct refusal: We cannot send you a price list, nor can we sell our lawn mowers directly to customers. We sell only through authorized dealers, and your dealer is HomeCo.

Implied refusal: Our lawn mowers are sold only through authorized dealers, and your dealer is HomeCo.

1. Unfortunately, we find it impossible to contribute to your excellent and worthwhile fund-raising campaign this year. At present all the funds of our organization are needed to lease equipment and offices for our new branch in Winnipeg. We hope to be able to support this commendable endeavour in the future.

2. We cannot ship our fresh fruit baskets c.o.d. Your order was not accompanied by payment, so we are not shipping it. We have it ready, though, and will rush it to its destination as soon as you call us with your credit card number.

3. Because of the holiday period, all our billboard space was used this month. Therefore, we are sorry to say that we couldn't give your charitable group free display space. However, next month, after the holidays, we hope to display your message as we promised.

▲ GRAMMAR/MECHANICS CHALLENGE 7

COMMAS 3

Review the Grammar/Mechanics Handbook Sections 2.10–2.15. Then study each of the following statements and decide where to insert necessary commas. In the space provided, write the number of commas you added; write *0* if no commas were needed. Also record the number of the G/M principle(s) illustrated. When you finish, compare your responses with those provided near the end of the book. If your responses differ, study carefully the principles shown in parentheses.

<u>2 (2.12)</u> **Example** It was the manager, not the president, who signed the cheque.

_____ 1. "A business that makes nothing but money" said Arlene Dickinson, "is a poor business."

_____ 2. We are required, at this time, to inspect all orders and confirm delivery dates.

_____ 3. We interviewed Shawna Patterson on June 2 didn't we?

_____ 4. Research shows that talking on a cell phone distracts drivers, and quadruples their chances of getting into accidents, such as rear-ending a car ahead of them.

_____ 5. The bigger the monitor the clearer the picture.

_____ 6. As you may already know information chips are encoded in the visas of people who need them for work, travel, or study in Canada.

_____ 7. We think, however, that the new passports will be issued only to diplomats, and other government employees beginning in August.

_____ 8. A widely discussed study of productivity, that was conducted by authoritative researchers, revealed that workers in Canada are slightly less productive than workers in Europe or Japan.

_____ 9. Canada's productivity deficits which were discussed in the report related to R&D and technology investment and spending.

_____ 10. As a matter of fact, the report said that Canada's productivity deficits resulted from bureaucratic, heavy-handed government oversight.

◣ EDITING CHALLENGE 7

To fine-tune your grammar and mechanics skills, in every chapter you will be editing a message. This price-increase message suffers from lapses in proofreading, spelling, grammar, punctuation, and other writing problems that require correction. Study the guidelines in the Grammar/Mechanics Handbook, as well as the lists of Confusing Words and Frequently Misspelled Words, to sharpen your skills.

Your Task. Edit the following message by correcting errors (a) in your textbook or (b) on a photocopy using proofreading marks from Appendix B.

ConnexCable The Nation's Largest Cable TV Producer
November 14, 2021
Mrs. Conchetta Stacko
467 17 Ave SW,
Calgary, AB, T3A 4B6

Dear Mr. Stacko:

As the nations leading producer of cable entertainment ConnexCable have been working continuous to bring you the highest-quality programming and cable features. Because many next generation technology features are available at this point in time we are investing in them to make sure of the fact that you have more programming choices and improvments in customer service.

Some of the recent improvements include a main dashboard layed out in a tile format. This will give you direct access to recorded and bookmarked shows as well as access to Facebook, Pandora and additional online media. Other improvements include voice commands on your remote control so that you can search with verbal commands for shows, movies, and Web videos based on title, topic, or actors. Our new system is four times faster then the current model and uses less energy then other cable boxs.

However these improvements, when combined with the rising costs of doing business and escalating programming charges has increased our operating budget. Although we are forced to make price adjustments in selected packages many adjustments are small and the cost of some programs in actuality really declines.

If you receive the Basic Cable package you wont see a price increase. Depending on where you live that package will remain at the price of $23 to $28 per month. If you receive the Digital Economy package you will see a rate decline, depending on you're package this decline will range from eight cents to ten dollars per month.

A complete schedule showing rate adjustments are enclosed. Although the cost of some packages are increasing you are receiving the best in voice, video and data transmission. Its a exceptional entertainment value and we are planning even more innovations for future programming. We appreciate you loyalty and we promise to continue to bring you the best in service and entertainment.

Sincerely,
Colson Bryant, President
Enclosure

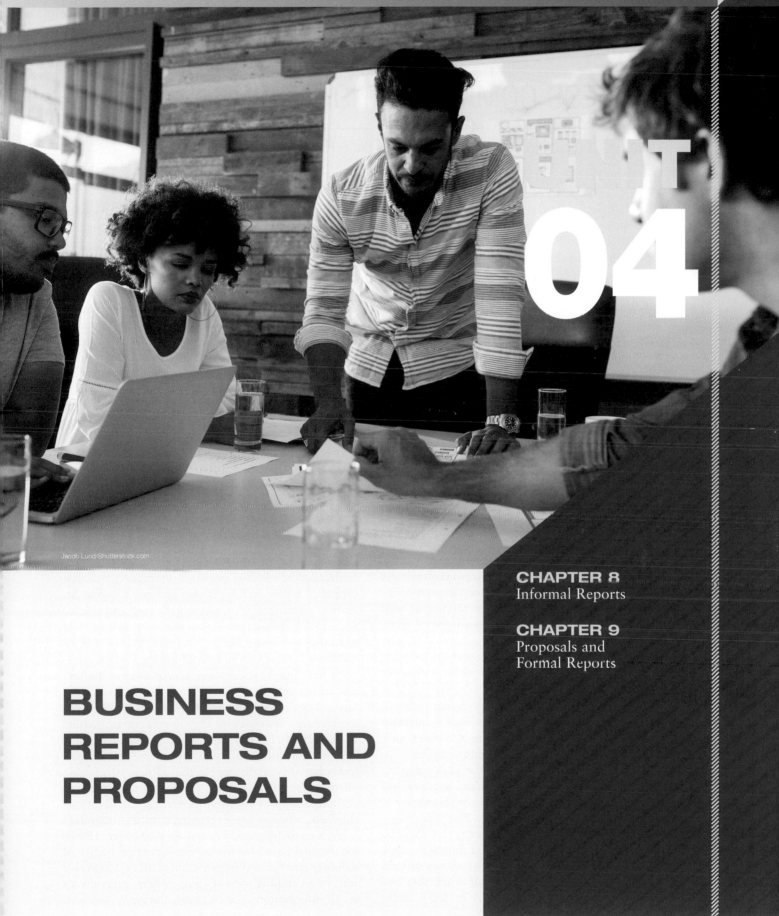

Jacob Lund/Shutterstock.com

UNIT
04

BUSINESS REPORTS AND PROPOSALS

BUSINESS COMMUNICATION RESEARCH UPDATE

Recreating the Scene: An Investigation of Police Report Writing.

Han Yu and Natalie Monas. (2020). Journal of Technical Writing and Communication, 50(1), 35–55.

Abstract: Police officers do a significant amount of high-stake writing in police reports, but report writing is given little attention in policy academies, and prevailing guidelines treat the task as a mechanical process of recording facts. As a result, officers are ill-prepared for this essential and inherently complex task. In this study, we interviewed officers to study what makes for a good police report. Our findings reveal that police reports are goal-directed genre actions. This understanding peers through the positivist emphasis on factual details to emphasize the social function of police reports in the criminal justice system. . . .

INTRODUCTION

Every police call involves paperwork. Generally referred to as police reports, this paperwork contains requisite forms as well as a narrative that describes the actions of the citizens involved, the actions of the officers involved, and various other information pertaining to the call. Because police calls are varied and involve a multitude of situations, so must police reports reflect those situations: from fender bender reports to fatality accident reports, from theft reports to burglary and robbery reports, from domestic violence reports to assault and battery reports, as well as death investigation, homicide, and use of force reports.

Being able to write successful reports is in many ways essential to officers' ability to perform their job and perform it well. In noncriminal cases such as an attempted suicide, writing a report that properly documents the mind-set of the individual in question and explains what protective action an officer took (or did not take) has important liability implications. In criminal cases, reports enable the police department and the court to use the officers' account and testimony to prosecute crimes (Beehr, Ivanitskaya, Glaser, Erofeev, & Canali, 2004). The report acts as a stand-in for the officer, allowing the court to discern what the officer experienced during the call. Reports are also a memory aid that allows officers to remember the specifics of a call when they are asked to testify in court, sometimes weeks, months, or years later. Last, reports serve as a way for police agencies to evaluate officers' work and ensure that officers appropriately handle calls by following agencies' standard operating procedure.

Given the importance of police report writing and its training reality, in this article, we interview police officers to study their experiences and perceptions of report writing. Our goal is to examine what makes police report writing challenging, what constitutes a successful police report, and subsequently, what knowledge and training may best prepare officers for report writing. This study not only sheds light on police report writing, it enriches technical communication literature. As a type of workplace writing that addresses complex situations, actions, and stakeholders, police reports are a uniquely important form of technical communication. Currently, they are missing from technical communication literature. Studying the ways these reports are conceived, composed, and taught contributes to our existing knowledge base. . . .

CURRENT LITERATURE ON POLICE WRITING

Reflecting the minimal emphasis on training, research on police report writing is also lacking. Existing literature prioritizes information gathering and studies such processes as interviews and note taking. For example, Milne and Bull (2006) state that during an interview, officers should avoid asking leading questions that "imply the answer and/or assume matters not earlier revealed" (p. 19). Similarly, officers are advised against asking yes/no questions to avoid the interviewees acquiesce to the officers' desire (Milne & Bull, 2006). Instead, officers are encouraged to ask open-ended questions, questions that "are worded in such a way as to enable the witness to provide an unrestricted response" (ABE, quoted in Milne & Bull, 2006). In addition to heeding the questions they ask, officers are encouraged to use cognitive interviews (Köhnken, Thürer, & Zoberbier, 1994). Established based on the psychological principles of memory storage and information retrieval, cognitive interviews employ memory aids to help interviewees recall information. For example, during a cognitive interview, interviewees are asked to mentally "reconstruct the context of the witnessed event, to form an image or impression of the environmental aspects of the scene, to remember their emotional feelings and their thoughts" (Köhnken et al., 1994, p. 15).

Contrasting with these studies is a lack of original research on the writing of police reports. When writing is discussed, it is mostly in terms of taken-for-granted guidelines, many of which assume that police report writing is a mechanical process of following rules or providing data according to checklists. Kanable (2005), for example, provides the following bulleted "pointers":

- Avoid jargon (police or technical) that a juror may not comprehend.
- Write in the first person.
- Use the active voice.
- Be as complete and detailed as possible.
- Use quotation marks to indicate what others have said. (p. 166) . . .

RESEARCH METHODS

To understand the various factors and knowledge that influence officers' report writing, we used open-ended, qualitative interviews. This research method allowed us to "capture how those being interviewed view their world, to learn their terminology and judgments, and to capture the complexities of their individual perceptions and experiences" (Patton, 2002, p. 348). In conducting the interviews, we used a list of prepared questions . . . ; at the same time, we remained flexible to ask follow-up questions.

Using a purposeful sampling method, we recruited typical case officers (Patton, 2002) who have different levels of experiences and are from different jurisdictions. We focused recruitment in one Midwestern state for practical reasons: given the sensitivity of police work, we anticipated difficulties in recruitment, so we leveraged one of the authors' prior contacts in police agencies in this area to recruit participants. As it turned out, this strategy was crucial. Wary of negative police coverage in the media, officers were generally suspicious of our study, especially since they were not familiar with the nature, intention, and publication venue of academic research. Despite this challenge, we were able to recruit six officers. . . .

Of the six interviews, one was conducted over the phone, two were face to face, and three were conducted using Skype. The length of the interviews ranged from 45 minutes to 75 minutes. This difference in length was, for the most part, caused by interviewees' varying levels of experiences. All interviewees answered all of the planned questions, and we made the same effort to ask follow-up questions, but because old-timers had more stories and experiences to draw upon, their interviews lasted longer. . . .

RESULTS AND DISCUSSION

Writing reports every day, often multiple ones (2–5) a day, interviewees all agreed that report writing is a huge part of their job, a bigger part than they thought it would be. The reports they write vary in length and complexity, ranging from one to a few pages and taking anywhere between 30 minutes to many hours to complete. All interviewees write criminal reports; Matt and Kathy also write informational reports such as responding to a broken water main. It is, however, apparent from the interviews that criminal reports are, by far, what is most important and challenging for these officers. In the following, we first report and discuss the challenges our interviewees encounter. We then propose, based on the interview findings, a genre-based approach to understanding police reports. Finally, we apply the genre approach to discuss how to enact effective police report writing and training. . . .

CHALLENGES IN WRITING POLICE REPORTS

All officers acknowledged that police report writing is challenging. Multiple factors complicate the task. Some are attributed to the officers themselves, but most are caused by external factors.

Time constraints. Time poses two constraints on police report writing. The first is the lag that can happen between the time an officer responds to a call and the time the officer sits down to report the call. Although officers can try to write in their patrol vehicles in between calls, that's not always possible. . . .

Lack of basic writing skills. Basic skills in punctuation, spelling, and sentence structuring are important in all professional writing. Their stakes are particularly high in police report writing. As our interviewees explained, crucial details can be misread if they are not properly punctuated or appear confusing due to grammatical errors. Even without comprehension issues, grammatical and spelling errors detract from an officer's professionalism and, by extension, their credibility in court.

"Messy" context. It probably goes without saying that police work can be "messy." To write a report for a call, officers may need to gather various details, take different evidence, and interview multiple

people—while trying to secure a scene, put victims at ease, or keep a watchful eye on an offender.

Stress. Police work is stressful because it deals with emotional and high-stake issues involving human lives and criminal offenses. That stress carries directly into report writing. As Kanable (2005) writes, "law enforcement writing is scrutinized more than most writing" (p. 168). . . .

POLICE REPORTS AS GENRE WITH GOAL-DIRECTED ACTION

At this juncture of our data analysis, it became clear that the concept of genre—even though our interviewees never used this term—is essential to understanding police reports. Genre has a significant influence on the teaching and research of workplace writing and technical communication. Many researchers adopt this concept to examine how the ideology of a social and discourse community shapes and is shaped by writing (Luzon, 2005). . . .

CONCLUSIONS AND IMPLICATIONS

Writing constitutes a significant part of police officers' work. Not only must officers write extensively, often under less-than-ideal logistic circumstances, their writing is of high stake. Understanding police reports via genre theories provides a useful way for officers to explicitly discuss and contemplate what makes report writing challenging, what makes for an effective report, and what their ethical and professional obligations are in writing reports. Rather than emphasizing facts and details to absolve human involvement and judgment, a genre approach openly admits reports' and, by extension, officers' goal-directed actions; gives officers the language to critically reflect on issues such as facts and opinions; and facilitates more effective and responsible report writing training.

To enact this genre-based training, police academies need to devote more time on report writing. Trainers, both in the academy and in the field, need to be trained to articulate their tacit knowledge in report writing. Rather than an isolated component, report writing training needs to be integrated into the teaching of the Constitution, the law, the criminal justice system, the elements of different crimes, and the day-to-day law enforcement activities. This training approach reflects the fact that police report writing is inherent in other aspects of police work and participates in constructing that work.

Genre-based training does not exclude mechanics or formal genre features such as using active voice and simple terminologies. But equally and more importantly, it frames the mechanics and formal features in terms of how they facilitate reports' social function. For example, issues in mechanics can create misunderstanding and detract from the credibility of an officer. Genre-based training, by emphasizing rather than hiding the rhetorical nature of police reports, highlights the crucial importance of ethics training in the police force. If reports are not truthful, then no amount of genre awareness will make them effective reports that serve the interests of the public, the criminal justice system, and, ultimately, the officers themselves.

Last, genre-based training embraces the fact that different police agencies may have different local requirements. As genre, police reports have typified commonalities but are also situated in the contexts of different crimes, police agencies, and local court systems. Genre-based training can build a strong foundation for officers to negotiate these different contexts and to transition from the academy to field work or from one work environment to another.

REFERENCES

Beehr, T. A., Ivanitskaya, L., Glaser, K., Erofeev, D., & Canali, K. (2004). Working in a violent environment: The accuracy of police officers' reports about shooting incidents. *Journal of Occupational and Organizational Psychology, 77*(2), 217–235.

Kanable, R. (September, 2005). Getting it write right: Convictions require good report writing. *Law Enforcement Technology,* 160–168.

Köhnken G., Thürer, C., & Zoberbier, D. (1994). The cognitive interview: Are the interviewers' memories enhanced, too? *Applied Cognitive Psychology, 8*(1), 13–24

Luzon, M. J. (2005). Genre analysis in technical communication. *IEEE Transactions on Professional Communication, 48*(3), 285–295.

Milne, B., & Bull, R. (2006). Interviewing victims of crime, including children and people with intellectual disabilities. In M. Kebbell & G. Davies (Eds.), *Practical psychology for forensic investigations and prosecutions* (pp. 7–23). Hoboken, NJ: John Wiley & Sons.

Patton, M. Q. (2002). *Qualitative research & evaluation methods* (3rd ed.). Thousand Oaks, CA: Sage

QUESTIONS

1. How does what you've learned in this article change your perception of business communication?

2. How might what you've learned in this article change your own communication style?

3. Come up with pro and con arguments for the following debate/discussion topic: Writing "event" reports—about trips, accidents, incidents, etc.—is difficult to do in a completely objective way, as the article shows. As a result, managers shouldn't expect complete objectivity from their employees.

INFORMAL REPORTS

> **BIZ COMM BYTE**
>
> Recent statistics from the Association of Workers' Compensation Boards of Canada show that in 2018 "lost time" claims due to illness, injury, and so on, are greatest in the health/social services and manufacturing sectors and lowest in the finance/insurance and fishing/trapping sectors. In Ontario lost time claims based on reported incidents have been rising each year since 2016, after almost ten years of annual decreases.
>
> Sources: Association of Workers' Compensation Boards of Canada. (2018). Lost time claims in Canada by industry. http://awcbc.org/?page_id=14; WSIB Ontario. (2020). Allowed claims and injury rates by injury/illness year. http://www.wsibstatistics.ca/S1/Claims%20_%20WSIB%20By%20The%20Numbers_P.php

8.1 The Function and Organization of Informal Reports

Good report writers are skilled at simplifying facts so that anyone can understand them. Collecting information and organizing it clearly and simply into meaningful reports are skills that all successful businesspeople today require. In this digital age of information, reports play a significant role in helping decision makers solve problems.

Because of their abundance and diversity, business reports are difficult to define. They may range in topic from an informal email trip report to an online-form report for a work compensation board detailing a work accident to a formal 200-page financial forecast. In terms of channel, reports may be presented orally in front of a group using PowerPoint or Infographics, whereas other reports are written and appear as emails, email attachments, online PDFs, template forms or lengthy, bound, book-like publications. Still others consist primarily of numerical data, such as tax reports or profit-and-loss statements.

Although reports vary in length, content, format, organization, channel of distribution, and level of formality, they all have one common purpose: they present well-organized data (and sometimes analysis/interpretation of data and recommendations based on analysis) so that decisions can be taken. Reports are informal if information included in them deals with routine or recurring events, or if decisions taken based on the report have a relatively low financial threshold. Decisions with large budgets attached usually come after a formal report has been researched and presented; you'll look at formal reports in Chapter 9.

8.1a Report Functions

Most reports can be classified into two functional categories: information reports and analytical reports.

INFORMATION REPORTS. Reports that present data without analysis or recommendations are primarily informational. Although writers collect and organize facts, they aren't expected to analyze the facts (i.e., say what the facts mean) for readers. A trip report describing an employee's visit to a conference, for example, simply presents information, though as we saw in the unit-opening research article, even the most objective of reports is going to include some level of unconscious bias. Other reports that present information without analysis could involve routine operations (e.g., an incident report in a fast-food restaurant), compliance with regulations (e.g., a status update on a new government regulation rollout in a bank), or company policies and procedures (e.g., a status update on employee reaction to enforcement of a new company policy in a manufacturing company).

ANALYTICAL REPORTS. Reports that provide analysis and conclusions as well as data are analytical. If requested, writers also supply recommendations. Analysis is the process of breaking down a problem into its parts to understand it better and solve it (e.g., each time you write an outline, as shown in Chapter 3, Figure 3.2, you are analyzing a problem). Analytical reports attempt to provide the insight necessary to persuade readers to act or change their opinions. For example, a recommendation report that compares several potential locations for an employee fitness club might recommend one site, but not until after it has analyzed and discussed the alternatives. This analysis should persuade readers to accept the writer's choice. Similarly, a feasibility report that analyzes the ability of a private chef school to open a satellite campus in a nearby city will either say *yes this can be done* or *no it can't*, but it will also discuss the alternative course of action.

8.1b Report Organization

Like the daily messages you studied in earlier chapters, reports can be organized using the direct or indirect method. The reader's expectations and the content of a report determine its pattern of development, as shown in Figure 8.1.

DIRECT STRATEGY. When the purpose for writing is presented close to the beginning, the organizational strategy is direct, as shown in Figure 8.1. Information reports are usually arranged directly. They open with an introduction, followed by the facts, which may be listed using headings for greater readability, and a summary.

Analytical reports may also be organized directly, especially when readers are supportive of or are familiar with the topic. Many busy executives prefer this pattern because it gives them the results of the report immediately. They don't have to spend time wading through the facts, findings, discussion, and analyses to get to the two items they are most interested in—the conclusions and recommendations. You should be aware, though, that unless readers are familiar with the topic, they may find the direct pattern confusing. Some readers prefer the indirect pattern because it seems logical and mirrors the way we solve problems.

Cengage

MINDTAP

In Mindtap go to the Whiteboard Animation for Chapter 8 and watch it now.

FIGURE 8.1 / Report Organization Based on Audience Analysis

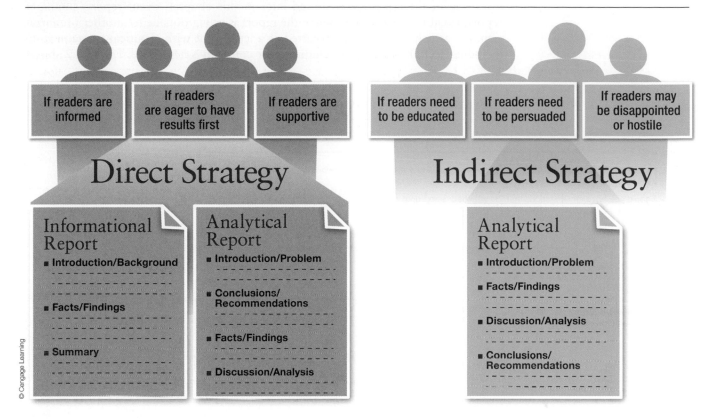

INDIRECT STRATEGY. Indirect-strategy reports, as shown in Figure 8.1, usually begin with an introduction or a description of the problem, followed by facts and interpretation from the writer. They end with conclusions and recommendations. This pattern is helpful when readers are unfamiliar with the problem. It is also useful when readers must be persuaded or when they may be disappointed in or hostile toward the report's findings. The writer is more likely to retain the reader's interest by first explaining, justifying, and analyzing the facts and then making recommendations. This pattern also seems most rational to readers because it follows the normal thought process: problem, alternatives (facts), solution.

8.2 Informal Formats and Headings

Because a report is by definition longer than a daily message, and because people's time is short these days, the design of a report needs to be visually appealing and professional-looking. The report should include a hierarchy of meaningful headings that highlight major points, allowing readers to see the flow of ideas. Some organizations use templates and reporting software to standardize the look of their reports.

8.2a Typical Report Channels

The decision about which channel to use to send your report is governed by the report's length, topic, audience, and purpose. After considering these elements, you'll probably choose from among the following five formats.

EMAIL REPORTS. In today's workplace informal reports are usually sent as emails. The report is either written in the body of the email (only if it's quite short), or more commonly it's attached to the email as a Word document, a PowerPoint deck, or a PDF version of Word or PowerPoint.

When the report is staying within your organization, the email attachment follows one of the report plans found later in this chapter: event report, summary report, feasibility report, etc. When the report is going outside to another organization, the attachment can be formatted as a letter (but with significant organization including section headings), including your company's letterhead. Figure 8.2 shows

▼ FIGURE 8.2 / Informal Report: Email and Letter Attachment

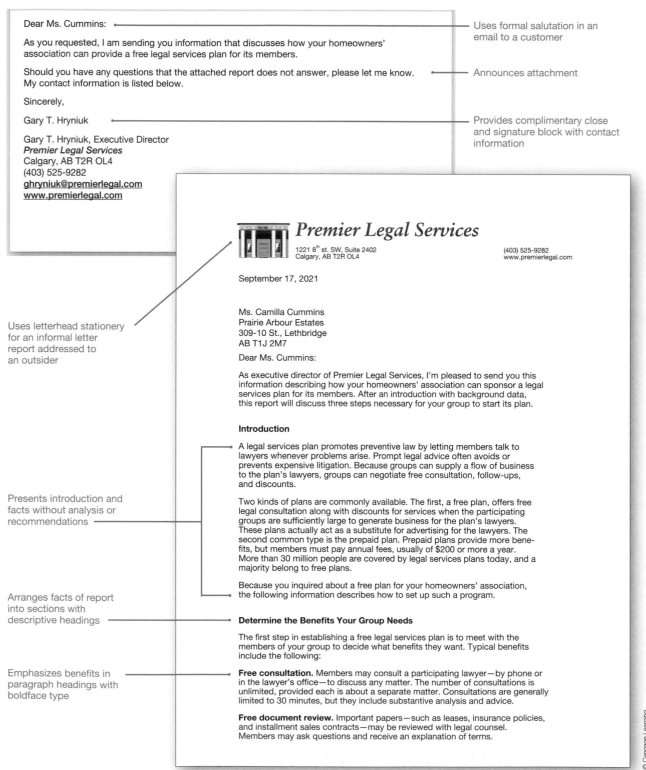

Dear Ms. Cummins: ●————————————————————— Uses formal salutation in an email to a customer

As you requested, I am sending you information that discusses how your homeowners' association can provide a free legal services plan for its members.

Should you have any questions that the attached report does not answer, please let me know. ●———— Announces attachment
My contact information is listed below.

Sincerely,

Gary T. Hryniuk ●————————————————————— Provides complimentary close and signature block with contact information

Gary T. Hryniuk, Executive Director
Premier Legal Services
Calgary, AB T2R OL4
(403) 525-9282
ghryniuk@premierlegal.com
www.premierlegal.com

Uses letterhead stationery for an informal letter report addressed to an outsider

Premier Legal Services

1221 8th st. SW, Suite 2402   (403) 525-9282
Calgary, AB T2R OL4   www.premierlegal.com

September 17, 2021

Ms. Camilla Cummins
Prairie Arbour Estates
309-10 St., Lethbridge
AB T1J 2M7

Dear Ms. Cummins:

As executive director of Premier Legal Services, I'm pleased to send you this information describing how your homeowners' association can sponsor a legal services plan for its members. After an introduction with background data, this report will discuss three steps necessary for your group to start its plan.

Introduction

Presents introduction and facts without analysis or recommendations

A legal services plan promotes preventive law by letting members talk to lawyers whenever problems arise. Prompt legal advice often avoids or prevents expensive litigation. Because groups can supply a flow of business to the plan's lawyers, groups can negotiate free consultation, follow-ups, and discounts.

Two kinds of plans are commonly available. The first, a free plan, offers free legal consultation along with discounts for services when the participating groups are sufficiently large to generate business for the plan's lawyers. These plans actually act as a substitute for advertising for the lawyers. The second common type is the prepaid plan. Prepaid plans provide more benefits, but members must pay annual fees, usually of $200 or more a year. More than 30 million people are covered by legal services plans today, and a majority belong to free plans.

Arranges facts of report into sections with descriptive headings

Because you inquired about a free plan for your homeowners' association, the following information describes how to set up such a program.

Determine the Benefits Your Group Needs

The first step in establishing a free legal services plan is to meet with the members of your group to decide what benefits they want. Typical benefits include the following:

Emphasizes benefits in paragraph headings with boldface type

Free consultation. Members may consult a participating lawyer—by phone or in the lawyer's office—to discuss any matter. The number of consultations is unlimited, provided each is about a separate matter. Consultations are generally limited to 30 minutes, but they include substantive analysis and advice.

Free document review. Important papers—such as leases, insurance policies, and installment sales contracts—may be reviewed with legal counsel. Members may ask questions and receive an explanation of terms.

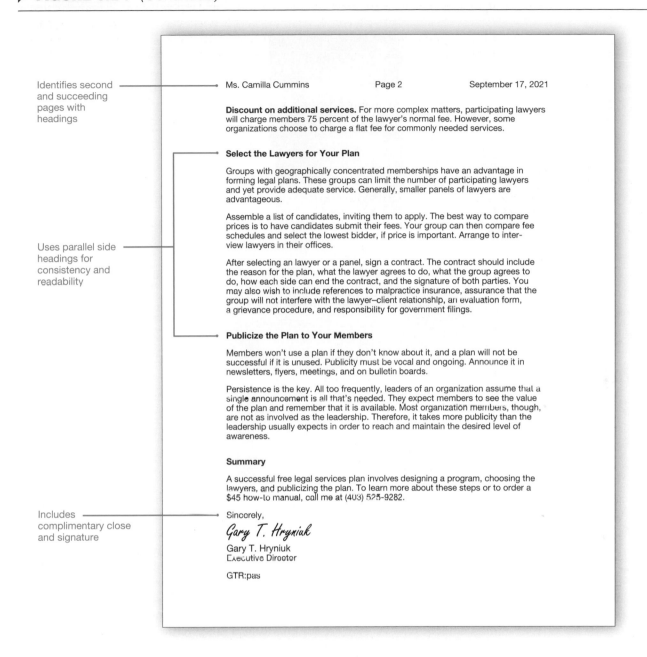

Identifies second and succeeding pages with headings

Uses parallel side headings for consistency and readability

Includes complimentary close and signature

Ms. Camilla Cummins   Page 2   September 17, 2021

Discount on additional services. For more complex matters, participating lawyers will charge members 75 percent of the lawyer's normal fee. However, some organizations choose to charge a flat fee for commonly needed services.

Select the Lawyers for Your Plan

Groups with geographically concentrated memberships have an advantage in forming legal plans. These groups can limit the number of participating lawyers and yet provide adequate service. Generally, smaller panels of lawyers are advantageous.

Assemble a list of candidates, inviting them to apply. The best way to compare prices is to have candidates submit their fees. Your group can then compare fee schedules and select the lowest bidder, if price is important. Arrange to inter- view lawyers in their offices.

After selecting an lawyer or a panel, sign a contract. The contract should include the reason for the plan, what the lawyer agrees to do, what the group agrees to do, how each side can end the contract, and the signature of both parties. You may also wish to include references to malpractice insurance, assurance that the group will not interfere with the lawyer–client relationship, an evaluation form, a grievance procedure, and responsibility for government filings.

Publicize the Plan to Your Members

Members won't use a plan if they don't know about it, and a plan will not be successful if it is unused. Publicity must be vocal and ongoing. Announce it in newsletters, flyers, meetings, and on bulletin boards.

Persistence is the key. All too frequently, leaders of an organization assume that a single announcement is all that's needed. They expect members to see the value of the plan and remember that it is available. Most organization members, though, are not as involved as the leadership. Therefore, it takes more publicity than the leadership usually expects in order to reach and maintain the desired level of awareness.

Summary

A successful free legal services plan involves designing a program, choosing the lawyers, and publicizing the plan. To learn more about these steps or to order a $45 how-to manual, call me at (403) 525-9282.

Sincerely,

Gary T. Hryniuk

Gary T. Hryniuk
Executive Director

GTR:pas

such a letter attachment report going to an outside organization. Increasingly, busi- nesses encourage employees to upload reports to the company intranet or sharing software (e.g., Google Docs) or cloud-based storage, especially for team-based writing.

DIGITAL SLIDE DECKS. Because reports are often presented within companies to managers and other employees, it's become quite common today for informal reports to be created as slides in PowerPoint or another presentation software. During a presentation, the slides are used to help the presenter discuss the report. But often the report isn't even presented orally: the visual nature of slides has simply begun, in some sectors, to overtake the traditional black-and-white written report. Creators of such slide deck/slide doc reports can choose to email or otherwise dis- tribute the slides before the presentation or afterward. An example of an informal report in slide format is shown in Figure 8.3. Notice the mix of pictures and graphs, as well as areas of relatively heavy analysis in traditional paragraphs.

FIGURE 8.3 / Informal Report: Slide Deck

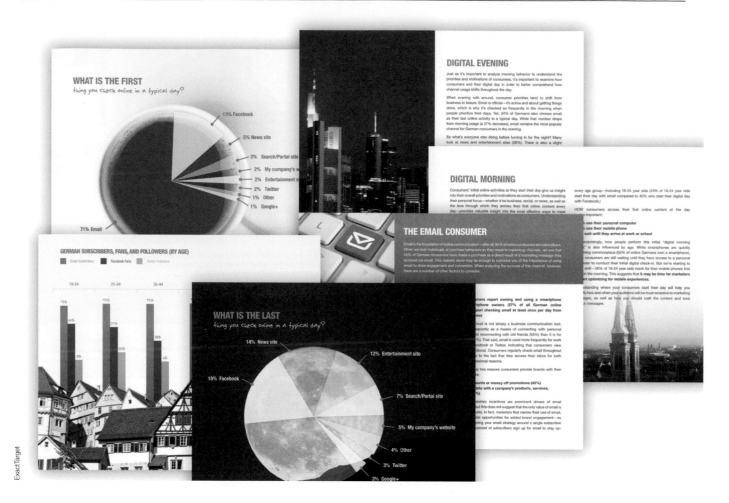

ExactTarget

INFOGRAPHICS. Infographics are visual representations of data or information. They're like a shortcut channel that displays complex information quickly and clearly, and in an easier to understand way than written text. Infographics are also affordable and easily shared on social media platforms. In fact, a good infographic can go viral when viewers embed and spread the word about it on their social media networks. Infographics can tell compelling stories that help all types of organizations attract and inform consumers. While they haven't yet taken over from traditional written reports or slide deck reports, they are starting to be a "nice to have" in certain industries. One issue with infographics is that their pictorial nature is sometimes seen as simplifying complex information too crudely—they shouldn't therefore be used in place of traditional reports that feature effective data and analysis. Figure 8.4 shows a sample infographic report from the Canadian government's Department of Agriculture.

TEMPLATES AND FORMS. Templates and forms (either company-produced or available online, for example, from Microsoft Word) are often used for regularly occurring situations, such as monthly sales reports, performance appraisals, merchandise inventories, expense claims, accident and incident reports, and personnel and financial reports. Standardized headings in these templates save time for the writer. Templates also make similar information easy to locate and ensure that all necessary information is provided.

BOUND AND PUBLISHED. For longer, more formal reports that are often created by government departments or by very large private-sector companies like banks, the writer uses a publishing format. Such reports look like books: they are bound with glue (or staples or coil binding), begin with a title followed by systematically

FIGURE 8.4 / Informal Report: Infographic

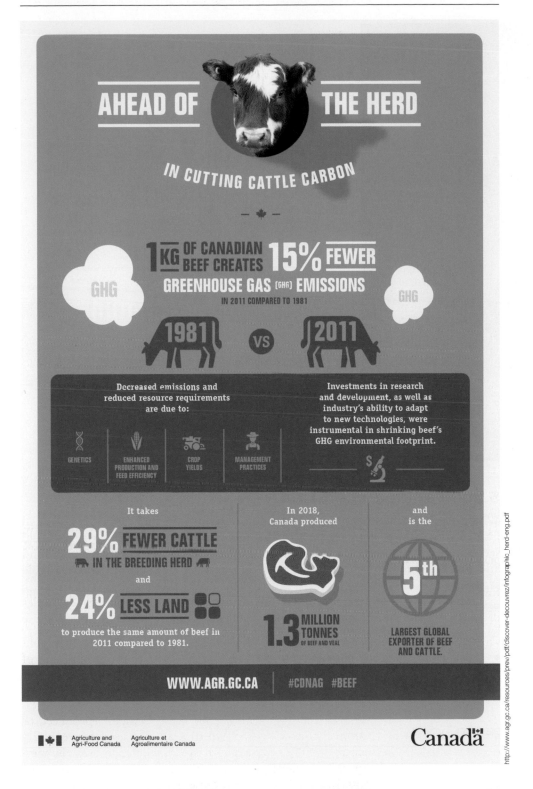

http://www.agr.gc.ca/resources/prev/pdf/discover-decouvrez/infographic_herd-eng.pdf

displayed headings and subheadings. A common time when a company uses the bound/published channel is for its corporate annual report or its corporate social responsibility report to shareholders and the media, although even in this case many organizations are acting more sustainably by not printing reports, instead posting them as PDFs on their website. A sample bound and published report in online PDF format is shown in Figure 8.5. You'll see an example of a formal report using bound and published format in Chapter 9.

FIGURE 8.5 / Informal Report: Bound and Published/Online PDF

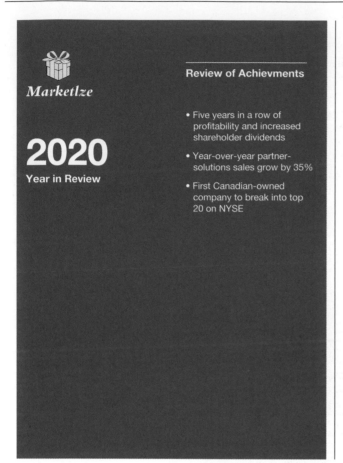

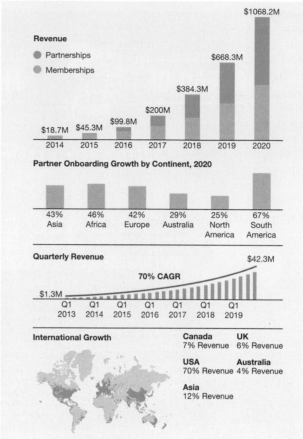

8.2b Effective Report Headings

Whatever channel you choose to communicate your informal report, it will need headings. Headings help readers understand the organization of a report and see major ideas at a glance. Also, headings provide resting points for the mind and the eye, breaking up large chunks of text into manageable and readable segments.

Report writers can use functional, talking, or combination headings, examples of which are shown in Figure 8.6. To create effective report headings, follow these basic guidelines:

- **Use a clear hierarchy of heading levels.** A hierarchy refers to the level of importance of the headings in a document. Some reports have one level of heading and others may have three. A heading's placement, size, and font should match those

FIGURE 8.6 / Report Heading Types

Functional Headings	Talking Headings	Combination Headings
• Background • Findings • Staffing • Production Costs	• Lack of Space and Cost Compound Parking Problems • Survey Shows Support for Parking Fees	• Introduction: Lack of Parking Reaches Crisis Proportions • Parking Recommendations: Shuttle and New Structures

© Cengage Learning

of the other headings in the same level. Writers can use varying font styles and sizes, but the hierarchy must be clear to the reader. Reports are easier to follow when they use three or fewer heading levels. Figure 8.7 shows the hierarchy of report heading levels.

- **Capitalize and emphasize carefully.** A writer can choose to use all capital letters for main titles, such as a report or chapter title. For first- and second-level headings, follow traditional rules for headings: capitalize the first letter of main words such as nouns, verbs, adjectives, adverbs, and so on. Don't capitalize articles (*a, an, the*), conjunctions (*and, but, or, nor*), and prepositions with three or fewer letters (*in, to, by, for*) unless they are the first or last words in the heading. Headings generally appear in bold font, as shown in Figure 8.7.
- **Create grammatically equal heading levels.** Create headings that are grammatically equal, or parallel, within the same level. For example, *Developing Product*

▛ FIGURE 8.7 / Report Heading Hierarchy

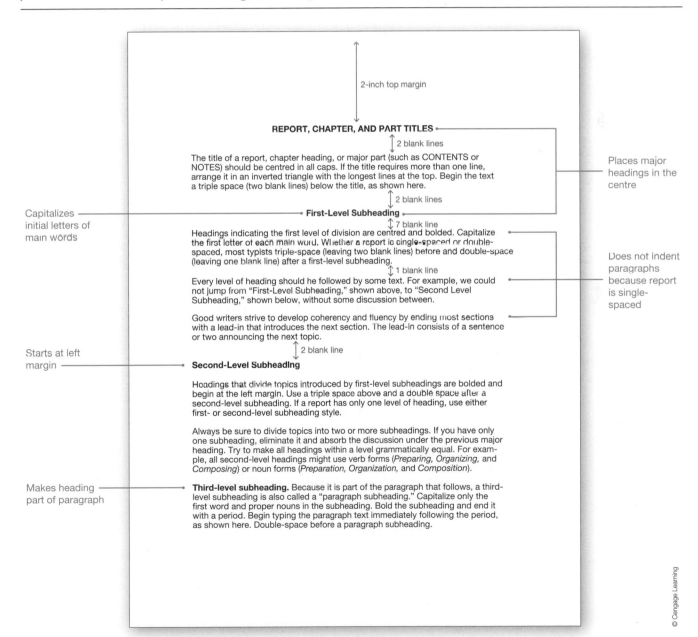

Teams and *Presenting Plan to Management* are parallel headings; they both begin with an action word ending in *-ing*. *Development of Product Teams* and *Presenting Plan to Management* are not parallel headings.

- **For short reports use one or two heading levels only.** In a short report, first-level headings might be bold and left-aligned; second-level headings might be bold paragraph headings.
- **Include at least one heading per report page, but don't end the page with a stand-alone heading.** Headings increase the readability and add visual appeal to report pages. Try to use at least one heading per page to break up blocks of text and reveal the content's topic. If a heading at the bottom of a page gets separated from the text that follows, move that heading to the top of the following page.
- **Punctuate correctly.** Stand-alone bold headings don't require end punctuation (i.e., a period). Paragraph headings, on the other hand, are followed by a period, which separates them from the text that follows.
- **Keep headings short but clear.** One-word headings are emphatic but not always clear. For example, the heading *Project* does not adequately describe the expectations of a summer internship project at an energy company. A better heading would be *(Company name)'s Internship Expectations*. Keep your headings brief (no more than eight words), but make them meaningful. Clarity is more important than brevity.

◣ 8.3 Determining the Problem and Purpose in Informal Reports

The following guidelines will help you plan your informal report and gather relevant data.

8.3a Problem and Purpose Statements

The first step in writing a report is figuring out the problem the report will address. Preparing a written problem statement helps clarify the task. Suppose a pharmaceutical company wants to investigate the problem of high transportation costs for its sales representatives. Some sales reps visit clients using company-leased cars; others drive their own cars and are reimbursed for expenses. The leasing agreements for 12 cars expire in three months. The company wants to investigate the transportation choices and report the findings before the leases are renewed. The following problem statement helps clarify the reason for the report:

> **Problem statement:** The leases on all company cars will expire in three months. We must decide whether to renew them or develop a new policy regarding transportation for sales reps. Expenses and reimbursement paperwork for employee-owned cars are excessive.

A statement of purpose defines the report's scope. To begin, develop questions that help clarify the purpose: Should the company compare the costs for buying and leasing cars? Should the company gather current data on reimbursement costs for those driving personal cars? Will the report writers evaluate the data and recommend a course of action? Should the sales reps' reactions be considered? Then write a statement of purpose that answers the questions:

> **Statement of purpose:** To recommend a plan that provides sales reps with cars. The report will compare costs for three plans: ownership, leasing, and compensation for employee-owned cars. Data will include the sales reps' reactions to each plan.

Preparing a written purpose statement is a good idea because it limits the scope and keeps the project on target. In writing purpose statements, choose action verbs that say what you intend to do: *analyze, choose, investigate, compare, justify, evaluate, explain,* and so on. Notice that the preceding purpose statement uses the action verbs *recommend* and *compare.*

Some reports require only a simple statement of purpose (e.g., to investigate expanded teller hours, to select a manager from among four candidates, to describe the position of accounts supervisor), whereas others require expanded purpose statements.

8.3b Gather Data

A professional report, even an informal one, is based on solid, accurate, verifiable facts found in primary and secondary research sources. Typical sources for informal reports include company records, observation, surveys, interviews, and secondary research from printed and digital sources like newspaper articles.

COMPANY RECORDS. Many business-related reports begin with an analysis of company files. From them you can observe past performance and methods used to solve previous problems. You can collect pertinent facts that will help determine a course of action. For example, if a telecommunications company is interested in revamping the design of the bills it sends to customers, the project manager assigned to this task would want to gather examples of previous bill designs to ensure that improvements are made and old designs aren't reused.

OBSERVATION. Another logical source of data for many problems lies in personal observation and experience. For example, if you were writing a report on the need for additional computer equipment, you might observe how much the current equipment is being used and for what purpose.

SURVEYS. Primary data from groups of people can be collected most efficiently and economically by conducting surveys. For example, if you were part of a committee investigating the success of a campus-wide recycling program, you might begin with a questionnaire on use of the program by students and faculty. You might also do some informal phoning or emailing to see if departments on campus know about the program and are using it.

INTERVIEWS. Talking with individuals directly concerned with the problem produces excellent primary information. For example, a food company adding a new low-fat organic bar to its nutrition bar line would solicit interview or focus-group feedback before releasing the new product to the market. Questions posed to people paid to taste the sample bar might include, "Did you find the bar tasty? Nutritious? Healthy?" and "Did you find the packaging attractive? Easy to open?"

SECONDARY RESEARCH. You'll probably be interested in finding examples from other organizations that shed light on the problem identified in your report. For example, an automobile parts manufacturer eager to drum up new business in the hybrid and electric vehicle market could do in-house research or pay for professional research into hybrid and electric vehicle manufacturing. Hundreds of articles on this topic are available electronically through library databases. Using search engines such as Google and Google Scholar will also yield hundreds of results on any topic.

When doing secondary research on the Internet, an extra step must be taken that isn't necessary when using library databases. You need to verify the accuracy of your sources. Because the Internet is a public space where anyone can post information, you should separate credible, useful information (e.g., from well-known sources like *The Globe and Mail* or *New York Times*) from opinion and noncredible sources.

WORKPLACE IN FOCUS

A type of reporting that's become increasingly, and unfortunately, frequent in Canadian workplaces is the incident, accident, or harassment report. In fact, *Canadian HR Reporter*, the trade publication that covers the human resources field in Canada, has published a number of articles in the past few years with titles like "Conducting Workplace Investigations" and "Never Too Busy for Investigations." In concert with law firm Hicks Morley, *Canadian HR Reporter* even offers a workplace investigation training seminar for employees who need to learn how to investigate and report on such incidents. One newsworthy incident in the Toronto area happened in 2016 when an employee of food producer Fiera Foods, Amina Diaby, was strangled when her headscarf got caught in the conveyor machine at which she was working. Cases like this are subject to internal and external reporting, first by the company's health and safety coordinator (usually an HR staffer) and then by the provincial or territorial Ministry of Labour, using forms like the one found in the image below. Fiera Foods eventually paid a fine that included a victim surcharge. *To what degree does the need to ensure profitability stand in the way of effective incident reporting in business, in your opinion and in your experience?*

Sources: Nathaniel Marshall. (2019, May 1). A quick guide for conducting workplace investigations. *Canadian HR Reporter*. https://www.hrreporter.com/employment-law/news/a-quick-guide-for-conducting-workplace-investigations/315946; Sara Mojtehedzadeh and Brendan Kennedy. (2018, April 9). This temp worker was being strangled by a machine. Her co-worker didn't know how to help. *Hamilton Spectator*. https://www.thespec.com/business/2018/04/09/this-temp-worker-was-being-strangled-by-a-machine-her-co-worker-didn-t-know-how-to-help.html; Worksafe BC. (2020). Employer incident investigation report (Form 52E40). https://www.worksafebc.com/en/resources/health-safety/forms/incident-investigation-report-form-52e40?lang=en

---

◥ 8.4 Writing Informal Informational Reports

Informational reports can describe periodic, recurring activities (such as monthly sales or weekly customer calls), as well as situational, nonrecurring events (such as accidents/incidents, conferences, and special projects). Short informational reports also include summaries of longer publications and of meetings.

Most informational reports have two things in common: they assume a neutral or receptive audience and they're written using a direct strategy. The readers of informational reports do not need to be persuaded; they simply need to be informed. Next we describe how to write four of the most common informal informational reports.

8.4a Event Reports

Employees sent on business trips to conventions and conferences typically submit reports to document the events they attended and what they learned. Employees who witness or are part of incidents or accidents at work typically submit reports (or participate in submission of reports) to document the incident or accident. Reports like these inform management, minimize risk, and maintain employee buy-in and morale.

When writing an event report, select the most relevant material and organize it coherently. For accident or incident reports, this usually means chronological sequencing (this happened, then that happened). For trip reports, it means a thematic focus (we learned about x, y, and z). The events or themes being discussed become the body of the report, and they're discussed as objectively as possible— without inserting your opinion or interpretation of the event. Then simply add an introduction and a closing, and your report is organized. Here is a general writing plan for event reports:

WRITING PLAN FOR AN EVENT REPORT

- **Opening:** Begin by identifying the event (name, date, and location) and preview briefly what happened.
- **Body:** Use a chronological or thematic organization strategy to explain the details of what took place. Try to maintain objectivity— that is, don't offer analysis or interpretation; keep to the facts.
- **Pleasant closing:** Be available to provide more information if requested.

Prakash Kohli was recently authorized to attend an IT conference in Germany. His boss, David Wong, asked Prakash to come back and explain what he learned from the experts. When he returns, Prakash writes the direct-strategy event report shown in Figure 8.8. He includes information that would most benefit the employees at Future Engine.

8.4b Progress and Status Reports

Continuing projects often require progress or status reports to describe what's been accomplished to date. When you or your team use project management principles, the report may be called a milestone report. Such reports may be external (telling customers how their projects are advancing) or internal (informing management of the status of activities). Here is a general writing plan for progress and status reports:

WRITING PLAN FOR A PROGRESS OR STATUS REPORT

- **Opening:** Begin by identifying the project, its purpose, and overall timeline.
- **Body:** Provide a summary of the work already completed; the work currently in progress (including personnel, methods, and obstacles and attempts to remedy obstacles); and a forecast of future activities still to be completed
- **Pleasant closing:** Be available to provide more information if requested.

In Figure 8.9 Avrom Gil explains progress on a market research project on the impact of a recent industry/consumer show. He begins with a statement summarizing the research project in relation to the expected completion date. He then updates the client with a brief summary of the project's progress. He emphasizes the

FIGURE 8.8 / Event Report

Hi, Dave! ●────────────────────────── Uses informal form of address

As you requested, I am sending you the attached trip report describing my amazing experiences
at the largest IT trade show in the world, the CeBIT. ●── Announces attachment

Thank you for the opportunity. I networked with a lot of people and had an enjoyable time. ●── Uses informal yet professional language

Cheers,
Prakash ●────────────────────────── Includes complimentary close and signature block

Prakash Kohli, Developer
Future Engine, Inc.
408.532.3434 Ext. 811
pkohli@future-engine.com
www.future-engine.com

FUTURE ENGINE, INC.
MEMORANDUM

Date: March 16, 2021

To: David Wong, IT Director

From: Prakash Kohli, Developer PK

Subject: Trip Report from the CeBIT Trade Show in Hannover, Germany

Identifies the event ──────

As you know, I attended the huge CeBIT computer show in Hannover on
March 4–9. CeBIT runs for six days and attracts almost 500,000 visitors from
Germany, Europe, and all over the world to the famed Hannover fairgrounds. It
features 27 halls full of technology and people. If you've been to Comdex Las
Vegas in the fall, think of a show that is easily five times larger. Let me describe
our booth, overall trends, and the contacts I made in Hannover.

Focuses on three main points ──────

Our Booth at the Fair

Our Future Engine booth spanned two floors. The ground floor had a theater
with large screen, demonstration stations, and partners showing their products
and services. Upstairs we had tables and chairs for business meetings, press
interviews, food, and drinks—along with a cooking area and a dishwasher.
Because no one has time to get food elsewhere, we ate in the booth.

Hot Tech Trends

Summarizes key information ──────

The top story at this year's CeBIT was Green IT. The expo management
decided to spotlight a range of topics dealing with Green IT, showcasing many
approaches in the Green IT Village in Hall 9. The main focus centered on highly
energy-efficient solutions and power-saving technologies and their contribution
to climate protection. *Green IT* is the big buzzword now and was even dubbed
the "Megatrend of this expo" by the organizer. Only the future will tell whether
Green IT will be able to spawn attractive new business areas.

Customers and Prospects

CeBIT is a fantastic way to connect with customers and prospects. Sometimes
it's a way of meeting people you only knew virtually. In this case, we had three
fans of our Internetpakt.com podcast visit us at the booth: Jürgen Schmidt, Karin
Richter, and Peter Jahn of MEGAFunk. All three came in our white FE T-Shirts,
which could only be rewarded with new black Internetpakt.com T-Shirts. All in
all, we made about 600 contacts and have 50 solid leads. The visit was definitely
worthwhile and will pay off very soon.

Highlights the value of the trip ──────

In closing, this was probably one of the best conference experiences I've ever
had. Customers and partners like FE; they are excited about our technology,
and they want more. Some know us because of our software solutions and were
surprised to learn that we sell hardware, too (this is a good sign). All want us to
grow and gain in influence.

Shows appreciation and mentions expenses ──────

Check out my CeBIT photo gallery on Flickr for some more impressions of our
booth at CeBIT with comments. Thank you for giving me the opportunity to
network and to experience one of the biggest trade shows in the business. My
itemized expenses and receipts are attached.

Tips for Trip Reports
- Use memo format for short informal reports sent within the organization.
- Identify the event (exact date, name, and location) and preview the topics to be discussed.
- Summarize in the body three to five main points that might benefit the reader.
- Itemize your expenses, if requested, on a separate sheet. Mention this in the report.
- Close by expressing appreciation, suggesting action to be taken, or synthesizing the value of the trip or event.

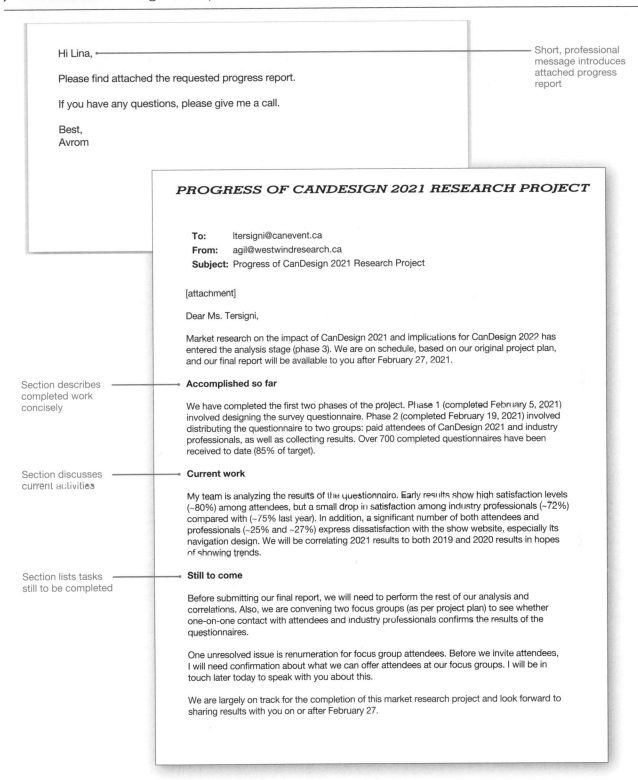

Hi Lina, ●————————————— Short, professional message introduces attached progress report

Please find attached the requested progress report.

If you have any questions, please give me a call.

Best,
Avrom

PROGRESS OF CANDESIGN 2021 RESEARCH PROJECT

To: ltersigni@canevent.ca
From: agil@westwindresearch.ca
Subject: Progress of CanDesign 2021 Research Project

[attachment]

Dear Ms. Tersigni,

Market research on the impact of CanDesign 2021 and implications for CanDesign 2022 has entered the analysis stage (phase 3). We are on schedule, based on our original project plan, and our final report will be available to you after February 27, 2021.

Accomplished so far

We have completed the first two phases of the project. Phase 1 (completed February 5, 2021) involved designing the survey questionnaire. Phase 2 (completed February 19, 2021) involved distributing the questionnaire to two groups: paid attendees of CanDesign 2021 and industry professionals, as well as collecting results. Over 700 completed questionnaires have been received to date (85% of target).

Current work

My team is analyzing the results of the questionnaire. Early results show high satisfaction levels (~80%) among attendees, but a small drop in satisfaction among industry professionals (~72%) compared with (~75% last year). In addition, a significant number of both attendees and professionals (~25% and ~27%) express dissatisfaction with the show website, especially its navigation design. We will be correlating 2021 results to both 2019 and 2020 results in hopes of showing trends.

Still to come

Before submitting our final report, we will need to perform the rest of our analysis and correlations. Also, we are convening two focus groups (as per project plan) to see whether one-on-one contact with attendees and industry professionals confirms the results of the questionnaires.

One unresolved issue is renumeration for focus group attendees. Before we invite attendees, I will need confirmation about what we can offer attendees at our focus groups. I will be in touch later today to speak with you about this.

We are largely on track for the completion of this market research project and look forward to sharing results with you on or after February 27.

Section describes completed work concisely

Section discusses current activities

Section lists tasks still to be completed

present status of the project and offers some preliminary data to build interest, then concludes by describing the next steps to be taken.

8.4c Minutes Reports

Minutes reports provide a summary of what happened in a meeting. Traditional minutes, illustrated in Figure 8.10, are written whenever a formal meeting has taken place. If you're the secretary or note taker of a meeting, you'll want to use the following writing plan to structure your report effectively:

WRITING PLAN FOR A MINUTES REPORT

- **Opening:** Begin by providing the name of the group, as well as the date, time, and place of the meeting. Also identify attendees and those absent, if necessary. If required, state what happened to previous minutes (e.g., accepted).
- **Body:** Make a note of all new business, announcements, and reports. Also include the precise wording of any motions (record the vote and action taken) and strong opinions.
- **Pleasant closing:** Conclude with the name and signature of the person recording the minutes (like a business memo, a minutes report doesn't have a polite signoff.)

FIGURE 8.10 / Minutes Report

Lor-Dan Produce Distribution
Safety Committee
Bi-annual Meeting Minutes
September 14, 2021

Present: A. Faccinelli, T. Loredan, M. Baransky, V. Singh

Absent: B. Fortier

Topics Discussed

1. Strategizing for our next Safe At Work inspection. Ministry of Labour officials will most probably be visiting the warehouse in early 2022 — we want to improve our scores. Should we hold a company-wide meeting, or rely on managers to filter down best practices within specific areas? Should we reach out to competitors who scored higher in 2019 to solicit advice?

2. Complying with Occupational Health and Safety Act provisions on Workplace Harrassment and Violence. We haven't drafted our policy yet, and are behind many of our competitors. Ministry of Labour regularly does blitz inspections looking for compliance in this area. Who should draft policy? Target dates? How do we make sure all Lor-Dan employees know and understand eventual policy?

Decisions

1. Hold company-wide meeting by November 1, 2021, to explain Safe at Work inspections and compliance. Reach out to two competitors by October 15, 2021, for advice on more successful compliance with Ministry inspections.

2. Harrassment and Violence policy should be drafted by subcommittee by October 15, 2021, for draft discussion at above meeting. Publish harassment and violence brochure and posters for distribution to employees and posting in warehouse.

Action Items

1. V. Singh and B. Fortier to organize meeting on or by November 1, 2021.
2. A. Faccinelli to contact competitors for advice by October 15, 2021.
3. T. Loredan, M. Baransky, and one employee to form subcommittee to draft harassment/violence policy by October 15, 2021.
4. Once above policy is finalized, ask C. Coletor (Director, HR) to print and distribute internally (estimated by November 15, 2021).

Next Meeting: March 15, 2022, Room and Agenda TBA

Notice in Figure 8.10 that the writer of the minutes summarizes discussions rather than capturing every comment. However, when a decision is made, it's recorded as close to verbatim (i.e., word for word) as possible.

In more formal meetings, before a decision is taken a *motion* must be called and that motion voted on by the majority in the room. A formal minutes report would list the motions (who made and seconded them, and the fact that they were passed), but few organizations use formal minutes any longer, except when the board of directors of the company is meeting.

8.4d Summary Reports

In today's economy, data drives organizations. Data is important because without it, business decisions are more difficult to make. Because a huge amount of data is available today on any given topic, senior managers who make decisions don't always have the time to read and review data on a particular problem, issue, or topic. Therefore, decision makers need the essential elements of an issue or a problem presented in a short, logical, easy-to-understand format that helps them quickly grasp what's vital.

Any time you take what someone else has written or said and reduce it to a concise, accurate, and faithful version of the original—in your own words—you are summarizing. Shown here is a writing plan for an effective summary report:

WRITING PLAN FOR A SUMMARY REPORT

- **Opening:** Begin by referencing the request for a summary and a brief overview of the topic, article, presentation, data set, etc.
- **Body:** State the important points (including important evidence or statistics) from the original source, mirroring the structure of the original material (i.e., if the original makes point X first, it should come first in your summary as well).
- **Pleasant closing:** State the conclusion from the original and offer more help if necessary.

In Figure 8.11, a new vice president of corporate social responsibility asks one of his managers to do research on the state of sustainability reporting in Canada, as the company they work for has been criticized for not producing such a report.

Bailey Bingley first reads the original source to understand it well, then she drafts her summary using the main points she's found, and she proofreads this draft until she's satisfied it's well organized and accurately written. She then sends it to her manager, John Swiderski.

8.5 Writing Informal Analytical Reports

Analytical reports differ significantly from informational reports. Although both seek to collect and present data clearly, analytical reports also evaluate the data and typically try to persuade the reader to accept conclusions and act on recommendations. Whereas informational reports are about stating facts; analytical reports are about saying what those facts mean and what should happen as a result.

In rare situations you'll organize analytical reports directly, with the conclusions and recommendations near the beginning. Directness is appropriate when the reader has complete confidence in the writer, based on either experience or credentials. Frontloading the recommendations also works when the topic is routine or familiar and the reader is supportive.

FIGURE 8.11 / Summary Report

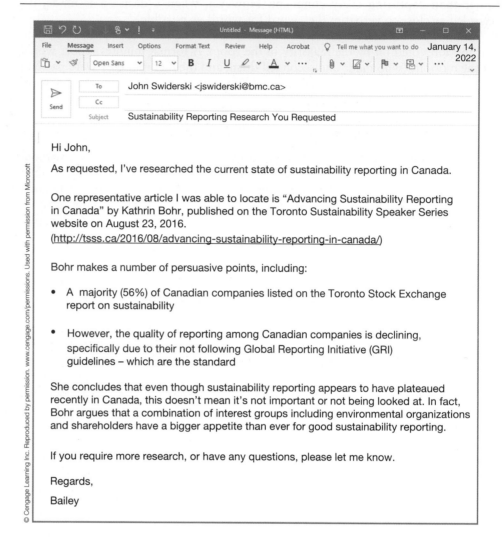

Directness can backfire, though. If you announce the recommendations too quickly, the reader may immediately object to a single idea. You may not have expected that this idea would trigger a negative reaction. Once the reader has an unfavourable mind-set, changing it may be difficult or impossible. A reader may also believe that you have oversimplified or overlooked something significant if you lay out all the recommendations before explaining how you arrived at them. When it's necessary to lead the reader through the process of discovering the solution or recommendation, use the indirect strategy: present conclusions and recommendations last.

Essentially, analytical reports answer questions about specific problems and aid in decision making (e.g., How can we use social media most effectively? Should we close the Moose Jaw plant? How can we improve customer service?).

8.5a Recommendation Reports

Both managers and employees sometimes need to write reports that justify or recommend something, such as buying equipment, changing a procedure, hiring an employee, consolidating departments, or investing funds. Large organizations sometimes have their own templates for this type of report. But sometimes, such reports aren't standardized and the writer must create the organization strategy.

For example, an employee takes it upon himself to write a report suggesting improvements in workplace safety because he feels strongly about it. When you're free to select an organizational plan yourself, however, let your audience and topic determine your choice of direct or indirect structure.

Shown here is a writing plan for an effective recommendation report:

WRITING PLAN FOR A RECOMMENDATION REPORT

- **Opening:** Identify the problem, need, or challenge.
- **Body:** *Direct strategy (for clearly supportive audiences)*: State the recommendation, solution, or action followed by reasoning to support (e.g., evidence, alternatives, potential courses of action). *Indirect strategy (for audiences needing convincing)*: State the evidence, alternatives, or possible courses of action with most realistic alternative or course of action last.
- **Pleasant closing:** *Direct strategy:* Summarize recommendation or actions to be taken. *Indirect strategy:* State conclusion and recommendations and action to be taken.

Lara Brown, executive assistant at a petroleum and mining company in Calgary, applied the preceding plan to write the recommendation report shown in Figure 8.12. Her manager, the director of human resources, asked her to investigate ways to persuade employees to quit smoking. Lara explained that the company had banned smoking many years ago inside the buildings but never tried very hard to get smokers to actually kick the habit. Lara's job was to gather information about the problem and learn how other companies have helped workers stop smoking. The report would go to her manager, but Lara knew he would pass it along to the management council for approval.

If the report was just for her manager, Lara would put her recommendation right up front using the direct strategy, because she was sure he would support it. But the management council is another story. The managers need to be persuaded because of the costs involved—and because some of them are smokers. Therefore, Lara uses the indirect strategy and puts the alternative she favours last. To gain credibility, Lara footnotes her sources. She has enough material for a ten-page report, but keeps it to two pages knowing that council members are busy and this topic might not be their priority.

8.5b Feasibility Reports

Feasibility reports look at the practicality and advisability of following a proposed course of action. They answer the question, Will this plan or proposal work? Feasibility reports are typically internal, and written to advise on matters such as consolidating departments, offering a wellness program to employees, or hiring an outside firm to handle a company's accounting or computing operations.

Sometimes, feasibility reports are written by consultants hired to investigate a problem. The focus in these reports is on the decision: saying yes or no to a proposed plan of action. Since your role isn't to persuade the reader to accept the decision, you'll want to present the decision immediately. When writing feasibility reports, use the following plan:

WRITING PLAN FOR A FEASIBILITY REPORT

- **Opening:** Using the direct strategy, announce your decision immediately along with a reminder of the background or problem that necessitated the proposal.
- **Body:** Discuss benefits of the proposal and any problems that may result. If appropriate, calculate costs associated with the proposal.
- **Pleasant closing:** Like a memo, a feasibility report doesn't have a summary or pleasant signoff. Instead, it ends by describing the time frame/schedule to get the work done.

Elizabeth Webb, customer service manager for an insurance company in London, Ontario, wrote the feasibility report shown in Figure 8.13. Because her company had been losing customer service reps (CSRs) after they were trained, she talked with the vice president about the problem. He didn't want her to take time away from her job to investigate what other companies were doing to retain their CSRs. Instead, he suggested that they hire a consultant to investigate. The vice president then wanted to know whether the consultant's plan was feasible. Although Elizabeth's report is only a page long, it provides all the necessary information: background, benefits, problems, costs, and time frame.

8.5c Yardstick Reports

Yardstick reports examine problems with two or more solutions, to determine the best solution. To make the comparison persuasive, the writer establishes criteria by which to compare the alternatives. The criteria then act as a yardstick against which all the alternatives are measured, as shown in Figure 8.14.

▶ FIGURE 8.12 / Recommendation Report

Date: October 11, 2021

To: Gordon McClure, Director, Human Resources

From: Lara Brown, Executive Assistant *LB*

Subject: Smoking Cessation Programs for Employees

At your request, I have examined measures that encourage employees to quit smoking. As company records show, approximately 23 percent of our employees still smoke, despite the antismoking and clean-air policies we adopted in 2020. To collect data for this report, I studied professional and government publications; I also inquired at companies and clinics about stop-smoking programs.

This report presents data describing the significance of the problem, three alternative solutions, and a recommendation based on my investigation.

Significance of Problem: Health Care and Productivity Losses

Employees who smoke are costly to any organization. The following statistics show the effects of smoking for workers and for organizations:

- Absenteeism is 40 to 50 percent greater among smoking employees.
- Accidents are two to three times greater among smokers.
- Bronchitis, lung and heart disease, cancer, and early death are more frequent among smokers (Arhelger, 2016, p. 4).

Although our clean-air policy prohibits smoking in the building, shop, and office, we have done little to encourage employees to stop smoking. Many workers still go outside to smoke at lunch and breaks. Other companies have been far more proactive in their attempts to stop employee smoking. Many companies have found that persuading employees to stop smoking was a decisive factor in reducing their health insurance premiums. Following is a discussion of three common stop-smoking measures tried by other companies, along with a projected cost factor for each (Rindfleisch, 2016, p. 4).

Alternative 1: Literature and Events

The least expensive and easiest stop-smoking measure involves the distribution of literature, such as "The Ten-Step Plan" from Smokefree Enterprises and government pamphlets citing smoking dangers. Some companies have also sponsored events such as the Great Canadian Smoke-Out, a one-day occasion intended to develop group spirit in spurring smokers to quit. "Studies show, however," says one expert, "that literature and company-sponsored events have little permanent effect in helping smokers quit" (Mendel, 2015, p. 108).

  Cost: Negligible

Avoids revealing recommendation immediately

Uses headings that combine function and description

Introduces purpose of report, tells method of data collection, and previews organization

Documents data sources for credibility; uses APA style citing author and year in the text

FIGURE 8.12 / *(Continued)*

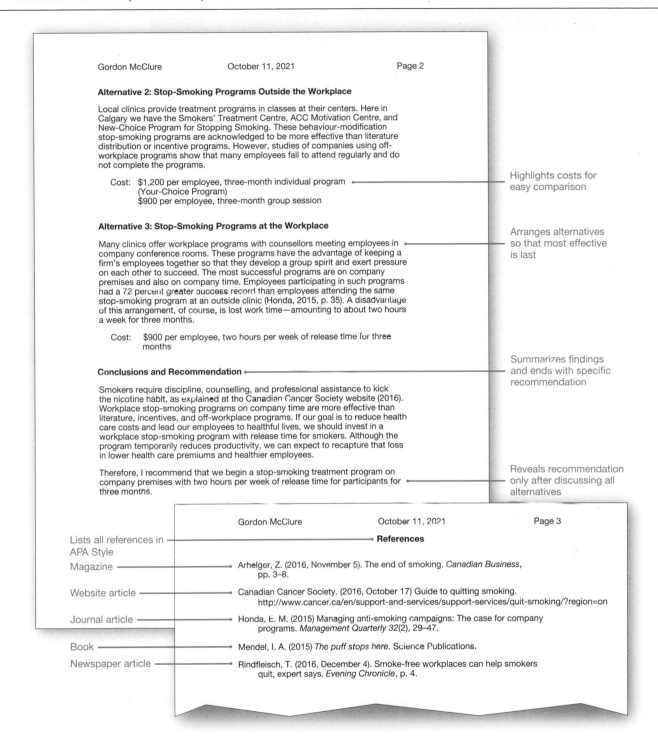

Gordon McClure   October 11, 2021   Page 2

Alternative 2: Stop-Smoking Programs Outside the Workplace

Local clinics provide treatment programs in classes at their centers. Here in Calgary we have the Smokers' Treatment Centre, ACC Motivation Centre, and New-Choice Program for Stopping Smoking. These behaviour-modification stop-smoking programs are acknowledged to be more effective than literature distribution or incentive programs. However, studies of companies using off-workplace programs show that many employees fail to attend regularly and do not complete the programs.

> Cost: $1,200 per employee, three-month individual program
>   (Your-Choice Program)
> $900 per employee, three-month group session

Highlights costs for easy comparison

Alternative 3: Stop-Smoking Programs at the Workplace

Many clinics offer workplace programs with counsellors meeting employees in company conference rooms. These programs have the advantage of keeping a firm's employees together so that they develop a group spirit and exert pressure on each other to succeed. The most successful programs are on company premises and also on company time. Employees participating in such programs had a 72 percent greater success record than employees attending the same stop-smoking program at an outside clinic (Honda, 2015, p. 35). A disadvantage of this arrangement, of course, is lost work time—amounting to about two hours a week for three months.

Arranges alternatives so that most effective is last

> Cost: $900 per employee, two hours per week of release time for three months

Conclusions and Recommendation

Summarizes findings and ends with specific recommendation

Smokers require discipline, counselling, and professional assistance to kick the nicotine habit, as explained at the Canadian Cancer Society website (2016). Workplace stop-smoking programs on company time are more effective than literature, incentives, and off-workplace programs. If our goal is to reduce health care costs and lead our employees to healthful lives, we should invest in a workplace stop-smoking program with release time for smokers. Although the program temporarily reduces productivity, we can expect to recapture that loss in lower health care premiums and healthier employees.

Therefore, I recommend that we begin a stop-smoking treatment program on company premises with two hours per week of release time for participants for three months.

Reveals recommendation only after discussing all alternatives

Gordon McClure   October 11, 2021   Page 3

References

Lists all references in APA Style

Magazine — Arhelger, Z. (2016, November 5). The end of smoking. *Canadian Business*, pp. 3–8.

Website article — Canadian Cancer Society. (2016, October 17) Guide to quitting smoking. http://www.cancer.ca/en/support-and-services/support-services/quit-smoking/?region=on

Journal article — Honda, E. M. (2015) Managing anti-smoking campaigns: The case for company programs. *Management Quarterly 32*(2), 29–47.

Book — Mendel, I. A. (2015) *The puff stops here*. Science Publications.

Newspaper article — Rindfleisch, T. (2016, December 4). Smoke-free workplaces can help smokers quit, expert says. *Evening Chronicle*, p. 4.

For example, a yardstick report could help a company decide on an inexpensive job perk. Perks are nontraditional benefits that appeal to current and future employees. Popular job perks include free food and beverages, flexible scheduling and telecommuting options, and onsite gyms and fitness classes.

A yardstick report might show that if the company wants to encourage long-term wellness, it can consider offering employees discounted fitness club memberships, on-site yoga classes, or ergonomic workstations (these are the alternatives). The report would then describe and compare the three alternatives in terms of three criteria: (a) costs, (b) long-term benefits, and (c) expected participation level.

FIGURE 8.13 / Feasibility Report

Untitled - Message (HTML)

File · Message · Insert · Options · Format Text · Review · Help · Acrobat · Tell me what you want to do

Open Sans · 12 · **B** *I* U

To: Shaun Clay-Taylor <sclaytaylor@bmc.ca>

Cc:

Subject: Feasibility of Progression Schedule for CSRs

Attached: CSR Progression Scale.docx

Hi Shaun,

Please find attached the feasibility report on our CSRs you asked for. If you need anything else, just let me know.

Best,

Elizabeth

[Memo starts here]
[Outlines organization of report]

The plan calling for a progression schedule for our customer service representatives is workable, and I think it could be fully implemented by April 1. This report discusses the background, benefits, problems, costs, and time frame involved in executing the plan.

[Reveals decision immediately]

Background: Training and Advancement Problems for CSRs. Because of the many insurance policies and agents we service, new customer service representatives require eight weeks of intensive training. Even after this thorough introduction, CSRs are overwhelmed. They take about eight more months before feeling competent on the job. Once they reach their potential, they often look for other positions in the company because they see few advancement possibilities in customer service. These problems were submitted to an outside consultant, who suggested a CSR progression schedule.

[Describes problem and background]

[Evaluates positive and negative aspects of proposal objectively]

Benefits of Plan: Career Progression and Incremental Training. The proposed plan sets up a schedule of career progression, including these levels: (1) CSR trainee, (2) CSR Level I, (3) CSR Level II, (4) CSR Level III, (5) Senior CSR, and (6) CSR supervisor. This program, which includes salary increments with each step, provides a career ladder and incentives for increased levels of expertise and achievement. The plan also facilitates training. Instead of overloading a new trainee with an initial eight-week training program, we would train CSRs slowly with a combination of classroom and on-the-job experiences. Each level requires additional training and expertise.

Problems of Plan: Difficulty in Writing Job Descriptions and Initial Confusion. One of the biggest problems will be distinguishing the job duties at each level. However, I believe that, with the help of our consultant, we can sort out the tasks and expertise required at each level. Another problem will be determining appropriate salary differentials. Attached is a tentative schedule showing proposed wages at each level. We expect to encounter confusion and frustration in implementing this program at first, particularly in placing our current CSRs within the structure.

Costs. Implementing the progression schedule involves two direct costs. The first is the salary of a trainee, at about $40,000 a year. The second cost derives from increased salaries of upper-level CSRs, shown on the attached schedule. I believe, however, that the costs involved are within the estimates planned for this project.

[Presents costs and schedule; omits unnecessary summary]

Time Frame. Developing job descriptions should take us about three weeks. Preparing a training program will require another three weeks. Once the program is started, I expect a breaking-in period of at least three months. By April 1 the progression schedule will be fully implemented and showing positive results in improved CSR training, service, and retention.

After interviewing employees and talking to people whose companies offer similar benefits, report writers would compare the alternatives and recommend the most workable job perk. Shown here is a writing plan for effective yardstick reports:

WRITING PLAN FOR A YARDSTICK REPORT

- **Opening:** Using the indirect strategy, begin by describing the problem or need.
- **Body:** Discuss possible solutions or alternatives, and introduce three criteria for comparing the alternatives. Explain why the criteria were selected. Evaluate each alternative using the criteria.
- **Pleasant closing:** Offer a conclusion and recommendation.

► FIGURE 8.14 / Yardstick Report

Date:	April 28, 2021
To:	Tony Marshall, Vice President
From:	Maria Rios, Benefits Administrator *M.R.*
Subject:	Selecting Outplacement Services

Here is the report you requested April 1 investigating the possibility of CompuTech's use of outplacement services. It discusses the problem of counselling services for discharged staff and establishes criteria for selecting an outplacement agency. It then evaluates three prospective agencies and presents a recommendation based on that evaluation.

Introduces purpose and gives overview of report organization

Problem: Counselling Discharged Staff

In an effort to reduce costs and increase competitiveness, CompuTech will begin a program of staff reduction that will involve releasing up to 20 percent of our workforce over the next 12 to 24 months. Many of these employees have been with us for ten or more years, and they are not being released for performance faults. These employees deserve a severance package that includes counselling and assistance in finding new careers.

Discusses background briefly because readers already know the problem

Solution and Alternatives: Outplacement Agencies

Numerous outplacement agencies offer discharged employees counselling and assistance in locating new careers. This assistance minimizes not only the negative feelings related to job loss but also the very real possibility of litigation. Potentially expensive lawsuits have been lodged against some companies by unhappy employees who felt they were unfairly released.

In seeking an outplacement agency, we should find one that offers advice to the sponsoring company as well as to dischargees. The law now requires certain procedures, especially in releasing employees over forty. CompuTech could unwittingly become liable to lawsuits because our managers are uninformed of these procedures. I have located three potential outplacement agencies appropriate to serve our needs: Gray & Associates, Right Access, and Careers Plus.

Uses dual headings, giving function and description

Announces solution and the alternatives it presents

Establishing Criteria for Selecting Agency

In order to choose among the three agencies, I established criteria based on professional articles, discussions with officials at other companies using outplacement agencies, and interviews with agencies. Here are the four groups of criteria I used in evaluating the three agencies:

1. <u>Counselling services</u>—including job search advice, résumé help, crisis management, corporate counselling, and availability of full-time counsellors
2. <u>Administrative and research assistance</u>—including availability of administrative staff, librarian, and personal computers
3. <u>Reputation</u>—based on a telephone survey of former clients and listing with a professional association
4. <u>Costs</u>—for both group programs and executive services

Tells how criteria were selected

Creates four criteria for use as yardstick in evaluating alternatives

© Cengage Learning

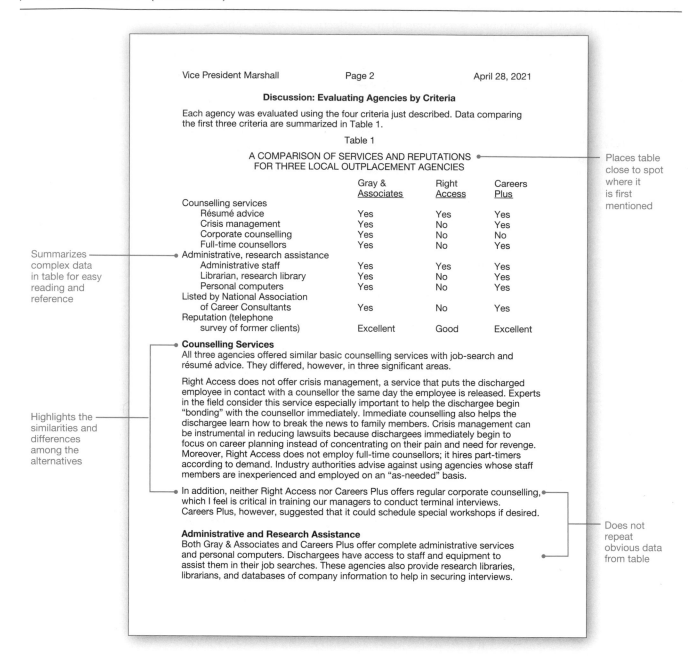

Vice President Marshall   Page 2   April 28, 2021

Discussion: Evaluating Agencies by Criteria

Each agency was evaluated using the four criteria just described. Data comparing the first three criteria are summarized in Table 1.

Table 1

A COMPARISON OF SERVICES AND REPUTATIONS
FOR THREE LOCAL OUTPLACEMENT AGENCIES

	Gray & Associates	Right Access	Careers Plus
Counselling services			
Résumé advice	Yes	Yes	Yes
Crisis management	Yes	No	Yes
Corporate counselling	Yes	No	No
Full-time counsellors	Yes	No	Yes
Administrative, research assistance			
Administrative staff	Yes	Yes	Yes
Librarian, research library	Yes	No	Yes
Personal computers	Yes	No	Yes
Listed by National Association of Career Consultants	Yes	No	Yes
Reputation (telephone survey of former clients)	Excellent	Good	Excellent

Places table close to spot where it is first mentioned

Summarizes complex data in table for easy reading and reference

Counselling Services

All three agencies offered similar basic counselling services with job-search and résumé advice. They differed, however, in three significant areas.

Right Access does not offer crisis management, a service that puts the discharged employee in contact with a counsellor the same day the employee is released. Experts in the field consider this service especially important to help the dischargee begin "bonding" with the counsellor immediately. Immediate counselling also helps the dischargee learn how to break the news to family members. Crisis management can be instrumental in reducing lawsuits because dischargees immediately begin to focus on career planning instead of concentrating on their pain and need for revenge. Moreover, Right Access does not employ full-time counsellors; it hires part-timers according to demand. Industry authorities advise against using agencies whose staff members are inexperienced and employed on an "as-needed" basis.

Highlights the similarities and differences among the alternatives

In addition, neither Right Access nor Careers Plus offers regular corporate counselling, which I feel is critical in training our managers to conduct terminal interviews. Careers Plus, however, suggested that it could schedule special workshops if desired.

Administrative and Research Assistance

Both Gray & Associates and Careers Plus offer complete administrative services and personal computers. Dischargees have access to staff and equipment to assist them in their job searches. These agencies also provide research libraries, librarians, and databases of company information to help in securing interviews.

Does not repeat obvious data from table

Maria Rios, benefits administrator for computer manufacturer CompuTech, was asked to write the report in Figure 8.14 comparing outplacement agencies and recommending one to management.

Maria gathered information about three outplacement agencies and wanted to organize it systematically. She chose to evaluate each agency using the following criteria: counselling services, administrative and research assistance, reputation, and costs.

She shows the results of her research in Table 1, using the criteria as row headings. She discusses how each agency meets, or fails to meet, each criterion. Making a recommendation is easy once Maria creates the tables and compares the agencies.

LEARNING SUMMARY

8.1 Explain informational and analytical business report functions and organization.

- Informational reports present data without analysis or recommendations, such as monthly sales reports, status updates, and compliance reports.
- Analytical reports provide data or findings, analyses, and conclusions. Examples include recommendation, feasibility, and yardstick reports.
- Audience reaction and content determine whether a report is organized directly or indirectly.
- Reports organized directly reveal the purpose and conclusions immediately; reports organized indirectly place the conclusions and recommendations last.
- Like other business messages, reports can range from informal to formal, depending on their purpose, audience, and situation.

8.2 Describe typical report formats including heading levels.

- Report formats vary, depending on the report's length, topic, audience, and purpose.
- Common report formats include email, template/form, PDF, and manuscript; digital reports can be created and shared as slide docks and infographics.
- Report headings add visual appeal and readability; they reveal the report's organization and flow of ideas.
- The hierarchy of heading levels should be clear to a reader; headings in the same level should use the same font size and style, placement, and capitalization.

8.3 Determine the problem to be addressed and the report's purpose.

- Clarifying the problem the report will address is the first step in writing a report.
- A purpose statement states the reasons for the report and answers the questions that prompted the report

- Typical sources of secondary information used in reports are company records, books, journals, magazines, newspapers, and Web resources.
- Typical sources of primary, or firsthand, information used in reports are personal observations, surveys, questionnaires, and interviews with topic experts.

8.4 Write informal informational reports.

- Informational reports provide information about recurring activities (e.g., monthly sales or project updates), as well as one-time events (e.g., trips, conferences, and special projects).
- Event reports include a summary of what happened, details about the event using either chronological or theme organization, and a conclusion with suggested action as a result.
- Progress reports include a project description, background information, work completed, work in progress, problems encountered, and future plans.
- Meeting minutes include the names of attendees and absentees, a discussion of old and new business, committee reports, and decisions made.

8.5 Write informal analytical reports.

- Analytical reports, such as recommendation, feasibility, and yardstick reports, evaluate information, draw conclusions, and make recommendations.
- Recommendation reports are organized directly when the reader is supportive and indirectly when the reader needs persuasion to accept the recommendations.
- Feasibility reports are written directly and examine the practicality and advisability of following a course of action.
- Yardstick reports examine problems by using a standard set of criteria to compare several alternatives before recommending a solution.

CHAPTER REVIEW

1. Explain the difference between providing information and providing an analysis of information. (Objs. 1, 4, 5)
2. Why are there two different patterns of organization for informal reports? (Obj. 1)
3. List the main report formats and when each should be used. (Obj. 2)
4. Describe functional and talking headings and give an example of each. (Obj. 2)
5. Define primary and secondary research and give two examples of each. (Obj. 3)
6. What three questions do progress reports typically address? (Obj. 4)
7. What is the purpose of a meeting minutes report? (Obj. 4)
8. What is the difference between a recommendation report and a feasibility report? (Obj. 5)
9. How can a yardstick report be useful to an organization? (Obj. 5)

CRITICAL THINKING

1. Why are many informal reports written using the direct strategy? (Obj. 1)

2. Is there a significant difference between a report that provides information and a regular email or text message that provides information? (Objs. 1, 2)

3. Is it a good idea to always provide analysis when asked to write reports, or are there times when it's okay to present information only? (Objs. 1, 3)

4. What technology trends do you think will affect business reporting and delivery in the future? (Obj. 2)

5. *Providing a summary is both an exercise in information gathering and an analytical task.* Discuss this statement and provide examples. (Objs. 4, 5)

ACTIVITIES AND CASES

8.1 EVALUATING HEADINGS AND TITLES (OBJ. 2)

Identify the following report headings and titles as *talking* or *functional/descriptive*. Discuss the usefulness and effectiveness of each.

1. Background

2. Oil Imports Slow in China

3. Discussion of Findings

4. Rosier Job Outlook: Emerging From the Crisis

5. Recommendation: Return to Stocks Is Paying Off Again

6. Adobe Exceeds Expectations on Creative Suite Sales

7. Best Android Apps for Business: CamScanner, Skype, and Slack

8. Budget

8.2 EVENT REPORT: LEARNING ABOUT FOOD IN NIAGARA FALLS (OBJS. 3, 4)

You're the general manager of the Milestones Restaurant in downtown Kingston, ON. Each year, one or two employees from each regional group within the restaurant chain are chosen to attend the annual Restaurants Canada Leadership Conference. This year, your district manager says that you can attend on behalf of the regional group. Excited, you check out the conference sessions online at www.rcshow.com. At the annual conference in downtown Toronto, you take part in three very stimulating sessions that offer all kinds of ideas for improving sales and customer experience at your location in Kingston. These sessions include Personalizing the Customer Experience, Millennials Are Massive, and Artificial Intelligence and Restaurants.

Your Task. The district manager asks you to create a 15-minute presentation with PowerPoint slides in which you can give a "topline" summary of what you learned in your three sessions. Create a conference report using PowerPoint. Use Google to search for information on the three session topics you took part in. The district manager also asks for a one-page conference report to be emailed to him a week before the presentation.

8.3 EVENT REPORT: SERVICING REPS IN THE FIELD (OBJS. 3, 4)

You are a corporate trainer for a well-known line of makeup and skin care products called Jeneuve. The products are sold across Canada in department stores and drug stores such as Hudson's Bay, Shopper's Drug Mart, and London Drugs. As the corporate trainer, a large part of your job is conducting training seminars across the country, once in the fall and once in the spring. During these training seminars, not only do you train customer service reps in the retail locations about your new products, changes in current products, etc., you also listen to their feedback about what's working and what's not, and take that feedback home to head office in Montréal.

Your Task. During your fall tour through Western Canada, things generally went well as you introduced reps to Jeneuve's new line of products for men including Beard Oil, Beard Balm, and Beard Protector, as well as products for women including Glitter-J tears, Juicy-J lipstick, and Colour-J eyeliner. The reps in large cities like Vancouver and Calgary were more enthusiastic about these new products than the reps in smaller cities like Lethbridge and Kelowna. At the same time, you heard some critical feedback from your large stores in the Greater Toronto Area. One complaint is that Jeneuve does not offer a line of women's cosmetics for women with darker skin tones. As usual after your fall trip, your VP, Sandy Fairchilde, requests a detailed report in memo format.

Related website: www.cosmopolitan.com/style-beauty/beauty/news/a50647/women-of-color-makeup-foundation/

8.4 MINUTES REPORT: RECORDING THE PROCEEDINGS OF A MEETING (OBJ. 4)

Ask your instructor to let you know when the next all-faculty or division or departmental meeting is taking place on your campus. Or ask your student association or student council representative to let you know when the next association or council meeting is taking place. Or next time you're at work or at your co-op job, ask your boss to let you sit in on a meeting. Or go to YouTube and search *Business meeting for minute taking*. Volunteer to act as note taker or secretary for this meeting.

Your Task. Record the proceedings of the meeting you attend in an informal meeting minutes report. Focus on reports presented, motions and action items, votes, and decisions reached.

8.5 MINUTES REPORT: ROLE-PLAY—EVERYONE'S TAKING MINUTES (OBJ. 4)

Next time you have a group or team related to one of your school assignments, make a video or an audio recording of one of your group or team meetings. Then turn that meeting into a scripted skit. Perform the skit in front of your class.

Your Task. As an audience member, watch the skit discussed above. Assume you are the note taker at the meeting. Create a minutes report for the meeting you just watched. Are there any elements of a meeting the group or team missed (e.g., motions, action statements)?

8.6 SUMMARY REPORT: FUTURE BUSINESS TECHNOLOGY TRENDS (OBJ. 4)

Like many executives, your boss is too busy to sift through all the articles describing current technology trends and predictions for the future. She has assigned the task to you. She asks you to search for articles about future technology trends and write a summary of two of the best articles you found.

Your Task. Write an article summary in memo format to Sandra Al-Khouri that addresses two articles on future technology trends. Include an introduction, such as *As you requested, I am submitting two article summaries.* Identify the author, article title, journal or website name, and date of publication for each article. Explain the purpose of each article and summarize three or four of its most important findings. Include an appropriate subject line and add meaningful headings. Your boss would also like a concluding statement indicating your overall reaction to the articles.

8.7 PROGRESS REPORT: MAKING HEADWAY TOWARD YOUR EDUCATIONAL GOAL (OBJ. 4)

You made an agreement with your parents (or spouse, relative, or partner) that you would submit a progress report at this time describing the headway you have made toward your educational goal (employment, certificate, diploma, degree).

Your Task. In memo format write a progress report that fulfills your promise to describe your progress toward your educational goals. Address your progress report to your parents, spouse, relative, or partner. In your memo (1) describe your goal; (2) summarize the work you have completed thus far; (3) discuss thoroughly the work currently in progress, including your successes and anticipated obstacles; and (4) forecast your future activities in relation to your scheduled completion date.

8.8 PROGRESS REPORT: DESIGNING A TEMPLATE FOR HR (OBJ. 4)

You are the assistant to the director of human resources at BASF's head office in Mississauga, Ontario. At a recent meeting of the management board, it was decided that the employee review process required an overhaul. Instead of once-yearly meetings with their immediate superior to discuss any issues, the company has decided to institute a more accountable process in which all employees (including managers) must write a yearly progress report.

Your Task. Develop a template report for your boss, Sue Swinton, director of Human Resources, that can be filled out by all BASF Canada employees at all ten locations once a year. Keep in mind that employees are generally unenthusiastic about the employee review process. In other words, your template must be easy to fill out and logical.

Related websites: BASF Canada's site is www.basf.ca. You may also want to research best practices in performance management and the employee review process.

8.9 PROGRESS REPORT: UPDATING YOUR SUPERVISOR (OBJ. 4)

As office manager for the Vancouver Humane Society (www.vancouverhumanesociety.bc.ca), an organization that rescues and finds homes for abandoned and abused animals, you have been asked to come up with ways to increase community awareness of your organization. For the past month, you have been meeting with business and community leaders, conducting Web research, and visiting with representatives from other nonprofit organizations. Your supervisor has just asked you to prepare a written report to outline what you have accomplished so far.

Your Task. In memo format write a progress report to your supervisor. In your memo (a) state whether the project is on schedule, (b) summarize the activities you have completed thus far, (c) discuss thoroughly the work currently in progress, and (d) describe your future activities. Also let your supervisor know any obstacles you have encountered and whether the project is on schedule.

8.10 RECOMMENDATION REPORT: WHAT IS IT ABOUT ADVERTISING? (OBJ. 5)

You are the Research manager of a midsized advertising agency named Slam! in Oakville, Ontario. Your company is in the enviable position of having secured the advertising contract for the next three years for Mini Canada, the car brand. The problem is, the company can't seem to keep employees around long enough to ensure continuity within projects. It seems as though the advertising business is a revolving door: new college and university graduates are eager to work for the company, but six months later, after they are trained, they leave for more lucrative jobs at other agencies. The CEO is too busy to figure out a solution or policy; in fact, she is so busy she hasn't got around to hiring a Human Resources manager. Instead she asks you rto write you a report on some possible solutions.

Your Task. As the research manager at Slam! research and write a short email recommendation report for CEO outlining some possible solutions to the revolving door problem. the CEO's thriftiness is well known, so you'll have to be careful about how you phrase any expensive solutions.

Related website: An article at strategyonline.ca/2016/11/25/brian-fetherstonhaugh-on-retaining-young-talent/ provides some suggestions about employee retention; however, you should also do other research on the topic of employee retention. Be careful not to plagiarize from your sources when completing this report. Information on Mini Canada can be found at www.mini.ca.

8.11 RECOMMENDATION REPORT: DEVELOPING A COMPANY SOCIAL MEDIA USE POLICY (OBJ. 5)

A social media use policy is a set of rules developed by organizations to regulate the use of social media by employees. As a manager in a midsized engineering firm, you see the need to draft such a policy. You have received reports that employees are using the Internet and social media sites during work hours to check Facebook and Twitter, look for jobs on LinkedIn, shop on eBay, and even play games online. You have also received reports that some employees have posted inappropriate comments about the company on Facebook. You have reason to worry about appropriate behaviour, declining productivity, security problems, and liability issues. The executive council now wants to establish a social media policy, in addition to the already existing Internet policy, to clarify their policies on social media use and acceptable behaviour. You are aware that the executive council needs to know that acceptable use of social media pertains to employees at work and at home. You decide to talk with other managers about the problem and to look at other companies' social media policies. You'll report your findings in a recommendation report.

Your Task. As a team, discuss the need for comprehensive social media use policies in general. Search for information about other firms' social media policies. Read about companies that are currently facing lawsuits over employees' inappropriate messages on social media networks. Find out what areas your policy should cover. Each member of the team should present and support his or her ideas regarding what should be included in the policy. Individually or as a team, write a convincing recommendation report in memo format to the executive council based on the conclusions you draw from your research and discussion. Because you are recommending action, decide whether your approach should be direct or indirect.

8.12 RECOMMENDATION REPORT: DIVERSITY TRAINING—DOES IT WORK? (OBJ. 5)

Employers recognize the importance of diversity awareness and intercultural sensitivity in the workplace because both are directly related to productivity. It is assumed that greater harmony also minimizes the threat of lawsuits. An interest in employee diversity training has spawned numerous corporate trainers and consultants, but after many years of such training, some recent studies seem to suggest that they may be ineffective or deliver mixed results at best. A 2009 article in the trade magazine *Canadian HR Reporter* concluded that diversity training does not necessarily change bias, for example, against lesbian, gay, and transgender employees.[1]

Search the Internet and your library's databases for information about diversity training. Examine articles favourable to diversity training and those that exhibit a more pessimistic view of such efforts.

Your Task. As a group of two to five members, write a memo report to your boss (address it to your instructor) and define diversity training. Explain which measures companies take to make their managers and workers culturally aware and respectful of differences. If you have personally encountered such training, draw on your experience in addition to your research. Your report should answer the question, *Does diversity training work?* If yes, recommend steps your company should take to become more sensitive to minorities. If no, suggest how current practices could be improved to be more effective.

8.13 FEASIBILITY REPORT: HEALTH AND WELLNESS PERKS (OBJ. 5)

Your company is considering adding some health and wellness perks that will interest current and future employees. Perks are benefits that are added beyond the normal medical coverage and sick pay. These wellness perks help in recruiting and retaining talented employees. You work for a smaller company that cannot compete with the great perks offered by giant companies such as Google and Amazon. However, small- and medium-sized companies are now adding health and wellness perks at little or no expense. You've been assigned to research and select three health and wellness perks that could be incorporated into your company's culture immediately. The company has a training room onsite for classes and a large lunchroom for lunchtime activities. You might consider the following options: a company-sponsored softball league, lunchtime walking groups, weekend hikes and bike trips, lunchtime classes on health and nutrition, or weekly yoga and cross-training classes. Search online for other possibilities, and be ready to suggest three company perks to your supervisor.

Your Task. Select three health and wellness perks that can be offered to employees at little or no cost. Write a memo report investigating the feasibility of adding the three perks. Begin by stating the decision to add the three perks. Then discuss the background leading up to the decision and the benefits of such programs. Estimate the approximate costs associated with each option, including administration costs, if any. Then suggest an appropriate time frame for implementation.

8.14 YARDSTICK REPORT: CHOOSING A LIVE CHAT SOLUTION (OBJ. 5)

As an intern for a midsized online marketing company that sells outdoor and recreational clothing and equipment, you are anxious to comply with a request from the vice president of Marketing. He wants to add a live chat feature on the company website to improve customer service with online shoppers. He is aware that online shoppers frequently accept invitations to chat live when they need help or have questions. What's more, they often turn into buyers. He asks you to research the most popular live chat software options, compare the features and monthly costs, and recommend one that the company could implement quickly.

Your Task. Write a memo yardstick report to vice president of Marketing, Jon Stokes, that compares the options. Search online for live chat support software, and look at several sources that list the most popular options for small and midsized companies. Choose five of the most frequently mentioned options, and compare them in terms of (a) monthly or yearly costs; (b) main features; and (c) ratings or reviews. Follow the instructions in the textbook for writing yardstick reports. Briefly discuss the background for the report, list the live chat alternatives, and compare them using the established criteria. Your comparison data may work best in a table. Draw conclusions and recommend a live chat solution that you believe will best meet the needs of the company.

8.15 YARDSTICK REPORT: WHERE TO BUILD A NEW CALL CENTRE (OBJ. 5)

You've recently been hired as director of Customer Experience at CanCommCo, a large telecommunications company. CanCommCo has hundreds of thousands of customers across Canada that purchase cell phones and plans, as well as television packages. A few months before you were hired, CanCommCo had the dubious distinction of winning the Worst Customer Service Award from the Consumers' Association of Canada (consumer.ca). Unfortunately, this news made it to the major media, and CanCommCo has been trying to figure out how to win back customers ever since.

Your Task. Create a PowerPoint yardstick report for the vice president of Total Customer Experience, Bernice Uglukak. Bernice has informed you that the senior management committee has decided that opening a new customer call centre somewhere in Canada will be a major part of CanCommCo's efforts to win back customer loyalty—many customers have complained over the years about the offshoring of CanCommCo's customer service to the Philippines. Bernice wants you to research three Canadian cities that seem to offer good prospects for a call centre: Moncton, NB; Ottawa, ON; and Winnipeg, MB. She asks you to use education and bilingualism, municipal incentives to new business, and quality of life as your criteria for assessing the three cities.

8.16 SUMMARY REPORT: CURRENT SOCIAL MEDIA MARKETING TRENDS (OBJS. 2, 4)

With the rise of social media in business, your supervisor wants to stay abreast of the latest social media marketing trends. He asks you to research this topic and list the current trends with a brief explanation of each. You will format this document as an article summary.

Your Task. Search for an article or infographic that addresses current or future social media marketing trends. In a memo report addressed to your manager, Jin Le, summarize the main ideas presented in the article or infographic. Be sure to identify the author, article title, publication name, and date of the article. If your source is an infographic, follow a similar procedure and identify the title, sponsoring website, source, and date, if available. Conclude with your overall opinion of the article or infographic.

8.17 LONGER REPORT: SOLVING A PROBLEM (OBJS. 1–5)

Choose a business or an organization with which you are familiar and identify a problem, such as poor quality, indifferent service, absenteeism at organization meetings, uninspired cafeteria food, outdated office equipment, unresponsive management, lack of communication, under-appreciated employees, wasteful procedures, or a similar problem.

Your Task. Describe the problem in detail. Assume you are to report to management (or to the leadership of an organization) about the nature and scope of the problem. Decide which kind of report to prepare (informational, analytical), and choose the format. How would you gather data to lend authority to your conclusions and recommendations? Determine the exact topic and report length after consultation with your instructor.

SEMICOLONS AND COLONS

Review Sections 2.16–2.19 of the Grammar/Mechanics Handbook. Then study each of the following statements. Insert any necessary punctuation. Use the delete symbol to omit unnecessary punctuation. In the space provided, indicate the number of changes you made. If you make no changes, write *0*. Also record the number of the G/M principle illustrated. This exercise concentrates on semicolon and colon use, but you will also be responsible for correct comma use. When you finish, compare your responses with those provided near the end of the book. If your responses differ, study carefully the principles in parentheses.

<u>2 (2.16a)</u>   **Example**   Jessica Mayer's task is to ensure that her company has enough cash to meet its obligations; moreover, she is responsible for finding ways to reduce operating expenses.

_____ 1. Short-term financing refers to a period of one year or less long-term financing on the other hand refers to a period of more than one year.

_____ 2. Jessica Mayer's firm must negotiate short-term financing during the following months October November and December.

_____ 3. Jessica was interested in her company's finances however she was also seeking information about improving her personal credit score.

_____ 4. Having a long history of making payments on time on all types of credit accounts is important to lenders therefore you should strive to make timely payments.

_____ 5. Two of the most highly respected and popular banks for short-term financing are: CIBC and TD Bank.

_____ 6. People with Fico scores of 700 to 800 are good credit risks people with scores of 400 or less are poor credit risks.

_____ 7. Jessica learned that three factors account for about a third of one's credit score (a) length of credit history (b) new credit and (c) type of credit.

_____ 8. She attended a credit conference featuring the following speakers Jonathon Cruz certified financial consultant Credit Specialist Margaret Lee founder Credit Solutions and Judith Plutsky legal counsel Liberty Financial.

_____ 9. Opening several new credit accounts in a short period of time can lower your credit score but scores are not affected by multiple inquiries from credit score agencies.

_____ 10. Your credit score ignores some surprising factors for example your age salary and occupation.

_____ 11. Credit Solutions which is a nonprofit counselling and debt management service says that two factors account for two-thirds of your credit score (1) your payment history and (2) the amount owed versus available credit.

_____ 12. If you want specific information from Credit Solutions send your request to Margaret Lee 3520 Troy Highway Simcoe Ontario K2D 1G8.

_____ 13. Margaret Lee who founded Credit Solutions employs an experienced courteous staff however she also responds to personal requests.

_____ 14. Interest rates are at historic lows they may never be this low again.

_____ 15. Margaret Lee said "If your goal is to increase your credit score take a look at folks with the highest credit scores. They have four to six credit card accounts no late payment and at least one installment loan with an excellent payment history."

EDITING CHALLENGE 8

The progress report shown below has proofreading, spelling, grammar, punctuation, wordiness, and other writing faults that require correction. Study the guidelines in the Grammar/Mechanics Handbook, as well as the lists of Confusing Words and Frequently Misspelled Words at the end of the book, to sharpen your skills. When you finish making corrections, your instructor can show you the revised version of this report.

Your Task. Edit the following message by correcting its errors (a) in your textbook or (b) on a photocopy using standard proofreading marks from Appendix B.

To: John Peters jpeters@zedfilms.ca December 10, 2021
From: Kalare Jegsee <kjegsee@zedfilms.ca>
Subject: Progress Report on Sites for "Great Canadian Cook Off" Series
Cc:
Bcc:
Attached:

This email will outline the progress of my location search for our Great Canadian Cook Off series, which begins to shooting in April. My location search has been undertaken in the downtown Toronto area, because the gratest number of restaurants are found there.

What I've done so Far: As requested by you, I've searched for restaurants that have a professional kitchen, that are not crampped in size, and which are avaliable for rental during our shoting period and renting for less than $1,000 per day. This required a week's worth of telephoning around the city to narrow down the possibilities. After my phoning I had narrowed down the search to five restaurants: Lisa's; On the Avenue; Trattoria Umberto, Avignon; and also the Mackenzie House. At this point I have had meetings with the owners of the first two restaurants named above. Bot Lisa's and On the Avenue fit our criterias, but Lisas is pretty cramped in size.

What I still Need To Do: As you can see from what I've said above, there are three restaurants I've yet to visit. I have meetings scheduled for this Thursday and Friday at all three. I realized while visiting Lisa's and On the Avenue that we should probably be add another criteria which is; what kind of front-of-house facilities do they have. In other words, if the dining area itself is not attractive (we may be using this for extra shots, e.g. one on one interviews), there isn't much points going with this location. So I will keep this extra criteria in mind when I meet with the other 3 restaurants.

I'll send u a final report narrowing my list of five down to 2 by early next week (probably Monday!). Please let me know if you have any questions.
Cheers,
Kalare

Saklakova/istock via Getty Images

OBJECTIVES

9.1 Write effective informal business proposals.

9.2 Follow a plan for writing formal reports.

9.3 Collect effective primary and secondary data for reports.

9.4 Document report sources effectively.

9.5 Convert report data into meaningful visuals.

9.6 Sequence a formal report effectively.

PROPOSALS AND FORMAL REPORTS

BIZ COMM BYTE

The average "win" rate—that is, the number of times a proposal is successful—is less than 5 percent. An organization that sends out 20 proposals will, on average, be successful with only one of them. As a result, working with a proposal template is essential as it can cut the time spent per proposal from 30 hours to 10 hours: a large gain in productivity.

Source: Andra Postolache. (2018, December 17). 13 Statistics about RFP responses for successful proposal managers. https://www.quandora.com/13-statistics-rfp-responses-successful-proposal-managers/

9.1 Writing Business Proposals

Proposals are persuasive written offers to solve problems, provide services, or sell equipment or other goods. From large aerospace and engineering firms to smaller businesses such as electricians, contractors, plumbers, and interior designers—all depend on proposals to sell their services and products.

Many organizations, including in the nonprofit sector, earn a sizable portion of their income from proposals (which are often called grant applications in the nonprofit sector).

In writing proposals, the most important thing to remember is that they constitute a type of sales presentation in which you offer a value proposition, so they must be persuasive, not merely mechanical descriptions of what you can do.

9.1a Types of Proposals

Writers create proposals for various reasons, such as asking for funds or promoting products and services to customers. All proposals share two significant characteristics: (1) they use easy-to-understand language, and (2) they show the value and benefits of the product or services being recommended. Proposals can be classified as (a) informal or formal, (b) internal or external, and (c) solicited or unsolicited.

INFORMAL OR FORMAL. Informal proposals are short documents of one to three pages, often formatted as memos or letters. An informal proposal usually includes the following parts: (a) an introduction or description of the problem; (b) pertinent background information or a statement of need; (c) the proposal benefits and schedule for completion; (d) the staffing requirements; (e) a budget; and (f) a conclusion that may include an authorization request.

Figure 9.1 shows an informal letter proposal to a dentist who sought to improve patient satisfaction. The research company submitting the proposal describes the benefits of a patient survey to gather data about the level of patient satisfaction.

Formal proposals are more complex and may range from 5 to 200 or more pages. For example, the train link to Toronto's Pearson Airport from downtown

Cengage

MINDTAP

In MindTap go to the Whiteboard Animation for Chapter 9 and watch it now.

▼ **FIGURE 9.1** / Informal "Letter" Proposal

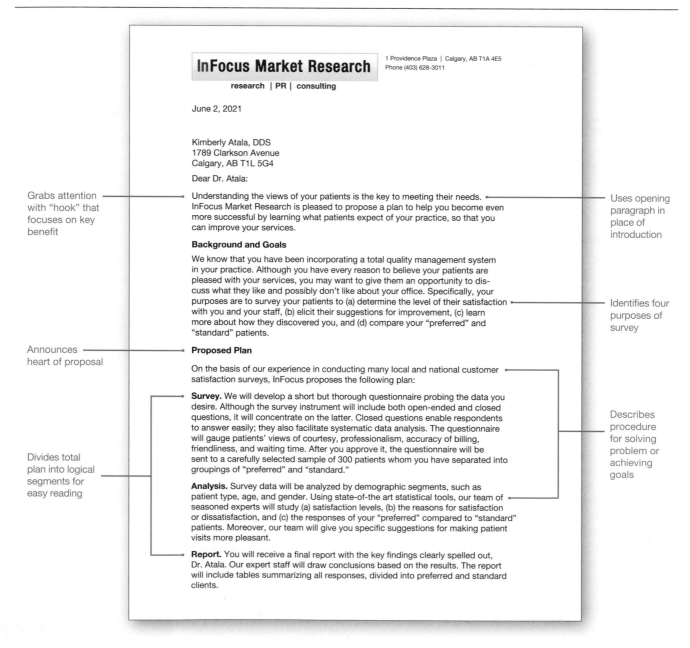

FIGURE 9.1 / *(Continued)*

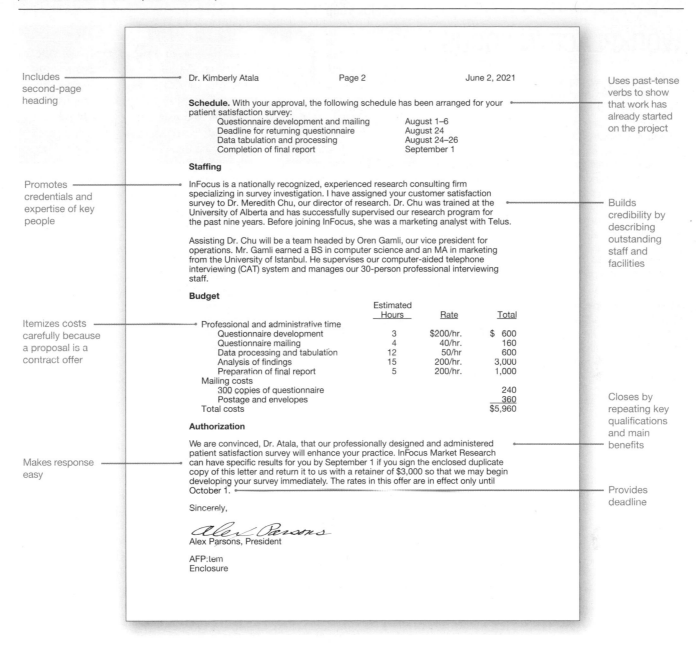

Includes second-page heading

Promotes credentials and expertise of key people

Itemizes costs carefully because a proposal is a contract offer

Makes response easy

Uses past-tense verbs to show that work has already started on the project

Builds credibility by describing outstanding staff and facilities

Closes by repeating key qualifications and main benefits

Provides deadline

(the Union Pearson Express) was a huge engineering and logistical undertaking. The proposals by AirLINX Transit Partners Inc. to build a station at the airport and 3 kilometres of track, and by Sumitomo Corporation of Americas to build the train cars,[1] were much longer than the two-page letter proposal in Figure 9.1.

In addition to the six basic parts just described, formal proposals contain some or all of the following additional parts: a copy of the request for proposal (RFP), a letter of transmittal, an abstract and/or executive summary, a title page, a table of contents, figures, and appendixes containing such items as detailed budgets and staffing information.

In this book we won't model formal proposals because it's unlikely that a business communicator in an entry-level position would write such a detailed proposal. Formal proposal writing is usually handled either by consultants or by employees with significant experience in this area.

Many organizations, especially those run on a consulting model, depend entirely on proposals to generate their income. Companies such as Phelps (mentioned in the Workplace in Focus box) employ numerous consultants who spend significant

WORKPLACE IN FOCUS

Phelps (phelpsgroup.ca) is an executive search and leadership advisory firm based in downtown Toronto. One of its main services is executive search, in which they support clients (usually government ministries, colleges and universities, large utilities, etc.) that have open high-level management positions (e.g., CEOs, VPs, and directors) to find and retain the right talent for those positions. Typically, firms like Phelps base their fees on a percentage of the projected first year's salary for the executives they successfully place with an organization. Although two-thirds of Phelps engagements are with repeat clients, an additional significant way in which Phelps creates new business is by writing proposals that are highly tailored to the requirements detailed in an RFP. For example, a large organization like the Liquor Control Board of Ontario (LCBO) will periodically advertise the need for "vendors of record" for search and recruitment. This means that the LCBO is looking for a firm to work exclusively for it on all of its executive hiring for a set number of years.

To win this potentially lucrative business from the LCBO, Phelps must create a highly professional and persuasive proposal—usually in PDF format with relevant content that addresses the needs of the client; full-colour graphics, pictures, and other illustrations; and all the elements outlined in this chapter (e.g., staffing, experience)—showcasing why it is the best executive search firm. *Most people use online job sites like Workopolis to find jobs. Why do you think executive search and recruitment is different? Is there something about humans finding and placing other humans in an organization (an old-fashioned-seeming idea) that's actually forward-thinking?*

time preparing proposals to compete for new business. For more information about industry standards and resources, visit the website of the Association of Proposal Management Professionals (www.apmp-mapleleaf.org).

INTERNAL OR EXTERNAL. Proposal writers can submit internal proposals to management when they see benefits in changing a company policy, purchasing equipment, or adding new products and services. A company decision maker will review the proposal and accept or reject the idea. Internal proposals resemble recommendation reports, discussed in Chapter 8. Most proposals, however, are external and addressed to potential clients, customers, and stakeholders outside the company. An external proposal to a client shows how the company's goods or services solve a problem or benefit the client.

Another type of external proposal is a grant request, written to obtain funding from an agency that supports the nonprofit sector. For example, Family Services of Greater Vancouver may submit yearly grant applications to United Way of the Lower Mainland for operating or special project expenses around reducing infant mortality.

SOLICITED OR UNSOLICITED. When government or business has a specific and complex need, an RFP is prepared—this is a document that specifies the requirements. Government and business use RFPs to solicit competitive bids from vendors. RFPs ensure that bids are comparable and that funds are awarded fairly.

For example, let's say that the City of Fredericton wants to upgrade the laptops and software at City Hall. After it knows exactly what it wants, it prepares an RFP specifying its requirements. It then publishes the RFP, and companies interested in bidding on the job submit *solicited* proposals. RFPs were traditionally publicized in newspapers (and known as *tenders* or *bids*), but today they're published on websites, such as www.merx.com, the best-known Canadian RFP site.

Enterprising companies or individuals looking for work might submit *unsolicited* proposals. For example, imagine you've just attended a conference on trends in digital marketing, at which a number of prospective clients was in attendance. As a

Cengage

MINDTAP

In MindTap, go to the Chapter 9 reading, section 9.1a, and watch the video of industry expert Jason John discussing best practices when creating proposals.

boutique digital marketing company, specializing in social media optimization, you might send out an unsolicited proposal to three to five potential clients you met at the conference to offer your services.

Not only do organizations want a good price from their project bidders, but they also want the legal protection offered by proposals, which are considered legal contracts.

9.1b Components of Informal Proposals

Informal proposals are often presented in letter format (or sometimes in a form, e.g., in a grant application). These "letter" proposals contain six parts, as shown in the writing plan: introduction, background, proposal or plan, staffing, budget, and authorization request. The informal proposal shown in Figure 9.1 illustrates these six parts, in the context of a proposal addressed to a Calgary dentist who wants to improve patient satisfaction.

WRITING PLAN FOR AN INFORMAL PROPOSAL

- **Opening:** Begin with an introduction that summarizes reasons for the proposal and your qualifications. Include a background section that shows you understand why the good or service is needed.
- **Body:** In this part of the proposal, include your plan or solution, information about staffing and relevant experience, and your budget.
- **Pleasant closing:** The proposal closes with a brief conclusion and a subtle request for authorization to go ahead with providing the good or service.

INTRODUCTION. The introduction states the reasons for the proposal and high-lights the writer's qualifications. To grab attention and be persuasive, the introduction contains a *hook*, such as:

- Hinting at extraordinary results with details to be revealed shortly
- Promising low costs or speedy results
- Mentioning a remarkable resource (well-known authority, new software, well-trained staff) available exclusively to you
- Identifying a serious problem (worry item) and promising a solution, to be explained later
- Specifying a key issue or benefit that you feel is the heart of the proposal

For example, in the proposal shown in Figure 9.1, writer Alex Parsons confidently focuses on a key benefit. She guesses that the potential client, Dr. Atala, will be most interested in receiving a concrete plan for making changes based on her patients' opinions. If this were a more complex (formal) proposal, the introduction would also describe the scope and limitations of the project.

BACKGROUND. The background section identifies the problem and discusses the goals or purposes of the project. The background is also the place to go over some recent history. In other words, briefly summarize what circumstances led to you writing the proposal, whether solicited or unsolicited. For example, in Figure 9.1, the "history" of the situation is alluded to in the sentence *We know that you have been incorporating a total quality management system in your practice*.

In a proposal, your aim is to convince the reader that you understand the need completely. Thus, if you are responding to an RFP, this means repeating its language. For example, if the RFP asks for the *design of a maintenance program for high-speed mail-sorting equipment*, you would use the same language in explaining the purpose of your proposal. This section might include segments entitled *Basic Requirements, Most Critical Tasks*, and *Most Important Secondary Problems*.

PLAN. In the plan section, you discuss your solution to the problem or need. In some proposals this is tricky: you want to disclose enough of your plan to secure the contract without giving away so much information that your services aren't needed. Without specifics about implementation, though, your proposal has little chance, so you must decide how much to reveal. Explain what you propose to do and how it will benefit the reader.

Remember, too, that a proposal is a sales presentation or value proposition. Sell your methods, product, and *deliverables*—items that will be left with the client. In this section some writers specify how the project will be managed, how its progress will be audited, and what milestones along the way will indicate the project is progressing as planned. Most writers also include a schedule or timeline showing when key events take place.

STAFFING. The staffing section describes the credentials and expertise of the project leaders and the company as a whole. A well-written staffing section describes the capabilities of the whole company. Although the example in Figure 9.1 doesn't do so, staffing sections often list other high-profile jobs that have been undertaken by the company as a way of building interest and reducing resistance. For example, before she mentioned Dr. Chu and Mr. Gamli, Parsons could have said, *Among our well-known past clients are Husky Energy and the Calgary Board of Education.*

The staffing section can also identify the size and qualifications of the support staff, along with other resources such as software and other analytical capabilities. In longer proposals, résumés of key people may be provided. The staffing section is a good place to endorse and promote your staff.

BUDGET. The most important item in proposals is the budget. You need to prepare this section carefully because it represents a contract; you can't raise the price later—even if your costs increase. You can—and should—protect yourself with a deadline for acceptance. In the budget section some writers itemize hours and costs; others present a total sum only. A proposal to install a complex IT system might, for example, contain a detailed line-by-line budget.

In the proposal shown in Figure 9.1, Parsons felt that she needed to justify the budget for her firm's patient-satisfaction survey, so she itemized the costs. But the budget included for a proposal to conduct a one-day seminar to improve employee communication skills might be a lump sum only. Your analysis of the project and your audience will help you decide what kind of budget to prepare.

AUTHORIZATION AND CONCLUSION. Informal proposals close with a request for approval or authorization and remind the reader of key benefits and motivate action. The closing might also include a deadline date beyond which the offer is invalid. Learning to write an effective authorization statement that finds a way of saying you want the job without appearing too greedy or needy is an important test of your persuasive abilities.

◣ 9.2 Writing Formal Business Reports

A formal report is as a document in which a writer analyzes findings, draws conclusions, and makes recommendations intended to solve a problem and help decision makers.

9.2a The Report Writing Process

Writing a formal report takes time. It requires planning, research, and organization. Because this is a complex process, writers are most successful when they follow specific steps, as outlined in the following sections.

DETERMINE THE PURPOSE AND SCOPE OF THE REPORT. Formal reports begin with a purpose statement. These statements are helpful in defining the focus of the report and providing a standard that keeps the project on target. Notice the use of action words (*adding*, *writing*, and *establishing*):

> **Simple purpose statement:** To recommend adding three positions to our sales team, writing a job description for the sales team leader, and establishing recruitment guidelines for sales team hiring.

You can determine the scope of a report by defining and limiting the problem or problems that will be researched and analyzed. Consider these questions: How much time do you have to complete the report? How accessible is the data you need? If interviews or surveys are appropriate, how many people should you contact, and what questions should you ask?

ANTICIPATE THE NEEDS OF THE AUDIENCE. Keep in mind that the audience may or may not be familiar with the topic. Your goal is to present key findings that are relevant to your audience. If you were reporting to a targeted audience of human resources managers, the following facts gathered from an employee survey would be considered relevant: *According to the company survey completed by 425 of our 515 employees, 72 percent of employees are currently happy with their health benefits package.*

DRAFT A WORK PLAN. A work plan guides the investigation. It should include a clear problem statement, a purpose statement, and a description of the research methods to be used. A good work plan also involves a tentative outline of the report's major sections and a logical work schedule for completion of major tasks.

CONDUCT RESEARCH USING PRIMARY AND SECONDARY SOURCES. Formal report writers conduct their research using *secondary sources*—information that has been previously published in books, articles, websites, podcasts, and annual reports for example. Writers may also conduct their research using primary sources—information and data gathered from firsthand experience. Interviews, observations, surveys, and focus groups are examples of primary research. Research methods are discussed in the section "Researching Report Data" later in this chapter.

ORGANIZE, ANALYZE, AND DRAW CONCLUSIONS. Formal report writers organize their information logically (see the organization strategies in Figure 9.2) and base their recommendations on solid facts to impress decision makers. All findings and analysis need to be relevant to the report's original purpose.

▼ FIGURE 9.2 / Strategies for Organizing Report Findings

STRATEGY TYPE	DATA ARRANGEMENT	USEFUL APPLICATION
Chronological	Arrange information in a time sequence to show history or development of topic	Useful in showing time relationships, such as five-year profit figures or a series of events leading to a problem.
Geographical	Organize information by geographic regions or locations	Appropriate for topics that are easily divided into locations, such as Atlantic Provinces, Central Canada, etc.
Topic/Function	Arrange by topics or functions; may use a prescribed, conventional format	Works well for topics with established categories or for recurring reports
Compare/Contrast	Present problem and show alternative solutions, use consistent criteria, and show how the solutions are similar and different	Best used for "before and after" scenarios or when comparing alternatives
Importance	Arrange from least to most important, lowest to highest priority, or lowest to highest value, etc.	Appropriate when persuading the audience to take a specific action or change a belief
Simple/Complex	Proceed from simple to more complex concepts or topics	Useful for technical or abstract topics
Best Case/Worst Case	Describe the best and the worst possible scenarios	Useful when dramatic effect is needed to achieve results; helpful when audience is uninterested or uninformed

Conclude the report by summarizing your findings, drawing conclusions, and making recommendations. The way you conclude depends on the purpose of your report and what the reader needs. A well-organized report with conclusions based on solid data will impress management and other decision makers.

DESIGN VISUALS TO CLARIFY THE REPORT'S MESSAGE. Presenting data visually helps your reader to understand information and accept your recommendations. Trends, comparisons, and cycles are easier to comprehend when they are expressed graphically. These visual elements in reports draw attention, add interest, and often help readers gain information quickly. Visuals include drawings, graphs, maps, charts, photographs, tables, and infographics. This topic is covered in more depth in the section "Converting Data Into Meaningful Visuals" later in this chapter.

9.2b Editing Formal Business Reports

The final step in preparing a formal business report involves editing and proof-reading. Because the reader is the one who determines the report's success, review the report as if you were the intended audience. Pay particular attention to the following elements:

- **Format.** Look at the report's format and assess its visual appeal.
- **Consistency.** Review the report for consistency in margins, page numbers, indents, line spacing, heading parallelism, and font style.
- **Graphics.** Make sure all visuals have meaningful titles, make written information clearer, and are placed in the report near the words that describe them.
- **Heading levels.** Check the heading levels for consistency in font style and placement. Headings and subheadings should be meaningful and help the reader follow the report's logic.
- **Accuracy.** Review the content for accuracy and clarity. Make sure all facts are documented.
- **Mechanics.** Correct all grammar, punctuation, capitalization, and usage errors. These errors will damage your credibility and might cause the reader to mistrust the report's content.

◣ 9.3 Researching Report Data

The most important step in writing a report is doing research that helps solve the business problem at hand. A report is only as good as its data, so you'll need to spend considerable time collecting data before you begin writing.

Data fall into two broad categories: primary and secondary. Primary data result from firsthand experience and observation. Secondary data come from reading what others have experienced and observed. Secondary data are easier and less expensive to develop than primary data, which could involve interviewing people, waiting for surveys questionnaires to be returned, etc.

9.3a Secondary Data

Reviewing secondary sources can save time and effort and help you avoid costly primary research to develop data that may already exist. Most secondary material is available in online databases.

BOOKS. Although sometimes outdated, depending on how quickly a particular body of knowledge changes, books provide excellent in-depth data and interpretation on many subjects. For example, if you are investigating best practices in website design, you will find numerous books with valuable information in your nearest library. Books are located through online catalogues that can be accessed in the library, on any campus computer, or from home with an Internet connection and valid password.

PERIODICALS. Magazines, newspapers, and journals are called periodicals because of their periodic publication (e.g., weekly, monthly, quarterly). Articles in journals and other periodicals will be extremely useful to you because they are limited in scope and are current, and they can supplement information in books. For example, if you want to understand the latest trends and research in the business communication field, you would browse through recent volumes of the *Journal of Business Communication*. And if you're studying the fluctuating prices of commodities like food and energy, a reputable newspaper's business section would be a good place to start to get oriented to the topic.

RESEARCH DATABASES. As a business report writer, you'll most likely do your secondary research using online research databases. Many researchers turn to databases first because they are fast, focused, and available online. Databases are exactly what they sound like: large collections of information in electronic format. In research databases, the information is almost every article published in every newspaper, magazine, academic journal, and trade journal—a huge amount of information, by any measure. By using these online resources you can look for the secondary data you require without ever leaving your office or home.

The strength of databases lies in the fact that they are current and field-specific. For example, if you go to the Mohawk College Library website (library.mohawk-college.ca/home), you'll instantly see the "Search all collections" search box and underneath it links that say "Library Catalogue" and "A–Z Databases." Clicking the databases link will give you options to see databases by subject, by database type, or by vendor or provider, or scroll down through the databases in alphabetical order.

If you click on "Canadian Business & Current Affairs," for example, you can view a database that focuses on business-related articles from Canadian sources, if you have a Mohawk ID. Libraries pay for these databases partly through your tuition fees. If in your workplace you don't have access to an institution's databases, your local public library (e.g., Vancouver Public Library) will have databases available (assuming you have a valid library card!).

Learning how to use an online database takes some practice. Go to your library's site and experiment with online databases. Choose a topic like *trends in business communication* and see what you come up with. Figure 9.3 shows a student doing just this, using Canadian Business & Current Affairs database.

The screen shots and their contents are published with permission of ProQuest LLC. Further reproduction is prohibited without permission.

Try to find one current article from a newspaper, a magazine, and a journal. Do you get better results when you use the basic or the advanced search function? Do you get better results by separating the topic into parts, for example, *trends* and

▼ **FIGURE 9.3 /** Conducting Secondary Research with a Research Database

business and *communication*, or by typing in the whole phrase at once? If you're having trouble, you can always sign up for a free guided seminar at your library, or ask a librarian for help next time you're there.

THE INTERNET. The Internet includes an enormous collection of pages created by people, organizations, and governments around the world. The Internet is interactive, mobile, and user-friendly. With trillions of pages of information available on the Internet, chances are that if you have a question, an answer exists online. To a business researcher, the Internet offers a wide range of information. You can find product and service facts, public relations material, mission statements, staff directories, press releases, current company news, government information, selected article reprints, collaborative scientific project reports, stock research, financial information, and employment information.

The Internet is unquestionably the greatest source of information now available to anyone needing facts quickly and inexpensively. But finding relevant, credible information can be frustrating and time-consuming. The constantly changing contents of the Internet and its lack of organization can irritate researchers. Moreover, content isn't always reliable. Anyone can publish content without any quality control or guarantee. To succeed in your search for high-quality information and answers, you need to understand how to browse the Internet and how to evaluate the information you find.

SEARCH ENGINE TIPS AND TECHNIQUES. To conduct a business research search using the leading search engine, Google, use these tips and techniques:

- **Consider Google Scholar.** If you'd like to find high-quality peer-reviewed sources from academic journals, start with Google Scholar before moving on to the regular Google search engine.
- **Understand case sensitivity.** Generally use lowercase for your searches, unless you are searching for a term that is typically written in upper- and lowercase, such as a person's name.
- **Use nouns as search words and as many as eight words in a query.** The right key words—and more of them—can narrow your search considerably. In other words *digital marketing* is a less effective search term than *digital marketing and search engine optimization.*
- **Use quotation marks.** When searching for a phrase, such as *cost-benefit analysis,* most search engines will retrieve documents having all or some of the terms. This and/or strategy is the default of most search engines. To locate occurrences of a specific phrase, enclose it in quotation marks.
- **Omit articles and prepositions.** Known as "stop words," articles and prepositions don't add value to a search. Instead of *request for proposal,* use *proposal request.*
- **Save the best.** To keep track of your favourite websites, save them as bookmarks or favourites.
- **Keep trying.** If a search produces no results, check your spelling. Try synonyms and variations on words. Try to be less specific in your search term. If your search produces too many hits, try to be more specific. Think of words that uniquely identify what you are looking for, and use as many relevant keywords as possible.

THE INTERNET AND CREDIBILITY. When searching online, you need to check the credibility and accuracy of the information you find. Anyone can publish online, and credibility can be difficult to determine. Unmoderated discussion forums are a case in point. The authorship may be unverifiable, and the credibility of the information may be questionable.

To assess the credibility of a Web page, scrutinize what you find using the following criteria:

- **Currency.** What is the date of the Web page? If the page you're looking at doesn't include date information for its content, the site is probably not reliable.

- **Authority.** Who publishes or sponsors this Web page? Is information about the author or sponsoring organization available on the About Us page? Can the author be contacted? Be skeptical about data and assertions from individuals and organizations whose credentials are not verifiable.
- **Content.** Is the purpose of the page to entertain, inform, convince, or sell? Is the purpose readily apparent? Who is the intended audience, based on content, tone, and style? Evaluate the overall value of the content and see how it compares with other resources on this topic.
- **Accuracy.** Do the facts that are presented seem reliable? Do you find errors in spelling, grammar, or usage? Do you see any evidence of bias? Are references provided? Do the external links work? Errors and missing references should alert you that the data may be questionable.

9.3b Primary Data

Providing answers to business problems often means generating primary data through surveys, interviews, focus groups, observation, or experimentation.

SURVEYS. Surveys collect data from groups of people. When companies develop new products, for example, they often survey consumers to learn their needs. The advantages of surveys are that they gather data economically and efficiently. Also, surveys are easy to respond to because they're designed with closed-ended, quantifiable questions. It's easy to pick an answer on a professionally designed survey, thus improving the accuracy of the data.

Surveys also have disadvantages. Most see them as an intrusion on our increasingly important private time, so response rates may be no higher than 10 percent. Furthermore, those who do respond may not represent an accurate sample of the overall population, thus invalidating generalizations for the group. Let's say that an insurance company sends out a survey questionnaire asking about provisions in a new policy. If only older retired people respond, the survey data can't be used to generalize what people in other age groups might think.

A final problem with surveys has to do with truthfulness. Some respondents exaggerate their incomes or distort other facts, thus causing the results to be unreliable. Nevertheless, surveys are still considered the best way to generate data for business and student reports.

Best practices in survey design are taught in research methods courses at colleges and universities. The basic rules—explain why the survey is being done, use a limited number of questions (usually fewer than ten), include questions that produce quantifiable answers, and avoid leading, biased, and ambiguous questions—should all be adhered to. These days, many students as well as professional researchers use free survey software by companies like SurveyMonkey to create and conduct their surveys. Figure 9.4 shows part of a survey created using SurveyMonkey's free software. You can find more information about survey design at the SurveyMonkey site: www.surveymonkey.com/mp/writing-survey-questions/.

INTERVIEWS. Some of the best report information, particularly on topics about which little has been written, comes from individuals. These individuals are usually experts in their fields. Tapping these sources will call for in-person, email, or telephone interviews. To create the most useful data in interviews, try the techniques discussed in Figure 9.5.

OBSERVATION AND EXPERIMENTATION. Some kinds of primary data can be obtained only through firsthand observation and investigation. How long does a typical caller wait before a customer service representative answers the call? How is a new piece of equipment operated? Are complaints of sexual harassment being taken seriously? Observation produces rich data but is especially prone to charges of subjectivity. One can interpret an observation in many ways. Thus, to make observations more objective, try to quantify them.

FIGURE 9.4 / Survey Creation Using SurveyMonkey

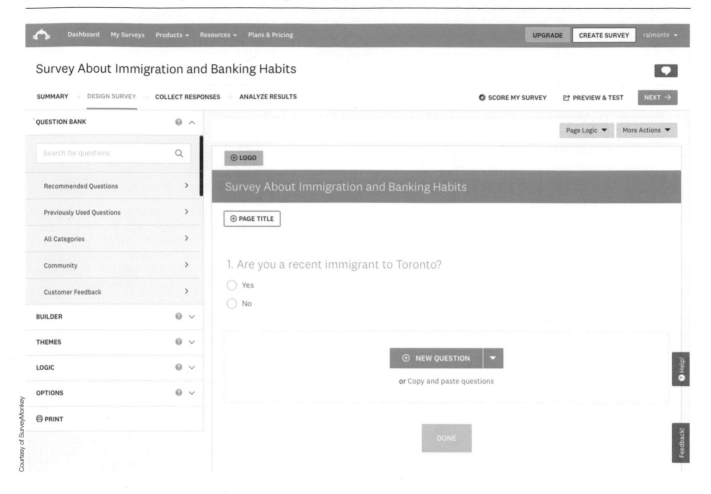

Courtesy of SurveyMonkey

For example, record customer telephone wait time for 60-minute periods at different times throughout a week. Or compare the number of sexual harassment complaints made with the number of investigations undertaken and the resulting actions.

When you observe, plan ahead. Arrive early enough to introduce yourself and set up whatever equipment you think is necessary. Make sure you've received permissions beforehand, particularly if you're recording. In addition, take notes, not only about the events or actions but also about the settings.

FIGURE 9.5 / How to Schedule and Conduct Interviews

Locate an Expert	Interview knowledgeable individuals who are experts in their field.
Prepare for the Interview	Read all you can about the topic you will discuss so you can converse intelligently. Learn the name and background of the individual you are interviewing. Be familiar with the terminology of the topic. Let's say you are interviewing a corporate communication expert about the advantages of creating a corporate blog. You ought to be familiar with terms such *as brand management, customer engagement, traffic,* and *damage control.*
Maintain a Professional Attitude	Call before the interview to confirm the appointment, and arrive on time. Be professional in your dress, language, and behaviour. If the interview is being conducted via email or Skype, send a reminder message the day before and ensure the recipient receives your interview questions the day before to prepare.
Ask Objective and Open-Ended Questions	Adopt a courteous, respectful attitude when asking questions. Open-ended questions encourage a variety of responses. Don't debate any issues and don't interrupt. You are there to listen, not to talk.
Watch the Time	Tell interviewees in advance how much time you'll need. Watch the clock and keep the interview discussion on track.
End Graciously	Conclude graciously with a general question, such as *Is there anything you'd like to add*? Express your appreciation, and ask permission to contact the interviewee later if necessary.

Experimentation produces data suggesting causes and effects. Informal experimentation might be as simple as a pretest and posttest in a college course. Did students expand their knowledge as a result of the course? More formal experimentation is undertaken by scientists and professional researchers who control variables to test their effects.

Imagine that Mordens' of Winnipeg Candy Manufacturing wants to test the *hypothesis* (which is a tentative assumption) that chocolate lifts people out of depression. An experiment testing the hypothesis would separate depressed individuals into two groups: those who ate chocolate (the experimental group) and those who did not (the control group). What effect did chocolate have? Such experiments are not done haphazardly, however. Valid experiments require sophisticated research designs, careful attention to matching the experimental and control groups, and ethical considerations.

9.4 Documenting and Citing Sources

In business reports, you'll often build on the ideas and words of others. In Western culture, whenever you "borrow" the ideas or words of others, you give credit to your information sources. This is called *documentation*. You can learn more about documentation (or citation) styles in Appendix C.

9.4a Documentation Guidelines

Whether you quote or paraphrase another person's words, you must document the source. To use the ideas of others skillfully and ethically, you need to know why, what, and how to document.

WHY DOCUMENT. As a careful business writer and presenter, you should document your data properly for the following reasons:

- **To strengthen your argument.** Including citations to reputable sources convinces readers of your credibility and the logic of your reasoning.
- **To protect yourself.** Acknowledging your sources keeps you honest. It's unethical and illegal to use others' ideas without proper documentation.
- **To instruct the reader or audience.** Citing sources enables readers and listeners to pursue a topic further and make use of the information themselves.

WHAT TO DOCUMENT. When you write reports, you're expected to conduct research, synthesize ideas, and build on the work of others. But you're also expected to give proper credit for borrowed material. To avoid plagiarism, give credit whenever you use the following:[2]

- Another person's ideas, opinions, examples, or theory
- Any facts, statistics, graphs, and drawings that are not common knowledge
- Quotations of another person's actual spoken or written words
- Paraphrases of another person's spoken or written words
- Visuals, images, and any kind of electronic media

Information that's common knowledge requires no documentation. For example, the statement *Many businesspeople agree that* Report on Business *is Canada's top business magazine* would require no citation. Statements that are not common knowledge, however, must be documented. For example, *Alberta is home to seven of Canada's top-ten fastest-growing large cities* would require a citation because most people don't know this fact (in this case the information came from a story on Huffingtonpost.ca quoting a recent Statistics Canada census). You probably already use citations to document direct quotations, but you must also cite ideas that you summarize in your own words.

HOW TO PARAPHRASE. When writing reports and using the ideas of others, you'll probably rely heavily on *paraphrasing*, which means restating already-published material in your own words and in your own style. To do a good job of paraphrasing, follow these steps:

1. Read the original material carefully to comprehend its full meaning.
2. Write your own version without looking at the original.
3. Avoid repeating the grammatical structure of the original and merely replacing words with synonyms.
4. Reread the original to be sure you covered the main points but didn't borrow specific language.

To better understand the difference between plagiarizing and paraphrasing, look at the following passages. Notice that the writer of the plagiarized version uses the same grammatical construction as the source and often merely replaces words with synonyms.

Original Source

We have seen, in a short amount of time, the disappearance of a large number of household brands that failed to take sufficient and early heed of the software revolution that is upending traditional brick-and-mortar businesses and creating a globally pervasive digital economy.[3]

Plagiarized Version

Many trusted household name brands disappeared very swiftly because they did not sufficiently and early pay attention to the software revolution that is toppling traditional physical businesses and creating a global digital economy (Saylor, 2012).

Effective Paraphrase

Digital technology has allowed a whole new virtual global economy to blossom and very swiftly wiped out some formerly powerful companies that responded too late or inadequately to the disruptive force that has swept the globe (Saylor, 2012).

HOW TO DOCUMENT. Documentation is achieved through citations. A citation is how you show your reader the borrowed idea or phrase or sentence. The original reason behind citations (before plagiarism became a big problem) was to allow anyone reading your work to find your sources should he or she want to do additional research. If someone says to you, "But you didn't cite it!" he or she means you didn't include a proper citation.

For example, in a report that reads: "Lemire and Gaudreault (2006) estimated that in 2003, Canada's road and highway network had over 50 percent of its useful life behind it, while federal and provincial bridges had passed the halfway mark of their useful lives,"[4] the APA-style citation is the combination of the lead-in phrase—*Lemire and Gaudreault . . . estimated*—and the bracketed date reference—*(2006)*. The basic elements of an APA-style (APA stands for the American Psychological Association) in-text citation are thus the author's name(s) + the date of publication in parentheses + a verb (e.g., *Almonte (2020) estimates*, *says*, *shows*, *argues*, *explains*). There will be times when you don't have these pieces of information.

For more information on such cases, as well as the two main citation methods—footnotes and endnotes (or Chicago style) and parenthetic (or author-date or APA style)—please read Appendix C. Besides in-text citations, you'll cite each source you've used (primary and secondary) at the end of your report on a page called the References page. There is a specific format for how this is done, also found in Appendix C.

▶ 9.5 Converting Data Into Meaningful Visuals

After collecting and interpreting information, you need to consider how best to present it. If your report contains complex numerical data, you should consider visuals such as tables and charts. They clarify your data, create visual interest for the reader, and make your numerical data meaningful. In contrast, readers tend to be bored and confused by text paragraphs packed with complex data and numbers. Use the following points as a general guide to creating effective visuals in a report:

- Clearly identify the contents of the visual aid with meaningful titles and numbering (e.g., *Figure 1: Social Media Use at Canadian Companies*).
- Refer the reader to the visual aid by discussing it in the text and mentioning its location and figure number (e.g., *as Figure 1 below shows . . .*).
- Locate the visual aid close to its reference in the text.
- Strive for vertical placement of visual aids. Readers are disoriented by horizontal pages in reports.
- Give credit to the source if appropriate (e.g., *Source: Statistics Canada*).

The same data can be shown in many forms. For example, a company's quarterly sales can be displayed in a chart, table, or graph. That's why you need to know how to match the appropriate graphic with your objective and how to incorporate it into your report.

9.5a Matching Visuals with Objectives

Before creating successful visuals, you should first decide what data you want to highlight and which visuals are most appropriate to your objectives. Figure 9.6 summarizes appropriate uses for each type of visual, and the sections that follow discuss each type in detail.

9.5b Creating Tables, Charts, and Infographics

The saying "a picture is worth a thousand words" definitely applies in business, where decision makers are pressed for time and need information in an easy-to-digest format.

▶ **FIGURE 9.6** / Matching Visuals With Objectives

Graphic		Objective
Table	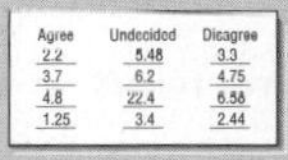	To show exact figures and values
Bar Chart		To compare one item with others
Line Chart	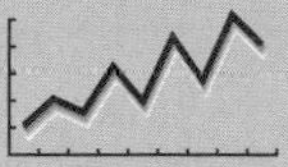	To demonstrate changes in quantitative data over time
Pie Chart		To visualize a whole unit and the proportions of its components
Flow Chart	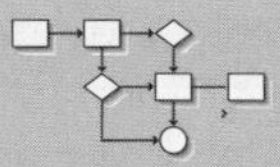	To display a process or procedure
Organization Chart	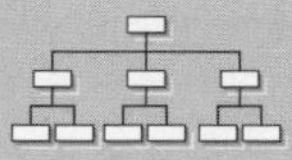	To define a hierarchy of elements
Photograph, Map, Illustration		To create authenticity, to spotlight a location, and to show an item in use

© Cengage Learning

FIGURE 9.7 / Table Summarizing Data

FIGURE 1 SATSUNO COMPUTING NUMBER OF TABLETS SOLD, 2021					
Region	**1st Qtr.**	**2nd Qtr.**	**3rd Qtr.**	**4th Qtr.**	**Yearly Totals**
Atlantic	13,302	15,003	15,550	16,210	60,065
Central	12,678	11,836	10,689	14,136	49,339
Prairie	10,345	11,934	10,899	12,763	45,941
Pacific	9,345	8,921	9,565	10,256	38,087
Total	45,670	47,694	46,703	53,365	193,432

For this reason report writers have moved away from large amounts of text and toward a more visual style of report writing in which tables, charts, PowerPoint slides, and infographics are prominently used to succinctly convey data.

TABLES. Probably the most frequently used visual aid in reports is the table. A table presents quantitative information in a systematic order of columns and rows. Here are tips for designing good tables, one of which is illustrated in Figure 9.7:

- Provide clear headings for the rows and columns.
- Identify the units in which figures are given (percentages, dollars, units per worker-hour, and so forth) in the table title, in the column or row head, with the first item in a column, or in a note at the bottom.
- Arrange items in a logical order (alphabetical, chronological, geographical, highest to lowest) depending on what you need to emphasize.
- Use *N/A* (not available) for missing data.
- Make long tables easier to read by shading alternate lines or by leaving a blank line after groups of five.

BAR CHARTS. Although they lack the precision of tables, bar charts enable you to make emphatic visual comparisons. Bar charts can be used to compare related items, illustrate changes in data over time, and show segments as part of a whole. Figures 9.8 through 9.11 show vertical, horizontal, grouped, and segmented bar charts that highlight income for an entertainment company called MPM. Note how the varied bar charts present information in different ways.

FIGURE 9.8 / Vertical Bar Chart

2021 MPM INCOME BY DIVISION

Source: Industry Profiles (New York: DataPro, 2017), p. 225. © Cengage Learning Inc.

FIGURE 9.9 / Horizontal Bar Chart

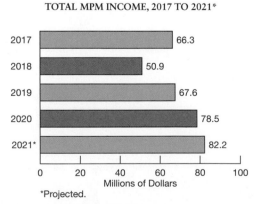

TOTAL MPM INCOME, 2017 TO 2021*

*Projected.

Source: Industry Profiles (New York: DataPro, 2017). © Cengage Learning

FIGURE 9.10 / Grouped Bar Chart

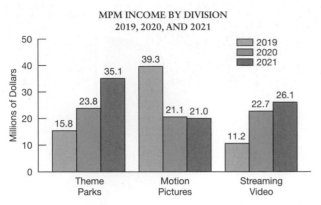

MPM INCOME BY DIVISION
2019, 2020, AND 2021

Source: Industry Profiles (New York: DataPro, 2017). © Cengage Learning

FIGURE 9.11 / Segmented 100 Percent Bar Chart

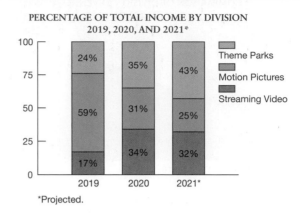

PERCENTAGE OF TOTAL INCOME BY DIVISION
2019, 2020, AND 2021*

*Projected.

Source: Industry Profiles (New York: DataPro, 2017). © Cengage Learning

Many suggestions for tables also hold true for bar charts. Here are a few additional tips:

- Keep the length of each bar and segment proportional.
- Include a total figure in the middle of a bar or at its end if the figure helps the reader and does not clutter the chart.
- Start dollar or percentage amounts at zero.

LINE CHARTS. The major advantage of line charts is that they show changes over time, indicating trends. Figures 9.12 through 9.14 show line charts that reflect revenue trends for the major divisions of MPM. Notice that line charts don't provide precise data. Instead, they give an overview or impression of the data. Experienced report writers use tables to list exact data; they use line charts or bar charts to spotlight important points or trends.

Simple line charts (Figure 9.12) show just one variable. Multiple line charts combine several variables (Figure 9.13). Segmented line charts (Figure 9.14), also called *surface charts*, illustrate how the components of a whole change over time.

Here are tips for preparing line charts:

- Begin with a grid divided into squares.
- Arrange the time component (usually years) horizontally across the bottom; arrange values for the other variable vertically.

FIGURE 9.12 / Simple Line Chart

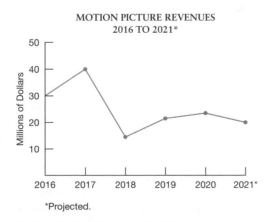

MOTION PICTURE REVENUES
2016 TO 2021*

*Projected.

Source: Industry Profiles (New York: DataPro, 2017). © Cengage Learning Inc.

FIGURE 9.13 / Multiple Line Chart

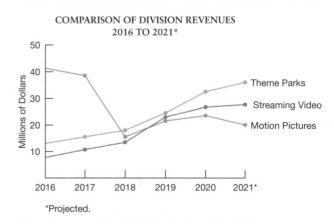

COMPARISON OF DIVISION REVENUES
2016 TO 2021*

*Projected.

Source: Industry Profiles (New York: DataPro, 2017). © Cengage Learning

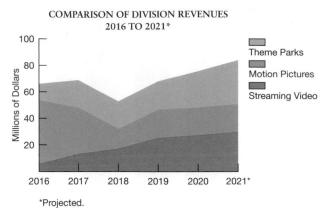

Source: Industry Profiles (New York: DataPro, 2017). © Cengage Learning

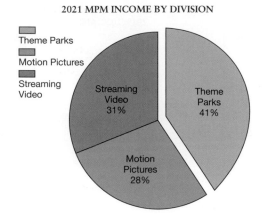

Source: Industry Profiles (New York: DataPro, 2017). © Cengage Learning

- Draw small dots at the intersections to indicate each value at a given year.
- Connect the dots and add colour if desired.
- To prepare a segmented (surface) chart, plot the first value (e.g., *streaming video*) across the bottom; add the next item (e.g., *motion picture income*) to the first figures for every increment; for the third item (e.g., *theme park income*) add its value to the total of the first two items. The top line indicates the total of the three values.

PIE CHARTS. Pie charts help readers visualize a whole and the proportion of its components, or wedges. Pie charts, though less flexible than bar or line charts, are useful in showing percentages, as Figure 9.15 illustrates. For the most effective pie charts, follow these suggestions:

- Begin at the 12 o'clock position, drawing the largest wedge first. (Software programs don't always observe this advice, but if you're drawing your own charts, you can.)
- Include, if possible, the actual percentage or absolute value for each wedge.
- Use four to eight segments for best results; if necessary, group small portions into one wedge called "Other."
- Distinguish wedges with colour, shading, or cross-hatching.
- Keep all labels horizontal.

FLOW CHARTS. Procedures are simplified and clarified by diagramming them in a flow chart, as shown in Figure 9.16. Whether you need to describe the procedure for handling a customer's purchase order or outline steps in solving a problem, flow charts help the reader visualize the process. Traditional flow charts use the following symbols:

- Ovals to designate the beginning and end of a process
- Diamonds to denote decision points
- Rectangles to represent major activities or steps.

ORGANIZATION CHARTS. Many large organizations are so complex that they need charts to show the chain of command, from the CEO down to managers and employees. Organization charts like the one in Figure 9.17 provide such information as who reports to whom, how many subordinates work for each manager (the span of control), and what channels of official communication exist. These charts may illustrate a company's structure—for example, by function, customer, or product. They may also be organized by the work being performed in each job or by the hierarchy of decision making.

USING SOFTWARE TO PRODUCE VISUALS. Designing effective visuals is easy with software. Spreadsheet programs such as Microsoft's Excel, as well as presentation programs such as Microsoft's PowerPoint, allow anyone to design quality visuals that can be printed for distribution in meetings, used in slides for presentations, or shared as PDFs.

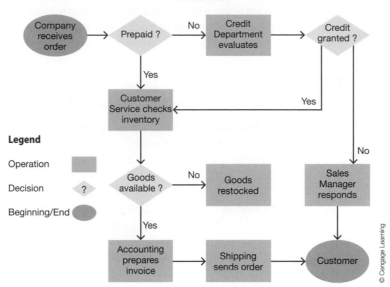

FLOW OF CUSTOMER ORDER THROUGH
ACME INC.

© Cengage Learning

An *infographic* is a visual representation of complex information in a format that's easy to understand. Compelling infographics tell a story by combining images and graphic elements, such as charts and diagrams. Free software from providers like piktochart.com, venngage.com, and canva.com allows anyone to create professional-looking infographics, like the one you encountered in Chapter 8 (Figure 8.4).

▟ FIGURE 9.17 / Organization Chart

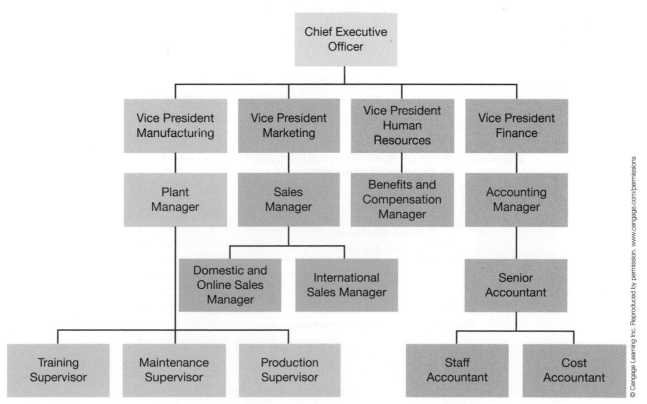

Organization Chart for XYZ Co.

© Cengage Learning Inc. Reproduced by permission. www.cengage.com/permissions

9.6 Sequencing the Report

Formal business reports with substantial research, analysis, and recommendations are organized into three major sections, as shown in the writing plan. Following the plan are detailed description of each section. Refer to the model formal report in Figure 9.18 for illustrations of these sections.

WRITING PLAN FOR A FORMAL REPORT

- **Front matter:** Before the actual report begins, several items are included such as a title page, a transmittal letter (if required), a table of contents, and an executive summary.
- **Body:** The report itself has three parts: an introduction, the findings, and the conclusion and recommendations.
- **Back matter:** After the actual report is over, a couple of items can be included such as a References list and appendixes.

9.6a Front Matter

Front matter items (everything before the body of a report) and back matter items (everything after the conclusions and recommendations) lengthen formal reports but enhance their professional tone and serve their multiple audiences. Formal reports may be read by many levels of managers, along with technical specialists and financial consultants. Therefore, breaking a long, formal report into small segments—and sometimes repeating the same information in different ways in these segments—makes a report more accessible and easier to understand.

TITLE PAGE. A report title page, as illustrated in the Figure 9.18 model report, begins with the name of the report typed in uppercase letters (no underscore and no quotation marks). Next comes *Prepared for* (or *Submitted to*) and the name, title, and organization of the individual receiving the report. Lower on the page is *Prepared by* (or *Submitted by*) and the author's name plus any necessary identification.

FIGURE 9.18 / Model Formal Report – Title Page

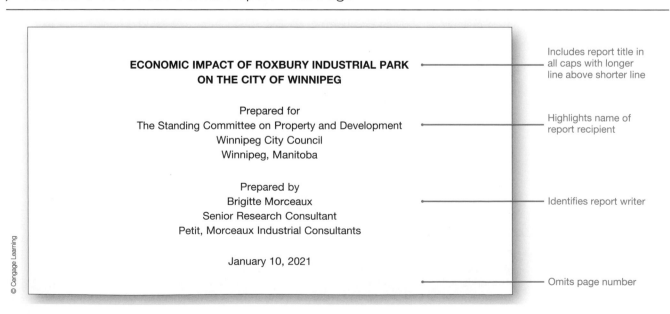

© Cengage Learning

ECONOMIC IMPACT OF ROXBURY INDUSTRIAL PARK
ON THE CITY OF WINNIPEG

Prepared for
The Standing Committee on Property and Development
Winnipeg City Council
Winnipeg, Manitoba

Prepared by
Brigitte Morceaux
Senior Research Consultant
Petit, Morceaux Industrial Consultants

January 10, 2021

Includes report title in all caps with longer line above shorter line

Highlights name of report recipient

Identifies report writer

Omits page number

FIGURE 9.18 / Model Formal Report - Transmittal

PETIT, MORCEAUX INDUSTRIAL CONSULTANTS

588 Main Street
Winnipeg, Manitoba R2L 1E6

www.petitmorceaux.com
(204) 549-1101

January 12, 2021

Councillor Richard Moody
Chairperson
Standing Committee on Property and Development
City of Winnipeg
Winnipeg, MB R2L 1E9

Dear Councillor Moody:

The attached report, requested by the Standing Policy Committee on Property and Development in a letter dated May 20, describes the economic impact of Roxbury Industrial Park on the City of Winnipeg. We believe you will find the results of this study useful in evaluating future development of industrial parks within the city limits.

This study was designed to examine economic impact in three areas:

(1) Current and projected tax and other revenues accruing to the city from Roxbury Industrial Park

(2) Current and projected employment generated by the park

(3) Indirect effects on local employment, income, and economic growth

Primary research consisted of interviews with 15 Roxbury Industrial Park tenants and managers, in addition to a 2017 survey of over 5000 RIP employees. Secondary research sources included the Annual Budget of the City of Winnipeg, other government publications, periodicals, books, and online resources. Results of this research, discussed more fully in this report, indicate that Roxbury Industrial Park exerts a significant beneficial influence on the Winnipeg metropolitan economy.

I would be pleased to discuss this report and its conclusions with you at your request. My firm and I thank you for your confidence in selecting our company to prepare this comprehensive report.

Sincerely,

Brigitte Morceaux

Brigitte Morceaux
Senior Research Consultant
bmonceaux@petitmonceaux.com

BM:mef

Attachment

Annotations (left margin):

- Announces report and identifies authorization
- Gives broad overview of report purposes
- Describes primary and secondary research
- Offers to discuss report; expresses appreciation

FIGURE 9.18 / Model Formal Report – Table of Contents

TABLE OF CONTENTS

LIST OF FIGURES

Uses leaders to guide eye from heading to page number

Indents secondary headings to show levels of outline

Includes tables and figures in one list for simplified numbering

iii

EXECUTIVE SUMMARY

Opens directly with major research findings

Winnipeg can benefit from the development of industrial parks like the Roxbury Industrial Park. Both direct and indirect economic benefits result, as shown by this in-depth study conducted by Petit, Morceaux Industrial Consultants. The study was authorized by the Standing Committee on Property and Development when Goldman-Lyon & Associates sought City Council's approval for the proposed construction of a G-L industrial park. The City Council requested evidence demonstrating that an existing development could actually benefit the city.

Identifies data sources

Our conclusion that Winnipeg benefits from industrial parks is based on data supplied by a survey of 5000 Roxbury Industrial Park employees, personal interviews with managers and tenants of RIP, City and Provincial documents, and professional literature.

Summarizes organization of report

Analysis of the data revealed benefits in three areas:

(1) Revenues. The City of Winnipeg earned nearly $1 million in tax and other revenues from the Roxbury Industrial Park in 2020. By 2024 this income is expected to reach $1.7 million (in constant 2020 dollars).

(2) Employment. In 2020 RIP businesses employed a total of 7035 workers, who earned an average wage of $28 120. By 2024 RIP businesses are expected to employ directly nearly 15 000 employees who will earn salaries totalling over $450 million.

(3) Indirect benefits. Because of the multiplier effect, by 2024 Roxbury Industrial Park will directly and indirectly generate a total of 38 362 jobs in the Winnipeg area.

Condenses recommendations

On the basis of these findings, it is recommended that development of additional industrial parks be encouraged to stimulate local economic growth.

iv

FIGURE 9.18 / Model Formal Report – Introduction

ECONOMIC IMPACT OF ROXBURY INDUSTRIAL PARK

Shortened report title repeated at beginning of Introduction

PROBLEM

This study was designed to analyze the direct and indirect economic impact of Roxbury Industrial Park on the City of Winnipeg. Specifically, the study seeks answers to these questions:

(1) What current tax and other revenues result directly from this park? What tax and other revenues may be expected in the future?

(2) How many and what kind of jobs are directly attributable to the park? What is the employment picture for the future?

Lists three problem questions

(3) What indirect effects has Roxbury Industrial Park had on local employment, incomes, and economic growth?

BACKGROUND

The Standing Committee on Property and Development commissioned this study of Roxbury Industrial Park at the request of Winnipeg City Council. Before authorizing the development of a proposed Goldman-Lyon industrial park, the City Council requested a study examining the economic effects of an existing park. Members of Council wanted to determine to what extent industrial parks benefit the local community, and they chose Roxbury Industrial Park as an example.

Describes authorization for report and background of study

For those who are unfamiliar with it, Roxbury Industrial Park is a 40-hectare industrial park located in Winnipeg about 2.5 kilometres from the centre of the city. Most of the area lies within a specially designated area known as Redevelopment Project No. 2, which is part of the Winnipeg Capital Region Development Commission's planning area. Planning for the park began in 2018; construction started in 2020.

1

FIGURE 9.18 / Model Formal Report – Findings

The park now contains 14 building complexes with over 25 000 square metres of completed building space. The majority of the buildings are used for office, research and development, marketing and distribution, or manufacturing uses. Approximately 5 hectares of the original area are yet to be developed.

Provides specifics for data sources

Data for this report came from a 2020 survey of over 5000 Roxbury Industrial Park employees, interviews with 15 RIP tenants and managers, the Annual Budget of the City of Winnipeg, current books, articles, journals, and online resources. Projections for future revenues resulted from analysis of past trends and *Estimates of Revenues for Debt Service Coverage, Redevelopment Project Area 2* (Miller, 2014, pp. 78–79).

APA-style (parenthetical) citation

DISCUSSION OF FINDINGS

The results of this research indicate that major direct and indirect benefits have accrued to the City of Winnipeg and surrounding municipal areas as a result of the development of Roxbury Industrial Park. The research findings presented here fall into three categories: (a) revenues, (b) employment, and (c) indirect effects.

Previews organization of report

Revenues

Roxbury Industrial Park contributes a variety of tax and other revenues to the City of Winnipeg. Figure 1 summarizes revenues.

Uses topical arrangement

Figure 1

Places figure close to textual reference

REVENUES RECEIVED BY THE CITY OF WINNIPEG
FROM ROXBURY INDUSTRIAL PARK

Current Revenues and Projections to 2024

	2020	2024
Property taxes	$604 140	$1 035 390
Revenues from licences	126 265	216 396
Business taxes	75 518	129 424
Provincial service receipts	53 768	92 134
Licences and permits	48 331	82 831
Other revenues	64 039	111 987
Total	$972 061	$1 668 162

City of Winnipeg Chief Financial Officer. (2020). 2021 annual financial report. Retrieved from http://www.winnipeg.ca/financials/2021

2

FIGURE 9.18 / Model Formal Report – Findings Continued

Sales and Use Revenues

As shown in Figure 1, the city's largest source of revenues from RIP is the property tax. Revenues from this source totalled $604 140 in 2021, according to the City of Winnipeg Standing Committee on Finance (City of Winnipeg, 2021, p.103). Property taxes accounted for more than half of the park's total contribution to the City of $972 061.

Continues interpreting figures in table

Other Revenues

Other major sources of City revenues from RIP in 2021 include revenues from licences such as motor vehicle in lieu fees, trailer coach licences ($126 265), business taxes ($75 518), and provincial service receipts ($53 768).

Projections

Total City revenues from RIP will nearly double by 2021, producing an income of $1.7 million. This projection is based on an annual growth rate of 1.4 percent in constant 2021 dollars.

Employment

One of the most important factors to consider in the overall effect of an industrial park is employment. In Roxbury Industrial Park the distribution, number, and wages of people employed will change considerably in the next five years.

Sets stage for next topics to be discussed

Distribution

A total of 7035 employees currently work in various industry groups at Roxbury Industrial Park, as shown below in Figure 2. The largest number of workers (58 percent) is employed in manufacturing and assembly operations. In the next largest category, the computer and electronics industry employs 24 percent of the workers. Some overlap probably exists because electronics assembly could be included in either group. Employees also work in publishing (9 percent), warehousing and storage (5 percent), and other industries (4 percent).

Although the distribution of employees at Roxbury Industrial Park shows a wide range of employment categories, it must be noted that other industrial parks would likely generate an entirely different range of job categories.

3

Pie chart shows proportion of a whole

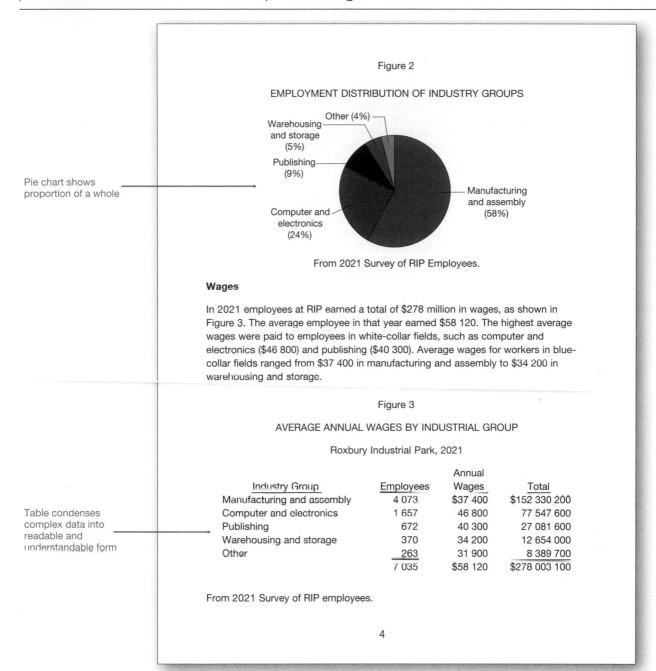

Figure 2

EMPLOYMENT DISTRIBUTION OF INDUSTRY GROUPS

From 2021 Survey of RIP Employees.

Wages

In 2021 employees at RIP earned a total of $278 million in wages, as shown in Figure 3. The average employee in that year earned $58 120. The highest average wages were paid to employees in white-collar fields, such as computer and electronics ($46 800) and publishing ($40 300). Average wages for workers in blue-collar fields ranged from $37 400 in manufacturing and assembly to $34 200 in warehousing and storage.

Figure 3

AVERAGE ANNUAL WAGES BY INDUSTRIAL GROUP

Roxbury Industrial Park, 2021

Industry Group	Employees	Annual Wages	Total
Manufacturing and assembly	4 073	$37 400	$152 330 200
Computer and electronics	1 657	46 800	77 547 600
Publishing	672	40 300	27 081 600
Warehousing and storage	370	34 200	12 654 000
Other	263	31 900	8 389 700
	7 035	$58 120	$278 003 100

Table condenses complex data into readable and understandable form

From 2021 Survey of RIP employees.

4

Projections

By 2021 Roxbury Industrial Park is expected to more than double its number of employees, bringing the total to over 15 000 workers. The total payroll in 2018 will also more than double, producing over $450 million (using constant 2021 dollars) in salaries to RIP employees. These projections are based on an 8 percent growth rate, along with anticipated increased employment as the park reaches its capacity (Miller, 2018, pp. 78–79).

Future development in the park will influence employment and payrolls. As Ivan Novak, RIP project manager, stated in an interview, much of the remaining five hectares is planned for medium-rise office buildings, garden offices, and other structures for commercial, professional, and personal services (September 2021). Average wages for employees are expected to increase because of an anticipated shift to higher-paying white-collar jobs. Industrial parks often follow a similar pattern of evolution (Badri, 2013, pp. 38–45). Like many industrial parks, RIP evolved from a ware-housing centre into a manufacturing complex.

Clarifies information and explains what it means in relation to original research questions

CONCLUSION AND RECOMMENDATIONS

Offers conclusion and recommendations

Analysis of tax revenues, employment data, personal interviews, and professional literature leads to the following conclusions and recommendations about the economic impact of Roxbury Industrial Park on the City of Winnipeg:

1. Property tax and other revenues produced nearly $1 million in income to the City of Winnipeg in 2021. By 2018 revenues are expected to produce $1.7 million in city income.

2. RIP currently employs 7035 employees, the majority of whom are working in manufacturing and assembly. The average employee in 2021 earned $38 120.

3. By 2021 RIP is expected to employ more than 15 000 workers producing a total payroll of over $450 million.

4. Employment trends indicate that by 2021 more RIP employees will be engaged in higher-paying white-collar positions.

On the basis of these findings, we recommend that the City Council of Winnipeg authorize the development of additional industrial parks to stimulate local economic growth.

5

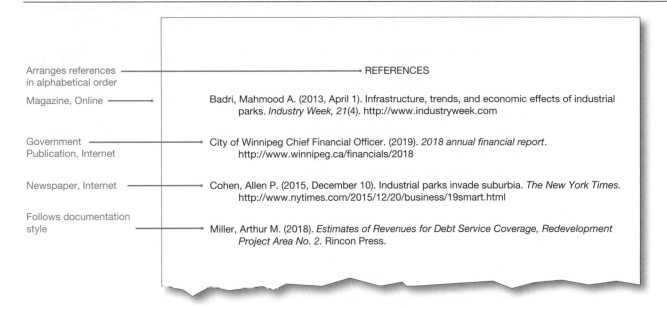

Arranges references in alphabetical order

Magazine, Online

Government Publication, Internet

Newspaper, Internet

Follows documentation style

REFERENCES

Badri, Mahmood A. (2013, April 1). Infrastructure, trends, and economic effects of industrial parks. *Industry Week, 21*(4). http://www.industryweek.com

City of Winnipeg Chief Financial Officer. (2019). *2018 annual financial report*. http://www.winnipeg.ca/financials/2018

Cohen, Allen P. (2015, December 10). Industrial parks invade suburbia. *The New York Times*. http://www.nytimes.com/2015/12/20/business/19smart.html

Miller, Arthur M. (2018). *Estimates of Revenues for Debt Service Coverage, Redevelopment Project Area No. 2.* Rincon Press.

The last item on the title page is the date of submission. All items after the title appear in a combination of upper- and lowercase letters. The information on the title page should be evenly spaced and balanced on the page for a professional look.

LETTER, MEMO, OR EMAIL OF TRANSMITTAL. Generally written on organization letterhead (unless being sent via email), a transmittal introduces a formal report. You'll recall that letters are sent to external audiences; memos, to internal audiences. A transmittal follows the direct strategy and is usually less formal than the report itself. For example, the letter or memo may use contractions and the first-person pronouns *I* and *we*. The transmittal typically (a) announces the topic of the report and tells how it was authorized; (b) briefly describes the project; (c) highlights the report's findings, conclusions, and recommendations, if the reader is expected to be supportive; and (d) closes with appreciation for the assignment, instructions for the reader's follow-up actions, acknowledgment of help from others, or offers of assistance in answering questions. If a report is going to various readers, a special transmittal should be prepared for each, anticipating how each reader will use the report.

TABLE OF CONTENTS. The table of contents shows the headings in a report and their page numbers. It gives an overview of the report topics and helps readers locate them. Wait to prepare the table of contents until after you've completed the report. For short reports you should include all headings. For longer reports you might want to list only first- and second-level headings. Leaders (spaced or unspaced dots) help guide the eye from the heading to the page number. Items may be indented in outline form or typed flush with the left margin.

LIST OF FIGURES. For reports with several figures or tables, include a list to help readers locate them. This list should appear on the same page as the table of contents, space permitting. For each figure or table, include a title and page number.

EXECUTIVE SUMMARY. The purpose of an executive summary is to present an overview of a longer report to people who may not have time to read the entire document. This time-saving device summarizes the purpose, key points, findings, and conclusions. An executive summary is usually no longer than 10 percent of the original document. Therefore, a 20-page report might require a two-page executive summary.

9.6b Report Body

The main section of a report begins with an introduction, includes a discussion of findings, and concludes with a summary and usually with recommendations.

INTRODUCTION. Formal reports start with an introduction that sets the scene and announces the subject. Because they contain many parts serving different purposes, the same information may be included in the letter or memo of transmittal, executive summary, and introduction. To avoid sounding repetitious, try to present the information slightly differently in each section.

A good report introduction typically covers the following elements, although not necessarily in this order:

- **Background:** Describe the events leading up to the problem or need.
- **Problem and purpose:** Explain the report topic and specify the problem or need that motivated the report.
- **Significance:** Say why the topic is important. You may want to quote experts or cite newspapers, journals, books, Web resources, and other secondary sources to establish the importance of the topic.
- **Scope and limitations:** Clarify the boundaries of the report, defining what will be included or excluded.
- **Sources and methods:** Describe your secondary sources (periodicals, books, databases). Also explain how you collected primary data, including survey size, sample design, and software used.
- **Definitions:** Define any terms you'll use in your findings section that may not be clear to every reader.
- **Organization:** Orient readers by giving them a road map that previews the structure of the report.

FINDINGS. This is the main section of the report and contains numerous headings and subheadings. It's not necessary to use the title *Findings*; many business report writers prefer to begin immediately with the major headings into which the body of the report is divided. Present your findings objectively, avoiding the use of first-person pronouns (*I, we*). Include tables, charts, and graphs to illustrate findings. Analytic and scientific reports may include another section entitled *Implications of Findings*, in which the findings are analyzed and related to the problem. Less formal reports contain the author's analysis of the research findings within the findings section itself. In other words, most business research reports present data and follow the presentation by analyzing what the data means.

CONCLUSION AND RECOMMENDATIONS. If the report has been largely informational, it ends with a summary of the data presented. However, the report will usually also analyze its research findings; in that case it should end with conclusions drawn from the analyses. An analytic report frequently poses research questions. The conclusion to such a report reviews the major findings and answers the research questions. If a report seeks to determine a course of action, it may end with conclusions and recommendations. Recommendations regarding a course of action may be placed in a separate section or incorporated with the conclusions. Recommendations should be numbered in order of descending importance (i.e., the most important recommendation first) and should begin with a present-tense verb (e.g., *Purchase, Inform, Reduce*).

9.6c Back Matter

The back matter of most reports includes a reference section and one or more appendixes. The reference section includes a bibliography of sources, and the appendix contains supplemental information or source documents. In organizing the back matter sections, use standard Arabic numerals to number the pages.

REFERENCES. If you use the APA format, like most business writers, list your sources in a section called *References*. Your listed sources must correspond to in-text citations in the report whenever you are borrowing words or ideas from published and unpublished resources.

APPENDIXES. If there is information that was too lengthy to include in the body of the report itself, but that would help a reader be persuaded by your conclusion and recommendations, include it in one or more appendixes. Examples of such material might be raw primary data (e.g., full interview responses, full survey responses).

9.6d Model Formal Report

In the formal report shown in Figure 9.18, Brigitte Morceaux, senior research consultant with Petit, Morceaux Industrial Consultants, examined the economic impact of a local industrial park on the city of Winnipeg, resulting in this formal report.

Brigitte's report illustrates the best practices discussed in this chapter. Although it's a good example of a traditional report format and style, it shouldn't be viewed as the only way to present a report. For example, as mentioned earlier in this chapter, many reports today have less text and more graphics than this model report; others are presented via PowerPoint slides or Infographics software.

Cengage

MINDTAP

In MindTap go to the Study Tools for Chapter 9 and complete the Practice Test.

■ LEARNING SUMMARY

9.1 Write effective informal business proposals.

- Proposals are written offers that solve problems, provide services, or sell products.
- Proposals may be solicited (requested by an organization) or unsolicited (written to offer a service, request funding, or solve a problem).
- Components of informal proposals often include an introduction; a background and purpose statement; a proposal, plan, and schedule; staffing requirements; a budget showing project costs; and a conclusion.
- Formal proposals often include additional components, such as a letter of transmittal, a title page, a table of contents, and an appendix.

9.2 Follow a plan for writing formal reports.

- Writers begin formal reports with a statement of purpose that defines the focus of the report.
- Report writers focus on their readers' needs and wants to present relevant findings.
- Researchers gather information from primary sources (firsthand observation, interviews, and surveys) and secondary sources (books, articles, journals, and the Internet).
- Writers proofread and edit formal reports by reviewing the format, spacing and font consistency, graphics placement, heading levels, data accuracy, and mechanics.

9.3 Collect effective primary and secondary data for reports.

- Writers gather most of their research from secondary sources by reading what others have published in books, scholarly journals, magazines, and Internet documents.
- Internet researchers find the information they want by using search terms and advanced search features to filter the results.
- Good writers assess the credibility of each Internet resource by evaluating its currency (last update), author or sponsoring organization, content, purpose, and accuracy.
- Report writers gather data from primary sources by distributing surveys, conducting interviews, and collecting data from firsthand observation.

9.4 Document report sources effectively.

- Documenting sources means giving credit to information sources to avoid plagiarism.
- The most common business citation format is from the American Psychological Association (APA style).

9.5 Convert report data into meaningful visuals.

- Visuals clarify data, add interest, and make complex data easy to understand; they should be placed close to where they are referenced.
- Tables show quantitative information in systematic columns and rows; they require meaningful titles, bold column headings, and a logical data arrangement (alphabetical, chronological, etc.)

- Bar charts and line charts show visual comparisons using horizontal or vertical bars or lines of varying lengths; pie charts show a whole and the proportion of its components; flow charts diagram processes and procedures.

- Infographics, popular in online environments, combine images and graphic elements to illustrate information in an easy-to-understand format.

9.6 Sequence a formal report effectively.

- Front matter components of formal reports include the following: title page, letter or memo of transmittal, table of contents, list of figures, and executive summary.

- Body components of formal reports include the introduction, the body, and the conclusions and recommendations.

- The body is the principal section of a formal report and discusses, analyzes, interprets, and evaluates the research findings before drawing conclusions.

- Back matter components of a formal report include a reference page and any appendixes.

◣ CHAPTER REVIEW

1. Who uses requests for proposals (RFPs) and why? (Obj. 1)

2. What are the principal parts and functions of an informal proposal? (Obj. 1)

3. Why is the budget section of a proposal especially important? (Obj. 1)

4. What is the first step in writing a formal report? (Obj. 2)

5. Why do formal report writers include visuals in reports? (Obj. 5)

6. List three sources of secondary report information, and be prepared to discuss how valuable each might be in writing a formal report about updating your company's travel policy. (Obj. 3)

7. Define these terms: *browser, URL, search engine.* (Obj. 3)

8. Explain plagiarism and how to avoid it. (Obj. 4)

9. What are the elements of a successful APA citation? (Obj. 4)

10. Pie charts are most helpful in showing what? (Obj. 5)

11. Line graphs are most effective in showing what? (Obj. 5)

12. List three reasons for documenting data in a business report. (Obj. 4)

13. What are some patterns you can use to organize your report's findings? (Obj. 2)

◣ CRITICAL THINKING

1. In what ways is a proposal similar to a sales message? (Obj. 1)

2. Why is proposal writing an important function in many businesses? (Obj. 1)

3. To what degree is information obtained on the Internet as reliable as information obtained from journals, newspapers, and magazines? Explain. (Obj. 3)

4. Should all reports be written so that they follow the sequence of investigation—that is, description of the initial problem, analysis of issues, data collection, data analysis, and conclusions? Why or why not? (Objs. 4, 6)

5. Are primary or secondary data more likely to be useful in a business report? Why? (Obj. 3)

6. Why is plagiarism a serious issue in the business world? Discuss. (Obj. 4)

7. Do visuals truly enhance a report or do they simply make its presentation livelier? (Obj. 5)

◣ ACTIVITIES AND CASES

9.1 INFORMAL PROPOSAL: PROPOSING A BUSINESS WRITING WORKSHOP (OBJ. 1)

Whether emailing status updates to team members, writing a Web article, preparing meeting agendas, or corresponding with potential customers, employees must write concise, coherent, clear, error-free documents and messages. As the founder of Business Writing Solutions, you offer one- and two-day business writing workshops for businesses and organizations. Your website features writing tips, workshop descriptions, and your contact information. These workshops are presented onsite in corporate training rooms.

You received an email inquiry from Human Resources Director Janet Somerfield, who is considering a one-day, onsite business writing workshop for employees in her midsized advertising agency. Janet is looking at several seminar companies who offer writing training. She asks about pricing, optimal class size, and course content. She also wants to know whether you can offer feedback on writing samples. Because Janet is considering other training options, you decide to respond with an informal proposal. Your goal is to meet her needs and win the contract.

Decide where it is appropriate to mention the following advantages of improving writing skills in business environments:

- Excellent writing skills help build trusting relationships, improve one's professional image, and add to the credibility of an organization.

- Business associates appreciate clarity, conciseness, and results-focused messages.

- Better writing skills help employees advance their careers, which in turn improves retention.

The one-day workshop is offered in two four-hour blocks in the client's training room. The course includes the following topics: (a) writing results-oriented email messages; (b) structuring routine, persuasive, and negative news messages; (c) reviewing the most common grammar errors; and (d) designing documents for readability. You will also offer feedback on brief writing samples furnished by the participants. Employees who attend the workshop will earn a certificate of completion.

The cost of the writing workshop is $175 per person. If 15 employees participate, the cost would be $2,625. The cost includes workbooks and writing supplies for each participant.

Your Task. Write an informal letter proposal promoting a one-day business writing workshop to Janet Somerfield, Director, Human Resources, The Buzz Agency, 211 Preston Avenue North, Saskatoon, SK S7N 4V2, jsomerfield@buzzagency.ca.

9.2 INFORMAL PROPOSAL: STUDENT VIEWS CONSULTING INC. (OBJ. 1)

Imagine you are in your last semester of college or university. As part of your business program, there is a course you can take called Consulting Business Simulation. This course allows students to simulate running a consulting business for a semester. You enrol in the course, and on the first day of class the instructor says, "There's only one requirement in this course, and it's worth 100 percent of your grade. You will design, conduct, and write a research proposal and project of your choice for this institution. You won't get paid for it, but you'll have gained a lot of experience that will look good on your résumé." You choose to work with two other students and you call yourselves Student Views Consulting Inc. You decide to tackle the problem of poor customer service at your institution.

Your Task. Write a proposal to the director of Student Services at your college or university. Propose that your consulting firm carry out a detailed study on current student satisfaction at your institution, which you understand has been problematic lately. For example, there have been questions about how effectively telephone, email, and in-person queries are being handled in various college departments and offices. Also, how the service level at your institution compares to that of competing institutions in the same area has been questioned. Describe the background of this problem and draft a schedule of the work to be done. Cost out this research realistically. When it comes to describing the prior work of Student Views Consulting Inc., make up a realistic list of prior work. Format this proposal as a letter to the director of Student Services.

9.3 INFORMAL PROPOSAL: IMPROVING THIS TEXTBOOK (OBJ. 1)

Textbooks like this one are revised every two to three years to try to stay ahead of the rapidly changing business communication environment. Still, the authors can't know everything, research everything, stay on top of all trends, etc. As a form of crowdsourcing, imagine the book's publisher asks for your help. Can you propose some ways to make this book and its companion MindTap a more effective learning tool?

Your Task. In teams of two to three, research trends in postsecondary textbook publishing and learning, as well as trends in business communication. Analyze what you find out and apply it to this textbook in particular. What's working? What should change? Why and how? Send a proposal to one of the Cengage Canada staff listed on page ii of this book, suggesting your team as consultants to be involved in the next revision of this textbook.

9.4 FORMAL BUSINESS REPORT: CHANGES IN THE URBAN LANDSCAPE (OBJ. 2)

Changes happen quickly in cities today, and often the change begins with reports being written for politicians to help set policy directions. For each of the following situations, do some secondary and primary research, analyze your results, draw conclusions, and make recommendations.

Your Task. Create mini formal reports—in written, PowerPoint, or Infographic format—for your city's Planning Committee (made up of city councillors from various parts of the city) on the following real-world issues facing your city:

City tax revenues have been falling for the past five years. It's been suggested one way to raise revenue is to allow a new megamall to be built somewhere in the city. Research the best location in your city for such a mall.

City tax revenues have been falling for the past five years. It's been suggested one way to raise revenue is to monetize certain services that have traditionally been free (e.g., library, parks, community centres, roads). Research the most appropriate services in your city to monetize.

City tax revenues have recently stabilized and even been growing. It's been suggested one worthwhile thing to do with the extra money is to increase municipal services. Research new areas for your city to provide services to its citizens.

9.5 FORMAL BUSINESS REPORT: GATHERING PRIMARY AND SECONDARY INTERCULTURAL DATA (OBJS. 3, 4, 5)

You work for auto parts manufacturer Linamar, a Canadian corporation with numerous overseas offices and manufacturing plants. As part of a "revisioning" of Linamar's international operations, the VP Strategy has asked you to collect information for a report focused on an Asian, Latin American, European, or African country where English is not regularly spoken. Try to ensure that the country you have selected is represented by a student in your class—you'll ideally interview someone from that country as part of your research.

Your Task. In teams, collect information about your target country from research databases, the Internet, and other sources. Then invite an international student from your target country to be interviewed by your group. As you conduct primary and secondary research, investigate two or three of the topics listed in Figure 9.19. Confirm what you learn in your secondary research by talking with your interviewee, or if this is not possible in your class, by using social media to find someone from the target country to approach. When you complete your research, write a report for the VP Strategy at Linamar. Assume that Linamar plans to expand its operations abroad. Your report should advise the company's executives on two to three topics related to the target country. Remember that your company's interests are business oriented; do not dwell on tourist information. Compile your results and write the report.

9.6 INFORMAL PROPOSAL: SUPPORTING A CHARITY (OBJ. 1)

Your uncle recently sold his start-up software company for $53 million. He plans to invest a portion of his money and retire early. He also plans to donate $5 million to a philanthropic charity. He is especially concerned about the environment. He has asked you to prepare an informal proposal to recommend three possible charities that could make a positive impact on the environment with his contribution. He wants to be certain that he is supporting a charity that is stable, accountable, and productive.

Your Task. Research three environmental charities, looking at their mission, structure, financial statements, and achievements. In addition to researching the charities' websites, consult other sites that monitor and evaluate charities, such as Charity Intelligence (www.charityintelligence.ca). Prepare an informal proposal for your uncle outlining your findings and recommendations.

9.7 INFORMAL PROPOSAL: SETTING UP AN APP (OBJ. 1)

As a consultant, you have been asked to investigate the cost of setting up an app for Arni Arason, who owns a small wine distribution business in Stratford, Ontario, named Fruit of the Gods Inc. He hopes to begin with a simple, basic app, but he wants it to be user friendly, and he wants customers (mostly local restaurants) to be able to buy wine from the site with a credit card. He also wants search engine optimization (SEO) to be part of the design.

FIGURE 9.19 / Intercultural Interview Topics and Questions

Social Customs

- How do people react to strangers? Are they friendly? Reserved? Cautious? Suspicious?
- What are appropriate topics of conversation in business settings? What topics should be avoided?
- What are the hours of a typical workday?
- What are the attitudes toward personal space and touching?
- Is gift-giving appropriate when invited to someone's home? If so, what gifts are appropriate?
- What facial expressions or gestures are considered offensive? Is direct eye contact appropriate?
- What is the attitude toward punctuality in social situations? In business situations?
- What gestures indicate agreement? Disagreement? Frustration? Excitement?

Family Life

- What is a typical family unit? Do family units include extended family members?
- Do women work outside the home? In what occupations?
- Are children required by law to attend school? Do families value education?

Housing, Clothing, and Food

- How does housing differ in urban and rural areas? How does housing differ among various socioeconomic groups?
- What special occasions require traditional or ceremonial clothing?
- What types of clothing are considered inappropriate or in poor taste?
- What is appropriate business attire for men? For women?
- What types of places, food, and drink are appropriate for business entertainment? Where is the seat of honour at a round table? At a rectangular table?

Class Structure

- Into what classes is society organized?
- Do racial, religious, or economic factors determine social status?
- Are there any minority groups? What is their social standing?

Political Patterns

- Are there any immediate threats or signs of political unrest in this country?
- How is political power manifested?
- What media channels are used for expressing political opinions?
- Is it appropriate to talk about politics in social situations?

Religious Preferences and Beliefs

- Are certain religious groups predominant?
- Do religious beliefs influence daily activities?
- Which places, objects, or animals are considered sacred?
- How do religious holidays affect business activities?

Economic Norms

- What are the country's principal exports and products?
- Are workers organized in unions?
- Are businesses owned by individuals, by large public corporations, or by the government?
- Do business associates normally socialize before conducting business?

Value Systems

- Is competitiveness or cooperation more prized?
- Is politeness more important than honesty?
- Do women own or manage businesses? If so, how are they treated?
- How do people perceive Canadians? What behaviours exhibited by Canadians are considered offensive?

Your Task. Use search engines on the Internet to locate information. Try *app development* as a search term. Visit several sites that offer to build apps. Focus on those that seem most professional. Look to see when the site was last updated. Read the promotional material and decide whether it's well written. Investigate the general characteristics of an app, how to create and promote an app, and how to maintain an app server. Mr. Arason wants a low-cost but high-quality app. Develop cost figures. Draw conclusions and make recommendations in a letter proposal to Mr. Arason.

Related website: Drinks Ontario (www.drinksontario.com), which Arni Arason hopes to join soon, has some brief background information about the wine distribution business.

9.8 UNSOLICITED PROPOSAL: WORKING FROM HOME (OBJ. 1)

You have been working as an administrative virtual assistant for your company since its inception in 2001. Every day you commute from your home, almost two hours round trip. Most of your work is done at a computer terminal with little or no human contact. You would prefer to eliminate the commute time, which could be better spent working on your programming. You believe your job would be perfect for telecommuting. With a small investment in the proper equipment, you could do all of your work at home, perhaps reporting to the office once a week for meetings and other activities.

Your Task. Research the costs and logistics of telecommuting, and present your proposal to your supervisor, Sidney Greene. Because this is an unsolicited proposal, you will need to be even more persuasive. Convince your supervisor that the company will benefit from this telecommuting arrangement.

9.9 DOING RESEARCH (OBJ. 3)

Like many business communication skills, research is one that only gets better when it is practised. In this activity you'll act as a consultant to your college or university, which needs some internal research done about the effectiveness of its policies, services, and procedures.

Your Task. Choose one of the research topics below and go through the following six-step procedure:

1. Create a five-question survey and a five-question follow-up interview.

2. After you've shown your survey and interview to your instructor, go out into the field and gather data. Try to get at least 15 completed surveys and two completed interviews.

3. Now that you have raw data, analyze the survey data by turning it into two or three of the types of illustration discussed in this chapter (e.g., bar chart, table, line chart).

4. Analyze your interview data by looking for similarities and differences between what the people you interviewed had to say.

5. Once you've completed your primary research and analysis, turn to secondary research. Find two newspaper or magazine articles, one academic article, one book, and one good website with information on your topic. How does this information compare with or help to illustrate the information you gathered in your primary research?

6. Finally, present all of the above in a two-page memo or email to your instructor.

7. Possible research topics:

   - Is the cost of tuition at your institution too high?

   - How well is your college or university doing in terms of customer service?

   - Does your college or university career centre do a good job?

   - Assess the usefulness of your college or university library.

   - Examine the success of your institution's physical plant: washrooms, hallways, stairwells, elevators, etc.

   - Choose a topic of your own in consultation with your instructor.

9.10 SELECTING VISUALS (OBJ. 5)

Your Task. In teams, identify the best visual (table, bar chart, line chart, pie chart, flow chart, organization chart) to illustrate the following data:

a. Instructions for workers telling them how to distinguish between worker accidents that must be reported to appropriate provincial or territorial agencies and those that need not be reported

b. Figures showing what proportion of every provincial tax dollar is spent on education, social services, health care, debt, and other expenses

c. Data showing the academic, administrative, and operation divisions of a college or university, from the president to department chairs and deans

d. Figures showing the operating profit of a company for the past five years

e. Figures comparing the sales of PVRs, flat-screen TVs, and personal computers for the past five years

f. Percentages showing the causes of forest fires (lightning, 73 percent; arson, 5 percent; campfires, 9 percent; and so on) in the Canadian Rockies

g. Figures comparing the cost of basic TV cable service in five areas of Canada for the past ten years (the manager wants to see exact figures)

9.11 EVALUATING VISUALS (OBJ. 5)

Your Task. From the online version of a business magazine like *Canadian Business*, *Businessweek*, or *The Economist*, or an online business news site like CNN money or CBC. ca/business, locate one example each of a table, a pie chart, a line chart, a bar chart, and an organization chart. Bring copies of these visual aids to class. How effectively could the data have been expressed in words, without the graphics? Is the appropriate graphic form used? How is the graphic introduced in the text? Your instructor may ask you to submit a short email recommendation report discussing how to improve visual aids.

9.12 VISUALS IN REPORTS: CREATING A BAR CHART AND WRITING A TITLE (OBJ. 5)

Your Task. You've written a report that compares corporate tax rates in various countries, using data available at https://home.kpmg/xx/en/home/services/tax/tax-tools-and-resources/tax-rates-online/social-security-employer-tax-rates-table.html. To help illustrate your findings, prepare a bar chart comparing the tax rates in eight industrial countries: Canada, 26.5 percent; France, 33.3 percent; Germany, 29.79 percent; Japan, 30.86 percent; Netherlands, 25 percent; Sweden, 22 percent; United Kingdom, 19 percent; United States, 40 percent. Arrange the entries logically. Write two titles: a talking head and a functional head. What should you emphasize in the bar chart and title?

9.13 ANNOTATED BIBLIOGRAPHY: THE FUTURE OF TECH (OBJ. 4)

Are you a member of the "thumb generation"? Can you work the keyboard of your smartphone faster than most people can speak? The term *thumb generation* was coined in South Korea and Japan and is applied to people under 25 who furiously use their handheld devices to text at lightning speeds.

You are one of several marketing interns at MarketNet Global, a worldwide e-commerce specialist. Your busy boss, Jack Holden, wants to be informed of cutting-edge technical and communication trends, especially those that could be successfully used in selling and marketing. Individually or as a team, you will research several cutting-edge technologies found on the MIT Technology Review website at https://forms.technologyreview.com/newsletters (try *The Download* newsletter). Use Google's search engine and your library's research electronic databases to find up-to-date information on each of these technologies.

Your Task. In teams or individually, write an email informational memo to Jack Holden (jack.holden@mnetglobal.com) that lists five of the ten new trends from the site above, followed by a brief explanation of the new technology, followed by at least two more sources Mr. Holden can look at for further reading on the trend. Use APA citation style when you list these sources for Mr. Holden.

9.14 FORMAL REPORT: IS VINYL BACK? (OBJS. 2, 3, 5)

Although you and fellow students were probably born long after the introduction of the CD in the early 1980s and regularly download music from iTunes to an MP3 player, something strange is afoot. Lately, sales of turntables and vinyl long-playing records (LPs) have been picking up. "Classic" bands such as the Beatles and Pink Floyd are not the only ones on vinyl. Contemporary artists such as the White Stripes, the Foo Fighters, and Metallica have released their music on vinyl to enthusiastic audiences. Listeners even claim that music sounds better on vinyl than it does on a CD. Perhaps most surprising, many vinyl fans are not nostalgic baby boomers but their teenage or twenty-something children.

Major music retailers have caught on to the trend. Although Amazon.ca has been selling vinyl records since its founding in 1994, it has recently begun to offer a vinyl-only section on its site. Now, your employer, Best Buy Company, is eager to test vinyl sales at some of its stores. Your manager, José Martinez, was asked by headquarters to explore the feasibility of offering a vinyl selection in his store, and he left this research job to you.

Your Task. This assignment calls for establishing primary data using a survey. Devise a questionnaire and poll young music consumers in your area to find out whether they enjoy and, more important, purchase vinyl records. Examine attitudes toward LPs in the populations and age groups most likely to find them intriguing. After collecting your data, determine whether your Best Buy store could establish a profitable vinyl business. Support your recommendation with conclusions you draw from your survey but also from secondary research detailing the new trend. To illustrate your findings, use pie charts for percentages (e.g., how many LPs are sold in comparison to CDs and other media), line graphs to indicate trends over time (e.g., sales figures in various consumer segments), and other graphics. Prepare a formal report for José Martinez, who will share your report with upper management.

9.15 FORMAL REPORT: QUICK-SERVICE RESTAURANT CHECKUP (OBJS. 2, 3)

The national franchising headquarters for a quick-service chain has received complaints about the service, quality, and cleanliness of one of its restaurants in your area. You have been sent to inspect and to report on what you see.

Your Task. Select a quick-service restaurant in your area. Visit on two or more occasions. Make notes about how many customers were served, how quickly they received their food, and how courteously they were treated. Observe the number of employees and supervisors working. Note the cleanliness of observable parts of the restaurant. Inspect the washroom as well as the exterior and surrounding grounds. Sample the food. Your manager is a stickler for details; he has no use for general statements like *The washroom was not clean*. Be specific. Draw conclusions. Are the complaints justified? If improvements are necessary, make recommendations. Address your report to Lawrence C. Shymko, president.

9.16 FORMAL REPORT: COMMUNICATION SKILLS ON THE JOB (OBJS. 2, 3)

Collect information regarding communication skills used by individuals in a particular career field (accounting, management, marketing, office administration, paralegal, and so forth). Interview three or more individuals in a specific occupation in that field. Determine how much and what kind of writing they do. Do they give oral presentations? Do they use PowerPoint? If so, what do they think of its effectiveness? How much time do they spend in telephone communication? How often do they use email? For what? Do they text or message at work? Do they find themselves communicating more or less than in past years? Are they happy or unhappy about the amount of communicating they have to do? What recommendations do they have for training for this position?

Your Task. Write a report that discusses the findings from your interviews. What conclusions can you draw regarding communication skills in this field? What recommendations would you make for individuals entering this field? Your instructor may ask you to research the perception of businesspeople over the past ten years regarding the communication skills of employees. To gather such data, conduct research database and Internet research.

9.17 FORMAL REPORT: SELECTING A LOCATION FOR A SATELLITE CAMPUS (OBJS. 2, 3, 6)

The college or university you attend has recently been experiencing unprecedented growth. Student enrollment has been up for five years in a row, research and donation money has been on the increase, and the number of international students applying for admission is also up. The board of directors has asked the director of development to look into the idea of planning a small satellite campus in an outlying area of the city. The question is, where to locate the satellite?

Your Task. Using your own college or university as the example for this report, research and write a formal report offering a recommendation about where to locate a satellite campus. What components (e.g., locations) will you choose to structure your report? What criteria would be important to the board of directors? Price of land? Proximity to public transportation? Proximity to other institutions? Proximity to a large population base? Where will you find data on these criteria?

◤ Grammar/Mechanics Challenge 9

APOSTROPHES

Review Sections 2.20–2.22 of the Grammar/Mechanics Handbook. Then study each of the following statements. Underline any inappropriate apostrophe form. In the space provided, write the correct form (or C if correct) and the number of the G/M principle illustrated. When you finish, compare your responses with those provided near the end of the book. If your responses differ, study carefully the principles in parentheses.

<u>years'</u> (2.20b)   **Example**   In just two <u>years</u> time, Marti earned her MBA degree.

_____	1.	Mark Hanleys smartphone was found in the conference room.
_____	2.	The severance package includes two weeks salary for each year worked.
_____	3.	In only one years time, her school loans totalled $5,000.
_____	4.	The board of directors strongly believed that John Petersons tenure as CEO was exceptionally successful.
_____	5.	Several employees records were accidentally removed from the files.
_____	6.	The last witness testimony was the most convincing to the jury members.
_____	7.	Everyone appreciated Robins careful editing of our report.
_____	8.	I always get my moneys worth at my favourite restaurant.
_____	9.	Three local companies went out of business last month.
_____	10.	In one months time, we hope to have our new website up and running.
_____	11.	I need my boss signature on this expense claim.
_____	12.	That legal secretarys credentials and years of experience qualified her for a higher salary.
_____	13.	In certain aerospace departments, new applicants must apply for security clearance.
_____	14.	Our companys stock price rose dramatically last year.
_____	15.	Several businesses opening hours will change in the next three months.

◣ EDITING CHALLENGE 9

The following executive summary has The message has proofreading, spelling, grammar, punctuation, wordiness, number form. and other writing faults that require correction. Study the guidelines in the Grammar/Mechanics Handbook, as well as the lists of Confusing Words and Frequently Misspelled Words at the end of the book, to sharpen your skills. When you finish making corrections, your instructor can show you the revised version of this summary.

Your Task. Edit the following message by correcting its errors (a) in your textbook or (b) on a photocopy using standard proofreading marks from Appendix B.

EXECUTIVE SUMMARY

Problem

The Canadian salmon industry must expand it's markets abroad particularly in regard to Japan. Although consumption of salmon is decreasing in Canada they are increasing in Japan. The problem that is for the canadian salmon industry is developing apropriate marketing strategies to boost its current sale in Japanese markets.

Summary of Findings

This report analyzes the Japanese market which currently consumes six hundred thousand tons of salmon per year, and is growing rapidly. Much of this salmon is supplied by imports which at this point in time total about 35% of sales. Our findings indicate that not only will this expand, but the share of imports will continue to grow. The trend is alarming to Japanese salmon industry leaders, because this important market, close to a $billion a year, is increasingly subject to the influence of foreign imports. Declining catches by Japans own Salmon fleet as well as a sharp upward turn in food preference by affluent Japanese consumers, has contributed to this trend.

Recommendations

Based on our analisys we reccommend the following 5 marketing strategys for the Canadian Salmon industry.

1. Farm greater supplys of atlantic farmed salmon to export.

2. We should market our own value added products.

3. Sell fresh salmon direct to the Tokyo Central Wholesale market.

4. Sell to other Japanese markets also.

5. Direct sales should be made to Japanese Supermarket chains.

Rawpixel.com/Shutterstock.com

PROFESSIONALISM AND SPEAKING SKILLS

CHAPTER 10
Communicating Professionally in Person

CHAPTER 11
Business Presentations

BUSINESS COMMUNICATION RESEARCH UPDATE

Prevention and Management of Unprofessional Behaviour Among Adults in the Workplace: A Scoping Review

Andrea C. Tricco,[1,2] Patricia Rios,[2] Wasifa Zarin,[2] Roberta Cardoso,[2] Sanober Diaz,[2] Vera Nincic,[2] Alekhya Mascarenhas,[2] Sabrina Jassemi,[2] Sharon E. Straus[2,3]*

1 Dalla Lana School of Public Health, University of Toronto, Toronto, Ontario, Canada, 2 Knowledge Translation Program, Li Ka Shing Knowledge Institute, St. Michael's Hospital, Toronto, Ontario, Canada, 3 Department of Medicine, University of Toronto, Toronto, Ontario, Canada

* sharon.straus@utoronto.ca

(2018). PLoS One, 13(7).

ABSTRACT
BACKGROUND

Unprofessional behaviour is a challenge in academic medicine. Given that faculty are role models for trainees, it is critical to identify strategies to manage these behaviours. A scoping review was conducted to identify interventions to prevent and manage unprofessional behaviour in any workplace or professional setting.

METHODS

A search of 14 electronic databases was conducted in March 2016, reference lists of relevant systematic reviews were scanned, and grey literature was searched to identify relevant studies. Experimental and quasi-experimental studies that reported on interventions to prevent or manage unprofessional behaviours were included. Studies that reported impact on any outcome were eligible. Two reviewers independently screened articles and completed data abstraction. Qualitative analysis of the definitions of unprofessional behaviour was conducted. Data were charted to describe the study, participant, intervention and outcome characteristics.

RESULTS

12,482 citations were retrieved; 23 studies with 11,025 participants were included. The studies were 12 uncontrolled before and after studies, 6 controlled before and after studies, 2 cluster-randomised controlled trials (RCTs), 1 RCT, 1 non-randomised controlled trial and 1 quasi-RCT. Four constructs were identified in the definitions of unprofessional behaviour: verbal and/or non-verbal acts, repeated acts, power imbalance, and unwelcome behaviour. Interventions most commonly targeted individuals (22 studies, 95.7%) rather than organisations (4 studies, 17.4%). Most studies (21 studies, 91.3%) focused on increasing awareness. The most frequently targeted behaviour change was sexual harassment (4 of 7 studies).

DISCUSSION

Several interventions appear promising in addressing unprofessional behaviour. Most of the studies included single component, in-person education sessions targeting individuals and increasing awareness of unprofessional behaviour. Fewer studies targeted the institutional culture or addressed behaviour change.

INTRODUCTION

Unprofessional behaviour, including bullying, has become a major issue in recent international news [1–3]. Academic medicine is not immune to unprofessional behaviour; it has been reported by medical students, residents and faculty [4–7]. A systematic review showed that almost 60% of medical students experienced at least one form of harassment or discrimination and the most common perpetrator was the consultant physician. Similarly, a review of resident mistreatment found that physicians of higher hierarchical power were the most common perpetrators [8]. Surveys of physicians in various countries [7, 9–12] have shown that up to 98% have experienced unprofessional behaviour in the workplace. While the commonest perpetrators are patients or their families, it is not uncommon for co-workers or supervisors to be the perpetrators [7, 9–12].

The impact of unprofessional behaviour on victims is widespread and concerning. Workplace abuse is associated with stress, depression, anxiety and absence from work in those who experience it [13–17]. Of particular concern in health care is the impact of unprofessional behaviour on role modeling for trainees and on patient care [14]. . . .

As such, the aim of this scoping review was to identify interventions to prevent and manage unprofessional behaviour among adults in any workplace or professional setting.

METHODS

We developed a protocol using the scoping review methods proposed by Arksey and O'Malley [19] and further refined by the Joanna Briggs Institute [20]. The review was conducted to inform the efforts of the Department of Medicine (DOM), University of Toronto, whose members provided feedback on the protocol. We registered the review through the Open Science Framework [21]. . . .

RESULTS

We retrieved 12,482 citations from the electronic database search (11,689), grey literature search (299), and reference scanning of relevant systematic reviews (515) . . . . Of these, 130 citations were potentially relevant and their full-texts were reviewed (102 citations from data base search, 25 from reference scanning, and 3 from grey literature). Subsequently, 23 articles met our eligibility criteria (17 articles from database search, 5 from reference scanning and 1 from grey literature). . . .

DISCUSSION

We identified 23 studies that described interventions for preventing or managing unprofessional behaviours in a variety of settings. Most of the studies included single component in person education sessions that targeted individuals, while fewer studies targeted both individuals and institutional culture and most focused on increasing awareness of unprofessional behaviour rather than effecting behaviour change. In studies that assessed the impact of interventions on outcomes such as reports or perceptions of unprofessional behaviour, results were mixed with some showing increases and some decreases following the intervention. These mixed results may be due to increased awareness of the unprofessional behaviour, leading to more comfort in reporting it. Overall, educational interventions may work but they need to be tailored to individual and organisational needs.

The culture of unprofessionalism in academic medicine may be perpetuated through the modelling of abuse that starts in training, thereby normalising the behaviour [18, 22–25]. Our scoping review identified few studies that have targeted academic centres to mitigate this culture. While studies from other fields such as private industry and government may be useful, there are unique aspects of the academic medicine setting that need to be considered when contextualising these interventions. For example, professional hierarchies within medical specialists, the high stress medical environment that includes long work hours and on-call responsibilities, and

the physician shortage in certain settings can all exacerbate the risk of unprofessional behaviour [14, 26–28]. Concerns about retaliation may also prohibit reporting of unprofessional behaviour, therefore allowing the behaviour to continue [14, 26–28].

Our scoping review identified a lack of consistency in definitions and terms used for unprofessional behaviour . . . . Unprofessionalism can include a wide range of behaviours that people perceive as hostile, abusive or humiliating [4]. The lack of agreement on the definitions, terms and behaviours make measuring the behaviour challenging. Thus measuring the impact of strategies to promote professionalism is problematic. Several studies have highlighted the challenge of assessing professionalism and the critical need for further work in this area [29– 33].

There are limitations to our scoping review that should be considered. First, our literature search was challenging because of the lack of agreement on the definition and terms used for unprofessional behaviour. . . .

We believe that the results of this scoping review can be used to target a full systematic review. Given that several relevant studies were identified, this systematic review could focus on studies conducted in health care organisations or educational settings. We also suggest that a realist review could be undertaken that would include the qualitative literature; this would be particularly helpful because of the need to contextualise the effectiveness of interventions. Specifically, a realist review would inform which circumstances and settings a particular intervention would work to mitigate unprofessional behaviour [34].

CONCLUSIONS

This is the first scoping review of strategies to mitigate professional behaviour in workplace settings. It identified where a future systematic review could inform practice in academic medicine and medical education. Most of the studies included single component, in-person education sessions targeting individuals and increasing awareness of unprofessional behaviour. There is limited evidence that printed education materials and large group education sessions substantially change physician behaviour [35, 36]. Given the need to effect individual behaviour change, strategies to increase awareness are likely not sufficient to address unprofessional behaviour and future primary studies should use behaviour change theory and evidence around what interventions work to effect behaviour change [37]. Moreover, the interventions need to target barriers to professionalism. As fewer studies targeted the institutional culture, this is a critical element to consider in future research.

REFERENCES

1. Bazelon E. Bullying in the Age of Trump The New York Times 2016. Available from: https://www.nytimes.com/2016/11/16/opinion/bullying-in-the-age-of-trump.html?_r=1.

2. Boyle T. Ontario doctors 'distressed' over wave of bullying, infighting: The Toronto Star; 2017. Available from: https://www.thestar.com/life/health_wellness /2017/02/27/ontario-doctors-distressed-over-waveof-bullying-infighting.html.

3. Farley SS, C. Culture of cruelty: why bullying thrives in higher education 2014 [cited 2017]. Available from: https://www.theguardian.com/higher-education-network/blog/2014/nov/03/why-bullying-thriveshigher-education.

4. Fnais N, Soobiah C, Chen MH, Lillie E, Perrier L, Tashkhandi M, et al. Harassment and discrimination in medical training: a systematic review and meta-analysis. Acad Med. 2014; 89(5):817–27. https://doi.org/10.1097/ACM.0000000000000200 PMID: 24667512

5. Rouse LP, Gallagher-Garza S, Gebhard RE, Harrison SL, Wallace LS. Workplace bullying among family physicians: A gender focused study. J Womens Health. 2016; 25(9):882–8.

6. Timm A. 'It would not be tolerated in any other profession except medicine': survey reporting on undergraduates' exposure to bullying and harassment in their first placement year. BMJ open. 2014; 4(7): e005140. https://doi.org/10.1136/bmjopen-2014-005140 PMID: 25009133

7. Miedema B, Hamilton R, Lambert-Lanning A, Tatemichi SR, Lemire F, Manca D, et al. Prevalence of abusive encounters in the workplace of family physicians A minor, major, or severe problem? Can Fam Physician. 2010; 56(3):e101–e8. PMID: 20228289

8. Leisy HB, Ahmad M. Altering workplace attitudes for resident education (A.W.A.R.E.): discovering solutions for medical resident bullying through literature review. BMC Med Educ. 2016; 16(1):127. https://doi.org/10.1186/s12909-016-0639-8 PMID: 27117063

9. Magin PJ, Adams J, Sibbritt DW, Joy E, Ireland MC. Experiences of occupational violence in Australian urban general practice: a cross-sectional study of GPs. Med J Aust. 2005; 183(7):352–6. PMID: 16201952

10. Phillips SP, Schneider MS. Sexual harassment of female doctors by patients. N Engl J Med. 1993; 329 (26):1936–9. https://doi.org/10.1056/NEJM199312233292607 PMID: 8247058

11. Gale C, Arroll B, Coverdale J. Aggressive acts by patients against general practitioners in New Zealand: one-year prevalence. N Z Med J. 2006; 119(1237).

12. Askew DA, Schluter PJ, Dick M- L, Re´go PM, Turner C, Wilkinson D. Bullying in the Australian medical workforce: cross-sectional data from an Australian e-Cohort study. Aust Health Rev. 2012; 36(2):197–204. https://doi.org/10.1071/AH11048 PMID: 22624642

13. Frank E, Carrera JS, Stratton T, Bickel J, Nora LM. Experiences of belittlement and harassment and their correlates among medical students in the United States: longitudinal survey. Bmj. 2006; 333(7570):682. https://doi.org/10.1136/bmj.38924.722037.7C PMID: 16956894

14. Miedema B, MacIntyre L, Tatemichi S, Lambert-Lanning A, Lemire F, Manca D, et al. How the medical culture contributes to coworker-perpetrated harassment and abuse of family physicians. Ann Fam Med. 2012; 10(2):111–7. https://doi.org/10.1370/afm.1341 PMID: 22412002

15. Zahid M, Al-Sahlawi K, Shahid A, Awadh J, Abu-Shammah H. Violence against doctors: 2. Effects of violence on doctors working in accident and emergency departments. Eur J Emerg Med. 1999; 6(4):305–9. PMID: 10646918

16. Ahmed I, Banu H, Al-Fageer R, Al-Suwaidi R. Cognitive emotions: depression and anxiety in medical students and staff. Journal of critical care. 2009; 24(3):e1–7. Epub 2009/08/12. https://doi.org/10.1016/j.jcrc.2009.06.003 PMID: 19664516

17. Heponiemi T, Kouvonen A, Virtanen M, Vanska J, Elovainio M. The prospective effects of workplace violence on physicians' job satisfaction and turnover intentions: the buffering effect of job control. BMC Health Serv Res. 2014; 14:19. Epub 2014/01/21. https://doi.org/10.1186/1472-6963-14-19 PMID: 24438449

18. Dorsey JK, Roberts NK, Wold B. Feedback matters: the impact of an intervention by the dean on unprofessional faculty at one medical school. Acad Med. 2014; 89(7):1032–7. https://doi.org/10.1097/ACM. 0000000000000275 PMID: 24979173

19. Arksey H, O'Malley L. Scoping studies: towards a methodological framework. Int J Soc Res Methodol. 2005; 8(1):19–32.

20. Peters M, Godfrey C, McInerney P, Soares C, Hanan K, Parker D. The Joanna Briggs Institute Reviewers' Manual 2015: Methodology for JBI Scoping Reviews. 2015.

21. Rios P, Tricco AC. Academic Bullying Open Science Framework2016. Available from: https://osf.io/cajy4/.

22. Cote L, Laughrea PA. Preceptors' understanding and use of role modeling to develop the CanMEDS competencies in residents. Acad Med. 2014; 89(6):934–9. Epub 2014/05/30. https://doi.org/10.1097/ACM.0000000000000246 PMID: 24871246

23. Bryden P, Ginsburg S, Kurabi B, Ahmed N. Professing professionalism: are we our own worst enemy? Faculty members' experiences of teaching and evaluating professionalism in medical education at one school. Acad Med. 2010; 85(6):1025–34. Epub 2010/01/14. https://doi.org/10.1097/ACM. 0b013e3181ce64ae PMID: 20068427

24. Park J, Woodrow SI, Reznick RK, Beales J, MacRae HM. Observation, reflection, and reinforcement: surgery faculty members' and residents' perceptions of how they learned professionalism. Acad Med. 2010; 85(1):134–9. Epub 2010/01/01. https://doi.org/10.1097/ACM.0b013e3181c47b25 PMID: 20042839

25. Quaintance JL, Arnold L, Thompson GS. What students learn about professionalism from faculty stories: an "appreciative inquiry" approach. Acad Med. 2010; 85(1):118–23. Epub 2010/01/01. https://doi. org/10.1097/ACM.0b013e3181c42acd PMID: 20042837

26. Manca D, Varnhagen S, Brett-MacLean P, Allan GM, Szafran O. RESPECT from specialists Concerns of family physicians. Can Fam Physician. 2008; 54(10):1434–5. e5. PMID: 18854474

27. Coverdill JE, Alseidi A, Borgstrom DC, Dent DL, Dumire RD, Fryer J, et al. Professionalism in the Twilight Zone: A Multicenter, Mixed-Methods Study of Shift Transition Dynamics in Surgical Residencies. Acad Med. 2016; 91(11 Association of American Medical Colleges Learn Serve Lead: Proceedings of the 55th Annual Research in Medical Education Sessions):S31–s6. Epub 2016/10/26. https://doi.org/ 10.1097/ACM.0000000000001358 PMID: 27779507

28. Sun NZ, Gan R, Snell L, Dolmans D. Use of a Night Float System to Comply With Resident Duty Hours Restrictions: Perceptions of Workplace Changes and Their Effects on Professionalism. Acad Med. 2016; 91(3):401–8. Epub 2015/10/22. https://doi.org/10.1097/ACM.0000000000000949 PMID: 26488569.

29. Young ME, Cruess SR, Cruess RL, Steinert Y. The Professionalism Assessment of Clinical Teachers (PACT): the reliability and validity of a novel tool to evaluate professional and clinical teaching behaviors. Advances in Health Sciences Education. 2014; 19(1):99–113. https://doi.org/10.1007/s10459-013-9466-4 PMID: 23754583

30. Hodges BD, Ginsburg S, Cruess R, Cruess S, Delport R, Hafferty F, et al. Assessment of professionalism: Recommendations from the Ottawa 2010 Conference. Medical teacher. 2011; 33(5):354–63. https://doi.org/10.3109/014215 9X.2011.577300 PMID: 21517683

31. Ginsburg S, Bernabeo E, Ross KM, Holmboe ES. "It depends": results of a qualitative study investigating how practicing internists approach professional dilemmas. Acad Med. 2012; 87(12):1685–93. Epub 2012/10/26. https://doi.org/10.1097/ACM.0b013e3182736dfc PMID: 23095932. Interventions for unprofessional behaviour

32. Ginsburg S, Lingard L. 'Is that normal?' Pre-clerkship students' approaches to professional dilemmas. Medical education. 2011; 45(4):362–71. Epub 2011/03/16. https://doi.org/10.1111/j.1365-2923.2010. 03903.x PMID: 21401684.

33. Bernabeo EC, Holmboe ES, Ross K, Chesluk B, Ginsburg S. The utility of vignettes to stimulate reflection on professionalism: theory and practice. Advances in health sciences education: theory and practice. 2013; 18(3):463–84. Epub 2012/06/22. https://doi.org/10.1007/s10459-012-9384-x PMID: 22717991.

34. Kastner M, Antony J, Soobiah C, Straus SE, Tricco AC. Conceptual recommendations for selecting the most appropriate knowledge synthesis method to answer research questions related to complex evidence. J Clin Epidemiol. 2016; 73:43–9. Epub 2016/02/26. https://doi.org/10.1016/j.jclinepi.2015.11. 022 PMID: 26912124.

35. Grudniewicz A, Kealy R, Rodseth RN, Hamid J, Rudoler D, Straus SE. What is the effectiveness of printed educational materials on primary care physician knowledge, behaviour, and patient outcomes: a systematic review and meta-analyses. Implementation science: IS. 2015; 10:164. Epub 2015/12/03. https://doi.org/10.1186/s13012-015-0347-5 PMID: 26626547; PubMed Central PMCID: PMCPMC4666153.

36. Forsetlund L, Bjorndal A, Rashidian A, Jamtvedt G, O'Brien MA, Wolf F, et al. Continuing education meetings and workshops: effects on professional practice and health care outcomes. The Cochrane database of systematic reviews. 2009;(2):Cd003030. Epub 2009/04/17. https://doi.org/10.1002/14651858. CD003030.pub2 PMID: 19370580.

37. Straus S, Tetroe J, Graham ID. Knowledge translation in health care: moving from evidence to practice. 2nd ed. Oxford, UK: John Wiley & Sons; 2013. Interventions for unprofessional behaviour

QUESTIONS

1. How does what you've learned in this article change your perception of business communication?

2. How might what you've learned in this article change your own communication style?

3. Come up with pro and con arguments for the following debate/discussion topic: The quality of our behaviour with others in real-time workplace situations is just as (or more) important than any writing we may do in the workplace

COMMUNICATING PROFESSIONALLY IN PERSON

OBJECTIVES

10.1 Apply professionalism skills in the workplace.

10.2 Engage in effective conversations.

10.3 Demonstrate professional telephone skills and voice mail etiquette.

10.4 Contribute positively to team performance.

10.5 Plan and participate in productive meetings.

BIZ COMM BYTE

According to research into workplace incivility and disrespectful behaviour, 96 percent of workers have experienced disrespectful behaviour in the workplace, and 94 percent of workers treated this way claim they've tried to get even with the people who treated them poorly.

Source: Statistics on Workplace Harassment. (2014, April 11). https://www.ilscorp.com/blog/7-statistics-workplace-harassment/

10.1 Professionalism, Business Etiquette, and Ethical Behaviour

You probably know that being *professional* is important. When you search for definitions, however, you'll find a wide range of meanings. Related terms such as *business etiquette, soft skills, social* or *emotional intelligence, polish,* and *civility,* may add to the confusion. However, they all have one thing in common: they describe desired workplace behaviour. Businesses desire workers who get along, make customers feel welcome, and deliver positive results that enhance profits and boost their image. As a new business professional, you have a stake in acquiring skills that will make you a strong job applicant and a valuable, successful employee.

In this chapter you'll learn which professional characteristics are most valued in workplace relationships. Next you'll be asked to consider the link between professional and ethical behaviour on the job. Finally, by knowing what recruiters want, you'll have the ability to shape yourself into the kind of professional they are looking to hire.

Cengage

MINDTAP

In MindTap go to the
Whiteboard Animation
for Chapter 10 and
watch it now.

10.1a Defining Professional Behaviour

Good relationships in the workplace and with business partners or the public are crucial for success. Unfortunately, as the unit-opening article shows, problematic behaviours like rudeness and bullying are a widespread phenomenon today, demonstrated in professional settings among employees, between managers and their employees, and between clients and employees.

As a result, some businesses have established procedures or policies to encourage civility. What are the behaviours that make up such procedures and policies? What follows is a list that defines professional behaviour you should engage in to foster positive workplace relations.

CIVILITY. Simply put, being civil with coworkers and clients means being respectful and considerate of them—not only of yourself. For an example of a policy encouraging civility, view Royal Bank of Canada's employee code of conduct (www.rbc.com/pdf /RBCCodeOfConduct.pdf). RBC is very clear about unprofessional and disrespectful behaviour, which when reported becomes the subject of disciplinary action. Most large organizations have similar enforceable policies.

POLISH. You may hear businesspeople refer to someone as being *polished* or displaying polish when dealing with others. In her book with the telling title *Buff and Polish: A Practical Guide to Enhance Your Professional Image and Communication Style*, Kathryn J. Volin focuses on nonverbal techniques and etiquette guidelines that are linked to career success. For example, she addresses making first impressions, shaking hands, improving one's voice quality, listening, and presentation skills.

SOCIAL INTELLIGENCE. Occasionally you'll encounter the expression *social intelligence*. One step beyond civility, social intelligence is shown when you proactively get along well with others and are able to get them to cooperate with and help you. Social intelligence points to a deep understanding of people and behaviour that helps you negotiate interpersonal situations. This type of intelligence can be much harder to acquire than simple etiquette. It requires us to interact well, be perceptive, show sensitivity toward others, and grasp a situation quickly and accurately.

SOFT SKILLS. Perhaps the most common term for positive interpersonal habits is *soft skills*, as opposed to *hard skills*, a term for the technical knowledge in your field. Soft skills are a whole cluster of personal qualities, habits, attitudes (e.g., likeability, problem-solving orientation), communication skills, and social graces. Employers want managers and employees who are comfortable with diverse coworkers, who are actively likeable with customers and colleagues, who can make eye contact, who display good workplace manners, and who possess a host of other interpersonal skills. These skills are immensely important not only to being hired but also to being promoted.

10.1b Ethics and Professional Behaviour

The wide definition of professionalism also encompasses another crucial quality in a businessperson: *ethics* or *integrity*. Not a day goes by without some business or business person being discussed in the news for committing some unethical action. However, for every company that captures the limelight for misconduct, thousands of others operate honestly and serve their customers and the public well. The overwhelming majority of businesses want to recruit ethical and polished graduates.

Ethics is the study of right and wrong behaviour, from both a theoretical point of view (normative ethics) and a practical point of view (applied ethics). Each day, we face decisions about how to act: should I give change to someone asking for it on the street, smile at a customer and maintain composure even after he has been slightly rude to me, etc.

All ethical theories, whether duty-based (do what's right in all cases), consequentialist-based (do what will make the most people happy), or social contract–based

Indigenous-owned and Calgary-based Indigenous advisory firm Cascade Projects Ltd. (www.cascadeprojects.ca) specializes in assisting clients with Indigenous engagement and economic inclusion for major projects across Western Canada. Indigenous engagement takes an intentional approach to building meaningful relationships, respecting the inherent and legal rights of Indigenous Peoples, their traditional practices, and their decision-making processes. Indigenous engagement includes facilitating interactions between industry (often in the natural resource sector, such as oil, gas, and mining) and Indigenous rights holders whose lands may be impacted by major project development, to build mutually beneficial outcomes. The process includes a number of intentional stages, such as listening constructively in organized in-person meetings with Indigenous leadership throughout the engagement process. As Cascade notes on its corporate website, the ability to build meaningful partnerships with Indigenous rights holders is based on

Memorandum of Understanding signing, February 2020 at Tsuut'ina Nation administration office. From left to right: Richard Piche (Cascade Projects Ltd.), Darrin Jamieson (Tsuut'ina Management Ltd.), and Darby Kreitz (Allnorth Consultants Ltd.)

principles that include respect, transparency, and listening. This type of commitment to reconciliation and better business practices is shifting the way in which industry and Indigenous Peoples work together. This requires skills like those discussed in many parts of this chapter, from how to respond effectively to criticism to how to run a meeting effectively. *Other than operating on an Indigenous rights holders or stakeholder group's legal and traditional territory, what other reasons might require a business to act in an ethical way?*

(do what's right because you live in a community and part of this means taking other people's needs into consideration), have one goal in mind: in your interactions with others, you shouldn't always think about things from your own point of view. Exercise empathy as often as you can—don't just do what's right for you, but as often as possible do what's right for the other person or people.

Clearly, there's a direct relationship between an ethical person and a professional person. Professionalism is essentially a type of applied ethics: it's applied because the respectful, pro-social behaviours are happening in a real-world setting, in this case in a business workplace. In effect, professionalism is made up of appearance aspects like dressing and sounding appropriate at work, as well as social aspects like treating the people around you with respect and consideration.

Figure 10.1 summarizes the six main components of professional workplace behaviour and for each component identifies behaviours you should be demonstrating to ensure your success on the job and increase the likelihood of promotion.

10.1c Professionalism Gives You an Edge

Professionalism is increasingly valuable in our digital economy and sets you apart in competition with others. Hiring managers expect you to have technical expertise in your field. A good résumé and interview may get you in the door. However, soft skills and professionalism will ensure your long-term success. Advancement and promotions may depend on your grasp of workplace etiquette and the ability to communicate with your manager, coworkers, and customers. You'll also earn recognition on the job if you prove yourself as an effective and contributing team member—and as a well-rounded professional overall.

Even in highly technical fields such as accounting and finance, employers are looking for professionalism and soft skills. Increasingly, finance professionals must be able to interact with the entire organization and various types of outsiders, view themselves as problem solvers, and explain terms without using financial jargon.

FIGURE 10.1 / The Six Dimensions of Professional Behaviour

Promptness

Giving and accepting criticism graciously

Apologizing for errors

Sincerity

Helpfulness

Showing up prepared

Delivering high-quality work

Dependability

Honouring commitments and keeping promises

Consistent performance

Dining etiquette

Good hygiene and grooming

Attractive business attire

Ability to compromise

Fair treatment of others

Self-control

Truthfulness

Respecting others

Fair competition

Empathy

Courtesy Respect

Collegiality Sharing

Reliability Diligence

Appearance Appeal

Tolerance Tact

Honesty Ethics

© Cengage Learning

Employers want team players who can work together productively. If you look at current job ads, chances are you'll find requirements such as the following examples:

- Proven team skills to help deliver on-time, on-budget results
- Strong verbal and written communication skills, as well as excellent presentation skills
- Excellent interpersonal, organizational, and teamwork skills
- Interpersonal and team skills plus well-developed communication skills
- Good people skills and superior teamwork abilities

In addition, most hiring managers are looking for new hires who show enthusiasm, are eager to learn, volunteer to tackle difficult tasks, and exhibit a positive attitude. You won't be hired to warm a seat.

Cengage

MINDTAP

In MindTap, go to the Chapter 10 reading, section 10.1c, and watch the video of industry expert Taylor Roberts discussing best practices when speaking in the workplace.

10.2 Face-to-Face Communication

Because technology provides many communication channels, you might think that face-to-face communication is no longer essential or even important in business and professional transactions. You've already learned that email is now the preferred communication channel. Yet despite their popularity and acceptance, new communication technologies can't replace the richness or effectiveness of face-to-face communication. Imagine that you want to tell your boss how you solved a problem. Would you settle for a one-dimensional email when you could step into her office and explain quickly in person?

Face-to-face conversation has many advantages. It allows you to be persuasive and expressive because you can use your voice and body language to make a point. You're less likely to be misunderstood because you can read feedback instantly and make needed adjustments. In a conflict situation, you can reach a solution more efficiently and cooperate to create greater levels of mutual benefit when communicating face to face. Moreover, people want to see each other to satisfy a deep human need for social interaction. For numerous reasons, communicating in person remains the most effective of all communication channels.

10.2a Your Voice as a Communication Tool

Celebrities, business executives, and everyday people consult voice and speech therapists to help them shake bad habits or help them speak so that they can be better understood and not sound less intelligent than they are. Below we discuss some useful tips for using your voice most effectively by learning how to control such elements as pronunciation, tone, pitch, volume, rate, and emphasis.

PRONUNCIATION. Pronunciation involves saying words correctly and clearly with the accepted sounds and accented syllables. You'll be at a distinct advantage in your job if, through training and practice, you learn to pronounce words correctly. At work you want to sound intelligent, educated, and competent. If you mispronounce words or slur phrases together, you risk being misunderstood as well as giving a poor impression of yourself. How can you improve your pronunciation skills? The best way is to listen carefully to educated people, read aloud from well-written newspapers like the *Globe and Mail* and the *National Post,* and listen to audio files from online dictionaries.

TONE. The tone of your voice sends a nonverbal message to listeners. It identifies your personality and your mood. Some voices sound enthusiastic and friendly, conveying the impression of an upbeat person who is happy to be with the listener. But voices can also sound controlling, patronizing, angry, or complaining. This doesn't mean that the speaker necessarily has that attribute. It may mean that the speaker is merely carrying on a family tradition or pattern learned in childhood. To check your voice tone, record your voice and listen to it critically. Is it projecting a positive quality about you?

PITCH. Effective speakers use a relaxed, controlled, well-pitched voice to attract listeners to their message. Pitch refers to sound vibration frequency; that is, it indicates the highness or lowness of a sound. Most speakers and listeners tend to prefer a variety of pitch patterns. Voices are most attractive when they rise and fall in conversational tones. Flat, monotone voices are considered boring and ineffectual.

VOLUME AND RATE. Volume indicates the degree of loudness or the intensity of sound. Just as you adjust the volume on your television, you should adjust the volume of your speaking to the occasion and your listeners. When speaking face to face, you generally know whether you are speaking too loudly or softly by looking at your listeners. To judge what volume to use, listen carefully to the other person's voice. Use it as a guide for adjusting your voice. Rate refers to the pace of your speech. If you speak too slowly, listeners are bored and their attention wanders. If you speak too quickly, listeners can't understand you. If you're the kind of speaker who speeds up when talking in front of a group of people, monitor the nonverbal signs of your listeners and adjust your rate as needed.

EMPHASIS. By emphasizing or stressing certain words, you can change the meaning you are expressing. For example, read these sentences aloud, emphasizing the italicized words:

> *Matt* said the hard drive crashed again. (Matt knows what happened.)
>
> Matt *said* the hard drive crashed again. (Or maybe he doesn't.)
>
> Matt said the hard drive crashed *again*? (Did he really say that?)

As you can see, emphasis affects the meaning of the thought expressed. To make your message effective, use emphasis appropriately so you're not confusing your listener. You can raise your volume to sound authoritative and raise your pitch to sound disbelieving. Lowering your volume and pitch makes you sound professional or reasonable.

10.2b Making Workplace Conversation Matter

In the workplace, conversations may involve giving and taking instructions, providing feedback, exchanging ideas on products and services, participating in performance appraisals, or engaging in small talk about such things as families and sports. Face-to-face conversation helps people work together harmoniously and feel that they are part of the larger organization. There are several ways to create positive workplace conversations, starting with using correct names and titles.

USE CORRECT NAMES AND TITLES. Although the world is increasingly informal, it's still wise to use titles and last names when addressing professional adults (*Mrs. Smith*, *Mr. Rivera*). In some organizations senior staff members will speak to junior employees on a first-name basis, but the reverse may not be encouraged. Probably the safest plan is to ask your managers how they want to be addressed. Customers and others outside the organization should always be addressed by title and last name.

When you meet strangers, do you have trouble remembering their names? You can improve your memory considerably if you associate the person with an object, a place, a colour, an animal, a job, an adjective, or some other memory hook. For example, *computer pro Kevin*, *Montréal Kim*, *silver-haired Mr. Lee*, *bulldog Chris*, *bookkeeper Lynn*, *traveller Ms. Janis*. The person's name will also be more deeply embedded in your memory if you use it immediately after being introduced, in subsequent conversation, and when you part.

CHOOSE APPROPRIATE TOPICS. In some workplace activities, such as social gatherings or interviews, you'll be expected to engage in small talk. Be sure to stay away from controversial topics with someone you don't know very well. Avoid politics, religion, or current events topics that might start arguments until you know the person better. Reading newspapers and listening to radio and TV shows that discuss current events will help you to initiate appropriate conversations. Make a mental note of items that you can use in conversation, taking care to remember where you saw or heard the news item so that you can report accurately and authoritatively. Try not to be defensive or annoyed if others present information that upsets you.

AVOID NEGATIVE REMARKS. Workplace conversations are not the place to complain about your colleagues, your friends, the organization, or your job. No one enjoys listening to whiners. And your criticism of others may come back to haunt you. A snipe at your boss or a complaint about a fellow worker may reach him or her, sometimes embellished or distorted with meanings you didn't intend. Be careful about publicizing negative judgments. Remember, some people love to repeat statements that will stir up trouble or set off internal workplace wars. It's best not to give them the ammunition.

LISTEN TO LEARN. In conversations with colleagues and customers, train yourself to expect to learn something from what you are hearing. Being attentive is not only instructive but also courteous. Beyond displaying good manners, you'll probably find that your conversation partner has information that you don't have. Being receptive and listening with an open mind means not interrupting or prejudging. Let's say you very much want to be able to work at home for part of your workweek. You try to explain your ideas to your manager, but he cuts you off shortly after you start. He says, "It's out of the question; we need you here every day." Suppose instead he says, "I have some reservations about telecommuting, but maybe you'll change my mind," and he settles in to listen to your presentation. Even if he decides against your request, you'll feel that your ideas were heard and respected.

GIVE SINCERE AND SPECIFIC PRAISE. Probably nothing promotes positive workplace relationships better than sincere and specific praise. Whether the compliments and appreciation are travelling upward to management or horizontally to colleagues, everyone responds well to recognition. Organizations run more smoothly and morale is higher when people feel appreciated. In your workplace conversations, look for ways to recognize good work and good people. Try to be specific. Instead of "You did a good job in leading that meeting," say something more specific, such as "Your leadership skills really kept that meeting focused and productive."

10.2c Responding Professionally to Workplace Criticism

When being criticized, you'll probably feel that you are being attacked. You can't just sit back and relax. Your heart beats faster, your temperature increases, your face reddens, and you respond with the classic *fight or flight* syndrome. You feel that you want to instantly retaliate or escape from the attacker. But focusing on your feelings distracts you from hearing the content of what's being said, and prevents you from responding professionally. Some or all of the following suggestions will guide you in reacting positively to criticism so that you can benefit from it:

- **Listen without interrupting.** Even though you might want to protest, make yourself hear the speaker out.
- **Determine the speaker's intent.** Unskilled communicators may throw "verbal bricks" with unintended negative-sounding expressions. If you think the intent is positive, focus on what's being said rather than reacting to poorly chosen words.
- **Acknowledge what you're hearing.** Respond with a pause, a nod, or a neutral statement such as "I understand." This buys you time. Don't disagree, counterattack, or blame, which may escalate the situation and harden the speaker's position.
- **Paraphrase what was said.** In your own words, restate objectively what you are hearing; for example, "So what you're saying is. . . ."
- **Ask for more information if necessary.** Clarify what's being said. Stay focused on the main idea rather than interjecting side issues.
- **Agree — if the comments are accurate.** If an apology is in order, give it. Explain what you plan to do differently. If the criticism is on target, the sooner you agree, the more likely you'll gain respect from the other person.
- **Disagree respectfully and constructively — if you feel the comments are unfair.** After hearing the criticism, you might say, "Can I tell you my perspective?" Or you could try to solve the problem by saying, "How can we improve this situation in a way we can both accept?" If the other person continues to criticize, say "I want to find a way to resolve your concern. When do you want to talk about it next?"
- **Look for a middle position.** Search for a middle position or a compromise. Be friendly even if you don't like the person or the situation.

Conflict is a normal part of every workplace, but it's not always negative. When managed properly, conflict can improve decision making, clarify values, increase group cohesiveness, stimulate creativity, decrease tensions, and reduce dissatisfaction. Unresolved conflict, however, can destroy productivity and seriously reduce morale.

10.2d Offering Constructive Criticism at Work

No one likes to receive criticism, and most of us don't like to give it either. But cooperation in the workplace demands feedback and evaluation. How are we doing on a project? What went well? What failed? How can we improve our efforts? Today's workplace often involves team projects. As a team member, you'll be called on to judge the work of others. In addition to working on teams, you can also expect to become a supervisor or manager one day. As such, you'll need to evaluate your direct reports.

Good employees seek good feedback from their supervisors. They want and need timely, detailed observations about their work to reinforce what they do well and help them overcome weak spots. But making that feedback palatable and constructive isn't always easy. Depending on your situation, you may find some or all of the following suggestions helpful when you need to deliver constructive criticism:

- **Mentally outline your conversation.** Think carefully about what you want to accomplish and what you'll say. Find the right words at the right time and in the right setting.
- **Generally, use face-to-face communication.** Most constructive criticism is better delivered in person rather than in emails. Personal feedback offers an opportunity for the listener to ask questions and give explanations. Occasionally, however, complex situations may require a different strategy. You might prefer to write out your opinions and deliver them by telephone or in writing. A written document enables you to organize your thoughts, include all the details, and be sure of keeping your cool. Remember, though, that written documents create permanent records—for better or worse.
- **Focus on improvement.** Instead of attacking, use language that offers alternative behaviour. Use phrases such as "Next time, it would be great if you could. . . ."
- **Offer to help.** Criticism is accepted more readily if you volunteer to help in eliminating or solving the problem.
- **Be specific.** Instead of a vague assertion such as "Your work is often late," be more specific: "The specs on the Riverside job were due Thursday at 5 p.m., and you didn't hand them in until Friday. This makes us look. . . ." Explain how the person's performance jeopardized the entire project.
- **Avoid broad generalizations.** Don't use words such as *should*, *never*, *always*, and other encompassing expressions. They may cause the listener to shut down and become defensive.
- **Discuss the behaviour, not the person.** Instead of "You seem to think you can come to work any time you want," focus on the behaviour: "Coming to work late means that someone else has to fill in until you arrive."
- **Use the word *we* rather than *you*.** "We need to meet project deadlines" is better than saying "You need to meet project deadlines." Emphasize organizational expectations rather than personal ones. Avoid sounding accusatory.
- **Encourage two-way communication.** Even if well-planned, criticism is still hard to deliver. It may surprise or hurt the feelings of the employee. Consider ending your message with "It can be hard to hear this type of feedback. If you'd like to share your thoughts, I'm listening."
- **Avoid anger, sarcasm, and a raised voice.** Criticism is rarely constructive when tempers flare. Plan in advance what you'll say and deliver it in low, controlled, and sincere tones.
- **Keep it private.** Offer praise in public; offer criticism in private. "Setting an example" through public criticism is never a wise management policy.

◤ 10.3 Phone and Voice Mail Etiquette

Despite our heavy reliance on email, the phone is still an extremely important piece of equipment in offices. As one telecom provider explains it, phone calls are still necessary for successful business because billions of people own and like using smartphones regularly (and not just for texting or browsing!), because the experience of a phone call is preferred by many customers when they have an important purchase or problematic issue to deal with, and because the combination of speaking to a real person and getting an issue dealt with in one interaction, without more back and forth, is appealing for consumers.[1] As a business communicator, you can be more productive, efficient, and professional on the phone by following some simple suggestions.

10.3a Making Professional Phone Calls

Before making a phone call, use the following suggestions to make it fully professional.

- **Plan a mini-agenda.** Have you ever been embarrassed when you had to make a second phone call because you forgot an important item the first time? Before placing a call, jot down notes regarding all the topics you need to discuss. Following an agenda guarantees not only a complete call but also a quick one. You'll be less likely to wander from business while rummaging through your mind trying to remember everything.

- **Use a three-point introduction.** When placing a call, immediately (1) name the person you are calling, (2) identify yourself and your affiliation, and (3) give a brief explanation of your reason for calling. For example: "Can I please speak to Pieter Kortenaar? This is Hillary Dahl at Evergreen, and I'm seeking information about Sinzer's impact measurement software." This kind of introduction enables the receiver to respond immediately without asking further questions.

- **Be quick if you're rushed.** For business calls when time is limited, avoid questions such as "How are you?" Instead, say, "Lisa, I knew you'd be the only one who could answer these two questions for me." Another efficient strategy is to set a "contract" with the caller: "Hi Lisa, I have only a few minutes, but I really wanted to get back to you."

- **Be cheerful and accurate.** Let your voice show the same kind of animation that it does when you greet people in person. In your mind try to envision the individual answering the phone. A smile can certainly affect the tone of your voice, so smile at that person. Moreover, be accurate about what you say. "Hang on a second; I'll be right back" is rarely true. Better to say, "It may take me two or three minutes to get that information. Would you prefer to hold or have me call you back?"

- **Bring it to a close.** The responsibility for ending a call lies with the caller. This is sometimes difficult to do if the other person rambles on. You may need to use suggestive closing language, such as "I've really enjoyed talking with you," "I've learned what I needed to know, and can move ahead with my work," "Thanks for your help," or "I need to go now, but can I call you again in the future if I need . . . ?"

- **Avoid phone tag.** If you call someone who's not in, ask when it would be best for you to call again. State that you'll call at a specific time—and do it. If you ask a person to call you, give a time when you can be reached—and then be sure you're available at that time.

- **Leave complete voice mail messages.** Remember that there's no rush when you leave a voice mail message. Always enunciate clearly. And be sure to provide a complete message, including your name, phone number, and the time and date of your call. Explain your purpose so that the receiver can be ready with the required information when returning your call.

10.3b Receiving Phone Calls Professionally

With a little planning, you can project a professional image and make your phone a productive, efficient work tool. Developing good phone manners also reflects well on you and on your organization. Try the following phone etiquette guidelines for receiving calls professionally:

- **Identify yourself immediately.** In answering your phone or someone else's, provide your name, title or affiliation, and, possibly, a greeting. For example, "Pieter Kortenaar, Sinzer Software. How can I help you?" Force yourself to speak clearly and slowly. Remember that the caller may be unfamiliar with what you are saying and will fail to recognize slurred syllables.

- **Be responsive and helpful.** If you're in a support role, be sympathetic to callers' needs. Instead of "I don't know," try "That's a good question; let me find out." Instead of "We can't do that," try "That's a tough one; let's see what we can do." Avoid "no" at the beginning of a sentence. It sounds especially abrasive and displeasing because it suggests total rejection.

- **Be cautious when answering calls for others.** Be courteous and helpful, but don't give out confidential information. Better to say "She's away from her desk" or "He's out of the office" than to report a colleague's exact whereabouts.
- **Take messages carefully.** Few things are as frustrating as receiving a potentially important phone message that's illegible. Repeat the spelling of names and verify telephone numbers. Write messages legibly and record their time and date. Promise to give the messages to intended recipients, but don't guarantee return calls.
- **Explain what you're doing when transferring calls.** Give a reason for transferring, and identify the extension to which you are directing the call in case the caller is disconnected.

10.3c Using Smartphones for Business

Smartphones are sophisticated mobile devices. They allow you to conduct business from virtually anywhere at any time. The smartphone has become an essential part of communication in the workplace and in our personal lives. While many Canadians still own landlines, there's a pronounced shift away from this "old" technology (especially among younger people) toward wireless phones only.

Today's smartphones can do much more than make and receive calls. They function very much like mini tablet computers. They can be used to store contact information, make to-do lists, keep track of appointments and important dates, send and receive email, send and receive text and multimedia messages, search the Web, get news and stock quotes from the Internet, take pictures and videos, synchronize with Outlook and other software applications, and many other functions. Thousands of applications ("apps") help people stay productive, informed, and entertained on the go.

Because so many people depend on their smartphones, it's important to understand proper use and etiquette. Most of us have experienced thoughtless and rude smartphone behaviour. Researchers say that the rampant use of technological devices has worsened workplace incivility, and employers say that the use of cell phones has worsened workplace productivity. To avoid offending, smart business communicators practise cell phone etiquette, as outlined in Figure 10.2. They're careful about location, time, and volume in relation to their calls.

LOCATION. Use good judgment in placing or accepting cell phone calls. Turn off your cell phone in your vehicle and when entering a conference room, an interview, a theatre, a place of worship, or any other place where it could be distracting or disruptive to others. Taking a call in a crowded place makes it difficult to hear and reflects poorly on you as a professional. A bad connection also makes a bad impression. Static or dropped signals create frustration and miscommunication. Don't sacrifice professionalism for the sake of a garbled phone call. It's smarter to turn off your phone in an area where the signal is weak and when you are likely to have interference. Use voice mail and return the call when conditions are better.

TIME. Often what you're doing is more important than whatever may come over the airwaves to you on your phone. For example, when you're having an important discussion with a business partner, customer, or manager, it's rude to allow yourself to be interrupted by an incoming call. It's also poor manners to practise multitasking while on the phone.

FIGURE 10.2 / Professional Cell Phone Use

Show courtesy

- Don't force others to hear your business.
- Don't make or receive calls in public places, such as post offices, banks, retail stores, trains, and buses.
- Don't allow your phone to ring in theatres, restaurants, museums, classrooms, and meetings.
- Apologize for occasional cellphone blunders.

Keep it down

- Speak in low, conversational tones. Cellphone microphones are sensitive, making it unnecessary to raise your voice.
- Choose a professional ringtone and set it on low or vibrate.

Step outside

- If a call is urgent, step outside to avoid being disruptive.
- Make full use of caller ID to screen incoming calls. Let voice mail take routine calls.

Drive now, talk and text later

- Talking while driving increases accidents almost fourfold, about the same as driving intoxicated.
- Texting while driving is even more dangerous. Don't do it!

© Cengage Learning

What's more, it's dangerous. Although you might be able to read and print out emails, deal with a customer at the counter, and talk on your wireless phone simultaneously, it's impolite and risky. If a phone call is important enough to accept, then it's important enough to stop what you're doing and attend to the conversation.

VOLUME. Many people raise their voices when using their cellphones. "Cell yell" results, much to the annoyance of anyone nearby. Raising your voice is unnecessary since most phones have excellent microphones that can pick up even a whisper. If the connection is bad, louder volume will not improve the sound quality. As in face-to-face conversations, a low, well-paced voice sounds professional and projects the proper image.

10.3d Making the Most of Voice Mail

Voice mail's popularity results from the many functions it serves, the most important of which is message storage. Because as many as half of all business calls require no discussion or feedback, the messaging capabilities of voice mail can mean huge savings for businesses. Incoming information is delivered without interrupting potential receivers and without all the niceties that most two-way conversations require. Voice mail messages allow communicators to focus on essentials. Voice mail also eliminates telephone tag, inaccurate message taking, and time-zone barriers.

However, voice mail shouldn't be overused. Individuals who screen all incoming calls cause irritation, resentment, and needless phone tag. Both receivers and callers can use etiquette guidelines to make voice mail work most effectively for them.

RECEIVING VOICE MAIL MESSAGES. Your voice mail should project professionalism and provide an efficient mechanism for your callers to leave messages for you. Here are some voice mail etiquette tips to follow:

- **Don't overuse voice mail.** Don't use voice mail to avoid taking phone calls. It's better to answer calls than to let voice mail messages build up.
- **Set the number of rings appropriately.** Set your voice mail to ring as few times as possible before picking up. This shows respect for your callers' time.
- **Prepare a professional, concise, friendly greeting.** Make your greeting sound warm and inviting, both in tone and content. Identify yourself and your organization so that callers know they have reached the right number. Thank the caller and briefly explain that you're unavailable. Invite the caller to leave a message or, if appropriate, call back. Here's a typical voice mail greeting: *Hello, this is Pieter Kortenaar at Sinzer Software, and I appreciate your call. You've reached my voice mailbox because I'm either working with customers or on the line at the moment. Please leave your name, number, and reason for calling so that I can be prepared when I return your call.* Give callers an idea of when you'll be available, such as *I'll be back at 2:30* or *I'll be out of my office until Wednesday, May 20.* If you screen your calls as a time-management technique, try this message: *I'm not near my phone right now, but I should be able to return calls after 3:30.*
- **Test your message.** Call your number and assess your message. Does it sound inviting? Sincere? Professional? Understandable? Are you pleased with your tone? If not, re-record your message until it conveys the professional image you want.
- **Change your message.** Update your message regularly, especially if you travel for your job.
- **Respond to messages promptly.** Check your messages regularly, and try to return all voice mail messages within one business day.
- **Plan for vacations and other extended absences.** If you won't be picking up voice mail messages for an extended period, let callers know how they can reach someone else if needed.

LEAVING VOICE MAIL MESSAGES. When leaving a voice mail message, follow these tips:

- **Be prepared to leave a message.** Before calling someone, be prepared for voice mail. Decide what you're going to say and what information you're going to include in your message. If necessary, write your message down before calling.
- **Leave a concise, thorough message.** When leaving a message, always identify yourself using your complete name and affiliation. Mention the date and time you called and a brief explanation of your reason for calling. Always leave a complete phone number, including the area code, even if you think the receiver already has it. Tell the receiver the best time to return your call. Don't ramble.
- **Use a professional and courteous tone.** When leaving a message, make sure that your tone is professional, enthusiastic, and respectful. Smile when leaving a message to add warmth to your voice.
- **Speak slowly and clearly.** You want to make sure that your receiver will be able to understand your message. Speak slowly and pronounce your words carefully, especially when providing your phone number. The receiver should be able to write information down without having to replay your message.
- **Be careful with confidential information.** Don't leave confidential or private information in a voice mail message. Remember that anyone could gain access to this information.
- **Don't make assumptions.** If you don't receive a call back within a day or two after leaving a message, don't get angry or frustrated. Call back and leave another message, or send the person an email.

◤ 10.4 Adding Value in Professional Teams

As we discussed in Chapter 1, the workplace and economy are changing. One significant recent change is the emphasis on teamwork. You might find yourself a part of a work team, project team, customer support team, supplier team, design team, planning team, functional team, cross-functional team, or some other group. All of these teams are formed to accomplish specific goals, and your career success depends on your ability to function well in a team-driven professional environment.

10.4a The Importance of Teams in the Workplace

Businesses are constantly looking for ways to do jobs in better ways at lower costs. They form teams for the following reasons:

- **Better decisions.** Decisions are generally more accurate and effective because group and team members contribute different expertise and perspectives.
- **Faster response.** When action is necessary to respond to competition or to solve a problem, small groups and teams can act rapidly.
- **Greater buy-in.** Decisions arrived at jointly are usually better received because members are committed to the solution and are more willing to support it.
- **Less resistance to change.** People who have input into decisions are less hostile, less aggressive, and less resistant to change.
- **Improved employee morale.** Personal satisfaction and job morale increase when teams are successful.
- **Reduced risks.** Responsibility for a decision is diffused, thus carrying less risk for any individual.

To connect with distant team members across borders and time zones, many organizations are creating *virtual teams*. These are groups of people who work interdependently with a shared purpose across space, time, and organization boundaries using technology.

Virtual teams may be local or global. Many workers today complete their tasks from remote locations, thus creating local virtual teams. Most major car companies exemplify virtual teaming at the global level. A company like Kia might complete engineering in Korea, research in Tokyo and Germany, styling in California, engine calibration and testing in Ontario, and heat testing in the Nevada desert. Members of its virtual teams coordinate their work and complete their tasks across time and geographic zones. Work is increasingly viewed as what you do rather than a place you go.

10.4b Positive and Negative Team Behaviour

How can you be a professional team member? The most effective teams have members who are willing to establish rules and abide by those rules. Effective team members can analyze tasks and define problems so that they can work toward solutions. They offer information and try out their ideas on the group to stimulate discussion. They show interest in others' ideas by listening actively. Helpful team members also seek to involve silent members. They help to resolve differences, and they encourage a warm, supportive climate by praising and agreeing with others. When they sense that agreement is near, they review significant points and move the group toward its goal by synthesizing points of understanding.

Not all teams, however, have members who contribute positively. Negative behaviour is shown by those who constantly put down the ideas and suggestions of others. They insult, criticize, and aggress against others. They waste the group's time with unnecessary recounting of personal achievements or irrelevant topics. The team joker distracts the group with excessive joke telling and inappropriate comments. Also disturbing are team members who withdraw and refuse to be drawn out. They have nothing to say, either for or against ideas being considered. To be a productive and welcome member of a team, be prepared to perform the positive tasks described in Figure 10.3. Avoid the negative behaviours.

10.4c Characteristics of Successful Teams

There's a general belief that teams allow workers to achieve more together than they might on their own. And yet many teams don't work well together. In fact, some teams can actually increase frustration, lower productivity, and create employee dissatisfaction. Experts who have studied team functioning and decisions have discovered that effective teams share some or all of the following characteristics.

BE SMALL AND DIVERSE. Teams can range from two to twenty-five members, although four or five is optimum for many projects. Larger groups have

FIGURE 10.3 / Positive and Negative Team Behaviours

Positive Team Behaviours
- ✓ Setting rules and abiding by them
- ✓ Analyzing tasks and defining problems
- ✓ Contributing information and ideas
- ✓ Showing interest by listening actively
- ✓ Encouraging members to participate

Negative Team Behaviours
- ✗ Blocking the ideas of others
- ✗ Insulting and criticizing others
- ✗ Wasting the group's time
- ✗ Making improper jokes and comments
- ✗ Failing to stay on task
- ✗ Withdrawing, failing to participate

© Cengage Learning

trouble interacting constructively, much less agreeing on actions. For the most creative decisions, teams generally have members of all genders who differ in age, ethnicity, social background, training, and experience. Members should bring complementary skills to a team. The key business advantage of diversity is the ability to view a project and its context from multiple perspectives. Teams with members from a variety of backgrounds can look at projects beyond the limited view of one culture. Many organizations find that diverse teams can produce innovative solutions with broader applications than homogeneous teams can.

AGREE ON PURPOSE. An effective team begins with a purpose. When the Great Lakes Coast Guard faced the task of keeping commerce moving when the lakes and rivers froze, it brought all the stakeholders together to discuss the mission. The Canadian Coast Guard, the U.S. Coast Guard, and the shipping industry formed a partnership to clear and flush ice from the Great Lakes and connecting rivers during winter months. Agreeing on the purpose was the first step in developing a concerted team effort. Preseason planning and daily phone conferences cemented the mission and gained buy-in from all stakeholders.[2]

AGREE ON PROCEDURES. The best teams develop procedures to guide them. They set up intermediate goals with deadlines. They assign roles and tasks, requiring all members to contribute equivalent amounts of real work. They decide how they'll communicate (e.g., Google Docs, email, weekly meetings) and reach decisions using one of the strategies discussed earlier. Procedures are continually evaluated to ensure movement toward the attainment of the team's goals.

CONFRONT CONFLICT. Poorly functioning teams avoid conflict through sulking, gossiping, or backstabbing. A better strategy is to acknowledge conflict and address the root of the problem openly using the plan shown in Figure 10.4. Although it may feel emotionally risky, direct confrontation saves time and enhances team commitment in the long run. To be constructive, however, confrontation must be task-oriented, not person-oriented. An open airing of differences, in which all team members have a chance to speak their minds, should centre on the strengths and weaknesses of the different positions and ideas—not on personalities. After hearing all sides, team members must negotiate a fair settlement, no matter how long it takes.

COMMUNICATE EFFECTIVELY. The best teams exchange information and contribute ideas freely in an informal environment. Team members speak

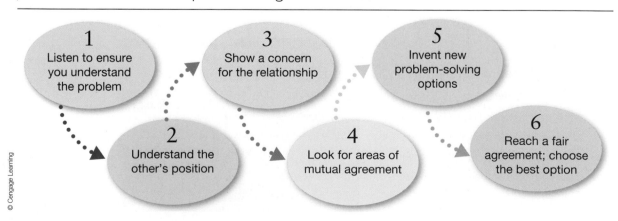

▶ **FIGURE 10.4 /** Six Steps for Dealing with Conflict

1 Listen to ensure you understand the problem

2 Understand the other's position

3 Show a concern for the relationship

4 Look for areas of mutual agreement

5 Invent new problem-solving options

6 Reach a fair agreement; choose the best option

Chapter 10: Communicating Professionally in Person

clearly and concisely, avoiding generalities. They encourage feedback. Listeners become actively involved, read body language, and ask clarifying questions before responding. Tactful, constructive disagreement is encouraged. Although a team's task is taken seriously, successful teams are able to inject humour into their interactions.

COLLABORATE RATHER THAN COMPETE. Effective team members are genuinely interested in achieving team goals instead of receiving individual recognition. They contribute ideas and feedback unselfishly. They monitor team progress, including what's going right, what's going wrong, and what to do about it. They celebrate individual and team accomplishments.

SHARE LEADERSHIP. Effective teams often have no formal leader. Instead, leadership rotates to those with the appropriate expertise as the team evolves and moves from one phase to another. Many teams operate under a democratic approach. This can achieve buy-in to team decisions, boost morale, and create fewer hurt feelings and less resentment. But in times of crisis, a strong team member may need to step up as leader.

ACCEPTANCE OF ETHICAL RESPONSIBILITIES. Team members have a number of specific responsibilities to each other, as shown in Figure 10.5. As a whole, teams have a responsibility to represent the organization's view and respect its privileged information. They shouldn't discuss with outsiders any sensitive issues without permission. In addition, teams have a broader obligation to avoid advocating actions that would endanger members of society at large.

The skills that make you a valuable and ethical team player will also serve you well when you run or participate in professional meetings.

▰ FIGURE 10.5 / Ethical Responsibilities of Team Members and Leaders

When people form a group or a team to achieve a purpose, they agree to give up some of their individual sovereignty for the good of the group. They become interdependent and assume responsibilities to one another and to the group. Here are important ethical responsibilities for members to follow:

- Determine to do your best. When you commit to the group process, you are obligated to offer your skills freely. Don't hold back, perhaps fearing that you will be repeatedly targeted because you have skills to offer. If the group project is worth doing, it is worth your best effort.

- Decide to behave with the group's good in mind. You may find it necessary to set aside your personal goals in favour of the group's goals. Decide to keep an open mind and to listen to evidence and arguments objectively. Strive to evaluate information carefully, even though it may contradict your own views or thwart your personal agenda.

- Commit to fair play. Group problem solving is a cooperative, not a competitive, event. Decide that you cannot grind your private axe at the expense of the group project.

- Expect to give and receive a fair hearing. When you speak, others should give you a fair hearing. You have a right to expect them to listen carefully, provide you with candid feedback, strive to understand what you say, and treat your ideas seriously. Listeners do not have to agree with you, of course. However, all speakers have a right to a fair hearing.

Rawpixel.com/Shutterstock.com

- Be willing to take on a participant and an analyst role. As a group member, it is your responsibility to pay attention, evaluate what is happening, analyze what you learn, and help make decisions.

- As a leader, be ready to model appropriate team behaviour. It is a leader's responsibility to coach team members in skills and teamwork, to acknowledge achievement and effort, to share knowledge, and to periodically remind members of the team's missions and goals.

10.5 Conducting Professional Business Meetings

Business meetings consist of three or more people who assemble to share information and solve problems via consensus. However, as growing numbers of employees work at distant locations, meetings have changed. Workers can't always meet face to face. To exchange information effectively and efficiently, you'll need to know how to plan and participate in face-to-face and *virtual meetings*.

Expect to attend meetings—lots of them! Estimates suggest that workers on average spend four hours a week in meetings and consider more than half of that time as wasted.[3] However, if meetings are well run, workers actually desire more, not fewer, of them.[4]

Also, meetings can be career-critical. Instead of treating them as thieves of your valuable time, try to see meetings as opportunities to demonstrate your leadership, communication, and problem-solving skills. To help you make the most of these opportunities, this section outlines best practices for running and contributing to successful meetings.

10.5a Preparing for Meetings

A face-to-face meeting provides the richest communication environment. Yet such meetings are also costly, potentially draining the productivity of all participants. As the meeting leader, to ensure productivity is maintained, do the following ahead of time: determine your purpose, decide how and where to meet, choose the participants, invite them using a digital calendar, and circulate an agenda.

DETERMINE THE PURPOSE OF THE MEETING. No meeting should be called unless the topic is important, can't wait, and requires an exchange of ideas. If the flow of information is strictly one way and no immediate feedback will result, then don't schedule a meeting. For example, if people are merely being advised or informed, send an email instead. Remember, the real expense of a meeting is the lost productivity of all the people attending. To decide whether the purpose of the meeting is valid, it's a good idea to consult the key people who'll be attending. Ask them what outcomes are desired and how to achieve those goals. This consultation also sets a collaborative tone and encourages full participation.

DECIDE HOW AND WHERE TO MEET. Once you're sure that a meeting is necessary, decide whether to meet face-to-face or virtually. If you decide to meet in person, reserve a room. If you decide to meet virtually, select the appropriate tool (e.g., Skype) and make any necessary arrangements for your voice conference, videoconference, or Web conference. These communication technologies are discussed in Chapter 1.

SELECT PARTICIPANTS. The number of meeting participants is determined by the purpose of the meeting, as shown in Figure 10.6. If the meeting purpose is motivational,

FIGURE 10.6 / Meeting Purpose and Number of Participants

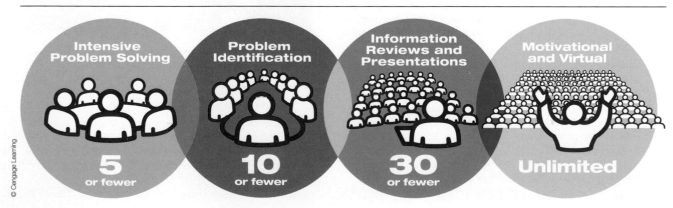

© Cengage Learning

such as an employee awards ceremony, then the number of participants is unlimited. But for making decisions, the best number is usually five or fewer participants. Ideally, those attending should be people who'll make the decision. Also attending should be people who'll implement the decision and who'll benefit from the decision.

USE DIGITAL CALENDARS TO SCHEDULE MEETINGS. Finding a time when everyone can meet is difficult. Fortunately, digital calendars make the task quicker and more efficient. Popular programs include Outlook Calendar, shown in Figure 10.7. Online calendars and mobile apps enable users to make appointments, schedule meetings, and keep track of daily activities. To schedule meetings, enter a new meeting request and add the names of attendees. Select a date, enter a start and end time, and list the meeting subject and location. Then send the meeting request to each attendee, making sure to ask for a response. Later you check the attendee availability tab to see a list of all meeting attendees. As the meeting time approaches, the program automatically sends reminders to attendees.

DISTRIBUTE AN AGENDA. At least one day before the meeting, email an agenda of topics to be discussed. Also attach any reports or materials that participants should consult in advance. For continuing meetings, you might also include a copy of the minutes of the previous meeting. To keep meetings productive, limit the number of agenda items. Remember, the narrower the focus, the greater the chances for success. A good agenda, as illustrated in Figure 10.8, covers the following information:

- Date and place of meeting
- Start time and end time

▶ FIGURE 10.7 / Using a Digital Calendar to Schedule a Meeting

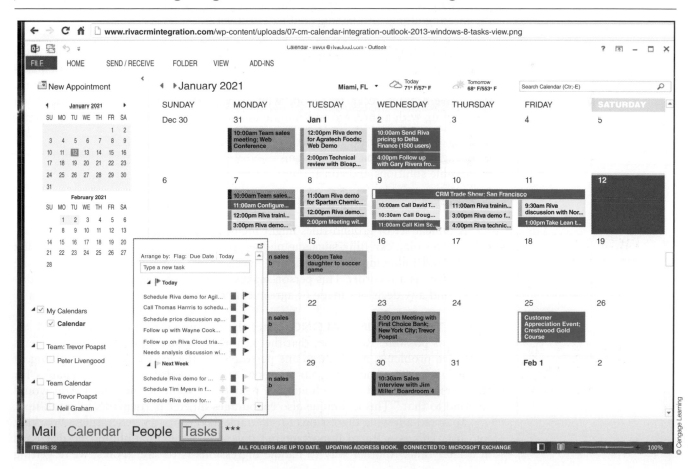

AGENDA
mAPP Dev™
Sales Department Meeting
November 15, 2021
9:30 a.m.–10:30 a.m.
Corporate Meeting Room

1. Sales update
    - Danny (10 mins.)
2. What's new and hot in the market
    - Monika (10 mins.)
3. Sales training tip of the week: Report on Mobile + WebDevCon 2021
    - Sasha (10 mins.)
4. Other updates: hires, products, etc.
    - Danny (5 mins.)
5. Morale boost: what's going well, where do we want to be, hero of the week
    - Danny + All (20 mins.)

- Brief description of each topic, in order of priority, including the names of individuals who are responsible for performing some action
- Proposed allotment of time for each topic
- Any pre-meeting preparation expected of participants

10.5b Managing the Meeting

Whether you're the meeting leader or a participant, it's important to act professionally during the meeting. Meetings are more efficient and productive if leaders and participants recognize how to get the meeting started, establish ground rules, move the meeting along, and handle conflict effectively.

GET STARTED AND ESTABLISH GROUND RULES. To avoid wasting time and irritating attendees, always start meetings on time—even if some participants are missing. Waiting for latecomers sets a bad precedent. For the same reasons, don't give a quick recap to anyone who arrives late. At the appointed time, open the meeting with a three- to five-minute introduction that includes the following:

- Goal and length of the meeting
- Background of topics or problems
- Possible solutions and constraints
- Tentative agenda
- Ground rules to be followed

A typical set of ground rules might include communicating openly, being supportive, listening carefully, silencing phones, participating fully, confronting conflict frankly, and following the agenda. The next step is to assign a participant to take minutes/act as a recorder. This person makes notes about the main ideas being discussed and any decisions made or agreements reached.

MOVE THE MEETING ALONG. After the preliminaries, the leader should say as little as possible. Remember that the purpose of a meeting is to exchange views and solve problems, not to hear one person, even the leader, do all the talking. If the group has one member who monopolizes, the leader might say, "Thanks for that perspective, Kurt. Please hold your next point while we hear how Ann would respond to that." This technique also encourages quieter participants to speak up.

To avoid allowing digressions to sidetrack the group, try generating a "parking lot" list. This is a list of important but divergent issues that should be discussed at a later time. Another way to handle digressions is to say, "Folks, we're getting off track here. Forgive me for pressing on, but I need to bring us back to the central issue of. . . ." It's important to adhere to the agenda and the time schedule. Equally important, when the group seems to have reached a consensus, summarize the group's position and check to see whether everyone agrees.

HANDLE CONFLICT. Conflict is natural and even desirable in workplaces, but it can cause awkwardness and uneasiness. In meetings, conflict typically develops when people feel unheard or misunderstood. If two people are in conflict, the best approach is to encourage each to make a complete case while group members give their full attention. Let each one question the other. Then, the leader should summarize what was said, and the group should offer comments. The group may modify a recommendation or suggest alternatives before reaching consensus on a direction to follow.

10.5c Ending with a Plan and Following Up

End the meeting at the agreed time or earlier if possible. The leader should summarize what's been decided, who's going to do what, and by what time. It may be necessary to ask people to volunteer to take responsibility for completing action items agreed to in the meeting. No one should leave the meeting without a full understanding of what was accomplished. One effective technique that encourages full participation is "once around the table." All attendees are asked to summarize briefly their interpretation of what was decided and what happens next. Of course, this closure technique works best with smaller groups. The leader should conclude by asking the group to set a time for the next meeting. The leader should also assure the group that a report will follow and thank participants for attending.

If minutes were taken, they should be distributed within a couple of days after the meeting. Figure 10.9 shows a minutes report generated using a meeting management program (there are also apps that produce similar reports). The key elements to

▼ FIGURE 10.9 / Email Meeting Minutes

Meeting proceedings are efficiently recorded in a template that provides subject, date, time, participant names, absentee names, meeting documents, and key decisions and action items.

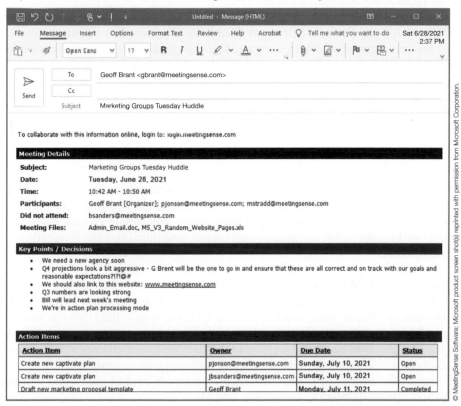

include are important points, decisions, and action items. It's up to the leader to see that what was decided at the meeting is accomplished. The leader may need to call or email people to remind them of their assignments and also to offer help if necessary.

10.5d Business Collaboration/Virtual Meeting Software

Another channel that has disrupted the transmission model of communication with its easy-to-identify sender and receiver is business collaboration/virtual meeting software. Popular examples include Google Docs, Microsoft Teams, Slack, and Zoom. Once you're logged into these platforms, you can work in real-time with multiple people to create and share documents. You can also hold virtual videoconferencing meetings and see your team in front of you on-screen.

ADVANTAGES OF THE SOFTWARE. Collaboration software has its advantages. When a team is working on a project, the ability to collaborate from different locations and at different times, but all in the same virtual space, makes work happen more quickly, and makes project management more streamlined, for example. This is because the collaboration software saves the most recent version of documents, shows who has made what additions, deletions, and changes, and allows for quick editing of documents.

HOW BUSINESSES USE THE SOFTWARE. As mentioned in Chapter 1, business has moved to a team-based, flattened management model for a while now. Given how busy this workplace style has made employees, it's natural that they can't physically be in the same place with each other all of the time. Collaboration software is a proxy for physical presence.

For example, a cross-functional team at the Saskatoon Symphony Orchestra is tasked with submitting an important annual grant application to the Canada Council for the Arts, a major funder. The grant is worth up to 25 percent of the orchestra's prior-year revenues, so it's a very important task. To get things started, the manager of development has posted the grant application on Microsoft Teams (the collaboration software used by the organization) and has divided the sections of the application among team members.

Team members can work on their individual parts of the grant application at their own pace. Because Microsoft Teams doesn't include a document management feature, team members are instructed to change the date each time they update the grant application, and to use their initials to show who's made the most recent changes. The application is downloadable from Microsoft Teams at any time in case someone needs to send it to a non-team member. Figure 10.10 is a schematic drawing of how collaboration/virtual meeting software works, and Figure 10.11 shows the actual interface of the Zoom virtual meeting software

10.5e Interacting Professionally in Virtual Meetings

Although the meeting management techniques discussed earlier for face-to-face meetings are useful for virtual meetings, additional skills and practices are important. To achieve the best results during virtual meetings, create ground rules, anticipate limited media richness, manage turn-taking, and humanize the interaction with remote members.

ESTABLISH GROUND RULES FOR VIRTUAL MEETINGS. Before beginning, explain how questions may be asked and answered. Many meeting programs allow participants to "raise their hands" with an icon on a side panel of the computer screen. Then they can type in their question for the leader and others to see. Unless the meeting involves people who know each other well, participants in audio conferences should always say their names before beginning to comment.

One of the biggest problems of virtual meetings is background noise from participants' offices or homes. You might hear dogs barking, telephones ringing, and

FIGURE 10.10 / Collaboration/Virtual Meeting Software in Action

Notice how team members can message and work with each other within software like MS Teams in real-time, and how the files they're working on are easily visible at the top of the screen.

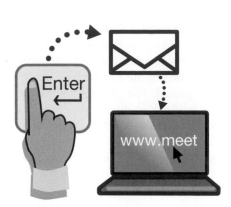  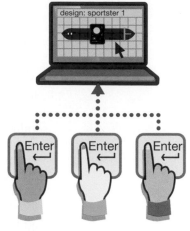

1. Email Contact

Alan T., president of Sportster Marketing, an athletic gear company in Kitchener, ON, sends an email to Meghan R., chief designer at NexxtDesign in Toronto, ON, to discuss a new sports watch. The email includes meeting date and time and a link to launch the session.

2. Virtual Meeting

When the Web conference begins, participants see live video of each other's faces on their screens. They look at photos of sports watches, share ideas, sketch designs on a shared "virtual whiteboard," and review contract terms.

3. Design Collaboration

NexxtDesign artists and Sportster Marketing managers use peer-to-peer software that allows them to share spaces on each other's computers. The software enables them to take turns modifying the designs, and it also tracks all the changes.

FIGURE 10.11 / Zoom Virtual Meeting Software in Action

Notice how team members can see each other in real-time, making for an effective meeting replacement when they can't be in the same place at the same time.

toilets flushing. Meeting planners disagree on whether to require participants to put their phones on mute. Although the mute button reduces noise, it also prevents immediate participation and tends to deaden the conference. Remind the group to silence all electronic alerts and alarms.

As a personal ground rule, don't multitask—and that includes texting and checking email—during virtual meetings. Giving your full attention is critical.

ANTICIPATE THE LIMITATIONS OF VIRTUAL TECHNOLOGY. Collaborating successfully in virtual meetings requires that you learn to manage limitations. Audioconferences in particular lack the richness that nonverbal cues provide during in-person meetings. Therefore, any small infraction or miscue can be blown out of proportion; words and tone can be easily misinterpreted. For example, when individuals meet face to face, they usually can recognize blank looks when people don't understand something being discussed. However, in virtual meetings participants and presenters can't always see each other.

As a result, when presenting ideas at a virtual meeting, you should be as precise as possible. Give examples and use simple language. Recap and summarize often. Confirm your understanding of what's being discussed. If you're a presenter, project an upbeat, enthusiastic, and strong voice. Without eye contact and nonverbal cues, the best way to keep the attention of the audience is through a powerful voice.

MANAGE TURN-TAKING AND OTHER MEETING PROCEDURES. To encourage participation and avoid traffic jams with everyone talking at once, experts suggest a number of techniques. Participants soon lose interest if the leader is the only one talking. Therefore, encourage dialogue by asking questions of specific people. Often you'll learn not only what the person is thinking but also what other participants feel but have not stated.

To elicit participation, go through the list of participants, inviting each to speak for 30 seconds without interruption. If individuals have nothing to say, they may pass when their names are called. Leaders should avoid asking vague and leading questions such as *Does everyone agree*? Remote attendees cannot answer easily without drowning out each other's responses.

Cengage

MINDTAP

In MindTap go to the Study Tools for Chapter 10 and complete the Practice Test.

◤ LEARNING SUMMARY

10.1 Apply professionalism skills in the workplace.

- Professionalism, good business etiquette, developed soft skills, social intelligence, polish, and civility are desirable workplace behaviours that are complemented by a positive online presence.

- Employers most want employees who can prioritize their work, work in teams, and exhibit a positive attitude in addition to displaying good workplace manners and other interpersonal skills.

- Professionalism means having integrity and being ethical; experts believe that no sharp distinction between ethics and etiquette exists. We should always treat others with respect.

- Practising business etiquette on the job and online can put you ahead of others who lack polish.

10.2 Engage in effective conversations.

- In-person communication is the richest communication channel; use your voice effectively by honing your pronunciation, voice quality, pitch, volume and rate, and emphasis.

- To excel in face-to-face conversations, use correct names and titles, choose appropriate topics, be positive, listen to learn, give sincere praise, and act professionally in social situations.

- When receiving criticism, avoid interrupting, paraphrase what you're hearing, agree if the criticism is accurate, disagree respectfully, look for compromise, and learn from criticism.

- When criticizing, plan your remarks, do it in person, focus on improvement, offer help, be specific, use the word *we*, encourage two-way communication, stay calm, and keep it private.

10.3 Demonstrate professional telephone skills and voice mail etiquette.

- When calling, follow an agenda, use a three-point introduction, be brisk, try to sound cheerful, be professional and courteous, avoid phone tag, and leave complete voice mail messages.

- When answering, be courteous, identify yourself, be helpful, be cautious when answering calls for others, be respectful when putting people on hold, and explain why you are transferring calls.

- Practise smartphone etiquette by being considerate, observing quiet areas, using your indoor voice, taking only urgent calls, not calling or texting while driving, and choosing a professional ring tone.

- Prepare a friendly voice mail greeting and respond to messages promptly; as a caller, plan your message, be concise, watch your tone, speak slowly, and don't leave sensitive information.

10.4 Contribute positively to team performance.

- Teams are popular because they lead to better decisions, faster responses, increased productivity, greater buy-in, less resistance, improved morale, and reduced risks.

- Virtual teams are collaborations among remote coworkers connecting with technology.

- Positive group behaviours include establishing and following rules, resolving differences, being supportive, praising others, and summarizing points of understanding.

- Negative behaviours include having contempt for others, wasting the team's time, and withdrawing.

- Successful teams are small and diverse, agree on a purpose and procedures, confront conflict, communicate well, don't compete but collaborate, are ethical, and share leadership.

10.5 Plan and participate in productive meetings.

- Before a meeting businesspeople determine its purpose and location, choose participants, use a digital calendar, and distribute an agenda.

- Experienced meeting leaders move the meeting along and confront any conflict; they end the meeting on time, make sure everyone is heard, and distribute meeting minutes promptly.

- Virtual meetings save travel costs but require attention to communication technology and to the needs of dispersed participants regarding issues such as different time zones and language barriers.

- Virtual meetings demand specific procedures to handle questions, noise, lack of media richness, and turn-taking.

CHAPTER REVIEW

1. How common is incivility in the workplace? What might be its costs? (Obj. 1)

2. Define the five traits and skills listed in the chapter that demonstrate professionalism. (Obj. 1)

3. Explain the advantages of face-to-face conversation over other communication channels. (Obj. 2)

4. Why is voice an important communication tool, and how can businesspeople use it effectively? (Obj. 2)

5. How can you ensure that your telephone calls on the job are productive? Provide at least six suggestions. (Obj. 3)

6. List at least five tips for receiving telephone calls professionally. (Obj. 3)

7. What are some of the reasons for the popularity of workplace teams? List at least five. (Obj. 4)

8. What is the best approach to address conflict in meetings? (Obj. 5)

9. What techniques can make virtual meetings as effective as face-to-face meetings? (Obj. 5)

CRITICAL THINKING

1. How can we square the empathy needed for ethical professionalism with the individualistic, sometimes greedy, nature of private enterprise (e.g., profit, advancement)? (Obj. 1)

2. Is face-to-face communication always preferable to one-dimensional channels of communication such as email? Why or why not? (Objs. 1, 2)

3. In what ways can conflict be a positive force in the workplace? (Objs. 2, 4, 5)

4. Commentators often predict that new communications media will destroy old ones. Do you think email, smartphones, and messaging/texting will replace phone calls? Why or why not? (Obj. 3)

5. Why do so many people hate voice mail when it's an efficient system for recording messages? (Obj. 3)

6. What's the right course of action when you're the only person on a team doing any actual work? (Obj. 4)

7. How can business meetings help you advance your career? (Obj. 5)

◣ ACTIVITIES AND CASES

10.1 RESEARCHING PROFESSIONAL WORKPLACE SKILLS AND PRESENTING ANNOTATED SOURCES (OBJ. 1)

You've seen that many definitions for *professionalism* exist. Recently, an opportunity to practise your research skills has arisen when your boss was invited to make a presentation to a group of human resources managers. He asked you and a small group of fellow interns to help him find articles about professionalism, soft skills, social intelligence, and other interpersonal qualities.

Your Task. As a team, divide your research in such a way that each intern is responsible for one or two search terms, depending on the size of your group. Look for articles with definitions of *professionalism*, *business etiquette*, *civility*, *business ethics*, *social skills*, *soft skills*, and *social intelligence*. Find at least three useful articles for each search term. If you get bogged down in your research, consult with a business librarian on campus or report to your instructor. After compiling your findings, present your annotated works-cited list as a team in an informational email or memo report to your boss, Ted Rollins.

10.2 INVESTIGATING SOFT SKILLS: EMPLOYER WISH LIST (OBJ. 1)

What soft skills do employers request when they list job openings in your field?

Your Task. Individually or in teams, check the listings at an online job board such as Monster, Workopolis, CareerBuilder, Indeed, or Charity Village. Follow the instructions to search job categories and locations. Also check college resources and local newspaper listings of job openings. Find five or more listings in your field. Print or otherwise save the results of your search. Examine the skills requested. How often do the ads mention communication, teamwork, and computer skills? What tasks do the ads mention? Discuss your findings with your team members. Then prepare a list of the most frequently requested soft skills. Your instructor may ask you to submit your findings or report to the class. If you are not satisfied with the job selection at any job board, choose ads posted on websites of companies you admire or on LinkedIn.

10.3 SOFT SKILLS: PERSONAL STRENGTHS INVENTORY (OBJ. 1)

When hiring, employers look for hard skills, such as mastery of software applications or accountancy procedures, as well as soft skills. Soft skills are personal characteristics, strengths, and other assets a person possesses.

Studies have divided soft skills into four categories:

- Thinking and problem solving
- Oral and written communication
- Personal qualities and work ethic
- Interpersonal and teamwork

Your Task. Using the preceding categories to guide you, identify your own soft skills, paying attention to attributes you think a potential employer would value. Prepare a list of at least four items for each of the four categories. For example, as evidence of problem solving, you might list a specific workplace or student problem you recognized and solved. You will want to weave these words and phrases into cover letters and résumés, which are covered in Chapter 12.

10.4 MAKING CONCESSIONS ON THE JOB (OBJ. 1)

Consider this statement from a young respondent in a recent survey of ethical decision making among young public relations professionals:

> At this point in my life, a job is a job, and in terms of ethics, I'll do what I have to do to keep my job; my personal feelings will take a back seat. With the economy so bad, it's just one of those things. I can't afford to let my personal feelings complicate my career.

Do you agree that personal ethics must not get in the way of one's career? Under what circumstances would you hold your tongue and keep your head down at work?

Your Task. Prepare a debate in which part of your team supports this view and part opposes it, in light of what you have read in this chapter about ethics and etiquette.

10.5 VOICE QUALITY (OBJ. 2)

Recording your voice gives you a chance to learn how your voice sounds to others and provides an opportunity for you to improve its effectiveness. Don't be surprised if you fail to recognize your own voice.

Your Task. Record yourself reading a newspaper or magazine article.

a. If you think your voice sounds a bit high, practise speaking slightly lower.

b. If your voice is low or expressionless, practise speaking slightly louder and with more inflection.

c. Ask a colleague, teacher, or friend to provide feedback on your pronunciation, pitch, volume, rate, and professional tone.

10.6 ROLE-PLAY: DELIVERING AND RESPONDING TO CRITICISM (OBJ. 2)

Develop your skills in handling criticism by joining a partner to role-play critical messages you might deliver and receive on the job.

Your Task. Designate one person A and the other B. Person A should make a list of the kinds of critical messages she or he is likely to receive on the job (e.g., *We need you to be on time regularly*) and identify who might deliver them (e.g., the shift manager). In Scenario 1, Person B should take the role of the critic and deliver the criticism in an unskilled manner. Person A should then respond using techniques described in this chapter. In Scenario 2, Person B again is the critic but delivers the criticism using techniques described in this chapter. Person A responds again. Then A and B reverse roles and repeat Scenarios 1 and 2.

10.7 ROLE-PLAY: DISCUSSING WORKPLACE CRITICISM (OBJ. 2)

In the workplace, criticism is often delivered thoughtlessly.

Your Task. In teams of two or three, describe a time when you were criticized by an untrained superior or colleague. What made the criticism painful? What goal do you think the critic had in mind? How did you feel? How did you respond? Considering techniques discussed in this chapter, how could the critic have improved his or her delivery? How does the delivery technique affect the way a receiver responds to criticism? Script the situation you've just discussed and present it to the rest of the class in a before-and-after scenario.

10.8 RESPONDING TO WORKPLACE CONFLICTS

Experts say that we generally respond to conflict in one of the following patterns: avoidance/withdrawal, accommodation/smoothing, compromise, competition/forcing, or collaboration/problem solving.

Your Task. For each of the following conflict situations, name the appropriate response pattern(s) and be prepared to explain your choice.

a. A company policy manual is posted and updated on an internal Web page. Employees must sign that they have read and understand the manual. A conflict arises when one manager insists that employees should sign electronically. Another manager thinks that a paper form should be signed by employees so that better records may be kept. What conflict response pattern is most appropriate?

b. Jeff and Mark work together but frequently disagree. Today they disagree on what tablets to purchase for an order that must be submitted immediately. Jeff insists on buying Brand X tablets. Mark knows that Brand X is made by a company that markets an identical tablet at a slightly lower price. However, Mark doesn't have stock numbers for the cheaper tablets readily available. How should Mark respond?

c. A manager and his assistant plan to attend a conference together at a resort location. Six weeks before the conference, the company announces a cutback and limits conference support to only one person. The assistant, who has developed a presentation specifically for the conference, feels that he should be the one to attend. Travel arrangements must be made immediately. What conflict response pattern will most likely result?

d. Two vice presidents disagree on a company instant messaging policy. One wants to ban personal messaging totally. The other thinks that an outright ban is impossible to implement. She is more concerned with limiting Internet misuse, including visits to online game, pornography, and shopping sites. The vice presidents agree that they need a policy, but they disagree on what to allow and what to prohibit. What conflict response pattern is appropriate?

e. Customer service rep Jackie comes to work one morning and finds Alexa sitting at Workstation 2. Although the customer service reps have no special workstation assigned to them, Jackie has the most seniority and has always assumed that Workstation 2 was hers. Other workstations were available, but the supervisor told Alexa to use Workstation 2 that morning because she didn't know that Jackie would be coming in. When Jackie arrives and sees "her" workstation occupied, she becomes angry and demands that Alexa vacate the station. What conflict response pattern might be most appropriate for Alexa and the supervisor?

10.9 CONSTRUCTIVE CRITICISM (OBJ. 3)

You work for a large company that is organized into work teams. Your work team, in the company's marketing department, meets weekly for a half-hour to review the week's activities and projects. The meetings are run by the team leader, Mandy Miller. The team leader is a position of extra responsibility with a higher salary than that of other marketing staffers. For the past three months, Mandy has been regularly missing or showing up late for meetings. No one has said anything but you. You had a conversation with Mandy in the cafeteria three weeks ago in which you relayed your concerns to her in as positive a way as possible. Mandy has again started to miss meetings. You feel it's appropriate to send an email to the director of the marketing department, letting him know what's been happening, that you've talked to Mandy, and that things haven't improved.

Your Task. Draft an email to your director about the situation with Mandy.

10.10 RULES FOR WIRELESS PHONE USE IN SALES (OBJ. 3)

As one of the managers of Wrigley Canada, a gum and confectionery company, you're alarmed at a newspaper article you just read. A stockbroker for BMO Nesbitt Burns was making cold calls on his personal phone while driving. His car hit and killed a motorcyclist. The brokerage firm was sued and accused of contributing to an accident by encouraging employees to use cellular telephones while driving. To avoid the risk of paying huge damages awarded by an emotional jury, the brokerage firm offered the victim's family a $500,000 settlement.

Your Task. Individually or in teams, write an email to Wrigley sales reps outlining company suggestions (or should they be rules?) for safe wireless phone use in cars. Check library databases for articles that discuss cell phone use in cars. Look for additional safety ideas. In your message to sales reps, try to suggest receiver benefits. How is safe cell phone use beneficial to the sales rep?

10.11 ROLE-PLAY: IMPROVING TELEPHONE SKILLS (OBJ. 3)

Acting out the roles of telephone caller and receiver is an effective technique for improving skills. To give you such practice, your instructor will divide the class into pairs.

Your Task. Read each scenario and rehearse your role silently. Then improvise the role with your partner. After improvising a couple of times, script one of the situations and present it to the rest of the class.

Partner 1

a. You are the HR manager of Datatronics, Inc. Call Elizabeth Franklin, office manager at Computers Plus. Inquire about a job applicant, Chelsea Chavez, who listed Ms. Franklin as a reference.

b. Call Ms. Franklin again the following day to inquire about the same job applicant, Chelsea Chavez. Ms. Franklin answers today, but she talks on and on, describing the applicant in great detail. Tactfully close the conversation.

Partner 2

a. You are the receptionist for Computers Plus. The caller asks for Elizabeth Franklin, who is home sick today. You don't know when she will be able to return. Answer the call appropriately.

b. You are now Ms. Franklin, office manager. Describe Chelsea Chavez, an imaginary employee. Think of someone with whom you've worked. Include many details, such as her ability to work with others, her skills at computing, her schooling, her ambition, and so forth.

c. You are now the receptionist for Tom Wing, of Wing Imports. Answer a call for Mr. Wing, who is working in another office, at Ext. 134, where he will accept calls.

d. You are now Tom Wing, owner of Wing Imports. Call your lawyer, Michael Murphy, about a legal problem. Leave a brief, incomplete message.

e. Call Mr. Murphy again. Leave a message that will prevent telephone tag.

c. You are now an administrative assistant for lawyer Michael Murphy. Call Tom Wing to verify a meeting date Mr. Murphy has with Mr. Wing. Use your own name in identifying yourself.

d. You are now the receptionist for lawyer Michael Murphy. Mr. Murphy is skiing in Mont-Tremblant and will return in two days, but he doesn't want his clients to know where he is. Take a message.

e. Take a message again.

10.12 MEETINGS: MANAGING DIFFICULT OR RETICENT TEAM MEMBERS AND OTHER CHALLENGES (OBJ. 4)

As you have learned, facilitating a productive meeting requires skills that may be critical to your career success.

Your Task. Individually or as a team, describe how you would deal with the following examples of unproductive or dysfunctional behaviour and other challenges in a team meeting that you are running. Either report your recommendations verbally, or, if your instructor directs, summarize your suggestions in an email or a memo.

a. Jimmy, a well-known office clown, is telling racist jokes while others are discussing the business at hand.

b. Anna is quiet, although she is taking notes and seems to be following the discussion attentively.

c. Peter likes to make long-winded statements and often digresses to unrelated subjects.

d. Carla keeps interrupting other speakers and dominates the discussion.

e. Ron and Mark are hostile toward each other and clash over an agenda item.

f. Elena arrives 15 minutes late and noisily unpacks her briefcase.

g. Kristen, Shelley, and Paul are texting under the table.

h. The meeting time is up, but the group has not met the objective of the meeting.

10.13 ANALYZING A MEETING (OBJ. 5)

You've learned a number of techniques in this chapter for planning and participating in meetings. Here's your chance to put your knowledge to work.

Your Task. Attend a structured meeting of a college, social, business, or other organization. Compare the manner in which the meeting is conducted with the suggestions presented in this chapter. Why did the meeting succeed or fail? Prepare a brief recommendation report for your instructor or be ready to discuss your findings in class.

10.14 PLANNING A MEETING (OBJ. 5)

Assume that at the next meeting of your Associated Students Organization (ASO), you will discuss preparations for a job fair in the spring. The group will hear reports from committees working on speakers, business recruiters, publicity, reservations of campus space, setup of booths, and any other matters you can think of.

Your Task. As president of your ASO, prepare an agenda for the meeting. Compose your introductory remarks to open the meeting. Your instructor may ask you to submit these two documents or use them in staging an actual meeting in class.

10.15 MANAGING A MEETING (OBJ. 5)

The best way to learn to manage a meeting is to actually do it.

Your Task. Using the agenda your team wrote in Activity 10.14, run part of your next class as a meeting. Many decisions will have to be made. Who will chair the meeting? (It does not necessarily have to be your instructor—in fact, it may be better if it's not.) What will the chair say to get the meeting started? What reports will be given at the meeting? How will you generate discussion at this meeting, considering that it's a mock meeting and the participants are your classmates, many of whom may be non-talkers? What will you do if the meeting gets off track? You may want to "plant" one of your team members as a disruptive meeting participant. Does the chair know how to deal with this disruptive person? Consider changing the normal seating arrangement of your class to more closely approximate that of a meeting. Who will take notes at this meeting? How will the meeting end and who will be in charge of following up?

10.16 SPOOFING MEETINGS (OBJ. 5)

One of the most popular ways to demonstrate to students the problems that can often occur in formal workplace meetings is to watch poorly run meetings on video.

Your Task. Search YouTube (www.youtube.com) for videos about poor meetings. You may also search Google using keywords like *spoof*, *meetings*, *bad business meetings*. Screen five to ten of the videos you find. Make a list of the most commonly shown "bad" meeting behaviours. Why do you think the makers of the videos included these behaviours? Are there other, more subtle bad behaviours that might be hard to represent on the screen but that can have a serious impact in meetings? Share your results in a presentation to your class or your instructor.

10.17 VIRTUAL MEETINGS: IMPROVING DISTANCE MEETING BUY-IN (OBJ. 5)

Marina Elliot works for a large insurance company at the headquarters in Waterloo, Ontario. Her position requires her to impose organizational objectives and systems on smaller groups that often resist such interference. Marina recently needed to inform regional groups that the home office was instituting a system-wide change to hiring practices. To save costs, she set up a Web conference between her office in Waterloo and regional offices in Vancouver, Calgary, and Winnipeg. Marina set the meeting for 10 a.m. Eastern Standard Time. At the designated date and hour, she found that the Vancouver team was not logged in, and she had to delay the session. When the Vancouver team finally did log in, Marina launched into her presentation. She explained the reasons behind the change in a PowerPoint presentation that contained complex data she had not distributed before the conference. Marina heard cellphone ringtones and typing in the background as she spoke. Still, she pushed through her one-hour presentation without eliciting any feedback.

Your Task. In teams, discuss ways Marina might have improved the Web conference. Prepare a list of recommendations from your team.

10.18 DISCUSSING A GROUP PROJECT OR CLASS ISSUE IN A VIRTUAL MEETING (OBJS. 4, 5)

Virtual meetings are extremely useful to dispersed workplace teams, and, yes, they may help harried college students. Some of them brave terrible traffic and commute vast distances to attend colleges and universities. When doing research for a group project, students often struggle to find a convenient time to meet because they may work on weekends or have family duties. Although software such as Google Docs can aid collaboration on shared files, a video chat conveys much more nuance than email or IM can. Real-time video chatting allows for a fast exchange of information with almost the media richness of face-to-face conversations.

Your Task. Settle on the type of communication software or app your team will use. Some popular group video chat applications are Skype, Google Hangouts, Fring, and WhatsApp. Following the guidelines in this chapter, prepare and conduct a virtual meeting with your collaborators. Ensure that everyone knows the technology; establish ground rules for the virtual meetings such as when to ask questions, letting everyone speak, and so forth. Your instructor may ask for deliverables by email or in memo form such as an agenda and meeting minutes. You could also be required to write a short memo report on the experience, summarizing what you did before, during, and after the virtual meeting.

◥ GRAMMAR/MECHANICS CHALLENGE 10

OTHER PUNCTUATION

Although this challenge concentrates on Sections 2.23–2.29 in the Grammar/Mechanics Handbook, you may also refer to other punctuation. Study each of the following statements. Insert any necessary punctuation and change any incorrect punctuation. In the space provided, indicate the number of changes you make. Count each mark separately; for example, a set of parentheses counts as two. If you make no changes, write *0*. Use underlining to show italics. Also record the number of the G/M principle illustrated. When you finish, compare your responses with those provided near the end of the book. If your responses differ, study carefully the principles in parentheses.

2 (2.27)   **Example** Current sales projections (see page 11 in the attached report) indicate a profitable year ahead.

_____ 1. Three outstanding employees Santiago Wilson, Rae Thomas, and Charles Stoop will receive bonuses.

_____ 2. Will you please Jonathan complete your assignment by six o'clock?

_____ 3. To determine whether to spell email with or without the hyphen be sure to consult our company style sheet.

_____ 4. Cargill, Koch Industries, and Royal Bank of Canada these are the most profitable private companies in North America.

_____ 5. (De-emphasize) Today's employers regularly conduct three kinds of background checks drug, credit, and criminal before hiring employees.

_____ 6. Was it Warren Buffet who said "The rearview mirror is always clearer than the windshield

_____ 7. Did you see the article titled Wireless Riches From Serving the Poor that appeared in The Toronto Star

_____ 8. (Emphasize) Three cities considered the best places in the world to live Vienna, Zurich, and Geneva are all in Europe.

_____ 9. Did you send invitations to Dr Lisa Uhl, Ms Ginger Ortiz, and Mr Orrin T Tapia

_____ 10. Our instructor recommended the chapter titled The Almost Perfect Meeting that appeared in Emily Post's book called The Etiquette Advantage in Business.

_____ 11. Incredible Did you see the price of gold today

_____ 12. Susan wondered what keywords would attract the most clicks in her Google ad?

_____ 13. The owner of Smash Party Entertainment found that the best keyword for her online ad business was party.

_____ 14. Is the reception scheduled to begin at 6 pm

_____ 15. The term autoregressive is defined as using past data to predict future data.

◥ EDITING CHALLENGE 10

The following report showing meeting minutes has proofreading, spelling, grammar, punctuation, wordiness, number form, and other writing faults that require correction. Study the guidelines in the Grammar/Mechanics Handbook, as well as the lists of Confusing Words and Frequently Misspelled Words at the end of the book, to sharpen your skills. When you finish making corrections, your instructor can show you the revised version of these minutes.

Your Task. Edit the following minutes by correcting its errors (a) in your textbook or (b) on a photocopy using proofreading marks from Appendix B.

Canadian Federation of Small Business
Policy Board Committee
February 4, 2021

Present: Debra Chinnapongse, Tweet Jackson, Irene Kishita, Barry Knaggs, Kevin Poepoe, and Ralph Mason

Absent: Alex Watanabe

The meeting was call to order by Chair Kevin Poepo at 9:02 a.m. in the morning. Minutes from the January 6th meeting was read and approve.

Old Business

Debra Chinnapongse discussed the cost of the annual awards luncheon. That honours outstanding members. The ticket price ticket does not cover all the expenses incured. Major expenses include: awards and complementary lunches for the judges, VIP guests and volunteers. CFSB can not continue to make up the difference between income from tickets and costs for the luncheon. Ms. Chinnapongse reported that it had come to her attention that other associations relied on members contributions for their awards' programs.

MOTION: To send a Letter to board members asking for there contributions to support the annual awards luncheon. (Chinapongse/Kishita). PASSED 6-0.

Reports

Barry Knaggs reported that the media relations committee sponsored a get acquainted meeting in November. More than eighty people from various agencys attended.

The Outreach Committee reports that they have been asked to assist the Partnership for Small Business, an Ottawa-based organization in establishing a speakers bureau of Canadian small business owners. It would be available to speak at schools and colleges about small business and employment.

New Business

The chair announced a Planning Meeting to be held in March regarding revising the agri-business plan. In other New Business Ralph Mason reported that the staff had purchased fifty tickets for members, and our committees to attend the Zig Ziglar seminar in the month of March.

Next Meeting

The next meeting of the Policy Boare Committee will be held in early Aprl at the Lord Elgin hotel, Ottawa. At that time the meeting will conclude with a tour of the seaway Networks inc. offices in Kanata.

The meeting adjourned at 10:25 am by Keven Poepoe.

Respectfully submitted,

BUSINESS PRESENTATIONS

BIZ COMM BYTE

According to research into eye tracking and gaze interaction, presenters can keep the attention of their audience in three important ways: speak off-PowerPoint (i.e. discuss material not in your slides), use humour, and move closer to your audience.

Source: School daze: Eye-tracking study reveals what earns student attention in the classroom. (2012, July 17). *Business Wire*. https://www .businesswire.com/news/home/20120717005219/en/School-Daze-Eye-Tracking-Study-Reveals-Earns-Student

11.1 Types of Business Presentation and Preparation

Organizations are interested in hiring people with good presentation skills. Why? The business world is changing. As you've seen, technical skills aren't enough to guarantee success. You also need to be able to communicate ideas effectively in presentations to customers, vendors, members of your team, and management.

11.1a Speaking Skills and Your Career

Speaking skills are useful at every career stage. Business communication researchers have found that the number one competency hiring managers look for in new employees is strong oral communication skills, including presentation skills. You might, for example, have to make a sales pitch before customers or speak to a professional gathering. You might need to describe your company's expansion plans to

Cengage
MINDTAP

In MindTap go to the Whiteboard Animation for Chapter 11 and watch it now.

your banker, or you might need to persuade management to support your proposed marketing strategy. Speaking skills rank very high on recruiters' wish lists. Almost 90 percent of executives consider oral communication skills very important for college and university graduates.

11.1b Understanding Presentation Types

A common part of a business professional's life is giving presentations. Some presentations are informative whereas others are persuasive. Some are face to face; others, virtual. Some are given before big audiences, and some happen with smaller groups. Some presentations are elaborate; others are simple. Figure 11.1 shows a sampling of business presentation types you may encounter in your career.

11.1c Preparing for a Presentation

In getting ready for a presentation, you may feel a lot of anxiety. For many people fear of speaking before a group is almost as great as the fear of pain. We get butterflies in our stomachs just thinking about it. For any presentation, you can reduce your fears and lay the foundation for a professional performance by focusing on five areas: preparation, organization, audience rapport, visual aids, and delivery. Preparation involves answering two important questions.

WHAT'S MY PURPOSE? The most important part of your preparation is deciding on your purpose. Do you need to sell a group insurance policy to a prospective client? Do you need to persuade management to increase the marketing budget? Do you need to inform customer service reps of three important ways to prevent miscommunication? Whether it's informing or persuading, by the end of your presentation, what do you want your listeners to remember or do?

Erick Rosan, a finance manager at AutoFleet, a car brokerage company, faced such questions as he planned a talk for a class in business communication. His business communication professor had invited him back to school as a guest speaker. He was asked to talk about what happened after he graduated, how he uses the skills

FIGURE 11.1 / Types of Business Presentations

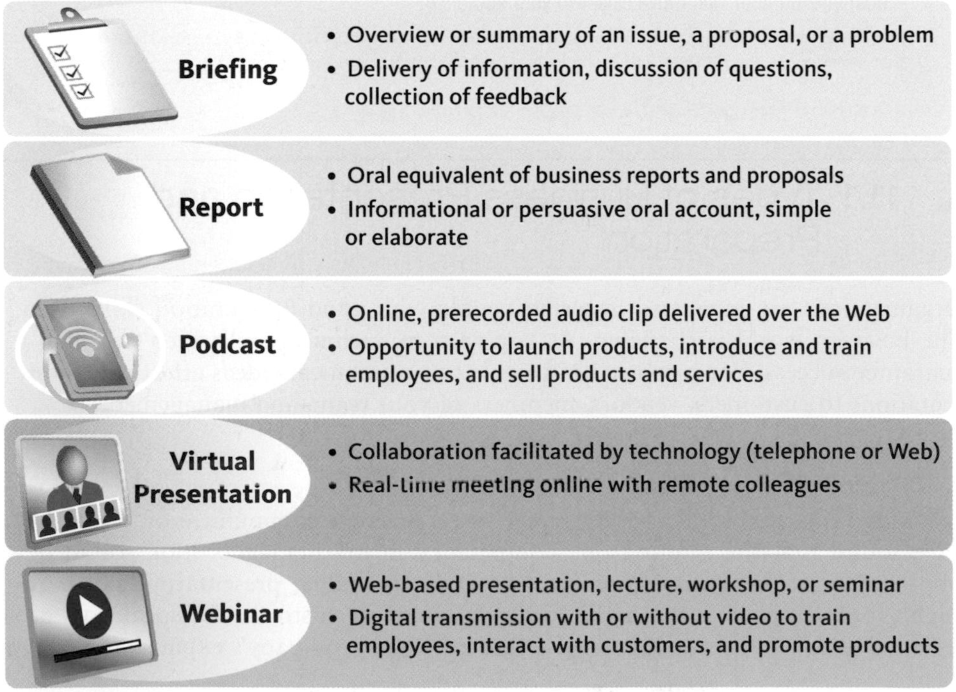

Briefing
• Overview or summary of an issue, a proposal, or a problem
• Delivery of information, discussion of questions, collection of feedback
Report
• Oral equivalent of business reports and proposals
• Informational or persuasive oral account, simple or elaborate
Podcast
• Online, prerecorded audio clip delivered over the Web
• Opportunity to launch products, introduce and train employees, and sell products and services
Virtual Presentation
• Collaboration facilitated by technology (telephone or Web)
• Real-time meeting online with remote colleagues
Webinar
• Web-based presentation, lecture, workshop, or seminar
• Digital transmission with or without video to train employees, interact with customers, and promote products

he gained in college in his current job, and what a "day in the life" of his job entails. (You can see the outline for his talk later in the chapter in Figure 11.4.) Because Erick obviously knows so much about this topic, he finds it difficult to extract a specific purpose statement for his presentation. After much thought he narrows his purpose to this: *To inform current business students about the realities of the post-college job market using my job as an example.* His entire presentation focuses on ensuring that the class members understand and remember three principal ideas.

WHO'S MY AUDIENCE? A second key element in preparation is analyzing your audience, anticipating its reactions, and adapting accordingly. Understanding four basic audience types, summarized in Figure 11.2, helps you decide how to organize your presentation. A friendly audience, for example, will respond to humour and personal experiences. A neutral audience requires an even, controlled delivery style. An uninterested audience that is forced to attend calls for brevity and a mix of humour, colourful visuals, and startling statistics. A hostile audience can be won over by a calm delivery style, objective data, and expert opinions.

Other elements, such as age, education, experience, and size of audience will affect your style and message content. Erick's analysis tells him that while students are "forced" to attend, they will also probably be friendly and eager because he'll be sharing information they may not be getting regularly from their professors. He decides he'll use some humour, but also maintain an even, professional tone. Answer the following questions to help you determine your organizational pattern, delivery style, and supporting material for any presentation.

- How will this topic appeal to this audience?
- How can I relate this information to their needs?

Cengage

MINDTAP

In MindTap, go to the Chapter 11 reading, section 11.1c, and watch the videos of industry experts Mike Draper discussing knowing your audience and Courtney Appleby discussing best practices when presenting to senior managers.

◢ FIGURE 11.2 / Succeeding With Four Audience Types

Audience Members	Organizational Pattern	Delivery Style	Supporting Material
Friendly			
They like you and your topic.	Use any pattern. Try something new. Involve the audience.	Be warm, pleasant, and open. Use lots of eye contact and smiles.	Include humour, personal examples, and experiences.
Neutral			
They are calm, rational; their minds are made up, but they think they are objective.	Present both sides of the issue. Use pro/con or problem/solution patterns. Save time for audience questions.	Be controlled. Do nothing showy. Use confident, small gestures.	Use facts, statistics, expert opinion, and comparison and contrast. Avoid humour, personal stories, and flashy visuals.
Uninterested			
They have short attention spans; they may be there against their will.	Be brief—no more than three points. Avoid topical and pro/con patterns that seem long to the audience.	Be dynamic and entertaining. Move around. Use large gestures.	Use humour, cartoons, colourful visuals, powerful quotations, and startling statistics.

> **Avoid** darkening the room, standing motionless, passing out handouts, using boring visuals, or expecting the audience to participate.

Hostile			
They want to take charge or ridicule the speaker; they may be defensive, emotional.	Organize using a noncontroversial pattern, such as a topical, chronological, or geographical strategy.	Be calm and controlled. Speak evenly and slowly.	Include objective data and expert opinion. Avoid anecdotes and humour.

> **Avoid** a question-and-answer period, if possible; otherwise, use a moderator or accept only written questions.

© Cengage Learning

- How can I earn respect so that they accept my message?
- What would be most effective in making my point? Facts? Statistics? Personal experiences? Expert opinion? Humour? Cartoons? Graphic illustrations? Demonstrations? Case histories? Analogies?
- How can I ensure that this audience remembers my main points?

◤ 11.2 Organizing Presentations for Impact and Rapport

After you've determined your purpose and analyzed the audience, you're ready to collect information and organize it logically. Good organization and conscious repetition are the two most powerful keys to audience comprehension and retention. In fact, many speech experts recommend the following repetitive, but effective, plan:

PLAN FOR A BUSINESS PRESENTATION
- **Opening:** Introduce yourself and tell the audience what you're going to say.
- **Body:** Explain your points persuasively using visual aids, some humour, and appropriate audience proximity, and by going off-slide a couple of times.
- **Pleasant closing:** Remind the audience of your main points and look forward to future interactions.

In other words, repeat your main points in the introduction, body, and conclusion of your presentation. Although it sounds boring, this strategy works surprisingly well. This is because in an increasingly wired, mobile, and distracting world, people may have trouble concentrating in face-to-face situations and need to be reminded of important points more than once.[1] Let's examine how to construct the three parts of an effective presentation: introduction, body, conclusion.

11.2a Capture Attention in the Introduction

How many times have you heard a speaker begin with *It's a pleasure to be here.* Or *I'm honoured to be asked to speak.* Boring openings such as these get speakers off to a dull start. Avoid such openings by striving to accomplish three goals in the introduction to your presentation:

- Capture listeners' attention and get them involved.
- Identify yourself and establish your credibility.
- Preview your main points.

If you're able to appeal to listeners and involve them in your presentation right from the start, you're more likely to hold their attention until the finish. Consider some of the same techniques that you used to open sales messages: a question, a startling fact, a joke, a story, or a quotation. Some speakers achieve involvement by opening with a question or command that requires audience members to raise their hands or stand up. You'll find additional techniques for gaining and keeping audience attention in Figure 11.3.

To establish your credibility, you should describe your position, knowledge, or experience—whatever qualifies you to speak. Try, as well, to connect with your audience by revealing something of yourself. Erick Rosan, for example, plans to talk a bit about his former extracurricular activities at the beginning of his upcoming presentation at his old college, as seen in Figure 11.4. Similarly, a consultant addressing

Experienced speakers know how to capture the attention of an audience and how to maintain that attention throughout a presentation. You can spruce up your presentations by trying these 12 proven techniques.

- **A promise.** Begin with a realistic promise that keeps the audience expectant (for example, *By the end of this presentation, you will know how you can increase your sales by 50 percent!*).

- **Drama.** Open by telling an emotionally moving story or by describing a serious problem that involves the audience. Throughout your talk include other dramatic elements, such as a long pause after a key statement. Change your vocal tone or pitch. Professionals use high-intensity emotions such as anger, joy, sadness, or excitement.

- **Eye contact.** As you begin, command attention by surveying the entire audience to take in all listeners. Give yourself two to five seconds to linger on individuals to avoid fleeting, unconvincing eye contact. Don't just sweep the room and the crowd.

- **Movement.** Leave the lectern area whenever possible. Walk around the conference table or down the aisles of the presentation room. Try to move toward your audience, especially at the beginning and end of your talk.

- **Questions.** Keep listeners active and involved with rhetorical questions. Ask for a show of hands to get each listener thinking. The response will also give you a quick gauge of audience attention.

- **Demonstrations.** Include a member of the audience in a demonstration (for example, *I'm going to show you exactly how to implement our four-step customer courtesy process, but I need a volunteer from the audience to help me*).

- **Samples/props.** If you are promoting a product, consider using items to toss out to the audience or to award as prizes to volunteer participants. You can also pass around product samples or promotional literature. Be careful, though, to maintain control.

- **Visuals.** Give your audience something to look at besides yourself. Use a variety of visual aids in a single session. Also consider writing the concerns expressed by your audience on a flipchart, a whiteboard, or a smart board as you go along.

- **Attire.** Enhance your credibility with your audience by dressing professionally for your presentation. Professional attire will help you look competent and qualified, making your audience more likely to listen and take you seriously.

- **Current events/statistics.** Mention a current event or statistic (the more startling, the better) that is relevant to your topic and to which the audience can relate.

- **A quote.** Quotations, especially those made by well-known individuals, can be powerful attention-getting devices. The quotation should be pertinent to your topic, short, and interesting.

- **Self-interest.** Review your entire presentation to ensure that it meets the critical *What's-in-it-for-me* audience test. People are most interested in things that benefit them.

iStock.com/Izabela Habur

© Cengage Learning

office workers might reminisce about how he started as a temporary worker; a CEO might tell a funny story in which the joke is on her.

After capturing attention and establishing yourself, you'll want to preview the main points of your topic, perhaps with a visual aid. You might put off actually writing your introduction until after you've organized the rest of the presentation and crystallized your principal ideas.

Look at Erick Rosan's introduction, shown in Figure 11.4, to see how he integrated all the elements necessary for a good opening.

11.2b Explain Persuasively in the Body of the Presentation

The biggest problem with most presentations is a failure to focus on a few main ideas. The body of your short presentation (20 or fewer minutes) should include

FIGURE 11.4 / Presentation Outline

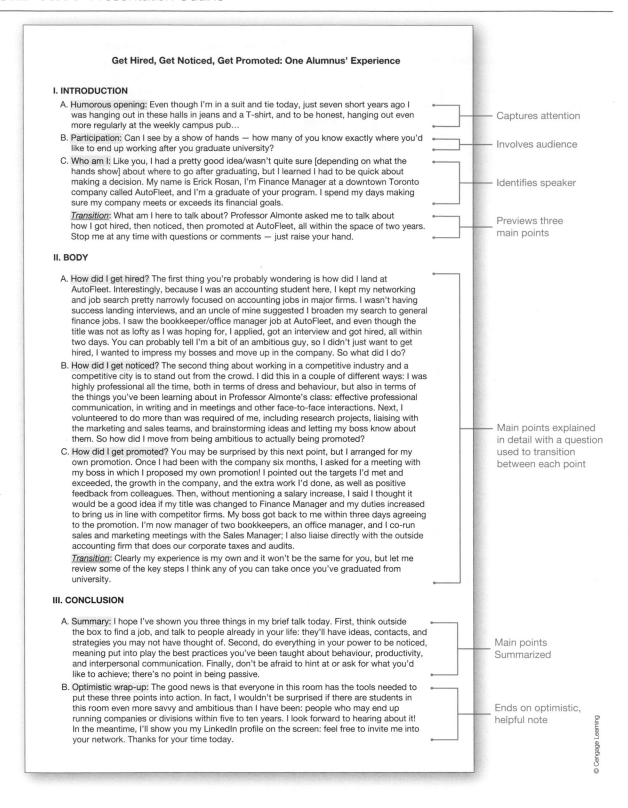

Get Hired, Get Noticed, Get Promoted: One Alumnus' Experience

I. INTRODUCTION

A. Humorous opening: Even though I'm in a suit and tie today, just seven short years ago I was hanging out in these halls in jeans and a T-shirt, and to be honest, hanging out even more regularly at the weekly campus pub… — Captures attention

B. Participation: Can I see by a show of hands — how many of you know exactly where you'd like to end up working after you graduate university? — Involves audience

C. Who am I: Like you, I had a pretty good idea/wasn't quite sure [depending on what the hands show] about where to go after graduating, but I learned I had to be quick about making a decision. My name is Erick Rosan, I'm Finance Manager at a downtown Toronto company called AutoFleet, and I'm a graduate of your program. I spend my days making sure my company meets or exceeds its financial goals. — Identifies speaker

Transition: What am I here to talk about? Professor Almonte asked me to talk about how I got hired, then noticed, then promoted at AutoFleet, all within the space of two years. Stop me at any time with questions or comments — just raise your hand. — Previews three main points

II. BODY

A. How did I get hired? The first thing you're probably wondering is how did I land at AutoFleet. Interestingly, because I was an accounting student here, I kept my networking and job search pretty narrowly focused on accounting jobs in major firms. I wasn't having success landing interviews, and an uncle of mine suggested I broaden my search to general finance jobs. I saw the bookkeeper/office manager job at AutoFleet, and even though the title was not as lofty as I was hoping for, I applied, got an interview and got hired, all within two days. You can probably tell I'm a bit of an ambitious guy, so I didn't just want to get hired, I wanted to impress my bosses and move up in the company. So what did I do?

B. How did I get noticed? The second thing about working in a competitive industry and a competitive city is to stand out from the crowd. I did this in a couple of different ways: I was highly professional all the time, both in terms of dress and behaviour, but also in terms of the things you've been learning about in Professor Almonte's class: effective professional communication, in writing and in meetings and other face-to-face interactions. Next, I volunteered to do more than was required of me, including research projects, liaising with the marketing and sales teams, and brainstorming ideas and letting my boss know about them. So how did I move from being ambitious to actually being promoted? — Main points explained in detail with a question used to transition between each point

C. How did I get promoted? You may be surprised by this next point, but I arranged for my own promotion. Once I had been with the company six months, I asked for a meeting with my boss in which I proposed my own promotion! I pointed out the targets I'd met and exceeded, the growth in the company, and the extra work I'd done, as well as positive feedback from colleagues. Then, without mentioning a salary increase, I said I thought it would be a good idea if my title was changed to Finance Manager and my duties increased to bring us in line with competitor firms. My boss got back to me within three days agreeing to the promotion. I'm now manager of two bookkeepers, an office manager, and I co-run sales and marketing meetings with the Sales Manager; I also liaise directly with the outside accounting firm that does our corporate taxes and audits.

Transition: Clearly my experience is my own and it won't be the same for you, but let me review some of the key steps I think any of you can take once you've graduated from university.

III. CONCLUSION

A. Summary: I hope I've shown you three things in my brief talk today. First, think outside the box to find a job, and talk to people already in your life: they'll have ideas, contacts, and strategies you may not have thought of. Second, do everything in your power to be noticed, meaning put into play the best practices you've been taught about behaviour, productivity, and interpersonal communication. Finally, don't be afraid to hint at or ask for what you'd like to achieve; there's no point in being passive. — Main points Summarized

B. Optimistic wrap-up: The good news is that everyone in this room has the tools needed to put these three points into action. In fact, I wouldn't be surprised if there are students in this room even more savvy and ambitious than I have been: people who may end up running companies or divisions within five to ten years. I look forward to hearing about it! In the meantime, I'll show you my LinkedIn profile on the screen: feel free to invite me into your network. Thanks for your time today. — Ends on optimistic, helpful note

© Cengage Learning

a limited number of main points, say, two to four. Develop each main point with adequate, but not excessive, explanation and details. Too many details can obscure the main message, so keep your presentation simple and logical. Remember, listeners have no pages to leaf back through should they become confused.

When Erick Rosan began planning his presentation, he realized that he could talk for quite a while on his topic. He also knew that listeners aren't good at separating major and minor points. So, instead of submerging his listeners in a sea of information, he sorted out a few principal ideas. First, college students, worried about where they might work after graduating, need concrete advice about how to become employable workers. Second, students need to be reassured that all the hard work they're currently doing (e.g., assignments, exams, research) is going to be useful in their jobs. Third, students need to understand what a day in the life of a professional is like: how it differs from that of a student or part-time worker (an experience most students already have).

These would become his main points, but Erick wanted to streamline them further so that his student audience would be sure to remember them. He summarized the three points as follows: *get hired, get noticed, get promoted*. As you can see in Figure 11.4, Erick prepared a sentence outline showing these three main ideas. Each is supported by examples and explanations.

How to organize and sequence main ideas may not be immediately obvious when you begin working on a presentation. In Chapter 9 you studied a number of patterns for organizing written reports. Those patterns, and a few new ones, are also appropriate for presentations:

- **Chronology.** A presentation describing the history of a problem, organized from the first sign of trouble to the present. We could argue that Erick Rosan's presentation is chronological: first get hired, then get noticed, and finally get promoted.
- **Geography/space.** A presentation about the changing diversity of the workforce, organized by regions in the country (Atlantic, Prairie, and so forth).
- **Topic/function/conventional grouping.** A report discussing mishandled airline baggage, organized by names of airlines. We could also argue that Erick's presentation is topical: topic 1 is getting hired, topic 2 is getting noticed, and topic 3 is getting promoted.
- **Comparison/contrast (pro/con).** A report comparing organic farming methods with those of modern industrial farming.
- **Journalism pattern.** A report describing how identity thieves can ruin your good name, organized by *who*, *what*, *when*, *where*, *why*, and *how*.
- **Value/size.** A report describing fluctuations in housing costs, organized by prices of homes.
- **Importance.** A report describing five reasons that a company should move its headquarters to a specific city, organized from the most important reason to the least important (using some criteria to judge importance, of course). Erick's presentation can also be seen as being organized this way; he leaves what he judges to be the most important topic (getting promoted) for last.
- **Problem/solution.** A company faces a problem such as declining sales. A solution such as reducing the staff is offered.
- **Simple/complex.** A report explaining genetic modification of plants, organized from simple seed production to complex gene introduction.
- **Best case/worst case.** A report analyzing whether two companies should merge, organized by the best-case result (improved market share, profitability, good employee morale) as opposed to the worst-case result (devalued stock, lost market share, poor employee morale).

When organizing presentations, prepare a little more material than you think you will actually need. Savvy speakers always have something useful in reserve (such as an extra handout or idea)—just in case they finish early.

11.2c Summarize in the Conclusion

Nervous speakers often rush to wrap up their presentations because they can't wait to flee the stage. But they forget that listeners will remember the conclusion more than any part of a speech. That's why you should spend some time to include an effective conclusion, even in a short presentation. Strive to achieve three goals:

1. Summarize the main ideas or points of the presentation.
2. Leave the audience with a specific or memorable takeaway.
3. Include a friendly statement as you leave the presentation area.

Some speakers end limply with comments such as *I guess that's it*. This leaves bewildered audience members wondering whether they should have bothered listening at all. Skilled speakers alert the audience that they are finishing. They use phrases such as *In conclusion, As I end this presentation,* or *It's time for me to stop, so let me repeat* . . . . Then they proceed immediately to the conclusion. Audiences become irritated with a speaker who announces the conclusion but then digresses with one more story or talks on for ten more minutes.

A concluding summary should review major points and focus on what you want the listeners to do, think, or remember. You might say, *In bringing my presentation to a close, I'll briefly repeat my main idea* . . . ; or *In summary, my major purpose has been to* . . . ; or *In support of my purpose, I have presented three major points. They are (a)* . . . , *(b)* . . . , *and (c)* . . . . Notice how Erick Rosan, in the planned conclusion shown in Figure 11.4, summarizes his three main points and provides a final focus for his audience.

If you're promoting a recommendation, you might end as follows: In conclusion, I recommend that we consider Moncton as the most appropriate home for our new customer service call centre. I make this recommendation using the criteria I've outlined, namely (a) there is an experienced, bilingual workforce available in Moncton, (b) the city is home to other call centres, fostering resource synergies, and (c) Moncton offers the most attractive tax and other municipal and provincial incentives among the cities we've considered.

In your conclusion you can also use an anecdote, an inspiring quotation, or a statement that ties in the attention-capturing opener and offers a new insight. Whatever strategy you choose, be sure to include a memorable take-away that indicates you're finished. For example, *This concludes my presentation. After investigating three qualified Canadian cities in detail, we are convinced that Moncton suits our customer service needs best. Your authorization of my recommendation will enable us to move forward quickly with this important infrastructure and productivity goal. Thank you.*

11.2d Build Audience Rapport

Good speakers know how to build audience rapport. Rapport is the bond formed with an audience; speakers with good rapport entertain as well as inform. How do they do it? Based on observations of successful and unsuccessful speakers, good speakers use a number of verbal and nonverbal techniques to connect with the audience. Some of these techniques include providing effective imagery, supplying verbal signposts such as transitions and repetition, and using body language strategically.

EFFECTIVE IMAGERY. You'll lose your audience quickly if your talk is filled with abstractions, generalities, and dry facts. To enliven your presentation and enhance comprehension, try using some of these techniques:

- **Analogies.** A comparison of similar traits between dissimilar things can be effective in explaining and drawing connections. For example, *Good customer service can be compared to hosting a good dinner party: people should leave the customer service interaction happier than when they arrived, wanting to come back again.*
- **Metaphors.** A comparison between otherwise dissimilar things without using the words *like* or *as* results in a metaphor. For example, *Those new drill sergeants in*

Accounting won't let me submit expense claims late, even by five minutes! or *My desk is a garbage dump.*

- **Similes.** A comparison that includes the words like or as is a simile. For example, *Building a business team is like building a sports team—you want people not only with the right abilities, but also with the willingness to work together.* Or, *Change management can be about as difficult as converting people to a new religion!*

- **Personal anecdotes.** Nothing connects you faster or better with your audience than a good personal story. In a talk about email best practices, you could reveal your own blunders that became painful learning experiences. In a talk to potential angel investors, the creator of a new app could talk about the cool factor of seeing an app he previously developed being used widely by young people.

- **Personalized statistics.** Although often misused, statistics stay with people— particularly when they relate directly to the audience. A speaker discussing job retraining might say, *If this is a typical workplace, I can safely say that half of the people in this room won't be here within three years—that's the rate of job change these days.* If possible, simplify and personalize facts. For example, *The sales of Creemore Springs Brewery totalled 5 million cases last year. That's a full case of Creemore for every man, woman, and child in the Greater Toronto Area.*

- **Worst- and best-case scenarios.** Hearing the worst that could happen can be effective in driving home a point. For example, *I don't want to sound alarmist, but if we don't listen more closely to consumers in terms of what products they want, we could be the next tech company to land in the graveyard of has-beens.*

- **Examples.** Finally, remember that an audience likes to hear specifics. If you're giving a presentation on interpersonal communication, for example, instead of just saying, *Rudeness in the workplace is a growing problem*, it's always better to say something like *Rudeness in the workplace is a growing problem. For example, we've heard from some of our clients that our customer service representatives are using an inappropriate tone of voice.*

VERBAL SIGNPOSTS. Presenters should remember that listeners, unlike readers of a report, cannot control the rate of presentation or flip back through pages to review main points. As a result, listeners get lost easily. Knowledgeable speakers help the audience recognize the organization and main points in an oral message with verbal signposts. They keep listeners on track by including helpful previews, summaries, and transitions, such as these.

- Preview
  The next segment of my talk presents three reasons for . . .
  I'll pass things off to Alia, who'll consider the causes of . . .

- Switch directions
  So far we've talked solely about . . . ; now let's move to . . .
  I've argued that . . . and . . . , but an alternative view holds that . . .

- Summarize
  Let me review with you the major problems I've just discussed.
  You can see, then, that the most significant factors are . . .

You can further improve any presentation by including appropriate transitional expressions such as *first, second, next, then, therefore, moreover, on the other hand, on the contrary*, and *in conclusion*. These expressions lend emphasis and tell listeners where you are headed. Notice in Erick Rosan's outline, in Figure 11.4, that his specific transition questions and other elements are designed to help listeners recognize each new principal point.

NONVERBAL MESSAGES. Although what you say is most important, the nonverbal messages you send can also have a potent effect on how well your message is received. How you look, how you move, and how you speak can make or break your presentation. The following suggestions focus on nonverbal tips to ensure that your verbal message is well received.

- **Look professional.** Like it or not, you'll be judged by your appearance. For everything but small, in-house presentations, be sure you dress professionally. The rule of thumb is that you should dress at least as well as the best-dressed person in the company.
- **Animate your body.** Be enthusiastic and let your body show it. Emphasize ideas with your hands to enhance points about size, number, and direction. Use a variety of gestures, but try not to consciously plan them in advance.
- **Punctuate your words.** You can keep your audience interested by varying your tone, volume, pitch, and pace. Use pauses before and after important points. Allow the audience to take in your ideas.
- **Get out from behind the lectern, table, or desk.** Avoid being planted behind the furniture. Movement makes you look natural and comfortable. You might pick a few places in the room to walk to. Even if you have to stay close to your visual aids, make a point of leaving them occasionally so that the audience can see your whole body.
- **Vary your facial expression.** Begin with a smile, but change your expressions to correspond with the thoughts you are voicing. You can shake your head to show disagreement, roll your eyes to show disdain, look skyward for guidance, or wrinkle your brow to show concern or dismay. To see how speakers convey meaning without words, mute the sound on your TV and watch the facial expressions of any well-known talk-show host.

◣ 11.3 Presentation Aids

Before you give a business presentation, consider this proverb: "Tell me, I forget. Show me, I remember. Involve me, I understand." Your goals as a speaker are to make listeners understand, remember, and act on your ideas. To get them interested and involved, include effective visual aids. Some experts say that we acquire 85 percent of all our knowledge visually. Therefore, an oral presentation that incorporates visual aids is far more likely to be understood and retained than one lacking visual enhancement.

Good visual aids have many purposes. They emphasize and clarify main points, improving comprehension and retention. They increase audience interest, and they make the presenter appear more professional, better prepared, and more persuasive. Visual aids are particularly helpful for inexperienced speakers because the audience concentrates on the aid rather than on the speaker. Good visuals also serve to jog the memory of a speaker, thus improving self-confidence, poise, and delivery.

11.3a Types of Visual Aids

Fortunately for today's presenters, many forms of visual media are available to enhance a presentation. Figure 11.5 describes a number of visual aids and compares their degree of formality and other considerations. Some of the most popular visual aids are PowerPoint or Prezi slides; infographics; a flipchart, blackboard, whiteboard, or smartboard; and handouts.

SLIDES. With today's excellent software programs—such as PowerPoint and Prezi—you can create dynamic, colourful presentations with your laptop or tablet. The output from these programs is usually shown on a screen, though sometimes on a TV monitor. With a little expertise and advanced equipment, you can create a slide presentation that includes professional sound, videos, and hyperlinks, as described in Figure 11.6. Slides can also be uploaded to a website or turned into podcasts to be broadcast live over the Internet. PowerPoint slides are linear whereas Prezi slides have a nonlinear, 3D interface that lends them an almost movie-like quality.

AID	PROS	CONS
PowerPoint or Prezi slides *Sebastien Decoret/123 RF*	Create professional appearance with many colour, art, graphic, and font options. Easy to use and transport via removable storage media, Web download, or email attachment. Inexpensive to update. Cinematic zoomable quality with Prezi slides.	Present potential incompatibility issues. Require costly projection equipment and practice for smooth delivery. Tempt user to include razzle-dazzle features that may fail to add value. Distract viewers during zooming or transitions.
Infographic *Antun Hirsman /Shutterstock.com*	Appealing visualization of data.	Oversimplification of complex ideas or concepts.
Flipcharts or boards *Antun Hirsman /Shutterstock.com*	Provide inexpensive option available at most sites. Easy to create, modify, or customize on the spot, record comments from the audience, combine with more high-tech visuals in the same presentation, create instant digital record of what happened during presentation.	Require graphics talent. Difficult for larger audiences to see. Prepared flipcharts are cumbersome to transport and easily worn with use. Smartboards take significant practice to master.
Handouts or speaker's notes *Grmgram/Shutterstock.com*	Encourage audience participation. Easy to maintain and update. Enhance recall because audience keeps reference material.	Increase risk of unauthorized duplication of speaker's material. Can be difficult to transport. May cause speaker to lose audience's attention.
Video *© Anikei/ Shutterstock*	Gives an accurate representation of the content; strong indication of forethought and preparation.	Creates potential for compatibility issues related to computer video formats. Expensive to create and update.
Props *© wavebreakmedia /Shutterstock*	Offer a realistic reinforcement of message content. Increase audience participation with close observation.	Lead to extra work and expense in transporting and replacing worn objects. Limited use with larger audiences.

► **FIGURE** 11.6 / ClearSlide Presentation

ClearSlide is a cloud-based presentation and sales management software. Like PowerPoint, it allows users to create slides, but it takes the emphasis off bullet points. Instead, ClearSlide offers numerous tools to help users create visually rich slides: stock photos, flash animation, 2D and 3D transitional effects, tables, and charts.

© Cengage Learning

INFOGRAPHICS. Infographics are a new way of visually displaying information. They take what's best about traditional graphics (i.e., graphs, charts, logos, icons) and meld it with what's best about cartoons and animations (i.e., faces, bodies, stick figures) to produce a new type of visual information. Almost any type of information or data set can be turned into an infographic, using software that is available on the Internet, some of which is free. Popular sites include Piktochart (piktochart.com) and Venngage (venngage.com). Infographics are usually added to a PowerPoint or Prezi slide presentation, but they can also be printed out as a handout.

FLIPCHART, WHITEBOARD, BLACKBOARD, OR SMARTBOARD. Even though it may seem old-fashioned, effective use of a blackboard and chalk, a whiteboard and dry-erase markers, or a paper flipchart and permanent markers is one of the best ways to teach a relatively small audience something so that it sticks in people's minds. If you think about it, the reason for this effectiveness is clear. Instead of just using your voice and assuming people will listen, understand, and take notes, writing down major headings, important concepts, new vocabulary words, and so on, gives the audience a double dose of information: orally through your voice and visually from your writing on the board. Another reason using these boards is effective: it makes you dynamic. You are *doing* something besides just talking.

Smartboards are now found in some classrooms and workplace meeting rooms—they take things one step further by allowing presenters to bring up and create new resources onsite. For example, a presenter can access a website on the smartboard and physically touch the screen to go to web links; save what's on the board and have it immediately translate into a file; or write on the board with a special stylus and save what's been written into a digital file.

HANDOUTS AND PROPS. You can enhance presentations by distributing pictures, outlines, brochures, articles, charts, summaries, or other supplements. Speakers who use slides often prepare a set of their slides (called a *deck*) along with notes to hand out to viewers, with mixed results. Often, the audience doesn't pay attention to the speaker but noisily flips through the printed-out pages of the slides. Timing the distribution of any handout is tricky. If given out during a presentation, your handouts tend to distract the audience, causing you to lose control. Thus, it's probably best to discuss most handouts during the presentation but delay distributing them until after you finish.

You can also use a prop during your presentation, which is one way of generating humour. A brick, for example, because it's heavy, can be used to make a joke about how cumbersome "bricks-and-mortar" retail locations have become in the new age of online shopping.

◣ 11.4 Designing Effective Presentations

Some presenters prefer to create their visuals first and then develop the narrative around their visuals. Others prepare their content first and then create the visual component. The risk associated with the first approach is that you may be tempted to spend too much time making your visuals look good and not enough time preparing your content. Remember that great-looking slides never compensate for thin content.

11.4a Analyze the Situation and Purpose

Making the best content and design choices for your visual presentation depends on your analysis of the presentation situation and its purpose. Will your visuals be used during a live presentation? Will they be part of a self-running presentation such as in a store kiosk? Will they be saved on a server so that those with Internet access can watch the presentation at their convenience? Will they be sent to a client—as an attachment instead of a hardcopy report? Are you converting slide shows into video

According to productivity and time-study consulting firm Pace Productivity, typical sales reps spend roughly 25 percent of their time each week selling to current and new (or "prospect") customers. Among the duties involved in selling are phone calls, emails, meetings, and presentations. When presenting to customers or prospects, the average time spent is 29 minutes with current customers and 51 minutes with prospects. Not all of that time will be formal presenting time, but if even 50 percent of the meeting time is spent presenting, that adds up to a lot of presenting each week and each month! Edmonton-based Aurora Cannabis, a leading producer and distributor of medical marijuana, recently advertised for a sales representative in its New Brunswick territory. Chief among the responsibilities of this prospective employee are the ability to "effectively lead industry and brand education sessions with key stakeholders." We can imagine that these sessions might include presentations to retailers, health care practitioners, and other groups and individuals. *What do you think the main difference is between presenting to current customers and prospective customers? What might you change in your sales presentation depending on the two audience types?* Sources: Mark Ellwood. (2020, April 19). How sales reps spend their time. https://www.paceproductivity.com/single-post/2017/02/09/How-Sales-Reps-Spend-Their-Time; Indeed, https://ca.indeed.com/Territory-Sales-Representative-jobs-in-New-Brunswick?vjk=31e230a24a7e4853, Accessed August 14, 2019.

podcasts using a program like Jing or Camtasia for viewing on the Internet via a laptop, tablet, or smartphone?

If you're emailing the presentation or posting it online as a self-contained file, the slides will typically feature more text than if they were delivered orally. If, on the other hand, you're creating slides for a live presentation, your analysis will include answering questions such as these: *Should I prepare speaker's notes pages for my own use during the presentation? Should I distribute hard copies of my slides to my audience?*

11.4b Anticipate Your Audience

Think about how you can design your visuals to get the most positive response from your audience. Audiences respond, for example, to the colours you use. Because the messages that colours convey can vary from culture to culture, colours must be chosen carefully. In the Western world, blue and white are the colours of credibility, transparency, tranquility, conservatism, and trust. As for slide text, adjust the colour so it provides high contrast and is readable. Black or blue, for example, usually work well on a white background.

Just as you anticipate audience members' reactions to colour, you can usually anticipate their reactions to special effects. Using animation and sound effects—flying objects, swirling text, and the like—only because they are available is not a good idea. But movement is a key component when it comes to attention. Indeed, you need only look at how Hollywood keeps our attention in movies by using short scenes and non-fixed camera positions. The "zooming" effect in Prezi can be very powerful in this way when used correctly as part of a journey that focuses or reveals pieces of content and information.[2] Special effects used without thought may distract your audience and draw attention away from your main points. Add animation features only if doing so helps to convey your message or adds interest to the content. When your audience members leave, they should be commenting on the ideas you conveyed—not the cool swivels and sound effects.

11.4c Slide Colour and Organization

As a general guideline, most graphic designers encourage the 6-x-6 rule: six bullets per screen, maximum; six words per bullet, maximum. You may find, however, that breaking this rule is sometimes necessary, particularly when your users will be viewing the presentation on their own with no speaker assistance.

If your company doesn't specify its own slide template, use PowerPoint or Prezi and choose a template with a light or white background with darker colour used for the text itself. Avoid using a dark font on a dark background, such as red text on a dark blue background. In the same way, avoid using a light font on a light background, such as white text on a pale blue background. Dark on dark or light on light results in low contrast, making the slides difficult to read.

When you create slides or infographics, you'll likely be translating your major headings into titles for slides or headings for infographics sections. Most times, you'll end up with an introduction slide, body slides, and a conclusion slide. In each of these slides, you'll then paste from your original Word files or else write directly in your slide software using short phrases.

In Chapter 4 you learned to improve readability by using graphic highlighting techniques such as bullets, numbers, and headings. In creating a slide presentation, you should put those techniques into practice. Unlike in emails and reports however, keep in mind that because so many slide presentations rely on bullets, they can sometimes become stale. Be creative in finding ways to present your points succinctly, but perhaps without always using bullet points.

11.4d Design Your Visuals

All presentation and infographic software requires you to (a) select or create a template that will serve as the background for your presentation and (b) add content (i.e., text, images, or links) to convey your message. In both PowerPoint and Prezi, as well as infographic software like Piktochart, you can use one of the templates provided with the software (see examples in Figure 11.7), download templates from the Internet, or create a template from scratch.

Most business communicators (unless they're in creative fields like design, advertising, or performing arts) usually choose existing templates because they're designed by professionals who know how to combine harmonious colours, borders, bullet styles, and fonts for pleasing visual effects. If you prefer, you can alter existing templates so that they better suit your needs. Adding a corporate logo, adjusting the colour scheme to better match the colours used on your organization's website, and selecting a different font are just some of the ways you can customize existing templates.

Be careful, though, of what one expert labels "visual clichés."[3] Overused templates and even clip art that come with slide software can weary viewers who have seen them repeatedly in presentations. Instead of always using a standard template, search *PowerPoint template* in Google. You'll see hundreds of template options available as free downloads. Unless your employer requires that presentations all have the same look, your audience may appreciate fresh templates that complement the purpose of your presentation and provide visual variety. That said, there's an argument to be made for consistency of slide appearance; for example, consistency connotes professionalism.

Experiment with graphic elements that will enhance your presentation by making your visuals more appealing and memorable. One of the simplest but most effective lessons to learn is to avoid long, boring bulleted lists like the one in the left slide of Figure 11.8.

If you look more closely at Figure 11.8, you'll notice that the listed items on the first slide are not parallel. The second and sixth bullet points express the same thought, that shopping online is convenient and easy for customers. Some bullet points are too

FIGURE 11.7 / Selecting Design Templates in PowerPoint and Prezi

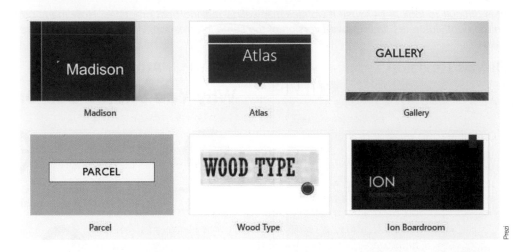

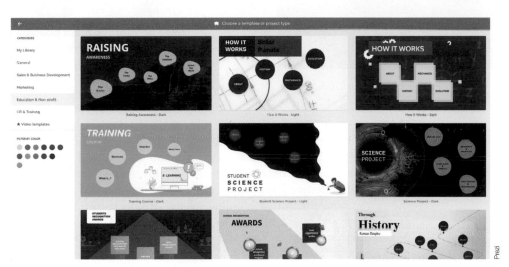

FIGURE 11.8 / Revising Slides for Greater Impact

The slide on the left contains bullet points that aren't parallel and that overlap meaning. The second and sixth bullet points say the same thing. Moreover, some bullet points are too long. After revision, the slide on the right has a more convincing title illustrating the "you" view. The bullet points are shorter, and each begins with a verb for parallelism. The photo adds interest. Both slides feature a contemporary and readable colour scheme.

Reasons for Selling Online

- Your online business can grow globally.
- Customer convenience.
- Conduct business 24/7.
- No need for renting a retail store or hiring employees.
- Reduce inquiries by providing policies and a privacy statement.
- Customers can buy quickly and easily.

Why You Should Sell Online

- Grow your business globally
- Provide convenience for customers
- Conduct business 24/7
- Save on rent and hiring
- Provide policies to reduce inquiries

FIGURE 11.9 / Revising Slides

The slide on the left is difficult to look at because it violates many slide-making best practices. How many problems can you detect? The slide on the right illustrates an improved version of the same information. Why do you think viewers would rather look at the revised slide?

Before Revision

Reasons for Selling Online

- Your online business can grow globally.
- Customer convenience.
- You can conduct your business 24/7.
- No need for renting a retail store or hiring employees.
- Reduce inquiries by providing policies and a privacy statement.
- Customers can buy quickly and easily.

After Revision

Why You Should Sell Online

| Grow business globally | Offer convenience to customers | Conduct business 24/7 |

| Save on rent and staff | Create policies to reduce inquiries |

long. The bullets on the improved slide (right side) are short, well within the 6-x-6 rule, although they are complete sentences and easy to read (because of the use of the bullets). The photo in the revised slide also adds interest and helps illustrate the point.

Another effective lesson when using slides is illustrated in Figure 11.9. The figure shows the same "reasons for online selling" from Figure 11.8, but has used an info-graphic/icon style to add variety to the presentation. This is just one of many diagram possibilities available in PowerPoint. Similar diagram options exist in Prezi and in infographic software. You can also animate each item in the diagram. As a best practice, try occasionally (e.g., once per presentation) to convert pure text and bullet points to diagrams, charts, and other images to add punch to your slide show. You'll keep your audiences interested and help them retain the information you are presenting.

Numeric information is more easily grasped in charts or graphs than in a listing of numbers. In most programs, you can also animate your graphs and charts. Say, for instance, you have four columns in a bar chart. You can control when each column appears to your audience by determining in what order and how each column appears on the screen. The idea is to use animation strategically to introduce elements of the presentation simultaneously as they are mentioned in your spoken remarks, as a way of adding suspense to your presentation. Figure 11.10 shows how a chart can be used in PowerPoint to illustrate the concept of selling online, which is being discussed in a presentation.

Remember that not every point or thought requires a visual. In fact, it's smart to switch off the slides occasionally and direct the focus to you—audiences remember these moments. Darkening the screen while you discuss a point, tell a story, give an example, say something humorous, or involve the audience will add variety to your presentation.

Create a slide only if the slide accomplishes at least one of the following purposes:

- Generates interest in what you're saying and helps the audience follow your ideas
- Highlights points you want your audience to remember
- Introduces or reviews your key points
- Provides a transition from one major point to the next
- Illustrates and simplifies complex ideas.

Here's a step-by-step process for creating a powerful presentation:

Start with the text
- Choose a simple but effective template.
- Express your ideas using clear, concise wording—one idea per slide.
- Ensure each slide has no more than five lines of text.

Select background and fonts
- Choose a simple but professional font, such as Arial or Times New Roman.
- Choose a point size between 24 and 36, with titles larger than the text font.
- Ensure the background colour is professional and easy to read (e.g., white or very light colours).

Choose images that help communicate your message
- Introduce images such as clip art, photographs, or maps to complement your text.
- If you copy images royalty-free from the Internet, ensure a source line is included, such as "Source: Google Images."

Create graphics
- Use your software's built-in tools to create graphs or infographics.
- Consider using graphics such as a flow chart, pie chart, bar chart, and so on.
- Ensure graphics are understandable even by someone with no knowledge of your presentation material. Keep it simple!

Add special effects
- Use your software's built-in tools to create effects like zooming, fading, wiping, animation, or audio.
- Use these effects only if they will make the presentation more persuasive.

Create hyperlinks to approximate the Web-browsing experience
- Paste appropriate Internet links into your presentation.
- Ensure the links are used sparingly—otherwise you'll dilute the persuasiveness of the presentation.

Engage your audience by asking for interaction
- Consider integrating audience response tools into your presentation.
- Free tools include Kahoot (for quizzes) and Socrative (for giving feedback).

Post your presentation to the Internet
- Consider posting your presentation to YouTube or your company's intranet.
- Free software like Jing allows you to record your presentation as a video with your voice recorded over it.

© Cengage Learning

11.4e Revise, Proofread, and Evaluate Your Slide Show

Before giving the presentation, build in time to focus on making your presentation as clear and concise as possible. In other words, just as you revise written messages, you also need to revise visual messages.

For example, if you're listing items in a slide, be sure that all items use parallel grammatical form. If you created your own slide template, be sure all slides have the same background colour. If you quickly created the presentation from scratch, make sure the slides are in the right order so they don't confuse your audience. If you haven't yet proofread the slides, do so to make sure there are no spelling, punctuation, grammar, or style errors.

Nothing is as embarrassing as projecting errors on a big screen in front of your audience. Do a final scan to ensure that basic slide best practices, such as number of bullet points per slide and length of sentence per bullet, are met, so as not to overwhelm your audience.

Review Figure 11.9 for tips on how to revise a typical slide to improve it for conciseness, parallelism, and other features.

As a last step before presenting, critically evaluate your slide show. Consider whether you've done all you can to use the tools PowerPoint or Prezi provide to communicate your message in a visually appealing way. In addition, test your slides on the equipment and in the room you'll be using during your presentation. Do the colours you selected work in this new setting? Are the font styles and sizes readable from the back of the room?

11.4f Use Slides Effectively in Front of an Audience

Many promising presentations have been sabotaged by technology glitches or by the presenter's unfamiliarity with the equipment. Fabulous slides are of value only if you can manage the technology expertly.

PRACTISE AND PREPARE. Allow plenty of time before your presentation to set up and test your equipment.[4] Confirm that the places you plan to stand are not in the line of the projected image. Audience members don't appreciate having part of the slide displayed on your body. Make sure that all video or Web links are working, that the sound level is appropriate (if audio is part of the slides), and that you know how to operate all features the first time you try. No matter how much time you put into preshow setup and testing, you still have no guarantee that all will go smoothly. Therefore, you should always bring backups of your presentation. Handouts of your presentation provide a good substitute. Transferring your presentation to a USB flash drive or storing it on the cloud at Dropbox or Google Cloud so you can run it from any available laptop might prove useful as well.

KEEP YOUR AUDIENCE ENGAGED. In addition to using the technology to enhance and enrich your message, here are additional tips for performing like a professional and keeping the audience engaged:

- Know your material so that you're free to look at your audience with only the occasional gaze at the screen, but not at your notes. Maintain genuine eye contact to connect with individuals in the room.
- As you show new elements on a slide or frame, allow the audience time to absorb the information. Then paraphrase and elaborate on what the listeners have seen. Don't insult your audience's intelligence by reading verbatim from a slide or frame.
- Leave the lights as bright as you can. Make sure the audience can see your face and eyes.
- Don't leave a slide on the screen when you're no longer discussing it. In PowerPoint, in Slide Show, View Show mode, strike *B* on the keyboard to turn off the screen image by blackening it (or press *W* to turn the screen white). Hit the key again to turn the screen back on.

Some presenters allow their slides or frames to steal their thunder. In developing visuals, don't expect them to carry the show.

You can avoid being upstaged by not relying totally on your visuals. Help the audience see your points by using other techniques. For example, drawing a diagram on a whiteboard or flipchart can be more engaging than showing slide after slide of static drawings. Demonstrating or displaying real objects or props is a welcome relief from slides. Remember that slides should be used only to help your audience understand the message and to add interest. You're still the main attraction! If in doubt, review the eight steps in Figure 11.10.

11.5 Polishing Your Delivery

After you've organized your presentation and prepared visuals, you're ready to practise delivering it. Below are suggestions on delivery methods, along with specific techniques to use before, during, and after your presentation.

11.5a Delivery Methods

Inexperienced speakers often feel that they need to memorize an entire presentation to be effective. Unless you're a professional performer, however, you'll sound unnatural. So memorizing an entire presentation isn't recommended. However, memorizing important parts—the introduction, the main points of the body, a memorable thought for the conclusion—is dramatic, impressive, and memorable.

On the other hand, reading to an audience is boring and highly ineffective. It suggests that you don't know your topic well, and the audience soon loses confidence in your expertise. Reading also prevents you from maintaining eye contact, which quickly leads to a loss of respect and attention from the audience.

Neither the memorizing nor the reading methods create convincing presentations. A better strategy plan by far is a *cue-card* method. As Erick Rosan, the guest speaker from earlier in this chapter did, plan your presentation carefully and then talk from cue cards that contain key sentences and major ideas. One of Erick's cue cards is shown below in Figure 11.11.

By preparing and then practising with cue cards, you can talk to your audience in a conversational manner. Your cards should contain phrases that help you introduce each major idea. Cue cards will keep you on track and prompt your memory, but only if you've rehearsed the presentation thoroughly.

11.5b Delivery Techniques

Nearly everyone experiences some stage fright when speaking in front of a group. But you can capitalize on the adrenaline that's coursing through your body by converting it into excitement and enthusiasm.

Being afraid is natural and results from physiological changes occurring in your body. Faced with a frightening situation, your body responds with the fight-or-flight response, discussed more fully in Figure 11.12. You can learn to control and reduce stage fright, as well as to incorporate techniques for effective speaking, by using the following techniques before, during, and after your presentation.

▼ FIGURE 11.11 / Sample Cue Card for Presentation

A. How did I get hired at AutoFleet?

- Looked at accounting jobs
- Talked to uncle; broadened search
- Applied, was interviewed, and hired at AutoFleet
- Wanted to impress boss

So what did I do?...

FIGURE 11.12 / How to Conquer Stage Fright

When you face a threatening or challenging situation, your body reacts with what psychologists call the fight-or-flight response. This physical reflex arouses your body for action by providing it with increased energy to deal with threatening situations. It also creates side-effect sensations—dry mouth, sweaty hands, increased heart rate, and stomach butterflies—collectively known as stage fright. You can reduce these side-effects with the following techniques:

Breathe deeply	Use deep breathing to ease your fight-or-flight symptoms. Inhale to a count of ten, hold this breath to a count of ten, and exhale to a count of ten. Concentrate on your counting and your breathing; both activities reduce your stress.
Convert your fear	Don't view your sweaty palms and dry mouth as evidence of fear. Interpret them as symptoms of exuberance, excitement, and enthusiasm to share your ideas.
Know your topic and come prepared	Feel confident about your topic. Select a topic that you know well and that's relevant to your audience. Test your equipment and arrive with time to spare.
Use positive self-talk	Remind yourself that you know your topic and are prepared. Tell yourself that the audience is on your side—because they are! Moreover, most speakers appear to be more confident than they feel. Make this apparent confidence work for you.
Take a sip of water	Drink some water to alleviate your dry mouth and constricted voice box, especially if you're talking for more than 15 minutes.
Shift the spotlight to your visuals	At least some of the time the audience will be focusing on your slides and not totally on you.
Ignore any stumbles	Don't apologize or confess your nervousness. If you keep going, the audience will forget any mistakes quickly.
Don't admit you're nervous	Never tell your audience that you're nervous. They will probably never notice!
Feel proud when you finish	You'll be surprised at how good you feel when you finish. Take pride in what you've accomplished, and your audience will reward you with applause and congratulations. Your body, of course, will call off the fight-or-flight response and return to normal.

BEFORE YOUR PRESENTATION

- **Prepare thoroughly.** One of the most effective strategies for reducing stage fright is knowing your subject thoroughly. Research your topic diligently and prepare a careful sentence outline. Those who try to "wing it" usually suffer the worst butterflies—and give the worst presentations.
- **Rehearse repeatedly.** When you rehearse, practise your entire presentation, not just part of it. Place your outline sentences on separate cards. Practise using transition phrases to help you move to the next topic. Use these cards as you practise, and include your visual aids in your rehearsal. If you're working with a team, give each other constructive criticism about what's going well and what can change.
- **Time yourself.** Most audiences tend to get restless during longer talks. Thus, try to complete your presentation in no more than 20 minutes. Set a timer during your rehearsal to measure your speaking time.
- **Request a lectern.** Every beginning speaker needs the security of a high desk or lectern from which to deliver a presentation. It serves as a note holder and a convenient place to rest wandering hands and arms.
- **Check the room.** Before you talk, make sure that a lectern has been provided. If you are using sound equipment or a projector, be certain it is operational. Check electrical outlets and the position of the viewing screen. Ensure that the seating arrangement is appropriate to your needs.
- **Greet members of the audience.** Try to make contact with a few members of the audience when you enter the room, while you are waiting to be introduced, or when you walk to the podium. Your body language should convey friendliness, confidence, and enjoyment.
- **Practise stress reduction.** If you feel tension and fear while you are waiting your turn to speak, use stress-reduction techniques, such as deep breathing. Additional techniques to help you conquer stage fright are presented in Figure 11.12.

DURING YOUR PRESENTATION

- **Begin with a pause.** When you first approach the audience, take a moment to adjust your notes and make yourself comfortable. Establish your control of the situation.
- **Present your first few sentences from memory.** By memorizing your opening, you can immediately establish rapport with the audience through eye contact. You'll also sound confident and knowledgeable.
- **Maintain eye contact.** If the size of the audience overwhelms you, pick out two individuals on the right and two on the left. Talk directly to these people.
- **Control your voice and vocabulary.** This means speaking in moderated tones but loudly enough to be heard. Eliminate verbal static, such as *ah, er, you know*, and *um*. Silence is preferable to meaningless fillers when you are thinking of your next idea.
- **Put the brakes on.** Many novice speakers talk too rapidly, displaying their nervousness and making it difficult for audience members to understand their ideas. Slow down and listen to what you are saying.
- **Move naturally.** You can use the lectern to hold your notes so that you are free to move about casually and naturally. Avoid fidgeting with your notes, your clothing, or items in your pockets. Learn to use your body to express a point.
- **Use visual aids effectively.** Discuss and interpret each visual aid for the audience. Move aside as you describe it so that the audience can see it fully. Use a pointer if necessary.
- **Avoid digressions.** Stick to your outline and notes. Don't suddenly include clever little anecdotes or digressions that occur to you on the spot. If it's not part of your rehearsed material, leave it out so that you can finish on time. Remember, too, that your audience may not be as enthralled with your topic as you are.
- **Summarize your main points.** Conclude your presentation by reiterating your main points or by emphasizing what you want the audience to think or do. After you have announced your conclusion, proceed to it directly.

AFTER YOUR PRESENTATION

- **Distribute handouts.** If you prepared handouts with data the audience will need, pass them out when you finish.
- **Encourage questions.** If the situation permits a question-and-answer period, announce it at the beginning of your presentation. Then, when you finish, ask for questions. Set a time limit for questions and answers.
- **Repeat questions.** Although the speaker may hear the question, audience members often do not. Begin each answer with a repetition of the question. This also gives you thinking time. Then, direct your answer to the entire audience.
- **Reinforce your main points.** You can use your answers to restate your primary ideas (*I'm glad you brought that up because it gives me a chance to elaborate on . . .*). In answering questions, avoid becoming defensive or debating the questioner.
- **Keep control.** Don't allow one individual to take over. Keep the entire audience involved.
- **Avoid "Yes, but" answers.** The word *but* immediately cancels any preceding message. Try replacing it with *and*. For example, *Yes, X has been tried. And Y works even better because . . . .*
- **End with a summary and appreciation.** To signal the end of the session before you take the last question, say something like *We have time for just one more question.* As you answer the last question, try to work it into a summary of your main points. Then, express appreciation to the audience for the opportunity to talk with them.

::: Cengage
—————
MINDTAP

In Mindtap go to the Study Tools for Chapter 11 and complete the Practice Test.
:::

◣ LEARNING SUMMARY

11.1 Differentiate between major presentation types.

- Excellent presentation skills are sought by employers and will benefit you at any career stage.
- Presentation types include briefings, reports, podcasts, and webinars; they can be informative or persuasive, face to face or virtual, and complex or simple.
- Savvy speakers know what they want to accomplish and are able to adjust to friendly, neutral, uninterested, and hostile audiences.

11.2 Organize a presentation effectively and build audience rapport.

- In the opening, capture the audience's attention, introduce yourself and establish your credibility, and preview your talk.
- Organize the body using chronology, space, function, comparison/contrast, a journalistic pattern, value/size, importance, problem/solution, simple/complex, or best case/worst case.
- In the conclusion, summarize the main topics of your talk, leave the audience with a memorable takeaway, and end with a statement that provides a graceful exit.
- Build rapport by using effective imagery, verbal signposts, and positive nonverbal messages.

11.3 Use presentation aids.

- Your audience is more likely to retain what you say if you use well-prepared visual aids.

- Good visuals emphasize and clarify main points, increase audience interest, prove you are professional, illustrate your message better than words alone, and serve to jog your memory.
- Common visual aids are multimedia slides, zoom presentations, videos, handouts, flipcharts and whiteboards, and props.
- Slides are vital presentation aids, and today the focus is on using more images and less text.

11.4 Design effective visual presentations.

- The purpose and the audience determine the slide design, which includes colour, images, and special effects.
- Building a presentation involves organizing and composing slide content, avoiding overused templates, and revising, proofreading, and evaluating the final product.
- The eight steps to creating impressive multimedia slides are as follows: start with the text, select a template, choose images, create graphics, add special effects, create hyperlinks, engage your audience with interaction, and consider posting online.

11.5 Deploy effective presentation delivery techniques.

- When giving a business presentation, don't memorize your talk or read from notes; instead, speak naturally using cue cards to help you remember main points.

- Before your presentation prepare and rehearse, time yourself, dress professionally, request a lectern, check the room, greet members of the audience, and practise stress reduction.
- During the presentation deliver your first sentence from memory, maintain eye contact, control your voice, show enthusiasm, slow down, move naturally, use visual aids skillfully, and stay on topic.
- After the presentation distribute handouts, encourage and repeat questions, reinforce your main points, avoid *Yes, but* answers, and end with a summary and appreciation.

◤ CHAPTER REVIEW

1. List and describe five types of presentations a business professional might make. (Obj. 1)

2. The age, gender, education level, experience, and size of the audience may affect your presentation style and message. List at least five questions you should answer to determine your organizational pattern, delivery style, and supporting material. (Obj. 1)

3. Which effective three-step organizational plan do many speech experts recommend, and why does it work well for oral presentations despite its redundancy? (Obj. 2)

4. What three goals should you accomplish in the introduction to your presentation? (Obj. 2)

5. Name at least eight techniques that can help you gain and keep audience attention. (Obj. 2)

6. List high-tech and low-tech visual aids that you can use when speaking to an audience. Which two are the most popular? (Obj. 3)

7. What is the 6-x-6 rule, and what might prompt a presentation slide creator to break it? (Obj. 4)

8. Which delivery method is best for persuasive business presentations? Explain why. (Obj. 5)

9. How can speakers overcome stage fright? Name at least six helpful techniques. (Obj. 5)

◤ CRITICAL THINKING

1. Why is repetition always a good idea in writing, but an excellent idea when presenting? (Objs. 1, 2)

2. Which of the visual aid options you learned about in this chapter is the most effective? Is using the same visual aid as everyone else necessarily the best choice in a presentation? (Obj. 4)

3. If PowerPoint, Prezi, and the use of infographics are so effective, why are people sometimes critical of their use in presentations? (Objs. 3, 4)

4. How can speakers prevent visuals from overtaking a presentation? (Objs. 3, 4)

5. To what degree do you think stage fright is real, as opposed to an excuse we make because of our discomfort? (Obj. 5)

◤ ACTIVITIES AND CASES

11.1 IT'S ALL ABOUT THE AUDIENCE (OBJ. 2)

As we saw at the beginning of this chapter, it's vital to think about your audience before developing a presentation. Depending on the type of audience, certain elements of your presentation will be emphasized, whereas others will be downplayed or eliminated altogether.

Your Task. Choose one of the presentation topics below and one of the audience sets below. Spend 15 minutes brainstorming what each presentation will look like; then, in front of a partner, a group, or the entire class, deliver a short improvised presentation in two different ways. After, see if your partner, group, or class can figure out what you've done differently and why you chose to do so.

Topics	Audience Sets
Surviving your first year of college/university	a) Your institution's board of governors b) Your institution's orientation day
The pros and cons of a particular piece of technology	a) A prospective customer b) Your parents
Your recent work experience	a) Your best friend b) A prospective employer
Choose a topic of your own with your instructor's permission	a) A formal audience b) An informal audience

11.2 FOLLOW YOUR FAVOURITE ENTREPRENEUR (OBJS. 2–5)

An important part of business today is using social media to enhance a brand. In this activity you'll research and present on how well-known business people use Twitter to enhance their own brands.

Your Task. If you don't already have a Twitter account, go to http://twitter.com and sign up so that you can follow businesspeople and examine the topics they like to tweet about. In the Search window at the top of the page, enter the name of the businessperson whose tweets you wish to follow. Arlene Dickinson, Richard Branson, Michele Romanow, Suze Orman, Guy Kawasaki, Kevin O'Leary, and other well-known businesspeople are avid Twitter users. Over the course of a few days, read the tweets of your favourite expert. After a while, you should be able to discern certain trends and areas of interest. Note whether and how your subject responds to queries from followers. What are his or her favourite topics? Report your findings to the class using notes or PowerPoint. If you find particularly intriguing tweets and links, share them with the class.

11.3 HOW MUCH SPEAKING CAN YOU EXPECT IN YOUR FIELD? (OBJS. 2, 4, 5)

It's common for job postings to ask for candidates with "excellent communication skills." Clearly, these ads mean oral and written communication.

Your Task. Interview one or two individuals in your professional field. How is oral communication important in this profession? Does the need for oral skills change as one advances? What suggestions can these people make to newcomers to the field for developing proficient oral communication skills? Discuss your findings with your class in a brief presentation. Try to use one visual aid you've not used before (e.g., Prezi, infographic).

11.4 SIZING UP YOUR AUDIENCE (OBJ. 2)

One of the best ways to profile your audience is to think about what they will find relevant and useful.

Your Task. Select a recent issue (paper or online) of *Report on Business Magazine*, *Canadian Business Magazine* (online only), *Bloomberg Businessweek*, *Fast Company*, *The Economist*, or another business magazine approved by your instructor. Based on an analysis of your classmates, select an article that will appeal to them and that you can relate to their needs. Submit to your instructor a one-page summary that includes the following: (a) the author, article title, source, issue date, and page reference; (b) a one-paragraph article summary; (c) a description of why you believe the article will appeal to your classmates; and (d) a summary of how you can relate the article to their needs.

11.5 PREPARING, REHEARSING, AND CRITIQUING A PRESENTATION (OBJS. 2–5)

Just as this book's chapters on business writing stress the importance of a revision stage, so too oral communication must be revised if it is to be effective. In other words, until you are a seasoned veteran, you should get into the habit of rehearsing your oral presentations. Likewise, you should get into the habit of offering constructive criticism to your peers and colleagues when they solicit it, and of accepting the same criticism when it is offered to you.

Your Task. In groups of four or five, select an issue with business ramifications that interests you. For example, people have strongly held views on the issue of whether or not Canada should allow privatized health care. Investigate your chosen issue in a couple of newspaper or magazine articles found through library online databases, and prepare an oral presentation based on your research. Rehearse the complete oral presentation in front of your group. Your audience members will politely raise their hand and interrupt your presentation each time they believe there needs to be improvement (e.g., your voice trails off, you mispronounce a word, you fidget nervously, your body language is sending the wrong signal, you've lost your train of thought). Accept their constructive criticism and keep rehearsing. Appoint someone to be note taker each time a presentation is being rehearsed so that, at the end, each of you has a list of notes—much like a theatre director would give to actors during rehearsal—that you can use to improve future presentations. Are there any common elements among the group members' notes?

11.6 TAMING STAGE FRIGHT (OBJ. 5)

What scares you the most about giving a presentation in front of your class? Being tongue-tied? Fearing all eyes on you? Messing up? Forgetting your ideas and looking silly?

Your Task. Discuss the previous questions as a class. Then, in groups of three or four, talk about ways to overcome these fears. Your instructor may ask you to write a memo (individual or collective) summarizing your suggestions, or you may break out of your small groups and report your best ideas to the entire class. Try using one visual aid you've not used before, such as Animoto or ClearSlide.

11.7 EXPLORING WEB CONFERENCING (OBJS. 1–5)

Your boss at Home Realty Company is interested in learning more about Web conferencing but doesn't have time to do the research herself. She asks you to find out the following:

a. In terms of revenue, how big is the Web conferencing industry?

b. Who are the leading providers of Web conferencing tools?

c. What are the typical costs associated with holding a Web conference?

d. What kind of equipment does Web conferencing usually require?

e. How are other realtors using Web conferencing?

Your Task. Using library research databases and the Internet, locate articles and sites that will provide good quality information in the areas your boss has outlined. Be prepared to role-play an informal presentation to your boss in which you begin with an introduction, answer the five questions in the body, and present a conclusion. Try using cue cards and not looking at the screen at all during this presentation.

11.8 INVITING A SPEAKER (OBJ. 2)

Speakers bureaus are companies that act as agents for professional speakers. If you are an organization that needs a speaker for a special event, you check out a speakers bureau website to see the list of clients.

Your Task. Your college or university is celebrating its 50th or 100th anniversary. As part of the celebrations, the Business School would like to invite a speaker to the school to give a talk on "business in the next 50 years." Go to the website of Canada's leading speakers bureau, Speakers Spotlight (www.speakers.ca), and click on the "Speakers" link then the "Topic" link. Under Topic, click "Future Trends." Watch five of the promotional videos available for each speaker. After you've watched the videos, decide which speaker you would like to invite. Create a presentation outline for a brief presentation you will give at an upcoming meeting of the Anniversary Committee that has several senior managers, including the dean. You are the only student on the committee. Persuade the committee to go with your choice of speaker. Try to use video during your presentation.

11.9 INVESTIGATING PRESENTATIONS IN YOUR FIELD (OBJ. 1)

One of the best sources of career information is someone already working in the field.

Your Task. Interview one or two individuals in your professional field. How are presentations important in this profession? Does the frequency of presentations change as one advances? What suggestions can these people make to newcomers to the field for developing proficient presentation skills? What are the most common reasons for giving presentations in this profession? Discuss your findings with your class.

11.10 OUTLINING A PRESENTATION (OBJ. 2)

For many people the hardest part of preparing a presentation is developing the outline.

Your Task. Select an oral presentation topic from the list in Activity 11.13 or suggest an original topic. Prepare an outline for your presentation using the following format.

Title	
Purpose	
	I. INTRODUCTION
Gain attention of audience	A.
Involve audience	B.
Establish credibility	C.
Preview main points	D.
Transition	
	II. BODY
Main point	A.
	1.
Illustrate, clarify, contrast	2.
	3.
Transition	
Main point	B.
	1.
Illustrate, clarify, contrast	2.
	3.
Transition	
Main point	C.
	1.
Illustrate, clarify, contrast	2.
	3.
Transition	
	III. CONCLUSION
Summarize main points	A.
Provide final focus	B.
Encourage questions	C.

11.11 USING INFOGRAPHICS SOFTWARE (OBJ. 3)

Today visual information can be communicated using infographics.

Your Task. Using the Internet, find a few classic graphs on a given topic in your area (e.g., graphs about salary trends for human resources, graphs about infectious disease rates for health care management, graphs about management expense ratios for financial planning). Then, sign up for a free account with Piktochart (piktochart.com) or Venngage (venngage. com). Turn the three classic graphs you located into a more updated type of visual: an infographic. What story are you trying to tell? Make sure your template matches the story. Present your infographic in a two-minute mini-presentation in front of your class.

11.12 RESEARCHING JOB-APPLICATION INFORMATION (OBJS. 2–5)

Your Task. Using your library's online databases, perform a subject search for one of the following topics. Find as many articles as you can. Then organize, create visuals for, and deliver a five- to ten-minute informative presentation to your class.

a. Do recruiters prefer one- or two-page résumés?

b. How do applicant tracking systems work?

c. How are inflated résumés detected, and what are the consequences?

d. What's new in writing cover letters in job applications?

e. What is online résumé fraud?

f. What are some new rules for résumés?

11.13 CHOOSING A TOPIC FOR A PRESENTATION (OBJS. 2–5)

Your Task. Select a topic from the list below. Prepare a five- to ten-minute oral presentation. Consider yourself an expert who has been called in to explain some aspect of the topic before a group of interested people. Since your time is limited, prepare a concise yet forceful presentation with effective visual aids.

a. What's the career outlook in a field of your choice?

b. How has the Internet changed job searching?

c. What are the advantages and disadvantages of instant messaging as a method of workplace communication?

d. Does social media drain productivity?

e. What is telecommuting, and for what kind of worker is it an appropriate work alternative?

f. To what degree is it necessary for parents to have choice in terms of where they send their children to school (e.g., public, private, religious, home schooling)?

g. What travel location would you recommend for college or university students at March Break (or another holiday period, or in summer)?

h. What's the economic outlook for a given product (such as domestic cars, laptop computers, tablets, fitness equipment, or a product of your choice)?

i. How can your organization or institution improve its image?

j. Why should people invest in a company or scheme of your choice?

k. What brand and model of computer and printer represent the best buy for college or university students today?

l. What franchise would offer the best investment opportunity for an entrepreneur in your area?

m. How should a job candidate dress for an interview?

n. What should a guide to proper cell phone use include?

o. Are internships worth the effort?

p. How is an administrative assistant different from a secretary?

q. Where should your organization hold its next convention?

r. What's your opinion of the statement "Advertising steals our time, defaces the landscape, and degrades the dignity of public institutions"?[5]

s. How can businesspeople reduce the amount of email spam they receive?

t. What's the outlook for real estate (commercial or residential) investment in your area?

u. What are the pros and cons of videoconferencing for [name an organization]?

v. Are today's communication technologies making us more productive or just more stressed out?

w. What kinds of gifts are appropriate for businesses to give clients and customers during the holiday season?

x. How are businesses and conservationists working together to protect the world's dwindling tropical forests?

y. Should employees be able to use computers in a work environment for anything other than work-related business?

11.14 CREATING A POWERPOINT OR PREZI PRESENTATION (OBJS. 3, 4)

You are a consultant who has been hired to improve the effectiveness of corporate trainers. These trainers frequently make presentations to employees on topics such as conflict management, teamwork, time management, problem solving, performance appraisals, and employment interviewing. Your goal is to teach these trainers how to make better presentations.

Your Task. Create six visually appealing slides. Base the slides on the following content, which will be spoken during the presentation titled "Effective Employee Training." The comments shown here are only a portion of a longer presentation.

Trainers have two options when they make presentations. The first option is to use one-way communication, where the trainer basically dumps the information on the employees and leaves. The second option is to use a two-way audience-involvement approach. The two-way approach can accomplish many purposes, such as helping the trainer connect with the employees, helping the trainer reinforce key points, increasing the employees' retention rates, and changing the pace and adding variety. The two-way approach also encourages employees to get to know each other better. Because today's employees demand more than just a "talking head," trainers must engage their audiences by involving them in a two-way dialogue.

When you include interactivity in your training sessions, choose approaches that suit your delivery style. Also, think about which options your employees would be likely to respond to most positively. Let's consider some interactivity approaches now. Realize, though, that these ideas are presented to help you get your creative juices flowing. After I present the list, we will think about situations in which these options might be effective. We will also brainstorm to come up with creative ideas we can add to this list.

- Ask employees to guess at statistics before revealing them.
- Ask an employee to share examples or experiences.
- Ask a volunteer to help you demonstrate something.
- Ask the audience to complete a questionnaire or worksheet.
- Ask the audience to brainstorm or list something as fast as possible.
- Ask a variety of question types to achieve different purposes.
- Invite the audience to work through a process or examine an object.
- Survey the audience.
- Pause to let the audience members read something to themselves.
- Divide the audience into small groups to discuss an issue.

11.15 LEARNING FROM THE BEST (OBJS. 2, 5)
TED is a nonprofit organization famous for creating short (up to 18 minutes) video "talks" in which an expert in some area delivers a highly impactful presentation that's posted on the TED website and on its YouTube channel. Over the 35 years of its existence, TED talks have been viewed more than 1 billion times, making them many people's ideal of what a presentation should look and sound like.

Your Task. Go to the TED website (ted.com) and use the search box to find the following TED talks: Tony Salvador's "The Listening Bias" and Thea Knight's "Lost in Translation: The Joy of a Jargon-Free World." Watch the talks, making notes about strengths and areas for improvement of each presenter. Then, deliver a short five-minute presentation in which you compare these two presenters' styles, discuss strengths and areas for improvement, and discuss how their techniques could be adapted to a more typical business presentation context.

11.16 TRAINING PRESENTATION (OBJS. 2–5)
A common situation in the workplace is the training seminar or presentation. A manager or team leader trains new hires in how to do a specific task or set of tasks necessary in the workplace. This could be anything from how to use a new piece of equipment in an industrial kitchen to how to deal effectively and thoughtfully with clients who don't identify with one of the binary genders (male and female). These types of presentations need to be persuasive, but it's more important that they be instructionally sound and clear.

Your Task. Imagine you are a manager at a large nonprofit or charity organization that employs teams of canvassers to solicit donations on busy street corners across Canada: Greenpeace, Red Cross, Amnesty International, and other organizations who participate in this sort of solicitation come to mind. The Federation of Canadian Municipalities (fcm.ca) has recently sent a letter of complaint to some of these organizations saying that their tactics are unnecessarily obtrusive. As a result, you decide you need to revise your standard training seminar for new street canvassers to become "kinder." Research canvassing strategies and techniques (as well as any laws that may apply to this activity in your part of the world) and then deliver a ten-minute training seminar with examples on how to be a kinder street canvasser.

◣ GRAMMAR/MECHANICS CHALLENGE 11

CAPITALIZATION

Review Sections 3.01–3.16 in the Grammar Review section of the Grammar/Mechanics Handbook. Then study each of the following statements. Draw three underlines below any letter that should be capitalized. Draw a slash (/) through any capital letter that you want to change to lowercase. Indicate in the space provided the number of changes you made in each sentence. If you made no changes, write 0. Also record the number of the G/M principle illustrated. When you finish, compare your responses with those provided near the end of the book. If your responses differ, study carefully the principles shown in parentheses.

5   **Example** The consumer product safety act was revised specifically to ensure the safety of Children's toys.

_____ 1. Employees of bank of montréal had to evacuate their Headquarters in suite 200 after the renfrew fire department units arrived.

_____ 2. Canadians are reluctant to travel to europe because of the weak dollar; however, more british and french citizens are travelling to Canada, according to Maurice Dubois, Vice President at Four Seasons Hotels and resorts.

_____ 3. Once the Management Team and the Union members finally agreed, mayor Faria signed the Agreement.

_____ 4. The boston marathon is an annual sporting event hosted by the city of boston on patriot's day.

_____ 5. Luis was disappointed when he learned that the univeroity of montréal eliminated italian from its curriculum; now he must take history, geography, and political science classes to learn about italy.

_____ 6. The most popular sites on the internet are those operated by google, facebook, and youtube.

_____ 7. According to a Federal Government report issued in january, any regulation of Provincial and Municipal banking must receive local approval.

_____ 8. The position of director of research must be filled before summer.

_____ 9. The Vice President of MegaTech Industries reported to the President that the Manitoba securities commission was beginning an investigation of their Company.

_____ 10. My Uncle, who lives near wasaga beach in simcoe county, says that the Moon and Stars are especially brilliant on cool, clear nights.

_____ 11. Our marketing director met with Adrienne Hall, Manager of our advertising media department, to plan an Adwords campaign for google.

_____ 12. During the Fall our Faculty Advisor explored new exchange and semester-abroad opportunities in asia, australia, and china.

_____ 13. Last february my Father and I headed south to visit the summer waves water park located on jekyll island in georgia.

_____ 14. On page 6 of my report, you will find a list of all instructors in our business division with Master's degrees.

_____ 15. Please consult figure 5.1 in chapter 5 of the book analysis of population growth for the latest Canadian census figures regarding non-english-speaking residents.

The following executive summary of a report has proofreading, spelling, grammar, punctuation, wordiness, number form and other writing faults that require correction. Study the guidelines in the Grammar/Mechanics Handbook, as well as the lists of Confusing Words and Frequently Misspelled Words at the end of the book, to sharpen your skills. When you finish making corrections, your instructor can show you the revised version of this abstract.

Your Task. Edit the following summary by correcting its errors (a) in your textbook or (b) on a photocopy using proofreading marks from Appendix B.

EXECUTIVE SUMMARY

Purpose of Report

The purposes of this report is (1) To determine the Sun coast university campus communitys awareness of the campus recycling program and (2) To recommend ways to increase participation. Sun Coasts recycling program was intended to respond to the increasing problem of waste disposal, to Fulfil it's social responsibility as an educational institution, and to meet the demands of legislation that made it a requirement for individuals and organizations to recycle.

A Survey was conducted in an effort to learn about the campus communities recycling habits and to make an assessment of the participation in the recycling program that is current. 220 individuals responded to the Survey but twenty-seven Surveys could not be used. Since Sun coast universitys recycling program include only aluminum, glass, paper and plastic at this point in time these were the only materials considered in this Study.

Recycling at Sun coast

Most Survey respondants recognized the importance of recycling, they stated that they do recycle aluminum, glass, paper and plastic on a regular basis either at home or at work.

However most respondants displayed a low-level of awareness, and use of the on campus program. Many of the respondants was unfamilar with the location of the bins around campus; and therefore had not participated in the Recycling Program. Other responses indicated that the bins were not located in convenent locations.

Reccommendations for increasing recycling participation

Recommendations for increasing participation in the Program include the following;

1. relocating the recycling bins for greater visability

2. development of incentive programs to gain the participation of on campus groups

3. training student volunteers to give on campus presentations that give an explanation of the need for recycling, and the benefits of using the Recycling Program

4. we should increase Advertising in regard to the Program

JPM/Getty Images

UNIT
06

COMMUNICATING FOR EMPLOYMENT

BUSINESS COMMUNICATION RESEARCH UPDATE

An Exploratory Study of the Influence of Soft and Hard Skills on Entry-Level Marketing Position Interviews

Deborah DeLong and Matthew Elbeck.
Department of Business, Chatham University, Pittsburgh, PA; Sorrell College of Business, Troy University–Dothan Campus, Dothan, AL.
Marketing Education Review, vol. 28, no. 3 (2018), pp. 159–169. Copyright 2018 Society for Marketing Advances. ISSN: 1052–8008 (print) / ISSN 2153–9987 (online). DOI: https://doi.org/10.1080/10528008.2017.1349475

This exploratory study looks at the relative impact of student soft and hard skills on entry-level marketing job interview success. Marketing professionals with hiring experience conducted pre-course and post-course structured interviews with students in a Principles of Marketing course using behaviorally anchored rating scales to tap soft and hard skills. Results indicate a significant hierarchical effect of soft skills beyond hard skills on a candidate's likelihood of being invited back for a second interview. . . .

Today's college graduates face a highly competitive job market with increasing rates of unemployment and underemployment. According to Yen (2012), half of U.S. college graduates are either jobless or underemployed in positions that do not fully use their skills and knowledge. Halimuddin (2013) reports that less than half (42%) of recent college graduates are working in jobs that require a college degree. Competitive marketplace realities are not lost on administrators and marketing instructors who are tasked with delivering effective programs to ensure their students' professional success. Scholars and professionals alike seek to better understand the factors that influence one of the most pervasive screening tools students are likely to encounter when pursuing employment, the job interview.

Many business schools are responding to industry expectations for both hard- and soft-skill competencies by incorporating a broader range of topics, teaching methods, and assessment into the curricula. Teaching both soft skills as well as hard skills is consistent with the Association to Advance Collegiate Schools of Business' (AACSB) flexibility in how business schools assess their learning goals (AACSB, 2010), and serves the additional benefit of demonstrating relevancy within the curriculum. Assessing the absolute and relative importance of soft and hard skills in an interview can provide guidance regarding their emphasis within the marketing and broader business curriculum. Ultimately, effective integration of soft- and hard-skill training may help align curricula with candidate as well as industry needs, preparing students to not only get a job but also keep it.

LITERATURE REVIEW

Hard Skills Defined

Dixon, Belnap, Albrecht, and Lee (2010) describe hard skills as "including the technical or administrative procedures that can be quantified and measured" (p. 35). Within a traditional marketing curriculum context, hard skills comprise the core topics of a typical introductory marketing course, laying a foundation of marketing knowledge to build on with further study within the discipline and affording assurances of learning to be demonstrated (LaFleur, Babin, & Burnthorne, 2009). . . .

Soft Skills Defined

Soft skills are described as the "interpersonal, human, people or behavioral skills needed to apply technical skills and knowledge in the workplace" (Weber, Finely, Crawford, & Rivera, 2009, p. 356). Dixon et al. (2010) identify soft skills as "a combination of interpersonal and social skills" (p. 35). Robles (2012) specifies the top 10 soft skills business executives consider most important: integrity, communication, courtesy, responsibility, social skills, positive attitude, professionalism, flexibility, teamwork, and work ethic. Finch, Nadeau, and O'Reilly (2013) provide an operational definition for each of these "meta skills," which are increasingly sought by employers in need of mature and socially well-adjusted employees.

Soft-skills training approaches are varied. Maurer, Solamon, Andrews, and Troxtel (2001) suggest that a combination of training components, model exposure, role playing, and videotape feedback is more effective for teaching soft skills than individual training components alone. Pope-Ruark

(2008) used interview projects where students plan, coordinate, conduct, transcribe, and synthesize interviews (with acquaintances or family members) to make tangible connections between course material and what the students consider "the real world."

Adoption of soft-skills training into business school curricula is on the rise, with 10% of required MBA programs teaching students about sensitivity in delivering and receiving feedback (Korn & Light, 2011) and offering courses in negotiation, persuasion, ethics, business writing, and the arts (Butler, 2007). Specific cases include ethics and team-oriented courses at Harvard Business School (Middleton & Light, 2011), meditation at Columbia Business School, "Touchy Feely" at Stanford Graduate School, and a personality awareness course at the University of California at Berkeley's Haas School of Business (Korn & Light, 2011).

The prevalence of hard- and soft-skills training integration in business curricula guides the first set of hypotheses:

H1: Hard skills can be improved by teaching the core content in an introductory marketing course.

H2: Soft skills can be improved with targeted training modules embedded in an introductory marketing course. . . .

METHODOLOGY

A multimethod hard- and soft-skills training and assessment program was implemented in three sections of a Principles of Marketing course (three consecutive semesters, N = 10 in each section; 75% female, 3.2 average GPA, 36% upper classmen, 86% business majors). All students in each section participated for course credit. The bias toward female participants is a result of the school's recent transition from all-female to coed enrollment. . . .

The marketing core curriculum served as the vehicle for hard-skills training, comprised of LaFleur et al.'s (2009) eight dimensions of hard skills within the marketing discipline: marketing fundamentals, understanding the customer, product concepts, pricing concepts, place concepts, promotion concepts, analyzing marketing problems, and the role of information. Multiple methods were used to teach hard skills, including assigned readings, in-class lectures, exams, homework, and a marketing-plan project spanning the length of the semester with sections corresponding with each core marketing concept. . . .

Soft skills were taught using modules designed to address Robles's (2012) 10 soft-skills dimensions.

Each training module was structured according to the principles of the theory of social learning (Bandura, 1971):

- Pre-assessment: preliminary mock interview to assess hard- and soft-skills performance.
- Conceptual learning: embedded modules of assigned readings, instruction, games, and discussion embedded at regular intervals within the course curriculum.
- Modeling: case analysis, videos, and vignettes used to illustrate positive and negative behavioral applications of each soft skill.
- Practice with feedback: managerial simulations, role plays, team projects, and other individual or group exercises, accompanied by verbal and/or written performance feedback.
- Application: follow-up mock interview to measure change in performance.

The position description was distributed to all the candidates both at the start of the course and at the end of the course. The interview included a series of behaviorally anchored rating scales (BARS) and observational measures to assess LaFleur et al.'s (2009) eight dimensions of hard-skills marketing knowledge and Robles's (2012) 10 dimensions of soft skills interpersonal qualities. Each BARS scale included descriptions of behaviors that typify the low, midpoint, and high end of each response scale to help standardize scoring across interviewers.

Prior to each interview, students read the entry level job description of assistant brand manager for a cosmetics manufacturer. Each interview lasted 20 minutes, during which time the interviewer greeted the candidate and read and scored all eight hard-skills items and 7 of the 10 soft-skills items as printed on the scoring sheet, scoring each one according to the behavioral anchors on each 5-point scale. The interviewer then scored the three remaining observational soft-skills items, using the behavioral anchors on each 5-point scale. Finally, the inter viewer scored on a 5-point scale the likelihood of inviting the interviewee back for a second interview. . . .

RESULTS

Two important insights are suggested by these findings. First, core marketing knowledge is captured by the hard-skills measure as a unique effect, separate from soft-skills variance. This means that each factor offers useful explanatory information for interview success not otherwise available and should be retained in the analysis. Second, it is possible that some portion of hard-skills performance is redundant with soft-skills performance, but an alternative explanation is the presence of halo error. Specifically, perceived hard skills may benefit or suffer from the individual's perceived soft skills, or vice versa. To test for a potential halo error effect and to control for an advantage gained via the order of variable entry, interview success scores are regressed on hard and soft skills in both directions as reported further on. . . .

DISCUSSION

This study is the first to empirically explore the simultaneous impact of soft and hard skills on job-interview success, using regression to infer importance and an authentic assessment of interview skills. This methodology is in stark contrast to the extant research that uses self-reported (indirect) importance measures (Gray, Ottesen, Bell, Chapman, & Whiten, 2007; Schlee & Harich, 2010; Wellman, 2010). The pattern of findings across multiple analyses reveal significant effects for the interviewee's hard and soft skills on the likelihood of being invited for a second interview.

Although both hard and soft skills significantly impact interview success, the relative impact of each skill set differs before and after training. Specifically, soft-skills performance is significantly more important than hard-skills performance for determining the likelihood of being invited back for a second interview when predictors are considered both alone and in combination. . . .

Our findings suggest a complimentary relationship between hard and soft skills such that both skill sets significantly impact interview outcomes; however, the relative impact of each skillset may depend on the interviewee's qualifications. Soft skills are considered "soft" because of their interpersonal, attitudinal, and disposition-oriented characteristics. Soft skills can also be considered soft because they fill in where the candidate's hard skills may be lacking or deficient, possibly by conveying the candidate's potential for acquiring these skills in time.

CONCLUSION

The results of this study offer compelling insight into the role of soft skills both alone and in combination with hard skills for interview success. Other studies imply the strategic importance of soft skills. For example, meta-studies (Cohen, 1984; Samson, Grave, Weinstein, & Walberg, 1984) suggest that the relationship between academic success (grades and test scores) and professional success is weak, perhaps highlighting the hitherto absence of soft skills that may well have a strong impact on professional success. The impact of formal soft-skills training may be reflected in sales programs where, according to Stevens and James (2015), sales students experience twice the national average for college graduate job placement. This outcome and this study's findings may well have substantive implications for professional accrediting agencies (e.g., AACSB, ACBSP, EQUIS) and regional accrediting commissions (e.g., SACS, WASC, NCACS) regarding the contribution and extent of soft skills training standards and evaluation to achieve accreditation. More research is needed to fully explore how soft skills contribute to interview success within a larger sample, at different job levels, and within different areas of marketing (e.g., qualitative versus quantitative orientation), as well as to test the effectiveness of different pedagogical methods.

The potential contribution of soft skills to interview success (and perhaps to one's career) reported in this article is worthy of reflection regarding ways to improve our student soft skills resulting in tangible interview success-rate improvement. . . .

REFERENCES

AACSB. (2010). Eligibility procedures and accreditation standards for business accreditation. Retrieved from http://www.aacsb.edu/accreditation/business/standards/

Bandura, A. (1971). Social learning theory. *General Learning Corporation*. Retrieved from http://www.jku.at/org/content/e54521/e54528/e54529/e178059/Bandura_SocialLearningTheory_ger.pdf

Butler, C. K. (2007, April). The soft side of the M.B.A. *U.S. News & World Report*, 142(12), 74.

Cohen, P. A. (1984). College grades and adult achievement: A research synthesis. *Research in Higher Education, 20*(3), 281–293. doi:10.1007/BF00983503

Dixon, J., Belnap, C., Albrecht, C., & Lee, K. (2010). The importance of soft skills. *Corporate Finance Review, 14*(6), 35–38.

Finch, D., Nadeau, J., & O'Reilly, N. (2013). The future of marketing education: A practitioner's perspective. *Journal of Marketing Education, 35*(1), 54–67. doi:10.1177/02734753 12465091

Gray, B. J., Ottesen, G. G., Bell, J., Chapman, C., & Whiten, J. (2007). What are the essential capabilities of marketers? A comparative study of managers', academics' and students' perceptions. *Marketing Intelligence & Planning, 25*(3), 271–295. doi:10.1108/02634500710747789

Halimuddin, S. (2013). College graduates face a dismal job market. *The Seattle Times*, June 8. Retrieved from http://seattletimes.com/html/opinion/2021142697_sandi-halimuddinopedxml.html

Korn, M., & Light, J. (2011). Business education: On the lesson plan: Feelings—"soft skills" business courses aim to prepare students for managerial roles. *Wall Street Journal*, B6.

LaFleur, E. K., Babin, L. A., & Burnthorne, L. T. (2009). Assurance of learning for principles of marketing students: A longitudinal study of a course-embedded direct assessment. Journal of Marketing Education, 31(3), 131–141. doi:10.1177/0273475309335242

Maurer, T. J., Solamon, J. M., Andrews, K. D., & Troxtel, D. D. (2001). Interviewee coaching, preparation strategies, and response strategies in relation to performance in situational employment interviews: An extension of Maurer, Solamon, and Troxtel (1998). Journal of Applied Psychology, 86(4), 709–717. doi:10.1037/0021-9010.86.4.709

Middleton, D., & Light, J. (2011). Business education: Harvard changes course—School's curriculum overhaul part of a push to alter elite B-school cultures. Wall Street Journal, B8.

Pope-Ruark, R. (2008). The interview project: Reinforcing business communication competence.

Business Communication Quarterly, 71(1), 63–67. doi:10.1177/1080569907312874

Robles, M. M. (2012). Executive perceptions of the top 10 soft skills needed in today's workplace. Business Communication Quarterly, 75(4), 453–465. doi:10.1177/1080569912460400

Samson, G., Grave, M., Weinstein, T., & Walberg, H. (1984). Academic and occupational performance: A quantitative analysis. American Educational Research Journal, 21(2), 311–321. doi:10.3102/00028312021002311

Schlee, R. P., & Harich, K. R. (2010). Knowledge and skill requirements for marketing jobs in the 21st century. Journal of Marketing Education, 32(3), 341–352. doi:10.1177/0273475310380881

Stevens, H. & James, G. (2015). Sales and Academia: Preparing Sales Professionals for a More Demanding Business Environment. Dayton, OH: Challey Group Worldwide.

Weber, M. R., Finely, D. A., Crawford, A., & Rivera, D. J. (2009). An exploratory study identifying soft skill competencies in entry-level managers. Tourism and Hospitality Research, 9(4), 353–361. doi:10.1057/thr.2009.22

Yen, H. (2012). In weak job market, one in two college graduates are jobless or underemployed. Huffington Post. Retrieved from http://www.huffingtonpost.com/2012/04/22/job-market-college-graduates_n_1443738.html

QUESTIONS

1. How does what you've learned in this article change your perception of business communication?

2. How might what you've learned in this article change your own communication style or strategy?

3. Come up with pro and con arguments for the following debate/discussion topic: Heading into a job interview, it's just as important to practise soft skills like positive attitude and friendliness as it is to prove your hard skills abilities relating to the potential job.

Antonio Guillem/Shutterstock.com

THE JOB SEARCH, RÉSUMÉS, AND COVER LETTERS

> **BIZ COMM BYTE**
>
> In 2018, according to research by Statistics Canada, 15 percent of the total Canadian workforce— roughly 3 million people—was self-employed. Of this number, 62 percent were men and 38 percent were women. Workers 55 and over were twice as likely (26 percent) to be self-employed as workers between the ages of 25 and 54 (14 percent).
>
> Source: Statistics Canada. (2019, May 28). Self-employment in Canada, 2018. https://www150.statcan.gc.ca/n1/pub/11-627-m/11-627-m2019040-eng.htm

12.1 Preparing for Employment

Whether you're applying for your first permanent position, competing for promotion, or changing careers, you'll be more successful if you understand employment communication and how to promote yourself with a winning résumé and related digital tools.

Employers today are most interested in how a candidate adds value to their organizations. That's why successful candidates customize their résumés to highlight their qualifications for each opening. In addition, career paths are no longer linear; most new hires won't start in a job and steadily rise through the ranks. Jobs are more short-lived and people are constantly relearning and retraining.

The résumé is still important, but it may not be the document that introduces the job seeker these days. Instead, the résumé may come only after the candidate has established a real-world relationship. Although we sometimes hear that the "print résumé is dead," the truth is that every job hunter needs one. Whether soft- or hardcopy, your résumé should always be available and current.

Analyze Yourself ■ Identify your interests and goals. ■ Assess your qualifications. ■ Explore career opportunities.	**Develop a Job-Search Strategy** ■ Search the open job market. ■ Pursue the hidden job market. ■ Cultivate your online presence. ■ Build your personal brand. ■ Network, network, network!	**Create a Customized Résumé** ■ Choose a résumé style. ■ Organize your info concisely. ■ Tailor your résumé to each position. ■ Optimize for digital technology.	**Know the Hiring Process** ■ Submit a résumé, application, or e-portfolio. ■ Undergo screening and hiring interviews. ■ Accept an offer or reevaluate your progress.

© Cengage Learning

It's natural to think that the first step in finding a job is to write a résumé. However, the employment communication process actually begins long before you're ready to prepare your résumé. Regardless of the kind of employment you seek, you should invest time and effort in getting ready, as outlined in Figure 12.1.

12.1a Identify Your Interests

Begin by looking inside yourself to analyze what you like and dislike so that you can make good employment choices. Career counsellors at your college or university can help you with this process, or you can do a self-examination online. For guidance in choosing a field that eventually proves to be satisfying, answer the questions below. You can use your responses to match the description of opportunities you come across in your job search. If a number of your responses appear in a particular job description, there's a good chance it might be a good fit for you.

- Do I enjoy working with people, data, or things?
- How important is it to be my own boss?
- How important are salary, benefits, and job stability?
- What type of working conditions, colleagues, and job stimulation am I looking for?
- Would I rather work for a large or small company?
- Must I work in a specific city, geographical area, or climate?
- Am I looking for security, travel opportunities, money, power, or prestige?
- How would I describe the perfect job, boss, and coworkers?

12.1b Assess Your Qualifications

In addition to your interests, assess your qualifications. Employers today want to know what assets you have to offer them. Your responses to the questions below will target your thinking as well as prepare a foundation for your résumé. As you'll see later in this chapter, there's room in a résumé to include answers to most of the questions below. Remember that employers seek more than empty assurances; they will want proof of your qualifications.

- What technology skills can I offer? (Name specific software programs and tools.)
- What other hard skills have I acquired in school, on the job, or through activities? How can I demonstrate these skills?
- What soft skills can I offer? Do I work well with people? What proof can I offer? (Consider extracurricular activities, clubs, and jobs.)
- Am I a leader, self-starter, or manager? A problem-solver? What evidence can I offer?
- Do I learn quickly? Am I creative? How can I demonstrate these characteristics?
- Do I communicate well in speech and in writing? How can I verify these talents?

Cengage

MINDTAP

In MindTap go to the Whiteboard Animation for Chapter 12 and watch it now.

12.1c Explore Career Opportunities

Today's job market is vastly different from that of a decade or two ago. The average Canadian can expect to change careers at least three times and change jobs at least seven times in a lifetime. As a student, you may not have yet settled on your first career choice; or you may be embarking on a second or perhaps third career. Although you may be changing jobs in the future, you still need to train for a specific career area now. When choosing an area, you'll make the best decisions if you can match your interests and qualifications with the requirements of specific careers. Here are some suggestions for finding career information:

- **Visit your campus career centre.** Most centres will have information on job-search techniques, workshops on résumé and cover-letter writing, information about local job fairs, and Internet connections that allow you to investigate any field you may be interested in.
- **Search the Internet.** Many job-search sites (e.g., Indeed, Workopolis, Monster, and Charity Village) offer career planning information and resources. For example, Workopolis's "Career Blog" link includes information on job search, résumé writing, and interviewing. A sample job site list of opportunities is shown in Figure 12.2.
- **Use your library.** Consult the latest edition of the Index of Occupational Titles and the Canadian government's National Occupational Classification (www.canada.ca/en/employment-social-development/services/noc.html) for information about career duties, qualifications, salaries, and employment trends.

▼ FIGURE 12.2 / Typical Job Site

Government of Canada Job Bank search results. URL: http://www.jobbank.gc.ca/job_search_results.do:jsessionid=70B 1BC28180A2852A768194992CF7B49.imnav2?searchstring=Canada&button.submit=Search. Employment and Social Development Canada, 2014. Reproduced with the permission of the Minister of Employment and Social Development Canada, 2014.

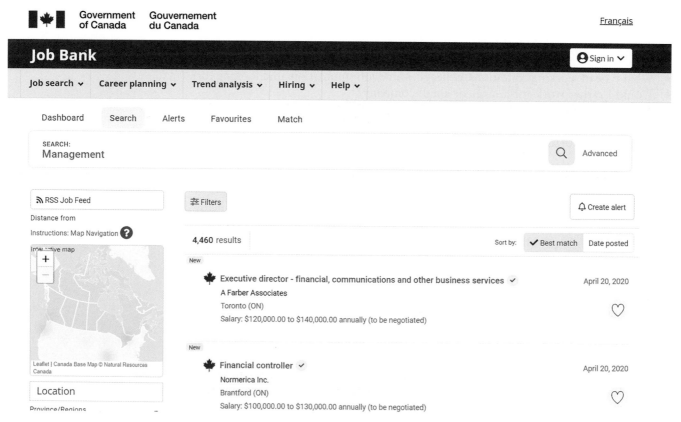

- **Take a summer job, an internship, or a part-time position in your field.** Nothing is better than trying out a career by actually working in it or in a similar area. Many companies offer internships or will let you create your own internship via networking. They may also offer temporary jobs to begin training students and to develop relationships with them (e.g., Indigo hires hundreds of holiday-season workers—a possible entry to a retail management career).
- **Volunteer with a nonprofit organization.** Many colleges and universities encourage service learning opportunities. In volunteering their services to nonprofit organizations in their city or town, students gain valuable experience. Nonprofits, in turn, appreciate the expertise and fresh ideas that students bring and are often happy to provide free training.
- **Interview someone in your chosen field.** People are usually flattered when asked to describe their careers. Once you've settled on your intended career or sector, use LinkedIn and Google to find names of leaders within local organizations. Then, send a polite email or voice mail in which you request an informational interview. In the interview, politely inquire about needed skills, required courses, financial and other rewards, benefits, working conditions, future trends, and entry requirements.
- **Monitor job ads.** Early in your postsecondary education career, begin monitoring company websites for job listings. Check job availability, qualifications sought, duties, and salary range. Don't wait until you're about to graduate to see how the job market looks.
- **Join professional organizations in your field.** Organizations like the Canadian Marketing Association (CMA) and the Human Resources Professionals Association (HRPA) are fantastic places to find out about your intended career. Frequently, these organizations offer student membership status and reduced rates for conferences and workshops. You'll get inside information on issues, career news, and possible jobs, as well as the opportunity to meet people who are working in the field you've identified as your future goal.

◣ 12.2 Searching for Jobs in the Open and Hidden Markets

Another significant change in the workplace involves the way we find jobs. Before the early 2000s, a job seeker browsed the local newspaper's classified ads, found a likely sounding job listing, prepared a résumé on paper, and sent it out by mail (and later by fax). Today, searching for a job online is the universal approach. That said, if you think that online job searching has totally replaced traditional methods, think again!

Although websites such as Workopolis and Indeed list millions of jobs, actually landing a job is much harder than just clicking a mouse. In addition, these job sites are facing competition from social networking sites such as LinkedIn and Facebook.[1]

Both recruiters and job seekers complain about employment sites. Corporate recruiters say that the big sites can bring a flood of candidates, many of whom aren't suited for the listed jobs. Workplace experts estimate that the average large corporation can be inundated with thousands of résumés a day. Job candidates grumble that listings are frequently out of date and fail to produce leads. Some career advisors call these sites "black holes" into which résumés vanish without a trace.

All that said, experts say that although internal referrals are still the source of about 25 percent of hires, employment sites account for just under 20 percent.[2] Clearly, a successful job search will come about through a combination of networking with people who already work inside companies, searching employment sites, and searching career sites on company and organization websites.

FIGURE 12.3 / Example of a Leading "Open Market" Job Site

12.2a Use "Open Market" Sites

Whether or not you end up landing an interview from a referral, a corporate site, or an employment site, you should definitely learn to use employment sites (if you haven't already!) to gather job-search information, such as résumé, interviewing, and salary tips. As seen in Figure 12.3, these sites can inform you about the kinds of jobs that are available, the skill sets required, and the current vocabulary of both job searching and the area you're looking in. Start your search at a few of the best-known online job sites:

- Workopolis (www.workopolis.com)
- Monster (www.monster.ca)
- Indeed (www.indeed.ca)
- Glassdoor (www.glassdoor.ca)
- Wowjobs (www.wowjobs.ca)
- Charity Village (www.charityvillage.com)

If you Google *Canadian employment sites*, you'll get a number of interesting hits, including Google's own job listings. For example, Eluta has a simple interface, whereas the federal government's Job Bank is more complex. You can also try a more specific search in Google, such as *hospitality jobs Canada*. One of the top hits is Hcareers (www.hcareers.ca), a reputable employment site exclusively targeted to jobs in the hospitality, tourism, and leisure industry. From this site you can also link to job boards in the public service, federal and provincial/territorial.

12.2b Go Beyond the Big Sites

Savvy candidates also know how to use the Internet to search for jobs at sites such as the following:

- **Company sites.** Next to internal referrals, probably the best way to find a job online is at a company's own website. Usually jobs are found at a link with the name "Employment" or "Careers" or "Work for us." One poll found that 70 percent of job seekers felt they were more likely to obtain an interview if they posted their résumés on company sites. In addition to finding a more direct route to decision makers, job seekers thought that they could keep their job searches more private at corporate websites than at big job board sites.[3]

- **Association websites.** Online job listings have proved to be the single most popular feature of many professional organizations such as the Canadian Apparel Federation. If you go to the association's website at www.apparel.ca you'll see that one of the six squares on the home page is the job board. Clicking here takes you to a job board with positions in apparel (clothing) companies across the country. To find a list of several industry associations in Canada, go to Charity Village's site on this topic, at https://charityvillage.com/cms/organizations/professional-associations. You can also enter a job category plus the words *association* and *Canada* and see what comes up; for example, *film editor* and *association*. Sometimes job boards at association sites are open only to fee-paying members, and you'll have to decide whether it's a good idea to join your target association, perhaps as a student member.

12.2c Use LinkedIn and Other Social Networking Sites

LinkedIn continues to dominate the world of job searching and recruiting. In a recent poll of 1,843 staffing professionals, 97 percent said they used LinkedIn as a recruiting tool.[4] At LinkedIn, job seekers can search for job openings directly, and they can also follow companies for the latest news and current job openings. (You'll learn more about using LinkedIn in the next section on networking.) Beyond LinkedIn, other social networking sites such as Facebook and Twitter also advertise job openings and recruit potential employees. Because organizations may post open jobs to their Facebook or Twitter pages before advertising them elsewhere, you might gain a head start on submitting an application by following them on these sites.

When posting job-search information online, it's natural to want to put your best foot forward and openly share information that will get you a job. The challenge is striking a balance between supplying enough information and protecting your privacy.

Thousands of employment sites listing millions of jobs now flood the Internet. The sobering reality, however, is that landing a job still depends largely on personal contacts. Researchers have found that 70 percent of jobs are discovered through traditional networking, that is, talking to people who work—or know others who work—in places you'd like to work.

12.2d Network to Find "Hidden Market" Opportunities

The most successful job candidates try to transform themselves from unknown into known quantities by networking. More jobs today are found through referrals and person-to-person contacts than through any other method. That's because people trust what they know. Therefore, your goal should be to become known to a large network of people, and this means going beyond close friends.

BUILD A PERSONAL NETWORK. Building a personal network involves meeting people you don't yet know and talking to them about your respective fields or industries so that you can gain information and locate possible job vacancies. Not only are many jobs never advertised, but some positions aren't even contemplated until the right person appears. One recent college graduate underwent three interviews for a position, but the company hired someone else. After being turned down, the grad explained why he thought he was perfect for this company but perhaps in a different role. Apparently, the hiring manager agreed and decided to create a new job (in social media) because of the skills, personality, and perseverance of this determined young graduate. Networking pays off, but it requires dedication. Here are three steps that will help you establish a network:

- **Step 1. Develop a contact list.** Make a list of anyone who'd be willing to talk with you about finding a job, including teachers, coworkers, former teachers and employers, neighbours, family members, and their friends. Even if you haven't talked with people in years, reach out to them in person or online. Consider asking your campus career centre for alumni willing to talk with students. Also dig into your social networking circles, which we'll discuss shortly.

- **Step 2. Make contacts in person and online.** Call the people on your list or connect online. To set up a meeting in person, say, *Hi _____. I'm looking for a job and I wonder if you could help me out. Could I come over to talk about it?* During your visit be friendly, well organized, polite, and interested in what your contact has to say. Provide a copy of your résumé, and try to keep the conversation centred on your job search. Your goal is to get two or more referrals. In pinpointing your request, say: *Do you know anyone who might have an opening for a person with my skills?* If the person does not, say: *Do you know of anyone else who might know of someone who would?*

- **Step 3. Follow up on your referrals.** Call or contact the people on your list. You might say something like: Hello. I'm Stacy Rivera, a friend of Jason Tilden. He suggested that I ask you for help. I'm looking for a position as a marketing trainee, and he thought you might be willing to spare a few minutes and steer me in the right direction. Don't ask for a job. During your referral interview, ask how the individual got started in this line of work, what he or she likes best (or least) about the work, what career paths exist in the field, and what problems must be overcome by a newcomer. Most important, ask how a person with your background and skills might get started in the field. Send an informal thank-you note to anyone who helps you in your job search, and stay in touch with the most promising people. Ask whether you could stay in contact every three weeks or so during your job search.

USE SOCIAL MEDIA TO NETWORK. Job searchers have a powerful new tool at their disposal: social media. These sites not only keep you in touch with friends but also function beautifully in a job search. If you just send out your résumé blindly, chances are good that not much will happen. However, if you have a referral, your chances of getting a job multiply. Today's expansion of online networks results in an additional path to developing coveted referrals.

LinkedIn is the top social media site for you to use. LinkedIn is where you can let recruiters know of your talents and where you begin your professional networking, as illustrated in Figure 12.4. For hiring managers to find your LinkedIn

---

▶ **FIGURE 12.4** / Branding Yourself to Land a Job

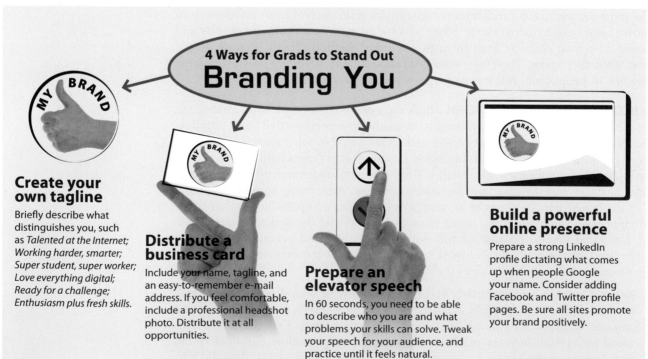

4 Ways for Grads to Stand Out
Branding You

Create your own tagline
Briefly describe what distinguishes you, such as *Talented at the Internet; Working harder, smarter; Super student, super worker; Love everything digital; Ready for a challenge; Enthusiasm plus fresh skills.*

Distribute a business card
Include your name, tagline, and an easy-to-remember e-mail address. If you feel comfortable, include a professional headshot photo. Distribute it at all opportunities.

Prepare an elevator speech
In 60 seconds, you need to be able to describe who you are and what problems your skills can solve. Tweak your speech for your audience, and practice until it feels natural.

Build a powerful online presence
Prepare a strong LinkedIn profile dictating what comes up when people Google your name. Consider adding Facebook and Twitter profile pages. Be sure all sites promote your brand positively.

© Cengage Learning

profile, however, you may need to customize your URL, which is the address of your page. To drive your name to the top of a Google search, advises career coach Susan Adams, scroll down to the LinkedIn "public profile" on your profile page, and edit the URL. Try your first and last name and then your last name and first name, and then add a middle initial, if necessary. Test a variety of combinations with punctuation and spacing until the combination leads directly to your profile.[5]

In writing your LinkedIn career summary, use keywords and phrases that might appear in job descriptions. Include quantifiable achievements and specifics that reveal your skills. You can borrow most of this from your résumé. In the Work Experience and Education fields, include all of your experience, not just your current position. For the Recommendations section, encourage instructors and employers to recommend you. Having more recommendations in your profile makes you look more credible, trustworthy, and reliable. The first few parts of a typical recent graduate's LinkedIn profile is shown in Figure 12.5.

One of the best ways to use LinkedIn is to search for a company in which you are interested. Try to find company employees who are connected to other people you know. Then use that contact as a referral when you apply. You can also send an email to everyone in your LinkedIn network asking for help or for people they could put you in touch with. Don't be afraid to ask an online contact for advice on getting started in a career and for suggestions to help a newcomer break into that

▶ FIGURE 12.5 / LinkedIn Profile/Résumé for New Graduate

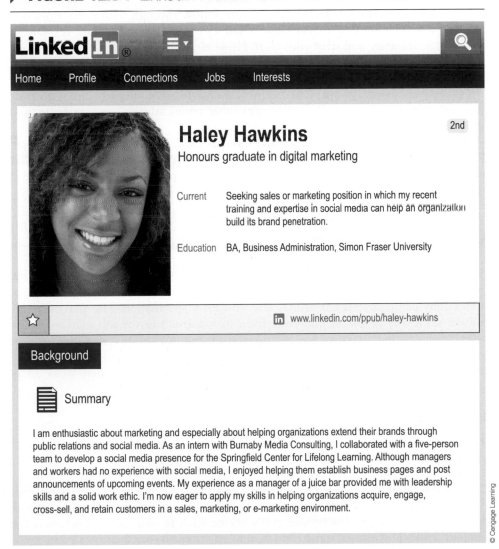

career. Another excellent way to use a contact is to ask that person to look at your résumé and help you tweak it. Like Facebook, LinkedIn has status updates, and it's a good idea to update yours regularly so that your connections know what's happening in your career search.

Employers often use social media sites to check the online presence of a candidate. In fact, one report claims that 91 percent of recruiters check Facebook, Twitter, and LinkedIn to filter out applicants.[6] Make sure your social networking accounts represent you professionally. You can make it easy for your potential employer to learn more about you by including an informative bio in your Twitter or Facebook profile that has a link to your LinkedIn profile. You can also make yourself more discoverable by posting thoughtful blog posts and tweets on topics related to your career goal.

12.2e Building a Personal Brand

A necessary part of your job-search strategy is seeing yourself as a brand. Even postsecondary graduates should seriously consider branding because finding a job today can be tough. Before you get into the thick of the job hunt, focus on developing your brand so that you know what you want to emphasize.

Personal branding involves deciding what makes you special and desirable in the job market. What's your unique selling point? What special skill set makes you stand out among all job applicants? What would your instructors or employers say is your greatest strength? Think about your intended audience. What are you promoting about yourself?

Try to come up with a tagline that describes what you do and who you are. Ask yourself questions such as these: Do you follow through with every promise? Are you a fast learner? Hardworking? What can you take credit for? It's OK to shed a little modesty and strut your stuff. However, keep your tagline simple, short, and truthful so that it's easy to remember. See Figure 12.4 for some sample taglines appropriate for new graduates.

Once you have a tagline, prepare a professional-looking business card with your name and tagline. Include an easy-to-remember email address such as *firstname. lastname@domain.com.*

Now that you have your tagline and business card, work on an elevator speech. This is a pitch that you can give in 30 seconds or less describing who you are and what you can offer, in case you bump into someone who's in a position to hire or recommend you. Tweak your speech for your audience, and practise until you can say it naturally.

◼ 12.3 Creating Persuasive Résumés

After reviewing employment ads, you can begin writing a persuasive résumé. This document does more than merely list your qualifications; it packages your assets into a convincing advertisement that sells you for a specific job. The goal of a persuasive résumé is to get an interview. Even if you aren't in the job market at this moment, preparing a résumé has advantages. Having a current résumé makes you look well organized and professional should an unexpected employment opportunity arise. Moreover, preparing a résumé early can help you recognize weak areas and give you time to bolster your credentials.

12.3a Choose a Résumé Style

Your qualifications and career goal will help you choose between three basic résumé styles: chronological, functional, or hybrid.

CHRONOLOGICAL. Most popular with recruiters is the chronological résumé, shown in Figure 12.6. It lists work history job by job, starting with the most recent position (i.e., starting in the present and working back to older jobs). Recruiters are familiar with the chronological résumé, and the majority of them prefer to see a

Casey J. Jepson
201–1300 John A. Macdonald Blvd.
Kingston, ON K3E 4A5

Email: cjepson82@gmail.com
Phone: 613–555–8876 http://www.youtube.com/watch?v=a2L8DHECtNj ·——— Includes URL of a video résumé posted on YouTube

SUMMARY OF QUALIFICATIONS	• Over two years' experience in customer service positions in major organizations • Excellent customer service skills including oral communication, listening, and written communication • Proven teamwork and interpersonal skills including leadership, cooperation, and on-time delivery • Mastery of computer skills (MOS certification) • Strengths in research, proofreading, coaching, and math
EXPERIENCE	Customer Service Representative, Co-op placement St. Lawrence College, Kingston, ON September 2020–present • Provide friendly, helpful senrice via face-to-face, phone, email, and messaging channels at a large urban college • File weekly incident/outlier reports • Work effectively in team of 15–20 co-op students and fulltime CSRs Front Desk Representative, part-time TD Canada Trust, Kingston, ON May 2018–June 2019 • Provide friendly, helpful face–to–face senrice at busy urban bank branch • Replace lost and stolen credit and debit cards for clients • Llaise with branch manager and tellers to increase branch profitability Customer Associate, part-time Sears, Kingston, ON May 2017–June 2017; December 2017 • Manage busy cash desk in women's clothing department • Provide friendly, helpful face–to–face answers to customer queries
EDUCATION	St. Lawrence College, Kingston, ON Major: Retail Management Advanced Diploma Graduation expected June 2021 Current average: A-
ACTIVITIES AND AWARDS	• Member of St. Lawrence Enactus team • Nominated for SLC Ambassador Award (recognizes outstanding students for excellence in and out of classroom) • Volunteer leader at annual student orientation (2019 & 2020)

candidate's résumé in this format. The chronological style works well for candidates who have experience in their field of employment and for those who show steady career growth. It's also the most honest form: it clearly shows what your work experience includes. Some students or new Canadians who lack extensive local experience may want to try the functional format, which is described below.

FUNCTIONAL. The functional résumé, shown in Figure 12.7, focuses attention on a candidate's skills rather than on past employment. Like a chronological résumé, the functional résumé begins with the candidate's name, address, telephone number, job objective, and education. Instead of listing jobs, though, the functional résumé lists skills and accomplishments, such as *Supervisory and Management Skills* or *Retail and Customer Service Experience*. This résumé style highlights accomplishments and can de-emphasize a negative or negligible employment history. People who have changed jobs frequently or who have gaps in their employment history may prefer the functional résumé. Be aware, though, that online employment sites may insist on chronological format. In addition, some recruiters may be suspicious of functional résumés, thinking the candidate is hiding something.

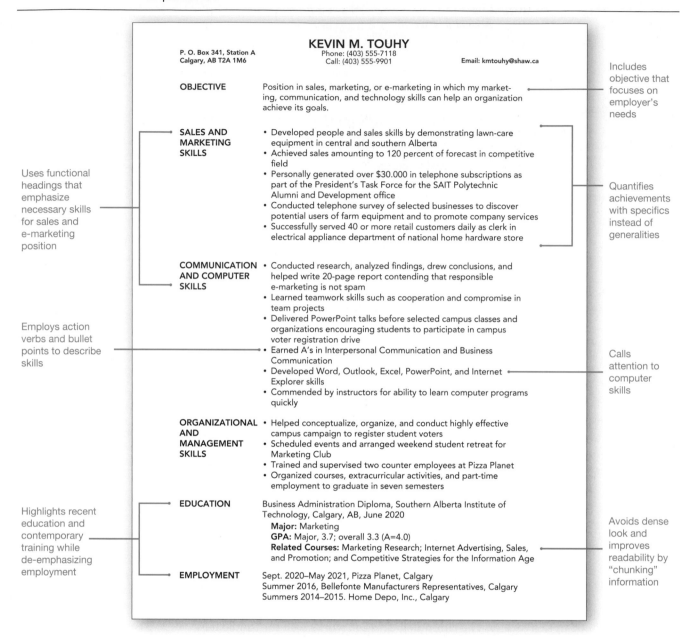

KEVIN M. TOUHY

P. O. Box 341, Station A
Calgary, AB T2A 1M6

Phone: (403) 555-7118
Call: (403) 555-9901

Email: kmtouhy@shaw.ca

Includes objective that focuses on employer's needs

Uses functional headings that emphasize necessary skills for sales and e-marketing position

OBJECTIVE
Position in sales, marketing, or e-marketing in which my marketing, communication, and technology skills can help an organization achieve its goals.

SALES AND MARKETING SKILLS
- Developed people and sales skills by demonstrating lawn-care equipment in central and southern Alberta
- Achieved sales amounting to 120 percent of forecast in competitive field
- Personally generated over $30,000 in telephone subscriptions as part of the President's Task Force for the SAIT Polytechnic Alumni and Development office
- Conducted telephone survey of selected businesses to discover potential users of farm equipment and to promote company services
- Successfully served 40 or more retail customers daily as clerk in electrical appliance department of national home hardware store

Quantifies achievements with specifics instead of generalities

COMMUNICATION AND COMPUTER SKILLS
- Conducted research, analyzed findings, drew conclusions, and helped write 20-page report contending that responsible e-marketing is not spam
- Learned teamwork skills such as cooperation and compromise in team projects
- Delivered PowerPoint talks before selected campus classes and organizations encouraging students to participate in campus voter registration drive
- Earned A's in Interpersonal Communication and Business Communication
- Developed Word, Outlook, Excel, PowerPoint, and Internet Explorer skills
- Commended by instructors for ability to learn computer programs quickly

Employs action verbs and bullet points to describe skills

Calls attention to computer skills

ORGANIZATIONAL AND MANAGEMENT SKILLS
- Helped conceptualize, organize, and conduct highly effective campus campaign to register student voters
- Scheduled events and arranged weekend student retreat for Marketing Club
- Trained and supervised two counter employees at Pizza Planet
- Organized courses, extracurricular activities, and part-time employment to graduate in seven semesters

EDUCATION
Business Administration Diploma, Southern Alberta Institute of Technology, Calgary, AB, June 2020
Major: Marketing
GPA: Major, 3.7; overall 3.3 (A=4.0)
Related Courses: Marketing Research; Internet Advertising, Sales, and Promotion; and Competitive Strategies for the Information Age

Highlights recent education and contemporary training while de-emphasizing employment

Avoids dense look and improves readability by "chunking" information

EMPLOYMENT
Sept. 2020–May 2021, Pizza Planet, Calgary
Summer 2016, Bellefonte Manufacturers Representatives, Calgary
Summers 2014–2015. Home Depo, Inc., Calgary

Recent graduate Kevin Touhy chose this functional format to de-emphasize his small amount of work experience and emphasize his potential in sales and marketing. This version of his résumé is more generic than one targeted for a specific position. Nevertheless, it emphasizes his strong points with specific achievements and includes an employment section to satisfy recruiters. The functional format presents ability-focused topics. It illustrates what the job seeker can do for the employer instead of narrating a history of previous jobs. Although recruiters prefer chronological résumés, the functional format is a good choice for new graduates, career changers, and those with employment gaps.

Although the functional résumé of Kevin Touhy shown in Figure 12.7 concentrates on skills, it does include a short employment section because he recognizes that recruiters expect it. Notice that Kevin breaks his skills into three categories. An easier method is to make one large list, perhaps with a title such as *Areas of Accomplishment, Summary of Qualifications,* or *Areas of Expertise and Ability.*

HYBRID. This type of résumé combines what's best about the two types above. It offers a chronological list of past employment but does so in a way that also highlights skills that are a significant part of your brand. This style makes sense when you have significant experience and want to show why you're right for this job while still displaying traditional résumé information.

12.3b Decide on Length

Conventional wisdom holds that recruiters prefer one-page résumés. Studies have however revealed that while they *claim* they prefer one-page résumés, they actually *choose* to interview applicants with two-page résumés. Recruiters who are serious about candidates often prefer a fuller picture with the kind of details that can be provided in a two-page résumé. On the other hand, recruiters are extremely busy, and concise résumés help speed up their work.

The best advice is to make your résumé as long as needed to sell your skills to recruiters and hiring managers. Individuals with more experience will naturally have longer résumés. Those with fewer than ten years of experience, those making a major career change, and those who have had only one or two employers will likely have a one-page résumé. Finally, some senior-level managers and executives with a lengthy history of major accomplishments might have a résumé that's three pages or longer.[7] Most recruiters now admit they look for résumés up to three pages for senior management positions, and two pages for entry-level positions.

12.3c Organize Your Information Under Headings

A résumé emphasizes skills and achievements aimed at a particular job or company. It shows a candidate's most important qualifications first, and it de-emphasizes any weaknesses. In organizing your information, create as few headings as possible; more than six generally looks cluttered. No two résumés are ever exactly alike, but job applicants usually include information under all or some of these headings: career objective; summary of qualifications; education; experience; capabilities and skills; awards and activities; personal information; and references. Besides these headings, a résumé always begins with a main heading.

MAIN HEADING. Keep the main heading of your résumé as uncluttered as possible. (Don't include the word *résumé* or *CV*; it's like putting the word *email* in the subject line of an email; i.e., it's redundant.) Begin with your name, add your middle initial for a professional look, and format it so that it stands out on the page. Following your name, list your contact information, including your complete address, area code and phone number (voice mail enabled), and email address. Some candidates now add links to their LinkedIn page or to a video résumé they've posted on a site like YouTube. If you do this, make sure these links lead to professional-looking and professional-sounding sites.

The recorded message at the phone number you list should be in your voice, mention your full name, and be concise and professional (e.g., "Thanks for your call. You've reached Casey Jepson. Please leave a message after the beep. I'll reply shortly."). If you're expecting an important recruiting call on your cell phone, pick up only when you're in a quiet environment and can concentrate.

Make sure your email address sounds professional and not something like *1foxylady@yahoo.com* or *hotdaddy@gmail.com*. Also be sure that you're using a personal email address. Putting your work email address on your résumé announces to prospective employers that you're using your current employer's resources to look for another job. See Figure 12.7 for an example of an effective main heading.

CAREER OBJECTIVE. Career objectives make the recruiter's life easier by quickly classifying the résumé. But such declarations may also disqualify a candidate if the stated objective doesn't match a company's job description.[8] A well-written objective customized for the job opening can add value to a résumé.

Cengage

MINDTAP

In MindTap, go to the Chapter 12 reading, section 12.3a, and watch the videos of industry experts Karen Richardson discussing the merits of templated versus creative résumés.

Your objective should focus on the employer's needs. Therefore, it should be written from the employer's perspective, not your own. Focus on how you can contribute to the organization, not on what the organization can do for you.

> **Ineffective:** To obtain a meaningful and rewarding position that enables me to learn more about the graphic design field and allows for advancement

> **Effective:** Position with advertising firm designing websites, publications, logos, and promotional displays for clients, where creativity, software knowledge, and proven communication skills can be used to build client base and expand operations

Also be careful that your career objective doesn't downplay your talents. For example, some consultants warn against using the words *entry level* in your objective, as they emphasize lack of experience or show poor self-confidence. Finally, your objective should be concise. Try to limit your objective to no more than two or three lines. Avoid using complete sentences and the pronoun *I*. A good example of a career objective can be found in Figure 12.7.

If you choose to omit the career objective, be sure to discuss your objectives and goals in your cover letter. Savvy job seekers are also incorporating their objectives into a summary of qualifications, which is discussed next.

SUMMARY OF QUALIFICATIONS. Recruiters are busy, and smart job seekers add a summary of qualifications to their résumés to save the time of recruiters and hiring managers. After a job is advertised, a hiring manager may get hundreds or even thousands of résumés in response. A summary at the top of your résumé makes it easier to read and ensures that a recruiter, who may be skimming résumés quickly, doesn't overlook your most impressive qualifications. A well-written summary motivates the recruiter to read further.

A summary of qualifications will include three to eight bulleted statements that prove you're the ideal candidate for the position. When formulating these statements, consider your experience in the field, your education, your unique skills, awards you've won, certifications, and any other accomplishments that you want to highlight. Include quantifiable accomplishments wherever possible (e.g., *Over five years' experience in* . . .). Target the most important qualifications an employer will be looking for in the person hired for this position. Examples of summaries of qualifications appear in Figures 12.6 and 12.11.

EDUCATION. The next component in a chronological résumé is your education—if it's more noteworthy than your work experience. In this section you should include the name and location of schools, dates of attendance, major fields of study, and certifications received (e.g., diplomas, degrees). Once you've attended college or university, you don't need to list high-school information on your résumé.

Although some hiring managers may think that applicants are hiding something if they omit a poor record of grades, others suggest leaving out a poor GPA. Instead, they advise that students try to excel in internships, show extracurricular leadership, and target smaller, lesser-known companies to offset low grades.

Refer to courses only if you can relate them to the position sought. When relevant, include certificates earned, seminars attended, workshops completed, and honours earned. If your education is incomplete, include such statements as *BBA degree expected May 2018*. Title this section *Education, Academic Preparation,* or *Professional Training*. If you're preparing a functional résumé, you'll probably put the education section below your skills summaries, as Kevin Touhy has done in Figure 12.7.

WORK EXPERIENCE OR EMPLOYMENT HISTORY. If your work experience is significant and relevant to the position sought, this information should appear before your education information. List your most recent employment first and work backwards, including only those jobs that you think will help you win the targeted position. A job application form may demand a full employment history, but your résumé may be selective. Be aware, though, that time gaps in your employment history will probably be questioned in the interview. For each position show the following:

- Employer's name, city/town, and province or territory
- Dates of employment (month and year)
- Most important job title
- Significant duties, activities, accomplishments, and promotions

Describe your employment achievements concisely but concretely to make what résumé consultants call a strong "value proposition." Avoid generalities by striving to be more specific.

Ineffective: Worked with customers

Effective: Served 40 or more retail customers a day; Successfully resolved problems about custom stationery orders; or Acted as intermediary among customers, printers, and suppliers

Whenever possible, quantify your accomplishments instead of making them sound vague.

Ineffective: Did equipment study; or Was successful in sales

Effective: Conducted study of equipment needs of 100 small businesses in Hamilton, ON; or Personally generated orders for sales of $90,000 annually

Professional recruiters routinely report that if they don't spot quantifiable results in the first ten seconds of reading your résumé, they'll move on to the next one.

Your employment achievements and job duties will be easier to read if you place them in a bulleted list. Don't try to list every single thing you've done on the job; instead, customize your information so that it relates to the target job. Ensure your list of job duties shows what you have to contribute and how you're qualified for the position you are applying for. Don't make your bullet points complete sentences, and avoid using personal pronouns (*I, me, my*) in them. If you've performed many of the same duties for multiple employers, you don't have to repeat them.

In addition to technical skills, employers seek individuals with developed soft skills. This means you'll want to select work experiences and achievements that illustrate your initiative, dependability, responsibility, problem solving, flexibility, creativity, leadership, and interpersonal communication strengths. One soft skill employers repeatedly ask for is people who can work together in teams.

Ineffective: Worked effectively in teams

Effective: Collaborated with interdepartmental five-person team to develop ten-page handbook for temporary workers

Statements describing your work experience can be made forceful and persuasive by using action verbs, such as those listed in Figure 12.8 and illustrated in Figure 12.9.

CAPABILITIES AND SKILLS. Recruiters want to know specifically what you can do for their companies. Therefore, list your skills, including your abilities with any technology tools such as apps, software, and social media.

Ineffective: Have payroll experience

Effective: Proficient/competent/experienced in preparing federal, provincial, and local payroll tax returns, as well as franchise and personal property tax returns

FIGURE 12.8 / Action Verbs to Strengthen a Résumé

COMMUNICATION SKILLS	TEAMWORK, SUPERVISION SKILLS	MANAGEMENT, LEADERSHIP SKILLS	RESEARCH SKILLS	CLERICAL, DETAIL SKILLS	CREATIVE SKILLS
clarified	advised	analyzed	assessed	activated	acted
collaborated	coordinated	authorized	collected	approved	conceptualized
explained	demonstrated	coordinated	critiqued	classified	designed
interpreted	developed	directed	diagnosed	edited	fashioned
integrated	evaluated	headed	formulated	generated	founded
persuaded	expedited	implemented	gathered	maintained	illustrated
promoted	facilitated	improved	interpreted	monitored	integrated
resolved	guided	increased	investigated	proofread	invented
summarized	motivated	organized	reviewed	recorded	originated
translated	set goals	scheduled	studied	streamlined	revitalized
wrote	trained	strengthened	systematized	updated	shaped

© Cengage Learning

FIGURE 12.9 / Action Verbs to Quantify Achievements

Identified weaknesses in internships and **researched** five alternative programs

Reduced delivery delays by an average of three days per order

Streamlined filing system, reducing 400-item backlog to zero

Organized holiday awards program for 1,200 attendees and 140 workers

Designed customer feedback form for company website

Represented 2,500 students on committee involving university policies and procedures

Calculated shipping charges for overseas deliveries and **recommended** most economical rates

Managed 24-station computer network linking data in three departments

Distributed and **explained** voter registration forms to over 500 prospective voters

Praised by top management for enthusiastic teamwork and achievement

Secured national recognition from Tree Canada for tree project

If you can speak any additional languages or use sign language, include it on your résumé. Describe proficiencies you've acquired through training and experience.

Ineffective: Trained in computer graphics

Effective: Certified in Adobe Photoshop and Illustrator and Web design through an intensive 350-hour classroom program

You'll also want to highlight exceptional skills, such as working well under stress, knowledge of coding, and strong sales abilities. If possible, provide details and evidence that back up your assertions; for example, *Led conflict resolution workshop through staff development department on 10 occasions for over 200 employees.* For recent graduates, this section can be used to give recruiters evidence of your potential. Instead of *Capabilities*, the section might be called *Skills and Abilities*.

Those job hunters preparing a functional résumé will place more focus on skills than on any other section. A well-written functional résumé groups skills into categories such as *Accounting/Finance Skills, Management/Leadership Skills, Communication/Teamwork Skills,* and *Computer/Technology Skills.* Each skills category includes a bulleted list of achievements and experience that demonstrate the skill, including specific quantifiable amounts (e.g., *20 seminars*) whenever possible. These skills categories should be placed at the beginning of the résumé where they'll be highlighted, followed by education and work experience. The action verbs shown in Figures 12.8 and 12.9 can also be used when constructing a functional résumé.

AWARDS, HONOURS, AND ACTIVITIES. If you have three or more awards or honours, highlight them by listing them under a separate heading. If not, put them with *Activities* or in the *Education* or *Work Experience* section if appropriate. Include awards, scholarships (financial and other), fellowships, dean's list, sports or other team affiliations, and so on.

> **Ineffective:** Recipient of King Scholarship

> **Effective:** Recipient of King Scholarship given by Macdonald College to outstanding graduates who combine academic excellence and extracurricular activities

It's also appropriate to include school, community, volunteer, and professional activities. Employers are interested in evidence that you are a well-rounded person. This section provides an opportunity to demonstrate leadership and soft skills. Strive to use specific action statements.

> **Ineffective:** Treasurer of business club

> **Effective:** Collected dues, kept financial records, and paid bills while serving as treasurer of 35-member business management club

PERSONAL DATA. Résumés omit personal data, such as birthdate, marital status, or national origin. Such information doesn't relate to occupational qualifications, and recruiters are legally barred from asking for this information. Some job seekers do, however, include hobbies or interests (such as skiing or photography) that might grab the recruiter's attention or serve as conversation starters. You could also indicate your willingness to travel or to relocate, since many companies will be interested.

REFERENCES. Recruiters prefer that you bring to the interview a list of individuals willing to discuss your qualifications. Therefore, you should prepare a separate list, such as that in Figure 12.10, when you begin your job search. Ask three of

▶ FIGURE 12.10 / Sample Reference List

your professors, your current employer or previous employers, colleagues, or other professional contacts whether they would be willing to answer inquiries regarding your qualifications for employment. Be sure to provide them with an opportunity to refuse. No reference at all is better than a negative one.

Don't include personal references, such as friends, family, or neighbours, because recruiters will rarely consult them. One final note: most recruiters see little reason to include the statement *References available upon request* at the end of your résumé. It's unnecessary and takes up precious space.

In Figures 12.6 and 12.7, shown earlier, you'll find models corresponding to the two main résumé types. Notice as you study the models that the chronological résumé (Figure 12.6) is for a current student with only one type of experience; the functional résumé (Figure 12.7) is for a recent graduate with largely unrelated work experience; and the third hybrid résumé (Figure 12.11) is for a graduate with significant related experience following her postsecondary education. Use the appropriate model to help you organize the content and format of your own persuasive résumé.

12.3d Online Résumé Reading Patterns

With increasing numbers of résumés being read online, it's wise for job applicants to know what researchers have found about how people read online text. Eye-tracking research reveals that people read text-based pages online in an F-shaped pattern.[9] That is, they read horizontally from the top of the page, concentrating on the top third and then focusing on the left side as they read downward. This roughly corresponds to the shape of a capital F. Smart applicants will arrange the most important information in the top section of the résumé. Additional significant information should appear at the beginning of each group down the left side.

12.3e Polish Your Résumé and Keep It Honest

As you continue to work on your résumé, look for ways to improve it. For example, consider consolidating headings. By condensing your information into as few headings as possible, you'll produce a clean, professional-looking document. Ask yourself what graphic highlighting techniques you can use to improve readability: capitalization, underlining, indenting, and bulleting. Experiment with headings and styles to achieve a pleasing, easy-to-read message. Moreover, look for ways to eliminate wordiness. For example, instead of *Supervised two employees who worked at the counter*, try *Supervised two counter employees*.

A résumé is expected to showcase a candidate's strengths and minimize weaknesses. For this reason, recruiters expect a certain degree of self-promotion. Some résumé writers, however, step over the line that separates honest self-marketing from deceptive half-truths and flat-out lies. Distorting facts on a résumé is unethical; lying may be illegal. Most important, either practice can destroy a career.

12.3f Proofread Your Résumé

After revising your résumé, you must proofread, proofread, and proofread again for spelling, grammar, mechanics, content, and format. Then have a knowledgeable friend or relative proofread it yet again. This is one document that must be perfect. Because the job market is so competitive, one typo, misspelled word, or grammatical error could eliminate you from consideration.

By now you may be thinking that you'd like to hire someone to write your résumé. Don't! First, you know yourself better than anyone else could know you. Second, you'll end up with either a generic or a one-time résumé. A generic résumé in today's highly competitive job market will lose out to a customized résumé nine times out of ten. Equally useless is a one-time résumé aimed at a single job. What if you don't get that job? Because you'll need to revise your résumé many times as you seek a variety of jobs, be prepared to write (and rewrite) it yourself.

Because Rachel has many years of experience and seeks executive-level employment, she highlighted her experience by placing it before her education. Her summary of qualifications highlighted her most impressive experience and skills. This hybrid two-page résumé shows the steady progression of her career to executive positions, a movement that impresses and reassures recruiters.

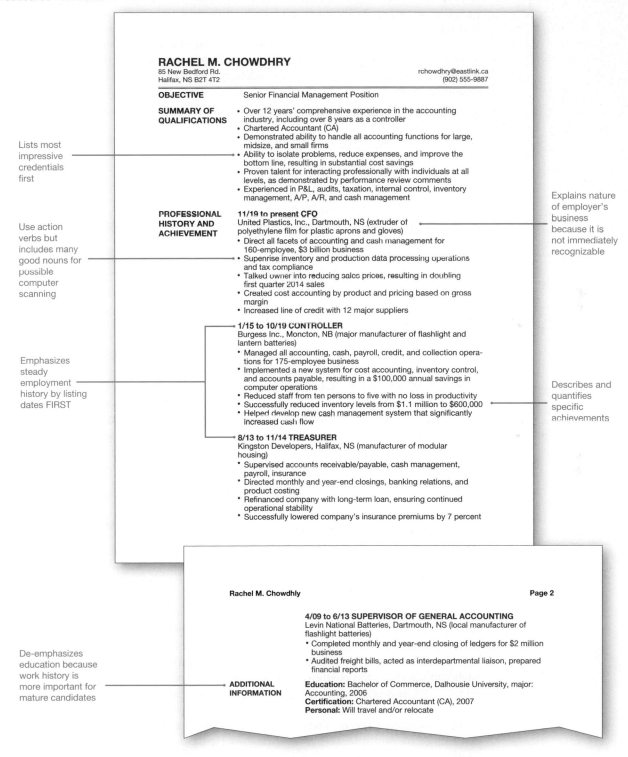

Lists most impressive credentials first

Use action verbs but includes many good nouns for possible computer scanning

Emphasizes steady employment history by listing dates FIRST

Explains nature of employer's business because it is not immediately recognizable

Describes and quantifies specific achievements

De-emphasizes education because work history is more important for mature candidates

RACHEL M. CHOWDHRY
85 New Bedford Rd.
Halifax, NS B2T 4T2

rchowdhry@eastlink.ca
(902) 555-9887

OBJECTIVE   Senior Financial Management Position

SUMMARY OF QUALIFICATIONS
- Over 12 years' comprehensive experience in the accounting industry, including over 8 years as a controller
- Chartered Accountant (CA)
- Demonstrated ability to handle all accounting functions for large, midsize, and small firms
- Ability to isolate problems, reduce expenses, and improve the bottom line, resulting in substantial cost savings
- Proven talent for interacting professionally with individuals at all levels, as demonstrated by performance review comments
- Experienced in P&L, audits, taxation, internal control, inventory management, A/P, A/R, and cash management

PROFESSIONAL HISTORY AND ACHIEVEMENT

11/19 to present CFO
United Plastics, Inc., Dartmouth, NS (extruder of polyethylene film for plastic aprons and gloves)
- Direct all facets of accounting and cash management for 160-employee, $3 billion business
- Supervise inventory and production data processing operations and tax compliance
- Talked owner into reducing sales prices, resulting in doubling first quarter 2014 sales
- Created cost accounting by product and pricing based on gross margin
- Increased line of credit with 12 major suppliers

1/15 to 10/19 CONTROLLER
Burgess Inc., Moncton, NB (major manufacturer of flashlight and lantern batteries)
- Managed all accounting, cash, payroll, credit, and collection operations for 175-employee business
- Implemented a new system for cost accounting, inventory control, and accounts payable, resulting in a $100,000 annual savings in computer operations
- Reduced staff from ten persons to five with no loss in productivity
- Successfully reduced inventory levels from $1.1 million to $600,000
- Helped develop new cash management system that significantly increased cash flow

8/13 to 11/14 TREASURER
Kingston Developers, Halifax, NS (manufacturer of modular housing)
- Supervised accounts receivable/payable, cash management, payroll, insurance
- Directed monthly and year-end closings, banking relations, and product costing
- Refinanced company with long-term loan, ensuring continued operational stability
- Successfully lowered company's insurance premiums by 7 percent

Rachel M. Chowdhly   Page 2

4/09 to 6/13 SUPERVISOR OF GENERAL ACCOUNTING
Levin National Batteries, Dartmouth, NS (local manufacturer of flashlight batteries)
- Completed monthly and year-end closing of ledgers for $2 million business
- Audited freight bills, acted as interdepartmental liaison, prepared financial reports

ADDITIONAL INFORMATION
Education: Bachelor of Commerce, Dalhousie University, major: Accounting, 2006
Certification: Chartered Accountant (CA), 2007
Personal: Will travel and/or relocate

◤ 12.4 Increasing Your Chances With Digital Tools

Just as digital media have changed the way candidates seek jobs, they've also changed the way employers select qualified candidates. For example, the first reader of your résumé may very well be applicant tracking system (ATS) software. Estimates suggest that as many as 90 percent of large companies use these systems.[10] ATS are favoured not only by large companies but also by job boards such as Monster to screen candidates and filter applications. You can expect to be seeing more of them with their restrictive forms and emphasis on keywords. Savvy candidates will learn to "game" the system by playing according to the ATS rules.

12.4a Get Your Résumé Selected: Maximize Keyword Hits

Job seekers can increase the probability of their résumés being selected by ATS through the words they choose. The following techniques, plus those cited earlier, can boost the chances of having your résumé selected:

- **Include specific keywords or keyword phrases.** Carefully study ads and job descriptions for the position you want. Describe your experience, education, and qualifications using terms associated with the job advertisement or job description for this position.
- **Focus on nouns.** Although action verbs will make your résumé appeal to a recruiter, ATS will be looking for nouns in three categories: (a) a job title, position, or role (e.g., *accountant*, *Web developer*, *team leader*); (b) a technical skill or specialization (e.g., *JavaScript*, *blog editor*); and (c) a certification, a tool used, or specific experience (e.g., *certified financial analyst*, *experience with WordPress*).
- **Use variations of the job title.** ATS may seek a slightly different job title from what you list. To be safe, include variations and abbreviations (e.g., *occupational therapist*, *certified occupational therapist*, or *COTA*). If you don't have experience in your targeted area, use the job title you seek in your objective.
- **Concentrate on the skills section.** A majority of keywords sought by employees relate to specialized or technical skill requirements. Therefore, be sure the skills section of your résumé is loaded with nouns that describe your skills and qualifications.
- **Skip a keyword summary.** Avoid grouping nouns in a keyword summary because recruiters may perceive them to be manipulative.[11]

12.4b Expand Your Résumé's Appeal: Add Video

Another way of strengthening your résumé and cover letter is to upload a video that profiles you and your skills to a site like YouTube or Vimeo. Video-sharing sites allow you to broadcast yourself and are incredibly powerful tools—a well-produced video résumé may open doors and secure an interview where other techniques have failed.[12] They allow candidates to demonstrate their public speaking, interpersonal, and technical skills more impressively than they can in traditional print résumés.

However, some recruiters are skeptical about video résumés because they fear that such applications will take more time to view than paper-based résumés do. Moreover, a lack of professionalism when creating video résumés can lead to embarrassment.

People who blog and write about video résumés suggest incorporating a number of best practices. These practices include ensuring excellent video quality; taking advantage of multiple authentic locations (your desk, outside a store you once worked at, etc.); using professional language; offering something unique from a traditional résumé; editing the sound and lighting so that there are no distractions; and limiting video length to between three and five minutes. Also, if you're satisfied with your video résumé, we suggest that you include a link to it in the heading of your traditional résumé, under your email address.

12.4c Translate Into Pictures: The Infographic Résumé

A hot trend in business is the infographic résumé. It uses colourful charts, graphics, and timelines to illustrate a candidate's work history and experience. "Anyone looking at it," says blogger Randy Krum, "is 650% more likely to remember it days later."[13] James Coleman, a graduating senior from the University of Saskatchewan, created an infographic résumé that secured him a job. Shown in Figure 12.12, James's résumé uses a timeline to track his experience and education. Colourful bubbles indicate his digital skills.

Most of us, however, aren't talented enough to create professional-looking infographics. To the rescue is infographic software such as Kinzaa.com, which lets you create a slick visual infographic-style résumé.

Will a dazzling infographic get you a job? Among hiring managers, the consensus is that infographic résumés help candidates set themselves apart, but such visual displays may not be appropriate for every job. In more traditional fields such as accounting and financial services, hiring managers want to see a standard print-based résumé. One hiring manager pointed out that traditional résumés evolved this way for a reason: they make comparison, evaluation, and selection easier for employers.[14]

12.4d Submitting Your Résumé

If you're responding to a job posting on a company website or a job site, be sure to read it carefully to make sure you know how the employer wants you to submit your résumé. Not following the employer's instructions can eliminate you from consideration before your résumé is even reviewed. Employers will ask you to submit your résumé in one of the following ways:

- **Word document.** Recruiters may ask applicants to attach their résumés as Word documents to an email. Alternatively, you may be asked to upload your Word file directly onto the recruiter's site.
- **PDF document.** For the sake of safety, many hiring managers prefer PDF (portable document format) files. A PDF résumé will look exactly like the original

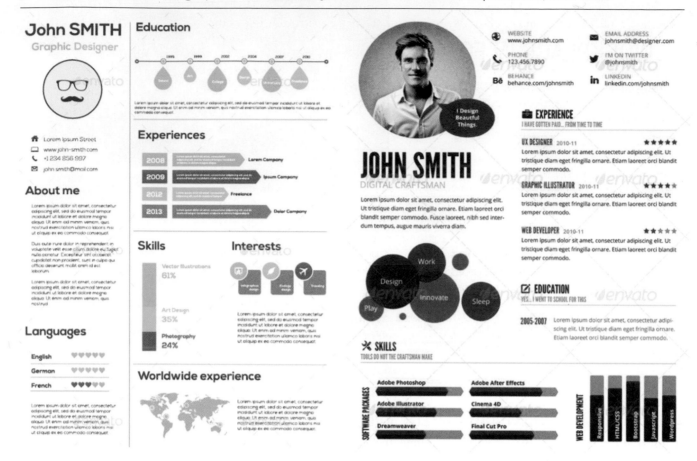

and cannot be easily altered. Save your Word résumé file as a PDF file (check for PDF under "Format" when you click "Save As") and keep it in the same folder as your Word version.

- **Company database.** Some organizations prefer that you complete an online form with your résumé information. This enables them to plug your data into their formats for rapid searching. You might be asked to paste your résumé into the form. In this case, save a separate version of the résumé as "Plain Text" before pasting it.
- **Fax or in person.** In rare cases, you may be asked to fax or drop off your résumé. When doing so, use at least a 12-point font to improve readability. Thinner fonts—such as Times, Palatino, New Century Schoolbook, Arial, and Bookman—are clearer than thicker ones. Avoid underlines, which may look broken or choppy when faxed.

Whichever method you use to submit your résumé, don't send it on its own. In almost all cases, a résumé is accompanied by a persuasive cover letter, discussed in the next section.

12.5 Persuasive Cover Letters

With your résumé, you'll send a persuasive cover letter. It introduces the résumé, highlights ways your strengths will benefit the reader, and helps obtain an interview by personalizing you. In many ways your cover letter is a sales letter; it sells your talents and tries to beat the competition. It therefore includes many of the techniques you learned for sales letters in Chapter 6.

Recruiters disagree on how long to make cover letters. Many prefer short letters of no more than three paragraphs; instead of concentrating on the letter, these readers focus on the résumé. Others desire longer letters that supply more information, thus giving them a better opportunity to evaluate a candidate's qualifications and gauge his or her personality. They argue that hiring and training new employees is expensive and time-consuming; extra data can guide them in making the best choice the first time. Use your judgment. If you feel, for example, that you need space to explain in more detail what you can do for a prospective employer, do so.

Regardless of length, a cover letter should have three primary parts: (a) an opening that gains attention, (b) a body that builds interest and reduces resistance by explaining why you're the right candidate for the role, and (c) a closing that motivates action.

12.5a Gain Attention in the Opening

The first step in gaining the interest of your reader is addressing that individual by name. Rather than sending your letter to the *human resources department*, find the name of the appropriate individual if it's not in the job posting. Call the organization for the correct spelling and the complete address. This personal touch distinguishes your letter and demonstrates your serious interest.

How you open your cover letter depends largely on whether your résumé is for a position that is solicited or unsolicited. If an employment position has been announced and applicants are being solicited, you can use a direct approach. If you don't know whether a position is open and you are prospecting for a job, use an indirect approach. Either way, strive for openings that are more imaginative than *I would like to apply for* . . . . Instead, you can say *I'm pleased to submit my application for the X position, to which I'm able to bring significant related experience.*

OPENINGS FOR SOLICITED JOBS. Here are some of the best techniques to open a cover letter for a job that's been posted:

- **Refer to the name of an employee in the company.** Remember that employers always hope to hire known quantities rather than complete strangers:

  > Mitchell Sims, a member of your customer service department, told me that DataTech is seeking an experienced customer service representative. The attached summary of my qualifications demonstrates my preparation for this position.

- **Refer to the source of your information precisely.** If you're answering an ad, include the exact position advertised and the name and date of the publication or site:

  > Your listing on Workopolis for a junior accountant (competition 15-003) greatly appeals to me. With my accounting training and computer experience, I believe I could serve the City of Richmond well.

  > Susan Butler, placement director at Carleton University, told me that Open Text Corporation has an opening for a technical writer with knowledge of Web design and graphics.

- **Refer to the job title and describe how your qualifications fit the requirements.** Recruiters are looking for a match between an applicant's credentials and the job needs:

  > Because of my in-depth training and experience in accounting at Simon Fraser University, I feel confident that I have the qualifications you described in your advertisement for a junior accountant.

OPENINGS FOR UNSOLICITED JOBS. If you're unsure whether a position exists, you can use a more persuasive opening. Since your goal is to convince this person to keep reading, try one of the following techniques:

- **Demonstrate interest in and knowledge of the reader's business.** Show the receiver that you've done your research and that this organization is more than a mere name to you.

Since the Canadian Automobile Association is putting together an IT team for its recently established group insurance division, could you use the services of a well-trained business analytics graduate who seeks to become a professional underwriter?

- **Show how your special talents and background will benefit the company.** Recruiters need to be convinced that you can do something for them.

I'm hoping that your rapidly expanding publications division can use the services of an editorial assistant who offers exceptional language skills, an honours degree from Brandon University, and two years' experience in producing a school publication.

In applying for an advertised job, Kendra Hawkins writes the solicited cover letter shown in Figure 12.13. Notice that her opening identifies the position and the job site completely so that the reader knows exactly what advertisement Kendra refers to. Using features of Microsoft Word, Kendra designs personal letterhead that uses her name and looks professionally printed.

◤ FIGURE 12.13 / Solicited Cover Letter

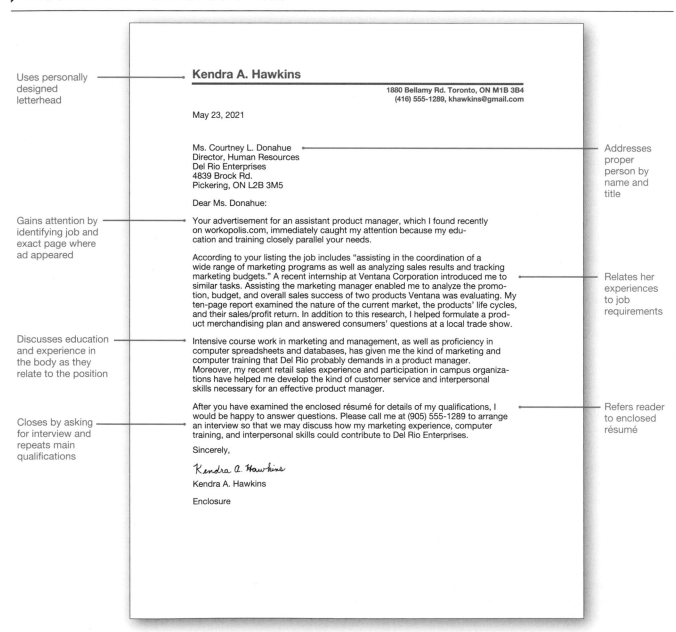

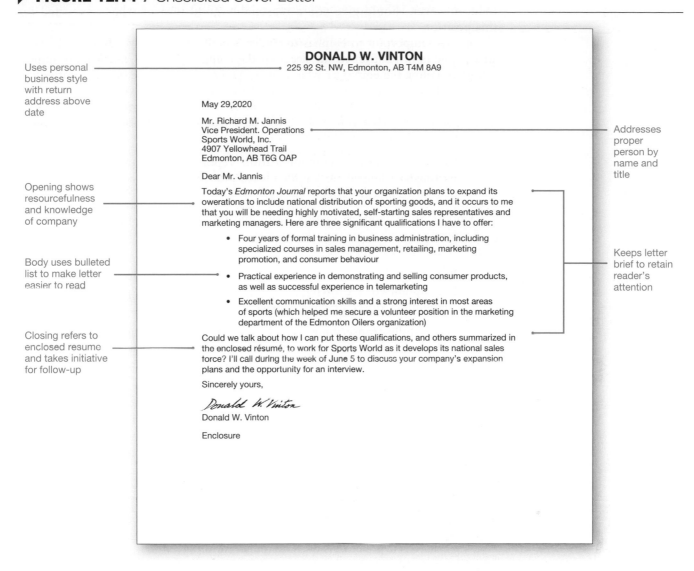

Uses personal business style with return address above date

Opening shows resourcefulness and knowledge of company

Body uses bulleted list to make letter easier to read

Closing refers to enclosed resume and takes initiative for follow-up

Addresses proper person by name and title

Keeps letter brief to retain reader's attention

DONALD W. VINTON
225 92 St. NW, Edmonton, AB T4M 8A9

May 29,2020

Mr. Richard M. Jannis
Vice President. Operations
Sports World, Inc.
4907 Yellowhead Trail
Edmonton, AB T6G OAP

Dear Mr. Jannis

Today's *Edmonton Journal* reports that your organization plans to expand its owerations to include national distribution of sporting goods, and it occurs to me that you will be needing highly motivated, self-starting sales representatives and marketing managers. Here are three significant qualifications I have to offer:

- Four years of formal training in business administration, including specialized courses in sales management, retailing, marketing promotion, and consumer behaviour

- Practical experience in demonstrating and selling consumer products, as well as successful experience in telemarketing

- Excellent communication skills and a strong interest in most areas of sports (which helped me secure a volunteer position in the marketing department of the Edmonton Oilers organization)

Could we talk about how I can put these qualifications, and others summarized in the enclosed résumé, to work for Sports World as it develops its national sales force? I'll call during the week of June 5 to discuss your company's expansion plans and the opportunity for an interview.

Sincerely yours,

Donald W. Vinton

Donald W. Vinton

Enclosure

More challenging are unsolicited letters of application, such as Donald Vinton's, shown in Figure 12.14. Because he's writing a cover letter where no advertised job exists, he's essentially hoping to create a job. For this reason his opening must grab the reader's attention immediately. To do this, he capitalizes on company information appearing in an online news story. Donald purposely keeps his application letter short and to the point because he anticipates that a busy manager will be unwilling to read a long, detailed letter. Donald's unsolicited letter "prospects" for a job. Some job candidates feel that such letters may be even more productive than efforts to secure advertised jobs, since prospecting candidates face less competition. Donald's letter uses a standard return address format, placing his name, street, city, province, and postal code above the date.

12.5b Build Interest in the Body

Once you've captured the attention of the reader, you can use the body of the letter to build interest and reduce resistance. Keep in mind that your résumé emphasizes what you've done in the past; your cover letter stresses what you can do in the future for the employer.

Your first goal is to relate your letter to a specific position. If you're responding to a listing, you'll want to explain how your preparation and experience fill the stated requirements. If you're prospecting for a job, you may not know the exact requirements. Your employment research and knowledge of your field, however, should give you a reasonably good idea of what's expected for this position.

It's also important to emphasize reader benefits. In other words, describe your strong points in relation to the needs of the employer. This is much more important than telling the employer what courses you took in college or what duties you performed in your previous jobs. Instead of simply saying what you've done—*I've completed courses in business communication, report writing, and technical writing*—say *how* what you've done will be useful in the position for which you're applying:

> Courses in business communication, report writing, and technical writing have helped me develop the research and writing skills required of your technical writers.

Choose your strongest qualifications and show how they fit the targeted job. And remember, students with little experience are better off spotlighting their education and its practical applications, as these candidates did:

> Because you're looking for an architect's assistant with proven ability, I've submitted a drawing of mine that won second place in the Algonquin College drafting contest last year.

> Successfully transcribing over 100 letters in my college transcription class gave me experience in converting the spoken word into the written word, an important communication skill demanded of your legal assistants.

In the body of your letter, you'll also want to discuss relevant personal traits. Employers are looking for candidates who, among other things, are team players, take responsibility, show initiative, and learn easily. Finally, in this section or the next, you should refer the reader to your résumé. Do so directly or as part of another statement, as shown here:

> Please refer to the attached résumé for additional information regarding my education and experience.

> As you'll notice from my résumé, I am graduating in June with a bachelor's degree in business administration.

12.5c Motivate Action in the Closing

After presenting your case, you should conclude with a spur to action. This is where you ask for an interview. However, never directly ask for the job. To do so would be presumptuous and naive. In indirectly requesting an interview, suggest reader benefits or review your strongest points. Be sincere and appreciative. Remember to make it easy for the reader to agree by supplying your phone number, email address, and the best times to call you. And keep in mind that some recruiters prefer that you take the initiative to call them. Here are possible endings:

> I hope this brief description of my qualifications and the information on my résumé indicate to you my genuine desire to put my skills in accounting to work for you. Please call me at (416) 488-2291 before 10 a.m. or after 3 p.m. to arrange an interview.

> To add a hard-working, experienced strategic communications practitioner to your team, please call me at (604) 492-1433 to arrange an interview. I can meet with you at any time convenient to your schedule.

> Next week, after you have examined the attached résumé, I will call you to discuss the possibility of arranging an interview.

12.5d Avoid *I* Dominance

As you revise your cover letter, notice how many sentences begin with *I*. Although it's impossible to talk about yourself without using *I*, you can reduce the number of sentences beginning with this pronoun by using two techniques. First, place *I* in the middle of sentences instead of dominating the opening. Instead of *I was the top salesperson in my department*, try *While working in X department, I did Y and Z*, or *Among 15 coworkers, I received top ratings from my managers*. Incorporating *I* into the middle of sentences considerably reduces its domination.

A second technique for avoiding *I* dominance involves making activities and outcomes, not you, the subjects of sentences. For example, rather than *I took classes in business communication and search optimization*, say *Classes in business communication and search optimization prepared me to . . . .* Instead of *I enjoyed helping customers*, say *Helping customers taught me to be patient under stress*.

12.5e Send Your Cover Letter by Email

Virtually all résumés these days arrive by email or by automatic upload at a company's site or recruitment site. Some applicants make the mistake of not including cover letters with their résumés when they submit them by email. An application submitted electronically should contain two separate files: a cover letter file and a résumé file. An application that arrives without a cover letter makes the receiver wonder what it is and why it was sent. Recruiters want you to introduce yourself, and they also are eager to see some evidence of your personality and that you can write. Some candidates either skip the cover letter or think they can get by with one-line email cover notes such as this: *Please see attached résumé, and thanks for your consideration.*

If you're serious about landing the job, take the time to prepare a professional cover letter. As illustrated in Figure 12.15, an electronic application includes a brief cover note, plus the two files mentioned above, as attachments.

Cengage

MINDTAP

In MindTap go to the Study Tools for Chapter 12 and complete the Practice Test.

FIGURE 12.15 / Job Application Sent Electronically

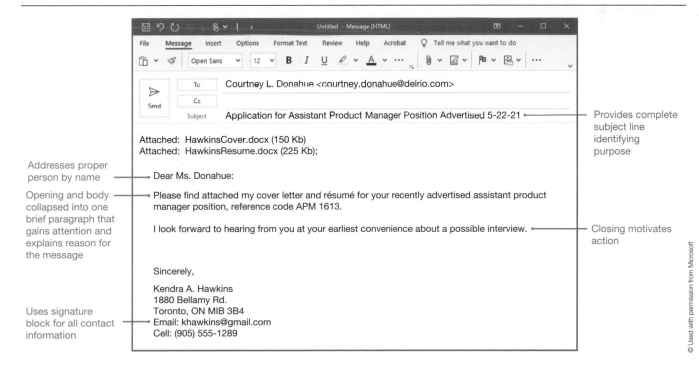

◤ LEARNING SUMMARY

12.1 Identify your employment interests and market requirements.

- Searching for a job has dramatically changed. Google, job sites, and social networks have all become indispensable tools in hunting for a job.

- Emphasis today is on what the employer wants, not what the candidate wants.

- Begin the job-search process by learning about yourself, your field of interest, and your qualifications. How do your skills match what employers seek?

- Search the Web, visit a campus career centre, take a summer job, interview someone in your field, volunteer, or join professional organizations.

- Identify job availability, the skills and qualifications required, duties, and salaries.

12.2 Use traditional and digital job-search techniques in the open and hidden markets.

- The primary sources of jobs today are networking (70 percent); job websites and company websites (20 percent); and recruitment agencies (10 percent).

- In searching the open job market—that is, jobs that are advertised—visit the big job sites, such as Indeed, Workopolis, and Charity Village.

- To find a job with a specific company, go directly to that company's website and check its openings and possibilities.

- Nearly all serious candidates today post profiles on LinkedIn.

- Estimates suggest that as many jobs are in the hidden job market—that is, unadvertised. Successful job candidates find jobs in the hidden job market through networking.

- An effective networking procedure involves (a) developing a contact list, (b) reaching out to contacts in person and online in search of referrals, and (c) following up on referrals.

- Because digital media and tools continue to change our lives, use social media networks—especially LinkedIn—to extend your networking efforts.

- Effective networking strategies include building a personal brand, preparing a professional business card with a tagline, composing a 30-second elevator speech that describes what you can offer, and developing a strong online presence.

12.3 Organize and format persuasive résumés.

- Because of intense competition, you must customize your résumés for every position you seek.

- Chronological résumés, which list work and education by dates, rank highest with recruiters. Functional résumés, which highlight skills instead of jobs, may be helpful for people with little experience, those changing careers, and those with negative employment histories.

Hybrid résumés use a chronological style but also highlight skills.

- In preparing a résumé, organize your skills and achievements to aim at a particular job or company.

- Study models to effectively arrange the résumé main heading and the optional career objective, summary of qualifications, education, work experience, capabilities, awards, and activities sections.

- The most effective résumés include action verbs to appeal to human readers and job-specific nouns that become keywords selected by applicant tracking systems.

- Look for ways to strengthen your résumé by polishing, proofreading, and checking for honesty and accuracy.

12.4 Use social media, video, and infographic résumés as alternatives to traditional résumés.

- To increase the probability of having your résumé selected by ATS, include specific keywords, especially nouns that name job titles, technical skills, and tools used or specific experience.

- A video résumé enables you to present your experience, qualifications, and interests in video form.

- An infographic résumé enables you to provide charts, graphics, and timelines to illustrate your work history and experience.

- Start with a basic print-based résumé from which you can make a plain-text résumé stripped of formatting to be embedded within email messages and submitted online.

12.5 Write a persuasive cover letter to accompany your résumé.

- Although cover messages are questioned by some in today's digital world, recruiters and hiring managers overwhelmingly favour them.

- Cover messages help recruiters make decisions, and they enable candidates to set themselves apart from others.

- In the opening of a cover message, gain attention by addressing the receiver by name and identifying the job. You might also identify the person who referred you.

- In the body of the message, build interest by stressing your strengths in relation to the stated requirements. Explain what you can do for the targeted company.

- In the body or closing, refer to your résumé, request an interview, and make it easy for the receiver to respond.

- If you're submitting your cover message by email, shorten it a bit and include your complete contact information in the signature block.

CHAPTER REVIEW

1. When preparing to search for a job, what should you do before writing a résumé? (Obj. 1)

2. What are the current trends in sources of new jobs? Which sources are trending upward and which are trending downward? (Obj. 2)

3. Although you may not actually find a job on the Internet, how can the big job sites be helpful to job hunters? (Obj. 2)

4. What is the hidden job market, and how can candidates find jobs in it? (Obj. 2)

5. In searching for a job, how can you build a personal brand, and why is it important to do so? (Obj. 2)

6. What is a customized résumé and why should you have one? (Obj. 3)

7. How do chronological and functional résumés differ, and what are the advantages and disadvantages of each? Is a hybrid résumé a better solution? (Obj. 3)

8. What is an ATS, and how does it affect the way you prepare a résumé? (Obj. 4)

9. How can you maximize the keyword hits in your résumé? What three categories are most important? (Obj. 4)

10. What are the three parts of a cover message, and what does each part contain? (Obj. 5)

CRITICAL THINKING

1. How has the concept of the job changed, and how will this affect your employment search? (Obj. 1)

2. To what degree is a social media profile (e.g., on LinkedIn or Facebook) a replacement for the traditional cover letter/résumé package? (Objs. 2, 4)

3. Is a résumé different from a job application form? (Obj. 3)

4. If a hybrid résumé combines the chronological and functional types, why isn't it the style everyone uses? (Obj. 3)

5. Some job candidates think that applying for unsolicited jobs can be more fruitful than applying for advertised openings. Discuss the advantages and disadvantages of letters that "prospect" for jobs. (Obj. 2)

6. **Ethical Issue:** At work, Karl confesses that he did not complete the degree he claims on his résumé. You've never liked Karl, but he does satisfactory work. You're both competing for the same promotion. You consider writing an anonymous note to the boss telling him to verify Karl's degree. Use Google or your library database to research Canadian guidelines for whistle-blowing at work. Based on your research, do you think your plan is a good one? (Objs. 1, 2)

7. A cover letter is a persuasive letter, but do you really want to reduce a potential employer's resistance? Why might this be dangerous? (Obj. 5)

ACTIVITIES AND CASES

12.1 INTERESTS AND QUALIFICATIONS INVENTORY (OBJ. 1)

It's often surprising what kind of information you can find out about your fellow classmates in a classroom setting. Imagine you are conducting a study for your college's co-op office or student association. The co-op office or student association wants to know the future career interests and aspirations of the college's students, as well as their current qualifications.

Your Task. Choose three people in your class (preferably classmates you don't know very well) and interview them. Ask them the questions listed in section 12.1a, "Identify Your Interests," and then the questions in section 12.1b, "Assess Your Qualifications." Develop a profile of each of your interviewees, and email this profile to your instructor. Your instructor may choose to share your inventory with you in a later class. How might you use this inventory for future networking purposes?

12.2 EVALUATING YOUR QUALIFICATIONS (OBJ. 1)

Your Task. Prepare four worksheets that inventory your own qualifications in the areas of employment; education; capabilities and skills; and honours and activities. Use active verbs when appropriate.

a. *Employment.* Begin with your most recent job or internship. For each position list the following information: employer; job title; dates of employment; and three to five duties, activities, or accomplishments. Emphasize activities related to your job goal. Strive to quantify your achievements.

b. *Education.* List degrees, certificates, diplomas, and training accomplishments. Include courses, seminars, or skills that are relevant to your job goal. Calculate your GPA in your major.

c. *Capabilities and skills.* List all capabilities and skills that recommend you for the job you seek. Use words such as *skilled*, *competent*, *trained*, *experienced*, and *ability to*. Also list five or more qualities or interpersonal skills necessary for a successful individual in your chosen field. Write action statements demonstrating that you possess some of these qualities. Empty assurances aren't good enough; try to show evidence (*Developed teamwork skills by working with a committee of eight to produce a . . .*).

d. *Awards, honours, and activities.* Explain any awards so that the reader will understand them. List school, community, and professional activities that suggest you are a well-rounded individual or possess traits relevant to your target job.

12.3 CHOOSING A CAREER PATH (OBJ. 1)

Your Task. Visit your school library, local library, or employment centre. Select an appropriate resource such as Employment and Social Development Canada's *National Occupational Classification* (https://www.canada.ca/en/employment-social-development/services/noc.html) to find a description for a position for which you could apply in two to five years. Photocopy or print the pages from the resource you chose that describe employment in the area in which you are interested. If your instructor directs, attach these copies to the cover letter you will write in Activity 12.10.Were you able to find the job that interests you? If not, where else can you find information on this job?

12.4 RÉSUMÉ RESEARCH (OBJ. 1)

By reading this chapter, you've learned about a number of different types of résumé. But what's reality like on the ground? Do employers care what the résumé looks like as long as it's well written? Or do they care a lot and have particular things they're looking for?

Your Task. Using the material from this chapter, develop a five- to ten-question survey about résumés. For example, do employers care what type of résumé applicants submit? What do employers look for in a résumé? What in a résumé turns them off a prospective candidate? Then identify three to five employers (people you know or who live in your area) and ask them to respond to your survey (this might be easier to do in person than over the phone or by email). Present the results of your primary research in a short memo or email or a presentation. Do your results corroborate or challenge what you learned in this chapter?

12.5 POSTING A RÉSUMÉ (OBJ. 1)

Learn about the procedure for posting résumés at job sites.

Your Task. Prepare a list of at least three online employment sites where you could post your résumé. Describe the procedure involved and the advantages of each site.

12.6 DRAFT DOCUMENT: RÉSUMÉ (OBJ. 3)

Analyze the following résumé. Discuss its strengths and weaknesses. Your instructor may ask you to revise sections of this résumé before showing you an improved version.

Winona Skudra
5349 Main Street
Saskatoon, SK S2N 0B4
Phone: (306) 834-4583 skudraw@lycos.ca.

Seeking to be hired at Meadow Products as an intern in Accounting

SKILLS: Accounting, Internet, MS Office 2013, Excel, PowerPoint, Freelance Graphics

EDUCATION

Now working on B.Comm. in Business Administration. Major, Management and Accounting; GPA is 3.5. Expect to graduate in June, 2021.

EXPERIENCE:

Assistant Accountant, 2014 to present. March and McLennan, Inc., Bookkeeping/Tax Service, Saskatoon. I keep accounting records for several small businesses accurately. I prepare 150 to 200 individual income tax returns each year. For Hill and Hill Trucking I maintain accurate and up-to-date A/R records. And I prepare payroll records for 16 employees at three firms.

Peterson Controls Inc., Saskatoon. Data Processing Internship, 2015 to present. I design and maintain spreadsheets and also process weekly and monthly information for production uptime and downtime. I prepare graphs to illustrate uptime and downtime data.

Saskatoon Curling Club. Accounts Payable Internship, 2015 to 2016. Took care of accounts payable including filing system for the club. Responsible for processing monthly adjusting entries for general ledger. Worked closely with treasurer to give the Board budget/disbursement figures regularly.

Saskatoon High School, Saskatoon. I marketed the VITA program to students and organized volunteers and supplies. Official title: Coordinator of Volunteer Income Tax Assistance Project.

COMMUNITY SERVICE: March of Dimes Drive, Central High School; All Souls Lutheran Church, coordinator for Children's Choir

12.7 DRAFT DOCUMENT: COVER LETTER (OBJ. 5)

Your Task. Analyze each section of the following cover letter written by an accounting major about to graduate.

Dear Human Resources Director:

Please consider this letter as an application for the position of staff accountant that I saw advertised in the Saskatoon *Star Phoenix*. Although I have had no paid work experience in this field, accounting has been my major in college and I'm sure I could be an asset to your company.

For four years I have studied accounting, and I am fully trained for full-charge bookkeeping as well as electronic accounting. I have completed 36 credits of college accounting and courses in business law, economics, statistics, finance, management, and marketing. In addition to my course work, during the tax season I have been a student volunteer for VITA. This is a project to help individuals in the community prepare their income tax returns, and I learned a lot from this experience. I have also received some experience in office work and working with figures when I was employed as an office assistant for Copy Quick, Inc.

I am a competent and responsible person who gets along pretty well with others. I have been a member of some college and social organizations and have even held elected office.

I feel that I have a strong foundation in accounting as a result of my course work and my experience. Along with my personal qualities and my desire to succeed, I hope that you will agree that I qualify for the position of staff accountant with your company.

Sincerely,

12.8 RÉSUMÉ (OBJ. 3)

Your Task. Using the data you developed in Activity 12.2, write your résumé. Aim it at a full-time job, part-time position, or internship. Attach a job listing for a specific position (from Activity 12.3). Revise your résumé until it is perfect.

12.9 COVER LETTER (OBJ. 5)

Your Task. Write a cover letter introducing your résumé from Activity 12.10. Revise your application letter until it is perfect in terms of written accuracy and formatting.

12.10 UNSOLICITED COVER LETTER (OBJ. 5)

As you read in this chapter, job applications are not always solicited. As part of your post-secondary education, you have no doubt come into contact with periodicals related to your field. For example, you may have read articles in *Canadian Business*, *Report on Business*, *HR Reporter*, *Marketing*, or any number of other magazines. In these magazines, you've come across the names of various businesspeople, either because they were featured in an article or because they were quoted as experts.

Your Task. Using your college or university library or local public library, read an issue of a business-related periodical or your local newspaper's business section. Look for a businessperson who is mentioned, quoted, or featured in that periodical. Write that person an unsolicited cover letter asking for an entry-level position or internship either for the summer or upon graduation. Make sure to revise this letter sufficiently, and hand it in to your instructor for comments before actually mailing it.

12.11 USING LINKEDIN TO ASSIST YOU IN YOUR JOB SEARCH (OBJ. 2)

LinkedIn is the acknowledged top site for job seekers and recruiters. It's free and easy to join. Even if you are not in the job market yet, becoming familiar with LinkedIn can open your eyes to the kinds of information that employers seek and also give you practice in filling in templates such as those that applicant tracking systems employ.

Your Task. To become familiar with LinkedIn, set up an account and complete a profile. This consists of a template with categories to fill in. The easiest way to begin is to view a LinkedIn video taking you through the steps of creating a profile. Search for *LinkedIn Profile Checklist*. It discusses how to fill in information in categories such as the following:

- **Photo.** Your photo doesn't have to be fancy. Just take a cell phone shot in front of a plain background. Wear a nice shirt and smile.
- **Headline.** Use a tagline to summarize your professional goals.
- **Summary.** Explain what motivates you, what you are skilled at, and where you want to go in the future.
- **Experience.** List the jobs you have held and be sure to enter the information precisely in the template categories. You can even include photos and videos of your work.

You can fill in other categories such as Organizations, Honours, Publications, and so forth. After completing a profile, discuss your LinkedIn experience with classmates. If you already have an account set up, discuss how it operates and your opinion of its worth. How can LinkedIn help students now and in the future?

12.12 TWEETING TO FIND A JOB (OBJ. 4)

Twitter résumés are a new twist on job hunting. While most job seekers struggle to contain their credentials on one page, others are tweeting their credentials in 140 characters or fewer! Here is an example from TheLadders.com:

> RT #SusanMoline seeks a LEAD/SR QA ENG JOB http://bit.ly/1ThaW @Talent-tEvolution - http://bit.ly/QB5DC @TweetMyJobs.com #résumé #QA-Jobs-QC

Are you scratching your head? Let's translate: (a) RT stands for retweet, allowing your Twitter followers to repeat this message to their followers. (b) The hashtag (#) always means *subject*; prefacing your name, it makes you easy to find. (c) The uppercase abbreviations indicate the job title, here *lead senior quality assurance engineer*. (d) The first link is a "tiny URL," a short, memorable Web address or alias provided free by TinyURL.com and other URL-shrinking services. It reveals the job seeker's Talent Evolution profile page. (e) The hashtags indicate the search terms used as seen here: name, quality assurance jobs in Québec, and the broad term *résumé*. When doing research from within Twitter, use the @ symbol with a specific Twitter user name or the # symbol for a subject search.

Your Task. As a team or individually, search the Web for *tweet résumé*. Describe to your peers the job-search process via Twitter presented on that website. Some services are free, whereas others come with charges. If you select a commercial service, critically evaluate its sales pitch and its claims. Is it worthwhile to spend money on this service? Do clients find jobs? How does the service try to demonstrate that? As a group or individually, share the results with the class.

12.13 EXPLORING INFOGRAPHIC RÉSUMÉS (OBJ. 4)
The latest trend in résumés is infographics. However, are they appropriate for every field?

Your Task. Do a Google search to locate 10 to 15 infographic résumés. Select your favourite three. Analyze them for readability, formatting, and colour. How many use timelines? What other similarities do you see? What career fields do they represent? Do you find any in your career field? In terms of your career field, what are the pros and cons of creating an infographic résumé? Do you think an infographic résumé would improve your chances of securing an interview? In an email to your instructor, summarize your findings and answer these questions.

12.14 E-PORTFOLIOS: JOB HUNTING IN THE TWENTY-FIRST CENTURY (OBJ. 4)
In high-tech fields digital portfolios have been steadily gaining in popularity and now seem to be going mainstream as universities are providing space for student job seekers to profile their qualifications in e-portfolios online. Although it is unlikely that digital portfolios will become widely used very soon, you would do well to learn about them by viewing many samples—good and bad.

Your Task. Conduct a Google search using the search term *student e-portfolios* or *student digital portfolios*. You will see long lists of hits, some of which will be actual digital document samples on the Web or instructions for creating an e-portfolio. Your instructor may assign individual students or teams to visit specific digital portfolio sites and ask them to summarize their findings in a memo or in a brief oral presentation. If this is your task, you could focus on the composition of the site, page layout, links provided, colours used, types of documents included, and so forth.

Alternatively, single groups or the whole class could study sites that provide how-to instructions and combine the advice of the best among them to create practical tips for making a digital portfolio. This option would lend itself to team writing, for example, with the help of a wiki. For either task a helpful place to start is the University of Toronto at Scarborough's Student Electronic Portfolio site at www.utsc.utoronto.ca/technology/student-electronic-portfolios.

12.15 COVER LETTER OPENING (OBJ. 5)

Your Task. James Nickson has just graduated from college with a three-year diploma in accounting. With the help of his college's career centre, James has begun applying for full-time employment. Below is the opening of one of James's cover letters. Analyze the letter, identify any problems, and rewrite this section of the letter following the guidelines in this chapter.

> To whom it may concern,
>
> It was a stroke of luck to find the job advertisement in the local newspaper last week for your company. I've always wanted to work for a company like yours, and this job opening may now give me the opportunity! My name is Jim Nickson and I just graduated in Accounting at a local college.

12.16 COVER LETTER BODY (OBJ. 5)

Your Task. Below is the body of James Nickson's cover letter. Analyze the letter, identify any problems, and rewrite this section of the letter following the guidelines in this chapter.

> As you can see from my enclosed résumé, I am a strong student, and I am also a good team player. I think these skills would be useful to me in your company. For example, I took a course in Auditing in which I received the highest GPA in the program. Finally, I have worked as a bookkeeper for the past two summers.

12.17 COVER LETTER CLOSING (OBJ. 5)

Your Task. The closing of James Nickson's cover letter is found below. Analyze the letter, identify any problems, and rewrite this section of the letter following the guidelines in this chapter.

> In closing, permit me to be blunt and say that there's nothing I'd like more than the opportunity to work for your company. I know I would be an asset to your organization. I look forward to hearing from you at your earliest convenience.
>
> Best,
> Jim Nickson

12.18 PRE-EMPLOYMENT TESTS (OBJ. 1)

As mentioned in the Workplace in Focus feature in this chapter, an important aspect of many recruitment scenarios today dis the pre-employment test. Broadly speaking, these tests, which happen as part of the interview process, fall into three types: specific skills tests (e.g. communication, math); personality tests (e.g. introversion versus extroversion); and situational tests (e.g. teamwork gone wrong, customer service problems). You can Google or Google Scholar *pre-employment test types* to find more information about these tools.

Your Task. Knowing that employers are generally looking for good communicators with strong interpersonal and soft skills, design two practice versions of a pre-employment test, one on communication skills and the other on interpersonal skills. Try not to make your tests multiple-choice tests. Instead, create situations or examples in which communication and soft skills are not happening effectively, and ask the test-taker to ensure that things improve. Once you've designed your tests, present them to the class or one on one to another student.

◤ GRAMMAR/MECHANICS CHALLENGE 12

NUMBER STYLE

Review Sections 4.03–4.13 of the Grammar/Mechanics Handbook. Then study each of the following pairs. Assume that these expressions appear in the context of letters, reports, or memos. In the answer spaces provided, write the preferred number style and the number of the G/M principle illustrated. When you finish, compare your responses with those provided near the end of the book. If your responses differ, study carefully the principles shown in parentheses.

<u>three (4.01a)</u>   **Example** He had (three, 3) cellphones.

_____	1. At least (20, twenty) candidates applied for the opening.
_____	2. The interview was on (Fourth, 4th) Street.
_____	3. Angelica saw (12, twelve) possible jobs listed on the Web.
_____	4. One job started on (June 1, June 1st).
_____	5. She filled her gas tank for ($40, forty dollars).
_____	6. She hoped to have a job by the (15th, fifteenth) of June.
_____	7. Her interview started at (3 p.m., 3:00 p.m.).
_____	8. The assistant edited (4 three-page, four 3-page) memos.
_____	9. She founded her company over (40, forty) years ago.

10. About (3 million; 3,000,000) people visited Monster.com.

11. (16, Sixteen) candidates applied for one open position.

12. I need (50, fifty) cents for the machine.

13. She graduated at the age of (21, twenty-one).

14. The interest rate on her loan was (7, seven) percent.

15. Only (4, four) of the 35 email messages were undelivered.

◣ EDITING CHALLENGE 12

The message has proofreading, spelling, grammar, punctuation, wordiness, number for, word use, wordiness, and other writing faults that require correction. Study the guidelines in the Grammar/Mechanics Handbook, as well as the lists of Confusing Words and Frequently Misspelled Words at the end of the book, to sharpen your skills. When you finish making corrections, your instructor can show you the revised version of this résumé.

Your Task. Edit the following message by correcting its errors (a) in your textbook or (b) on a photocopy using proofreading marks from Appendix B.

MEGAN A. Kozlov
245 Topsail Street
St. John's, Newfoundland A1B 3Z4
makozlov@hotmail.com

EDUCATION
Memorial University, St. John's, Newfoundland. Bachelor of Arts Degree expected in June 2022. Major English.

EXPERIENCE:
- Administrative Assistant. Host Systems, St. John's. 2017 too pressent. Responsible for entering data on the computer. I had to insure accuracy and completness of data that was to be entered. Another duty was maintaining a clean and well-organized office. I also served as Office Courier.

- Lechter's Housewares. Outlook Newfoundland. 2015-2018. 2nd Asst. Mgr I managed store In absence of mgr. and asst. mgr. I open and close registers. Ballanced daily reciepts. Ordered some mds. I also had to supervise 2 employes, earning rabid promotion.

- Office Assistant. Sunshine Travel Outlook. 2014–2015. (part time) Entered travel information onto a spreadsheet. Did personalized followup emails to customer inquirys. Was responsible for phones. I also handled all errands as courier.

STRENGTHS
Microsoft Office Applications, transcription, poofreading.
Can input 50 words/per/minute.
I am a fast learner, and very accurate.
Msoffice 2017 including Excell, Access, and Outlook,

© Olena Yakobchuk/Shutterstock

OBJECTIVES

13.1 Explain the purposes and types of job interviews.

13.2 Know what to do before an interview to make an impressive initial contact.

13.3 Know what to do during an interview to create a favourable impression.

13.4 Know what to do immediately after an interview to maintain the positive impression you've created.

13.5 Prepare useful employment-related documents.

INTERVIEWS AND FOLLOW-UP

▶ BIZ COMM BYTE

According to research published on careergeekblog.com, the most common nonverbal mistakes made by candidates (as reported by recruiters) during job interviews are, first, at 67 percent, not making eye contact with the interviewers; second, at 47 percent, having little to no knowledge of the company at which you're interviewing; and third, at 38 percent, not smiling at the people interviewing you.

Source: Faizan Patankar. (nd). Statistics behind what happens in a job interview. https://www.careergeekblog.com/what-happens-in-job-interview/

◢ 13.1 Purposes and Types of Employment Interviews

Whether you're completing your education and searching for your first full-time position or in the workforce and striving to change jobs, a job interview can be life changing. Because employment is a major part of everyone's life, job interviews take on enormous importance.

Most people consider job interviews to be extremely stressful. However, the more you learn about the process and the more prepared you are, the less stress you'll feel. Also, a job interview is a two-way street. It's not just about being judged by the employer. You, the candidate, will be using the job interview to evaluate the employer and find out if you really want to work for this organization.

Clearly, job interviews are intimidating for most of us. No one enjoys being judged and possibly rejected. Everyone is uneasy about being scrutinized and questioned. But think of how much more nervous you'd be if you had no idea what to expect in the interview and were unprepared.

You can also expect to succeed in an interview when you know what's coming and when you prepare thoroughly. Remember, it's often the degree of preparation as well as the appearance of confidence that determines who gets the job.

13.1a Purposes of Employment Interviews

An interview is your opportunity to (a) convince the employer of your potential, (b) learn more about the job and the company, and (c) expand on the information in your résumé. This is the time for you to gather information about whether you would fit into the company culture. You should also be thinking about whether this job suits your career goals.

From the employer's perspective, the interview is an opportunity to (a) assess your abilities in relation to the requirements for the position; (b) discuss your training, experience, knowledge, and abilities in more detail; (c) see what drives and motivates you; and (d) decide whether you would fit into the organization.

13.1b Types of Employment Interviews

Job applicants generally face two interviews: screening interviews and hiring/placement interviews, as shown in Figure 13.1. You must succeed in the first to proceed to the second. After you make it to the hiring/placement interview, you'll find a variety of interview styles, including one-on-one, panel, group, sequential, stress, and online interviews. You'll be better prepared if you know what to expect in each type of interview.

SCREENING INTERVIEWS. Screening interviews eliminate candidates who fail to meet minimum hard skill requirements. Companies use screening interviews to save time and money by weeding out lesser-qualified candidates before scheduling face-to-face interviews. Although some screening interviews are conducted during job fairs or on college campuses, many screening interviews take place on the telephone, and some take place online; for example, by using conversational chatbots.

Today, screening interviews are often completed using specialized software. Companies like Self Management Group sell simulation software to organizations in various sectors, such as banking and retail. According to the sales pitch for these products, they can help these companies "make better hiring decisions and select candidates who are more likely to stay, perform, and deliver results."[1]

In essence, the screening software experience is like taking a test in an online course or when applying for a driver's licence. During a screening interview, the interviewer will probably ask you to provide details about the education and experience listed on your résumé; therefore, you must be prepared to promote your qualifications. Remember that the person conducting the screening interview is trying to determine whether you should move on to the next step in the interview process.

A screening interview may be as short as five minutes. Even though it may be short, don't treat it casually. If you don't perform well, it may be your last interview with that organization. You can use the tips that follow in this chapter to succeed during the screening process.

HIRING/PLACEMENT INTERVIEWS. The most promising candidates selected from screening interviews will be invited to hiring/placement interviews. Hiring managers want to learn whether candidates are motivated, qualified, and a good fit for the position. Their goal is to learn how the candidate would fit into their organization. Conducted in depth, hiring/placement interviews may take many forms.

ONE-ON-ONE INTERVIEWS. This is the most common interview type. You can expect to sit down with a company representative (or two) and talk about the job and your qualifications. If the representative is the hiring manager, questions will be specific and job-related. If the representative is from the human resources department, the questions will probably be more general.

Cengage

MINDTAP

In MindTap go to the Whiteboard Animation for Chapter 13 and watch it now.

1. Know the interviewing sequence

- Expect a telephone screening interview.
- If you are successful, next comes the hiring interview.
- Be prepared to answer questions in a one-on-one, panel, group, or video interview.

2. Research the target company

- Study the company's history, mission, goals, size, and management structure.
- Know its strengths and weaknesses.
- Try to connect with someone in the company.

3. Prepare thoroughly

- Rehearse detailed but brief success stories.
- Practise stories that illustrate dealing with a crisis, handling tough situations, juggling priorities, and working on a team.
- Clean up your online presence.

4. Look sharp, be sharp

- Suit up! Dress professionally to feel confident.
- Be ready for questions that gauge your interest, explore your experience, and reveal your skills.
- Practise using the STAR method to answer behavioral questions.

5. End positively

- Summarize your strongest qualifications.
- Show enthusiasm; say that you want the job!
- Ask what happens next.

6. Follow up

- Send a note thanking the interviewer.
- Contact your references.
- Check in with the interviewer if you hear nothing after five days.

PANEL INTERVIEWS. Panel interviews are typically conducted by people who'll be your supervisors and colleagues. Usually seated around a table, interviewers may take turns asking questions. Panel interviews are advantageous because they save time and show you how the staff works together. For these interviews, you can prepare basic biographical information about each panel member. When answering questions, maintain eye contact with the questioner and with the other team members. Try to take notes during the interview so that you can remember each person's questions and what was important to that individual.[2]

GROUP INTERVIEWS. Group interviews occur when a company interviews several candidates for the same position at the same time. Some employers use this technique to measure leadership skills and communication styles. During a group interview, stay focused on the interviewer and treat the other candidates with respect. Even if you're nervous, try to remain calm, take your time when responding, and express yourself clearly. The key during a group interview is to make yourself stand out from the other candidates in a positive way.[3]

SEQUENTIAL INTERVIEWS. In a sequential interview, you meet individually with two or more interviewers over the course of several hours or days. For example, you may meet separately with human resources representatives, your hiring manager, and potential future supervisors and colleagues in your division or department. You must listen carefully and respond positively to all interviewers. Promote your qualifications to each one; don't assume that any interviewer knows what was said in a previous interview. Keep your responses fresh, even when repeating yourself many times. Subsequent interviews also tend to be more in-depth than first interviews, which means that you need to be even more prepared and know even more about the company.

ONLINE, VIDEO, AND VIRTUAL INTERVIEWS. Many companies today use technology to interview job candidates from a distance. Although conference call interviews have a long tradition, today's savvy companies use webcams and video-conferencing software to conduct interviews.

Using Skype and a webcam saves job applicants and companies time and money, especially when applicants are not in the same geographic location as the company. Even though your interview may be online, conducted with videoconferencing software and a webcam, don't take it any less seriously than a face-to-face interview.

Despite the technical ability to conduct interviews online through videoconferencing, there is evidence that, although flexible and time-saving, these types of interviews are not viewed in as positive a light (by both employers and candidates) as traditional in-person interviews.[4]

◤ 13.2 Before the Interview

Being active in the job market means that you must be prepared to be contacted by potential employers. As discussed earlier, employers use screening interviews to narrow the list of candidates. If you do well in the screening interview, you'll be invited to an in-person or online meeting. Below are tips for how to prepare yourself before an interview.

13.2a Use Professional Phone Techniques

Even with the popularity of email, many employers still contact job applicants by phone to set up interviews. Employers can judge how well applicants communicate by hearing their voices, expressions, and tone over the phone. Therefore, once you are actively looking for a job, remember that any time the phone rings it could be a potential employer. Don't make the mistake of letting an unprofessional voice mail message or an unfriendly-sounding roommate ruin your chances. Here's how you can avoid such problems:

- Make sure that your voice mail instructions are concise and professional, with no distracting background sounds. If your home voice mail instructions are for your entire family, consider offering only your personal cell phone number on your résumé. The instructions should be in your own voice and include your full name for clarity.
- Tell anyone who might answer your phone about your job search. Explain to them the importance of acting professionally and taking complete messages. Family members or roommates can affect the first impression an employer has of you.
- Don't answer your cell phone unless you're in a quiet enough location to have a conversation with a prospective employer. It's hard to pay close attention when you're in a noisy restaurant or on a crowded bus. That said, if you do answer the phone in a noisy situation and find an employer on the other end, say hello politely, identify yourself, apologize for the noise, and ask whether the employer wants to continue the conversation or have you call back shortly.

13.2b Make the First Conversation Impressive

Whether you answer the phone directly or return an employer's call, make sure you're prepared for the conversation. Remember that this is the first time the employer has heard your voice. How you conduct yourself on the phone will create a lasting impression. To make that first impression a positive one, follow these tips:

- Keep a list near or in your phones of the positions for which you've applied.
- Treat any call from an employer just like an interview. Use a professional tone and appropriate language. Be polite and enthusiastic, and sell your qualifications.
- If caught off guard by the call, ask whether you can call back in a few minutes. Organize your materials and yourself.
- Have a copy of your résumé available so that you can answer any questions that come up. Also have your list of references, a calendar, and a notepad handy. If you're talking on a smartphone, you'll be able to access a calendar and notepad on the phone itself.
- Be prepared to undergo a screening interview. As discussed earlier, this might occur during the first phone call.
- Take notes during the phone conversation. Obtain accurate directions, and verify the spelling of your interviewer's name. If you'll be interviewed by more than one person, get all of their names.
- Before you hang up, reconfirm the date and time of your interview. You could say something like *I look forward to meeting with you next Wednesday at 2 p.m.*

13.2c Research the Target Company

After you've scheduled an in-person or online interview, start preparing for it. One of the most important steps in effective interviewing is gathering detailed information about a prospective employer. Never enter an interview cold. Recruiters are impressed by candidates who have done their homework.

Search the potential employer's website, Google, and trade publications.[5] Learn all you can about the company's history, mission and goals, size, geographic locations, number of employees, customers, competitors, culture, management structure, reputation in the community, financial condition, strengths and weaknesses, and future plans, as well as the names of its leaders. Also, learn what you can about the industry in which the company operates. Visit the library and explore your campus career centre to find additional information about the target company and its field, service, or product.

Analyze the company's advertising. One candidate spent a great deal of time poring over brochures from an aerospace contractor. During his initial interview, he shocked and impressed the recruiter with his knowledge of the company's guidance systems. The candidate had, in fact, relieved the interviewer of his least-favourite task—explaining the company's complicated technology.

Talking with company employees is always a good idea, if you can manage it. They are probably the best source of inside information. Try to speak to someone who's currently employed there, but not working in the immediate area where you want to be hired. You may be able to find this person by using LinkedIn. Remember, however, that asking favours of someone who doesn't know you is a risky proposition and is best handled with complete transparency.

Finally, you may also want to connect with the company through social media. "Like" the company on Facebook and comment shrewdly on the organization's status updates and other posts. You may hear about vacancies before they're advertised. If you follow the company and its key people on Twitter, you may draw some positive attention to yourself and perhaps even hear about up-to-the-minute job openings. If you know the interviewers' names, look up their profiles on LinkedIn but don't try to connect with them before actually meeting them.[6]

In learning about a company, you may uncover information that convinces you that this is not the company for you. It's always better to learn about negatives early in the process. More likely, though, the information you collect will help you tailor your interview responses to the organization's needs. Employers are pleased when job candidates take an interest in them. Be ready to put in plenty of effort in investigating a target employer because this effort really pays off at interview time.

In addition, one of the best things a job seeker can do is to get into the habit of reading the newspaper regularly. The best place to go for current information on Canadian companies is the business sections of the two national newspapers: nationalpost.com and www.theglobeandmail.com. Your local city or town newspaper will occasionally profile local businesses.

13.2d Prepare and Practise

After you've learned about the target organization, study the job description. As mentioned earlier, successful job candidates never go into interviews cold. They prepare success stories and practise answers to typical questions. They also plan their responses to any problem areas on their résumés. As part of their preparation before the interview, they decide what to wear, and they gather the items they plan to take with them, such as a portfolio of projects completed.

REHEARSE SUCCESS STORIES. To feel confident and be able to sell your qualifications, prepare and practise success stories. These are specific examples of your educational and work-related experience that demonstrate your qualifications and achievements. Look over the job description and your résumé to determine what skills, training, personal characteristics, and experience you want to emphasize during the interview. Then prepare a success story for each one. Quantify whenever possible, for example, by mentioning dollars saved or percentage of sales increased. Your success stories should be detailed but brief. Think of them as 30-second sound bites.

Practise telling your stories until you can tell them fluently and they sound natural. Then in the interview be certain to find places to insert them. Tell stories about (a) dealing with a crisis, (b) handling a tough interpersonal situation, (c) successfully juggling many priorities, (d) changing course to deal with changed circumstances, (e) learning from a mistake, (f) working on a team, and (g) going beyond expectations.

PRACTISE ANSWERS TO POSSIBLE QUESTIONS. Imagine the kinds of questions you may be asked and work out sample answers. Although you can't anticipate precise questions, you can expect to be asked about your education, skills, experience, and availability. Practise answering some typical interview questions aloud, either in a mirror, with a friend, while driving in your car, or before going to bed. Keep practising until you have the best responses memorized. Consider recording a practice session to see and hear how you answer questions. Do you look and sound enthusiastic?

CLEAN UP DIGITAL DIRT. A study showed that 45 percent of employers screen candidates using Google and social networking sites such as Facebook, LinkedIn, and Twitter.[7] Even more important, 70 percent of recruiters have found something online that caused them not to hire a candidate.[8] The top reasons for not considering an applicant after an online search are that the candidate (a) posted provocative or inappropriate photographs or information; (b) posted content about drinking or doing drugs; (c) talked negatively about current or previous employers, colleagues, or clients; (d) exhibited poor communication skills; (e) made discriminatory comments; (f) lied about qualifications; or (g) revealed a current or previous employer's confidential information.

For example, the president of a small consulting company was about to hire a summer intern when he discovered the student's Facebook page. The candidate described his interests as "smoking' blunts [cigars hollowed out and stuffed with marijuana], shooting people and obsessive sex." The executive quickly lost interest in this candidate. Even if the student was merely posturing, his page showed poor judgment. Teasing photographs and provocative comments about drinking, drug use, and sexual exploits make students look immature and unprofessional. Follow these steps to clean up your online presence:

- **Remove questionable content.** Delete incriminating, provocative, or distasteful photos, content, and links that could make you look unprofessional to potential employers.
- **Stay positive.** Don't complain about things in your professional or personal life online. Even negative reviews you've written on various sites can turn employers off.
- **Be selective about who's on your list of friends.** You don't want to miss an opportunity because you seem to associate with negative, immature, or unprofessional people. Your best bet is to make your personal social media pages private.

Cengage

MINDTAP

In MindTap, go to the Chapter 13 reading, section 13.2c, and watch the video of industry expert Candice Wong discussing best practices when preparing for job interviews.

- **Avoid joining groups or pages that may be viewed negatively.** Remember that online searches can turn up your online activities, including group memberships, blog postings, and so on. If you think any activity you are involved in might show poor judgment, remove yourself immediately.
- **Don't discuss your job search if you're still employed.** Employees can find themselves in trouble with their current employers by writing status updates or sending tweets about their job search.
- **Set up a professional social media page or create your own personal website.** Use Facebook, LinkedIn, or other social networking sites to create a professional page. Many employers actually find information during their online searches that convinces them to hire candidates. Make sure your professional page demonstrates creativity, strong communication skills, and well-roundedness.[9]

EXPECT TO EXPLAIN PROBLEM AREAS ON YOUR RÉSUMÉ. Interviewers are certain to question you about problem areas on your résumé. If you have little or no experience, you might emphasize your recent training and up-to-date skills. If you have gaps in your résumé, be prepared to answer questions about them positively and truthfully. If you were fired from a job, accept some responsibility for what happened and explain what you gained from the experience. Don't criticize a previous employer, and don't hide the real reasons. If you earned low grades in one term, explain why and point to your improved grades in subsequent terms.

DECIDE HOW TO DRESS. What you wear to a job interview still matters. Even if some employees in the organization dress casually, you should look qualified, competent, and successful. When in doubt, a suit is a good idea as it will probably be expected. Avoid loud colours; strive for a coordinated, natural appearance. Favourite colours for interviews are grey and dark blue. Don't overdo jewellery, and make sure that what you do wear is clean, pressed, odour-free, and lint-free. Shoes should be polished and scuff-free, and they should be "dress" shoes, not running shoes.

GATHER ITEMS TO BRING. Decide what you should bring with you to the interview, and get everything ready the night before. You should plan to bring copies of your résumé, your references list, a pad of paper and pen, money for parking or for public transit, and samples of your work, if appropriate. If you deem the workplace to be tech savvy, bring along your smartphone or tablet if you own one, just in case. Place everything in a businesslike bag, briefcase, or folder to add a final professional touch to your look.

13.2e Get to Your Interview

The big day has arrived! Ideally you're fully prepared for your interview. Now you need to make sure that everything goes smoothly. That means arriving on time and handling that fear you're likely to feel.

On the morning of your interview, give yourself plenty of time to groom and dress. Then give yourself ample time to get to the employer's office. If something unexpected happens that will cause you to be late, such as an accident or a transit issue, call the interviewer right away to explain what's happening. On the way to the interview, don't smoke, don't eat anything messy or smelly, and don't use perfume or cologne. Arrive at the interview five or ten minutes early.

When you enter the office, be courteous to everyone. Remember that you're being judged not only by the interviewer but by the receptionist and anyone else who sees you before and after the interview. They'll notice how you sit, what you read, and how you look. Introduce yourself to the receptionist if there is one, and to whomever else you may bump into, and wait to be invited to sit.

Greet the interviewer confidently, and don't be afraid to initiate a handshake, if appropriate. Doing so exhibits professionalism and confidence. Extend your hand, look the interviewer directly in the eye, smile pleasantly, and say, *I'm pleased to meet you, Mr. Thomas. I'm Constance Ferraro.* A firm but not crushing handshake sends a nonverbal message of assurance. Once introductions have taken place, wait for the interviewer to offer you a chair. Make small talk with upbeat comments, such as *This is a beautiful headquarters* or *I'm very impressed with the facilities you have here*. Don't immediately begin rummaging in your briefcase, bag, or folder for your résumé. Being at ease and unrushed suggest that you're self-confident.

13.2f Fight Fear

Expect to be nervous before and during the interview: it's natural! Other than public speaking, employment interviews are some of the most anxiety-inducing events in people's lives. One of the best ways to overcome fear is to know what happens in a typical interview. You can further reduce your fears by following these suggestions:

- **Practise interviewing.** Try to get as much interviewing practice as you can—especially with real companies. The more times you experience the interview situation, the less nervous you'll be. If offered, campus mock interviews also provide excellent practice, and the interviewers will offer tips for improvement.
- **Prepare thoroughly.** Research the company. Know how you'll answer the most frequently asked questions. Be ready with success stories. Rehearse your closing statement. One of the best ways to reduce butterflies is to know that you've done all you can to be ready for the interview.
- **Understand the process.** Find out ahead of time how the interview will be structured. Will you be meeting with an individual, or will you be interviewed by a panel? Is this the first of a series of interviews? Don't be afraid to ask about these details before the interview so that an unfamiliar situation won't catch you off guard.
- **Dress professionally.** If you know you look sharp, you will feel more confident.
- **Breathe deeply.** Take deep breaths, particularly if you feel anxious while waiting for the interviewer. Deep breathing makes you concentrate on something other than the interview and also provides much-needed oxygen.
- **Know that you are not alone.** Everyone feels some level of anxiety during a job interview. Interviewers expect some nervousness, and a skilled interviewer will try to put you at ease.
- **Remember that an interview is a two-way street.** The interviewer isn't the only one who's gleaning information. You have come to learn about the job and the company. In fact, during some parts of the interview, you'll be in charge. This should give you courage.

◤ 13.3 During the Interview

During the interview you'll be answering questions and asking some of your own. Your behaviour, body language, and other nonverbal cues will also be on display. The interviewer will be trying to learn more about you, and you should learn more about the job and the organization. Although you may be asked some unique questions, many interviewers ask standard, time-proven questions, which means that you can prepare your answers ahead of time.

13.3a Send Positive Nonverbal Messages and Act Professionally

You've already sent nonverbal messages to your interviewer by arriving on time, being courteous, dressing professionally, and greeting the receptionist confidently.

Continue to send positive nonverbal messages throughout the interview. Remember that what comes out of your mouth and what is written on your résumé are not the only messages an interviewer receives from you. Here are suggestions that will help you send the right nonverbal messages during interviews:

- **Control your body movements.** Keep your hands, arms, and elbows to yourself. Don't lean on a desk. Keep your feet on the floor. Don't cross your arms in front of you. Keep your hands out of your pockets.

WORKPLACE IN FOCUS

Despite the advice and best practices discussed so far in this chapter—all of which is important and useful—a growing number of Canadian organizations are using conversational artificial intelligence (AI) to replace the traditional human interaction in a job interview. Conversational AI, like other chatbot situations (e.g., customer service help chatbots, library help chatbots) puts candidates in front of a chatscreen, and the chatbot—not a human recruiter—engages the candidates in conversational questions that constitute a job interview. Where a human-to-human interview allows for and is highly influenced by factors such as nervousness, smiles, handshakes, clothing, and getting comfortable in a chair, a human-to-chatbot situation is different. There isn't time for or benefit in any of the above behaviours. Instead, candidates need to get their answers typed into the chat box efficiently and effectively. This means using the kinds of streamlining techniques discussed earlier in this book, such as using graphic highlighting (numbering, listing) and using verbal cues such as *first*, *second*, and *third*. Knowing you might face a chatbot

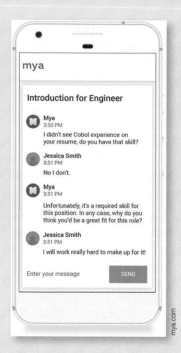

instead of a human recruiter at your next job interview, how might you change your strategy for describing yourself and your experiences?

Source: HR Daily Advisor. (2018, July 23). Is conversational AI a recruiting revolution? https://hrdailyadvisor.blr.com/2018/07/23/conversational-ai-recruiting-revolution/

- **Exhibit good posture.** Sit erect, leaning forward slightly. Don't slouch in your chair; at the same time, don't look too stiff and uncomfortable. Good posture demonstrates confidence and interest.
- **Practise appropriate eye contact.** A direct eye gaze, at least in North America, suggests interest and trustworthiness. If you're being interviewed by a panel, remember to maintain eye contact with all interviewers.
- **Use gestures effectively.** Nod to show agreement and interest. Gestures should be used as needed, but don't overdo it.
- **Smile enough to convey a positive attitude.** Have a friend give you honest feedback on whether you generally smile too much or not enough.
- **Listen attentively.** Show the interviewer you're interested and attentive by listening carefully to the questions being asked. This will also help you answer questions appropriately.
- **Turn off your devices.** Avoid the embarrassment of allowing your phone to ring, or even to buzz, during an interview. Turn phones off completely; don't just switch them to vibrate.
- **Don't chew gum.** Chewing gum during an interview is distracting and unprofessional.
- **Sound enthusiastic and interested—but sincere.** The tone of your voice has an enormous effect on the words you say. Avoid sounding bored, frustrated, or sarcastic during an interview. Employers want employees who are enthusiastic and interested.
- **Avoid "empty" words.** Filling your answers with verbal pauses such as *um*, *uh*, *like*, *totally* and *basically* communicates that you're not prepared. Also avoid annoying distractions such as clearing your throat repeatedly or sighing deeply.

Above all, remember that employers want to hire people who have confidence in their own abilities. Let your body language, posture, dress, and vocal tone prove that you're self-assured.

13.3b Answer Typical Questions Confidently

The way you answer questions can be almost as important as what you say. Use the interviewer's name and title from time to time when you answer: *Ms. Lyon, I'd be pleased to tell you about . . . .* People like to hear their own names. But be sure you're pronouncing the name correctly. Avoid answering questions with a simple *yes or no*; elaborate on your answers to better promote yourself and your assets. Keep answers positive; try not to criticize anything or anyone.

Occasionally it may be necessary to clarify vague questions. Some interviewers are inexperienced in the role. You may have to ask your own question to understand what was asked: *By . . . do you mean . . . ?*

Consider closing some of your responses with Does that answer your question? or Would you like me to elaborate on any particular experience?

Always aim your answers at the key characteristics interviewers seek: expertise and competence, motivation, interpersonal skills, decision-making skills, enthusiasm for the job, and a pleasing personality. And remember to stay focused on your strengths. Don't reveal weaknesses, even if you think they make you look human. You won't be hired for your weaknesses, only for your strengths.

Enunciate clearly: remember that you'll be judged by how well you communicate. Avoid slurred words such as *gonna* and *y'know*, as well as slangy expressions such as *yeah*, *like*, and *awesome*. Also eliminate verbal static (*ah* and *um*). As you practise for the interview, a good idea is to record answers to expected interview questions. Is your speech filled with verbal static?

You can't expect to be perfect in an employment interview. No one is. But you can increase your chances of success by avoiding the behaviours described in Figure 13.2.

The following section presents questions that are often asked during employment interviews. To get you thinking about how to respond, we've provided an answer or discussion for the first question in each group. As you read the remaining questions in each group, think about how you could respond most effectively.

▼ **FIGURE 13.2 /** Interview Actions to Avoid

A survey of recruiters showed that between 26 percent and 65 percent of candidates commit these errors during interviews.

The Six Most Common Interview Mistakes to Avoid

65% Failing to make eye contact

36% Failing to smile

33% Playing with something on the table

30% Having bad posture

29% Fidgeting too much in their seat

26% Crossing their arms over their chest

Data courtesy of CareerBuilder

QUESTIONS TO GET ACQUAINTED. After introductions, recruiters generally start the interviewing with personal questions that put the candidate at ease. They're also striving to gain a picture of the candidate to see if he or she will fit into the organization's culture.

1. Tell me about yourself.

   Experts agree that you must keep this answer short (one to two minutes, tops) but on target. Try practising this formula: "My name is _____. I've completed a _____ degree with a major in _____. Recently I worked for _____ as a _____. Before that I worked for _____ as a _____. My strengths are _____ (interpersonal) and _____ (technical)." Try rehearsing your response in 30-second segments devoted to your education, your work experience, and your qualities and skills. Some candidates end with "Now that I've told you about myself, can you tell me a little more about the position?"

2. What are your greatest strengths?
3. Do you prefer to work by yourself or with others? Why?
4. What was your major in college, and why did you choose it?
5. What are some things you do in your spare time?

QUESTIONS TO GAUGE YOUR INTEREST. Interviewers want to understand your motivation for applying for a position. Although they realize you're probably interviewing for other positions, they still want to know why you're interested in this particular position with this organization. These types of questions help them determine your level of interest.

1. Why do you want to work for (*name of company*)?

   Questions like this illustrate why you must research an organization thoroughly before the interview. The answer to this question must prove that you understand the company and its culture. This is the perfect place to bring up the company research you did before the interview. Show what you know about the company, and discuss why you'd like to become a part of this organization. Describe your desire to work for this organization not only from your perspective but also from its point of view. What do you have to offer?

2. Why are you interested in this position?
3. What do you know about our company?
4. Why do you want to work in the _____ industry?
5. What interests you about our products (services)?

QUESTIONS ABOUT YOUR EXPERIENCE AND ACCOMPLISHMENTS. After questions about your background and education, the interview generally becomes more specific, with questions about your experience and accomplishments.

1. Why should we hire you when we have applicants with more experience or better credentials?

   In answering this question, remember that employers often hire people who present themselves well instead of others with better credentials. Emphasize your personal strengths that could be an advantage with this employer. Are you a hard worker? How can you demonstrate it? Have you had recent training? Some people have had more years of experience but actually have less knowledge because they have done the same thing over and over. Stress your experience using new technologies and equipment. Be sure to mention any software you can use effectively. Emphasize that you're open to new ideas and learn quickly.

2. Describe the most rewarding experience of your career so far.
3. How have your education and professional experiences prepared you for this position?
4. What were your major accomplishments in each of your past jobs?
5. What was a typical workday like?
6. What job functions did you enjoy most? Least? Why?
7. Tell me about your technology skills.
8. Who was the toughest boss you ever worked for and why?
9. What were your major achievements in college?
10. Why did you leave your last position? OR: Why are you leaving your current position?

QUESTIONS ABOUT THE FUTURE. Questions that look into the future tend to stump some candidates, especially those who haven't prepared adequately. Some of these questions give you a chance to discuss your personal future goals, and others require you to think on your feet and explain how you would respond in hypothetical situations.

1. Where do you expect to be five (or ten) years from now?

   Formulate a realistic plan with respect to your present age and situation. The important thing is to be prepared for this question. Show an interest in the current job and in making a contribution to the organization. Talk about the levels of responsibility you'd like to achieve. One employment counsellor suggests showing ambition but not committing to a specific job title. Suggest that you hope to learn enough to have progressed to a position in which you will continue to grow. Keep your answer focused on educational and professional goals, not personal goals.

2. If you were hired for this position, what would you do to be sure you fit in?
3. This is a large (or small) organization. Do you think you'd like that environment?
4. Do you plan to continue your education?
5. What do you predict for the future of the _____ industry?
6. How do you think you can contribute to this company?
7. What would you most like to accomplish if you get this position?
8. How do you keep current with what's happening in your profession?

CHALLENGING QUESTIONS. The following questions may make you uncomfortable, but the important thing to remember is to answer truthfully without dwelling on your weaknesses. As quickly as possible, convert any negative response into a discussion of your strengths.

1. What are your greatest weaknesses?

   It's amazing how many candidates knock themselves out of the competition by answering this question poorly. Actually, you have many choices. You can present a strength as a weakness (*Some people complain that I'm a workaholic or too attentive to details*). You can mention a corrected weakness (*I found that I really needed to learn about the Internet, so I took a course*). You can cite an unrelated skill (*I really need to brush up on my French*). You can cite a learning objective (*One of my long-term goals is to learn more about international management. Does your company have any plans to expand overseas?*). Another possibility is to reaffirm your qualifications (*I have no weaknesses that affect my ability to do this job*). Be careful that your answer doesn't sound like a cliché (*I tend to be a perfectionist*) and instead shows careful analysis of your abilities.

2. What type of people do you have little patience for?
3. If you could live your life over, what would you change and why?
4. How would your former (or current) supervisor describe you as an employee?
5. What do you want the most from your job?
6. What's your grade point average, and does it accurately reflect your abilities?
7. Who in your life has influenced you the most and why?
8. What are you reading right now?
9. Describe your ideal work environment.
10. Is the customer always right?
11. How do you define success?

SITUATIONAL QUESTIONS. Questions related to situations help employers test your thought processes and logical thinking. When using situational questions, interviewers describe a hypothetical situation and ask how you'd handle it. Situational questions differ based on the type of position for which you are interviewing. Knowledge of the position and the company culture will help you respond favourably to these questions. Even if the situation sounds negative, keep your response positive. Here are a few examples:

1. You receive a call from an irate customer who complains about the service she received last night at your restaurant. She's demanding her money back. How would you handle the situation?

   When answering situational questions, it's always a good idea to tie your answer to a real experience from your past. You could say, for example, that you experienced a similar situation in one of your retail positions, and then explain the similarity. Tell the interviewer that you learned to first agree with the complaining customer to validate her complaint. Your next step would be to remedy the complaint, which does not necessarily mean giving the complaining customer what she is asking for. For example, in this case, based on restaurant policy, you could say politely that while you cannot refund her money, you can offer a two-for-one coupon valid for a year and a promise that service will be exemplary next time.

2. If you were aware that a coworker was falsifying data, what would you do?
3. Your manager has just told you that she's dissatisfied with your work, but you think it's acceptable. How would you resolve the conflict?
4. Your manager has told you to do something a certain way, and you think that way is wrong and that you know a far better way to complete the task. What would you do?
5. Assume that you're hired for this position. You soon learn that one of the staff is extremely resentful because she applied for your position and was turned down. As a result, she's being unhelpful and obstructive. How would you handle the situation?
6. A colleague has told you in confidence that she suspects another colleague of stealing. What would your actions be?
7. You've noticed that communication between upper management and entry-level employees is eroding. How would you solve this problem?

BEHAVIOURAL QUESTIONS. Instead of traditional interview questions, you may be asked to tell stories. The interviewer may say, *Describe a time when . . .* or *Tell me about a situation in which . . . .* To respond effectively, learn to use the storytelling technique. Ask yourself what the situation or task was, what action you took, and what the results were. Practise using this method, illustrated in Figure 13.3, to recall specific examples of your skills and accomplishments. To be fully prepared, develop a coherent narrative for every bullet point on your résumé. When answering behavioural questions, describe only educational and work-related

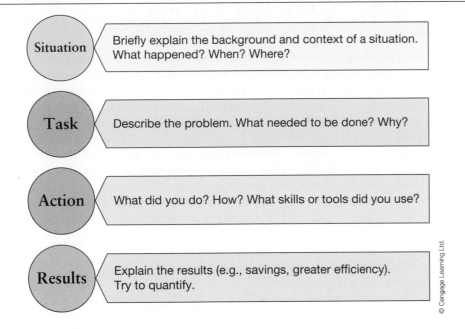

situations or tasks, and try to keep them as current as possible. Here are a few examples of behavioural questions:

1. Tell me about a time when you solved a difficult problem.

   Tell a concise story explaining the situation or task, what you did, and the result. For example, When I was at Ace Products, we continually had a problem of excessive back orders. After analyzing the situation, I discovered that orders went through many unnecessary steps. I suggested that we eliminate much of the paperwork. As a result, we reduced back orders by 30 percent. Go on to emphasize what you learned and how you can apply that learning to this job. Practise your success stories in advance so that you'll be ready.

2. Describe a situation in which you were able to use persuasion to successfully convince someone to see things your way.
3. Describe a time when you had to analyze information and make a recommendation.
4. Describe a time that you worked successfully as part of a team.
5. Tell me about a time you dealt with confidential information.
6. Give me an example of a time when you were under stress to meet a deadline.
7. Tell me about a time when you had to go beyond the call of duty to get a job done.
8. Tell me about a time you were able to successfully deal with another person even when that person may not have liked you (or vice versa).
9. Give me an example of an occasion when you showed initiative and took the lead.
10. Tell me about a recent situation in which you had to deal with an upset customer or coworker.

ILLEGAL AND INAPPROPRIATE QUESTIONS. Because human rights legislation protects job applicants from discrimination, interviewers may not ask questions such as those in the following list. Nevertheless, you may face an inexperienced or unscrupulous interviewer who does ask some of these questions. How should you react? If you find the question harmless and if you want the job, go ahead and answer. If you think that answering would damage your chance to be hired, try to deflect the question tactfully with a response such as *Could you tell me how my marital status relates to the responsibilities of this position?* Or you could use the opportunity to further emphasize your strengths. An older worker responding to a question about age might mention experience, fitness, knowledge, maturity, stability, or extensive business contacts. You might also wish to reconsider working for an organization that sanctions such procedures.

Here are some illegal or inappropriate questions that you may or may not want to answer:

1. Are you married, divorced, separated, single, or living common law?
2. Is your spouse subject to transfer in his or her job? Tell me about your spouse's job.
3. What's your corrected vision? (But it's legal to ask about the quality of your vision if visual acuity is directly related to safety or some other factor of the job.)
4. Do you have any disabilities? Do you drink or take drugs? Have you ever received psychiatric care or been hospitalized for emotional problems? Have you ever received workers' compensation? (But it's legal to ask if you have any condition that could affect your ability to do the job or if you have any condition that should be considered during selection.)
5. Have you ever been arrested? Have you ever been convicted of a crime? Do you have a criminal record? (But if bonding is a requirement of the job, it's legal to ask if you are eligible.)
6. How old are you? What's your date of birth? Can I see your birth certificate? (But it's legal to ask *Are you eligible to work under Canadian laws pertaining to age restrictions?*)
7. In what other countries do you have a current address? (But it's legal to ask *What's your current address, and how long have you lived there?*)
8. What's your maiden name? (But it's legal to ask *What's your full name?*)
9. What's your religion? How often do you attend religious services? Would you work on a specific religious holiday? Can you provide a reference from a clergyperson or religious leader?
10. Do you have children? What are your child-care arrangements? (But it's legal to ask *Can you work the required hours?* and *Are you available for overtime?*)
11. Where were you born? Were you born in Canada? Can you provide proof of citizenship? (But it's legal to ask *Are you legally entitled to work in Canada?*)
12. Were you involved in military service in another country? (But it's legal to ask about Canadian military service.)
13. What's your first language? Where did you receive your language training? (But it's legal to ask if you understand, read, write, and speak the language[s] required for the job.)
14. How much do you weigh? How tall are you?
15. What's your sexual or gender orientation?
16. Are you under medical care? Who's your family doctor? Are you receiving therapy or counselling? (But it's legal to make offers of employment conditional on successful completion of a medical exam that's relevant to that job.)

13.3c Ask Your Own Questions

At some point in the interview, you'll be asked if you have any questions. The worst thing you can say is no. Instead, ask questions that will help you gain information and will impress the interviewer with your thoughtfulness and interest in the position. Remember that the interview is an opportunity for you to see how you would fit with the company. Use it to find out whether this job is right for you. Be aware that you don't have to wait for the interviewer to ask you for questions. You can ask your own questions throughout the interview to learn more about the company and position. Here are some questions you might ask:

1. What will my duties be (if not already discussed)?
2. Tell me what it's like working here in terms of the people, management practices, workloads, expected performance, and rewards.
3. What training programs are available from this organization? What specific training will be given for this position?
4. Who would be my immediate supervisor?
5. What is the organizational structure, and where does this position fit in?

6. Is travel required in this position?
7. How is job performance evaluated?
8. Assuming my work is excellent, where do you see me in five years?
9. How long do employees generally stay with this organization?
10. What are the major challenges for a person in this position?
11. What do you see in the future for this organization?
12. What do employees say they like best about working for this organization?
13. May I have a tour of the facilities?
14. When do you expect to make a decision?

Do not ask about salary or benefits, especially during the first interview. It's best to let the interviewer bring those topics up first.

13.3d End Positively

After you've asked your questions, the interviewer will signal the end of the interview, usually by standing up or by expressing appreciation that you came. If not addressed earlier, you should find out what action will follow. Demonstrate your interest in the position by asking when it will be filled or what the next step will be. Too many candidates leave the interview without knowing their status or when they'll hear from the recruiter. Don't be afraid to say that you want the job!

Before you leave, summarize your strongest qualifications, show enthusiasm for obtaining this position, and thank the interviewer for a constructive interview and for considering you for the position. Ask the interviewer for a business card, which will provide the information you need to write a thank-you letter, which is discussed next. Shake the interviewer's hand with confidence, and acknowledge anyone else you see on the way out. Be sure to thank the receptionist if there is one. Leaving the interview gracefully and enthusiastically will leave a lasting impression on those responsible for making the final hiring decision.

◣ 13.4 After the Interview

After leaving the interview, immediately write down key points that were discussed, the names of people you spoke with, and other details in case you're called back for a second interview. Ask yourself what went really well and what could have been improved. Next, note your follow up plans. To whom should you send thank-you messages? Will you contact the employer by phone? If so, when? Then be sure to follow up on those plans, beginning with writing a thank-you message and contacting your references.

13.4a Thank Your Interviewer

After a job interview you should always send a thank-you message, also called a follow-up message. This courtesy sets you apart from other applicants, some of whom will not bother. Your message also reminds the interviewer of your visit and suggests your good manners and genuine enthusiasm for the job.

Follow-up messages are most effective if sent immediately after the interview. Experts believe that a thoughtful follow-up note carries as much weight as the cover letter does. The vast majority of senior executives say that in their evaluation of a job candidate, they are swayed by a written thank you. In your thank-you message refer to the date of the interview, the exact job title for which you were interviewed, and the specific topics discussed. Don't get carried away after a successful interview and send a poorly planned thank-you email that reads like a text message or sounds too chummy. Smart interviewees don't ruin their chances by communicating with recruiters in hasty text messages.

In addition to being respectful when following up after an interview, try to avoid worn-out phrases, such as *Thank you for taking the time to interview me.* There are better ways of expressing the same idea. Try *Today's interview was enjoyable; thank you for the opportunity.* Be careful, too, about overusing *I*, especially

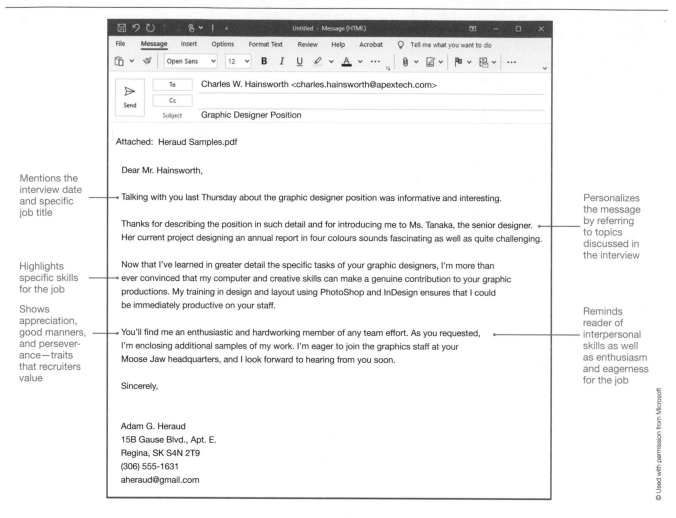

Mentions the interview date and specific job title

Highlights specific skills for the job

Shows appreciation, good manners, and perseverance—traits that recruiters value

Personalizes the message by referring to topics discussed in the interview

Reminds reader of interpersonal skills as well as enthusiasm and eagerness for the job

To Charles W. Hainsworth <charles.hainsworth@apextech.com>

Subject Graphic Designer Position

Attached: Heraud Samples.pdf

Dear Mr. Hainsworth,

Talking with you last Thursday about the graphic designer position was informative and interesting.

Thanks for describing the position in such detail and for introducing me to Ms. Tanaka, the senior designer. Her current project designing an annual report in four colours sounds fascinating as well as quite challenging.

Now that I've learned in greater detail the specific tasks of your graphic designers, I'm more than ever convinced that my computer and creative skills can make a genuine contribution to your graphic productions. My training in design and layout using PhotoShop and InDesign ensures that I could be immediately productive on your staff.

You'll find me an enthusiastic and hardworking member of any team effort. As you requested, I'm enclosing additional samples of my work. I'm eager to join the graphics staff at your Moose Jaw headquarters, and I look forward to hearing from you soon.

Sincerely,

Adam G. Heraud
15B Gause Blvd., Apt. E.
Regina, SK S4N 2T9
(306) 555-1631
aheraud@gmail.com

to begin sentences. Most important, show that you really want the job and that you're qualified for it. Notice how the thank-you email in Figure 13.4 conveys both enthusiasm and confidence.

If you've been interviewed by more than one person, send a separate message to the two most important people in the room (e.g., hiring manager; human resources recruiter). These days most follow-up messages are sent by email, so make sure to get the correct addresses before you leave the interview. One job candidate summarizes her method for sending follow-up emails in this way: thank the employer for the interview opportunity, very briefly summarize what was discussed during the face-to-face interview, and add a bit of information you didn't get to mention during the interview.[10]

13.4b Contact Your References

After you've thanked your interviewer, it's time to alert your references that they may be contacted by the employer. You might also have to request a letter of recommendation to be sent to the employer by a certain date. As discussed earlier, you should already have asked permission to use these individuals as references, and you should have supplied them with a copy of your résumé and information about the types of positions you're seeking.

To provide the best possible recommendation, your references need information. What position have you applied for and with what company? What should they stress to the prospective employer?

Let's say you're applying for a specific job that requires a letter of recommendation. Professor Orenstein has already agreed to be a reference for you. To get the best letter of recommendation from Professor Orenstein, help her out. Send her an email telling her about the position, its requirements, and the recommendation deadline. Attach a copy of your résumé. You might remind her of a positive experience with you that she could use in the recommendation. Remember that recommenders need evidence to support generalizations, as the student has provided in the following request:

Dear Professor Orenstein:

Recently I interviewed for the position of administrative assistant in the human resources department of Host International. Because you kindly agreed to help me, I'd like to ask you to be available by phone to provide a recommendation to Host.

The position calls for good organizational, interpersonal, and writing skills, as well as computer experience. To help you review my skills and training, I enclose my résumé. As you may recall, I earned an A in your business communication class last fall, and you complimented my research report for its clarity and organization.

You can expect to hear from James Jenkins at Host International (jjenkins@hinternational.com) before July 1. He said he'd call in the morning before 10 a.m. I'm grateful for your support, and I promise to let you know the results of my job search.

13.4c Follow Up

If you don't hear from the interviewer within five days, consider following up. The standard advice to job candidates is to call to follow up a few days after the interview. However, some experts suggest that cold calling a hiring manager is risky. You may be putting a busy recruiter on the spot and forcing him or her to search for your application. In addition, remember that you're not the only candidate; multiply your phone call by the dozens of applicants whom some hiring managers interview. Therefore, you don't want to be a pest. Sending an email to find out how the decision process is going may be best because such a message is much less intrusive.

However, if you believe it's safe to follow up by phone, or if the recruiter suggested it, practise saying something like I'm wondering what else I can do to convince you that I'm the right person for this job, or I'm calling to find out the status of your search for the _____ position. When following up, it's important to sound professional and courteous. Sounding desperate, angry, or frustrated because you've not been contacted can ruin your chances. The following follow-up email would impress the interviewer:

Dear Ms. Kahn:

I enjoyed my interview with you last Thursday for the receptionist position. You should know that I'm very interested in this opportunity with Coastal Enterprises. Because you mentioned that you might have an answer this week, I'm eager to know how your decision process is coming along. I look forward to hearing from you.

Sincerely,

Depending on the response you get to your first follow-up request, you may have to follow up additional times. Keep in mind, though, that some employers won't tell you about their hiring decision unless you're the one hired. Don't harass the interviewer, and don't force a decision. If you don't hear back from an employer within several weeks after following up, it's best to assume that you didn't get the job and to continue with your job search.

◣ 13.5 Other Employment Documents

Although the résumé and cover letter are vital, other important documents and messages are often required during the employment process. Because each of them reveals something about you and your communication skills, you'll want to put your best foot forward. These documents often subtly influence company officials to offer a job.

13.5a Application Form

Some organizations require job candidates to fill out job application forms instead of, or in addition to, submitting résumés. This practice lets them gather and store standardized data about each applicant. Whether the application is on paper or online, follow the directions carefully and provide accurate information. The following suggestions can help you be prepared:

- Put your résumé on your smartphone. If you don't have a smartphone, carry a card that has some basic information written on it, such as graduation dates; beginning and ending dates of all employment; salary history; full names, titles, and present work addresses of former supervisors; full addresses and phone numbers of current and previous employers; and full names, occupational titles, occupational addresses, and telephone numbers of persons who have agreed to serve as references.
- Look over all the questions before starting.
- Fill out the form neatly, using blue or black ink. Print your responses.
- Answer all questions honestly. Write *Not applicable* or *N/A* if appropriate.
- Use accurate spelling, grammar, and punctuation.
- If asked for the position desired, give a specific job title or type of position. Don't say, *Anything* or *Open*. These answers will make you look unfocused; moreover, they make it difficult for employers to know what you're qualified for or interested in.
- Be prepared for a salary question. Unless you know what comparable employees are earning in the company, the best strategy is to suggest a salary range or to write *Negotiable* or *Open*.
- Be prepared to explain the reasons for leaving previous positions. Use positive or neutral phrases such as *Relocation, Seasonal, To accept a position with more responsibility, Temporary position, To continue education,* or *Career change*. Avoid words or phrases such as *Fired, Quit, Didn't get along with supervisor,* or *Pregnancy*.
- Look over the application before submitting to make sure it's complete and that you've followed all instructions. Sign and date the application.

13.5b Application or Résumé Follow-Up Message

If your résumé or application generates no response within a reasonable time, you may decide to send a short follow-up email such as the following. Doing so (a) jogs the memory of the human resources staff, (b) demonstrates your serious interest, and (c) allows you to emphasize your qualifications or to add new information.

> Dear Ms. Lavecchia:
>
> Please know I am still interested in becoming an administrative support specialist with Quad, Inc.
>
> Since submitting my application [or résumé] in May, I've completed my degree and have been employed as a summer replacement for office workers in several downtown offices. This experience has honed my communication and project management skills. It has also introduced me to a wide range of office procedures.
>
> Please keep my application in your active file and let me know when I may put my formal training, technical skills, and practical experience to work for you.
>
> Sincerely,

13.5c Rejection Follow-Up Message

If you didn't get the job and you think it was perfect for you, don't give up. Employment specialists encourage applicants to respond to a rejection. The candidate who was offered the position may decline, or other positions may open up. In a rejection follow-up email, it's okay to admit you are disappointed. Be sure to add, however, that you're still interested and will contact the company again in a month in case a job opens up. Then follow through for a couple of months—but don't overdo it. You should be professional and persistent, but not a pest. Here's an example of an effective rejection follow-up message:

> Dear Mr. O'Neal:
>
> Although I'm disappointed that someone else was selected for your accounting position, I appreciate your promptness and courtesy in notifying me.
>
> Because I firmly believe that I have the technical and interpersonal skills needed to work in your fast-paced environment, I hope you'll keep my résumé in your active file. My desire to become a productive member of Deloitte staff remains strong.
>
> I enjoyed our interview, and I especially appreciate the time you and Ms. Chu spent describing your company's presence in international markets. To enhance my qualifications, I've enrolled in a CFA program.
>
> If you have an opening for which I am qualified, please reach me at (519) 555-3901. In the meantime, I'll call you in a month to discuss employment possibilities.
>
> Sincerely,

13.5d Job Acceptance and Rejection Messages

You'll eventually be offered a position you want. Although you'll likely accept the position over the phone, it's a good idea to follow up with an acceptance email to confirm the details and to formalize the acceptance. Your acceptance message might look like this:

> Dear Ms. Madhumali:
>
> It was a pleasure talking with you earlier today. As I mentioned, I am delighted to accept the position of web designer with Innovative Creations, Inc., in your Richmond office. I look forward to becoming part of the IC team and to starting work on a variety of exciting and innovative projects.
>
> As we agreed, my starting salary will be $76,000, with a benefits package including health and life insurance, retirement plan, stock options, and three weeks of vacation per year.
>
> I look forward to starting my position with Innovative Creations on September 15, 2021. Before that date I'll send you the completed tax and insurance forms you need. Thanks again for everything, Ms. Madhumali.
>
> Sincerely,

If you must turn down a job offer, show your professionalism by writing a sincere email. This message should thank the employer for the job offer and explain briefly that you're turning it down. Taking the time to extend this courtesy could help you in the future if this employer has a position you really want. Here's an example of a job rejection message:

Dear Mr. Opperman:

Thank you very much for offering me the position of sales representative with Bendall Pharmaceuticals. It was a difficult decision to make, but I have accepted a position with another company.

I appreciate your taking the time to interview me, and I wish Bendall much success in the future.

Sincerely,

13.5e Resignation Letter

After you've been in a position for a time, you may find it necessary to leave. Perhaps you've been offered a better position, or maybe you've decided to return to school full-time. Whatever the reason, you should leave your position gracefully and tactfully. Although you'll likely discuss your resignation in person with your supervisor, it's a good idea to document your resignation by writing a formal letter. Some resignation letters are brief, others others contain great detail. Remember that many resignation letters are placed in human resources files; therefore, it should be formatted and written using the professional business letter-writing techniques you learned earlier. Here's an example of the body of a basic letter of resignation:

Dear Ms. Patrick:

This letter serves as formal notice of my resignation from Allied Corporation, effective Friday, August 15. I have enjoyed working as your office assistant for the past two years, and I am grateful for everything I have learned during my employment with Allied.

Please let me know what I can do over the next two weeks to help you prepare for my departure. I would be happy to help with finding and training my replacement.

Thanks again for providing such a positive employment experience.

Sincerely,

Although this employee gives a standard two-week notice, a longer notice may be necessary. The higher and more responsible your position (and depending on the contract you might have signed), the longer the notice you must give your employer.

Writing job acceptance, job rejection, and resignation messages requires effort. That effort is worth it because you're building bridges that may carry you to even better jobs in the future.

Cengage

MINDTAP

In MindTap go to the Study Tools for Chapter 13 and complete the Practice Test.

◼ LEARNING SUMMARY

13.1 Explain the purposes and types of job interviews.

- An interviewer wants to (a) find out whether your skills are right for the job, (b) discuss your abilities in detail, (c) probe for motivation, and (d) see whether you would fit into the organization.

- An interviewee has a chance to (a) show potential, (b) learn about the job and company, and (c) elaborate on the information in the résumé.

- Screening interviews help companies weed out lesser-

qualified candidates before scheduling face-to-face hiring/placement interviews with the most promising applicants.

- Hiring interviews include one-on-one, panel, group, sequential, stress, and online or virtual interviews.

13.2 Know what to do before an interview to make an impressive initial contact.

- Aim to make a good first impression on the phone by being polite and enthusiastic, recording a professional voice mail greeting, and alerting any housemates that a potential employer may call.

- Research the company on the Web, analyze its advertising and media presence, and try to locate insider information; then prepare by rehearsing success stories and cleaning up any digital dirt.

- Allow plenty of time for travelling to the interview; greet the interviewer politely and be pleasant.

- Fight fear by preparing thoroughly and dressing professionally; remember to breathe.

13.3 Know what to do during an interview to create a favourable impression.

- Be aware of your body language, exhibit good posture, maintain eye contact, use gestures effectively, listen, smile, turn off your cell phone, don't chew gum, use proper speech, and be confident.

- Aim your answers at the key characteristics interviewers seek; focus on your strengths.

- Expect questions designed to get acquainted, gauge your interest, determine your accomplishments, probe for future plans, and challenge you; anticipate situational, behavioural, and inappropriate questions.

- Demonstrate interest by asking your own questions; end positively and say goodbye graciously.

13.4 Know what to do immediately after an interview to maintain the positive impression you've created.

- Send a thank-you note, email, or letter immediately after the interview to each interviewer, but do not text message; reiterate your interest and qualifications, but avoid overused phrases.

- Alert your references to expect recruiter calls, and give them the appropriate information so they can support generalizations about you with specific evidence.

- A few days after the interview, follow up by email or by calling the recruiter, if you believe it's safe, but don't be a pest. If you call, be professional and courteous.

13.5 Prepare useful employment-related documents.

- Follow-up messages reveal a lot about you and your communication skills; prepare each with care.

- To fill out application forms neatly and accurately, carry records summarizing your vital statistics.

- In an application or résumé follow-up message, remind the recruiter of your application, demonstrate serious interest, and emphasize your qualifications.

- Even if you didn't get the job, write a follow-up email or letter; be persistent yet not annoying.

- When accepting a job, follow up in writing to confirm what was discussed; when declining an offer, be professional and sincere. Thank the interviewer and courteously turn down the position.

- If you decide to resign, write a graceful and tactful formal letter to document your decision.

CHAPTER REVIEW

1. Name the main purposes of interviews—for job candidates and for employers. (Obj. 1)

2. If you've sent out your résumé to many companies, what information should you keep handy and why? (Obj. 2)

3. Briefly describe the types of hiring or placement interviews you may encounter. (Obj. 1)

4. How can you address problem areas on your résumé such as lack of experience, being fired, or earning low grades? (Obj. 3)

5. Name at least six interviewing behaviours you can exhibit that send positive nonverbal messages. (Obj. 3)

6. What's your greatest fear of what you might do or what might happen to you during an employment interview? How can you overcome your fears? (Obj. 3)

7. Should you be candid with an interviewer when asked about your weaknesses? (Obj. 3)

8. How can you clarify vague questions from recruiters? (Obj. 3)

9. How should you respond to questions you believe to be illegal? (Obj. 3)

10. List the steps you should take immediately following your job interview. (Obj. 4)

11. Explain the various kinds of follow-up employment messages. (Obj. 5)

CRITICAL THINKING

1. Online questionnaires are a trend in recruiting. Employers can ask how applicants would handle tricky situations, how happy they are, and how much they may have stolen from previous employers. Multiple-choice format makes it tricky for applicants to know whether to be truthful or to say what the prospective employer wants to hear. What's wrong with this type of screening activity? (Obj. 1)

2. Is it normal to be nervous about an employment interview? What can be done to overcome this fear? (Obj. 2)

3. What can you do to improve the first impression you make at an interview? (Obj. 2)

4. In employment interviews, do you think that behavioural questions (such as *Tell me about a business problem you have had and how you solved it*) are more effective than traditional questions (such as *Tell me what you are good at and why*)? (Obj. 3)

5. If you're asked an illegal interview question, why is it important to first assess the intentions of the interviewer? (Obj. 3)

6. Why is it important to ask your own questions of the interviewer? (Obj. 3)

7. Why is it a smart strategy to thank an interviewer, to follow up, and even to send a rejection follow-up message? Are any risks associated with this strategy? (Obj. 4)

◣ ACTIVITIES AND CASES

13.1 RESEARCHING AN ORGANIZATION (OBJ. 2)

Often graduates find employment through co-op placements or through family networks. However, it's equally possible to find employment by researching organizations with which you've had no contact.

Your Task. Choose an organization where you would like to be employed. Assume you've been selected for an interview. Using resources described in this chapter, locate information about the organization's leaders and their business philosophy. Find out about the organization's accomplishments, setbacks, finances, products, customers, competition, and advertising. Prepare a summary report documenting your findings.

13.2 LEARNING WHAT JOBS ARE REALLY ABOUT THROUGH BLOGS, FACEBOOK, AND TWITTER (OBJ. 2)

Blogs and social media have become important tools in the employment search process. By accessing blogs and social media, job seekers can learn more about a company's culture and day-to-day activities.

Your Task. Using the Web, locate a blog that is maintained by an employee of a company where you would like to work. Monitor the blog for at least a week. Also, access the company's Facebook page and monitor its Twitter feeds for at least a week. Prepare a short report that summarizes what you learned about the company through reading the blog postings, status updates, and tweets. Include a statement of whether this information would be valuable during your job search.

13.3 BUILDING INTERVIEW SKILLS (OBJ. 2)

Successful interviews require diligent preparation and repeated practice. To be prepared, you need to know what skills are required for your targeted position. In addition to software and communication skills, employers generally want to know whether a candidate works well with a team, accepts responsibility, solves problems, is efficient, meets deadlines, shows leadership, saves time and money, and is a hard worker.

Your Task. Consider a position for which you are eligible now or one for which you will be eligible when you complete your education. Identify the skills and traits necessary for this position. If you prepared a résumé in Chapter 12, be sure that it addresses these targeted areas. Now prepare interview worksheets listing at least ten skills (both technical and other skills) or traits a recruiter will want to discuss in an interview for your targeted position, and provide examples of how you are proficient at these skills.

13.4 SCRIPTING ANSWERS TO TYPICAL INTERVIEW QUESTIONS (OBJ. 2)

Your Task. You've probably already been through a number of job interviews in your life, but they may not have been formal like the interviews you will go through when you start applying for post-college or -university jobs. Script a one- to two-minute answer to the following interview question, and memorize it. Do not use the template from this chapter. Then practise speaking the answer in a natural voice so that you don't appear to have memorized it. Consider filming yourself and posting the video on YouTube so it can be shared with your instructor and classmates.

Question: Tell me about yourself and your previous work experience.

13.5 SCRIPTING ANSWERS TO TYPICAL INTERVIEW QUESTIONS (OBJ. 2)

Your Task. Script a one- to two-minute answer to the following typical interview question, and memorize it. Then practise speaking the answer in a natural voice so that you don't appear to have memorized it. Consider filming yourself and posting the video on YouTube so it can be shared with your instructor and classmates.

Question: Tell me about a time in a previous job when you faced a difficulty, a criticism, or a problem and how you dealt with it.

Follow-Up Question: What would you do differently if this problem happened again?

13.6 SCRIPTING ANSWERS TO TYPICAL INTERVIEW QUESTIONS (OBJ. 2)

Your Task. Script a one- to two-minute answer to the following typical interview question, and memorize it. Then practise speaking the answer in a natural voice so that you don't appear to have memorized it. Consider filming yourself and posting the video on YouTube so it can be shared with your instructor and classmates.

Question: Tell me about a former boss or coworker whom you admire and why you admire him or her.

Now that you've memorized these three answers, practise interviewing a partner. As you ask each other questions, surprise each other by slightly modifying the questions so they're not exactly as printed above. This modification will force you to improvise on the spot, a valuable interviewing skill.

13.7 PREPARING SUCCESS STORIES (OBJ. 2)

You can best showcase your talents if you are ready with your own success stories that show how you have developed the skills or traits required for your targeted position.

Your Task. Prepare success stories that highlight the required skills or traits. Select three to five stories to develop into answers to potential interview questions. For example, here's a typical question: *How does your background relate to the position we have open?* A possible response: "As you know, I have just completed an intensive training program in _____. In addition, I have over three years of part-time work experience in a variety of business settings. In one position I was selected to manage a small business in the absence of the owner. I developed responsibility and customer-service skills in filling orders efficiently, resolving shipping problems, and monitoring key accounts. I also inventoried and organized products worth over $200,000. When the owner returned from a vacation trip to Florida, I was commended for increasing sales and was given a bonus in recognition of her gratitude." People relate to and remember stories. Try to shape your answers into memorable stories. Consider filming yourself and posting the video on YouTube so it can be shared with your instructor and classmates.

13.8 CLEANING UP DIGITAL DIRT (OBJ. 2)

Before embarking on your job hunt, you may want to know what employers might find if they searched your personal life in cyberspace, specifically on Facebook, Twitter, Instagram, and so forth. Running your name through Google and other search engines, particularly enclosed in quotation marks to lower the number of hits, is usually the first step. Assembling a digital portrait of an applicant is easier than ever thanks to spy-worthy websites such as Snitch. name and PeekYou—that collect information from a number of search engines, websites, and social networks.

Your Task. Use Google or Snitch.name to search the Web for your full name, enclosed in quotation marks. In Google, don't forget to run an image search at www.google.ca/images to find any photos of questionable taste. If your instructor requests, share your insights with the class—not the salacious details, but general observations—or write a short memo summarizing the results.

13.9 PRE-EMPLOYMENT SCREENING TESTS (OBJ. 2)

What do PetSmart, Radio Shack, Walmart, and Burger King have in common? They use pre-employment testing to identify applicants who will fit into the organization. Unlike classical aptitude tests that began in the military, today's online multiple-choice tests assess integrity, collegiality, and soft skills in general. To give you a flavour of these talent assessments, here are three typical scenarios:

1. You've learned that eye contact is important in communication. How much eye contact should you have when conversing with someone in a professional environment?

   A. At all times. You want to make sure the person knows you are paying attention.

   B. About 60–70 percent of the time.

   C. Every now and then. You don't want to make the other person uncomfortable.

   D. About half the time.

2. You're attending an important meeting with colleagues who are more senior than you are. How much should you speak at the meeting?

   A. You should look very interested but not speak at all unless they request it.

   B. You should speak only when the topic is within your expertise.

   C. You should try to talk as much as possible to show your knowledge.

   D. You should speak in the beginning of the meeting and every now and then.

3. You just found out that people at work are spreading a bad rumour about you that is untrue. How would you respond?

   A. Tell everybody that it is not true. You need to clear your name.

   B. Don't react to it at all. It'll blow over eventually.

   C. Find out who started it and talk to them to make sure that they will never do it again.

   D. Talk to others about another coworker's rumour so people will forget about yours.

Your Task. Answer the questions; then compare your answers with those of your classmates. Discuss the scenarios. What specific skills or attributes might each question be designed to measure? Do you think such questions are effective? What might be the best way to respond to the scenarios? Your instructor may share the correct answers with you. If your instructor directs, search the Web for more talent assessment questions. Alternatively, your instructor might ask you to create your own workplace (or college or university) scenarios to help you assess an applicant's soft skills. As a class you could compare questions or scenarios and quiz each other.

13.10 APPROPRIATE INTERVIEW ATTIRE (OBJ. 3)

As you prepare for your interview by learning about the company and the industry, don't forget a key component of interview success: creating a favourable first impression by wearing appropriate business attire. Job seekers often have nebulous ideas about proper interview wear. Some wardrobe mishaps include choosing a conservative "power" suit but accessorizing it with beat-up casual shoes or a shabby bag. Grooming glitches include dandruff on dark suit fabric, dirty fingernails, or mothball odour. Women sometimes wrongly assume that any black clothing items are acceptable, even if they are too tight, revealing, sheer, or made of low-end fabrics. Most image consultants agree that workplace attire falls into three main categories: business formal, business casual, and casual. Only business formal is considered proper interview apparel.

Your Task. To prepare for your big day, search your library databases and the Web for descriptions and images of *business formal*. You may research *business casual* and *casual* styles, but for an interview, always dress on the side of caution—conservatively. Search peer-reviewed journals in the fields of business communication and psychology to see if anyone is doing academic research on the effectiveness of and changes to business attire. Share your findings (notes, images, statistics, etc.) with the class and your instructor. Consider using Infographic software for your response.

13.11 CREATING AN INTERVIEW CHEAT SHEET (OBJ. 2)

Even the best-rehearsed applicants sometimes forget to ask the questions they prepared, or they fail to stress their major accomplishments in job interviews. Sometimes applicants are so rattled they even forget the interviewer's name. To help you keep your wits during an interview, make a "cheat sheet" that summarizes key facts, answers, and questions. Review it before the interview and again as the interview is ending to be sure you have covered everything that is critical.

Your Task. Prepare a cheat sheet with the following information:

- Day and time of interview:
- Meeting with: [Name of interviewer(s), title, company, city, province or territory, postal code, telephone, cell, email]
- Major accomplishments: (four to six)
- Management or work style: (four to six)
- Things you need to know about me: (three to four items)
- Reason I left my last job:
- Answers to difficult questions: (four to five answers)
- Questions to ask interviewer:
- Things I can do for you:

13.12 ROLE-PLAY: PRACTISING ANSWERING INTERVIEW QUESTIONS (OBJ. 2)

One of the best ways to understand interview dynamics and to develop confidence is to role-play the parts of interviewer and candidate.

Your Task. Choose a partner from your class. Make a list of five interview questions from those presented in this chapter. In team sessions you and your partner will role-play an actual interview. One acts as interviewer, the other as the candidate. Before the interview, the candidate tells the interviewer what job he or she is applying for, at which company. For the interview, the interviewer and candidate should dress appropriately and sit in chairs facing each other. The interviewer greets the candidate and makes him or her comfortable. The candidate gives the interviewer a copy of his or her résumé. The interviewer asks three (or more, depending on your instructor's time schedule) questions from the candidate's list. The interviewer may also ask follow-up questions if appropriate. When finished, the interviewer ends the meeting graciously. After one interview, reverse roles and repeat.

13.13 ANSWERING QUESTIONS IN A VIRTUAL INTERVIEW (OBJS. 2, 3)

Numerous websites offer excellent interview advice. For instance, Monster Career Advice articles, such as the one at www.monster.ca/career-advice/article/skype-interview-ca, can help you improve your interviewing skills in virtual interviews, but the site doesn't allow you to actually practise.

Your Task. Using Google, find at least three high-quality sites that offer *free practice* in virtual interviewing. Try each site. You may need to create a profile and login credentials. Then, choose criteria by which to rate such sites and rate your top sites. Briefly explain why you chose the site you did, and explain the best piece of advice you find on the site. Show the class your results in a creative format such as video, animation, or infographic.

13.14 HANDLING DIFFICULT INTERVIEW QUESTIONS (OBJ. 3)

Although some questions are not appropriate in job interviews, many interviewers will ask them anyway—whether intentionally or unknowingly. Being prepared is important.

Your Task. How would you respond in the following scenario? Let's assume you are being interviewed at one of the top companies on your list of potential employers. The interviewing committee consists of a human resources manager and the supervising manager of the department where you would work. At various times during the interview the supervising manager has asked questions that made you feel uncomfortable. For example, he asked whether you were married. You know this question is illegal, but you saw no harm in answering it. But then he asked how old you were. Since you started college early and graduated in two years, you are worried that you may not be considered mature enough for this position. But you have most of the other qualifications required, and you are convinced you could succeed on the job. How should you answer this question?

13.15 SAYING THANKS FOR THE INTERVIEW (OBJ. 4)

You've just completed an exciting employment interview, and you want the interviewer to remember you.

Your Task. Write a follow-up thank-you email to Ronald T. Ranson, human resources manager, Electronic Data Sources, ranson@eds.ca (or a company of your choice).

13.16 TURNING A NEGATIVE OUTCOME INTO A POTENTIAL OPPORTUNITY (OBJ. 5)

After an excellent interview with Electronic Data Sources (or a company of your choice), you're disappointed to learn that it hired someone else. But you really want to work for the company.

Your Task. Write a follow-up email to Ronald T. Ranson, human resources manager, Electronic Data Sources, ranson@eds.ca (or a company of your choice). Indicate that you are disappointed but still interested.

13.17 FOLLOWING UP AFTER SUBMITTING YOUR RÉSUMÉ (OBJ. 5)

A month has passed since you sent your résumé and cover letter in response to a job advertisement. You are still interested in the position and would like to find out whether you still have a chance.

Your Task. Write a follow-up letter that won't offend the reader or damage your chances of employment.

13.18 REQUESTING A REFERENCE (OBJ. 4)

Your favourite professor has agreed to be one of your references. You have just arrived home from a job interview that went well, and you must ask your professor to write a letter of recommendation.

Your Task. Write to the professor requesting that a letter of recommendation be sent to the company where you were interviewed. Explain that the interviewer asked that the letter be sent directly to him. Provide data about the job description and about yourself so that the professor can target its content.

13.19 SAYING YES TO A JOB OFFER (OBJ. 5)

Your dream has come true: you have just been offered an excellent position. Although you accepted the position on the phone, you want to send a formal acceptance letter.

Your Task. Write a job acceptance letter to an employer of your choice. Include the specific job title, your starting date, and details about your compensation package. Make up any necessary details.

13.20 HUMOUR AND JOB INTERVIEWS (OBJ. 2)

Job interviews can be stressful occasions, so it's no surprise that comedians have for a long time used job interviews in their routines. YouTube has a number of postings under the category *job interview funny*.

Your Task. Do some research on YouTube by watching a few funny interview clips. Develop a three- to five-minute presentation in which you use part of a YouTube clip to illustrate a useful strategy or insight you can teach the rest of your class. Remember, humour has to be used carefully in a classroom or workplace. You're using the humour to make a point, not just to get laughs from your audience.

GRAMMAR/MECHANICS CHALLENGE 13

TOTAL REVIEW

This exercise reviews all of the guidelines in the Grammar/Mechanics Handbook as well as the lists of Confusing Words and Frequently Misspelled Words. The following sentences contain errors in grammar, punctuation, capitalization, number style, usage, and spelling. Write a corrected version of each sentence. When you finish, compare your responses with those provided near the end of the book.

1. In the evening each of the female nurses are escorted to there cars.

2. It must have been him who received the highest score although its hard to understand how he did it.

3. Our Office Manager asked Rachel and I to fill in for him for 4 hours on Saturday morning.

4. Working out at the Gym and jogging twenty kilometres a week is how she stays fit.

5. 3 types of costs must be considered for proper inventory controll, holding costs, ordering costs and stockout costs.

6. If I was him I would fill out the questionaire immediately so that I would qualify for the drawing.

7. Higher engine revolutions mean better acceleration, however lower revolutions mean the best fuel economy.

8. Our teams day to day operations include: setting goals, improving customer service, manufacturing quality products and hitting sales targets.

9. If I had saw the shippers bill I would have payed it immediately.

10. When convenent will you please send me 3 copys of the companys color logo?

11. Do you think it was him who left the package on the boss desk.

12. About 1/2 of Pizza Huts slx thousand outlets will make deliverys, the others concentrates on walk in customers.

13. Every thing accept labor is covered in this five year warranty.

14. Our Director of Human Resources felt nevertheless that the applicant should be given a interview.

15. When Keisha completes her degree she plans to apply for employment in: Calgary, Toronto and Halifax

---

EDITING CHALLENGE 13

The following interview thank-you email has proofreading, spelling, grammar, punctuation, wordiness, and other writing faults that require correction. Study the guidelines in the Grammar/Mechanics Handbook, as well as the lists of Confusing Words and Frequently Misspelled Words at the end of the book, to sharpen your skills. When you finish making corrections, your instructor can show you the revised version of this email.

Your Task. Edit the following message by correcting its errors (a) in your textbook or (b) on a photocopy using proofreading marks from Appendix B.

To: <AMasters@Biolage.ca>   June 4, 2021
From:
Subject: Interview
Cc:
Bcc:
Attached:

Dear Mr. Masters:

I appriciate the opportunity for the interview yesterday for the newly-listed Position of Sales Trainee. It was really a pleasure meeting yourself and learning more about Biolage Enterprises, you have a fine staff and a sophisticated approach to marketing.

You're organization appears to be growing in a directional manner that parralels my interests' and career goals. The interview with yourself and your staff yesterday confirmed my initale positive impressions of Biolage Enterprises and I want to reiterate my strong interest in working with and for you. My prior Retail sales experience as a sales associate with Sears; plus my recent training in Microsoft Word and Excel would enable me to make progress steadily through your programs of training and become a productive member of your sales team in no time at all.

Again, thank-you for your kind and gracius consideration. In the event that you need any additional information from me, all you have to do is give me a call me at (405) 391-7792.

Sincerly yours,

A Guide to Document Formats

Business communicators try to produce documents and messages with standardized formats. Becoming familiar with these formats is important because documents and messages actually say two things about the writer. Meaning is conveyed by the words chosen to express the writer's ideas, and a sense of trust and credibility is conveyed by the appearance of a document and its adherence to recognized formats.

You'll want to give special attention to the appearance and formatting of your emails, letters, envelopes, and memos. While we don't cover texts and social media posts here, as you learned earlier, these short messages should have a professional tone when sent at work, meaning they shouldn't contain slang or other inappropriate language, they should be short and to the point, and they should deal with one issue at a time.

 ## EMAILS

Email has been around now for about 25 years; as a result, certain formatting and usage norms have developed. The following suggestions, illustrated in Figure A.1 and also in Figure 5.1, can guide you in setting up the parts of an email. Always check, however, with your organization so that you follow its practices.

FIGURE A.1 / Effective Email

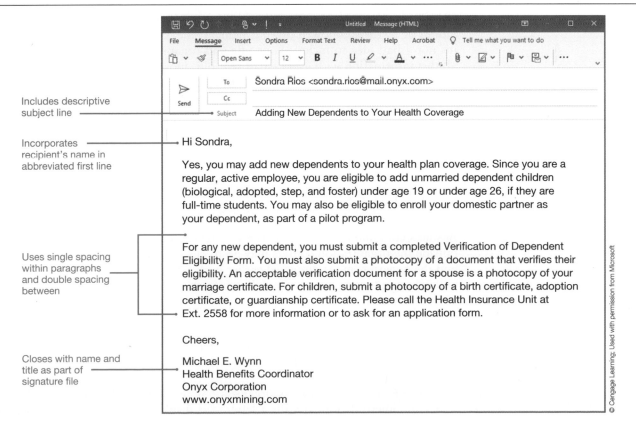

Includes descriptive subject line

Incorporates recipient's name in abbreviated first line

Uses single spacing within paragraphs and double spacing between

Closes with name and title as part of signature file

© Cengage Learning; Used with permission from Microsoft

TO LINE. Type the receiver's email address after To. If replying to an email, your software will fill in the address once you click on Reply. If responding to someone you once were in touch with, you can either click Reply in an old saved email from that person, or type in the address once again.

CC AND BCC. Insert the email address of anyone who is to receive a copy of the message. Cc stands for *carbon copy* or *courtesy copy*. Don't be tempted, though, to send needless copies just because it's so easy. Some organizations develop an internal style in which anyone cc'd on an original email should be cc'd on the response. Other organizations ask employees to only cc when it's necessary. Check with your manager or experienced coworker.

Bcc stands for *blind carbon copy*. Some writers use bcc to send a copy of the message without the addressee's knowledge. Writers also use the bcc line for mailing lists. When a message is being sent to a number of people and their email addresses should not be revealed, the bcc line works well to conceal the names and addresses of all receivers.

SUBJECT. Identify the subject of the email with a brief but descriptive summary of the topic. Be sure to include enough information to be clear and compelling. Capitalize the initial letters of principal words.

SALUTATION. Include a brief greeting. Some writers use a salutation such as *Dear Selina* followed by a comma or a colon. Others are more informal with *Hi Selina!* or *Good morning* or *Greetings*. Some writers simulate a salutation by including the name of the receiver in an abbreviated first line, as shown in Figure A.1. Other writers treat an email like a memo and skip the salutation entirely or include only a brief salutation consisting of the recipient's name, such as *Dave*.

MESSAGE. Cover just one topic in your email, and try to keep your total message under one screen long. Single space and be sure to use both upper- and lowercase letters. Double space between paragraphs, and use graphic highlighting (bullets, numbering) whenever you are listing three or more items.

CLOSING. Conclude your email with a short expression such as *Cheers* or *Best wishes* or *Regards* followed by your name. If the recipient is unlikely to know you, it's not a bad idea to include your title and organization. To avoid having to type all this information with every email sent out, most professional email users create an email signature that includes name, title, and department or company name, and that can also be embellished with an electronic business card, hyperlink (e.g., to the company's website), and a picture. Use restraint, however, because email signatures take up precious space. Within organizations you may omit a closing especially if this isn't your first message to your receiver.

◥ LETTERS

Business communicators write business letters primarily to correspond with people outside the organization. Letters may go to customers, vendors, other businesses, and the government, as discussed earlier in this book. The following information will help you format your letters following conventional guidelines.

Letter Parts

Following is a discussion of how to use letter parts properly. Figure A.2 illustrates the parts in a block-style letter.

LETTERHEAD. Most business organizations use 8.5-by-11-inch paper (215.9 by 279.4 millimetres) printed with a letterhead displaying their official name, street address, website address, email address, and telephone number. The letterhead may also include a logo and an advertising tag line such as *Ebank: A new way to bank*.

DATELINE. On letterhead paper you should place the date two blank lines below the last line of the letterhead or five centimetres from the top edge of the paper (line 13). On plain paper, place the date immediately below your return address. Since the date goes on line 13, start the return address an appropriate number of lines above it. The most common dateline format is as follows: *June 9, 2021*. Don't use *th* (or *rd*) when the date is written this way. For European or military correspondence, use the following dateline format: *9 June 2021*. Notice that no commas are used.

ADDRESSEE AND DELIVERY NOTATIONS. Delivery notations such as *FAX TRANSMISSION, CONFIDENTIAL*, or *CERTIFIED MAIL* are typed in all capital letters two blank lines above the inside address.

INSIDE ADDRESS. Type the inside address—that is, the address of the organization or person receiving the letter—single-spaced, starting at the left margin. The number of lines between the dateline and the inside address depends on the size of the letter body, the type size (point or pitch size), and the length of the typing lines. Generally, two to ten lines is appropriate.

Be careful to duplicate the exact wording and spelling of the recipient's name and address on your documents. Usually you can copy this information from the letterhead of the correspondence you are answering. If, for example, you're responding to *Jackson & Perkins Company*, don't address your letter to *Jackson and Perkins Corp.*

Always be sure to include a courtesy title such as *Mr., Ms., Mrs., Dr.,* or *Professor* before a person's name in the inside address—for both the letter and the envelope. Although many women in business today favour *Ms.*, you'll want to use whatever title the addressee prefers.

In general, avoid abbreviations (such as *Ave.* or *Co.*) unless they appear in the printed letterhead of the document being answered.

ATTENTION LINE. An attention line allows you to send your message officially to an organization but to direct it to a specific individual, officer, or department. However, if you know an individual's complete name, it's always better to use it as the first line of the inside address and avoid an attention line. Here are two common formats for attention lines:

MultiMedia Enterprises
931 Calkins Avenue
Toronto, ON M3W 1E6

Attention Marketing Director

MultiMedia Enterprises
Attention: Marketing Director
931 Calkins Avenue
Toronto, ON M3W 1E6

Attention lines may be typed in all caps or with upper- and lowercase letters. The colon following *Attention* is optional. Notice that an attention line may be placed two lines below the address block or printed as the second line of the inside address. You'll want to use the latter format if you're writing on a computer, because the address block may be copied to the envelope and the attention line will not interfere with the last-line placement of the postal code. (Mail can be sorted more easily if the postal code appears in the last line of a typed address.)

SALUTATION. Place the salutation two lines below the last line of the inside address or the attention line (if used). If the letter is addressed to an individual, use that person's courtesy title and last name (*Dear Mr. Lanham*). Even if you're on a first-name basis (*Dear Leslie*), be sure to add a colon (not a comma or a semicolon) after the salutation, unless you're using open punctuation. Do not use an individual's full name in the salutation (e.g., *Dear Mr. Leslie Lanham*) unless you're unsure of gender identity (*Dear Leslie Lanham*).

SUBJECT AND REFERENCE LINES. Although traditionally the subject line is placed one blank line below the salutation, many businesses actually place it above the salutation. Use whatever style your organization prefers. Reference lines often show policy or file numbers; they generally appear two lines above the salutation.

BODY. Most business letters and memos are single-spaced, with double line spacing between paragraphs. Very short messages may be double-spaced with indented paragraphs.

COMPLIMENTARY CLOSE.
Typed two lines below the last line of the letter, the complimentary close may be formal (*Yours truly*) or informal (*Sincerely* or *Respectfully*). The simplified letter style omits a complimentary close.

SIGNATURE BLOCK. In most letter styles, the writer's typed name and optional identification appear three to four blank lines below the complimentary close. The combination of name, title, and organization information should be arranged to achieve a balanced look. The name and title may appear on the same line or on separate lines, depending on the length of each. Use commas to separate categories within the same line, but not to conclude a line.

Sincerely,

Jeremy M. Wood

Jeremy M. Wood, Manager
Technical Sales and Services

Respectfully,

Casandra Baker-Murillo

Casandra Baker-Murillo
Executive Vice President

Some organizations include their names in the signature block. In such cases the organization name appears in all caps two lines below the complimentary close, as shown here:

Sincerely,
LITTON COMPUTER SERVICES

Shelina A. Simpson

Ms. Shelina A. Simpson
Executive Assistant

REFERENCE INITIALS. If used, the initials of the typist and writer are typed two lines below the writer's name and title. Generally, the writer's initials are capitalized and the typist's are lowercased, but this format varies.

ENCLOSURE NOTATION. When an enclosure or attachment accompanies a document, a notation to that effect appears two lines below the reference initials. This notation reminds the writer to insert the enclosure in the envelope, and it reminds the recipient to look for the enclosure or attachment. The notation may be spelled out (*Enclosure, Attachment*), or it may be abbreviated (*Enc., Att.*). It may indicate the number of enclosures or attachments, and it may also identify a specific enclosure (*Enclosure: Form 1099*).

COPY NOTATION. If you make copies of correspondence for other individuals, you may use *cc* to indicate carbon copy, *pc* to indicate photocopy, or merely *c* for any kind of copy. A colon following the initial(s) is optional.

SECOND-PAGE HEADING. When a letter extends beyond one page, use plain paper of the same quality and colour as the first page. Identify the second and succeeding pages with a heading consisting of the name of the addressee, the page number, and the date. Use either of the following two formats:

Ms. Rachel Ruiz   2   May 3, 2021

Ms. Rachel Ruiz
Page 2
May 3, 2021

Both headings appear on line 7, followed by two blank lines to separate them from the continuing text. Avoid using a second page if you have only one line or the complimentary close and signature block to fill that page.

PLAIN-PAPER RETURN ADDRESS. If you prepare a personal or business letter on plain paper, place your address immediately above the date. Don't include your name; you will type (and sign) your name at the end of your letter. If your return address contains two lines, begin typing it on line 11 so that the date appears on line 13. Avoid abbreviations other than the two-letter province or territory abbreviation.

580 East Leffels Street
Dartmouth, NS B6R 2F3
December 14, 2021

Ms. Ellen Siemens
Retail Credit Department
Union National Bank
1220 Dunsfield Boulevard
Halifax, NS B4L 2E2

Dear Ms. Siemens:

For letters prepared in the block style, type the return address at the left margin. For modified block-style letters, start the return address at the centre to align with the complimentary close.

Letter and Punctuation Styles

Business letters are generally prepared in either block or modified block style, and they generally use mixed punctuation.

BLOCK STYLE. In the block style, shown in Figure A.2, all lines begin at the left margin. This style is a favourite because it's easy to format.

MODIFIED BLOCK STYLE. The modified block style differs from block style in that the date and closing lines appear in the centre, as shown at the bottom of Figure A.2. The date may be (a) centred, (b) begun at the centre of the page (to align with the closing lines), or (c) backspaced from the right margin. The signature block—including the complimentary close, writer's name and title, or organization identification—begins at the centre. The first line of each paragraph may begin at the left margin or may be indented five or ten spaces. All other lines begin at the left margin.

Most businesses today use mixed punctuation, shown with the modified block-style letter at the bottom left of Figure A.2. This style requires a colon after the salutation and a comma after the complimentary close. Even when the salutation is a first name, the colon is appropriate.

Letterhead

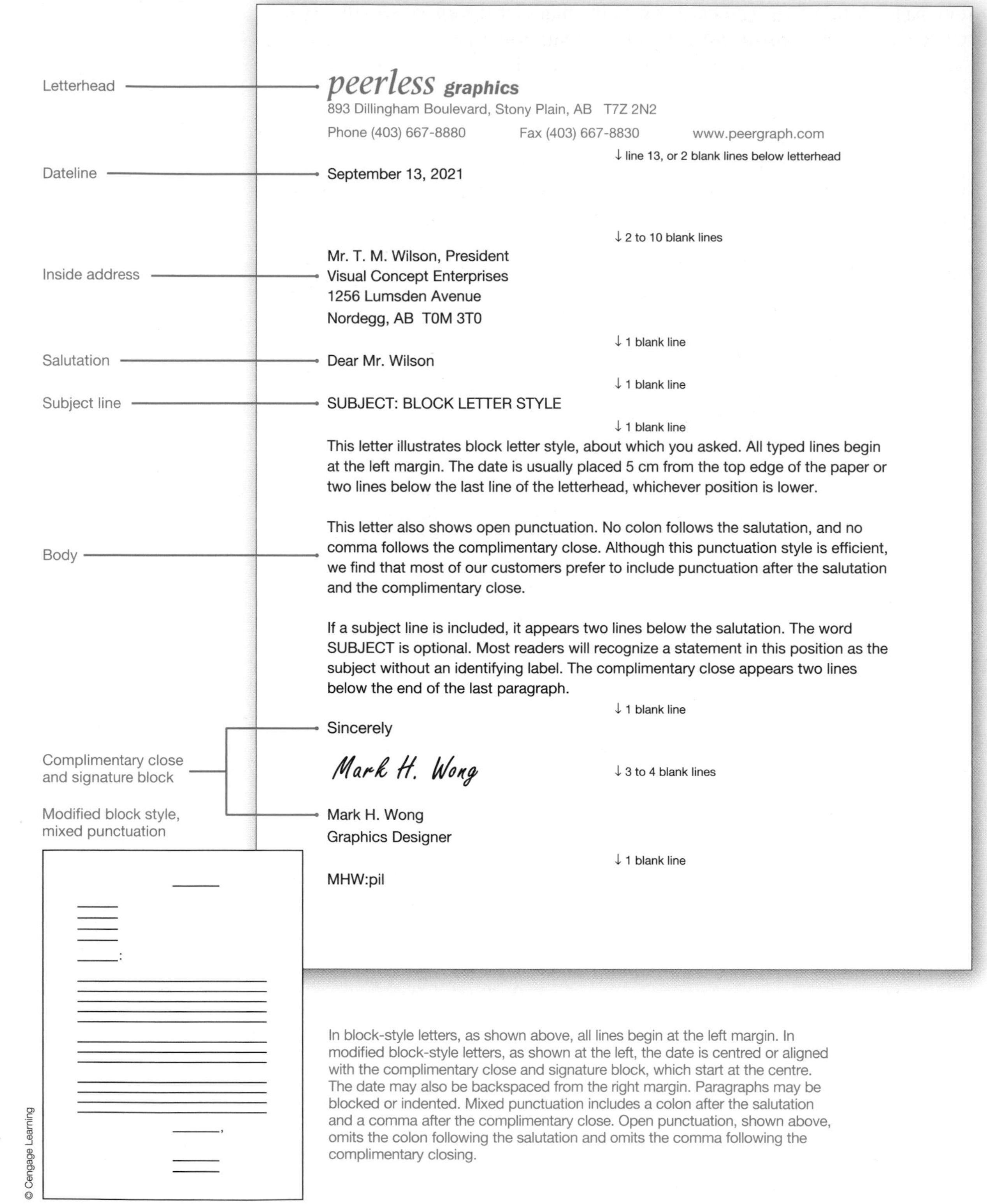

peerless **graphics**
893 Dillingham Boulevard, Stony Plain, AB   T7Z 2N2
Phone (403) 667-8880   Fax (403) 667-8830   www.peergraph.com
↓ line 13, or 2 blank lines below letterhead

Dateline

September 13, 2021

↓ 2 to 10 blank lines

Inside address

Mr. T. M. Wilson, President
Visual Concept Enterprises
1256 Lumsden Avenue
Nordegg, AB T0M 3T0

↓ 1 blank line

Salutation

Dear Mr. Wilson

↓ 1 blank line

Subject line

SUBJECT: BLOCK LETTER STYLE

↓ 1 blank line

This letter illustrates block letter style, about which you asked. All typed lines begin at the left margin. The date is usually placed 5 cm from the top edge of the paper or two lines below the last line of the letterhead, whichever position is lower.

Body

This letter also shows open punctuation. No colon follows the salutation, and no comma follows the complimentary close. Although this punctuation style is efficient, we find that most of our customers prefer to include punctuation after the salutation and the complimentary close.

If a subject line is included, it appears two lines below the salutation. The word SUBJECT is optional. Most readers will recognize a statement in this position as the subject without an identifying label. The complimentary close appears two lines below the end of the last paragraph.

↓ 1 blank line

Sincerely

Mark H. Wong

↓ 3 to 4 blank lines

Complimentary close and signature block

Mark H. Wong
Graphics Designer

↓ 1 blank line

Modified block style, mixed punctuation

MHW:pil

In block-style letters, as shown above, all lines begin at the left margin. In modified block-style letters, as shown at the left, the date is centred or aligned with the complimentary close and signature block, which start at the centre. The date may also be backspaced from the right margin. Paragraphs may be blocked or indented. Mixed punctuation includes a colon after the salutation and a comma after the complimentary close. Open punctuation, shown above, omits the colon following the salutation and omits the comma following the complimentary closing.

© Cengage Learning

◣ ENVELOPES

An envelope should be of the same quality and colour of stationery as the letter it carries. Because the envelope introduces your message and makes the first impression, you need to be especially careful in addressing it. Moreover, how you fold the letter is important.

RETURN ADDRESS. The return address is usually printed in the upper left corner of an envelope, as shown in Figure A.3. In large companies some form of identification (the writer's initials, name, or location) may be typed or handwritten above the company name and return address. This identification helps return the letter to the sender in case of nondelivery.

On an envelope without a printed return address, single space the return address in the upper left corner. Beginning on line 3 on the fourth space (approximately 1.25 centimetres or 0.5 inch) from the left edge, type the writer's name, title, company, and mailing address.

MAILING ADDRESS. On legal-sized No. 10 envelopes (10.5 by 24 centimetres), begin the address on line 13 about 11.5 centimetres from the left edge, as shown in Figure A.3. For small envelopes (7.5 by 15 centimetres), begin typing on line 12 about 6.2 centimetres from the left edge.

Canada Post recommends that addresses be typed in all caps without any punctuation. This postal service style, shown in the small envelope in Figure A.3, was originally developed to facilitate scanning by optical character readers (OCRs). Today's OCRs, however, are so sophisticated that they scan upper- and lowercase letters easily. Many companies today prefer to use the same format for the envelope

▶ FIGURE A.3 / Envelope Formats

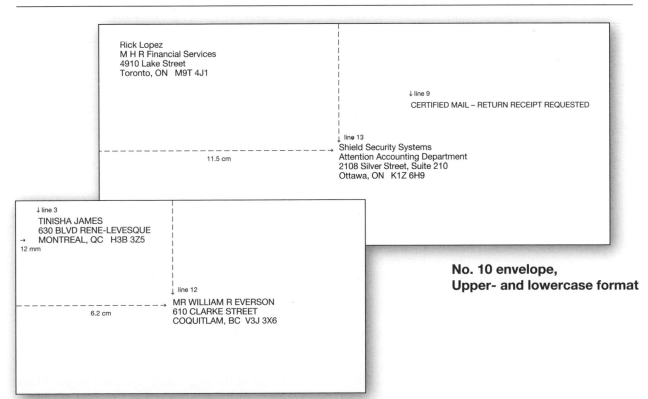

**No. 10 envelope,
Upper- and lowercase format**

No. 6¾ envelope, uppercase format

© Cengage Learning

as for the inside address. If the same format is used, writers can take advantage of word-processing programs to copy the inside address to the envelope, thus saving keystrokes and reducing errors. Having the same format on both the inside address and the envelope also looks more professional and consistent. For these reasons you may choose to use the familiar upper- and lowercase combination format. But you'll want to check with your organization to learn its preference.

In addressing your envelopes for delivery in North America, use the two-letter province, territory, and state abbreviations.

FOLDING. The way a letter is folded and inserted into an envelope sends an additional credibility signal about a writer's professionalism and carefulness. Your goal in following the procedures shown here is to produce the least number of creases that may distract readers.

For traditional business letter envelopes, begin with the letter face up. Fold slightly less than one third of the sheet toward the top, as shown in the diagram. Then fold down the top third to within 6 to 7 millimetres of the bottom fold. Insert the letter into the envelope with the last fold toward the bottom of the envelope.

For smaller personal note envelopes, begin by folding the bottom up to within 6 to 7 millimetres of the top edge. Then fold the right third over to the left. Fold the left third to within 6 to 7 millimetres of the last fold. Insert the last fold into the envelope first.

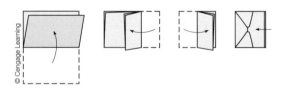

◤ MEMOS

Memos are still important business documents where they're used, but they've been largely replaced by mass emails in many organizations. For example, in the past if a company wanted to announce an important policy change to its employees, it would send out a hardcopy memo to each employee's mailbox (or desk or workstation). Today, it's increasingly rare to receive hard-copy memos. Nevertheless, you may still find it necessary to create a memo on occasion.

The easiest route is to choose a memo template in Microsoft Word, but if you'd like to design your own memo, follow these instructions:

- Open a Word document and begin typing three centimetres from the top of the page.
- Right and left margins may be set at four centimetres (1.5 inches).
- Include an optional company name and the word MEMO or MEMORANDUM as a heading. Leave two blank spaces after this heading.
- Create four subheadings on the left side of the page, each separated by one blank line: DATE, TO, FROM, and SUBJECT. The information that comes after each of these subheadings should be stated as clearly and succinctly as possible.

- After the SUBJECT subheading, leave one or two blank lines and begin typing the content of your memo. Single space between lines and double space between paragraphs.
- Don't include a closing salutation or signature. This is one of the major differences between emails and letters and faxes and memos. Because you've included the FROM subheading at the top, you don't need to repeat your name again at the end of a memo or fax.

Correction Abbreviations and Proofreading Marks

When marking your hard-copy assignments, your instructor may use the following symbols or abbreviations to indicate writing areas for improvement. You may also see them in the workplace when proofreading written documents.

The abbreviations refer to style issues discussed in Appendix D or in the Grammar/Mechanics Handbook at the end of this book. The symbols are proofreading marks used by professional editors (although their usage is diminishing because of the widespread use of software tools such as Microsoft Word's Track Changes feature). Knowing this information is valuable because part of your career may involve reviewing documents for others.

◤ CORRECTION ABBREVIATIONS

For an explanation of the errors covered by the 11 abbreviations below, consult Chapter 4, the Grammar/Mechanics Handbook, or Appendix D.

ART   An article has been used incorrectly or is missing.

AWK   Your sentence is awkwardly written (see also PREC).

PA   A pronoun doesn't agree with its antecedent (the noun it replaces).

PREC   Your sentence is imprecise.

PUNCT   A punctuation mark has been used incorrectly or is missing.

RO   Your run-on sentence has two or more independent clauses without a conjunction or semicolon, or it uses a comma to join the clauses.

SF   Your sentence is actually a fragment of a sentence; either a subject or a verb is missing.

SV   The subject and verb in your sentence don't agree.

WORDY   Your sentence includes repetition or redundancy.

VPR   A pronoun in your sentence is vague.

VT   One of your verbs is in the wrong tense, or you've shifted its tense unnecessarily.

PROOFREADING MARKS

PROOFREADING MARK	DRAFT COPY	FINAL COPY
꞊ Align horizontally	TO: Rick Munoz	TO: Rick Munoz
‖ Align vertically	‖166.32 132.45	166.32 132.45
≡ Capitalize	Coca-cola	Coca-Cola
⌒ Close up space	runs on android	runs on Android
⊐⊏ Centre	meeting at 3 p.m.	meeting at 3 p.m.
ℛ Delete	⊐ Recommendations ⊏	Recommendations
ᵛ Insert apostrophe	in my final judgement	in my judgment
⋏ Insert comma	our companys product	our company's product
⋏ Insert semicolon	you will of course	you will, of course,
꞊ Insert hyphen	value;therefore, we feel	value; therefore, we feel
⊙ Insert period	tax free income	tax-free income
ᵛ᾽ Insert quotation mark	Ms Holly Hines	Ms. Holly Hines
# Insert space	shareholders receive a bonus	shareholders receive a "bonus"
/ Lowercase (remove capitals)	downloadapps	download apps
⊏ Move to left	the Vice-President	the vice-president
⊐ Move to right	HUMAN RESOURCES	Human Resources
⊖ Spell out	⊏ I. Labour costs	I. Labour costs
	A. Findings of study ⊐	A. Findings of study
	aimed at ②depts	aimed at two departments
¶ Start new paragraph	¶Keep the screen height at eye level.	Keep the screen height at eye level.
⋯ Stet (don't delete)	officials talked openly	officials talked openly
∼ Transpose	accounts recievable	accounts receivable
⌇⌇⌇ Use boldface	Conclusions	**Conclusions**
— Use italics	The Perfect Résumé	*The Perfect Résumé*
⌐ Start new line	Globex, 23 Acorn Lane	Globex 23 Acorn Lane
⌒ Run lines together	Invoice No. 122059	Invoice No. 122059

Documentation Formats

Professional writers have many reasons to make sure they properly document any data appearing in reports or messages. Citing sources strengthens a writer's argument, as you learned earlier in this book. Acknowledging sources also shields writers from charges of plagiarism and the loss of reputation that may follow. Moreover, clear references help readers pursue further research. Fortunately, word-processing software has taken much of the pain out of documenting data, particularly for footnotes and endnotes.

◤ SOURCE NOTES AND CONTENT NOTES

Before we discuss specific documentation formats, you should know the difference between source notes and content notes. Source notes (also called in-text citations) identify quotations, paraphrased passages, and author references. They lead readers to the sources of cited information, and they must follow a consistent format. Content notes, on the other hand, allow writers to add comments, explain information not directly related to the text, or refer readers to other sections of a report.

◤ TWO DOCUMENTATION METHODS FOR SOURCE NOTES

For years researchers have struggled to develop the perfect documentation system—one that's efficient for the writer and clear to the reader. Most of these systems can be grouped into two methods: the footnote or endnote method and the parenthetic method.

Footnote or Endnote Method

Writers using footnotes or endnotes insert a small superscript (raised) numeral into the text close to the place where a reference is mentioned. This number leads the reader to a footnote at the bottom of the page or to an endnote at the end of the document. Footnotes or endnotes contain a complete description of the source document. In this book we've used the endnote method. We chose this style because it is least disruptive to the text.

In referring to a previously mentioned footnote, cite the page number along with the author's last name or a shortened form of the title if no author is given. The Latin forms *ibid.*, *op. cit.*, and *et al.* are rarely seen in business reports today. A portion of a business report using the endnote method for source citation is found in Figure C.1. Figure C.1 demonstrates the endnote method for source citation, given in the traditional style suggested in *The Chicago Manual of Style*, 17th ed. (Chicago: The University of Chicago Press, 2017). Most of the individual citation formats in this book most closely follow the American Psychological Association (APA) style, and you'll find a comparison of these two citation styles below.

Parenthetic Method

Many academic writers prefer to use a parenthetic style to cite references. In this method a reference to the author appears in parentheses close to the place where it's mentioned in the text. Some parenthetic styles show the author's last name and date of publication (e.g., *Cook 2000*), whereas others show the author's last name

These changes are introducing challenges to companies operating both in Canada and abroad. Obviously, all of these employees need specific business and technology skills, but they also need to be aware of, and be sensitive to, the cultures in which they are living and working.[1] The Bank of Montreal has targeted several of these areas in which to enhance services. Chinese-Canadian business has increased 400 percent in the last five years.[2]

Women are increasing their role as both customer and worker. By the year 2011 women are expected to compose 48 percent of the labour force in Canada, as compared with 27 percent in 1961.[3] However, women hold only about 20 percent of the top management positions in organizations in the industrialized world.[4]

Companies that focus on diversity are improving their bottom line. Recently, Federal Express was named in the *Financial Post* as one the 100 best companies to work for in Canada. Canadian Pacific Forest Products received recognition for ensuring that selection committees had diverse membership, for their development of antiharassment policies, and for other diversity initiatives.[5]

Notes

1. Brenda Lynn, "Diversity in the Workplace: Why We Should Care," *CMA Management Accounting Magazine* 70, no. 5 (June 2010): 9–12.

2. Richard Sommer, "Firms Gain Competitive Strength from Diversity (Says Report by Conference Board of Canada)," *Financial Post,* May 9, 2011, 31.

3. British Columbia, Ministry of Education, Skills, and Training, *The Impact of Demographic Change* (Victoria: Ministry of Education, Skills, and Training, 2012), 35.

4. R. J. Burke and C. A. McKeen, "Do Women at the Top Make a Difference? Gender Proportions and the Experiences of Managerial and Professional Women," *Human Relations* 49, no. 8 (2012): 1093–1104.

5. British Columbia, 36.

and page cited (e.g., *Cook 24*). One of the best-known parenthetic systems is the Modern Language Association (MLA) format. The long report shown in Chapter 9 illustrates this format. Below we'll discuss both MLA and APA formats.

Which Method for Business?

Students frequently ask, "What documentation system is most used in business?" While we can't know which style is used in all businesses, anecdotal evidence shows that MLA format is considered more appropriate for humanities subjects, and that for business (both academic and real-world), the APA format, in which the year of publication is mentioned along with the author name, has become generally accepted and expected.

APA STYLE—AMERICAN PSYCHOLOGICAL ASSOCIATION

Popular in the social and physical sciences, and increasingly the standard in business writing, the American Psychological Association (APA) documentation style uses parenthetic citations. That is, each author reference is shown in parentheses when cited in the text. Following are selected features of the APA style. For more information see the *Publication Manual of the American Psychological Association,* seventh edition.

In-Text Citation

In-text citations consist of the author's last name, year of publication, and sometimes specific parts of a source (e.g., page number). These items appear in parentheses, usually at the end of a clause or end of a sentence in which material is cited. This parenthetic citation, as shown in the following illustration, directs readers to a reference list at the end of the report where complete bibliographic information is recorded.

> The strategy of chicken king Don Tyson was to expand aggressively into other "center-of-the-plate" proteins, such as pork, fish, and turkey (Berss, 2010, p. 64).

One of the paragraphs from the report in Figure C.1, with the citation style changed from Chicago to APA, would look like this:

> These changes are introducing challenges to companies operating both in Canada and abroad. Obviously, as Brenda Lynn (2010) argues, all of these employees need specific business and technology skills, but they also need to be aware of, and be sensitive to, the cultures in which they are living and working. The Bank of Montreal has targeted several of these areas in which to enhance services. Chinese-Canadian business has increased 400 percent in the last five years (Sommer, 2011).

Reference List

All reference sources are alphabetized in a list entitled "References." Below are selected guidelines summarizing important elements of the APA reference list format:

- Include authors' names with the last name first followed by initials, such as: **Smith, M. A.** First and middle names are not used.
- Show the year of publication in parentheses, such as: **Smith, M. A. (2011).**
- Italicize the titles of books and use sentence-style (sometimes called *down style*) capitalization. This means that only the first word of a title, proper nouns, and the first word after an internal colon or dash are capitalized. Book titles are followed by the publisher's name, such as **Smith, M. A. (2011).** *Communication for managers.* **Pergamon Press.**
- Type the titles of magazine and journal articles without italics or quotation marks. Use sentence-style capitalization for article titles. However, italicize the names of magazines and journals and capitalize the initial letters of all important words. Also italicize the volume number, such as **Oliveira, T., & Dhillon, G. (2015). From adoption to routinization of B2B e-commerce: Understanding patterns across Europe.** *Journal of Global Information Management,* 23(1), 24–43. ["*23*(1), 24–43" indicates volume 23, issue 1, pages 24 to 43.]
- Many publications now contain a digital object identifier (DOI), an alphanumeric string that makes them easier to find online. If a DOI is shown, include it instead of a URL.
- Don't include personal communications (such as interviews, telephone conversations, email, and messages from nonarchived discussion groups and online forums) in the reference list, since they aren't retrievable.

Electronic References

When print information is available, APA suggests placing it first followed by online information. For example, a newspaper article: Schellhardt, T. D. (2009, March 4). In a factory schedule, where does religion fit in? *The Wall Street Journal,* B1, B12.

References

Online annual report	Air Canada. (2014). *2014 annual report*. http://www.aircanada.com/en/about/investor/index.html#reports
Magazine article	Berss, M. (2010, October 24). Protein man. *Forbes, 154,* 64–66.
Journal article with volume and issue numbers and DOI	Gill, A., & Biger, N. (2012). Barriers to small business growth in Canada. *Journal of Small Business and Enterprise Development, 19*(4), 656–668. https://doi.org/10.1108/14626001211277451
Newspaper article, no author	Globalization often means that the fast track leads overseas. (2012, June 16). *The Financial Post,* A10.
Magazine article in online research database	Jahl, A. (2013, November 24). PowerPoint of no return. *Canadian Business*. Retrieved from CBCA database, George Brown College Library.
Newspaper article, one author	Lancaster, H. (2012, February 7). When taking a tip from a job network, proceed with caution. *The Wall Street Journal,* B1.
Website, no author, no publication date	Communication Theory. (n.d.). *Lasswell's model*. http://communicationtheory.org/lasswells-model/
Online newspaper article	Markoff, J. (2009, June 5). Voluntary rules proposed to help ensure privacy for Internet users. *The New York Times*. http://www.nytimes.com
Online magazine article	Murphy, H. L. (2008, August 31). Saturn's orbit still high with consumers. *Marketing News Online*. http://www.ama.org/pubs/mn/0818n1.htm
Brochure	Pinkerton Investigation Services. (2008). *The employer's guide to investigation services* (3rd ed.) [Brochure]. Pinkerton Information Center.
Book, two authors	Rose, R. C., & Garrett, E. M. (2008). *How to make a buck and still be a decent human being*. HarperCollins.
Government publication	Public Health Agency of Canada. (2018). *Key health inequalities in Canada: A national portrait*. https://www.canada.ca/content/dam/phac-aspc/documents/services/publications/science-research/key-health-inequalities-canada-national-portrait-executive-summary/hir-full-report-eng.pdf

© Cengage Learning

http://interactive.wsj.com. For additional discussion and examples, visit the APA website (www.apastyle.org/apa-style-help.aspx).

Figure C.2 shows the format of an APA References List.

◣ MLA STYLE—MODERN LANGUAGE ASSOCIATION

The MLA citation style uses parenthetic author references in the text. These in-text citations guide the reader to a bibliography called "Works Cited." Following are selected characteristics of the MLA style. For more information, consult The Modern

Language Association of America, *MLA Handbook for Writers of Research Papers*, eighth edition (New York: The Modern Language Association of America, 2016).

In-Text Citations

Within the text the author's last name and relevant page reference appear in parentheses: *(Chartrand 310).* In-text citations should be placed close to the reference they cite. Notice that no separating comma appears. If the author's name is mentioned in the text, cite only the page number in parentheses. If you don't know the author's name (e.g., when quoting from a website or blog), use the title of the website section or blog entry you took the information from in your in-text citation. Your goal is to avoid interrupting the flow of your writing. Thus, you should strive to place the parenthetical reference where a pause would naturally occur, but as near as possible to the material documented. Note the following examples:

Author's Name in Text

Peters also notes that stress could be a contributing factor in the health problems reported thus far (135).

Author's Name Unknown

One website goes so far as to claim that new communication technologies such as BlackBerrys and multipurpose cell phones will soon make in-person conversations "a thing of the past" ("Talking Not Cool").

Author's Name in Reference

The study was first published in 1958 (Peters 127–35).

Authors' Names in Text

Others, like Bergstrom and Voorhees (243–51), support a competing theory.

Authors' Names in Reference

Others support a competing theory (e.g., Bergstrom and Voorhees 243–51).

When citing an entire work—whether a print source, a nonprint source such as a film, a television program, or a Web source that has no pagination or any other reference numbers—MLA style recommends that you include in the text, rather than in a parenthetical reference, the name of the person or organization that begins the corresponding entry in the works-cited list.

Electronic Source With Author

William J. Kennedy's *Bits and Bytes* discusses new computer technologies in the context of the digital telecommunications revolution. (In the "Works Cited" list, the reader would find a complete reference under the author's name.)

Electronic Source Without Author

More companies today are using data mining to unlock hidden value in their data. The data mining program "TargetSource," described at the Tener Solutions Group website, helps organizations predict consumer behaviour.

In the "Works Cited" list, the reader would find a complete reference under "Tener Solutions Group," the organization that owns the website.

Works Cited List

In-text citations lead the reader to complete bibliographical citations in the "Works Cited." This alphabetical listing may contain all works consulted or only

Works Cited

Air Canada. *2014 Annual Report*, 10 Feb. 2015, www.aircanada.com/ en/about/investor/documents/2014_ar.pdf. Accessed 14 July 2019. — Online annual report

Beresford, Marcia. "The Shift in Profit." *Maclean's,* 24 Oct. 2011, pp. 25–26. — Magazine article

"Clementine@work." *SPSS*, 15 May 2014, www.spss.com/customer/clem_stories. Accessed 7 Sept. 2019. — Company website, no author

Gill, Amarjit, and Nahum Biger. "Barriers to Small Business Growth in Canada." *Journal of Small Business and Enterprise Development,* vol. 19, no. 4, 2012, pp. 656–668. doi.org/10.1108/14626001211277451. — Journal article with volume and issue numbers and DOI

"Globalization Often Means That the Fast Track Leads Overseas." *The Globe and Mail*, 16 June 2012, p. A10. — Newspaper article, no author

Harris, Rebecca. "It's All About Value for Today's Consumers (Study)." *Marketing,* 20 Oct. 2015, www.marketingmag.ca/consumer/its-all-about-value-for-todays-consumers-study-159542. Accessed 14 July 2019. — Online magazine article

The Impact of Demographic Change. British Columbia Ministry of Education, Skills and Training, 2012. — Government publication (organization is both author and publisher)

Jahl, Andrew. "PowerPoint of No Return." *Canadian Business*, 24 Nov. 2013. *ProQuest,* ezproxy.library.yorku.ca/login?url=http://search.proquest.com .ezproxy.library.yorku.ca/docview/221427923?accountid=15182. — Online research database magazine article, where *ProQuest* is the research database

Lancaster, Hal. "When Taking a Tip From a Job Network, Proceed With Caution." *The Wall Street Journal*, 7 Feb. 2012, p. B1. — Newspaper article, one author

"Lasswell's Model." *Communication Theory*, communicationtheory.org/ lasswells-model/. Accessed 11 Dec. 2017. — Website, no author, no date

Pinnacle Security Services. *What Employers Should Know About Employees*. 2nd ed., Pinnacle Information Centre, 2012. — Brochure

Rivers, John. Interview by Susan Smith. 16 May 2015. — Interview

Rose, Richard C., and Echo Montgomery Garrett. *How to Make a Buck and Still Be a Decent Human Being*. HarperCollins Publishers, 2008. — Book, two authors

Wingrove, Josh. "How New Laws Are About to Change Your Privacy." *The Globe and Mail,* 9 June 2014, www.theglobeandmail.com/news/politics/how-new-laws-are-about-to-change-your-privacy/article19054653/. — Online newspaper article

those mentioned in the text. Check with your instructor or editor to learn what method is preferred. Below are selected guidelines summarizing important elements of the MLA format for Works Cited, as shown in Figure C.3.

HANGING INDENTED STYLE. Indent the second and succeeding line for each item. MLA format suggests double-spacing for the entire paper, including the works-cited list. However, Figure C.3 is single-spaced to represent preferred business usage.

BOOK AND WEBSITE TITLES. Italicize the titles of books and use headline style for capitalization. This means that the initial letters of all main words are capitalized:

Lewe, Glenda, and Carol D. MacLeod. *Step Into the World of Workplace Learning: A Collection of Authentic Workplace Materials.* Nelson Thomson Learning, 2011.

"ACE Aviation to Take Minority Stake in Merged U.S. Airline." *CBC,* 19 May 2015, www.cbc.ca.

MAGAZINE TITLES. For the titles of magazine articles, include the date of publication but omit volume and issue numbers:

Lee, Mary M. "Investing in International Relationships." *Business Monthly* 18 Feb. 2010, pp. 25–27.

JOURNAL ARTICLES. For journal articles, follow the same format as for magazine articles except include the volume number, issue number, and the year of publication:

Collier, Roger. "Morals, Medicine, and Geography." *Canadian Medical Association Journal,* vol. 179, no. 10, 2014, pp. 996–98.

ITALICS AND UNDERLINING. MLA style now recommends italicizing book, magazine, and journal titles (instead of underlining).

Electronic References

The objective in citing sources, whether print publications or electronic publications, is to provide enough information so that your reader can locate your sources.

The eighth edition of the *MLA Handbook* makes the following recommendations for citing Web publications:

- Give the same information for electronic sources as you would if you were citing a print publication (e.g., author name, title, page number).
- Give all relevant dates. Because electronic sources can change or move, cite the date the document was produced (if available; if not, omit it) as well as the date you accessed the information. The date of access is helpful because multiple versions of an electronic work may be available, and any version may vary from previous or future versions.
- Include the electronic address or universal resource locator (URL). It should appear immediately after the publication date, followed by a period, and should be the complete address, if possible (exclude "http://" or "https://"), and be followed by a period. If the URL needs to be divided at the end of a line, do so only after the double slashes or a single slash. Never add a hyphen (or allow your word processor to add one) to mark a break in the address.
- If the publisher has assigned a digital object identifier (DOI) to the publication, cite it instead of the URL.
- Download or print (for future reference) any Web material you use, as online resources frequently move or even disappear.

Article in an Online Journal

Chrisman, Laura, and Laurence Phillips. "Postcolonial Studies and the British Academy." *Jouvert,* vol. 3, no. 3, 1999, english.chass.ncsu.edu/jouvert/index.htm.

Brown, Ronnie R. "Photographs That Should Have Been Taken." *Room of One's Own,* vol. 18, no. 3, Summer 1995, roommagazine.com.

Article in an Online Newspaper or on a Newswire

These sites change very frequently—in some cases daily—so it is a good idea to download or record citation information (and URL, if needed) immediately.

Scarth, Deborah. "Many Top University Students Use Tutors to Keep an Edge." *The Globe and Mail,* 4 June 2000. theglobeandmail.com.

"Canada's Unemployment Rate Dips." Canadian Broadcasting Corporation, 4 June 2000. CBCnews.ca.

Article in an Online Magazine

Campbell, Colin. "Making Bad Times Good." *Maclean's*, 26 Feb. 2009, macleans.ca.

Professional or Personal Website

List the publication information in the following order: the name of the creator of the site, the title of the site (italicized), a version number (for example, edition, posting date, volume or issue number), publisher or sponsor of the site (the name of the organization affiliated with the site), the date of publication (day, month, year, as available; if citing an entire website, cite a range of dates—scroll down and check the bottom of the screen; if no date is available, omit it), the electronic address, and the date you accessed the information. If some of this information is unavailable, cite whatever is available.

Canadian Tire Corporation Limited. *Investor Relations*. 1997–2017, investors. canadiantire.ca.

Ellison, Sara. *Sara's Home Page*. U of Victoria, orca.phys.uvic.ca/~sara/. Accessed 29 July 2015.

Online Book

Many books are now available electronically, either independently or as part of a scholarly project. Some have appeared previously in print, while others exist only on the Web. Follow the general recommendations for citing books in print, but include the additional information required for electronic citations, as outlined here.

If a book that you are citing has appeared in print, it may be important to include the print version of the publication information (e.g., if the book was scanned as part of an online database). In that case, give the name of the author first, if it is available; if not, give the name of the editor, translator, or compiler, followed by a comma and then the appropriate descriptive label (*editor*, *translator*, or *compiler*). Next give the title of the work (italicized if the work is independent; in quotation marks if the work is part of a larger work); the name of the editor, translator, or compiler (if relevant); the edition or version used; followed by the publication information for the printed version (name of the publisher and year of publication). Then add the following information: the title of the website or database (italicized), the URL, and the date you accessed the information.

If the book you are citing has not been previously published, follow the instructions above regarding the name of the author, editor, translator, or compiler, and the title of the work. Follow that information with the title of the website (italicized); the edition or version used; the publisher or sponsor of the website (if available; if not, omit it); the date of publication (day, month, year, if available; if not, omit it); the URL; and the date you accessed the information (if needed).

Montgomery, Lucy Maud. *Anne of Green Gables*. 1908. *The Literature Network*, www.online-literature.com.

Dewey, John. *Democracy and Education*. Macmillan, 1916. *Wikisource*, 20 Mar. 2016, 06:23 a.m., en.wikisource.org/wiki/Democracy_and _Education. Accessed 22 Nov. 2016.

Other Nonprint Sources

The citations for other nonprint sources will follow the recommendations for print versions, with some additional required information. If you are citing an online posting, you may need to include the URL, as it could otherwise be difficult for your reader to find the posting.

Television/Radio Episode

"Sears Saga." *The National*, narrated by Peter Mansbridge, CBC, 4 June 2014.

Television/Radio Episode Found Online

"CRA to Review Disability Tax Credit Applications." *The National*, CBC, 8 Dec. 2017, www.cbc.ca/news/thenational/cra-to-review-disability-tax -credit-applications-1.4441165?autoplay=true.

Email Communication

Pen Canada. "Your Inquiries to PEN." Received by author, 3 July 2016.

Online Posting

Matus, Roger. "Another University Sends False Admission Emails." *Robert Matus's Death by Email*, InBoxer Inc., 6 Apr. 2009, inboxer.typepad.com/ deathbyemail/. Accessed 7 April 2014.

Material From an Online Research Database

Online services such as ProQuest and LexisNexis provide a variety of databases that your college or university library will have. Give the name of the service (in italics) before the URL and the date you accessed the information (if necessary).

Golden, Anne. "Do Our Foreign Investment Laws Still Have Legs?" *The Globe and Mail*, 1 Dec. 2004, p. A23. *CBCA Current Affairs*, www.proquest.com/ libraries/academic/databases/cbca.html.

Podcast

"Cartoonist Lynda Barry on Reclaiming the Art of Child's Play." *Writers and Company*, hosted by Eleanor Wachtel, CBC, 29 May 2016, www.cbc.ca /radio/writersandcompany/cartoonist-lynda-barry-on-reclaiming-the-art-of- child-s -play-1.4262131.

Tweet

Include the full text of the tweet in place of a title, and provide the time of posting in addition to the date.

@JustinTrudeau. "Today, we pause to remember the Canadians who've served our country and stood on guard for us: http://bit.ly/2htdEyq." Twitter, 11 Nov. 2017, 5:21 a.m., twitter.com/JustinTrudeau/status/929338309024694272.

Style in Writing

Professional writers strive to develop an effective style. While all business writers should be able to write simple declarative sentences (*The stock market is down today*) or even more complex sentences (*The stock market is down today, despite the higher employment numbers*), more experienced writers recognize certain "tricks of the trade" that lend their writing an even more professional, persuasive tone. Some of these tricks are discussed below. Try incorporating them into your work as you progress through your course and your future career.

◣ EMPHASIS

When you are talking with someone, you can emphasize your main ideas by saying them loudly or by repeating them slowly. You could pound the table if you wanted to show real emphasis. Another way you can signal the relative importance of an idea is by raising your eyebrows, shaking your head, or whispering. But when you write, you must rely on other means to tell your readers which ideas are more important than others. Emphasis in writing can be achieved in two ways: mechanically and stylistically.

Emphasis Through Mechanics

To emphasize an idea, a writer may use any of the following devices:

Underlining	<u>Underlining</u> draws the eye to a word.
Italics and boldface	Use *italics* or **boldface** for special meaning and emphasis.
Font changes	Changing from a large font size to a smaller font size or to a *different font* adds interest and emphasis.
All caps	Printing words in ALL CAPS is like shouting them.
Dashes	Dashes—if used sparingly—can be effective in capturing attention.
Tabulation	Listing items vertically makes them stand out:

1. First item

2. Second item

3. Third item

Other means of achieving mechanical emphasis include the arrangement of space, colour, lines, boxes, columns, titles, headings, and subheadings. Today's software and colour printers provide a wide choice of capabilities for emphasizing ideas.

Emphasis Through Style

Although mechanical means are occasionally appropriate, a good writer more often achieves emphasis stylistically. That is, the writer chooses words carefully and constructs sentences skillfully to emphasize main ideas and de-emphasize minor or negative ideas. Here are four suggestions for emphasizing ideas stylistically:

USE VIVID WORDS. Vivid words are emphatic because the reader can picture ideas clearly.

> **General** One business uses personal selling techniques.
>
> **Vivid** Avon uses face-to-face selling techniques.
>
> **General** A customer said that he wanted the contract returned soon.
>
> **Vivid** Mr. LeClerc insisted that the contract be returned by July 1.

LABEL THE MAIN IDEA. If an idea is significant, tell the reader.

> **Unlabelled** Explore the possibility of leasing a site, but also hire a consultant.
>
> **Labelled** Explore the possibility of leasing a site, but most important, hire a consultant.

PLACE THE IMPORTANT IDEA FIRST OR LAST IN THE SENTENCE. Ideas have less competition from surrounding words when they appear first or last in a sentence. Observe how the concept of productivity is emphasized in the first and second examples:

> **Emphatic** Productivity is more likely to be increased when profit-sharing plans are linked to individual performance rather than to group performance.
>
> **Emphatic** Profit-sharing plans linked to individual performance rather than to group performance are more effective in increasing productivity.
>
> **Unemphatic** Profit-sharing plans are more effective in increasing productivity when they are linked to individual performance rather than to group performance.

PLACE THE IMPORTANT IDEA IN A SIMPLE SENTENCE OR IN AN INDEPENDENT CLAUSE. Don't dilute the effect of the idea by making it share the spotlight with other words and clauses.

> **Emphatic** You are the first trainee we have hired for this program. (Use a simple sentence for emphasis.)
>
> **Emphatic** Although we considered many candidates, you are the first trainee we have hired for this program. (The independent clause contains the main idea.)
>
> **Unemphatic** Although you are the first trainee we have hired for this program, we had many candidates and expect to expand the program in the future. (Main idea is lost in a dependent clause.)

When to De-emphasize

To de-emphasize something, such as bad news, try one of the following stylistic devices:

USE GENERAL WORDS.

> **Vivid** Our records indicate that you were recently fired.
>
> **General** Our records indicate that your employment status has changed recently.

PLACE THE BAD NEWS IN A DEPENDENT CLAUSE CONNECTED TO AN INDEPENDENT CLAUSE WITH SOMETHING POSITIVE. In sentences with dependent clauses, the main emphasis is always on the independent clause.

Emphasizes bad news We cannot issue you credit at this time, but we do have a plan that will allow you to fill your immediate needs on a cash basis.

De-emphasizes bad news We have a plan that will allow you to fill your immediate needs on a cash basis since we cannot issue credit at this time.

◤ ACTIVE AND PASSIVE VOICE

In sentences with active-voice verbs, the subject is the doer of the action. In passive-voice sentences, the subject is acted upon.

Active verb Mr. Wong completed the tax return before the April 30 deadline. (The subject, *Mr. Wong*, is the doer of the action.)

Passive verb The tax return was completed before the April 30 deadline. (The subject, *tax return*, is acted upon.)

In the first sentence, the active-voice verb emphasizes Mr. Wong. In the second sentence, the passive-voice verb emphasizes the tax return. In sentences with passive voice verbs, the doer of the action may be revealed or left unknown. In business writing, and in personal interactions, some situations demand tact and sensitivity. Instead of using a direct approach with active verbs, we may prefer the indirectness that passive verbs allow. Rather than making a blunt announcement with an active verb (*Gunnar made a major error in the estimate*), we can soften the sentence with a passive construction (*A major error was made in the estimate*).

Here's a summary of the best use of active- and passive-voice verbs:

- Use the active voice for most business writing. It clearly tells what the action is and who is performing that action.
- Use the passive voice to emphasize an action or the recipient of the action. *You have been selected to represent us.*
- Use the passive voice to de-emphasize negative news. *Your watch has not been repaired.*
- Use the passive voice to conceal the doer of an action. *A major error was made in the estimate.*

How can you tell if a verb is active or passive? Identify the subject of the sentence and decide whether the subject is doing the acting or being acted upon. For example, in the sentence *An appointment was made for January 1*, the subject is *appointment*. The subject is being acted upon; therefore, the verb (*was made*) is passive. Another clue in identifying passive-voice verbs is that they generally include a *to be* helping verb, such as *is*, *are*, *was*, *were*, *being*, or *been*.

◤ PARALLELISM

Parallelism is a writing technique that creates balanced writing. Sentences written so that their parts are balanced or parallel are easy to read and understand. To achieve parallel construction, use similar structures to express similar ideas. For example, the words *computing, coding, recording,* and *storing* are parallel because they all end in *-ing*. To express the list as *computing, coding, recording, and storage* is disturbing because the last item is not what the reader expects. Try to match nouns with nouns, verbs with verbs, and clauses with clauses. Avoid mixing active-voice verbs with passive-voice verbs. Your goal is to keep the wording balanced in expressing similar ideas.

Lacks parallelism The market for industrial goods includes manufacturers, contractors, wholesalers, and those concerned with the retail function.

Revision The market for industrial goods includes manufacturers, contractors, wholesalers, and retailers. (Parallel construction matches nouns.)

Lacks parallelism Our primary goals are to increase productivity, reduce costs, and the improvement of product quality.

Revision Our primary goals are to increase productivity, reduce costs, and improve product quality. (Parallel construction matches verbs.)

Lacks parallelism We are scheduled to meet in Toronto on January 5, we are meeting in Montreal on the 15th of March, and in Burlington on June 3.

Revision We are scheduled to meet in Toronto on January 5, in Montreal on March 15, and in Burlington on June 3. (Parallel construction matches phrases.)

Lacks parallelism Mrs. Chorney audits all accounts lettered A through L; accounts lettered M through Z are audited by Mr. Faheem.

Revision Mrs. Chorney audits all accounts lettered A through L; Mr. Faheem audits accounts lettered M through Z. (Parallel construction matches active-voice verbs in balanced clauses.)

In presenting lists of data, whether printed horizontally or tabulated vertically, be certain to express all the items in parallel form.

Parallelism in Vertical Lists

Three primary objectives of advertising are as follows:

1. Increase the frequency of product use.
2. Introduce complementary products.
3. Enhance the corporate image.

◤ UNITY

Unified sentences contain thoughts that are related to only one main idea. The following sentence lacks unity because the first clause has little or no relationship to the second clause:

Lacks unity Our insurance plan is available in all provinces and territories, and you may name anyone as a beneficiary for your coverage.

Revision Our insurance plan is available in all provinces and territories. What's more, you may name anyone as a beneficiary for your coverage.

The ideas in a sentence are better expressed by separating the two dissimilar clauses and adding a connecting phrase. Three writing faults that destroy sentence unity are imprecise writing, mixed constructions, and misplaced modifiers.

Imprecise Writing

Sentences that twist or turn unexpectedly away from the main thought are examples of imprecise writing. Such confusing writing may result when too many thoughts are included in one sentence or when one thought does not relate to another. To rectify an imprecise sentence, revise it so that the reader understands the relationship between the thoughts. If that is impossible, move the unrelated thoughts to a new sentence.

Imprecise writing I appreciate the time you spent with me last week, and I have purchased a computer and software that generate graphics.

Revision I appreciate the time you spent with me last week. As a result of your advice, I have purchased a computer and software that generate graphics.

Imprecise writing The stockholders of a corporation elect a board of directors, although the chief executive officer is appointed by the board and the CEO is not directly responsible to the stockholders.

Revision The stockholders of a corporation elect a board of directors, who in turn appoint the chief executive officer. The CEO is not directly responsible to the stockholders.

Mixed Constructions

Writers who fuse two different grammatical constructions destroy sentence unity and meaning.

Mixed construction The reason I am late is because my car battery is dead.

Revision The reason I am late is that my car battery is dead. (The construction introduced by *the reason is* should be a noun clause beginning with *that*, not an adverbial clause beginning with *because*.)

Mixed construction When the stock market index rose five points was our signal to sell.

Revision When the stock market index rose five points, we were prepared to sell. Or: Our signal to sell was an increase of five points in the stock market index.

Dangling and Misplaced Modifiers

For clarity, modifiers must be close to the words they describe or limit. A modifier dangles when the word or phrase it describes is missing from the sentence. A modifier is misplaced when the word or phrase it describes is not close enough for the relationship to be clear. The solution is to position the modifier closer to the word(s) it describes or limits, or to introduce the word that's missing, often a person or place. Introductory verbal phrases are particularly dangerous; be sure to follow them immediately with the words they logically describe or modify.

Dangling modifier To win the lottery, a ticket must be purchased. (Purchased by whom? The verbal phrase must be followed by a subject.)

Revision To win the lottery, you must purchase a ticket.

Dangling modifier Driving through Tetrahedron Plateau, the ocean suddenly came into view. (Is the ocean driving through Tetrahedron Plateau?)

Revision Driving through Tetrahedron Plateau, we saw the ocean suddenly come into view.

Try this trick for detecting and remedying dangling modifiers. Ask the question *who or what?* after any introductory phrase. The words immediately following should tell the reader who or what is performing the action. Try the test on the previous danglers.

Misplaced modifier Seeing his error too late, the envelope was immediately resealed by Adrian. (Did the envelope see the error?)

Revision Seeing his error too late, Adrian immediately resealed the envelope.

Misplaced modifier A wart appeared on my left hand that I want removed. (Is the left hand to be removed?)

Revision I want to remove the wart that appeared on my left hand.

Misplaced modifier The busy human resources director interviewed only candidates who had excellent computer skills in the morning. (Were the candidates skilled only in the morning?)

Revision In the morning the busy human resources director interviewed only candidates who had excellent computer skills.

◤ PARAGRAPH COHERENCE

A paragraph is a group of sentences with a controlling idea, usually stated first. Paragraphs package similar ideas into meaningful groups for readers. Effective paragraphs are coherent; that is, they hold together. But coherence does not happen accidentally. It is achieved through effective organization and (1) repetition of key ideas, (2) use of pronouns, and (3) use of transitional expressions.

Repetition of Key Ideas or Key Words

Repeating a word or key thought from a preceding sentence helps guide a reader from one thought to the next. This redundancy is necessary to build cohesiveness into writing.

> **Effective repetition** Quality problems in production are often the result of inferior raw materials. Some companies have strong programs for ensuring the quality of incoming production materials and supplies.

The second sentence of the preceding paragraph repeats the key idea of quality. Moreover, the words incoming production materials and supplies refer to the raw materials mentioned in the preceding sentence. Good writers find similar words to describe the same idea, thus using repetition to clarify a topic for the reader.

Use of Pronouns

Pronouns such as his, her, their, *this*, *that*, *they*, *these*, and *those* promote coherence by connecting the thoughts in one sentence to the thoughts in a previous sentence. A pronoun without a clear antecedent can be annoying. That's because the reader doesn't know precisely to what the pronoun refers.

> **Faulty pronoun use** When company profits increased, employees were given either a cash payment or company stock. This became a real incentive to employees. (Is *This* the cash or the stock or both?)

> **Revision** When company profits increased, employees were given either a cash payment or company stock. This profit-sharing plan became a real incentive to employees.

Use of Transitional Expressions

One of the most effective ways to achieve paragraph coherence is through the use of transitional expressions. These expressions act as road signs: they indicate where the message is headed and they help the reader anticipate what is coming. Here are some of the most effective transitional expressions. They are grouped according to use.

TIME ASSOCIATION	CONTRAST	ILLUSTRATION
before, after	although	for example
first, second	but	in this way
meanwhile	however	
next	instead	
until	nevertheless	
when, whenever	on the other hand	
CAUSE, EFFECT	**ADDITIONAL IDEA**	
consequently	furthermore	
for this reason	in addition	
hence	likewise	
therefore	moreover	

PARAGRAPH LENGTH

Although no rule regulates the length of paragraphs, business writers recognize the value of short paragraphs. Paragraphs with eight or fewer printed lines look inviting and readable. Long, solid chunks of print appear formidable. If a topic can't be covered in eight or fewer printed lines (not sentences), consider breaking it into smaller segments.

WRITING IMPROVEMENT EXERCISES

Emphasis

For each of the following sentences, circle (a) or (b). Be prepared to justify your choice.

1. Which is more emphatic?
   a. We need a faster, more efficient distribution system.
   b. We need a better distribution system.

2. Which is more emphatic?
   a. Increased advertising would improve sales.
   b. Adding $50,000 in advertising would double our sales.

3. Which is more emphatic?
   a. The committee was powerless to act.
   b. The committee was unable to take action.

4. Which sentence puts more emphasis on product loyalty?
   a. Product loyalty is the primary motivation for advertising.
   b. The primary motivation for advertising is loyalty to the product, although other purposes are also served.

5. Which sentence places more emphasis on the seminar?
   a. An executive training seminar that starts June 1 will include four candidates.
   b. Four candidates will be able to participate in an executive training seminar that we feel will provide a valuable learning experience.

Active-Voice Verbs

Business writing is more forceful if it uses active-voice verbs. Revise the following sentences so that the verbs are in the active voice. Put the emphasis on the doer of the action. Add subjects if necessary.

Example The computers were powered up each day at 7 a.m.
Revision Kamal powered up the computers each day at 7 a.m.

1. Initial figures for the bid were submitted before the June 1 deadline.
2. New spices and cooking techniques were tried by South St. Burger to improve its hamburgers.

◤ PASSIVE-VOICE VERBS

When indirectness or tact is required, use passive-voice verbs. Revise the following sentences so that they are in the passive voice.

Example Sade did not submit the accounting statement on time.
Revision The accounting statement was not submitted on time.

1. Andreas made a computational error in the report.
2. We cannot ship your order for 10 monitors until June 15.
3. The government first issued a warning regarding the use of this pesticide over 15 months ago.

Parallelism

Revise the following sentences so that their parts are balanced.

1. (Hint: Match verbs.) Some of our priorities include linking employee compensation to performance, keeping administrative costs down, the expansion of computer use, and the improvement of performance review skills of supervisors.
2. (Hint: Match active voice of verbs.) Yin Huang, of the Red River office, will now supervise our Western Division; the Eastern Division will be supervised by our Ottawa office manager, David Ali.
3. (Hint: Match nouns.) Word processing software is used extensively in the fields of health care, by lawyers, by secretaries in insurance firms, for scripts in the entertainment industry, and in the banking field.
4. If you have decided to cancel our service, please cut your credit card in half, and the card pieces should be returned to us.

Sentence Unity

The following sentences lack unity. Rewrite, correcting the identified fault.

Example (Dangling modifier) By advertising extensively, all the open jobs were filled quickly.
Revision By advertising extensively, we were able to fill all the open jobs quickly.

1. (Dangling modifier) To open a money market account, a deposit of $3,000 is required.
2. (Mixed construction) The reason why Ms. Rutulis is unable to travel extensively is because she has family responsibilities.
3. (Misplaced modifier) Identification passes must be worn at all times in offices and production facilities showing the employee's picture.

Coherence

Revise the following paragraphs to improve coherence. Be aware that the transitional expressions and key words selected depend largely on the emphasis desired. Many possible revisions exist.

Example Computer style-checkers rank somewhere between artificial intelligence and artificial ignorance. Style-checkers are like clever children: smart but not wise. Business writers should be cautious. They should be aware of the usefulness of style-checkers. They should know their limitations.

Revision Computer style-checkers rank somewhere between artificial intelligence and artificial ignorance. For example, they are like clever children: smart but not wise. For this reason, business writers should be cautious. Although they should be aware of the usefulness of these software programs, business writers should also know their limitations.

1. Our database includes all customer data. It provides space for name, address, and other vital information. It has an area for comments. The area for comments comes in handy. It requires more time and careful keyboarding, though.

2. No one likes to offer poor products. We began highlighting recurring problems. Employees make a special effort to be more careful in doing their work right the first time. It doesn't have to be returned to them for corrections.

GRAMMAR/MECHANICS HANDBOOK

▶ INTRODUCTION

For students who need a quick review of basic grammar and mechanics, the Grammar/Mechanics Handbook offers a rapid, systematic review, consisting of four parts:

- **Grammar/Mechanics Diagnostic Test.** This 65-point pre-test helps you assess your strengths and weaknesses in eight areas of grammar and mechanics. Your instructor may later give you a posttest to assess your improvement.
- **Grammar/Mechanics Profile.** The G/M Profile enables you to pinpoint specific areas in which you need remedial instruction or review.
- **Grammar/Mechanics Review.** A concise review of basic principles of grammar, punctuation, capitalization, and number style. The Review also provides reinforcement and quiz exercises that help you interact with the principles of grammar and test your comprehension. The guidelines not only provide a study guide for review but will also serve as a reference manual throughout the course. The Review can be used for classroom-centred instruction or for self-guided learning.
- **Confusing Words and Frequently Misspelled Words.** A list of selected confusing words, along with a list of 160 frequently misspelled words, completes the Handbook.

Begin your systematic review of grammar and mechanics by completing the following diagnostic pretest.

▶ GRAMMAR/MECHANICS DIAGNOSTIC PRETEST

Name_____

This diagnostic pretest is intended to reveal your strengths and weaknesses in using the following:

plural nouns	adjectives	punctuation
possessive nouns	adverbs	capitalization style
pronouns	prepositions	number style
verbs	conjunctions	

The pretest is organized into sections corresponding to the preceding categories. In Sections A through G, each sentence is either correct or has one error related to the category under which it is listed. If a sentence is correct, write C. If it has an error, underline the error and write the correct form in the space provided. When you finish, check your answers with your instructor and fill out the Grammar/Mechanics Profile at the end of the test.

A. Plural Nouns

<u>companies</u>   **Example**   Large <u>companys</u> hire numerous CPAs and accountants.

_____   1. All job candidates are asked whether they can work on Saturday's.

_____ 2. Two students discussed the pro's and con's of using laptops and cell phones in their classes.

_____ 3. Both of Jeff's sister-in-laws worked as secretaries at different facilities.

_____ 4. Neither the Parvezes nor the Harris's knew about the changes in beneficiaries.

_____ 5. Since the early 2000s, most judicial systems and lawyers have invested in packages that detect computer viruses.

B. Possessive Nouns

_____ 6. We sincerely hope that the jurys judgment reflects the stories of all the witnesses.

_____ 7. In a little over two months time, the analysts finished their reports.

_____ 8. Ms. Porters staff is responsible for all accounts receivable for customers purchasing electronics parts.

_____ 9. At the next stockholders meeting, we will discuss benefits for employees and dividends for shareholders.

_____ 10. For the past 90 days, employees in the sales department have complained about Mr. Navetta smoking.

C. Pronouns

me   **Example** Whom did you ask to replace Francisco and <u>I</u>?

_____ 11. The chief and myself were quite willing to send copies to whoever requested them.

_____ 12. Much of the project assigned to Samantha and I had to be reassigned to Matt and them.

_____ 13. Although it's marketing spend is relatively low, Nk'Mip Cellars continues to grow sales.

_____ 14. Just between you and me, only you and I know that she will be transferred.

_____ 15. My friend and I applied at Loblaws because of their excellent benefits.

D. Verb Agreement

has   **Example** The list of payments <u>have</u> to be approved by the boss.

_____ 16. This cell phone and its calling plan costs much less than I expected.

_____ 17. A description of the property, together with several other legal documents, were submitted by my lawyer.

_____ 18. There are a wide range of proposals for reducing email overload.

_____ 19. Neither the manager nor the employees in the office think the solution is fair.

_____ 20. Because of the holiday, our committee were unable to meet.

E. Verb Mood, Voice, and Tense

_____ 21. If I was in charge, I would certainly change things.

_____ 22. To make a copy, first open the disk drive door and then you insert the disk.

_____ 23. If I could chose any city, I would select Hong Kong.

_____ 24. Those contracts have laid on his desk for more than two weeks.

_____ 25. The auditors have went over these accounts carefully, and they have found no discrepancies.

F. Adjectives and Adverbs

_____ 26. Until we have a more clearer picture of what is legal, we will proceed cautiously.

_____ 27. Britney thought she had done good in her job interview.

_____ 28. A recently appointed official was in charge of monitoring peer to peer file-sharing systems.

_____ 29. Robert only has two days before he must submit his end-of-the-year report.

_____ 30. The architects submitted their drawings in a last-minute attempt to beat the deadline.

G. Prepositions and Conjunctions

_____ 31. Can you tell me where the meeting is scheduled at?

_____ 32. It seems like we have been taking this pre-test forever.

_____ 33. Our research shows that Zoom meetings may be less productive then regular meetings.

_____ 34. My courses this semester are totally different than last semester's.

_____ 35. Do you know where this shipment is going to?

H. Commas

For each of the following sentences, insert any necessary commas. Count the number of commas that you added. Write that number in the space provided. All punctuation must be correct to receive credit for the sentence. If a sentence requires no punctuation, write C.

<u>1</u>   **Example**   Because of developments in theory and computer applications‸management is becoming more of a science.

_____ 36. For example management determines how orders assignments and responsibilities are delegated to employees.

_____ 37. Your order Ms. Lee will be sent from Niagara Falls Ontario on July 3.

_____ 38. When you need service on any of your equipment we will be happy to help you Mr. Lemieux.

_____ 39. Michelle Wong who is the project manager at TeleCom suggested that I call you.

_____ 40. You have purchased from us often and your payments in the past have always been prompt.

I. Commas and Semicolons 1

Add commas and semicolons to the following sentences. In the space provided, write the number of punctuation marks that you added.

_____ 41. The salesperson turned in his report however he did not indicate the time period it covered.

_____ 42. Interest payments on bonds are tax deductible dividend payments are not.

_____ 43. We are opening a branch office in Brandon and hope to be able to serve all your needs from that office by the middle of January.

_____ 44. As suggested by the committee we must first secure adequate funding then we may consider expansion.

_____ 45. When you begin your secondary research consider many sources of information namely think about using the Internet, books, periodicals, government publications, and databases.

J. Commas and Semicolons 2

_____ 46. After our chief had the printer repaired it jammed again within the first week although we treated it carefully.

_____ 47. Our experienced courteous staff has been trained to anticipate your every need.

_____ 48. In view of the new law that went into effect on April 1 our current liability insurance must be increased therefore we need to adjust our budget.

_____ 49. As stipulated in our contract your agency will develop a social media program and supervise our media budget.

_____ 50. As you know Ms. Okui we aim for long-term business relationships not quick profits.

K. Other Punctuation

Each of the following sentences may require colons, question marks, quotation marks, periods, parentheses, and underlining, as well as commas and semicolons. Add the appropriate punctuation to each sentence. Then in the space provided, write the total number of marks that you added or changed.

2   **Example**   Fully recharging your digital camera's battery (see page 6 of the instruction manual) takes only 90 minutes.

_____ 51. The following members of the department volunteered to help on Saturday Kim Carlos Dan and Sylvia.

_____ 52. Todd Phillips, Pixie Reed, and Marijela Garcia usually arrive at the office by 8:30 a m.

_____ 53. We recommend that you use hearing protectors see the warning on page 8 when using this electric drill.

_____ 54. Did the CEO really say "All employees may take Friday off

_____ 55. We are trying to locate an edition of _Canadian Business_ with an article titled Who Is Reading Your Texts

L. Capitalization

For each of the following sentences, underline any letter that should be capitalized. In the space provided, write the number of words you marked.

4   **Example**   vice president kumar devised a procedure for expediting purchase orders from area 4 warehouses.

_____ 56. although english was his native language, he also spoke spanish and could read french.

_____ 57. on a trip to the east coast, uncle henry visited peggy's cove.

_____ 58. karen enrolled in classes in history, german, and sociology.

_____ 59. the business manager and the vice president each received a new dell computer.

_____ 60. james lee, the president of kendrick, inc., will speak at our conference in the spring.

M. Number Style

Decide whether the numbers in the following sentences should be written as words or as figures. Each sentence either is correct or has one error. If it is correct, write C. If it has an error, underline it and write the correct form in the space provided.

five   **Example** The bank had 5 branches in three suburbs.

_____ 61. More than 3,000,000 people have visited the Parliament Buildings in the past five years.

_____ 62. Of the 28 viewer comments we received regarding our online commercial, only three were negative.

_____ 63. We set aside forty dollars for petty cash, but by December 1 our fund was depleted.

_____ 64. The meeting is scheduled for May fifth at 3 p.m.

_____ 65. In the past five years, nearly fifteen percent of the population changed residences at least once.

◤ GRAMMAR/MECHANICS PROFILE

In the spaces place a check mark to indicate the number of correct answers you had in each category of the Grammar/Mechanics Diagnostic Pretest.

		NUMBER CORRECT*				
		5	4	3	2	1
1–5	Plural Nouns	___	___	___	___	___
6–10	Possessive Nouns	___	___	___	___	___
11–15	Pronouns	___	___	___	___	___
16–20	Verb Agreement	___	___	___	___	___
21–25	Verb Mood, Voice, and Tense	___	___	___	___	___
26–30	Adjectives and Adverbs	___	___	___	___	___
31–35	Prepositions and Conjunctions	___	___	___	___	___
36–40	Commas	___	___	___	___	___
41–45	Commas and Semicolons 1	___	___	___	___	___
46–50	Commas and Semicolons 2	___	___	___	___	___
51–55	Other Punctuation	___	___	___	___	___
56–60	Capitalization	___	___	___	___	___
61–65	Number Style	___	___	___	___	___

***Note:** 5 = have excellent skills; 4 = need light review; 3 = need careful review; 2 = need to study rules; 1 = need serious study and follow-up reinforcement.

◤ GRAMMAR/MECHANICS REVIEW

Parts of Speech (1.01)

1.01 Functions English has eight parts of speech. Knowing each part's function helps writers to better understand how words are used and how sentences are formed.

a. **Nouns.** Name persons, places, things, qualities, concepts, and activities (e.g., _Kevin, Lethbridge, computer, joy, work, banking_)

b. **Pronouns.** Substitute for nouns (e.g., _he, she, it, they_)

c. **Verbs.** Show the action of a subject or join the subject to words that describe it (e.g., _walk, heard, is, was jumping_)

d. **Adjectives.** Describe or limit nouns and pronouns and often answer the questions _what kind? how many?_ and _which one?_ (e.g., _red_ car, _ten_ items, _good_ manager)

e. **Adverbs.** Describe or limit verbs, adjectives, or other adverbs and frequently answer the questions *when? how? where?* or *to what extent?* (e.g., *tomorrow, rapidly, here, very*)

f. **Prepositions.** Join nouns or pronouns to other words in sentences (e.g., desk *in* the office, ticket *for* me, letter *to* you)

g. **Conjunctions.** Connect words or groups of words (e.g., you *and* me, Mark *or* Jill)

h. **Interjections.** Express strong feelings (e.g., *Wow! Oh!*)

Nouns (1.02–1.06)

Nouns name persons, places, things, qualities, concepts, and activities. Nouns may be classified into a number of categories.

1.02 Concrete and Abstract Concrete nouns name specific objects that can be seen, heard, felt, tasted, or smelled. Examples of concrete nouns are *telephone, dollar, Shopify,* and *tangerine.* Abstract nouns name generalized ideas such as qualities or concepts that are not easily pictured. *Emotion, power,* and *tension* are typical examples of abstract nouns.

Business writing is most effective when concrete words predominate. It is clearer to write *We need 16-pound copy paper* than to write *We need office supplies.* Chapter 4 provides practice in developing skill in the use of concrete words.

1.03 Proper and Common Proper nouns name specific persons, places, or things and are always capitalized (*Lululemon Athletica, Kamloops, Jennifer*). All other nouns are common nouns and begin with lowercase letters (*company, city, student*). Rules for capitalization are presented in Sections 3.01–3.16.

1.04 Singular and Plural Singular nouns name one item; plural nouns name more than one. From a practical view, writers rarely have difficulty with singular nouns. They may need help, however, with the formation and spelling of plural nouns.

1.05 Guidelines for Forming Noun Plurals

a. Add -s to most nouns (chair, chairs; mortgage, mortgages; Monday, Mondays).

b. Add -es to nouns ending in s, x, z, ch, or sh (bench, benches; boss, bosses; box, boxes; Parvez, Parvezes).

c. Change the spelling in irregular noun plurals (*man, men; foot, feet; mouse, mice; child, children*).

d. Add -*s* to nouns that end in *y* when *y* is preceded by a vowel (*journey, journeys; valley, valleys*).

e. Drop the *y* and add -*ies* to nouns ending in *y* when *y* is preceded by a consonant (*company, companies; city, cities; secretary, secretaries*).

f. Add -*s* to the principal word in most compound expressions (*editors in chief, fathers-in-law, bills of lading, runners-up*).

g. Add -*s* to most numerals, letters of the alphabet, words referred to as words, degrees, and abbreviations (*5s, 2000s, Bs, ands, CPAs, lbs.*).

h. Add '*s* only to clarify letters of the alphabet that might be misread, such as *A's, I's, M's, U's, i's,* and *p's* and *q's.* An expression like *c.o.d.s* requires no apostrophe because it would not easily be misread.

1.06 Collective Nouns Nouns such as *staff, faculty, committee, group,* and *herd* refer to a collection of people, animals, or objects. Collective nouns may be considered singular or plural depending on their action. See Section 1.10i for a discussion of collective nouns and their agreement with verbs.

Review Exercise A—Nouns

In the spaces write *a* or *b* to complete the following statements accurately. When you finish, compare your responses with those provided. Answers are provided for odd-numbered items. Your instructor has the remaining answers. For items you need to review, consult the numbered principle shown in parentheses.

_____ 1. Two of the contest (a) *runner-ups*, (b) *runners-up* protested the judges' choice.

_____ 2. Please write to the (a) *Davis's*, (b) *Davises* about the missing contract.

_____ 3. That accounting firm employs two (a) *secretaries*, (b) *secretarys* for five CPAs.

_____ 4. The home was constructed with numerous (a) *chimneys*, (b) *chimnies*.

_____ 5. We asked the (a) *Parvez's*, (b) *Parvezes* to contribute to the fund-raising drive.

_____ 6. The stock market is experiencing abnormal (a) *ups and downs*, (b) *up's and down's*.

_____ 7. This office is unusually quiet on (a) *Sundays*, (b) *Sunday's*.

_____ 8. Two major (a) *countries*, (b) *countrys* will participate in arms negotiations.

_____ 9. The (a) *board of directors*, (b) *boards of directors* of all the major companies participated in the surveys.

_____ 10. When shipping we are careful to include all (a) *bill of sales*, (b) *bills of sale*.

---

1. b (1.05f) 3. a (1.05e) 5. b (1.05b) 7. a (1.05a) 9. b (1.05f) (Only odd-numbered answers are provided. Consult your instructor for the others.)

◤ GRAMMAR/MECHANICS CHECKUP 1

Nouns

Review Sections 1.01–1.06. Then study the following statements. Underline any mistakes and write a correction in the space provided. Record the appropriate Handbook section and letter that illustrates the principle involved. If a sentence is correct, write C. When you finish, compare your responses with those provided in the Answer Key. If your answers differ, carefully study the principles shown in parentheses.

<u>companies (1.05e)</u> **Example** Two surveys revealed that many <u>companys</u> will move to the new industrial park.

_____ 1. Counter business is higher on Saturday's, but online business is greater on Sundays.

_____ 2. Some of the citys in Kevin's report offer excellent opportunities.

_____ 3. Frozen chickens and turkies are kept in the company's lockers.

_____ 4. Only the Nashs and the Lopezes brought their entire families.

_____ 5. In the 2000's profits grew rapidly; in the 2010's investments lagged.

_____ 6. Both editor in chiefs instituted strict proofreading policies.

_____ 7. That font makes it difficult to distinguish between *o's* and *a's*.

_____ 8. Both runner-ups complained about the winner's behaviour.

Pronouns (1.07–1.09)

Pronouns substitute for nouns. They are classified by case.

1.07 Case Pronouns function in three cases, as shown in the following chart.

Nominative Case	Objective Case	Possessive Case
(Used for subjects of verbs and subject complements)	*(Used for objects of prepositions and objects of verbs)*	*(Used to show possession)*
I	me	my, mine
we	us	our, ours
you	you	your, yours
he	him	his
she	her	her, hers
it	it	its
they	them	their, theirs
who, whoever	whom, whomever	whose

1.08 Guidelines for Selecting Pronoun Case

a. Pronouns that serve as subjects of verbs must be in the nominative case:

> *He* and *I* (not *Him* and *me*) decided to apply for the jobs.

b. Pronouns that follow linking verbs (such as *am, is, are, was, were, be, being, been*) and rename the words to which they refer must be in the nominative case.

> It must have been *she* (not *her*) who placed the order. (The nominative-case pronoun *she* follows the linking verb been and renames *it*.)

> If it was *he* (not *him*) who called, I have his number. (The nominative-case pronoun *he* follows the linking verb *was* and renames *it*.)

c. Pronouns that serve as objects of verbs or objects of prepositions must be in the objective case:

> Mr. Andrews asked *them* to complete the proposal. (The pronoun *them* is the object of the verb *asked*.)

> All media requests are sent to *him*. (The pronoun *him* is the object of the preposition *to*.)

> Just between you and *me*, profits are falling. (The pronoun *me* is one of the objects of the preposition *between*.)

d. Pronouns that show ownership must be in the possessive case. Possessive pronouns (such as *hers, yours, ours, theirs*, and *its*) require no apostrophes:

> I bought a cheap cell phone, but *yours* (not *your's*) is impressive.

> All parts of the machine, including *its* (not *it's*) motor, were examined.

> The house and *its* (not *it's*) contents will be auctioned.

> Don't confuse possessive pronouns and contractions. Contractions are shortened forms of subject–verb phrases (such as *it's* for *it is*, *there's* for *there is*, and *they're* for *they are*).

e. When a pronoun appears in combination with a noun or another pronoun, ignore the extra noun or pronoun and its conjunction. In this way pronoun case becomes more obvious:

> The manager promoted Jeff and *me* (not *I*). (Ignore *Jeff and*.)

f. In statements of comparison, mentally finish the comparative by adding the implied missing words:

Next year I hope to earn as much as *she*. (The verb *earns* is implied here: . . . *as much as she earns*.)

g. Pronouns must be in the same case as the words they replace or rename. When pronouns are used with appositives, ignore the appositive:

A new contract was signed by *us* (not *we*) employees. (Temporarily ignore the appositive *employees* in selecting the pronoun.)

We (not us) neighbours have formed our own organization. (Temporarily ignore the appositive *neighbours* in selecting the pronoun.)

h. Pronouns ending in *self* should be used only when they refer to previously mentioned nouns or pronouns:

The CEO *himself* answered the telephone.

Robert and *I* (not *myself*) are in charge of the campaign.

i. Use objective-case pronouns as objects of the prepositions *between*, *but*, *like*, and *except*:

Everyone but John and *him* (not *he*) qualified for the bonus.

Employees like Jess Gillis and *her* (not *she*) are hard to replace.

j. Use *who* or *whoever* for nominative-case constructions and *whom* or *whomever* for objective-case constructions. In making the correct choice, it's sometimes helpful to substitute *he* for *who* or *whoever* and *him* for *whom* or *whomever*:

For whom was this book ordered? (This book was ordered for him/whom?)

Who did you say would drop by? (*Who/He . . . would drop by?*)

Deliver the package to *whoever* opens the door. (In this sentence the clause *whoever opens the door* functions as the object of the preposition *to*. Within the clause itself, *whoever* is the subject of the verb *opens*. Again, substitution of he might be helpful: *He/Whoever opens the door*.)

1.09 Guidelines for Making Pronouns Agree With Their Antecedents Pronouns must agree with the words to which they refer (their antecedents) in gender and in number.

a. Use masculine pronouns to refer to masculine antecedents, feminine pronouns to refer to feminine antecedents, and neuter pronouns to refer to antecedents without gender:

The man opened *his* office door. (Masculine gender applies.)

A woman sat at *her* desk. (Feminine gender applies.)

This software and *its* mobile apps fit our needs. (Neuter gender applies.)

b. Use singular pronouns to refer to singular antecedents:

Common-gender pronouns (such as *him* or *his*) traditionally have been used when the gender of the antecedent is unknown. Sensitive writers today prefer to recast such constructions to avoid gender-biased pronouns. Study these examples for bias-free pronouns:

Each student must submit *a* report on Monday.

All students must submit *their* reports on Monday.

Each student must submit *his or her* report on Monday. (This alternative is least acceptable since it is wordy and calls attention to itself.)

c. Use singular pronouns to refer to singular indefinite subjects and plural pronouns for plural indefinite subjects. Words such as *anyone*, *something*, and *anybody* are considered indefinite because they refer to no specific person or object. Some indefinite pronouns are always singular; others are always plural.

Always Singular		**Always Plural**	
anybody	either	nobody	both
anyone	everyone	no one	few
anything	everything	somebody	many
each	neither	someone	several

Somebody in the group of touring women left *her* (not *their*) purse in the museum.

Either of the companies has the right to exercise *its* (*not their*) option to sell stock.

d. Use singular pronouns to refer to collective nouns and organization names:

The engineering staff is moving *its* (not *their*) facilities on Friday. (The singular pronoun its agrees with the collective noun *staff* because the members of *staff* function as a single unit.)

Jones, Cohen, & Chavez, Inc., *has* (not *have*) cancelled *its* (not *their*) contract with us. (The singular pronoun *its* agrees with *Jones, Cohen, & Chavez, Inc.*, because the members of the organization are operating as a single unit.)

e. Use a plural pronoun to refer to two antecedents joined by *and*, whether the antecedents are singular or plural:

Our company president and our vice president will be submitting *their* expenses shortly.

f. Ignore intervening phrases—introduced by expressions such as *together with*, *as well as*, and *in addition to*—that separate a pronoun from its antecedent:

One of our managers, along with several salespeople, is planning *his* retirement. (If you wish to emphasize both subjects equally, join them with *and*: One of our managers *and* several salespeople are planning *their* retirements.)

g. When antecedents are joined by *or* or *nor*, make the pronoun agree with the antecedent closest to it.

Neither Jackie nor Kim wanted *her* (not *their*) desk moved.

Review Exercise B—Pronouns

In the spaces write *a*, *b*, or *c* to complete the statement accurately. When you finish, compare your responses with those provided. For items you need to review, consult the numbered principle shown in parentheses.

_____ 1. Send email copies of the policy to the manager or (a) *me*, (b) *myself*.

_____ 2. A lot of preparation for the seminar was done by Sally Cho and (a) *I*, (b) *me* before the brochures were sent out.

_____ 3. A number of inquiries were addressed to Jeff and (a) *I*, (b) *me*, (c) *myself*.

_____ 4. When you visit Western Financial, inquire about (a) *its*, (b) *their* GICs.

_____ 5. Apparently one of the applicants forgot to sign (a) *her*, (b) *their* application.

_____ 6. I've never known any man who could work as fast as (a) *him*, (b) *he*.

_____ 7. Give the supplies to (a) *whoever*, (b) *whomever* ordered them.

_____ 8. When he finally found a job, Dante, along with many other recent graduates, described (a) *his*, (b) *their* experience in an employment blog.

_____ 9. Any woman who becomes a charter member of this organization will be able to have (a) *her*, (b) *their* name inscribed on a commemorative plaque.

_____ 10. Everyone has completed the reports except Debbie and (a) *he*, (b) *him*.

1. a (1.08h) 3. b (1.08c, 1.08e) 5. a (1.09b) 7. a (1.08j) 9. a (1.09b)

◣ GRAMMAR/MECHANICS CHECKUP 2

Pronouns

Review Sections 1.07–1.09. Then study the following statements. In the space provided, write the word that completes the statement correctly and the number of the Handbook principle illustrated. When you finish, compare your responses with those provided in the Answer Key again. If your responses differ, carefully study the principles in parentheses.

<u>its (1.09d)</u> **Example**   The Recreation and Benefits Committee will be submitting (*its*, *their*) report soon.

_____ 1. I was expecting the manager to call. Was it (*he*, *him*) who left the message?

_____ 2. A serious disagreement between management and (*he*, *him*) caused his resignation.

_____ 3. It looks as if (*her's*, *hers*) is the only report that cites up-to-date sources.

_____ 4. My friend and (*I*, *me*, *myself*) were also asked to work on Saturday.

_____ 5. Give the budget figures to (*whoever*, *whomever*) asked for them.

_____ 6. Everyone except the broker and (*I*, me, *myself*) claimed a share of the commission.

_____ 7. No one knows that problem better than (*he*, *him*, *himself*).

_____ 8. Investment brochures and information were sent to (*we*, *us*) shareholders.

◣ CUMULATIVE EDITING QUIZ 1

Use proofreading marks (see Appendix B) to correct errors in the following sentences. All errors must be corrected to receive credit for the sentence. Check with your instructor for the answers.

Example   Max and ~~her~~ started ~~there~~ own company in early 2000s.
              she   *their*

1. Neither the citys nor the countys would take responsibility for there budget overruns.

2. Can we keep this matter just between you and I?

3. Only a few secretarys took the day off, despite the storm.

4. Our staff committee gave their recommendation to the president and I as soon as they finished deliberating.

5. Theres really no excuse for we employees to have no voice in the matter.

6. The manager and myself will deliver supplies to whomever ordered them.

7. Many basketball and hockey star's earn huge salarys.

8. Are you sure that this apartment is their's?

9. Each student must submit their report on Monday.

10. Both the network administrator and myself are concerned about the increase in personal internet use and it's tendency to slow productivity.

Verbs (1.10–1.15)

Verbs show the action of a subject or join the subject to words that describe it.

1.10 Guidelines for Agreement With Subjects One challenging area in English is subject–verb agreement. Note the following guidelines for making verbs agree with subjects.

a. A singular subject requires a singular verb:

> The stock market *opens* at 10 a.m. (The singular verb *opens* agrees with the singular subject *market*.)

> He *doesn't* (not *don't*) work on Saturday.

b. A plural subject requires a plural verb:

> On the packing slip several items *seem* (not *seems*) to be missing.

c. A verb agrees with its subject regardless of prepositional phrases that may intervene:

> This list of management objectives *is* extensive. (The singular verb *is* agrees with the singular subject *list*.)

> Every one of the letters *shows* (not *show*) proper form.

d. A verb agrees with its subject regardless of intervening phrases introduced by *as well as*, *in addition to*, *such as*, *including*, *together with*, and similar expressions:

> An important deal memo, together with several contracts, *is* missing. (The singular verb *is* agrees with the singular subject *deal memo*.)

> The president as well as several other top-level executives *approves* of our proposal. (The singular verb *approves* agrees with the subject *president*.)

e. A verb agrees with its subject regardless of the location of the subject:

> Here *is* one of the contracts about which you asked. (The verb *is* agrees with its subject *one*, even though it precedes *one*. The adverb *here* cannot function as a subject.)

> There *are* many problems yet to be resolved. (The verb *are* agrees with the subject *problems*. The word *there* does not function as a subject.)

> In the next office *are* several printers. (In this inverted sentence, the verb *are* must agree with the subject *printers*.)

f. Subjects joined by *and* require a plural verb:

> Analyzing the reader and deciding on a strategy *are* the first steps in message writing. (The plural verb *are* agrees with the two subjects, *analyzing* and *deciding*.)

> The tone and the wording of the message *were* persuasive. (The plural verb *were* agrees with the two subjects, *tone* and *wording*.)

g. Subjects joined by *or* or *nor* may require singular or plural verbs. Make the verb agree with the closer subject:

> Neither the memo nor the report *is* ready. (The singular verb *is* agrees with *report*, the closer of the two subjects.)

h. The following indefinite pronouns are singular and require singular verbs: *anyone, anybody, anything, each, either, every, everyone, everybody, everything, many a*, neither, *nobody, nothing, someone, somebody*, and *something*:

> Either of the alternatives that you present *is* acceptable. (The verb *is* agrees with the singular subject *either*.)

i. Collective nouns may take singular or plural verbs, depending on whether the members of the group are operating as a unit or individually:

> Our management team *is* united in its goal.

> The faculty *are* sharply divided on the tuition issue. (Although acceptable, this sentence sounds better recast: The faculty *members* are sharply divided on the tuition issue.)

j. Organization names and titles of publications, although they may appear to be plural, are singular and require singular verbs.

> Bergeron, Anderson, and Horne, Inc., *has* (not *have*) hired a marketing consultant.

> *Thousands of Investment Tips is* (not *are*) again on the bestseller list.

1.11 Voice Voice shows whether the subject of the verb acts or is acted upon. Active-voice verbs direct action from the subject toward the object of the verb. Passive-voice verbs direct action toward the subject.

Active voice:	Our employees *send* many emails.
Passive voice:	Many emails *are sent* by our employees.

Business writers should generally use active-voice verbs because they are specific and forceful. However, passive-voice constructions can help a writer be tactful. Chapter 3 presents strategies for effective use of active- and passive-voice verbs.

1.12 Mood Three verb moods express the attitude or thought of the speaker or writer toward a subject: (a) the *indicative* mood expresses a fact; (b) the *imperative* mood expresses a command; and (c) the *subjunctive* mood expresses a doubt, a conjecture, or a suggestion.

Indicative:	I am looking for a job.
Imperative:	Begin your job search by networking.
Subjunctive:	I wish I were working.

Of the three, the subjunctive mood creates the most problems for majority of speakers and writers. The most common use of subjunctive mood occurs in clauses including *if* or *wish*. In such clauses substitute the subjunctive verb *were* for the indicative verb *was*:

> If he *were* (not *was*) in my position, he would understand.

> Nathan Simon acts as if he *were* (not *was*) the boss.

> I wish I *were* (not *was*) able to ship your order.

The subjunctive mood can maintain goodwill while conveying negative information. The sentence *I wish I were able to ship your order* sounds more pleasing to a customer than *I cannot ship your order*. However, for all practical purposes, both sentences convey the same negative message.

1.13 Tense

Verbs show the time of an action by their tense. Speakers and writers can use six tenses to show the time of sentence action; for example:

Present tense:	I *work*; he *works*.
Past tense:	I *worked*; she *worked*.
Future tense:	I *will work*; he *will work*.
Present perfect tense:	I *have worked*; he *has worked*.
Past perfect tense:	I *had worked*; she *had worked*.
Future perfect tense:	I *will have worked*; he *will have worked*.

1.14 Guidelines for Verb Tense

a. Use present tense for statements that, although introduced by past-tense verbs, continue to be true:

> What did you say his name *is*? (Use the present tense *is* if his name has not changed.)

b. Avoid unnecessary shifts in verb tenses:

> The manager *saw* (not *sees*) a great deal of work yet to be completed and *stayed* back to do it herself.

Although unnecessary shifts in verb tense are to be avoided, not all the verbs within one sentence have to be in the same tense; for example:

> She *said* (past tense) that she *likes* (present tense) to work late.

1.15 Irregular Verbs Irregular verbs can cause difficulty. Unlike regular verbs, irregular verbs do not form the past tense and past participle by adding *-ed* to the present form. Here is a partial list of selected irregular verbs. Consult a dictionary if you are in doubt about a verb form.

Irregular Verbs

Present	**Past**	**Past Participle (*always use helping verbs*)**
begin	began	begun
break	broke	broken
choose	chose	chosen
come	came	come
drink	drank	drunk
go	went	gone
lay (to place)	laid	laid
lie (to rest)	lay	lain
ring	rang	rung
see	saw	seen
write	wrote	written

a. Use only past-tense verbs to express past tense. Notice that no helping verbs are used to indicate simple past tense:

> The auditors *went* (not *have went*) over our books carefully.

> He *came* (not *come*) to see us yesterday.

b. Use past-participle forms for actions completed before the present time. Notice that past-participle forms require helping verbs:

Steve *had gone* (not *had went*) before we called. (The past participle *gone* is used with the helping verb *had*.)

c. Avoid inconsistent shifts in subject, voice, and mood. Pay particular attention to this problem area because undesirable shifts make your writing appear less persuasive.

Inconsistent:	When Ms. Thobani read the report, the error was found. (The first clause is in the active voice; the second, passive.)
Improved:	When Ms. Thobani read the report, she found the error. (Both clauses are in the active voice.)
Inconsistent:	The clerk should first conduct an inventory. Then supplies should be requisitioned. (The first sentence is in the active voice; the second, passive.)
Improved:	The clerk should first conduct an inventory. Then he or she should requisition supplies. (Both sentences are in the active voice.)
Inconsistent:	All workers must wear security badges, and you must also sign a daily time log. (This sentence contains an inconsistent shift in subject from *all workers* in the first clause to *you* in the second clause.)
Improved:	All workers must wear security badges, and they must also sign a daily time log.
Inconsistent:	Begin the transaction by opening an account; then you enter the customer's name. (This sentence contains an inconsistent shift from the imperative mood in the first clause to the indicative mood in the second clause.)
Improved:	Begin the transaction by opening an account; then enter the customer's name. (Both clauses are now in the imperative mood.)

Review Exercise C—Verbs

In the spaces write *a* or *b* to complete the statement accurately. When you finish, compare your responses with those provided. For item you need to review, consult the numbered principle shown in parentheses.

_____ 1. Our database of customer names and addresses (a) *was* (b) *were* out-of-date.

_____ 2. Improved communication technologies and increased global competition (a) *is*, (b) *are* changing the world of business.

_____ 3. Yesterday Ravinder (a) *choose*, (b) *chose* a new office on the second floor.

_____ 4. Our management team and our lawyer (a) *is*, (b) *are* researching the privacy issue.

_____ 5. If you had (a) *saw*, (b) *seen* the rough draft, you would better appreciate the final copy.

_____ 6. Although we have (a) *began*, (b) *begun* to replace outmoded equipment, the pace is slow.

_____ 7. Changing attitudes and increased job opportunities (a) *is*, (b) *are* resulting in increased numbers of female executives.

_____ 8. If I (a) *was*, (b) *were* you, I would ask for a raise.

_____ 9. The hydraulic equipment that you ordered (a) *is*, (b) *are* packed and will be shipped Friday.

_____ 10. Either of the proposed laws (a) *is*, (b) *are* going to affect our business negatively.

---

1. a (1.10c) 3. b (1.15a) 5. b (1.15b) 7. b (1.10f) 9. a (1.10a)

Review Exercise D—Verbs

In the following sentence pairs, choose the one that illustrates consistency in use of subject, voice, and mood. Write *a* or *b* in the space provided. When you finish, compare your responses with those provided. For items on which you need review, consult the numbered principle shown in parentheses.

_____ 1. (a) You need more than a knowledge of technology; one also must be able to interact well with people.

(b) You need more than a knowledge of technology; you also must be able to interact well with people.

_____ 2. (a) Tim and Jon were eager to continue, but Bob wanted to quit.

(b) Tim and Jon were eager to continue, but Bob wants to quit.

_____ 3. (a) The salesperson should consult the price list; then you can give an accurate quote to a customer.

(b) The salesperson should consult the price list; then he or she can give an accurate quote to a customer.

_____ 4. (a) Read all the instructions first; then you install the printer program.

(b) Read all the instructions first, and then install the printer program.

_____ 5. (a) She was an enthusiastic manager who always had a smile for everyone.

(b) She was an enthusiastic manager who always has a smile for everyone.

1. b (1.15c) 3. b (1.15c) 5. a (1.14b)

◣ GRAMMAR/MECHANICS CHECKUP 3

Verbs

Review Sections 1.10–1.15. Then study each of the following statements. Underline any verbs that are used incorrectly. In the space provided, write the correct form (or *C* if correct) and the number of the Handbook principle illustrated. When you finish, compare your responses with those provided in the Answer Key. If your responses differ, carefully study the principles in parentheses.

<u>was (1.10c)</u> **Example** Our inventory of raw materials <u>were</u> presented as collateral for a short-term loan.

_____ 1. Located across town is a research institute and our product-testing facility.

_____ 2. Can you tell me whether a current database of customers' names and addresses have been sent to marketing?

_____ 3. The credit union, along with 20 other large national banks, offer a variety of savings plans.

_____ 4. Locating a bank and selecting a savings/chequing plan often require considerable research and study.

_____ 5. If he had chose the Maximizer Plus savings plan, his money would have earned maximum interest.

_____ 6. Nadia acts as if she was the manager.

_____ 7. One of the reasons that our Nunavut branches have been so costly are the high cost of living.

In the space provided, write the letter of the sentence that illustrates consistency in subject, voice, and mood.

_____ 8. (a) If you will read the instructions, the answer can be found.

             (b) If you will read the instructions, you will find the answer.

◤ CUMULATIVE EDITING QUIZ 2

Use proofreading marks (see Appendix B) to correct errors in the following sentences. All errors must be corrected to receive credit for the sentence. Check with your instructor for the answers.

1. The production cost and the markup of each item is important in calculating the sale price.
2. Safi acts as if he was the manager, but we know he is not.
3. The committee are reconsidering their decision in view of recent health care legislation.
4. My brand new tablet and it's lightweight keyboard is sleek but difficult to use.
5. Waiting in the outer office is a job applicant and a sales representative who you told to stop by.
6. Each applicant could have submitted his application online if he had went to our website.
7. One of the reasons she applied are that she seen the salarys posted at our website.
8. Either of the options that you may chose are acceptable to Jake and myself.
9. Although there anger and frustration is understandable, both editor in chiefs decided to apologize and reprint the article.
10. The Lopez'es, about who the article was written, accepted the apology graciously.

Adjectives and Adverbs (1.16–1.17)

Adjectives describe or limit nouns and pronouns. They often answer the questions *what kind? how many?* or *which one?* Adverbs describe or limit verbs, adjectives, or other adverbs. They often answer the questions *when? how? where?* or *to what extent?*

1.16 Forms Most adjectives and adverbs have three forms, or degrees: *positive, comparative,* and *superlative.*

	Positive	**Comparative**	**Superlative**
Adjective:	clear	clearer	clearest
Adverb:	clearly	more clearly	most clearly

Some adjectives and adverbs have irregular forms:

	Positive	**Comparative**	**Superlative**
Adjective:	good	better	best
	bad	worse	worst
Adverb:	well	better	best

Adjectives and adverbs composed of two or more syllables are usually compared by the use of *more* and *most*; for example:

The Accounting Department is *more efficient* than the Shipping Department.

Accounting is the *most efficient* department in our organization.

1.17 Guidelines for Use

a. Use the comparative degree of the adjective or adverb to compare two persons or things; use the superlative degree to compare three or more:

> Of the two plans, which is *better* (not *best*)?
>
> Of all the plans, we like this one *best* (not *better*).

b. Do not create a double comparative or superlative by using *-er* with *more* or *-est* with *most*:

> His explanation couldn't have been *clearer* (not *more clearer*).

c. A linking verb (*is, are, look, seem, feel, sound, appear,* and so forth) may introduce a word that describes the verb's subject. In this case be certain to use an adjective, not an adverb:

> The characters on my monitor look *bright* (not *brightly*). (Use the adjective *bright* because it follows the linking verb *look* and modifies the noun *characters*.)
>
> The company's letter made the customer feel *bad* (not *badly*). (The adjective *bad* follows the linking verb *feel* and describes the noun *customer*.)

d. Use adverbs, not adjectives, to describe or limit the action of verbs:

> The business is running *smoothly* (not *smooth*). (Use the adverb *smoothly* to describe the action of the verb *is running. Smoothly* explains how the business is running.)
>
> Don't take his remark *personally* (not *personal*). (The adverb *personally* describes the action of the verb *take*.)
>
> Drishti said she did *well* (not *good*) on the test. (Use the adverb *well* to tell how she did.)

e. Two or more adjectives that are joined to create a compound modifier before a noun should be hyphenated:

> The *four-year-old* child was tired.
>
> Our agency is planning a *coast-to-coast* campaign.

Hyphenate a compound modifier following a noun only if your dictionary shows the hyphen(s):

> Our speaker is very *well-known*. (Include the hyphen because most dictionaries do.)
>
> The tired child was four years old. (Omit the hyphens because the expression follows the word it describes, *child*, and because dictionaries do not indicate hyphens.)

f. Keep adjectives and adverbs close to the words they modify:

> She asked for a cup of hot coffee (not a hot cup of coffee).
>
> Patty had only two days of vacation left (not only had two days).
>
> Students may sit in the first five rows (not in five first rows).
>
> He *has saved almost* enough money for the trip (not *has almost saved*).

g. Don't confuse *there* with the possessive pronoun *their* or the contraction *they're*:

> Put the documents *there*. (The adverb *there* means "at that place or at that point.")
>
> *There* are two reasons for the change. (The pronoun *there* is used as function word to introduce a sentence or a clause.)

We already have *their* specifications. (The possessive pronoun *their* shows ownership.)

They're coming to inspect today. (The contraction *they're* is a shortened form of *they are*.)

Review Exercise E—Adjectives and Adverbs

In the spaces write *a*, *b*, or *c* to complete the statement accurately. If two sentences are shown, select *a* or *b* to indicate the one expressed more effectively. When you finish, compare your responses with those provided. For items on which you need review, consult the numbered principle shown in parentheses.

_____ 1. After the interview, Yoshi looked (a) *calm*, (b) *calmly*.

_____ 2. Because we appointed a new manager, the advertising campaign is running (a) *smooth*, (b) *smoothly*.

_____ 3. Darren completed the employment test (a) *satisfactorily*, (b) *satisfactory*.

_____ 4. Which is the (a) *more*, (b) *most* dependable of the two cars?

_____ 5. Of all the copiers we tested, this one is the (a) *easier*, (b) *easiest* to operate.

_____ 6. (a) We only thought that it would take two hours for the test.

   (b) We thought that it would take only two hours for the test.

_____ 7. (a) The committee decided to retain the last ten tickets.

   (b) The committee decided to retain the ten last tickets.

_____ 8. The time passed (a) *quicker*, (b) *more quickly* than we expected.

_____ 9. Today the financial news is (a) *worse*, (b) *worst* than yesterday.

_____ 10. You must check the document (a) *page by page*, (b) *page-by-page*.

1. a (1.17c) 3. a (1.17d) 5. b (1.17a) 7. a (1.17f) 9. a (1.17a)

◤ GRAMMAR/MECHANICS CHECKUP 4

Adjectives and Adverbs

Review Sections 1.16 and 1.17. Then study each of the following statements. Underline any inappropriate forms. In the space provided, write the correct form (or *C* if correct) and the number of the Handbook principle illustrated. You may need to consult your dictionary for current practice regarding some compound adjectives. When you finish, compare your responses with those provided in the Answer Key. If your answers differ, carefully study again the principles in parentheses.

<u>live-and-let-live (1.17e)</u>   **Example**   He was one of those individuals with a <u>live and let live</u> attitude.

_____ 1. Many of our long time customers have PayPal accounts.

_____ 2. The supplier supplied the answer so quick that we were all amazed.

_____ 3. He only had $5 in his pocket.

_____ 4. Although the e-bike was four years old, it was in good condition.

_____ 5. Of the two colours, which is best for a website background?

_____ 6. Channel 12 presents up to the minute news broadcasts.

_____ 7. The conclusion drawn from the statistics couldn't have been more clearer.

_____ 8. If you feel badly about the transaction, contact your portfolio manager.

Prepositions (1.18)

Prepositions are connecting words that join nouns or pronouns to other words in a sentence. The words *about*, *at*, *from*, *in*, and *to* are examples of prepositions.

1.18 Guidelines for Use

a. Include necessary prepositions:

> What type *of* software do you need (not *What type software*)?

> I graduated *from* high school two years ago (not *I graduated high school*).

b. Omit unnecessary prepositions:

> Where is the meeting? (Not *Where is the meeting at?*)

> Both printers work well. (Not *Both of the printers . . .*)

> Where are you going? (Not *Where are you going to?*)

c. Avoid the overuse of prepositional phrases.

> **Weak:** We have received your application for credit at our branch in the Windsor area.

> **Improved:** We have received your recent credit application.

d. Repeat the preposition before the second of two related elements:

> Applicants use the résumé effectively by summarizing their most important experiences and *by* relating their education to the jobs sought.

e. Include the second preposition when two prepositions modify a single object:

> George's appreciation *of* and aptitude *for* coding led to a promising career.

Conjunctions (1.19)

Conjunctions connect words, phrases, and clauses. They act as signals, indicating when a thought is being added, contrasted, or altered. Coordinating conjunctions (such as *and*, *or*, *but*) and other words that act as connectors (such as *however*, *therefore*, *when*, *as*) tell the reader or listener what direction a thought is heading. They are like road signs signalling what's ahead.

1.19 Guidelines for Use

a. Use coordinating conjunctions to connect only sentence elements that are parallel or balanced.

> **Weak:** His report was correct and written in a concise manner.

> **Improved:** His report was correct and concise.

> **Weak:** Management has the capacity to increase fraud, or reduction can be achieved through the policies it adopts.

> **Improved:** Management has the capacity to increase or reduce fraud through the policies it adopts.

b. Do not use the word *like* as a conjunction:

> It seems as *if* (not *like*) this day will never end.

c. Avoid using when or where inappropriately. A common writing fault occurs in sentences with clauses introduced by is when and is where. Written English ordinarily requires a noun (or a group of words functioning as a noun) following the linking verb is. Instead of acting as conjunctions in these constructions, the words where and when function as adverbs, creating faulty grammatical equations (adverbs cannot complete equations set up by linking verbs). To avoid the problem, revise the sentence, eliminating is when or is where.

Weak:	A bullish market is when prices are rising in the stock market.
Improved:	A bullish market is created when prices are rising in the stock market.
Weak:	A flow chart is when you make a diagram showing the step-by-step progression of a procedure.
Improved:	A flow chart is a diagram showing the step-by-step progression of a procedure.
Weak:	A podcast is where a pre-recorded audio program is posted to a website.
Improved:	A podcast is a pre-recorded audio program posted to a website.

A similar faulty construction occurs in the expression *I hate when*. English requires nouns, noun clauses, or pronouns to act as objects of verbs, not adverbs.

Weak:	I hate when we're asked to work overtime.
Improved:	I hate it when we're asked to work overtime.
Improved:	I hate being asked to work overtime.

d. Don't confuse the adverb *then* with the conjunction *than*. *Then* means "at that time"; *than* indicates the second element in a comparison:

> We would rather remodel *than* (not *then*) move.

> First, the equipment is turned on; *then* (not *than*) the program is loaded.

Review Exercise F—Prepositions and Conjunctions

In the spaces write *a* or *b* to indicate the sentence that is expressed more effectively. When you finish, compare your responses with those provided. For items on which you need review, consult the numbered principle shown in parentheses.

_____ 1. (a) The chief forgot to tell everyone where today's meeting is.
  (b) The chief forgot to tell everyone where today's meeting is at.

_____ 2. (a) Josh Samuels graduated college last June.
  (b) Josh Samuels graduated from college last June.

_____ 3. (a) Both employees enjoyed setting their own hours.
  (b) Both of the employees enjoyed setting their own hours.

_____ 4. (a) What style of typeface should we use?
  (b) What style typeface should we use?

_____ 5. (a) Mediation in a labour dispute occurs when a neutral person helps union and management reach an agreement.
  (b) Mediation in a labour dispute is where a neutral person helps union and management reach an agreement.

_____ 6. (a) We expect to finish up the work soon.
  (b) We expect to finish the work soon.

_____ 7. (a) Your client may respond by email or a telephone call may be made.
  (b) Your client may respond by email or by telephone.

_____ 8. (a) Sara exhibited both an awareness of and talent for developing innovations.
  (b) Sara exhibited both an awareness and talent for developing innovations.

_____ 9. (a) An ombudsman is an individual hired by management to investigate and resolve employee complaints.
  (b) An ombudsman is when management hires an individual to investigate and resolve employee complaints.

_____ 10. (a) By including accurate data and by writing clearly, you will produce effective messages.
  (b) By including accurate data and writing clearly, you will produce effective messages.

---

1. a (1.18b) 3. a (1.18b) 5. a (1.19c) 7. b (1.19a) 9. a (1.19c)

Prepositions and Conjunctions

Review Sections 1.18 and 1.19. Then study each of the following statements. Write *a* or *b* to indicate the sentence in which the idea is expressed more effectively. Also record the number of the Handbook principle illustrated. When you finish, compare your responses with those provided in the Answer Key. If your answers differ, carefully study again the principles shown in parentheses.

<u>b (1.18a)</u>   **Example** (a)   Raoul will graduate college this spring.

(b)   Raoul will graduate from college this spring.

_____ 1. (a)   DataTech enjoyed greater profits this year then it expected.

(b)   DataTech enjoyed greater profits this year than it expected.

_____ 2. (a)   Dr. Vitautas has a great interest and appreciation for the study of robotics.

(b)   Dr. Vitautas has a great interest in and appreciation for the study of robotics.

_____ 3. (a)   Gross profit is where you compute the difference between total sales and the cost of goods sold.

(b)   Gross profit is computed by finding the difference between total sales and the cost of goods sold.

_____ 4. (a)   We advertise to increase the frequency of product use, to introduce complementary products, and to enhance our corporate image.

(b)   We advertise to have our products used more often, when we have complementary products to introduce, and we are interested in making our corporation look better to the public.

_____ 5. (a)   What type printer do you prefer?

(b)   What type of printer do you prefer?

_____ 6. (a)   The sale of our Halifax office last year should improve this year's profits.

(b)   The sale of our office in Halifax during last year should improve the profits for this year.

_____ 7. (a)   Do you know where the meeting is at?

(b)   Do you know where the meeting is?

_____ 8. (a)   They printed the newsletter on yellow paper like we asked them to do.

(b)   They printed the newsletter on yellow paper as we asked them to do.

► CUMULATIVE EDITING QUIZ 3

Use proofreading marks (see Appendix B) to correct errors in the following sentences. All errors must be corrected to receive credit for the sentence. Check with your instructor for the answers.

1. Her new tablet is definitely more faster then her previous tablet.

2. Max said that he felt badly that he missed his appointment with you and myself.

3. Neither the managers nor the union are happy at how slow the talks are progressing.

4. Just between you and I, we have learned not to take the boss's criticism personal.

5. After completing a case by case search, the consultant promised to send his report to Carlos and I.

6. If you was me, which of the two job offers do you think is best?

7. Did your team members tell you where there meeting is at?

8. Jason felt that he had done good on the three hour certification exam.

9. It seems like our step by step instructions could have been more clearer.

10. hate when I'm expected to finish up by myself.

◤ PUNCTUATION REVIEW

Commas 1 (2.01–2.04)

2.01 Series Commas are used to separate three or more equal elements (words, phrases, or short clauses) in a series. To ensure separation of the last two elements, careful writers use a comma before the conjunction in a series:

> Business letters usually contain a dateline, address, salutation, body, and closing. (This series contains words.)

> The job of an ombudsman is to examine employee complaints, resolve disagreements between management and employees, and ensure fair treatment. (This series contains phrases.)

> Interns complete basic office tasks, marketing coordinators manage author events, and editors proofread completed projects. (This series contains short clauses.)

2.02 Direct Address Commas are used to set off the names of individuals being addressed:

> Your inquiry, *Mrs. Johnson*, has been referred to me.

> We genuinely hope that we may serve you, *Mr. Zhou*.

2.03 Parenthetical Expressions Skilled writers use parenthetical words, phrases, and clauses to guide the reader from one thought to the next. When these expressions interrupt the flow of a sentence and are unnecessary for its grammatical completeness, they should be set off with commas. Examples of commonly used parenthetical expressions follow:

all things considered	however	needless to say
as a matter of fact	in addition	nevertheless
as a result	incidentally	no doubt
as a rule	in fact	of course
at the same time	in my opinion	on the contrary
consequently	in the first place	on the other
hand		
for example	in the meantime	therefore
furthermore	moreover	under the
circumstances		

> *As a matter of fact*, I wrote to you just yesterday. (Phrase used at the beginning of a sentence.)

> We will, *in the meantime*, send you a replacement order. (Phrase used in the middle of a sentence.)

Your satisfaction is our first concern, *needless to say*. (Phrase used at the end of a sentence.)

Do not use commas if the expression is necessary for the completeness of the sentence:

Kimberly had *no doubt* that she would finish the report. (Omit commas because the expression is necessary for the completeness of the sentence.)

2.04 Dates, Addresses, and Geographical Items When dates, addresses, and geographical items contain more than one element, the second and succeeding elements are normally set off by commas.

a. Dates:

The conference was held February 2 at our home office. (No comma is needed for one element.)

The conference was held February 2, 2021, at our home office. (Two commas set off the second element.)

The conference was held Tuesday, February 2, 2021, at our home office. (Commas set off the second and third elements.)

In February 2021 the conference was held. (This alternate style omitting commas is acceptable if only the month and year are written.)

b. Addresses:

The letter addressed to Jim W. Ellman, 600 Ellerby Trail, Calgary, Alberta T4E 8N9, should be sent today. (Commas are used between all elements except the province or territory and postal code, which in this special instance act as a single unit.)

c. Geographical items:

She moved from Whitehorse, Yukon, to Toronto, Ontario. (Commas set off the province or territory unless it appears at the end of the sentence, in which case only one comma is used.)

In separating cities from provinces or territories and days from years, many writers remember the initial comma but forget the final one, as in the examples that follow:

The package from Sydney, Nova Scotia{,} was lost.

We opened June 1, 2009{,} and have grown steadily since.

Review Exercise G—Commas 1

Insert necessary commas in the following sentences. In the spaces write the number of commas that you add. Write *C* if no commas are needed. When you finish, compare your responses with those provided. For items that you need to review, consult the numbered principle shown in parentheses.

_____ 1. As a rule we do not provide complimentary tickets.

_____ 2. I have no doubt that your calculations are correct.

_____ 3. Every accredited TV newscaster radio broadcaster and blogger had access to the media room.

_____ 4. The employees who are eligible for promotions are Terry Evelyn Vicki Rosanna and Steve.

_____ 5. Many of our customers include architects engineers attorneys and others who are interested in customer management programs.

_____ 6. The new book explains how to choose appropriate legal protection for ideas trade secrets copyrights patents and restrictive covenants.

_____ 7. You may however prefer to be in touch directly with the manufacturer in China.

_____ 8. The rally has been scheduled for Monday January 12 in the campus stadium.

_____ 9. Goodstone Tire & Rubber for example recalled 400,000 steelbelted radial tires because some tires failed their rigorous tests.

_____ 10. In the meantime thank you for whatever assistance you are able to furnish.

1. (1) rule, (2.03) 3. (2) newscaster, radio broadcaster, (2.01) 5. (3) architects, engineers, attorneys, (2.01) 7. (2) may, however, 9. (2) Rubber, for example, (2.03)

◣ GRAMMAR/MECHANICS CHECKUP 6

Commas 1

Review Sections 2.01–2.04. Then read each of the following statements and insert necessary commas. In the spaces write the number of commas that you add; write *0* if no commas are needed. Also record the number of the Handbook principle illustrated. When you finish, compare your responses with those in the Answer Key. If your answers differ, carefully study again the principles shown in parentheses.

2 (2.01)   **Example**   In this class students learn to write clear and concise business letters, memos, and reports.

_____ 1. We do not as a rule allow employees to take time off for spa appointments.

_____ 2. You may be sure Ms. Schwartz that your car will be ready by 4 p.m.

_____ 3. Anyone who is reliable conscientious and honest should be very successful.

_____ 4. We are relocating our distribution centre from Calgary Alberta to La Salle Quebec.

_____ 5. The last meeting recorded in the minutes was on February 4 2011 in Windsor.

_____ 6. The package mailed to Ms. Leslie Holmes 3430 Larkspur Lane Regina Saskatchewan S5L 2E2 arrived three weeks after it was mailed.

_____ 7. Eric was assigned three jobs: checking supplies replacing inventories and distributing delivered goods.

_____ 8. We will work diligently to retain your business Mr. Fuhai.

Commas 2 (2.05–2.09)

2.05 Independent Clauses An independent clause is a group of words that has a subject and a verb and that could stand as a complete sentence. When two such clauses are joined by *and*, *or*, *nor*, or *but*, use a comma before the conjunction:

> We can ship your merchandise July 12, but we must have your payment first.

> Net income before taxes is calculated, and this total is then combined with income from operations.

Notice that each independent clause in the preceding two examples could stand alone as a complete sentence. Do not use a comma unless each group of words is a complete thought (i.e., has its own subject and verb).

Our accountant calculates net income before taxes *and* then combines that figure with income from operations. (No comma is needed because no subject follows *and*.)

2.06 Dependent Clauses Dependent clauses do not make sense by themselves; for their meaning they depend on independent clauses.

a. **Introductory clauses.** When a dependent clause precedes an independent clause, it is followed by a comma. Such clauses are often introduced by *when*, *if*, and *as*:

> *When your request came*, we responded immediately.

> *As I mentioned earlier*, Clementine James is the manager.

b. **Terminal clauses.** If a dependent clause falls at the end of a sentence, use a comma only if the dependent clause is an afterthought:

> We have rescheduled the meeting for October 23, *if this date meets with your approval*. (Comma used because dependent clause is an afterthought.)

> We responded immediately *when we received your request*. (No comma is needed.)

c. **Essential versus nonessential clauses.** If a dependent clause provides information that is unneeded for the grammatical completeness of a sentence, use commas to set it off. In determining whether such a clause is essential or nonessential, ask yourself whether the reader needs the information contained in the clause to identify the word it explains:

> Our district sales manager, *who just returned from a trip to the Northern Ontario District*, prepared this report. (This construction assumes that there is only one district sales manager. Because the sales manager is clearly identified, the dependent clause is not essential and requires commas.)

> The salesperson *who just returned from a trip to the Northern Ontario District* prepared this report. (The dependent clause in this sentence is necessary to identify which salesperson prepared the report. Therefore, use no commas.)

> The position of assistant sales manager, *which we discussed with you last week*, is still open. (Careful writers use which to introduce nonessential clauses. Commas are also necessary.)

> The position *that we discussed with you last week* is still open. (Careful writers use *that* to introduce essential clauses. No commas are used.)

2.07 Phrases A phrase is a group of related words that lacks both a subject and a verb. A phrase that precedes a main clause is followed by a comma if the phrase contains a verb form or has five or more words:

> *Beginning November 1*, Worldwide Savings will offer two new combination chequing/savings plans. (A comma follows this introductory phrase because the phrase contains the verb form *beginning*.)

> *To promote our plan*, we will conduct an extensive social media advertising campaign. (A comma follows this introductory phrase because the phrase contains the verb form *to promote*.)

> *In a period of only one year*, we were able to improve our market share by 30 percent. (A comma follows the introductory phrase—actually two prepositional phrases—because its total length exceeds five words.)

In 2014 our organization installed a multiuser system that could transfer programs easily. (No comma needed after the short introductory phrase.)

2.08 Two or More Adjectives Use a comma to separate two or more adjectives that equally describe a noun. A good way to test the need for a comma is this: Mentally insert the word *and* between the adjectives. If the resulting phrase sounds natural, a comma is used to show the omission of *and*:

> We're looking for a *versatile, error-free* operating system. (Use a comma to separate *versatile* and *error-free* because they independently describe *operating system*. *And* has been omitted.)

> Our *experienced, courteous* staff is ready to serve you. (Use a comma to separate *experienced* and *courteous* because they independently describe *staff*. *And* has been omitted.)

> It was difficult to refuse the *sincere young* caller. (No commas are needed between *sincere* and *young* because *and* has not been omitted.)

2.09 Appositives Words that rename or explain preceding nouns or pronouns are called *appositives*. An appositive that provides information not essential to the identification of the word it describes should be set off by commas:

> James Wilson, *the project director for Sperling's*, worked with our architect. (The appositive, *the project director for Sperling's*, adds nonessential information. Commas set it off.)

Review Exercise H—Commas 2

Insert only necessary commas in the following sentences. In the spaces indicate the number of commas that you add for each sentence. If a sentence requires no commas, write C. When you finish, compare your responses with those provided. For items that you need to review, consult the numbered principle shown in parentheses.

_____ 1. A corporation must register in the province in which it does business and it must operate within the laws of that province.

_____ 2. If you will study the cost analysis you will see that our company offers the best system at the lowest price.

_____ 3. The salesperson who amasses the greatest number of sales points will win a bonus trip to Montreal.

_____ 4. On the basis of these findings I recommend that we retain Jane Rada as our counsel.

_____ 5. The bright young student who worked for us last summer will be able to return this summer.

_____ 6. We will be able to process your application when you return the completed form.

_____ 7. Knowing that you wanted this merchandise immediately I took the liberty of sending it by FedEx.

_____ 8. A tax credit for energy-saving homes will expire at the end of the year but Ottawa might extend it if pressure groups prevail.

_____ 9. For the benefit of employees recently hired we are offering a two-hour seminar regarding employee benefit programs.

_____ 10. The meeting has been rescheduled for September 30 if this date meets with your approval.

1. (1) business, (2.05) 3. C (2.06c) 5. C (2.08) 7. (1) immediately, (2.07) 9. (1) hired, (2.07)

Commas 2

Review Sections 2.05–2.09. Then read each of the following statements and insert necessary commas. In the space provided, write the number of commas that you add; write *0* if no commas are needed. Also record the number of the Handbook principle(s) illustrated. When you finish, compare your responses with those provided in the Answer Key. If your answers differ, carefully study again the principles shown in parentheses.

__1 (2.06a)__   **Example** When businesses encounter financial problems‸they often reduce their administrative staffs.

_____ 1. As stated in the warranty this printer is guaranteed for one year.

_____ 2. Today's profits come from products currently on the market and tomorrow's profits come from products currently on the drawing boards.

_____ 3. One large automobile manufacturer which must remain nameless recognizes that buyer perception is behind the success of any new product.

_____ 4. The imaginative promising agency opened its offices April 22 in Cambridge.

_____ 5. Ian Sims our sales manager in the North Bay area will present the new sales campaign at the June meeting.

_____ 6. To motivate prospective buyers we are offering a cash rebate of $25.

Review of Commas 1 and 2

_____ 7. When you download the application please fill it out and submit it before Monday January 3.

_____ 8. On the other hand we are very interested in hiring hard-working conscientious individuals.

Commas 3 (2.10–2.15)

2.10 Degrees and Abbreviations Degrees following individuals' names are set off by commas. Abbreviations such as *Jr.* and *Sr.* are also set off by commas unless the individual referred to prefers to omit the commas:

> Anne G. Turner, *MBA*, joined the firm.

> Michael Migliano, *Jr.*, and Michael Migliano, *Sr.*, work as a team.

> Anthony A. Gensler *Jr.* wrote the report. (The individual referred to prefers to omit commas.)

The abbreviations *Inc.* and *Ltd.* are set off by commas only if a company's legal name has a comma just before this kind of abbreviation. To determine a company's practice, consult its stationery or a directory listing:

> Firestone and Blythe, *Inc.*, is based in Waterloo. (Notice that two commas are used.)

> Computers *Inc.* is extending its franchise system. (The company's legal name does not include a comma before *Inc.*)

2.11 Omitted Words A comma is used to show the omission of words that are understood:

> On Monday we received 15 applications; on Friday, only 3. (Comma shows the omission of *we received.*)

2.12 Contrasting Statements Commas are used to set off contrasting or opposing expressions. These expressions are often introduced by such words as *not*, *never*, *but*, and *yet*:

> The prime minister suggested cutbacks, *not* layoffs, to ease the crisis.

> Our budget for the year is reduced, *yet* adequate.

> The greater the effort, the greater the reward.

If increased emphasis is desired, use dashes instead of commas, as in *Only the sum of $100—not $1,000—was paid on this account.*

2.13 Clarity Commas are used to separate words repeated for emphasis. Commas are also used to separate words that may be misread if not separated:

> The building is a long, long way from completion.

> Whatever is, is right.

> No matter what, you know we support you.

2.14 Quotations and Appended Questions

a. A comma is used to separate a short quotation from the rest of a sentence. If the quotation is divided into two parts, two commas are used:

> The manager asked, "Shouldn't the managers control the specialists?"

> "Perhaps the specialists," replied Tim, "have unique information."

b. A comma is used to separate a question appended (added) to a statement:

> You will confirm the shipment, won't you?

2.15 Comma Overuse Do not use commas needlessly. For example, commas should not be inserted merely because you might drop your voice if you were speaking the sentence:

> One of the reasons for expanding our East Coast operations is{,} that we anticipate increased sales in that area. (Do not insert a needless comma before a clause.)

> I am looking for an article entitled{,} "State-of-the-Art Communications." (Do not insert a needless comma after the word *entitled*.)

> Customers may purchase many food and nonfood items in convenience stores *such as*{,} 7-Eleven and Couche-Tard. (Do not insert a needless comma after *such as*.)

> We have{,} at this time{,} an adequate supply of parts. (Do not insert needless commas around prepositional phrases.)

Review Exercise I—Commas 3

Insert only necessary commas in the following sentences. Remove unnecessary commas with the delete sign (℘). In the spaces indicate the number of commas inserted or deleted in each sentence. If a sentence requires no changes, write C. When you finish, compare your responses with those provided. For items that you need to review, consult the numbered principle shown in parentheses.

_____ 1. We expected Anna Wisniowska not Tyler Rosen to conduct the audit.

_____ 2. "We simply must have" said Brian "a bigger budget to start this project."

_____ 3. You returned the merchandise last month didn't you?

_____ 4. The better our advertising and recruiting the stronger our candidate pool will be.

_____ 5. "On the contrary" said Kamal Stevens "we will continue our proven marketing strategies."

_____ 6. What we need is more not fewer suggestions for improvement.

_____ 7. "Canada is now entering" said Minister Saunders "the Age of Innovation."

_____ 8. The talk by D. A. Spindler PhD was particularly difficult to follow because of his technical and abstract vocabulary.

_____ 9. We are very fortunate to have, at our disposal, the services of excellent professionals.

_____ 10. Emily Sandoval was named legislative counsel; Sam Freeman executive adviser.

1. (2) Wisniowska, Rosen, (2.12) 3. (1) month, (2.14b) 5. (2) contrary," Stevens, (2.14a) 7. (2) entering," Saunders, (2.14a) 9. (2) have at our disposal (2.15)

◣ GRAMMAR/MECHANICS CHECKUP 8

Commas 3

Review Sections 2.10–2.15. Then read each of the following statements and insert necessary commas. In the space provided, write the number of commas that you add; write *0* if no commas are needed. Also record the number of the Handbook principle(s) illustrated. When you finish, compare your responses with those provided in the Answer Key. If your answers differ, carefully study again the principles shown in parentheses.

2 (2.12)   **Example**   It was Lucia Bosano, not Melinda, Ho who was given the Kirkland account.

_____ 1. "The choice of a good name" said President Etienne "cannot be overestimated."

_____ 2. Hanna H. Cox PhD and Katherine Meridian MBA were hired as consultants.

_____ 3. The bigger the investment the greater the profit.

Review Commas 1, 2, 3

_____ 4. We think however that you should reexamine your website and that you should consider redesigning its navigation system.

_____ 5. Our convention will attract more participants if it is held in a resort location such as Collingwood the Laurentians or Banff.

_____ 6. A recent study of productivity that was conducted by authoritative researchers revealed that Canadian workers are more productive than workers in Europe or Japan.

_____ 7. The report concluded that Canada's secret productivity weapon was not bigger companies more robots or even brainier managers.

_____ 8. As a matter of fact the report said that Canada's productivity resulted from unprotected hands-off competition.

Use proofreading marks (see Appendix B) to correct errors and omissions in the following sentences. All errors must be corrected to receive credit for the sentence. Check with your instructor for the answers.

1. Emails must be written clear and concise, to ensure that receivers comprehend the message quick.

2. Our next sales campaign of course must target key decision makers.

3. In the meantime our online sales messages must include more then facts testimonials and guarantees.

4. The Small Business Administration which provide disaster loans are establishing additional offices in High River Calgary and Lethbridge.

5. Because we rely on email we have reduced our use of faxes, and voice messages.

6. In business time is money.

7. "The first product to use a bar code" said Alice Beasley "was Wrigley's gum."

8. In 1912, the Model 41 Touring went into production in Sam McLaughlin's plant in Oshawa Ontario.

9. As Professor Payne predicted the resourceful well trained graduate was hired quick.

10. The company's liability insurance in view of the laws that went into effect January 1 need to be increased.

Semicolons (2.16)

2.16 Independent Clauses, Series, Introductory Expressions

a. **Independent clauses with conjunctive adverbs.** Use a semicolon before a conjunctive adverb that separates two independent clauses. Some of the most common conjunctive adverbs are *therefore*, *consequently*, *however*, and *moreover*:

> Business messages should sound conversational; *therefore*, writers often use familiar words and contractions.

> The bank closes its doors at 5 p.m.; *however*, the ATM is open 24 hours a day.

Notice that the word following a semicolon is *not* capitalized (unless, of course, that word is a proper noun).

b. **Independent clauses without conjunctive adverbs.** Use a semicolon to separate closely related independent clauses when no conjunctive adverb is used:

> RRSPs are taxed upon redemption; TFSAs are not.

> Ambient lighting fills the room; task lighting illuminates each workstation.

Use a semicolon in *compound* sentences, not in *complex* sentences:

> After one week the paper feeder jammed; we tried different kinds of paper. (Use a semicolon in a compound sentence.)

> After one week the paper feeder jammed, although we tried different kinds of paper. (Use a comma in a complex sentence. Do not use a semicolon after *jammed*.)

The semicolon is very effective for joining two closely related thoughts. Don't use it, however, unless the ideas are truly related.

c. **Independent clauses with other commas.** Normally, a comma precedes *and*, *or*, and *but* when those conjunctions join independent clauses. However, if either clause contains commas, the writer may elect to change the comma preceding the conjunction to a semicolon to ensure correct reading:

Our primary concern is financing; and we have discovered, as you warned us, that capital sources are quite scarce.

d. **Series with internal commas.** Use semicolons to separate items in a series when one or more of the items contains internal commas:

> Delegates from Charlottetown, Prince Edward Island; Moncton, New Brunswick; and Truro, Nova Scotia, attended the conference.

> The speakers were Kevin Lang, manager, Riko Enterprises; Henry Holtz, vice president, Trendex, Inc.; and Margaret Woo, personnel director, West Coast Productions.

e. **Introductory expressions.** Use a semicolon when an introductory expression such as *namely*, *for instance*, *that is*, or *for example* introduces a list following an independent clause:

> Switching to computerized billing are several local companies; namely, Ryson Electronics, Miller Vending Services, and Black Home Heating.

> The author of a report should consider many sources; for example, books, periodicals, databases, and newspapers.

Colons (2.17–2.19)

2.17 Listed Items

a. **With colon.** Use a colon after a complete thought that introduces a formal list of items. A formal list is often preceded by such words and phrases as *these*, *thus*, *the following*, and *as follows*. A colon is also used when words and phrases like these are implied but not stated:

> Additional costs in selling a house involve *the following*: title examination fee, title insurance costs, and closing fee. (Use a colon when a complete thought introduces a formal list.)

> Collective bargaining focuses on several key issues: cost-of-living adjustments, fringe benefits, job security, and work hours. (The introduction of the list is implied in the preceding clause.)

b. **Without colon.** Do not use a colon when the list immediately follows a *to be* verb or a preposition:

> The employees who should receive the preliminary plan are James Sears, Monica Spees, and Rose Lopretti. (No colon is used after the verb *are*.)

> We expect to purchase equipment for Accounting, Legal Services, and Payroll. (No colon is used after the preposition *for*.)

2.18 Quotations Use a colon to introduce long one-sentence quotations and quotations of two or more sentences:

> Our consultant said: "This system can support up to 32 users. It can be used for decision support, computer-aided design, and software development operations at the same time."

2.19 Salutations Use a colon after the salutation of a business letter:

> Dear Ms. Seaman:

> Dear Jamie:

Review Exercise J—Semicolons, Colons

In the following sentences, add semicolons, colons, and necessary commas. In the spaces indicate the number of punctuation marks that you add. If a sentence requires no punctuation, write *C*. When you finish, compare your responses with those provided. For items that you need to review, consult the numbered principle shown in parentheses.

_____ 1. Technological advances have made full-motion video viewable on small screens therefore mobile phone makers and carriers have rolled out new services and phones.

_____ 2. The sedan version of the car is available in these colours Olympic red metallic silver and Aztec gold.

_____ 3. The individuals who should receive copies of this announcement are Jeff Wong Alicia Green and Kim Doogan.

_____ 4. Many of our potential customers are in Southern Ontario therefore our promotional effort will be strongest in that area.

_____ 5. Three dates have been reserved for initial interviews January 15 February 1 and February 12.

_____ 6. Several staff members are near the top of their salary ranges we must reclassify their jobs.

_____ 7. If you apply for an Advantage Express card today we will waive the annual fee moreover you will earn 10,000 bonus miles and reward points for every $1 you spend on purchases.

_____ 8. Monthly reports are missing from the Legal Department Human Resources Department and Engineering Department.

_____ 9. The convention committee is considering Victoria British Columbia Whistler British Columbia and Canmore Alberta.

_____ 10. Sherry first asked about salary next she inquired about benefits.

1. (2) screens; consequently, (2.16a) 3. (2) Wong, Alicia Green, (2.01, 2.17b) 5. (3) interviews: January 15, February 1, (2.01, 2.17a) 7. (3) today, fee; moreover, (2.06a, 2.16a) 9. (5) Victoria, British Columbia; Whistler, British Columbia; Canmore, (2.16d)

◣ GRAMMAR/MECHANICS CHECKUP 9

Semicolons and Colons

Review Sections 2.16–2.19. Then read each of the following statements. Insert any necessary punctuation. Use the delete symbol to omit unnecessary punctuation. In the space provided, indicate the number of changes you made and record the number of the Handbook principle(s) illustrated. (When you replace one punctuation mark with another, count it as one change.) If you make no changes, write 0. This exercise concentrates on semicolon and colon use, but you will also be responsible for correct comma use. When you finish, compare your responses with those shown in the Answer Key. If your responses differ, carefully study again the specific principles shown in parentheses.

<u>2 (2.16a)</u>   **Example**   Hans Wellworth's job is to make sure that his company has enough cash to meet its obligations⁀moreover⁀he is responsible for locating credit when needed.

_____ 1. We must negotiate short-term financing during the following months September October and November.

_____ 2. Although some firms rarely, if ever, need to borrow short-term money many businesses find that they require significant credit to pay for current production and sales costs.

_____ 3. A grocery store probably requires no short-term credit, a greeting card manufacturer however typically would need considerable short-term credit.

_____ 4. The prime interest rate is set by the Bank of Canada and this rate goes up or down as the cost of money to the bank itself fluctuates.

_____ 5. Most banks are in business to lend money to commercial customers for example retailers service companies manufacturers and construction firms.

_____ 6. When Avionics, Inc., was refused by Business Development Bank of Canada its financial managers submitted applications to the following Worldwide Investments, Dominion Securities, and Mid Mountain Group.

_____ 7. The cost of financing capital investments at the present time is very high therefore Avionics' managers may elect to postpone certain expansion projects.

_____ 8. If interest rates reach as high as 18 percent the cost of borrowing becomes prohibitive and many businesses are forced to reconsider or abandon projects that require financing.

Apostrophes (2.20–2.22)

2.20 Basic Rule The apostrophe is used to show ownership, origin, authorship, or measurement.

Ownership:	We are looking for _Brian's keys_.
Origin:	At the _president's suggestion_, we doubled the order.
Authorship:	The _accountant's annual report_ was questioned.
Measurement:	In _two years' time_ we expect to reach our goal.

a. **Ownership words not ending in** _s_. To place the apostrophe correctly, you must first determine whether the ownership word ends in an _s_ sound. If it does not, add an apostrophe and an _s_ to the ownership word. The following examples show ownership words that do not end in an _s_ sound:

the employee's file	(the file of a single employee)
a member's address	(the address of a single member)
a year's time	(the time of a single year)
a month's notice	(notice of a single month)
the company's building	(the building of a single company)

b. **Ownership words ending in** _s_. If the ownership word does end in an _s_ sound, usually add only an apostrophe:

several employees' files	(files of several employees)
ten members' addresses	(addresses of ten members)
five years' time	(time of five years)
several months' notice	(notice of several months)
many companies' buildings	(buildings of many companies)

A few singular nouns that end in _s_ are pronounced with an extra syllable when they become possessive. To these words, add _'s_.

my boss's desk   the waitress's table   the actress's costume

Use no apostrophe if a noun is merely plural, not possessive:

All the sales representatives, as well as the assistants and managers, had their names and telephone numbers listed in the directory.

2.21 Names Ending in s or an s Sound The possessive form of names ending in *s* or an *s* sound follows the same guidelines as for common nouns. If an extra syllable can be pronounced without difficulty, add *'s*. If the extra syllable is hard to pronounce, end with an apostrophe only.

Add apostrophe and s	Add apostrophe only
Russ's computer	New Orleans' cuisine
Bill Gates's business	Los Angeles' freeways
Mrs. Jones's home	the Morrises' family
Mr. Lopez's desk	the Lopezes' pool

Individual preferences in pronunciation may cause variation in a few cases. For example, some people may prefer not to pronounce an extra *s* in examples such as *Bill Gates' business*. However, the possessive form of plural names is consistent: *the Joneses' home, the Burgesses' children, the Bushes' car*. Notice that the article *the* is a clue in determining whether a name is singular or plural.

2.22 Gerunds Use *'s* to make a noun possessive when it precedes a gerund, a verb form used as a noun:

> Ken Smith's smoking prompted a new office policy. (Ken *Smith* is possessive because it modifies the gerund *smoking*.)

> It was Betsy's careful proofreading that revealed the discrepancy.

Review Exercise K—Apostrophes

Insert necessary apostrophes and corrections in the following sentences. In the spaces write the corrected word. If none were corrected, write C. When you finish, compare your responses with those provided. For items you need to review, consult the numbered principle shown in parentheses.

_____ 1. In five years time, Lisa hopes to repay all of her student loans.

_____ 2. All the employees personnel folders must be updated.

_____ 3. The Harrises daughter lived in Halifax for two years.

_____ 4. Both companies headquarters will be moved within the next six months.

_____ 5. Some of their assets could be liquidated; therefore, a few of the creditors received funds.

_____ 6. The package of electronics parts arrived safely despite two weeks delay.

_____ 7. According to Mr. Parvez latest proposal, all employees would receive an additional holiday.

_____ 8. His supervisor frequently had to correct Jacks financial reports.

_____ 9. Mr. Jackson estimated that he spent a years profits in reorganizing his staff.

_____ 10. The contract is not valid without Mrs. Harris signature.

---

1. years' (2.20b) 3. Harrises' (2.21) 5. C (2.20b) 7. Parvez's (2.21) 9. year's (2.20a)

◣ GRAMMAR/MECHANICS CHECKUP 10

Possessives

Review Sections 2.20–2.22. Then read each of the following statements. Underline any inappropriate form. Write a correction in the space provided, and record the number of the Handbook principle(s) illustrated. If a sentence is correct, write C.

When you finish, compare your responses with those in the Answer Key. If your answers differ, carefully study again the principles shown in parentheses.

years' (2.20b)   **Example**   In just two <u>years</u> time, the accountants and managers devised an entirely new system.

_____   1. Two supervisors said that Leo Ruskins work was excellent.

_____   2. None of the employees in our Logistics Department had taken more than two weeks vacation.

_____   3. All the secretaries agreed that Cindy Lanhams suggestions were practical.

_____   4. After you obtain your boss approval, send the application to Human Resources.

_____   5. Despite Kaspar grumbling, his wife selected two bonds and three stocks for her investments.

_____   6. In one months time we hope to be able to complete all the address files.

_____   7. Marks salary was somewhat higher than David.

◣ CUMULATIVE EDITING QUIZ 5

Use proofreading marks (see Appendix B) to correct errors and omissions in the following sentences. All errors must be corrected to receive credit for the sentence. Check with your instructor for the answers.

1. Mark Zuckerberg worked for years to build Facebook however it was years' before the company made a profit.

2. E-businesses has always been risky, online companys seem to disappear as quick as they appear.

3. According to a leading data source three of the top live entertainment companys are the following Double Fusion, Jerusalem, Israel, Echovoc, Geneva, Switzerland, and IceMobile, Amsterdam, The Netherlands.

4. By the way Tess email was forwarded to Jims incoming box in error and she was quite embarrassed.

5. The OSCs findings and ruling in the securitys fraud case is expected to be released in one hours time.

6. Only one hospitals doctors complained that they were restricted in the time they could spend listening to patients comments.

7. Any one of the auditors are authorized to conduct an independent action however only the CEO can change the councils directives.

8. Charles and Les mountain bicycles were stole from there garage last night.

9. Five of the worst computer passwords are the following your first name, your last name, the Enter key, *Password*, and the name of a sports' team.

10. On January 15 2021 we opened an innovative fully equipped fitness centre.

Other Punctuation (2.23–2.29)

2.23 Periods

a. **Ends of sentences.** Use a period at the end of a statement, command, indirect question, or polite request. Although a polite request may have the same structure as a question, it ends with a period:

> Corporate legal departments demand precise skills from their workforce. (End a statement with a period.)

Get the latest data by reading current periodicals. (End a command with a period.)

Mr. Rand wondered whether we had sent any follow-up literature. (End an indirect question with a period.)

Would you please re-examine my account and determine the current balance. (A polite request suggests an action rather than a verbal response.)

b. **Abbreviations and initials.** Use periods after initials and after many abbreviations.

R. M. Johnson	c.o.d.	Ms.
p.m.	a.m.	Mr.
Inc.	i.e.	Mrs.

The latest trend is to omit periods in degrees and professional designations: BA, PhD, MD, RN, DDS, MBA. Use just one period when an abbreviation falls at the end of a sentence:

Guests began arriving at 5:30 p.m.

2.24 Question Marks Direct questions are followed by question marks:

Did you send your proposal to Datatronix, Inc.?

Statements with questions added are punctuated with question marks.

We have completed the proposal, haven't we?

2.25 Exclamation Points Use an exclamation point after a word, phrase, or clause expressing strong emotion. In business writing, however, exclamation points should be used sparingly:

Incredible! Every terminal is down.

2.26 Dashes The dash (constructed at a keyboard by striking the hyphen key twice in succession) is a legitimate and effective mark of punctuation when used according to accepted conventions. As a connecting punctuation mark, however, the dash loses effectiveness when overused.

a. **Parenthetical elements.** Within a sentence a parenthetical element is usually set off by commas. If, however, the parenthetical element itself contains internal commas, use dashes (or parentheses) to set it off:

Three top salespeople—Tom Yashimoto, Gary Templeton, and Mona Judkins—received bonuses.

b. **Sentence interruptions.** Use a dash to show an interruption or abrupt change of thought:

News of the dramatic merger—no one believed it at first—shook the financial world.

Ship the materials Monday—no, we must have them sooner.

Sentences with abrupt changes of thought or with appended afterthoughts can usually be improved through rewriting.

c. **Summarizing statements.** Use a dash (not a colon) to separate an introductory list from a summarizing statement:

Sorting, merging, and computing—these are tasks that our data processing programs must perform.

2.27 Parentheses One means of setting off nonessential sentence elements involves the use of parentheses. Nonessential sentence elements may be punctuated in one of three ways: (a) with commas, to make the lightest possible break in the normal flow of a sentence; (b) with dashes, to emphasize the enclosed material; and (c) with parentheses, to de-emphasize the enclosed material. Parentheses are frequently used to punctuate sentences with interpolated directions, explanations, questions, and references:

> The cost analysis (which appears on page 8 of the report) indicates that the copy machine should be leased.

> Units are lightweight (approximately 1 kg) and come with a leather case and operating instructions.

> The latest laser printer (have you heard about it?) will be demonstrated for us next week.

A parenthetical sentence that is not embedded within another sentence should be capitalized and punctuated with end punctuation:

> The Model 20 has stronger construction. (See a Model 20 brochure by clicking the "Model 20" icon.)

2.28 Quotation Marks

a. **Direct quotations.** Use double quotation marks to enclose the exact words of a speaker or writer:

> "Keep in mind," Kelly Frank said, "that you'll have to justify the cost of upgrading company iPhones."

> The boss said that AI integration was inevitable. (No quotation marks are needed because the exact words are not quoted.)

b. **Quotations within quotations.** Use single quotation marks (apostrophes on the keyboard) to enclose quoted passages within quoted passages:

> In her speech, Marge Deckman remarked, "I believe it was the poet Robert Frost who said, 'All the fun's in how you say a thing.'"

c. **Short expressions.** Slang, words used in a special sense, and words following *stamped* or *marked* are often enclosed within quotation marks:

> Jeffrey described the damaged shipment as "gross." (Quotation marks enclose slang.)

> Students often have trouble spelling the word "separate." (Quotation marks enclose words used in a special sense.)

> Jobs were divided into two categories: most stressful and least stressful. The jobs in the "most stressful" list involved high risk or responsibility. (Quotation marks enclose words used in a special sense.)

> The envelope marked "Confidential" was put aside. (Quotation marks enclose words following *marked*.)

In the four preceding sentences, the words enclosed within quotation marks can be set in italics instead, if italics are available.

d. **Definitions.** Double quotation marks are used to enclose definitions. The word or expression being defined should be underscored or set in italics:

> The term *penetration pricing* is defined as "the practice of introducing a product to the market at a low price."

e. **Titles.** Use double quotation marks to enclose titles of literary and artistic works, such as magazine and newspaper articles, chapters of books, movies, television shows, poems, lectures, and songs. Names of major publications—such as books, magazines, pamphlets, and newspapers—are set in italics (underscored).

Particularly helpful was the chapter in Smith's *Effective Writing Techniques* entitled "Right Brain, Write On!"

John's article, "Email Blunders," appeared in *The Globe and Mail*; however, we couldn't locate it online.

f. **Additional considerations.** Periods and commas are always placed inside closing quotation marks. Semicolons and colons, on the other hand, are always placed outside quotation marks:

Sandra said, "I couldn't find the article entitled 'Cell Phone Etiquette.'"

The director asked for "absolute security": All written messages were to be destroyed.

Question marks and exclamation points may go inside or outside closing quotation marks, as determined by the form of the quotation:

Sales Manager Martin said, "Who placed the order?" (The quotation is a question.)

When did the sales manager say, "Who placed the order?" (Both the incorporating sentence and the quotation are questions.)

Did the sales manager say, "Ryan placed the order"? (The incorporating sentence asks a question; the quotation does not.)

"In the future," shouted Bob, "ask me first!" (The quotation is an exclamation.)

2.29 Brackets Within quotations, brackets are used by the quoting writer to enclose his or her own inserted remarks. Such remarks may be corrective, illustrative, or explanatory:

My professor said that "CSIS [the Canadian Security Intelligence Service] is becoming one of the most controversial and secretive of the federal government agencies."

Review Exercise L—Other Punctuation

Insert necessary punctuation in the following sentences. In the spaces indicate the number of punctuation marks that you added. Count sets of parentheses, dashes, and quotation marks as two marks. Emphasis or de-emphasis will be indicated for some parenthetical elements. When you finish, compare your responses with those provided. For items you need to review, consult the numbered principle shown in parentheses.

_____ 1. Will you please send me a link to your latest catalogue

_____ 2. (Emphasize) Three of my friends Irina Volodyeva, Stan Meyers, and Ivan Sergo were promoted.

_____ 3. Mr Lee, Miss Evans, and Mrs Rivera have not responded.

_____ 4. We have scheduled your interview for 4 45 p m

_____ 5. (De-emphasize) The appliance comes in limited colours black, ivory, and beige, but we accept special orders.

_____ 6. The expression de facto means exercising power as if legally constituted.

_____ 7. Who was it who said "This, too, will pass

_____ 8. Should this package be marked Fragile

_____ 9. Did you see the Macleans article titled How Far Can Wireless Go

_____ 10. Amazing All sales reps made their targets

(1). catalogue. (2.23a) 3. (2) Mr.; Mrs. (2.23) 5. (2) colours (black, ivory, and beige) (2.26a) 7. (3) said,; pass"? (2.28f) 9. (4) *Maclean*'s; "How Go?" (2.28e)

Other Punctuation

Although this checkup concentrates on Sections 2.23–2.29, you may also refer to other punctuation principles. Insert any necessary punctuation. In the spaces indicate the number of changes you make and record the number of the Handbook principle(s) illustrated. Count each mark separately; for example, a set of parentheses counts as 2. If you make no changes, write *0*. When you finish, compare your responses with those provided in the Answer Key. If your responses differ, carefully study again the specific principles shown in parentheses.

<u>2 (2.27)</u>   **Example**   (De-emphasize.) The consumption of cereal products is highest in certain provinces (Manitoba, Saskatchewan, Alberta, and Newfoundland), this food trend is spreading to other parts of country.

_____ 1. (Emphasize.) The convention planning committee has invited three managers Yu Wong, Frank Behr, and Yvette Sosa to make presentations.

_____ 2. (De-emphasize.) A second set of demographic variables see Figure 13 on page 432 includes nationality, religion, and race.

_____ 3. Recruiting, hiring, and training these are three important functions of a human resources officer.

_____ 4. Have any of the research assistants been able to locate the article entitled How Tax Reform Will Affect You

_____ 5. Have you sent invitations to Mr Kieran E Manning, Miss Kathy Tanguay, and Ms Petra Bonaventura?

_____ 6. James said, "I'll be right over" however he has not appeared yet.

_____ 7. Because the work was scheduled to be completed June 10 we found it necessary to hire temporary workers to work June 8 and 9.

_____ 8. Hooray I have finished this checkup haven't I

Punctuation Review

Review Sections 1.19 and 2.01–2.29. Then read the groups of sentences. In the spaces write the letter of the sentence that is correctly punctuated. When you finish, compare your responses with those in the Answer Key. If your responses differ, carefully study again the principles in parentheses.

_____ 1. (a)   Our accounting team makes a point of analyzing your business operations, and getting to know what's working for you and what's not.

   (b)   We are dedicated to understanding your business needs over the long term, and taking an active role when it comes to creating solutions.

   (c)   We understand that you may be downsizing or moving into new markets, and we want to help you make a seamless transition.

_____ 2. (a)   The competition is changing; therefore, we have to deliver our products and services more efficiently.

(b) Although delivery systems are changing; the essence of banking remains the same.

(c) Banks will continue to be available around the corner, and also with the click of a mouse.

_____ 3. (a) We care deeply about the environment; but we also care about safety and good customer service.

(b) The president worked with environmental concerns; the vice president focused on customer support

(c) Our website increases our productivity, it also improves customer service.

_____ 4. (a) All assistants' computers were equipped with MS Office.

(b) Both lawyers statements confused the judge.

(c) Some members names and addresses must be rekeyed.

_____ 5. (a) The package from Albany, New York was never delivered.

(b) We have scheduled an inspection tour on Tuesday, March 5, at 4 p.m.

(c) Send the cheque to M. E. Williams, 320 Summit Ridge, Elizabethtown, Ontario K6T 1A9 before the last mail pickup.

_____ 6. (a) If you demand reliable, competent service, you should come to us.

(b) We could not resist buying cookies from the enthusiastic, young Girl Guide.

(c) Our highly trained technicians, with years of experience are always available to evaluate and improve your network environment.

_____ 7. (a) Their wealthy uncle left $1 million to be distributed to Hayden, Carlotta, and Susanna.

(b) Their wealthy uncle left $1 million to be distributed to Hayden, Carlotta and Susanna.

(c) Our firm will maintain and upgrade your computers, printers, copiers and fax machines.

_____ 8. (a) We specialize in network design, however we also offer troubleshooting and consulting.

(b) We realize that downtime is not an option; therefore, you can count on us for reliable, competent service.

(c) Our factory-trained and certified technicians perform repair at your location, or in our own repair depot for products under warranty and out of warranty.

◤ CUMULATIVE EDITING QUIZ 6

Use proofreading marks (see Appendix B) to correct errors and omissions in the following sentences. All errors must be corrected to receive credit for the sentence. Check with your instructor for the answers.

1. We wondered whether Dr Ellen Hildago would be the speaker at the Kingston Ontario event?

2. Our operating revenue for 2021 see Appendix A exceeded all the consultants expectations.

3. Four features, camera, text messaging, Web access, and voice mail—are what Canadians want most on there cell phones.

4. Serge Laferia CEO of Imperial Tobacco said "We're being socially responsible in a rather controversial industry.

5. Kym Andersons chapter titled Subsidies and Trade Barriers appears in the book How to Spend $50 Billion to Make the World a Better Place.

6. Wasnt it Zack Tesar not Ellen Trask who requested a 14 day leave.

7. Was it Oprah Winfrey who said that the best jobs are those we'd do even if we didn't get paid.

8. The word mashup is a technology term that is defined as a website that uses content from more then one source to create a completely new service.

9. Miss. Rhonda Evers is the person who the employees council elected as there representative.

10. Would you please send a trial subscription to Globex, Inc

---

◤ STYLE AND USAGE

Capitalization (3.01–3.16)

Capitalization is used to distinguish important words. However, writers are not free to capitalize all words they consider important. Rules or guidelines governing capitalization style have been established through custom and use. Mastering these guidelines will make your writing more readable and more comprehensible.

3.01 Proper Nouns Capitalize proper nouns, including the *specific* names of persons, places, schools, streets, parks, buildings, holidays, months, agreements, websites, software programs, historical periods, and so forth. Do not capitalize common nouns that make only *general* references.

Proper nouns	Common nouns
Lisa LaFlamme	well-known news anchor
Mexico, U.S.A.	Canadian trading partners
Algonquin College	a community college
Parc Lafontaine	a park in the city
Rideau Room, Royal York Hotel	a meeting room in the hotel
Family Day, New Year's Day	two holidays
Google, Facebook, Wikipedia	popular websites
Burlington Skyway	a bridge
Consumer Protection Act	a law to protect consumers
Halifax Chamber of Commerce	a chamber of commerce
Billy Bishop Airport	a municipal airport
January, February, March	months of the year

3.02 Proper Adjectives Capitalize most adjectives that are derived from proper nouns:

Greek symbol	British thermal unit
Roman numeral	Freudian slip
Xerox copy	Hispanic community center

Do not capitalize the few adjectives that, although originally derived from proper nouns, have become common adjectives through usage. Consult your dictionary when in doubt:

manila folder	diesel engine
venetian blinds	china dishes

3.03 Geographic Locations Capitalize the names of *specific* places such as continents, countries, provinces, mountains, valleys, lakes, rivers, oceans, and geographic regions:

Quebec City	Lake Athabasca
Rocky Mountains	Pacific Ocean
Annapolis Valley	Bay of Fundy
the East Coast	the Prairie provinces

3.04 Organization Names Capitalize the principal words in the names of all business, civic, educational, governmental, labour, military, philanthropic, political, professional, religious, and social organizations:

Bombardier	Board of Directors, Scotiabank
The Montreal Gazette*	Vancouver Art Gallery
Toronto Stock Exchange	Bank of Canada
United Way	Canadian Union of Public Employees
Al Purdy A-Frame Association	Canadian Association of Retired Persons

3.05 Academic Courses and Degrees Capitalize particular academic degrees and course titles. Do not capitalize general academic degrees and subject areas:

Professor Bernadette Ordian, *PhD*, will teach *Accounting* 221 next fall.

Julia Snyder, who holds *bachelor's* and *master's degrees*, teaches *marketing* classes.

Pablo enrolled in classes in history, business English, and management.

3.06 Personal and Business Titles

a. Capitalize personal and business titles when they precede names:

Vice President Ames	Uncle Edward
Board Chairman Frazier	Councillor Herbert
Premier Thurmond	Sales Manager Klein
Professor Mahfouz	Dr. Samuel Washington

b. Capitalize titles in addresses, salutations, and closing lines:

Mr. Juan deSanto	Very truly yours,
Director of Purchasing	
Space Systems, Inc.	Clara J. Smith
Madoc, ON K0K 2K0	Supervisor, Marketing

c. Generally, do not capitalize titles of high government rank or religious office when they stand alone or follow a person's name in running text.

The prime minister conferred with the armed forces council and many senators.

Meeting with the chief justice of the Supreme Court were the senator from British Columbia and the mayor of Vancouver.

Only the cardinal from Montreal had an audience with the pope.

d. Do not capitalize most common titles following names:

The speech was delivered by Robert Lynch, *president*, Academic Publishing.

Lois Herndon, *chief executive officer*, signed the order.

---

*Note: Capitalize *the* only when it is part of the official name of an organization, as printed on the organization's stationery.

e. Do not capitalize common titles appearing alone:

> Please speak to the *supervisor* or to the *office* manager.

> Neither the *president* nor the *vice president* could attend.

However, when the title of an official appears in that organization's minutes, bylaws, or other official document, it may be capitalized.

f. Do not capitalize titles when they are followed by appositives naming specific individuals:

> We must consult our *director of research*, Ronald E. West, before responding.

g. Do not capitalize family titles used with possessive pronouns:

my mother	your father
our aunt	his cousin

h. Capitalize titles of close relatives used without pronouns:

> Both *Mother* and *Father* must sign the contract.

3.07 Numbered and Lettered Items
Capitalize nouns followed by numbers or letters (except in page, paragraph, line, and verse references):

Flight 34, Gate 12	Plan No. 2
Volume I, Part 3	Warehouse 33-A
Invoice No. 55489	Figure 8.3
Model A5673	Serial No. C22865404-2
Provincial Highway 10	page 6, line 5

3.08 Points of the Compass
Capitalize *north*, *south*, *east*, *west*, and their derivatives when they represent *specific* geographical regions. Do not capitalize the points of the compass when they are used in directions or in general references.

Specific Regions	General References
from the South	heading north on the highway
living in the West	west of the city
Easterners, Westerners	western Ontario, southern Saskatchewan
going to the Middle East	the northern part of province
from the East Coast	the east side of the street

3.09 Departments, Divisions, and Committees
Capitalize the names of departments, divisions, or committees within your own organization. Outside your organization capitalize only *specific* department, division, or committee names:

> The inquiry was addressed to the Legal Department in our Consumer Products Division.

> John was appointed to the *Employee Benefits Committee*.

> Send your résumé to their *human resources division*.

> A *planning committee* will be named shortly.

3.10 Governmental Terms
Do not capitalize the words *federal*, *government*, *nation*, *province*, or *territory* unless they are part of a specific title:

> Unless *federal* support can be secured, the *provincial* project will be abandoned.

> The *Council of the Federation* promotes inter-provincial cooperation.

3.11 Product Names Capitalize product names only when they refer to trademarked items. Except in advertising, common names following manufacturers' names are not capitalized:

Magic Marker	Lululemon pants
Kleenex tissues	Swingline stapler
Q-tip swab	ChapStick lip balm
Levi's 501 jeans	Excel spreadsheet
DuPont Teflon	Roots sweatshirt

3.12 Literary Titles Capitalize the principal words in the titles of books, magazines, newspapers, articles, movies, plays, songs, poems, and reports. Do not capitalize articles (*a, an, the*), short conjunctions (*and, but, or, nor*), and prepositions of fewer than four letters (*in, to, by, for*) unless they begin or end the title:

Jackson's *What Job Is for You?* (Capitalize book titles.)

Gant's "Software for the Executive Suite" (Capitalize principal words in article titles.)

"Performance Standards to Go By" (Capitalize article titles.)

"The Improvement of Fuel Economy With Alternative Fuels" (Capitalize report titles.)

3.13 Beginning Words In addition to capitalizing the first word of a complete sentence, capitalize the first word in a quoted sentence, independent phrase, item in an enumerated list, and formal rule or principle following a colon:

The business manager said, "*All* purchases must have requisitions." (Capitalize first word in a quoted sentence.)

Yes, if you agree. (Capitalize an independent phrase.)

Some of the duties of the position are as follows:

1. *Editing* and formatting Word files
2. *Arranging* video and teleconferences
3. *Verifying* records, reports, and applications (Capitalize items in a vertical enumerated list.)

One rule has been established through the company: No smoking is allowed in open offices. (Capitalize a rule following a colon.)

3.14 Celestial Bodies Capitalize the names of celestial bodies such as *Mars*, *Saturn*, and *Neptune*. Do not capitalize the terms *earth*, *sun*, or *moon* unless they appear in a context with other celestial bodies:

Where on *earth* did you find that manual typewriter?

Venus and *Mars* are the closest planets to *Earth*.

3.15 Ethnic References Capitalize terms that refer to a particular culture, language, or race:

Asian	Hebrew
Caucasian	Indian
Latino	Japanese
Persian	Judeo-Christian

3.16 Seasons Do not capitalize seasons:

> In the *fall* it appeared that *winter* and *spring* sales would increase.

Review Exercise M—Capitalization

In the following sentences, correct any errors that you find in capitalization. Underscore any lowercase letter that should be changed to a capital letter. Draw a slash (/) through a capital letter that you wish to change to a lowercase letter. In the spaces indicate the total number of changes you have made in each sentence. If you make no changes, write *0*. When you finish, compare your responses with those provided.

5   **Example**   Bill McAdams, currently Assistant Manager in our Compensation division, will be promoted to Manager of the Employee Services division.

_____ 1. The copyright modernization act, passed in 2011, has been seen as taking away rights from content creators.

_____ 2. Marilyn Afraz, mba, received her bachelor's degree from Queen's university in kingston.

_____ 3. Please ask your Aunt and your Uncle if they will come to the Lawyer's office at 5 p.m.

_____ 4. Once we establish an organizing committee, arrangements can be made to rent holmby hall.

_____ 5. Either the President or the Vice President of the company will make the decision about purchasing xerox copiers.

_____ 6. Some individuals feel that canadian companies do not have the sense of loyalty to their employees that japanese companies do.

_____ 7. The prime minister recently said, "we must protect our domestic economy from Foreign competition."

_____ 8. All marketing representatives of our company will meet in the empire room of the red lion motor inn.

_____ 9. The special keyboard for the Dell Computer must contain greek symbols for Engineering equations.

_____ 10. In the Fall our organization will move its corporate headquarters to the franklin building in downtown winnipeg.

---

1. (3) Copyright Modernization Act (3.01) 3. (3) aunt uncle lawyer's (3.06e, 3.06g) 5. (4) president vice president Xerox (3.06e, 3.11) 7. (2) We foreign (3.10, 3.13) 9. (3) computer Greek engineering (3.01, 3.02, 3.11)

◣ GRAMMAR/MECHANICS CHECKUP 13

Capitalization

Review Sections 3.01–3.16. Then read each of the following statements. Underscore any lowercase letter that should be changed to a capital letter. Draw a slash (/) through any capital letter that you wish to change to lowercase. Indicate in the space provided the number of changes you made in each sentence and record the number of the Handbook principle(s) illustrated. If you made no changes, write *0*. When you finish, compare your responses with those provided in the Answer Key. If your responses differ, carefully study again the principles in parentheses.

<u>4 (3.01, 3.06a)</u> **Example** After consulting our ~~A~~ttorneys for ~~L~~egal advice, Vice
president Fontaine signed the ~~C~~ontract.

_____ 1. Personal tax rates for japanese citizens are low by International
standards; rates for japanese corporations are high, according to
Iwao Nakatani, an Economics Professor at Osaka university.

_____ 2. Did you see the *Maclean's* article entitled "Careers in horticulture
are nothing to sneeze at"?

_____ 3. Although I recommend Minex Printers sold under the brand-
name MPLazerJet, you may purchase any Printers you choose.

_____ 4. According to a Federal Government report, any development of
Provincial waterways must receive an environmental assessment.

_____ 5. My Mother, who lives near Plum Coulee, reports that protection
from the Sun's rays is particularly important when travelling to
the South.

_____ 6. Next week, Editor in Chief Mercredi plans an article detailing the
astounding performance of the euro.

_____ 7. To reach Terrasse Vaudreuil park, which is located on an Island
in the St. Lawrence river, tourists pass over the vanier bridge.

_____ 8. On its website you will see that the computer science department
is offering a number of courses in programming.

◣ CUMULATIVE EDITING QUIZ 7

Use proofreading marks (see Appendix B) to correct errors and omissions in the
following sentences. All errors must be corrected to receive credit for the sentence.
Check with your instructor for the answers.

1. wonder whether ceo Jackson invited our Marketing Vice President to join the
   upcoming three hour training session?

2. Our Sales Manager said that you attending the two day seminar is fine however
   we must find a replacement.

3. The boston marathon is an annual Sporting Event hosted by the City of Boston,
   Massachusetts on the third monday of April.

4. Steve Chen one of the founders of YouTube hurried to gate 44 to catch flight
   246 to north carolina.

5. Jake noticed that the english spoken by asians in hong kong sounded more
   british than north american.

6. Good Friday is a Statutory holiday therefore banks will be closed.

7. Because the package was marked fragile the mail carrier handled it careful.

8. Money traders watched the relation of the american dollar to the chinese yuan,
   the european euro and the canadian dollar.

9. My Aunt and me head South each Winter to vacation in the okanagan with our
   friends the Perry's.

10. Jim Balsillie former Co-CEO of Research in motion (inventors of the blackberry)
    now serves as Chair of the Board of the centre for International Governance
    Innovation in waterloo.

Number Style (4.01–4.13)

Usage and custom determine whether numbers are expressed in the form of figures
(e.g., 5, 9) or in the form of words (e.g., *five, nine*). Numbers expressed as figures are
shorter and more easily understood, yet numbers expressed as words are necessary

in certain instances. The following guidelines are observed in expressing numbers in written sentences. Numbers that appear on business documents—such as invoices, monthly statements, and purchase orders—are always expressed as figures.

4.01 General Rules

a. The numbers *one* through *ten* are generally written as words. Numbers above *ten* are written as figures:

> The bank had a total of *nine* branch offices in *three* suburbs.

> All *58* employees received benefits in the *three* categories shown.

> A shipment of *45,000* lightbulbs was sent from *two* warehouses.

b. Numbers that begin sentences are written as words. If a number beginning a sentence involves more than two words, however, the sentence should be revised so that the number does not fall at the beginning.

> *Fifteen* different options were available in the annuity programs.

> A total of 156 companies participated in the promotion (not *One hundred fifty-six companies participated in the promotion*).

4.02 Money Sums of money $1 or greater are expressed as figures. If a sum is a whole dollar amount, omit the decimal and zeros (whether or not the amount appears in a sentence with additional fractional dollar amounts):

> We budgeted *$300* for a digital camera, but the actual cost was *$370.96*.

> On the invoice were items for *$6.10*, *$8*, *$33.95*, and *$75*.

Sums less than $1 are written as figures that are followed by the word *cents*:

> By shopping carefully, we can save *15 cents* per unit.

4.03 Dates In dates, numbers that appear after the name of the month are written as cardinal figures (*1*, *2*, *3*, etc.). Those that stand alone or appear before the name of a month are written as ordinal figures (*1st*, *2nd*, *3rd*, etc.):

> The Workplace Safety Committee will meet *May 7*.

> On the *5th* day of February and again on the *25th*, we placed orders.

In Canadian business documents, dates generally take the following form: *January 4, 2021*. An alternative form, used primarily in military and foreign correspondence, begins with the day of the month and omits the comma: *4 January 2021*.

4.04 Clock Time Figures are used when clock time is expressed with *a.m.* or *p.m.* Omit the colon and zeros in referring to whole hours. When exact clock time is expressed with the contraction o'clock, either figures or words may be used:

> Mail deliveries are made at 11 *a.m.* and 3:30 *p.m.*

> At *four* (or *4*) *o'clock* employees begin to leave.

4.05 Addresses and Telephone Numbers

a. Except for the number *one*, house numbers are expressed in figures:

540 Queen Street	17802 8th Avenue NW
One René Lévesque Boulevard	2 Highland Street

b. Street names containing numbers *ten* or lower are written entirely as words. For street names involving numbers greater than *ten*, figures are used:

330 Third Street	3440 Seventh Avenue
6945 East 32nd Avenue	4903 West 23rd Street

c. Telephone numbers are expressed with figures. In some jurisdictions, area codes are essential parts of phone number and are placed preceding the telephone number:

> Please call us at *519-347-0551* to place an order.

When area codes are nonessential parts of phone number, they often appear in parentheses:

> Brian Sims asked you to call (604) 554-8923, Ext. 245, after 10 a.m.4.06 Related Numbers.

d. Numbers are related when they refer to similar items in a category within the same reference. All related numbers should be expressed as the largest number is expressed. Thus if the largest number is greater than *ten*, all the numbers should be expressed in figures:

> Only *5* of the original *25* applicants completed the processing. (Related numbers require figures.)

> The *two* plans affected *34* employees working in *three* sites. (Unrelated numbers use figures and words.)

> Beaver Drilling operated *14* rigs, of which *3* were rented. (Related numbers require figures.)

> The company hired *three* accountants, *one* customer service representative, and *nine* sales representatives. (Related numbers under ten use words.)

4.07 Consecutive Numbers When two numbers appear consecutively and both modify a following noun, generally express the first number in words and the second in figures. If, however, the first number cannot be expressed in one or two words, place it in figures also (*120 85-cent* stamps). Do not use commas to separate the figures.

> Historians divided the era into *four 25-year* periods. (Use word form for the first number and figure form for the second.)

> We ordered *ten 30-page* colour brochures. (Use word form for the first number and figure form for the second.)

> Did the manager request *150 100-watt* bulbs? (Use figure form for the first number since it would require more than two words.)

4.08 Periods of Time Seconds, minutes, days, weeks, months, and years are treated as any other general number. Numbers above ten are written in figure form. Numbers below ten are written in word form unless they represent a business concept such as a discount rate, interest rate, or warranty period.

> This business was incorporated over *50* years ago. (Use figures for a number above ten.)

> It took *three* hours to write this short report. (Use words for a number under ten.)

> The warranty period is limited to 2 years. (Use figures for a business term.)

4.09 Ages Ages are generally expressed in word form unless the age appears immediately after a name or is expressed in exact years and months:

> At the age of *twenty-one*, Elizabeth inherited the business.

> Wanda Tharp, *37*, was named acting president.

> At the age of *4 years and 7 months*, the child was adopted.

4.10 Round Numbers Round numbers are approximations. They may be expressed in word or figure form, although figure form is shorter and easier to comprehend:

> About *600* (or *six hundred*) stock options were sold.

> It is estimated that *1,000* (or *one thousand*) people will attend.

For ease of reading, round numbers in the millions or billions should be expressed with a combination of figures and words:

> At least *1.5 million* readers subscribe to the ten top magazines.

> Deposits in money market accounts totalled more than *$115 billion*.

4.11 Weights and Measurements Weights and measurements are expressed with figures:

> The promotional bookmark measures *2* by *6 inches*.

> Her new suitcase weighed only *1.5 kilograms*.

> Toronto is *70 kilometres* from Oshawa.

4.12 Fractions Simple fractions are expressed as words. Complex fractions may be written either as figures or as a combination of figures and words:

> Over *two thirds* of the stockholders have already voted.

> This software will execute the command in *1 millionth* of a second. (A combination of words and numbers is easier to comprehend.)

> She purchased a *one-fifth* share in the business.*

4.13 Percentages and Decimals Percentages are expressed with figures that are followed by the word *percent*. The percent sign (%) is used only on business forms or in statistical presentations:

> We had hoped for a *7 percent* interest rate, but we received a loan at *8 percent*.

> Over *50 percent* of the condo owners supported the plan.

Decimals are expressed with figures. If a decimal expression does not contain a whole number (an integer) and does not begin with a zero, a zero should be placed before the decimal point:

> The actuarial charts show that *1.74* out of *1,000* people will die in any given year.

> Inspector Norris found the setting to be *.005* centimetre off. (Decimal begins with a zero and does not require a zero before the decimal point.)

> Considerable savings will accrue if the unit production cost is reduced *0.1* percent. (A zero is placed before a decimal that neither contains a whole number nor begins with a zero.)

Quick Chart—Expression of Numbers

Use Words	Use Figures
Numbers *ten* and under	Numbers *11* and over
Numbers at beginning of sentence	Money
Ages	Dates
Fractions	Addresses and telephone numbers
	Weights and measurements
	Percentages and decimals

---

*Note: Fractions used as adjectives require hyphens.

Review Exercise N—Number Style

Write the preferred number style in the spaces. Assume that these numbers appear in business correspondence. When you finish, compare your responses with those provided. For items you need to review, consult the numbered principle shown in parentheses.

_____	1. (a)	2 alternatives	(b) two alternatives
_____	2. (a)	sixty sales reps	(b) 60 sales reps
_____	3. (a)	forty dollars	(b) $40
_____	4. (a)	at 2:00 p.m.	(b) at 2 p.m.
_____	5. (a)	at least 15 years ago	(b) at least fifteen years ago
_____	6. (a)	twelve cents	(b) 12 cents
_____	7. (a)	ten percent interest rate	(b) 10 percent interest rate
_____	8. (a)	the rug measures one by two metres	(b) the rug measures 1 by 2 metres
_____	9. (a)	at eight o'clock	(b) at 8 o'clock
_____	10. (a)	three laptops for twelve people	(b) three laptops for 12 people

1. b (4.01a) 3. b (4.02) 5. a (4.08) 7. b (4.13) 9. a or b (4.04)

◣ GRAMMAR/MECHANICS CHECKUP 14

Number Style

Review Sections 4.01–4.13. Then read each of the following pairs. Assume that these expressions appear in the context of letters, reports, or emails. Write *a* or *b* in the space provided to indicate the preferred number style and record the number of the Handbook principle illustrated. When you finish, compare your responses with those in the Answer Key. If your responses differ, carefully study again the principles in parentheses.

a (4.01) **Example** (a) six investments (b) 6 investments

_____	1. (a)	sixteen credit cards	(b) 16 credit cards
_____	2. (a)	July eighth	(b) July 8
_____	3. (a)	twenty dollars	(b) $20
_____	4. (a)	at 4:00 p.m.	(b) at 4 p.m.
_____	5. (a)	3 200-page reports	(b) three 200-page reports
_____	6. (a)	over 18 years ago	(b) over eighteen years ago
_____	7. (a)	2/3 of the emails	(b) two thirds of the emails
_____	8. (a)	two extensions for 15 employees	(b) 2 extensions for 15 employees

◣ CUMULATIVE EDITING QUIZ 8

Use proofreading marks (see Appendix B) to correct errors and omissions in the following sentences. All errors must be corrected to receive credit for the sentence. Check with your instructor for the answers.

1. My partner and myself will meet at our lawyers office at three p.m. on June ninth to sign our papers of incorporation.

2. Emily prepared 2 forty page business proposals to submit to the Senior Account Manager.

3. Of the 235 emails sent yesterday only seven bounced back.

4. Your short term loan for twenty-five thousand dollars covers a period of sixty days.

5. Each new employee must pick up their permanent parking permit for lot 3-A before the end of the 14 day probationary period.

6. 259 identity theft complaints were filed with the Competition bureau on November second alone.

7. Robertas 11 page report was more easier to read then Davids because her's was better organized and had good headings.

8. Every morning on the way to the office Tatiana picked up 2 lattes that cost a total of ten dollars.

9. Taking 7 years to construct the forty thousand square foot home of Olexiy Karpolin reportedly cost more then fifty million dollars.

10. Many companys can increase profits nearly ninety percent by retaining only 5% more of there current customers.

Confusing Words

accede:	to agree or consent	*cereal:*	breakfast food
exceed:	over a limit	*serial:*	arranged in sequence
accept:	to receive	*cite:*	to quote; to summon
except:	to exclude; (prep.) but	*site:*	location
adverse:	opposing; antagonistic	*sight:*	a view; to see
averse:	unwilling; reluctant	*coarse:*	rough texture
advice:	suggestion, opinion	*course:*	a route; part of a meal; a unit of learning
advise:	to counsel or recommend	*complement:*	that which completes
affect:	to influence	*compliment:*	(n.) praise, flattery; (v.) to praise or flatter
effect:	(n.) outcome, result; (v.) to bring about, to create	*conscience:*	regard for fairness
all ready:	prepared	*conscious:*	aware
already:	by this time	*council:*	governing body
all right:	satisfactory	*counsel:*	(n.) advice, lawyer; (v.) to give advice
alright:	unacceptable variant spelling	*credible:*	believable
altar:	structure for worship	*creditable:*	good enough for praise or esteem; reliable
alter:	to change	*desert:*	arid land; to abandon
appraise:	to estimate	*dessert:*	sweet food
apprise:	to inform	*device:*	invention or mechanism
ascent:	(n.) rising or going up	*devise:*	to design or arrange
assent:	(v.) to agree or consent	*disburse:*	to pay out
assure:	to promise	*disperse:*	to scatter widely
ensure:	to make certain	*elicit:*	to draw out
insure:	to protect from loss	*illicit:*	unlawful
capital:	(n.) city that is seat of government; wealth of an individual; (adj.) chief	*envelop:*	(v.) to wrap, surround, or conceal
capitol:	building that houses U.S. state or national lawmakers	*envelope:*	(n.) a container for a written message

every day:	each single day	*personnel:*	employees
everyday:	ordinary	*plaintiff:*	(n.) one who initiates a lawsuit
farther:	a greater distance		
further:	additional	*plaintive:*	(adj.) expressive of suffering or woe
formally:	in a formal manner		
formerly:	in the past	*populace:*	(n.) the masses; population of a place
grate:	(v.) to reduce to small particles; to cause irritation; (n.) a frame of crossed bars blocking a passage	*populous:*	(adj.) densely populated
		precede:	to go before
		proceed:	to continue
		precedence:	priority
great:	(adj.) large in size; numerous; eminent or distinguished	*precedents:*	events used as an example
		principal:	(n.) capital sum; school official; (adj.) chief
hole:	an opening		
whole:	complete	*principle:*	rule of action
imply:	to suggest indirectly	*stationary:*	immovable
infer:	to reach a conclusion	*stationery:*	writing material
lean:	(v.) to rest against; (adj.) not fat	*than:*	conjunction showing comparison
lien:	(n.) a legal right or claim to property	*then:*	adverb meaning "at that time"
liable:	legally responsible	*their:*	possessive form of they
libel:	damaging written statement	*there:*	at that place or point
		they're:	contraction of they are
loose:	not fastened	*to:*	a preposition; the sign of the infinitive
lose:	to misplace		
miner:	person working in a mine	*too:*	an adverb meaning "also" or "to an excessive extent"
minor:	a lesser item; person under age		
patience:	calm perseverance	*two:*	a number
patients:	people receiving medical treatment	*waiver:*	abandonment of a claim
		waver:	to shake or fluctuate
personal:	private, individual		

160 Frequently Misspelled Words

absence	desirable	independent	prominent
accommodate	destroy	indispensable	qualify
achieve	development	interrupt	quantity
acknowledgment	disappoint	irrelevant	questionnaire
across	dissatisfied	itinerary	receipt
adequate	division	judgment	receive
advisable	efficient	knowledge	recognize
analyze	embarrass	legitimate	recommendation
annually	emphasis	library	referred
appointment	emphasize	license (v.) licence (n.)	regarding
argument	employee	maintenance	remittance

automatically	envelope	manageable	representative
bankruptcy	equipped	manufacturer	restaurant
becoming	especially	mileage	schedule
beneficial	evidently	miscellaneous	secretary
budget	exaggerate	mortgage	separate
business	excellent	necessary	similar
calendar	exempt	nevertheless	sincerely
cancelled	existence	ninety	software
catalogue	extraordinary	ninth	succeed
changeable	familiar	noticeable	sufficient
column	fascinate	occasionally	supervisor
committee	feasible	occurred	surprise
congratulate	February	offered	tenant
conscience	fiscal	omission	therefore
conscious	foreign	omitted	thorough
consecutive	forty	opportunity	though
consensus	fourth	opposite	through
consistent	friend	ordinarily	truly
control	genuine	paid	undoubtedly
convenient	government	pamphlet	unnecessarily
correspondence	grammar	permanent	usable
courteous	grateful	permitted	usage
criticize	guarantee	pleasant	using
decision	harass	practical	usually
deductible	height	prevalent	valuable
defendant	hoping	privilege	volume
definitely	immediate	probably	weekday
dependent	incidentally	procedure	writing
describe	incredible	profited	yield

Challenge 1

1. countries (1.05e) **2.** CEOs (1.05g) **3.** employees (1.05a) **4.** Sundays, Mondays (1.05a) **5.** turkeys (1.05d) **6.** Alvarezes (1.05b) **7.** 1990s (1.05b) **8.** brothers-in-law (1.05f) **9.** klutzes (1.05b) **10.** inquiries (1.05e) **11.** Anthonys (1.05a) **12.** C (1.05d) **13.** liabilities (1.05e) **14.** C (1.05h) **15.** women (1.05c)

Challenge 2

1. she (1.08b) **2.** his (1.09c) **3.** him (1.08d) **4.** Whom (1.08j) **5.** yours (1.08d) **6.** me (1.08c) **7.** I (1.08a) **8.** its (1.08d) **9.** whoever (1.08j) **10.** me (1.08i) **11.** he (1.08f) **12.** us (1.08g) **13.** her (1.09c) **14.** its (1.09c) **15.** he and I (1.08a)

Challenge 3

1. is (1.10c) **2.** has (1.10i) **3.** offers (1.10d) **4.** are (1.10e) **5.** has (1.10i) **6.** were (1.12) **7.** C (1.10h) **8.** gone (1.15) **9.** lain (1.15) **10.** is (1.10h) **11.** believe (1.10b) **12.** b (1.15c—matches active voice) **13.** b (1.15c—matches subjects) **14.** a (1.15c—matches active voice) **15.** a (1.14b—matches verb tense)

Challenge 4

1. tried-and-true (1.17e) **2.** ten-year-old (1.17e) **3.** bright (1.17c) **4.** quickly (1.17d) **5.** clearer (1.17b) **6.** work-related (1.17e) **7.** their (1.17g) **8.** spur-of-the-moment (1.17e) **9.** spur of the moment (1.17e) **10.** well-thought-out (1.17e) **11.** change-of-address (1.17e) **12.** case-by-case (1.17e) **13.** nearer (1.17b) **14.** bad (1.17c) **15.** smoothly (1.17d)

Challenge 5

1. a (1.19d) **2.** b (1.19c) **3.** b (1.19d) **4.** b (1.19c) **5.** b (1.19a) **6.** a (1.18a) **7.** b (1.18b) **8.** b (1.18c) **9.** b (1.18a) **10.** b (1.18e) **11.** b (1.19a) **12.** a (1.19b) **13.** b (1.19c) **14.** a (1.18b) **15.** b (1.19c)

Challenge 6

1. 1: desperate, (2.06a) **2.** 1: aggressive, (2.05) **3.** 0 (2.05) **4.** 2: Wang, firm, (2.09) **5.** 1: reliable, (2.08) **6.** 1: months, (2.07) **7.** 2: manager, months, (2.06c) **8.** 0 (2.06c) **9.** 1: candidate, (2.06a) **10.** 0 (2.06c) **11.** 4: company, releases, reports, coverage, (2.01 and 2.07) **12.** 3: hired, Monday, 15, (2.04 and 2.07) **13.** 2: pay, interview, (2.06c) **14.** 1: fact, (2.03) **15.** 3: opportunity, Tuesday, 3, (2.04 and 2.06)

Challenge 7

1. 1: money," (2.14a) 2. 2: delete commas after *required* and *time* (2.15) 3. 1: 2, (2.14b) **4.** 2: delete commas after *drivers* and *accidents* (2.15) **5.** 1: monitor, (2.12) **6.** 1: know, (2.06a, 2.01) **7.** 1: delete comma after *diplomats* (2.03, 2.15) **8.** 1: delete comma after *productivity* (2.15) **9.** 2: deficits, report, (2.06c) **10.** 0: (2.03, 2.08)

Challenge 8

1. 3: less; financing, hand, (2.16b, 2.03) **2.** 3: months: October, November, (2.17a, 2.01) **3.** 2: finances; however, (2.16a) **4.** 2: lenders; therefore, (2.16a) **5.** 1: are: (2.17b) **6.** 1: risks; (2.16b) **7.** 3: score: history, credit, (2.17a, 2.01) **8.** 6: speakers: Cruz, consultant; Lee, Solutions; Plutsky, (2.17a, 2.09, 2.16d) **9.** 1: score, (2.05) **10.** 4: factors; example, age, salary, (2.16e, 2.01) **11.** 3: Solutions, service, score: (2.06c, 2.17a) **12.** 4: Solutions, Lee, Highway, Simcoe, (2.06a, 2.04d) **13.** 5: Lee, Solutions, experienced, staff; however, (2.09, 2.08, 2.16a) **14.** 1: lows; (2.16b) **15.** 4: said: score, accounts, late payment, (2.18, 2.06a, 2.01)

Challenge 9

1. Hanley's (2.20a) **2.** weeks' (2.20b) **3.** year's (2.20a) **4.** Peterson's (2.20a) **5.** employees' (2.20b) **6.** witness's (2.20b) **7.** Robin's (2.22) **8.** money's (2.20a) **9.** C **10.** month's (2.20a) **11.** boss's (2.20b) **12.** secretary's (2.20a) **13.** C **14.** company's (2.20a) **15.** businesses' (2.20b)

Challenge 10

1. 2: employees— Stoop— (2.26a) **2.** 3: please, Jonathan, o'clock. (2.02, 2.23a) **3.** 1: hyphen, (2.06a) **4.** 1: Bechtel— (2.26c) **5.** 2: (drug criminal) (2.27) **6.** 4: said, "The windshield"? (2.14, 2.24, 2.28a, 2.28f) **7.** 4: "Wireless Poor" The Toronto Star? (2.24, 2.28e) **8.** 2: live— Geneva— (2.26a) **9.** 5: Dr. Ms. Mr. T. Tapia? (2.23b, 2.24) **10.** 3: "The Meeting" The Etiquette Advantage in Business (2.28e) **11.** 2: Incredible! today? (2.25, 2.24) **12.** 1: ad. (2.23a) **13.** 1: party (2.28c; can be italics or in quotation marks) **14.** 3: p.m.? (2.23b, 2.24) **15.** 3: autoregressive "using data." (2.28d)

Challenge 11

1. 7: Bank Montreal headquarters Suite 200 Renfrew Fire Department (3.03, 3.07) **2.** 6: Europe British French vice president Resorts (3.01, 3.02, 3.15) **3.** 6: management team union members Mayor agreement (3.06a, 3.09) **4.** 6: Boston Marathon City Boston Patriot's Day (3.01, 3.03) **5.** 4: University Montreal Italian Italy (3.01, 3.05, 3.15) **6.** 5: Internet Google Facebook YouTube (3.01, 3.04) **7.** 5: federal government January provincial and municipal (3.01, 3.10) **8.** 0: (3.06f) **9.** 5: vice president president Securities Commission (3.01, 3.06e) **10.** 7: uncle Wasaga Beach Simcoe County moon stars (3.01, 3.03, 3.06g, 3.14) **11.** 6: manager Advertising Media Department Adwords Google (3.01, 3.02) **12.** 6: fall faculty advisor Asia Australia China (3.01, 3.03, 3.06e, 3.16) **13.** 9: February father Summer Waves Water Park Jekyll Island Georgia (3.01, 3.03, 3.04, 3.06g) **14.** 3: Business Division master's (3.05, 3.07, 3.09) **15.** 6: Figure Chapter Analysis Population Growth non-English-speaking (3.07, 3.12, 3.15)

Challenge 12

1. 20 (4.01a) **2.** Fourth (4.05b) **3.** 12 (4.01a) **4.** June 1 (4.03) **5.** $40 (4.02) **6.** 15th (4.03) **7.** 3 p.m. (4.04) **8.** four 3-page (4.07) **9.** 40 (4.08) **10.** 3 million (4.10) **11.** Sixteen (4.01b) **12.** 50 (4.01a) **13.** twenty-one (4.09) **14.** 7 (4.13) **15.** 4 (4.06)

Challenge 13

1. In the evening each of the female nurses is escorted to her car.
2. It must have been he who received the highest score, although it's hard to understand how he did it.
3. Our office manager asked Rachel and me to fill in for him for four hours on Saturday morning.
4. Working out at the gym and jogging twenty kilometres a week is how she stays fit.
5. Three types of costs must be considered for proper inventory control: holding costs, ordering costs, and stockout costs.
6. If I were him, I would fill out the questionnaire immediately so that I would qualify for the drawing.
7. Higher engine revolutions mean better acceleration; however, lower revolutions mean the best fuel economy.
8. Our team's day-to-day operations include setting goals, improving customer service, manufacturing quality products, and hitting sales targets.
9. If I had seen the shippers bill, I would have paid it immediately.
10. When convenient, will you please send me three copies of the company's colour logo?
11. Do you think it was he who left the package on the boss's desk?
12. About half of Pizza Hut's six thousand outlets will make deliveries; the others concentrate on walk-in customers.
13. Everything accept labour is covered in this five-year warranty.
14. Our director of Human Resources felt, nevertheless, that the applicant should be given an interview.
15. When Keisha completes her degree, she plans to apply for employment in Calgary, Toronto, and Halifax.

Checkup 1

1. Saturdays (1.05a) **2.** cities (1.05e) **3.** turkeys (1.05d) **4.** Nashes (1.05b) **5.** 2000s/2010s (1.05g) **6.** editors in chief (1.05f) **7.** C (1.05h) **8.** runners-up (1.05f)

Checkup 2

1. he (1.08b) **2.** him (1.08c) **3.** hers (1.08d) **4.** I (1.08a) **5.** whoever (1.08j) **6.** me (1.08i) **7.** he (1.08f) **8.** us (1.08g)

Checkup 3

1. *are* for *is* (1.10e) **2.** *has* for *have* (1.10c) **3.** *offers* for *offer* (1.10d) **4.** C (1.10f) **5.** chosen (1.15) **6.** *were* for *was* (1.12) **7.** *is* for *are* (1.10c) **8.** b (1.15c)

Checkup 4

1. long-time (1.17e) **2.** quickly (1.17d) **3.** had only (1.17f) **4.** C (1.17e) **5.** better (1.17a) **6.** up-to-the-minute (1.17e) **7.** couldn't have been clearer **8.** feel bad (1.17c)

Checkup 5

1. b (1.19d) **2.** b (1.18e) **3.** b (1.19c) **4.** a (1.19a) **5.** b (1.18a) **6.** a (1.18c) **7.** b (1.18b) **8.** b (1.19b)

Checkup 6

1. (2) not, as a rule, (2.03) **2.** (2) sure, Mrs. Schwartz, (2.02) **3.** (2) reliable, conscientious, (2.01) **4.** (3) Calgary, Alberta, La Salle, (2.04c) **5.** (2) February 4, 2011, (2.04a) **6.** (4) Holmes, Lane, Regina, Saskatchewan S5L 2E2, (2.04b) **7.** (2) supplies, replacing inventories, (2.01) **8.** (1) business, (2.02)

Checkup 7

1. (1) warranty, (2.06a) **2.** (1) market, (2.05) **3.** (2) manufacturer, nameless, (2.06c) **4.** (1) imaginative, (2.08) **5.** (2) Sims, area, (2.09) **6.** (1) buyers, (2.07) **7.** (2) application, Monday, (2.06a, 2.04a) **8.** (2) hand, hard-working, (2.03, 2.08)

Checkup 8

1. (2) name," Etienne, (2.14a) **2.** (4) Cox, PhD, Meridian, MBA, (2.10) **3.** (1) investment, (2.12) **4.** (2) think, however, (2.03) **5.** (2) Collingwood, Laurentians, (2.01, 2.15) **6.** (0) (2.06c) **7.** (2) companies, robots, (2.01) **8.** (2) fact, unprotected, (2.03, 2.08)

Checkup 9

1. (3) months: September, October, (2.01, 2.17a) **2.** (1) money, (2.06a, 2.16b) **3.** (3) short-term credit; manufacturer, however, (2.03, 2.16a) **4.** (1) Canada, (2.05) **5.** (5) customers; for example, retailers, service companies, manufacturers, (2.16e) **6.** (2) Bank of Canada, applications to the following: (2.06a, 2.17a) **7.** (2) high; therefore, (2.16) **8.** (2) 18 percent, prohibitive; (2.06a, 2.16c)

Checkup 10

1. Leo Ruskin's (2.20a, 2.21) **2.** weeks' (2.20b) **3.** Cindy Lanham's (2.21) **4.** boss's (2.20b) **5.** Kaspar's (2.22) **6.** month's (2.20a) **7.** Mark's, David's (2.20a)

Checkup 11

1. (2) managers—Yu Sosa—(2.26a, 2.27) **2.** (2) variables (see Figure 13 on p. 432) (2.27) **3.** (1) training—(2.26c) **4.** (3) "How You"? (2.28e, 2.28f) **5.** (3) Mr. Kieran E. Manning, Miss Kathy Tanguay, and Ms. Petra (2.23b, 2.24) **6.** (2) over"; however, (2.16, 2.28f) **7.** (1) June 10; (2.06) **8.** (3) Hooray! checkup, haven't I? (2.24, 2.25)

Checkup 12

1. c (2.05) **2.** a (2.16a) **3.** b (2.16b) **4.** a (2.20) **5.** b (2.04a) **6.** a (2.08) **7.** a (2.01) **8.** b (2.16)

Checkup 13

1. (6) Japanese international Japanese economics professor University (3.01, 3.02, 3.04, 3.06d) **2.** (5) Horticulture Are Nothing Sneeze At (3.12) **3.** (2) printers printers (3.11) **4.** (3) federal government provincial (3.10) **5.** (2) mother sun's (3.03, 3.06g, 3.08, 3.14) **6.** (1) Euro (3.02) **7.** (5) Park island River Vanier Bridge (3.01, 3.03) **8.** (3) Computer Science Department (3.05, 3.07, 3.09)

Checkup 14

1. b (4.01a) **2.** b (4.03) **3.** b (4.02) **4.** b (4.04) **5.** b (4.07) **6.** a (4.08) **7.** b (4.12) **8.** a (4.06)

Notes

Chapter 1

1 O'Rourke, J. (2012). *Managerial communication* (5th ed.). Upper Saddle River, NJ: Prentice Hall.

2 MetLife. (2011, May). The MetLife Survey of the American Teacher: Preparing students for college and careers. Retrieved from http://files.eric.ed.gov/fulltext/ED519278.pdf

3 Our Work: Livewire Communications. (n.d.). Retrieved from http://www.livewireinc.com/our-work/

4 Robert Half. (2016). CEOs seek finance professionals with mix of hard and soft skills. Retrieved from https://www.roberthalf.ca/en/research-and-insights/media-room/cfos-seek-finance-professionals-with-mix-of-hard-and-soft-skills

5 Driver, S. (2018, October 7). Keep it clean: Social media screenings gain in popularity. BusinessNewsDaily.com. Retrieved from https://www.businessnewsdaily.com/2377-social-media-hiring.html

6 English, A. (2012, October). What makes a great techie? *IBM Systems Magazine*. Retrieved from http://www.ibmsystemsmag.com/aix/trends/whatsnew/great_techie

7 Davenport, T. (2015, January 22). Why data storytelling is so important—And why we're so bad at it. *Deloitte Insights, 24*(50). Retrieved from https://www2.deloitte.com/insights/us/en/topics/analytics/data-driven-storytelling.html

8 Mitchell, G. A., Skinner, L. B., & White, B. J. (2010) Essential soft skills for success in the twenty-first-century workforce as perceived by business educators. *The Delta Pi Epsilon Journal, 52*(1). Retrieved from https://www.scribd.com/document/286348027/Essential-Soft-Skills-For-success-in-the-twenty-first-century-workforce-pdf

9 McEwen, B. C. (2010). Cross-cultural and international career exploration and employability skills. *National Business Education Association Yearbook 2010: Cross-Cultural and International Business Education, 48*, 142.

10 Rampell, C. (2013, February 19). College premium: Better pay, better prospects. Economix Blogs, The New York Times. Retrieved from http://economix.blogs.nytimes.com/2013/02/19/college-premium-better-pay-better-prospects/

11 Shah, N. (2013, April 2). College grads earn nearly three times more than high school dropouts. *WSJ Blogs*. Retrieved from http://blogs.wsj.com/economics/2013/04/02/college-grads-earn-nearly-three-times-more-than-high-school-dropouts

12 Employers rank top 5 candidate skills. (2011, September 3). Retrieved from http://wildcat-career-news.davidson.edu/internships/employers-rank-top-5-candidate-skillsqualities-sought-in-job-candidates/

13 Ligaya, A. (2017, October 26). Demand skyrockets for coworking office space: Experts. *CTV News*. Retrieved from https://www.ctvnews.ca/business/demand-skyrockets-for-coworking-office-space-experts-1.3650335

14 Edmondson, A. C. (2012, April). Teamwork on the fly. *Harvard Business Review*. Retrieved from http://hbr.org/2012/04/teamwork-on-the-fly/ar/1

15 Watzlawick, P., Beavin-Bavelas, J., & Jackson, D. (1967). Some tentative axioms of communication. In: *Pragmatics of human communication: A study of interactional patterns, pathologies and paradoxes*. New York: W. W. Norton.

16 Bentley, A. (2018, March 27). New research reveals facial expressions as tools for social influence. Retrieved from https://medicalxpress.com/news/2018-03-reveals-facial-tools-social.html

17 Hall, E. T. (1966). *The hidden dimension*. Garden City, NY: Doubleday, pp. 107–122.

18 Davis, T., Ward, D. A., & Woodland, D. (2010). Cross-cultural and international business communication—Verbal. *National Business Education Association Yearbook: Cross-Cultural and International Business Education, 3*; Hall, E. T., & Hall, M. R. (1990). *Understanding cultural differences*. Yarmouth, ME: Intercultural Press, pp. 183–184.

19 Chaney, L. H., & Martin, J. S. (2011). *Intercultural business communication* (5th ed.). Upper Saddle River, NJ: Prentice Hall, p. 93.

20 Hofstede, G. (2015). National differences in communication styles. In: D. Brzozowska & W. Chlopicki (Eds.), *Culture's software: Communication styles*. Newcastle Upon Tyne, England: Lady Stephenson Library, pp. 1–15. Retrieved from https://books.google.ca/books

21 Klass, P. (2012, January 9). Seeing social media more as portal than as pitfall. *The New York Times*. Retrieved from http://www.nytimes.com/2012/01/10/health/views/seeing-social-media-as-adolescent-portal-more-than-pitfall.html

22 Cain, S. (2013). *Quiet: The power of introverts in a world that can't stop talking*. New York: Crown Publishing.

23 Carter, J. F. (2010, October 14). Why Twitter influences cross-cultural engagement. *Mashable Social Media*. Retrieved from http://mashable.com/2010/10/14/twitter-cross-cultural

24 Krys, K., et al. (2016). Be careful where you smile: Culture shapes judgment of intelligence and honesty of smiling individuals. *Journal of Nonverbal Behavior, 40*, 101–116. Retrieved from https://www.ncbi.nlm.nih.gov/pmc/articles/PMC4840223/

25 Quan, D. (2014, June 27). Have Canada's changing demographics made it time to retire the concept of "visible minority"? *National Post*. Retrieved from http://news.nationalpost.com/news/canada/have-canadas-changing-demographics-made-it-time-to-retire-the-concept-of-visible-minority

26 Bellemare, A. (2017, April 25). Diversity good for Canadian businesses, says new CIGI report. *CBC News*. Retrieved from https://www.cbc.ca/news/canada/kitchener-waterloo/diversity-good-business-cigi-waterloo-report-1.4084341

[27] DeMers, J. (2018, April 16). How "groupthink" can cost your business (and 3 corporate examples). Retrieved from https://www.entrepreneur.com/article/311864

Chapter 2

[1] Shannon, C., & Weaver, W. (1949). *The mathematical theory of communication*. Urbana, IL: University of Illinois Press.

[2] McLuhan, M. (1964). *Understanding media: The extensions of man*. New York: McGraw-Hill.

[3] Employee communications during times of change linked to job satisfaction: Report. (2013, July 5). *Canadian HR Reporter*. Retrieved from http://www.hrreporter.com/article/17937 -employee-communications-during-times-of-change-linked-to -job-satisfaction-report/

[4] Personal communication with Mary Ellen Guffey, January 30, 2012.

[5] Foulk, T., et al. (2016, January). Catching rudeness is like catching a cold: The contagion effects of low-intensity negative behaviors. *Journal of Applied Psychology*, 101(1), 50–67.

[6] Link, S. (2012, May 2). Use "person first" language. [Letter to editor]. *USA Today*, p. 6A.

Chapter 3

[1] Based on Willerton, A. (2018, May 23). Inside Benevity's dog -friendly, mural-filled Office in Bridgeland. Retrieved from https://www.avenuecalgary.com/City-Life/Office-Space /Inside-Benevity-Office-Calgary/

Chapter 4

[1] Aaserud, K. (2016, July 20). How offices can use instant messaging to truly get more done. *Canadian Business*. Retrieved from https://www.canadianbusiness.com/innovation /how-offices-can-use-instant-messaging-to-truly-get-more-done/

[2] Sword, H. (2012, July 25). Zombie nouns. Retrieved from http://www.3quarksdaily.com/3quarksdaily/2012/07/zombie -nouns.html

Chapter 5

[1] Plantronics. (2010). How we work: Communication trends of business professionals. Retrieved from http://www.plantronics .com/media/howwework/brochure-role-of voice.pdf

[2] Middleton, D. (2011, March 3). Students struggle for words. *The Wall Street Journal*. Retrieved from http://online.wsj.com /article/SB10001424052748703409904576174651780110 970.html

[3] Gill, B. (2013, June). Vision statement: E-mail: Not dead, evolving. *Harvard Business Review*. Retrieved from http://hbr.org/2013/06/e-mail-not-dead-evolving

[4] Orrell, L. quoted in Tugend, A. (2012, April 21). What to think about before you hit "send." *The New York Times*, p. B5.

[5] Kupritz, V. W., & Cowell, E. (2011, January). Productive management communication: Online and face-to-face. *Journal of Business Communication*, 48(1), 70–71.

[6] Dulek, R., & Campbell, K. (2015) On the dark side of strategic communication. *International Journal of Business Communication*, 52(1), 122–142.

[7] MacLeod, M. (2019, May 10). Quebec furniture maker recalls dresser sold in Canada, US after toddler's death. CTV News. Retrieved from https://www.ctvnews.ca/canada/quebec -furniture-maker-recalls-dresser-sold-in-canada-u-s-after -toddler-s-death-1.4416765

[8] Radicati, S. (2012, November 15). Statistics anyone? Retrieved from http://www.radicati.com/?p=8417

[9] Plantronics. (2010). How we work: Communication trends of business professionals. Retrieved from http://www.plantronics .com/media/howwework/brochure-role-of-voice.pdf

[10] Pazos, P., Chung, J. M., & Micari, M. (2013). Instant messaging as a task-support tool in information technology organizations. *Journal of Business Communication*, 50(1), 78.

[11] Marketing News Staff. (2010, March 15). Digital dozen. AMA. Retrieved from https://archive.ama.org/archive /ResourceLibrary/MarketingNews/Pages/2010/3_15_10 /Digital_Dozen.aspx

[12] Skinner, C. A. (2008, July 16). UK businesses ban IM over security concerns. CIO. Retrieved from http://www.cio.com /article/437910/UK_Businesses_Ban_IM_over_Security _Concerns

[13] Flynn, N. (2012, May 23). Social media rules: Policies & best practices to effectively manage your presence, posts & potential risks. The ePolicy Institute. Retrieved from http://www.epolicyinstitute.com /social-media-risks-rules-policies-procedures

[14] Pearson, M. (2016, August 2). Why corporate blogging is on the rebound. *The Globe and Mail*. Retrieved from http://www.theglobeandmail.com/report-on-business/small -business/sb-managing/why-corporate-blogging-is-on-the -rebound/article10003057/

[15] Westergaard, N. (2013, August 18). Social media: Don't fear negative content. *The Gazette*. Retrieved from http:// thegazette.com/2013/08/18/social-media-dont-fear -negative-content

[16] Devaney, T., & Stein, T. (2012, December 19). How to turn your online critics into fans. *Forbes*. Retrieved from http://www.forbes.com/sites/capitalonespark/2012/12/19 /how-to-turn-your-online-critics-into-fans

[17] Live blog: Wildfire in Fort McMurray, AB. (2016, August 2). Retrieved from http://blog.allstate.ca/cat_events/wildfire-in -fort-mcmurray/

[18] Lindstrom, M. (2012, July 3). How many lives does a brand have? Fast Company. Retrieved from http://www.fastcompany .com/1841927/buyology-martin-lindstrom-lives-of-brands -china-marketing

[19] What is customer experience? (n.d.). Ameyo. Retrieved from https://www.ameyo.com/customer-engagement/what-is -customer-experience

[20] Social media copywriter job description.Retrieved from https://resources.workable.com/social-media-copywriter-job -description

[21] Zantal-Wiener, A. (2018, May 15). Social media copywriting: How to compose text for 5 different channels. Retrieved from https://blog.hubspot.com/marketing/social-media -copywriting

[22] Mullaney, T. (2012, May 16). Social media is reinventing how business is done. *USA Today*. Retrieved from http:// usatoday.com/money/economy/story/2012-05-14 / social-media-econony-companies/55029088/1

[23] Success story: Driving in-restaurant sales. (2016, August 2). Retrieved from https://www.facebook.com/business /success/a-w-canada

[24] Nova Scotia Human Rights Commission. (n.d.). *Know Your Rights*. Retrieved from https://humanrights.novascotia.ca/

Chapter 6

[1] Simpson, J. (2017, August 25). Finding brand success in the digital world. *Forbes*. Retrieved from https://www.forbes .com/sites/forbesagencycouncil/2017/08/25/finding-brand -success-in-the-digital-world/#3c9ed227626e

[2] Yamakami, T. (2013). Toward mass interpersonal persuasion marketing: design guidelines for a new type of Internet marketing. In: *Proceedings. Fifteenth International Conference on Persuasive Technology 2013*. Retrieved from http://www.icact.org/upload/2013/0279/20130279_Abstract_B.pdf

[3] Discussion based on Perloff, R. M. (2010). *The dynamics of persuasion: Communication and attitudes in the twenty-first century* (4th ed.). New York: Routledge, pp. 4–5.

[4] Perloff, R. M. (2010). *The dynamics of persuasion: Communication and attitudes in the twenty-first century* (4th ed.). New York: Routledge, p. 9.

[5] Ibid.

[6] Engaging millennials through direct mail. (2018, November 2). Retrieved from https://www.printaction.com/mailing/engaging-with-millennials-through-direct-mail-5219?jjj=1560609484455

[7] Reynolds, C. (2015, June 8). Direct mail vs. email—Who is king? Socialmediaweek.org. Retrieved from https://socialmediaweek.org/blog/2015/06/direct-mail-vs-email-king/

[8] McGee, M. (2012, April 5). 77 percent of us want to get marketing messages via email & there's no close second place, study says. MarketingLand. Retrieved from http://marketingland.com/77-percent-of-us-want-to-get-marketing-messages-via-email-theres-no-close-second-place-study-says-9420

[9] Kopecky, J. (2013, January 10). An investigation into the ROI of direct mail vs. email marketing. *Hubspot Marketing*. Retrieved from https://blog.hubspot.com/blog/tabid/6307/bid/34032/ an-investigation-into-the-roi-of-direct-mail-vs-email-marketing-data.aspx

[10] Cited in Rubel, S. (2010, August 9). Hot or not: Email marketing vs. social-media marketing. *Advertising Age*. Retrieved from http://adage.com/digital/article?article_id=145285

[11] Burson-Marsteller. (2011, October 25). *Asia-Pacific corporate social media study*. Retrieved from https://issuu.com/bursonmarsteller/docs/b-m_asiapacific_corporate_social_media_study_2011

[12] Jackson, D. (2017, May 30). The complete guide to Twitter marketing. *Sprout Social Blog*. Retrieved from https://sproutsocial.com/insights/twitter-marketing/

[13] Edwards, L. (2012, March 5). Are brands turning people into adverts with social media? *Socialmedia Today*. Retrieved from http://socialmediatoday.com/laurahelen/462175/are-brands-turning-people-adverts-social-media

[14] Zbar, J. D. (2001, March). Training to telework. *Home Office Computing*, p. 72.

[15] Canadian Fitness and Lifestyle Research Institute. (2003, January 1). 2002 physical activity monitor. Canadian Fitness and Lifestyle Research Institute. Retrieved from http://72.10.49.94/node/595

Chapter 7

[1] Rodger, R. (2011, June 30). Communicating in a crisis. Step Two Designs. Retrieved from http://www.steptwo.com.au/papers/kmc_crisis/index.html

[2] Webber, L. (2013, July 18). Text from the boss: U R fired. *The Wall Street Journal*. Retrieved from http://blogs.wsj.com/atwork/2013/07/18/text-from-the-boss-u-r-fired

[3] Canavor, N. (2012). *Business writing in the digital age*. Thousand Oaks, CA: Sage, p. 62.

[4] Tjan, A. (2017, April 12). This is how you apologize to your flyers. Retrieved from https://www.linkedin.com/pulse/how-you-apologize-your-fliers-anthony-tjan

[5] Sample collection (Dunning) letters. (n.d.). Credit Guru. Retrieved from https://www.creditguru.com/index.php/collection-management/collection-correspondence-dunning-letters/sample-collection-dunning-letters

[6] Woodward, L. (2016, December 7). Shopify tops tech-heavy ranking of best places to work in 2017. http://www.bnn.ca/shopify-tops-tech-heavy-ranking-of-best-places-to-work-in-2017-1.625348

Chapter 8

[1] Klie, S. (2009, July 13). LGBT employees still face barriers. *Canadian HR Reporter*, p. 13. Retrieved from CBCA Business (Proquest).

Chapter 9

[1] Union Pearson Express. (n.d.). *Metrolinx*. Retrieved from http://www.metrolinx.com/en/projectsandprograms/upexpress/upexpress.aspx

[2] Writing Tutorial Services, Indiana University. (2011). Plagiarism: What it is and how to recognize and avoid it. Retrieved from http://www.indiana.edu/~wts/pamphlets/plagiarism.shtml

[3] Saylor, M. (2012). *The mobile wave: How mobile intelligence will change everything*. New York: Vanguard Press.

[4] Broadbent Institute. (September 2015). *The economic benefits of infrastructure spending in Canada*. Retrieved from https://d3n8a8pro7vhmx.cloudfront.net/broadbent/pages/4555/attachments/original/1441907687/The_Economic_Benefits_of_Public_Infrastructure_Spending_in_Canada.pdf?1441907687

Chapter 10

[1] 5 reasons why phone calls are still important for businesses. (2018, August 7). Retrieved from https://www.datakom.co.uk/2018/08/5-reasons-why-phone-calls-are-still-important-for-businesses/

[2] Callahan, D. (2009, April 21). Breaking the ice: Success through teamwork and partnerships. Retrieved from http://greatlakes.coastguard.dodlive.mil/2009/04/breaking-the-ice-success-through-teamwork-and-partnerships

[3] Phillips, A. (2012, May 9). Wasted time in meetings costs the UK economy £26 billion. *Business Matters Magazine*. Retrieved from http://www.bmmagazine.co.uk/in-business/wasted-time-in-meetings-costs-the-uk-economy-26-billion

[4] Rogelberg, S. G., Shanock, L. R., & Scott, C. W. (2012). Wasted time and money in meetings: Increasing return on investment. *Small Group Research*, 43(2), 237. https://doi.org/10.1177/1046496411429170

Chapter 11

[1] Dassanayake, D. (2013, October 2). Just Google it: Britons lose ability to remember key dates because of search engines. *Express*. Retrieved from http://www.express.co.uk/news/science-technology/433898/Just-Google-it-Britons-lose-ability-to-remember-key-dates-because-of-search-engines

[2] Arts and Science Support of Education through Technology (ASSETT), University of Colorado. (n.d.). Prezi vs. SlideShare. Retrieved from http://assett.colorado.edu/prezi-vs-slideshare

[3] Sommerville, J. (n.d.). The seven deadly sins of PowerPoint presentations. *About.com: Entrepreneurs*. Retrieved from http://entrepreneurs.about.com/cs/marketing/a/7sinsofppt.htm

[4] See TLC Creative Services Inc. (n.d.). PowerPoint pre-show checklist. Retrieved from http://www.tlccreative.com/images/tutorials/PreShowChecklist.pdf

5 Jackson, M., quoted in (1992, December). Garbage in, garbage out. *Consumer Reports*, p. 755.

Chapter 12

1 Social media vs. job boards—The future of recruiting. (2015, March 11). Onrec. Retrieved from http://www.onrec .com/news/statistics-and-trends/social-media-vs-job-boards -the-future-of-recruiting

2 Haun, L. (2013, March 22). Source of hire report: Referrals, career sites, job boards dominate. ERE.net. Retrieved from http://www.ere.net/2013/03/22/source-of-hire-report-referrals -career-sites-job-boards-dominate

3 Pratt, S. (2016, May 7). Source of hire 2016 (Infographic). Retrieved from https://www.socialtalent.co/blog /source-of-hire-2016-infographic

4 Adams, S. (2013, February 5). New survey: LinkedIn more dominant than ever among job seekers and recruiters, but Facebook poised to gain. *Forbes*. Retrieved from http:// www.forbes.com/sites/susanadams/2013/02/05/new-survey -linked-in-more-dominant-than-ever-among-job-seekers-and -recruiters-but-facebook-poised-to-gain

5 Adams, S. (2012, March 27). Make LinkedIn help you find a job. *Forbes*. Retrieved from http://www.forbes.com/sites /susanadams/2012/04/27/make-linkedin-help-you-find-a-job-2

6 Swallow, E. (2011, October 23). How recruiters use social networks to screen candidates. Mashable. Retrieved from http://mashable.com/2011/10/23/how-recruiters-use-social -networks-to-screen-candidates-infographic

7 Isaacs, K. (n.d.). How long should my resume be? Monster. Retrieved from http://career-advice.monster.com/resumes -cover-letters/resume-writing-tips/how-to-decide-on-resume -length/article.aspx

8 Hansen, K. (n.d.). Your job-search resume needs a focal point: How job-seekers can add focus to resumés. Retrieved from https://www-cms.livecareer.com/quintessential/resume -objectives

9 Diaz, C. (2013, December). Updating best practices: Applying on-screen reading strategies to résumé writing. *Business Communication Quarterly*, 76(4), 427–445; see also Nielsen, J. (2006, April 17). F-shaped pattern for reading web content. Retrieved from http://www.nngroup.com/articles/f -shaped-pattern-reading-web-content

10 Struzik, E., IBM expert, quoted in Weber, L. (2012, January 24). Your résumé vs. oblivion. *The Wall Street Journal*, p. B6.

11 Optimalresume.com. (n.d.). Optimizing your résumé for scanning and tracking. Retrieved from https://admin .optimalresume.com/upload/ResourceFile_university _keywords.pdf

12 Saltpeter, M. (2012, August 17). How a good video resume leads to a good job. *U.S. News & World Report*. Retrieved from http://money.usnews.com/money/blogs/outside-voices -careers/2012/08/17/how-a-good-video-resume-leads-to-a -good-job

13 Krum, R. (2012, September 10). Is your resume hopelessly out of date? Retrieved from http://infonewt.com/blog/2012/9/10 /infographic-resumes-interview-by-the-art-of-doing.html

14 Larsen, M. (2011, November 8). Infographic resumes: Fad or trend? Retrieved from http://www.recruiter.com/i/infographic -resumes

Chapter 13

1 Wilmott, N. (n.d.). Interviewing styles: Tips for interview approaches. About.com. Retrieved from http://humanresources .about.com/cs/selectionstaffing/a/interviews.htm

2 Smith-Proulx, L. (2011, November 12). Five tips to ace the panel job interview. Retrieved from https://www.hcareers.com /article/career-advice/5-tips-to-ace-the-panel-job-interview

3 Cristante, D. (n.d.). How to succeed in a group interview. Career FAQs. Retrieved from http://www .careerfaqs.com.au/careers/interview-questions-and-tips /how-to-succeed-in-a-group-interview

4 Ovsey, D. (2013, July 29). Study shows job interviews done via video conference put both applicants and interviewers at a disadvantage. *Financial Post*. Retrieved from http://business .financialpost.com/executive/business-education/study-shows -job-interviews-done-via-video-conference-put-both -applicants-and-interviewers-at-a-disadvantage

5 Rossheim, J. (n.d.). Do your homework before the big interview. Monster. Retrieved from http://career-advice .monster.com/job-interview/interview-preparation/do-your -homework-before-interview/article.aspx

6 Bowles, L. (n.d.). How to research a company for a job search. eHow. Retrieved from http://www.ehow.com/how_7669153 _research-company-job-search.html

7 CareerBuilder. (2016, April 28). Number of employers using social media to screen candidates has increased 500 percent over the last decade. Retrieved from http://www.careerbuilder .ca/share/aboutus/pressreleasesdetail.aspx?sd=4%2F28%2F20 16&id=pr945&ed=12%2F31%2F2016

8 Guiseppi, M. (2010, April 30). Microsoft study finds online reputation management not optional. Executive Career Brand. Retrieved from http://executivecareerbrand. com/microsoft-study-finds-online-reputation-management -not-optional

9 CareerBuilder. (2016, April 28). Number of employers using social media to screen candidates has increased 500 percent over the last decade. Retrieved from http://www.careerbuilder. ca/share/aboutus/pressreleasesdetail.aspx?sd=4%2F28%2F201 6&id=pr945&ed=12%2F31%2F2016

10 Green, A. (2010, December 27). How to follow up after applying for a job. *U.S. News & World Report*. Retrieved from http://money.usnews.com/money/blogs/outside-voices -careers/2010/12/27/how-to-follow-up-after-applying-for-a-job

Index

Effective
Communication for the
Technical Professions

Effective Communication for the Technical Professions

Second Edition

Jennifer MacLennan

OXFORD
UNIVERSITY PRESS

OXFORD
UNIVERSITY PRESS

8 Sampson Mews, Suite 204, Don Mills, Ontario M3C 0H5
www.oupcanada.com

Oxford University Press is a department of the University of Oxford.
It furthers the University's objective of excellence in research, scholarship,
and education by publishing worldwide in

Oxford   New York

Auckland   Cape Town   Dar es Salaam   Hong Kong   Karachi
Kuala Lumpur   Madrid   Melbourne   Mexico City   Nairobi
New Delhi   Shanghai   Taipei   Toronto

With offices in

Argentina   Austria   Brazil   Chile   Czech Republic   France   Greece
Guatemala   Hungary   Italy   Japan   Poland   Portugal   Singapore
South Korea   Switzerland   Thailand   Turkey   Ukraine   Vietnam

Oxford is a trade mark of Oxford University Press
in the UK and in certain other countries

Published in Canada
by Oxford University Press

Copyright © Oxford University Press Canada 2009

Library and Archives Canada Cataloguing in Publication

MacLennan, Jennifer
Effective communication for the technical professions / Jennifer
MacLennan. — 2/e

Includes index.
ISBN 978-0-19-544468-1

1. Communication of technical information—Textbooks.
2. Technical writing—Textbooks. I. Title.

T11.M32 2008   808'.0666   C2008-903598-4

Cover image: Shaun Lowe/iStockphoto

This book is printed on permanent acid-free paper.

Printed and bound in Canada.

2 3 4 – 12 11 10

Contents

Introduction

The first task I was given when I joined the College of Engineering ten years ago as D.K. Seaman Chair in Professional and Technical Communication was to overhaul the ailing communication course. All students in engineering programs across Canada are required by the Canadian Engineering Accreditation Board to complete such a course; most follow a fairly standard curriculum using similar textbooks. Like its counterparts in most engineering faculties, the course in our college emphasized regular practice through a variety of written assignments, weekly speeches, and regular examinations.

As in most such courses, however, this practice was taking place without reference to any underlying principles or theoretical framework. At the time when the course was created, the teaching of technical and professional communication was seen largely as a matter of showing students how to stuff facts into one of a limited number of standard formats—memos, reports, letters, log-books, e-mail messages. Not surprisingly, students were emerging from these courses with little more than a few precepts ('adopt a you-attitude' or 'remember your purpose'), and certainly without the skill to assess and respond appropriately to complex or unfamiliar situations. When their memorized templates proved inadequate, they were left with no strategies of invention or response.

For years, our faculty had been dissatisfied with the results of the course, and they hoped that I would be able to provide something better. I knew that the problem lay with 'the standard textbooks and the standard curriculum', which, as Cezar Ornatowski points out, emphasize stylistic values of 'objectivity, clarity, and neutrality' while saying nothing about the political, interpersonal, or ethical demands of writing in a professional workplace (2003: 172). Improving on this standard approach meant incorporating the theoretical foundations of rhetoric, the discipline that traditionally deals with the strategies of creating effective and appropriate discourse.

Our new course, piloted in 2001, made explicit use of rhetorical principles and theory in a way that was still very new in the teaching of technical communication to students in the professions. The success of that course—now known as *RCM 300: Foundations of Professional Communication*—was immediate and obvious, and it quickly won the support of our engineering faculty, who witnessed a dramatic improvement in students' communicative judgement and abilities.

During the first year or two, we managed with one of the standard texts, but it was clear that existing books were inadequate for our needs; instead, we would require a new textbook with an explicitly rhetorical orientation. Unlike most technical communication texts then available, the first edition of *Effective Communication for the Technical Professions* placed practice firmly on a foundation of underlying principles and theory; it explicitly emphasized rhetorical reasoning; it included a meaningful discussion of ethics in communication (as opposed to professional ethics); and it asked students to understand not only what format to use for a message, but why.

In the years since that book appeared, RCM 300 has undergone some refinement and some streamlining. Our commitment to its rhetorical foundations is stronger than ever, but our methods and approach have gained more finesse. Our students no longer refer to their required course in communication as 'speak and spell', the dismissive epithet applied to its predecessor. Instead, our rhetorical approach has become a fixture in student discussions of and reflection upon their own message-making. We've changed, too; our required course is more explicitly than ever about the formation of good rhetorical judgement, and application is always founded on the principles articulated by MacLennan's Nine Axioms, Bitzer's rhetorical situation, and Booth's rhetorical stance.

This new edition shows the marks of our refined approach. Although those who have used the first edition will find the structure and many of the writing samples familiar, the book has been completely rewritten to reflect changes in professional practice and to make the application chapters more explicitly rhetorical in approach. Some of the specific changes include the following:

- The chapters on style and strategy have been overhauled to incorporate a more explicit 'levels of edit' approach coherent with the 'problem-solving' rubric advanced in the first edition.
- Communication ethics has been given a fuller treatment, with a broader discussion of ethics in professional practice for those who wish to increase their coverage of this important aspect of professional communication practice.
- The chapters on reports have been redesigned and some new material added on technical instructions and minute-taking; the treatment of informal, semi-formal, and formal report formats has been consolidated into a separate chapter.
- The job application and interview chapters have been tightened and elaborated, with several new résumés added to the mix of samples.
- New critical readings in each chapter explicitly address and respond to issues in communication that directly affect our students.

Finally, this new edition includes a new chapter of communication scenarios and case studies of the sort that have proven so effective for our students in RCM 300. These are intended to provide a foundation for discussion and analysis, as well as for writing, and will add to the students' understanding of communication as a political, interpersonal, and ethical interaction.

Since the publication of the first edition, there has been dramatic growth in scholarly activity around the study and practice of technical communication generally. In response to these developments, professional programs in both colleges and universities have begun to redesign their introductory offerings to give them more theoretical integrity. Students are being asked to read with more critical awareness, to become more sensitive to interpersonal and social dimensions of professional interaction, and to exercise more thoughtful judgement. This new edition of *Effective Communication for the Technical Professions* is therefore timely; its purpose is to reinforce and support this richer approach to the teaching of technical communication.

Jennifer MacLennan
Saskatoon, Saskatchewan
19 May 2008

Acknowledgements

As public an act of communication as a book is, it is also a very personal thing: a product of your own hands and mind. It is also something of a leap of faith—faith in your vision, faith in your insights, and faith, finally, in your readers. Coming to the end of the process of writing offers a chance to pause, to reflect, and to give thanks to those whose contributions and support have made that leap possible.

I have been lucky to be surrounded by many such friends and colleagues in my work and in my life generally, and I am immensely grateful to all of them. I begin with those whose direct contributions have helped to bring this new edition into being. I would like to thank Burton Urquhart of the Ron and Jane Graham Centre for his assistance with various matters related to the production of the manuscript; his help is indispensable, as always. I am thankful too to everyone who contributed written pieces to the book, and especially to those whose submissions appear for the first time in this book: John Moffatt, Janelle Hutchinson, Brahm Neufeld, Debora Rolfes, Sandra Terry, and Jeanie Wills.

I am also grateful for the many good-humoured and helpful exchanges I have had with my editors at Oxford University Press: Dina Theleritis, Cliff Newman, David Stover, and the skilled and tactful Jessie Coffey, whose attentions to my manuscript have saved it from my lapses in sense and grammar. I would like to thank reviewers who took the time to make thoughtful and helpful comments on the manuscript; their advice has guided me in making the book a better resource for students and instructors. I would also like to express my gratitude to Gwen MacLennan, who prepared the materials for the online instructor's manual.

I have been most fortunate in the colleagues and friends I have found in the College of Engineering, who have given so freely of their time and their advice whenever I've asked for it. My time here has been immeasurably enriched by the friendship and mentoring of David Male, Emeritus Professor of Mechanical Engineering; John Thompson, Emeritus President of St Thomas More College; and Richard Burton, Professor of Mechanical Engineering. I have also been fortunate in having the continued support of former Deans of our college, Claude Lagüe and Franco Berruti, and I will always be grateful for their counsel and their insights.

I have been privileged too in those who have willingly served on the Advisory Committee to the D.K. Seaman Chair: its current members Gord Putz, Professor of Civil Engineering, and Allan Dolovich, Associate Professor of Mechanical Engineering; former members Ron Bolton, Professor of Electrical Engineering, and Lee Barbour, Professor of Civil Engineering.

Finally, this book, like all of the rest of my work, has been possible only with the continued belief and support of David Cowan, who is the source of all good things in my life, including the gifts of commitment and of joy. He's stood with me through challenging times, including the storms of the past several months. I know that, whatever may come, he'll be there right to the end. May it be a long time coming.

To Ron and Jane Graham
and Daryl K. Seaman
for whom I will always do my best

Chapter 1

Understanding the Communicative Situation

Learning Objectives

- To understand the nature and importance of communication.
- To learn the Nine Axioms that govern all communication activity.
- To become acquainted with the rhetorical foundations of communication.
- To understand the role of situation in shaping human interaction.

© iStockphoto.com/Marcus Clackson

Why Communication Matters

It may surprise you to learn that, of all the daily tasks performed by a technical professional, none is more important than effective communication. On the job, you may interact daily with dozens—or even hundreds—of people, communicating by letter, memorandum, telephone, and electronic mail. In fact, recent trends suggest that skill in communication—an ability to connect with others, understand their concerns, forge effective professional relationships, and motivate them to achieve their best—is regarded by employers as an essential ingredient in professional success.

Such an understanding isn't new, especially in the professions. As long ago as 1984, James McAlister argued that skill in communication is 'more important than technical skills' in establishing technical professionals as 'someone with potential' in the eyes of their supervisors (1984: 47–9). McAlister pointed to poor relationships on the job, an inability to work effectively with other members of a team, an unwillingness to consult, and general ineptness in communication as chief among the career problems encountered by technical specialists. And long before McAlister, Elmer Lindseth, then president of the Cleveland Electric Company, observed that a technical professional's effectiveness 'can be completely offset by a breakdown in human relations and communication' (1955).

One measure of the importance of communication is the amount of time we devote to it. One study estimates that we spend more than 25 per cent of our entire lives communicating with others—a close second to the roughly 30 per cent we spend sleeping (Jones, 2004). Others suggest that as much as 75 per cent of the average person's waking time is spent communicating in some way. As one expert has put it, 'we listen a book a day, we speak a book a week, read the equivalent of a book a month, and write the equivalent of a book a year' (Loban, in Berko, Brooks, and Spielvogel, 1995: 1).

While you are a student, you will spend 68 per cent of your communication time on speaking and listening, 17 per cent on reading, and 14 per cent on writing (Barker, et al., 1980). But your need to communicate effectively doesn't end when you graduate; indeed, it will likely escalate. Those in scientific or technical professions are reported to spend anywhere from 50 per cent to 90 per cent or more of their work time engaged in some form of communication—and this is true even at the entry level. For this reason, nearly all practitioners in the technical professions list communication among the essential skills for new graduates and experienced practitioners alike. When the Association of Professional Engineers and Geoscientists of Saskatchewan (APEGS) asked practising engineers to identify important areas for career development (Hein, 1998) under the guidelines for 'continuing competence' provided by the Canadian Council of Professional Engineers, nearly all the respondents identified communication skill development as a main priority.

The survey also asked respondents to list qualities they would use to judge each other's professional competence. As we will see, nearly all the categories identified by the engineers involved skill in communicating effectively. For instance, 'experience' and 'knowledge' represent competence only if they can be effectively communicated to others; 'approach' and 'attitude' are clearly measures of a professional's interpersonal skill. A separate study by the US Department of Labor showed similar results, identifying sixteen qualities for high job performance in any field. Ten are communication skills: listening, speaking, creative thinking, decision-making, problem solving, reasoning, self-esteem, sociability, self-management, and integrity/honesty (1991: vii).

Research and anecdotal reports alike affirm that skills in writing, speaking, listening, and critical reading are valued by employers, by the professions themselves, and by society at large. It seems clear that any new graduate who can demonstrate a mastery of these desirable communication skills will be considered more attractive to an employer. For example, consider some of the skills included in the following paragraph, which I have seen featured in numerous job postings for a variety of technical and other positions over the past five years:[1]

> Ability to read, analyze, and interpret common scientific and technical journals, financial reports, and legal documents. Ability to respond to common inquiries or complaints from customers, regulatory agencies, or members of the business community. Ability to write speeches and articles for publication that conform to prescribed style and format. Ability to effectively present information to top management, public groups, and/or boards of directors. Ability to define problems, collect data, establish facts, and draw valid conclusions. Ability to interpret an extensive variety of technical instructions in mathematical or diagram form and deal with several abstract and concrete variables.

Although it has been used for a variety of senior posts, I originally saw this formulation in an advertisement for an entry-level position in a technical field (Trane, Inc., 2001). It struck me then as quite a remarkable list, in that it calls for several sophisticated communication skills: analytical reading and interpretive skills, speech-writing, persuasion, and adapting messages for complex and varied audiences. Few technical programs adequately prepare their graduates for such demanding communication tasks;[2] in fact, even experienced technical specialists might find it a challenge to measure up to the complete list. However, the fact that this skill set was included in a job ad targeted to recent graduates not only points to the employer's scale of values, but suggests that any applicant who could demonstrate mastery of these skills would have a distinct advantage over the competition.

Unfortunately, many graduates of engineering and other technical programs are ill-prepared in skills like the ones listed, partly because technical students often don't realize the extent to which their career success will depend on their ability to communicate effectively. Even worse, some faculty, assuming that students will automatically pick up such skills along the way, fail to emphasize the importance of acquiring them.

However, employers like the company that ran this ad recognize that, in our highly complex and demanding workplaces, skill in communication at all levels is essential; they know that clear and easy-to-understand messages will be dealt with efficiently and promptly, while those that are unclear, incomplete, or discourteous will be set aside for later—or possibly disregarded entirely. These employers recognize the value of skills like leadership, cooperation, flexibility of attitude, and responsibility; they are well aware of the importance of being able to interact effectively with people whose priorities, values, and experience are different from our own; they know, too, that writing clearly and speaking persuasively are just as important as technical expertise to any job. And finally, they know all too well that people whose communication is unclear, incomplete, or discourteous will be ineffective and possibly costly to the company in time, money, and customer relations. For this reason, significant effort has been spent in documenting the need for strong communication skills among technical professionals (Buonopane, 1997; Beer and McMurrey, 1997; Barchilon, 1998), and in discussing ways in which such skills might be implemented across the engineering curriculum (Flemming and Wacker, 1980; Staples and Ornatowski, 1997; MacIsaac and McLean, 1998; MacLennan, 2001). Those who can bring such skills to the workplace have an edge in any job market.

Exactly how are graduates measuring up? One answer can be found in a study conducted by the University of North Carolina. Researchers asked the employers of recent university graduates to assess their new employees in both technical preparedness and communication skill, and then to rate the importance of both kinds of skills to the job being performed. The study showed that in specialized and technical skills, the new graduates consistently exceeded employer expectations and job requirements. However, their communication skills were not so well developed. In the four areas of writing, reading, listening, and public speaking, the employers consistently rated actual ability of the students significantly *lower* than the level of skill required by their jobs (Hoey, 2001).

Those who hope some day to advance to management have added reason for attending carefully to communication skills. Another recent survey listed managerial communication skills as the single most important factor in creating an effective workplace environment. Managers who are good communicators aid employee retention by helping employees to understand how their work contributes to the organization's goals, thereby increasing their sense of value and commitment to the organization. Since recruiting and training new employees is much more expensive than retaining those already on the job, hiring managers who communicate effectively is a sound investment.

Most people recognize that any professional's ability to communicate highly technical subjects in a clear and understandable way is important, but they may not realize that good communication involves more than simply information transfer. Instead, it requires careful attention not only to the clarity of the message itself, but also to satisfying the needs of the audience and to establishing the speaker's credibility. This is a greater challenge than it may appear, since most technical professionals must communicate regularly with non-specialists whose technical expertise varies widely—clients, support staff, managers, and administrators. While communicating with others who share the same level of technical training is usually quite straightforward, it is actually the exception for most professionals, who communicate as often, or more often, with lay people than with others in their field of specialization.

The successful professional must therefore be able to present specialized information in a manner that will enable non-specialist readers to make policy, procedural, and funding decisions. In order to do this, a technical specialist's communication, like that of any other professional, must establish and maintain credibility and authority with those who may be unfamiliar with technical subjects. Because such lay readers cannot directly judge technical skill, they will instead rely on the clarity and confidence of a professional's communication as a basis for judging technical competence. Thus, skill in communicating specialized information often becomes the measure of a professional's competence, irrespective of this person's actual technical expertise.

The course in which you are reading this book is intended to accomplish two tasks. First, it will enhance your practical communication skills in four areas of communication: writing, speaking, critical reading, and listening. More important, it will help to improve your ability to communicate by building a foundation for making effective judgements in the various kinds of communication situations you face on the job. For this reason, before considering the specific techniques of professional and technical communication, we will take time to explore some theoretical principles that form the foundation of communication effectiveness.

What Is Communication?

Most people, when asked to define communication, would produce something like the following definition: 'the transmission of information by speaking, writing, or other means' (Barber, 1998). This conception of communication, known as the 'bullet' or radio-transmission model, has its basis in information theory and can be illustrated by a diagram known as the **Shannon–Weaver model** (Figure 1.1).

According to this model, a 'sender' transmits a message to a 'receiver' through a 'channel'. Notice that the message, or the sender's meaning, is treated as a separate entity, independent of the sender and the receiver. The sender 'encodes' this meaning into a form (for instance, an off-the-cuff remark, a thoughtful conversation, a quick follow-up e-mail to confirm an earlier exchange, a formal report) appropriate to the chosen 'channel' (for instance, a telephone call, a face-to-face meeting, an e-mail message, an annual report to shareholders). As it travels through the channel, the message may encounter 'noise' or interference, which may make it difficult for the receiver to interpret what has been said or written or recorded. The model includes the possibility of feedback from the receiver to the sender, which allows the sender to receive confirmation and inquiries from the receiver.

However, while it may be easy to visualize and understand, this model of communication is ultimately inadequate, since it implies that communication is little more than an exchange of information. By emphasizing the centrality of the message over the **interaction** between the people involved, the Shannon–Weaver model provides an incomplete understanding of what actually takes place when two people communicate, whether they do so professionally, socially, or personally.

In practice, communication is less like a process of information exchange than it is like a process of negotiation, which almost always involves the interplay of assumptions, values, ethics, public or professional status, self-definition, personal feelings, and social needs. Because the Shannon–Weaver model tends to obscure the human dimensions of interaction by reducing people to 'senders' and 'receivers' of information, it can't satisfactorily account for all the complexities that come into play when people communicate.

Throughout this book, we will assume that communicating effectively means not only making a message clear, but also creating an appropriate and effective relationship with the person or persons you are addressing, and establishing or maintaining personal credibility.

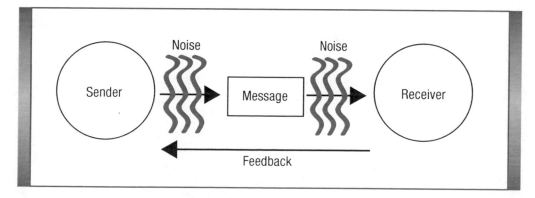

Figure 1.1

Source: Adapted from Shannon and Weaver, *The Mathematical Theory of Communication* (Urbana, IL: University of Illinois Press, 1949). Copyright © 1998 Board of Trustees. Used with permission of the author and the University of Illinois Press.

The Roots of Communication Study

People have been thinking about communication in a systematic way for a long time, perhaps longer than they've been studying anything else. For example, the oldest book in existence (dating to 2675 BCE) is a collection of tips on effective communication.[3] Probably the most influential book on communication in all of history was a textbook—not unlike this one—geared to teaching people practical strategies for communicating more effectively. Written nearly 2500 years ago (*c.* 330 BCE) by Aristotle, the *Rhetoric* combined theory and application, with an analysis of the principles that govern all communication and lots of practical advice on how to apply them. Although today's study of communication is different in some ways from the book Aristotle wrote, it still deals with the practical reasons why people communicate and the strategies they use to make their communication effective.

Aristotle's primary interest was in understanding how we **influence** each other through our public messages, how we establish credibility and authority to speak, how we accommodate our different audiences, and how we can best structure our messages to win a hearing from those with whom we wish to communicate. His insights are still useful to those who would like to communicate more effectively, thoughtfully, and ethically in all situations.

From the standpoint of practical usefulness, one of the most important parts of Aristotle's theory is a model of communication that has come to be known as the **rhetorical triangle**, illustrated in Figure 1.2. In contrast to the Shannon–Weaver model we saw earlier, the rhetorical triangle emphasizes the dynamic, interactional nature of communication. Like many contemporary theorists, Aristotle understood that effective communication involves observation, judgement, and adaptation, and that it is an interaction rather than a simple transaction or exchange of static information.

Aristotle began his discussion by observing that all communication involves three essential elements: a speaker, an audience, and a message to be communicated. While at first glance we might be inclined to think that the most important element of any communication is the quality of the message itself, Aristotle emphasized that a communicator who wishes to be understood, respected, and heeded must pay careful attention to all three key components of effective communication. He recognized the

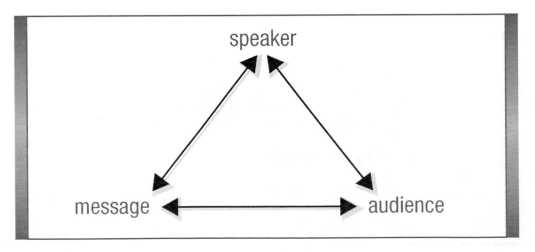

Figure 1.2

influence of each component upon the others, and showed how an understanding of each element can actually help a speaker to identify relevant arguments and prepare an appropriate response.

Aristotle understood, for example, that it is frequently the speaker's credibility that most determines the way a message is received. This feature of effective communication, which he named '**ethos**', refers to what is revealed about a speaker or writer by the style and tone of the message. Aristotle recognized that people establish or confirm their public character through the content and manner of the things they say, and that this public character affects the way their messages are received. He knew that believability depends as much on our confidence in a speaker's character as it does on the quality of the message content.

Aristotle showed that anyone who wishes to be listened to and taken seriously by others must demonstrate three important qualities. These are (1) **good will**, by which he meant genuine respect and concern for others' interests and views; (2) **good judgement** of the situation and issues, which includes a sensible and reasonable point of view based on a full understanding of what is at stake, and (3) **good character**, that is, integrity and credibility. As Aristotle pointed out, an audience will be unlikely to trust a speaker who does not demonstrate these qualities, and will therefore be inclined to doubt or even reject such a person's message, no matter how accurate it may otherwise be.

As an indicator of the importance of ethos in technical communication, consider once more the APEGS survey mentioned earlier. When asked to identify 'categories used to describe competence', the professional engineers who took part in the survey identified seven qualities that reflect the same qualities of good judgement, good will, and good character that Aristotle noted as important to effective communication.[4] These seven measures are quickly recognizable as aspects of ethos. For example, the top two categories, 'experience' and 'knowledge', assess the candidate's demonstration of good judgement, as does the category 'publications, patents, awards'. 'Approach' and 'attitude' are measures of good will, while 'professional association', 'references', and 'clean record' offer evidence of good character.

The rhetorical model of communication in Figure 1.2 also shows the importance of the relationship a speaker forms with the audience, since it can also influence how the message is heard and whether it is accepted. In addition to establishing credibility, a successful communicator must establish a bond with the audience. To do so, a writer or speaker needs to demonstrate an understanding of the audience by recognizing and affirming the things that they value, need, hope for, fear, or care about. A communicator must also exhibit respect and concern for the audience. Aristotle called this aspect of communication '**pathos**', so named for its recognition of the feelings and concerns of others. You may recognize this word as the root of English words like 'empathy' and 'sympathy', and it may help you to think of pathos as a form of empathy.

Finally, Aristotle argued that an effective communicator must construct the message with care, being sure to provide reasonable and logically sound arguments. A speaker or writer must demonstrate a thorough knowledge of the issues being discussed, show a command of both style and subject matter, and avoid logical inconsistencies. This aspect of effective communication Aristotle called '**logos**', a word that meant both 'logic' and 'word'. In other words, to be an effective communicator, a speaker or writer must attend carefully both to the quality of the arguments and evidence offered, and to the language in which the arguments are made. A communicator who is verbally or logically sloppy will cause readers and listeners to doubt her judgements and competence.

In the remainder of this chapter, and indeed in the remainder of this book, we will explore the way in which the three forms of appeal identified by Aristotle—the good will, good judgement, and good character of the speaker (ethos), a clear and well-constructed message (logos), and a recognition of and accommodation to audience (pathos)—provide a foundation for building effective professional communication in any situation. Let's begin with Nine Axioms that can help us to understand exactly how effective communication functions.

Nine Axioms of Communication

An **axiom** is a universal principle or foundational truth that operates across cases or situations. In other words, it's a proposition that holds no matter who the communicators are or what the circumstances are. The Nine Axioms that follow are not 'tips' or things you can do to improve your professional communication, although understanding them will help you to communicate more thoughtfully and effectively. Instead, they offer a way of conceptualizing how communication works. Although they are not intended as a direct method or strategy for improving practice, they are still useful because they provide a foundation for devising effective practical strategies to help ensure that your communication is more effective.

Axioms are not features that you can incorporate into your communication or leave out if you wish. Instead, they are principles that govern and influence all of your communication, whether you are aware of them or not.

These axioms about the practice of communication arise out of Aristotle's three principles of communication effectiveness. Some of them may surprise those who are used to thinking of communication as primarily information exchange, but they make sense once we recognize that communication is about more than just the content of a message. It is also about building relationships.

Box 1.1   Nine Axioms of Communication

1. Communication is not simply an exchange of information, but an interaction between people.
2. All communication involves an element of **relation** as well as content.
3. Communication takes place within a **context** of 'persons, objects, events, and relations'.
4. Communication is the principal way by which we establish ourselves and maintain credibility.
5. Communication is the main means through which we exert influence.
6. All communication involves an element of interpersonal risk.
7. Communication is frequently ambiguous: what is unsaid can be as important as what is said.
8. Effective communication is audience-centred, not self-centred.
9. Communication is pervasive: you cannot not communicate.

1. Communication is not simply an exchange of ideas or information, but an interaction between people

This most fundamental of the Nine Axioms emphasizes the dynamic nature of communication represented by the rhetorical triangle. Communication is not simply something you do (an action), nor is it an exchange (a transaction). Instead, communication is a living process in which two or more people participate together (an interaction). This Axiom is also intended to remind us that all genuine communication—even when it occurs through e-mail or the Internet, and even when it is as impersonal as a form letter—nevertheless has a personal dimension and a personal impact. Finally, it emphasizes that messages are not simply static commodities in an exchange; their meanings are negotiated, understood, interpreted, and 'spun' in complex ways by the participants in an interaction.

It is true that, for the sake of consistency, efficiency, or simplicity, some routine communicative tasks can be formalized, decontextualized, and depersonalized—the standardized forms we use for many purposes, from job applications to insurance claims to incident reports, are examples. The primary goal of these standardized devices is efficiency; they enable their users to process large amounts of information quickly and easily, and make categorization and filing easier.

If communication were simply about exchanging and processing information, this bureaucratic approach would be appropriate for all our interactions. But communication, even in a professional or technical context, is about much more than exchanging information.

The economic metaphor of communication as the 'exchange' of a commodity of information is one we have come to take for granted; however, because it tends to obscure the human element of the interaction, it is a flawed understanding of communication. You will quickly recognize how important this element of human contact is to communication as soon as you have to deal with a bureaucracy. Consider, for instance, the last time you received correspondence from your college or university, from a government agency, an insurance company, the military, or any other bureaucracy. Chances are it was a form letter or some other standardized message.

What is your typical response to receiving such messages? Do you feel that you've been heard? That your specific concerns have been understood and addressed? That any real communication even occurred? In all likelihood, the answer is no, since form letters treat you as 'typical' rather than individual, and the frustration you feel in such situations is a natural response to the absence of real human contact.

Imagine, instead, receiving correspondence genuinely addressed to you from someone in an organization who has taken time to deal directly with your request or situation. Even if the message content is negative—a rejection letter for the job you applied for or a denial of your application for a loan, for example—the sense that you have been acknowledged and your feelings considered goes a long way to promoting good will. It can even take some of the sting out of a rejection.

But, you might protest, the government, the university, the insurance company, the military are all bureaucracies, and processing information efficiently is what bureaucracies do. They *have* to reduce every individual case to the simplest common denominator, because to do otherwise would slow the process to unacceptable levels. We shouldn't take it personally.

Or should we? The problem with this view is that communication is *always* personal, in the sense that it always has an impact on the individuals it affects. We need to be wary of simply accepting bureaucratic practices without thinking much about them, because the values that underlie them have a way of creeping into our everyday interactions and our attitude toward those we work with. Placing efficiency before every other concern means tacitly accepting the view that communication is about content only, and that 'fairness' involves treating individuals as though they are identical. When we allow efficiency to trump other concerns, we encourage ourselves to ignore the human being on the other end of the interaction, to depersonalize others into categories without regard to the individual human beings we are dealing with.

Fortunately, most of us don't behave like bureaucratic entities—or at least we don't intend to do so. But we are surrounded by bureaucratese, and if we aren't vigilant, our interactions with others can become tainted by the same kinds of assumptions about communication, about fairness, and about responsibility and ethical interaction.

Because of its role in creating connection between people, communication has been described as a process of 'building community by exchanging symbols' (Hart, 1997: 36). This definition rightly emphasizes the relationships that are formed when we communicate, rather than the information exchanged. Our professional effectiveness and social success alike often depend on such relationships, and every time we communicate, whether in face-to-face exchanges, by telephone, via e-mail, or through letters or reports, we should ask ourselves what kind of workplace or professional communication we are helping to build. The second of the Nine Axioms focuses on this process.

2. All communication involves an element of relation as well as content

When we understand communication as an interaction between people rather than simply an exchange of information, we can begin to understand that all communication, on the job and elsewhere, involves building or maintaining human relationships. This element of a message is called the *relation*, and it is frequently as important as—and sometimes more so than—the content or information that the message contains. In fact, ignoring this quality of relation is one reason that many workplace messages fail.

All communication establishes some kind of relationship, or footing, between the participants.[5] **Footing** refers to the foundation upon which your credibility rests in a given interaction. For instance, if you are my supervisor, you may have the footing, or authority, to advise me, to give me direction, or to correct my work. If you are my subordinate, however, you probably do not have the footing to tell me what to do. Footing always depends on several factors, including not only your formal role as supervisor or subordinate, colleague or partner, but also your relationship with your listeners, your knowledge and understanding of the issues, and the level of trust between you and those you are communicating with.

Obviously, not all professional relationships are equal. The relationship we are building may be a formal, official relationship; it may be a cordial, collegial relationship; it may be a supportive, mentoring relationship. It may be characterized by admiration, respect, liking, and good feelings.

Unfortunately, however, the relationship established by our communication isn't always positive and rewarding. Messages can also create unpleasantness between participants through a mismanagement or disregard of relation, and the footing we create may be characterized by condescension, dislike, hostility, defiance, and discomfort. A message may, for example, communicate an air of superiority or disdain; it may indicate a lack of consideration or a disregard for the feelings of another; it may even imply contempt for another's concerns, intelligence, or values. This negative relation may be unintentional, or it may be deliberately encoded in a message; it may even be the inadvertent result of attempting to contain or eliminate personal engagement.

It is true that many organizations, and even some individuals, attempt to depersonalize their communication and neglect its relational component. However, although this practice is all too common, it actually displays a *failure* to communicate because it refuses to really engage the reader or hearer. Many writers and language specialists, among them the noted Canadian cultural critic Northrop Frye and essayist and social commentator George Orwell, have condemned this bureaucratic use of language as 'dead, senseless, sentenceless, written pseudo-prose that surrounds us like a boa constrictor, which is said to cover its victims with slime before strangling them' (Frye, 1963: 37).

Organizations and bureaucratic structures sometimes indulge in this kind of 'dead, senseless' language in the mistaken belief that doing so will make their communication sound more professional. However, since depersonalizing means treating others as if they are objects rather than beings, things rather than people, there is nothing professional about it. In fact, we need to be very clear that such officiousness is not a sign of professionalism or sophistication in communicating; in fact, by refusing to really engage another person, such messages are actually the *opposite* of communication. Although this depersonalized style may be an attempt to contain or eliminate the personal, it is important to realize that these messages don't make relation disappear; instead, they simply establish a negative, unproductive footing.

Part of the function of every professional message, no matter how routine, is to create and maintain an effective working relationship between the writer and the reader. Thus, you need to think as you write not only about the content of your message but about how you are building and shaping your professional relationships through your communication with your clients, colleagues, and managers. In the long run, such neglect will undermine your firm's relationships with its clients, and eventually will compromise its professional standing. E-mail, as we will later see, is especially prone to failures of relation-building because of the depersonalizing effect of the technology, and needs to be handled with particular care.

There are two final characteristics of relation that you need to be aware of. First, the impact of relation on communication is intense and long-lasting, and when it goes wrong, it leaves a persistent, often permanent, impression. Years after an unpleasant interaction, long after people have forgotten the specific details of what happened, the resentment of a soured relationship will remain strong. Second, although there are some reparative strategies you can employ to try to restore damaged relation, you should keep in mind that it is not always possible to 'fix' a communication interaction that has gone wrong. However, it *is* always possible, through a mishandling of a touchy situation, to make things worse. For both of these reasons, you should try to establish, and to maintain, as positive a relation as you can, even in difficult circumstances. You will find more on this delicate topic later in the book.

3. All communication takes place within a context of 'persons, objects, events, and relations'

This Axiom reminds us that our messages do not stand alone; they are all products of their social, historical, professional, and personal **context**. If we are to be successful, we must consider not only the informational requirements of our communication, but also the background, history, interpersonal qualities, professional **constraints**, and social consequences of the situation into which they are introduced.

The context for understanding a message may be public or private; it may be political or historical; it may be legally bound or discipline-specific; it may be professional or personal; it may be conventional or original; it may be a combination of these and other factors. But make no mistake: messages *always* arise in some kind of context, and cannot be understood without reference to that context.

Similarly, the context in which we are communicating shapes the kinds of things we say and do. We adapt and adjust our messages to the place and time when we are communicating, to the needs and expectations of the person with whom we are communicating, to the relational history we have with that person, to the rest of the people who may be present, and to a host of other constraints.

In fact, the ability to accommodate your communication content, tone, and style to the situation in an appropriate way is an important measure of your personal and professional judgement and competence. Those who are unable, or unwilling, to moderate their communication in this way are generally judged to be ineffective or incompetent as communicators, and perhaps professionally or socially inept, even dysfunctional.

No communicator who hopes to be effective can afford to ignore the situation in which any message must function. If we wish to improve our own communication and our understanding of the communication of others, we need to recognize how much our professional, social, cultural, political, historical, and interpersonal circumstances contribute to the way we make our messages and to the way they are received and interpreted by others.

4. Communication is a principal way of establishing ourselves and maintaining credibility

Whether we like it or not, people judge us by how effectively we communicate. In fact, a professional's ability to communicate is frequently the *only* basis others have for assessing that person's competence and authority. This is easy enough to demonstrate: consider how you yourself determine the skill and competence of other professionals: your physician or dentist, your mechanic, your MP or MLA, your professors, your lawyer, your clergyperson, or your veterinarian. Few of us are qualified to directly assess the skills of specialists in other fields; instead, we form our impressions of their credibility and knowledge based almost entirely on how well they communicate, on the quality of their messages, and on the respect and good will they extend to us.

Even in cases where we feel we are sufficiently qualified to assess someone else's expertise, we rarely have the opportunity to do so directly. For example, your classmates have training and experience roughly equivalent to your own. You probably have an impression of how smart or how skilled they are, but on what basis have you made these judgements? Since it is unlikely that you have actually evaluated their technical work, your assessments are more likely based on the way they have communicated to you in class, in labs, and in person.

A person's professional reputation—a version of what Aristotle meant by ethos—is based on the competence and authority others perceive that person to have. We all wish to achieve and maintain the regard and respect of those around us. But doing so isn't simply a matter of technical mastery in our respective fields of expertise. Instead, it rests on the respect of colleagues, clients, and the public, who for the most part have no means to assess our ability apart from what they see in our public communication. An ability to communicate clearly, competently, and respectfully is indispensable to a successful career, not least because it is the chief means we have to demonstrate our professionalism and our competence.

5. Communication is the main means through which we exert influence

Influence—the ability to gain cooperation and compliance from others—is a fundamental requirement for our survival, comfort, and success. It's easy enough to see how our physical survival and comfort depend on cooperation. For example, few of us are skilled enough to provide all the necessities of life for ourselves. The food we eat, the homes in which we live, the clothing we wear, the roads we travel, the vehicles we drive, and many other goods and services, large and small, are substantially provided for us by others. To have these needs fulfilled, we rely on a network of social cooperation that extends well beyond our own immediate circle of family and friends. It's not surprising that some theorists, such as linguist S.I. Hayakawa, identify cooperation—not competition, as many people think—as the fundamental principle of human survival (Hawayaka and Hayakawa, 1990: 5). As professionals, we also rely on cooperation, since it allows us to coordinate efforts so we can accomplish large or complex tasks. Cooperation, in turn, depends on effective and ethical persuasion, an issue we will explore in greater detail throughout this book.

Relation is not something we can achieve as readily as we can satisfy our physical and survival needs. For example, if we have the financial means, we can easily purchase food, clothing, and shelter without ourselves having to do the work necessary to create them. But when it comes to the relationships that make professional success and effectiveness possible, we cannot rely on anyone else to build them for us. Instead, we must be able to forge appropriate bonds with others on our own. If we cannot do so, we will fail no matter how technically expert we may be.

Virtually all influence in the contemporary world—with the exception of that exercised by criminal action or by military force—is achieved through communication, whether it takes place organizationally, politically, interpersonally, or through the mass media. We exert persuasive influence daily in many ways, large and small, and we do it through nearly all of our interaction with others.

Consider a simple and immediate example. In order to acquire the qualifications needed for a professional position, you must satisfy a series of officials that you have mastered the fundamental skills you need. You do this by communicating your understanding in exams and assignments, persuading your examiners to grant you the degrees and credentials you require. After graduation, you will continue to exercise influence—an effective résumé, a well-prepared application form, and a successful interview will persuade an employer to hire you. Once on the job, you will exert influence through reports, e-mails, letters, phone calls, meetings, conversations, and presentations that must convincingly convey your professionalism and expertise to a series of audiences, causing them to respect and accept the advice, ideas, policies, or actions that you recommend. And if your profession requires you to obtain a professional licence, you will have to communicate your expertise convincingly to the licensing body.

What is true of our professional lives is also true in our personal and social lives: satisfaction and success depend on our ability to achieve the cooperation of others. For this reason, our professional and personal success and fulfilment are directly dependent on the quality of our communication.

6. All communication involves an element of interpersonal risk

This Axiom recognizes the close relationship between credibility and communication. Because so much of our worthiness as professionals and as individuals is judged by how effectively we communicate, it is not surprising that every time we interact with others, our professional and personal reputations are at stake. We all wish to establish, and to maintain, a good name and professional reputation, to communicate competence and integrity, to receive the respect of others. These things, in turn, depend on the quality of our communication.

Those who already know us expect to see our character reinforced; new acquaintances need to see a demonstration of our credibility and worthiness. Both our self-worth and our sense of public affirmation—the positive social value that communication theorist Erving Goffman calls '**face**'—depend on the continued good will of those with whom we interact. As Goffman explains, whether we are aware of doing so or not, we tend to act and communicate so as to support and maintain that approval. Each time we enter into a new interaction, we encounter what Goffman calls '**face risk**'—the risk of being judged and possibly rejected. Thus, each encounter with others carries the risk of 'losing face', an experience that can shame and discredit us (Goffman, 1967).[6]

For example, in a job interview where a potential employer is meeting you for the first time, you strive to create a positive impression in appearance, attitude, and knowledge so that the employer will take you seriously as a potential employee. Once you have obtained the position, such assessments continue, both formally and informally, and you act so as to maintain the good impression that you established in the initial contact.

It is important to remember that all communication, not just interviews, involves similar risks of being judged and possibly rejected. Consider the face risk inherent in other frequent communication activities—seeking a favour from a friend, inviting an acquaintance on a date, requesting a raise, applying for a loan, phoning a stranger, selling an item door-to-door, canvassing for a charity, or giving a speech. Face risk is part of what makes such activities intimidating for many people. We wish to establish, and maintain, an air of competence and integrity; we wish to be accepted and respected. Each interaction presents a danger that this public image may be compromised, and thus each contact involves risk.

7. Communication is frequently ambiguous: what is unsaid can be as important as what is said

All human communication is complex, and involves much more than the explicit verbal content of any message. A range of motives, interests, and perceptions, some of which are never made explicit, shapes the relational dynamic of communication. In other words, the real meaning of your interactions is often located in its unexpressed and frequently unacknowledged subtext. For example, you may never say to an obnoxious co-worker, 'I don't like you', but he may nevertheless be aware of your dislike; you may never explicitly tell the boss, 'I don't understand what you want done with this project', yet she may be aware enough of your confusion to invite you in for a consultation.

Although our focus in this book is on explicit verbal communication—written and spoken (oral) messages—it is important to remember that all communication also contains significant unstated elements that we might think of as '**the message behind the message**'.

Some of the unspoken content of a message is contained in nonverbal cues such as eye contact, facial expression, vocal tone, gestures, physical movement, stance and posture, manner of dress, personal hygiene, or overall attractiveness. Nonverbal expressions, commonly referred to as 'body language', can communicate trust, happiness, contentment, approval, affection, or delight, or they can exhibit distrust, unhappiness, anger, disapproval, dislike, or disappointment. They can display assertiveness, confidence, self-possession, energy, enthusiasm, cooperativeness, reliability, and truthfulness—or their opposites. And, while our written communication doesn't offer any opportunity for the reader to judge us on our personal appearance or physical presentation, it does provide plenty of nonverbal information about our attitudes and commitment through such additional elements as diction, sentence structure, grammar, spelling, punctuation, handwriting, and document design, combined with the tone and style we choose.

The 'message behind the message' is also communicated at the relational level as an implicit display of our attitudes toward both the task at hand and the audience. Those who are paying attention to such matters can gauge the depth of our engagement with the content of our messages and the quality of the relationship we seek to establish with our readers or listeners. They can even 'read' us for evidence of our view of ourselves and our footing with the intended audience.

Emphasis, elision, positioning, and word choice, in combination with habitual patterns of figurative language, can carry clues to the unspoken assumptions on which our communication is based. Even the things we choose to leave out of our messages can reveal much about our assumptions. These implicit attitudes may never be stated or acknowledged, even to ourselves, in part because we take them so much for granted that we may not even recognize they are there. Nevertheless, they can be powerful factors in how others receive and interpret our communication.

The study of nonverbal communication and of the implicit values embedded in our messages can be quite complex. In general, however, you should remember that such nonverbal cues are always present, and can either complement or contradict the explicit verbal message. Nonverbal signals or implied values that do not seem to coincide with the explicit content of our messages can discredit our communication. Although it is not possible to completely control your nonverbal messages, you can learn to pay closer attention to the way you colour your messages, both orally and in writing, through unconscious nonverbal cues and implicit meanings that may create unintended implications in the minds of your readers.

8. Effective professional communication is audience-centred, not self-centred

Another way of putting this Axiom is that effective professional communication is *rhetorical*. This means two things: first, that it has a practical purpose, and second, that it is addressed to an audience. **Rhetoric** is the word we use to describe communication intended to 'produce action or change in the world' (Bitzer, 1968: 4) by appealing to those who are in a position to make this change; it is the means by which we exercise influence in order to get things done. For this reason, rhetorical communication always depends on engaging an audience, motivating their concern, and enabling them to make decisions or take an action that the speaker believes to be essential or desirable. To do so, it must be audience-focused rather than speaker- or writer-focused.

Unfortunately, however, too many of us approach day-to-day communication with our focus squarely on ourselves and on what we want to say rather than thinking explicitly about what our audience needs to hear. Many workplace messages fail for exactly this reason, because they focus on the speaker or writer's interests at the expense of the audience's needs and expectations.

This is not to say that communication can never function as a way of expressing our own needs or interests. Clearly, it can. In times of celebration or in times of crisis, we use our communication to express and deal with our joys and disappointments. Perhaps I have just passed my licensing exam, and I want to share this good news with my supervisor and my colleagues; the company's new product has had record sales in its first month, and everyone has received a bonus; our division has just completed a major contract a month ahead of schedule, and we're arranging a celebration. Or perhaps there has been a downturn in our business, and we've just received news that layoffs are likely, so our work group has an impromptu meeting to commiserate, or we've just learned that a colleague has suffered a terrible accident, so we have gathered in the boardroom for a few minutes of public mourning.

These forms of expressive communication serve an important function. However, in a professional context, the majority of our communication is purposeful rather than expressive, seeking someone else's cooperation, approval, or action. In such cases, a failure to focus on the interests and needs of the audience will result in failure, since we will be unable to inspire audience confidence or collaboration.

If we are interested in engaging others, in moving them to acceptance or action, we must consciously train ourselves to take the audience's point of view as we design oral and written messages, placing the audience's needs, expectations, and perspective ahead of our own.

9. Communication is pervasive: you cannot not communicate

The last of the Nine Axioms recognizes the pervasiveness of communication in every aspect of our experience. It also accounts for the inescapable human need to interpret symbolic meanings. Interestingly, even non-messages are typically read as having communicative meaning.

For example, imagine you have interviewed for a job. If a length of time passes without your hearing from the employer, you will undoubtedly interpret this lack of communication as itself a negative message, even though nothing negative has actually been said. This simple example demonstrates that once a channel of exchange has been opened, anything that occurs—even if it is nothing at all—will be read as a message. As soon as we have entered into any form of interaction with others, we are engaged in a relationship in which non-communication becomes impossible.

Channels can be opened not only by choice, as in the interview scenario, but also by coincidence—as long as you live, work, attend school, socialize, or shop where there are other human beings, you are immersed in a social environment filled with messages. Participating in this pervasive environment is inevitable, because each action of yours will be read by others for its communicative meaning. Even a refusal to participate in communication becomes a form of communication that others will interpret, just as we read meaning in the non-messages of others.

For example, suppose that the apartment across the hall from you is occupied by a man with whom you have never spoken. You see each other every day as you come and go from the building, and yet he barely makes eye contact, and never greets or acknowledges you. Although he has said nothing to you, you will soon begin to infer meaning from his uncommunicative actions: at the very least, you might consider him shy, unfriendly, a loner or a snob. At worst, you might even begin to wonder whether he is antisocial, possibly even dangerous. Your inferences may or may not be accurate, but some form of inference will be inescapable, because the man's resistance to normal social interaction itself constitutes a message, whether or not he intended it to do so.

Once a context for communication has been established, there is no possibility of noncommunication. Every action you perform will send messages that will be understood—or in some cases misunderstood—by others.

Although the Nine Axioms are not recipes for communication success, they are nevertheless useful because they provide a foundation for understanding what takes place beneath the surface when people interact. Keeping them in mind can assist us in communicating more appropriately and effectively and in adapting our responses to the demands of the situation and the priorities of the audience.

Since so much of our professional contact with others takes place through the things we write, whether they are distributed electronically or in 'hard copy', much of this book focuses on written messages. However, because professionals increasingly need to communicate clearly, engagingly, and effectively in presentations, briefings, interviews, and meetings, you will also find segments devoted to these skills.

Whenever we are communicating with others on practical issues, we will enhance our skill if we remember to consider the expectations, needs, and interests of those we hope to engage, and if we can keep the purpose of our communication clearly in view. As you read, you should remember that all your communication—not just the communication you do on the job—could be improved by understanding the Nine Axioms of Communication and applying them through the concrete strategies you will learn in the rest of this book.

Critical Reading

Lloyd F. Bitzer, 'The Rhetorical Situation'
Until his retirement in the early 1990s, Lloyd F. Bitzer taught rhetoric and communication at the University of Wisconsin, where he is now Professor Emeritus. Our selection, a portion of Bitzer's famous and influential essay, originally appeared in the inaugural issue of the learned journal *Philosophy and Rhetoric* (1968: 1–14). Here, Bitzer discusses the ways in which a message is shaped by the context in which it is spoken or written, by the participants in the interaction, and by limitations encountered through the interaction of physical, political, social, personal, or professional considerations.

Although the article covers some of the same ground covered in the chapter, it differs significantly from the chapter in its treatment of the subject matter. As you read, consider why these differences might exist, and use the principles you have learned about communication to understand how the article and the chapter function differently. Questions about audience, purpose, and author credibility will help you to understand both this reading in particular and communication in general.

The Rhetorical Situation

If someone says, That is a dangerous situation, his words suggest the presence of events, persons, or objects which threaten him, someone else, or something of value. If someone remarks, I find myself in an embarrassing situation, again the statement implies certain situational characteristics. If someone remarks that he found himself in an ethical situation, we understand that he probably either contemplated or made some choice of action from a sense of duty or obligation or with a view to the Good. In other words, there are circumstances of this or that kind of structure which are recognized as ethical, dangerous, or embarrassing. What characteristics, then, are implied when one refers to 'the rhetorical situation'—the context in which speakers or writers create rhetorical discourse? Perhaps this question is puzzling because 'situation' is not a standard term in the vocabulary of rhetorical theory. 'Audience' is standard; so also are 'speaker', 'subject', 'occasion', and 'speech'. If I were to ask, 'What is a **rhetorical audience**?' or 'What is a rhetorical subject?'—the reader would catch the meaning of my question.

When I ask, What is a **rhetorical situation**?, I want to know the nature of those contexts in which speakers or writers create rhetorical discourse: How should they be described? What are their characteristics? Why and how do they result in the creation of rhetoric? By analogy, a theorist of science might well ask, What are the characteristics of situations which inspire scientific thought? A philosopher might ask, What is the nature of the situation in which a philosopher 'does philosophy'? And a theorist of poetry might ask, How shall we describe the context in which poetry comes into existence?

The presence of rhetorical discourse obviously indicates the presence of a rhetorical situation. The Declaration of Independence, Lincoln's Gettysburg Address, Churchill's Address on Dunkirk, John F. Kennedy's Inaugural Address—each is a clear instance of rhetoric and each indicates the presence of a situation. While the existence of a rhetorical address is a reliable sign of the existence of situation, it does not follow that a situation exists only when the discourse exists. Each reader probably can recall a specific time and place when there was opportunity to speak on some urgent matter, and after the opportunity was gone he created in private thought the speech he should have uttered earlier in the situation. It is clear that situations are not always accompanied by discourse. Nor should we assume that a rhetorical address gives existence to the situation; on the contrary, it is the situation which calls the discourse into existence. Clement Attlee once said that Winston Churchill went around looking for 'finest hours'. The point to observe is that Churchill found them—the crisis situations—and spoke in response to them.

I hope that enough has been said to show that the question—What is a rhetorical situation?—is not an idle one. I propose in what follows to set forth part of a theory of situation. This essay, therefore, should be understood as an attempt to revive the notion of rhetorical situation, to provide at least the outline of an adequate conception of it, and to establish it as a controlling and fundamental concern of rhetorical theory.

I

It seems clear that rhetoric is situational. In saying this, I do not mean merely that understanding a speech hinges upon understanding the context of meaning in which the speech is located. Virtually no utterance is fully intelligible unless meaning-context and utterance are understood; this is true of rhetorical and non-rhetorical discourse. Meaning-context is a general condition of human communication and is not synonymous with rhetorical situation. Nor do I mean merely that rhetoric occurs in a setting which involves interaction of speaker, audience, subject, and communicative purpose. This is too general, since many types of utterances—philosophical, scientific, poetic, and rhetorical—occur in such settings. Nor would I equate rhetorical situation with persuasive situation, which exists whenever an audience can be changed in belief or action by means of speech. Every audience at any moment is capable of being changed in some way by speech; persuasive situation is altogether general.

Finally, I do not mean that a rhetorical discourse must be embedded in historic context in the sense that a living tree must be rooted in soil. A tree does not obtain its character-as-tree from the soil, but rhetorical discourse, I shall argue, does obtain its character-as-rhetorical from the situation which generates it. Rhetorical works belong to the class of things which obtain their character from the circumstances of the historic context in which they occur. A rhetorical work is analogous to a moral action rather than to a tree. An act is moral because it is an act performed in a situation of a certain kind; similarly, a work is rhetorical because it is a response to a situation of a certain kind.

In order to clarify rhetoric-as-essentially-related-to-situation, we should acknowledge a viewpoint that is commonplace but fundamental: a work of rhetoric is pragmatic; it comes into existence for the sake of something beyond itself; it functions ultimately to produce action or change in the world; it performs some task. In short, rhetoric is a mode of altering reality, not by the direct application of energy to objects, but by the creation of discourse which changes reality through the mediation of thought and action. The rhetor alters reality by bringing into existence a discourse of such a character that the audience, in thought and action, is so engaged that it becomes mediator of change. In this sense rhetoric is always persuasive.

To say that rhetorical discourse comes into being in order to effect change is altogether general. We need to understand that a particular discourse comes into existence because of some specific condition or situation which invites utterance.

Hence, to say that rhetoric is situational means: (1) rhetorical discourse comes into existence as a response to situation, in the same sense that an answer comes into existence in response to a question, or a solution in response to a problem; (2) a speech is given *rhetorical* significance by the situation, just as a unit of discourse is given significance as answer or *as* solution by the question or problem; (3) a rhetorical situation must exist as a necessary condition of rhetorical discourse, just as a question must exist as a necessary condition of an answer; (4) many questions go unanswered and many problems remain unsolved; similarly, many rhetorical situations mature and decay without giving birth to rhetorical utterance; (5) a situation is rhetorical insofar as it needs and invites discourse capable of participating with situation and thereby altering its reality; (6) discourse is rhetorical insofar as it functions (or seeks to function) as a fitting response to a situation which needs and invites it. (7) Finally, the situation controls the rhetorical response in the same sense that the question controls the answer and the problem controls the solution. Not the rhetor and not persuasive intent, but the situation is the source and ground of rhetorical activity—and, I should add, of rhetorical criticism.

II

Let us now amplify the nature of situation by providing a formal definition and examining constituents. Rhetorical situation may be defined as a complex of persons, events, objects, and relations presenting an actual or potential exigence which can be completely or partially removed if discourse, introduced into the situation, can so constrain human decision or action as to bring about the significant modification of the exigence. Prior to the creation and presentation of discourse, there are three constituents of any rhetorical situation: the first is the *exigence*; the second and third are elements of the complex, namely the *audience* to be constrained in decision and action, and the *constraints* which influence the rhetor and can be brought to bear upon the audience.

Any *exigence* is an imperfection marked by urgency; it is an obstacle, something waiting to be done, a thing which is other than it should be. In almost any sort of context, there will be numerous exigences, but not all are elements of a rhetorical situation—not all are rhetorical exigences. An exigence which cannot be modified is not rhetorical; thus, whatever comes about of necessity and cannot be changed—death, winter, and some natural disasters, for instance—are exigences to be sure, but they are not rhetorical. Further, an exigence which can be modified only by means other than discourse is not rhetorical; thus, an exigence is not rhetorical when its modification requires merely one's own action or the application of a tool, but neither requires nor invites the assistance of discourse. An exigence is rhetorical when it is capable of positive modification and when positive modification requires discourse or can be assisted by discourse. For example, suppose that a man's acts are injurious to others and that the quality of his acts can be changed only if discourse is addressed to him; the exigence—his injurious acts—is then unmistakably rhetorical. The pollution of the air is also a rhetorical exigence because its positive modification—reduction of pollution—strongly invites the assistance of discourse producing public awareness, indignation, and action of the right kind. Frequently rhetors encounter exigences which defy easy classification because of the absence of information enabling precise analysis and certain judgement—they may or may not be rhetorical. An attorney whose client has been convicted may strongly believe that a higher court would reject his appeal to have the verdict overturned, but because the matter is uncertain—because the exigence *might* be rhetorical—he elects to appeal. In this and similar instances of indeterminate exigences the rhetor's decision to speak is based mainly upon the urgency of the exigence and the probability that the exigence is rhetorical.

In any rhetorical situation there will be at least one controlling exigence which functions as the organizing principle: it specifies the audience to be addressed and the change to be effected. The exigence may or may not be perceived clearly by the rhetor or other persons in the situation; it may be strong or weak depending upon the clarity of their perception and the degree of their interest in it; it may be real or unreal depending on the facts of the case; it may be important or trivial; it may be such that discourse can completely remove it, or it may persist in spite of repeated modifications; it may be completely familiar—one of a type of exigences occurring frequently in our experience—or it may be totally new, unique. When it is perceived and when it is strong and important, then it constrains the thought and action of the perceiver who may respond rhetorically if he is in a position to do so.

The second constituent is the *audience*. Since rhetorical discourse produces change by influencing the decision and action of persons who function as mediators of change, it follows that rhetoric always requires an audience—even in those cases when a person engages himself or ideal mind as audience. It is clear also that a rhetorical audience must be distinguished from a body of mere hearers or readers: properly speaking, a rhetorical audience consists only of those persons who are capable of being influenced by discourse and of being mediators of change.

Neither scientific nor poetic discourse requires an audience in the same sense. Indeed, neither requires an audience in order to produce its end; the scientist can produce a discourse expressive or generative of knowledge without engaging another mind, and the poet's creative purpose is accomplished when the work is composed. It is true, of course, that scientists and poets present their works to audiences, but their audiences are not necessarily rhetorical. The scientific audience consists of persons capable of receiving knowledge, and the poetic audience, of persons capable of participating in aesthetic experiences induced by the poetry. But the rhetorical audience must be capable of serving as mediator of the change which the discourse functions to produce.

Besides exigence and audience, every rhetorical situation contains a set of *constraints* made up of persons, events, objects, and relations which are parts of the situation because they have the power to constrain decision and action needed to modify the exigence. Standard sources of constraint include beliefs, attitudes, documents, facts, traditions, images, interests, motives and the like; and when the orator enters the situation, this discourse not only harnesses constraints given by situation but provides additional important constraints—for example his personal character, his logical proofs, and his style. There are two main classes of constraints: (1) those originated or managed by the rhetor and his method (Aristotle called these 'artistic proofs'), and (2) those other constraints, in the situation, which may be operative (Aristotle's 'inartistic proofs'). Both classes must be divided so as to separate those constraints that are proper from those that are improper.

These three constituents—exigence, audience, constraints—comprise everything relevant in a rhetorical situation. When the orator, invited by situation, enters it and creates and presents discourse, then both he and his speech are additional constituents.

III

In the best of all possible worlds, there would be communication perhaps, but no rhetoric—since exigences would not arise. In our real world, however, rhetorical exigences abound; the world really invites change—change conceived and effected by human agents who quite properly address a mediating audience. The practical justification of rhetoric is analogous to that of scientific inquiry: the world presents objects to be known, puzzles to be resolved, complexities to be understood—hence the practical need for scientific inquiry and discourse; similarly, the world presents imperfections to be modified by means of discourse—hence the practical need for rhetorical investigation and discourse. As a discipline, scientific method is justified philosophically insofar as it provides principles, concepts, and procedures by which we come to know reality; similarly, rhetoric as a discipline is justified philosophically insofar as it provides principles, concepts, and procedures by which we effect valuable changes in reality. Thus rhetoric is distinguished from the mere craft of persuasion which, although it is a legitimate object of scientific investigation, lacks philosophical warrant as a practical discipline.

Lloyd F. Bitzer. 1968. 'The Rhetorical Situation', *Philosophy and Rhetoric* 1 (Winter): 1–14.

Points to Remember

1. As much as 75 per cent of the average person's day is spent communicating. Those in technical jobs are estimated to spend between 50 per cent and 90 per cent of their work-day engaged in communication tasks.

2. All communication involves a speaker or writer, an audience, and a message.
3. Communication is a dynamic process that involves adapting your message to suit the needs and expectations of the audience, while at the same time recognizing that your message has the power to influence and change the attitudes of the people who hear it.
4. All communication involves relation as well as content.
5. Your credibility depends on the quality of your communication.
6. All communication involves influence and risk.
7. Nonverbal and other unspoken elements can enhance or detract from verbal messages.
8. Communication always takes place in a context of persons, events, and relationships.

Key Concepts

axiom	footing	pathos
constraints	good character	relation
context	good judgement	rhetoric
ethos	good will	rhetorical audience
exigence	influence	rhetorical situation
face	interaction	rhetorical triangle
face risk	logos	Shannon–Weaver model

Assignments and Exercises

1. At intervals during the term, and again at the end of the term, your instructor may require you to submit a course portfolio consisting of all of the writing you have produced over the term, including diagnostic tests, regular course assignments, ungraded reflective writing, in-class exercises, and exams. The portfolio should be organized in some kind of binder, with a clear table of contents and section divisions, and should be submitted for assessment periodically during the term, as your instructor directs. The portfolio allows both you and your instructor to track your progress and provides a vehicle for reflection; it will also provide you with a record of your improvement as a writer, as well as evidence that you could take with you to a job interview. Your instructor may also regularly assign brief reflective or analytical writing tasks specifically for inclusion in the portfolio. Your portfolio should present a professional image, while at the same time showcasing your personality. It should represent you at your professional best. Finding a balance between professionalism and personality is one of the challenges of selecting and preparing your work for presentation to any professional audience, and the portfolio is intended to give you some practice in this reflective process. You can read more about preparing the portfolio in the article by Jeanie Wills on page 182 in this book.
2. Prepare a short written self-introduction (100–250 words) that will help your instructor become acquainted with you. In it, outline your goals as a professional communicator and indicate in what ways your instructor may be able to assist you

in meeting these goals. The specific content and the approach are up to you, but bear in mind that you are helping to set the tone for the professional relationship between yourself and the instructor over the course of the term.

3. Introduce yourself to the class in a two-minute impromptu speech, following directions you will receive in class. Keeping in mind that you are setting the stage for your in-class interactions with your colleagues and instructor for the remainder of the term, what is at stake? When the exercise is over, consider the following questions. This exercise is more anxiety-producing for some than for others; how difficult did you and your classmates find this exercise? Apart from the usual nervousness arising from speaking in public, did you feel any added pressure during this exercise? Why might that have been? What did you learn from watching the other speakers? Be prepared to answer these questions in writing or as part of class discussion, or both, as directed by your instructor.

4. Think about the last time you dealt with a representative of a bureaucracy: a clerk in a government office, an administrative functionary in the university or college where you go to school, a representative of an insurance company or a bank. Did you feel satisfied with the way in which your concerns were handled? If so, what elements of the communication made you feel this way? If not, why not? In what ways do the Nine Axioms of Communication help to explain what took place? Be prepared to present your analysis in writing or as part of class discussion, as directed by your instructor.

5. Consider the following communication challenges; which involve the greater risks? Make a list of these experiences (and add others that occur to you), ranking them in order from the highest to the lowest level of risk.

- returning an item to a store
- attending a job interview with one interviewer
- attending a job interview with a panel of interviewers
- sending back a poorly cooked meal in a restaurant
- asking a neighbour whom you do not know to turn down loud music
- asking a neighbour you know to turn down loud music
- telephoning a stranger
- telemarketing
- asking an acquaintance for a favour
- asking a friend for a loan
- criticizing a friend's schoolwork
- saying no to a classmate who asks to copy your homework
- asking a professor to reconsider a grade on your assignment
- inviting an acquaintance on a first date
- arranging a date with your regular boyfriend or girlfriend
- making a television appearance
- making a speech in front of family and friends
- making a speech in front of strangers
- going on a blind date
- giving a presentation in class
- persuading someone to take an action you have taken
- persuading someone to take an action you have not taken
- requesting a raise

- canvassing for charity door-to-door
- canvassing for charity by telephone
- receiving an award in public

Compare your list with that of others in the class. How much consensus was there? What differences did you discover? To what extent does this exercise suggest that communication apprehension (the fear of face risk) is situational, cultural, or individual? Summarize the results of the class discussion and write a short memo report for your instructor. Submit the report via e-mail if your instructor directs you to do so.

6. After reading 'The Rhetorical Situation', compare Bitzer's discussion to the treatment of similar material in this chapter. What are the central principles emphasized by both the article and the chapter materials? Describe at least two major differences that you see in the treatment of their subject matter. Given what both the chapter and the article say about the nature of successful communication, why do you think the two are so different in approach?

7. Write a memo to your instructor in which you discuss how Bitzer's article illustrates any three of the Nine Axioms. Be sure to provide specific examples from Bitzer's work to support your argument.

8. Answer the following questions about Bitzer's essay, as directed by your instructor. Submit your responses via e-mail or in memo format.

   a. According to Bitzer, what is rhetoric? What is meant by his term 'rhetorical situation'? What does he identify as the three constituents of the rhetorical situation?

   b. Who do you think are Bitzer's intended readers of this article? How can you tell? What assumptions does Bitzer make about the reader's needs, expectations, prior experience, or concerns? Given his intended audience, are these assumptions reasonable?

   c. If all communication is a product of its situation, as Bitzer contends, is his own essay also a product of its particular context? Can you point out any evidence that this is so?

   d. How difficult was it to read Bitzer's essay? Compare it with the information presented in the chapter. Which is more difficult? Can you suggest why that might be?

Writing Samples for Discussion and Analysis

The writing samples that follow are flawed in some way. Drawing on the Nine Axioms, explain why the messages will fail to achieve what the writers want. What kind of relation does each message establish? How well has each writer understood and accommodated the rhetorical situation in which he or she is writing? Are there any ways in which the message has potentially worsened the situation or undermined the writer's credibility? If the writers had sought your advice before writing, what would you have advised each to do? Be prepared to present your analysis in writing or in class discussion, as directed by your instructor.

Writing sample #1

Subject:	**problems with last lab assignment**
Date:	september 30, 2008
From:	jms@stu.wpu.ca
To:	r.wolfchild@mechtech.wpu.ca

dear dr wolfchild:

we would like to get together with you to discuss the marks we received on the last lab --
everybody in the class is upset with their grades and we don't think you explained clearly
enough what you wanted anyway we want to meet with you thurs. on your lunch hour to
settle this problem. please give us an answer in tommorrow's class.

Jim Shenassa, esq.
class rep

Figure 1.3:   How effectively has Jim Shenassa considered the constraints of his rhetorical situation in writing to his mechanical engineering professor? Why might this e-mail message fail to resolve the issues the class has with Professor Wolfchild?

Writing sample #2

First-year university students wrote the following self-introductions. The writers were
responding to Assignment #2, above (page 22), given as an in-class writing task on the
first day of their communication course. Keeping in mind the purpose of a self-introduction and the constraints facing the students in this situation, assess these self-introductions for the kind of relation that each establishes, or attempts to establish, with the
instructor. What does each say about the student who wrote it?

> I'm here in Communication Foundations Sec. E because during my May registration,
> my time table was prepared for me. I am taking Pre Engineering and this coarse is
> required. I want to be remembered by my stunning good looks, intellect, and my ten-
> dency to over exagerate.

> Greetings, Professor:
> I'm Ted Dhartman. I hail from the town of Rat's Pass, New Brunswick. If you would
> care to know where Rat's Pass is located, please consult the atlas conveniently stapled
> to this note. (In the event that such an atlas is not attached, please take up the argu-
> ment with the staple company.) This is my first year (or week) in university. I'm a
> computer science major. I have terrible handwriting and have generally blamed it
> upon my parents' genes (their mailing address is the same as my permanent address

if you'd like to send them an abrasive note because you can't read this assignment.) I'm taking this communication course because communication is, in my opinion, a highly valuable skill in any job and one can never have too much practice.

My name is Christopher Summerville and I am here because I am in the witness relocation program. I'm just joking of course. Actually, my story is quite contrary to that written above. Recently, I escaped from jail after serving only four years of my life sentence. When I'm not attending classes here at the university, I spend my spare time selling drugs to elementary school kids. I also enjoy playing monopoly and knitting.

I am in this class for one main reason. I am in the pre-Engineering program at the university. The university set up a schedule for me and in order to be sure I got in all the classes I needed, they said I had to take this class at this time [3-4:30 pm]. In order to avoid a long tedious ordeal trying to get an earlier class, I just took this one. Something memorable about myself is that I tend to not blink my eyes very much. However, when I am tired I keep my eyes shut. I also always look tired. I am constantly chewing 'stuff' whether it is gum, my pen cap or both.

I was born in Winkler, Manitoba, on the fourth of April 1991. I don't know how much I weighed or what my first word was or any of that stuff. What I do know is that I think there was a mix-up in the hospital because I don't look anything like my parents, and my parents often argue about what exactly my first word was. The fact of the matter is, I don't like my parents much. My dad is difficult to live with and all my mom does is complain about how much she hates being married to him.

Chapter 2

Planning and Drafting Technical Messages

Learning Objectives

- To understand the two basic principles of effective communication.
- To learn how to use a problem-solving approach to message design.
- To understand how to plan your message and produce a preliminary draft.
- To discover the importance of rhetorical balance in all communication.

© iStockphoto.com/Dmitriy Shironosov

The Nine Axioms of Communication covered in the previous chapter provide a foundation for understanding how to communicate more effectively in any situation, from written reports and e-mail messages to oral presentations and briefings, from communicating on the job to social and interpersonal interactions. Since our interest in this book is communication on the job, most of our discussion and examples will involve professional communication, but the principles and practices we will discuss can easily extend to other areas of your experience.

As the Axioms make clear, the quality of our communication has a profound influence on our quality of life; for instance, it is well known that those who communicate well have more fulfilling personal lives and enjoy greater career success. Because communication tasks make up a large proportion of the working life of any professional, those who write and speak clearly, coherently, and respectfully are more effective than those who cannot do so. Because their messages are easier to grasp and thus are dealt with more promptly, they seem to get more accomplished. They know the secret of good writing: they approach their written works not as ends, but as means to ends; not as products, but as part of a process of communication between people.

There are at least three reasons that you need to write clearly and courteously in your professional life: so that others can understand and heed your messages, so that you can establish positive working relationships, and so that you can maintain your credibility and professionalism. Stating your meaning coherently and editing your messages carefully will help to prevent misunderstandings or delays that can cost time and money, or cause embarrassment to the profession and to your own credibility.

Box 2.1   Three Reasons to Write Clearly and Courteously

- To enable others to understand and heed your messages
- To establish positive working relationships
- To maintain credibility and professionalism

Achieving the clear, crisp style that professional writing requires is not easy, especially for a novice, but with a bit of effort almost anyone can learn to write more effective professional messages. As you will discover throughout this book, the formats and structures of professional writing are actually designed to help you to communicate clearly and succinctly with your intended audiences.

This book will help you to master the standardized forms of technical writing, but before we turn to them, we will take a closer look at two important principles of communication that will help you to accomplish your professional goals.

Two Basic Principles of Effective Communication

All good communicators, whether instinctively or by design, have learned to do two essential things whenever they write or make a presentation:

1. focus clearly on their purpose and make sure that everything in the message contributes to achieving it; and
2. shape the message to accommodate the reader's needs, interests, priorities, expectations, background knowledge, concerns, and professional relationship to you.

Box 2.2   **Two Principles of Written Communication**

1. Focus clearly on your purpose and make sure that everything in your message contributes to achieving it.
   a. Put the main point first.
   b. Be as specific as possible.
   c. Simplify your message.

2. Shape your message to accommodate the reader's:
   a. needs,
   b. interests,
   c. priorities,
   d. expectations,
   e. background knowledge,
   f. concerns, and
   g. professional relationship to you.

Paying conscious attention to your purpose and your audience is a kind of 'best practice' approach to communication, since it will help you to apply the rhetorical principles identified by Aristotle and confirmed by the Nine Axioms: maintaining personal credibility, establishing a coherent and sound message, and accommodating your audience's priorities and concerns. Let's take a closer look at what it means to keep purpose and audience in mind as you plan and draft your messages.

Focus clearly on your purpose

Before you begin writing any e-mail, letter, memo, or report, be sure you know exactly why you are writing. You can't make any message clear to a reader unless you know, before you begin to write, what you want your message to accomplish. What do you want the reader to understand, to accept, or to do? What kind of relationship are you forging? What image of yourself, your company, and your profession do you hope to convey or maintain? Is your primary aim to pass on information or do you wish to persuade your reader to take action or to believe something? What goal will your message help to fulfill?

A clearly defined purpose is critical; whether you are writing an ordinary letter of request or an application for a job, and whether your document is a simple e-mail message, a more formal letter, or a lengthy report, there are several specific steps you can take to ensure that your purpose will be clear to the reader.

Put your main point first

Professional or technical writing differs from other kinds of writing—novels, feature articles in magazines, advice columns, news stories, even comic books. At this point in your education, you are likely more familiar with these other kinds of writing than you are with technical reports or formal correspondence, and that poses a bit of a challenge as you learn to write technical documents.

What these other forms of writing have in common is that they are usually organized chronologically; that is, they start at the beginning of a process or an event and follow the plot to a satisfying conclusion. In other words, they unfold almost naturally in a kind of story form. The fact is that we live our lives surrounded by stories, or by story-like messages, and as a result we have all learned to expect—and to write in—the same more or less chronological sequence in which the desired result, the inevitable outcome, or the most powerful insight is delayed until the end, when the sequence is complete: the hero vanquishes the enemy or triumphs over adversity; the advice columnist provides an answer; the news item describes what occurred.

However, while this chronological arrangement is ideal for a comic book, a novel, or a news story, it is *not* the best way to approach most work-related writing. Technical and professional documents such as reports, memos, and e-mail messages typically follow a sequence that violates all our narrative expectations. Instead of a plot that fulfills itself at the end, a professional or technical document supplies the most important and critical information at the beginning, in a summary of recommendations, a 'Re' line, or the reverse chronology of a résumé. In other words, in most instances a professional message is organized counter to your natural expectations.

To understand why business and professional writing has developed such different conventions from all the other messages we experience, think for a moment about why we write on the job at all, and about the situation your reader is in. The recipient of your report, e-mail, or job application likely has many time demands, and probably receives several dozen or more e-mail messages, memos, and letters daily, in addition to numerous reports. All of these messages require attention, decisions, and action. Even if this busy reader wanted to follow the plot to the end to find out what the point is, she doesn't have the time. Instead, she needs to know right away exactly what the message is about, and what has to be done to respond to it.

In fact, she has so little time to devote to your message that she would find a plot-based approach irritating and wouldn't read all the way to the end; she can't wait until you finally decide to reveal what the point is. As a result, your report sits unread, your proposal gets ignored, your résumé goes into the trash. In business and in the professions, a message that doesn't get to the point is a waste of the reader's time.

To succeed in writing as a professional, the first thing you need to do is train yourself to put the main message at the beginning, preferably in a subject (or 'Re') line. You can remind yourself to do this by beginning your rough drafts with the clause, 'The most important thing I want you to know is that . . .'. This strategy will help you to stay focused on your main message. Be sure to edit out this clause in subsequent drafts.

Be specific

Before you begin writing any professional document, make sure you can clearly answer two questions: (1) What *exactly* do I want my reader to know?, and (2) What do I want my reader to do about it? Be as concrete and specific as possible, and provide sufficient detail for the reader to act. Provide reference and file numbers, quantities, prices, and dates; name the relevant parties who have an interest or involvement in the issue; spell out the anticipated results; provide direction as to what remains to be done; suggest a first step to action. Let your reader know exactly what the problem or issue is, what has been done about it so far, what you propose to do yourself, and what you would like him to do in response to your message. The more specific you are, the more likely it is that your message will be understood and acted upon. Don't waste your reader's time; get to the point quickly, and provide as much concrete detail as is necessary to get the job done.

Simplify your message

Try to keep your e-mail messages, letters, and memos as simple as possible by eliminating irrelevant information. Anything that isn't essential to your reader's understanding or that does not contribute to furthering your purpose is irrelevant to the message, no matter how intrinsically interesting it may be to you. Provide only the details your reader will need to fully understand the situation; eliminate anything that doesn't serve your immediate purpose. Many technical writing experts suggest that you distinguish between those details that a reader will 'need to know' and those that are simply 'nice to know', including only the 'need to know' material in the final draft that goes to the reader.

If you can, stick to one main topic per e-mail message or letter, and make sure the subject line of e-mail messages and memos clearly indicates what the message is about so that the reader can easily file and locate it. Longer documents may deal with more than one topic, but if you must deal with several topics in one document, be sure that each is dealt with fully before moving to the next issue. Cluster related information and get to the point as quickly as possible.

Remember your reader

If it is to be effective, professional writing has to catch and maintain a reader's attention and interest long enough to get its points across and to motivate action. It seems obvious that you won't be able to engage your reader if you don't understand the person's expectations, priorities, and concerns. Why should this reader care about your message? What is the reader's interest in the information? What background does this person have? What will the reader need to know to make a decision?

Part of the aim of any professional communication is to demonstrate to your intended reader that your recommendations are both sensible and necessary. To achieve this end, you must present the information in a manner most likely to convince that specific reader.

As Axiom #8 reminds us, good communication puts the reader's needs first. It focuses not so much on what the *writer* feels like saying, but on the things the *reader* needs to hear to make an informed decision. In order to communicate effectively, you need to identify your reader's needs, background knowledge, priorities, expectations, and concerns. You must also attend to the relationship your organization or company has had with this reader. Without this information you cannot hope to create a message that will effectively motivate and enable your reader to respond to your request, proposal, or notice.

Needs

As you adapt your message to your intended audience, consider first the information that your reader needs in order to make a decision. What is the reader's interest in this subject? What will the reader be doing with the information? How much detail will the reader need in order to act? Leave out any information that is not immediately relevant to the reader's needs, no matter how interesting it may seem from your point of view. If you are to communicate your point successfully, you must recognize and respond to what the reader needs from the information you are providing.

Background knowledge

Keep in mind your reader's level of expertise or familiarity with your subject. If you are writing to someone who has no prior knowledge of your field of specialization or who is unfamiliar with your specific project, you will need to explain substantially more than if you are writing to someone who is an expert, or who is well acquainted with what you're doing.

Remember that even if your reader is generally familiar with the contents and context of your report, the specific details will not be as familiar to the reader as they are to you. In such instances, it is courteous to help the reader along by contextualizing and clarifying as necessary, reminding the reader of pertinent details that may have been forgotten.

On the other hand, pointing out details to a reader who is very familiar with the project could come across as a condescending waste of the reader's valuable time; telling the reader what she already knows instead of getting to what she needs to know will reflect poorly on your judgement of the situation.

Obviously, before you begin to write, you need to have a clear idea of exactly what information your reader may already have and what information needs to be provided in your report. The kind of prior knowledge your audience brings can influence the way you choose to present your information as well as the amount or kind of information to present. Provide your reader with sufficient context and background to interpret your information accurately, without overburdening him with material he already knows.

Priorities

In addition to taking into account the audience's level of expertise or knowledge and their need for the information you are providing, you should also pay attention to their priorities, which may be quite different from your own. Even people who are interested in the same problem can have very different views of how it should be approached or solved, particularly in instances where different values may have to be accommodated. For example, imagine a contractor who is doing renovations to a client's house. The client has asked the contractor to purchase and install new flooring, and has a particular colour scheme in mind.

At the flooring supplier, the contractor discovers two carpets of comparable quality. One fits exactly with the colour palette that the client has selected. The colour of the other is not quite so perfectly matched, but it is a slightly better carpet and is on sale for $10 less per metre, a significant enough amount that buying it would save the client more than enough to cover the cost of installation. The contractor, seeing a good deal that he's sure the client will also appreciate, decides to purchase the less expensive carpet that isn't quite a colour match.

Imagine his dismay when he returns to the job site and discovers that the client's priorities are quite different. It turns out that this is the client's dream home, and he wants it to be perfect; hence, the colour match is a very high priority. In the larger scale of the cost of the entire renovation, a few hundred dollars saved isn't all that significant compared to the satisfaction of seeing the renovation done exactly as he envisioned. The contractor could have saved himself a lot of bother, expense, and hard feelings if he had first developed a better understanding of the client's priorities.

We are often tempted, like the contractor, to position the message according to our own priorities rather than taking the time to understand and accommodate those of our readers. However, if we are to communicate effectively, we should arrange and position our messages according to the reader's scale of value rather than our own. As you prepare your message, ask yourself what the *reader* is likely to value most highly, and organize your message accordingly. Your approach should show how your message responds to the problem as the reader conceives of it rather than how it accommodates your own priorities.

Expectations

What you say, and how you say it, will be very much affected by what the reader is expecting from your work. A reader who is anticipating a positive outcome will be pleased when you're able to satisfy those expectations, while a reader who has been expecting a negative outcome but receives positive news instead is likely to be relieved and delighted. A reader who has been anticipating a negative response probably won't be thrilled by having his expectations fulfilled, but at least he's likely to be resigned to the outcome. Finally, a reader who has been anticipating positive results is likely to be disappointed and frustrated if those expectations are not met.

Communicating bad news, whether it was anticipated or not, is always a delicate challenge. In order to avoid turning frustration into anger or disappointment into bitterness, you need to moderate your words and your tone so as to accommodate the reader's feelings. Ignoring or overlooking a reader's frustrated expectations when you write will only worsen an already difficult situation, and may damage both your credibility and your relationship with your correspondent.

On the other hand, sincerely and appropriately acknowledging a reader's legitimate disappointment can help to cushion the impact of bad news and emphasize your professional concern and interest in the reader's viewpoint. Such positive reinforcement can go a long way in cementing effective professional relationships, as we will see in greater detail when we deal with communicating 'bad news'.

Concerns

Just as important as reader expectations are the things that the reader is worried or concerned about. Perhaps she fears costs escalating out of control, or problems meeting deadlines; perhaps he is worried about how a negative result might affect the company's reputation. Try to be attuned to the kinds of concerns that your intended reader—whether that person is a client or a supervisor—might be expected to have. Although it may not always be appropriate to address such fears directly, concerns should at least be indirectly accommodated by providing appropriate information and assurances that will help the reader see that you are sensitive to the context and the situation into which the report or message will be delivered. Your job is to help dispose your reader to understand and accept your message, and acknowledging reader concerns is one important part of doing so.

Relationship

A large part of the context in which the message will be read is the existing relationship with the audience. Is the reader of your message a long-time client who knows your firm and its reputation, or someone new, for whom your credibility is unknown? Is the reader a client, a colleague, a subordinate, or a superior? Is the message going to someone with whom you have a personal relationship, or to someone with whom you have had no previous personal contact? Have former interactions been cooperative and pleasant, or contentious? Is this reader likely to be compliant or challenging? While you should be courteous and polite to all of these potential readers, you may require an additional element of polite deference when communicating with those whose authority or professional rank is higher than your own.

As Axiom #2 reminds us, all communication involves an element of relation. In order to make the communication a success, it is the writer's responsibility to pay attention to the relational level of the message as well as to its content. To create and maintain effective relationships within your professional circle, you will need to think carefully about the needs and expectations of the reader who will receive your communication. If you do this each time you create an e-mail, a memo, a letter, or a report, you will not only communicate your content more effectively, but you will also maintain more successful interactions with clients and colleagues.

Professional Writing as Problem Solving

As a form of systematic problem solving, writing well follows thoughtful steps of invention and assessment. Like other forms of practical troubleshooting, designing an effective message cannot be done in one pass, except perhaps for the most routine communicative tasks. The more sensitive the situation or complex the task, the more demanding the writing process, as might be the case, for example, with a formal report to head office or an assessment of unsatisfactory work by a colleague. In most cases, the writing task is usually more manageable and ultimately results in a more effective message if it is carried out in stages.

The stages of writing well are very like those you may have encountered in other areas of your professional training. A framework known as the **problem-solving cycle** enables a practitioner in fields such as design, accounting, mediation, engineering, media production, or medicine to approach problems in a structured, repetitive pattern. You have likely learned a similar process in your technical courses. The problem-solving cycle includes studying the problem, analyzing its components, and considering all possible solutions, eliminating those that are not workable.

When all the steps in the problem-solving process have been completed and a preliminary solution developed, these practitioners do not consider their work finished. Instead, they typically start again at the beginning of the cycle, reconsidering the original problem in order to decide whether the draft solution will actually resolve the problem or accomplish the task. If it is not, they repeat the steps in the problem-solving process as many times as necessary to refine their solution until it is comprehensive and satisfactory. Writing, particularly in longer formats like reports, involves a similar process of 're-seeing'—or revising—until the proposed document is as effective as it can be.

Just as an engineer, a physician, or a crime scene profiler studies a problem and then draws upon theory and experience to design an appropriate intervention, a good writer considers the demands of the communication problem—its intended audience, the purpose of the message, and the best way to establish credibility—and then draws upon the principles of effective communication in order to create an appropriate message. The same problem-solving approach applies to communication, using the following steps:

- Identify the problem you are responding to, and state it clearly. Then determine the specific purpose of your message, making sure you are clear about exactly how your message responds to the situation.
- Figure out who exactly your audience is for this message; you will want to target your communication to the person or persons who are best positioned to act on it. Consider your own footing with respect to this audience.
- Consider more than one possible way of understanding the situation; brainstorm ideas to help you identify as many possible interpretations as you can, no matter how unlikely they may initially appear. Revisit your initial assessment of the audience, the purpose of the message, and the relational context. Restate the purpose to include any new information that emerges from this process of reconsideration.
- Identify the constraints you face in preparing an appropriate message; consider the context and history of the situation, the face needs of the individuals involved, your own footing and credibility, the expectations of your intended readers, the kind and positioning of your message; consider, too, any limitations of time, funding, policy, or personnel that might affect what you can or can't say.
- Use the constraints you have identified to analyze and assess your initial plan and content; separate relevant details from irrelevant information, and categorize relevant information into essential and non-essential details.
- Order your information into a logical sequence that privileges relevant information and write the first draft of your message.
- Once you have produced a draft, reconsider your message and edit it using the 'levels of edit' approach outlined in the next chapter.

Box 2.3 Communication as Problem Solving

- State the problem and determine the purpose of the message.
- Consider other possible ways of understanding the situation and brainstorm ideas.
- Identify constraints and limitations.
- Analyze the alternatives and eliminate unlikely or unnecessary details.
- Select the best organization and write the draft.
- Reconsider your message and edit until it is as effective as possible.

One of the greatest challenges for any communicator is to appropriately balance the competing demands of the communication situation, so as to accommodate audience needs, message development, and speaker's credibility. Finding this appropriate balance means learning to understand the particular challenges of an individual communication scenario, and using your knowledge of effective communication principles to prepare a solution that is effectively adapted to the situation. The problem-solving cycle can help to identify such imbalances so they can be corrected before the message goes to its intended readers.

To use the cycle in this way, you need to keep in mind the three principal influences that shape what a writer or speaker can choose to say in any given situation; these influences define what is or is not appropriate. These three sources of influence are the problem or obstacle that prompts the communication in the first place; the nature and proclivities of the audience who must be addressed; and the constraints imposed by the context or situation in which the communication occurs. Just as the nature of any problem and the situation in which the solution must function shape any design process, these three factors together help to determine the kind of message that will be considered appropriate to the situation. This complex of factors make up what Lloyd Bitzer refers to as **the rhetorical situation**.[1]

It's obvious to most of us that the audience for whom you are writing exerts an influence on how you express yourself. You shape your message differently if it is intended for your grandmother's bridge club than if it is directed to a class of elementary school children; you speak differently to the police officer who stops you for speeding than you do to a classmate who hails you in the parking lot; you choose your words differently in a job interview than you do in a conversation with your friends over coffee, even if the topic under discussion is identical.

Your choice of what to say is also influenced by the reason you're writing in the first place. Persuasive writing, for instance, involves a different approach than informative writing; touchy situations require face-saving strategies that need not be considered in situations where the communication is routine. For example, you wouldn't, or at least you shouldn't, begin a message of condolence by remarking that the reader's loved one is better off dead; you wouldn't begin a message of apology by blaming the person to whom you're supposed to be apologizing; and finally, you wouldn't begin a rejection letter to a job candidate by observing that he didn't get the position because he's incompetent. You need to give thought to your choice of words and phrasing in all of your written communication, of course, but the touchier the situation, the more demanding the communication, and the more carefully you need to think about what you should or should not say and about what is appropriate to your purpose.

Similarly, a primarily informative message requires different strategies than an explicitly persuasive one, though all messages are implicitly persuasive in the sense that they encourage a particular view of how the facts should be interpreted or what they mean. How you present your information is also implicitly persuasive, in that you are also presenting a view of the situation, of yourself, and of your audience that you are asking them to accept. Nevertheless, if you wish to explicitly persuade—to move your readers to action, convince them of a point of view, or encourage them to accept a change in plans, for example— you need to make use of persuasive techniques. These are covered in greater detail in Chapter 5.

Finally, in addition to the influence exerted by the audience and the purpose of the communication, every context imposes expectations and limitations—constraints—on what can and can't be said. These may arise from the physical setting in which the communication occurs, the historical, social, professional, or personal context, and the manner in which the message must be communicated. In addition, as you are already aware, influences are always exerted by the needs and priorities of the audience, by the form and structure of the message itself, and the speaker's character and experience. As in all human experience, some constraints also arise from moral, legal, and ethical considerations, as well as from technical or communicative limitations.

As in any problem-solving process, a problem presents itself and the reflective practitioner draws upon experience and good judgement to create a solution that fits the constraints of the particular situation. For example, in solving a design challenge, a careful engineer redefines the original problem so as to ensure that all constraints have been identified and considered; in diagnosing what a patient's symptoms mean, a thoughtful physician considers all possible causes, until the correct cause is identified. Similarly, a technical writer or speaker who is planning a message does not stop at the first solution that occurs; instead, an effective writer reviews the problem and the written response several more times to be sure that the problem has been properly understood and adequately addressed. The writer edits and revises the document in light not only of the original request or situation but also with an eye to crafting a message that appropriately addresses the intended audience and that communicates clearly. Seeing writing as a form of problem solving will help you to keep in mind all of the elements of effective communication.

Plan, Produce, and Polish Your Message: The Three Ps

The writing process, like any design process, can be divided into three main stages: an initial planning stage, a preparation or draft stage, and a polishing or editing stage. During the **planning** stage, you define your task by analyzing your purpose, your audience, and your own credibility requirements. At this stage you should sketch a brief outline of your main points. A draft or **production** stage follows, during which you create a series of rough drafts, reviewing each to ensure that you have fully addressed the issue, that you have adequately considered your audience's interests and needs, and that you have effectively established your **ethos**.

The **polishing**, or editing, stage involves several levels of re-reading and revising the message for clarity, completeness, conciseness, coherence, correctness, courtesy, and credibility. This stage follows the completion of a more or less finished draft, and the whole process may be repeated several times until a satisfactory message has been produced.

These three general stages can be broken down further into manageable steps. Though following these steps will initially seem more time-consuming than what you currently do, mastering this process will, in the long run, actually save you time—and potential embarrassment—by enabling you to produce more efficient, competent messages. Careful planning, production, and polishing can help to ensure that your communication achieves its purpose. In this chapter we will focus on the planning and production stages of writing; the next chapter provides guidance for editing and giving your work a final polish.

Stage I: Plan your message

1. Sketch out a writing plan

Before you begin to write, you should sketch out a plan for your communication. Why are you writing? Who is it for? What do you want this person to do as a result of your message? You can use a device such as the Professional Writing Planner (Figure 2.1) as a guide to help you draw up a preliminary overview of your task. If you answer the questions as fully and completely as you can, the planner will assist you in understanding the context in which your message will be received, and in identifying the important elements of your message and the probable needs and expectations of your reader.

Box 2.4   The Three 'Ps' of the Writing Process

Stage I: Plan Your Message
 1. Sketch a writing plan.
 2. Generate ideas.
 3. Outline and organize.

Stage II: Produce a Draft
 1. Start with the main message.
 2. Keep the audience in mind.
 3. Focus on your purpose.
 4. Commit to an organizational pattern.
 5. Build cohesiveness.
 6. Break up the task.

Stage III: Polish Your Writing Style
 1. Let it sit for a while.
 2. Run the spell-checker and grammar-checker.
 3. Read your words out loud.
 4. Apply the 'levels of edit'.
 5. Seek help from others.
 6. Ask style questions.

Professional Writing Planner
Before beginning your letter or memo, consider these points carefully.

1. What is the topic of this letter or memo?
2. What is my focus or purpose? Am I providing information? Promoting an idea? Proposing an action?
3. What is the single most important piece of information I hope to communicate to my reader?
4. Who is my reader? What is his or her interest in this subject? What does my reader already know and what further information will be needed or wanted? What is the reader's likely attitude to this information?
5. What do I know about my reader's priorities that might have an effect on the way I position my message?
6. What background information does my reader need as preparation for what I am going to say?
7. What are my primary supporting points? Which details are important? Have I answered any Who, What, When, Where, Why, and How questions the reader might have?
8. What, if any, action do I wish my reader to take after reading my letter or memo? Have I made it possible for her or him to do so?
9. How do I wish to be perceived by the reader of this message?

Figure 2.1:   A **writing planner** can help you in all your written communication. Your instructor can provide you a copy of this form on a handout. A similar planner for writing reports can be found in Chapter 5.

2. *Generate ideas*

If the writing task is short—an e-mail message, letter, or memo—you may be able to keep track of all the points that you hope to cover, without writing them down. However, most people find it useful to jot their main points on scrap paper or on the computer screen before they begin writing. At this point, you should write down everything that seems relevant; as you work through subsequent drafts, you can always eliminate any information that becomes unnecessary.

Once you have assembled the major ideas you wish to cover, shift them about to achieve the most logical order. Consider eliminating those that don't seem relevant; if you're unsure about any of them, you can retain them into the next writing stage, when it will be clearer whether they need to be incorporated or scrapped. The assembled ideas need not be arranged into a formal outline; they are simply intended to help you remember your points and to provide an overview of the message as a whole so that you can structure your communication in an understandable way. This kind of 'scratch outline' is particularly useful for planning longer messages.

3. *Outline and organize*

Once you've assembled and selected the ideas you need to communicate and established a preliminary structure, move your attention from the gathering of content and focus more fully on clustering your ideas into a sequence of logically ordered parts. The general shape of your message as a whole should, of course, follow a standard, and at this stage you should certainly be thinking about how your proposed message fits into that general shape.

However, the body or discussion portion of your message will also need its own appropriate internal structure so that your reader can make sense of your argument. For example, a technical description may be best written using a top-to-bottom or left-to-right order; an incident report may employ a chronological or cause-to-effect arrangement; a process analysis is usually presented chronologically, with greater or lesser detail depending on whether the reader is expected merely to understand the process or to actually reproduce it; a site analysis may move from general to specific or from perimeter to centre. As you order the points for the discussion segment of your message, try to think in terms of how they will most effectively communicate what you want to say. Several common **organizational patterns** are shown in Box 2.5.

During this planning stage, your primary goal is to identify one or more appropriate organizational patterns as a way of helping you to develop your argument. You should aim for a sequence that will make clear to the reader the details and intent of the message and that will help you to distinguish between main ideas and supporting details. As you begin to order the points, you should also consider whether any elements can be eliminated and which need to be further supported.

As you sequence your thoughts, keep your purpose clearly in mind. The action you require should make sense to the reader by the time he or she reaches the end of the message, and your structure should help to engage attention and motivate the reader to action. As you work, you should be prepared to shift some of the ideas to fit the revised sequence. Some writers find that simply numbering the scratch outline points into the new sequence is enough at this early stage; however, taking the time to rewrite your list into the new sequence will provide you with a better visual sense of the whole message, and will make it easier for you to identify ideas that are misplaced or superfluous.

Box 2.5   Common Organizational Patterns

- Chronological (beginning to end)
- Sequential (first to last)
- Order of importance (least to most *or* most to least)
- Spatial order (top to bottom, bottom to top, right to left, and left to right)
- Cause to effect
- Problem to solution
- Thematic (tracing a particular idea through a sequence of cases)
- General to specific *or* specific to general
- Comparison or contrast
- Size (large to small *or* small to large)
- Function
- Levels of complexity (most to least *or* least to most)

Stage II: Produce the draft(s)

1. Start with the main message

After developing your scratch outline, write your initial draft. Start your first paragraph with 'The most important thing I want you to know is that. . .'. Beginning your rough draft in this way will help remind you to put the most important piece of information—your purpose—at the beginning, and will help you to keep it in view as you develop the draft. As you revise subsequent drafts, you should edit out this clause, but use it in the beginning to help you focus your message, and keep it in place until you're sure that you've maintained that focus in the entire document.

2. Keep your audience in mind as you write

As is probably clear to you by now, audience is one of the most important influences on the success of any communication. But though we have already covered this point more than once, it bears repeating because a surprising number of people forget all about the audience once they start the task of writing. Instead, they become preoccupied with the message itself or with their own writing challenges.

Not just at the very beginning, but throughout the writing process, each time you take a break, each time you read through your draft, you should make it a habit to return your thoughts to the person or persons who will be reading your message. Try to imagine their reactions to what you are telling them and to the way you are presenting the information. Reconsider all the important features of your audience: What do these people need to know? What is their interest in the information you are providing them? What are they likely to be worried about, excited over, moved by? Do they have any concerns that need to be addressed? What are their priorities for this information? How are they likely to react to the message as you have written it? Is there anything that the reader might find confusing, offensive, or inappropriate? Are they likely to resist any of the ideas you're advancing? Is there any way to make your message clearer, more acceptable, less confusing?

3. Keep the focus on your purpose

You started your draft with the main idea you wanted to communicate; this is a good beginning. But it's also important to continue thinking consciously about what you want the message to accomplish. Do this not only at the beginning, but also throughout the writing and editing process. As you re-read and re-write your drafts, keep clearly in mind your reason for writing in the first place. What do you want your message to accomplish? Has it achieved that purpose? Is there some way to make it better? What do you hope your audience will do with the information? Have you made it possible for them to make the decision or take the action that you want made or done? Does every statement in your draft contribute to fulfilling your intended purpose? As you read each sentence, look for ways to make it do its job better, listen for ways to make your message clearer and more convincing, and check that you have achieved the purpose for which you are writing.

4. Commit to an organizational pattern

Reconsider the organizational pattern you have selected for your message. Is it doing the job you thought it would do when you selected it? Is it turning out to be appropriate to the subject you're writing about? Is it making your message clearer for its intended audience? Is it helping you to get the job done? If you find that you are having real difficulty in making your information conform to the organizational pattern you have selected, it could be that the organizational pattern you started with isn't the best one for your purposes. For example, perhaps you have been trying to develop your site report using a chronological order when a spatial order would have been preferable; perhaps your incident report would be better written with a thematic rather than a chronological order.

In some cases, two or even more modes of organization may need to be combined. For example, a technical description of a complex piece of equipment may need two patterns of organization to be understandable: it can be organized from general information to specific detail, and also by function. In such a case, the device is described initially according to its general or overall operation; then each of the parts in turn is treated as to its specific function within the whole. For example, a guitar may be described as to type (acoustic or electric; bass, rhythm, or steel), overall appearance (size, shape, material, colour), and general performance or range of sound. Then its individual parts—sound box, fingerboard, or string configuration—can be described, along with the contribution that each makes to the overall function and sound of the instrument. Similarly, a site analysis that compares two potential building sites might combine both spatial and general-to-specific patterns, as well as a comparison–contrast structure.

Review what you have written to ensure that the pattern, or combination of patterns, that you have chosen is one that appropriately accommodates your purpose and the needs or interests of your audience; if it isn't working, or if it isn't making your writing task more manageable, consider revamping your organizational approach.

5. Build in cohesiveness

Although a sensible and appropriate organizational pattern will go a long way toward developing an understandable structure for your message, you also need to attend to its cohesiveness—the way the individual parts of the message are connected—so that the whole makes sense to your reader. Cohesive texts are more coherent and easier to understand than fragmented texts, and readers generally experience them as better written (and their authors as more competent and credible). There are two primary principles of cohesiveness, and several specific linking devices you can use to build this quality into your messages.

Box 2.6   Two Principles of Cohesiveness

1. Place familiar information before new information in sentences, paragraphs, and documents.
2. Connect every sentence in some explicit way to the sentence that went before, and connect every paragraph in some explicit way to the paragraph that went before.

The first principle of cohesiveness has to do with something called the **known–new contract**. This is the expectation that, in any argument, information that is known to the reader will be presented both logically and chronologically *before* information that is new to the reader. If you want to explain an idea to someone, start with what she already knows and move from there to the part that she doesn't yet understand; if you want to persuade someone, start with things he already cares about and show how your message addresses those concerns. Building in just the appropriate amount of planned redundancy—a kind of review of what the reader already knows—will help make your meaning clearer to those you hope to influence by connecting your points to things they already understand and accept.

Virtually all messages provide some new information, but too many of them fail to tell readers why they should care, or how this new data connects to what they already know. To test out the pervasiveness of the known–new contract, look at any well-written document you have at hand; you will immediately see that nearly every sentence presents the known information in the subject of the sentence and the new information in the predicate; every paragraph begins with familiar or established facts before moving on to new data. Finally, individual segments of the document (summary, introduction, discussion, and so on), as well as the document as a whole, do the same. If it is to be understood and accepted by your readers, every message you write should *always* be arranged with familiar information first.

Here's how the known–new contract might operate in a report. Suppose you are introducing your reader to a new concept or idea. The first time you use the term you will need to define it and provide synonyms or examples. Subsequent uses—especially if brief reminders or quick summative statements accompany them—reinforce the explanation. Finally, when the new term itself has become familiar enough to be considered known information, it can in turn be used to introduce other new information.

For example, recall the introduction of the term 'ethos' in Chapter 1. We began with a definition: the term 'ethos' refers to the speaker's character as it is revealed in the style and tone of the message. This definition was augmented with synonyms such as 'credibility' to further clarify and cement the meaning of the concept. Examples drawn from common experience—the way in which we assess the professionalism and expertise of our colleagues, for instance—helped to reinforce this new-found knowledge, as did continued repetition of the idea through the chapter. Finally, your familiarity with the concept of ethos was used to introduce two other forms of appeal—'**logos**', the quality of the message, and '**pathos**', adapting the argument to the needs and expectations of the audience.

If you look at any of your textbooks—including those from mathematics or science courses—you will find a similar pattern of development. In fact, mathematical arguments always honour the known–new contract: they typically begin with what is given (the known information) and proceed to the proof of a theorem (the new information). Good writers in all disciplines instinctively adhere to the known–new contract; writers in all fields who ignore the known–new contract typically confuse and alienate their readers.

Adhering consciously to the known–new contract is an important first step in improving the logical coherence of what you write, but there is more you can do to ensure that your readers find your words understandable and clear. As you will learn in more detail in Chapter 3, you can also use **devices of cohesiveness** to link every single sentence in some *explicit* way to the sentence that went before it, and connect every single paragraph in some *explicit* way to the paragraph that went before by repeating a key word or idea, by using a word or idea that calls the key word vividly to mind, or by employing a specific linking word such as 'next', 'because', or 'therefore'. To achieve its purpose, the linking device should be placed close to the beginning of the new sentence or paragraph, where it can help the audience to pick up the thread of your argument and so stay on track to the end. These devices will be discussed in detail when we turn to the editing process in the next chapter.

Box 2.7   Devices of Cohesiveness

- Repeat a key word.
- Use a pronoun that refers to a key word.
- Use a synonym for a key word.
- Use an antonym for a key word.
- Use a word commonly paired with a key word.
- Use an explicit connecting word.
- Use grammatical parallelism.

6. Break up writing sessions into smaller periods, and divide a large task into smaller ones

If you're writing a message longer than a few lines, you'll probably do a better job if you don't try to write the whole thing in one sitting. Try instead to spread out the task over a longer period of time. For example, if your deadline is two weeks away, try to devote an hour or more per day to the writing, rather than leaving everything to the day before the report is due. Even if your deadline is only two days away, you can still use this method; try writing for shorter periods of half an hour or forty-five minutes; then take a short break of five or ten minutes so that you can return to the task at least somewhat refreshed.

In addition to dividing up the time spent, you can also make your writing less painful by splitting the task itself into more manageable bits. Try dividing a large task into smaller ones; for example, write the introduction and the conclusion as separate tasks; write the discussion in several sections; write the recommendations as the last stage before you write the summary.

It's human nature to put things off, but if you can get started early, you can intersperse writing with other regular tasks. That way, each time you return to the job of writing you will bring a fresh perspective that will help you to understand the problem anew. Spreading out the writing task also means that you will come to a fuller understanding of how to achieve your purpose. Some nuances of a communication problem won't be clear to you until you have had a chance to think about the challenges through several drafts.

When you have a first complete draft of your report, you can turn your attention to the final stage in the writing process: polishing your work into a clear and effective instrument for achieving your purpose. Editing is more than simply proofreading and running the spell-check program on your computer, though it involves both of those steps. It's not just about correcting errors in fact or in grammar. Instead, it's a process of re-seeing what you have written, of asking questions about how close your document is likely to come to accomplishing its purpose.

The editing process, like the planning and production of a draft document, is best carried out in stages known as the 'levels of edit'. The stages of editing are the subject of the next chapter of this book.

Critical Reading

Wayne C. Booth, 'The Rhetorical Stance'

Until his death in 2005, Wayne Booth was George M. Pullman Professor Emeritus of English from the University of Chicago. The author of more than 15 books, Booth wrote widely on subjects from teaching and critical thinking to music and ethical criticism, but he is best known for his works on rhetoric. Among these are *The Rhetoric of Fiction* (1961), *A Rhetoric of Irony* (1974), *Modern Dogma and the Rhetoric of Assent* (1974), and *The Rhetoric of Rhetoric: The Quest for Effective Communication* (2004). Our selection holds the distinction of being the most frequently reprinted article from the journal *College Composition and Communication*, where it first appeared in 1964.

In it, Booth probes the question of what it means to achieve an appropriate **rhetorical balance** in writing, a quality quite apart from correctness in grammar, sentence structure, and spelling. Booth is one of many contemporary theorists who have defined rhetoric quite broadly as encompassing the process of human communication. 'The Rhetorical Stance' discusses the relationship among speaker, audience, and message that creates the dynamic known as the 'rhetorical triangle'.

Like Lloyd Bitzer's 'The Rhetorical Situation' in Chapter 1, Booth's article deals with similar material as that discussed in this chapter, and makes similar arguments, but it differs significantly from the chapter in its treatment of the subject matter. As you read, consider why these differences might exist, and use the principles you have learned about communication to understand how the two readings function.

The Rhetorical Stance

Last fall I had an advanced graduate student, bright, energetic, well-informed, whose papers were almost unreadable. He managed to be pretentious, dull, and disorganized in his paper on *Emma*, and pretentious, dull, and disorganized on *Madame Bovary*. On *The*

Golden Bowl he was all these and obscure as well. Then one day, toward the end of term, he cornered me after class and said, 'You know, I think you were all wrong about Robbe-Grillet's *Jealousy* today.' We didn't have time to discuss it, so I suggested that he write me a note about it. Five hours later I found in my faculty box a four-page polemic, unpretentious, stimulating, organized, convincing. Here was a man who had taught freshman composition for several years and who was incapable of committing any of the more obvious errors that we think of as characteristic of bad writing. Yet he could not write a decent sentence, paragraph, or paper until his rhetorical problem was solved—until, that is, he had found a definition of his audience, his argument, and his own proper tone of voice.

The word 'rhetoric' is one of those catch-all terms that can easily raise trouble when our backs are turned. As it regains a popularity that it once seemed permanently to have lost, its meanings seem to range all the way from something like 'the whole art of writing on any subject', as in Kenneth Burke's *The Rhetoric of Religion,* through 'the special arts of persuasion', on down to fairly narrow notions about rhetorical figures and devices. And of course we still have with us the meaning of 'empty bombast', as in the phrase 'merely rhetorical'.

I suppose that the question of the role of rhetoric in the English course is meaningless if we think of rhetoric in either its broadest or its narrowest meanings. No English course could avoid dealing with rhetoric in Burke's sense, under whatever name, and on the other hand nobody would ever advocate anything so questionable as teaching 'mere rhetoric'. But if we settle on the following, traditional, definition, some real questions are raised: 'Rhetoric is the art of finding and employing the most effective means of persuasion on any subject, considered independently of intellectual mastery of that subject.' As the students say, 'Prof. X knows his stuff but he doesn't know how to put it across.' If rhetoric is thought of as the art of 'putting it across', considered as quite distinct from mastering an 'it' in the first place, we are immediately landed in a bramble bush of controversy. Is there such an art? If so, what does it consist of? Does it have a content of its own? Can it be taught? Should it be taught? If it should, how do we go about it, head on or obliquely?

Obviously it would be foolish to try to deal with many of these issues in twenty minutes. But I wish that there were more signs of our taking all of them seriously. I wish that along with our new passion for structural linguistics, for example, we could point to the development of a rhetorical theory that would show just how knowledge of structural linguistics can be useful to anyone interested in the art of persuasion. I wish there were more freshman texts that related every principle and every rule to functional principles of rhetoric, or, where this proves impossible, I wish one found more systematic discussion of why it is impossible. But for today, I must content myself with a brief look at the charge that there is nothing distinctive and teachable about the art of rhetoric.

The case against the isolability and teachability of rhetoric may look at first like a good one. Nobody writes rhetoric, just *as* nobody ever writes writing. What we write and speak is always *this* discussion of the decline of railroading and *that* discussion of Pope's couplets and the other argument for abolishing the poll-tax or for getting rhetoric back into English studies.

We can also admit that like all the arts, the art of rhetoric is at best very chancy, only partly amenable to systematic teaching; as we are all painfully aware when our 1:00 section goes miserably and our 2:00 section of the same course is a delight, our own rhetoric is not entirely under control. Successful rhetoricians are to some extent like poets, born, not made. They are also dependent on years of practice and experience. And we can finally admit that even the firmest of principles about writing cannot be taught in the same sense that elementary logic or arithmetic or French can be taught. In my first year of teaching, I had a student who started his first two essays with a swear word. When I suggested that perhaps the *third* paper ought to start with something else, he protested that his high school teacher had taught him always to catch the reader's attention.

Now the teacher was right, but the application of even such a firm principle requires reserves of tact that were somewhat beyond my freshman.

But with all of the reservations made, surely the charge that the art of persuasion cannot in any sense be taught is baseless. I cannot think that anyone who has ever read Aristotle's *Rhetoric* or, say, Whateley's *Elements of Rhetoric* could seriously make the charge. There is more than enough in these and the other traditional rhetorics to provide structure and content for a year-long course. I believe that such a course, when planned and carried through with intelligence and flexibility, can be one of the most important of all educational experiences. But it seems obvious that the arts of persuasion cannot be learned in one year, that a good teacher will continue to teach them regardless of his subject matter, and that we as English teachers have a special responsibility at all levels to get certain basic rhetorical principles into all of our writing assignments. When I think back over the experiences which have had any actual effect on my writing, I find the great good fortune of a splendid freshman course, taught by a man who believed in what he was doing, but I also find a collection of other experiences quite unconnected with a specific writing course. I remember the instructor in psychology who pencilled one word after a peculiarly pretentious paper of mine: *bull.* I remember the day when P.A. Christensen talked with me about my Chaucer paper, and made me understand that my failure to use effective transitions was not simply *a* technical fault but a fundamental block in my effort to get him to *see* my meaning. His off-the-cuff pronouncement that I should never let myself write a sentence that was not in some way explicitly attached to preceding and following sentences meant far more to me at that moment, when I had something I wanted to say, than it could have meant as part of a pattern of such rules offered in a writing course. Similarly, I can remember the devastating lessons about my bad writing that Ronald Crane could teach with a simple question mark on a graduate seminar paper, or a pencilled 'Evidence for this?' or 'Why this section here?' or 'Everybody says so. *Is* it true?'

Such experiences are not, I like to think, simply the result of my being a late bloomer. At least I find my colleagues saying such things as 'I didn't learn to write until I became a newspaper reporter', or 'The most important training in writing I had was doing a dissertation under old *Blank*.' Sometimes they go on to say that the freshman course was useless; sometimes they say that it was an indispensable preparation for the later experience. The diversity of such replies is so great as to suggest that before we try to reorganize the freshman course, with or without explicit confrontations with rhetorical categories, we ought to look for whatever there is in common among our experiences, both of good writing and of good writing instruction. Whatever we discover in such an enterprise ought to be useful to us at any level of our teaching. It will not, presumably, decide once and for all what should be the content of the freshman course, if there should be such a course. But it might serve as a guideline for the development of widely different programs in the widely differing institutional circumstances in which we must work.

The common ingredient that I find in all of the writing I admire—excluding for now novels, plays, and poems—is something that I shall reluctantly call the **rhetorical stance**, a stance which depends on discovering and maintaining in any writing situation a proper balance among the three elements that are at work in any communicative effort: the available arguments about the subject itself, the interests and peculiarities of the audience, and the voice, the implied character, of the speaker. I should like to suggest that it is this balance, this rhetorical stance, difficult as it is to describe, that is our main goal as teachers of rhetoric. Our ideal graduate will strike this balance automatically in any writing that he considers finished. Though he may never come to the point of finding the balance easily, he will know that it is what makes the difference between effective communication and mere wasted effort.

What I mean by the true rhetorician's stance can perhaps best be seen by contrasting it with two or three corruptions, unbalanced stances often assumed by people who think they are practicing the arts of persuasion.

The first I'll call the **pedant's stance**; it consists of ignoring or underplaying the personal relationship of speaker and audience and depending entirely on statements about a subject—that is, the notion of a job to be done for a particular audience *is* left out. It is a virtue, of course, to respect the bare truth of one's subject, and there may even be some subjects which in their very nature define an audience and a rhetorical purpose so that adequacy to the subject can be the whole art of presentation. For example, an article on 'The relation of the ontological and teleological proofs' in a recent *Journal of Religion,* requires a minimum of adaptation of argument to audience. But most subjects do not in themselves imply in any necessary way a purpose and an audience and hence a speaker's tone. The writer who assumes that it is enough merely to write an exposition of what he happens to know on the subject will produce the kind of essay that soils our scholarly journals, written not for readers but for bibliographies.

In my first year of teaching I taught a whole unit on 'exposition' without ever suggesting, so far as I can remember, that the students ask themselves what their expositions were *for*. So they wrote expositions like this one—I've saved it, to teach me toleration of my colleagues: the title is 'Family relations in More's *Utopia*'. 'In this theme I would like to discuss some of the relationships with the family which Thomas More elaborates and sets forth in his book, *Utopia*. The first thing that I would like to discuss about family relations is that overpopulation, according to More, is a just cause of war.' And so on. Can you hear that student sneering at me, in this opening? What he is saying is something like 'you ask for a meaningless paper, I give you a meaningless paper.' He knows that he has no audience except me. He knows that I don't want to read his summary of family relations in *Utopia*, and he knows that I know that he therefore has no rhetorical purpose. Because he has not been led to see a question which he considers worth answering, or an audience that could possibly care one way or the other, the paper is worse than no paper at all, even though it has no grammatical or spelling errors and is organized right down the line, one, two, three.

An extreme case, you may say. Most of us would never allow ourselves that kind of empty fencing? Perhaps. But if some carefree foundation is willing to finance a statistical study, I'm willing to wager a month's salary that we'd find at least half of the suggested topics in our freshman texts as pointless as mine was. And we'd find a good deal more than half of the discussions of grammar, punctuation, spelling, and style totally divorced from any notion that rhetorical purpose to some degree controls all such matters. We can offer objective descriptions of levels of usage from now until graduation, but unless the student discovers a desire to say something to somebody and learns to control his diction for a purpose, we've gained very little. I once gave an assignment asking students to describe the same classroom in three different statements, one for each level of usage. They were obedient, but the only ones who got anything from the assignment were those who intuitively imported the rhetorical instructions I had overlooked—such purposes as 'Make fun of your scholarly surroundings by describing this classroom in extremely elevated style', or 'Imagine a kid from the slums accidentally trapped in these surroundings and forced to write a description of this room.' A little thought might have shown me how to give the whole assignment some human point, and therefore some educative value.

Just how confused we can allow ourselves to be about such matters is shown in a recent publication of the Educational Testing Service, called 'Factors in Judgements of Writing Ability'. In order to isolate those factors which affect differences in grading standards, ETS set six groups of readers—business men, writers and editors, lawyers, and teachers of English, social science, and natural science—to reading the same batch of papers. Then ETS did a hundred-page 'factor analysis' of the amount of agreement and disagreement, and of the elements which different kinds of graders emphasized. The authors of the report express a certain amount of shock at the discovery that the median correlation was only 0.31 and that 94% of the papers received either 7, 8, or 9 of the 9 possible grades.

But what *could* they have expected? In the first place, the students were given no purpose and no audience when the essays were assigned. And then all these editors and businessmen and academics were asked to judge the papers in a complete vacuum, using only whatever intuitive standards they cared to use. I'm surprised that there was any correlation at all. Lacking instructions, some of the students undoubtedly wrote polemical essays, suitable for the popular press; others no doubt imagined an audience, say, of *Reader's Digest* readers, and others wrote with the English teachers as implied audience; an occasional student with real philosophical bent would no doubt do a careful analysis of the pros and cons of the case. This would be graded low, of course, by the magazine editors, even though they would have graded it high if asked to judge it as a speculative contribution to the analysis of the problem. Similarly, a creative student who has been getting As for his personal essays will write an amusing colourful piece, failed by all the social scientists present, though they would have graded it high if asked to judge it for what it was. I find it shocking than tens of thousands of dollars and endless hours should have been spent by students, graders, and professional testers analyzing essays and grading results totally abstracted from any notion of purposeful human communication. Did nobody protest? One might as well assemble a group of citizens to judge students' capacity to throw balls, say, without telling the students or the graders whether altitude, speed, accuracy, or form was to be judged. The judges would be drawn from football coaches, hai-lai experts, lawyers, and English teachers, and asked to apply whatever standards they intuitively apply to ball throwing. Then we could express astonishment that the judgements did not correlate very well, and we could do a factor analysis to discover, lo and behold, that some readers concentrated on altitude, some on speed, some on accuracy, some on form—and the English teachers were simply confused.

One effective way to combat the pedantic stance is to arrange for weekly confrontations of groups of students over their own papers. We have done far too little experimenting with arrangements for providing a genuine audience in this way. Short of such developments, it remains true that a good teacher can convince his students that he is a true audience, if his comments on the papers show that some sort of dialogue is taking place. As Jacques Barzun says in *Teacher in America*, students should be made to feel that unless they have said something to someone, they have failed; to bore the teacher is a worse form of failure than to anger him. From this point of view we can see that the charts of grading symbols that mar even the best freshman texts are not the innocent time savers that we pretend. Plausible as it may seem to arrange for more corrections with less time, they inevitably reduce the student's sense of purpose in writing. When he sees innumerable W13's and P19's in the margin, he cannot possibly feel that the art of persuasion is as important to his instructor as when he reads personal comments, however few.

This first perversion, then, springs from ignoring the audience or overreliance on the pure subject. The second, which might be called the **advertiser's stance**, comes from undervaluing the subject and overvaluing pure effect: how to win friends and influence people.

Some of our best freshman texts—Sheridan Baker's *The Practical Stylist,* for example— allow themselves on occasion to suggest that to be controversial or argumentative, to stir up an audience is an end in itself. Sharpen the controversial edge, one of them says, and the clear implication is that one should do so even if the truth of the subject is honed off in the process. This perversion is probably in the long run a more serious threat in our society than the danger of ignoring the audience. In the time of audience-reaction meters and pre-tested plays and novels, it is not easy to convince students of the old Platonic truth that good persuasion is honest persuasion, or even of the old Aristotelian truth that the good rhetorician must be master of his subject, no matter how dishonest he may decide ultimately to be. Having told them that good writers always to some degree accommodate their arguments to the audience, it is hard to explain the difference between justified accommodation—say changing *point one* to the final position—and the kind of accommodation that fills our popular magazines, in which the very substance of what is said is accommodated to some preconception of what will sell. 'The publication of *Eros* [magazine] represents a major breakthrough in the battle for the liberation of the human spirit.'

At a dinner about a month ago I sat between the wife of a famous civil rights lawyer and an advertising consultant. 'I saw the article on your book yesterday in the Daily News', she said, 'but I didn't even finish it. The title of your book scared me off. Why did you ever choose such a terrible title? Nobody would buy a book with a title like that.' The man on my right, whom I'll call Mr. Kinches, overhearing my feeble reply, plunged into a conversation with her, over my torn and bleeding corpse. 'Now with my *last* book', he said, 'I listed 20 possible titles and then tested them out on 400 businessmen. The one I chose was voted for by 90 per cent of the businessmen.' 'That's what I was just saying to Mr. Booth', she said. 'A book title ought to grab you, and *rhetoric* is not going to grab anybody.' 'Right', he said. 'My *last* book sold 50,000 copies already; I don't know how this one will do, but I polled 200 businessmen on the table of contents, and . . .'.

At one point I did manage to ask him whether the title he chose really fit the book. 'Not quite as well as one or two of the others', he admitted, 'but that doesn't matter, you know. If the book is designed right, so that the first chapter pulls them in, and you *keep* 'em in, who's going to gripe about a little inaccuracy in the title?'

Well, rhetoric is the art of persuading, not the art seeming to persuade by giving everything away at the start. It presupposes that one has a purpose concerning a subject which itself cannot be fundamentally modified by the desire to persuade. If Edmund Burke had decided that he could win more votes in Parliament by choosing the other side—as he most certainly could have done—we would hardly hail this party-switch as a master stroke of rhetoric. If Churchill had offered the British 'peace in our time', with some laughs thrown in, because opinion polls had shown that more Britons were 'grabbed' by these than by blood, sweat, and tears, we could hardly call his decision a sign of rhetorical skill.

One could easily discover other perversions of the rhetorician's balance—most obviously what might be called the **entertainer's stance**—the willingness to sacrifice substance to personality and charm. I admire Walker Gibson's efforts to startle us out of dry pedantry, but I know from experience that his exhortations to find and develop the speaker's voice can lead to empty colorfulness. A student once said to me, complaining about a colleague, 'I soon learned that all I had to do to get an A was imitate Thurber.'

But perhaps this is more than enough about the perversions of the rhetorical stance. Balance itself is always harder to describe than the clumsy poses that result when it is destroyed. But we all experience the balance whenever we find an author who succeeds in changing our minds. He can do so only if he knows more about the subject than we do, and if he then engages us in the process of thinking—and feeling—it through. What makes the rhetoric of Milton and Burke and Churchill great is that each presents us with the spectacle of a man passionately involved in thinking an important question through, in the company of an audience. Though each of them did everything in his power to make his point persuasive, including a pervasive use of the many emotional appeals that have been falsely scorned by many a freshman composition text, none would have allowed himself the advertiser's stance; none would have polled the audience in advance to discover which position would get the votes. Nor is the highly individual personality that springs out at us from their speeches and essays present for the sake of selling itself. The rhetorical balance among speakers, audience, and argument is with all three men habitual, as we see if we look at their non-political writings. Burke's work on the Sublime and Beautiful is a relatively unimpassioned philosophical treatise, but one finds there again a delicate balance: though the implied author of this work is a far different person, far less obtrusive, far more objective, than the man who later cried *sursum corda* to the British Parliament, he permeates with his philosophical personality his philosophical work. And though the signs of his awareness of his audience are far more subdued, they are still here: every effort is made to involve the *proper* audience, the audience of philosophical minds, in a fundamentally interesting inquiry, and to lead them through to the end. In short, because he was a man engaged with men in the effort to solve a human problem, one could never call what he wrote dull, however difficult or abstruse.

Now obviously the habit of seeking this balance is not the only thing we have to teach under the heading of rhetoric. But I think that everything worth teaching under that heading finds its justification finally in that balance. Much of what is now considered irrelevant or dull can, in fact, be brought to life when teachers and students know what they are seeking. Churchill reports that the most valuable training he ever received in rhetoric was in the diagramming of sentences. Think of it! Yet the diagramming of a sentence, regardless of the grammatical system, can be a live subject as soon as one asks not simply 'How is this sentence put together', but rather 'Why is it put together in this way?' or 'Could the rhetorical balance and hence the desired persuasion be better achieved by writing it differently?'

As a nation we are reputed to write very badly. As a nation, I would say, we are more inclined to the perversions of rhetoric than to the rhetorical balance. Regardless of what we do about this or that course in the curriculum, our mandate would seem to be, then, to lead more of our students than we now do to care about and practice the true arts of persuasion.

Wayne C. Booth. 1963. 'The Rhetorical Stance', *College Composition and Communication* 14 (3) Annual Meeting Los Angeles, 1963: Toward a New Rhetoric (October 1963): 139–45.

Points to Remember

1. Start with a writing plan, and use the Professional Writing Planner to assist you.
2. Be clear about your main purpose, and know who your audience is.
3. Begin with your main idea; put it into a subject (or 'Re') line where possible.
4. Break up the writing into smaller tasks, and take breaks.
5. Always be prepared to write more than one draft.

Key Concepts

advertiser's stance	organizational patterns	rhetorical situation
devices of cohesiveness	pathos	rhetorical stance
entertainer's stance	pedant's stance	two basic principles of communication
ethos	plan, prepare, polish	writing planner
known–new contract	problem-solving cycle	
logos	rhetorical balance	

Assignments and Exercises

1. It's been three weeks since you began your summer job as a research assistant for one of the senior professors in your program, Dr. David Stover. Your duties include data collection and analysis for crystal diffraction and immunomagnetic separation. You have fallen into the habit of taking lunch at your desk, and today you accidentally knocked over a full super-sized container of cola onto a pile of irreplaceable printouts from the diffractometer. Unfortunately, you didn't notice the spill right away, and most of the data have been obliterated. The printouts were the only record of the data, and the accident means that the experiments that produced them will have to be re-run. This mishap has caused a loss of all the work you have so far accomplished. Using the Professional Writing Planner on page 38, strategize the way in which you would respond to this sensitive communication situation. Be sure to consider all aspects of the problem, and in particular, to evaluate the needs and expectations of your audience. If your instructor directs you to do so, write a memo justifying the approach you have taken to the problem. Be prepared to discuss your responses with the class.

2. Compare Wayne Booth's discussion of rhetorical balance to the treatment of similar material in this chapter. Write a memo to your instructor in which you describe the central principles emphasized by both the article and the chapter materials, and describe at least two major differences that you see in the treatment of their subject matter. Given what both the chapter and the article say about the nature of successful communication, why do you think the two are so different in approach?

3. After writing your memo, think about the following and be prepared to discuss it in class: which reading—Booth or the chapter—did you find more accessible? Why? For whom was each written? What is the purpose of each? Do these factors make a difference?

4. Answer the following questions about Booth's essay, as directed by your instructor. Submit your responses via e-mail or in memo format.

a. What are three components of any communication situation, according to Booth? How may these be perverted?

b. Who are the intended readers of Booth's essay? How can you tell? Are the readers of this book among them? What value is there in reading something that was originally written for a different audience?

c. What devices does he use to capture and retain their interest? Do they work? How can you tell?

d. Booth's essay started out as a conference talk. To what extent does it retain elements of its oral nature? What does this do to the style of the passage?

Writing Samples for Discussion and Analysis

The writing samples that follow contain multiple weaknesses. Drawing on what you have learned so far, evaluate their effectiveness and identify what could be done to improve the clarity and professionalism of each message. How well has each writer understood and accommodated the critical elements of the rhetorical situation? In what ways has each message failed? Are there any ways in which the message has potentially worsened the situation? If the writers had sought your advice before writing, what would you have advised each to do? Be prepared to present your analysis in writing or in class discussion, as directed by your instructor.

Writing sample #1

Dave Storer is an instructor of technical communication at Waskasoo University College. It's near the end of term, and the students in the Fundamentals of Professional Communication course are preparing their final reports, which are due at the end of this week.

In setting the formal report assignment, Professor Storer and his colleagues have established several constraints for student research. At least half of the research must be drawn from credible print sources. The instructors have also stipulated that any online research sources must be authoritative: refereed electronic journals, reliable news sources, or other scholarly research sites. They have specifically disallowed such unreliable sources as blogs or Wikipedia.

This morning, Professor Storer received the following e-mail from a student in his class.

Subject: **Wikipedia**
From: Schuler Uhsholy <sbu123@stud.wuc.ca>
Date: 2 April 2011
To: Dave Storer <dstorer@sci.wuc.ca>

Hey there

you need to know that some of us are objectionable to your deniel of us using wikipedia for our report reference. I relaize it's along time since you where in school and that books were what got used i the olden days but this is modern times and studnets expect more upto date methods.

What you need to undestand is that wikipedia is a great referance for studnts to use that are to bussy to go to the library for books like you said we have to. I now its to late to help us for this years report, but I am writting this so you wont make the same mistake next year for the future students who can benifit from this advise.

In fact its also good for you to reckonize that old fashion methods do'nt work anymore and so you can be upto date in youre classrom.

If you need anymore help or questions, please don't hesitate to contact myself.

Figure 2.2:   Following the guidelines above, make note of the weaknesses you see in this message. Be prepared to discuss your assessment with the group or to present your analysis in writing, as directed by your instructor.

Writing sample #2

Laura Patterson is a Senior Technical Writer with Urquhart-Wills Consulting Services. Recently, she received the following e-mail message out of the blue. Patterson had never met or heard of Tyler Ketchley before receiving his message; what appears below is exactly how he initiated contact with her.

Subject: **help**
From: tyler@innovativethinker.ca
Date: 26/09/10
To: <lpatters@urquhart-wills.com>

---

hello laura,
your info was passed on to me by a friend who said you might be able to help me. i'm writing a short business proposal and would like some help with communicating my idea clearly and concisely. i've got a rough draft already made and just need to go over it with someone who is good at communications. do you deal with communications? would you be willing to go through it with me? its only a couple pages and would only take like an hour at the most. please let me know if your interested.

thanks.
tyler ketchley.

— SUBLIME
www.innovativethinker.ca
tyler@innovativethinker.ca
306/299/8391

Figure 2.3:   Considering what you have learned so far, assess this message as professional communication. What inferences can be made about Tyler's ethos? His professionalism? His attitude? His maturity? If you were offering any advice to Tyler as to how to approach a senior professional, what would you tell him? (It might help you to know that when Laura mentioned this message to some colleagues at a local meeting of the Professional Writers' Guild, two of them reported receiving exactly the same message from Tyler.)

Writing sample #3

Adam Adamson is a third-year student at Central Maritime University who had the following exchange of e-mails with the Student Services Department.

Subject:	**Problems with Online Registration**
From:	Adam Adamson <ada321@stid.cmu.ca>
Date:	3 July 2010
To:	Student Services <std-servs@cmu.ca>
Re:	Student # 555999

I am having trouble registering on line for classes for the fall 2010 term, and I hope that you can help me resolve the problem.

When I try to register for any class, I receive the following error message:
>Registration denied. Student has outstanding tuition dobt that must be paid.

I am fairly certain that this is an error, since I checked my online status after I finished finals in the spring, and it showed that my account was paid in full. As far as I know, I do not owe any money to the university. I have a printout of the relevant page, dated April 27 of this year, showing a zero balance on my account.

I need to have this issue resolved as quickly as possible so that I can register in classes before they fill. Please let me know what I can do to help clear up this misunderstanding.

Thank you for your help.

Adam Adamson

Figure 2.4

Subject: Problems with Online Registration
From: Student Services <std-servs@cmu.ca>
Date: 5 Jul 2010
To: Adam Adamson <ada321@stid.cmu.ca>

Adam:

Your account is in arrears in the amount of $108.32. If you do not pay this amount immediately, you will not be able to register in classes for the fall term.

These are fees owing from the last term, January to April. These are manually assessed student fees, but due to an administrative backlog, these fees were not assessed until the 24th of May. That is why your online account information showed no outstanding fees as of April.

These fees should not have come as a surprise to you, as all students know that they owe student fees for every term they are registered. Weren't you curious why you had paid no student fees for the second term of last year? It is your responsibility to stay apprised of your student account status and to rectify any outstanding debts.

Our records show that payment to your account is already several months overdue. To ensure that you will not be prevented from registering in fall classes, you must immediately pay this debt at Student Services. Further delay will result in suspension of your eligibility for enrolment and will require that you re-apply for admission.

Please see that this matter is rectified right away.

Figure 2.5:   The very next day after receiving this response from the university, Adam received a mail-out from the university, consisting of a glossy brochure advertising its new 'user-friendly' Student Services Department and inviting students to take advantage of its supportive, student-centred atmosphere. Drawing on what you have so far learned about communication, assess the appropriateness and the effectiveness of the message Adam received from Student Services. What is its intended purpose? Is the message suitable, given the constraints of its context? In what ways might it be said to have failed? In what ways might the clerk's response have worsened the situation for Adam? What, if any, long-term consequences might there be for the university? Be prepared to present your analysis in writing or in class discussion, as directed by your instructor.

Chapter 3

Editing Your Technical Writing Style

Learning Objectives

- To learn effective strategies for editing your professional messages.

- To master the Seven Cs of professional writing.

- To examine several common causes of unclear professional writing and learn how to edit them out of your own writing.

- To understand how to use common organizational patterns and devices of cohesiveness.

O nce you have produced an acceptable draft of your report and checked it over to see that it is complete, you can turn to the final—and arguably most important—stage of the writing process: polishing your draft into a finished document with a crisp, professional style.

Editing is more than a process of proofreading to catch errors; it is also more than simply running the spell- and grammar-check programs on your computer (although you should do this, too). Instead, **editing** means thoughtfully reconsidering your message with an eye to its overall purpose, its suitability to the writing situation, its accommodation of audience needs, and its presentation of a credible and authoritative writer. Editing is the process of giving focus and sharpness to your writing, of trimming off the loose and rough bits, of clearing away the debris. It's essential to achieving **clarity** and purpose. Quite simply, nobody writes crisply and effectively without editing.

Like the planning and production stages of writing, the editing stage is carried out in several steps, outlined below.

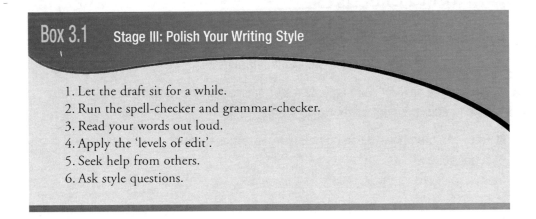

Box 3.1   Stage III: Polish Your Writing Style

1. Let the draft sit for a while.
2. Run the spell-checker and grammar-checker.
3. Read your words out loud.
4. Apply the 'levels of edit'.
5. Seek help from others.
6. Ask style questions.

Step III: Polish Your Writing Style

1. Let the draft sit for a while

If you can, take a break from your writing task once you have finished each full draft. If the document is complex, you might even want to take a break when you have finished each major segment. In any case, you should try to set your work aside and turn your attention to something else. When you return to read through your document, you will be better able to see your words as the reader will see them, and you may be able to see any weaknesses and correct them before you send out the message. The length of this break will depend on the time available and the complexity of the message, but if you can, try to let your document sit at least overnight so you can approach it with a fresh perspective.

2. Run the spell-checker and grammar-checker

Use both, but recognize their limitations. Although helpful, these programs do not catch mistakes in diction, and can even introduce new errors into your writing. The spell-checker will change specialized words it does not recognize into similar words that are in its dictionary, turning sense into nonsense; the grammar-checker, by its limited list of common grammatical rules, will frequently recommend changes that are simply wrong. Discerning good advice from bad requires informed judgement by the writer, and if you are unfamiliar with grammar principles, you may end up following recommendations that actually compromise the clarity or correctness of your writing.

On the positive side, when they are used judiciously, these programs can help you to catch typos and other small errors that you might otherwise miss, so you should make use of them. But you should not rely on them exclusively; be sure to proofread on your own as well. Don't automatically assume that any changes these programs suggest are for the best; use your own judgement too. If you're uncertain about a spelling or grammar point, you should check a dictionary or grammar handbook to be sure.

3. Read your words out loud

Editing involves reading through your work to ensure that it makes sense, that it addresses its readers appropriately, that it displays a confident and capable writer, and that it accomplishes its purpose. Reading silently will, of course, reveal some of these considerations, but hearing the message read out loud can sometimes be more effective at revealing flaws in reasoning or wording. When you read to yourself, your eye tends to see what you wanted to say rather than what you did say, and hearing your words out loud will help you to locate weaknesses before the message goes to your audience. While you may not wish to read an entire lengthy report aloud, you should use this technique for any segments of the document in which you are having difficulty with organizing or wording.

4. Apply the 'levels of edit'

The 'levels of edit' concept, described in greater detail below, approaches the job of revision as a complex of tasks rather than a single task. Instead of trying to edit every aspect, or level, of your message in one pass, this multi-phase approach requires several readings, each one focusing on a different aspect of the message. While technical editors and writing scholars have advanced several different versions of the levels-of-edit approach since it was first made popular in the early 1980s, the one described in this book is a rhetorical model that emphasizes the usability and effectiveness of the document.

As you will learn in the next section of this chapter, the rhetorical levels-of-edit approach focuses your attention on the effectiveness of each of the following, in turn: context, reader accommodation, writer's credibility, and clarity of language and meaning. Depending on the available time, the importance of the document, and the situation, you should read through the document several times, each time with a different end in view. One read-through focuses on how effectively the document fulfills its intended purpose. A second considers the kind of relationship that is assumed and maintained with the intended reader. A third reading looks only at the credibility and footing of the writer. The final stage is a close reading of the document that looks carefully at such issues as word choice and usage, sentence structure and complexity, paragraph coherence and development, and the clarity and organizational patterns of individual sections and of the document as a whole.

Although the levels-of-edit approach may sound like a lot more work than you're doing now, it is actually a much more efficient way of polishing your documents because it focuses your attention on each of the individual aspects of the message that affect its overall credibility and persuasiveness. Specific guidelines for the rhetorical levels-of-edit approach are provided later in this chapter.

5. Seek help from others

If you can, have someone else read your work for you. Ask your reader to note anything that is out of place, confusing, inaccurate, or incomplete. Be sure to choose someone who will appraise your style honestly rather than someone who will simply flatter your ego with praise whether you deserve it or not. The more experience you gain in having someone else review your work, the more distance you will develop and the better you will become at editing your own work and seeing it as a reader might see it.

6. Ask style questions

At last, when you think you have reached the final draft of your work, read it again as you ask yourself the following questions:

1. Will my opening catch the attention of the person with whom I want to communicate?
2. Is my argument clear and direct?
3. Is the material presented in a logical manner?
4. Does my writing have a clear beginning, middle, and end?
5. Is it easy for a reader to follow along?
6. Have I put myself in my reader's place?
7. Is the report interesting enough to make people want to read all the way through?
8. Is my main point or request obvious?
9. Does my conclusion follow from what I've presented, or does it seem to come out of left field?
10. Would people who have read this report likely want to take the action I've recommended and be willing to encourage others to do so?

Answer these questions as honestly as you can; if you have a friend who is willing to read the document through for you, have her answer these questions as well. If you can honestly answer 'yes' to all of these, your draft is probably ready to go to the reader.

Strategies of Editing

The levels of edit

The 'levels of edit' concept was originated by Mary Ann Buehler and Robert VanBuren, who wrote an influential primer on technical editing for use at the Jet Propulsion Laboratory in Los Alamos (1980). Their work showed that editing, the process of re-reading and re-thinking a document to improve its clarity and effectiveness, should be understood not as a single task but as a collection of several distinct tasks.

In their original handbook, Buehler and VanBuren identified eight separate tasks that a professional editor completes in conducting a thorough edit of any written document.

Their different levels involve a variety of management functions (coordination, policy, document integrity, and screening) as well as several document correction functions (including formatting, mechanics, language, and content). The editor may complete any or all of these separate tasks for a given document; the intensiveness of the edit depends upon several factors, such as the purpose and audience for which the document was written, as well as the time and money available for editing.

Buehler and VanBuren developed their model as a guideline for professional editors, rather than for other kinds of professionals who have to write as part of their jobs, but their multi-stage approach appealed to writing experts, and several others offered their own versions of the process (see Plotnik, 1996; Rude, 1998). Not surprisingly, our own 'levels of edit' model is a rhetorical one that reiterates the theoretical orientation of this book.

Whatever the details of the specific model you are following, the overall goal of the levels-of-edit process is the same: to improve the document's usability and comprehensibility. The process involves making several passes through your final draft, considering different elements of the document each time. The important outcome of this kind of substantive editing is that it considers the document not according to some rigid notion of 'correctness', but as a working instrument—as it will actually be read and used by its intended audience. Such comprehensive editing doesn't focus on line-by-line proofreading. Instead, its focus is on *how effectively the document is adapted to its goals and context.*

The levels-of-edit approach involves scrutinizing your document for different features on each read-through. On the first pass, focus *only* on the context in which the message has to function. Use your intended purpose as a measure to determine how successfully you have adapted your document to its function. Consider the task that the document is supposed to fulfill; have you positioned it as effectively as possible to achieve your aims? On this pass, you should be evaluating how effectively you have accommodated the constraints of the situation in which your document will be read.

On the second read-through, you should focus exclusively on the reader's needs and expectations, priorities and concerns, knowledge and interests. Does your document take all of these issues into account, for all of your intended readers? Are there any political issues that have to be considered in the positioning of the document, such as turf wars, testy relationships, or workplace power struggles? Try to put yourself into the shoes of your readers; think about how they are likely to view your message. Think especially about how they will react to the way you've positioned the message; if there is anything that will unnecessarily provoke them, you should modify your style and wording to reduce a negative reaction. Pay attention to the language you've used and to the way you have implicitly characterized your reader.

The third pass should focus on your own ethical stance, footing, and credibility. Have you represented the situation and the issues fairly and ethically? What is the basis for your authority to address the issue? Does your document demonstrate a sufficiently full understanding of the issues? What is your organizational or experiential status relative to that of your reader? Have you accommodated these differences? Is the **tone** of the document reasonable and appropriate? Does your handling of the content and style demonstrate credibility and competence, or do you sound as though you're out of your depth? Is your argument coherent and sensible, or does it make you sound foolish? What relation is established or invited by the way you have positioned yourself? Is it appropriate to the task you hope to accomplish?

The final read-through is devoted to message quality and effectiveness; at this level you are looking to eliminate lapses in grammar, spelling, and tone. This reading may be conducted in one pass, or it may require more than one, depending on your command of such issues as spelling, usage, and grammar. You should examine your document minutely, considering the language you've chosen: have you avoided overuse of **jargon** and **acronyms**? Have you used your words appropriately and correctly? Have you taken care with your tone?

Message quality and effectiveness depend not only on individual words, but also on grammatical and syntactical correctness, forcefulness, emphasis, and coherence. You should read your sentences individually to eliminate awkwardness, wordiness, and over-writing. You should aim for coherence and appropriateness of tone.

You can also evaluate the document paragraph by paragraph and section by section, looking at the development and support of your argument. Your concern as you examine the report at this level is to ensure that each paragraph or segment has a clear relationship to the overall purpose of the document, and that each flows sensibly from the previous one.

Finally, you should examine the entire document to evaluate its overall impact, considering such issues as formatting, structure, the use of headings and section divisions, and whether the document actually accomplishes the purpose for which it was written. At this stage, too, you should consider the visuals you have chosen to support your document. Are they sufficiently clear and uncomplicated? Do they contribute to the reader's understanding? Are they placed where they will assist the reader to get the point?

The following box provides a handy summary of the stages in the rhetorical levels-of-edit process. You will notice as you scan it that 'tone' appears as an item at several levels. This is not an accident; tone—the writer's attitude toward the reader, the message, or the context—is affected by the choices a writer makes at every level of the document, and because it is an expression of relation, it is of critical importance in communicating the message. As you consider your document through each successive reading, you should also be on the alert for any factors that might undermine the relationship that you are building with your reader.

Mastering the Seven Cs of Professional Writing

The levels-of-edit approach provides guidance for evaluating the quality and effectiveness of your message through several readings, with the goal of achieving a keen and functional technical writing style. But what are the qualities of such a style, and what would it actually sound like?

Effective professional and technical messages feature several identifiable stylistic characteristics that I have named the 'Seven Cs': **completeness**, **conciseness**, **clarity**, **coherence**, **correctness**, **courtesy**, and **credibility**. These principles can be used as guidelines as you edit your writing to give it the crisp, authoritative style that marks a competent professional.

1. Completeness

At each stage of the writing process, and at every level of editing, you should always check to be sure that no important details have been overlooked and that you have included all relevant information. To ensure that you have included all of the information your reader will need in order to understand and act on your message, always revisit

> ## Box 3.2   The Rhetorical Levels of Edit
>
> *Step One: Read for Context*
> - purpose for which the document is intended; number of readers; political climate and constraints; time limitations; economic limitations; use to which it will be put
>
> *Step Two: Read for Reader Accommodation and Relationship*
> - expectations; probable attitude to message; receptiveness; knowledge base; interests; needs; level of understanding; existing stance on issue; respect; conciliation; relational history; status needs; face issues
>
> *Step Three: Read for Writer's Credibility*
> - ethical stance; basis of authority; organizational or experiential status; tone; accuracy; logic; command of material and of style; language and usage; clarity of argument; relation established or invited
>
> *Step Four: Read for Message Quality and Effectiveness*
> - At the *word* level, check for:
>   - spelling, word choice, correct usage, accuracy, political correctness, jargon, technical language, acronyms, consistency, Canadian/American spelling, tone
> - At the *sentence* level, check for:
>   - grammatical correctness, sentence structure, syntactical variety and complexity, coherence, forcefulness, emphasis, awkwardness, wordiness, overwriting, style, audibility, tone
> - At the *paragraph* level, check for:
>   - topic focus, link to overall purpose, movement of the argument, sentence-to-paragraph coherence, paragraph-to-paragraph coherence, paragraph-to-document coherence, full development of appropriate detail, ordering of paragraph relative to the rest of the segment, tone
> - At the *section* level, check for:
>   - section-to-section coherence, section-to-document coherence, placement of section within document, logical structure of section, **parallelism**, completeness, topic focus
> - At the *document* level, check for:
>   - overall impact, coherence of overall document, parts complete and in order, structure, conformity to standards of formatting, fulfillment of purpose, appropriateness of title, credit given, correctness of references
> - With respect to *visuals*, check for:
>   - clarity, simplicity, correctness, ease of understanding, placement and positioning, contribution to understanding, readily reproducible by available technology

the issue of completeness, to double-check that no critical information has been accidentally eliminated during the editing process.

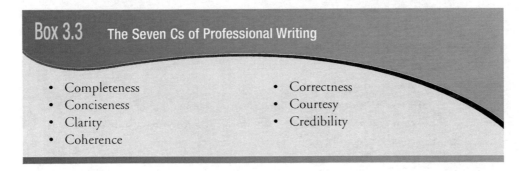

Box 3.3   The Seven Cs of Professional Writing

- Completeness
- Conciseness
- Clarity
- Coherence

- Correctness
- Courtesy
- Credibility

At each stage, look again at the purpose that you want your document to achieve, and think about the information that your audience will require in order to make a decision. You can use the following questions as a guideline to ensure that you have included all the information your reader needs. Be sure you have answered any that are relevant:

| Who? | What? | How many? | When? |
| Where? | How? | Why? | How much? |

Finally, always double-check that you have included any attachments (electronic or 'hard' copy) that you intended to send with your message. If you're e-mailing a document that is to contain an attachment, make it a habit to attach the file before you write the message so that you won't be as likely to hit 'send' before the appropriate files are appended.

2. Conciseness

Good technical writing is concise without being curt or unnecessarily blunt. Ideally, you should aim to cover everything you need to in as little space as possible without compromising your tone or the reader's understanding. Achieving conciseness without sacrificing completeness is more difficult than it initially sounds, because it involves more than just brevity. Although you do want to eliminate unnecessary information, you must at the same time preserve whatever details are necessary to the reader's full understanding, and you have to take care to establish and maintain an appropriate tone.

Once you have completed your first draft, and have made certain that all essential information is included, you should aim to eliminate any *irrelevant* information that has crept into your message, and to remove any unnecessary wordiness. Be ruthless as you consider each detail: ask yourself whether it is essential to the reader's understanding. If the answer is no, then cut it. Don't, however, cut in such a way that your tone is compromised and your document is rendered impolite or overly directive. Below are some of the causes of wordiness in technical documents, along with some tips on how to correct them.

Eliminate unnecessary passive voice

One of the most common causes of wordiness in technical writing is the over-use of a grammatical feature known as **passive voice**. Grammatical 'voice' refers to the relationship between the subject of a sentence and the action of the verb. The passive voice expresses not action done *by* the subject (as in the sentence 'Kenneth kicked the dog' or 'The dog bit Kenneth'), but action done *to* the subject (as in the sentence 'The dog was

Box 3.4 Improving Clarity

- Eliminate unnecessary passive voice.
- Eliminate unnecessary repetition.
- Where possible, replace phrases and clauses with a single word.
- Eliminate inflated expressions and buzzwords.

kicked by Kenneth' or 'Kenneth was bitten by the dog'). This change in arrangement may seem minor, but it makes a crucial difference to the forcefulness of the statement. Not only is the passive version longer and wordier, it also changes the focus of reader attention away from the agent and onto the receiver of the action. In fact, a passive construction allows a writer to hide agency altogether by simply removing the phrase that refers to who or what performed the action, as in 'The dog was kicked' or 'Kenneth was bitten.' A sentence that uses active voice is almost always stronger, more concise, and much more vivid. For example, a sentence like 'Your request was received yesterday. . .' is almost always better written, 'I received your request yesterday.'

There are some exceptions. In certain types of very formal writing, and in some (but not all) scientific disciplines, the use of passive voice is considered not only appropriate but essential, particularly in cases where an emphasis on scientific objectivity is the stylistic goal. For example, a chemist reporting laboratory results will likely write 'The experiment was conducted under controlled conditions' instead of 'My associates and I conducted the experiment under controlled conditions.' Passive voice can appear to be more 'objective' because it allows you to report that an action occurred, while downplaying the role of the agent who actually performed it, making it seem as though it happened almost without human intervention or cause. Most scientists would find the second of the two sample sentences inappropriate because of its unaccustomed emphasis on the actions of the associates, instead of on the unfolding of the experiment.

Although scientific writing conventions are not usually employed to deceive the reader, passive voice is sometimes used (along with vague and clichéd wording) as a deliberate strategy by writers who want to avoid acknowledging responsibility for an action or who wish to confuse or obfuscate: bureaucratic documents and administrative memos are often written in such opaque language. Consider, for example, the sentence, 'An error in measurement was observed.' There is no indication of who made the error or how it happened, and therefore no indication where responsibility for this mistake rests. In fact, because the 'error' is the subject of the sentence, it may even come to seem that it somehow caused itself.

At times this sort of rhetorical sleight-of-hand is legitimate and desirable. For example, although it should be used only sparingly, at times passive voice may be legitimately employed to preserve relation and save face for someone else. For example,

'George misplaced the Ferguson project file.'

is more likely to cause a loss of face to George than is

'The Ferguson project file has been misplaced.'

Similarly,

'John's tardiness has caused a delay to the design phase of the project.'

may unfairly blame John, while

'A delay has occurred in the design phase of the project.'

will avoid unnecessarily apportioning blame to anyone.

Remember that, although the passive voice may be used legitimately in some circumstances, you can usually make your own writing more powerful and concise by eliminating it wherever possible. Documents that are written mostly in passive voice obscure your meaning and deaden your prose. If the situation isn't contentious or sensitive, or if you are not writing in a context where convention demands its use (as in certain scientific disciplines), you should prefer the active voice. In most situations, you will want your writing to stand out for its clarity, directness, and human connection; overuse of the passive voice in ordinary professional reports and correspondence distances writer from reader, deadens style, and often causes a loss of clarity.

Consider how much more vivid and powerful, not to mention shorter, the following sentences are when they are written in active voice.

'Larry completed our report.'

is more concise than

'The report that we were working on has been completed by Larry.'

'Shirley conducted the required tests.'

is less wordy than

'The tests that were required have been conducted by Shirley.'

'Doug hired John Smith to complete the project tender assessment.'

is more direct than

'John Smith was hired by Doug for the completion of the assessment for the project tender process.'

'We have evaluated your application.'

is more personal than

'Your application has been evaluated by us' or 'Your application has been evaluated.'

Unless there is a legitimate, ethical reason for refocusing the reader's attention away from the agency in a sentence, you should generally prefer active to passive constructions in the things you write in order to develop a more energetic, engaging style.

Eliminate unnecessary repetition

A second cause of wordiness is unnecessary repetition of ideas or phrasing. Repetition can be a powerful tool for persuasion; when it is used effectively and deliberately, it can engage attention, stir emotion, and motivate an audience into action. However, two things must be said about repetition as a strategy: first, effective repetition is primarily an oral device that rarely achieves quite the same effects in writing, where subtlety is more effective. Too much repetition in writing is often cumbersome and unworkable; it may even seem unnatural and overdone. In professional writing, where the goal is to communicate efficiently and clearly, unnecessary repetition can actually undermine the impact of your message.

In an e-mail, memo, or letter, you need to say what you mean in as little space as possible. To avoid unnecessary repetition, cluster related information and make each point only once. If you say it clearly the first time, you can eliminate the useless and often confusing repetition that weakens your writing and obscures your message. Use repetition only where necessary for clarity and cohesiveness; in general, you should avoid using it for emphasis. Reading out loud will help you to identify these lapses so that you can trim them away.

Where possible, replace phrases and clauses with a single word
We all occasionally find ourselves using several words when we could have used just one, but a good writer will use the editing process to cut the clutter and simplify sentences. Believe it or not, long, windy sentences are actually easier to create than clear, concise ones because they don't demand as much care or attention to meaning, and they require little concern for the audience's needs. But they can also make your documents unnecessarily tedious to read, and busy readers might not bother. An unread message can't fulfill its purpose or achieve its writer's goals. Unnecessarily long or overwritten sentences may sound impressive to an inexperienced writer, but they reduce the forcefulness and effectiveness of your communication.

Excessive use of phrasal and clausal modifiers is among the most common causes of this kind of wordiness, and when it is combined with the passive voice (as in the examples above) it can also be confusing. As a rule, you should not use several words when a few, or even one, will do the job. See how much more concise the following examples can be.

- the project I am working on (my project)
- the equipment that our department recently purchased (our recently purchased equipment)
- the store on the corner (the corner store)
- the tender submission belonging to this consultant (this consultant's tender submission)
- the reason for which I am writing (my reason for writing)
- the project files that I recently acquired (my recently acquired project files)
- property that belongs to the government (government property)
- a friend whom I have known for a long period of time (a long-time friend)

Watch, in particular, for an overuse of the word 'of' (or other prepositions) and the conjunctive pronouns 'which', 'that', or 'whom'. All of these signal a phrase or clause that could probably be rewritten more simply. Rewrite such phrases or clauses into one or two words whenever you can do so without a loss of precision or thought.

Eliminate inflated expressions and buzzwords
The most problematic and most persistent cause of wordiness in workplace writing is the prevalence of wordy or inflated expressions, **clichés**, meaningless jargon, and organizational buzzwords such as those shown in the boxes below.

Box 3.5   Wordy and Inflated Expressions

- at the present time
- at the end of the day
- at this point in time
- at your earliest convenience
- basically speaking
- due to the fact that
- due to the foregoing consideration
- enclosed herewith find
- give consideration to
- if this proves to be the case
- in accordance with your request
- in the amount of
- in the event that
- in the near future
- in today's society
- in view of the foregoing

- it has come to my attention that
- it is probable that
- it will be our earnest endeavour
- make a decision about
- on or before
- please do not hesitate to
- postpone until later
- reach a decision
- revisit this later
- send you herewith
- under separate cover
- until such time as
- whether or not
- with reference to

Box 3.6   Buzzwords and Clichés

- achieve forward mobility
- client-focused service
- down-sizing
- elephant in the room
- fast track
- get with the program
- give a heads-up
- herding cats
- hit it out of the ball park
- incentivize
- joined-up thinking
- know where all the bodies are buried
- leveraging business synergies
- looking to the future going ahead
- manage a change event
- managed separation
- mindset
- mover and shaker
- no-brainer
- on point
- out of the loop

- play hardball
- proactive
- push the envelope
- put that one to bed
- quality-driven
- right-sizing
- run it up the flagpole
- stay in the bandwidth
- stick a couple of ideas into your intellectual toaster and see what pops out
- stick with the game plan
- strategic fit
- sweet spot
- synergy
- team player
- that's chewing gum in the hair
- think outside the box
- touch base
- value-added
- walk the talk
- win–win solutions

Professional and organizational writing is especially prone to such inflated phrases and buzzwords, to jargon and acronym, and to vaguely legalistic language and clichéd phrases that substitute for thinking, instead of clarifying ideas. Inexperienced writers often imagine that workplace writing is supposed to sound bloated, because so much of it does, and many writers, not knowing what else to do, fall back on the clichés they have seen in the writing of others.

It's probably impossible to *completely* avoid clichés and buzzwords in your professional writing, but you should make the effort anyway, since such thoughtless words and phrases actually can impair your readers' understanding and undermine their interest. It's not hard to see why; what does it really mean to speak of 'running an idea up the flagpole' or 'thinking outside the box' or 'circling the wagons'? Probably the metaphor of 'an elephant in the room' was cute the first time someone used it, but it's already lost its ability to stimulate fresh understanding. Now it's just a tired phrase that suggests a writer is too lazy to come up with her own description of the situation.

In addition to such trendy buzz phrases, there are many other pat formulations like those shown that have been circulating in professional correspondence for decades. They are no longer fresh or meaningful, and they are far from original, but they persist because some writers mistakenly believe they are somehow more professional than clear language, or that they are proper to workplace writing. Instead, they are nothing more than a form of verbal padding, a signal that the writer is not thinking carefully about the message or about the reader who will receive it. Instead, she is reaching for a ready-made phrase that is a substitute for having to think through the ideas herself. Much simpler language—in many cases, a single word that communicates much more forcefully and directly—can often replace these cumbersome and meaningless expressions. For example, 'at this point in time' could be replaced by 'now'; 'if this proves to be the case' could be written simply as 'if'; 'postpone until later' should simply be 'postpone'. Some of these expressions, such as 'it has come to my attention that', can be eliminated completely without any loss of meaning.

The clichés and jargony phrases we are discussing should not be confused with **idiomatic expressions**, which are phrases that function linguistically as a single unit whose meaning cannot easily be expressed in any other way. Idiomatic expressions such as 'My favourite jeans *wore out*', 'The robber *held up* the bank', 'John *turned in* for the night', or 'Dad *pulled through* after the operation' have a specific linguistic function that is different from the meaning of the individual words that make them up. Consider, by contrast, 'I wore my favourite jeans out to the park', 'I held the curtain up so the dancers could pass through', or 'I pulled the cord through the keyhole'. Though these usages may appear similar to the idiomatic expressions above, they are not the same kind of linguistic units. The words that make up a true idiom cannot be split apart within the sentence; for instance, it would not make sense to say 'Dad pulled after the operation through' or 'In John turned for the night'.

While idiomatic expressions are an indispensable part of the way we speak, the clichés of business writing do little more than puff up simple ideas unnecessarily. Because these clichés of business language add words without adding meaning or clarity, because they say in several words what could more clearly be said in one, and because they frequently obscure rather than clarify your meaning, they are bad writing. You will do yourself, and your readers, a favour if you avoid this trap. Always check your own writing for such phrases and replace them with more direct language.

3. Clarity

Technical writing cannot do its job if its meaning is ambiguous or obscure. Professional correspondence is typically intended to prompt a specific kind of action from the reader: you are writing because you want results. Your purpose and desired action should be clear to the reader on the first brief reading. This information should be established early in the document, and it should be expressed in a way that your reader will immediately understand.

Although as a writer you may feel that the appropriate course of action is obvious, what you want done may not be quite so clear to the reader, whose idea of a suitable solution may differ from yours. Don't expect your reader to come automatically to the same conclusion you have reached about what must be done. State directly, in clear and specific language, what you expect the reader to do. If there are several steps to be taken, list and enumerate them for the reader's convenience. Your reader should never have to puzzle out your meaning and should have no unanswered questions after reading your correspondence.

As you edit, consider each sentence, each paragraph, and each section of the document. Ask yourself whether it communicates exactly what you want to say, whether it can easily be understood by its intended reader, and whether it leads naturally to the sentence, paragraph, or section that follows it. If a sentence does not accomplish these tasks, rewrite it until it does. If there are lapses in logic from one paragraph to the next, rewrite them both until the argument is transparent. If an idea seems to come out of nowhere, without connection to what preceded it or what follows, remove it or revise it until it carries your argument forward as it needs to do.

Clarity is not only a matter of detail and organization, but also of the language you use. Your meaning will be clearer if you avoid heavy use of technical terminology or jargon that may not be familiar to your reader. While it's true that mastering a specialized vocabulary is an important part of every profession, and that using the language of the profession is one way to help establish yourself as credible in the eyes of your peers, that same technical jargon can quickly become a barrier to understanding when you are communicating with those outside your immediate field of expertise. Of course, some technical language may be essential, but frequently, much of what you need to say can be expressed more simply in language that your reader will be able to understand. Consider the agronomist who writes a report for management or the board of directors, the engineer who produces specifications for the marketing department, the technologist who creates user's manuals for the public, the accountant who writes economic forecasts for investors, the academic who writes a textbook in her field for use by first-year undergraduates, the publisher who must lead a first-time author through the editing and production process. Like most specialists, these experts write most often for audiences far removed from their own field of specialization; such writers have to master the skill of writing about technical subjects in language that can be understood by non-experts. Providing a glossary of technical terms is a partial solution to the problem of opaque language, but it isn't a substitute for writing more concretely, and it will be of little use if your reader is overwhelmed by too many unfamiliar terms.

Similarly, if you wish to write clearly, you should avoid acronyms as far as possible. These abbreviated forms are much loved by technical specialists, but they can be impenetrable for the reader, in part because the same acronym can stand for several different meanings. For instance, the simple acronym ABC could refer to the Australian Broadcasting Corporation or the American Broadcasting Corporation; it could stand for the Association of Business Communicators or for a computer programming language; it could refer to an organization called the Audit Bureau of Circulations or another entitled Associated Builders and Contractors. Before the dissolution of the USSR, the acronym CSSR stood for the Czech and Slovakia Socialist Republic; it also refers to the Congregation of the Most Holy Redeemer (Congregatio Sanctissimi Redemptoris). Canadian academics might know it as the Canadian Society for the Study of Rhetoric, or perhaps as the Canadian Society for the Study of Religion. Confusingly, it might also refer to the Council of Societies for the Study of Religion, of which the Canadian group might be a member. It could refer to the Center for the Study of Science and Religion at Columbia University, or the Center for Social Services Research at Berkeley. Similarly, the acronym AVP could refer to the Associate Vice President of a company or organization, or to either of two anti-violence movements: the Alternatives to Violence Project or the Anti-Violence Project. It could even mean Avon Products Inc. Choose nearly any acronym and check for yourself with a quick Internet search: you'll no doubt find numerous possibilities, even within the same field.

And it's not just non-expert readers who find an overuse of acronyms confounding. Listen to what the distinguished engineering professor Richard Burton has to say about their proliferation in his own field of specialization:

> I have just finished reading a graduate thesis that had over 25 acronyms on a single page. Even with a reference page beside me, I could not decipher the writer's meaning, and I finally gave up. Too bad for me, you might say. But it's too bad for him if his thesis fails because the committee could not understand what he had written. (2008: 107–8)

As a rule, you should employ acronyms only if they are absolutely unavoidable. If you must use them, be sure to employ the full phrase on each new page.

4. Coherence

In order to get the job done, your professional documents need to 'hold together'; the parts should logically follow one from the other so that the pattern of argument is easy to follow and clear to the reader. Coherence is the product of four elements:

- sensible organization,
- effective use of standard formats,
- adherence to the known–new contract, and
- explicit linking strategies that help the reader to follow your reasoning.

We have already discussed several patterns of organization that can help to establish coherence in a document; you should carefully choose a pattern that is suited to the kind of information you are communicating: for example, problem–solution for a design report, spatial order for a site analysis, general to specific for a technical description.

It may seem obvious, but as you organize your message, be sure to place related points together: jumping back and forth is unnecessarily confusing to the reader. For instance, if you are writing to obtain registration information for a technical conference, and to inquire about submitting a paper to the convention program, it would make sense to put all information pertaining to the registration into one paragraph and your query about the paper submission into another. But although that sounds simple enough, writers don't always remember to do it, adding details as they think of them and failing to edit so that the related information is grouped more sensibly. If you find yourself writing the phrase 'as I said above. . .' you probably need to do more to cluster the related information.

The standard formats of professional communication also aid you in developing a coherent document. The standard parts of a business letter, the subject-date-from-to structure of an e-mail message, the chronological arrangement of a résumé, the SIDCRA format of a formal report—all of these assist your reader in making sense of your message. These formats provide coherence in part because their highly conventionalized structure is already familiar to the reader, who knows exactly what to expect from them.

The known–new contract, discussed in the previous chapter, also contributes to the coherence of your document, and the ease of reader understanding. You will recall that the known–new contract refers to the expectation that familiar information will be presented both logically and chronologically *before* information that is new to the reader.

Finally, coherence is a product of deliberate strategies that explicitly create links between ideas and statements. In a coherent document, each sentence is linked to the subsequent sentence, each paragraph to the subsequent paragraph, and each part of the correspondence to the overall purpose or focus of the message. These **devices of coherence** are described in the next section of this chapter.

5. Correctness

Correctness is one of the most important indicators of credibility and competence. A document containing errors in fact or detail, in grammar or usage, or in spelling will immediately mark you as a person who either can't get things right or can't be bothered to do so: in other words, that you are unprofessional, unreliable, or sloppy. It can cause readers to question your competence, your intelligence, and your self-discipline. In turn, a poorly written letter makes inappropriate demands on the reader's patience and understanding, and is therefore also discourteous. For all these reasons, failure to proofread for correctness and accuracy could be costly.

You may think that only your communication professor cares about a few mistakes in grammar or spelling, and that employers or other professionals won't be quite so picky. In fact, the reverse is true: your communication professor *has* to read your document all the way through in order to grade it, even if it doesn't make sense. He's skilled at figuring out obscure or ambiguous meaning. An employer or potential employer, on the other hand, has no such imperative, and a lot less indulgence. She can simply pitch sloppy applications, funding proposals, or reports straight into the garbage.

What you may not realize is that nearly everyone—including those who aren't perfect writers themselves—will quickly see, judge, and frequently condemn the errors in someone else's writing. Your written documents speak for you when you're not there to speak for yourself. Just as you wouldn't dream of wearing a coffee-stained shirt to a job interview or addressing a meeting with a big piece of spinach stuck in your teeth, you should never let your written documents go out into the world with the equivalent flaws.

Because others will form impressions of your competence based on what your writing says about you, you should always check the accuracy of all information—names, dates, places, receipt numbers, measurements, lab results, prices—that you include in any correspondence. Try to make it a habit never to send a written message of any kind—including e-mail—without proofreading it first and checking its tone. Run your spell- and grammar-check programs, and proofread carefully yourself.

6. Courtesy

As Axiom #2 reminds us, relation is an important element in all communication. In professional life, as in all human interactions, things usually go more smoothly if people are pleasant and courteous to one another. Your relationships with clients and colleagues are very important, and, as we will continue to emphasize throughout this book, every communication you send can enhance or undermine those relationships. Since your attitude is displayed clearly in your writing and will affect the relational level of your message, it's important to pay close attention to tone in what you write.

Tone refers to the attitude of the writer toward the audience and also toward the topic of the message. It is reflected in the words you choose, in the structure of your sentences, and in the assumptions you take for granted. In general, you should try to make it a habit to be respectful and positive in your professional communication. Do not presume too far on others' time or good will, and be sure to thank your correspondents for any services or favours requested or received. In particular, avoid **sarcasm**, which—though it can satisfy our immediate expressive needs—will nearly always be read by the target as hurtful and offensive. *It therefore has no place in professional correspondence.*

Even if you are writing to someone whom you believe has done you wrong, give this person the benefit of the doubt, at least initially: allow the recipient to save face by taking the attitude that the error was the unintentional result of a misunderstanding. This approach will be much more effective in resolving difficulties than will a confrontational, accusatory, or sarcastic tone. Although a courteous writer naturally avoids giving offense, courtesy means much more than simply avoiding insult. Your writing should leave the reader feeling positive about the encounter.

To check this important aspect of your own professional communication, always read over your work carefully, putting yourself in the place of the reader. If you are uncertain whether you've achieved an appropriate tone, ask someone you trust to read the message for you. If you're not sure whether the message could be taken the wrong way, assume that it will be, and rewrite rather than send it.

7. Credibility

As we have already established, one of the most important features of effective communication is the projection of credibility—the quality that Aristotle called 'ethos'. As you know by now, the way in which others judge you as a professional depends on how you communicate with them, and your correspondents will judge your professionalism, expertise, and competence by the clarity and attention to detail revealed in your writing.

Credibility involves demonstrating to your reader your good judgement, good will, and good character, just as Aristotle outlined. You do this in part through the appropriateness of your style, diction, tone, emphasis, and sentence structure. You also demonstrate your judgement by your understanding of the issues, by the details you choose to include, by the reasonableness of your solutions, and by your command of the facts, as well as through correct spelling, grammar, and punctuation. You demonstrate good will through the way you address your readers and attend to their needs. Attention to the first six Cs on the list will actually help to establish the seventh by contributing to the reader's perception of your competence, judgement, and attitude.

Credibility also involves the presentation of the message in appropriate format, layout, and structure. Letters, memos, and reports are fairly standardized in their appearance, and a reader will expect yours to conform to these accepted standards. Letters, memos, or reports that do not observe the conventions of professional format may suggest a sloppy or unprofessional writer.

E-mail messages, of course, are far less consistent in their format: some writers, perceiving e-mail to be a casual medium of communication, habitually ignore all conventions of punctuation, spelling, and capitalization. However, you should know that not all readers appreciate *receiving* such unconventional messages; they can hinder understanding by being much more difficult and time-consuming to decipher. It is much better, from the point of view of reader consideration, to observe the conventions of spelling, punctuation, and grammar than to take the chance of annoying or alienating a correspondent. Many workplaces have established standards for e-mail correspondence, both in format and in content. Whether your workplace has such a policy or not, you should do your best to maintain a professional manner and style in all your messages.

When it comes to both printed and PDF documents, appearance and layout also contribute to your credibility. Generous margins, consistent fonts, bullets, and appropriate visuals can all contribute to the professional appearance of your document, making it both more attractive and easier to read. You will find more on document design in Chapter 7.

Devices of Cohesiveness

One of the most important principles of good writing that you will ever learn is this one: always explicitly link every sentence to the sentence that preceded it, and explicitly link every paragraph you write to the paragraph that preceded it by placing a linking device close to the beginning of the sentence or paragraph. The linking device helps the audience to pick up the thread of your argument by helping to fulfill the known–new contract. All good writing follows this principle, a fact that you can easily check by turning to any piece of prose that you consider well written. You will find at least one, and frequently more than one, of the following devices in every sentence of the text. Interestingly, though these devices are easy to find once you know what to look for, and may strike you as cumbersome when you are learning to use them, they pass unnoticed by the average reader, who simply experiences the writing as especially clear. You can make your own writing similarly lucid by mastering the seven explicit strategies explained below.

The examples below show linking strategies from sentences in this book; you can find others if you look for them. Some of the examples show connections between clauses rather than separate sentences, but the principles of linkage are the same in both cases.

Box 3.7   **Devices That Create Cohesiveness**

- Key words
- Pronouns
- Synonyms
- Antonyms
- Commonly paired words
- Connecting words
- Parallel structure

1. Repeat a key word from the previous clause or sentence in the new clause or sentence

Do not overuse the device of repetition, but employ enough 'planned redundancy' to make your text readable.

Nonverbal cues such as eye contact, facial expression, vocal tone, gestures, physical movement, stance and posture, manner of dress, personal hygiene, or overall attractiveness communicate personal traits. Your nonverbal expressions can display assertiveness, confidence, self-possession, energy, enthusiasm, cooperativeness, reliability, and truthfulness—or their opposites.

2. Use a pronoun in the new clause or sentence to refer to a specific noun or noun phrase in the previous clause or sentence

Avoid using pronouns such as 'it' or 'this' unless they clearly point to a preceding noun; pronouns with no identifiable antecedent can actually undercut the cohesiveness of your text.

Your need to communicate clearly doesn't end when you graduate; indeed, it will likely escalate.

3. In the new clause or sentence, use a synonym for a key word or phrase in the previous clause or sentence

Make sure that the synonym fits the context, and that your reader will connect the two; remember to place the synonym near the beginning of the second clause or sentence.

Unfortunately, many graduates of engineering programs are ill-prepared in skills like the ones listed, partly because technical students often don't realize the extent to which their career success will depend on their ability to communicate effectively.

4. In the new clause or sentence, use an antonym for a key word or phrase in the previous clause or sentence

The principle of contrast helps your audience to link two thoughts and to follow the thread of your argument. Contrast may be combined with parallelism (device #7) for greater effect.

Although 'communication' is frequently thought of as simply the 'transmission of information by speaking, writing, or other means' (Barber, 1998: 287), it is actually a much more complex process than this characterization would lead us to believe.

5. Use a word in the new clause or sentence that is closely associated with a word in the previous clause or sentence

The link appears similar to the synonym, but differs in that the paired items are words that have become yoked by habit or convention, rather than synonyms in meaning: cats and dogs; salt and pepper; trains, planes, and automobiles; lions and tigers and bears.

Ethos helps to build the relationship with the reader. Pathos performs the same function.

Readers will expect a text to be clear. Writers need to respond to this expectation.

6. Use a specific connecting word or phrase

If you have organized your ideas well, cohesiveness (and hence coherence) can be enhanced by adding explicit connective words and expressions. Some of these are shown in the box below.

Box 3.8 Connecting Words and Expressions

- after
- afterwards
- also
- as a matter of fact
- as a result
- as well as
- because
- consequently
- first this; second, this
- following
- for example

- for instance
- for this reason
- furthermore
- however
- in addition to
- in the end
- moreover
- naturally
- nevertheless
- of course
- once again
- on the other hand

- since
- subsequently
- such as
- then
- therefore
- thus
- whenever
- when it was completed
- when it was over

You may be able to think of other words and short phrases that perform this linking function. Any word that explicitly signals a movement in your thought from cause to effect, problem to solution, first to last, front to back, and so on, is considered a connective.

In many technical jobs, for example, 50 per cent or more of your work can involve communicating, persuading, and cooperating with others. For this reason, nearly all practitioners in the technical professions list communication among the essential skills for new graduates and experienced engineers alike.

Because lay readers cannot directly judge technical skill, they will instead rely on the clarity and confidence of a professional's communication as a basis for judging technical competence. Thus, skill in communicating specialized information often becomes the measure of an engineer's competence, irrespective of his or her actual technical expertise.

7. Place ideas in a parallel structure

Parallel structure is a form of arrangement that increases coherence by placing ideas in identical configurations. This means that phrases, clauses, sentences, paragraphs, or sections of the document should be arranged in the same structural or organizational pattern.

In many technical jobs, for example, 50 per cent or more of your work can involve <u>communicating</u>, <u>persuading</u>, and <u>cooperating</u> with others.

The example demonstrates a list of three items arranged in parallel structure; all three words are '–ing' formations. However, the same device of parallelism can also be used to unify sentences, paragraphs, or even sections of a document.

You have probably already used parallel structure as an organizational device if you have ever written a résumé. Recall that you created several sections, such as education, volunteer activities, and work experience. When you organized the information within these sections, you likely repeated the same pattern of arrangement in order to help your reader to make sense of the information you were providing. Parallel structure assists the reader in making sense of unfamiliar information and provides part of the structural glue that makes a document coherent.

Use one or more of these devices for every sentence you ever write in your professional correspondence. Using explicit writing strategies to create cohesiveness will help to keep you from drifting or jumping around, and will ensure that your readers perceive you as a competent and considerate writer.

Your goal in editing your reports and other documents is to ensure that they are rhetorically effective: that they accommodate audience needs, that they are appropriately adapted to the constraints of the situation, and that they establish you as a credible and competent professional. In order to achieve your goals, the document has to engage its readers, motivate them to accept its arguments, and enable them to take the necessary action.

Learning strategies for effectively editing your own work will improve your writing and make your messages easier to understand and act upon. While the 'levels of edit' approach may seem like a lot of extra work at the beginning, it will become a time-saver when you master it, because it will help to guarantee that your messages do the work they are intended to do. You only once have to experience the fall-out from a poorly positioned or badly written document to appreciate the importance of learning this process. Taking the time to master these strategies now is a small investment that will pay large dividends when you're faced with writing tasks on the job.

Critical Reading

G. John Moffatt, 'A Precision Instrument: Word Choice and Effective Communication'
G. John Moffatt is Associate Professor in the Ron and Jane Graham Centre for the Study of Communication in the College of Engineering, University of Saskatchewan, where his research and teaching focus on the history and structure of the English language, the English language in Canada, the language of Canadian identity, and heritage language preservation and revivalism. The premiere of his theatrical adaptation of *The Canterbury Tales* recently took place before sell-out crowds at UCFV Theatre in Chilliwack, BC, in Fall 2007.

A Precision Instrument: Word Choice and Effective Communication
Right now you are operating the most sophisticated piece of equipment you will ever use in your professional life. It's not your computer, or some expensive laboratory instrument.

It's more portable than the most wafer-thin laptop, and costs almost nothing to operate. It exerts a direct and powerful impact on everyone and everything around you whenever you use it. You switched it on the moment you woke up and it will keep running until it follows you into sleep mode at the end of the day, and even then it will keep functioning while you dream. In the meantime, you'll use it to process thousands of pieces of information as you go about changing the world before bedtime.

I'm talking, of course, about language.

Changing the world? An exaggeration, surely? Not at all. Changing the world is what we humans spend most of our time doing, and we do it with language. Every time we speak or write with any expectation of being heard or read, we are changing the world. We speak or write to someone in order to make something happen that wouldn't otherwise happen, and language is the tool for the job.

Most people will agree that some tools are better than others for certain tasks: to turn a bolt, you could use your fingers, a pair of pliers, an adjustable wrench, or a socket wrench, depending on the situation. While in some cases it might be *possible* to use any of the above, a wrench with the right size of socket will work well every time.

Words are like those sockets; their small differences can have a huge impact. Specific language tasks require particular word structures. This should sound like simple common sense, but it's surprising how little attention gets paid to language education as part of professional training. The popular wisdom is that if you can spell, avoid glaring grammar mistakes, and recognize some standard document formats, then you're in control of all the language you'll need in your professional life. Those skills are essential, but if you don't know *why* you're doing *what* you're doing with language, the assembly will likely be a little shaky, with quite a few bolts stripped, loose, or missing.

The English language is an incredibly precise instrument. It has the largest vocabulary of any language in the history of this planet, with at least 600,000 words. Selecting the right word from this huge menu is a challenge we face every day. Think of the distinctions between *strength, power, might,* and *capability,* for example. They can all be used to say roughly the same thing. Consider this example:

They have the _____ *to achieve their goal.*

We could put any of the above words into the blank space and make ourselves understood, generally speaking. But are we equally happy with all the choices? Does *power* sound better than *strength* to you? Is there any word here that you would hesitate to use in this sentence?

If the answer to either of these questions is 'yes', or even 'maybe', you've recognized some important facts. You've noted that a word's meaning works on two levels. The *denotation* is the basic idea that the word represents. In this case all five words denote the same thing, the qualities and resources that allow whoever 'they' are to achieve their goal. At the same time, each word can have several *connotations,* which are associations that make a word appropriate in some situations but not in others. A word's connotation is based on our experience of its use; in language as elsewhere, we learn by doing. As we learn words by speaking and reading and writing them, we also learn about the company they usually keep. We learn to recognize the signs that tell us if a word's connotations are right for our needs. Will the word lead the audience to make the exact connection you want? Or does it 'slip' a little? Could the reader take some different, unintended meaning from the words you've used? If so, what is causing the slippage? Why won't this word fit snugly over want you want to say?

You have already learned about the importance of *context* to the rhetorical situation. Audiences look to the context for information about a word's intended connotation, and your job is to make sure that the context supports your word choice. If you answered 'maybe' to the questions about filling in the blank space in our example, it was probably because you felt there wasn't enough information to let you decide. It's like being asked, 'Which tool would you use to put a fastener on these two things?' You would probably want to know what materials you were working with. Are we talking about nails, screws, bolts, rivets, or thumbtacks? Are you fastening sheets of wood, steel, drywall, paper, or some combination of the above?

Normally, we would only write or say something like *They have the* _____ *to achieve their goal* as part of a sequence of other sentences. Their content would influence how we choose to fill in the blank. In fact, if you go ahead and select one of the words from the list without further information, then your choice is based on what you think the most likely context will be.

Try adding a descriptive modifier to the noun you've chosen. Your choice will say a lot about the meaning you see behind the words. Here's a list of adjectives: *technological, political, physical, military*. Insert one into each of these sentences.

They have the _____ *strength to achieve their goal.*
They have the _____ *power to achieve their goal.*
They have the _____ *might to achieve their goal.*
They have the _____ *capability to achieve their goal.*

Do some of these adjectives pair more readily with some words than with others? If you think so, then your own experience of language use is picking out patterns, words that you've commonly seen or heard together. Chances are, if you recognize that pattern, so will your audience. Here again, context should help you choose. For example, think of how much easier it would be to fill in both sets of blanks in our sentence if, instead of ending with the very general phrase *to achieve their goal*, it read:

They have the _____ _____ *to support the weight of the whole structure.*
They have the _____ . ____ *to defeat the government in the next election.*
They have the _____ _____ *to launch an invasion.*
They have the _____ _____ *to implement improvements in the emissions control system.*

You still have some choice. However, you'll probably find that certain pairings (*physical strength; technological capability*) fit a little better in some cases than the others do. For example, *emissions control system* invites the use of *technological*; the scientific tone suggests the fairly neutral term *capability*. By contrast, the word *invasion* connects logically with *military*, and we associate both words with the old-fashioned but emotionally 'loaded' use of *might*. Literal meaning and emotional association combine to create an exact fit.

We can often make these choices automatically and unselfconsciously as we speak or write. Still, the better we understand the choices we make, and know our options, the more confident we can be that we're making the right decisions. After all, why fiddle with the 5/32 socket when the 1/8 will do it right the first time?

Points to Remember

1. Always take time to edit your writing to achieve a crisp and authoritative professional style.
2. Use the spell-check and grammar-check programs, but recognize that they are not enough on their own.
3. Use the 'levels of edit' approach to review your document for audience adaptation, clarity of purpose, writer's credibility, and stylistic effectiveness.
4. Always check and double-check your tone.
5. Try reading your work out loud to catch errors that your eye will miss.
6. Repeat the editing process until the message is as effective as you can make it.

Key Concepts

acronyms	credibility	sarcasm
clarity	devices of coherence	Seven Cs
clichés	editing	SIDCRA
coherence	idiomatic expression	Three Ps: Plan your writing, Produce
completeness	jargon	a draft, Polish your style
conciseness	levels of edit	tone
correctness	parallelism	
courtesy	passive voice	

Assignments and Exercises

1. Following your instructor's directions, select a page or two of text from this or another of your textbooks, from one of the critical readings, or from any source that you consider to be well written. Following the list on page 74, identify all the linking strategies that are used in your selection. To what extent do these strategies affect your understanding? How easy would the text be to read if these strategies were removed?

2. Revisit a piece of your own writing. Any piece of writing that falls into the broad and rather loosely defined category of 'professional' writing will do: one of your regular assignments from this course, a cover letter you wrote for a job, a short report you wrote for another course, a essay answer from an exam for a course you've completed. It may be graded or ungraded, but it should be something you can revisit with some distance from the original context in which it was written. Your selection should be substantial enough to provide a foundation for analysis, and at least 500 words but no more than 1,500 words long. Drawing on your newfound expertise as a professional writer, assess your chosen piece of writing. You do not need to edit the document itself, but you should give an overview of what aspects of the document *should* be edited. Before proceeding to the appraisal itself, be sure to establish a context for the document: identify its purpose, its intended readers, the use to which it will be put, and the footing it was meant to establish. Your assessment should address the overall character of the communication—that is, it should address how well the document fulfilled its intended purpose. You should evaluate the quality of the mes-

sage, its positioning, the appropriateness and calibre of its appeal to its intended audience, its effectiveness at establishing the writer's credibility, and its overall stylistic quality. Finally, you should address any editing issues at all levels of the document: its diction and word choice and correctness; its syntax and sentence quality; the coherence and clarity of its paragraphs, the force and impact of its voice and style, the attractiveness and effectiveness of its layout. Write a brief report of approximately 300–500 words that provides an assessment of this work and some specific recommendations about how the document might be improved.

3. In his famous essay 'Politics and the English Language', George Orwell rewrites a familiar passage from *Ecclesiastes* into what he calls 'modern' language. Here is the original, followed by Orwell's rewritten version:

> I returned and saw under the sun, that the race is not to the swift, nor the battle to the strong, neither yet bread to the wise, nor yet riches to men of understanding, nor yet favour to men of skill; but time and chance happeneth to them all.

Compare Orwell's version, rewritten in modern English:

> Objective considerations of contemporary phenomena compels the conclusion that success or failure in competitive activities exhibits no tendency to be commensurate with innate capacity, but that a considerable element of the unpredictable must invariably be taken into account (1956: 360).

Of course, Orwell's point is to demonstrate how much less clear the modern language is than the original. As a class, compare Orwell's passage with the passage from Ecclesiastes and explain why the original is more effective.

4. Just for fun, try your hand at this reverse process by rewriting some clear passages into 'modern' language, using the clichés and abstract phrases we have been discussing. Try rewriting some familiar or popular text in this manner—perhaps a fairy tale such as the 'The Three Little Pigs', a job advertisement, or one of Rick Mercer's 'rants'.[1] Compare and discuss your choices with those of the other members of the class.

5. Revise the following sentences, taken from actual memos and letters, to make them clearer and more concise.

a. Please be advised that interested parties who wish to apply must consider that documents for application should meet the deadline of submission which is August 31.

b. I have a colleague of mine, Brian Quigley, who passed on to myself the facts and details contained in the information you provided.

c. In the event that any employee should be the final individual to exit the premises of this firm on the eve of any given working period, it would be greatly appreciated by management as a gesture of fiscal responsibility if such individuals should leave the offices in a state of darkness.

d. The full and complete application materials she submitted on behalf of herself have received a nod of acceptance.

e. Please be advised that I would like to express my interest in consideration to being interviewed for this very attractive opening that is currently available for hire in your firm.

f. Please accept this letter as formal notice of the fact that the scholarship award of which you had expectation of confirmation has received a negative decision in the form of a rescindment.

g. Due to the difficulties involved with the aforementioned request, the writer would like to take this opportunity to thank you in advance for your assistance in this difficult matter.

h. A cheque for the amount specified to cover the loss experienced due to the above incident of April 30 has been prepared by this office. The appearance of yourself is requested at your earliest convenience to complete the necessary paperwork and receive such payment. We trust this is in order.

i. With reference to your communication of the above-referenced date, enclosed herewith find the documents which you requested at that point in time.

j. In the event of circumstances beyond our control which affect delivery of this service, some alteration to the planned schedule may be required.

5. John Moffatt argues that language is a kind of instrument, or tool, for making changes in the world. What method does Moffatt use to make his point? What does it add to his argument? Explain your reasoning to your instructor in a memo of approximately 250 words.

6. Take another look at the sample sentences in Moffatt's essay. Why does he include them? How do they help him make his argument? Be prepared to discuss your assessment with the class or to submit your comments in writing, as your instructor directs.

7. If you have read Lloyd Bitzer's 'The Rhetorical Situation', what similarities do you see between Bitzer's concept of the 'situatedness' of communication and Moffatt's treatment of language? What do these similarities tell you about the nature of communication? Write your analysis in a short memo report addressed to your instructor.

Writing Samples for Discussion and Analysis

The following real examples contain weaknesses similar to those we've discussed above. As you read, look for ways in which each could have been improved. Ask yourself whether the writer in each case has attended to content and relation, established credibility and professionalism, and developed an understandable, clear message. Identify any ways in which the writers violate the Seven Cs. What is your impression of each? Be prepared to discuss the flaws in each example and to offer suggestions as to how to correct them. If your instructor asks you to do so, edit the samples to improve their ethos, clarity of content, and audience relation.

Writing Sample #1

Park Estates Development Inc
Your Home is Our Business

25 April 2003
Mr. Bob Loblaw, MPP
2345 Eglinton Avenue, East
Toronto, Ontario M3R 5T6

   Dear Bob,

   Hi, You don't know me but Thanks for an insightful and interesting speech this afternoon at the Bakery Road - Service Club whose guest I was of John Cookman of the American BAnk of Canada at Pope and Lottery Avenue.

   As I listened to some of the questions especially Development that were directed at you after your speech, the thought occured to me to ask about this issue which is herewith included and alarmed me when I first read about it recently. An excerpt from Harold Blossomb's April Fool Edition of the Saturday World.

   I could not remember all the details at the time during the luncheon speech you were making, but I do remember tearing this section of the leftover World while I patiently awaited a haircut the other day at the Pickborough Mall, and the thought still remained to whom could I take this issue if in fact there was any truth to it!!

   Although I work in a field directly related to Devlopment, Construction, the imediate thoughts that go through ones mind when reading something like this. First of all every once and awhile I personally enjoy using our national parks and especially in the summer they make good picnic grounds for large clubs and family outings and company gatherings and personally in my opinion I would not like to see even one of these wonderful natural resources tampered with in any negative way!

   The second thing is I very much respect your 'Lowly Politicians Job' as you so aptly put it but hope you will continue to carry on the superb responsibilities you have so admirably taken on that I am wondering why you would not be seriously interested in being willing to take over where Mr. Harrass is leaving off? I hope you would be willing to answer these questions either personally or or a province wide level-entirely your choice!

                                             Thanks Again.
                                             Yours Professionally,

---

Figure 3.1:   If you were Mr. Loblaw, what would you make of this letter? Has this writer established credibility? Is he respectful of his audience? Is his message clear? If not, why not?

Writing sample #2

2419 LeRoy St
Truro, Nova Scotia B2S 6M7

February 10 2010

Dear Sir or Madam:

Re: Summer Student Position

Based on the qualifications listed in your posting I am the person you are looking for.

I am currently in my third year of college. During my time in school I have aquired many assets including multi-tasking, time management, and inter-personal skills. Scholastically I have gained valuable knowledge, both technical and practical. I have taken multiple classes designed to simulate real situations in the working world.

Through previous work experience I have shown that I can responsibly work indpeendently or as part of a group. By applying my skills in past experiences, I have been able to achieve most of my goals.

I feel that I am a strong candidate for the position of summer student. Both my technical and practical knowledge in combination with my experiences make me an ideal employee. I invite you to call if you have further questions or wish to arrange a meeting. Feel free to contact me at (902) 353-7865 or by e-mail at <ron.boyle @cenmar.u.ca>. Thank you for your time and considering my application.

Sincerly

Ron Boyle

Figure 3.2: How persuasive is Ron's letter of application? How effectively has he considered the reader's needs and expectations? Does his letter observe the Seven Cs of professional communication? Is he likely to be called for an interview? Why or why not?

Chapter 4

Ethics in Professional Communication

Learning Objectives

■ To understand the role and importance of ethics in effective professional communication.

■ To distinguish between a code of ethics and a code of conduct.

■ To learn and apply the Communication Code of Ethics.

■ To understand the practical implications of ethical communication.

Our actions and our messages frequently can have a substantial impact on others, influencing them in sometimes profound ways. Through the messages we create, we have the power to affect the interests and well-being of others, their choices and their actions, their understanding of their professional role and relationships. It is this potential to influence, shape, and constrain the experience and behaviour of other people that introduces a special level of ethical responsibility into the study and practice of professional communication.

Like other human choices and actions, professional communication is shaped by a host of influences and considerations, among them scientific validity, professionalism, public welfare, factual accuracy, and truthfulness. Our choices as we communicate in a professional context are also affected, both consciously and unconsciously, by more personal factors, including self-interest, security concerns, status, power politics, **face**, and commitment to a particular way of doing things. They can even be influenced by feelings of pride, affection, greed, or fear. As a result of these influences, professional communication, like any other form of human interaction, can be honest or dishonest; it can be helpful or harmful; it can be ethical or unethical.

The link between **ethics** and communication has been understood at least since Aristotle, who insisted that the study of communication, and particularly of persuasion, could best be understood as a form of ethical studies (Aristotle, 1954).[1] In fact, the word 'ethics' is derived from the same source as Aristotle's concept of **ethos**, or public character (Halloran, 1982). Contemporary communication scholars have also recognized how important ethics is in technical communication practice, as well as its role in how we understand the functions of technical communication, how we assess its **effectiveness** in fulfilling its purpose, and how we manage its impacts on its human audiences. As Paul Dombrowski observes, confirming Axiom #3, technical communication 'is intertwined in its social context', a context that includes people, society, and a range of assumed values that govern what is viewed as 'right and good' (2000: ix). As soon as we communicate with others at all, and particularly when we use our speech and writing to guide others, to advise them, to persuade or influence them, to shape their behaviour and their understanding, we are inevitably in the realm of ethical decision-making.

What Is Ethics?

Ethics refers to the process by which we choose between right and wrong, between competing 'goods', between self-preservation and the possibility of harm to others. Ethical principles are the precepts or values that guide our actions—the foundation upon which we make decisions and choose how we will respond in a certain situation, and in particular, how we treat others.

For many of us, the word 'ethics' still carries some of the flavour of the original meaning of *ethos*; for example, we still recognize ethical behaviour as a key component of good character (Kilpatrick, 1992). As it's used now, the word 'ethics' has at least two distinct, though related, meanings, both of which retain a clear relationship to its Greek origins.

First, 'ethics' refers to a branch of academic study that concentrates on understanding exactly how people make decisions between right and wrong, on how we choose between two conflicting values, and on how deeply-held principles actually guide our choices and our actions. Although this kind of academic study is usually thought of as a specialization within philosophy or theology, it may also be carried out in the context of specific professions, such as law, medicine, engineering, or business. In these contexts, ethicists not only study values and their sources, but also conduct analyses of various cases to identify the pertinent issues that shape decision-making in particular fields and situations (see Sommerville, 2002).

The word 'ethics' is also used in a second, more practical or applied sense. In addition to referring to the formal study of the way people reason and choose between right and wrong, 'ethics' also refers to the systems of values or principles that we have evolved to help us make reasonable and effective choices as we live, work, and socialize with other people. Codes of ethics articulate these principles explicitly, as guides to help us assess and respond to the situations that we encounter, and in particular to guide us in our treatment of other people. To act ethically is to act responsibly and with good judgement, taking into account not only our own wants, but also the needs and the autonomy of others, as well as the obligations we may have to our own character, to our families, to our employers, to our profession, or to our community. To act ethically is to respect and interact with other people not as objects to be dismissed or manipulated for our own benefit, but as beings whose interests must be considered. Ethical systems, even ethical codes specific to professions, have evolved to help us to make decisions in keeping with this fundamental principle of respect and consideration for the interests of others.

It is important to understand that individuals do not invent their own ethical codes, nor are ethical codes ever exclusively 'personal'. Although each of us is free to evaluate and respond to situations using our own judgement and values, ethics is not simply a matter of doing what you feel like. It is also not a matter of expediency or convenience or social conformity or self-gratification.[2] From time to time we are all subject to motives like these, but the fact that they play a part in why we do what we do does *not* make them part of an ethical process. Instead, true ethical decision-making is a thoughtful, **deliberative** process and not an automatic, accidental, or unintentional outcome of serving our own self-interest.

Although people may exercise individual choice and act according to personal conscience, ethical systems do not originate with individuals. Instead, codes of ethics are always social or communal in origin, and typically find their justification in some authority beyond the individual: the authority of religious belief; the wisdom of a distinguished moral leader such as Buddha, Jesus, the Dalai Lama, or Mohammed; the sanction of society; the traditions of a culture; the collective experience of a profession. Thus, while our interactions with others at all levels are shaped by cultural norms and religious beliefs, by social custom, by family tradition, by law, by church doctrine, by the code of a profession, and even by standards of conduct within a given workplace, all ethical systems have a strong collective component; they are based on interests broader than those of the individual, and are not simply a matter of personal whim.[3] Instead, ethical practice in all contexts invites us to transcend our individual wants and to take into account interests beyond our own.

A sense of appropriateness, of right and wrong, of ethical conduct, permeates all human interaction, whether it occurs in the workplace or in social situations. For example, consider two of the theoretical constructs we learned in Chapter 1: both the **Nine Axioms** of Communication and Aristotle's rhetorical triangle implicitly assume a **code of ethics**; both have at their centre an emphasis on respect for others. Similarly, the notion of **rhetorical balance** advanced by Wayne Booth (see page 44) and the theory of the **rhetorical situation** articulated by Lloyd Bitzer (see page 17) also assume a level of ethical responsibility on the part of a communicator who must devise a 'fitting' response to the situation and achieve an 'appropriate' balance in constructing the message. An ethical code is implied, too, by Erving Goffman's (1959, 1967) theory of face, also discussed in Chapter 1. In fact, Goffman's study of face behaviour is in many respects a study of unspoken ethical codes that seem to transcend all cultures.

Most professions, too, have developed explicit codes of ethics to guide their members in carrying out their responsibilities;[4] many organizations, including universities,[5] provide codes of conduct for their members that implicitly assume an ethical standard.

Some Universal Ethical Principles

Interestingly, although there are variations in the specific precepts of different ethical systems, there are some universal principles that they all seem to share. At the heart of all ethical codes is some form of the principle that we have been calling respect: regard and honour for others with whom we interact. This principle of respect for others permeates all ethical codes, including those of the professions, and can be seen in the celebrated Confucian principle known as the **golden rule**, which is most frequently stated as 'do unto others as you would have them do unto you'. The best-known and longest-standing code of professional ethics, the **Hippocratic oath** of physicians, implicitly embodies this same principle of respect in its admonition to 'first, do no harm'.

A **code of ethics** is not a cookie-cutter recipe for how to act. A true code of ethics (as opposed to a **code of conduct**) is meant to assist, and not replace, human assessment and choice. Its purpose is not to directly regulate behaviour, but to provide a foundation for thoughtfully evaluating and judging the situations in which we must act. As the ethicist Andrew Olson explains, the purpose of a code of ethics is not to tell us what to do, but to give us a foundation for deciding for ourselves what we must or should do. According to Olson, 'a code of ethics increases ethical sensitivity and judgement, strengthens support for individuals' moral courage, and helps to hone an organization's sense of identity' (Olson, n.d.).

By contrast, a code of conduct attempts to regulate behaviour directly, usually by prohibiting or 'outlawing' certain specific actions. An example of a code of conduct might be the 'pool rules' posted by the local condo association.

Box 4.1   General Pool Rules

- Everyone who enters the pool facility must pay an entrance fee.
- Swimmers must shower before entering the pool.
- Conversation with the lifeguards should be limited. Please refer questions and concerns to the staff in the office. Patrons will not obstruct the lifeguards' view.
- Groups of 20+ need prior approval to attend recreation swim at least two weekdays in advance.
- Aluminum lawn chairs are permitted on the lawn area.
- The pool may close due to inclement weather.

- All patrons will comply with the directions of the Lifeguards and Aquatics Staff. Failure to comply will result in dismissal from the facility.
- Food and drink are not permitted in the facility.
- Clear plastic water bottles containing water are okay. Coolers may contain only water and are subject to inspection.
- Children must be 48" tall to ride the slide. NO exceptions.

Unlike a code of conduct, a code of ethics is not a list of regulations. Instead, it provides guidelines rather than specific rules, and leaves to the individual the ultimate responsibility for choosing how to act. Because the situations in which we have to make judgements are not always clear-cut, because they are not entirely predictable, and because each is unique, we must draw on our understanding to make choices that will best fulfill our obligations to our listeners, our messages, and ourselves. A code of ethics is intended to help us do that.

Professional Codes of Ethics

Many professions have developed codes of behaviour by which their members are bound. Some of these are closer to a code of conduct than to a code of ethics, since they address specific actions that must be performed or avoided, while others are true codes of ethics, providing general principles to guide decision-making.

If you study the codes of a number of professions and organizations, you will be initially struck by the range of variation in the specific details each addresses. However, despite their outward variations, the majority of such codes share striking similarities.

Box 4.2   Two Features of Professional Codes of Ethics

- A sense of obligation or responsibility
- Regard for the sanctity of human life and autonomy

Two features in particular stand out: first, professional codes of ethics focus not on the benefits to individual practitioners, but on the obligations and responsibilities of practitioners to those they serve, to society, to the profession or organization of which they are a part, or to some other higher good. In a study of professional codes of ethics, Cristina Sewerin (2004) notes that responsibility to the public is the primary component of professionalism, and explains that 'a key role of licensure and of licensing bodies is to set across-the-board standards on which the public can rely.'

The language of the codes themselves typically emphasizes service, focusing on values like duty, responsibility, or obligation. Sewerin, for example, points to the Canadian Medical Association's emphasis on 'the ethic of service' as a 'key feature of medical professionalism', and observes that '[t]wo relationships are considered crucial: the relationship between a physician and a patient, and the social contract between physicians and society.' Like the CMA, the Canadian Council of Professional Engineers also takes seriously 'the overriding duty to serve and protect the public interest' (Sewerin, 2004), and their code of ethics reflects that fact. First among the values articulated in the code is the principle that engineers must 'hold paramount the safety, health and welfare of the public and the protection of the environment and promote health and safety within the workplace'. They are also admonished to 'conduct themselves with fairness, courtesy and good faith towards clients, colleagues and others, give credit where it is due, and accept, as well as give, honest and fair professional criticism' (Canadian Council of Professional Engineers, n.d.).

But it's not just in medical and engineering codes of professional ethics that duty and service are emphasized. Ethical codes in virtually every profession, from accountancy to nursing, from veterinary medicine to university teaching, emphasize responsibility to a public and to the profession itself. The following excerpt from the Statement of Professional Ethics of the American Association of University Teachers is a typical example:

> As teachers, professors encourage the free pursuit of learning in their students. They hold before them the best scholarly and ethical standards of their discipline. Professors demonstrate respect for students as individuals and adhere to their proper roles as intellectual guides and counsellors. Professors make every reasonable effort to foster honest academic conduct and to ensure that their evaluations of students reflect each student's true merit. They respect the confidential nature of the relationship between professor and student. They avoid any exploitation, harassment, or discriminatory treatment of students. They acknowledge significant academic or scholarly assistance from them. They protect their academic freedom. (American Association of University Teachers, 1987)[6]

Similarly, the Purchasing Management Association of Canada's (PMAC) code of ethics emphasizes several core values, including:

- 'Honesty/Integrity', which is defined as 'Maintaining an unimpeachable standard of integrity in all their business relationships both inside and outside the organizations in which they are employed';
- 'Professionalism', described as 'Fostering the highest standards of professional competence amongst those for whom they are responsible'; and
- 'Serving the Public Interest', elaborated as 'Not using their authority of office for personal benefit, rejecting and denouncing any business practice that is improper'. (PMAC, n.d.)

The American Society of Agronomy defines the concept of professionalism as a form of ethical responsibility, noting that 'the privilege of professional practice imposes obligations of responsibility as well as professional knowledge' (American Society of Agronomy, n.d.). Interestingly, most of the precepts given in this document emphasize responsible communication as the key to professional conduct.

Finally, even librarians, whose profession would seem to involve limited interaction with the public, describe their profession in terms of 'an obligation to maintain ethical standards of behaviour in relation to the governing authority under which they work, to the library constituency, to the library as an institution and to fellow workers on the staff, to other members of the library profession, and to society in general' (American Library Association, 1939).

The second important feature of all ethical codes, including those of the professions, is respect for others: regard for human life, concern for public safety, and recognition of individual liberty. While these values are not always explicitly stated in the codes of professional ethics, they are always assumed to underlie the precepts that are stated. Thus, in addition to their emphasis on service and social obligation, ethical codes take for granted that human life, and the interests of individual human beings, are innately worthy of our consideration as we make decisions that might affect their well-being.

A Communication Code of Ethics

Like other forms of ethical conduct, ethical communication involves genuine regard for your audience. It also involves respect for the other components of interaction: a sincere commitment to what you are saying and authentic respect for your own integrity. We communicate ethically when we choose a course of action that limits the unnecessary harm done to others; when we take responsibility for our choices and actions; and when we do not knowingly deceive or misrepresent facts, beliefs, or actions. While you may not always be able to achieve these ideals, you should strive as far as possible to fulfill them in all of your communication with others.

The ethical principles of communication—credibility, sincerity, and integrity—are anchored in the participatory process of building connections with other people. Let's consider the three principles of our ethical code in greater detail, along with examples of how they might translate into specific behaviour.

Box 4.3   A Communications Code of Ethics

1. I will take responsibility for my words and my actions.
2. I will take care not to misrepresent myself or my message.
3. I will avoid unnecessary hurt to others by my words or my tone.

---

1. I will take responsibility for my words and my actions.

I will acknowledge and honour my obligation to stand behind my words. I will do my best to ensure the validity of my interpretations. I will not present interpretations and judgements as if they are simple reports. I will keep my word. If I do not know the answer to a question, I will acknowledge it rather than trying to bluff my way through. I will focus on accommodating others' need for understanding, information, and support before indulging my own need for self-expression. I will hold myself responsible for how well someone else understands my message. When I am wrong, I will admit it. If an **apology** is owed, I will apologize, sincerely and with good grace. I will not divulge things said to me in confidence. I will offer advice only when it is asked for. I will do my best to listen genuinely in the spirit of understanding. I will keep in mind that my assessments are provisional and can be altered by subsequent information. I will try to recognize and defuse defensive reactions before conflict escalates.

2. I will take care not to misrepresent myself or my message.

I will strive to communicate clearly, simply, and tactfully. I will not pretend to be something I am not. I will not assume authority that I do not legitimately merit or claim expertise that I do not possess. I will choose my words with care and precision. I will not distort or misrepresent issues in order to win a point. I will label inferences and judgements as such, and not present them as fact. I will present my thoughts in my own language, and will not present the ideas or thoughts of others as though they are my own. I will know the source of information that I use, and I will be able to explain how and why it is credible. I will recommend to others only actions that I have myself taken, or genuinely would take. I will not make promises I cannot keep. I will pay attention to what I may be communicating nonverbally.

3. I will avoid unnecessary hurt to others by my words or tone.

I will respect others as autonomous human beings and treat them with courtesy. I will assume good will on the part of others, and act with good will in return. I will listen to others as carefully as I expect them to listen to me. I will treat others as I would like to be treated in their place. I will follow through on my promises to others. I will avoid causing face loss to others, and will give face when necessary. I will make reasonable requests. If I must criticize others, I will speak with tact and generosity of attitude. Where an apology is due, I will apologize to others genuinely and sincerely. I will accept with good grace the sincere apologies of others. I will avoid repeating unfounded gossip. If a conflict arises, I will do my best to avoid escalating it. I will try not to say things in anger that I may later regret.

Ethics in Practice: Civility

Even though we cannot always fully accommodate the needs of others, we nevertheless have a fundamental obligation to behave in ways that respect their face needs and their autonomy (Goffman, 1967: 5). For various reasons, however, people sometimes behave in ways that violate their ethical obligations to those around them. Disregard of others' interests may be unintentional, such as when an attempt to save face for ourselves inadvertently causes someone else to lose face, or it may be the product of deliberate acts of disrespect or hostility, such as the desecrating of the local mosque in the wake of 9/11. It may be a minor infraction, as when the clerk in the registrar's office places policy above the needs of the person standing in front of her, or it may be an action bordering on the criminal, as when someone is made the victim of a hate crime.

It's relatively simple for most of us to recognize ethical failures when they take place on a large scale of social and political action. We easily reject and condemn policies that dehumanize and treat others as objects rather than people, such as, for instance, race-based immigration policies or mass-sterilization of the mentally challenged.[7]

What may be less obvious is that the small-scale incivilities that occur in many workplaces are also forms of dehumanization. When a supervisor reams out an employee in front of other workers; when a member of the project team refuses to pitch in on a task because it's 'not in his job description'; when a student hands in work completed by someone else; when a bully humiliates a victim in the cafeteria at school—all of these are examples, on a small, individual scale, of the ways we routinely disrespect and objectify each other and disregard each other's face needs.

Civility is behaviour that displays fundamental respect for others' well-being. It is more than mere politeness; instead, it requires a genuine commitment to collegiality and a cooperative self-restraint (Burgess and Burgess, 1997). According to civility expert P.M. Forni (2003): 'We are civil when we believe that other people's claim to comfort and happiness is as valid as our own, and we back up belief with action.' In other words, civility is the golden rule applied in our everyday interaction.

Unfortunately, however, many experts believe that there has been a general erosion of civility in everyday life and in the workplace (Jacoby, 1999; Truss, 2005), a fact that has led to an increase in abusive, confrontational behaviour (Keashly, Trott, and MacLean, 1994; Shaw, 1998), which in turn contributes to employee stress and lost productivity that are estimated to cost Canadian businesses millions of dollars annually (Centre for Suicide Prevention, 2000; Urbanski, 2002; BBC News, 2005; Scott, 2006; McCormick, 2007).

Most of us don't set out to offend others, to treat them as objects, to dehumanize them or cause them to lose face. However, in many ways our contemporary lives encourage depersonalization, either for the sake of **efficiency** and objectivity, or because of a faulty conception of fairness that mistakes uniformity for equality or professionalism. For instance, you apply for a job, and the employer insists that everyone fill out an identical form rather than considering résumés on a case-by-case basis. You are not granted an interview, and instead of a personalized rejection, you are sent a form letter. Worse, perhaps you receive no acknowledgement at all, since 'only those who are selected for an interview will be contacted.'

You telephone the university, and get caught up in a voice-mail system that never connects you to another human being. You get into a disagreement with a colleague in a meeting, and when you return to your desk you discover he has flamed you by e-mail. When you go to lunch, you have to wait in line at the single open cash, even though there are three clerks chatting idly nearby. You go for some routine medical tests and find yourself standing at the check-in for 15 minutes while the admitting nurse who is right across the counter ignores you completely and continues to type on her computer. You answer the phone when you arrive home after a long day, only to be confronted with a telemarketer who reads a canned spiel that doesn't even pretend to take into account that either of you is a human being.

Such aggravations are familiar to all of us as the stuff of contemporary life; in fact, most of us have become more or less resigned to such impersonal treatment. After all, we understand the pressures of too much work, too fast a pace, too many things to get done and too little time. Good manners are a dispensable luxury, and besides, it's just too much work to interact meaningfully with everyone we come into contact with. Isn't it?

There is much evidence to suggest that making the effort to be civil is worth it. An uncivil workplace is not simply a harmless annoyance; it is costly, not only in dollar terms but in productivity, job satisfaction, and employee health. The increasing depersonalization in public interaction generally, and especially in the workplace, is known to have a number of negative effects on individuals (Forni, 2002; Jarecke and Plant, 2006), including an upswing in stress-related mental health issues (Freeman, n.d.; Valle, n.d.; Cairney, 2003; Ambert, 2007). Seemingly innocuous examples like the ones above contribute to workplace stress and to a decline in professionalism (Durham, 2007), as well as to the erosion of public civility and communal identity (Spanier, 2000; Gandhi, 2007; *Montreal Gazette*, 2007).

Clearly, then, if we are to communicate successfully, we need to take care of the quality of relation that our messages establish and maintain. Our professional messages always contribute to some form of relation, and we will all be better served if that relation is positive and rewarding; as a result, we should strive to behave respectfully toward each other, in small ways and large. The practice of treating others as we would like to be treated, familiar to us from the golden rule, is known as the '**ethic of reciprocity**' (Mitchell, 2003), and is one of the markers of professionalism.

To help us negotiate the risks inherent in interaction, and to assist us in according to others the appropriate levels of respect, most cultures have evolved unspoken standards or codes of politeness (Brown and Levinson, 1987). More explicitly formulated behavioural rules, known as **etiquette**, provide guidelines for everything from how to write a thank you letter to how to make introductions (see Post, 2004). Although most of us associate the concept of etiquette with social situations, there is a longstanding tradition of advice-giving that deals with how to conduct oneself in a professional context (see, for example, Carnegie and Associates, 1995; Casperson, 1999; Bixler and Dugan, 2000; Greene and Burleson, 2003; Whitmore, 2005).

The rules of etiquette are not the equivalent of an ethical system, since they offer specific regulations for behaviour, often in the form of 'dos' and 'don'ts'; some of these precepts can even be overly picky, even arbitrary. However, despite these quibbles, in general the purpose of etiquette guidelines is to help preserve a minimum level of civility in how we behave to each other. The specific behaviour itself is not as important as the underlying attitude of mutual respect and professionalism that it represents.

The display of mutuality and respect is just as important in our day-to-day interactions with colleagues, clients, and the public as it is in written messages such as reports and correspondence, or in more formal interactions like interviews and public presentations. The following discussion provides some suggestions for establishing and maintaining civility in our encounters with colleagues, clients, and supervisors in the workplace.

Civility in face-to-face interaction

Respect for professional colleagues is a matter, in part, of understanding and observing personal boundaries and autonomy. Even in a relatively 'open' workplace, each of us needs a degree of privacy and personal space, a sense of appropriate distance and formality, and the authority to make choices about how 'close' someone else can get, both in terms of physical proximity and in terms of social intimacy.

While most of us recognize the inappropriateness of overtly aggressive behaviour, such as shouting or swearing at a co-worker, issuing threats, physically pushing another, or interfering with another's property, we may be less aware of the damaging impact of inconsiderate behaviour, such as borrowing someone's belongings without permission, leaving dirty dishes lying around the lunch room, gossiping, playing loud music that can be heard outside your space, taking the last cup of coffee without making a new pot, and dozens of other acts that betray a lack of concern for others (Holmvall and Francis, 2007). Respectful professional behaviour means acknowledging and appropriately honouring others' personal dignity, territorial needs, positional authority, organizational rank, experience, and seniority.

We live in a culture that encourages easy familiarity, and that stresses notions of egalitarianism and self-esteem, sometimes at the expense of professional and personal boundaries (Glossop, 2002). We communicate more and more through electronic media, which distance us from the immediate impact of our words on others and thus encourage depersonalization. For the past several decades, employee workloads have escalated, leaving us with little energy or time to behave considerately to others. Whatever the reasons, researchers argue that incivility is on the rise (Cortina, Magley, Williams, and Langhout, 2001; Harvey and Keashly, 2005; Truss, 2005), with potentially disastrous consequences to both individuals and organizations.

Perhaps not surprisingly, contemporary employers frequently observe that new graduates do not always know how to interact in the workplace, and especially how to behave respectfully to co-workers, particularly to those who are senior to them in age or experience. To the employers, this inability to interact effectively represents a failure of professionalism that can have serious implications for a junior employee's career prospects.

Recognizing others' boundaries is an essential part of demonstrating appropriate respect. Consider the case of Barbara, who was one of three junior consultants hired a year ago in the training and development division of Dolovich and Cowan. During their first week with the company, a senior colleague, Bruce, extended the hand of friendship and offered to show the new people the ropes. True to his word, Bruce toured Barbara and the others around the office complex and introduced them to other staff. He emphasized the collegial environment of the unit, and explained the group's tradition of offering coaching and support for new employees. Bruce explained how the whole group is invested in each other's success, and pointed out that they frequently collaborate on and share handout materials. He ended the tour by showing the new hires where to find the originals of existing handout materials and explaining the procedure for getting copies printed for their own workshops. On their way past his cubicle, Bruce explained his practice of preparing handouts in advance of his upcoming workshops, and pointed out his own stockpile of printed training materials.

Faced with organizing her first couple of workshops within two weeks of her arrival, Barbara found herself grateful for the materials the group had already developed. On the days of her workshops, she helped herself to the printed handouts from Bruce's filing cabinet, taking enough to supply her two groups of trainees. The sessions went off without a hitch, and Barbara was thrilled with her success.

Arriving at the office on a Monday morning a week later, however, she encountered a tense situation. It took a little while for Barbara to get the details, since Bruce never did raise the issue with the new hires, but the story circulating through the office grapevine was that Bruce's weekend training session for an important new group of high-profile clients had blown up. Apparently, when Bruce went to retrieve the handout materials he had had printed in advance for this important workshop, he discovered that his stockpile was nearly depleted. It was too late to do anything about the missing materials, and Bruce had to adjust his plan on the fly. As senior trainer, he was experienced enough to proceed without all the materials, but things were far from satisfactory. Though Bruce had hastily made photocopies of some of the handouts, the participants didn't have all of the necessary worksheets and supplementary materials, and in the end Bruce had to cut the whole workshop short, sending people on their way without the printed 'take-aways' that always accompany training events.

As a result, the workshop evaluations were very poor, and several of those who had travelled a long distance to attend were irritated enough to complain via e-mail to their own management, who in turn contacted Bruce's boss to say that they would not be requiring any further training from the department.

Bruce never did figure out for sure who had raided his stash of materials, and Barbara was too embarrassed to admit she was the one who had done it. Bruce and several other members of the department started locking their filing cabinets, and though no one was ever overtly impolite to her or any of the other new hires, the camaraderie Barbara had anticipated never really materialized. Just short of a year on the job, Barbara left Dolovich and Cowan to take a job at another company.

Barbara now realizes that she misjudged her new situation in several ways. For example, while the members of the department freely shared their originals, each trainer was responsible for arranging to get handouts printed for her own workshops. Barbara ignored this basic principle of civility when she helped herself to Bruce's printed handouts, without his permission and even without his knowledge. She erred even further when she neglected to order replacements to replenish the stash.

Finally, as soon as she realized her mistake, Barbara should have apologized, and she should have offered to explain her mistake to their manager who had received complaints from Bruce's trainees. Instead, Barbara took no responsibility for the loss of face she had caused to Bruce, and had remained silent in the hope that the situation would simply resolve itself. As a result, she inadvertently created a sense of distrust with her new colleagues, and her actions compromised the open sharing that had previously been the norm in the department.

Recognizing and honouring others' boundaries is symbolized not only by how we acknowledge physical space and property, but also by how we speak to each other. Contemporary culture encourages us to address everyone on a first-name basis, whether we have been invited to or not. Telemarketers address their targets by first name; wait staff introduce themselves to restaurant diners as familiarly as though they are guests at the table; checkout clerks are encouraged to refer to customers by name. Receptionists in medical offices routinely call patients, including those much older than themselves, by first names; physicians do the same (though you may note that they are careful to insist on using their own titles in conversation with those same patients). This phenomenon of '**fake personalization**' may be intended to suggest human connectedness, but as the psychoanalyst and sociologist Hendrik Ruitenbeek (1965) has pointed out, it actually is a sign of incivility, since it so clearly emphasizes the extent to which our culture has lost its 'real regard for persons' (98).

Despite this pervasive cult of familiarity, there are still those who prefer to set a slightly more formal tone in their work and business dealings. For example, the president of the company may be 'Jerry' to his contemporaries and long-time associates, but may nevertheless expect the new hire to address him as 'Mr. Purcell', at least until they are better acquainted. While you are usually safe to address your immediate colleagues by first name without being invited to do so, you should consider using surname and title when addressing those senior to you in rank, status, experience, or age, unless or until they invite you to call them by their first names.

University and college students are sometimes uncertain how to address or refer to their professors, particularly since some professors prefer the formality of surnames and titles, while others encourage students to call them by their first names. As in the workplace, it's more respectful and more considerate to opt for formality in a situation where expectations are unclear. Even if you happen to know your professor's first name, even if you have heard other students use it, and even if you are on a first-name basis with other professors, you should not call a professor by first name unless you have been explicitly invited to do so. If you are uncertain as to what honorific is appropriate, 'Professor' plus the surname is the safest bet for both female and male professors.

Receiving clients with civility

All organizations involve face-to-face contact at some level between clients and company representatives. In some businesses or organizations, drop-in service is a normal part of the working day, and whatever your position, you may occasionally find yourself the first point of contact between a client and your company.

Even if reception isn't your primary job, you should consider it part of your responsibility to make your clients feel valued and welcomed. If you happen to be at a reception desk or front counter when the client enters, greet the person promptly in a pleasant and professional manner. If receiving clients is part of your job, make eye contact as soon as the client approaches you, and smile. Ask 'How can I help you?' or 'May I help you?'

No matter how important your other tasks may be, never leave an unacknowledged client standing at the counter or reception area while you take care of filing, telephone calls, or other administrative details. If you are genuinely busy with a task that must be completed immediately, take a moment to acknowledge the client and say 'I'll be right with you' or 'Someone will be with you in a moment.' If it is appropriate, ask the person to have a seat, and offer coffee if there is some available.

Finally, you should never ignore or interrupt a person who is standing in front of you in order to take a call. If answering the telephone is part of your job, excuse yourself politely and do so, but put the caller on hold until you have completed your business with the human being in front of you. A person who has taken the trouble to meet with you personally should always take precedence over one who contacts you by telephone.

Handling face-to-face complaints

If you interact with clients in any capacity, you will from time to time find yourself dealing with someone who is disgruntled, frustrated, or angry with your company or its service. People who have been inconvenienced, who have a legitimate gripe about your products and service, who have been waiting a long time to speak to someone in authority, or who are just plain frazzled or annoyed may take their feelings out on the nearest representative of the company. If that's you, as it may occasionally be, you will need to have some skills for dealing with grumpy or frustrated people.

It is normal to respond to someone else's rudeness by being rude in return. However, as you know by now, responding in kind will only aggravate the situation for both you and the client. Furthermore, the memory of the unpleasantness will remain even after the content of the exchange is forgotten, and may sour your relationship with the client or with their organization.

The most important principle is to try to maintain your cool and be pleasant even when others are rude. Try not to take the client's frustration personally, and try your best to put yourself in the other person's position. Keep in mind that there's nearly always some good reason for the person's frustration; try to understand why the person is feeling upset. Remember that, though you may not be able to resolve the situation, you could well inflame it if you respond rudely to someone who has been curt to you.

Most angry people simply want to feel that their concerns are being heard, and are able to be reasonable once they've had a chance to calm down. Listen attentively; even if the client's position initially seems unreasonable, remember that the feelings of frustration and anger are genuine (and often legitimate). An upset client is unlikely to cooperate in finding a resolution to a difficulty; someone whose interests have been acknowledged is more likely to be interested in finding a reasonable compromise. If you can remain calm and respond with genuine concern, you can usually keep a difficult situation from escalating and becoming impossible; you may even be able to resolve the problems and preserve the client relationship.

Civility in telephone communication

Even in this age of e-mail, business is still frequently conducted via telephone. Nearly everyone these days carries a cell phone, and almost all of us are accessible at all hours to professional and business contacts. However, the ubiquity of telephones doesn't always mean that people know how to conduct their business in a respectful and civil manner. While some of the following principles may seem like 'common sense', it is surprising how often these basic manners are violated, both by callers and by those who are answering the phone.

Placing a call

If you are placing a call to someone, be sure to let the phone ring long enough for the person to reach it if she doesn't happen to be standing beside her desk when it rings. Nothing is more frustrating than to have to run from the photocopy room or the next office, only to have the person hang up on the second ring before you can hope to reach the instrument. Cell phones may take a few minutes to extract from a pocket or case, or may require that a person driving a car pull over before answering.

Identify yourself by name before proceeding to your business. Someone answering the telephone has a right to know right away to whom he is speaking. When the person answers the telephone, clearly identify yourself, by name and title, state the name of the company or firm you represent, and briefly explain the purpose of your call. Do this first, and in a pleasant tone, before asking 'How are you?' or otherwise exchanging greetings. Even if you are telephoning someone you know, you should still say who is calling. A delay in identifying yourself can cause the recipient of the call to respond defensively or even to hang up.

When you telephone someone else, never begin the interaction by asking 'Who is this?' Expecting the recipient of a call to identify herself by name to an unknown caller is simply rude, and invites rudeness in return. As the caller, you should know whom you called; identify *yourself* first, and then ask by name for the person you wish to speak with.

Remember that the people you are speaking to have other duties to take care of. Unless you are calling a help line or customer service desk where the person's main job is to answer the telephone, an unexpected telephone call is *always* an interruption to the person who has answered; do not automatically assume that the person can take time to respond immediately to your questions. Always ask if the person has time to speak with you; if he is busy, offer to call back when it is more convenient. If the person is free to take your call, respect the fact that you are encroaching on that individual's work time. Make your business calls brief and avoid detaining people for too long on the phone.

As a general rule, you should avoid telephoning people on business when they are at home. If you must make a business-related call to someone at home, you should consider that you are not only imposing on her personal time, but in a sense you are also invading her privacy. Acknowledge the intrusion and offer your apology; even if the person welcomes the call, your polite recognition of the interruption will be appreciated.

If you must leave a message on an answering machine or voice mail, leave a short, business-like message, stating your name and contact number clearly and distinctly so that the person hearing the message can get it down in one pass. Repeat your name and number at the end of the message to assist the recipient in recording them correctly. If you realize that you have mistakenly dialled the wrong number, do not hang up without speaking. Instead, politely apologize and terminate the call.

Receiving a call

In telephone calls, as in writing, your priority should be to maintain both a respectful, polite tone and good will. Being polite over the phone doesn't take a lot of effort, but it can be a very important element in an overall professional demeanour.

Try to establish a policy of handling all your calls during the same period each day, if your schedule allows. Let your contacts know you'll be available to take calls during that time, and make it a practice to return all your calls in that time period. If you can establish this routine, your colleagues will get to know the best time to phone you, and you will be able to keep telephone interruptions to a minimum during the rest of the day.

Make a habit of answering the telephone politely. The tone of your voice can set the tone for the call. Try to cultivate a pleasant telephone manner, even if you aren't feeling particularly cheerful. Remember that the person on the other end will make inferences about your attitude and professionalism based on how you sound. Barking rudely into the phone is unlikely to represent your organization, or your own character, very positively.

If you happen to work in a setting where several people must share a phone, it is customary to answer by stating the name of your department or division, followed by your name: 'Research and Development, Brian Lau speaking' or 'Claims, Demetrice here' or 'Engineering, Wing Chiu'. You can answer your own extension in whatever manner you prefer, from a simple 'hello' to a more elaborate professional greeting that includes your name or title. One colleague answers the phone by crisply stating his last name: 'Tobias'. Another sets an entirely different tone by answering 'Hi, you've reached Special Undergraduate Programmes, this is Ken'. Still another says 'Good morning. Coordinator of Finance, Roxanne speaking'. Any of these is appropriate, and should accord with the conventions of your workplace and with your own manner and style.

You should never take calls while you are in a face-to-face meeting with someone else. Instead, turn off your cell phone and let your desk phone ring through to reception or voice mail. If you must pick up the instrument, explain briefly that you are engaged, and offer to return the call when you are available. Then do it.

Taking calls during classes, meetings, presentations, or performances is always rude. Leave your cell phone at home or turn it off for the duration of the event. If you are dealing with a crisis that entails taking an emergency call, such as a medical situation, you should probably not be present at the meeting or event in any case. If you must attend the event, but also must be available in case of emergency, set your phone to 'vibrate' so that it doesn't disturb anyone else, then quietly slip out of the room to answer the call. Otherwise, put your cell phone away and turn your attention to the event you are attending.

Never give out personal information, including your name, to a caller who has not self-identified. Instead, politely ask, 'Who is calling, please?' or 'Whom were you hoping to speak to?' Most people will immediately tell you who they are, but if you should encounter a caller who is reluctant to identify himself, or who uses cagey responses such as 'Don't you know who this is?' or 'It's a good friend of yours', politely respond 'I'm sorry, I don't recognize you', and terminate the call immediately.

While it is permissible to provide a caller with a colleague's work extension number, or to transfer a call directly to your colleague, you should *never* give out someone else's personal information—including a personal cell phone number, home phone number, or home address—without that person's explicit permission. Doing so could subject your co-worker to harassment, identity theft, or worse, and you or your company could be liable if something were to happen as a result of your disclosure. If a caller requests personal contact information for a colleague, offer to take the caller's name and number and pass it on to the person concerned. That way, if the request is legitimate, your colleague can make the choice to contact the individual.

Civility in e-mail correspondence

The many advantages of e-mail as a means of communication—its speed, its ease of use, and its cost-effectiveness—can sometimes blind us to its shortcomings when it comes to civility. In fact, the very things that make e-mail so useful can also make it prone to misunderstanding and relational disaster: because we can send information to someone without having to actually face the person or hear a human voice, it's easy to overlook the kinds of polite gestures we would normally employ in face-to-face or telephone interaction.

We are often admonished to keep our e-mail messages brief. In general, that's good advice, but unless brevity is tempered by courtesy, it can come off as unfriendly or even just plain rude. It's a good idea, therefore, to remember the human being on the other end of the interaction, and to build in some of the polite gestures we routinely employ in more traditional business correspondence, or in face-to-face encounters. Just as a letter begins with a salutation, an e-mail message should use a brief greeting and the person's name. It doesn't take much longer to type a friendly opener that personalizes the message for the recipient and establishes a human touch. If you're initiating contact with someone who doesn't know you, it's also polite to clearly state who you are and why you're writing to them; give your reader sufficient context to understand your message. Be sure to provide your complete contact information.

Just as you would in a letter, make use of the words 'please' and 'thank you' for favours requested or provided. These gestures serve to establish a level of civility by conveying respect and courtesy to the recipient. Remember also to close the message with some kind of sign-off, such as 'thanks very much' or 'sincerely', depending on how well you know the person. Sign with your full name.

When you are communicating by e-mail, pay attention to the little things: run your spell-checker. Proofread carefully and check your grammar. Don't write your messages without capitals or punctuation—reading such messages places an unreasonable burden on the recipient because the meanings are much more difficult to decipher. Don't send attachments to someone you don't know until after you have established initial contact and the person has signalled a willingness to receive them. When you do send attachments, make sure they are actually attached so that your reader doesn't have to send you another message in order to secure the documents you intended to send. Finally, AVOID WRITING YOUR MESSAGE IN ALL CAPS, which gives the unpleasant impression of shouting.

To some, e-mail may seem like a good way to avoid a face-to-face confrontation when contentious issues arise. Unfortunately, far from easing the tension, e-mail can often make things worse. It's all too easy, especially when we are angry, to dash off a message and hit send without pausing to reflect carefully on positioning, relation, wording, or tone. Without the added information provided by voice inflection, facial expression, gesture, and other nonverbal cues, we can easily misunderstand someone else's intention; it's also much more difficult to gauge the impact of our own words, which may come across more forcefully in writing.

The ability to respond quickly, afforded to us so readily by e-mail, is really a double-edged sword. Its swift pace can get things done more rapidly, but that same quickness can lead to mistakes and hurt feelings. Because so little time is required to create an e-mail, we can react hastily when our feelings are strongest, often without considering the long-term impact of our messages. In cases where we actually have to face the individual, or where we have to print out a letter, place it into an envelope, and walk it to the mailbox, we might have pause to hesitate and reconsider our reactions, but e-mail allows us to respond almost right away, often without having time to calm down or think things through. Many misunderstandings are created when we react too quickly without taking time to reflect, and unfortunately, once the message has been sent, there's no way to recall our ill-thought words.

If you have to deal with a contentious issue, consider first whether it would be better to speak to the person face to face. If doing so is logistically impossible (not just uncomfortable) and you must resort to e-mail, take the time to compose yourself before you write. Ask someone you trust to read and assess the tone of the message before you send it. Take the time to calm down and think carefully about the long-term implications of the message you're composing; does the issue really need to be addressed at all? If so, is your e-mail going to help resolve the problem, or will it inflame the situation unnecessarily? Every message we send either builds relation or destroys it, and while it might initially feel good to 'get this off your chest', will that 30 seconds of release be worth the long-term effects?

If you must confront a difficult issue via e-mail, you will need to be very careful to manage your tone effectively. Don't personalize the issue or insult the other person's character, work ethic, or personal habits. Give the person an opportunity to save face. Take responsibility for your part in the dynamic by explaining the effects of the situation on you. Do your best to create common ground, and ask for a shared solution.

The Ethics of Apology

No matter how much care we take with our communication, mistakes can happen: we may inadvertently cause hurt to someone else through a thoughtless act or word; we may misunderstand a situation and respond in a way that turns out to be ill-chosen; we may, in an attempt to save face for ourselves, cause someone else to lose face. In such situations, or in any case where someone else has suffered embarrassment, face loss, or hurt from our actions or words, we have the ethical obligation to apologize, sincerely and appropriately.

It may initially strike you as odd that an apology is regarded primarily as an ethical act; however, the three principles of the **Communication Code of Ethics** make clear why this is so. First, the willingness to apologize for hurt done to another, whether or not that injury was intentional and whether or not you were the cause of the damage, means that you must take full responsibility for the harm that someone else suffered. Apologizing requires you to place another's need for acknowledgement and reparation above your own need to defend yourself or save face. A genuine apology is an act of contrition that is full of risk because it makes you vulnerable.

Like many ethical actions, making an apology can also be difficult, in part because the act must take place in uncomfortable circumstances. Chances are that hard feelings have already been created and expressed, and that the person with whom you are communicating is feeling upset, disappointed, or angry. A sincere apology must acknowledge the legitimacy of those feelings and reactions, and take responsibility without criticism, qualification, or blame.

A sincere apology is also an ethically motivated act because it honours our obligation to avoid unnecessary harm to others. In this case, of course, some harm has already been done, but the act of contrition involved in an apology recognizes that inflicting damage upon others is wrong, and that a gesture of reparation for that harm must be made. Apologizing carries ethical responsibility because it is an attempt to put right what has gone wrong, and it takes upon ourselves the responsibility for doing so. A failure to apologize when an apology is warranted is unethical, both because it denies responsibility for the effects of your words and actions and because it escalates the harm done to another.

An apology must be sincerely given. An insincere apology not only will not repair the damage, but can actually further the harm done; it makes a mockery of your obligation to another, and ultimately misrepresents your own motives and interests. An apology is not simply saying the words 'I'm sorry', but meaning them and demonstrating a genuine commitment to making amends.

A sincere apology is also given with humility and an openness to further dialogue. This is something that Ram Dharmaratnam, a technician in a large research facility, has found difficult to master. Ram understands that apologies are sometimes required in a professional setting, and he's learned to say the words 'I'm sorry' when he has messed up. But Ram's apologies are not always well received, and he's had some trouble figuring out why that is.

Part of the problem is that Ram just can't bring himself to be genuinely humble; his apologies are often phrased in a way that appears to blame the other person. Recently, for instance, Ram was sent to retrieve a piece of specialized glassware from the lab next door to the one where he normally works. While chatting idly with the female technician, Ram absent-mindedly turned on the faucet in a nearby lab sink, spilling water into the beaker directly below. The other technician gasped. The beaker had contained a sensitive experiment that had been processing for several weeks; the senior researcher to whom it belonged had left it in the sink so it wouldn't be accidentally knocked over.

Ram had clearly violated accepted protocol, which was that you never touch or otherwise interfere with *anything* in someone else's lab. When he was called to account by the senior research chemist, Ram immediately responded with the following: 'I'm sorry for what happened, and it's my fault, but it wouldn't have happened if you hadn't left a sensitive experiment in the sink.' To Ram's surprise, the researcher seemed disinclined to accept his apology; when she asked whether he understood the standing protocol or its importance, or if he appreciated the gravity of his action, Ram declared, 'Look, I've already apologized, and I'm not going to say it again.'

Given what you know about communication, can you guess why Ram is having some difficulty in his professional relationships? First, the wording of Ram's original apology is problematic: it seems to shift responsibility for Ram's actions onto the senior chemist, a gambit which is unlikely to inspire either trust in his good will or faith in his competence.

Second, the researcher's request for a further explanation was a signal that Ram's gesture was incomplete; something more would be needed to re-establish the good will that was damaged by his action. But Ram seems to view the words 'I'm sorry' as a means of curtailing discussion, not an opportunity for further discussion and genuine understanding. Far from confirming Ram's professionalism, his defensive response was likely perceived by the senior researcher as defiance and insubordination. What do you think might be the outcome?

Does all of this mean that you cannot offer a sincere apology to someone with whom you still disagree? Certainly not. An apology is not necessarily about whether you agree on the facts of the case; instead, it is about how you handle the disagreement itself. What you are apologizing for is not disagreeing, but causing someone else to be hurt or to lose face or to be unnecessarily inconvenienced or embarrassed. You can, and should, find ways to disagree with someone's ideas without denigrating the person's judgement, intelligence, or humanity.

Because it is part of taking responsibility, the ability to apologize effectively is a key component of professionalism, as well as an important quality of leadership. An ethical professional is not someone who never makes errors in dealing with others, or who never hurts another's feelings. An ethical professional is someone who, when mistakes happen, acknowledges the hurt, takes responsibility for his or her own part in it, and takes responsibility for making it right. To apologize effectively, we must personally and sincerely express regret, and must recognize and take responsibility for the actual or potential pain, damage, or inconvenience that our words or actions may have caused to the other person.

In addition to being able to make an appropriate apology when one is warranted, an ethical professional is also willing to accept another's sincere gesture of apology. When the gesture is genuinely made, it is not only rude to refuse, but also an act of hostility, since such a refusal causes the other person to lose face, destroys trust, and escalates hard feelings. If the apology is sincere and genuinely given, you will help to restore a positive relation by accepting graciously.

Box 4.4   An Effective Apology

To be effective, an apology must do the following:

- Acknowledge the wrong done to the injured party.
- Recognize the legitimacy of feelings of hurt, anger, frustration, disappointment, or betrayal.
- Take responsibility for any damage inflicted to the individual or to the relationship.
- Never blame the recipient.
- Sincerely apologize, on a personal level.
- Offer a gesture of support and compensation, if possible.

Effective and ethical communicators are much in demand in the technical workplace, and are valued as colleagues and managers. Effective communicators are those who listen, those who respect others, those who can adapt their words and actions appropriately to the situation, but above all, effective communicators are those who behave ethically and with civility toward others.

Whatever the circumstances, we need to be very clear that whenever we choose to disregard the welfare and face of others, when we treat others simply as things that can be used for our own purposes and then brushed aside, when we serve ourselves at the expense of others' welfare, when we attempt to influence others without regard to their well-being, we are choosing to behave unethically, just as much as when we lie, cheat, steal, or betray others.

Critical Reading

Tania Smith, 'Three Aims and Evaluation Criteria for Persuasion'

Tania Smith is Assistant Professor of Professional Communication in the Faculty of Communication and Culture at the University of Calgary. With a background in English literature and Rhetoric and Composition, she teaches courses in Rhetorical History and Theory, Professional and Technical Communication, and Written and Oral Discourse. Her current research activities focus on the ways language creates communities and identities in higher education settings, and how individuals in the eighteenth century advanced rhetorical abilities without formal academic training. She supports teaching and learning enhancement programs at universities that promote experiential, interactive learning and reflection, such as community service learning, peer mentoring programs, and inquiry-based learning.

Three Aims and Evaluation Criteria for Persuasion

In this document I summarize a simple rhetorical theory that I call the 3 'Es' of Persuasion: Efficiency, Effectiveness, and Ethics. Unlike the Aristotelian appeals of ethos, logos, and pathos, this view of persuasion does not advise us regarding particular strategies for persuasion. However, a 3E analysis does help us to distinguish among three general intentions and results of a particular persuasive program or tactic.

Persuasion is 'successful' to the degree that it aims to be, and is:

- EFFICIENT (limiting the expenditure of time and money, and increasing the inflow of benefits to the persuader, for every persuasive act)
- EFFECTIVE (achieving the desired effect on the audience)
- ETHICAL (using language to build community and uphold social and moral values)

A person or organization who desires to persuade may prioritize each of these aims in a different hierarchy. While the best rhetorician desires to maximize all three aims, often one aim will be emphasized to the detriment of the other two.

Efficiency is a starting point for communication: in order for persuasion to happen at all, before we even consider its effectiveness, it needs to be minimally efficient in terms of being physically or technologically possible for A to get his/her message across to B. Nobody will make the effort of trying to persuade if there is little chance of their message being heard or understood; nobody will bother listening for long if the message is too difficult or impossible to decode. In addition, altering communication tools and technologies, as well as audience size, distribution, and diversity, will alter the possibilities for efficient persuasion—obviously the inventions of print, telecommunications and the Internet has improved efficiency in terms of enhancing the ability of one person to communicate with many with little effort.

Standardization and authority are the basic means of efficiency. To communicate efficiently, a society must establish and protect conventional or agreed-upon uses of language and symbols, and ensure compatibility and support of its media systems. But merely having the ability to communicate clearly to another person does not necessarily result in persuasive effectiveness, that is, achieving the desired results in the audience. Efficiency is the usual priority of organizational management and political governance, since it is associated with existing power and authority, and focuses on reducing costs in terms of time, energy, and money. Efficiency usually accompanies messages from the more powerful to the less powerful, and messages about activities that are already presumed by most people to be necessary and beneficial. Efficiency creates simplicity and clarity of messages, but when overemphasized, it tends to reinforce the status quo and consolidate power, can result in an audience's unthinking obedience, inattentiveness, or extreme resistance, and is limited in its ability to enhance dialogue, critical thinking, and education. If no kind of communication were permitted but that which was the most efficient, it would oversimplify communication to a mere act of factual transmission, it would limit spontaneity and emotion, and put people on 'auto pilot.'

Effectiveness is the most complex term of the three because it depends so much on situational dynamics and the personal limitations and the free will of audiences. An excessive desire to be effective can lead to manipulation on the one hand, or spineless people-pleasing and conformity on the other hand. Effectiveness is the usual first priority of advertising, as well as of ardent political and religious persuasion, whenever there is controversy and doubt in the audience at the same time as the persuaders experience a strong drive to increase the number of believers and supporters. We cannot ultimately control people's thoughts and actions through persuasion: the audience and the constraints of a situation have a great deal of power to render the best-designed appeal relatively ineffective. There is no way of ensuring 100 per cent effectiveness for persuasive appeals, nor any conclusive and final measurement of effectiveness. Effectiveness is qualitative, not just quantitative, encompassing not just observable and countable effects in the short term, but the indirect and subconscious effects on people over time. To the degree we fail to persuade, we can still fail gracefully—without needlessly causing a waste of time and money, or causing social harm.

When evaluating our communication after some of its effects can be measured, if effectiveness criteria are the only criteria in use, we will be unable to improve our future effective strategies so that they are also ethical and efficient. However, it is unwise to boast of having used effective strategies that are ethically suspicious or liable to fall into disuse because they are inefficient. Therefore, in order to increase the overall quality of rhetoric, it is very important to examine effectiveness in terms of the social values of efficiency and ethics.

Ethics is listed last not because it is least important, but because it is the most controversial. Because the pressures to be efficient and effective are usually high, ethics can be the most difficult to keep in view when creating rhetoric. Despite the fact that ethical perfection is unattainable, it is an honourable and worthwhile goal. Ethical persuasion is often associated with education because it presumes that ethical persuaders humbly and continually seek to understand what is good, true, honourable, and just—it continually seeks to understand how to build communities at the same time as preventing or reducing harm to individuals.

It seems that efficiency and ethics are usually two ends of a spectrum (although they need not always be). Arguments which are the most efficient or efficiency-driven are perceived to be more likely to be unethical, for several reasons. (1) It is always easier to destroy than to build—for example, harming someone else's image is quick and easy in comparison to building up one's own reputation on valid grounds. (2) Short-cuts in persuasion are often unethical because they omit important steps in reasoning or questioning. These tactics at their worst are deceptive and at the very best may keep the audience in a state of ignorance. They take advantage of an audience's laziness and habitual thinking instead of calling them to rise to the challenge of careful consideration. (3) The efficiency goal is a built-in bias: it prioritizes the persuader's self-interest and power, whereas ethics involves sharing respect and power with one's audience.

Less successful persuasion may come in any of these forms:

- **Effective but unethical** (Your company convinces people to sign up for a credit card by hiding the fact that you'll sell their personal information.)
- **Effective but inefficient** (Student's Union candidates personally visit 20 classrooms to talk for 5 minutes in each; as a result, SU election votes for those candidates increase in those faculties.)
- **Efficient but unethical** (Politicians discuss their views on an issue with peers and civil service workers, but do not take the time to consult with their constituents.)
- **Efficient but ineffective** (A company sends spam emails to inform people that a new store has been opened, but then research discovers that few actual customer visits to the store were motivated by this email campaign.)
- **Ethical but inefficient** (To redesign a university course, a teacher enlists the assistance of administrators, advisors, students, and teaching assistants over a period of six months, making sure it is a course that meets everyone's needs; in the process, he educates his collaborators and himself about the best way to run the course, but they had less time and energy to devote to other projects in the mean time.) An increase in ethics usually reduces efficiency in the communication process, because it usually means doing more research, verifying sources, creating time and forums for ethical reflection such as peer review and revision, talking and listening to audiences, etc.
- **Ethical but ineffective** (A candidate hosts an open and honest dialogue with voters, yet it does not result in increased votes for the candidate because voters at the event were enlightened and actually discovered more reasons not to vote for the candidate.)

There are already many incentives to make persuasion more effective and efficient. The challenge for society is to move ethical persuasion further into the realm of everyday practice. One can do this on an individual level by more often exercising one's ethical awareness, engaging in dialogue about ethics, and submitting oneself to ethical peer review, thus building ethical persuasive aims into one's identity, habits, and consciousness.

The primary way for our society to make ethical persuasion more frequent in practice is to remove or lower the efficiency barrier: to discover how to make it more efficient, not only more effective. Within organizations, communities and nations, societies can invest time in research and dialogue to discover methods to encourage ethical reflection and ethical persuasion in education, public media, and political and legal forums. A society can manage its culture and technology so that they give easier access to ethical persuasion strategies that otherwise would be less efficient. This strategy would be analogous to building wheelchair ramps up to building entrances—the initial costs would be recouped over time by social benefits.

Society could also introduce deterrents by increasing the time and money required to practice unethical persuasion, but these sanctions would require yet more time investment in policymaking, policing, and legal proceedings. Rules and sanctions carelessly made or applied could result in injustice and further conflict. We already have laws to enforce ethical behavior, if not ethical persuasion, in the general populace. It is likely that only smaller organizations or communities will find it efficient or beneficial to establish and enforce codes of conduct regarding ethical rhetoric. Communities often do so indirectly through the norms of their culture.

Points to Remember

1. Communication always involves others' feelings, attitudes, experiences, and concerns, as well as our own expectations and the quality of what we say.
2. Because our communication affects the interests and well-being of others, it always involves a question of ethics.
3. Communication, like all our interactions with others, is shaped by ethical codes based on cultural, familial, religious, or professional values and customs.
4. All ethical systems have a strong collective, or social, component.
5. Ethical communication involves taking responsibility for our words and actions, avoiding misrepresentation of ourselves or our messages, and limiting unnecessary harm done to others.
6. People tend to respond in kind. Defensive or rude behaviour will invite similar behaviour from others; polite, considerate behaviour will invite polite behaviour in return. Keep your cool and try to be pleasant even when others are rude.
7. What people want more than anything is for their concerns to be heard. If you can learn to listen to relation as well as content, you can dramatically improve your communication with others.
8. The ability to sincerely apologize, and the willingness to accept the sincere apologies of others, is a key component of ethical professionalism and workplace civility.
9. Communication that over-emphasizes efficiency is more likely to be unethical; while you wish to be concise and not squander your time, be sure not to compromise ethics for the sake of efficiency as you design your messages.

Key Concepts

apology	efficiency	fake personalization
civility	ethic of reciprocity	golden rule
code of conduct	ethics	Hippocratic oath
code of ethics	ethos	Nine Axioms
Communication Code of Ethics	etiquette	rhetorical balance
deliberative	face	rhetorical situation
effectiveness		

Assignments and Exercises

1. In a recent interview, a senior student interviewing for his first professional position was asked the following question:

   > If a situation arose in which you were asked to violate company policy, under what circumstances would you do so?

   Consider your response to the ethical issues this question raises, and your own potential answer to the question. Prepare to discuss with the class, or write a memo to your instructor, regarding the following issues:
   a) Would it matter what the policy was?
   b) Are there any special circumstances that might warrant breaking company rules? Do you think your boss would agree?
   c) How accurately does your hypothetical answer to the question reflect your past experience? Is a hypothetical answer ethical? Is the question itself ethical?

2. Surveys and anecdotal reports suggest that academic cheating among university students is widespread. However, there is some disagreement about what counts as cheating, or whether it should be considered a serious academic violation. Consider the following scenarios, some of which are explicitly disallowed by the codes of student conduct at various universities. Which of these do you consider to be cheating? Which are clearly not cheating? Which are questionable, but permissible in some circumstances, or justified by the workload in your program? Which are never acceptable in any situation? Rank these in order from acceptable to unacceptable, and be prepared to defend your answer in class discussion.

   - Copying routine assignments from someone else and handing them in as your own
   - Fudging lab results
   - Changing the results of calculations to coincide with answers given in the book before handing them in
   - Buying assignments from a website
   - Copying from someone else in an examination
   - Studying from a pirated copy of last year's exam
   - Having a friend sign in and write your exam in your place
   - Secretly taking notes into an exam, though they have been specifically disallowed
   - Handing in the same report in two different classes without the instructors' approval
   - Having someone else edit your written report
   - Hiring a tutor for help with mathematics or writing
   - Sharing the workload in a study group for an assignment that will be handed in individually
   - Writing on your own the project report that the entire group was supposed to write
   - Handing in a report that a friend or relative wrote for the same class a couple of years before
   - Downloading a report from the web and submitting it as your own for an assignment
   - Storing information in your calculator to take into an exam without your instructor's approval
   - Passing answers to a friend during an exam

- Lending your finished assignment to a friend two hours before it's due
- Copying from a friend's work without her knowledge and submitting it for grading as your own
- Copying from a friend's work, with her approval, and submitting it for grading as your own
- Copying a report or assignment from a textbook or other published source
- Copying a technical design from another source without acknowledgement and including it as your own in your report
- Knowingly letting a friend copy your assignments
- Including large chunks of downloaded material in your report without citing the source
- Letting another student dictate the problem-solving steps for an assignment while you type or write
- Copying (electronically or by hand) someone else's computer file, modifying it, and handing it in as your own work
- Having someone load his/her assignment into the computer, then modifying it and handing it in as your own work
- Posting your work to a website or to an electronic bulletin board, or similar medium, for reference by others

Compare your list with that of others in the class. How much consensus was there? What differences did you discover? Both individually and as a class, consider whether you would change your opinion if the course in question were: a required elective; a free elective; a required core course. How should your university or college deal with plagiarism and cheating? Should students be expelled for handing in the work of others as if it is their own? Would such measures curb cheating? Summarize the results of the class discussion into a code of ethics, and write them up in a short memo report for your instructor. Submit the report via e-mail if your instructor directs you to do so.

3. You've just graduated and are seeking a permanent job, but you have been offered a second summer internship with the company where you worked last summer. It's a great job, and you've been told that there's the serious possibility that this position will become full-time when the summer is over. This year, they will be hiring a second intern, and you have been invited to participate in screening the applications for the job. Your boss has let you know that your recommendation will strongly influence the decision about whom they will interview.

In the applicant pool, you discover a submission from someone else in your college program. Judging from the applications, he is the best-qualified candidate for the position. As well, you know from being in classes with him that he would do a very good job—as good as you can do yourself. Unfortunately, though you have nothing personal against the guy, you know that there will be only one permanent job when the summer ends, and you fear that, should they hire your acquaintance for the summer post, he will be your chief rival for the permanent position. Using the principles of ethical communication as a guideline, what should you tell your boss? In what sense is this scenario strictly a communication dilemma? In what sense is it an ethical dilemma? To what extent are the two mixed? Be prepared to discuss your reactions with the class or to submit your response to your instructor in a memo or e-mail.

4. In a recent high-profile case, a Canadian university professor was removed from her job for misrepresenting her academic qualifications and research. In interviews contained in the news coverage of the incident, the students in the department where she taught for two years expressed outrage at this deception, and said they feared that this act of misrepresentation by their instructor would compromise the value of their university education. Do you agree? How serious is this breach of communication ethics? Should this professor have lost her job for her action? Why or why not? Be prepared to defend your argument using what you have learned about communication in this course.

5. If you read Bitzer's 'The Rhetorical Situation' in Chapter 1, use the theory of the rhetorical situation to help you to identify the controlling exigence and any relevant constraints in the scenario 'Sam Spade and University Ace Painters' on page 356. In what sense is the situation described in the scenario an ethical dilemma? Why? What responsibilities does Sam have, apart from returning the client's deposit? How can Sam be held responsible for problems caused by the weather? Considering the circumstances, was it ethical for Wells to have lodged a formal complaint? Why or why not? To whom is ethical responsibility owed?

6. Go to the section of your college or university calendar or website that deals with student rights and responsibilities. Based on what we have discussed in this chapter, does the material contained there constitute a code of ethics? To what extent is it a guideline for ethical communication? Most codes of ethics balance a sense of duty or obligation with freedom of choice; which of the two (obligation and choice) does your college's behavioural code emphasize? How prescriptive is it? Write your analysis into a brief informal report and submit it to your instructor in hard copy or electronic form.

7. Turn again to your responses to problem #2 and problem #4. Did you apply the same ethical standard in both cases? If not, why not? What is the relationship between students who resort to plagiarism and faculty who do the same? Should one be punished more severely than the other? Why or why not?

8. What relationship does Tania Smith posit between ethics and efficiency? Why are these two values potentially in conflict? What remedy does Smith imply? Be prepared to defend your position in class discussion.

9. What 'built-in bias' exists in the value of efficiency? What remedies does Smith suggest to correct this bias? Do you think they are workable? Why or why not? Explain your findings in a memo report of approximately 250 words addressed to your instructor.

Writing Samples for Discussion and Analysis

The following real examples violate the standards of ethics or workplace civility. As you read, ask yourself whether the writer in each case has attended to content and relation, established credibility and professionalism, or developed an understandable, clear message. Identify any ways in which the writers violate the principles of courtesy and civility discussed here and in Chapter 1. What is your impression of each message, and of its writer? Be prepared to discuss the flaws in each example and to offer suggestions as to how to correct them. If your instructor asks you to do so, edit the samples to improve their ethos, civility, clarity of content, and audience relation.

Writing sample #1

From: Madan Tupgar <Mr-T@whoopie.com>
To: Professor McAllister <hmcallister@wpu.ca>

Hey prof harding:

sorry i missed class. my assingment is attatched all u have to do is print it out.

i do not like the approach used in teh book. . . . so i did not do the assignment u gave.

this is how i have always do these kind of assignmnts and i decided to turn it in instead. I think u must not be familar with the approach we learned in High School. its much better. u should study it. u could learn something for next years class.

please feel free to contact me if u would like more infomration about hot its done.

madan tupgar
'Mr.-T'

Figure 4.1: In how many ways has Madan Tupgar failed to be civil in this e-mail to his professor? How do you think Dr. Harding McAllister will react to this message? What implications might there be for Madan?

Writing sample #2

The passage below appeared in the syllabus for a third-year university course:

Guidelines for Classroom Behaviour

Disruptive classroom behaviour, defined as 'any behaviour that a reasonable person would view as substantially or repeatedly interfering with the conduct of a class,' can negatively affect the classroom environment as well as the educational experience for students enrolled in the course. Therefore, disruptive behaviour such as the following will be considered childishly irritating and will not be tolerated: habitual lateness, 'texting' or surfing the Internet, talking to classmates, reading the paper or doing homework for another course, sleeping, eating, handing in late assignments, coming to class unprepared, being generally disengaged or inattentive, or interrupting my lecture with questions.

As your instructor, it is my responsibility to ensure that the class atmosphere is conducive to learning at all times. I claim the right to impose a seating chart on the class, or on a subset of the class; to remove offending students from the room at my discretion; or to otherwise publicly challenge and curb inappropriate behaviour whenever it occurs.

Persons who are unwilling to govern themselves in a manner appropriate to the post-secondary classroom are welcome to transfer to another course or class section.

Figure 4.2: How likely is this passage to promote a civil classroom atmosphere? As a student, how would you respond if you saw it in a course syllabus? What responsibility does the instructor have to enforce classroom civility? Will this document contribute to that purpose? Why or why not?

Chapter 5

Professional Correspondence

Learning Objectives

- To learn common types of professional correspondence and when to use them.

- To learn the standard parts and formats for letters and memos.

- To learn judicious care in dealing with electronic communication.

- To learn to select writing formats appropriate to audience and context.

E-mail, Letters, and Memos

Routine correspondence—by e-mail, letter, or memo—remains the most common form of business communication. While information can also be exchanged by telephone, written messages create a permanent record and allow a precision not always possible in oral exchanges.

Professional correspondence may be distributed electronically or in hard copy, by e-mail or fax, by 'snail mail' or inter-office mail, within an organization or to clients and associates outside. Although e-mail has not yet entirely replaced the formal business letter, in most organizations it has overtaken the traditional memorandum for most routine purposes.

The advantages of e-mail are obvious. It provides a quick and inexpensive means of communicating with people within an organization or with other people and organizations around the world, and makes it easy to send identical information to many recipients. You can send a query in the morning and receive an answer by the afternoon. You can easily transmit documents or pictures to anyone, in any location. You can even collaborate on documents with someone miles away. In these regards, e-mail can be seen as a way of bringing people closer together, of bridging the distances between countries, cultures, and individuals.

E-mail has become so ubiquitous and convenient that we tend to take it for granted. We use it casually, even carelessly at times. However, although e-mail is quick and convenient, inexpensive, and nearly ubiquitous, it is not the casual medium that we sometimes assume, and the implications of its widespread use are significant for professional communicators. First, e-mail is not a secure forum for discussing sensitive or personal issues, as it may be viewed by management or accessed by someone else on the system. As well, although we think of it nonchalantly as almost the equivalent of conversation, e-mail is far from being a transient or fleeting form. In fact, it is in many ways as permanent as hard copy and infinitely simpler to distribute more widely and indiscriminately. E-mail messages, once sent, can easily be passed on by the recipient to readers you never imagined would see your words. Ironic, humourous, or off-hand comments may easily be misread, particularly if they are seen by someone other than the intended readers. For this reason alone, we should always, but often don't, exercise caution in our electronic comments.

Though we think of it as a way of bringing people together, the overuse of e-mail can actually create relational distance, as when we send an e-mail to someone in the next office rather than simply stepping next door to communicate in person. And because we do not have to face those we interact with via e-mail, we may not choose our words as carefully or manage **tone** as deftly as we ought to do, with the result that e-mail can lead to misunderstandings and hurt feelings.

Finally, e-mail may be unsuitable for conveying important information simply because of sheer volume. If you have had an e-mail account for any length of time, you already know that you can easily receive thirty or more messages per day, many of them from unwanted sources—scam and advertising clutter; stale jokes that acquaintances habitually circulate to larger and larger lists; routine mailings to everyone in the organization that may have no direct relevance to you. Many professionals automatically delete e-mails of this kind, and may inadvertently delete important messages as they routinely clear their queues. You should be aware, too, that many employers regularly monitor e-mail communication; according to a survey by the American Management Association (2006), some 26 per cent of employers surveyed 'have terminated employees for e-mail misuse'.

Two increasingly common forms of electronic communication that also have implications for the workplace are web diaries, or blogs, and social networking sites like Facebook.com or Myspace.com. Although you may tend to think of your blog or your networking account as private communication, you need to bear in mind that the information you post to these sites is public, and can be read by nearly anyone—including clients, employers and prospective employers, and parents (CollegeRecruiter.com, 2006; Jackson Lewis LLP, 2006; Johnson, 2006; Mitrano, 2006; Millar, 2007). As a result, these forms of interaction have implications for your professional credibility and success, as well as for the increasingly common crime of identity theft or other victimization such as stalking (Abrahamson, 2005; Waite, 2006).

You should realize, as well, that things you post to your blog or networking page are permanent, even if you change your mind or take them down (Blogscholar.com, 2007; Facebook.com, 2007). The Internet contains permanent archives dating to the late 1990s, and any information posted online since then can be located and viewed by nearly anyone without your permission or your knowledge (Lasica, 1998a, 1998b). Also, of course, anything that you post or send electronically can also be snagged and saved by someone else and redistributed widely. Information you post to blogs or send in private e-mail can thus have serious and irrevocable implications for your professional communication. In recognition of this fact, many workplaces have developed policies on employees' computer usage—including the use of work-related information on personal home-based blogs (American Management Association, 2006). You should therefore exercise caution and good judgement about what you place online; your words create an indelible record for which you may be held legally or otherwise responsible, not just now but years from now.

In the workplace, you should be cautious about using e-mail communication for sensitive or confidential messages unless you can ensure that they will be securely encrypted and decoded only by the intended recipient. Even then, you should remember that the recipient may indefinitely retain anything you send via e-mail, or may forward the material without your knowledge or permission to someone else virtually anywhere in the world. If your message is official or formal, or involves legal liabilities, consider writing a letter or a memo rather than an e-mail; busy people who are inundated with dozens of e-mail messages a day may not give an important piece of communication the attention it deserves if it arrives amid a hail of spam messages. A telephone call or even a personal note will suffice if the information is for one person only, if no copies will be distributed elsewhere, and if it is not for the record.

When formal letters and memos were the dominant modes of workplace correspondence, consistent standards of content, format, and style evolved to make the task of writing—and reading—easier. Though the bulk of your correspondence may now be carried on electronically, there are still good reasons for observing conventional standards in your written messages. Doing so will not only help to make your messages more easily understood, but will also create a positive impression and help to establish your credibility as a professional. E-mail messages that ignore conventions of capitalization, spelling, or punctuation are likely to brand you as careless or lazy, incompetent or boorish. All your written messages should get to the point and not waste the reader's time, while at the same time conveying a courteous and respectful manner and tone. To be effective, they must be accurate, clear, and written in an acceptable format. In the remainder of this chapter we will consider general guidelines for the content of your professional correspondence, and then we will learn the standard formats used for formal correspondence.

The Functions of Professional Correspondence

In the workplace we write formal and informal correspondence for a multitude of purposes, from providing information to soliciting financial support. Whether your message is delivered by e-mail or in a letter or memo, it may carry **good news** or bad news and will usually fall into one of two broad categories: request and response. A **request** is any message through which you initiate an interaction; a **response** is a message produced as the second stage of an interaction initiated by someone else.

Making a request

A request may be written for any number of purposes: to order merchandise; to request information or documentation (such as printed materials, specifications, user's manuals); to book an appointment; to reserve a conference or hotel room; to apply for a job; to ask for favours (a reference, for instance); to submit a tender or funding application; or to invite donations. Basically, a request is any message that initiates contact with another person. In it, the writer should aim to establish an effective working relationship between correspondents.

Request messages should observe the **Seven Cs**: completeness, conciseness, clarity, coherence, correctness, courtesy, and credibility. As you plan your message, keep in mind that a major part of courtesy is making reasonable requests—don't ask the person to whom you are writing to do your work for you. Here are some questions to ask yourself before you write.

1. Have I provided appropriate context for the person to know who I am and why I am contacting him or her?
2. Have I established an appropriate footing from which to make the request?
3. Am I being specific about what I want to know or what I'd like done?
4. Is this request going to inconvenience the person in any unreasonable way?
5. Am I asking someone else to find information or perform a task that I could easily accomplish myself or that I should be doing for myself?
6. Have I taken sufficient care to be respectful in my tone and word choice?
7. If I received a similar request from someone else, would I feel it an unreasonable imposition?

Bear in mind that a request, no matter how simple, is always to some extent an imposition on someone else's time or expertise. Always provide sufficient context for the request, and approach the person with appropriate respect and courtesy. If you can easily find out the information you need from the Internet, a library, or other source, if you are vague about exactly what you want, if your request will cause the other person an unreasonable amount of inconvenience or effort, or if you are requesting services that you would normally have to pay for, you should reconsider your request carefully. Do not compromise your ethos by asking others to do for you what you could easily do for yourself, or by presuming upon others' time and expertise. Always thank the person sincerely for any help you have received or expect to receive.

Writing a response

A response is any message written in reply to someone else's request, in reaction to a situation, or in response to an advertisement. These might include letters of recommendation, information, congratulation or condolence, adjustment, refusal, or complaint.

In addition to observing the Seven Cs, an effective response to a reasonable request is both prompt and helpful. Always give the reader a positive impression and make sure your answer is complete and understandable. If you do not have time to deal with the request right away, provide a timeline as to when the person might expect a fuller response.

Not all requests are reasonable. These days, thanks to the easy access provided by e-mail, you may receive requests for information or assistance from people you do not know, or requests for what amounts to free consultation on professional matters. Despite the fact that the writers are looking for a favour, some of these can be discourteous in content, tone, or expectation. You are not obliged to respond to rude overtures, and, while it can be tempting to send a curt answer, you should certainly resist responding in kind. It is usually better to simply ignore over-the-top requests and send no reply than to confirm their rudeness by being unpleasant in return.

Positive and Negative Messages

The purposes and the possible contexts in which we communicate are too numerous to itemize in detail. However, it is useful to consider the difference between messages that convey negative information (**bad news messages**) and those that carry neutral or positive information (**good news messages**). Messages that carry positive news, such as congratulations or recommendations, or those whose content is emotionally neutral, such as a notice of a meeting or a cover letter for the company's staff directory, make it easy to establish a positive writer–reader relationship. However, messages that must convey negative, disappointing, or contentious information—**messages of complaint** or **refusal**, for example—demand more careful handling.

All messages, whether they carry positive, neutral, or negative information, should adhere to the standards of completeness, conciseness, coherence, correctness, clarity, and competence. In addition, while all your correspondence should be polite, negative messages also require special attention to courtesy. In a difficult or challenging situation, especially one in which bad news is being presented, it is particularly important to be courteous to your correspondents in order to ensure cooperation and good will.

Be sure to moderate your tone when delivering bad news. Don't make an uncomfortable situation worse by antagonizing the reader with insensitive or unsuitable language or a flippant attitude. Your tone should be respectful and calm rather than angry or insincerely positive. Be especially careful to avoid suggesting or implying that the other person is somehow responsible for the situation, even if you believe this to be the case, and avoid making light of a situation your reader will feel is serious. Always assume that you could be mistaken, and give your correspondent the benefit of the doubt if you can. Be pleasant and take care to avoid a sarcastic tone. What you really want is to resolve the problem, and creating unnecessary bad feelings will only lessen the chances of this happening.

The following discussion outlines several common writing situations encompassing both positive and negative messages. Messages of congratulations, fundraising appeals, and public service announcements could be considered generally positive or neutral messages, while messages of complaint or refusal are considered negative. The models below show these types of messages in a variety of formats. While all such messages could be delivered by e-mail, more formal messages are still likely to come by letter or memo.

Box 5.1   **The Functions of Professional Correspondence**

- Acceptances, Congratulations, Acknowledgements
- Complaints
- Conciliations and Apologies
- Refusals and Rejections

Acceptances, congratulations, or acknowledgements

The letter of **acceptance**, **congratulation**, or **acknowledgement** is the most pleasant to write of the four types we will consider. Such a 'good news' letter, memo, or e-mail message may be written to an employee, a colleague, or a client on the occasion of achievement or accomplishment. Perhaps someone you know has graduated from college, obtained a great job, been accepted to a specialized training program, received an award, earned a promotion, made a significant contribution to an important project, published a book or article, or simply provided long or effective service. Whatever the occasion, the letter of acknowledgement or congratulations should be warm in tone and to the point. Such messages should be:

- specific (identify the achievement or occasion);
- positive (make sure your tone is warm and your language complimentary);
- sincere (nothing is more insulting than congratulations that sound insincere, overly effusive, or ironic); and
- appropriately brief (many people ruin effective acknowledgement or congratulation messages by not knowing when to quit).

Of course, your message should also observe the Seven Cs; a sloppy, error-filled letter undercuts the sincerity of the congratulations and compromises your credibility.

Figure 5.1 contains a message of acknowledgement from a supervisor to a staff member who has contributed an extraordinary year's work to the company. Figure 5.2 is a message expressing congratulations to a colleague who has received the company's Employee of the Year award. Compare the two to see which is the more effective.

Messages of complaint

Unfortunately, the task of delivering negative messages is much more common than writing messages of acknowledgement, partly because none of us is immune to error. We do the wrong thing, say the wrong words, break the rules, fail to deliver on our obligations, and make mistakes. Mix-ups occur, documents get misplaced, cheques can be lost, computer files erased, wrong parts sent, or mailings waylaid.

Dolovich and Cowan Technical Services

internal correspondence

DATE: April 14, 2009
TO: Gwynne Nishikawa, Management Team
FROM: Allan Dolovich, President
RE: Appreciation of your contributions during the 2008/2009 fiscal year

Just a note to say thank you for all the work you have done on Project Management this past year. I have especially appreciated your willingness to aid in the vacation period when I needed someone to fill in for ill personnel, and to take on an extra project when one of our engineers left the company.

Considering that you also managed to design a new training program for Staff Development, your contribution has been truly commendable and beyond any requirements of your job description.

Thank you for all that you have done and for your valuable assistance. Few, if any, members of the management team have done more to make this a successful year.

Please accept my heartfelt thanks for a job well done.

cc.   Personnel File
      AD:jm

Figure 5.1:   Note how Allan Dolovich's warm tone and use of specific details make his letter of congratulation effective.

Most of us—and most organizations—do our best to keep such occurrences at a minimum, since life functions more smoothly for all of us when things run smoothly. Despite all our good intentions, however, problems can crop up anyway. But, although you can't always prevent mistakes from happening, you can help to keep them from becoming a major inconvenience if you always make it a rule to assume, at least initially, that the mix-ups you encounter in your professional dealings are honest errors. This only makes sense; few of us want to cause upset to our colleagues and clients. If you treat such incidents as unintentional and try to maintain a positive attitude, it's likely that your complaints will be dealt with more promptly and positively.

The first rule for messages of complaint is to be especially courteous. No one wants to receive abusive, sarcastic, or threatening messages; phrase your bad news in as calm and neutral terms as possible. Avoid inflaming the situation by name-calling or blaming others. Problems will be more easily solved if you allow your correspondents room to save face, and to correct the situation without making them look foolish. They will be more interested in helping you and they will be more anxious to maintain your good will if you approach them in a friendly, non-threatening manner.

It is also important that in a complaint you specifically identify the nature of the problem and the action you wish taken. For example, if you have ordered technical manuals and, after waiting a reasonable length of time, have not received your order, you may wish to contact the supplier. You will need to be able to identify the missing items by name, catalogue or item number, catalogue issue, and page number. You should state the date of your order, the cheque number, if there is one, and the amount of the order. If you have

---

Subject: Employee of the Year Award
Date: January 25, 2010
From: <Randy_Alexander@dolovicow.ca>
To: <Peter_Holowaczok@dolovicow.ca>

Congratulations on winning the Employee of the Year Award. It doesn't usually go to somebody who has been in the company only two years—you must really be something special. I have been here for four years and though my work is really deserving, nobody seems to notice. I haven't even been nominated. I suppose I haven't made friends with the right people; I never was much good at lobbying.

I have heard it said that the work you've been doing in Public Relations is really outstanding, especially that slick brochure you produced for the new Project Management Strategies campaign. Most everybody believes that it's really well designed. I saw it—it is pretty good, but could I give you a little advice? I didn't think that the photo of Dolovich and Cowan cutting the ribbon on the plant project was appropriate for the cover. I have a talent for graphic design, and it's not what I would have chosen.

Please let me know if you'd like to get together sometime to talk about layout; I took a course in graphic art in college and could probably pass on a few useful hints. Also, I'd like to have a chance to talk with the new golden boy from PR.

Congratulations again on winning the award.

Sincerely,

Randy

Figure 5.2:   In what ways is this message of congratulation flawed? (Consider both content and relation.) What does it suggest about its author?

---

a standing account with the firm, cite your account number. Be sure that all of this information is correct. Be sure also that you tell the reader exactly what you want done about the problem, since the reader's idea of a satisfactory solution may differ from yours. For example, the supplier may think the best course of action is to send the missing manuals, but if you have already had to obtain them from another source, you will need to make it clear that what you want is a refund.

Finally, once you have drafted your letter of complaint, let it sit for a day, and then, before you send it, take another look at what you've said and how you've said it. Messages composed in the heat of the moment are rarely effective, and may even unintentionally inflame the situation. Give yourself a chance to cool down, and always reconsider your tone before you send the message. No matter how irritated you feel, or how in the right you may be, the situation is unlikely to be resolved with an angry exchange.

Below are the points to remember for messages of complaint.

- Phrase your comments neutrally.
- Avoid blaming your correspondent.
- Be sure to identify the exact nature of the problem immediately.
- Provide all relevant details.

- Request specific action.
- Be courteous. Thank correspondents for their help.
- Avoid angry, accusatory, or sarcastic language or tone.
- Always allow a 'cool-down' period, and reconsider your complaint before you send it.

In Figure 5.3, Lam Huan is making a complaint regarding an error in the processing of a scholarship award. Note that though the awards officer is at fault, Huan wisely does not cause more difficulty by being sarcastic or abusive.

---

90 Victoria Crescent
Bruce Mines, ON
N2E 2R4

November 20, 2009

Talya Melniczok, Awards Officer
Student Awards and Services
Science Division, Northwoods College
Box 456
Bruce Mines, Ontario N0E O4O

Dear Ms. Melniczok:

Re: Scholarship for 2009-2010
        Student number: 987-451-03

I have just received word from the Office of Student Accounts that my entrance scholarship, which came into effect in 2009-2010, has been discontinued. The clerk I spoke to told me that their records indicate that the award was for one year only, and that I am liable for full tuition payments for this academic year.

I am certain there has been an error in communication between your office and the Accounts office. I have attached a copy of the original letter I received from your office, which clearly states that the scholarship will automatically be renewed for subsequent years if my grade average is above 80% and if no individual grade is below 75%. I believe you will find that I have met these requirements; I have attached a photocopy of my grade report showing that my average for last year stands at 86%, and that the lowest grade I received in any course was 79%.

I hope you can assist me in straightening out this error. Would it be possible for you to contact the Accounts office to confirm that the scholarship is still in effect? The person who is handling my case is Vasjli Gajic.

Thanks very much for your assistance. If you need any further information from me, I can be reached at <lph123@std.northwoods.cc.ca> or by phone at 546-7089.

Sincerely,

Lam Huan

Lam Huan

Figure 5.3: What features make Lam Huan's request for adjustment effective? Compare Huan's letter with the letter in Figure 5.4; in what ways does Ing Jang violate the principles of effective professional writing?

22 Ulethe Crescent
Calgary, Alberta
T3R 5Q8

November 14, 2009

Registrar
Western Plains University
PO Box 666
Calgary, AB T2K 3M4

Dear Registrar:

The other day I was in the office to pick up a transcript that I need for an internship job I'm applying for. If I don't send it right away I can't be considered. So anyway I talked to this clerk of yours who should be fired for her rudeness to me. Who do you people think pays for your salary?

She told me that the transcript costs eight dollars. Eight dollars! For what? And anyway she said I couldn't have it because of this so-called library fine that she said was outstanding from last term. I needed to have that book to study for my final exam and then I accidentally left it home when I came back here in September. It's not like anybody was reading it over the summer anyway, and now she tells me that the fine is seventy-five dollars. So this means it's going to cost me eighty-three dollars to get a stupid transcript.

Well, you can imagine I wasn't very happy about that. But she had no right to call the security people. It was only a joke when I said I know where she parks her car. She embarrassed me half to death. Now how am I going to apply for my internship? If I don't have enough money for next term it will be your fault, and anyway this business of having to wait for a week to get a lousy transcript is stupid.

I think you should fire the woman I spoke to and anybody else who is rude to students. After all, this is a public institution, so as a student you people work for me. I hope I don't see her anymore.

Sincerely,

Ing Jang

Ing Jang

Figure 5.4: How effective is this letter of complaint? Can you think of any ways it could be improved?

Messages of conciliation or apology

Because of the centrality of relation to professional communication, the ability to sincerely apologize is of central importance to anyone who hopes to be successful. When things have gone wrong, we need to create messages that will put things right, make amends, and repair shattered relationships. **Messages of apology** or **conciliation** are particularly challenging to write because they are typically written in circumstances in which hard feelings have already been created and expressed. Normally, the readers to whom these messages are directed are feeling upset, disappointed, or angry, and these feelings of hurt or frustration must be dealt with explicitly before the rest of the issue can be attended to. If they are ignored, the apology will be rejected as insincere, and the situation may be further inflamed.

A message of apology or conciliation must recognize the violation that has been done to the relationship of professional trust between the reader and the writer or the organization; if it does not do so, it will not only fail to correct the situation, it may even escalate it by hardening attitudes even further. An apology thus requires careful attention to the relational element of the message—that is, it must deal forthrightly and sincerely with the hurt and disappointment of the reader. A sincere and effective apology genuinely recognizes these feelings and supports the reader's expression of them.

Most important to an effective message of conciliation is that the writer must also be prepared to take responsibility, either personally or on behalf of the company or organization, for whatever part was played in causing the upset. The responsibility may be diffuse across the company or organization, or may rightly belong to some junior member of the staff, but for the apology to be effective, the writer must personally express regret, and must recognize the actual or potential pain, damage, or inconvenience that the action has caused to the reader. If possible, the writer should offer a gesture of conciliation—perhaps the original damage cannot be withdrawn or corrected, but some compensatory measure can be made. Without these gestures, sincerely given, rifts may not be healed and divisions may be increased and irrevocably entrenched.

A message of conciliation or apology, therefore, must do the following:

- Acknowledge the wrong done to the injured party.
- Recognize the legitimacy of feelings of hurt, anger, frustration, disappointment, or betrayal.
- Take responsibility for any damage inflicted to the individual or to the relationship.
- Never blame the recipient.
- Sincerely apologize, on a personal level.
- Offer a gesture of support and compensation, if possible.

Below are two messages of apology, one ineffective and the other effective. The ineffective letter (Figure 5.5) responds to the communication scenario 'An Engineering Prank Goes Wrong' (Assignment #17 on page 145 in this chapter).

The effective letter (Figure 5.6) deals with a missed deadline. Sine Eyeour was initially flattered when she was asked by one of her professors to contribute an essay on effective studying for a student handbook the professor was writing. Unfortunately, getting it done turned out to be more difficult than she had thought, especially given everything else she had to do. Embarrassed, Sine compounded her mistake by procrastinating until she received a final e-mail from her professor asking politely for her contribution and informing her that her lateness threatened to hold up the entire project. Compare the two letters; what differences can you see immediately? What other, more subtle differences are there? What role does tone play in each? Explain, if you can, the strategies that make the successful letter more effective than the weak one.

Engineering Students Society
Western Plains University
PO Box 666 Calgary, AB T2K 3M4

September 13, 2010

Valerie Price, Vice President
Student Affairs and Services
Western Plains University
PO Box 666
Calgary, AB T2K 3M4

Dear Mrs. Price:

It has come to my attention that you complained about the recent prank by two engineering students. The dean of Engineering said I had to write to you about it.

I am unable to reinmburse you because WPESS policy doesnt require us to take responsibility for your problem, and anyway we have'nt got sufficient funds available to cover the incident. And besides, the students were'nt representing WPESS, so it's not really our problem.

If you want to recover the money, I suggest that you return the new binders to Office World. If you want I can give you the names of the two students involved in the prank but other then that I do not see what else you expect.

Thank you for your time and attention to this matter.

Sincerly,

Marv Gryphon, Esq.
President

Figure 5.5:   How effectively has Marv Gryphon assessed the situation? In what ways is his letter of apology flawed? Is it likely to satisfy Dr. Price and the Dean of Engineering?

Refusals and rejections

Turning down a legitimate request or application, whether it has come from a candidate for employment or from a client who wants an adjustment of a fee or a resolution to a conflict, is a delicate challenge requiring considerable diplomacy. Diplomacy is particularly critical when you write the subject line, since you should avoid unnecessary bluntness. Rather than

To:	Professor Mok <MMok@wpu.ca>
From:	Sine Eyeour <sae987@studs.wpu.ca>
Date:	October 1, 2012
Re:	My essay on study skills for your book

Dear Professor Mok:

Please accept my sincere apologies for my lateness in submitting my essay on study skills for your book *How to Succeed at College: Making the Most of Your First Year*. I am very sorry for, and very embarrassed by, the inconvenience I've caused you.

I never intended to hold up the project; the problem is that I do really want to contribute this essay, so instead of doing what I should have done long ago and relinquishing it to someone else, I kept hoping that I would be able to get to it. But each time I started working on it, something more immediately urgent moved it to the bottom of the pile. I put off e-mailing you because I hoped to be able to send the article with my message. Then it just became ridiculously and embarrassingly late. Nevertheless, my delay is inexcusable, and in your place I would be furious.

This is no excuse, but in my own defence, I will say that the past year has been exceptionally difficult for me. I know that all students claim to be busy, but I had no idea what the word meant until I took a position on the executive of WPESS in the same year that I was completing my senior design elective, while also continuing to hold down a part-time job. To add to my difficulties, my father was diagnosed last fall with MS, and I've been helping my mother to care for him.

However, those are my troubles, and however much they might explain my lateness, knowing about them doesn't solve your publication deadline issues. The bottom line is this: if you are willing to allow me to do so, I would still like to write the essay and will pledge to have it to you in one week from today, come hell or high water. However, if you feel that you've already given me enough rope to hang myself, I can recommend another person who would be in a position to write a very good article on this subject for you. Again, you have my most humble apology, though I know that it can't possibly be enough to erase my embarrassment for placing you in this predicament.

Sincerely,
Sine Eyeour

Figure 5.6:   How effectively has Sine handled this awkward situation? How has she conveyed her sincerity and her humility?

a subject line that reads 'Rejection of your application' or 'Refusal to grant your request', in this case it would probably be more tactful to write 'Your application' or 'Your request' so that you do not give the impression of shoving the **rejection** in the person's face.

As in all negative messages, tone is important to a refusal. You should be tactful in refusing to provide the service or approve the request, and you should aim to preserve the other person's good will as far as possible under the circumstances. You should use as positive terms as you can to cushion the impact of the refusal; while you do not want to trivialize or underplay a difficult situation, you also don't want to exaggerate it through unnecessarily negative language. Be sure especially to avoid sarcasm or accusation. State the message briefly and then politely explain your reasons in terms that will allow your reader to preserve face.

At least initially, it is best to avoid placing responsibility for the refusal on the reader, even in cases where that person shares part of the responsibility. It rarely helps to point fingers at anyone; it is preferable instead to stress your own inability to comply with the request. Keep in mind that your most important goal is maintaining good will. For example, if you are writing a letter of refusal to someone who has been turned down for a job, stress that the position was offered to another candidate because, for instance, that individual more closely suited your needs, not because the person you are writing to is inadequate. Likewise, if you are refusing a reference, it is better to stress your inability to supply it, rather than to suggest that the person is flawed. The following are some points to keep in mind when writing a letter of refusal.

- Word the subject line tactfully, avoiding a blunt refusal.
- Stress your inability to comply with the reader's request, using as positive terms as possible and doing so as briefly as possible.
- State your reasons simply, taking responsibility for your refusal.
- Avoid sarcasm or accusation.
- Be polite and sincere.
- Suggest someone else your correspondent might approach for assistance, if possible.
- Offer the person your best wishes for better success elsewhere if it's appropriate to do so.

In the letter of refusal in Figure 5.7, the impact of the **bad news** has been cushioned with positive comments, and the reader has been invited to reapply for a future training session. As well, the writer has recommended additional steps that might enlarge the candidate's skill base in preparation for future training intakes. Contrast it with Figure 5.8; both have a similar message to relate. Which of the two would you rather receive?

Remember, no matter what kind of message you are writing, be sure to identify your main point first and communicate your message as clearly and concisely as possible, maintaining a polite tone throughout.

Persuasive Messages

The success of any professional writing depends on understanding and accommodating the reader's needs, expectations, priorities, concerns, and interests. Such an understanding of your reader is always important, but it is critical when you move from primarily informative to explicitly persuasive writing. Persuasive messages invite the reader not only to comprehend but also to accept and act on the information they contain. Such messages must engage the attention and interest of the intended audience and motivate that audience to behave as requested. As well, an effective persuasive message should help to guide the reader to the appropriate action through an enabling strategy, a device that makes it easy and convenient for the reader to take the requested or recommended action.

When you write to persuade, you are not only asking the reader to make sense of your message, but inviting the person to respond with action. A persuasive message must influence your readers, motivating them to adopt a proposal, accept a tender, donate to a cause, volunteer time or resources, or provide some authorization or sanction. Grant applications, research proposals, tenders, and design reports are among the forms of persuasive writing in the technical professions; you may have seen others.

Testamek Engineering Ltd.
64 Weniam Street — Vancouver, British Columbia — V1R 9V1
www.testamek.com

February 15, 2009

Ms. Molly Crump
55 Elwood Close
Calgary, Alberta
T5W 3F6

Dear Ms. Crump

Thank you for participating in our recent screening session for our Technical Management Trainee Programme. Although the interviewers felt your qualifications and aptitude tests showed solid potential, I am afraid we will not be able to offer you a spot in the programme for this year's intake.

This decision is not meant to reflect on your management potential; rather, it is an indication of the large number of very fine applicants who participated in this year's screening interviews. We simply could not accommodate all who applied.

We would like to encourage you to reapply for next year's intake. In the meantime, we suggest further upgrading your communication skills, either through additional courses or through one of the many commercial training programmes available. We believe such an experience would enhance your readiness for the demands of management training.

We extend our best wishes and look forward to seeing you again next year.

Sincerely

Lazar LaFleur
Training Director

Figure 5.7: What strategies did Lazar LaFleur use to soften the news of rejection for Molly Crump? Contrast this example with the e-mail message in Figure 5.8. Which would you prefer to receive?

In order to persuade effectively, you need to establish a human connection with the reader through the relational aspect of your message; to do this, you must demonstrate credibility through a positive, rhetorically balanced approach that is above all honest and sincere. Outline to the reader the advantages of the course of action you are advocating, and don't bully, patronize, or pander to the reader. Finally, to demonstrate credibility and courtesy, you must avoid obvious gimmicks.

In order to persuade, you must first capture and hold the attention and interest of your readers—**engage** them with your ideas and your enthusiasm, and with your obvious command of the situation. Second, you must find a way to **motivate** your audience's interest and action by showing the connection between your proposal and their needs or concerns and by emphasizing what they will gain or how they will benefit from

Subject: Your submission to The Collegian
Date: 1 April 2010
From: editor@collegian.waskcc.on.ca
To: <Gaetan Jamberneau> gfj589@waskcc.on.ca

We have received your latest 'experimental' close-up photos of the gadgets in the engineering building. As you know, the *Collegian*'s editorial staff usually welcome submissions from students and members of the community at large.

We would prefer, however, not to receive any more strange photos from you. Although I admit that we published one of your photos last year, you should know that 'art' photography is not really our 'thing' and we used the other shot only because we were short on submissions and had some extra space to fill.

We are more interested in other kinds of submissions—cartoons, normal photos of stuff on campus, and articles written by the college community; I am pretty sure that our readers don't know much about experimental photography and don't really want to see these weird extreme closeups in the Collegian. If they did want to look at such stuff, they could take an art course! After all, we are interested in things that are relevant to real life and most people agree that technical devices are boring. Besides, I'm not even sure how to judge the quality of your work, since I don't know what you mean by 'chiaroscuro' or whatever you called it.

I hope you won't be too upset by my letter, but I thought you would want to hear the truth. If you decide to take up a more interesting kind of photography, please let us know. We might like to have something else from you.

Sincerely,

David Kaminski, Editor
The *Collegian*: The Voice of Waskasoo College
Student Union Building, C-870

Figure 5.8: How might Gaetan Jamberneau respond to this letter? Suggest some ways David Kaminski's message might be improved.

what you propose. Finally, you need to **enable** your readers to act on the information you have provided; give them the means to do what you have encouraged by showing them how it can be achieved and by outlining the first steps they need to take to get the plan underway.

Persuasive messages may be sent to colleagues, clients, or managers who are already positively disposed to your project, or to those who are not 'in the loop'. You will sometimes have to find ways to persuade those who are not already disposed to accept your ideas, or who are actually opposed to them. Naturally, your approach will have to be adjusted to suit the circumstances. The following are some of the things your persuasive message should do if it is sent to someone who isn't familiar with your project or who may not already be supportive:

Box 5.2   Three Steps in Persuading Others

- Engage reader attention
- Motivate reader interest
- Enable reader action

- Engage the reader's attention quickly. You may do this with a question, a statement of an intriguing problem, a surprising fact, or a brief case study. If you are offering a solution to a problem the reader faces, make that clear right away. The point is to make a connection with the reader's interests, expectations, immediate challenges, or needs.
- Motivate the reader to respond by demonstrating clearly *how* your idea will help to solve a problem for the reader, fulfill a pressing need, remove a difficulty, or satisfy expectations. Link your proposal to the reader's concerns by showing how it will help to fulfill, alleviate, or resolve them; show her how she will benefit.
- Make it easy for the reader to respond to your suggestion or implement your plan. Be sure to provide a description of what specific action should be taken to get the plan moving. If the audience cannot clearly see exactly what they must do, they may be unmoved to action; even if they are convinced by your argument but unsure of your ability to follow through, their commitment may be lost. The audience will expect a proposal to hold out a reachable goal and show a plausible first step.
- Do your homework. Be able to demonstrate that your idea has merit and that you have a concrete plan for implementing it. Point to the success of similar ideas or to an existing track record. Let the reader see that you know what you're talking about.
- Show that you understand both the situation and the reader by countering probable objections before the reader has a chance to raise them. A reader unfamiliar with or unsupportive of your proposal will be able to think of reasons why it won't be feasible. If you think ahead to the reader's probable objections and provide solutions to them, you will remove them as obstacles and build confidence that you know what you're doing.
- Keep a positive, enthusiastic tone. Aim to resolve difficulties, not to intensify them through a negative approach. Your recommendation should clearly and explicitly offer advantages to the reader, either by solving an existing problem, or by enhancing a current method or system.
- Communicate your sincerity and commitment. No matter how earnest you feel, your reader will reject your message if you don't sound as though you mean what you say or if you seem uncertain about how your plan will be realized. Be sure that your sincerity is reflected in what you write. Especially avoid the standard clichés of professional writing, which will make you sound insincere or even phony.

If you are writing for someone who is already familiar with and supportive of your work, you must still engage interest, motivate action, and instill confidence, but the task will be a little easier because the reader is already with you:

- Someone already familiar with and positively disposed to your ideas will be more inclined to read your message through, so engaging attention and interest will be simpler. Make a connection with what you know the reader cares about.
- Your established contacts have already shown commitment to your ideas; briefly remind them of the advantages of your idea. If relevant, outline your achievements to date. Remind your supporters of the benefits of the proposal and the ways it will help to serve their needs.
- Be enthusiastic. Outline advantages in a positive tone.
- Communicate your sincerity by addressing the reader directly and genuinely.
- Show your commitment with a concrete plan for implementing and completing your project.

All persuasive correspondence must appeal to the reader strongly enough to make that person respond actively. It should be positive, warm, and persuasive, appealing to the needs, interests, and expectations of the reader.

Persuasion, Manipulation, and the 'Hard Sell'

In the course of my work, I routinely encounter students who mistakenly regard all persuasion as an inherently manipulative and unethical activity. This attitude isn't entirely surprising: after all, we live in a world surrounded by unwelcome and often ethically questionable persuasive messages: fundraising appeals, television commercials, pop-up ads on the web, product placements in TV shows and movies, Internet and e-mail scams. Some of these appeals employ ethically questionable strategies: instead of identifying and responding to an existing need, for instance, they rely on creating a false sense of urgency or fear, or manipulate readers by appealing to their greed or pandering to their secret doubts. Little wonder, then, that many people have learned to be suspicious of attempts to persuade. Little wonder, too, that writing overtly persuasive messages can be challenging.

However, before you decide that you can't, or shouldn't, write persuasively, and before you dismiss the idea of persuasion as inherently bad, you should be aware that you already practice persuasion. You should be aware, too, that not all persuasion is manipulative, unethical, or even unwelcome; in fact, the majority of the persuasion we encounter is beneficial, even essential to our well-being. For example, persuasion is present in admonitions from parents, advice from dentists or physicians, guidance from teachers, or instructions from police officers at a traffic accident. It is present when we write a résumé, interview for a job, petition for a change of grade, or approach the boss for a raise. Even writing an exam is an act of persuasion in which you hope to convince the professor that you've mastered the course material.

When you undertake to persuade others, you do have an ethical responsibility, as we learned in Chapter 4, to represent your message and yourself honestly and accurately, and to exercise concern for the well-being of your reader. This means, among other things, that you don't submit the work of others as if it is your own; you don't misrepresent your credentials or experience on your résumé; you don't pander to or falsely flatter your reader so as to obtain the ends you seek. In other words, you do not compromise your own credibility or your audience's commitment by overstating or misrepresenting your case for persuasion.

If you wish to move your readers to action, convince them of a point of view, or encourage them to accept a change in plans, you will need to make use of legitimate persuasive techniques, keeping the needs and expectations of your audience firmly in mind and accommodating those without compromising either your own integrity or that of the message. Contemporary readers, who are overwhelmed with persuasive messages from the Internet, television, films, and print media, are sophisticated about pushy '**hard sell**' approaches to persuasion. They may be wary and suspicious of such methods, and will reject your message as insincere if they detect such an attitude. Remember to keep your tone positive and warm, not crass or offensive, and to keep your audience's concerns genuinely in focus. As well, be on the lookout for unintentional phrases that might undercut the effectiveness of your message.

The following example of an effective persuasive appeal (Figure 5.9) encourages donations for a public cause. Contrast it with the letter circulated in a downtown neighbourhood to advertise a new security service that has just opened (Figure 5.10).

West Coast College

PO Box 4646, Burnaby, BC V6J 2T7
www.wcc.bc.ca

April 29, 2010

Dear Friend:

Like many of us who live in the city of Burnaby, you may have fond memories of playing at the old City Recreation Park. Unfortunately, in the last ten years the park has fallen into disrepair and is no longer a place where children and families can go for recreation and fun. With your help, that can change. This spring students from the Civil Technology Program at West Coast College have been at work on a special project: with permission of the mayor and city councillors, they have begun to refurbish the old recreation park. They have already embarked on a clean-up of the site, where they plan to establish a playground, picnic park, and games field.

As you may know, what is left of the old playground equipment is in dire need of repair. The students have donated their time to the clean-up and have organized teams to help with the building of new facilities and the repair of any of the old equipment that can be salvaged. Once the park is rebuilt, the mayor has promised to fund supervised recreational activities for children throughout the summer.

Unfortunately, all this hard work leads nowhere without financial support. That's where you come in: the Civil Technology Student Society of West Coast College invites you to participate in this worthwhile project with a donation of equipment, materials, or money to assist the students in rebuilding the park into a site we can all enjoy and be proud of. Our goal is to raise $5000 in corporate and private donations to support the work the students are doing. Donations of any amount will be welcomed.

We hope you will come out to the site to see the progress we have already made, and that you will be able to assist us in our efforts to complete this worthwhile project. Cash donations may be sent directly to the CTSS or dropped off at any Benjamin's Drug Store location. To donate materials or equipment, please contact Louis Mfu-Mansa, Chair of the Civil Technology Department.

Sincerely,

Jerry Maniel, President

Louis Mfu-Mansa, Faculty Advisor

Figure 5.9: What are the qualities that make this fundraising letter effective? What methods do Maniel and Mfu-Mansa use to engage readers' interest and gain their support?

Get the Feeling
SOMEBODY'S WATCHING YOU
555 Broadway, Whitney Pier NS
(902) 345 2473

Dear Neighbour:

We are recent graduates of the Electronic Technology Program at East Coast College, and we have just opened our very first home security service to offer you the best in up-to-date remote-observation electronic household security. In school, we learned just about every technique imaginable for electronic and computer monitoring, and we are anxious to try them out on your home. Take a chance with your security: Try us!

As the new kids on the block, we are anxious to make a go of this venture, and we think it will be good for you to try somebody new for a change. We need to establish a clientele or we won't be able to stay in business for long, so we hope you will try us out.

To make our new service more attractive to you, bring this letter with you when you come in to register your home for a security check. We will perform a free 'casing' service of your belongings, and will give you 5% off your first month's rates. Also, we guarantee to satisfy your security needs, so if there is a theft while we are monitoring your property, we promise we will provide an additional three months' outstanding service for no cost. So instead of going with the old-fashioned security companies, come in and try us. We're anxious to please you and to have a chance to practice our various computer-based techniques. We think you'll be really surprised at the quality of our service.

Sincerely,

Ali Mahoud

Kevin Heppner
Co-Owners

Figure 5.10: A promotional letter like this one is a good idea for a new service, but these writers could use a little help. What improvements to their letter would you suggest?

The Formats of Professional Correspondence

Although much professional correspondence is now conducted by e-mail, business letters are still used for formal purposes, and professionals are expected to be aware of the conventions of formatting these important standard documents. Whether they are sent by ordinary post, via fax, or as an e-mail attachment, all letters consist of the same standard parts and are laid out according to a conventional format that includes single-spacing.

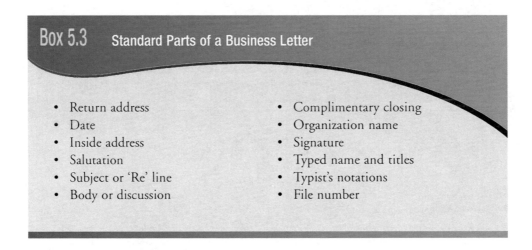

Box 5.3   Standard Parts of a Business Letter

- Return address
- Date
- Inside address
- Salutation
- Subject or 'Re' line
- Body or discussion

- Complimentary closing
- Organization name
- Signature
- Typed name and titles
- Typist's notations
- File number

The parts of a business letter

Return address or letterhead
This is the mailing address of the writer of the letter; it does not normally include the writer's name, which customarily appears below the signature. In a personal letter, your home address serves as the return address. If you are writing on behalf of your organization, it is the organization's name and address. If you are using company letterhead, you do not need to include a separate return address.

Date
All correspondence should be dated. If possible, write out the date in full to avoid confusion, since styles of numerical dating vary. There are currently three forms in use:

Canadian	12/06/10	Day/Month/Year
American	06/12/10	Month/Day/Year
'Metric'	10/06/12	Year/Month/Day

Looking at these examples, you can immediately see how confusing numerical dating can be. The date shown is 12 June 2010, but if you saw '12/06/10' written on a document and had no other cues for interpretation, this same configuration could also be read as 6 December 2010 or 6 October 2012, and you would have no way to be sure. If your employer prefers numerical dating, you should use the format the company uses, but otherwise, avoid this unnecessary confusion by writing the date out in full.

Inside address

This is an important part of the business letter for filing and legal purposes; since it provides a record of the company and the individual to whom it was sent. The inside address consists of the following elements:

Name and title	Professor Louis Mfu-Mansa, Chair
Name of organization	Civil Technology Program
	West Coast College
Address of organization	PO Box 4646
	Burnaby, BC
	V6J 2T7

If the person's title is very long, it might be placed on a separate line, but the order of the parts remains the same.

Name	Ms. Soo Liang Chan
Title	Assistant Manager, Human Resources
Name of organization	Waskasoo College
Address of organization	PO Box 1977
	Forestville, ON
	P6R 2T7

Salutation

The salutation is the conventional form of address that opens a business letter. Traditionally, it is 'Dear' plus the title and name of the person you are writing to, as in 'Dear Dr. Berutti' or 'Dear Ms. Wills'. Note that the standard form of address for women in contemporary business is 'Ms.'; do not use 'Mrs.' or 'Miss' unless you know for a fact that your correspondent prefers it. In North American usage, the correct title for those who hold the degrees PhD, DSc, DVM, DMD, or MD is 'Dr.'. University professors are properly addressed as 'Dr.' or 'Professor', as in 'Dear Dr. MacLennan' or 'Dear Professor Urquhart'. A member of the administration may be addressed by either of these honorifics or as 'Dean Lague', 'Vice President Barber', or 'President MacKinnon'.

If you don't know the person's name and it is important that you have it (for instance, in a job application letter), check the company website, or telephone the organization and ask for the person's name. If you are unable to obtain the name by these means, you could substitute the job title, as in 'Dear Personnel Manager' or 'Dear Department Head'. If this isn't possible, you may wish to delete the salutation altogether, an option that has become more acceptable in modern correspondence. You should probably avoid using 'Dear Sir' if you don't know the name; your correspondent may well turn out to be a woman who may resent the assumption that only males hold positions of organizational importance.

Note that in Canada, unless you are already on friendly personal terms, it is *never* proper to address a professional correspondent by first name. 'Dear Barbara' or 'Dear Mai Li' is considered an inappropriate usage in formal correspondence, especially for a person you do not know well. Instead, always use the person's title and surname, as in 'Dear Dr. Warnick' or 'Dear Ms. Chiu'. If you are corresponding with a person who gives only a first initial or whose given name you cannot readily identify as male or female—for example, K. Barnett, Terry Ferguson, Inderjit Bhanot, Saran Narang, or Pat Androgue—you may wish to write the full name in the salutation rather than risking 'Mr.' or 'Ms.': 'Dear K. Barnett' or 'Dear Inderjit Bhanot'.

The salutation normally ends with a colon, as in 'Dear Dr. Cowan:' or 'Dear Mr. MacLean:'. It may, however, be left without punctuation; if so, the complimentary closing should also be left without punctuation.

Subject or 'Re' line

The subject line has become a useful part of the contemporary business letter. It refers the reader immediately to the main purpose of the correspondence. This line should be brief and to the point, and should indicate clearly what the letter is about. It usually consists of a single phrase or two.

Body or discussion

This portion of your correspondence contains the main information you wish to communicate, in as clear a form as possible. It begins with an introductory statement or paragraph that briefly outlines the situation or problem. It is followed by pertinent details, carefully selected and organized so that the reader may easily understand your message. Finish with a concluding statement or paragraph that outlines what you expect of the reader.

The body of the letter is single spaced and divided into brief paragraphs for ease of reading. The number of paragraphs can vary, as can the length of the letter, depending on the complexity of the subject matter. Some letters are two or three pages long, but most are one page. Whatever the length of the letter, its message should be easily grasped on one reading. If your reader must reread the letter several times simply to understand it, it is poorly composed and ineffective.

Complimentary closing

By far the most commonly used standard closing is 'Sincerely' or perhaps 'Yours sincerely'. 'Yours truly', although not incorrect, is used less frequently than it once was. Whichever you use, be sure to note its correct spelling. If you are on friendly terms with your correspondent, you may even wish to use a more familiar closing, such as 'Cordially' or 'Best wishes' or even (if you are very well acquainted) 'Cheers', but you should avoid these in formal correspondence.

Normally a comma follows the complimentary closing, unless you are employing what is known as 'open' punctuation. In that case, both salutation and complimentary closing are unpunctuated.

Organization name

This feature is optional and is used only in limited circumstances to signify that a letter written on organization letterhead was in fact written on behalf of the organization. The organization's name, in block letters, is placed immediately below the complimentary closing, above the writer's signature. This precaution is observed to clarify responsibility for legal purposes. At one time, it was safe to assume that anything written on the company's letterhead was written on behalf of the firm, but frequent use of letterhead for personal correspondence has made this assumption impractical. Nowadays writers may take this extra measure to emphasize that the contents of the letter are indeed a matter of company business. It is not necessary to include this line in your business letters unless it is common practice in your organization.

Yours sincerely,
DOLOVICH AND COWAN

Aidan Terry

Writer's signature

All formal correspondence is signed by the writer. The signature normally is the legal or preferred name of the writer; it does not include nicknames, titles, or degrees. A professional should use a consistent signature, not Jennifer in one letter and Jen or Jenny in the next. Choose one form of your name and use it consistently for your professional correspondence. Unless you are well known by a diminutive or a nickname (Gordie Howe, Woody Allen), you probably shouldn't use either as your signature.

Typed name and titles

Since signatures can be difficult to decipher, a courteous writer types the name in full beneath the signature, along with the person's job title, if it is relevant. If you wish to list any degrees or honorifics, type them along with your name. (These, you will remember, are never part of the signature.) If you typically sign your name with initials, or if it is otherwise hard to distinguish, or if you prefer an honorific that is different from the norm, you may wish to indicate, in parentheses, which you prefer. A woman who signs herself as J. MacLennan, for example, should not be surprised or offended if some correspondents make the incorrect assumption and address her as 'Mr.'. A man who uses only an initial should similarly not be surprised to be addressed occasionally as 'Ms.'.

Nancy Black, MD
Chief of Staff

Terry Lansdown (Mrs.)
Client Services

Saran Narang, PhD, P.Eng.
Editor in Chief

Soo Liang Chan (Ms.)
Assistant Manager, Human Resources

Typist's notations

As with the inside address, the typist's notation is useful for record purposes; it is sometimes important to know who typed the correspondence, whether any enclosures or attachments were included, and whether any other people received carbon copies or photocopies. The notations appear in the lower left of the page and are as follows.

/jml   Typist's initials are included if someone other than the writer typed the letter. Some organizations use this form to indicate that the typist actually composed the correspondence on behalf of the writer, though this is not the case in every office.

DFC/jm   Writer's initials/typist's initials. The notation may be written this way to indicate that an assistant typed what someone else wrote.

encl:2	Enclosure notation, with number of enclosures. In this example, two items were enclosed with the package.
attach:3	Attachment notation, with the number of attachments. This notation is identical to an enclosure notation, but suggests that the items were appended to the letter with a clip or staple. In this example, there were three.
cc. R. Burton R. Vandeven	Correspondence notation. The people named received copies of the correspondence. The notation 'cc' originally meant carbon copy, the method used for creating copies of documents before photocopiers and computers became indispensable office equipment. Although no one now uses carbon copies, the notation 'cc' continues to be used whenever copies, however generated, are sent to other individuals in addition to the addressee. This notation occasionally still appears as 'pc' for photocopy, but this attempt at updating never really caught on. In either case, its meaning is the same.

File number

The file number appears as a combination of letters and numbers either at the lower left of the page below the cc notation or, more commonly, at the upper right of the page. This is a reference number that assists the business in filing copies of correspondence in the appropriate location.

The parts of a memo or e-mail message

If you have used e-mail, you are already familiar with the structure of a standard memo, on which e-mail layout is based. Although the letter and memo serve similar purposes and may carry similar kinds of messages, a memo is intended to remain inside the company or organization, and this fact affects its structure. It has no need of an inside address, return address, or salutation; instead, it uses the four standard headings familiar to you from your electronic mail: 'To', 'From', 'Date', and 'Subject' (or 'Re', which stands for 'in reference to').

These labels are usually arranged vertically at the top left-hand side of the memo, although the layout of these parts may vary slightly. Unless the memo form is being used for a short informal report, the body of the memo is single-spaced. Paragraphs are typically not indented, and are separated by a single skipped line.

To, From, Date, Subject

This compact form replaces the return and inside addresses and the salutation; since the memorandum is intended for internal mail and does not normally go outside the company, the detailed information provided by these parts of a formal business letter is not required.

Like the letter, however, a memo includes both date and subject lines, and may include additional notations to aid in filing. The 'To' line takes the place of the salutation and identifies, by name and title, the person or persons to whom the memo is directed, while the 'From' line identifies, again by name and title, the person who wrote the memo. As in the letter, the 'Re' or 'Subject' line tells the reader exactly what issue the memo or e-mail message addresses and what you wish to say about that issue. This crucial line of your memo should contain the main point you have identified in your rough draft with the key words, 'The main information I want to tell you is that. . .'. Busy people should not have to scan the entire memo to find the gist of your message. Often they decide whether to take the time even to read the memo by glancing at the subject line, so make sure yours is specific.

This line is especially important in an e-mail message; regular users of e-mail can receive as many as twenty or thirty messages every day. Most don't have time to carefully read all of these, and some even delete those that look unimportant without reading them at all. If you want to make sure your message gets read, supply a subject line that makes clear to the reader what the message involves.

Body or discussion

The body of the memo, normally without a salutation, follows the headings; it may be separated from them by a solid line if you wish. Like the body of the letter, it contains the main information you wish to communicate, in as clear a form as possible. It is single-spaced and deals with the situation or problem as specifically as possible. The body of the e-mail message is similar to that of the memo, although many people like to personalize this impersonal form of communication by adding a salutation. If your e-mail message is to someone you know well and with whom you're on friendly terms, this salutation may be as familiar as 'Hi, Gail'. If you are corresponding via e-mail to a professional colleague or client, you may wish to use the same form of salutation that is used in a letter: 'Dear Franco,' or the more formal 'Dear Dr. Berruti'.

Like a letter, a memo or e-mail may deal with issues of varying complexity. Memos used for simple issues are usually less than a page long, but the memo format may also be used for a short report dealing with more complex situations. (Informal memo reports are discussed in Chapter 6). Whatever its purpose, the memo or e-mail message, like the letter and report, provides specifics to support the main point given in the subject or 'Re' line. However, because these messages are often very short and to the point, they risk being curt or abrupt in tone. Be especially careful to observe courtesy in a memo or e-mail message in order to avoid offending your reader.

Use a memo for information that might be considered 'official'; a casual message may be better delivered by telephone, by e-mail, or by a brief personal note. As a gesture of courtesy and respect to your correspondents, you should avoid contributing to the flurry of unnecessary memos or e-mails and refrain from cluttering others' e-mail queues with mass e-mailings of trashy messages; if others send these to you, avoid passing them on.

Initial or signature

No complimentary closing is normally required for a memo, but it may be initialled or signed if you wish or if the practice at your company dictates. Though a signature is not essential on all memos, it is becoming more common to sign them, particularly if they are intended to confirm official arrangements or if they must record authorization for a project or procedure. Your initials may be placed adjacent to your name at the top, or they may be placed at the bottom following the message. There is no need to type your name again under your signature.

Typist's notations

Since memos serve the same purposes as letters, they make use of the same notations, especially typist's initials and carbon copy designations. If it is appropriate, copies may be sent to superiors or other interested parties within the company. For example, a supervisor who writes a memo commending an employee for work well done might direct a copy to the personnel file; the head of a departmental committee might direct a copy of a meeting announcement to the department head to let that individual know that the committee is getting on with its work. Memos, like letters, may also contain file numbers for easy reference. E-mail messages may be sent to several people simultaneously; if so, their e-mail addresses appear in the 'To' portion of the message rather than in a copy notation at the bottom of the page.

Full block layout in letters and memos

Contemporary business letters and memos use a layout known as **full block format**, in which all parts of the letter are aligned to the left margin. You may still occasionally see letters using an older format in which the return address, date, and complimentary closing are placed to the right of centre, but this older form is rarely used anymore.

When you set up your letters, you should follow the contemporary standard and align everything to begin at the left margin. The entire body of the letter is single-spaced. Paragraphs are not indented, and they are separated by a single skipped line. Figure 5.11 shows the standard layout of the business letter.

You may also have noticed that the examples in this book use different punctuation styles. Some use an 'open' style, with no punctuation marks at the end of the salutation or complimentary closing; others use 'closed' punctuation, with a colon following the salutation and a comma after the complimentary closing. Either punctuation style is acceptable in any of the formats, but do not mix open and closed styles within a single letter.

A standard memorandum also uses the full block style, aligning everything to the left margin. As in the letter, the body of the memo is single-spaced, and a single skipped line separates paragraphs.

In both letters and memos, the impression of clarity is enhanced by an attractive arrangement of the letter or memo on the page. Leave generous margins—at least 1" on all sides—and place the printed material as near as possible to the vertical centre of the page. Try not to crowd your letter or memo too close to the top of the page; unless it is very brief, you should space your letter so that approximately half of the print falls within the lower half of the page.

Another important factor in creating an attractive and readable layout is the font you select from those available in your word processor program. In general, a serif font (such as Times or Roman) is easier on the eye in a lengthy printed document than is a sans serif font (such as Helvetica). Script fonts, especially in smaller sizes, are also difficult to read, as are many decorative or novelty fonts. Avoid using these for formal correspondence as they also risk looking too 'cutesy' and may undercut your ethos. Finally, always select a font large enough to be read comfortably. Most are pre-set at 12; you may go slightly larger than this for headings, but do not reduce the font in the body of your document below 12. Compare the following examples for visual appeal and professionalism:

Times	The quick brown fox jumps over the lazy dog. The lazy dog does not respond. The fox disappears through a hole in the hedge.
Palatino	The quick brown fox jumps over the lazy dog. The lazy dog does not respond. The fox disappears through a hole in the hedge.

Helvetica   The quick brown fox jumps over the lazy dog. The lazy dog does
                              not respond. The fox disappears through a hole in the hedge.

Comic Sans   The quick brown fox jumps over the lazy dog. The lazy dog
                              does not respond. The fox disappears through a hole in
                              the hedge.

---

980 Main Street
Saint John, NB
E1G 2M3
[1]
January 21, 2010
[2]

David Cowan, President of Operations
Dolovich and Cowan Technical Services
403 Reindeer Street
Vancouver, BC V3A 4D4
[2]

Dear Dr. Cowan
[1]
Re: Full Block Letter Format
[1]
This is an example of the full block style; note how all the parts begin at the left margin. Paragraphs are
not indented, and lines are skipped between them.
[1]
The standard parts of the business letter are also differentiated by skipped lines. The normal number of
lines skipped is indicated by the bracketed numbers printed in blue in this letter. If my letter is short, I
can balance the layout of my text by skipping extra lines between parts. I do not normally add skipped
lines between paragraphs.
[1]
Also, you will notice that this letter is single spaced, as all business letters should be. Note, too, the
optional use of open punctuation in this letter—this means no punctuation at the end of the salutation
or the complimentary closing. Of course, if you wish, you may use a colon after the salutation and a
comma following the complimentary closing.
[1]
Sincerely
[1]
MEDIACORP LTD
[2]

Stan Cherniowsky

[2]
Stan Cherniowsky
Communication Manager
[2]

cc.   Ian Hauen, Ryker Sheepskin Products Ltd.
      SC/jm
[1]
05-01-SD

Figure 5.11: This sample letter shows the parts and spacing of a letter in full block format.

Critical Reading

Joe Lau and Lusina Ho, 'Writing Proper E-mails to Teachers'
Joe Lau (PhD, MIT) is an Associate Professor in the Philosophy Department at the University of Hong Kong. His research area is in the philosophy of mind and cognitive science. He also teaches critical thinking and logic.

Lusina Ho (BCL, Oxford) is a Professor in the Faculty of Law at the University of Hong Kong. She specializes in restitution and trusts. She received an Outstanding Young Researcher Award in 2006.

Writing Proper E-mails to Teachers
Why bother?

When you write to friends you can be as informal as you wish. But when you write to your teacher, you should use proper and polite language. Why? You can communicate more effectively, and it gives people a better impression of your manners and abilities, which might be important if your teacher has to write a reference for you in the future. Also, by training yourself to write properly, you develop skills necessary to deal with future clients and supervisors, who are unlikely to tolerate bad e-mail manners.

Commonsense, politeness, and correct grammar and spelling are the basic ingredients of a proper e-mail. It does not have to be very formal. I have compiled a list of reminders below, which I hope you will find useful.

Some students might find this list ridiculous, and in a way it is. However, the problem is that very few students observe such rules, and yet respectable employers and companies often expect you to know these things. In any case, if you can leave a better impression at very little cost to yourself, why not do it?

Points to Note
1. Avoid abbreviations and ICQ English. So do not use expressions such as 'giv 2 u' or 'b4'. Always use capital 'I' to refer to yourself. Use capital letters properly ('Dear Jimmy' and not 'dear jimmy'). Otherwise you are giving the impression that the other person is not worth your time to write properly.
2. A proper e-mail should begin with an appropriate salutation. For example, 'Dear Dr. Suzuki,'; 'Dear Miss Chan'. Avoid 'Hi/Hey/Dear Sir' if you know the name of the addressee. You might skip the salutation only if you have exchanged a few e-mails on this topic already, and an informal e-mail is appropriate for the context.
3. After the salutation, begin the body of the e-mail with an explanation of why you are sending the e-mail, or explain the request that you are making.
4. If you have a question about a course, say which course it is. This is because a teacher usually teaches more than one course each term. Give enough context so the teacher knows where your question is coming from.
5. If you have a request, say it politely. You can start with 'I would like to. . .', 'I wonder if you can. . .', 'May I. . .', 'Is it possible to. . .', 'Do you mind. . .'. NOT: 'I want to know. . .', 'I want you to. . .', 'Send this to me. . .', 'Tell me when. . .'.
6. Remember that just because you use the word 'please', it does not mean that you are being polite. 'Please' can be used in commands, e.g., 'Please behave yourself', 'Please finish the project tomorrow.'

7. After stating your request, never say 'Please reply'; 'Please reply as soon as possible.' Even if a matter is urgent, it is very rude to say so, because these statements read more like commands than requests. Just explain that the matter is urgent, and the teacher/administrator will understand.

8. If a teacher has responded to your request, always send a return e-mail saying 'Thank you.' Otherwise you would appear to be rude.

9. If you would like to make an appointment with the teacher/administrator, write it politely. For example, 'I wonder if I could make an appointment with you. . .', but not 'May I have an appointment with you so that you may have a chance to help.'

10. When making an appointment, you can suggest a few time slots, but always say something like 'If these times do not suit you, please feel free to let me know any other time that you prefer/is convenient to you.'

11. If you cannot make the date suggested, say 'I am sorry I cannot come to see you on [Monday].' Never say 'I am not available on [Monday]' (teachers can say that to you, but not vice versa).

12. If you have a suggestion for the teacher, avoid saying 'I suggest you [do this or that]', 'Send me XXX before YYY', 'You may e-mail the notes to me.' (These are polite commands.)

13. If you have a course tutor, try consulting your tutor first. Don't ask questions if you can find out the answers by yourself. Ask your classmates, and check the department website or the course website first.

14. You should close an e-mail properly, e.g. 'Best wishes, Lala / Dada Wong', 'Sincerely yours, Lala', 'Regards, Lala', 'Best, Lala' (the last one is more informal). Give your true name, never say 'A student of PHIL1006', 'Your tutee'. Never leave the e-mail unsigned.

15. Always re-read your e-mails and check for spelling and grammatical mistakes before sending them.

Points to Remember

1. Professional correspondence can either initiate or respond to contact, and can contain positive or negative messages.

2. Do not use e-mail for messages that are confidential or that contain important or sensitive information.

3. Apply the Seven Cs of professional writing to all e-mail messages, letters, and memos.

4. Make sure your letter contains all the appropriate parts, whether you are sending it by fax or by conventional mail: return address, date, inside address, salutation, subject line, body, complimentary closing, organization name, signature, typed name, notations, and file number.

5. In a memo, the 'To', 'From', 'Date', and 'Re' or 'Subject' information appears first.

6. Be sure to provide a clear and relevant 'Re' line on all correspondence.

7. Recognize reader needs, expectations, priorities, knowledge, concerns, and relationships, and always avoid sarcasm.

8. Always be professional in tone and attitude.

9. Avoid contributing to e-mail clutter.

Key Concepts

acceptance, message of
acknowledgement, message of
apology, message of
bad news
complaint, message of
conciliation, message of

congratulation, message of
engage, motivate, enable
full block format
good news
hard sell
refusal, message of

rejection, message of
request message
response message
Seven Cs
tone

Assignments and Exercises

1. Write a letter to a former instructor or employer, requesting permission to name that person as a reference in a job application. Be sure to include all the information the person will need in order to comply with your request.

2. You are working on a project for which you need a quantity of fasteners called Chicago screws. After researching suppliers online, you have decided to go with a Canadian supplier, Stephens Rivet and Machine, in Brampton, Ontario. These fasteners are available in a variety of materials, including stainless steel, anodized aluminum (available in all colours), and plastic (available in black and white only). You will be needing the fasteners in quantity and have more or less decided to go with a 1¼" anodized aluminum in blue. You expect to be placing an order for approximately 25,000, but before you make your final order you would like to see some samples of the product. Compose the e-mail you would send to the order desk at Stephens Rivet <info@stephensrivet.com> requesting samples of the appropriate product in all three materials.

3. Your department chair has been arranging mock job interviews for the students in your program in order to give them experience in interviewing. The interviews are to be conducted by professionals in your future field who have agreed to come to the college to participate in the exercise. Your program chair has impressed upon all of you how important these practice interviews are. Yours is set for next Thursday at 2:00 pm. Since you made this appointment, however, you have had a real job interview scheduled for 2:30 pm that same day. You can't make it to both interviews. If you are successful in the actual interview, the job will give you experience directly related to your college program. Write a memo to your program chair with a copy to Allan Goren, the person who was to have conducted your mock interview, cancelling your appointment and explaining why you can't be there.

4. You and a friend have recently found yourselves in competition for a plum internship in your field. You feel certain that you are the better qualified candidate, since your grades are slightly better than your friend's, and you have a full year more experience in this kind of position. Nevertheless, you have just learned that your friend has been offered the job, while you have received a polite letter of rejection. You are happy for your friend, but disappointed for yourself. Write a letter of congratulation to send to your friend. Invent any details you need.

5. You are the former instructor of Pat Yorgason, who has just written to you asking for a letter of reference. It has been three years since Pat was in your class, and you have taught 300 students per year since then. You never knew Pat well and you

can't picture a face to go with the name; all you can recall is the impression of an indifferent student. A check of your records confirms that impression: Pat's grade in your communications class was C–, but otherwise nothing much jogs your memory. In fact, you have taught lots of 'Pats', both male and female, but you have no clear recollection of Pat Yorgason. For this reason, you don't feel that you are the best choice to write a recommendation for him or her. Write a letter to Pat politely explaining why another referee might be a better choice. Pat Yorgason, PO Box 75, Okotoks, Alberta, T0K 0K0.

6. You've been working for the summer in the textbook division of your college bookstore, where you've been tracking orders and unpacking books for the coming school year. It's now the first week of August, and the textbook orders for the fall have started to come in. Just this morning, you received a shipment from the publishing house MacDonald-Bain, containing books for your college's required course in technical communication. As this is a course you have to take yourself, you look closely at the book as you unpack the boxes. According to what's written on the packing slip, the boxes should contain 300 copies of *Communication for Technical Professionals*, but when you open the box, what's inside is *Communication for Social Workers*. You double-check the ISBN code on the back of the books (0-536-43810-2) against the one given on the packing slip and discover they match. Theoretically, and according to the procedure the bookstore uses to verify stock, you've done all you're required to do, and the books should be cleared for shelving. But the book titles don't match the title shown on the packing slip, and you happen to know that the students who take the course are enrolled in engineering, agriculture, and geological sciences, not social work. You are certain that this is the wrong book, so you decide to go online to confirm the ISBN for the technical communication title. You discover that the number given on the packing slip is indeed wrong: the correct ISBN for the technical communication book is 0-536-08297-9. It's not clear where along the line that the mistake happened, but it has to be corrected in time for the start of classes in September. Compose an e-mail to the manager of the textbook division, Murdena Maclardy, explaining the situation.

7. Re-read the story of Ram Dharmaratnam, as told on pages 102–103 in Chapter 4, and write the apology that Ram should have made to the senior research chemist. Format your message as a memo addressed to your communication instructor.

8. You've recently become interested in genealogy and have been researching your family tree. As you gather your information, you find that you would like to have copies of some of the birth, marriage, and death certificates for your ancestors. Select a parent or grandparent and write a correctly formatted business letter requesting a copy of the birth certificate for your relative. Address your letter to the appropriate registry of vital statistics in the relevant province or country and be sure to provide, in a readable fashion, all of the details that the registry will need to locate the records. You will need the person's full birth name, the city or town of birth, the names of both parents, and the date.

9. Along with three other members of your communication class, you are interested in forming a public speaking club for students in your program. Your communication instructor has agreed to act as faculty sponsor, but in order for your group to be allowed to hold events on campus, you have to be ratified by the Students' Association. Ratification requires a membership list of at least 15 people. Compose an e-mail message to all students in your program encouraging them to join your

club. Be sure to include a listing of the advantages of such an organization, the deadline for ratification, fees or start-up costs, and a deadline for signing up. If you plan to post or circulate a sign-up sheet, tell your audience where and when they can sign. Send a copy of your memo to the chair of your department.

10. As you have been discovering, the way you communicate has a profound impact on your career success; many studies have shown that employers in all fields—including engineering—rank communication high among the skills they seek in new recruits. Suppose you have applied for a job with such an employer. In the course of the interview process, you have been asked to identify three important principles of communication and show how they have contributed to your own effectiveness as a communicator. Present your discussion in standard memo format and address it to your communication instructor.

11. You've been out of school for two years, but you remember your college experience fondly. In particular, you recall one professor who really made a difference to your work and your life, though you never really thought to say so at the time; in fact, you are fairly certain you would not have been able to pass your senior year without this person's intervention. Just this morning, however, you received an e-mail from a former classmate to let you know that your mentor has passed away suddenly. This news has hit you very hard, since only last month you were reminiscing about your school days with another friend, and your thoughts and conversation had turned to your former professor. At the time it occurred to you, as it has from time to time since graduation, that you should maybe write a note to let your professor know what a difference those extra efforts made in your life, but you just didn't seem to get around to it, and now it's too late. However, in the midst of your own sorrow you realize that the grief of the professor's family must be even more devastating than your own, and you decide to write a letter of condolence to let them know just what this person's work and friendship has meant in your life.

12. Turn again to the scenario in Assignment #9. You're still trying to set up your public speaking club, but your e-mail hasn't brought the response you'd hoped for, so you've decided you need to visit the communication classes in person to talk to your target audience face-to-face. Write an e-mail message to the head of the communication department requesting permission to visit the classes and circulate your sign-up sheet.

13. You are nearing graduation and have been conducting a job search. You are lucky enough to have been offered two positions. The first is with the small firm where you completed an internship last year; the other is a more promising position with a multinational. The small company offers better pay initially, but the multinational firm offers better prospects for promotion and benefits over the long term, and after carefully considering the two, you have decided to accept the position with the multinational. Write the letter to your internship supervisor thanking him for the offer, but politely refusing the job. He is: Gene Kirk, Testamek Engineering Ltd, 64 Weniam Street, Vancouver, British Columbia, V1R 9V1.

14. Recently you deposited in person $300 into your bank account. A week later, on checking your balance at the bank machine, you discover that the $300 has not appeared. When you visit the bank, the teller, Baghwan Dua, discovers that the money has been placed into another customer's account. The person has the same surname as yours, but the account numbers are significantly different. Dua arranges to correct the error, but he is quite unapologetic and even implies that the

mistake is somehow your fault. Write to the manager of your bank, Ramona Chief Calf, to register your complaint.

15. You and a friend spent last summer operating a small manufacturing and retailing business to market a series of topological puzzles that you designed. The designs were your idea, but you needed a partner and your friend, a business major, seemed eager to be involved. The puzzles proved popular and the business was a success. You did not bother to draw up a formal business agreement, but it seemed a good partnership, and the plan is to repeat the experience next year. At the end of the summer you returned to the city to find an apartment while your friend stayed behind in Banff to wrap up the business over the Labour Day weekend. Your understanding was that you would split the remaining profits of the business in three ways: one-third to each of you, and one-third as seed capital for next summer. You haven't seen your friend since school began, and you still don't have a cheque for your portion, which should be $4,500. You also haven't been advised about whether your friend has banked the seed capital. It's early in the term yet, and you know that the delay could be simply the result of hectic pace of back-to-school, but you're getting a little nervous and you really need the money. You don't want to undermine the partnership or sour the friendship, especially if it's just a misunderstanding, but you do want to know where you stand. Write an e-mail message to your friend requesting that he provide this information, and your cheque, as soon as possible.

16. Your friend Ing Jang is a student at Western Plains University. He has recently had an encounter with the staff of the registrar's office that turned out very wrong, as you can see from Ing's letter (Figure 5.4). Ing wants to register his complaint, but before sending his letter on to the Registrar's office, he has forwarded it to you for your comments. After reading the letter, analyze Ing's communication situation in order to answer the following questions: Should Ing write a letter at all? If so, what should its purpose be? Describe the likely expectations, needs, and attitudes of the intended audience. Given what took place, what challenges does Ing face in repairing his credibility? What strategies can he adopt to manage the situation effectively? What elements of the current letter might actually inflame the situation further? Write your analysis as a letter of advice to Ing Jang.

17. Scenario: An Engineering Prank Goes Wrong

At Western Plains University, the Engineering Students Society has always been actively involved in the university-wide orientation program for new students, which is organized and coordinated through Student Affairs and Services, under the authority of the Director of Student Retention, Joanna Davidson. In addition to coordinating all the events, Davidson's office also prepares a package of materials for each student who participates in orientation, delivered in a presentation binder featuring the university's logo. The binders are fairly costly even at the bulk rate ($2.50 per student); the inserts cost $3 apiece for photocopying, and the binders are assembled by hand.

Orientation for this year took place last Saturday, and Davidson's staff were busy with preparations until well into Friday evening. Right before she was ready to leave the campus at about 9:30 pm, Davidson did one last check to ensure that everything was in order. To her horror, she discovered that she was short three cartons of binders—thirty-six in all. She searched everywhere she could think of, but to no avail: the binders had apparently vanished.

Unable to spend any more precious time searching, Davidson and her assistant Paul Pavlova got to work reprinting and organizing materials to be put into replacement binders, a task that took them until past 1:00 am. Early the next morning, before orientation was set to begin at 10:00 am, Pavlova had to purchase thirty-six binders at full price from an office supply store. By working frantically, they were able to get the extra binders assembled for the 10:00 start-up, but the last-minute replacements have cost them in total $12 per student instead of the $5.50 they had planned upon. Davidson can't figure out where the error occurred, but it has driven up their costs by more than $230, not counting the additional time and aggravation to get the additional binders together at the last minute. This is a serious overrun since their entire Orientation budget is only $1,500.

At 10:45 Saturday morning, an exhausted Davidson and Pavlova gathered the Orientation staff and volunteers for one last briefing session before kick-off. When they recounted their travails of the previous evening, the two engineering volunteers burst into laughter. Stunned, Davidson asked to know what they thought was so funny. Between guffaws, the engineers confessed that they had hidden the three boxes of binders 'for a prank'. Davidson and her office staff were understandably annoyed: they had spent several extra hours replacing the missing materials and now would be stuck with three-dozen binders of material that they couldn't use and that cost them over twice the budgeted price.

When Davidson is asked to explain the budget overrun to her supervisor, Dr. Valerie Price, University Vice President of Student Affairs and Services, Dr. Price is far from amused. She contacts the Dean of Engineering, Dr. R. Billinton, to register her complaint and to ask for reimbursement of this significant cost. The Dean feels that the matter should be handled by the WPESS, and he assigns the task of writing a letter of apology to the WPESS President, Marv Gryphon.

Drawing on the principles of effective communication taught in this book, evaluate the situation and explain the constraints that Marv faces. What kind of letter should he write? What is his footing? How will he establish his credibility and repair the relation between the Vice President and the College of Engineering? What should his letter contain? What pitfalls should it avoid? Why should Marv have to write a letter at all? Write your analysis in a memo directed to your communication instructor. (If you're interested in how Marv handled this challenge, you can find his letter on page 123.)

Writing Samples for Discussion and Analysis

The following real examples violate the principles of effective professional communication that we have learned so far. What is your impression of each message, and of its writer? As you read, ask yourself whether the writer in each case has attended to content and relation, established credibility and professionalism, or developed an understandable, clear message. Be prepared to discuss the flaws in each example and to offer suggestions as to how to correct them. Identify any specific ways in which the writers violate the Seven Cs of completeness, conciseness, clarity, coherence, correctness, courtesy, and credibility discussed in Chapter 1. If your instructor asks you to do so, edit the samples to improve their ethos, civility, clarity of content, and audience relation.

Writing sample #1

2100 Allendon Crescent
Peachvale, Ontario
L7B 3Z9

March 14, 2011

Ms. Kara Exner
90 Main Street
Oshawa, Ontario M6K 3D4

My dearest Kara

Our class just heard the news from Professor Bolton that students from your little communication class are going to present papers at the Maritime Communication Association Conference in April.

I know just how you feel—I did a presentation for one of my classes last week too, and I'm sure it's good enough to present at a conference if I wanted to submit it (conferences can be such a mind-numbing experience, can't they?) And Halifax, what a place, it almost makes you think you should find somewhere interesting to go!

However, it is an accomplishment, dear—and who knows? Maybe someday you'll be shaking my hand as a fellow conference presenter!

Yours very sincerely

Donna Skreyuw

Donna Skreyuw

Figure 5.12: This letter violates the guidelines for a letter of congratulations. What impression does it make on the reader?

Writing sample #2

To:	students@cenmar.u.ca, faculty@cenmar.u.ca, staff@cenmar.u.ca
From:	Phyllis Golemiec <Phyllis.Golemiec@cenmar.u.ca>
Date:	October 1, 2012
Re:	Town Hall Meeting on Student Computing

On Wednesday, October 10, 2004, there will be a 'Town Hall' meeting on Student Computing sponsored by the Vice President of Information and Communication Technology. This event will be held in room 107 Billinton Hall. All students, staff, and faculty are welcome to attend.

The purpose of this meeting is to provide an opportunity for students to ask questions and discuss issues relating to computing and technology at Central Maritime University. Computer facility managers and members of the Information Technology Services and other technology-related departments will be in attendance and will participate in the discussion.

Please plan to attend this event.

Figure 5.13: What common error renders this simple message ineffective?

Writing sample #3

31 March 2010

Prentice Truell
45 Masih Blvd
Sudbury, ON P3Q 1R5

RE: Mechanical Engineering Technology — Statement of Interest

Over the last term, I have had the opportunity to take a senior high school science course with labs taught by Mr. Xiang. The coursework and the labs have left me with a feeling of wanting more; wanting to obtain an understanding of science projects that goes deeper than the material in the course. Pursuing a college diploma is that next logical step in learning more about not only projects, but furthering the education I have received in the past four years in high school. I am excited to have the opportunity to go to college in the fall, and ready for the challenges that lie ahead.

Sincerely,

Prentice Truell

Figure 5.14: A 'statement of intent' letter such as this is primarily a persuasive document. It is normally submitted as part of an application package, and its purpose is to establish the writer's credibility and suitability for the program he hopes to enter. Given the likely expectations of his readers, how effective is Prentice's letter? Does it do a good job of establishing his ethos? How might he improve it?

Writing sample #4

To: allstaff@dolocow.com
From: Ivana Petrovic <ivanapet@dolocow.com>
Date: July 29, 2009
Re: Arrangements for Annual Centre Employee Picnic

This is to inform you that the arrangements for this year's annual company picnic are final and complete at long last. After lots of hard work and planning by this committee, it was decided that it will be on Saturday, August 9.

As you know, we needed to ask for volunteers to lend us various types of equipment for playing sports and games, and we also had to arrange for barbecues to be brought to the site. Luckily we have lots of willing volunteers who can help us out with these requests and they have agreed to bring their equipment for us all to use.

If you are one of those generous people who have agreed to volunteer to us any sports or games supplies or a barbecue or any other kind of item we will be needing, those who have done so are asked by your dedicated committee to arrive one half hour early. The entertainment subcommittee and the food committee, including myself among many other dedicated individuals will be on hand by 10 am to get things rolling right along.

The picnic begins properly at 11, though you can plan to arrive with your family anytime between 10 and 11, unless you are one of our volunteers mentioned above. As has been the case with our many previous successful annual company picnics, this one is to be held as usual at Ellsworth Conservation Park.

If you need directions how to get to the park, just contact me or anyone else on the social committee. Plan to bring everyone in your whole family for a super fun-filled day.

See you all there.
Ivana Petrovic, Social Committee Chairperson

Figure 5.15: Convoluted wording makes it difficult to pick out the important information from this e-mail message. How would you improve it?

Chapter 6

Writing Reports

Learning Objectives

■ To understand the purposes for which reports are written.

■ To learn the standard parts of all reports: Summary, Introduction, Discussion, Conclusion(s), Recommendation(s), and Appendices.

■ To know how to use the Report Writing Planner to plan your report and select appropriate information.

■ To learn about writing an effective technical description and technical instructions.

■ To understand the purpose and focus of a proposal.

© iStockphoto.com/Wendell Franks

Technical occupations typically involve a large amount of paperwork. Regular project reports, incident reports, memos, minutes, funding proposals, tenders, log book entries, lab reports, and other forms of correspondence form a large part of the routine responsibilities of these positions.

Like other communication, reports are not produced in isolation. They are the product of a dynamic interaction between a writer and an intended audience, between the writer and the situation in which the writer must function, between the situation and the audience, and between the message content and the audience. They contribute to a company's professional image and they keep the wheels of industry turning by ensuring that the necessary information reaches those who need to turn ideas into action.

Reports perform a variety of functions in an organization or workplace and come in a huge range of formats, from standardized application forms to comprehensive annual reports, from a two-page memo report to a formal document of several hundred pages. Reports can establish or undermine a company's professionalism; they can make or break the reputation of a researcher; they can help decision-makers to act wisely and well. They may be matters of routine information management, or they may signal the beginning of innovative developments that will change the shape of an organization. In all their diversity, reports really are the currency of business, industry, and the professions.

Why Write Reports?

Writing reports on the job is one of the most important of all the tasks performed by a technical professional. Reports are written for a variety of reasons, but their primary function is to pass on information to supervisors and co-workers. For example, routine incident reports provide an account of what occurred and a record of the action that was taken at the time of the incident. They allow staff to communicate with others in the organization about incidents or situations that might require further action.

Box 6.1   Why Write Reports?

- Pass on information
- Keep permanent records
- Provide an overview of trends and developments
- Enable effective decision-making

Reports also provide a permanent record of events; as such, they function as a kind of diary of the company, of various departments or divisions within the company (for instance, personnel or payroll), or of a chain of events leading to a particular decision or result. They provide a record of project work, of interactions with clients, and of strategic planning at the department level; they are essential for continuity should personnel or circumstances change. Often, reports constitute an important foundation for future decisions or actions, recording the details of project decisions or interactions with staff, clients, or the public. They can also form a record of how the company has carried out its business in accord with statutes or government policy.

Apart from their role in record-keeping, reports provide an overview of company operation. Management rely on the information supplied in the routine reports of various employees to help them keep track of trends and developments in the workplace. The larger the organizational structure, the more significant are individual reports to the functioning of the whole company. Reports from those who deal with the day-to-day personnel, business, managerial, or technical issues can help upper management to assemble an overview of the operation of the company, can flag small problems before they turn into big ones, and can alert officials to the need for policy or procedure changes.

Finally, reports are a critical element in corporate or organizational decision-making, since they provide the information necessary for managers to make effective decisions by reporting actions and details as objectively as possible. A well-written report distinguishes between observed facts and inferences or interpretations; analysis and judgements are clearly labelled as such. By reading such objective reports from a variety of sources in the institution over a period of time, a manager can be assured of acting in the best interests of clients and personnel.

The reports you write as a routine part of your job may also be significant if you hope to be promoted, since, especially in a large organization, your superiors may know you *only* through the reports you write. If you wish to advance in your chosen career, you will need to report accurately, carefully, and clearly. Furthermore, if you are employed in a licensed profession such as engineering, or in a government position, your reports are legal documents, and may be used as evidence in a court case or be required in an investigation, inquiry, or inquest. For all these reasons, your reports require careful attention to detail and clarity.

As a technical professional, you will be required to write numerous reports and to read the reports of others; when you are faced with piles of paperwork on the job, you will appreciate the skills of conciseness, completeness, and accuracy, both as a writer who produces reports for others to read, and as a reader who must plough through the written work of others. Since writing reports will be such an important part of your professional life, you should cultivate these skills while you are still in training for your future career.

The Parts of a Report

All reports feature a conventional structure that readers have learned to both expect and welcome. This standard structure contains several parts, differentiated according to their function and presented in the same order in every message. There are four essential parts and two optional parts to this standard structure; the more formal and lengthy the report, the more likely it is to contain all six.

Box 6.2   The Standard Parts of a Report (SIDCRA)

- Summary
- Introduction
- Discussion

- Conclusion(s)
- Recommendation(s)
- Appendices

In lengthy or formal documents, each of the six parts has its own section heading. In shorter, informal correspondence, the parts are not given headings and are simply indicated by paragraph breaks. The more formal the report, and the longer it is, the more likely it will be to employ formal section headings and subheadings, to include appendices, and to feature formal recommendations for action. All of these parts are intended to assist the reader in following the direction and purpose of a complex message.

Summary

Since reports are longer than most other forms of professional communication, and since their intended readers are typically very busy, the report writer should include a **summary** or **abstract**. The purpose of the summary is to provide an overview of the contents of the report and to outline its recommendations. In a very short report, the summary statement can be as short as a sentence or two; in a long report, it can be as long as several pages. In a formal report, this section is normally set apart with its own heading of 'Summary' or 'Abstract', and provides an overview of the report's conclusions and recommendations. After reading the summary, the reader should know what the recommendations are, and what, in general, to expect from the introduction, discussion, and conclusion of the document.

The summary of the report is written for the least expert of your intended readers, so it should make clear the substance and the direction of your findings in terms that can be understood by a lay reader. Further, the language of the summary (along with that of the introduction, conclusion[s], and recommendation[s]), should be straightforward and should avoid technical jargon. The length of the summary varies with the length of the report, and though there is no set standard, a good guideline is roughly one-tenth as long as the report itself. For example, a ten-page report may have a summary of approximately one page, while the summary of a fifty-page formal report should be expected to be around five pages. The summary for a short informal report in memo or letter format could consist of a subject line and a brief initial paragraph.

Although the summary is the first part of a report that the audience reads, it is normally the last part to be written. Because it provides an overview of the findings, it usually cannot be written until after the report is finalized. The summary of a report is directed at the least specialized of its intended readers, and provides a general sense of the purpose, constraints, outcomes, and recommendations that will follow.

Introduction

Every professional document contains an **introduction**. The purpose of the introduction is to let the reader know the focus and scope of the document. It is also intended to capture attention by engaging the reader with the problem or issue under discussion, and to give the reader an indication of what follows in the body of the document.

The introduction should set out as clearly as possible the problem or situation being examined, and should provide any necessary background information to help the reader understand the report's context, purpose, and function. The introduction may also set out the writer's assumptions and approach to the problem, and should spell out the limits of the report's coverage. In short, the function of the introduction is to prepare the reader for the discussion of the possible outcomes or solutions offered in the report. In semi-formal or formal reports, the introduction is set apart under the heading 'Introduction'.

Discussion

The **discussion**, or body of the work, contains what is known as the 'full development' of the report. This segment provides all necessary background, context, facts, and details, organized in an order appropriate to the content and the purpose of the report.

The discussion is the longest and most detailed part of your report, and is normally written first. It is typically made up of several sections, each with its own heading. Unlike the introduction, the word 'discussion' itself rarely appears as a heading; instead, it is a general term that is used to denote everything in the report between the introduction and the conclusion. The headings used for the discussion section are specific to the content and method of the report in question.

The discussion segment of any report provides additional details about the problem or situation that is being examined. It describes the writer's method of research or assessment (including the criteria used to evaluate possible solutions), any constraints that affected the research, and the steps that led to the report's recommendations and conclusions. Technical calculations and specialized data that are essential to the reader's understanding may also be included as part of the discussion. In contrast to the summary, which is aimed at your least specialized readers, the discussion is aimed at the most knowledgeable of your expected readers.

The headings that are used in the discussion section are specific to the contents of the report and can vary widely, so it's difficult to generalize in a meaningful way. However, as an example, a report that evaluates a training program offered by a local consulting firm might use these section headings within the discussion:

> Our Training Needs
> Description of the Program
> Requirements and Prerequisites
> Costs
> Advantages of the Program
> Limitations of the Program
> Resources Required

Conclusion(s)

The **conclusion** of a report brings the report to an appropriate close. The purpose of the conclusion is to remind your reader of your main purpose and should outline any implications or results that you expect or intend. It should interpret the meaning of your findings for the reader, laying out the judgements that can be made based on the facts presented in the discussion. It presents the logical outcomes of your investigation or evaluation, and should present no surprises for your reader, who has been led by your discussion to expect certain results. For example, if your report evaluates three different computer systems that the company is considering for purchase, your conclusion should indicate which best meets the company's needs.

Depending on the complexity of the situation you are investigating or evaluating, you may have to provide several possible outcomes or implications. If so, you should discuss each in turn, interpreting the meaning of your findings for the reader.

The conclusion is distinct from the recommendations that follow it because, though it draws together the information that was presented in the body of the report, it does not spell out recommendations for action.

Recommendation(s)

The role of the **recommendation**(s) section is to clearly spell out the action desired as a result of the information presented in the discussion. Whereas the conclusion says 'here's what all this means', the role of the recommendation(s) section is to tell the reader 'here's what we should do about it'.

For example, I may write a report that concludes that technical education in contemporary universities is failing to prepare students for the complex communicative demands of their future careers; on the basis of those findings, I can then recommend specific changes to the programming offered in my own college, perhaps in the form of additional courses or an alteration to existing courses. You should think of the recommendations as providing specific direction for the reader as to how to respond to the information you have presented. For instance, your report evaluating the computer systems should clearly recommend the system, or combination of components, that the company should purchase.

Your recommendation(s) section may even include actions you intend to perform yourself; for example, as a result of my report on the state of technical education, I may recommend several new communication courses that I propose to implement in the college. In a formal document, recommendations for action normally appear in their own headed section following the conclusion.

Appendices

An **appendix** is additional material or information that is attached to or included with a report to assist your reader in fully understanding your information. An appendix is a separate document, complete in itself. It should therefore be designed so that it could be read on its own if required. It is not considered a part of the report itself, but it provides additional support or explanation for points in the discussion. Generally, such appended documents contain facts, details, calculations, or research findings that were referred to in the body of the report but are not central to the reader's understanding.

In the process of composing a report, the writer sifts information to determine which details are necessary to the reader's understanding and which may be safely left out. Although the discussion segment of the report is aimed at the most technically specialized of your readers, you should not allow overly detailed technical information to overwhelm the argument. If, for instance, you have a large number of calculations to present, or pages of specifications that would be useful to the reader but are not essential to the argument, you may wish to outline them briefly in the discussion and refer the reader to an appropriate appendix, where they can be presented in greater detail.

For example, if I am writing a report that evaluates training options for our staff, I may begin by establishing what our needs are. Assume that, as part of the process of ascertaining our training needs, I circulated a survey and tabulated the results, which I then summarized as part of my supporting argument in favour of the training program. Because this summary has direct bearing on the argument that I am making, it is included in the discussion segment of the report. Although some of my readers may be interested to read the survey questions themselves and look at participants' actual responses, including them in the discussion would drag me off topic and potentially overwhelm my argument. However, I can include that information as an appendix so that those readers who wish to do so can consult the primary documents for themselves.

In short, an appendix contains any relevant supporting information that, for reasons of space or complexity, has not been dealt with in the discussion section of the report. Your report may require one appendix or several appendices, or it may include none at all. Whether your report requires appendices depends on whether there are reference documents or additional information that would assist your reader in appreciating the full context within which you are writing. Formal reports are more likely than informal ones to include appendices.

You can remember these standard parts of a technical report by the acronym SIDCRA. When you are writing, you can use the SIDCRA structure as an outline device to help you organize your ideas; jotting down your main points can make the writing process easier because you will be able to approach your task with a clearer sense of what you wish to say. It is your responsibility as a writer to help your reader understand your meaning and purpose, and following this structural outline will allow you to make your meaning clearer to those who must make use of the information.

No matter what the subject of your report, from a government white paper to a technical report, it should conform to this general structure. Once you are on the job, your employer may require a specific structure or organization pattern that differs in detail from the advice presented in this book, which is necessarily general. If this is the case, you should follow the requirements of your employer. However, as a general guideline, you can always rely on the SIDCRA structure to help you organize your materials for presentation.

Planning and drafting your report

Reports, like other effective written communication, should be carefully planned and drafted using the communication problem-solving approach described in Chapter 2; such a process is especially useful for writing longer documents such as reports, and you should refer to that chapter as you begin to plan and organize your materials. As well, the Report Writing Planner (Figure 6.1) on page 158 will help you to identify the important elements of your message and the probable needs and expectations of your reader.

Following the strategies outlined in Chapter 2, assemble the main information to be covered in the discussion segment of your report, keeping your reader's needs, attitudes, expectations, and purposes clearly in mind. Be sure to follow the problem-solving approach to drafting and editing your report and to attend to all three of the keys to effective communication: effective audience appeal, a coherent and sound message, and personal credibility.

Following the steps in planning and preparing your report, develop the relevant details, giving enough information to enable your reader to make an informed decision. Consider carefully the way in which the points in your discussion can be presented, choosing your words with care as you work and selecting an appropriate organizing principle. Then write the rough draft of your discussion, beginning with the summary statement.

Once you have developed a reasonable draft of the discussion, plan and write the conclusion, recommendations, and introduction. Let the document sit for a while, then read it from beginning to end, revising as you go using the 'levels of edit' approach described in Chapter 3. When you have a nearly complete draft of the report, write the summary.

As in all your professional communication, you will find the writing process easier if you define the purpose before you begin, keeping in mind the goals of the communication, the probable needs, concerns, and expectations of the intended audience, the relationship between yourself, the reader, and the issue under discussion, and the most likely use to which the report will be put. The Report Writing Planner (Figure 6.1) will help with these tasks.

Report Writing Planner
Before beginning your report, answer these questions as fully as possible.

1. What is the topic of this report?
2. What is going to be done with this report? Why is it needed? Who asked for it?
3. Who are my readers? What are their interests in this subject? What background information is already known to them and what will I have to fill in so that my report may be understood and acted on? What is the readers' likely attitude to this information?
4. What is my main message? What will my Summary Statement be?
5. Can I briefly outline my introduction, providing the appropriate background information?
6. Can I outline my discussion, providing any relevant main points and details?
7. Can I clearly state my conclusion and recommendation(s)?

Figure 6.1:   Use this planner to identify your main message and your reader's needs and expectations.

Common Report Situations

In the initial chapters of this book, you learned the importance of the Seven Cs of effective professional writing: completeness, conciseness, clarity, coherence, correctness, courtesy, and credibility. These qualities of effective style remain as important in a report as in any other job-related correspondence. However, in work settings involving the application of government standards or regulations, routine report writing takes on an added element of legal responsibility. In such a case, the correctness and completeness of the information you provide is not only desirable, but crucial, since your report forms part of the legal record of the company.

Reports may be written in a variety of situations and for a variety of purposes. However, the most frequent types written as a matter of daily routine can be classified into one of the following categories.

Box 6.3   Common Report Situations

- Log books
- Lab reports
- Incident or occurrence reports
- Minutes
- Accident or injury reports
- Assessment or evaluation reports

- Progress, status, or project completion reports
- Investigative or analytical reports
- Research reports
- Proposals

Log books

You may not think of the **log book** as a report, since it is routinely seen only by the individual who writes it. Nevertheless, a log book provides a record of the research being conducted or of the development of a project. In some research and development environments, this log book is a legal document, and as such it must be readable by other engineers and specialists. Because it performs many of the functions of a report, a log book is considered to fit into this category.

The purpose of a log book is to keep a record of the daily research and design activities of a practising engineer, a research scientist, or other technical professional. It is the raw data from which a formal report may be written at the conclusion of the project, or upon which regular progress reports will be based. It is normally updated every day. This practice gives the engineer or technical support staff a record of the activity that went into a particular design, but it also does much more. Because the log book is a legal record, it can become a crucial piece of evidence in legal disputes over patents or design rights. In such cases, the log book entries establish a date, or even in some cases a time, at which a critical insight or idea was first noted. Such evidence can be critical in establishing ownership of an idea, technique, or device in patent decisions or other legal proceedings.

In preparing your log book, you must observe the following critical requirements. The log book must be a bound notebook from which pages cannot be easily detached. (A coil-bound notebook from which pages can be torn will not serve this purpose, nor will any stapled or temporarily bound notebook.) Every page must be numbered consecutively, and no pages may be removed from the book. Every entry must be dated, and there may be no significant blank spaces between entries where information could be inserted at a later time. Any such blank spaces should be blocked off with a stroke or an 'x' through them to show that they were intentionally left blank. Entries may—and in some cases should—include calculations, thumbnail design sketches, diagrams, or charts. These too should be dated. Finally, the log book should be written in indelible ink and should not contain any obliterations or adjustments in correction fluid. Any corrections that are made should be crossed out neatly with a single pen stroke so that they remain legible. In many firms, the writer must sign and date every page as it is completed.

Though there is no set layout or format for the log book, it should be kept as ordered and readable as possible so it can serve as a clear future reference or legal evidence if the need should arise. The dates and details should be consistently presented and easy to find. The book is useless as a legal submission if there are obliterations, if pages are torn out, if it cannot be understood by anyone other than the writer, or if there are gaps into which information could be inserted at a later time. The records may be kept on both sides of the page, or on one side only. If you choose to write on one side of the page only, you must be consistent; never enter any information onto the back-side of a page for all the reasons already given.

The log book should also be carried to technical meetings where the design project will be discussed so that the discussion may be recorded. Most engineers keep their log books handy at work, and make time each day to record what has been thought, said, and done. The log book should record all your ideas, calculations, diagrams, experiments, and tests relating to the project you're working on. It should be clear and detailed enough to allow another engineer to understand and recreate your work. The full book should be stored in a safe place.

Lab reports

Lab reports differ from log books in that they are clearly intended for a reader other than the writer, and that they report the findings of a single experiment or a connected series of experiments. These are used in university classes for training scientists, agronomists, engineers, and other specialists, or in technical environments such as research centres, hospitals, engineering firms, and computer companies to record findings from laboratory work. They may be forwarded as part of a longer research report or kept on file locally. The lab report write-up is normally a more formal presentation of material already recorded in the log book.

The format used for lab reports can vary somewhat from one employer to another, from one discipline to another, or even from one college course or instructor to another. Most laboratories have developed a set format that is used for their lab reports, and you should follow the format that your employer or instructor prefers. In general, however, despite variations in structure, the lab report is fairly consistent in content, and if you have not been given any other guidelines, the format described here is the one you should use.

The lab report presents information on why the experiment was conducted, how the work was carried out (the equipment and method used), the findings, any problems that occurred, the results that were produced, and the implications of these findings for future experimentation. The headings used in a lab report normally reflect the steps outlined above, so that the general structure of the lab report follows some variation of the following headings:

- Purpose (Statement of Problem)
- Procedures
- Equipment
- Problems Encountered
- Results or Findings
- Implications for Future Work

You should note that these headings, though they use different terminology from the SIDCRA outline we have been discussing, present the same kinds of information in the same general order. As in the SIDCRA structure, introductory information precedes the fuller discussion, which is followed by conclusions and recommendations.

Incident or occurrence reports

The incident or **occurrence report** is probably the single most common type of report after lab reports and logs, since it is used in nearly every profession and field. Written in response to an unexpected (usually problematic) incident, this report is primarily an informative one that outlines details of an unusual event, recording exactly what happened and what the circumstances were. It may suggest ways in which the event has influenced work currently in progress and outline the steps that are being taken to correct the setback. Incident reports cover any atypical occurrence even if it seems minor at the time it occurred; over a period of time, a series of minor incidents may point to a significant pattern or reveal a failure of a particular procedure or practice. This report provides details of the event as completely and fully as possible.

An incident report requires complete information. To ensure that you have included all the necessary detail, use the questions below as a guideline. Providing the answers to such questions is essential in an incident report; complete information will make future decisions and actions easier and more effective. Keeping these prompts in mind will help ensure that nothing is left out of your report.

- *When?* Record the exact day, date, and time of the incident.
- *Where?* Describe the location in as much detail as necessary for officials to reconstruct the incident should it be necessary to do so.
- *What?* Explain exactly what occurred from the moment you became aware of the situation until its completion. What did you hear? What did you actually see? What action did you take?
- *Who?* Identify those who were directly involved in the incident and those who were present at the scene.
- *Why?* It may not be possible in every circumstance to answer this question, but if you have access to such information, you should include it in your report. If the statement of motive or cause is the result of your own inference, you should clearly label it as such in the report.
- *How?* You may not be able to answer this question with certainty, but in some situations (for example, an equipment failure or security breach that is the result of faulty maintenance practices) such information may be crucial if future occurrences are to be prevented.

In addition to the standards of completeness that apply to all of your professional correspondence, the incident reports that you write should adhere to a further standard of objectivity because, like your log books, they are part of the legal record. When reporting an accident, injury, or unusual occurrence in the workplace, you should refrain from making unwarranted inferences, recording only what you know for certain happened and avoiding speculation about who was at fault or what caused the mishap. A useful guideline for writing such reports is the formula '**I was, I saw, I did**.'

'I was' records where you were and what you were doing at the time of the incident. It clearly sets the scene for the reader, allowing a clear understanding of the circumstances surrounding the occurrence.

'I saw' records exactly what you personally observed; it does not involve judgements or inferences you have made about the circumstances. For example, you may be driving in a convoy of vehicles heading for a work site. It is winter, and the roads are icy. As you round a corner, you observe that one of the trucks that had been ahead of you is now lying in the ditch. When you stop your vehicle and go to investigate, you discover that the truck has collided with another vehicle that is also in the ditch. The driver of the car is injured and your own driver is unconscious. You are not an accident specialist, but it looks to you as though your driver ploughed into a car that had already been in the ditch when he rounded the corner. You guess that he was momentarily distracted by the sight of the first vehicle and lost control on the ice. However, even if it seems clear to you that this is what occurred, you should realize that this is a conclusion you have drawn from the circumstances. Write in your report only those events that you observed for yourself; if you must include your conclusions, be sure to clearly label the additional information as an inference or judgement.

'I did' tells of the actions you performed in response to the incident: did you handle the situation yourself? If so, what exactly did you do? Did you call in your supervisors, medical personnel, or the police? Record every detail of your actions with respect to the incident so that others will be able to understand clearly the sequence of events that occurred.

An effective incident report records only information that the writer knows for certain to be accurate. Keeping to the 'I was, I saw, I did' formula will assist you in maintaining objectivity in your incident reports and will ensure that your report records as fact only what you actually observed.

Minutes of meetings

Meeting minutes are a form of routine occurrence report intended to record the decisions made in the regular meeting of any formal department, research unit, group, union, or organization. Like lab reports, minutes are used to keep track of important information in the life of a department or of a project group. They are intended primarily to provide a record of discussions and other group decisions or action so that these may be reviewed and referred to in the future.

Some groups, such as a university Board of Governors or a government ministry, may have a recording secretary whose job is to take minutes. Such a person observes and records, but does not participate in, the meeting. In smaller departments or organizations, the task of taking minutes may fall to one of the members of the unit.

Like lab reports, minutes usually follow a standardized structure that varies only slightly from organization to organization. Should you be assigned the task of taking minutes, you will need to familiarize yourself with the specific layout used in your organization. Like all incident reports, minutes record the name of the organization, where and when the meeting occurred, who was in attendance, what items were discussed, what decisions were made, what motions were proposed and passed, and any action that is expected as follow up to the meeting.

If you are charged with the responsibility for taking minutes, you should review the agenda before the meeting begins, along with any supporting documents that have been circulated to the membership so that you will be familiar with the items for discussion. At the meeting, sit close by the chair so as to obtain clarification of items if needed. You should record the name of the organization at the top of the page, following the phrase 'Minutes of the Meeting of . . .'. Record the date, time, and place of the meeting, and the names of those in attendance. If regular members of the group are absent, record their names as well. If the meeting is large or contains people you do not know, circulate an attendance sheet and ask people to sign it. It may be useful as well to quickly make a map of the seating arrangement to help you identify speakers and keep track of those who propose or second motions.

Your notes should be organized by numbered agenda items, written in the order in which they are discussed. Normally items are discussed in the order in which they appear on the agenda, but occasionally the order is changed in the course of discussion so that, for example, agenda item 5 is dealt with before agenda item 3. If this occurs, keep the original item number 5, but record it at the point where discussion took place.

As you record the major points in the discussion, be aware that taking minutes is not like taking dictation; your goal is not to capture every word spoken. Instead, your aim is to record major discussion points, decisions, and motions. Concentrate on getting the gist of the discussion and taking enough notes to summarize it later. Take your notes as objectively as possible, and avoid editorializing. If you are also expected to participate in the discussion, you may find it challenging to take minutes, but bear in mind that, as minute-taker, your goal is to capture the spirit and direction of the discussion rather than the specific details of who said what. Briefly summarize your own contributions and move on.

Most commonly, minutes are written in draft form and then formally transcribed later. If this is the case, you should choose whatever recording method is most comfortable for you, a notepad, loose-leaf sheets, or a laptop computer. If you know shorthand, you may wish to use it in taking your notes. In some organizations, you may be able to use a tape recorder to help you remember details, but be sure to get everyone's permission first. In any case, recording the meeting still means you'll have to take notes later anyway, so it's not necessarily a time-saver and may be useful only if the discussion is likely to be complicated and you need to record specific details.

As you record information about each agenda item, be sure to note any motions proposed and voted upon, or any follow-up actions that are expected. Motions that are passed, or carried, form the policy record of the organization, and should be recorded distinctly in the minutes, showing who proposed and who seconded the motion (usually written with the name of the proposer followed by the name of the seconder), its exact wording, and the vote tally. Many organizations use a format such as that shown below.

> MOTION: MacLennan/Moffatt
> That the new course, entitled 'Language Structure for Professional Communication', be offered as part of the Communication Option beginning in the upcoming winter term.
> CARRIED UNANIMOUSLY (by show of hands).

If you are responsible for transcribing the minutes, do so as soon after the meeting as possible, so that your memory of the event is still fresh. Be sure to follow the format used in previous minutes of the organization, and attach as appendices any relevant supplementary material that may be needed to clarify the information. Write 'Submitted by' and then sign your name and the date.

Once you have finished with the draft of the minutes, be sure to double-check it for typographical errors before sending it to the participants. It is probably wise to keep all rough notes until the minutes have been approved. Once all of the participants have signed off on the draft, you can finalize the minutes and throw your notes away.

While most minutes are typed up following the meeting, a few smaller organizations may still employ a minutes book, into which the recording secretary writes directly. Like a log book, a minutes book is a bound notebook from which pages cannot be easily detached. Every page must be numbered consecutively, and no pages may be removed from the book. Every entry must be dated, and there may be no significant blank spaces between entries where information could be inserted at a later time. Any such blank spaces should be blocked off with a stroke or an 'x' through them to show that they were intentionally left blank. Finally, just like a log book, entries to a minutes book should be written in indelible ink and should not contain any obliterations or adjustments in correction fluid. Any corrections that are made should be crossed out neatly with a single pen stroke so that they remain legible. The minute-taker may be expected to sign and date every page as it is completed.

Box 6.4   The Structure of Meeting Minutes

- Meeting of [Organization Name]
- Date
- Members in attendance
- Members sending regrets
- Agenda items (in numerical order)
- General gist of discussion, recorded by each agenda item in turn
- Motions, showing names of those who proposed and seconded

Accident or injury reports

An accident or **injury report** is a special kind of incident report written when an accident or injury has occurred in the workplace. Like the incident report, it records the details of the accident, the action that followed, and the treatment that was provided. It follows the same pattern of information as that provided in the incident report: it identifies the day, date, time, and location of the accident, the series of events that took place, the observations of the report writer, and the resulting action. Because an accident or injury in the workplace is a serious occurrence, it may involve police investigation, a workers' compensation claim, or an insurance claim or investigation. The writer of an accident or injury report must be sure to include all known details as accurately and as clearly as possible. This report, like the occurrence report, should answer all pertinent questions—when, where, what, who, why, and how—and follow the formula 'I was, I saw, I did.'

Assessment or evaluation reports

An **assessment report** or **evaluation report**, unlike the various types of incident report, does more than record information. In contrast to the incident report, in which the writer refrains from offering inferences or judgements, the entire point of an assessment report is that the writer makes a judgement or offers a professional opinion of a situation, an action, or a client. Assessment reports draw upon the experience and training of the technical professional in order to evaluate what action, response, or intervention is needed.

Evaluation reports may be specially commissioned as part of the investigation of a proposed course of action or an existing situation. In this case, the writer is asked to assess the likely outcome of a proposed policy change or to investigate the nature of a problem and suggest possible solutions. The evaluation report may be used whenever more information is needed, either on its own to evaluate an existing situation or proposed action, or as a follow-up report to evaluate the recommendations made by another report. Rather than analyzing causes and effects, this latter type of report usually measures a solution or a situation against a set of explicitly stated criteria in order to determine the suitability or unsuitability of that solution or situation. Its conclusions are based on a careful comparison between the initial criteria (usually identified by the person who commissioned the report) and the suggested action or solution.

Unlike an incident report, which outlines the facts of the case and describes the action already taken, an assessment report calls for the writer to apply professional judgement, and usually involves recommendations for future action.

Progress, status, or project completion reports

A **progress report**, also known as a **status report** or a **project completion report**, is a kind of assessment report that details the movement or development of a long-term project or program over a period of time. The project completion report is the final progress report for a given project; as is obvious from its title, it is written when the project has been completed.

Progress reports are of two types. The first, the *periodic report*, is delivered at regular time intervals—every two weeks, for example, or for very long-term projects, every few months. In a college or school, students receive periodic reports of grades at the completion of each term. A company's annual report is another example of a periodic progress report.

The second type, the *occasional progress report*, is delivered whenever a milestone is reached, and the time interval between reports may vary. For instance, if I am overseeing the construction of a new facility, I may write reports only when significant stages are completed; since each part of the project takes a different amount of time to complete, my reports will be delivered at irregular time intervals.

Progress reports are part of the record-keeping function of a business or organization.

Box 6.5   **Structure of a Typical Progress Report**

- Project title
- Period covering [start date] to [end date]
- Work completed
- Obstacles encountered
- Work remaining
- Anticipated date of completion
- Overall assessment

Progress reports are used for other purposes besides tracking engineering projects; they may also be used to assess a new program, method, or system. As well, the annual professional development reports that you might prepare on the job are progress reports, as are the performance evaluations that your supervisor provides.

Investigative or analytical reports

The **investigative report** (or **analytical report**) is usually commissioned or requested by someone other than the writer, and examines and analyzes a particular problem or question that has been identified by management. An investigative report may even be the result of a government commission or enquiry, such as the 2001 report of the Saskatchewan Commission on Medicare (Fyke Commission), the 1997 report of the Commission of Inquiry on the Blood System in Canada (Krever Commission), or the influential 1949 report of the Royal Commission on National Development in the Arts, Letters and Sciences (Massey Commission).

An investigative report is forensic in focus, in that it evaluates causes and effects, frequently offers solutions to the difficulty, and may even apportion blame. Its conclusions are based on careful research, such as results from a controlled scientific experiment or data collected from testimony, interviews, surveys or questionnaires. Such reports are generally beyond the scope of the daily routine for most employees; nevertheless, their recommendations may have implications for the way your company carries out its activities.

Research reports

The **research report**, like the investigative report, examines a particular question of scientific or other importance. However, the research report differs from the investigative report in that it does not necessarily seek to resolve a specific problem or assess cause and effect for a product failure. Research reports fall into two broad categories, which are quite distinct. They may report the results of experimental research, such as you might submit for a senior design report or an MSc thesis, or they may survey and synthesize the results of existing work in the field and offer a summary of current thought, practices, or ideas. Academic writing in the technical professions frequently combines these two functions.

Even when it is used for the second of these two purposes, the research report does not attempt to resolve a specific organizational problem. Instead, it aims at increased understanding by gathering information helpful to the company in making decisions about its future goals and directions, such as developing a new product or line, changing or streamlining a procedure or policy, or reframing the organizational structure.

The major function of this kind of report is to present the findings from your research, whether it covers experimental or qualitative research; the report may or may not offer recommendations based on its results. As part of your college program, you may be assigned a research report of either type. You may have to report on the results of your own experimental research, or you may be required to consult research sources in order to determine the importance of a particular issue to your field of study. The credibility of such a report may depend to a large degree on the thoroughness and authority of your research sources.

If your report draws on material from outside sources—others' research, government documents, books and professional journals, articles in the popular press, Internet sources—this material should be properly documented, according to standards appropriate to your field of study. You will find more information on documentation in Chapter 7, on page 200.

Proposals

The **proposal** is a kind of report intended specifically to persuade; its goal is to stimulate action by its intended reader. A proposal may be initiated by the writer who has a good idea for a positive change or innovation that the company should adopt; it may offer a course of action that solves an existing or potential difficulty; or it might request approval or funding for a new or existing project. For instance, I might write a proposal to create an innovative program in my department, or I might propose a policy change that would solve an administrative difficulty. Alternatively, a proposal may be requested by management, or may be developed in response to a client's request for a service. For example, I might propose a computer-training seminar specifically because a client asked for one.

Proposals can also be written to secure funding. For example, a researcher may submit a funding proposal to a government granting agency such as the National Science and Engineering Research Council (NSERC) outlining the kind of research that is being undertaken and its value for the advancement of scientific discovery in Canada; a university may approach wealthy alumni or corporate partners with a proposal to secure funding for a new program or facility; a charity may write a proposal to gain government or corporate support.

Proposals may be directed to readers within the company—to immediate managers who have the power to approve or reject the project—or they may be submitted to agencies or readers outside the organization. They are written in a variety of situations, and may take the form of tenders, grant applications, project proposals, or marketing summaries. These may be initiated by you or invited by someone else, or they may respond to a general call for submissions.

Proposals may have multiple readers: a proposal for an innovative program, for instance, may go from the writer to the department head, from department head to upper management, from upper management to an advisory or administrative committee, and from there to a budget committee. A funding proposal from a university researcher may have to go through the department, the university's research office, the committee at NSERC, and several reviewers before being approved for funding.

Because a proposal is intended to solicit authorization or funding for the writer's project, it must be sufficiently detailed and convincing to gain the acceptance and approval of all of its readers; like other reports, it must answer the significant questions of when, where, what, who, why, and how.

A proposal is particularly challenging to write because you must not only provide all necessary information, but also influence your reader to approve the project or implement the plan you're putting forth. In writing proposals, as in all persuasive writing, you will therefore need to develop skill in identifying and accommodating the reader's needs, expectations, concerns, and interests.

For example, suppose I plan to write a book such as the one you are reading. I would begin by writing a project proposal to the publishing house. I may do this on my own, as a result of an original idea I have for a book, or I may be approached by a representative of the publisher who specifically invites me to consider writing a book on this topic. Finally, I may even respond to a general call for submissions. In each case, my submission follows a set of general guidelines laid out by the company or organization to whom I am submitting the proposal, with variations depending on whether I have initiated the process or the publisher has done so.

The main parts of a proposal—summary, introduction, discussion, conclusion, recommendations, and appendices—are the same as for any other report, and as in other reports, the headings in the discussion section reflect the specific subject matter of the proposal. Because a proposal asks the reader to act on what is recommended, to support the idea with approval, a contract, or funding, you must be sure to demonstrate the value of what is proposed and show how it fulfills the reader's interests and needs. You must establish your credibility by displaying an understanding of the challenges of the situation and the details of implementation, including costs and obstacles.

Above all, as the writer of a proposal, you must demonstrate that you really know what you're talking about and have done your homework thoroughly. You may believe that your proposal is sound, but unless you can convince your reader that you have thought the project through and have anticipated any problems, you will not gain that person's confidence, approval, or funding. Don't expect the reader to act on faith if your presentation is incomplete or unclear. Do your research.

Here are some elements to consider in the writing of a proposal:

- If the granting agency, publisher, or company has provided guidelines for proposal submissions, be sure to follow them exactly, and to clearly identify what is being proposed.
- Demonstrate the need for the action you are proposing, particularly if the proposal originated with you. If you are responding to a call for tenders or submissions, indicate as much in your proposal.
- Communicate the advantages of the proposed action or change. If it will solve an existing difficulty; if it will save the reader time, work, or money; or if it will increase sales, efficiency, or profits, show how.
- If your proposal responds to an invitation for submissions, be sure to show how your proposed action offers the best means of reaching your reader's desired object-ives. Because the reader has requested a proposal designed to meet specific needs, you must make sure that the details of your proposal match those requirements.
- Make it easy for the reader to implement the proposal. Give all pertinent details of the situation and point out any existing resources that can be put to use. Try to anticipate any questions your reader will have and answer them in advance.
- Present information positively, even when outlining disadvantages. Naturally you feel that the advantages of your proposal outweigh any disadvantages it may have. Your task is to make your reader share this view.
- Indicate the steps to be taken to bring about the proposal. Remember that to help your reader accept your project, you must show how it can be done.
- For tenders and grant applications, and for some project proposals, including a projected budget is mandatory. Be sure to think through all aspects of the project, and provide a budget that indicates as accurately as possible what implementation will cost. Remember as you draft your budget that people may be more willing to commit money, time, or effort after they have been convinced of the worth and viability of the project.

At times, you will be invited to submit a proposal for implementation of a project someone else has suggested. As with original proposals, you must still present all the information the reader will need to evaluate your suggestions, but in this case the proposal will differ slightly, since you will be responding to requirements that the reader has outlined for you.

Remember that a proposal, whether originated by you or requested by someone else, must be especially persuasive to convince a reader to implement the very good idea you've presented.

Writing Technical Descriptions

Description, or making pictures with words, is part of all good writing. Description is designed to create an image in the mind of the reader of the thing being discussed. In technical writing, description is often accompanied by labelled diagrams, line drawings, or photographs.

In a professional or technical document, description is meant to clarify and convince. It should capture the details that would be observed in a visual inspection of the site, product, object, or patient. A **technical description** may stand alone as an informal report, with its own introduction, discussion, and conclusion; it may be incorporated into the discussion of a longer formal report; or it may be attached as an appendix to a long report.

The description is not merely informative; it is also partly analytical. In addition to providing the reader with details of a physical layout, the size, shape, and function of a device or object, or the dynamics of a situation, a technical description also interprets the meaning of these details with respect to the problem that is being discussed. In this way, description helps engineers, designers, and architects to establish the importance of a project under development; medical personnel to monitor a patient's condition; manufacturers and retailers to sell their products; contractors or businesses to secure a bank loan; or filmmakers to get financial backing.

Apart from its usefulness as a device for clarification of detail, description is also an important part of demonstration and persuasion. If you hope to motivate a reader to act on a proposal or recommendation, a description can help that person visualize and understand what you are proposing or asking for. A person who can readily visualize the outcome will be more likely to act on the recommendation. For instance, an architect or interior designer will want to help the client to envision the finished room, building, or landscape design in order to convince that person to engage the firm. A detailed description, accompanied by clear floor plans and different views of the finished room or building, will help the customer understand what is being proposed.

Finally, in cases where a reader must be able to carry out a task based on your instructions, description is an important strategy for enabling your reader to perform the action you are requesting or recommending. Many a convincing proposal fails in its purpose because the reader is not made clearly aware of what is to be done next or how it may be accomplished. In many circumstances, a description can help to make clear the steps that the reader must follow in order to carry out its recommendations, rendering the report or proposal much more effective and convincing.

The content of a technical description

Description provides the answer to questions about the nature and function of a device or object, or the general structure of a geographical or architectural layout. It answers several specific questions and follows a systematic organization. A description should communicate clearly to the reader the character and purpose of the item, its appearance, and (if appropriate) its assembly. The questions that a description should answer are described below.

Box 6.6   Questions Answered by an Effective Technical Description

- What is it? What is it used for? What does it do?
- What does it look like? What is it made of?
- How does it work?
- How was it put together? How is it to be assembled?

What is it? What is it used for? What does it do?

Before you can effectively describe the item in detail, you must establish for the reader its general nature: the item to be described is a computer program, an accounting system, an industrial sewing machine, a metal lathe, a can opener, an adhesive, a paint, an item of protective clothing, an anti-theft device for a vehicle, a high-speed cutting tool. The layout shown is for a kitchen renovation, a medical office, a classroom, an artist's studio, a woodworking shop, a business office. Without this general orientation of understanding, it will be impossible for the reader to figure out what is being presented.

All descriptions begin by letting the reader know exactly what is about to be described. Often, this task is performed by identifying the use to which the object or device or layout will be put, by emphasizing its function (a fastening device, a floor plan, or a solar cooker) or showing its uses (screws are used to firmly fasten objects to wood surfaces; a polymer stamp platemaker allows small-scale manufacture of rubber stamps; a personal organizer is a small computer that stores appointment, contact, and scheduling information).

What does it look like? What is it made of?

Normally, a description provides information about the dimensions and fabrication of the object. For example, a real estate listing normally describes the property in terms of its square footage before moving on to provide other details about number of rooms, special features, location, or price. If the description is of an object or device, the user or reader will need to know precisely how large the item is, or its operational capacity, or both, in order to make a determination about its suitability for purchase. For instance, a coffee maker that is 15" high by 10" wide by 17" deep may fit the available counter space in my staff room, but if it makes only five cups of coffee at a time instead of the twelve I require, it may not meet my needs.

The client or customer will also need to know the number of parts, the material of which the device is constructed, and, if it is relevant, the design and colour of the object. The specific details of appearance and construction that are required in a description will depend upon the use to which the object is to be put. For example, a plastic housing may be preferable to cast iron for a portable household sewing machine, but in an industrial machine, where durability is more of an issue, the cast iron head may be preferable. The purpose for which the description has been written—as instructions for assembly, perhaps, or as a sales document—will also influence the kind of information it includes.

How does it work?

Depending on what the object is, and the purpose of the description, the reader may need to know whether the item is electronic or manual, whether it is digital or analogue, whether it runs on electricity or compressed air, whether it can be plugged in or must be supplied with batteries, whether it has a timer, a delay setting, auto-defrost, a water-saver function, a remote starter, a safety-lock operating switch, an instant-on feature, or an automatic power-surge protector. To operate the device effectively, the client will need to know exactly how it is used, the sequence of steps involved in operating it, how to troubleshoot problems, and how to refine its use to achieve more sophisticated effects. If the operation of the device is simple (for instance, a set of locking pliers or a vegetable peeler), the description may be brief. However, if the device is complex (for instance, a polymer stamp platemaker or a computerized engraving machine), the description may take up a substantial portion of a user's manual.

How was it put together? How is it to be assembled?

Like the other elements of description, these questions may be answered depending on the nature of the device and the purpose of the description. If the description is part of a set of instructions for assembling an item of furniture, a bicycle, an appliance, or an instrument, for example, the description would certainly involve step-by-step set-up instructions. Similarly, if the description is part of the training of an operator who does not have to assemble the machine but who needs to know exactly how it functions, it should provide an analysis of the components of the machine, instructions on its disassembly for cleaning or maintenance, advice on routine replacement of worn parts (a furnace filter, guitar strings, printer cartridges, band saw blades), and a description of the function of each of its parts.

An effective professional description, like **incident reports** and **accident reports**, should be as objective and impartial as possible. It should filter out personal impressions, judgements, and reactions, focusing instead on visible (or audible) details that will be evident to other observers and that will assist readers in visually reconstructing the scene or object.

Specifications

Many devices and structures we use every day must comply with particularly precise and exacting descriptions known as **specifications**, which set standards for safety, quality, and performance. Specifications provide requirements for the design, construction, use, and maintenance of a particular product. In construction and manufacturing industries, specifications may be set and controlled by professional standards and by law. Because those who use the product could suffer injury or death if it should fail, manufacturers or contractors who 'cut corners' on meeting specification requirements are liable under the law if the equipment, device, or structure should malfunction.

Specifications for most products, from children's toys to lawn furniture, from electrical appliances to sports equipment, from office buildings to aircraft, from meat products to cereals, provide standards governing the following aspects of manufacture and installation:

- the methods used to build, install, or manufacture the product;
- the materials and equipment that may be used;
- the conditions under which the product may be manufactured; and
- the size, weight, strength, and shape of the finished product.

Specifications detail what is to be done and how it is to be done. Because specifications will be interpreted, assessed, and applied by diverse audiences, these detailed descriptions must be written clearly and unambiguously enough to ensure identical understanding and interpretation by a wide range of possible readers, who may include

- the client or end user, who has a vision of what the product can do;
- the designer or architect who develops the product within the limits, or constraints, of the specifications;
- the contractor, builder, or manufacturer whose company produces the product;
- the supplier of parts to the manufacturer, whose products must meet the particular requirements of the device or building in which they will be used (for example, building materials that are considered adequate and safe for residential use may not stand up to the heavier requirements of industrial or commercial buildings);

- the labourers who work on the actual construction or assembly;
- the inspectors who approve the final product; and
- the advertisers who market the product to the public.

Each of these participants in the process of product development, manufacture, and marketing is required to adhere to the standards laid out in the specifications. The safety and welfare of the general public and the solvency and success of the company rely on these standards, which in many instances are set and protected by law.

The structure of a technical description

Whether your technical description is a stand-alone document or is to be attached as an appendix to a longer report, it should be given its own separate organizational structure. Normally the technical description includes a title, an overview of appearance and parts, some accompanying illustrations and visuals, a description of the functions of each part, and any appropriate details that the reader needs to understand the nature and operation of the device in question.

Box 6.7   The Structure of a Technical Description

- Clear and specific title
- Overall appearance and component parts
- Illustrations or visuals
- Functions of all parts
- Appropriate details

Clear and specific title
You should provide a title that will immediately communicate to your reader what you are describing. A title that mystifies unnecessarily, or that does not specify the item described, will render your description confusing and ineffective.

Overall appearance and component parts
Most descriptions employ a general-to-specific pattern, beginning with an overall depiction of the thing to be described. The reader needs to have a general sense of what the object or product is and how it functions, or of the size and layout of the site or building, before turning to the specific details of the description. Present your audience with a general overview before you get to the details.

Illustrations or visuals
As you are already aware, descriptions of products, objects, or layouts are made much clearer if they are accompanied by illustrations. These diagrams, drawings, or photographs can be labelled to show the location of each significant component or part. Illustrations should be clear and easy to understand; they should correspond to the object in a way that is obvious and recognizable to the reader. You will find more information on visuals in Chapter 7.

Functions of all parts

The description should appropriately explain the purpose, dial settings, and operation of each part, clarifying what each does and showing how it relates to the whole. For instance, a polymer stamp platemaker uses a process similar to the development of black and white photographs. The ultraviolet lights inside the unit are used to expose a photosensitive liquid acrylic material through a photographic negative. The exposed photosensitive material hardens, forming a stamp that can be used for hand printing on paper and fabrics.

Appropriate details

Technical descriptions are as various as the objects they describe, so no two will include identical details. Your description should present the necessary details in order to help the reader understand what must be known. As a user, I do not need to know how ultraviolet bulbs are manufactured for my polymer plate-making machine; I don't even need to know what ultraviolet light *is*. However, I do need to know the bulbs' function, position, and operation details with respect to the machine I own, and I need to know how to remove them and install replacements when they have burned out.

The details given in your description should be presented in the clearest sequence or organizational pattern. Though there are several organizational patterns to choose from, only three of these are generally useful for organizing a description: a spatial pattern, a functional sequence, or a chronological order. The first might be best suited to a description of a site or room layout; the second to a complex machine or device with several operations; and the third for describing steps that must be performed in sequence, as in the assembly of a device or object. A description of a complex mechanism might employ a combination of these. You can find more on organizational patterns in Chapter 3.

Summary and operating description

Your description should conclude by explaining, where appropriate, how the parts work together to make the whole item function. The summary and operation details serve as the conclusion to your technical description report.

Writing Technical Instructions

Technical instructions are, by far, the most common and the most familiar application of technical writing. These step-by-step explanations of how to assemble, operate, maintain, or repair things are all around you, in everything from the user's manual for your band saw to the operating instructions for your digital camera, from advice on the best way of cracking a lobster tail to the safety guidelines in the seat pouch on an airline, from the assembly guide for your new desk to the online help function of the latest computer program. Unlike many other forms of technical writing, which are encountered only by those who work in technical fields, instructions are used by just about everyone, on an almost daily basis.

As a user of technical instructions, you already know that they are not all equal in helpfulness, clarity, understandability, or detail. When the instructions are clear, specific, and correctly sequenced, with each step explained in an understandable way, the reader can proceed with confidence, completing the task in a reasonable time and without errors. On the other hand, because instructions are frequently among the worst written of technical documents, it's likely that you've had the opposite experience: instructions that are too vague, that leave out important steps, or worse, that contain errors in sequence or detail. Poorly written instructions waste valuable time, frustrate the reader, and can even lead to costly mistakes.

Because writing instructions is the most common writing task facing a technical professional, it's an important and useful skill for you to learn. However, learning to write technical instructions can be challenging. Perhaps even more than other forms of technical writing, instructions have to be reader-centred to be effective, since the audience must not only be able to make out your meaning, but must actually apply the information to successfully perform a task. Good instruction writing features all of the virtues of good technical writing that we have already discussed:

- a crisp, uncluttered writing style;
- a focus on the reader's needs and ability;
- a clear statement of the purpose of the instructions;
- a thorough understanding of the task or procedure, including all of the required steps; and
- a willingness to test the instructions with a representative reader.

To accomplish their task effectively, your instructions must be complete, correctly sequenced, and presented in small, clearly defined steps. They should be clear enough to produce the desired results without frustration when the reader tries to replicate the process. Effective instructions must also feature an appropriately authoritative voice that will inspire your reader's confidence and trust.

Before you set out to write a set of technical instructions, you must first take the time to clarify three things: what the instructions will be used for (for assembly, for operation, for maintenance); who the intended or likely reader is (the general public; an experienced operator; a maintenance technician); the exact nature and details of the process you will be explaining, and the steps involved in reproducing it. As you write, you need to keep your audience's needs clearly in mind, as well as accommodate your purpose, context, and the complexity of your task. The specific content of your instructions must be tailored to all of these constraints.

A crisp, uncluttered writing style

Instructions require clarity and certainty if they are to be effective. Your style should be direct, concrete, and specific. For example, 'The plastic tubing should be attached to the nozzle on the front of the device' sounds clear enough to a writer who understands that this is actually an instruction that should be followed, who is certain which section of tubing is required, who knows which side of the device is the 'front', and who knows exactly where on the device the protruding nozzle is located and how to distinguish it from other protrusions such as the rivets that hold the device together.

However, as part of a set of instructions, the statement fails. It is clear only to someone who is already intimately familiar with the process being explained and for whom such details are 'common sense'; other readers will be lost and confused. The example violates the Seven Cs of professional style described in Chapter 3, primarily because it lacks both clarity and certainty. First, the statement that 'the plastic tubing should be connected to the nozzle . . .' isn't clearly an instruction to the reader to perform a task; for instance, it could be read to mean that the tubing should already be in place and the reader just needs to find it.

Instructions should always be written in the imperative mood—that is, they should explicitly tell the reader what to do. 'Connect the plastic tubing to the nozzle on the front of the device' is therefore a better beginning. However, although this improved version is more directive, it still lacks clarity. The reader may need help in figuring out which side of the device is the front, in locating the nozzle and distinguishing it from other protrusions, such as rivets, that might be visible on the surface of the device, and in choosing the correct piece of tubing. Consider the following improvements:

Step 2: Attach the 24" length of clear 3/8" plastic tubing to the air nozzle on the front of the device. Rotate the device so that the grey panel is facing you. You will see the platen opening (a rectangular cavity 12" wide and 1" high) positioned 5" below and parallel to the top of the device. Locate the air nozzle directly below and to the right of the platen opening. The nozzle is a hollow conical protrusion 3/8" high and is located 2" from the right edge of the grey panel and 1" above the bottom. Friction-fit the 24" length of tubing by pushing the end of the tubing onto the nozzle. It should fit snugly.

The additional detail and directive tone of these revised instructions will help the reader to proceed confidently with this stage of assembly.

This revised version is an improvement over the original version for several reasons. First, it is more complete, containing details that will help the novice reader to perform the task correctly. It is also more courteous because it more appropriately addresses the reader's needs. Finally, it succeeds where the earlier version fails because it satisfactorily establishes the writer's authority and credibility, thus helping to ensure the reader's confidence.

A focus on the reader's needs and ability

All good technical writing considers and accommodates the reader's needs, expectations, ability, and background knowledge. However, this consideration of audience is especially important to the writing of technical instructions, since your reader must not only be able to make out your meaning, but must actually use your instructions to successfully complete a task.

As with all technical writing, you need to try to put yourself into the shoes of your readers; think about what information they need in order to accomplish the task, what their purpose is in seeking instruction in the first place, and how they are likely to receive your direction. In order to write your instructions effectively, you need to consider exactly who your intended readers are. Are you writing for a brand new user who may be completely unfamiliar with the process you're explaining? For a technician who understands the process in general and needs only enough guidance to work with this specific device? For maintenance personnel who have to assemble and then repair the device? The reader's needs and orientation will help to shape the instructions in both content and detail. As you write, pay attention to the language you've used and to the way you have implicitly characterized your reader. Make it clear for whom the instructions are intended.

A clear statement of purpose

The purpose of a set of technical instructions is partly a function of who the target audience is: a brand new user who is unfamiliar with the operation of the device or product obviously needs a different kind of guidance than is required by a more specialized and technically sophisticated user, though in both of these cases and in every case in between, your instructions should aim to help that person understand and reproduce the process without error or confusion.

The purpose for which the description has been written—as instructions for assembly, perhaps, or as a sales document—will also influence the kind of information it includes. A set of instructions that is intended primarily to sell a product may emphasize results or ease of use, but need not actually educate the reader as to the detailed uses or steps involved. On the other hand, instructions in an operating manual must explain exactly what the device does, how it is used, the sequence of steps involved, how to troubleshoot problems, and how to refine its use to achieve more sophisticated effects.

All technical instructions begin by letting the audience know exactly what they will be able to do after reading and following your guidelines: they will learn how to import java scripts into a website; they will master the steps for changing the oil in their car; they will learn how to turn a photograph into a machine embroidery design using a computer digitizing program; they will learn how to change the blade on a table saw; they will be able to make perfect pocket welts for a tailored jacket.

This statement of purpose should be direct and plainly worded, either in the form of an explicit purpose statement such as 'This manual will demonstrate how to load and play a DVD in your new BRS Model 100 DVD player', or in the document title: 'Operating Instructions for the Brother PR600 Home Embroidery Machine' or 'Troubleshooting Guide for the Boomerang 750 Polymer Stamp Platemaker'. Failure to provide this general orientation is one of the most common faults of ineffective instructions.

Similarly, if your instructions are intended for an operator who does not have to assemble the machine but who needs to know exactly how it functions, they should include an analysis of the components of the machine, instructions on its dis-assembly for cleaning or maintenance, advice on routine replacement of worn parts (a furnace filter, guitar strings, printer cartridges, band saw blades) and a description of the function of each of its parts.

A thorough understanding of the task or procedure

Before you can write a set of instructions, you must have a clear grasp of all of the steps that the task or procedure requires. When you are familiar with a process, it's easy to take steps for granted if they seem obvious to you, and to inadvertently leave out information that may turn out to be essential for your reader. To see how this might work, consider the following instructions for using an ordinary stapler:

Make sure there are staples in the stapler. Load staples into the chamber if required. Insert paper and press down on the end.

Are these instructions adequate even for a reader who is generally familiar with how to use a stapler? What does this writer assume about the reader's knowledge and existing skills? What makes these instructions problematic?

The goal of all instructions is to enable the reader to reproduce the task without error and without frustration. You cannot do this unless you conduct a task analysis first. A **task analysis** evaluates the task to identify all of the necessary steps and their appropriate sequence. If you are intimately familiar with the task you will be explaining, it's possible to conduct your task analysis by mentally walking yourself through the process. However, your very familiarity can sometimes be a hazard if it causes you to leave out steps that have become second nature to you. If you are able to do so, it's always better to conduct your analysis while you are actually performing the task. That way, it will be easier to ensure that you have identified and included all of the necessary steps, and that you have placed them into the correct sequence.

With your computer or notebook handy, assemble all of the tools, equipment, and materials you need to perform the task. Make a note of all of these items so you can provide materials and equipment lists at the beginning of your instructions. As you begin, note down each separate task you perform, no matter how small it may be. Pay attention to each step as you perform it, and consider how much detail your intended reader will need (Will she know without being told which side is the 'front'? Will he understand the technical names of the items you are using? Will she need assistance in locating the relevant part on the device? Will he need to be told whether to turn the valve clockwise or counter-clockwise? If so, then be sure to put this information into your list of steps).

Once you have completed and recorded all the steps, go back over your notes and visualize the process again as you read. Try to imagine yourself as a reader unfamiliar with the steps and their sequence. Do your notes provide sufficient information and detail for a reader to reproduce the process without errors and without frustration? If so, then number your steps in the sequence in which they are performed, and edit them for readability and clarity.

The structure of technical instructions

Technical instructions are typically written and formatted as a stand-alone document. This document is always given its own separate organizational structure, which can vary depending on the specific purpose of the instructions and the complexity of the task or process described. While instructions for a simple process or task may occupy only a single page, instructions for more complex devices or processes may be several pages, or even several hundred pages. These longer documents are usually presented in formal report format, complete with a table of contents, an overview of purpose, a list of parts or materials, some accompanying illustrations and visuals, and any appropriate details that the reader needs to understand the nature and operation of the process.

Box 6.8   The Structure of Technical Instructions

- Clear and specific title
- Table of contents
- Introduction and statement of purpose
- Diagrams and illustrations
- List of parts, required materials, equipment, or methods, if appropriate
- Section headings, as appropriate
- Numbered steps
- Failsafe statements, as appropriate
- Operational check and troubleshooting information

Clear and specific title

You should provide a title that will immediately communicate to your reader what process or task is being explained. The title for a set of instructions need not be elaborate or clever; a simple declaration is more effective: 'Assembly and Operation of the Boomerang 750' or 'How to Make Hawaiian Chicken'.

Table of contents

If you are writing instructions for a multi-stage process, or if you are creating an operating manual for a product that has several functions, your document should be divided into relevant sections and should include a table of contents to guide the user in finding the information she needs. However, if the instructions are very brief, such as might be the case if you are explaining a simple technique of one or two steps (such as a baking recipe or the assembly instructions for a simple bookcase), you would not need to provide a table of contents. But more complicated documents, such as operating instructions for a device with multiple functions or directions for a complex process that involves many stages, should also include a table of contents so that the reader can locate exactly the information that she requires to get the specific job done. For example, a reader who wishes to change the ink cartridge in his printer or someone who wants to know how to load pictures from her digital camera into a computer should be able to easily find the specific instructions needed to complete this single task, without having to read the entire set of instructions for everything the device can do.

Introduction and statement of purpose

Provide the reader with a brief introduction and overview of the process or device that you are explaining. The reader needs to have a general sense of what the object or product is and how it functions, or of the size and layout of the site or building, before turning to the specific steps and details of the process.

    After reading your statement of purpose, the reader should understand very clearly what is and is not covered in the manual, and what he will be able to accomplish by following your instructions. The introduction should be clear enough to be grasped easily by your intended reader and should be direct enough to inspire confidence.

Diagrams and illustrations

It is often said that a picture is 'worth a thousand words', and nowhere is this more true than in the case of writing instructions. As in the technical description, a clear photograph, diagram, or illustration can help the reader to see exactly what is being referred to, what the step should accomplish, and what the result should look like.

    Use graphics to illustrate any key actions or objects. Illustrations should be clear and easy to understand; they should correspond to the object in a way that is obvious and recognizable to the reader. Clear diagrams and illustrations can help to clarify and can sometimes communicate details that are difficult to explain in words. While you usually can't rely on pictures alone to make your instructions clear, you certainly can, and should, employ illustrations and diagrams wherever they will aid you in making your meaning clearer to the reader.

List of parts, required materials, equipment, or methods

Depending on the purpose and complexity of your instructions, provide the reader with a list of the materials required to complete the project, with the equipment that will be used in the assembly of the device, or with the methods the reader will need to employ to bring about the desired results.

You might notice that in this respect technical instructions resemble a lab report. Both are a kind of **process analysis**: that is, both analyze a process. However, their focus is rather different; where the lab report details how something is done so that the reader can understand how the result was arrived at, technical instructions explain how the reader can actually reproduce the procedure.

Section headings, as appropriate

Obviously a simple one-step process has no need of sections and headings, but you can help your reader to understand complex instructions if you cluster information into relevant sections, each with its own appropriate heading, just as you might do in any other formal report. For example, during my years as a soft toy design engineer, I created many sets of assembly instructions to accompany my work when it appeared in books and magazines. Each design was assembled in stages, and each stage of the assembly was given its own heading—Legs, Arms, Ears, or Body—and each headed section included the instructions for creating the relevant part.

The 'sectioning' of the instructions in this way is intended to assist the reader in successfully recreating the design, by placing related information together and by breaking down a fairly complex process into more manageable steps. In a highly complex document, you may need to divide your information further: each headed section is divided in turn into smaller chunks with their own subheadings.

Numbered steps

While it is not essential to number the steps in your technical instructions, doing so can be helpful to the reader, not only because the numbers help to organize the material into a sequence, but because the numbers serve as a visual cue for the reader. A numbered sequence helps keep the reader on track and makes it easier to refer to the instructions while working your way through the process that is being explained.

Failsafe statements, as appropriate

The more complex a process, the more it is prone to error. It can be helpful to your reader if you can provide failsafe warnings or statements at critical points in the instructions: at places where misunderstandings are likely to occur or in instances where there may be some danger to the user. Failsafe warnings should be highly visible to the reader; it can be helpful to set them apart in shaded boxes or to print them in colour.

WARNING: Turn off power before changing blade.

Figure 6.2

Operational check and troubleshooting information

As a final step, particularly if you are writing assembly instructions, you may wish to provide an operational check. Direct the reader to try the device to make sure it has been assembled correctly and that it will function as it is supposed to. If it does not function, provide a list of the common problems and how to correct them.

Test the instructions with a representative reader

When you have completed your writing, ask a friend or colleague to read through your instuctions to ensure that they are clear and understandable. Ideally, have the person perform the task following what you have written. This process will help you to identify any areas that need further clarification.

Writing technical instructions requires careful attention to detail and clarity. You should avoid ambiguity by providing specific details: measurements, colours, placement, and orientation of relevant parts and steps. Your instructions will be more user-friendly and helpful if you explain the process in bite-sized steps and if you can provide diagrams or pictures wherever they would help to clarify the information you are presenting.

Standardized Report Forms

Although some reports are comprehensive formal documents that are as long as this book, most are brief, routine documents with highly prescribed structure. Many common types of short day-to-day reports are submitted on **standardized report forms**, which can make the job of managing routine information easier for both reader and writer. Instead of having to invent a report structure for each client interview or incident that occurs, the writer simply fills in the blanks using the appropriate form provided by his agency or organization.

Report forms ensure consistency in cases where large numbers of reports containing similar information must be kept by many people as a matter of routine. Nearly any kind of report filled out on a regular basis can be organized into a standard form. Frequently the information is entered directly into a computerized report form on your screen. In cases where the kind of information required is the same, a form helps to ensure that each person applies the same standards and collects the same details in the same order. In this way, too, much repetitive work is eliminated. The questions are designed to prompt the writer to provide the information pertinent to each type of report, and the reader knows just where to find important facts in every case.

Insurance claim forms, student grade reports, workers' compensation forms, income tax forms, registration forms, hospital charts, requisition forms, travel claims, some project status reports, and even job application forms are some common examples of standardized report forms. Other types that are often standardized in large organizations include occurrence or incident reports, accident or injury reports, and performance reviews. Figure 6.3 shows a performance evaluation report form; Figure 6.4 shows a sample project completion report form of the sort that might be used in an engineering firm.

CAREER PROGRESS REPORT

Evaluation for the Period: _____ To: _____

EMPLOYEE'S NAME: _____

Department: _____

Position Duties: _____

Additional Responsibilities since Last Assessment:
Achievements:

EVALUATION SUMMARY	Superior	Competent	Developmental
Overall performance	[ ]	[ ]	[ ]
Job-related goals	[ ]	[ ]	[ ]
Development of others' goals	[ ]	[ ]	[ ]
Relationship goals	[ ]	[ ]	[ ]
Potential for advancement	[ ]	[ ]	[ ]

MERIT INCREASE RECOMMENDED   [ ] yes   [ ] no

NARRATIVE STATEMENT OF ASSESSMENT:

Suggestions for Professional Development:

SUPERVISOR: _____   Date: _____
Signature:

Employee's Comments:

I have read this summary and enclosed comments and discussed them with my supervisor.

Employee's Signature: _____   Date: _____

Figure 6.3: A career progress report is a periodic assessment report that may be completed annually, semi-annually, biennially, or quarterly, depending on the job in question.

DOLOVICH AND COWAN
Project Completion Report

Department: . . . .   Date:. . . . .

Project title:. . . . .

Project number (as per inventory): . . . .   Location:. . . . .

Project manager(s): . . . .

. . . .

Affiliation:. . . . .

Date of approval:. . . . .   Initiation date: . . . .

Scheduled completion date:. . . . .   Completion date: . . . .

Funding source:. . . . .

Completion report done by: . . . .

Parent projects: . . . .

. . . .

Related projects: . . . .

. . . .

Abstract: attached ☐   Rationale: attached ☐

Methodology: attached ☐   Benefits/Accomplishments: attached ☐

Publications/Presentations: attached ☐

Key words:. . . . .

. . . .

Signature of reporting personnel . . . .

Figure 6.4:   This is a sample project completion report form, such as might be used in any engineering firm. Note that the form standardizes the information that is invited, and provides a checklist for attachments. It also carries the signature of the person who submits it, and, like all important documents, is dated.

Critical Reading

Jeanie Wills, 'Creating an Exceptional Writing Portfolio: Fine Tuning Your Voice with the Nine Axioms'

Jeanie E. Wills is Assistant Professor of Communication in the Ron and Jane Graham Centre for the Study of Communication in the College of Engineering, University of Saskatchewan. A former advertising copywriter, Wills' academic interests range from the rhetoric of advertising to theories of audience, and her recent papers have addressed such diverse topics as the role of sasquatch in the Canadian imagination and an analysis of the rhetoric of Saskatchewan politician Jim Pankiw.

Creating an Exceptional Writing Portfolio: Fine Tuning Your Voice with the Nine Axioms

Constructing a **portfolio** of your work may well be one of the most valuable communication exercises you'll ever undertake, since it gives you the opportunity to gain perspective on where you've been and where you're going, on what you've achieved so far and what remains to be done, on your strengths and on your weaknesses. Portfolios of work function much as a résumé functions, as an instrument through which you can showcase your skills, achievements, and potential, and may be used in a variety of professional activities, from photography to teaching, from music to acting, from commercial art to technical design. In all cases, the purpose of the portfolio is not simply to gather random bits and pieces of your work, but instead to create a coherent message that communicates the personality and ability of its creator. Although the fundamental principles outlined here apply to all portfolios, we will concentrate our attention on the preparation of a communication or writing portfolio.

You may be asked to create a writing portfolio to fulfill a course requirement, or you may simply plan to showcase your skills for an employer; either way, creating a writing portfolio will teach you how to organize samples of your work into a form that will present you and your skills in a meaningful way to your intended reader. It will give you practice in preparing a cover letter or memo that introduces a work and draws the reader's attention to the highlights of the compilation. But most important of all, the act of putting together a portfolio allows you to reflect on the strengths and weaknesses of your own work, helping you to understand what you've accomplished and identify what you've yet to work on.

Despite the value of reflecting on your achievements and your goals through the preparation of a portfolio of work, students who are assigned such a task sometimes miss the real value of doing it. After all, how hard is it to throw together all the course assignments or gather a bunch of writing samples and hand them in? If understood in this way, it might seem that the only challenge is rounding up all the term's assignments to put them into a folder!

However, approaching the task of preparing a writing portfolio in such a haphazard manner won't get you a job, earn you marks, give you practical organizational experience, or demonstrate your creative problem-solving skills. Like any other piece of technical writing, a portfolio is a solution to a problem, or a remedy for a rhetorical exigence. The exigence comes from needing to showcase your ability to judge a situation and address it appropriately. To your professor, you want to demonstrate that you have absorbed the theoretical principles taught in the course and can apply your new-found understanding to the special constraints of this assignment. To an employer, you want to demonstrate your competence and credibility as a professional who can communicate effectively in writing. The writing portfolio will test your judgement of the communicative situation, your understanding of your audience, and your awareness of how to relate effectively to that audience. My purpose in this essay is to give you several methods to help you excel at these tests.

So, how does a portfolio manage all these tasks? First, the portfolio serves a persuasive purpose. It aims to convince your instructor or a potential employer that you can negotiate the complex demands imposed by the situation and to encourage her to give you an exceptional mark or hire you into your dream job. To be successful in this persuasive task, you must understand that its constraints, while imposing limits, also provide you opportunities to make your voice heard and stand out as unique.

As in any technical document, some of the conventions of the portfolio itself will limit your choices. For example, you must use a binder or folder to present the material, and provide standardized elements such as a table of contents, a pattern of organization, dividers between sections, and a covering document that introduces the contents of the portfolio and points to the document's significance. These standardized elements assist the reader in making sense of your submission, even as they place limitations on what your portfolio should include.

Everyone who is submitting a portfolio faces similar limitations. For example, if the portfolio is part of a communication course, all the students have done the same assignments and so the contents of the portfolios will be similar; the table of contents format has only so many variations; and only so many possibilities exist for organizing material within a binder or between report covers.

However, despite the limiting nature of the constraints you face, they also present you with all sorts of opportunities and possibilities to have your voice heard clearly and distinctly. Instead of focusing on the ways in which the format makes your work look similar to that of others, you should think of the portfolio as an opportunity to demonstrate your creativity and individuality despite its standardized conventions. In fact, mastering the conventions while being unique within them gives definition to your creative task by focusing not on the elements that appear in every portfolio, but on the elements that appear only in your collection of work. Preparing a portfolio gives you a chance to exercise your creative problem-solving skills. How do you make your portfolio stand out among all the other portfolios your instructor or employer has to read? One very good way is to employ the Nine Axioms of Communication to help shape your approach the task.

Perhaps the Axiom that is most relevant to the creation of a writing portfolio is the one that reminds us of the connection between communication and credibility—Aristotle's conception of ethos. The good judgement you demonstrate in the more mechanical aspects of format and layout—such as organization, binding, and table of contents design—will have an impact on how your reader views your character, your attitude, and your overall competence. Depending on your situation, these elements may enhance your credibility, affirm it, or damage it. The judgement you use in working with design elements helps you to prove your commitment to the task and your understanding of its purpose, as well as to acknowledge the professional relationship that you hope to establish with your new employer or the relationship that you have been developing with your professor over the course of the term. In turn, as you establish your credibility, you also increase your potential to influence how your reader perceives and assesses you as a professional.

In addition to helping you establish credibility and exert influence, the writing portfolio—like all professional writing—is also part of an interaction that establishes relation as well as communicates content. To demonstrate these Axioms, let me share the story of one student who was a remarkably bad speller. While he was adept at applying theory to analyze and examine case studies, his spelling was atrocious. He was likely to spell 'persuasive' as 'persusive', 'ambiguous' as 'umbigus', and 'rhetoric' as 'retric'. In out-of-class writing, he coped with his spelling difficulties by proofreading carefully and using a spell-checker, but in-class assignments posed a very different challenge. After marking his midterm exam, I had a discussion with him about his spelling, and I suggested some methods he could use to improve it.

When this student handed in his course portfolio, the title page looked like this:

~~PURTFULEO~~

~~PORTFUULEO~~

~~PORTFOOLEO~~

~~PORTFOLEO~~

PORTFOLIO

This strategy had two immediate effects: it both built and depended on relation, since it leveraged his weakness and our discussion of it to create a kind of shared 'inside joke'. By so doing, he acknowledged my concerns and proved his grasp of the interactional element of communication. But his creativity and his cementing of relation didn't stop there.

Like any formal report, the portfolio was divided into sections with separate headings. Each of the section headings had been given a similar treatment, with several misspelled versions crossed out, followed by the corrected heading. The repetition of this same dramatic device in each subsequent section grabbed my attention as I flicked through the binder. Then I noticed that the strikethroughs, indicating spelling errors, were fewer and fewer in each section until the very last section heading, which showed no strikethroughs at all. His creative use of this device not only invoked, and thus built upon, our interactions over the term, but it also cleverly communicated their impact by visually representing the improvement of his skills over the term. Additionally, his use of this clever device acknowledged our friendly footing by taking a bit of a risk.

The creator of this portfolio also demonstrated his understanding that effective professional communication is 'audience-centred'. His reference to our shared communication showed me that he had listened and heard, and would act upon, what he had been learning. Because the course-writing portfolio is in part an assessment report on the writer's progress over the term, his creativity also provided the information I needed to make my evaluation of the quality and effect of the presentation. His portfolio was effective not only because it was complete and well organized, but also because his creative design acknowledged his willingness to improve his performance by using the tools I had given him.

While this 'misspelling' device wouldn't be appropriate in every writing portfolio, it demonstrates a number of the qualities that make a good portfolio: an acknowledgement of relation, an accommodation of audience, a unique and personal expression of the writer's character and concerns, and a level of creativity and originality. The best writing portfolios I've received over the years have not always come from those who were the most grammatically proficient or who were technically the 'best' writers. Instead, they have come from those who were willing to put something of themselves into their work, who could communicate a unique personality by approaching the challenge with creativity and individuality.

When I take up a writing portfolio that clearly amplifies the writer's individual voice, I feel as though I can hear her in the room with me, talking me through the plan for the portfolio and proudly telling me both what she has learned and what she has discovered that she needs to work on. When I am evaluating an entire class group of portfolios, all in binders, all with the 'same' table of contents, identical writing samples, and similar organization, I listen carefully for the individual's voice. When I hear it, I am pleased to have the company of its creator as I read through the assembled work of a unique mind.

Points to Remember

1. An effective report is carefully planned and clearly organized.
2. Be sure to identify the purpose of your report or the action you wish the audience to take.
3. Consider the context in which the report will be received, and what is to be done with the information it contains.

4. Use the problem-solving approach to define the communication challenge and develop your report content, and keep your reader's needs in sight as you work.
5. Answer the questions When? Where? What? Who? Why? and How? in each report.
6. Follow the 'I was, I saw, I did' formula for writing incident, accident, or misconduct reports.
7. Where it is appropriate, use the standardized forms supplied by your employer or instructor.

Key Concepts

abstract	investigative or analytical report	recommendation
accident report	I was, I saw, I did	research report
appendix	lab report	SIDCRA
assessment report	log book	specifications
conclusion	occurrence report	standardized report forms
discussion	portfolio	status report
evaluation report	process analysis	summary
incident report	progress report	task analysis
injury report	project completion report	technical description
introduction	proposals	technical instructions

Assignments and Exercises

As you prepare to write the following reports, you should make use of the Report Writing Planner (Figure 6.1) to outline your two principal elements: reader and main message. Be sure to edit your work carefully.

1. Progress reports are routine in many professional occupations; some jobs even require that you submit an annual self-assessment report detailing your achievements for the past year. Your task for this assignment is to prepare such a report outlining and evaluating your progress in your professional communication course. This informal report of approximately three pages should include such topics as your initial objectives or expectations, your achievements thus far, any failings or obstacles you have encountered and what you have done (or plan to do) to overcome them, the work that has yet to be done, and your expected grade or performance. You may wish to supplement your report with evidence such as midterm or assignment grades, course projects, and topics covered. Keep in mind that you are not evaluating the course, but your own progress in and commitment to the course.

   Although the assignment is intended to focus on your professional communication course, you may wish to use another of your courses instead. If you want to do this, get the approval of your instructor.

2. The dean of your college is conducting a study of the first-year experience with an eye to dealing with a number of concerns, including heavy workload, class sizes, and opportunities for co-op. In the course of this investigation, the dean has called for contributions from students. You have decided to offer some comments about

areas of your program that you feel should be improved and areas that should remain unchanged. Assemble your comments into a short informal report addressed to Dean Colin Snowsell.

3. Write a set of technical instructions for a common item that you use every day or for a familiar process, such as how to tie your shoes, how to operate a stapler, how to load paper into a photocopier, how to insert a pair of contact lenses, or how to change the blade in a table saw. Have your instructor approve your choice before you begin to write. Remember that the purpose of your instructions is to enable the reader to replicate the process, not simply to explain how the process is done. Present your instructions in semi-formal or formal format, as your instructor directs.

4. Assume that you have been asked to present a five-minute persuasive speech of the type described in Chapter 8, Assignment #5 (page 269). To assist you in preparing for that assignment, and to enable your instructor to give you specific guidance for that assignment, you are asked to complete a speech strategy report using the standardized form on page 188. Your strategy report should contain at least three of the research sources that you plan to consult in preparing your speech. In addition, the outline of the speech that you attach to the strategy report should include specific details: the exigence, the speech's purpose, the proposal, and the points and details that support the proposal.

Answer all the questions fully and specifically, using the theoretical principles discussed in class and in the text. Your strategy report must be detailed, thorough, thoughtful, and specific. Give concrete examples of the strategies that you intend to use to engage your audience's attention, to motivate them to action, and to enable them to act as you are advising.

In order to better understand and assess the constraints that you face in giving your persuasive speech, you may wish to consult the description of the speech assignment in Chapter 8 (Assignment #5 on page 269).

Date _____   Name _____

Complete this form and submit it to your instructor as your speech strategy report.

1. What action do you wish your audience to take as a result of hearing your speech? In other words, what is the purpose of the speech? (I want my audience to _____ [insert verb.])

2. What is the exigence to which your speech responds, or the problem that your audience is asked to solve? In what sense is this problem urgent?

3. How does the issue you are researching affect your audience personally, politically, or professionally? Why should your audience care about the problem? Why should they be interested in taking action? (In other words, 'Why us?' and 'Why now?')

4. How exactly will your audience benefit from taking the action you are recommending?

5. What constraints are imposed by your purpose or by your rhetorical situation (audience, time limit, delivery requirements, structural expectations, feedback process)?

6. What specific strategies will you use to appeal to your audience?

7. What common interest do you share with your audience that can help you to frame your persuasive appeal? How will you appeal to that common interest?

8. What evidence and examples will you use to support your argument?

9. What pattern of organization will you employ in your speech?

10. What is your own interest in or commitment to this topic?

11. Please correctly cite at least three of the sources you consulted as part of your research for your report, selecting those that are immediately relevant to the focused speech topic. Use any standard documentation format. You may list no more than ONE interview, and this must be with an authority on the subject. (If you choose to use an interview, please identify, by name and title, the person you have interviewed, so that it is clear how this person's comments are relevant.)

12. Please attach an outline of your speech as an appendix to your report.

Figure 6.5

Chapter 7

Formal, Semi-formal, and Informal Reports

Learning Objectives

■ To learn the basic parts and formats of informal, semi-formal, and formal reports.

■ To learn how to select the format appropriate for the report you are writing.

■ To learn about the use of visuals in a formal report.

■ To study models of formal, semi-formal, and informal reports.

© iStockphoto.com/Marcin Balcerzak

Because they are used in a wide variety of contexts and for a wide variety of purposes, reports can vary significantly in length, appearance, and complexity. Their structure may be highly formal or relatively informal, or they may strike a balance between the two with a semi-formal format.

Although the differences are not absolute, length and layout are the most visible distinctions between report types. The **formal report** is normally at least twenty pages long, and can sometimes run to as long as several hundred pages. In addition to the six standard parts of a report described in Chapter 6, the formal report includes some additional features, including a bound cover, a cover letter known as a **letter of transmittal**, a **table of contents**, lists of tables and figures, an **acknowledgements** page, and **references**.

By contrast with the formal report, the **informal report** is usually very brief, with an average length of three to five pages, and is normally structured in memo or letter format. It deals with more routine and less complex matters than the formal report, and is therefore far less detailed, with fewer distinct parts and a less elaborate layout. It can, but normally does not, make use of section headings.

The **semi-formal report** is not so much a distinct type as a variation of the informal report. The semi-formal report is typically quite short, normally under fifteen pages long, but contains complex or significant content that merits a more formal treatment than the informal report provides. Since the organizational apparatus of the formal report can overwhelm a shorter report, and since a memo or letter format could seem an overly casual treatment of your information, the semi-formal structure offers an appropriate compromise.

Rather than opening with a memo or letter-like format, the semi-formal report usually features the title, author's name, and date centred at the top of the first page. The semi-formal report typically does make use of section divisions with headings to assist the reader in making sense of the information.

Choosing a Format for Your Report

In writing your reports, remember that format is meant to serve function, and select a format that delivers your message most effectively in the context in which it will be read. The formal report format allows clearer organization of large amounts of material, while short reports may be better presented simply. Generally, the longer and more complex the material dealt with in the report, the more formal its presentation should be, and the more likely it will be to use headings and other organizational devices to assist the reader in understanding the material presented.

Although routine reporting tasks can be, and often are, standardized on forms such as those shown in the previous chapter (Figures 6.3 and 6.4), not all situations can be predicted or standardized. For non-routine tasks, where standardized forms are inappropriate or unavailable, you will need to generate your own structure, as well as to identify exactly what information should be included to 'flesh out' the body of the report by appropriately answering the questions of who, what, when, where, why, how, and how much.

Although some organizations have specific formatting requirements, it is just as likely that you will be expected to choose your own format, according to the content and purpose of your document. How do you know whether to arrange your material into a formal, an informal, or a semi-formal report? Asking yourself the following questions may help you to decide.

1. *What is your purpose?* If you are addressing a relatively minor or routine issue, your report will most likely be informal; if the situation is complex or important, your report will be semi-formal or even formal.
2. *Who is your audience?* The more distinguished or the wider your audience, the more formal your presentation should be. A brief document to your immediate supervisor that no one else is likely to read will probably be informal; a detailed proposal being sent to the company president and advisory board, or outside the company, is likely to be formal.
3. *How detailed is your analysis?* The more complex the problem or issue and the more detailed and thorough your presentation, the more carefully you will have to organize your information, and the more likely you will need to use the titles, headings, table of contents, and support materials of the formal report.

In choosing a report format, you should be guided by the complexity of the problem or issue—that is, how much detail or research is required—and the intended audience or readers of the report. The more important your purpose, or the larger or more distinguished your audience, the more likely you will choose a semi-formal style over the informal one. If the report is over ten pages long but the issue presented is fairly straightforward and direct, the semi-formal format is more appropriate. If your report is likely to be more than ten pages and is divided into many complex sections, you should consider using a formal format. Anything over 20 pages should employ a formal report structure.

Figure 7.1, the Report Format Decision Scale, provides an at-a-glance guideline to help you decide whether your report should be informal, semi-formal, or formal.

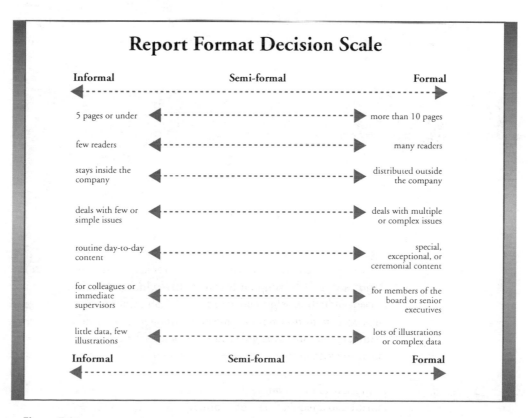

Figure 7.1

To use the Report Format Decision Scale shown in Figure 7.1, put an 'x' on each line of the scale to indicate the probable characteristics of your report. If most of your marks are to the far left of centre, your report should likely be informal in structure; if most of your marks fall to the far right, the report should be formal. If the marks tend to cluster in the middle, you should probably write your report in a semi-formal format.

Informal reports

The informal report format is commonly used for regular progress reports, incident reports, evaluative reports, and informal proposals. In structure, the informal report begins as a memo or a business letter. The standard format of the memo (To, From, Date, Subject) or letter (return address or letterhead, date, and inside address) identifies the primary reader, the writer, and the date. The subject or 'Re' line states the report's primary **recommendation**.

Informal reports are normally printed on one side of the page only, observing standard margins: 1" at top, right, and bottom, and 1" or 1½" at left. Remember that informal reports, like all other types, may be double- or single-spaced, according to the preference of your employer. The first page of the report may be printed on company letterhead or the internal correspondence form used for memos, and is not numbered. Subsequent pages are printed on plain paper and the pages are numbered, either in the upper right corner or at the bottom centre of the page.

An informal report has no title page or table of contents, and is not usually complex enough to require section headings, references, or **appendices**, although any of these could be included if they were needed. If the report is under three pages, section headings are not used. If the report is longer than five pages, you should use headings. Look closely at the parts of the informal report shown below to see how closely they conform to the SIDCRA structure we have been discussing.

Box 7.1   The Parts of the Informal Report

- Memo or letter opening
- Statement of recommendation(s) contained in subject or 'Re' line
- Brief summary statement
- Introduction
- Discussion:
    - Background to issue or situation
    - Outline of important facts and details
    - Possible outcomes, results, or solutions
- Conclusion
- Recommendation(s)
- Appendices (optional):
    - Charts
    - Supporting data
    - Diagrams

Sample informal report

Informal reports normally use memo format, though business letter format may also be used. The class observation report in Figure 7.2, a variation of the assessment report, is written in letter format. Had the writer chosen to do so, it could also have been format-ted as a memo and sent as an attachment to a letter or an e-mail message.

Semi-formal reports

The semi-formal report format is used whenever your reports require a more formal appear-ance than a memo or letter, but are not long enough or complex enough to require the full treatment of a formal report. Semi-formal reports usually run between five and ten pages, though the format can be used for reports up to twenty pages long. Contents are usually divided into short sections headed with appropriate titles. Regular progress reports, incident reports, evaluation reports, and proposals may also be presented as semi-formal reports.

The most obvious difference between the informal report and the semi-formal report is the more formal appearance of its first page. Instead of using memo or letter format, the semi-formal report is given a title, and displays the names of both the author and the com-pany or organization of origin at the top of the first page, along with the date of submis-sion. This information may be centred or placed at the left margin.

The semi-formal report does not employ a 'Re' line. Instead, the **summary** of recom-mendations is given in a short paragraph at the beginning of the report.

Like all reports, the semi-formal report is printed on one side of the page only, observ-ing the same standard margins as the informal report, and may be double- or single-spaced, depending on the preference of your employer. The first page is not numbered, but subsequent pages are numbered in either the upper right or the bottom centre.

Because the semi-formal report is a variation of the informal report, the distinctions between them are not entirely clear-cut; in some cases, the same material could be presented in either format, depending on the circumstances. A sample semi-formal report is shown in Figure 7.3.

Box 7.2   Contents of the Semi-formal Report

- Report title, author's name and title, and date at top of page one
- Summary
- Introduction
- Discussion:
  - Background to issue or situation
  - Outline of important facts and details
  - Possible outcomes, results, or solutions
- Conclusion
- Recommendation(s)
- References/Bibliography (optional)
- Appendices (optional):
  - Charts
  - Supporting data
  - Diagrams

Department of Civil Engineering
Central Maritime University

Box 5005 Truro, Nova Scotia B2S 4M3
<www.cenmar.u.ca>

26 February 2010

Veronica Scott
Dolovich and Cowan Technical Services
Eastern Office: 403 Frederick Street,
Halifax NS B3A 4D4

Dear Ms. Scott:

Re: Seminar Observation Report

Thank you for contributing a session to our third-year Professional Practice course. I found the session both interesting and informative, and am happy to contribute this observation report for your files.

The session I saw was conducted with a group of a dozen or so students, along with yourself, seated around a large central table in a seminar room. The principal method you employed was organized discussion. Though you had a clear agenda for the session, the students also seemed to feel free to ask questions and contribute to the table talk—and they did so freely. Your written outline on the board behind you served to both structure the session and keep the discussion on track.

I found your interaction with the group to be very professional, striking exactly the right balance of cooperation and respect. I noted that you established a warm and supportive atmosphere by sitting at the table with the students, a move that signalled your respect for them as future colleagues, and encouraged their engagement and active participation. As well, your willingness to share your personal experiences as a student, an intern, and a partner confirmed the friendly professionalism of your approach, and I'm sure the students will benefit from your generous advice regarding the selection of technical electives, the identification of firms offering professional internships, and other details of their remaining education.

As a practising engineer yourself, you were able to draw extensively on direct knowledge of the kinds of preparation and experience they've had to date, and on what lies ahead for them as they undertake their first jobs. You offered a very helpful framework to assist them in assessing their own interests and selecting a position that will be right for them. Your extensive experience, your level-headed advice, and your genuine enthusiasm helped to make the session a valuable and helpful one for all the students.

Overall, I came away from your session impressed with your ability to reach the students at their own level of concern and need, a factor that in my view indicates your strong commitment to the welfare of these young professionals. The presentation was clear, organized, thoughtful, and genuinely useful. We are delighted that practising professionals like yourself are willing to take the time to share their insights and advice. I know that the students join me in expressing my thanks, and in extending an invitation to return next year. Thank you very much for your contribution to making CivEng 351 a success.

Sincerely,

[CATCH – please insert a hand-written signature]

Alphonso Malle
Associate Professor of Civil Engineering and
Coordinator, CivEng 35

Figure 7.2: This example of an informal report offers a brief assessment of the seminar conducted by a visiting professional engineer as part of the Department of Civil Engineering's Professional Practice course. Though the report is presented using a letter format, it could as well have been presented in memo form.

Sample semi-formal report

The semi-formal report shown below is a proposal for a new course to be offered as part of the Engineering Communication Option in the Ron and Jane Graham Centre for the Study of Communication at the University of Saskatchewan. As you read, notice that the headings used in the body of the report are structured to answer the reader's probable questions. The section headings are designed to tell them quickly what they need to know to gauge the viability of the new course and the rationale for its being added to the curriculum. Although the report is shown here in semi-formal format, the information it contains could also be presented in a standardized form of the sort that most universities use for new course proposals.

New Course Proposal
Submitted by
Jennifer MacLennan, Professor and
D.K. Seaman Chair, Professional and Technical Communication
Academic Director, Ron and Jane Graham Centre
College of Engineering
April 2006

Summary

This proposal describes *RCM 405: Communication Ethics*, a new course for the Engineering Communication Option (ECO). The course is planned for implementation in 2008.

Introduction

The ECO provides engineering undergraduates with the opportunity to enhance their technical education with an additional specialization in communication. The need for individuals who can deal thoughtfully and ethically with the demands of their professions is widely recognized. Although communication ethics is already part of the curriculum of our *Foundations of Professional Communication* course, students taking the ECO will require deeper consideration of the issues surrounding the ethics of how and what we choose to communicate.

Calendar Description

The proposed calendar description for *RCM 405: Communication Ethics* will read as follows.
    As a social practice that affects the interests and well-being of others, communication is
    inescapably concerned with ethical decision-making, both in the content of our messages and in
    the strategies we use to exert influence over our audiences. Communication ethics therefore
    considers the relationship among character, social values, and professional practices in human
    communication, both public and private.

Prerequisite and Co-requisite Requirements

The normal prerequisite for *RCM 405: Communication Ethics* will be *RCM 300: Foundations of Professional Communication*. Any other courses in the ECO series would also be helpful. Permission of the instructor may be granted for those outside of engineering who have not taken RCM 300.

Topics and Methods

The course will begin by establishing a theoretical framework through reading, lecture, and class discussion. Topics to be covered in RCM 405 include the following:
   • The Social Nature of Ethics
   • What is Ethical Practice?
   • Ethics, Propriety, and Expediency
   • Consequentialism and Ethical Decision-making
   • Ethical Standards and Universals

- Ethics in Context
- Ethics and the Nine Axioms
- The Rhetorical Nature of Ethics
- An Ethical Code for Communicators

The remainder of the course will proceed by the case study method; students will analyze, discuss, and defend the various courses of action possible in a given situation. Discussion will aim to establish a thoughtful understanding of the facts presented in each case study and of the implications of each possible course of action, taking into consideration a) the requirements of ethical responsibility, relation, ethos, rhetorical balance, and purpose; b) the potential risks associated with various options; c) any constraints present in the situation, and how these might apply; d) the personal and/or institutional values involved; e) the effect on individuals/groups to whom loyalties are owed.

Additional Resources

No new resources will be required; this course will be taught by faculty in the Ron and Jane Graham Centre for the Study of Communication and offered as part of the ECO.

Conclusion

The purpose of the ECO is to provide undergraduates in professional and technical programs the opportunity to expand their understanding of human communication and to obtain a valuable specialization in this area. RCM 405 will provide an opportunity to deepen their understanding of ethical practice and to develop their skills in the deliberative process of ethical decision-making.

Recommendation

That *RCM 405: Communication Ethics* be added to the current offerings in the ECO series, and that it be piloted in 2008.

Figure 7.3: A semi-formal report offers a more formal appearance than that of the informal memo report, and is therefore more suitable for complex analyses or issues.

Formal reports

Formal report format is used for lengthy, complex, or important documents, and is normally reserved for reports more than ten pages long. The formal report employs the same six standard parts as make up shorter reports, but its physical structure is more highly elaborate, employing a title page, table of contents, lists of figures and tables, and section headings. It is also bound in a cover that bears the company name, the title of the report, the author's name, and the date.

A formal report is expected to reflect the organization's professionalism and public ethos, and to conform to standard conventions of layout and structure. It should be error free and written on one side of the page only, with standard margins of 1" at top, right, and bottom of the page and 1½" at the left side. The text may be single- or double-spaced, according to your company's practice, though double spacing is more common. The writing style of a formal report is crisp and professional without being curt, and the document employs figures, **charts**, **diagrams**, and illustrations wherever these would serve to make the meaning clearer.

Because the formal report must manage several levels of complex information, it employs headed sections that are assembled in a conventional order. The parts of a formal report, in the order of presentation, are as follows.

| Box 7.3 | The Parts of a Formal Report |

- Cover
- Letter of transmittal
- Cover page
- Summary
- Table of contents
- List of tables and figures
- Acknowledgements
- Introduction
- Discussion
- Conclusion
- Recommendations
- References
- Appendices

Cover

The cover does more than simply enclose a formal report; it helps to establish its professionalism and the credibility of its author. Some corporate reports may have specially designed covers that display the company's name and logo, but most will be presented in standard purchased covers. A plain-coloured, good-quality cover is best. Like the work inside, the cover should make as professional an impression as possible, and a plain gray, black, or navy makes a more dignified impression than a gaudy picture or design.

Letter of transfer or transmittal

The letter is a formal business letter from the writer (you) to the person or persons to whom the report is addressed. It should briefly outline the reason for the report and point out some of its important findings or features. The letter of transmittal may be attached to the outside of the report cover, or bound inside the cover just ahead of the title page, depending on your company's preference. Like all business letters, the letter of transmittal is normally single-spaced.

Title page

The formal report should always contain a separate title page, whether or not the title appears on the cover of the report. The title page is never numbered. It displays the name of the company or institution, the title and subtitle of the report, the name(s) and title(s) of person(s) who commissioned the report, the name(s) of author(s) and their title(s), and the date. If your employer provides you with a cover page format, follow that; otherwise use the format shown in the sample title page on page 214 of this chapter.

The title of your report should be carefully chosen to reflect the content and focus of the report; it should be neither too long nor too brief, and may include a subtitle for clarity.

Summary of recommendations

Also known as the **executive summary** or **abstract**, this section usually precedes the table of contents in a standard formal report, although some report formats place it afterwards. The summary, as discussed in Chapter 6, is a brief overview of all of the recommendations and their rationale. After reading your summary, even your least expert reader should have a clear idea of your findings and your approach.

Although there is no strict guideline about the length of the executive summary, it should normally be no longer than one-tenth the length of the report as a whole; that is, a ten-page report would likely feature a summary of one page, while the summary of a hundred-page report could be as long as ten pages. The summary is not considered part of the report proper, and so is not numbered as part of the main text.

Table of contents

This is a detailed listing of numbered sections and the pages on which these are to be found. It is designed to help the reader locate information in the body of the report. Sections are listed in order, and may or may not be numbered. The sections of a very lengthy report may be further divided into subsections; if so, these should also be listed in the table of contents. Like the summary, the table of contents page is front matter and is not considered part of the actual body of the report, so it is not numbered along with the main content. However, if desired, front matter (summary, table of contents, list of illustrations, glossary, and acknowledgements) may be numbered separately using lower-case Roman numerals at the bottom centre of each page.

List of tables and figures or list of illustrations

Depending on the contents of your report, either or both of these may follow the table of contents, especially in a technical report. They list, by number and title, the figures and tables or the illustrations presented in the report, along with the corresponding numbers of pages on which they appear. These lists, like the table of contents, are an aid to the reader who wishes to quickly locate information in the body of the report.

Glossary or list of technical terms

Also known as '**nomenclature**', a **glossary** may follow the **list of illustrations** if the report is highly technical or extremely complex. In general, this section is used for technical or specialized terminology that is essential to the report; unnecessary jargon should be minimized or avoided where possible.

Such a list provides an at-a-glance reference for specialized terminology, making a complex report more reader-friendly and usable. Terms should be defined clearly and in a manner that will allow the reader a quick grasp of meaning. If there are relatively few, but essential, technical terms, this segment may be placed in the body of the report rather than as a separate section.

Acknowledgements

If they are appropriate to your report, **acknowledgements** are placed on a separate page following the various lists of contents. Here the authors of the report may recognize and thank any individuals or groups who assisted in the preparation of the report, or contributed to the project it discusses.

The acknowledgements page is considered front matter and, like the table of contents page, the list of illustrations, and the glossary, is not numbered as part of the main text. It may, like other front matter, be numbered with lower-case Roman numerals.

Introduction

This section begins the report proper, and its first page is considered the first page of the report. As you will recall from the discussion in Chapter 6, the **introduction** not only introduces the subject matter of the report, but also prepares the reader for the report's particular focus and its findings. It also briefly outlines any necessary background information, states the problem or issue, describes the situation, and sets out any limitations that might have been imposed on the investigation or analysis, as well as giving specifics about the direction that the analysis has taken. It is not meant to do any of these things in depth, but to prepare the reader for what will come in the body of the report.

The introduction may occupy between one-tenth and one-fifth of the report proper; that is, the introduction to a hundred-page report will likely be between ten and twenty pages. Its first page is numbered '1', usually at the bottom centre of the page.

Discussion

The main body of the report, or **discussion**, sets out the writer's method (including the criteria used to evaluate possible results, solutions, or outcomes) and presents a detailed analysis of the problem, issue, or situation that led to the conclusions and recommendations offered in the report. It should discuss the important facts of the situation, including relevant history, details, formulae, calculations, and examples. As well, it should itemize any possible outcomes or courses of action, indicating the one that has been recommended and detailing the reasons for rejecting the others.

The discussion is divided into headed subsections, each of which begins on a new page. The word 'discussion' is not normally used as a heading.

Conclusion

As you will recall from the last chapter, the **conclusion** summarizes the findings of the report and should be a natural result or extension of the point of view presented in the discussion. It should not contain any unexpected revelations or outcomes. Instead, it should satisfy the expectations created by the rest of the report, and draw together the arguments that have been presented in the discussion. Like the introduction, the conclusion of the report generally occupies between one-tenth and one-fifth of the report, so that the conclusion of a hundred-page report would generally be between ten and twenty pages long. It begins on a separate page under the heading 'Conclusion'.

Recommendations

The recommendations spell out the action that the report writer expects will be taken on the conclusions presented. If a conclusion says 'this is what I think about this situation', the recommendation says 'here's what we should do about it'. The recommendation may include several steps that the reader is expected to follow; if so, these should be listed and numbered individually so that they are easy to identify and follow. This headed section begins on a separate page.

References or bibliography

Reports that are intended to influence policy, corporate vision, workplace practices, or product design strategies frequently draw on material from outside sources—others' research, government documents, books and professional journals, articles in the popular press, and Internet sources—in order to assist managers and administrative officers in making informed decisions about the future of the company or organization. If your report makes use of such materials, a citation list should be included.

Some style guides use the terms '**references**' and '**bibliography**' interchangeably; others insist that 'references' should include only those sources directly quoted in the discussion of the report, while 'bibliography' is usually understood to also include sources consulted but not directly quoted. You may wish to resolve this difficulty by listing as 'references' only those sources from which you have quoted, which is the path many researchers take.

However, you may find that you have made use of research sources that, though not cited, helped to shape your understanding of the issue or problem, and many believe these should be also acknowledged. In such a case, you may wish to divide your references into two lists, one showing 'sources cited' and the other indicating 'sources consulted'. Either way, your list of references is intended to provide the reader with the information needed either to do further reading on the subject of the report or to check the accuracy of the writer's interpretations of previous research.

Documenting your sources

The credibility of a research report can depend to a large degree on the thoroughness and authority of your sources. For this reason, all sources you consult, including Internet sources, should be properly documented, according to standards appropriate to your field of study. Once you have determined that the information you have collected is reliable and authoritative (an issue of particular importance in dealing with websites), you should be able to record all the information your readers would require to locate the cited sources for themselves if they should need to do so.

When you refer to your research sources in the body of your report, you may use one of two methods. The first of these is a format known as author-date, which places the last name of the author and the year in parentheses immediately following the relevant statement, as in (Urquhart 2008). The reader may then refer to an alphabetical list of references at the end of the report to find the complete documentation information for Urquhart's work. This format is currently the most widely used in nearly all fields.

A second method commonly used in mathematics and the natural sciences also employs an alphabetical list of references at the end of the report. The difference is that items in this list are numbered, so that instead of placing the author's name and the date in parentheses, the writer places the relevant number in parentheses immediately following the quoted material, as in (1). The reader then refers to the numbered alphabetical list to find the complete documentation information.

Documentation information for research sources is intended to assist your readers in locating the information for themselves, if they wish to do so. Each entry is like a mini report that identifies who, what, where, and when; thus, all **citation formats** include information about author, title, place of publication, publisher, and date. For Internet sources, you should identify the author, the name of the posting or website, and either the date on which the material was posted to the web, if it is available, or the date on which you accessed the information, along with the electronic address (URL). Below are several examples of source citations using the author-date arrangement recommended for the natural and social sciences, which can be found, for example, in the *Chicago Manual of Style*. Even if you number your references, the information they contain can still be presented using this format. A style manual will provide you with more detailed guidelines, along with samples of layout.

Print Sources

A book or book-length work:

> MacLennan, J.M. 2008. *Interpersonal Communication for Canadians*. Toronto: Oxford University Press Canada.

An article or chapter in an edited book:

> Urquhart, B.L. 2008. Bridging gaps, engineering audiences: Understanding the communicative situation. In *Readings for Technical Communication*. Ed. Jennifer MacLennan. Toronto: Oxford University Press Canada. 196–202.

Electronic Sources

An article in an electronic scholarly journal:

> Wills, J.E. 'Telling it like it is': Jim Pankiw and the politics of racism. *Rhetor* 2 (2007). Online: <uregina.ca/~rheaults/rhetor/2007/wills.pdf>

A page or entry on an Internet site:

> MacLennan, J.M. 2007. Academic and professional programs in the Ron and Jane Graham Centre. Online: <grahamcentre.usask.ca/programs.html>

An e-mail message:

> Snowsell, C. 2008. RSA conference registration. E-mail to Jennifer MacLennan (24 January).

There are many acceptable styles for reference entries in addition to the ones shown, and, though no one style is more 'correct' than another, the particular citation format you choose should conform to that preferred by your academic discipline, employer, instructor, or editor. You should select the appropriate format and use it accurately and consistently throughout your document.

Appendices

Attachments or appendices are often employed in a formal report, since the information presented there is sometimes quite complex. Supporting data that are either too cumbersome or too complicated to be included in the body of the report, such as detailed charts or diagrams, calculations and derivations, or data derived from a survey, should be attached as **appendices**.

Appendices should be inserted into the report in the order in which they were referred to in the discussion. The first to be mentioned is labelled 'Appendix A', the second is labelled 'Appendix B', and so on. Each appendix should be clearly labelled and given its own title. Although it is an attachment to your formal report, an appendix should also function as a self-contained document, with its own brief introductory paragraph and its own conclusion.

Assembling the Report

The parts of the formal report are usually arranged in the order listed, beginning with the front matter (letter of transmittal, title page, summary, table of contents, list of illustrations, acknowledgements). Front matter is not numbered as part of the body of the report, but may be numbered using lower case Roman numerals placed in the centre bottom of the page. After you have assembled the front matter, you should assemble the main report itself. Each of the parts in the main report (the introduction, the sections of the discussion, the conclusion, and the recommendations) normally begins with its own title on a new page, almost like a chapter of a book. Starting at the introduction, the pages of the report are numbered using Arabic numerals (1, 2, 3 . . .). The first page of each section may be numbered or left without a number.

Although the usual placement of page numbers in the bulk of the text is in the upper right corner of the page, your company's format may centre them at top or bottom of each page. Use the format recommended or required by your college or your employer.

Page numbers in a report consist of numbers alone; they are not accompanied by the word 'page'.

Remember that part of the effectiveness of a formal report, as of any professional communication, depends on its visual appeal, so it is important that your report be printed in a professional manner. Follow an accepted format carefully, and take great care that no spelling, grammatical, or typing errors mar the quality of your report.

Formal reports also make use of frequent paragraphing and employ headings and subheadings to assist the reader in following the reasoning of the writer. As in all professional communication, layout is part of your organization, so you should use white space effectively and choose a readable font, preferably a serif font in 12-point. Do not make corrections to a formal report in ink or pencil; instead, reprint the page. Always make corrections using the same font as you used for the rest of the report.

Using Visuals in a Formal Report

A well-written formal report should contain straightforward, readily understandable explanations, but your words need not work alone to communicate your message. Instead, they are frequently augmented by visuals—graphic or pictorial material used to simplify or clarify the verbal material. You should try to translate your written information into visuals wherever they will help you to clarify and enhance your discussion. Well-chosen visual aids can help to communicate your message more effectively, and they should be carefully selected to fulfill this purpose.

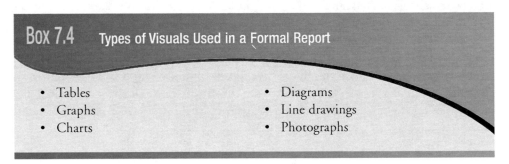

Box 7.4   Types of Visuals Used in a Formal Report

- Tables
- Graphs
- Charts

- Diagrams
- Line drawings
- Photographs

Visuals can include **tables**, **graphs**, charts, diagrams, **line drawings**, and photographs that are designed to help the reader understand what is being discussed. In many cases, they serve not only as handy presentation devices, but also as aids to analysis.

However, you should never use visuals simply to decorate your reports. Tables that are overly cluttered, diagrams or charts that present an incomprehensible jumble of acronyms and detail, photographs that are muddy or indistinct, or drawings that do not isolate the information they are meant to communicate are detrimental to the clarity and effectiveness of the report. If your visuals are not immediately understandable to the intended audience, consider redesigning them, replacing them with something else, or eliminating them completely. Never allow your visuals to unduly complicate your information or confuse your reader, or distract from your message. If they do not focus and communicate clearly, they are not fulfilling their purpose.

Depending on their size, comprehensiveness, and immediate relevance to the written material, visuals may be placed either within the body of the report or in an appendix at the end. If they are necessary to the reader's immediate understanding and if they are simple enough, visuals should be positioned close to the appropriate paragraph in the report, preferably on the same page or on the page immediately following. Some experts advise that visuals may even be placed on the back of the preceding page so that they face the text where they are discussed. Large visuals may be rotated 90° with the top toward the left side of the page, so that it is caught in the bound edge.

Number visuals sequentially (Figure 1, Figure 2, and so on) and identify each with an appropriate title and brief caption, positioned beneath the visual. The report text should refer to the visual by figure number and title when discussing the material it illustrates, and the discussion should occur as close as possible to the placement of the visual in the text.

If the visual is very complex, or if it is not immediately necessary to the reader's grasp of the situation, it could be placed in an appendix. If it is very complex but necessary to the reader's immediate understanding, the complex version could be placed in the appendix and a simplified version placed in the body of the report. Below is a discussion of when and how to use different types of visuals.

Tables

Tables are widely used by writers of reports to help consolidate, present, and analyze comparative information. They are especially useful for comparing large amounts of material in a small space. While tables cannot take the place of your discussion, they do allow you to organize and effectively present information in a format that is readily grasped by your readers. In fact, you should expect that some readers will turn first to the table for an overview of the facts, before they read the discussion of the details. For this reason, the tables need to be clear and easily understandable, presenting complex information according to some clear comparative principle.

Most word-processing packages allow you to design and insert tables right into the text of your report. If your program does not allow you to do this, you can create tabular columns using the tab key. Here are some guidelines for creating an effective table:

- Provide a heading for your table that includes a number and a suitable caption.
- Space items so that they are not too cramped.
- If the table becomes too wide for the page, turn it 90 degrees, with the top of the table toward the bound side of the page.
- Design and place your table so that it fits on one page.
- Label all parts of the table clearly so that readers will know what they are looking at.
- Keep your table simple so that readers can apprehend the information quickly. A table that takes ten minutes to decipher is not fulfilling its purpose.
- Number your tables in the order in which they are presented in the text.
- Numbers and captions for a table are placed above the table; for other illustrative material, they are placed below.
- If possible, compare information vertically (in columns) rather than horizontally (in rows). People can scan vertical information more easily than horizontal information.

Tables 7.1 and 7.2 both deal with educational attainment in Canada, but communicate different information. Note how the arrangement of the table is adapted to the table's purpose.

Tables allow us to compare large amounts of information conveniently and clearly. Comparisons may be made along only one variable (for instance, by year), but more commonly, tables compare information along two variables, as shown in Table 7.1, which compares educational attainment by both year and level of schooling.

Table 7.1 Canadian Population by Highest Level of Schooling (percentage)							
	1976	1981	1986	1991	1996	1999	2001
Less than grade 9	25.4	20.7	17.7	14.3	12.4	11.0	9.8
Grades 9 to 13	44.1	43.7	42.5	42.6	40.4	37.7	21.5
Some post-secondary education	24.1	27.6	30.2	31.7	33.9	36.6	16.8
College or trades diploma							18.9
University degree	6.4	8.0	9.6	11.4	13.3	14.8	15.4

Population over the age of 15.
Source: © Census of Canada, Statistics Canada. Available at http://www40.statcan.ca/l01/cst01/educ43a.htm.

Tables are effective for communicating more complex comparisons in a relatively compact space, and for making statistical information easier to grasp.

Table 7.2 Undergraduate Degrees Granted in Canada, by Field of Study					
	2001	2002	2003	2004	2005
Education	22,350	23,664	24,864	25,401	25,191
Visual and performing arts, communications technologies	5,904	5,958	6,708	7,554	7845
Humanities	19,902	20,571	22,227	22,485	23,904
Social and behavioural sciences, and law	35,784	37,026	38,613	41,346	42,069
Business, management and public administration	34,791	37,581	40,944	44,295	45,318
Physical and life sciences and technologies	14,967	14,460	14,865	15,408	15,921
Mathematics, computer and information sciences	9,009	10,008	10,602	11,040	9,993
Architecture, engineering and related technologies	13,842	14,769	16,389	17,502	17,988
Agriculture, natural resources and conservation	3,888	3,660	3,771	3,615	3,303
Health, parks, recreation and fitness	16,314	17,286	18,222	20,244	21,903
Personal, protective, and transportation services	228	270	270	360	327
Other instructional programs	1,122	900	1,050	1,248	1,581
Total, all instructional programs	178,101	186,153	198,525	210,504	215,367

Source: © Statistics Canada. Available at http://www40.statcan.ca/l01/cst01/educ52a.htm.

Graphs

Graphs provide a visual means to display relationships between variables. Line graphs plot one variable as a function of the other, with the vertical axis representing one of the variables and the horizontal axis representing the other. Since line graphs are frequently used to display successive change or growth over time, a convention has developed for orienting them. The notches along the horizontal axis (bottom) of the graph typically represent time periods (days, weeks, or months); the notches indicated on the vertical axis (up the left side of the graph) normally represent growth units (pounds, number of items, or profits). Growth is represented by a line that slopes either upward (for an increase) or downward (for a decrease) inside the graph.

For example, you could use a graph to track weight gain or loss, showing the time interval along the bottom (horizontal axis) and the weights along the left side (vertical axis); you might use it to track temperature change in a wet-lab chemistry experiment, showing the time interval along the horizontal axis and the temperature range along the vertical axis; you might use it to compare sales figures for a product, indicating the time periods along the horizontal axis and the number of units sold along the vertical axis. Or you might use it to display changes in the educational attainment of Canadians over a span of decades, as in the example below. In each of these examples, the time intervals recorded along the horizontal axis of the graph would differ significantly: for weight gain or loss, relevant intervals might be measured in days or weeks; for the chemistry experiment, meaningful intervals would be minutes or even seconds; for sales figures, significant intervals might be measured in months, quarters, or even years.

Graphs may also show a comparison of two or even three growth lines, but any more than three or four can be confusing. For instance, when you keep track of your own weight loss or gain, if you also record a friend's progress on the same graph, you are using it comparatively.

Although they can be hand-drawn, most graphs are produced on a computer. Software for making presentation slides (such as PowerPoint) and even most word processing programs will generate professional-quality graphs from a data set. Unless you are a graphic artist, it's unlikely that you could produce graphs of comparable quality to those generated by your software. The challenge is to select the kind of graph that will display your information most clearly and understandably to the reader. Most programs allow for elaborate shading, colouring, and three-dimensional effects, all of which can enhance the appearance and clarity of your report, provided the graphs can be clearly reproduced using the method you intend to use for copying the report.

However, though fancy graphs and diagrams are attractive and can be fun to create by computer, it's sometimes easy to get carried away with visual effects and lose sight of their primary purpose. It is tempting at times to include fancy visuals just because they look attractive rather than considering whether they really serve to communicate information clearly. Keep in mind that a graph is meant to provide an easy way for the reader to visualize significant information by providing a quick overview. If you decide to create and include graphs in your report, ask yourself honestly whether they will do the job you want them to do. Some graphs, although attractive to the eye, can actually complicate rather than clarify information that the reader needs. Graphs that force the reader to puzzle through complicated information are ultimately detrimental to the impact of the report.

Don't try to make a graph do too much. If you use a graph to show comparisons in weight loss or gain, drug dosages, sales figures, absenteeism, or costs of training, for example, you could use a different colour to represent each of the items compared (absenteeism in four different departments, costs of two different training programs, weight loss for

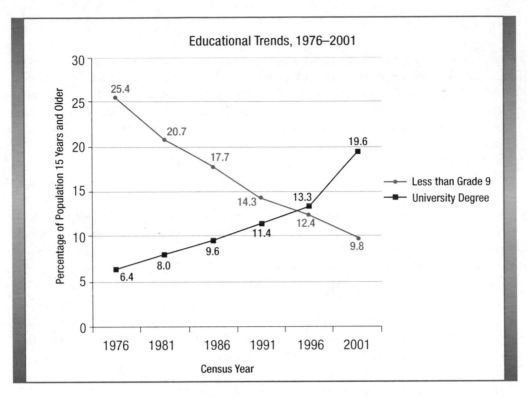

Figure 7.4: A graph enables the reader to easily perceive general trends in the educational attainments of Canadians over time.

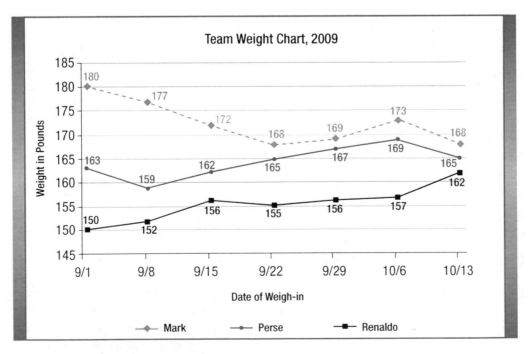

Figure 7.5: A graph may also be used to track the relative weight gain (or loss) of members of a sports team.

four individuals). Although coloured lines can be used effectively to differentiate tracks on a single comparative graph, you should avoid using colour unless your report is being printed and copied in colour, or unless you are making only a few copies and can draw all the lines by hand after the report is copied and assembled. If your report is to be photocopied on a black and white copier, show comparisons by using lines of varying thickness or a combination of broken, dotted, and solid lines.

Charts

Like graphs, charts are used to communicate comparative information quickly and clearly. They simplify complex information into an immediately understandable visual form. Charts come in different types, the most common of which are **bar charts**, **pie charts**, and flow charts. **Bar graphs** are used to compare a single significant aspect of two or more items; each bar on the chart represents one of the items being compared. The length of the bars may be easily compared and give the reader a quick impression of the difference among items. Bar charts may be drawn vertically or horizontally. The vertical bar chart (Figure 7.6) is a visual representation of data from Table 7.2, showing undergraduate degrees, by field, granted in Canada in 2004.

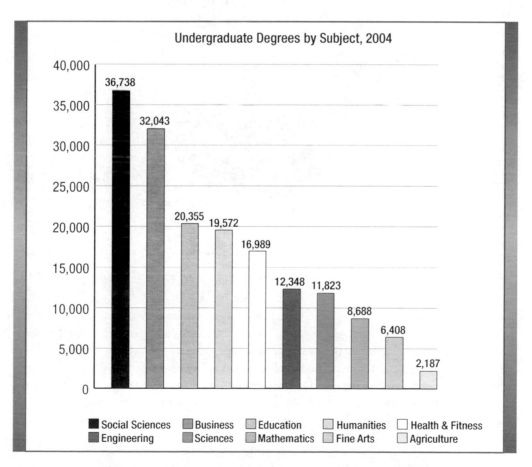

Figure 7.6:   A bar graph can be used to highlight dramatic comparisons in a highly visual way. Because it simplifies the information it presents, a bar chart is best for illustrating large differences in scale.

Pie charts are used to show percentages or parts of a whole: how a budget is spent, the percentage of employees who have college diplomas, the breakdown of total business expenditures, or the percentage of total sales made up by sales of one item. This kind of chart is best suited to emphasizing proportional relationships, as is suggested by Figure 7.7. The pie chart shown presents data from Table 7.2, showing undergraduate degrees awarded in each category as percentages of the total number of degrees granted in Canada during 2004.

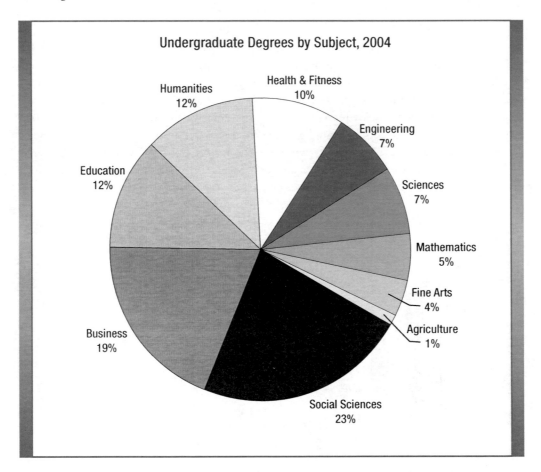

Figure 7.7: A pie chart shows the relationships of the parts to the whole. The reader can see at a glance the percentage of total degrees granted in each area or field.

Photographs

Whenever you must describe a site, a scene, or a product, a good-quality photograph can aid your reader's understanding, provided it is clear and detailed enough to display the information you require. Digital cameras, scanners, colour laser printers, and colour photocopying can make it easy and relatively inexpensive to include both colour and black-and-white photographs in your day-to-day reports.

However, obtaining a good photograph is harder than it sounds, since it must be sharp, with no fuzziness or unnecessary clutter in its composition, and it must be focused tightly enough to communicate the information it is intended to communicate. Finally, it must reproduce clearly when it is copied. Remember that only the sharpest and clearest photos will reproduce well; others may be rendered muddy or unclear. Make sure that the photograph you select is detailed enough to show clearly the information you intend it to communicate. If the shot is cluttered or indistinct, or taken from too far away, you should choose a different method of illustration.

Always try making a copy of the photo using the method you will be using to reproduce the report. When they are reproduced, even clear photographs may become blurred, losing the very detail that you want them to communicate. As well, you should be aware that standard black and white photocopying will not produce sufficiently clear prints, even of black and white photos. If the photograph you have chosen will not reproduce clearly enough using the printing options available to you, you might consider printing the appropriate number of copies of the photograph itself and pasting them into position in each copy of the finished report. You may decide for yourself how many reports you are prepared to assemble by hand like this; obviously it would be suitable only when your report contains few photos and you are making few copies. An advantage of this hand-assembly is that it may allow you to use colour photographs of high quality in a report that is otherwise simply photocopied.

Line drawings

When the information a reader needs from the visual is likely to be unclear in a photograph, or if a photograph would be unsuitable, a line drawing may be a better option. Line drawings, or technical drawings, can be used to illustrate any item, in any scale and from any angle. They can be as simple or as complex as required, and they retain their clarity with standard photocopying. For this reason, they can be extremely valuable for communicating complex visual detail. A line drawing may be used, for example, to illustrate items in a parts list, to show detail in a particular construction, to demonstrate the layout of a building or work site, or to display the package design for a new product. Such drawings are often used in technical manuals or reports to illustrate parts, products, or design details; they may also be used in assembly instructions for furniture or equipment; in film-making to outline the sequence of scenes and action; and in architecture to show the proposed appearance of a finished building.

Line drawings, or technical drawings, are used when photographic illustration would be too expensive or insufficient to communicate the kind of information you require. You need not be a professional artist or technical draftsperson to do a simple line drawing, especially with the help of computer-aided design packages. Whether produced on your printer or by hand, your work must be neat and easy to read. It should be drawn with black ink and clearly labelled, and should be as uncluttered as possible. Figure 7.8 illustrates the parts and lock-washer assembly for attaching eyes to children's toys; Figure 7.9 shows one stage in an assembly diagram for a desk-bookshelf combination; and Figure 7.10 shows a view of a staircase and windowed wall in a proposed house addition.

Diagrams

Unlike line drawings, which show realistic detail, diagrams are usually simplified illustrations designed to highlight one or two aspects of a site, object, or process. Diagrams are particularly useful if your report explains how something works or is assembled. They are

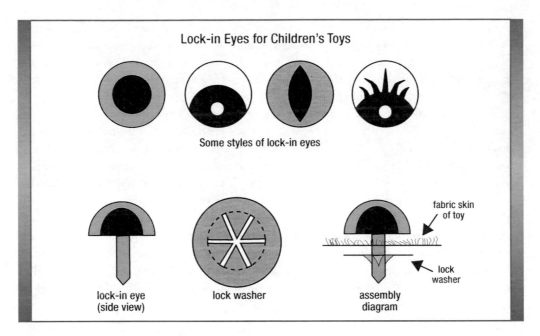

Figure 7.8: A line drawing can be used to illustrate detail in situations where photographs may be insufficient to capture certain types of detail, as in the assembly of these child-safe plastic lock-in eyes for children's toys.

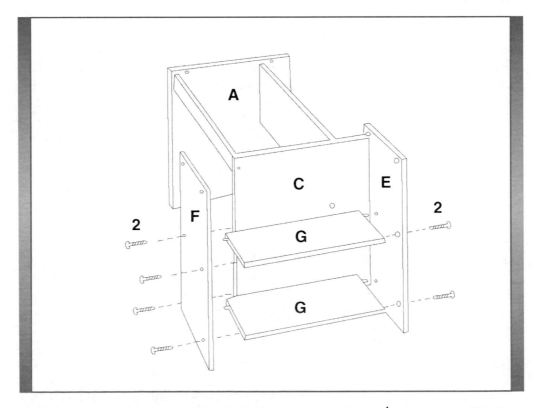

Figure 7.9: A line drawing can clearly show steps in a construction process that may be difficult to capture in a photograph.

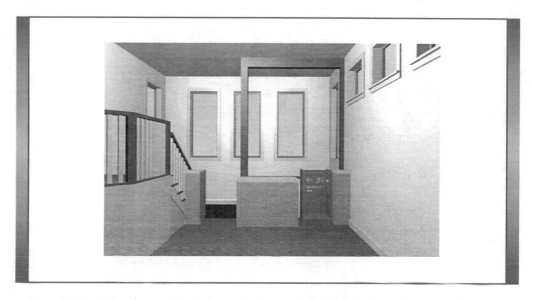

Figure 7.10: A drawing can also help us visualize what doesn't yet exist, as it does in this architect's rendering of one view in a recreation room addition.

not meant to show what the object in question looks like in any realistic way; instead, they are a simplification of some particular feature of the item or process that is being illustrated. For example, a diagram may show the floor plan of the company's proposed new office space, it may lay out the circuitry in an electrical system, or it may illustrate the operation of a nuclear reactor or distilling process.

Diagrams, like line drawings, should be clearly drawn in plain black ink. Though colour may be used effectively, you should avoid it if your report will be photocopied on a black and white copier. Shading, stippling, and cross-hatching can be used instead. Be sure to clearly label all elements of the diagram so that the reader can apprehend quickly the information that you want to communicate. The diagram in Figure 7.11 shows the floor plan for the house addition pictured in 7.10. Figure 7.12, a circuit diagram, demonstrates how a diagram can be used to present intricate detail.

Critical Reading: Sample Formal Report

A formal report may be used for any number of purposes. Annual reports, research reports, some progress reports, evaluation reports, proposals, and feasibility studies are some types. The following example shows a project status report, but the format is similar to that of any other type of formal report.

The report below was written specifically as a model for this book. The report is fictionalized, but its contents are based on an actual site in eastern Canada.

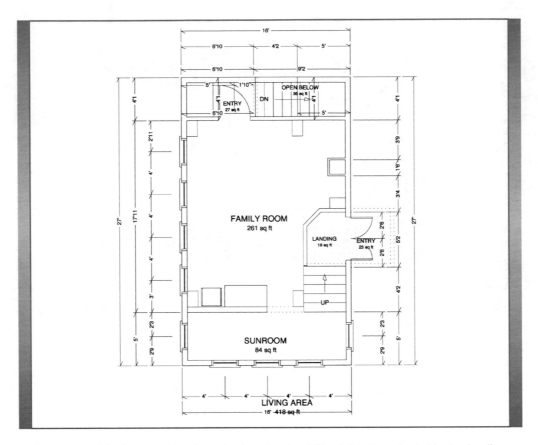

Figure 7.11: This diagram of the floor plan for a house addition helps the householder to visualize the architect's plans for the family room and sunroom additions.

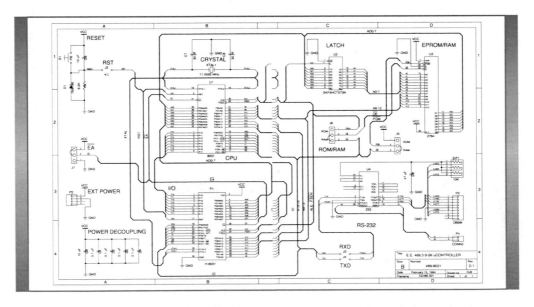

Figure 7.12: Reading a wiring diagram requires special expertise, but its symbols are clear to those who are trained to understand it. A simplified version of a highly complex circuit diagram would likely appear in the body of the report, while this complex version might be placed in an appendix.

Dolovich and Cowan Technical Services

Eastern Office: 403 Frederick Street, Halifax NS B3A 4D4 (902) 987 6543

February 14, 2011
Richard Hynes, Chair
Sherman Bay Watershed Cleanup Consortium
PO Box 959
Sherman Bay, NS

Dear Mr. Hynes:

We have attached the project status report for the Murdoch Creek Watershed Cleanup Project

The report details progress made so far in the jointly funded hazardous waste cleanup and decontamination project. It sets out a description of the challenges inherent in such a project, outlines the strategies to be undertaken, and describes the tasks so far completed; it also provides an overview of budget expenditures to date.

In our recent meetings, you also asked that we consider the extent to which costs may exceed the current budget; we have attempted to estimate the potential overrun, but because the exact nature of the contaminants is still unknown, such an estimate is necessarily sketchy.

However, as this report indicates, there is little likelihood that the contamination can be contained or removed within the budget restrictions we currently face; when this project has come to a close, it is likely that the 'Scum Dump' problem will remain a serious environmental and health issue for years to come.

We will be present at the next meeting of the Consortium Board and will be prepared to answer questions on this report or any other aspect of the Watershed Cleanup Project.

Sincerely,

Bruce James

Bruce James, Project Manager

J.M. Neilands

Jennifer Neilands, Consulting Engineer

Figure 7.13a: The letter of transmittal. Note that this cover letter normally precedes the title page of the report.

Murdoch Creek Watershed Cleanup Project

Status Report

Prepared for the Sherman Bay Watershed Cleanup Consortium
by
Bruce James, Project Manager
Jennifer Neilands, Consulting Engineer

Dolovich and Cowan Technical Services
Eastern Office
403 Frederick Street
Halifax NS B3A 4D4
(902) 987 6543

Figure 7.13b: The title page of the report also shows the company's name, the client, and the names of the report's authors.

SUMMARY

Sherman Bay, Nova Scotia's infamous 'Scum Dump' area is Canada's worst hazardous waste site, containing over 700,000 tonnes of toxic sludge. Toxicity tests conducted in the nearby neighbourhood showed levels of at least a dozen toxic chemicals well above those permitted by the CCME (Canadian Council of Ministers of the Environment).

In May 2005, federal, provincial, and municipal governments announced a $62 million cost-share agreement to fund activities recommended by a Watershed Cleanup Consortium formed of members from the surrounding communities, government, technical specialists, and volunteers. The present report presents a summary of activities and achievements to date.

i

Figure 7.13c: The summary precedes the table of contents, and may or may not be numbered with lower-case Roman numerals.

Murdoch Creek Watershed Cleanup Project

TABLE OF CONTENTS

ii

Figure 7.13d: The table of contents for the formal report.

1

INTRODUCTION

Sherman Bay, Nova Scotia's infamous 'Scum Dump' area is Canada's worst hazardous waste site, containing over 700,000 tonnes of toxic sludge—over 20 times the amount of toxic waste in New York's infamous Love Canal. Among these are polychlorinated biphenyls (PCBs), arsenic, lead, and benzene, all at levels well above those permitted by the CCME (Canadian Council of Ministers of the Environment).

The entire area is bordered by residential and commercial sites. A large number of health problems, including elevated rates of cancer, asthma, and other life-threatening conditions, combined with the extent and nature of the contamination, add to the urgency and challenge of cleanup at this site.

The process of cleanup is underway. This progress report details strategies that have been implemented to date and outlines work to be completed. It also recommends further study of and action to resolve this complex and dangerous contamination.

Figure 7.13e: The introduction is the first page of the report proper.

BACKGROUND: SITE DETAILS

For nearly a century, Sherman Bay, Nova Scotia, was the site of a large steel making and coking operation situated near Murdoch Creek in what has become the centre of the city. The plants have been closed for nearly a decade, but the site they occupied, and its nearby 'Scum Dump', today constitute Canada's worst hazardous waste site.

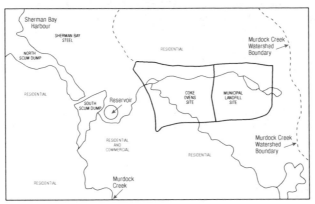

Figure 1: Area surrounding the 'Scum Dump'.

The area known to local residents as the 'Scum Dump' is, in fact, an estuary opening into Sherman Bay Harbour at the mouth of Murdoch Creek. Although at one time it used to accommodate large sailing ships, today this estuary is narrow and shallow, filled with at least 700,000 tonnes of highly toxic by-products of coking and steel-making accumulated over 80 years of dumping from the nearby plants. The estuary daily receives additional tonnes of untreated sewage from 30 outlets that drain into Murdoch Creek. An unlined municipal dump sits at the head of Murdoch Creek and also leaches into it. In all, the 200-hectare site is estimated to contain over 20 times the amount of toxic waste of New York's infamous Love Canal.

It is known that at least 40,000 tonnes of this waste is polychlorinated biphenyls (PCBs). It is also known that the coke plant's benzene tank leaked for years, saturating the surrounding ground. A remaining tank, open to the air, contains an unknown mix of these and other chemicals, and piles of coal, coke, and sulphur also remain at the site. Beneath the old coke plant site, 160 kilometres of underground pipes carry more deadly chemicals. The soil around the area regularly erupts in flames, which cannot be extinguished, and authorities fear that attempts to dismantle the pipes may cause an explosion.

Toxicity tests conducted on the site and surrounding area showed high levels of arsenic, molybdenum, benzopyrene, antimony, naphthalene, lead, toluene, tar, benzene, kerosene, copper, and polyaromatic hydrocarbons (PAHs). All are at levels well above those permitted by the CCME (Canadian Council of Ministers of the Environment). For example, the concentration of arsenic has been shown to be 18.5 times higher than acceptable levels under federal/provincial guidelines; naphthalene levels are 8.9 times higher, and molybdenum and benzopyrene levels are six times the recommended limit.

Above the coal plant is a century-old dump, originally used for slag and other hazardous wastes from the steel mill, which continues to serve as a clandestine junkyard; every week unrecorded industrial discards are dropped amid the slag. An aging incinerator on the site emits mercury, and a brook that flows through it runs a bright shade of rust. When it rains, puddles turn fluorescent green.

The entire area is bordered by residential and commercial development containing homes, ball fields, playgrounds, schools, supermarkets, and even restaurants. Recent (one year ago) tests have shown that the surrounding land, the groundwater, and a brook where children play have all become contaminated with a variety of toxins known to cause various cancers, birth defects, heart disease, kidney disease, brain damage, immune deficiencies, and skin rashes.

Figure 7.13f

3

CONTAMINANT TEST RESULTS

Over 1,000 samples of soil, surface water, and groundwater have been collected at the 'Scum Dump' and coke plant sites to determine the nature and extent of contamination. Samples were compared with provincial and Canadian Council of Ministers of the Environment (CCME) guidelines to determine if further study is needed.

Preliminary findings of soil and groundwater analyses reveal:

- PAH levels in some surface soil samples above CCME guidelines;
- metals, including arsenic and lead, at levels above CCME guidelines;
- impact on groundwater, primarily in samples taken near the landfill site;
- discolouration and levels of iron and manganese in groundwater exceeding CCME guidelines.

These latter features—discolouration and high metal levels—are not considered a health issue because they are common to the area.

Figure 7.13g

4

HEALTH IMPLICATIONS

Recent studies have confirmed the presence of polycyclic aromatic hydrocarbons (PAHs) at concentrations of up to 8,000 ppm; concentrations of PCBs range from 50 to 1,000 ppm. Exposure to both chemicals, and to the heavy metal contaminants at the site, has been linked in lab animals to cancer, liver damage, birth defects, heart disease, kidney and skin diseases, brain damage, immune deficiencies, and reproductive malfunctions.

Cancer rates in the area have never been adequately documented, but some estimates place them at almost double the national average. A study of the medical history of 117 deceased long-term steel plant employees found that an alarming 63 per cent were treated for some form of cancer prior to their death. Current residents complain of 'sore throats, dry eyes, nausea, headaches and a long list' of other ailments (Shawn, 2000), including 'watering eyes, scratchy throat, and shortness of breath' (Toxins cloud history, 2000) and 'asthma, ear infections, eye infections ... bronchitis' (Unknown dangers, 2001).

Figure 7.13h

5

STRATEGIES IMPLEMENTED TO DATE

1. Preparations for Site Demolition

Before extensive decontamination can be carried out, stacks, buildings, and other structures remaining at the site must be dismantled. As well, piles of coal, coke, and sulfur must be carefully removed so as to prevent further distribution of pollutants. During demolition and removal, 'separation zones', which have been determined based on the nature of the contaminants at the site, will be used to establish safe distances for the protection of those who live and work nearby. Work methods will be carefully controlled so as to minimize the possibility of additional contamination. A new access road, designed to divert traffic from residential areas, is currently under construction, as is a pad for washing vehicles and equipment. When these accommodations are complete, demolition will begin. The first of the demolition activities will be to remove the two remaining stacks and derelict buildings.

2. New Fencing

To ease residents' concerns about children and pets wandering onto the demolition site, construction of 3.5 km of new fencing around the site was completed in January of this year. The entire site is now enclosed and the fencing will remain in place throughout the cleanup.

3. Air Monitoring Program

An expanded air-monitoring program has been implemented to measure both 'real-time' and long-term air quality during site demolition and beyond. Hand-held monitors will allow an immediate response to changes in air quality during on-site work. A mobile unit will be transported to sites around the area as an extra safety measure.

4. Landfill Closure

The landfill, which sits at the top of a hill overlooking the main site, contains nearly a century of industrial and household waste. The landfill has been closed and sealed to public access in preparation for site containment procedures, the goal of which is to stop the flow of contaminants from the landfill into the coke plant site. Plans include capping the site and diverting the brook that runs through the area. Construction of a clay landfill cap is underway. The landfill containment is expected to be complete within a year of the date of this report. A leachate management plan—to keep contaminants from leaving the site—will also be implemented.

Figure 7.13i

6

5. Diversionary Sewer Project Phase I: Design
Complicating the cleanup operation is the fact that at least 30 sewer outfalls feed into Murdoch Creek. To deal with this large volume of wastewater, which includes storm and sanitation sewers, a diversionary sewer will be constructed to redirect wastewater to an area off nearby Lookout Point where a water treatment plant development is planned. Design plans for the diversionary sewer are complete, with construction set to begin immediately, weather permitting. Construction is expected to take eight to ten months.

As an added precaution, soil removed to make way for the underground pipes will be tested for contaminants prior to disposal. Contaminated soil will be treated according to environmental regulations.

6. Heritage Resources Impact Statement
The new diversionary sewer will be routed through a portion of Lookout Point thought to be one of Sherman Bay's first settlements. A Heritage Resources Impact Assessment revealed that a military hospital was formerly located in the area, possibly with an on-site cemetery. An archaeological dig will be required to ensure that no burial ground will be disturbed during construction.

Figure 7.13j

7

SUMMARY OF BUDGET AND EXPENSES TO DATE

The $62-million cost-share agreement for the Murdoch Creek Watershed Cleanup Project is managed by Dolovich and Cowan, with the assistance of the provincial government. Approximately $16.4 million has been spent to date (Figure 2). This has covered extensive fieldwork and design plans for the landfill closure, the construction of the fence, purchase of an emergency response vehicle, and plans for the diversionary sewer. A complete budget may be found in Appendix A.

Budget Allocations to Date (in millions of dollars)

Environmental Studies and Assessments	6.0
Identifying Cleanup Technology and Strategies	1.2
Emergency Response Equipment and Training	0.3
Site Separation (includes past relocations)	1.1
Site Security Fencing and On-Site Patrols	1.9
Health Studies	0.4
Landfill Closure	1.5
Regulatory Environmental Health Assessments	0.5
Secretariat and Activities	1.0
Project Management and Public Communication	2.5
Total expended to date	16.4
Total budget allocation	62.0

Figure 2: Murdoch Creek Watershed Cleanup Project: Budget expenditures to date.

Figure 7.13k

8

WORK REMAINING

1. Diversionary Sewer Construction
An archaeological dig will be conducted in the Lookout Point area to ensure that no burial ground will be disturbed during construction; a further assessment will be designed to confirm that no munitions were buried in the area. Construction of the diversionary sewer will begin later this year when these assessments have been completed.

2. Demolition of Remaining Structures
The first of the demolition activities will be to remove the two stacks and the by-products building which still remain on the site. This work will begin when the road and washing pad construction is complete. These are expected to be complete within four months of the date of this report.

3. Decontamination Proposals
Total cleanup of the Sherman Bay 'Scum Dump' is still far from complete. The extent of contamination at the site will require further study beyond that budgeted for in this project, in order that strategies for decontamination may be identified and carefully assessed. Further environmental and health impact studies must be carried out, and appropriate technology for dealing with extensive soil and water contamination at the site will have to be identified and implemented.

Figure 7.13l

9

CONCLUSION

The Murdoch Creek Watershed Cleanup remains on schedule, and several strategies identified in the original proposal have been implemented. Demolition, site closure, containment, and construction of the diversionary sewer can continue to move ahead as soon as preliminary adjustments to the site are carried out. Removal of structures and surface contaminants will follow. However, total cleanup of the Sherman Bay 'Scum Dump' is still far from a reality. It's too soon to determine which technology will be found to be most appropriate for decontamination procedures, or to foresee what further complications may emerge as the site structures are dismantled. It is estimated that cleanup may take ten or more years and cost up to $1 billion.

Figure 7.13m

10

RECOMMENDATIONS

The recommendations arising from this project status report are as follows:

1. that the Murdoch Creek Watershed Cleanup Project, under its current consortium and budget, move ahead as planned;
2. that further plans be made to commit an additional budget of at least $40,000 for implementation of appropriate and extensive decontamination proposals;
3. that pyroengineering specialists be brought into the consortium to deal with the explosive and flammable potential of unknown combustibles at the site;
4. that testing of various decontamination methods begin as soon as possible, so that they may be implemented when preliminary demolition and removal of waste materials has been completed;
5. that a strategic plan be developed for handling unknown chemicals in the tank on the site.

Figure 7.13n

11

REFERENCES

Cancer study left in federal hands. *Sherman Bay Record*, 19 November 1999.

Environment Canada. Government support to Murdoch Creek watershed initiatives. 12 October 2001. Online. <http://www.ec.gc.ca/murdo.htm>.

Fact sheet on the infamous Sherman Bay 'scum dump.' *Enviro Club Canada*. Press Release, 24 July 2000.

Hare, Brenda. Coke plant cleanup group awaits word on next step. *Enviro Club Canada*, 16 January 1999. Online. <http://www.murdo.htm>.

Losing patience on 'scum dump'. *Nova Scotia Chronicle*, 23 November 2000.

Shawn, Gwen. Sherman Bay 'scum dump': It's time to clean up Canada's 'national shame.' *Environmental Hazards Magazine*, April/May 2000.

Toxins cloud history of Sherman Bay street. *The World Post*, 20 July 2000.

Unknown dangers lurk in toxic wasteland. *The Toronto Comet*, 20 July 2001.

Figure 7.13o

12

APPENDIX A: BUDGET

Murdoch Creek Watershed Cleanup Project Current Budget

Item/Category of Expenditures	Allocated	Expended	Remaining
Environmental Studies and Assessments	8.2	6.0	2.2
Demolition and Coke Plant Cleanup Activities	13.0	0.0	13.0
Identifying Cleanup Technology and Strategies	5.0	1.2	3.8
Emergency Response Equipment and Training	1.5	0.3	1.2
Site Separation (includes past relocations)	1.7	1.1	0.6
Site Security Fencing and Security Patrols	1.9	1.9	0.0
Health Studies	1.7	0.4	1.3
Landfill Closure	12.5	1.5	11.0
Regulatory Environmental Health Assessments	3.5	0.5	3.0
Secretariat and Activities	3.5	1.0	2.5
Project Management and Public Communication	9.5	2.5	7.0
Total Budget	62.0	16.4	45.6

Figure 7.13p

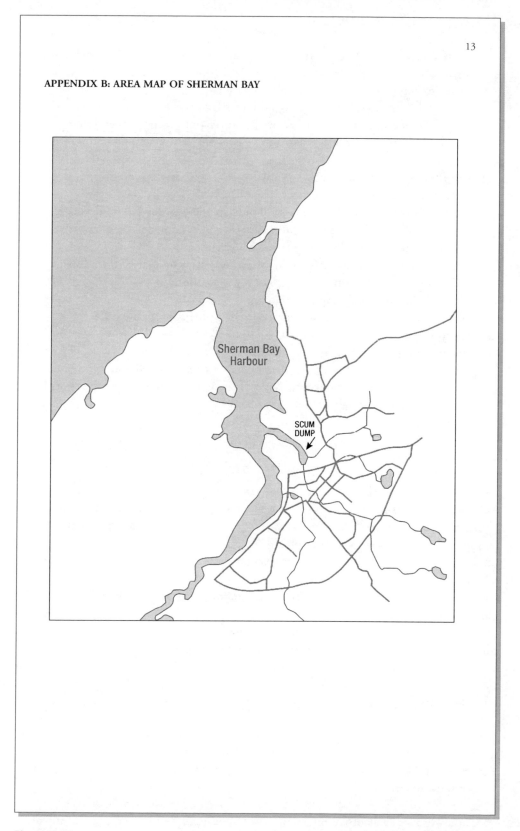

Figure 7.13q

Points to Remember

1. No matter what kind of report you are writing, you must prepare thoroughly and organize carefully. Be sure to refer again to Chapters 2 and 3 before starting to write any report.
2. Identify the purpose of your report and understand the use to which it will be put.
3. Identify your reader and his or her needs, expectations, concerns, and knowledge.
4. Define the writing challenge and the constraints of the situation in which the report will be read.
5. Use the Report Format Decision Scale to select the appropriate format: formal, informal, or semi-formal.
6. Adopt a problem-solving approach to planning, producing, and polishing your report.
7. Choose an appropriate organizational pattern, and build in devices of cohesiveness.
8. Develop your points fully and observe the Seven Cs.
9. Use charts, diagrams, pictures, and tables as necessary to clarify information.
10. Edit your report carefully.
11. Correctly document all research sources.
12. Make sure the parts of your formal report are in the appropriate order.
13. Proofread carefully.
14. In choosing a report format, you should be guided by the complexity of the problem or issue—that is, how much detail or research is required—and the intended audience or readers of the report. Most of the reports you will be writing will be informal or semi-formal.

Key Concepts

abstract	formal report	nomenclature
acknowledgements	executive summary	pie chart
appendix/appendices	glossary	recommendation
bar graph	graphs	references
bibliography	informal report	semi-formal report
charts	introduction	SIDCRA
citation format	letter of transmittal	summary
conclusion	line drawings	table of contents
diagrams	list of illustrations	tables
discussion	list of technical terms	visuals

Assignments and Exercises

The following report situations require a formal report or a proposal. Using the report preparation form in the previous chapter to outline your approach, and employing the strategies for writing developed in Chapter 3, follow your instructor's directions to write one of these reports.

1. You work for Dolovich and Cowan, where several people have expressed an interest in upgrading their skills in professional communication, preferably through obtain-

ing a certificate or diploma in the field. You have been asked to identify the options available to your colleagues, either through your local college or university or through an online certificate program. Investigate at least three possibilities for your colleagues, and write up your findings into a formal report addressed to the President of the company, David Cowan. You will outline for these prospective students all they will need to know regarding the basics of the program (including admission requirements, duration, courses, any practicum or co-op experience or special courses, and advanced standing), as well as the general facilities offered by various institutions (student services, library facilities, recreational facilities, and any special assistance for mature students). You will also want to draw up a study of costs. Evaluate the programs according to their appropriateness for people who are working full time and who wish to achieve certification as professional communicators.

2. Choose any topic in the broadly defined area of technical or professional communication as the focus of your formal report. If you prefer, you may work with *one* of the topics on the list below rather than selecting your own. Drawing on all available research sources, survey the current trends in thinking on the topic you have chosen. Write a formal report that answers the following questions.

   a. Briefly, what major trends appear to be current in this area of communication? Is there a particular emphasis that seems to be especially important?

   b. Has there been any significant change in focus or direction of conventional thinking on communication in business or the professions, as a result of new technologies?

   c. What impact has this trend or these developments in technology had on the practice of your profession?

   d. What conclusions can you draw from your research into this topic? What are the implications of this information for others who wish to pursue careers in your field?

   Here are several topics that have received attention in the recent past, though you are certainly not limited to these. You may choose your own topic if you find something of greater interest to you.

   a. Virtual Office/Home Office
   b. Telecommuting
   c. Job Sharing
   d. Team Building Exercises
   e. Cross-cultural Communication in the Technical Workplace
   f. Corporate Retreats
   g. 'Opting Out'
   h. 'Outsourcing'
   i. Ethics in Communication Practice
   j. Communication 'Coaching'

   Your research should include a minimum of ten sources, and may include interviews or Internet sites as well as library journals and books. You need not provide an exhaustive analysis of the importance of this topic. Instead, present a convincing overview of what is being done and published in the field, and what the major trends appear to be. This analysis must be firmly anchored in sufficient research to make your findings credible.

3. One of the most challenging tasks facing an engineer is communicating technical information to non-specialists. Since budget and contract decisions are frequently made by non-engineers, it is imperative that all technical specialists be able to

explain their projects in clear, non-specialized language. This assignment is designed to help you learn to do just that by having you adapt a report on your current work for a non-technical audience of the general public. You may choose to report on work you have done for a class in which you are currently enrolled, such as an engineering design report or a lab report. You do not need to, though you may choose to, research a new topic for this assignment. However, the report you submit for this class must be written specifically for your communication course and not simply copied from what you submitted in another course.

Your information should be presented in formal report format, and must be written for a lay audience of non-specialists. Although it may be based on the same research as a report you've written for one of your business classes, it must be written specifically for this audience. The body of your report should be organized in the order that best supports your focus and that best serves the needs of your intended reader. Use appropriate section headings for each part of your report. Be sure to correctly document any research sources, and supplement your textual material with appendices where appropriate; you may also provide visual support in the form of photos, graphs, or charts wherever they will enhance understanding or clarify information.

4. On occasion, your formal report will be preceded by a proposal for the written work that is to be submitted. This proposal is the advance work for your formal report and will give your instructor an opportunity to offer guidance for the report itself. The proposal should be descriptive, briefly outlining the report you will be presenting at the end of this course. Like the final report, the proposal should be presented as a formal report, approximately 3–5 pages long, typed or word-processed, and double-spaced. It should include the following sections, with headings.

   a. Identify the report focus. In this section, you must name the topic that you are researching and briefly describe its importance to the field. What makes it significant for your audience of fellow students, to members of the profession in general, or to me, as your professor? What do you hope to demonstrate or reveal in your report?

   b. State the purpose of or need for the report. What is the primary purpose of your report? Why is such an investigation needed? Ideally, the report should contribute something to our understanding of the profession of engineering. What do you hope to learn, discover, reveal, or contradict?

   c. Identify the main section headings or topics that will be covered in the report. Given the topic you are researching, and the nature of the question you hope to answer, what are the major sub-topics you'll be discussing? On what elements will you focus? In other words, what headings do you expect to use in your discussion? You should briefly provide some reasons for your choice of focus, and show how this approach will best answer the question you have posed.

   d. Suggest an outcome (results or conclusions) for your research. Because you won't know for sure what your analysis will establish until it's completed, you should not write this proposal until much of your preliminary research and reading is completed. You will therefore need to be well into your work, at least the preparation, when you do this assignment. Suggest the probable outcome for your analysis: what, exactly, do you anticipate this analysis will establish? What conclusions do you expect to be able to draw from your analysis? What, if any, contributions do you hope to make to the understanding of the profession as a whole? What recommendations will result from your report?

Chapter 8

Oral Reports and Technical Presentations

Learning Objectives

- To master the four common types of oral presentations: impromptu; manuscript; memorized; and extemporaneous.

- To learn how to prepare an oral report for extemporaneous delivery.

- To master elements of vocal and visual presence so as to deliver your message effectively and confidently.

- To learn how to incorporate visuals into your presentation.

© iStockphoto.com/Ben Blankenburg

More and more often, professionals in all fields are called upon to present materials orally, whether in workshops, seminars, design presentations, technical briefings, or staff meetings. Inexperienced speakers often find these public-speaking situations unnerving, and may even try to avoid them whenever possible. However, anyone who wants to advance in business or the professions will sooner or later have to face an audience.

An oral report or briefing, like a written report, should be carefully thought out, well organized, and clearly presented. It should be addressed appropriately and effectively to its intended audience, engaging their attention, motivating them to take the action recommended, and providing a means by which that action can be achieved. It should contribute effectively to the sense of human connection that is at the heart of all communication, and it should establish the speaker as a person of good judgement, good character, and good will.

Think of the last time you heard a talk or presentation that engaged and motivated you, that captured and held your attention, that challenged and delighted you. Chances are you can't name a single one. In fact, far too many speeches are lacklustre efforts in which the speaker is more concerned with surviving the experience than with actually communicating with the audience. Sadly, too many of us feel we have done a satisfactory job as speakers if we got through the speech without major embarrassment.

Because we so rarely hear a really outstanding talk, few of us understand what to aim for; as a result, we prepare inexpertly and inadequately, focusing on our own concerns for saving face rather than on connecting with the audience. Fear of public exposure, combined with a lack of outstanding models for speaking, leaves us without skill in this indispensable form of communication.

However, as this chapter will demonstrate, no matter how uncomfortable you are at the thought of public speaking, you can learn to give an effective speech or presentation. No matter what kind of speech, technical talk, or presentation you are asked to do, it is possible to plan an effective talk, organize your materials carefully, and **practise** successfully. As an added bonus, you will find that the fear associated with public speaking will actually fade if you gain control over your subject matter and focus on communicating your message to your audience instead of on your own performance anxiety.

One big difference between oral presentations or reports and the written variety is the advantage of meeting your audience face-to-face. Though it may be intimidating to stand before a group of your peers or your supervisors, you should remember that it's also a lot easier to establish rapport with someone who is in the same room with you than it is to engage and motivate the readers of a written report. If you can think of the opportunity for oral communication as an advantage rather than a burden, you will find it easier to prepare for the experience.

Four Foundations of Effective Speaking

In order to take full advantage of the opportunity to speak directly to your audience, you will need to think about your speech in a different manner than you may have been accustomed to doing. A speech is not about you and your performance; it is about connecting and communicating with a group of other people. Public speaking is communication, and no talk need ever bore the audience if the speaker approaches the task with genuine enthusiasm and an intent to communicate with them.

As with all professional communication, there are four fundamental principles that underlie every successful speech: put the audience first, focus on your purpose, attend to your credibility, and identify the speaking context.

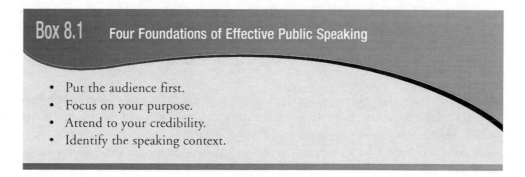

Box 8.1   Four Foundations of Effective Public Speaking

- Put the audience first.
- Focus on your purpose.
- Attend to your credibility.
- Identify the speaking context.

Put the audience first

Remember that you are giving this speech in order to communicate with an audience, that someone thought it was important for you to deliver your message in person rather than in written form. For this reason, you need to provide the connection that only a face-to-face meeting can achieve. This principle, as you know, is the key to all effective communication; unfortunately, it is also a principle that many speakers forget as they focus on their own anxieties and concerns. As you prepare, think clearly about how you will accommodate the needs and interests of those who are taking the time and trouble to come to hear your presentation: To whom are you speaking? Are you delivering material to your peers? Your subordinates? A group of visitors? The Board? What is the audience's interest in your project? How much information do they already have? What do they want or need to know? How much depth do they expect? As you consider these expectations and needs, adapt your report presentation as closely as possible to your audience's expectations. Recognize that some things you consider important may have to be left out if they are not as significant to your audience.

Focus on your purpose

If your presentation is to be successful, you need to think about exactly what it is intended to accomplish. Why are you speaking at all, rather than providing a written report? As well, you need to understand just what, and how much, you can accomplish in the time available. Should you give a quick overview of your project, or should you present an in-depth analysis of your work? Are you expected to outline, support, or justify what you've been doing? Do you have to persuade your audience to accept a new point of view or course of action? Will you face questions from your listeners? What are your own expectations? At the planning stage, you will need to shape your speech to reflect the face-to-face task it is meant to accomplish.

Attend to your credibility

Remember that you build credibility as a direct result of the quality of respect you demonstrate, both for your listeners and for the focus and **structure** of the speech itself. Your credibility depends on your demonstrating an understanding of the situation, of the audience's needs and expectations, and of your own role as a professional. It will be portrayed in the level of preparation you bring to the presentation and in the quality of your **delivery**—confident, clear, and engaging. This chapter presents strategies for preparation and delivery that will assist you in establishing yourself as a credible, competent speaker who can connect effectively with the audience.

Identify the speaking context

One of the things that make oral communication different from written work is the fact that it is presented face-to-face in a physical setting. A speech is not simply reading aloud to an audience who could easily have read the report for themselves. You are giving your information in person for a reason. Be sure to take full advantage of the opportunity to build a genuine connection with your audience.

The size of your audience, the room in which you are speaking, and the limits of time are among the factors that will influence how you build that connection. Where will you be giving your presentation? How big is the room? What facilities are available? How far will you be from your audience? Will you be using a microphone? Overhead cameras? Computer slides? How much time will you have to make your connection with the audience? If you have prepared a forty-five-minute presentation only to find that you're expected to give a three-minute overview of your project as visitors are paraded past your desk, you'll have a difficult time—though perhaps not as difficult as if you're in the reverse situation! Make sure you know how much time you're expected to fill, and tailor your speech accordingly.

Like all effective professional communication, oral communication depends on building appropriate relations with your audience. It also means staying focused on your communicative purpose, and taking care to present your message in an understandable and engaging manner. Finally, when you are preparing an oral presentation, you should also think about the constraints of the physical setting and historical, interpersonal, or professional context in which your report will be given. As you prepare your presentation, and as you deliver it, you should be demonstrating your credibility and good will through your consideration of all these elements.

Four Methods of Speech Delivery

Oral presentations vary not only in length and formality, but also in the style of delivery. There are four main types of speech delivery, but not all are suited to every occasion. Be sure to choose the one that is most appropriate for the requirements of your situation.

Impromptu

This kind of speech is given on the spur of the moment: the speaker is called upon to speak without warning and without any prepared notes. This type of presentation is most commonly used as an exercise in public speaking classes or groups, or it may occur when a party guest who wasn't expecting to be honoured is called upon to say a few words. For obvious reasons, the **impromptu speech** is usually short (under two minutes); a suitable

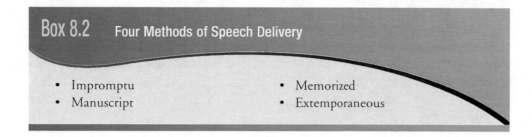

Box 8.2   Four Methods of Speech Delivery

- Impromptu
- Manuscript

- Memorized
- Extemporaneous

topic for such a speech is one on which almost anyone could speak without having to prepare. The speaker isn't expected to provide new information; at best, she may simply give us a new way of looking at something we all know. This style of delivery is not suitable for any occasion where the speaker had reason to know that a presentation would be required, nor is it appropriate for a longer presentation, since few people—including experienced speakers—can generate more than one or two minutes of coherent remarks, even on familiar topics, without advance preparation.

Manuscript

This presentation style involves reading word for word from a printed document that is the result of extensive research and thoughtful organization by the speaker. A **manuscript speech** has limited usefulness, and is most appropriate in situations where exact wording is important due to legal or political considerations (a judge rendering a decision on a precedent-setting case, a lawyer making a submission to the supreme court, or an elected official issuing policy might use this form). This kind of speech is, in ordinary circumstances, not particularly effective, since it is difficult to maintain audience engagement when you're focused on a manuscript in front of you instead of on your listeners. If you aren't focused on the audience, you won't hold their attention, and if you lose their attention, you can't hope to move them.

As well, the act of giving a speech is an oral event, a dynamic interaction for both speaker and listeners. Unfortunately, written text just doesn't have the same sound, **immediacy**, or power of engagement that is evident in words spoken directly to an audience for whom the message is shaped even as it is being delivered. Reading from a prepared text turns the audience from participants into observers, and turns the speech from an event into an artefact, and thus deadens the engagement that your audience will feel. For this reason, reading from a manuscript is discourteous to the people who have come to hear you in person, since they have gathered to hear you—your enthusiasm and engagement, your commitment and investment in the topic and in them. Even if you are very accomplished at reading aloud (most people are not), you may have trouble keeping your audience's attention if you attempt to read to them from a written script.

Despite these warnings, you may be tempted to resort to a written manuscript in your talks because reading something you have written out in advance seems easier than talking more naturally with your audience. Before you do that, consider what happened to you the last time you had to listen to someone read aloud from a report or a paper that you could easily have read for yourself. You already know how unpleasant that experience can be for the audience. It's just plain boring to listen to, and a bored audience is not engaged, not motivated, and not persuaded. They may even be irritated or insulted by your lack of respect and engagement. No matter how much easier it might seem to prepare a manuscript in advance, and no matter how many times you may have seen others do just that, boring your audience is not a style you should want to emulate. To keep your audience with you, you need to focus on communicating clearly with them and making a personal connection. Focusing your attention on the printed page at the expense of your audience connection will result in failure.

Memorized

Rather than bore the audience by reading to them, some speakers simply memorize a written script that they have prepared in advance. However, you may already have guessed that this process deadens audience connection just as surely as reading does—perhaps even more so. While you may be able to maintain the appearance of eye contact as you gaze over the crowd, your attention will not be with your audience. Instead, your focus will be on the text in your head as you reach for exact phrasing. If you've written something and then memorized it, it will sound like exactly that—a prefabricated message that does not respond to the audience's needs or build the interaction.

Do not imagine you can memorize your speech and then fake the audience connection; experienced listeners will be able to hear in your voice the flattening of inflection and enthusiasm that mark a **memorized presentation**. As well, since you're reaching for exact wording rather than for ideas, a slip of memory can leave you gasping. You may not be able to recover your train of thought without repeating phrases you've already spoken. Finally, as you focus on remembering exactly what you were going to say next, you lose the contact that's vital to the communication interaction. Unless you are acting in a play, there is rarely a reason to memorize your message verbatim; doing so will in fact cost you the connection that is necessary to effective, natural communication with your audience.

Extemporaneous

Instead of reading from a manuscript, or delivering a memorized monologue, a speaker delivering an **extemporaneous speech** carries one **notecard** on which is written only enough, in a scratch outline form, to jog her memory of the points she wants to make. Working from this outline, the speaker expands the details from her knowledge of the topic, rather than from a memorized script.

A well-delivered extemporaneous speech sounds natural and conversational, but don't make the mistake of thinking that it is unprepared or 'ad-libbed'. It isn't. In fact, like all good reports, extemporaneous presentations require as much—if not more—detailed planning and advance organization as any manuscript or memorized speech. They also require practice, since the speaker needs sufficient command of the topic and the speech structure to speak naturally to the audience without exceeding or falling too far short of the time allowed for the speech.

The key to an effective extemporaneous speech is that it gives the speaker a chance to establish and maintain an effective relationship with the audience while still providing a clear, explicit structure and a clearly articulated purpose. The speaker's ability to speak comfortably about the topic rests on the thorough research and preparation that preceded the presentation. When well-done, extemporized speeches appear natural, even casual—so much so that they may even fool an inexperienced observer into thinking they are completely spontaneous. One of my former students recently gave a presentation in a senior class. A classmate astonished her by remarking, 'I can't believe that you were winging it like that, and it came out so well!'

She was not winging it, of course. Instead, she is a very accomplished speaker who has mastered the art of extemporaneous speaking. She prepares meticulously, researches thoroughly, and practises her speeches repeatedly in order to achieve the command of her topic that enables her to speak naturally to her audience. All that effort, however, was invisible to her classmate, who saw only the natural, comfortable delivery of an effective extemporaneous speech. That's what your audience should see also—a credible speaker who knows the subject well enough to interact naturally with the audience.

Extemporaneous speaking keeps both speaker and audience 'in the moment' so that both experience the speech as an event in which they are participants. The result is a more engaging, effective oral presentation. Because it allows the speaker to stay connected with the audience and to adapt to the situation as it unfolds, extemporaneous delivery is preferable for nearly all speaking situations. Of the four types of speech delivery described here, this is the one that you will find most useful. For that reason, it is the one we will explore in the remainder of this chapter. Before turning to the process of preparing the speech and making the notecard, we will spend some time discussing **topic invention**.

Choosing and Positioning Your Speech Topic

Clearly, one of the first things you must do in preparing for a speech, whether it's in the classroom or the boardroom, is to select and properly focus your topic. The latitude you have for topic selection can vary considerably. In the classroom or on the job, you may be assigned a topic; more likely, you will be given at least some degree of choice, for instance, even on the job you will sometimes be faced with opportunities to educate others about the work you do, the projects you are involved with, or the nature of the profession in which you work. You may also be asked to give a talk of this kind as part of a job search, or you may be involved in outreach programs to local high schools.

Remember: no topic is by nature boring; it becomes so only in the hands of an underprepared, unenthusiastic speaker who has not found a link with the audience. Whether you are assigned a subject or are free to choose for yourself, you should be careful to focus and position your topic in a way that is interesting and important to you and that can be made accessible and relevant for your audience. Also, if you can approach the topic in a way that unites your interests and those of your audience, your enthusiasm will show in your presentation, making it more dynamic and engaging. Speakers who are bored by their own speeches cannot help but bore their audiences with dull presentations.

Box 8.3   Elements of a Good Speech Topic

- Immediate and relevant to the audience
- Engages your passionate interest
- Offers new information or a fresh approach

In order to discuss the process of topic invention, let's assume that you are free to choose your own topic and approach for an upcoming speech. Perhaps you're interested in some large social or political issues: greenhouse emissions, the building of community pride, apathy among young voters, the impact of low science enrolments on Canada's future competitiveness and prosperity, the increasingly public nature of social interaction, the construction of a space elevator. How do you make such topics both manageable and interesting for yourself and your audience?

First, you should strive to give your speech a sense of immediacy; if possible, it should show how the topic affects them directly. While 'big' topics can make good speeches, your topic does not need to be world-shaking to be a good choice for a presentation. What's more important is that it affects your audience in some significant and immediate way. The newspaper magnate William Randolph Hearst knew the importance of giving the audience something relevant to their lives; he is reported once to have declared that a dog-fight in your own neighbourhood is more interesting than a full-scale war half a world away. While wars across the globe are of course important, Hearst's principle is a good one: people are more engaged by topics that have some impact on their lives.

Here's an example of immediacy. One of my students, who was concerned about green-house emissions, decided to provide his classmates with a simple action they could perform to reduce energy use. He undertook to persuade them not to use the school elevators unnecessarily. Because student tuition costs had taken a sharp rise just previous to his pres-entation, he used as his focal point the cost of maintenance contracts for operating the ele-vators at their current rate of use—more than a full year's salary for one extra professor. His research showed that reducing the use of the elevators would in turn reduce the cost of these contracts, thus saving the university money. By avoiding the use of the elevators, he argued, the students could contribute a cost-saving gesture that would cut down the school's environmental 'footprint', while at the same time offer the possible benefit of increasing the number of course offerings, or preventing an additional scheduled tuition increase. These outcomes affected all the students in the class, and dealt with something of immediate interest and importance to them. They couldn't help but be interested.

Another student read about a type of 'grassroots' community activism in her political studies course. She was intrigued by how residents in low-income neighbourhoods had transformed their communities by clearing debris out of abandoned lots and providing green space. As she walked past a small snack bar in one of the main hallways, she noticed with some annoyance the amount of debris that littered the surrounding area—candy wrappers, chip bags, pop cans, and pizza boxes. She picked some of it from the floor to put into the trash, and as she asked herself silently why nobody else was doing the same, she recalled those community activists and realized she'd found a subject for a persuasive speech. She set about to investigate it: how much time did the maintenance staff spend cleaning up garbage that careless students left behind? What other chores were neglected because the staff was occupied by this task? How did the dirty hallways affect the students who lived in the residence wing? In what way could her student audience benefit by help-ing to keep the area tidy? The answers to these questions, which she obtained by doing some library research on the psychology of physical surroundings and by interviewing the head of Maintenance Services, provided the basis for a powerful speech persuading her classmates to put their own garbage into the trash cans, and to pick up just two pieces of litter from the floor each time they walked along the hall.

The second important quality of a good speech topic is that it reflects some interest and involvement of the speaker. The famed public speaking expert Dale Carnegie reports hearing and evaluating approximately six thousand speeches per year at the height of his career. In one of his several books on public speaking, he emphasizes more than anything else the urgent necessity of 'having something clear and definite to say, something that has impressed one, something that won't stay unsaid. Aren't you unconsciously drawn to the speaker who, you feel, has a real message in his head and heart that he zealously desires to communicate to your head and heart? That is half the secret of speaking (Carnegie, 1955: 29). Speaking about something that genuinely interests you, and that you genuinely want to share with your audience, will help to make your speech livelier and more engaging.

An effective speaker is passionate and enthusiastic about the topic, and it is that enthusiasm that connects with and convinces an audience. The most important thing you can do for yourself and your audience is to pick something that holds *your* interest as well as theirs, then find areas of common ground between your own interests and those of your listeners, and build the structure of your speech on these. If you can't interest yourself in your topic, you're not going to succeed in holding the interest of an audience. You'll be bored, and that boredom will be evident to your listeners.

Speech topics are everywhere. As long as there are problems to be solved, new ideas to be communicated, actions to take, there will be subjects for speeches. It's up to you to find one that you care about, and are committed to, and that will interest your audience.

There's one other rule to picking a topic that you should consider: you should bring something fresh and new to your speech, either in topic or in approach. Some subjects, such as recycling and exercise, have been overworked. Try instead to pick something a little different from the same few tired topics. Chances are that, if an idea comes easily to your mind, it has likely crossed the minds of everyone else in your audience, and it will be difficult to give the subject a fresh twist. Unless you can find some brand new information and focus on a specific connection to them, you will probably lose your audience in the first few minutes of your speech. Give them something unusual, original, and exciting. As an additional rule of thumb, if you heard about the topic on a television talk show, it's probably been overdone, and you should not choose it for your speech.

It is possible, however, to give a familiar topic a fresh perspective. One of my students decided to speak on becoming an organ donor. This topic, as important as it is, has received a lot of recent exposure, and it's hard to think of how to make it more immediate for the audience. But my student had a personal experience with organ donation, since her father had received a kidney transplant that saved his life. To open her speech, she held up an 11x17" colour enlargement of herself, her fiancé, and her parents at her recent engagement dinner. In a dramatic gesture, she tore her dad from the photo, telling her audience that, had it not been for his transplant, he would have been torn from her life exactly as he had just been torn from the photo. This approach, based on her own direct experience and including a dramatic action, brought life to a topic that to most of the audience had been an abstraction.

Strategies for Topic Invention

Many people have difficulty coming up with a good speech topic or figuring out how to approach an assigned topic. The suggestions below are intended to stimulate your thinking if you have to generate your own topic, and the same strategies can help you to narrow down a technical topic or tailor it to a particular audience.

- Freewriting
- Brainstorming
- Challenging the status quo

Freewriting

Freewriting is a technique you can use to help generate ideas for speech topics, or to come up with an angle for your speech on an assigned topic. Simply sit down with pen and paper or in front of your computer and start writing. The trick is to force yourself to keep on writing, no matter what, for at least 15 minutes without stopping. Set a timer and don't pause for anything. It doesn't matter what you write at the beginning. You can either begin with a specific topic area and try to jot down everything you know about it, or—if you're using the method to invent a topic area—you can begin with nearly any thought that pops into your head.

As you freewrite, think mainly about what you can say about your topic that will be of value to your audience. Even if you have to write something like "This is stupid! I can't think of anything to say!", you will find that pretty soon your thoughts will swing around to the task at hand and ideas will start to occur to you. Once you begin to generate ideas, you'll likely find that plenty of possible topics start to occur to you. When your time is up, you can go over them to consider their possibilities for developing your speech.

Brainstorming

If you have to come up with a topic from scratch, you might want to try a **brainstorming** approach. The process is similar to freewriting except that it is a bit more structured. Begin by making a list of all the subjects you know about. Don't worry at first if they seem inappropriate or too broad for a speech; selecting and narrowing your topic to a specific purpose will come later. As you begin to brainstorm topic areas you should write down all the ideas that come to you, no matter how silly they may seem. You can always cross the weak ones out later. Your list may look like the sample.

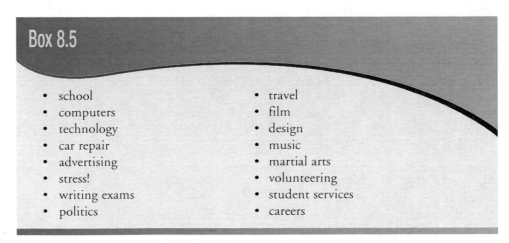

Box 8.5

- school
- computers
- technology
- car repair
- advertising
- stress!
- writing exams
- politics
- travel
- film
- design
- music
- martial arts
- volunteering
- student services
- careers

Once you've got a list, ask yourself if any of these subjects contain possibilities. Select a few that seem likely and set the rest aside. Once you've narrowed your initial list, take the possibilities and repeat the brainstorming process for each in turn, developing all of the sub-topics you can think of for each one. For example, let's say you have chosen 'school' from the first list; from it you have generated a second list of topics.

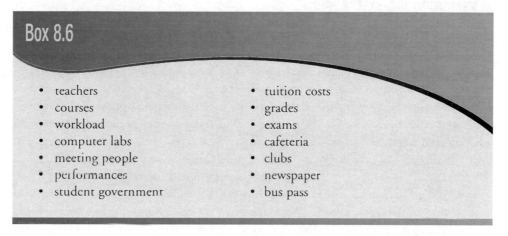

Box 8.6

- teachers
- courses
- workload
- computer labs
- meeting people
- performances
- student government

- tuition costs
- grades
- exams
- cafeteria
- clubs
- newspaper
- bus pass

Select from this second list any topics that offer interesting possibilities for you and your audience. You will need to find a 'hook' that will catch your audience's attention and link the speech to them. If you need to, generate a third list, and then a fourth—each time becoming more specific. If you selected 'student newspaper' from your second list, for instance, your third list might look like the one shown.

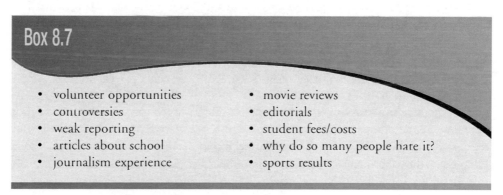

Box 8.7

- volunteer opportunities
- controversies
- weak reporting
- articles about school
- journalism experience

- movie reviews
- editorials
- student fees/costs
- why do so many people hate it?
- sports results

This strategy works surprisingly well, and can actually generate more than one topic. After we made just such a list in class, one of my students decided to give a speech encouraging her classmates to read the school newspaper regularly. Another chose to speak about why the class should boycott the newspaper entirely. And yet another encouraged people in the class to join the writing staff at the paper, citing the experience in journalism that could be gained.

The subject of student newspapers, of course, isn't the only topic that can be mined this way. One of my students gave an excellent speech encouraging her classmates to volunteer for the university's late-night escort program. Another offered a speech inviting the class to nominate a favourite instructor for a teaching award by pointing out how doing so might help to retain good teachers on staff and would pay something back to someone who had contributed in an important way to their education. Yet another student taught his classmates a do-it-yourself method for increasing reading speed and comprehension. By emphasizing the amount of reading they were faced with in the current term, as well as the overall reading load in their program, he was able to convince many of them to try the method he advocated, and he offered handouts describing the method in detail.

Challenging the status quo

A third possibility for discovering or inventing a speech topic is to consider **challenging the status quo**. Most of us take certain social attitudes for granted: walk instead of taking the elevator, recycle, get more exercise, wear a certain brand of clothing, eat more vegetables. You can catch and hold an audience's attention sometimes just by taking an approach contrary to what the audience expects. The trick to this approach is to concentrate your efforts very specifically: not simply global resistance to commercial culture, for example, but a speech on why you should NOT wear a certain brand of shoes or jeans, on why you should NOT take the stairs instead of the elevator, or why you should NOT recycle. Of course, you will still need to support your argument and be sure your evidence is convincing. It's not enough simply to disagree with received wisdom; you must prove your case. However, many issues—even ones that everyone takes for granted—can be considered from a new angle. This approach can yield a really challenging and interesting speech if you think it through carefully.

The best topics are personal: Try this
If your topic is one of your own choosing and you're having some difficulty in identifying something to talk about, you might keep in mind the principle that the best speeches have a personal dimension, establishing a bond between speaker and audience. This doesn't mean that your best strategy is to adopt the unbalanced rhetorical stance that Wayne C. Booth calls the entertainer, focusing on yourself instead of on the audience or on the topic of your speech. Instead, a good speech brings something of the speaker's passion and experience to help connect with the audience.

At least two areas of everyone's experience can profitably be 'mined' for topics. First, consider recommending to your audience a product, a book, a movie, or a magazine that you have found entertaining or effective: I have heard excellent speeches inviting the audience to subscribe to the speaker's favourite magazine, recommending a favourite recipe, encouraging the audience to incorporate spinach into their diet. Any product that you have used that you think is good—perhaps a metal polish for removing rust from your bicycle, or a particular brand of jeans—can be made the basis for a persuasive or informative speech.

Second, you may wish to invite your audience to participate in an activity or join an association that you belong to. The activity may be socially significant, such as volunteering at the local hospital or donating to the food bank, or it may be personally relevant, such as participating in a new sport, joining a particular student club at your college, or trying a new hobby. I have heard some great speeches on rock climbing, juggling, participating in the 24-hour famine program, and taking a particular elective course. Once again, this method of topic invention is a good foundation for both persuasive and informative speeches.

Whichever of these methods you use for choosing a topic, or if you use another method, be sure to evaluate your choice in light of the course requirements, the probable interests of your audience, your own interests, and the demands of the assignment. Ask yourself what approach you could take to each subject, and consider where you might turn to research them further. If your presentation date is only a week away, you may not want to pick a subject that will require a trip to a distant library or a lengthy wait for inter-library loans.

Planning and Preparing a Speech

Once you've identified your topic and your purpose, you will have to develop your presentation. The first point to remember is that, no matter how personal it may be, a speech is a form of report, and as such it must provide convincing arguments supported by appropriate details and facts. Although your speech should aim to establish a personal connection with your audience, it will still require careful planning and preparation, just like any other report.

Like a written report, an oral presentation is developed through a succession of three main stages: an initial planning stage, a preparation or draft stage, and a polishing or practice stage. These stages are similar to those used in formulating a written report, as described in Chapters 2 and 3, but with some significant differences. Just as in a written report, the **planning** stage for an oral presentation involves defining the communication task: analyzing your purpose, your audience, and your own credibility requirements. At this stage also, you should carry out the necessary research and begin to develop the outline that will form the framework of your speech.

Unless the speech you are presenting is a simple story of your own experiences, don't make the mistake of assuming you can give an effective speech without conducting research. Unless you are a recognized expert on your topic, you will not be able to make a convincing argument if you do not provide evidence to support your claims. In fact, even recognized authorities rarely rely exclusively on their own expertise to persuade others; they bolster their arguments with evidence from other sources. You need to do the same.

Take a good look at your topic, and consider all subjects that are relevant to it. Search the catalogues in your library using these relevant topics as search terms. For example, if you are speaking about education, include words like 'school', 'teaching', 'learning', and 'teachers' in your search. Look for relevant (and reliable) materials on the Internet. Ask the research librarian for help if you need it. Just as you would for any other report, you should look for information that will offer support for your ideas and assist you in making your argument. Gather information that will help you to engage your audience and convince them to take the action you intend to ask for.

Don't expect to find ready-made arguments for your exact topic, however. Obviously you won't be able to find articles urging people to read your college's student newspaper, or to take part in your specific student society—but you can find information about the role of newspapers in general and why they are valuable parts of our mass media, and you can find information about the value of campus involvement as a broader issue. Your job as a speaker is to link your research to the specific action you want your audience to take.

Once you've gathered the necessary information, you should begin to draft the speech. *Do not write out the speech as you would a report or essay*, instead, develop an outline only. List, in point form, several main ideas that strike you as significant. Consider your speech purpose and speaking situation and evaluate each of the ideas you've jotted down. Some will turn out to be useful for persuading your audience toward your goal; others will have to be discarded. Return to the strategies for composition discussed in Chapter 4, and use those same methods to plan and prepare your speech.

Although in the planning stage the preparation for a speech is very similar to that for a written report, the difference between the two tasks becomes apparent in the draft or **preparation** stage that follows, primarily because an extemporaneous speech is developed from the beginning as an outline only, and that outline is pared down as you practise through the material until it is simply a cue to memory; it is *never* written out fully, even during the early stages.

Instead, once you've completed your research and sifted the evidence, prepare a preliminary speaking outline. Your outline should have a clear and explicit structure, with a focused introduction, an organized discussion, and a tight conclusion. Your goal in this stage is to create a framework for what you will say without ever writing a complete script. Instead of working through a series of written drafts, you will be working with an outline only, trimming, tightening, and ordering it.

The structure of your speech should follow a **survey–signpost–summary** pattern: first, survey or preview the purpose of your speech and the main points you will cover. Then, as you discuss each point in turn, provide verbal signposts to the audience to let them know where you are in the speech. Use the signposts to signal transitions between points in your argument, and to remind listeners of how each point links to the purpose and to the other points in your discussion. Finally, you should conclude with a brief summary of your argument, drawing all the points together in support of your purpose.

Box 8.8   Speech Structure

- Survey: Preview your purpose and main points.
- Signpost: Link each point to the purpose and to each other with a clear transition statement as you move from point to point.
- Summary: Restate your purpose and summarize the main points.

This overt structure may seem awkward to you at first because it's a more explicit method than you would ever use in a written report; however, an explicit structure is an aid to audience attentiveness and understanding, and will make your speech much more effective. Keep in mind that your audience for your speech will hear the material only once as you speak. Because they will need to pick up the structure and purpose as you go, and they will not be able to turn back to an earlier point for clarification, your structure should not be too subtle. State your purpose clearly at the outset, and use your transitional statements to remind the audience of that purpose as you move through the body of the speech. When you conclude, use the opportunity to review your points one more time, and to restate your purpose.

Once you have a reasonable outline of what you will speak about, talk your way through it, listening for lapses in coherence or fullness, or for places where you stumble over an idea. Strive to correct these, adding and cutting as required, so that your outline is coherent and comfortable for you to work with, but not so full that you find yourself reading from it. The point of these early, informal rehearsals is not to master your delivery, but to solidify your structure and content. Work at an outline level only, and pare that down as much as possible as you practise, turning sentences into phrases and phrases into single words wherever possible. Adjust anything that needs to be changed or reorganized, cut unnecessary details, and trim the outline as far as you can. Use cue words that are meaningful enough to remind you of what you want to discuss. As you talk through your speech, pay attention to whether you have fully addressed the pertinent issues, adequately considered your audience's interests and needs, and effectively established your ethos.

The final stage of polishing your speech consists of the formal practising you will need to achieve a professional level of delivery. Once you have reached a nearly finished version of your speech, you should transfer your outline to your final 3x5" notecard and start practising, out loud, all the way through without stopping. Stand up as you rehearse so as to more closely approximate the conditions under which you'll be speaking, and time your talk. Your goal in this stage is to improve your grasp of the main ideas in your speech, so you can talk about them naturally. As you work, you should aim for mastery of ideas rather than memorization of particular phrases or sentences. Keep practising until you can consistently finish within your allotted time.

Making the Notecard

An effective notecard is the key to a successful extemporaneous speech. When you have enough mastery of your information, but before you're through practising, you should make up the final version of your card. Your card should be so pared down that it would be useful only to the person who has done the research for the speech and who has practised delivering it. If the card has enough information that someone who had not researched the material could present your speech, it contains too much detail.

Make the card once you have arrived at your final bare outline; jot it on a single note-card no larger than 3x5". Use the card in portrait orientation, with the 3" edges at top and bottom. Each point you write down is intended to provide a cryptic signal to you to trigger your memory of the materials and help you organize your comments during the presentation. It isn't meant to record details or exact phrasing.

Unless your speech is very lengthy (longer than twenty-five minutes), you should be able to fit sufficient information onto one card. You may use both sides of the card, but don't be tempted to write down too much detail. Remember, your card should contain only a brief outline that will serve to remind you of your main points.

Preparing your notecard well is one way of ensuring that your presentation will be successful, since it is the only text you will have with you at the front of the room. If you have practised effectively, you will never need to read directly from the card, unless you are citing quotations or statistics, and these should be used sparingly. Consult the card only as a reminder of your organization: it is a tool but not a crutch. The words on the card should be written as large as possible, in bold ink; you may wish to use highlighters or coloured ink to colour-code your main points. If you wish to include a brief quotation in your speech, or cite statistics, these may also be written on the card.

Why should you use a card rather than a page? A card is preferable first because its small size forces you to write down only main points, so you can expand the details from memory (that is, extemporize) as you speak. Your outline should never contain a complete script of what you intend to say, and the small card will help to ensure you do not write too much. It is meant to prompt you, and give you something to rely on should your memory fail you because of nervousness.

In addition, the small size of the card enables you to palm it quite easily, so that it is inconspicuous in your hand. By contrast, a full page is too large to be used unobtrusively and can actually serve as a distraction. It can rattle and shake if your hands tremble, communicating your nervousness to your audience and emphasizing it to yourself.

The sample card below (Figure 8.1) is one I used for a half-hour presentation given at the official opening of the Ron and Jane Graham Centre for the Study of Communication. The audience was made up of dignitaries from the university, the Graham Centre, and the engineering profession, including the Graham family, the dean of engineering, and the president of the university. The process I used for preparing the outline and the card are the same ones we are discussing here. Because the speech was a half hour, I have used both sides of the card.

Don't be alarmed if you can't understand what is meant by all the points listed—if you could reconstruct the speech from the card alone, without having heard it delivered, the card would not have served its purpose. The example is intended to show how individual and personal an effective card should be.

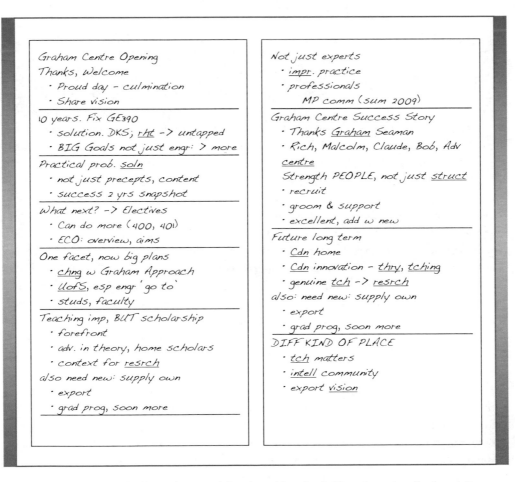

Figure 8.1: The sample shows the material on two sides of a 3x5" card, used as the foundation for a speech of approximately thirty minutes. Note that I use the card lengthwise, in portrait orientation, to accommodate all of my notes, and to keep myself from writing too much.

Elements of Delivery

Preparation and organization are, of course, the foundation of any oral presentation, and you should never step up to speak without a clear purpose, solid research, and an effective structure. However, it is not until you actually face your audience that these efforts can be fully realized. No matter how masterful your preparation, weak delivery can completely undermine your effectiveness and alienate your audience

Good delivery isn't accidental. Like an effective structure or topic positioning, it is the result of focused effort. Just as you edit your writing, you also 'edit' your speech by practising your delivery until it becomes second nature. We all have been bored to near distraction by speakers who may have had valuable information to share, but who lost us with unimpressive presence or distracting mannerisms that compromised their delivery. None of us should wish to repeat these mistakes. Unfortunately, if you do not practise effective delivery, you will find yourself unconsciously reproducing the bad habits of speakers you have seen in the past.

The purpose of delivery is to engage your audience and keep their attention on your speech. Your delivery should not call attention to itself at the expense of what you are saying, distracting the audience from the message you hope to convey. An audience that is not paying attention to your words cannot possibly be persuaded by your speech; they will also be more likely to doubt your credibility. While thoughtful planning and topic positioning will help to forge a link with the audience, that link can only be maintained with a polished, professional delivery. Without the credible presence that cements your connection with the audience, your presentation will fail to communicate, no matter how well planned and researched it may be.

Delivery is not simply a performance, like acting in a play; in fact, if you treat it as such, you will introduce a quality of insincerity to your presentation. However, because the effectiveness of your message depends in part on your self-possession and the professionalism of your demeanour, you do need to pay attention to how you appear and sound to your audience. Every element of your presentation should enhance the overall impact of your message. Sometimes this simply means not calling attention to weaknesses, but just as often it means taking care to create definite strengths in your presentation. In order to speak effectively, you need to take account of two major aspects of effective speech delivery—what the audience hear and what they see. As you claim your place at the front of the room, your **vocal and visual presence** are the most important factors in successful delivery. Here are some of the elements of delivery that can make or break your speech.

Vocal presence: The sound of your presentation

Although in these days of television, we tend to think of sound as less powerful than appearance, it is in fact the central element in any oral presentation, since your voice is the primary medium through which your information is transmitted. Your **vocal presence** must be confident and steady; it should not detract from your presentation. There are some common flaws to which first-time speakers are subject, but with awareness and practice you can eliminate them from your presentation style.

Box 8.9   Establish an Effective Vocal Presence

- Maintain reasonable volume.
- Speak clearly.
- Pace yourself.
- Avoid fillers or speech tags.
- Watch your pitch.
- Maintain a pleasant voice tone.
- Avoid grammatical errors, profanity, slang, or jargon.

Maintain a reasonable volume

Most inexperienced speakers speak too softly to be heard. Of course you should not shout at your audience, but you should ensure that your voice is loud enough to be heard by everyone, especially those in the back row. If you can, practise your speech in the room where it will be delivered, having a friend sit at the very back to determine whether you can be heard. If you absolutely cannot project your voice that far, try to arrange for a microphone, and practise so that you can use the device confidently and smoothly. The members of your audience will not be attentive if they cannot hear you clearly.

Speak clearly

Enunciate your words carefully. Far too many speakers swallow the last half of their words, or run over them too quickly. These habits make a speaker extremely unpleasant to listen to and difficult to understand. Before you even get up to give a speech, start paying attention to your speech habits; ask those you know to tell you honestly if you have a tendency to mumble or chew your words. If you discover that you are not as careful as you could be, then start taking more care with the way you speak every day so that careless enunciation does not become an impediment when you speak in public.

Check your pronunciation too, particularly if your topic involves words with which you are unfamiliar. I recently heard a student presentation on organ transplantation in which the speaker repeatedly used the word 'cadaver'. Throughout the speech, he pronounced it as 'cad-uh-VARE'. This slip utterly destroyed his credibility, as his audience struggled at first to figure out what word he was using, and then doubted that he really understood his topic since he obviously didn't even have command of its basic vocabulary. Similarly, when I was a student myself, I listened to a classmate give a half-hour presentation about the play *Doctor Faustus*, in which the learned doctor bargains with one of Satan's agents for possession of his soul. Throughout the presentation, this student pronounced the name of Mephistopheles as 'muh-FIST-uh-flees'. After he had finished speaking, not a single person in the room, including the professor, could remember anything else about the presentation, and nobody thought he had done a good job. Mispronunciations of important words will harm your credibility with your audience.

Pace yourself

Although you don't want to pause for too long between words, far more speakers are inclined to speak too quickly than too slowly. Don't rush through your material. Your audience will appreciate a brief pause here and there to allow them time to grasp your points, and you will speak more effectively if you take the time to catch your breath.

Avoid fillers or speech tags

Don't say UM! (Or 'okay', 'like', 'you know', or 'really'.) These can be so distracting that an audience may actually begin to count them and thus lose the thread of your speech (Did you know she said 'um' 37 times in ten minutes?). Don't be afraid to simply pause if you need a few seconds to collect your thoughts; you need not make sounds all the time. Speech that is riddled with 'ums' or 'uhs' will communicate little to the audience except the speaker's nervousness and lack of command of self and situation; littering your presentation with 'like' or 'ya know' will undercut your credibility, because it sounds as though you lack the vocabulary to make your point articulately.

These words are, of course, the mainstay of some people's vocabulary, and are sprinkled throughout their speech every time they open their mouths. If that sounds like you, or if you find that you tend to use fillers when you make a presentation, the best way to avoid them in your formal speaking is to practise eliminating them from your everyday speech. Start today and keep at it until you no longer need to pad your talk with fillers.

If you can't always hear these sounds in your own speech, ask your family and friends to gently alert you when they hear you saying 'um' or 'like'. Consciously allow yourself to pause and take a breath instead. Getting rid of fillers takes practice, but it is possible to eliminate them almost entirely from your speech.

Watch your pitch

A common weakness among inexperienced speakers is raising voice pitch at the end of statements as if to ask a question. In fact, this voice tic—known as 'uptalk'—*is* a form of questioning—a plea for the audience's constant support and reassurance. Unfortunately, when used repeatedly, it makes a speaker sound nervous and uncertain. State your points confidently, dropping your pitch decisively and naturally at the end of each sentence.

Maintain a pleasant tone

Voice quality is another factor that can influence a speaker's effectiveness. Try to cultivate a voice that is pleasant to listen to: a voice that is piercing or nasal, for example, may irritate listeners and prevent your message from getting through. As well, try to project some animation into your voice. A deadpan delivery in a monotonous voice tone is just as annoying to the audience as a grating, nasal tone.

Avoid any obvious grammatical errors, profanity, slang, or inappropriate technical jargon

Audiences should be intrigued by your presentation, not put off by it. Slang and profanity are never appropriate, and technical jargon should be avoided unless the audience is made up of people from the same profession. Even then, it should be used judiciously. Remember that your most important task is to communicate your ideas to your audience. You cannot do this if your language is inappropriate.

Visual presence: The sight of your presentation

Many people don't realize how powerful a visual impression can be, and in an oral presentation it can be crucial. The speaker may be in front of an audience for anywhere from five minutes to two hours. The attention of audience members is concentrated on the speaker; listeners, without necessarily being completely aware that they are doing so, often take in every idiosyncrasy of the speaker's behaviour and every detail of appearance. You can test the validity of this point by asking yourself what small peculiarities you have noticed in your instructors—details of behaviour, expression, or dress. You'll be surprised how much you have noticed without necessarily intending to, and without being aware of doing so. For example, students in my classes, when asked, have even been able to tell me what colour socks one of their other professors had worn that same day.

While you can't control everything about your appearance as a speaker, there are many details you can take care of consciously that will help you to present a confident and capable visual presence to your audience.

Box 8.10   Create a Confident Visual Presence

- Dress appropriately.
- Stay calm.
- Maintain eye contact.
- Employ appropriate facial expressions.
- Create energy with appropriate movements and gestures.
- Support your talk with appropriate **visual aids**.

Dress appropriately for the occasion

Wear clothing that is appropriate to the speaking situation. Don't wear clothing you will feel uncomfortable in, and avoid pulling at or adjusting your collar, sleeves, waistband, or any other part of your costume. At the same time, don't expect to be taken seriously if you show up in sweatpants. Even if the venue for your presentation is one of your university classes, dress up a bit.

Remember, too, that unless you are speaking about fashion, conservative dress is usually preferable to flamboyant or scruffily casual outfits. You want to be memorable for the quality of what you say, not for the outrageousness or inappropriateness of what you wear, and clothing that attracts attention away from your speech will undercut your effectiveness.

Stay calm

Approach the lectern calmly and pause briefly before beginning to speak, so as to give yourself a chance to catch your breath. Don't rush to the podium and immediately begin to speak. Give yourself time to relax and your listeners a chance to get used to your presence. Likewise, don't rush away from the lectern just as your last words are leaving your mouth. Give the audience a few seconds to recognize that your speech has ended. Allow for questions if it's appropriate to do so.

Maintain eye contact

Eye contact is one of the chief means by which a speaker can create a bond with listeners; it helps to engage and maintain their interest. Your goal should be to meet the eyes of every member of the audience at some point in your speech. Of course, it may be impossible to do this if your audience is very large, but you should try so that you are able to establish a visual connection with your audience. Although public speaking is frightening for most people, you should not be afraid to meet your listeners' eyes. Making the effort to connect with those who have come out to hear you speak can actually help to calm your nerves.

You may have heard of speaking coaches who advise nervous speakers to fix their eyes on a point on the back wall, gazing just over the heads of the audience. Don't be tempted to take this advice, because your audience will not be fooled by this gambit. They may even begin to wonder what you are looking at so intently, and turn to stare too. You should also avoid looking for extended periods at your notecard. By all means glance down at the card if you need to remind yourself of your next point—after all, it is intended to aid your memory. But if you stare at it for a long time you may make your audience, and yourself, uncomfortable. If you have practised effectively, you should have sufficiently mastered your material so that you will not need to do this.

Employ appropriate facial expressions

People who are nervous sometimes betray their lack of confidence by giggling or grinning inappropriately, even when the speech is serious, or by glaring defensively at the audience. Try to relax and keep your expression consistent with the material you are delivering. It is perfectly correct to smile at appropriate moments in the speech, and to maintain a pleasant expression the rest of the time, but the important thing is to demonstrate that you are in command of yourself and your facial expressions.

Create energy with appropriate movements and gestures

You should appear comfortable and self-possessed. Stand straight, but not stiffly, keeping your body weight distributed evenly on both feet, using gestures to emphasize your points. As well, though you will likely feel vulnerable, don't lean on or hide behind the lectern.

You should not be afraid to move about comfortably in front of your audience, but avoid flinging your arms about wildly, fidgeting, or shifting uncomfortably from one foot to the other. Such extravagant movements are likely to detract from your presentation (your audience may begin to count your unconscious gestures: Did you notice how many times she pushed her glasses up? Did you see him jiggling the change in his pockets?) At the same time, you do not wish to appear physically rigid or stiff, since a lack of movement may communicate fear to the audience and exaggerate it to yourself.

If you watch carefully, you will notice that a skilled speaker neither avoids nor overuses gestures and movement. Instead, such a person uses controlled movements and gestures to create energy in the delivery. An effective speaker knows how distracting unnecessary movements can be, and at the same time how horribly dull it can be to watch someone who does not move about at all.

Support your talk with appropriate visual aids

Of course, one of the most important of the visual factors of your presentation is your use of visual aids. When used effectively, these can enhance and strengthen your presentation. However, if they are overused, or used inappropriately, they can exaggerate weaknesses in content and delivery, and can even bore your audience into unconsciousness. Visual aids should be simple, readable, and well-timed, and they should be smoothly incorporated into the talk. Below you will find more detailed information on the appropriate use of a variety of visual aids.

Visual Aids in Oral Presentations

The impact you make on your audience can be enhanced by the effective use of visual aids; in fact, visual aids are one of the most useful means of demonstrating a point to your audience, since people tend to learn more easily and remember better when a demonstration accompanies the explanation. Even a chart or slide showing the main points of your talk can help to fix your points firmly in the minds of your listeners. Further, visual aids not only can help to make your presentation clearer to the audience, but can also serve as an aid to your own memory.

These days, when we think of visuals for a speech, most of us think immediately of computer-generated slide programs such as PowerPoint. Actually, however, the range of possible visual aids is much greater, as the list below suggests.

Box 8.11   **Types of Visual Aids**

- an object
- a scale model
- photos, sketches, or drawings
- charts and graphs
- videos and films
- blackboard or flip chart
- demonstration
- computer-generated slides (PowerPoint)

For example, you may wish to display the actual object that you are discussing in your speech, if it is large enough to be seen and portable enough to be carried around. Incorporating the item into your speech can help to attract and hold your audience's attention; an actual prototype not only clarifies the information you are presenting, but boosts your credibility.

However, you should not bring live animals with you to display during your speech. They are likely to be made skittish and frightened by the situation and can be very difficult to manage. Their unpredictability has implications for the **timing** and control of your speech, as well as for your own nervousness, because you cannot anticipate how the situation may affect them and their nervous antics can be disruptive.

If you can't bring the object itself because of size or unmanageability, you may wish to provide a scale model, for example, a small-scale version of the CN Tower or a large-scale model of the DNA molecule. A scale model can assist you in explaining your points and can boost your audience's grasp of your meaning. It can also, if well used, help to make your presentation easier to follow.

If the object you're discussing is impossible to bring and no model is available, you can enhance your impact and the audience's understanding by effectively incorporating other visual materials such as photographs, drawings, or sketches. Pictures may be enlarged to make posters, or may be presented as conventional slides, on overheads, or as PowerPoint slides. In all cases, though, your pictures should be large enough to be seen by the audience and clear enough to communicate your points, and you should be careful not to allow them to upstage you.

Large, simple, and colourful charts or graphs can also enhance the communication of certain types of information, provided they are well designed and effectively incorporated into your discussion. Like photos or drawings, these may be presented on posters, slides, overheads, or computer projections, and should be large and simple enough to communicate effectively with the audience.

Brief video or film clips can sometimes be useful in a speech longer than fifteen minutes, though they are too unwieldy to be effective in a short speech. Remember that they are there to support and reinforce your message, not to overwhelm or displace it. Use them judiciously and only in cases where the information they contain cannot be communicated any other way. Video clips should never be allowed to replace the speaker or become the entire focal point of the presentation.

For some kinds of presentations, the best visual aid may be a blackboard or a flip chart. If you want your presentation to be interactive, if you need to pace the presentation to the speed of the audience's understanding, if the intent of the presentation is deliberative (as, for example, a college class is), or if you can't predict ahead of time exactly what you may need to write down, these means are ideal. Their flexibility and pacing are two reasons why these devices remain popular for teaching: while pre-prepared visuals can 'shut out' the audience and risk turning the presentation from an event into an artefact, the use of a blackboard or flip chart can involve the audience, as they see the event taking shape before them and their own ideas incorporated into the proceedings. Because it takes time to write things down, a blackboard presentation isn't the best choice for a five-minute talk, but if your talk is thirty minutes or longer, you might consider incorporating such a visual aid.

If your speech discusses how to do something or how something is done, you can use the objects, models, or clear diagrams and pictures to demonstrate the process step by step.

Finally, you may wish to augment your presentation with well-designed computer-generated slides such as those created with PowerPoint. The ease with which these can be created and displayed makes them very popular as visual aids in corporate settings, but this same ease can also make them a speaker's downfall. There is just too great a temptation to make too many slides with too much information and too many effects on each. As a rule of thumb, the number of PowerPoint slides in your talk should number no more than half the length of your presentation, in minutes. In other words, a ten-minute talk should feature a maximum of five slides, and these should be simple, clear, and easily readable from anywhere in the room.

Guidelines for the use of visual aids

Decide on the type of visual aid you will employ (model, demonstration, chart, drawing, photograph, poster showing a list of main points, computer-generated slides, etc.), prepare whatever needs to be designed in advance, and incorporate the visual into your practice sessions. Because a poorly designed or poorly used visual can actually compromise rather than enhance the effectiveness of your speech, you need to be sure that your visuals are clear and understandable enough to be easily followed by your audience. Complex or overly detailed visuals, or visuals that are too small to read, will do nothing to clarify the information you are presenting and may just confuse your audience. If you are using an interactive visual such as a blackboard or write-able overhead, you may wish to write some of your material before beginning your speech and keep the interactional nature of the presentation fresh by adding additional relevant material as you go along.

Be sure to work with the visual in practise so that you can manage it with confidence and skill during the actual presentation.

Box 8.12   Guidelines for Using Visual Aids

- Prepare them in advance.
- Make sure they're large enough.
- Remember to show them as you speak.
- Use them sparingly.
- Speak to the audience and not to the visual.
- Do not pass objects around among the audience while you speak.

Your visuals will be useless unless they are large enough to be seen by your audience. A 3x5" photo from your album may be interesting to you, and may perfectly capture the spirit of your speech, but it is unlikely to be of any value to your audience members who cannot see it from their seats. You cannot solve this problem by passing the photo among the audience while you speak; not only is it distracting and potentially disruptive, but most of the audience will be unable to see the image at the point where it is mentioned in the speech, and they will have trouble paying attention to you as the object comes round. If you are to be persuasive and convincing, you will need to keep your listeners' eyes and interest fixed on you. Instead, enlarge the image in some manner so that everyone in the room can see it easily.

You should always be sure to display your visual aids while you speak about them (believe it or not, some people forget to show their carefully prepared charts, drawings, or models at the appropriate moment because of nervousness or poor planning) and be sure to speak about them once you have displayed them. Nervous or inexperienced speakers sometimes display very intriguing-looking visuals and forget completely to refer to them during the presentation. Never let your visuals take the place of your spoken voice, nor assume that they speak for themselves; instead, always incorporate reference to them into your speech.

Visual aids should be used sparingly—don't overwhelm your audience with so much visual material that your presentation is lost. Too much visual material can detract from your speech, and visual aids cannot by themselves serve as a substitute for an effective presentation. Remember that these are aids to your speech; the speaker should remain the focal point in an oral presentation and all visual aids should support and enhance the message.

Finally, while showing your visuals, remember to speak to the audience and not to the picture or chart you are discussing. Avoid turning your back to your audience as you speak so as to maintain your relationship with them throughout your speech. Be especially careful of this point if you are using a blackboard or flow chart while speaking, or if you are presenting visual material by computer projection. There is a temptation to look at the screen of your laptop instead of at your audience. When you practise delivering your presentation, be sure to practise using the visual aid in such a way that it will not cause you to lose your connection with the audience.

Working with computer-generated visuals, overheads, and slides

In contemporary business and the professions, talks are frequently given with PowerPoint or other computer-generated visual aids. It's easy to fall into the trap of thinking that a talk will be improved by flashy, impressive visuals with lots of technical enhancements. Unfortunately, this is rarely the case. A poorly prepared or ill-considered talk cannot be salvaged by flashy visuals, and many a good talk is ruined by speakers who allow the devices to take over. In such a case, the visuals can actually impose a barrier between speaker and audience.

In my work as a consultant to government, business, and industry, I have heard from many professionals about what they call the 'PowerPoint nap'. It's not hard to understand what they mean. Picture a late afternoon meeting in an overheated conference room: the dim lighting, the hum of the equipment, the drone of a speaker who isn't concerned with making an audience connection, the confident knowledge that you can always download the slides afterwards if you miss anything. . . zzzzzzzz. Students report that some professors who rely on PowerPoint have resorted to gimmicks to force students to pay attention; for instance, they may leave key words blank so that the students have to attend the lecture in order to 'fill in' the missing information. This tactic is obviously not an effective way to engage an audience meaningfully in what's going on; in my view, it's little better than a trick, and constitutes an admission that a flashy collection of slides is no substitute for forging an effective connection with the audience.

This is not to say that there is no role for such technology in a presentation; in fact, there is nothing better than PowerPoint or similar devices if you wish to incorporate photographs, maps, exploded diagrams, line drawings, or other visual material into your speech. But those who load their slides with textual material and then read it to the audience are doing their listeners a disservice and, frankly, wasting their time. At best, reading to the audience is merely inefficient: after all, there is no need to gather people together if the point is to read a written document; it would be better, and likely more effective, to send the text directly to them and let them read it for themselves. They could read at their own pace, take notes on critical points right on the document, and flip back to an earlier point if they lose the thread of the argument.

At worst, it is inconsiderate. If there is no real reason for gathering people together, if the information you're disseminating could as easily be read by your audience on their own, then you have taken up their valuable time without any appreciable benefit. A presentation should be an event in which you and your listeners are participants, rather than an artefact for which they are merely spectators. Its primary benefit is that you and your audience are actually gathered in each other's *presence*. If what you have prepared doesn't take advantage of that opportunity for interaction, then it is a waste of your audience's time as well as your own.

Although it's very easy to put lots of verbal information on computer-generated slides, and to incorporate movement and colour, you should think twice about overwhelming your message with visual gimmicks. Concentrate instead on creating an engaging, interesting speech that addresses the audience's needs and concerns, and about creating a human connection with them. Use the visuals to support this connection, and don't allow them to replace or undercut it. Apart from the barest outline of your main points, which is permissible, slides should also not be used to present primarily textual information. Visual aids are best used to communicate *visual* information—pictures or diagrams, useful charts or maps—not verbal information. Any text you do display should use a font no smaller than 30-point, since anything smaller will be difficult for the audience to see and will tempt you to cram too much information onto the slide.

PowerPoint, like other visual aids, should never be more than simply a tool to help you deliver your message and make your audience connection. It should never be used in such a way as to upstage you or dominate your presentation. For this reason, and for the comfort of the audience, you should strictly limit the number of slides (no more than one slide per two minutes of talk, or a maximum of ten slides for a twenty-minute talk).

Below are some tips for working with computer-generated visuals, overheads, and slides.

Designing your slides

1. Make sure each slide is large and clear enough to read easily from the back of the room. You should never use a type smaller than 30-point; a 36- or 40-point is even better.

2. Avoid crowding too much text on a slide—a few lines is plenty. If you are tempted to reduce the font to a size smaller than 30-point in order to squeeze in more text, you are putting too much on your slide.

3. Never, ever put every word of your talk on slides or computer-generated visuals: if you are presenting a complex argument and need to put some of your message before the audience in writing, limit yourself to main points or highlights only.

4. Put on the slide only the necessary information or main points, and use your talk to elaborate the details. Never post an entire script of a presentation.

5. Limit the number of slides you use—too many can be distracting. How many is too many? Unless your talk is a slide show, allow approximately two minutes per slide—which means that, in a ten-minute talk, you should prepare no more than five slides. There are very few exceptions to this rule, and only when the information is highly visual; in most cases, you should aim to use far fewer.

6. Avoid light print on dark background, except for headings; it is harder for the eye to process, especially from a distance.

7. If you need to use coloured fonts, be sure to allow sufficient contrast between font and background: avoid blue on green, red on orange or purple, yellow on white, or purple on red. These are impossible to read.

8. Avoid placing print on patterned or 'busy' backgrounds.

9. Never make slides that will compete with you for attention: the slides will win, and they will compromise your audience relationship. Limit special effects such as animation; if over-used, these special effects may actually distract your audience and undercut your presence.

10. Never use a slide to present information that is primarily verbal; use visuals to communicate visual information.

11. Always proofread your slides for spelling, grammar, punctuation, and accuracy of facts and figures.

12. Prepare your talk so that it can be presented without the slides, in case of equipment failure.

Using slides in a talk can be tricky; they need to be incorporated smoothly into your presentation so that the two fit together as a seamless whole. For this reason, you need to incorporate your visuals into your practice sessions, so that you can operate the necessary equipment with ease when the time comes.

As well, as you prepare your talk, you should also ready yourself with a back-up plan to accommodate for equipment failure, which happens more frequently than you might expect. When you are delivering a talk with slides, you should try to check the system or equipment before your speech begins, to ensure that it is working properly, that it is focused, and that your slides can be seen clearly from every point in the room.

During your presentation
1. If the equipment is not working, deliver the talk without the slides. Delays to tinker with faulty slides or equipment can compromise your authority and credibility, they can cut into the time allotted to the speakers who follow you, and they can annoy the audience. Spend no more than three minutes of a twenty-minute talk trying to get the equipment to function; if your talk is shorter than twenty minutes, go ahead immediately without the slides.
2. Never, ever read from the slide. If you find yourself doing this in a talk, you have put too much information on your slide or are insufficiently practised. Learn from your mistake and correct it for the next talk.
3. Maintain eye contact with the audience throughout the talk—look at them, not at the slides or computer screen.
4. Never let the slides dominate your talk; the audience should see and connect with *you* first, not with the slide, and it should never upstage you.
5. Be sure to discuss each slide as you display it, and to display each slide as you talk about the point it supports.
6. Never display slides that you aren't going to discuss—they may distract the audience from the talk.
7. Make sure that you do not block the audience's view of your slides while you are discussing them. Try to place the screen where everyone can see it easily no matter where they are seated in the room.

Always keep in mind that your best visual aid is your own enthusiasm and energy. Be sure to move around freely, to smile, and to make eye contact with your audience. If you respond to their presence with vitality and engagement, they will be more attentive and involved. They will find your message more convincing and influential, and you more credible, if you make a human connection with them.

No matter what style of visual you choose to support your talk, you should remember that its role is exactly that: to support, and not to replace, the connection you make with your audience when you stand before them. Since communication is about relation as much as it is about content, your goal should be to engage the audience with you in exploring the matter you are discussing.

The Importance of Practice

The importance of practice to an effective extemporaneous speech cannot be overstated; in the absence of a script, it is practice that will provide mastery of your information and enable you to deliver your speech within your allotted time. Learning to practise effectively is the key to proficiency and skill, and it will also pay off in helping you to gain control of your nerves.

You should begin to practise as soon as you have organized your presentation and selected and prepared your visual aids. Do not wait until the night before your speech is due; instead, spread your practice sessions over several days. Cramming them together in a short space of time will not only be ineffective but will lead you to memorize particular phrases before you have actually mastered the ideas.

If you can, set up conditions as close as possible to those in which you will be speaking. Actually deliver your presentation several times, out loud, to master your timing, your command of your material, your delivery, and your use of visual aids. You will have enough to worry about as you step up to speak, without worrying about whether you know your stuff. You will feel much less nervous if you are well prepared and can concentrate on projecting a positive, confident image.

If you have access to video equipment, have your practice presentation recorded and then watch it to see if you can identify elements that need improvement. You can also audiotape your speech, or practise in front of a mirror as a way of monitoring your delivery. Don't rely on these methods alone, however; if you can, try to practise your speech in front of a live audience in order to gauge how it registers on actual listeners. Have a friend or someone else you trust listen to your presentation and give you honest feedback.

Practise delivering your speech out loud until speaking about this topic is as natural to you as breathing, but stop before you begin to memorize particular turns of phrase. Your audience will be able to spot a memorized presentation, and the quality of your speech will suffer for it.

In addition to improving your delivery, practice will also tell you whether your presentation fits the time you've been allowed. Think about how much time you have: a short time limit means you'll have to be selective about the details you include. On the other hand, you will need to make sure that you have enough material to fill the time allotment. Keep some extra points in reserve in case you speak more quickly during the actual delivery than you did during practice, as sometimes happens when a speaker is nervous. Managing your timing effectively is one way to show respect and consideration for the audience and for speakers who might follow you.

As I write this, I have just awarded the first failing grade of the term to a five-minute speech assignment in my communication class. The speaker managed only two minutes and twenty-five seconds. She had chosen a poor topic and had done practically no research. Like many inexperienced speakers, she underestimated how nervous she would feel, and despite all of my urging, she assumed she would be able to ad lib material while she was standing in front of the class and didn't take the time to practise sufficiently. She was mistaken, and in addition to earning a poor grade on the assignment, she also embarrassed herself in front of her classmates.

Don't let this happen to you. An inexperienced speaker cannot possibly invent material on the spot that will be sufficient to present a coherent, organized, and convincing speech of five minutes. Without appropriate preparation and practice, most people cannot even manage to speak for a full minute. Unless you practise your speech out loud and fully master its content, you will find it difficult to accurately gauge or fill your allotted time.

Practise your delivery, and to be sure you have estimated correctly how long your presentation will take. You don't want to be in the uncomfortable situation of running out of material, or of being cut off because your speech is too long. If you find that your speech is not long enough, you will need to develop your points with further research. If it comes out too long, you will need to cut some material. Don't wait until the morning of your speech to find out that you didn't prepare properly—practise in enough time to make any adjustments that are needed.

When you are practising, resist the temptation to write out all or part of your presentation in full, just to capture a particular turn of phrase. If you do this, you will condition yourself to rely on a script, or to memorize. A written text just doesn't sound like the spoken word, and both of these will deaden your delivery and almost certainly bore your audience. Not only should you always practise from the single notecard that you intend to use in the final speaking situation, but you should also try to word your speech slightly differently each time you practise. Aim to capture the ideas, not the particular phrasing. If you work with the card you will actually use in the speech, it will be familiar to you by the time of the presentation and will serve as an additional aid to memory, resulting in a much smoother presentation.

Preparing a Technical Briefing

In your technical training courses, or on the job, you will not always have complete freedom in selecting your topic; more likely, you will be required to speak about a project you're working on, or some other aspect of your work. This kind of presentation, often referred to as a briefing, is similar to the kind of presentation outlined above, but may differ in the exact steps you follow to prepare your materials.

The exact shape and structure of your talk will vary depending on the dynamics of your communication situation. For example, as part of my professional role, I give many talks, seminars, and training workshops on communication. However, each is different from the previous ones according to the demands of the particular setting and audience. Professional alumni of the college, government employees taking part in a work retreat, new graduate student teaching assistants, undergraduates participating in a leadership program, professional surveyors, veterinarians, and engineers, or students of our Foundations of Professional Communication course all have different needs, interests, and levels of expertise which must be taken into consideration as I prepare my talk. Similarly, a technical professional faces different constraints in presenting a talk to other technical specialists than in speaking to sales staff, managers, or to a group of students at a career fair.

Many professional talks are based on research and project reports that have already been prepared and circulated. The speaker in these situations must simplify and adapt the findings to fit the time available, the interests and expertise of the audience, and the purpose of the talk. Like the summary of a formal report, the technical briefing should be geared for the least technically specialized of the expected audience, with technical details kept to a minimum. A ten-minute presentation of research findings even to a specialized audience cannot be expected to cover all the complexities of a lengthy research report. It can only hit the highlights, intriguing the audience enough so that they will read the details in the written report. If the audience for a design presentation is made up of clients or end users of the device, the speaker should keep technical details to a minimum and focus on how the project satisfies the original design constraints. Finally, in a talk to the marketing department, the research and development team must emphasize elements of the design upon which the sales staff can build a marketing strategy rather than focusing on its scientific merit.

Let's consider the strategies used by Jennifer Varzari in preparing a briefing for the Board of Directors at Dolovich and Cowan on the training workshops her department hoped to develop for new employees. Because Jennifer's presentation involves a specific aspect of her work, she does not need to brainstorm topic ideas. However, she does need to clearly define her audience, her purpose, and her speaking context. To do so, she uses a process similar to the topic invention strategies outlined at the beginning of this chapter.

Audience

Jennifer knows that her audience, the company's Board of Directors, have the power to approve or veto her proposal. They are an important group in the company, with greater authority than she has as manager of her department. Because they have already received and read her written proposal, she can assume that they are generally familiar with what she hopes to do. She can also assume that they are favourably disposed to the project, since they have indicated their interest by inviting her to attend their meeting to discuss the proposal and answer their questions.

Purpose

Jennifer must convince the Board of Directors that her proposal is worth implementing. She knows that they want to do what is best for the company, so she must show them that this project is to the firm's benefit. Because they have already read the proposal, her introductory remarks can be a quick overview of the project, emphasizing the company's need for improved training in this area. She can tailor her remarks to the probable interests of the board members, emphasizing the project's potential benefits and its reasonable implementation cost.

Speaking context

Jennifer has been allotted a half hour at the beginning of the board's regular monthly meeting, which is held in an executive meeting room that seats twenty people. There is no lectern; Jennifer will be seated at a meeting table with the members of the group. It will be a relatively informal setting, and Jennifer is expected to present a brief introductory presentation followed by questions from the group.

Jennifer will want to bring support materials with her to the meeting—the survey results, copies of the materials to be used in the training, perhaps a cost-benefit analysis, and an outline of the implementation procedure. She should also prepare a notecard to help her frame her initial remarks. She can use an outline based on her written proposal as the notecard, but because her audience has already seen the full proposal, she must not simply read from it or repeat materials they have already read. Given the audience's interests, Jennifer should emphasize the company's need for report-writing training, the failures of the current system, and the advantages of the new one. Figure 8.2 shows the outline Jennifer developed for her presentation.

Introducing and Thanking a Speaker

At formal gatherings, a featured speaker is normally introduced to the audience and thanked afterward by a member of the organization, department, or unit. The purpose of introductory remarks is to provide some context for the speaker's contributions to the meeting of the organization and some background so that the audience will be better prepared to receive the message in its appropriate context.

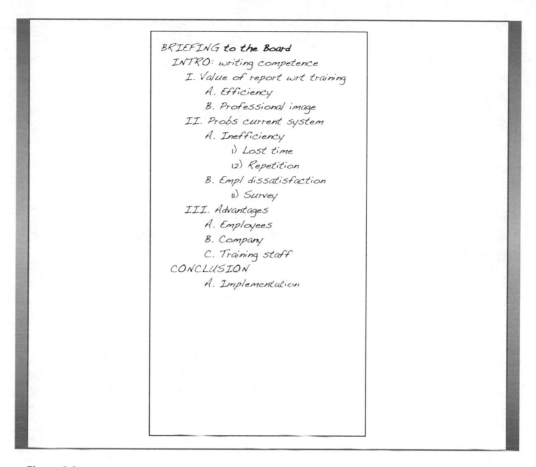

BRIEFING *to the Board*
  INTRO: writing competence
    I. Value of report wrt training
      A. Efficiency
      B. Professional image
    II. Probs current system
      A. Inefficiency
        1) Lost time
        12) Repetition
      B. Empl dissatisfaction
        11) Survey
    III. Advantages
      A. Employees
      B. Company
      C. Training staff
  CONCLUSION
      A. Implementation

Figure 8.2

Introducing a speaker

In order to introduce the speaker effectively you will need to obtain the appropriate information; most speakers are happy to provide a title and abstract for the speech, along with a brief résumé of their relevant experience. You can draw on both of these to frame your introduction; it's also polite, if you have the opportunity, to speak briefly with the speaker in order to confirm that your introduction is both accurate and appropriate.

Your introduction is intended to present the speaker to the audience and to establish the person's credibility to speak on the chosen topic. The introduction should also indicate the title and focus of the speech to follow, particularly if the audience has not seen an abstract. Even if they have had a chance to read about the speech beforehand, your introduction should aim to remind them of the relevance of the speech to their interests and needs.

As you prepare and deliver your introduction, keep in mind that the focus of the introduction should be on the speaker rather than on yourself. Your brief words are purely a formality designed to provide a frame for the speaker.

The introductory remarks should always be brief, but they should be in scale with the length of the speech. For a speech of twenty minutes to an hour, your introduction should be no more than five to ten minutes; if the speech itself is under ten minutes, however, your introduction should be two minutes or less. After all, imagine how absurd it would be if the speaker's introduction were longer than the speech itself.

The introduction should establish the speaker's credibility. What qualifies the person to speak on this topic? What's the speaker's interest in or commitment to the subject? Why should we be interested in what this person has to say?

Finally, your introduction should set the tone for the speech and help to create realistic expectations without giving away the force of the speech. If your speaker agrees, you can identify exactly what problem the speech will address.

Thanking a speaker

Like the introduction, the thank you should focus on the speaker. It should pick up a theme or comment from the speech and make a brief statement connected to the speaker's main point.

In planning your thanks, it is possible to prepare only a structural outline and then flesh out your remarks from the introduction and from the speech itself as you listen to them. And, of course, you may consult beforehand with the speaker and with the person introducing the speaker so that you can, if you wish, prepare some of your material ahead of time.

The thanks extended to a speaker should be brief. The audience has just finished listening to a speech; they don't need to hear another one. You should focus briefly on what the speaker has achieved in the speech and any particularly noteworthy or interesting element in it. Sometimes this can't be prepared in advance, but will have to be gleaned from the speech as it is delivered. Don't be afraid to take advantage of any unexpected events, if they seem worth commenting on.

However, you should avoid mentioning any gaffes or obvious failings in the speech; the audience will already be painfully aware of anything of this nature, and so will the speaker, and mentioning it further would be unforgivably rude. Better to dwell on the positive.

Finally, your remarks should end on a positive note, thanking the speaker warmly and sincerely for giving the speech.

Critical Reading

Sandra Terry, 'Giving Speech Feedback in an Oral Critique'
Sandra Terry is an Instructor of Professional Communication in the Ron and Jane Graham Centre for the Study of Communication in the College of Engineering, University of Saskatchewan. Terry's academic experience includes work as a correspondence instructor, English language researcher, writing centre consultant, and instructor of composition and English language. In addition to her post-secondary teaching, she has conducted writing workshops for varied audiences, from new instructors to senior secondary school students.

Giving Speech Feedback in an Oral Critique
Over the course of your professional career, whether as a supervisor or a team leader, or even simply as a respected professional, you will often be called upon to assess and evaluate another's work. In fact, the ability to give criticism is one of the principles of the Canadian Engineering Code of Ethics, which reminds engineering professionals that they

must be able to 'accept, as well as give, honest and fair professional criticism' (Canadian Council of Professional Engineers, n.d.).

Providing a critique of someone else's efforts, especially an oral critique, is a delicate task, perhaps one of the most difficult you will face in your professional life. If your remarks are to be helpful, it is essential that you deliver your message in a thoughtful and helpful manner that respects both the person's efforts and her need to preserve face.

Fortunately, the skills you have been learning with the help of this book provide a foundation for delivering evaluative messages to someone else, especially in situations where those messages must be delivered in public, as is the case when you provide feedback on someone else's in-class presentation. To assist you in delivering fair and useful criticism that will benefit and guide the other person, you can draw upon the lessons of the Nine Axioms of Communication, practise Booth's concept of rhetorical balance, and apply the principles of the Communication Code of Ethics. If you can incorporate these principles into your feedback, you are on the way to becoming a more successful communicator, colleague, and leader.

As you set out to provide feedback on someone else's work, it is essential to remember the Nine Axioms of Communication so that your message will be taken seriously. For example, you will be more influential as a leader and more respected as a colleague if you treat each interaction as a conversation between two people, rather than simply as an opportunity to deliver a set of 'facts'. As you have learned by studying the principles in this book, the relation you establish with your listener and the kind of interaction you encourage are just as important as, and perhaps more so than, the content of your message—and this is especially true in face-to-face interaction. You should always aim to establish a positive and constructive relation and to preserve the other person's dignity, even when you have suggestions to make. You can do this in part by affirming some strengths of the other person's work and by making some favourable observations. Then you can cement this positive relation by referring to fundamental values, experiences, or expectations that you and your listener share.

Giving criticism, especially when it is done publicly, involves a lot of face risk to both the presenter and the recipient. You might find that you are tempted to minimize your own face risk with strategies that absolve you of responsibility for your remarks and that, in effect, place blame on the other person for any communication failure that has occurred. Although you should not shy away from giving advice that will genuinely help others to do better, you should also realize that negative feedback, no matter how deserved, may be experienced by the recipient as an attack. Even in situations where you have been granted the authority or the footing to deliver a critique of someone else's work, such as when you are playing a leadership role, it does not follow that your message will automatically be welcomed. For this reason, in order to provide useful and helpful feedback, it is important to minimize the other person's face risk as far as possible.

Place yourself into the other person's shoes and consider carefully how you can position your message so that it will be heard and accepted. Ensure that your remarks have a solid basis, and that they will be genuinely helpful to the other person. You can help make your points clearer if you can provide examples and a sense of direction for the person being critiqued. Being able to provide concrete evidence will increase your confidence in your message and will help to lessen your own face risk. Use humour, where appropriate, to lighten the situation, but above all, remember to allow the person time to respond to your comments, and re-establish their own sense of self-worth in the interaction.

An important part of giving feedback is identifying areas for improvement. In fact, this is the main reason for providing feedback at all: to assist the other person in identifying ways to improve a particular piece of work. As you frame your remarks, keep this purpose clearly in mind, and take some time to think about how your objective can best be accomplished. What does the other person need to hear for your input to be meaningful and welcome? The person you are critiquing will be less likely to become defensive and more likely to welcome your input if you put your remarks into a helpful professional perspective. Frame your suggestions as ways to overcome weaknesses in the audience's discernment rather than to fix problems in the speaker's work. Once the person feels comfortable that you genuinely intend your remarks helpfully rather than disparagingly, he will be much more willing to listen to the rest of your message.

Understanding and incorporating the principles learned from the Nine Axioms will help you to deliver your criticism more effectively and to establish your credibility and authority to deliver this message. If the recipient is made to feel belittled or defensive, or if she senses your own indifference or biases, she will most likely lose respect for you and your message.

In addition to incorporating lessons from the Nine Axioms, you can improve your chances of being heard if you remember to strive for a balanced rhetorical stance, as Wayne Booth advises. To do so, you need to find the right combination of appeals based on your content, your listener's needs, and your own footing in the situation. This balance is essential if you want the other person to learn from your criticism.

Of course, if your message is entirely positive and flattering, it will be relatively easy to position it effectively and to maintain face. However, most critiques point to elements in the other person's work that require improvement. In such a case, you need to think more carefully about how to balance your information with the person's need to preserve face and with your own need to establish a credible footing.

Remember that your message is communicated through channels other than simply the words you use. Be aware that your nonverbal cues such as facial expression, eye contact, gesture, and tone also communicate volumes to someone else, and your message will be more powerful and more believable when the nonverbal and the verbal content are complementary. Accordingly, your verbal communication must mirror your nonverbal communication. Your message must be honest (no matter how difficult the message), and it must be audience-centred (no matter how focused you are on its content). Your message must be both honest and respectful if you want the person you are critiquing to trust you and accept your criticism.

Finally, when preparing your critique of someone else's work, you should bear in mind the principles of the Communication Code of Ethics. The first of these requires that you take responsibility for both the content and the manner of your remarks. For example, the other person will be more open to your critique if you acknowledge that your inability to understand something may be a result of your own failings rather than simply attributing the lack to flaws in his skills. Do not try to displace responsibility for your critique onto others, onto the speaker, or onto the rest of the audience; instead, take ownership of your own failure to understand. Taking responsibility also applies to the manner in which you frame your remarks. You should emphasize that you intend them as suggestions for further improvement rather than as attacks on the person's efforts.

Ethical communication also entails making sure that you don't misrepresent your message. It can be very difficult to deliver criticism of someone's work, but as a credible professional you need to learn how to do so with grace and tact. While you need to take care to present your critique in a way that respects the other person's efforts no matter how far short they may have fallen, lying to someone about the quality of her work, letting her believe a weak presentation was good enough, is both irresponsible and dishonest. You should also be careful about disguising your real message behind vague phrasing or euphemistic language. Attempting to sugar-coat your remarks may help to limit your own sense of risk in the situation, but it may also mislead your listener, cheating her out of assistance that would genuinely help her to improve.

The third principle of the Communication Code of Ethics directs you to avoid causing unnecessary harm through your words or actions. Of course, you cannot always avoid giving people bad news or serious criticism when it is warranted, but even when your message is challenging to deliver, you need to find a way to preserve good will and communicate your genuine investment in the other person's success. Offering a critique of someone else's work is already threatening and uncomfortable for him, and though you may be tempted to use humour in an already difficult situation, you should keep in mind that sarcasm is never audience-centred and is always hurtful and belittling. Remember always to provide the opportunity for your listener to maintain a sense of self-worth even while receiving criticism. Remember, too, that an effective leader and communicator maintains an ethical stance in all situations.

Face-to-face criticism is never an easy task, but if you remember to maintain a balance between your message, your listener's needs, and your own sense of purpose in the situation, your message will be more valuable for the other person, and you will emerge as a more credible professional and a more effective leader. The Nine Axioms of Communication are vitally important as you craft your criticism of someone else's work or ideas. Use them to help you maintain your rhetorical balance. Finally, ensure that your message is ethically grounded: fair, honest, and sincere.

Points to Remember

An oral presentation needs as much care and attention in its organization and preparation as a written report. Here, briefly, are the things to remember when getting ready for a presentation.

1. Choose a topic or aspect of a topic that you are interested in and familiar with; in a professional speech about some aspect of your work, select details and an approach that will appeal most effectively to your intended audience.
2. Focus your topic to suit your audience, according to their needs, their expectations, their concerns, and their prior knowledge.
3. Tailor your topic and your approach to the purpose and the setting of the presentation.
4. Prepare your topic so you can cover it adequately in the time you have been allotted for speaking.
5. Select and prepare at least one appropriate visual aid.
6. Deliver your speech extemporaneously, unless there is some particular reason why it must be memorized or read from a script. (Your own nervousness or discomfort is not a sufficient reason.)
7. Practise your delivery and your use of visuals. Practise your timing!
8. Remember that every element in your presentation should support, and not detract from, your presentation. Avoid inappropriate gestures, mannerisms, or visual items that will distract your audience from the message.

9. Never let visual aids impose a barrier between you and your audience. Choose them wisely, and use them sparingly.

10. Manage your nervousness with specific strategies to help you gain control of yourself and your message.

Key Concepts

brainstorming	manuscript speech	topic invention
challenging the status quo	memorized presentation	visual aids
delivery	notecard	visual presence
extemporaneous speech	planning, preparation, practice	vocal presence
freewriting	structure	
immediacy	survey–signpost–summary	
impromptu speech	timing	

Assignments and Exercises

1. Prepare a two-minute self-introduction in which you help your classmates and instructor to get to know you better. Identify yourself by name and major; describe your hometown, family, and hobbies or interests; tell the class your goals for developing your communication skills; or outline your biggest concern about public speaking. Select any or all of these details, or something else of relevance to your audience to help give them a sense of your interests and character. Do not exceed the two-minute time limit.

2. Prepare a ten-minute presentation for your classmates, employing at least one visual aid, in which you provide them with tips on *one* of the following.
   a. Incorporating visual data into a report presentation (briefing or written format).
   b. Applying standard report writing structure—SIDCRA—to a specific report situation.
   c. Conducting library research for a report on any topic (identify a specific topic and show samples).
   d. Distinguishing between a proposal and an ordinary report in purpose and organization.
   e. Writing a self-evaluation report.
   f. Organizing and presenting a briefing.

3. Prepare and present, in extemporaneous form, a five-minute demonstration speech in which you explain clearly how to do something. Your goal is not merely to demonstrate how something is done, but to enable your audience to reproduce the action for themselves.

   You are free to choose your own topic, provided it can be reasonably handled within the available time. You should be sure to provide all the necessary steps, in order, and employ appropriate visual aids. When the speech is complete, your audience ideally should be able to perform the task you have demonstrated.

   As in all speeches, your presentation should establish some common ground between you and the audience, and contain a clear, explicit value or benefit to the audience; establish your own authority and ethos as speaker (good will, good judgement, and good character); demonstrate an effective construction of audience; and come within 10 seconds of the time limit either way (that is, your time must fall between 4:50 and 5:10).

4. Prepare and present, in extemporaneous form, a five-minute informative speech designed to assist your audience in understanding something new—to teach them something they did not know before. In this speech, you may speak on any topic familiar to you, as long as it will provide your audience with new insights or understanding.

   Your goal is to engage the audience with some new concept, process, idea, or insight, not simply lay out facts. You will therefore need to employ strategies to attract and hold your audience's attention; communicate the relevance of your information; and show them how they will benefit from the insights you will provide.

   As in all speeches, your presentation should establish some common ground between you and the audience, and contain a clear, explicit value or benefit to the audience; establish your own authority and ethos as speaker (good will, good judgement, and good character); demonstrate an effective construction of audience; and come within 10 seconds of the time limit either way (that is, your time must fall between 4:50 and 5:10).

5. Prepare and present, in extemporaneous form, a five-minute persuasive speech in which you propose a specific action for your audience to take. Your goal is not merely to provide information to your audience, nor simply to ask them to change their views on the topic; instead, you must exhort them to undertake a particular, clearly identified action.

   You are free to choose your own topic, provided it displays a clear exigence: an urgent problem in the world which must be solved and for which this group is an appropriate rhetorical audience in the sense that Lloyd Bitzer uses the term. Don't ask the audience to pretend that they are someone else (a grade 4 class or a group of parents at a PTA meeting, for instance).

   Do not assume that your audience will be moved to act simply because you have laid some information before them. You will need to employ strategies which will attract and hold your audience's attention; communicate the urgency of the exigence and show them how they will benefit by taking the action you propose; make it easy, or possible, for them to take the action you are asking for. You should make your appeals as specific as possible to *this* audience (including your instructor), and you should identify the action they must take as a result of hearing you speak. The more specific the resulting action, the more targeted your appeals, and the easier it will be for you to persuade.

   As in all speeches, your presentation should establish some common ground between you and the audience, and contain a clear, explicit value or benefit to the audience; establish your own authority and ethos as speaker (good will, good judgement, and good character); demonstrate an effective construction of audience; and come within 10 seconds of the time limit either way (that is, your time must fall between 4:50 and 5:10).

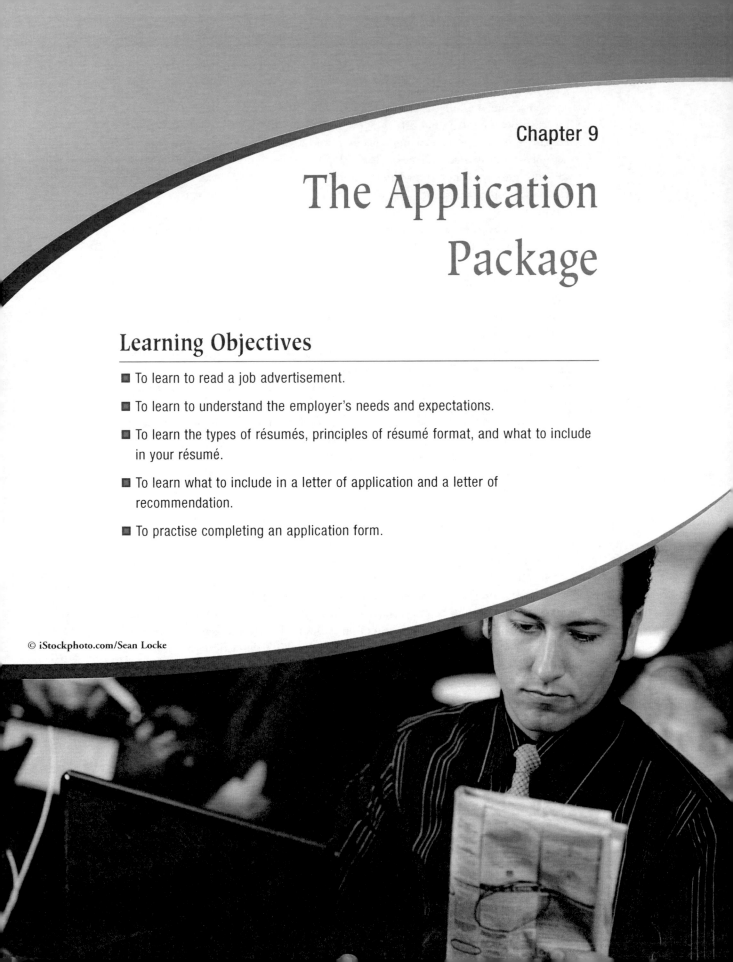

The Application Package

Learning Objectives

- ◾ To learn to read a job advertisement.
- ◾ To learn to understand the employer's needs and expectations.
- ◾ To learn the types of résumés, principles of résumé format, and what to include in your résumé.
- ◾ To learn what to include in a letter of application and a letter of recommendation.
- ◾ To practise completing an application form.

© iStockphoto.com/Sean Locke

As your first step from college or university into the professional workplace, the job application package may well be the most important writing you will do in your professional program. Whether you are competing for your first career position, an internship, or a plum placement, everything depends on communicating effective ethos, so your application must be as effective as possible.

Like all other professional communication, the job application has a clear, specific **purpose**. In it (perhaps more than in any other kind of professional writing), you must acknowledge and respond to the reader's needs. The job application is a special kind of persuasive report; its task is to convince an employer that you are a good fit for her workplace: competent, reliable, and cooperative. In order to achieve this purpose, you need to focus not simply on what you have done in your previous jobs, but on what your experience will enable you to do in your new job, and on what that prospective employer wants, expects, or needs to hear. You must also tailor your application to suit the job you're applying for and the person who will be reading it.

Your submission must be appropriately adapted to its purpose in three respects. First, it must be adapted in **content**, so that it provides the information that the employer needs to make a decision to interview you. Second, it must be adapted to the **needs and expectations** of the employer. You can figure out what the employer is interested in by taking time to read the job advertisement carefully. You can then use that knowledge to shape your application so that you can draw from your experience to emphasize the skills that the employer will find relevant. Finally, your application should **establish you as a credible and competent professional** who understands the purpose of the application process as well as the demands of the job, and who has demonstrated care in preparing the résumé and letter. In other words, your résumé should establish effective appeals based on **ethos** (your credibility), **logos** (appropriate content and purpose), and **pathos** (audience's needs and expectations). These factors will help establish the employer's confidence in your suitability for employment.

Understanding the Employer

There are two ways to gain a better understanding of the employer's needs. The first is to recognize the qualities that all employers are looking for, and the second is to read the job posting carefully.

There are several general characteristics that all employers consider desirable in job applicants—qualities that they want to see in the people they are considering for hire. These include stability, initiative, dependability, responsibility, loyalty, honesty, personability, energy, and enthusiasm. **Stability** is a quality of character marked by balance in your communication and behaviour. An employer will judge your personal and professional stability by the steadiness of your employment or school record, by how you deal with receptionists or support staff during the interview and probationary period, by your balanced approach to workplace demands, and by your reaction to stressors.

Initiative indicates a high level of motivation, and the ability and willingness to see what needs doing and then do it. Initiative also means you can carry tasks to completion without constant supervision. **Dependability** is a measure of commitment to the job and to the quality of your work, no matter what the task. It is measured by punctuality, self-discipline, and reasonable professional goals.

Employers will also be looking for indications that you can take **responsibility** for your work, not only for your achievements but also for your mistakes, and that you do not make excuses or blame others. They want employees who display **loyalty** to their profession, to their employer, and to their co-workers.

Needless to say, **honesty** is an essential quality, and misrepresentations or inconsistencies in the application process will destroy your credibility permanently. Employers also respond well to positive personality traits like **energy**, **enthusiasm**, and **personability**; they will judge these qualities by your courtesy, confidence, general friendliness, and tactfulness. In other words, employers are looking for evidence of convincing ethos throughout the application and interview process, and they are often quite skilled at discerning it.

The second way you can learn about the employer's needs is to read the job posting carefully. Better yet, read several postings for jobs similar to the one you're applying for. Doing so will give you an indication of skills and qualities that are currently in demand, and allow you to emphasize the appropriate aspects of your own experience as you create your résumé. As you study the ads, you will notice patterns of skills and requirements that seem to be common to all. You can best pick out these patterns by surveying at least half a dozen ads for jobs in your field using a technique known as **key terms analysis**. As you read, look for skills that recur with frequency. The repetition of these terms can tell you where the employer is placing emphasis. The patterns of skills identified in the job postings will give you an idea how to build your résumé and application materials so as to showcase those elements most attractive to the employer.

For example, ads for technical positions frequently emphasize qualities such as the following: 'personal attributes that enable you to make a significant contribution. . . including the ability to listen to client needs and a commitment to strive to quality, team spirit, and creativity', 'superior interpersonal/communication skills as well as superior skills in oral presentation, judgement/problem solving/decision making', 'excellent customer service skills and leadership/coaching skills', or 'the ability to persuade or influence others who may be angry, frustrated, rude, upset, difficult to work with, in order to reach mutually acceptable or workable solutions/agreements'. All are communication skills, and these and more requirements like them can be found in ads for professional positions at all levels. The pattern of these concerns in job advertisements tell us that employers are particularly interested in applicants' communication skills. You should be sure to emphasize your own communication strengths on your résumé, and you should make sure that the quality of the résumé itself reinforces that emphasis.

Preparing the Résumé

A résumé is a kind of persuasive report that outlines the information an employer will want or need to ascertain your suitability for a job. The primary purpose of a résumé is to establish the applicant's professional ethos: good judgement, or professional competence; good character, or attitude; and good will, the ability to get along with others. You can think of a résumé as 'you' on paper—or at least, the professional 'you'— and you want to make the best possible impression. Remember that the résumé and application are the first step in establishing a professional relationship with your prospective employer. In a résumé, even more than anywhere else, all the virtues of professional writing are important: understanding your reader and your purpose and applying the Seven Cs of professional writing—completeness, conciseness, clarity, coherence, correctness, courtesy, and of course credibility. Remember that the nonverbal aspects of the résumé, its organization and accuracy, its clarity, and its tone all contribute to establishing an effective writer–reader relationship.

You should be aware also that the résumé you submit will not be read in isolation. It will be considered against as many as two hundred other applications for the same job. It is important therefore to think of the impact of your documents on the person who is screening the pile of applications; such a person is likely taking time away from other duties in order to complete this task, so your submission must communicate, in a reader-friendly way, the information that the recruiter needs. If the résumé fails to distinguish you significantly from the competition, or if it is confusing or unclear, it will be set aside.

Visual impact (layout) also makes a big difference as to how you will be perceived. A pleasing balance between white space and print is important; a résumé should display its essential information without crowding or obscuring any part. As you have already discovered, effective layout is part of your organization, and assists in communicating your information. Your résumé should call attention to your strengths and should help to distinguish you from other applicants with similar experience. For this reason, I do not recommend using any standardized template, including the résumé 'wizard' found in some word processing packages. A template may help you to organize your information initially, but its final effect is to produce a résumé identical in appearance and structure to that of everyone else who uses it. When several such résumés are read in sequence, as would be the case when the résumés are being screened, well-qualified individuals may get lost in the shuffle simply because their résumés look exactly like everyone else's. As in all other communication situations, an effective message relies on the writer's good judgement in understanding the unique requirements of the situation and responding with an appropriately adapted message. It's very easy for a recruiter to reject a cookie-cutter résumé without giving it serious consideration, because, in the context of all those other cookie-cutter résumés, it appears to reflect little thought or effort on the writer's part. It is the person who has responded thoughtfully and creatively who stands out.

Since readability is especially important in an application, you should choose a font that is easy on the eye. In general, a serif font (such as Times) is easier to read on a printed page than a sans serif font (such as Helvetica), although some of these can be quite clear if your résumé is short. Avoid script-style or cutesy fonts or those that look like hand printing, and avoid mixing several fonts in one document. Choose an attractive 12-point font for your résumé, and use the same font for your **letter of application** so that the two will be visually unified.

Finally, there is one other nonverbal element that you should consider if you smoke in your home or if you live with people who do. Do not smoke while you are preparing your résumé and application package, and do not keep your résumé paper in a room or in an apartment where smoking takes place. Paper readily absorbs odours, and cigarette smoke is no exception. While someone who is used to smoke may not notice the scent in his workspace, those who open the envelope in a non-smoking office environment will certainly notice it. Stale cigarette smoke is not only unattractive, it is also an allergen for many people, and it could cause your application to be rejected before it is even read. If you're not certain whether your own paper has picked up the scent of second-hand smoke, take your résumé to school or to a printing service, and print your materials onto clean, fresh paper. It will be worth the slight cost to ensure that your submission is not rejected for reasons that have nothing to do with its content.

The résumé introduces you to a prospective employer and should encourage that employer to want to speak with you. That is its only function, and you will be called for an interview only if it fulfills this purpose effectively. For this reason, it should make a very good impression. A good résumé combines organized content with effective visual arrangement so that the layout actually becomes part of the organization, and it organizes information so that the employer can quickly grasp the relevant information.

Types of résumés

There are three main types of résumés: the **functional** (or skills-oriented), the **chronological** (or data sheet), and the **analytical** (also known as the 'crossover' or 'targeted' résumé). The functional résumé is sometimes recommended for people who have little formal education or experience; because it emphasizes employable skills instead of positions held or training completed, it is thought to be useful for obscuring gaps in an employment or education history.

Box 9.1   Types of résumés

- Functional
- Chronological
- Analytical or targeted

However, there are a couple of reasons why you might not want to choose a purely functional style. First, it often obscures or omits dates, names, or locations that could be verified by the recruiter, so its claims may appear unsubstantiated. Worse, the strategy of using the functional style to gloss over a problematic or sketchy work history has made employers wary or suspicious about what is left unsaid. Thus, while this format may appear to serve the *writer's* needs—to make a lack of experience or gaps in work history less obvious, for example—it may actually backfire because it doesn't usually provide the details an employer needs to make an informed assessment. As a result, because it does not effectively serve the needs of the person screening the applications, this kind of résumé may be set aside without serious consideration. The first draft of Samantha Arar's résumé (Figure 9.5) shows the skills-based emphasis of the functional approach.

The more traditional chronological résumé has been widely used and is probably the format you learned in high school. It is generally more readily accepted than the functional: it presents your training and experience chronologically, always beginning with the most recent and working backwards. The information is organized under fairly standard headings and focuses on facts and details, without elaboration or interpretation. However, while employers usually prefer this chronological organization over the functional format, the brief bare-facts outline provided by the chronological résumé alone may not be enough to convince a prospective employer to take a closer look at the applicant.

Even when the economy is strong, the competition for the most desirable jobs is always intense, and many employers want more of a 'sense' of the applicant before they decide to invest time in an interview. For this reason, the analytical or targeted résumé (which blends the most effective features of the chronological and functional approaches) is usually the best choice, because it is adapted to the specific job applied for and because it effectively accommodates both the employer's needs and the applicant's background.

Targeting simply means adapting the content of your résumé to the context, audience, and purpose, just as you have learned to do for all of your reports. Effective targeting depends on two principles, which should always govern the content and arrangement of your résumé: **recency** and **relevance**. As in the chronological résumé, information about employment and education is clustered into categories, and entries in each category are arranged in **reverse chronological order**, so that older information follows more recent experience. However, the difference between the targeted and the strictly chronological résumé format is that the categories themselves are redefined: selected, titled, and ordered according to the candidate's most *relevant* experience.

Box 9.2   The Principles of Targeting

- Recency
- Relevance

A targeted approach allows the candidate to cast emphasis on relevant experience without sacrificing the chronological organization that appeals to employers. For instance, when Samantha Arar was laid off by the high-tech firm where she had worked for three years following her graduation from a computer technician program, she took on some menial work rather than sit idle. However, when she updated her résumé, she ran into difficulty with the strictly chronological approach she had been taught. Using this format meant that her technical experience was displaced by her more recent experience and buried later in the résumé, where it was overlooked by recruiters who were reading quickly to eliminate unqualified candidates. However, when Sam learned to use the principles of targeting, she was able to give her technical experience a more prominent place on her résumé by subdividing her employment into two categories: 'Relevant Experience' and 'Additional Experience'. She placed all of her technical experience into the 'Relevant' category and positioned it at the beginning of the résumé, where it is more likely to catch the employer's eye, and moved the remaining category to the end. As a result of this creative re-thinking, Sam was offered an interview and a position with the next company she applied to.

You will see how these two principles of 'targeting' can improve the presentation of content, the adaptation to audience, and the establishment of credibility when we consider several of the sample résumés, including Sam's, at the end of this chapter.

A closer look: The parts of the résumé

A résumé typically contains a survey of an applicant's education, work history, achievements, and skills. However, far from indiscriminately listing every job-related experience you have ever had, no matter what it is, an effective résumé is selective, both in terms of what it includes and in how that material is organized. A résumé, like other kinds of reports, is a form of communication with a very specific purpose; its job is to get you an interview, and it is effective only if it achieves that goal. Since it is the *reader's* needs that will determine who is interviewed, the résumé should be designed and focused to meet those needs. Although the résumé does contain standard sections, its contents are also, to some extent, flexible and what you choose to include will depend partly on your experience and partly on the position you are seeking.

Although everyone's résumé should be tailored to suit the candidate's specific combination of education and experience, there are some standard features that every reader will expect to see in your résumé. All résumés feature sections showing personal information, education, employment experience, and skills. Entries within these categories are always arranged in reverse chronological order, preferably with dates displayed for the convenience of the reader.

Personal Information

This section identifies you by name and provides contact information: your address, a phone number where you may be reached, your e-mail address, and a website address if you have one. Do not include an e-mail or website address that will soon be defunct, however. For instance, if your e-mail and website are based on college accounts that will disappear after you graduate, do not invite your prospective employer to contact you this way. Also, if you are using an e-mail address on a commercial server, you should avoid silly or suggestive names such as 'sexybeast' or 'headlice'. Your e-mail address, like everything else about your application, should project an air of professional competence, and—although they may be amusing—silly or off-colour names may portray you as sophomoric to a potential employer.

As you know, many employers now search out potential employees on the Internet, including social networking websites such as MySpace or Facebook. If you have a presence on such sites, you should probably consider how your postings might look to a possible employer. Since so many employers now search on these sites for information about potential hires, some job coaches advise using the sites to establish yourself as a professional, listing the kinds of interests and accomplishments that would appeal to an employer rather than bragging about your exploits in the local bar. At the very least, as more and more employers suss out applicants on the Internet, you will want to turn a critical eye on how you are 'marketing' yourself online.

You will notice from the sample résumés that personal information should be displayed in an eye-catching position on the first page. You may even wish to use a desktop publishing program to design an appealing personal letterhead to use as the first page of your résumé. You can then use the same format for your letter of application. This type of letterhead can be very effective if well designed, but you should avoid cutesy graphics or too many combined effects such as boldfacing, italics, block capitals, and underlining. A slightly conservative design makes a more professional impression than one that displays a whole range of visual effects in a single heading.

At one time, résumés commonly included personal details such as age, height, weight, social insurance number, state of health, marital status, and citizenship. However, this kind of information has not been considered appropriate to include for at least 25 years. You definitely should not include such sensitive information as religious affiliations and racial or cultural origin, unless, of course, they are directly relevant to the job for which you're applying, or you have chosen to self-identify under employment equity guidelines. If you wish to include such information, place it near the end of your résumé—don't take up valuable space on the front page.

As a general rule, leave out any personal information that has no bearing on your ability to perform the job or that may invite prejudice; unless a piece of information will help to establish your professionalism and credibility, leave it out of your résumé.

Career objective

The **career objective** or job target statement is a phrase, sentence, or brief paragraph that links your career aspirations to the position you are applying for. Although it's optional for candidates whose experience is directly related to the job, a career objective statement can help with the task of targeting, particularly if your experience is diverse. Here are some instances in which a career objective statement can prove useful.

- If you are aiming at a specific position or type of position and are not interested in any other kind of work, you may wish to focus on this aim in a career objective.
- If you have spent some time out of the workforce—to travel or to raise a family, for example—a career objective can explain the gap in your employment history.
- If you are changing careers, this statement can serve as a link between your aspirations and your experience.

New graduates from a technical program that has specifically trained them for the position they seek may find a statement of objective unnecessary. However, if you decide to use a career objective statement, you must be clear and specific; avoid such statements as 'I am seeking a challenging position that will make use of my skills and offer room for advancement.' Such a vague statement takes up room without adding anything valuable to your résumé. It is better left out.

Education

For a student or a recent graduate, or in cases where a particular credential (degree, diploma, or certificate) is a minimum qualification for the job, education follows immediately after personal information. In such a case, retain education as the first category even after you've been working for several years, so as to prevent being disqualified by a recruiter who makes an initial decision based on the first page.

Dated information on a résumé is always given in reverse chronological order. Your educational history should include the following information, beginning with the most recent experience: dates attended; name and location of institution; diploma, certificate, or degree obtained or expected; and some brief detail about your particular program of study. Mention grades only if they are outstanding.

List everything back to high school, but no further. Do not include high school information if you possess or are in the process of obtaining a second degree or diploma, or if you have been working for a period longer than two years following graduation from college or university. Be selective: remember that the employer needs to know only what is relevant and useful in making the decision to interview you. Anything else is clutter.

Employment

For most people, this category follows education, although it may be placed first on the résumé if your experience is impressive and the position you are seeking doesn't require a particular credential. Beginning with your most recent position, in reverse chronological order list dates, place of employment, job title, and responsibilities or achievements. Provide a quick outline of the job, emphasizing any skills you can bring to the new position. Again, always be forward-looking, focusing on the requirements of the job you want rather than on those of your old job.

As you plan your résumé, but before you write the first draft, list all the duties you performed as part of each job. Once you have a complete list, reorder them according to how relevant they are to the new job, and then delete those at the bottom of the list, leaving only the top three or four.

In all cases, your goal is to use your résumé to emphasize knowledge or skills that are relevant to the job you seek. For instance, few students have had work experience in their field; most have held part-time and summer positions in the retail sector that may have little relevance to the position they will be seeking on graduation. In this case, the fact that you worked while also going to school is more important to the employer as a measure of your work ethic and character than it is as an illustration of your specific job-related skills. Rather than taking up a lot of space on the résumé listing each position, you could try the cluster technique. For instance, if you have had a series of similar or related jobs—for instance, if you worked part-time in several different restaurants—you could cluster them into one listing, or even delete some less important or short-term jobs. Instead of a separate listing for each restaurant position, you could create a single entry called 'Restaurant Server', showing the inclusive dates for all positions, and then list all the employers under that one entry. This strategy can reduce repetition and save valuable space on the résumé if you have a lot of information to include. The entry might look something like this:

2008–2010   **Restaurant Server**
              Chez Martinique, Calgary, AB
              Lou's Prime Rib, Calgary, AB
              Chow Down, Calgary, AB
                  Duties: Greeting customers, taking food orders, serving food

Skills

Skills are generalized abilities that may be transferred with relative ease from one situation to another. A segment that elaborates on your skills can be a useful device, especially for a recent graduate who may have little directly relevant employment background, because it provides an opportunity to emphasize relevant abilities, regardless of your past experience, and can help to distinguish you from other similarly qualified applicants. Use this segment of your résumé to promote your unique combination of skills, but make sure it is focused for the job you seek.

In the sample résumés, you will notice a variety in the ways that the skills are clustered and presented; each person has selected a method that shows his or her skills to best advantage and that best suits the job sought, and each has titled the section accordingly.

Employable skills are of four general types:

- **specialized or technical skills**, which may include operation of equipment (for example, a computerized milling machine), knowledge of specific procedures (such as WHMIS, CPR, drafting, quality control, or bookkeeping), mastery of certain kinds of software packages (web design, desktop publishing, PowerPoint, or statistics packages), or any other specialized ability (public presentation, training skills);

- **general aptitude or practical abilities**, which address how you handle tasks in the workplace and include such qualities as punctuality, conscientiousness, organizational ability, ability to work to deadlines, and efficiency;
- **communication and interpersonal skills**, which are concerned with how effectively you manage information or handle your professional relationships, and include not only writing, public speaking, listening, and critical reading, but also interpersonal skills such as tact, diplomacy, leadership, motivational skills, cooperation, and teaching ability; and
- **creativity, artistic flair, or innovative problem-solving skills**, which may include specific abilities such as design, technical illustration, drafting, document paste-up and layout, and photography, or a more general ability to develop original and creative solutions to problems. To showcase some of these skills, you should prepare a portfolio of your work to bring with you to the interview.

Like the writers of the sample résumés, you should choose the format that displays your skills and experience most effectively. As you identify your skills and list them for your résumé, be sure you can provide concrete examples and describe a situation in which you demonstrated each one. An employer may ask you for such an example in an interview.

Although the skills section can be positioned at the beginning of the résumé, it functions more effectively when placed at the end, where it supports the information given in the rest of the résumé. The prospective employer then comes on it after reading the details of your employment and education history.

Box 9.3   Classifying Employable Skills

- Specialized or technical skills
- General aptitude or practical abilities
- Communication and interpersonal skills
- Creativity, artistic flair, or innovative problem-solving skills

---

References

Prepare a list of two or three names of people who are willing to provide references for you, and include this list with your résumé. If you have copies of letters from former employers or professors, you may even include photocopies of these along with your submission. Never send your original file copy, as it will not be returned.

References should be obtained from those acquainted with your work, such as former employers, supervisors, or teachers or professors. Personal references are of limited value to employers, and should be avoided unless a character reference is specifically requested. Letters or testimonials from friends, family, or fellow students are not appropriate for a job search. You will find more information on references in the section on letters of recommendation later in this chapter.

Optional résumé categories

The résumé is a flexible instrument that can, and should, be tailored to your individual combination of education and experience and to the demands of the job you want. In addition to featuring essential information about education and experience, your résumé can include a variety of optional categories that will help you to display your unique background to best advantage. The list below shows the most common categories, but there is nothing to prevent your creating others specifically adapted to your particular needs and experience.

Scholastic awards

Use this category to list, in reverse chronological order, any academic awards or scholarships, giving dates, institutions, and titles of awards. Awards received for achievements other than academic ones should be listed under 'Achievements' or 'Accomplishments'.

Extracurricular activities

List in this category any *significant* contributions to school-related activities; membership in academic or athletic clubs or teams, participation in student council, yearbook, or newspaper activities, and so on. This segment is useful mainly for students or recent graduates, and will be less relevant after you've been out of school for two or more years. College experiences have greater longevity on a résumé than high school ones; as a general guideline, delete this section if it describes high school experience more than three years old or college experience more than six years old, unless your achievements are especially outstanding or relevant to the job you seek, and have not been replaced or surpassed by anything else.

Additional courses/Training

Use this category to list courses or certifications that are outside of your main education but which could contribute skills to the job. Perhaps you are formally trained in agricultural economics, but have supplemented your education with additional courses in management. Perhaps you are an electrical engineering technician, but have training in computer programming, or perhaps you are a mechanical engineer with expertise in web design. Perhaps you have taken a pilot's licence, first aid courses, mediation training, or a desktop publishing certificate. If so, include this information on your résumé. You may not wish to include general interest or non-credit courses unless they are in some way relevant to your job search. Once again, list in reverse chronological order the dates, institutions, and titles of the courses.

Volunteer experience

Use this category to showcase significant or substantial volunteer experience, especially if it is relevant to the job you want or to establishing your ethos. Arrange your entries in reverse chronological order and outline major responsibilities, just as you would for a paid position.

Community service/Professional memberships/Professional service

You can include membership in service clubs, organization of community events, or service in civic positions, if these contribute meaningfully to your résumé. It is usually considered best to leave out organizations of a strictly religious nature, unless the job for which you are applying is with a religious organization. List dates, name and location of organization, position title, and any relevant duties.

If the organizations to which you belong are professional associations and are not unions (the Canadian Society of Chemical Engineering, the Canadian Council on Social Development, the Canadian Communication Association, and the Canadian Healthcare Association are some examples), you could re-title this category 'Professional Service' rather than 'Community Service'. If your experience is evenly mixed and significant in both professional and community service categories, you could include both categories on your résumé. If the listings are primarily memberships in organizations of a professional or service nature, you may even want to call the category simply 'Memberships'.

Achievements/Accomplishments

Use this category to feature relevant accomplishment not covered in any previous section. It may include awards other than scholastic ones (for instance, Citizen of the Year), relevant certification of some form (pilot's licence, WHMIS, or drafting certificate), publication of a book or article, a presentation at an academic or professional conference, or a special achievement in your work. Once again, in reverse chronological order, include dates; name and location of institution, agency, or publisher; and nature of certificate, award, or publication. List such achievements only if they help qualify you for the job you seek or contribute to your professional ethos.

Websites/Desktop publishing

Finally, if you have significant experience in developing websites or in publishing newsletters, pamphlets, or other documents using a desktop publishing program, you might want to feature these in their own category on your résumé. For each entry, list the title, place, and date of publication, or the URL. If they are few, these items can instead be included in one of the other categories such as 'Achievements'.

Layout and visual appeal

The appearance of the résumé—its visual appeal—is almost as important as its content. The résumé is seen by an employer before you are; it should therefore make a positive impression and establish your credibility. Just as you wouldn't dream of going to an interview with an unkempt appearance or a smudge on your face, you should never introduce yourself to a prospective employer via an unattractive, disorganized, or cookie-cutter résumé. Few employers will be interested enough to interview an applicant whose résumé is poorly constructed; to them a weak résumé suggests a lazy or unmotivated individual—not, of course, the kind of person they want to hire.

Your command of **nonverbal cues** such as diction, sentence structure, grammar, spelling, punctuation, style, tone, and document design is part of the appeal of your résumé. These elements can help to portray you positively to the employer as confident, enthusiastic, thorough, and reliable—or they can communicate the reverse by betraying a lack of skill and command. After all, if you cannot effectively manage the information on your own résumé, or if you have not taken care in preparing such an important document, the employer may doubt your motivation, your commitment to your tasks, or your understanding of the demands of the situation.

An effective layout builds visual appeal, and credibility, by contributing to your organization and by creating a pleasing balance between white space and printed elements, with reasonable margins on all sides (1" to 1¼" at top, bottom, and both sides is standard). A consistent format also lends a professional appearance, as it does to all work-related writing: major headings should begin at the left margin, lining up neatly beneath one another. The headings should all be in parallel format (all capitalized, for example, or all underlined). Entries within each category should be indented so they line up consistently throughout the résumé, and they should also be uniformly treated (all italicized, for example). Use consistent spacing between sections: for example, you might skip two lines between major categories and one line between entries within a category. This consistency is not only attractive, but, because the layout is also part of your organization, it actually helps the reader to make sense of the information you are presenting, and increases your credibility by revealing you as disciplined and capable.

Use capital letters, underlining, or boldfacing to set apart important details, but use these features uniformly and sparingly. In general, you should not combine underlining with capital letters or with boldfaced or italicized type. Other combinations (boldfacing and block capitals, italics and boldfacing, italics and block capitals) are permissible, though these too should be used sparingly and consistently to help your reader make sense of the information on your résumé. A little of each goes a long way and overuse will destroy the effectiveness of these visual devices. For example, if too much of the résumé is printed in capital letters, it is not only harder to read, but important information no longer stands out.

In general, it is also not good practice to combine several different fonts in a single document, and you should especially avoid fonts that are difficult to read—calligraphic and script fonts, or those designed to look like hand-printing, are typically harder on the eye than a simple serif font; even some sans serif fonts are tiring if the document is lengthy. These should therefore be avoided in a résumé or application letter, which will risk being thrown out if it is difficult to read.

Avoid mixing font sizes as well; at most, you may want to use a slightly larger font for headings and a smaller one for information within categories. Finally, be sure to choose a font in a readable size for the body of your document—12-point type may take up more space than a smaller font, but it is much easier to see. Never reduce the font to try to crowd more information onto the page. It is in your interest to design your résumé so that it's easy for readers to find the information they need to make a decision in your favour; a cramped font will not kindly dispose a reader toward your application.

It should go without saying that visual appeal also means a good quality print job with sharp, clear type. Don't send out a résumé with faint, spotty, or blurred print; the employer may simply discard the whole thing rather than struggle to read it. If possible, you should also send an original résumé, tailored to the job, with every application you submit. Any photocopies you do provide should be perfectly clean.

There are nearly as many varieties of résumé layout as there are people to give advice, but some are better than others. How can you tell a good layout from one that is not so good? One way to check the effectiveness of a layout is to hold the résumé away from you. A good layout is appealing to look at even when it is held too far away for you to read the print, because the print and white space are balanced and the important information stands out from the rest of the material on the page. A good résumé format is also effective close up: it is easy to scan for important information and should be appealing to look at. Here are some characteristics of an effective résumé format. The examples that follow meet these criteria.

A good layout:

- maintains consistent margins and indentations throughout;
- uses white space effectively so that nothing is crowded or cramped, and everything is readable;

- is easily skimmed for main points;
- uses visual effects and indentation to make significant information easily available to the eye so that the reader quickly get the gist of the applicant's work history without having to read every detail (though necessary details are given too, of course); and
- is professional-looking, but also flexible enough to be arranged to suit an individual applicant.

Never underestimate the importance of an attractive layout; your communication instructor may be willing to struggle to read your résumé through to the end, but an employer does not have to do so. In fact, many employers can rapidly cut down a pile of résumés from two hundred to a short list of ten or twenty by immediately discarding unattractive résumés—without even reading them. Remember that, at least initially, the reader of your résumé is seeking reasons to *eliminate* your application, not reasons to keep it.

Why Résumés Get Rejected

Recruiters reject application packages for many reasons, some of which might strike you as unfair. But in order to understand how the process works, and to give your own résumé a better chance to surviving the first cut, you need to recognize the context in which the submissions are read. Always remember that the reader has many résumés to consider and is looking for some key information. You should construct your materials to make that information readily accessible.

First, the employer is looking for evidence of competence, integrity, and the ability to work well with others. Such a reader also expects the résumé to communicate in the voice of the candidate, and will usually not be impressed by cookie-cutter productions. It is useful, too, to keep in mind that the recruiter will not read your résumé in isolation, the way you wrote it, but in the company of several dozen—even several hundred—other submissions. Thus, the reading of a résumé by its audience is always comparative, and a résumé that looks just like all the rest of the pile will not attract attention. Finally, the recruiter is seeking a candidate who closely conforms to the expectations that have been laid out in the job posting.

Unless your résumé reveals a person who is both capable of performing the required job and willing to meet its demands, a person who took care preparing the résumé submission, it will in all likelihood be rejected. Just as you did when you read the job posting, the recruiter is looking for several key items; she is interested in how closely the candidate's qualifications match with the employer's needs, and as a result her first scan of the résumé is focused on the key items sought: required qualifications, competent presentation and written communication, and an understanding of the nature of the job. If the information the recruiter needs is not easy to pick out on the first reading, if the résumé does not establish the writer's competence, or if the whole thing lacks focus, it will likely be rejected.

After the first read-through, résumés that made the cut are subjected to a more thorough scrutiny. At this stage, the recruiter is looking for consistency; he may check timelines and evaluate the applicant's claims to skills and experience. Does the résumé itself confirm the writer's competence, or does it raise doubts? In this pass, the recruiter is looking for confirmation of his first assessment, but he is also looking to reduce the pile of potential candidates even further. Careless errors, lack of clarity, inflated claims, or jarring inconsistencies will cause the recruiter to eliminate the résumé from the pile.

Depending on how many résumés have passed the first cut and how many need to be eliminated, the recruiter may make several more passes through the pile, each time scrutinizing the documents more closely and looking for further reasons to reject. Only those candidates whose résumés survive this rigorous process will be offered an interview; the rest will be rejected. Below are some of the more common reasons employers give for rejecting applications.

- Required credentials not evident on first page (check the ad and make sure your relevant credentials are prominently displayed)
- Difficult to scan or locate details, dates, or relevant categories
- Scant or underdeveloped information; lack of detail
- Claims are unsupported by facts
- Listed skills are too general and not targeted to the job sought (check the ad, which will often tell you what skills the employer is interested in)
- Disorganized presentation (too many bullets, unclear divisions between categories, confusing margins, too many visual devices)
- Font too small (12-point is easiest to read)
- No clear relationship to the job sought
- Too much irrelevant information
- Obvious lack of care: errors, inconsistencies, contradictions, grammar or spelling mistakes
- Cookie-cutter structure
- Appears to have been prepared by a résumé service
- No cover letter accompanies the résumé
- Unprofessional message on the answering machine when the employer calls to set an interview

Sample Résumés—Ineffective and Effective

The following résumés illustrate the principles discussed in this chapter (Figures 9.1 to 9.6). The first résumé of each pair is weak and in need of improvement; the second is an improved version. While the weak examples violate principles of relevance or recency and generally offer a poor layout, all of the samples of effective résumés follow the principles of effective layout. Study the before-and-after examples below, taking a critical look at what makes an effective layout and what looks unattractive.

The first example is the résumé of Shawn Horton. Study the sample before reading the analysis. As you read, consider the following: How focused is Shawn's message? Is the résumé easy to scan? Do you know right away what kind of work he is qualified to do?

The problem

The primary flaw in Shawn's résumé is that he has failed to address the probable needs of his potential employer, and he has not effectively targeted his résumé to the job he is seeking. Shawn created his résumé using a template that accompanied his word-processing package; unfortunately for him, the effect of this template has been to make him appear very much like every other candidate in the competition.

Shawn Horton
1234 - 5th St W
Fredericton, NB
E8J 0S3
(506) 345-6789

EDUCATION

2007–09	Faculty of Engineering, ***Central Maritime University*** Mechanical Engineering
2006–07	Faculty of Arts and Sciences, ***Central Maritime University***
2006	Graduated with distinction, and as class valedictorian from Willis Bowler High School, Hindenberg, NB
2008	St. John's CPR, and Safety Oriented First Aid. TDG, WHMIS H2S Alive–H2S gas safety training.

EMPLOYMENT HISTORY

May 1 to Sept 10 2008	*North American Resources, Saint John, NB* *Summer Student.* Duties included the operation of various water injection plants and oil batteries. A large amount of responsibility and trust was placed on my behalf, as I spent most of the time working independently (having to make my own decisions), with expensive and dangerous equipment. I was also entrusted with a company vehicle for the summer.
May 2 to Sept 8 2007	*Bob's Building, Saint John, NB* *Assistant Carpenter.* Free use of all tools. Often worked independently.
2007	*A Buck or Two, Edmunston, NB* Ran till, stocked shelves, aided customers.
2007	*Oscar's General Merchants, Edmunston, NB* Ran till, stocked shelves, aided customers.

Figure 9.1a: The first draft of Shawn Horton's résumé has some flaws that undercut his credibility. Can you pick them out?

Shawn has also fallen into the trap of including details that are not relevant to the employer. For example, Shawn entered engineering after his second year of study, a common path at many universities. That detail isn't of particular interest to an employer, who is more concerned with the degree he will have at the end. The multiple entries take up unnecessary room without communicating any significant information; in fact, an

---

Shawn Horton
1234 - 5th St W
Fredericton, NB
E8J 0S3
(506) 345-6789

SKILLS

Team skills	Enjoy working with parteners. Am able to work efficiently within a group, and able to motivate if necessary.
Independent	Able to make independent decisions based on my evaluation of the situation.
Intelligent	70% avg. last term in Engineering (full course load).
Leadership	Ability to take charge when it becomes necessary. Have organized campus intramural teams, high school SRC vice-president, coached junior soccer, junior leader in 4-H, Social Coordinator for Clegg Hall Residence, engineering 'Peer Mentor Program.'
Computer skills	Experience with a large amount of applications (both DOS and Windows,) programming (FORTRAN, C/C++), hardware (from drivers to installation).
Problem solving skills:	Find solving problems enjoyable and rewarding.

EXTRA CURRICULAR

Sports	Soccer, hockey, fastball, volley ball, cross-country, mtn. biking, skiing.
Interests	Electronics, programming, mechanics, music, reading.
Organizations	UCESS, 4-H Alumni, National Geographic Society
Volunteer	Meals-on-Wheels, coached junior soccer

REFERENCES
available on request

Figure 9.1b

employer who is skimming the résumé on the first read-through could even get the impression of a spotty school background.

Shawn needs to run his spell-checker and proofread more carefully. As well, he needs to consider the effect on an employer of some of what he's said on his résumé: under skills, for example, he's listed 'intelligent', a claim that might strike the reader as immodest or even arrogant. And consider this: What if the employer graduated from engineering with an average of 95 per cent? Is such a person likely to find 70 per cent impressive? What about an employer who graduated with 50 per cent? Would this person feel that grades are a reliable indication of intelligence? Since it can potentially be taken negatively, Shawn would do well to eliminate this problematic statement entirely.

SHAWN HORTON
1234 - 5th St. W., Fredericton, NB E8J 0S3
(506) 345-6789   <shorton@atlantis.nb.ca>

EDUCATION

2009   **BSc, Mechanical Engineering**
                        Faculty of Engineering, Central Maritime University
                        • 70% avg. last term in engineering (full course load)

2006   **High School Diploma** (with distinction)
                        Willis Bowler High School, Hindenberg, NB
                        • class valedictorian

CERTIFICATES

2008   St. John's CPR, and Safety Oriented First Aid
                        TDG, WHMIS
                        H2S Alive–H2S gas safety training

RELEVANT EXPERIENCE

Summer   **Engineering Summer Student**
2008   North American Resources, Saint John, NB
                        • operated water injection plants and oil batteries
                        • worked independently with expensive and dangerous equipment
                        • entrusted with a company vehicle

Summer   **Assistant Carpenter**
2007   Bob's Building, Saint John, NB
                        • skilled on various construction and woodworking tools
                        • frequently worked independently

Figure 9.2a: Shawn has redrafted his résumé to better present himself and his skills to an
employer. What improvements can you see?

The Solution

Shawn's improved résumé is much easier for the employer to scan for relevant information, and is targeted to catch the reader's attention. Shawn has also improved the focus and impact of his résumé by including the design experience gained in his classes.

He could have chosen to leave out his grade average entirely, but he feels it's important to mention; however, instead of featuring it awkwardly under the heading of 'Intelligent', he has placed it more naturally along with his degree as part of his education.

Shawn Horton (506) 345-6789

DESIGN PROJECT EXPERIENCE

2009   **Free-Motion Wheelchair Stabilizing Mechanism**
- judged top design in internal competition
- involved analysis, testing, and fabrication of prototype
- formally presented to a public audience

SKILLS
- teamwork
- leadership
- public speaking
- troubleshooting and problem-solving
- computer programming (FORTRAN, C++)
- clear and effective writing

ACTIVITIES
- Mentor for Faculty of Engineering 'Peer Mentor Program'
- Social Coordinator for Clegg Hall Residence
- organized campus intramural teams
- Meals-on-Wheels volunteer
- coached junior soccer
- Student Council vice-president, high school
- junior leader in 4-H
- enjoys sports, including soccer, hockey, fastball, mountain-biking, skiing

REFERENCES

Professor C.S. Major   **(902) 555 6789**
Department of Mechanical Engineering
Central Maritime University
Box 5005, Truro, NS B2S 4M3

Professor D.A. Broker   **(902) 555 0987**
English Language and Linguistics
Central Maritime University
Box 5005, Truro, NS B2S 4M3

Figure 9.2b

Note, too, that Shawn has moved the industrial certificates into their own category, since they aren't properly classified as 'education', and he has focused his skills to better serve the employer's needs.

Abilities and Skills
-familiar with use of an Excell spreadsheet
-honesty and integrity are regarded highly
-have excellent social skills
-have typing training
-have experience dealing with dangerous goods
-familiar with the operation of a forklift
-possess an air brake endorsement on a class 5 licence

Education
June 2005 Grade 12 – with honours
     Rosston Central High School

Sept 05- Dec 05	All Gospel Bible Institute
	Bible Knowledge Program
	Glory, SK
Sept 06- Present	Tyrell University
	College of Engineering
	Pursuing a Bachelor's Degree in
	Chemical Engineering

Personal Interests
-enjoy basketball and other such sports
-enjoy playing pool
-enjoy walking, biking, swimming, and other physical activities
-enjoy listening to music

Reference

Kurt Dedalopolous
President of Dedalopolous and Associates - Biggar
(306) 882-3575   (Home)

Figure 9.3a: What flaws can you spot immediately in this weak résumé?

The Problem

This is a very disappointing résumé from someone who is actually very capable. Not only is the format confusing and hard to read, but the applicant has failed to provide his name and contact information on a prominent page. It's hard to tell which is the first page of the résumé, and an employer is unlikely to spend any time trying to figure it out.

Work Experience
September 2008-August 2009Chem-Tech of Calgary

Position: Intern

Duties:-Apply advanced computing skill to design and implement new software technology in the
         Delphi (Object Pascal) programming environment.
         -Identify and solve engineering and software problems.
         -Pinpoint sources of error by debugging the software code and examining simulation results.
         -Work as part of a high performance team committed to producing high quality engineering
         software.

May 2008- August 31 2008   Transportation Department, Lougheed Transit Services

Position: Utility Person - Maintenance

Duties:- Responsible to clean the interiors of city buses
        - Assist in the changing and retorqueing of tires
        - Perform general custodial duties in the garage and maintenance shop
        - Safely operate the buses about the city and in the garage
        - Assist in ensuring that bus shelters are clean and free of safety hazards

Supervisor: Devorek Andrusiak   (306) 864-4245

April 2007- September 2007   Tyrell University

Posiion: Research Assistant

Duties:- Develop software package
        - Write proposal for project
        - Prepare final report and presentation

Supervisor: Prof. Sipursky

May 2006-September 2006   Lougheed Transportation Company, Lougheed Depot

Position: Express Services Attendant I

Duties:- Responsible to assist in the loading of buses
        - Responsible to assist in the sorting and putting away of freight
        - Responsible to serve customers at the front counter

Figure 9.3b

Even a reader who is willing to plough through the rest of this 'no-name' résumé would
soon bog down in irrelevant detail, because the writer has not provided sufficient focus to
target the content to a technical position.

The writer needs to provide contact information and display it prominently on the first
page, so that the employer is familiar with his name right from the start. He also

February 2005- August 2005   Biggar Petro Canada Service Station and
December 2005- May 2006   RTC bus depot

Position: Manager of Depot / Gas Attendant

Duties:-Responsible to make sure that people and business are informed of newly arrived parcels.
        -Responsible to send, receive, and sort freight.
        -Responsible to give information upon request concerning arrival and departure times of bus
        routes, passenger ticket prices, and shipping costs.
        -Performed Gas Attendant duties and some custodial duties.

September 2003-February 2005   Biggar Burger Queen

Position: Cook

Duties:-Preparation of hot food and ice cream products.
        -Operation of cash register
        -General Cleaning.

July 2002- June 2003   Biggar Co-operative Grocery Store

Position: Grocery Packer

Duties:-Bagging groceries and taking them to customer's vehicles on request
           Stocking Shelves and working with fresh produce and dairy shelves

For further information please contact me at:
        Phone: (306) 373-3313
        Email: klh117@stdnts.tyrellu.ca

Figure 9.3c

desperately needs to do some editing to de-emphasize or delete the irrelevant information, leaving only the content that demonstrates how he has prepared himself specifically
for a career in chemical engineering. He should also focus the remaining information to
accommodate the employer's needs, and he should polish his format to communicate
important details more clearly and effectively. Turn to the improved version (Figure 9.4)
to see how effectively he has accomplished these goals.

KIRO HATZITOLIOS
#2 – 2710 Main St., Regina, SK S4R 0M3
Email: <klh117@stdnts.tyrellu.ca> Phone: (306)343-0213

EDUCATION

Tyrell University, Lougheed, SK   2006–Present
BE, Chemical Engineering

Achievements:
- member, Golden Key National Honour Society
- improved my academic performance each year
- 84% avg. last year

Relevant Skills:
- work productively in a fast-paced environment
- strong problem-solving ability
- advanced programming skills

Graduation:
- expected May 2010

RELATED EXPERIENCE

Chem Tech Ltd., Calgary, AB   2008–2009
Intern Engineer in Batch Design Kit (BDK) Development

Responsibilities:
- design and implement new software in Delphi (Object Pascal) programming environment
- identify and solve engineering and software problems
- pinpoint sources of error and debug software
- part of a high-performance team producing engineering software

Tyrell University, Lougheed, SK   2007 (Summer)
Undergraduate Research Assistant, Chemical Engineering

Responsibilities:
- develop software package to model a Packed Bed Biofilm Reactor
- create a proposal outlining the goals of the project
- correspond frequently with Saskatchewan Research Council
- prepare final report and formal presentation describing the software and proving the integrity of the mathematical model

Figure 9.4a: How much better is Kiro's improved résumé?

The Solution

Kiro's dramatically improved résumé now communicates professional credibility in its content, organization, and design, and is more likely to attract the attention of an employer who hopes to fill an entry-level engineering position.

Kiro's strengths are much more visible in this well-designed résumé that will help to distinguish him from other applicants who have relied on a cookie-cutter approach. Notice

Kiro Hatzitolios (306)343-0213 /2

PRESENTATIONS AND TECHNICAL PAPERS

A Computer Model for Characterizing the Packed Bed Biofilm Reactor
Canadian Society for Chemical Engineering Conference   2004
Saskatoon, SK (October) *Third Place Winner*

Communicating Value: Rhetoric and the Undergraduate Degree.
Communicating across Boundaries Conference   2008
(Panel participant) Tyrell University, Lougheed, SK (September)

ENGINEERING PROJECTS

Knock Out of H$_2$S in Vent Gas   Ongoing
GEng 465, Tyrell University

  Responsibilities: • design a method of removing H$_2$S from the vent gas of a local
                           canola crushing plant
                         • work with all involved to provide an effective, economic, and
                           practical solution
                         • present final design to colleagues, college professors, and industry
                           professionals

Preliminary Economic Feasibility Analysis   2009
GEng 365, Tyrell University

  Responsibilities: • evaluate economic feasibility of trucking coal from a mine to
                           seaport
                         • merge reports of members of design group to create final report
                         • carefully show all calculations and assumptions

  REFERENCES   *A list of those who have agreed to supply references is attached to this application.*

Figure 9.4b

in particular how Kiro has selected categories that display his background to greatest advantage, and how he has arranged them in order of relevance to the job he seeks.

Finally, the layout allows the reader to scan quickly to achieve an overview of the candidate's background, but also allows for additional information to support and elaborate the information provided in the headers. The new résumé is not only more informative and selective, but it is also more readable and more credible than Kiro's initial attempt.

SAMANTHA ARAR

354 Acadabra Street, Brampton, ON L8W 2T1

905 429-1873

samantha.arar@wahoo.ca

ACQUIRED SKILLS

Writing and Information Management

- Experience in researching, writing, and editing reports and other complex documents
- Excellent grammar, spelling and proofreading skills
- Efficient sorting and filing of information
- Ability to interpret documents and follow written instructions
- Skilled at writing instruction manuals for computer programs
- Act as resource person, problem solving for users
- Above average computer skills, operate computer equipment, install software

Organizational and Problem-solving

- Good planning and organizing skills
- Able to manage priorities effectively
- Well-developed problem-solving skills
- Work well in a fast-paced environment

EXPERIENCE

Housekeeper   2009-2010

Bon Ami Hotels Inc.   Brampton, ON

- Performed housekeeping services for staff and guest areas
- Used cleaning equipment

Janitor   2008

First Choice Janitorial Services   Brampton, ON

- Performed Janitorial services for offices, classrooms, cafeterias and washrooms
- Cleaned and maintained building common areas

HP Technical Support Agent   2007-2008

DFS Canada   Brampton, ON

- Phone support to HP Pavilion Desktop Customers
- Logged calls using People Soft Program

Technical Support/Revision Control Manager and Programmer   2004-2007

Tektonix Inc.   Mississauga, ON

- Researched and wrote product proposals and product evaluation reports
- Regularly edited documents written by others
- Wrote and edited user documentation for computer products
- Maintained document and software libraries
- Managed technical support and product fulfillment departments

Figure 9.5a

The Problem

Sam is highly skilled and fully certified in computer programming and technical support; she worked for three years with the same tech company before it closed down. Economic conditions in her area made it difficult for her to immediately find a similar position, but Sam isn't one to sit idle while waiting for something appropriate to crop up. She took work where she could find it while she continued to look for a position more closely suited to her experience and skills.

Unfortunately, Sam's work ethic, combined with a conventional approach to résumé preparation, has left her in something of a bind: the first work experience recruiters now

Samantha Arar 306 429-1873 \2

Programmer
Sasktek
- Revised and edited existing programs
- Ported programs to other languages
- Wrote and edited user documentation for software

1996
Etobicoke, ON

Cashier/ Sales Representative
Buck or Two Stores Ltd.
- Performed Cash and Credit transactions
- Maintained Ladies Wear Stock
- Designed Displays

1992-1995

EDUCATION

Small Business Bookkeeping
Mohawk College

2008
Hamilton, ON

Income Tax Preparation Course
H & R Block

2008
Brampton, ON

Introduction to Novell Networking
Mohawk College

2006
Hamilton, ON

A+ Certification Course
University of Guelph

2004 – 2005
Guelph, ON

Information Systems Programming Certificate
Mohawk College

2004
Hamilton, ON

Business Computer Programming Certificate
Mohawk College

1996
Hamilton, ON

RELATED TRAINING

WHMIS Training, First Aid /CPR Training, Driver Training, Beginner Sign Language

REFERENCES
Available on Request

Figure 9.5b

see when they look at her résumé is entirely irrelevant to the work she is looking for. Recruiters tend not to read very far before they make their initial decision about whether to reject a submission, and, based on the first couple of entries on Sam's résumé, they have been tossing her application into the round file.

On the advice of a consultant, Sam tried to remedy the situation with a functional approach, listing her skills first. But this strategy backfired, since her skill set appeared to be so out of line with the listed work experience. The mismatch actually had the effect of undermining rather than bolstering her ethos, since at best it looks like exaggeration and at worst it might cause an employer to wonder what's wrong with her, that someone so highly qualified is working so far beneath her potential.

SAMANTHA ARAR
354 Acadabra Street, Brampton, ON L8W T51
905 429-1873
samantha.arar@wahoo.ca

Information current as of January 2010

HIGHLIGHTS

- Above-average computer skills (including programming and user-support experience)
- Experience in researching, writing, and editing reports and other complex documents
- Outstanding grammar, spelling, and proofreading skills
- Efficient sorting, filing, and retrieval of information
- Professional appearance and manner

PROGRAMMING AND USER-SUPPORT EXPERIENCE

HP Technical Support Agent   2007-2008
  DFS Canada, Brampton, ON
  - User support to HP Pavilion Desktop customers
  - Logged calls using PeopleSoft

Technical Support/Revision Control Manager and Programmer   2004-2007
  Tektonix Inc., Mississauga, ON
  - Researched and wrote product proposals and product evaluation reports
  - Edited documents written by others
  - Wrote and edited user documentation
  - Maintained document and software libraries
  - Managed technical support and product fulfillment departments

Computer Programmer   1996
  Ontek, Etobicoke, ON
  - Revised and edited existing programs
  - Ported programs to other languages
  - Wrote and edited user documentation for software

TECHNICAL EDUCATION

Introduction to Novell Networking   2006
  Mohawk College, Hamilton, ON

A+ Certification   2004-2005
  University of Guelph, Guelph, ON

Figure 9.6a

Sam's challenge is to position her technical experience so that it catches the recruiter's eye, and to give the entire document an overhaul so that, instead of simply listing the things she has done, it has a more focused appearance that will get her the job she wants. Take a look at her improved résumé to see how she solved her difficulties through effective targeting.

The Solution

Sam's résumé has been dramatically improved with the use of targeting, and by overhauling its formatting to make it easier to read and to scan.

Samantha Arar /2

Information Systems Programming Certificate	2004
Mohawk College, Hamilton, ON	
Business Computer Programming Certificate	1996
Mohawk College, Hamilton, ON	

SOFTWARE PACKAGES (selected)

- MS Word
- PowerPoint
- QuickBooks
- Excel
- Front Page
- Installshield
- Access
- PeopleSoft
- Perforce
- Rational Rose
- Delphi
- PE Design

BUSINESS CERTIFICATION

Small Business Bookkeeping	2008
Mohawk College, Hamilton, ON	
Income Tax Preparation	2008
H&R Block, Brampton, ON	

ADDITIONAL EXPERIENCE

2008-Present I was among the last to be laid off when Tektonix closed its doors in 2007, and remain hopeful of finding another position that will make best use of my office experience and technical training. I am not afraid of hard work, and rather than sit idle I have been employed in housekeeping services for Bon Ami Hotels Inc. (2009-Present) and First Choice Janitorial Services (2008).

OFFICE SKILLS

- Scheduling appointments, maintaining records, sorting and filing of information
- Invoicing and ordering of supplies
- Providing basic information to clients and the public
- Good basic math skills (calculation, estimation, data analysis)
- Ability to interpret documents and follow written instructions
- Can take initiative and work without supervision

REFERENCES

- A list of references is attached.

Figure 9.6b

The new version uses two strategies to make it more forceful and effective. First, splitting her work history into two separate categories (one 'relevant' and one 'other') has enabled Sam to move her technical experience to the beginning of the résumé, where it will have more impact on the reader. As well, this move has enabled her to better focus the résumé so that it more effectively targets the kind of job she seeks. As the recruiter scans the résumé, everything she sees is directly relevant, and each entry reinforces the picture of a competent technical professional that Sam wishes to convey.

Second, Sam has not only moved the janitorial entries to the end of her résumé, where they are far less prominent, but she has reduced their impact even further by placing the information into a paragraph, where it is available but not dominant. These strategies of presentation help to place the janitorial work into an appropriate relation to her technical experience: because they are given much less importance both visually and positionally, the recruiter will be less inclined to overemphasize them when evaluating Sam's qualifications.

Finally, Sam's list of skills has been shortened considerably, and is more convincing because it is immediately followed up by experience that reinforces the skill set she claims. A visual updating provides a final polish. The new approach strengthens and reinforces Sam's credibility and professionalism.

With this improved résumé, Sam was able to obtain an interview and a job offer for a position more closely aligned with her abilities and training.

Writing the Cover Letter

A letter of application, also called a **cover letter**, always accompanies a résumé. Its function, like the letter of transmittal for the formal report, is to introduce the résumé and focus the reader's attention on its relevant details. Even if you are submitting your résumé as an electronic attachment, you should still include a properly formatted cover letter as a separate attachment. Your e-mail message then functions as a letter of transmittal for the entire package. Like all professional correspondence, a job application letter must follow the **Seven Cs**: it must be complete, concise, clear, coherent, correct, and courteous, and it must also establish your professional credibility.

In format, the cover letter is arranged like any standard letter using full block style. If you have developed a letterhead-style header for your résumé, you should employ the same header for your letter of application so that the two are unified visually. As well, use the same font for the text of your letter as you used in the body of your résumé, and in the same size.

Two types of application letter

An application letter may be written in either of two circumstances, roughly corresponding to the request/response categories outlined in Chapter 5. In other words, you may *respond* to an existing job advertisement with a **solicited** letter of application, or you may *request* to be considered for a position if one becomes available by way of an **unsolicited** letter. The advantage of the second, if your timing is right, is obvious: there will be less competition than for an advertised position. However, the risk is that there may not be a job available.

Both letters perform essentially the same task, and the process of writing them may be broken down into steps. How many paragraphs each step takes will depend on the background of the individual and the nature of the job applied for, but as a general guideline, you may assume that each step is treated in a separate paragraph.

Remember that the application letter, like all professional writing, must be carefully directed to your reader's requirements and expectations. Its sole purpose is to engage the reader's attention and direct it toward your résumé. Thus, what you might want to say is not as important as what the employer needs to hear. Draw on the information you gathered from your survey of advertisements and position descriptions to help you shape your information. Always ask yourself what questions an employer will want your application to answer. Targeting the letter effectively to the reader and the job will help to demonstrate your own good judgement and professional credibility.

The following steps can serve as a guideline; you could plan to allow one paragraph for each step, though each step may be shorter or longer than a paragraph.

Step 1: Identify the purpose

The first thing an employer will want to know upon receiving a letter is 'What is this about?' As in all professional communication, you need to put your main message first. Begin by identifying your reason for writing. If you are answering an advertisement, state the title of the position you are applying for, quoting the competition number if there is one, and the source and date of the advertisement. For an unsolicited letter, state clearly the type of work you desire and enquire whether such a position is currently open or soon to become available. You may wish to use a 'Re' or subject line for both types of letters to identify the message by title or type of position sought.

Step 2: Outline relevant qualifications

The next thing the employer will want to know is, 'Is this applicant qualified for the job?' Whether your letter is solicited or unsolicited, you should briefly highlight your qualifications and your reasons for applying for this position, adapting the information to the job requirements. This section need not be elaborate—your résumé will take care of the details—but it should convince the employer that you are a suitable candidate based on how well your skills and education fit the position as described in the advertisement. Remember that the purpose of the letter is to direct the employer's attention to your résumé, which accompanies the letter, and to motivate the employer to read it. In this paragraph, you may wish explicitly to refer the employer to the résumé.

Step 3: Emphasize your strengths

An employer will also be interested in what distinguishes you from other similarly qualified candidates. Highlight relevant skills and details from your résumé, qualifying these with brief examples appropriate to the job you seek. Be specific about the close match between your skills and those sought by the employer.

Step 4: Refer the reader to your résumé

If you have not yet referred the employer to your résumé, do so at this stage; mention also that you have attached letters of recommendation or other documentation (if you have done so) or invite the employer to contact the references you have listed.

Step 5: Request an interview

Close with a statement of confidence in your abilities; thank the employer for considering you and ask for an interview. You might even say that you will call the employer on a specified date to set up an interview. This is a good move if you can carry it off. However, if the idea of cold-calling an employer to request an interview makes you uncomfortable, and you really can't imagine yourself making such a call, don't say that you will do so. Instead, request an interview at the employer's convenience. Provide a telephone number where you may be reached or where a message may be left, and then make sure that the message on your answering machine conveys a suitably professional image.

Sample letters of application

Figures 9.7 and 9.8 are effective examples of the solicited and unsolicited application letter.

#2 – 2710 Main St.
Regina, SK S4R 0M3

3 March 2011

Wayne Chiu, Manager
Chem-Tech Ltd.
3267 Periphery St.
Calgary, AB T2X 6L7

Dear Mr. Chiu:

Re: Chemical Engineering Internship Opportunity

If you are looking for a committed chemical engineering student with strong technical and lab skills to fill this position, you'll want to put me on your interview list. In addition to a solid academic record (85% overall this year, 87.5% in my engineering courses), I bring an unusual level of determination and self-discipline. Let me give you an example of what I mean: when I began my engineering studies, my lack of high school calculus put me at a disadvantage. Consequently, I left first year with a 62.5% average in math. However, once I saw what was needed, I rolled up my sleeves and got to work, and within a year I had pulled up my grade to 85% – an increase of more than 20% when others' grades were falling. This is the same level of discipline and commitment I can bring to an internship position with Chem-Tech.

In addition to determination, I can bring solid technical skills developed from course work in my engineering program. I have learned to think through problems logically and to propose solutions based on sound application of mathematical and chemical principles, and have performed at the top of my class in fluid flow, thermodynamics, and mass balances. I am experienced in object-oriented programming, and have used both Delphi and Visual Basic.

My communication skills have been sharpened both through a course in oral and written communication and through my work experience to date. I have functioned as part of an effective unit, and I'm comfortable working with a variety of people.

As my résumé illustrates, I am ready and willing to put my skills and enthusiasm to work for you. I would very much appreciate the opportunity to speak with you in an interview, and may be reached at (306) 343-0213 or by e-mail at <klh111@stdnt.uregina.ca>.

Sincerely,

Kiro Hatzitolios

Kiro Hatzitolios

Figure 9.7: This solicited letter of application will certainly stand out from the others that the employer is likely to have received. How effectively does it target the employer's needs? What risks does it take? Would it work for all applicants? Why or why not?

1234 - 5th St W
Fredericton, NB E8J 0S3

June 27, 2004

Eastern HR Consulting Ltd.
FAX: (506) 215-2151
Email: careers@easternhr.com

Re: Quality Assurance Specialist

Based on the qualifications outlined in your posting for this position, I believe I may be the person you're seeking. Please add my application to the list.

I graduated in June with a degree in Mechanical Engineering from the Central Maritime University, where I've been fortunate to receive a first-class technical education that has provided a strong knowledge base and advanced problem-solving skills. My technical course work has included materials and manufacturing, mechanics of materials, and two courses in engineering and industrial design. Lab work involved analysis and fabrication to client specifications, including troubleshooting and diagnostics.

In addition to this technical education, I believe communication and report writing are also highly important. I've had the opportunity to extend my communication and leadership skills through advanced study and through participation in the UNB Speakers Club, where I sit on the executive. Engineering students are required to take an oral and written communication course as part of their program of study; however, I was able to take advantage of two advanced courses in communication theory and practice, from which I gained additional experience in writing and public speaking, as well as in understanding the dynamics of communication interaction generally.

If you are seeking a capable communicator who brings solid technical background in product fabrication, I would be pleased to hear from you when you begin interviewing for this position. I may be reached at (506) 345-6789 or by e-mail at <shorton@atlantis.nb.ca>. Thank you for considering my application.

Sincerely,

Shawn Horton

Figure 9.8: What features of Shawn's letter enable him to target the needs and expectations of the employer? Compare his letter with the one written by Kiro Hatzitolios; what differences can you see?

The Application Form

Completing an application form may seem relatively straightforward once you have finished preparing your résumé, since you may assume that you can simply cut and paste from one document to the other. However, despite the similarities in the two documents, a résumé and an application form perform their tasks in different ways, and therefore require somewhat different strategies.

Like the résumé, the application form is a kind of report. However, unlike the résumé, which is a flexible document that can be adapted to your particular experience and requirements, an application form is a standardized instrument whose purpose is to make it easier for an employer to compare applicants' qualifications. It does this, in part, by forcing everyone's information into an identical format.

From the applicant's perspective, the application form is not so advantageous, since it minimizes your ability to adapt format to context and experience. Though it may seem to you like an unnecessary overlap in information, you may sometimes be asked to complete a standard application form in addition to a résumé. In some firms, the two are used for different purposes and kept on file in different locations: the résumé goes to the department in which you would be working if you were hired, while the application form is kept on file in the personnel department, where it is used for human resources purposes.

Forms vary considerably in their thoroughness. Some are little more than data sheets that allow no room for elaboration. These are normally used in conjunction with the résumé and cover letter. Others are more detailed, with sections that allow you to present additional information. It is the latter kind with which we are concerned here.

Some employers use a form produced by their own company, whereas others use a standardized form such as the one created by the Canadian Association of Career Educators and Employers. A copy of this detailed application form may be required by the firm to which you are applying; if so, you can find it online at http://www.cacee.com. A copy of the form is reproduced on the following pages.

Though completing this kind of form can be demanding, it generally offers an advantage over briefer versions because it allows room to communicate any special skills and abilities that might be overlooked on a shorter form. It can thus help you to make a stronger impression on the employer. However, this advantage exists only if you take the opportunity to showcase your unique abilities and to make yourself stand out from the competition. Be sure to take the time to complete all the sections thoughtfully and carefully.

Your instructor will likely require you to complete the CACEE form as part of your résumé submission. Complete all sections as fully as possible, taking special care to fill in areas asking for elaboration on the form's standard questions, such as 'Summary' and 'Educational Experiences and Accomplishments'. It is important to take advantage of these sections, not only because they allow you to distinguish yourself from other applicants, but also because employers frequently complain about applicants' failure to fill out forms completely.

It is especially important to complete the flexible categories of 'Summary' and 'Educational Experiences and Accomplishments'. They are areas that you can use to your advantage, elaborating on strengths that may not have shown up clearly in the rest of the application form. When completing the narrative sections of the form, do not simply cut and paste from your résumé and cover letter. Instead, rewrite the information in other words, so that an employer reading the submission will see that you have taken the time to complete the form thoughtfully. If you are completing the form by hand, write in ink. Check your spelling and grammar, and the accuracy of all your details. Finally, be sure to sign and date the form where indicated.

Page 1 of 5

Approved By

CACEE Application for Employment

☐ Full-time
☐ Summer
☐ Co-op
☐ Internship
☐

Name of Organization	Position(s) Sought

Name of Educational Institution

General Information

Surname	Given Name(s)

Address until	No.	Street	Tel.
City	Province/State	Postal Code	E-mail

Permanent Address (if different from above)	No.	Street		Tel.
	City	Province/State	Postal Code	E-mail

Are you legally eligible to accept employment in Canada?

Yes ☐   No ☐

Would you accept employment anywhere in Canada?

Yes ☐   No ☐

When are you available to start work?

Preferred Location(s)
1.
2.
3.

Education

Post Secondary or other institutions attended. Begin with most recent.	Faculty, Department, Division, or School	Discipline or Program (Major)	Degree Certificate	/Diploma/ or expected	Date obtained

G.P.A. for your most recently completed academic year   on a scale of   (Percentage or letter equivalent:).

G.P.A. for all courses completed to date (cumulative average)   on a scale of   (Percentage or letter equivalent:).

Highlight skills relevant to the position(s) sought.

Figure 9.9a

Educational Experiences and Accomplishments

Describe your relevant courses, project work, theses, publications, and presentations. Include awards and scholarships.

Extracurricular Activities

Describe your extracurricular activities including class or campus offices held, volunteer experience, memberships in clubs or organizations, leadership roles, sports activities, hobbies, etc. (You are not required to mention the names of organizations that indicate race, ancestry, place of origin, colour, ethnic origin, citizenship, creed, sex, sexual orientation, age, marital status, family status, political beliefs or disabilities).

Figure 9.9b

Work Experience		
Describe all work experience (paid and unpaid) starting with most recent.		

Position   Name of Organization

☐ Summer
☐ Part-time

City   Province/State   Dates   (# of hours/wk   )

☐ Co-op

Duties:

☐ Internship
☐ Volunteer
☐ Full-time
☐ Other: (specify)

Position   Name of Organization

☐ Summer
☐ Part-time

City   Province/State   Dates   (# of hours/wk   )

☐ Co-op

Duties:

☐ Internship
☐ Volunteer
☐ Full-time
☐ Other: (specify)

Position   Name of Organization

☐ Summer
☐ Part-time

City   Province/State   Dates   (# of hours/wk   )

☐ Co-op

Duties:

☐ Internship
☐ Volunteer
☐ Full-time
☐ Other: (specify)

Position   Name of Organization

☐ Summer
☐ Part-time

City   Province/State   Dates   (# of hours/wk   )

☐ Co-op

Duties:

☐ Internship
☐ Volunteer
☐ Full-time
☐ Other: (specify)

Figure 9.9c

Work Experience		

Describe all work experience (paid and unpaid) starting with most recent.

Position   Name of Organization   ☐ Summer

                                                                    ☐ Part-time

City   Province/State   Dates   (# of hours/wk   )

                                                                    ☐ Co-op

Duties: ☐ Internship

                                                                    ☐ Volunteer

                                                                    ☐ Full-time

                                                                    ☐ Other: (specify)

Position   Name of Organization   ☐ Summer

                                                                    ☐ Part-time

City   Province/State   Dates   (# of hours/wk   )

                                                                    ☐ Co-op

Duties: ☐ Internship

                                                                    ☐ Volunteer

                                                                    ☐ Full-time

                                                                    ☐ Other: (specify)

Position   Name of Organization   ☐ Summer

                                                                    ☐ Part-time

City   Province/State   Dates   (# of hours/wk   )

                                                                    ☐ Co-op

Duties: ☐ Internship

                                                                    ☐ Volunteer

                                                                    ☐ Full-time

                                                                    ☐ Other: (specify)

Position   Name of Organization   ☐ Summer

                                                                    ☐ Part-time

City   Province/State   Dates   (# of hours/wk   )

                                                                    ☐ Co-op

Duties: ☐ Internship

                                                                    ☐ Volunteer

                                                                    ☐ Full-time

                                                                    ☐ Other: (specify)

Figure 9.9d

Summary

Demonstrate your suitability for position(s) sought, by outlining your career objectives and elaborating on the factual material already presented. Show how your experience (educational, extracurricular and work) is relevant to the position(s), organization, and/or field of work for which you are applying.

I understand that any omission or misrepresentation with respect to this information may be cause for denial or immediate termination of employment.

Date

_____
Signature

Figure 9.9e

The Letter of Recommendation

As part of your application, employers will usually ask you to include references from people who have known you professionally, either as an employee or as a student. Sometimes you can simply append a list of names and contact information to your résumé, but you may also be asked to have each referee provide a letter describing the person's impressions of you.

Although letters may be sent directly to the employer by the referee, you may wish to start your own collection of letters from people who have overseen your work. Whenever you leave a job or an educational institution, consider requesting a generic letter of recommendation. Then, when you are job-hunting, you can submit a photocopy of pertinent letters with your application package as additional substantiation of your claims. That way, a prospective employer can get a stronger impression of your strengths right away, a factor that might influence the decision to interview you.

There are several reasons why it can be a good idea to get copies of reference letters for your own files, particularly in the early stages of your career: people who know you and are familiar with your accomplishments can move on, retire, get promoted, or even pass away; they might also just plain forget you. A letter written when your performance is current and fresh in the person's mind will also be more enthusiastic and sound more genuine than a vague recollection written long after they are no longer seeing you every day. Finally, the act of writing a letter for you creates a record of the referee's impressions of your experience and capabilities. Then, should you later need to contact that same person for a reference, you can provide her with a copy of the earlier letter, which will refresh her memory should it have been a long time since she worked with you.

Employment references come from someone who has supervised you either at school or on the job and who is familiar enough with you and your work to provide meaningful feedback about your abilities and attitude. Prospective employers are mainly interested in your ability to do a job, and they will want this information from as objective and reliable a source as possible. Most employers no longer accept personal 'character references'.

When you are arranging for letters of recommendation, it is courteous to allow your referees plenty of time to prepare them. Since your former employers and professors are likely to be very busy, and a thoughtful and careful letter takes time to compose, last minute requests for letters may lead to disappointment. Give your referees enough time to write as carefully and thoughtfully as you, and they, would like.

The format for a recommendation letter is identical to that of other professional letters. If you are writing a letter for someone else, naming the person about whom you are writing in a 'Re' or subject line will help the reader more easily identify who is being described in the letter. The writer of a letter of recommendation should take care that the content and focus of the letter demonstrate the writer's own credibility. The referee must also consider the needs of the reader and provide answers to the questions the employer is most concerned about. No matter who is writing the letter of recommendation, its contents are approximately the same.

1. *How long, and in what context, have you known the person you are writing about?*
   The writer must indicate their relationship (supervisor? employer? instructor? academic advisor?) to the job applicant, and the length of time that the writer served in that capacity.

2. *What is your estimation of this person as an employee or a professional or, if it's an educational reference, as a student?* The writer should provide some specific examples—mention grades achieved, work completed, duties performed in the position, record of advancement, quality of work, or outstanding achievements.
3. *What is your estimation of the subject's personality?* Employers want to know what kind of person they are considering for a position. Will she get along with others? Is he flexible? Cooperative? Reliable? Personable? Stable? Motivated?
4. *Close with a strong statement of recommendation for the person* and invite the employer to contact you for further information. A reference writer who can't strongly recommend the applicant should not be writing the letter in the first place.

When you are applying for work and considering your choices for referees, you should approach only those who know your work and who are in a position to offer a positive assessment. Be sure that the person approached can and will give you a positive recommendation; a lukewarm or unenthusiastic letter can be worse than a negative evaluation.

If the person is unsure of what should go into the letter, don't be afraid to offer some guidance. Suggest that the person comment upon the three major areas above and emphasize any qualities that are important to the job you will be seeking. To assist your referee in writing knowledgeably and convincingly about your suitability for the job, provide a copy of the job advertisement or description, along with a copy of your transcript and updated résumé and any other information that is required.

If the letter is to be sent directly to the employer, make sure your referee has the correct name and address of the person, and offer to supply pre-addressed envelopes and postage. If you are collecting the letter for your own files, ask for a general letter addressed 'To Whom It May Concern', and explain to the referee that the letter will be kept for your own files and potentially used for future job searches.

Recognize that the person who writes a letter of recommendation for your job search is doing you a favour. Be sure not to take this support for granted; always thank those who have written you letters.

After you have been working for a few years, you may well be in the position to write letters for others, just as your referees are now doing for you. When that day comes, you should try to adhere to the following principles:

1. Avoid writing letters of recommendation for someone you cannot recommend positively. If you don't feel you can write enthusiastically in the person's behalf, politely suggest that the person contact someone else.
2. Follow the guidelines above to help you decide what to say in your letter of recommendation. As well, ask the applicant to provide you with a copy of the job posting, an up-to-date résumé, and any additional information about what is expected.
3. Be sure the applicant has provided you with the correct name and address of the person to whom the letter is addressed, if it is to be sent directly; if not, address your letter 'To Whom It May Concern'.

Sample letters of recommendation

Figure 9.10 demonstrates an ineffective letter of recommendation; Figures 9.11 and 9.12 show effective letters.

Bob's Building

2450 Schindelhauer Hill Road • Saint John, NB • E6Y 4R7 • (506) 234 5098

To: Whom It May Concern
From: Robert Clowney, Jr., Foreman and Manager

The purpose of this correspondence is to verify the employment of Mr. Shawn Horton with our firm.

Mr. Horton, was in our employ during summer, 2002. During this time he performed the duties assigned to him. His personnel file contains no records of complaints received about his work.

Mr. Horton seeks another position. Because of the usual vagaries of construction considerations, not the least of which, the fiscal restraints have mitigated against a permanent position at our facility. I share Mr. Horton's anxiety for his security.

Sincerely,

Robert Clowney

Robert Clowney, Jr
Foreman and Manager

Figure 9.10:   What qualities make this letter unsuitable for Shawn to include with his applications?

City Electrical
4531 Victoria Avenue
Vancouver, BC V7J 4T6

April 12, 2010

To Whom It May Concern:

Re: Ghirmay Zakaluzny

As Manager of City Electrical, I have had the pleasure of supervising Ghirmay during his apprenticeship from the Electrical Engineering Technician Program at West Coast College.

Since joining our firm two years ago, Ghirmay has been consistently dedicated and eager to learn. He has willingly taken on all jobs assigned to him and has been quick to learn new techniques. Despite the rapid expansion in his skills, he is both efficient and reliable, and has performed well above the recommended standard for apprentice electricians. He has even offered some valuable suggestions for improving our job tracking and scheduling process.

I have been thoroughly satisfied with Ghirmay's work and his professionalism. He is cooperative, dedicated, and personable, and he interacts effectively with customers and staff alike. His good humour is apparent in everything he does, and his skill in handling customer enquiries and complaints has earned him extra respect from his co-workers.

I can recommend Ghirmay, without hesitation, as an outstanding employee and co-worker, and would be pleased to elaborate on these comments by phone. I may be reached at (604) 897-0612.

Sincerely,

Mike Dharmaratnan

Figure 9.11: Note that this letter satisfies the questions an employer is likely to have and that it supports its claims with examples.

Western Plains University
PO Box 666, Calgary, AB T2K 3M4

Dr. P. Ramamurthy
Department of Mechanical Engineering
McMaster University
Hamilton, ON L8N 3T2

April 2, 2011

Dear Dr. Ramamurthy,

Re: Cameron Britten

In response to your e-mail of March 25, I am happy to recommend Cameron for a research assistantship.

I had the pleasure of teaching Cam in several courses in mechanical engineering, including MEng 351 — Engineering Design II. I was impressed from the start with Cam's technical competence and troubleshooting skills; he was able to grasp the problem quickly and isolate the issues that would be most challenging. He assumed leadership of his design group, and they produced one of the better solutions to their particular problem, building a full-scale prototype of their design for an automated tray-mover for a medical research lab. I believe that Cam and his team have been working with the client to create a modified version of the initial device that will be used in the lab. This group's design is among the best student work I've encountered in ten years in the program.

In addition to his technical skill, Cam also communicates effectively with others, particularly in a team environment. His presentations are also engaging and technically sound. He is not as strong a writer as some, but takes direction well and willingly edits. I am confident that, with time, his writing skills will develop the polish necessary for advancement in professional engineering.

If you're looking for a technically outstanding research assistant, a willing and disciplined worker, and a personable individual, I recommend Cameron Britten most highly. Please call me if you'd like to discuss his skills further.

Sincerely,

G.M. Hardbody
Department of Mechanical Engineering

Figure 9.12: A specific letter of recommendation is addressed to a particular individual, but it covers the same kinds of material as the general letter shown in Figure 9.11.

Your Online Job Search

Many contemporary employers use the Internet as part of their recruiting strategy. Job hunters, too, make use of websites and even social networking sites to help get their qualifications out there. Preparing an electronic application package requires similar care to creating a 'hard' copy, but there are a few differences that you will likely want to consider.

Posting your résumé to a website

If you decide to post your résumé on the Internet, whether to your own website or to a job-search site, you should probably choose a PDF format. That way, you can ensure that the page is readable and attractive, as well as consistent with the print version.

A major difference between distributing your print résumé to prospective employers and posting it online is the potential for violations of your privacy. An employer to whom you have sent a hard copy does not have a legal right to distribute or divulge the information on your résumé to anyone else without your explicit permission. By contrast, a résumé on a website is vulnerable to anyone who has access to the Internet. Once you have 'published' online, your work history and educational experience, along with every other piece of information contained in your résumé, are no longer private.

You may feel this to be a good thing if it brings you to the attention of an employer who wouldn't otherwise have seen your résumé; however, the risks may far outweigh the benefits. Even if it got you a dream job, placing private information on public view can have some negative, and even potentially disastrous, consequences, from identity theft to victimization by predators. Even in a hot job market, there is really little incentive for employers to cruise the web seeking unsolicited résumés, especially for entry-level positions. It is more efficient, and usually more effective, for them to post the job and wait for the candidates to come to them. The only people actively seeking your details may be those who hope to exploit the information for their own gain. For all of these reasons, you should exercise some caution about what you place online.

If you do decide to post your information, you should leave out details that might make it easy for someone to assume your identity or get access to your home address. For example, you should remove all contact information except your e-mail address. Criminals have been known to make use of personal information to establish false identities, potentially destroying the victim's credit rating, job prospects, or clean record.

As well, you may want to provide incomplete information about your credentials, to prevent others from securing copies of your degrees or transcripts or claiming these for their own, as recently happened in a highly publicized case at a Canadian university. For your own safety and security, you should not provide any information that might make you vulnerable to unwanted harassment or credential theft.[1] Instead, post an abridged version of the résumé and offer to provide a more detailed one should an employer be interested enough to contact you.

Searching the job market online

Although posting your résumé to a website and waiting for prospective employers to come to you is risky and most likely futile, the same cannot be said for using the Internet as a tool for your job search. Nearly all businesses post job openings on their websites, as do colleges, universities, and both provincial and federal governments. Many newspapers make their classified advertisements, including job ads, available online, and generic employment sites like <monster.ca> and <yahoojobs> list positions all over the country (though they may not have access to the best postings). Other possibilities for an online job search include professional and trade journals and magazines, and the websites of professional organizations, many of which regularly feature job ads for career-specific positions. There are also databases to which you can subscribe online that feature current job listings in a given field. Not all websites are completely reliable; you should make it a policy not to pay for access to job listings.

One very nice advantage of using the Internet to look for job opportunities is that you can locate openings not just locally but also in other cities or provinces, or even in the US or other foreign countries. Once you've found a position that interests you, you may even be able to submit your application online by sending your résumé and application letter as document attachments to an e-mail message.

If you are submitting an application electronically, you should be aware that many of the firms that accept electronic applications use search engines, rather than human readers, to screen résumés. You will want to be sure to include in your submission the key words employed in the posting for the job, or those that are currently 'hot' in the field in which you are applying; if the search engine does not pick these out, the résumé will be discarded.

You may wish to send your résumé in PDF format in order to preserve its appearance for the end reader. If the advertisement specifies that the file must be sent as a document file or RTF, you may wish to reconsider its layout; extensive formatting may not survive the translation from one word-processing program to another or from HTML format to text. In that case, try to simplify the layout and design so as not to rely on textual features like boldfacing, italics, or a variety of fonts, since these may not translate effectively, and may render your carefully worded application into gibberish. Simple effects like underlining and indentation will usually survive the translation into RTF format, and since this format can be opened successfully in any program, it's a good idea to send it as an RTF attachment if PDF is not acceptable.

Finally, try to keep your résumé as brief and simple as possible; the longer the document, the more likely there will be a problem with transmitting it, and the less likely that it will receive appropriate consideration at the other end. As well, always be sure to submit a cover letter along with the résumé, even for an electronic submission, since to neglect this important part of the application is to risk rejection. While there are currently no fixed standards for electronic submission, for reasons of consistency you should write a letter and send it as an attachment. This way, it's easier for the recipient to simply save and print without having to translate from an e-mail program to a word processor.

If you are looking for a position in another province or country, you should probably remember that some employers may still be reluctant to consider applicants who have to travel a long distance to the interview and may for this reason prefer local candidates. Nevertheless, the access to job listings provided by the Internet can be a major convenience for the applicant. While the Internet should probably not be the only resource you use for searching out employment opportunities, it is a useful source of information that can aid you in your job search. Even if you use it only as a research tool for gathering information about potential careers, the Internet can be a valuable addition to your job-seeking strategies.

If your application has been successful, the employer will be interested in talking with you about the position and will invite you for an interview. This second stage of the job-search process is every bit as important as the résumé preparation stage, and will be dealt with in the next chapter.

Critical Reading

Jennifer M. MacLennan and Brahm Neufeld, 'Showcasing Leadership Skills in the Résumé: A Case Study'
Jennifer M. MacLennan is the founding Academic Director of the Ron and Jane Graham Centre for the Study of Communication in the College of Engineering, University of

Saskatchewan, where she is also the first occupant of the D.K. Seaman Chair in Communication. Her research interests are wide-ranging, from exploring how rhetorical theory can enhance communication practice to studying how identity is formed and maintained on both personal and cultural levels. MacLennan is the author of seven communication textbooks and two practical books on design. She regularly presents talks and workshops on communication to a variety of professional, academic, and student groups and gatherings.

Brahm Neufeld is pursuing a bachelor's degree in Electrical Engineering at the University of Saskatchewan, and is enrolled in the Engineering Communication Option offered by the Graham Centre for the Study of Communication. He has spent four years (and counting) as a leader with Sci-Fi Science Camps, a non-profit, student-powered organization operated through the College of Engineering. The program's mission is to have all Saskatchewan youth experience science and technology through fun, hands-on activities, and reached nearly 13,000 youth in 2007 alone. In his spare time, Brahm enjoys playing soccer, database and web programming, and the electric guitar.

The case study below was developed for a course in Leadership as Communication. Students were asked to review and rank the résumés as if they were on the search committee, and then make their recommendations in a report to the FYep Coordinator, Corey Owen. Brahm Neufeld's report appears below.

The Scenario

Recently, Western Plains University advertised several student employment opportunities for peer advisors in the university's First Year Experience Program. These positions, aimed at second- and third-year students, will be part-time for the next academic year. The job of peer advisor involves leading a weekly one-hour seminar for a group of first-year students, in which the PA acts as a sort of mentor and academic coach. The PA is expected to teach study skills, provide information about university services, conduct field trips, host guest speakers from the university faculty and administration, and, of course, command the respect and confidence of the first-year charges. The advertisement emphasized the importance of leadership skills for these positions.

Among the applications received were the three résumés below. The FYep Coordinator directed the committee, which included several of last year's peer advisors, to evaluate the résumés on the basis of leadership potential or achievement, and asked them to look for evidence of the following specific qualities:

- initiative
- confidence
- articulateness
- decisiveness
- organizational skill
- integrity

- compassion
- humour
- character (ethos)
- skill/knowledge
- self-discipline
- honesty

- authority
- communication skill
- sociability
- empathy
- trustworthiness

The résumés themselves are shown below, just as the committee received them. Read them carefully and make your own judgement about how effectively they communicate the candidate's leadership potential. Before reading Brahm Neufeld's essay (page 321), record your impressions of these three candidates. Compare your assessments with Neufeld's.

Joe Blow
Box 123 Noseworthy Hall,
Calgary AB T1A 2B3
(403) 966-1234
<job123@wpu.ca>

Education:
   2008 Wayne Gretzky High School
       -Industrial Arts
   2008-Present Western Plains University
       -Second year in Agriculture program

Relavent Experience:
   May-August 2009 General labourer, Parks Department, Lloydminster
       Duties: Floating Ball Diamonds, mowing lawnblowing coarse, irrigation,
            maintenance of facilitys and machinery, grounds keeping, labourer on
            various projects, training new employees.

   June-August 2008 House construction; Columbine Zukovny,
       Duties: Wall consturction, cement pouring, shingling, hanging drywall, operating
            bobcat, errant running

   2003-2009 Farm labourer; Rod Mungo, Bach SK
       Duties: Operating tractors (rock picking, cultiovating, harrow-packing, stacking
            bales, and pull-tupe comgines), maintainence of vehicles and chores

References:
   Mr. Wade Grandoni
       Teacher-Wayne Gretzky High School
       454-5665

   Mr. Jim Drimble
       Labourer-Parks Dept: City of Red Deer
       998-3434

   Mr. Columbine Zukovny
       Carpenter-self-employed
       554-3332

Reggie Armbruster   Home: (905) 424-7669

183 Haggarty St., Oster, ON L2Z 4B5   Cell: (905) 222-1718

Education

2008-Present   **Electrical Engineering**
Sept 2002-Dec 2003   Central Maritime University, Truro, NS
                                    Course completed:
                                    • Computer Science
                                    • Microprocessor Hardware & Software
                                    • Hardware Descriptive Languages
                                    • Power Systems 1
                                    • Spectrum Analysis & Discrete Time Systems
                                    • Electronic Devices
                                    • Several mathematics classes
                                    • Engineering Design II
                                    • Electrical Engineering Lab II
                                    Currently enrolled in:
                                    • Electric Machines 1
                                    • Communication Systems
                                    • VLSI Circuit Design

Skills
Technical:
• Able to perform lab tests (measuring current, voltage, change in states, etc) on both analog and digital electrical components (resistors, transistors, integrated circuits etc)
• Able to build, simulated and tested multiple FPGA programs
• Able to program and debug Intel 8051 and Motorola 68HC11 microprocessors
• Trained to solder and inspect electronig assemblies to Class 2 specifications

Computer:
· Programming in C++, Visual C++, Visual Basic, and Verilog
· Proficient in Windows 9x/XP, MS Office, Matlab, Autodesk Inventor 9.0, and Maple

Relevant Experience:
   Jan 2008   **ABC Industries**
   Sep 2008   Assistant Shop Manager
                                    • Responsible for operations on production line
                                    • Maintain shop equipment
                                    • Trained in use and maintenance of CNC router
                                    • Trained in forklift operations

- Received training in lean manufacturing procedures and applications

Jan2006-
Jan 2007
Redline Cabs
Computer Programmer
- Responsbile for designing, programming, debugging and updating receipt database

Additional Experience:

Jan 2004-
Present
Railway Gas and Convenience
Cashier

Dec 2003-
Aug 2007
McDonalds
Crew Person
- Trained in grill, drive thru and shipment
- Operated POS cash system
- Trained in WHIMS safety procedures
- Member of Occupational Health & Safety Committee

Volunteer Experience

2009
Lounge Director
Central Maritime Engineering Students Society

2008
Group Leader for Orientation 2005
Central Maritime University

Interests:

- Electronics
- Skiing
- Reading·

- Car audio & security
- Car restoration
- Photography

References

Wayne Loftus, Shop Supervisor, ABC Industries

Bus: (905) 656 9897
Home: (905) 222 8728

Claudio Melina, Operations Manager, Redline Cabs

Bus: (905) 442 7683
Home: (905) 733 2875

Leona Wiley, 1st Assistant Manager, Macdonald's

Bus: (905) 599 5579
Home: (905) 561 7022

Jeanine Alteen

Current Address (until May 12, 2007)	**Permanent Address:**
Box 292, Campus Residence	21 Rook St
West Coast University College	Innisfree, AB T9P 1W9
Burnaby, BC V6J 2T7 Canada	
Phone: N/A	(403) 345-1267
sea459@wcuc.ca	

Education

West Coast University College, Burnaby BC   2009-Present
Major: Criminology

James Barber Comprehensive High School   2005-2009
High School Diploma and International Baccalaureate Diploma

Relevant Experience

General Service Employee
Innisfree Fair Grounds, Innisfree AB
   -Set up and take down for events including horse shows, banquets, concerts and the Three
   Hills Exhibition and Fair
   -Operated forklifts and floor scrubbers
   -Performed minor maintenance where ever needed

Lifeguard/Instructor
Innisfree Aquatics Centre, Innisfree AB
   -Performed regular lifeguard duties which focused on safety
   -Cleaning duties included staff area, pool deck, change rooms & bathrooms
   -Public relations such as pool bookings, answering phones and dealing with complaints
   -Performed minor maintenance

Bay Attendant
Jumbo Carwash, Innisfree AB
   -Washed bays with a pressure washer
   -Dealt with customer complaints
   -Performed minor maintenance such as repairing pressure washer guns

Relevant Skills

Safety

Awards are not current:
- -National Lifeguard Service
- -First Aid and CPR C
- -Water Safety Instructor

Communication Skills
- -Currently taking Public Speaking and Professional Communication courses
- -Able to work in groups or independently
- -Experience with public relations

Volunteering
- -Innisfree Regional Hospital   September 2009-June 2009

References

Maude MacLeod	Craig Steel	Roberta Greenwood
Aquatics Director	Asst. Operations Manager	Owner
Town of Innisfree	Innisfree Fair Grounds	Jumbo Carwash
Innisfree, AB	Innisfree, AB	Innisfree, AB
(403) 727-3836	(403) 434-6700	(403) 434-5300

Brahm Neufeld, 'An Assessment of Candidate Résumés for the FYep Program'

TO: Corey Owen, First Year Experience Program
FROM: Brahm Neufeld
RE: Peer Advisor Candidates

After reviewing the résumés of Joe, Reggie, and Jeanine I am hesitant to recommend that you interview any of them for the peer advisor position. If you are unable to repost the job, or if we simply must interview one of the three, I would recommend you interview Jeanine, followed by Reggie if Jeanine is unavailable. We do not need to interview Joe. I'll explain my rationale starting from the bottom, up.

I could go through your bulleted list of characteristics one-by-one for Joe Blow, but I'll save the printer toner and simply say that his application lacked meaningful content across the board. His one redeeming point was that he 'trained new employees' while he was a labourer for the Parks Department, but given that he did not expand on that point I can't assume it included any significant amount of leadership or effort. I did also not see any evidence of achievement in his résumé, academic or otherwise, unless you count his specialization in 'Industrial Arts' in his five-year high school career.

Reggie's application was significantly better, but Joe was not much of a benchmark. I appreciate Reggie including his academics—at least it shows he (probably) knows something about study skills. I would have liked for him to give us an indication of his academic standing, and also expand more on his group leader position for Orientation in 2002. What made me raise an eyebrow—the reason I believe Reggie isn't much of a leader—is that he spent six years working at McDonald's as just a crew person. Overall I saw some hints of sociability and trustworthiness/dependability in his application, but not much else.

Jeanine's résumé was the best of the three applications but far from the best I have ever seen. Her life-guarding achievements show self-discipline, authority, and empathy, and we know that her communication classes will hopefully make her a more skilled communicator than her peers. She has some volunteer experience and some public relations experience. On the other hand, I'd like to review the job posting we sent out because I don't find fork-lifting and floor scrubbing 'relevant experience' for peer advising.

If Jeanine's application was the best one we received, we need to review how we advertise these positions. Having a job posting that clearly states some basic requirements would be a good start and having an information session for potential applicants may also be a good idea. In that session we would be able to go over many aspects of the job including our expectations—this will give candidates a chance to deliver some very custom-tailored résumés that highlight nothing but their relevant experience. We should interview Jeanine if we have to, but I believe we will have better luck by re-posting the job.

Improved Résumés for the FYep Candidates

Below you will see improved résumés for each of the three candidates, showing how each might better have showcased the leadership skills required for the position of peer advisor. Although intangibles like leadership are challenging to establish through a résumé, these improved versions show that it is possible to do a much better job than any of the three did in their original submissions. Nothing has been added to the students' experience; the changes have all been in emphasis, wording, and targeting.

Compare these improved documents with the originals to see what changes have been made.

Joe Blow
Box 123 Noseworthy Hall, Calgary, AB T1A 2B3
(403) 966-1234   <job123@wpu.ca>

Education

2008– Present	**Agricultural Science Program** Western Plains University, Calgary, AB • Currently in second year (will graduate in 2008) • Relevant courses include Foundations of Professional Communication and Introduction to Business Management
2008	**High School Diploma** Wayne Gretzky High School, Lloydminster, AB • Graduated with distinction

Work Experience

Summer 2009	**Outdoor Maintenance** Parks Department, Lloydminster, AB • Duties primarily included maintenance and groundskeeping • Participated in the training of other employees
Summer 2008	**Construction Assistant** Zukovny Renovations, Lloydminster, AB • Drywalling, carpentry, and general labour on construction sites • Operated heavy machinery
2003– 2009	**Farm Labourer** Rod Mungo, Bach, SK • Operated tractors for a variety of farm-related tasks • Performed routine maintenance of vehicles

Comments

• Worked part time throughout high school to save for university
• Self-supporting in university (personal savings and scholarships; no student loans)
• Disciplined and motivated worker

References

Attached

Reggie Armbruster

Home: (905) 424-7669

183 Haggarty St., Oster, ON L2Z 4B5

Cell: (905) 222-1718

EDUCATION

2008–
Present

Electrical Engineering
Central Maritime University, Truro, NS
Currently in 3rd year
Scheduled to graduate in 2009

SKILLS

Detail-oriented (trained to perform sensitive laboratory and inspection tests)
Proficient in several computer languages and software packages
Experienced in managing a workplace environment
Experienced student leader

VOLUNTEER EXPERIENCE

2009

Lounge Director
Central Maritime Engineering Students Society
- Responsible for open/close of facility
- Responsible for keeping users from getting too rowdy

2008

Group Leader for Orientation 2005
Central Maritime University
- Directed a group of Orientation Volunteers
- Participated in Volunteer Training

EMPLOYMENT

Jan 2009–
Present

Railway Gas and Convenience
Cashier
- Handled cash, credit cards, and general business transactions
- Responsible for open/close

Jan 2008–
Sep 2008

ABC Industries
Assistant Shop Manager
- Responsible for operations on production line
- Trained in lean manufacturing procedures and applications

Jan2006–
Jan 2007

Redline Cabs
Computer Programmer
- Responsbile for designing, programming, debugging, and updating receipt database

Dec 2001–	**McDonald's**
Aug 2007	Crew Person

- Worked throughout high school
- Trained in WHIMS safety procedures
- Member of Occupational Health & Safety Committee

REFERENCES

Wayne Loftus, Shop Supervisor, ABC Industries   Bus: (905) 656-9897
Home: (905) 222-8728

Claudio Melina, Operations Manager, Redline Cabs   Bus: (905) 442-7683
Home: (905) 733-2875

Leona Wiley, 1st Assistant Manager, McDonald's   Bus: (905) 599-5579
Home: (905) 561-7022

Jeanine Alteen

Current Address (until May 12, 2007):
Box 292, Campus Residence
West Coast University College
Burnaby, BC V6J 2T7
Phone: N/A
sea459@wcuc.ca

Permanent Address:
21 Rook St
Innisfree, AB T9P 1W9
Canada
(403) 345-1267

Education

West Coast University College, Burnaby BC   2009–Present
Major: Criminology
Relevant Courses: Developmental Psychology, Sociology, Introduction to Professional
Communication, Public Speaking

James Barber Comprehensive High School   2005–2009
High School Diploma and International Baccalaureate Diploma

Relevant Experience

Lifeguard/Instructor   2003–2009
Innisfree Aquatics Centre, Innisfree, AB
Relevant Responsibilities: Supervising pool users to ensure public safety; providing swimming
and pool-safety instruction

Other Experience

Volunteer   Sept.–June 2008
Innisfree Regional Hospital

General Service Employee   Summer 2004
Innisfree Fair Grounds, Innisfree, AB

Bay Attendant   Summer 2003
Jumbo Carwash, Innisfree, AB

Relevant Skills

- Have completed courses in First Aid, CPR, and Water Safety Instruction
- Currently taking Public Speaking and Professional Communication courses
- Experience in handling customer complaints and in working with groups and the public

References

Maude MacLeod	**Craig Steel**	**Roberta Greenwood**
Aquatics Director	Asst. Operations Manager	Owner
Town of Innisfree	Innisfree Fair Grounds	Jumbo Carwash
Innisfree, AB	Innisfree, AB	Innisfree, AB
(403) 727-3836	(403) 434-6700	(403) 434-5300

Points to Remember

1. The purpose of the application package is to secure an interview by persuading the employer of your suitability for the job.
2. An effective résumé is always 'targeted' to the reader's needs, values, and expectations; study job postings in your field to help out with this process.
3. Prepare your résumé and application letter carefully to showcase your strengths, not emphasize your weaknesses.

4. Use the principles of relevance and recency to organize your résumé. Choose appropriate categories, and arrange information in reverse chronological order within each.
5. Be sure to provide a focus for your résumé, tailored to the job you seek.
6. Remember that your résumé will not be read in isolation; it will always be compared to those of other applicants for the same job.
7. Always proofread carefully, and remember to apply the Seven Cs of professional writing.
8. If you are submitting an application electronically, use PDF format. If you must submit a document file, simplify your document design, use RTF format, and be sure to include both a résumé and a letter as part of your package.
9. Exercise caution about the amount of detailed information you post online.

Key Concepts

analytical résumé	initiative	relevance
career objective	key terms analysis	responsibility
chronological résumé	letter of application	reverse chronological order
content	logos	Seven Cs
cover letter	loyalty	skills
dependability	needs and expectations	solicited
energy	nonverbal cues	stability
enthusiasm	pathos	targeted résumé
ethos	personability	targeting
functional résumé	purpose	unsolicited
honesty	recency	visual impact

Assignments and Exercises

1. Collect as many job advertisements as you can find from newspapers, flyers, websites, or the placement office of your college. You can look only at jobs related to your field or scan a broad cross-section in all fields. Study them carefully and circle key words—that is, those that appear most frequently and that seem to be most important. Based on your survey, what are the skills that employers seem to value most? Which ones are in greatest demand in your field? Compare your findings with those of others in your class; what implications can you draw for preparing your own job application?
2. Prepare your own application package, including a complete application letter, a résumé of your experience and education, a completed job application form, and a letter of recommendation. Be sure to provide your instructor with a copy of the position advertisement.

Chapter 10

The Job Interview

Learning Objectives

- To learn what employers are looking for in interviews.
- To become familiar with typical job interview situations.
- To learn common interview questions and strategies for answering them.
- To learn what goes into the follow-up letter of thanks.

© iStockphoto.com

Once you have submitted your application package, you will wait anywhere from two weeks to two months for a response. In some cases, you will hear from the employer only if the company has decided to interview you. If they are interested in speaking with you regarding an interview, a representative of the company will likely telephone you.

The interview process begins as soon as the employer calls you to set up a meeting. For this reason, while you are conducting a job search, it's a good idea to think about the professional impression created by the message on your answering machine, or by those who may answer the phone at the contact number you have provided to employers. Caution everyone that you are seeking work, and that employers may telephone looking for you, and ensure that each person knows to take a message for you detailing the name of the caller and the company he or she represents, the telephone number where that person may be reached, and the time of the call. Ask them to record any other information that is provided, and to be sure to leave the message where you can readily find it so that you can respond promptly.

If you use an answering machine, here's something to consider. An employer I recently interviewed had just telephoned a job applicant, only to find herself confronted with a long and inane answering machine message. Like many busy employers, she resented the waste of her time. The effect on her opinion of the candidate could not have been worse, since it undermined the person's credibility by creating the impression that he lacked professional **judgement**. This employer did not leave a message; instead, she telephoned the second candidate on her list and offered that person an interview. I am sure that the first candidate still has no idea why he did not get a call.

A good rule to follow is this: a contact number left for work purposes should not waste the caller's time with 'humourous' messages. At least while you are job hunting, keep the message on your answering machine simple and professional. Silly messages, especially if they are long, may make a negative impression on an employer who has not yet met you. Don't risk losing an interview by frustrating someone who calls for work reasons.

We have already considered the implications of social networking sites and weblogs for your professional communication, and particularly for your job search. Despite claims to the contrary, you should always consider the information you post to these sites to be public because they can easily be accessed and read by nearly anyone. As well, because material posted on the Internet is permanent, you should exercise caution and good judgement about what you place online; your words create an indelible record that can affect how you are seen by employers and potential colleagues and clients, not just now but years from now. Don't jeopardize your future professionalism and success by carelessly placing online things that could compromise your ethos. No matter how private your enclave on Facebook may seem, it is public space, and you should not post anything that you would not be happy to see broadcast on television or displayed in a store window.

The Interview

The interview is the employer's chance to get to know you in person, to determine if you are right for the job. Typically you will meet face to face with one or more people, who will ask you questions and possibly have you complete some technical tasks or write some tests. Interviews can last anywhere from fifteen minutes to several hours, or they can stretch over several days.

In the interview, you will want to maintain the positive impression you created with your résumé and application, since the employer's first impression of you will strongly influence any decision to hire you. This decision is made in many cases within the first minute of the interview, during the employer's first reaction to you; if this impression is negative, the employer may spend the rest of the interview looking for faults to justify this dislike. It's obviously in your best interest to make the employer's first response to you a positive one. You should do all you can to prepare yourself, and thus give yourself an advantage.

A successful interview, like other effective professional communication, depends partly on your preparation. Before your interview, think carefully about the needs and interests of your audience—the person who may be paying your salary. What does that person want in an employee? What will the recruiter be looking for?

Although you cannot completely predict the interviewer's response to you, there are three aspects of that initial impression that you can control so as to make it a good one: your **appearance**, your **attitude**, and your **background knowledge**.

Appearance

An employer is seeking indications that you can demonstrate professional and appropriate judgement in a work situation. One of the easiest ways for the recruiter to assess your professionalism is to assess your appearance. Here are some tips for making a positive impression.

Dress appropriately

For an interview, you should wear slightly more formal attire than you would wear on the job. For professional or office jobs, wear relatively conservative clothes: a suit is fine for both men and women, though a jacket and dress pants or a dress and jacket may serve the purpose. If you are applying for a labour or other blue-collar job, or for a technical position in the field, a suit might be considered overdressed. Instead, wear dress casuals and a shirt or sweater. In every case, your clothes should also be comfortable enough that you don't have to repeatedly adjust or fiddle with them. No matter what you're wearing, be sure you're neat and clean; avoid splashy colours or unusual hairdos, and leave the nose ring at home.

Be punctual

Arrive at the interview with a few minutes to spare, but not more than 15 minutes early. Know how long it will take you to arrive by whatever means you're travelling and allow yourself enough time for delays. Be sure to take a watch.

Occasionally, there may be a legitimate reason why you have to be late—car trouble, an accident, or an illness. If this happens to you, telephone the interviewer immediately to explain the situation and politely request a later interview. If you miss your interview, you should not count on being given a second chance; sometimes the employer will be unable or unwilling to reschedule, and you will just have to give up on that job. You should also be aware that even legitimate lateness may create a negative impression that damages your chances, so allow extra time just to be safe. Sleeping in or misjudging how long it takes to get to the interview are *not* acceptable reasons for being late.

Go alone to the interview

An interview is a formal meeting, not a social event, and bringing someone with you may cause the interviewer to question your maturity or your awareness of appropriate professional behaviour. A confident applicant is more likely to get the job, and you won't look confident if you bring someone else along.

Shake hands when offered

It is considered rude to refuse a **handshake** for other than religious reasons. Use a firm, confident grip; don't let your hand hang limply, but be sure not to grip too tightly either. As silly as it sounds, it's a good idea to practise your handshake with a friend before going to your first interview.

Do not chew gum or expect to smoke

Gum-chewing is just tacky, and smoking is never permitted in today's smoke-free workplaces. If you are a smoker, expect to go for long periods without a cigarette. As well, you should try not to smoke just before going in to the interview. Non-smoking interviewers can be put off by the reek of second-hand smoke on a candidate.

Make eye contact

Though some people avoid eye contact simply because they are nervous, this habit can make a very negative impression on an interviewer. It can suggest uncertainty or even dishonesty, neither of which will further your chances. Don't stare at the floor or ceiling or avoid meeting the interviewer's eyes; instead, make eye contact frequently and comfortably, but do look away occasionally to avoid appearing overly aggressive.

Speak clearly and use correct grammar

Employers do judge applicants' intelligence and education by the way they speak. Don't mumble or chew your words; instead, pay attention to your enunciation, and avoid littering your comments with fillers. Poor grammar is another pet peeve of interviewers. Watch out for such pitfalls as 'I seen', 'I done', 'I did good in that course', or 'between you and I', and avoid slang expressions.

Watch your body language

Sit comfortably without slumping in your chair or hooking your feet around the chair legs. Don't fidget, tap your fingers, or fiddle with your clothes. You should appear self-controlled, and any of these is a clear message that you are unduly nervous or inexperienced. Excessive fidgeting can actually compromise your credibility because it signals that you are not in command of the situation or of yourself. Don't block your view of the employer, or the employer's of you, with a large briefcase or other unnecessary props. If you are carrying supporting materials in a briefcase, place the case on the floor beside you rather than in the way on the desk.

Attitude

Many interviewers agree that a good attitude is one of the most important things an applicant can bring to the interview. You should appear confident and positive. Although you will most likely feel, and the employer will expect, a little nervousness, you should try to be as relaxed and comfortable as you can. Be yourself—at your very best.

Avoid bragging or overstating your abilities

Employers will be put off by displays of arrogance. Be alert and attentive to questions, enthusiastic and sincere in your answers. Show a willingness to learn and grow with the organization; no matter how much you feel you already know, there is always something else to learn.

Avoid one-word responses

Try to answer questions fully; one-word answers may seem curt or uncooperative. At the same time, don't take over the interview with rambling or overly long replies. Watch the interviewer for cues that will signal when to stop speaking.

Show some interest and direction

You should display an interest in the profession itself or in the organization where you are interviewing, and a sense of what you want from your career over the long haul. Employers like someone who has thought about the future and can show some direction. You may display ambition, but don't give the impression that you expect to run the company right away. Indicate a willingness to work hard and start at a reasonable level.

Don't appear obsessed with money, benefits, or vacations

Remember that the goal of the interviewer is to find out what you can do for the company, not to hear what it can do for you. In most cases, you should not raise the question of salary or benefits until you have received an offer of employment.

Emphasize what you can offer, not what you can gain

Although you will want to demonstrate drive and a reasonable level of ambition, you should avoid stressing how you can benefit from the position at the expense of showing how you can contribute to the company. You should especially avoid talking about how much you need the job. Desperation in a candidate is a huge turn-off for the interviewer.

Be courteous at all times

Don't do or say anything that could be considered rude or discourteous. Remember this especially when you enter and are met by a receptionist or an administrative assistant: rudeness to these people can cost you the job offer, since they often are part of the screening process. Among other things, the employer wants to know how well you will get along with other people in the organization, and one measure of this is how you treat people you meet on the way in. Always remember that first impressions count!

Background knowledge

Employers are interested in discovering just how well you understand what will be expected of you in the position you've applied for; they will want you to demonstrate the skills that you have claimed on your résumé. You should naturally be prepared to discuss your experience, always remembering to show how it is relevant to the position you are looking for.

But there's much more on the employer's mind. Although primarily interested in what you know about the duties of the job, your prospective employer will be impressed if you can demonstrate knowledge of the company's mission or mandate. Try to learn as much as you can about the firm before the interview, for example, how large it is and what products or services it offers. You can find out a little about the company by checking on the Internet or looking in your local library. Here are some questions you might consider answering for yourself before the interview.

1. What is the exact nature of the company—who are their clients, and what do they make or do?
2. Is it a local firm, a national company, or a multinational?
3. What is the company's mission statement?
4. How extensive is their client base?
5. How long has the company been in operation?
6. What is their organizational style?

An annual report (often found online) will give you this information and more that might be useful. If you know someone who works for the organization, try to talk to that person before your interview. Visit the company website when you are preparing for the interview. It will provide you with important information about how the company sees itself. Find out as much as you can. Though you may not be asked such questions in the interview, the more you know when you go in, the more confident you will be and the better impression you will make. You can adapt your answers to highlight your commitment to the company's ethos.

Typical Interview Questions

Although the list of typical interview questions is very long, in fact there are only three things that an employer really wants to know, and all of the recruiter's questions are aimed at answering one or more of these questions. These three factors are:

1. *Can you do the job?* That is, do you have not only the necessary education, but also the aptitude and ability to do what the job requires? Not everyone with the same qualifications on paper is equally qualified for the position, and the interview is designed to assess your level of ability and skill.
2. *Are you a willing worker?* That is, do you have a good work ethic, and the **self-discipline** and commitment to carry through on what you are assigned to do? Employers also want some indication that you are self-aware, that you know yourself and have thought about your goals, and that you have realistic expectations. They will also be interested to see if you can effectively solve the problems you are likely to face on the job.
3. *Are you a good fit?* In other words, do you have a positive attitude, and can you fit in with the existing personnel and culture? All the technical skill in the world won't make up for an employee with a bad attitude, who can't get along with co-workers, who will not cooperate, and who whines and blames others. Every employer knows that such people are far more trouble than they are worth.

Box 10.1   Three Things Every Employer Wants to Know

- Can you do the job?
- Are you a willing worker?
- Are you a good fit?

Thus, though every interview is different, and interviewers have different styles, there are some questions that occur regularly in one form or another. You will find that many interviews focus more on your personal qualities than on your particular specialized or technical qualifications, which are spelled out in the résumé and application materials you've submitted beforehand, and which are also guaranteed by your professional or technical training or education. Although it is possible that you may face an aptitude or skills test of some form in the interview process, employers are often more interested in using the opportunity of a face-to-face meeting to explore the kind of employee you will be than they are in assessing your technical knowledge. Among the qualities that an employer is seeking are **motivation**, **maturity** and **self-reflectiveness**, **leadership** and **interpersonal skills**, an ethical orientation, and effective communication abilities. As a result, they will often employ questioning strategies that are designed to elicit information about your attitudes, your priorities, and your **self-awareness**.

As you read through the questions below, you should carefully consider what the employer may be interested in learning from your answer; chances are it's not factual information as much as information about your general attitude, **self-knowledge**, work ethic, and ability to work well with others. As you consider how you would answer each of the following, think about the probable needs and interests of the employer, and try to tailor your response to fit the job you're applying for.

You should never memorize a prepared answer or try to bluff the employer by pretending to be something you're not; instead, think of strategies you would use for answering each question and consider specific examples from your experience that would serve as concrete illustrations of the qualities the employer is seeking. When you're at the interview, be sure to answer each question as fully and sincerely as possible, and be sure to provide an example from your background that supports your answer.

Finally, if you're applying for a position in a technical field, you may have assumed that questions about philosophy, cultural interests, or pleasure reading are irrelevant. You couldn't be more wrong. In many cases, you will be interviewed by non-technical people whose job is to determine such intangibles as attitude and ability to interact effectively with co-workers, management, and clients. Such questions offer a very effective way for an employer to probe these qualities and to gauge your ability to get along with others.

Below are some samples of favourite employer questions, with strategies for answering them. If you think about these, and about some potential answers, before you go to any interview, you will have a better chance of handling the questions effectively. Remember that the employer is looking for someone who is motivated, capable, and able to get along with other employees. You should try to respond in ways that will showcase your abilities to do those things, and always support your answers with specific examples from your experience.

Questions about self-knowledge and awareness

Employers often begin an interview with a question designed to elicit information about your level of self-knowledge, and then follow up with several more over the course of the interview. Personal attitude can be probed using questions about your general approach to life. Once again, these questions have no simple 'right' answer, but the way in which you choose to respond will tell the employer much about what you think is important, about the kind of person you are and the general attitudes of tolerance, cooperation, reliability, tenacity, and good will you bring to the job.

Box 10.2   Self-knowledge and Awareness Questions

- Tell me about yourself.
- How would your friends describe you?
- Do you have a personal philosophy? What is it?
- Have you ever been under pressure? How do you handle it?
- Describe your strengths. How do you know these are strengths of yours?
- What are your weaknesses? What are you doing to correct them?
- What can you bring to this job that nobody else can?
- What strategies do you use to adapt to change?
- How do you like to spend your leisure time?
- If you could leave me with one lasting impression, what would you want that impression to be?
- Why should we hire you?

In answering any of these questions, keep in mind the probable needs and interests of all employers: they will be looking for someone who is confident and capable, but not arrogant or self-absorbed. In inviting you to talk about yourself, an employer is interested primarily in information relevant to the position you've applied for, your work attitude, and your ability to adapt to the vision of the organization. Be honest and appropriately modest, but not overly so; be confident, but not arrogant. Show that you have both strengths and weaknesses, but that your weaknesses are not serious and can be overcome. Don't cite weaknesses or flaws in character that are likely to damage your employment chances.

When responding to a question such as 'tell me about yourself', avoid the temptation to deliver the epic of your life. You might present a brief summary of educational and employment highlights, as they have prepared you for the job in question, or you could choose to focus on a dominant interest that has guided your career choices so far, such as 'My primary motivation is my love of building things' or 'All my life, in one way or another, I have been a coach and trainer.' Follow up this initial claim with a few examples.

As for strengths and weaknesses, a mature person knows what his or her strong points are and can state them briefly without either bragging or understating them; such a person is also able to acknowledge weaknesses and take responsibility for them. Before heading to the interview, take some time to identify the things you do really well; go back over the skills section of your résumé and be ready with some examples. When it comes to identifying weaknesses, you should use good judgement; avoid describing yourself in terms that would make an employer think twice about hiring you: such comments as 'I have trouble finishing what I start' or 'I can't get motivated in the morning' may put an employer off. Instead, try to follow up with a statement about how you are working to overcome the weaknesses you have identified, balancing the negative with a positive. For example, 'I sometimes find it hard to take criticism, but even though I find it difficult to hear, I usually end up benefiting from constructive comments', or 'I'm not really a morning person, but I find that using that time for routine tasks helps me to get focused on the big jobs when I get to them later in the day.'

Finally, you should avoid giving an overused, predictable response, such as 'I'm a workaholic.' Every recruiter has heard this same claim from so many applicants that it's hard to take it seriously, even in cases where it may be true. Above all, make sure you are sincere in your answers. An experienced interviewer can recognize phoney or insincere answers and will reject an applicant she believes is misrepresenting herself.

Questions about work ethic and self-discipline

Box 10.3 Work Ethic and Self-discipline Questions

- Why do you want this job?
- Why do you want to work for us?
- In what ways do you think you can contribute to our mandate?
- What qualities of yours make you the best candidate for this position?
- What made you choose this field as your career?
- What job have you had that you've liked the least? The most? Why?
- What was your favourite subject in college, university, or school? Your least favourite?
- Why are your grades only average?
- What strategies do you use to adapt to change?
- What is your biggest criticism of your college program?
- What specific strategies do you use to organize your time?

While there are no 'correct' answers to these questions, you should pay attention to the sincerity and credibility of your answers, and to the likely interests, needs, and expectations of the person who is asking the question. Your research into the company will give you some information that may help you to develop your response. You should never identify pay or benefits as a primary reason for your choice of career, nor should you suggest that you've chosen your path simply because 'This is the field my dad [or mom] works in.' Instead, show that you have put some thought into your choice, and emphasize the intrinsic appeal of the work itself or its fit with your particular abilities and interests.

Frequently, questions that ask you to pass judgement or assess the value of some experience or event are intended to elicit information about your attitude and judgement and your willingness to take responsibility. Weak answers typically blame others or show a lack of insight or exaggerated sense of entitlement. They may also reveal whether a candidate is a chronic complainer. Consider what the following responses would sound like to an employer:

- 'Working at the burger joint is an okay part-time job for other people, but I knew I was better than that.'
- 'I hated my last job because I worked with a bunch of jerks.'
- 'I didn't like Statistics because my professor was so terrible.'

Questions about general attitude, judgement, and maturity

> ### Box 10.4   General Attitude, Judgement, and Maturity Questions
>
> - What was the last book you read purely for personal interest?
> - Give me an example of a situation in which you faced and resolved an ethical dilemma.
> - Describe an instance in which you handled criticism.
> - Have you ever been under pressure? How did you handle it?
> - Have you ever made a serious mistake? What was it, and how did you respond?
> - Are your grades a good indication of what kind of employee you will be?
> - What did your college program fail to teach you that you should have learned? What did they teach you that you didn't need to know?
> - Would you be comfortable as the only woman working in an all-male (or the only man working in an all-female) environment? What challenges do you think this situation would present?

Personal attitude, maturity, and judgement can be probed with questions such as these. Once again, these questions have no simple 'right' answer, but the way in which you choose to respond will tell the employer much about the kind of person you are and the general attitudes of reliability, tenacity, cooperation, tolerance, and good will you bring to the job. Remember that the employer is looking for someone who is motivated, capable, and able to get along with other employees. You should try to respond in ways that will showcase your abilities to do those things, and you should always support your answers with specific examples from your experience.

In answering any of these questions, keep in mind the probable needs and interests of all employers: they will be looking for someone who is confident and capable, but not arrogant or self-absorbed. They want employees who can demonstrate and act with respect for others and who will take responsibility for their words and actions. Admit to mistakes, but show that you have learned from them and can handle criticism effectively. Be honest and appropriately modest, but not overly so; be confident, but not arrogant.

Questions about ethics and motivation

Employers are interested in how much thought you've given to your goals and to your life in general; they are interested in your ethical judgement and in the principles that drive you. Questions like those in Box 10.5 provide insight into these things and into your understanding of the demands of a professional career. Responses that suggest indecision or immaturity, or that reveal a thoughtless individual who doesn't know why he has made the choices he has, are likely to be rejected by a recruiter.

As you answer questions about your future plans, try to show that you have given some consideration to the future, but that you are flexible and able to adjust your goals as well.

Box 10.5   Ethics and Motivation Questions

- What motivates you? What drives you crazy?
- Describe the biggest risk you have ever taken.
- Describe an achievement you are proud of.
- What would you like to be doing in five years? Ten?
- Do you have plans to further your education? Would you be interested in doing so?
- How long do you think you'd be happy in this job before you started thinking about promotion?
- If a situation arose in which you might have to violate company policy, would you do so? How would you decide?
- Have you ever cheated on an assignment? If you saw someone else cheating, would you report that person?
- What are you doing right now to improve yourself?
- Are you usually right? Are other people's ideas as important as yours?

When it comes to questions about furthering your education or experience, you should never close any door on yourself. You could indicate that you are willing to take further training if necessary. Even if you don't think right now that you would ever go back to school, remember that with time you might change your mind. On the other hand, you might also want to reassure the employer that you're not going to quit this job as soon as you're trained in order to return to school.

Questions about **ethics** are tricky; your best bet is to spend some time before you go to the interview reflecting on the choices you have made in your life and why you have done so. Then answer as candidly and thoughtfully as you can. The material in Chapter 4 will help you to obtain clarity about what it means to act ethically and the challenges associated with doing so.

Questions about leadership

The cluster of personal characteristics that we associate with leadership tops the wish list of every interviewer, no matter what job is being filled. Although not all positions directly involve the supervision of others or the leading of a team, nearly every job makes use of qualities of decisiveness, problem-solving, initiative, an ability to manage conflict, and the capacity to take responsibility. As we learned in Chapter 1, these attributes are highly prized by employers and are very much in demand. At the same time, they are relatively rare, especially in new graduates, so anyone who can display them in an interview has a decided advantage over the competition.

As with the previous lists of questions, there are no single 'correct' answers to these, since situations and individuals can vary quite dramatically. However, in general, the employer will be looking for evidence that you have reflected on your experiences, that your judgements are based on a solid foundation, and that you can manage your reactions

Box 10.6 Leadership Questions

- What are the qualities of a good leader? A good boss? How many of them do you possess?
- How would you describe a good employee? Are you a good employee?
- Describe the most challenging (or highly technical) project you have ever worked on. Was it a team project? What was your role?
- Give me an example of a situation in which you initiated change. How successful was it?
- If you had an idea for improving one of our procedures, how would you proceed?
- Have you ever had a conflict with a colleague? How did it arise? How did you resolve it?
- What did your college program fail to teach you that you should have learned? What steps have you taken to learn it on your own?
- What have you left unfinished in your life? Why?

so as not to inflame situations that could have been resolved. A candidate who has never taken any time to evaluate past experiences or to consider their meaning can't answer questions like these satisfactorily, and a failure to answer effectively will reveal a great deal to an experienced interviewer.

Before you head out to an interview, think through this list and try to discern what the employer needs to hear from you. Think about your experiences and draw upon them to develop a thoughtful approach to each of these questions, so that you reveal yourself to the employer as a person of good judgement, good character, and good will.

Questions about communication and interpersonal skills

Your ability to communicate effectively will be assessed throughout the interview, since nearly all of the probable questions deal either directly or indirectly with communication. However, an interviewer may also ask you to speak directly about your communication experience. Once again, the goal is more to uncover your assumptions, attitudes, judgement, thoughtfulness, and capacity to accept responsibility for your words and actions than it is to elicit information.

There are no right answers for these questions, but as you may have guessed, there are some wrong ones. Poor answers would be those that cast blame on others, that show an inability to 'think on your feet', that show little evidence of insight into your own character or experience, or that reveal a shallow or immature level of understanding.

Your experiences in the course in which you are using this book can provide you with some fodder for developing your answers to questions about your **communication skills** and understanding. Take some time to review the Nine Axioms and the material on ethical communication in Chapter 4. Answers that reveal a familiarity with these concepts and ideas will demonstrate good judgement to the interviewer who asks about your communication.

Box 10.7   Communication and Interpersonal Skills Questions

- You have one minute. Sell yourself to me.
- Tell me a joke.
- What did you do to prepare for this interview?
- Describe your experience in making formal (or technical) presentations. Give an example.
- What's the most important presentation (or assignment, or task) you've ever completed?
- What advice would you give to a colleague on how to handle criticism? Do you have any experience in doing so?
- Describe a situation in which you resolved an interpersonal conflict.
- Tell me about a situation in which you were unable to resolve an interpersonal conflict.
- Have you ever worked with a difficult person? Tell me about that.
- How do you know that you're not someone else's 'difficult person' to work with?

What to Expect in the Interview

Interviews can vary not only in the type and number of questions that employers ask, but in other ways as well. As you may already have guessed, there is no set pattern for interviews and no 'right' way to conduct them with respect to length or number of screenings. Employers tend to base their selection process on questions and procedures that best suit their needs, and the more interviews you go to, the greater variety you will see.

For example, the length of time you spend in an interview may be anywhere from twenty minutes to two or even three hours, depending on the type of position and the number of applicants. An acquaintance of mine recently attended an interview where the process lasted seven hours! The last one I went to stretched over two days, but I have been to interviews as short as twenty minutes. Often the person who telephones you to set up the interview will indicate how long it will take; if he or she doesn't volunteer the information, ask for an estimate of how long the interview will last. If you're not sure, allow yourself at least two hours, just to be safe.

You may be interviewed by one person, by two or three together, or even by a committee of five or more; the more responsible the position, the more likely there will be more than one interviewer. Again, you may be told this ahead of time. But whether you are told or not, be prepared for the possibility that you may be interviewed by a committee.

In some organizations or institutions, two or three people interview you separately, then compare impressions. These meetings may take place on the same day (you may spend twenty to forty minutes with three different people successively, for instance) or on subsequent days. You may also be individually interviewed, or you may be part of a cluster of interviewees who are put through a formal process as a group. These differences are neither good nor bad; they merely show the employer's personal preference.

In any of these cases, don't be thrown off by interviewers taking notes while you speak. Remember that they have seen several different people in a short space of time and are merely interested in keeping track of what was said. The note-taking is really for your benefit—you wouldn't want an interviewer to forget you or confuse you with someone else.

Skills or aptitude tests

Sometimes, depending on the employer and on the position, you may be asked to complete some form of testing. Occasionally these tests will be vocationally specific—you may be asked to explain some important concepts in the field; to give a presentation; to write a report or memo; or to solve a mathematical or technical problem. In these cases, the interviewer is interested in knowing that you really do have the level of technical skill needed for the job. Try to remain calm and just do the best you can. The other candidates will be asked to complete the same tasks and will likely be just as nervous as you are.

There are other kinds of tests that you may be asked to take: general aptitude or even psychological tests. These are tests you can't really prepare yourself for; they are thought by some to reveal your general intelligence, attitude, or aptitude for the position you are interested in. Like all trends, aptitude testing goes in and out of favour, and is used more in some fields than in others. Even when they are popular, such tests are not universally employed by all organizations; slightly under half of all applicants report being asked to complete personality testing of some kind during an interview. However, employers who choose to use aptitude testing generally believe it is useful.

Your best bet if you are asked to write one of these tests is to be as honest and forthright as you can. Most of the tests are designed to double-check your responses by asking several questions aimed at the same information, so keep in mind that it's difficult to try to second-guess the tests. Fudged answers can usually be identified by the cross-questions. Simply try to relax as much as possible and do your best. There is nothing to be frightened of, and you will do better if you can keep from being too upset.

There is much talk these days about poor writing skills among college and university graduates, and many employers have expressed concern over such weaknesses. As a result, occasionally an employer will ask applicants to write a piece of professional correspondence—a letter, memo, or short report—right on the spot, in response to a situation such as the ones given in earlier chapters of this book. You should be prepared to write if necessary; to prepare, you might review the chapters on the letter and the memo before you go to the interview. In this case, the employer will be looking not only for proper letter or memo format, but also for correct grammar and sentence structure, and the other Seven Cs of professional writing, as well as for how well you handle the situation.

Problem questions

Employers are forbidden by law to ask an applicant questions about age, marital status, religious affiliation, ethnic background, sexual orientation, or family relationships. Nevertheless, occasionally you will encounter an interviewer who asks you such questions anyway, either because of inexperience or because of deliberate disregard for the law. This kind of slip doesn't happen often anymore, but if it does happen to you it could be rather awkward.

You are obviously not obliged to answer questions like these, but if you wish to preserve good will in the interview, your options may be somewhat limited. You must be able to balance your need for the job against your willingness to field inappropriate questions. This is entirely a judgement call, and it's important to know for yourself how much is too much. A direct refusal may be awkward and uncomfortable, since it poses a face threat to the interviewer. If you declare that you don't see the relevance of the question to the job, you will probably cause the person to become defensive, especially if the action was a faux pas rather than a deliberate offense.

You could simply choose to go ahead and answer the question if you are comfortable doing so. For example, perhaps you aren't bothered by a question about your marital status or your family life, and you may wish to answer it even though, strictly speaking, it's not appropriate for the employer to ask.

Sometimes such questions are unthinking expressions of other employer concerns; when this is the case, you will sometimes be able to determine the employer's train of thought from the context of the remark. An employer may really be thinking about overtime and may ask about your marital status because he or she feels overtime might be more difficult for a person with a family. If you think this might be what's going on, you could choose to answer the implied question rather than the explicit one, and phrase your response to address the employer's concern directly. For example, a prospective employer may ask if you are married. You could answer: 'If you're concerned about my willingness to work overtime, I am willing to put in all the time the job requires.'

Most interviewers want to see you at your best and will try very hard to put you at ease. However, if you do run into a difficult situation, know how much of such behaviour is tolerable to you, and don't be afraid to leave if you have to. If the interview is that unpleasant, it's unlikely that you would want to work for this company anyway.

After the Interview

Following the formal interview, you may be taken to lunch or dinner. If this occurs, remember that it's still part of the interview process, even though the formal questions are over. Although by this point you will have established a good impression, you will want to maintain your professional demeanour. Be careful to order food that is easy to manage—stay away from messy sauces or sloppy finger food. Recognize that the conversation will continue during the meal; pause occasionally as you eat, so that you will be able to respond naturally.

While the occasion may appear purely social, remember that you are still subject to the judgement of those who may become your future employers. If you are at dinner, you may wish to order an alcoholic drink, but if you do so, be sure that you limit yourself to one, or at most two, drinks. Take your cue from the interviewers, but don't overdo it. Continue to behave courteously and professionally, and be careful not to say anything that may be judged inappropriate. You should be friendly in your manner, but not so much so that you appear to be presuming you have clinched a job offer.

The letter of thanks

After the interview process is complete, you may wish to send the employer a polite **letter of thanks**. While this courtesy is not required, it provides a final gesture of professionalism and good will that contributes to your overall ethos. It need not be lengthy, but it should express your sincere appreciation for the effort that went into interviewing you.

The letter of thanks should also express your continued interest in the position, but you should not appear to assume you've got a job you haven't yet been offered. You will need to strike a balance between friendly courtesy and unwarranted expectation; the best way to do this, as you have already learned, is to put yourself in the audience's place. Figure 10.1 shows a sample letter of thanks.

1234 5th St W
Fredericton, NB
E8J 0S3

May 15, 2011

Sven Runkvist, Managing Director
Eastern Passage Technical Services
PO Box 930
Halifax, NS
B2G 0X0

Dear Mr. Runkvist:

Thank you very much for the opportunity to meet with you for an interview for the Quality Assurance Specialist position in your Halifax office. I enjoyed meeting all the staff, and appreciated their friendly courtesy during the whole process.

I particularly appreciated the chance to demonstrate my problem-solving and design skills in developing plans for a pattern-cutting system for Ceejay-Maritime Toy Mfg.

Whether or not I am successful in the competition for this position, I am grateful for the chance to speak with you and to learn more about the operation of a large full-service engineering firm. Thank you again for the very positive experience, and for the enjoyable staff luncheon.

Yours truly,

Shawn Horton

Shawn Horton

Figure 10.1: How effectively does Shawn's letter adhere to the principles of effective business communication we have been learning?

Why Didn't I Get the Job I Interviewed For?

Even when the job market is excellent, 60 to 80 per cent or more of the people who are selected for an interview fail to secure a job offer. As you search for the ideal position, you will certainly find yourself in this situation some of the time. Of course, there are many reasons why people who are interviewed don't get an offer, and many of these are beyond the candidate's control—internal competition, someone with slightly more experience, a transfer from another branch of the same company, the timing of the interview.

However, some fail in the interview because of factors that need not have presented a problem; they fail because they have made one or more of the common mistakes that lead to rejection. These factors are ones you can bring under your control, and while managing these elements effectively won't guarantee an offer, doing so will help to ensure that you won't be dismissed before you have had a chance to demonstrate your suitability for the job.

In general, you should avoid any behaviour in the extreme, and in particular, be sure to respond openly and willingly to questions, since a pattern of unresponsiveness suggests an uncooperative, even hostile personality. Extremes of any behaviour—talking too much or not enough, laughing too much or not at all, making eye contact or failing to do so, refusing to shake hands or doing so limply—could cost you a job offer, because extremes always suggest you are not entirely in control of yourself or the situation; similarly, being too animated or too stiff implies extreme nervousness out of proportion to the stress of an interview, and suggests an inexperienced or incompetent applicant.

An inability to stay focused on one point or one question will also make a bad impression; do your best to concentrate on the questions you are being asked, and ask for clarification occasionally if you do not understand the direction the question is taking. Even something as simple as failing to smile or even smiling too much can be a sign to an employer that you are not at your ease. Finally, any indication of disorganization beyond the norm, such as not being able to find essential papers or a pen in your briefcase, purse, or pocket, forgetting significant documents at home, or being unable to recall details of past employment, will make an employer hesitate.

The following are some of the specific reasons employers have given for rejecting people who, on paper, were appealing enough to be invited for an interview.

1. Arrived late to the interview
2. Was inappropriately dressed
3. Was poorly groomed
4. Was rude to the receptionist
5. Chewed gum
6. Refused a handshake when offered
7. Had a limp handshake
8. Seemed excessively nervous or uncomfortable
9. Fidgeted; did not appear in command of self or situation
10. Lacked energy or enthusiasm
11. Didn't answer questions fully, or rambled on too long or pointlessly
12. Was unforthcoming in answering questions
13. Could not provide examples to support claims in the résumé
14. Was aggressive, arrogant, or self-important
15. Displayed a sense of entitlement beyond what was merited by experience or skill

16. Attempted to dominate the interview
17. Was dismissive of work done by professionals in fields other than his or her own
18. Appeared more interested in pay or benefits than in the work itself
19. Criticized former employers or professors
20. Was unable or unwilling to provide references
21. Spoke poorly, with noticeable errors in grammar or diction
22. Knew nothing about the company or was uninformed about the profession or field
23. Was unfamiliar with current trends in the profession
24. Had exaggerated on the application or résumé
25. Displayed ambitions or expectations far beyond abilities
26. Lacked clear goals or professional interests
27. Appeared whiny or unmotivated
28. Was a complainer
29. Did not take responsibility for weaknesses or mistakes; blamed others
30. Was defensive when answering questions
31. Was unwilling to start at the entry level
32. Had a poor school record and could not offer an explanation
33. Was insincere or glib
34. Seemed to rely too much on charm
35. Lied in the application or interview

Interviewing, like everything else in this book, is a skill you can learn and polish. You can do this best by practising. Go to as many interviews as you can, even if you're not sure you would want the job in question. You can never get too much experience, and every interview you go to will make the next one easier. You might even find that a job that didn't appear so attractive on paper turns out to be just the position you were seeking.

Critical Reading

Craig Silverman, 'The Traditional Job Interview: That's So Yesterday'
Craig Silverman, a freelance journalist from Montreal, is founder of *Regret the Error*, an award-winning website that tracks and reports on accuracy and media corrections. His book, *Regret the Error: How Media Mistakes Pollute the Press and Imperil Free Speech*, appeared in 2007. Silverman is the author of two weekly columns, 'The Office' in *The Globe and Mail*, and 'The Explainer' for *Hour.ca*. His work has also appeared in venues from *The New York Times* and the *International Herald Tribune* to the *Montreal Gazette*, *Report On Business*, and *Report On Small Business*.

The Traditional Job Interview: That's So Yesterday
MONTREAL—Along with attending classes, running for student council at the University of Toronto, and holding down a part-time job, 20-year-old Aidan Nulman spent the last few weeks obsessing over a four-page document that could land him his dream job for the summer.

The position is a paid internship in New York with Seth Godin, the acclaimed market-ing guru and best-selling author of books such as *Meatball Sundae: Is Your Marketing Out of Sync?* The sole application requirement is to send a PDF document of no more than four pages. 'You decide what's on it; that's part of the application,' Mr Godin wrote when he announced the job.

While the majority of companies still adhere to the standard practice of sitting a candidate in a room and giving him or her canned questions, innovation and creativity have begun to creep into the process. In today's job market, candidates are more likely than ever to be thrown a curveball when applying for work.

Though undoubtedly a unique hiring process, Mr Godin's internship application is not a departure for a man who once wrote a blog post that declared, 'I've been to thousands of job interviews (thankfully as an interviewer mostly) and I have come to the conclusion that the entire effort is a waste of time.'

Reached by phone, he elaborated. 'If you use a standard interviewing process, then the people you hire will by definition be good at the standard interview process,' he says. 'But there are very few jobs where being good at a job interview is what you do for a living.'

Mr Godin and others like him are doing their best to evangelize for the end of the typical job interview. They see it as a structure that rewards candidates who do well in interviews, as opposed to in the job itself. It appears the message is getting through to some Canadian companies.

'Some of the younger organizations like 1-800-GOT-JUNK?, who are entrepreneurial and high-growth, are embracing a lot more untraditional techniques,' says Drew Railton, a partner at The Caldwell Partners International, the country's largest executive search firm, and president of the BC Human Resources Management Association. 'They will bring five or six candidates in a room at the same time and interview them en masse to see who performs best.'

Even seemingly staid professions such as finance and accounting are changing things up. Jean-Philippe Gauthier, recruiting director for Robert Half Finance & Accounting, a placement firm for finance and accounting workers, says the scarcity of talent has led companies to evolve their hiring practices.

'One of the things people started to do is speed interviewing,' he says, noting that companies can't slowly evaluate finance candidates over weeks or months because others will hire them first. 'Companies take four or five candidates and interview them for 30 or 40 minutes. If a candidate fits the bill, they bring them back for a long interview.'

That longer interview, currently the standard, has some flaws. Mr Gauthier says studies show interviewers make up their minds within the first 12 minutes of the discussion, so much of the interview can be a waste of time. Recent Canadian research identified other problems.

'We found that 78 per cent of interviewers are actually prompting people [with hints] in interviews,' says Geoffrey Smith, the assistant dean of the college of management and economics at the University of Guelph. Along with Sheldene Simola and Simon Taggar, two colleagues from other Canadian universities, he studied how job interviews were conducted in Canada. Their research was published in the *Canadian Journal of Administrative Sciences* last year.

Mr Smith says 75 per cent of interviewers added new questions for some candidates, meaning not all were evaluated based on the same information, which is the point of a structured interview process.

Still, 'you can't dispense with the traditional interview,' Mr Smith says. 'But you can certainly add to it.'

The new methods also have their unique flaws. Mr Gauthier recalls one person who interviewed via a webcam and appeared on screen wearing a shirt and tie. 'Then they stood up at the end and were wearing shorts,' he says.

In the end, Mr Nulman's document is set up like a pitch for a film—a film that just happens to be 'about a student at the University of Toronto named Aidan Nulman and his desire and dedication to making people's lives better,' among other things. Mr Nulman also embedded video clips.

It's been a lot of work, but the non-standard job application/interview process appears to be in his blood. His father, Andy Nulman, is the president and chief marketing officer of Montreal technology company Airborne Mobile. When he oversaw hiring for the company, he ditched the job interview and told candidates to do something to prove they were right for the position. One candidate for a marketing position launched a campaign that saw his friends and contacts send Nulman e-mails with the subject line, 'Hire Jonathan Karpfen: He'll Help You Put FUN in PHONE.'

'My process was, show me you want the job,' he says. 'Formulas are for scientists or for babies. . .they are definitely not for hiring human beings.'

Naturally, he's proud of what his son pulled together for the internship. 'The stuff my son sent me was so good it knocked me down,' he says. 'Right now, whether he gets this particular job is moot.'

Aidan Nulman agrees his submission has other uses.

'Aside from the cover page, I don't see a single thing on this that could not be reworked for getting some other kind of creative job,' he says.

Over the past decade, companies have begun conducting 'behavioural-based' interviews. Drew Railton of The Caldwell Partners International says this puts an emphasis on 'what have you done and how have you done it.'

'If you're trying to understand how a candidate works with conflict, you will ask them to describe a situation where they had to manage or lead through conflict,' he says. 'You have them tell you the situation, their specific actions and the impact it had on the organization. They have to walk you through their mindset.'

At the core of this approach is the belief that past action and behaviour are a good predictor of future performance. Employers want to know how you work, as opposed to just looking at skills listed on a résumé.

'The majority of people are hired for skills and fired for personality,' he says.

From *The Globe and Mail*, 7 April 2008. Available at http://www.theglobeandmail.com/servlet/story/RTGAM.20080407.wlintvu07/BNStory/lifeWork/home/.

Points to Remember

1. Manage your online presence so as to portray yourself professionally.
2. Take the goofy messages off your answering machine.
3. Remember that the employment interview is an opportunity for you to display your suitability for the job.
4. Review typical questions beforehand, and develop strategies for answering them, but don't memorize pat answers.
5. Always arrive on time to the interview.
6. Listen carefully to questions so as to respond effectively to the concerns and interests of the interviewer.
7. Answer questions willingly and completely, but do not go on for too long, and use examples to illustrate your skills wherever possible.

8. Show respect for others in both your actions and your comments.
9. Make eye contact appropriately, smile, and avoid fidgeting or adjusting clothing.
10. Always be polite to receptionists, office staff, and others you meet in the course of the interview.
11. Develop a strategy for handling inappropriate questions, should they arise.
12. Following the interview, write a note of thanks to the interviewer.

Key Concepts

appearance
attitude
background knowledge
body language
communication skills
ethics

handshake
interpersonal skills
judgement
leadership
letter of thanks
maturity

motivation
self-awareness
self-discipline
self-knowledge
self-reflectiveness

Assignments and Exercises

1. Consider the job you applied for when you wrote your résumé package in Chapter 9. From the lists of common interview questions given in this chapter, and based on the posting or advertisement for that position, select five questions that you feel would be likely to come up in an interview for this job. Develop some effective strategies for answering these appropriately. In a memo to your instructor, or as part of a brief oral presentation, discuss the ways in which your strategies demonstrate the principles of effective communication.

2. Study the sample questions in this book and select three that seem most challenging. Exchange your list with a classmate, and then interview each other using these questions. Note carefully the strategies used by your partner, paying attention to strengths in the person's interview and to areas that might be improved. Be prepared to report your observations in written or oral form.

3. Your instructor may organize practice interviews to take place in class; in this exercise, each person in the class is interviewed in turn, with the rest of the class looking on. Your instructor may choose questions at random, or allow you to identify five of your own choosing, selecting one or more of these for your interview. After your interview, give a brief assessment of your own performance, and then listen to comments from your classmates and instructor. Be prepared to discuss the experience with the rest of the class.

4. Which of the interview questions seem to you most difficult to answer? Why? What do such questions teach us about the nature and importance of communication?

5. In what ways does the interview constitute a nearly perfect illustration of the Nine Axioms of Communication that we learned in Chapter 1? Prepare a short oral report that may be delivered to the class in which you identify these features and suggest some implications for our study of communication.

Appendix A

Communication
Case Studies

Your instructor may use the case studies in this Appendix as a basis for class discussion or as a foundation for written assignments, or both. The scenarios presented in the case studies are of several types: some feature sample written documents that you are asked to analyze, respond to, or edit; others describe an unresolved situation that requires a response, either in writing or in person. Still others ask you to choose among several possible responses, and to justify that choice based on the principles of communication you have been learning in this course.

In working with the scenarios, your instructor may ask you to apply material from a specific chapter, or to incorporate all of the reading you have done so far; in every case, however, you should make explicit use of the theory and concepts you have learned to give the fullest explanation you can of the interaction described in the case study.

As you prepare to analyze and respond to the scenarios, you should consider the following:

1. What is the exigence that the communication addresses? What issues seem to be at stake? Why?
2. What constraints does the situation present to the speaker or writer? Did he or she take them into account sufficiently?
3. Have any misunderstandings occurred? What seems to have caused them?
4. Did the writer or speaker effectively establish or in any way compromise credibility or professionalism? How?
5. Did the message achieve an appropriate rhetorical balance? Why or why not?
6. What role, if any, has been played by face risk, footing, and relation?
7. To what extent does the scenario present an ethical dilemma? Why or why not?
8. To what extent has context shaped the communication?
9. Is there any way in which the message could worsen the situation? What, if anything, could be done to prevent the situation from deteriorating further?

Case Study 1: Communication for the Future Challenge

As government funding diminishes, colleges and universities increasingly rely on gifts from alumni and friends, which are raised through fundraising appeals such as the one in the letter below. Take a close look at the message, keeping in mind what you have learned about effective communication. Does this letter accomplish what the writer intended? What weaknesses do you see in the letter?

The letter, recently circulated to alumni of a Canadian college, was very likely written for the dean by a member of his administrative staff. Nevertheless, the dean is the one who signed the letter. How responsible is he for the quality of this message that went out to alumni with his signature attached?

Many people mistakenly assume that only fussy writers notice others' mistakes, and that their own readers will forgive any weaknesses in style. The reply to the dean's letter, on page 352, shows that even those who do not write especially well themselves can notice and criticize the mistakes of other writers.

If you were one of the alumni who received this letter from the dean of their college, what would have been your reaction? Would you have donated to the communication fund? If not, why not? Consider your own reaction to the letter, then compare it with the actual letter written by one of the college's alumni, shown after the dean's letter.

Waskasoo College
Office of the Dean of Student Services, Division of Science and Technology
PO Box 1977, Forestville ON P6R 2T7
www.waskasooc.on.ca/sci-tech/htm

The 'Communication for the Future' Challenge
April 2009

Dear Waskasoo Alumni:

Exciting, challenging, and innovative are the words to best describe the 'Communication for the Future Challenge'. At the close of this first campaign for the CFFC fund we have reached the $45,000 mark of donations matched by contribution from an alumni who wishes to remain anonymous. I would like to take this opportunity to thank you for your gift which enabled us to get this fund off the ground.

As we pass the close of an old century and the beginning of a new millennium, we are taking positive steps necessary with the Communication for the Future Challenge Fund to ensure that each and every one of our students receives the appropriate training in communication that they so richly deserve and which are our continuing priority. This year, we would like to build the 'Communication for the Future Challenge Fund' into a stable source of funding. The accumulated interest income o this endowment fund, which will not only allow the Division to have some flexibility, but ensures delivery of the best possible educational experience to our students.

The Curriculum Committee of the Division of Science and Technology has been working labouriously to implement a new communication program revisions into the curriculm at all levels. The need for program changes is necessary as academic and continuing competence demands escalate. The size of student enrolment has increased at the same time as allocated resources decreasing. We all face the challenge of doing more with less, putting our shoulders to the wheel, and striving toward the future. Whjle we acknowledge with undying gratitude, support from our alumni, industry and friends combined with the commitment to dedication, hard work and loyalty demonstrated by our instructors and staff, the circumstances we confront every year signal us to continue the vigil of trying to keep up with ever-changing societal demands.

The Division of Science and Technology continues to maintain its commitment to provide each and every student the highest possible quality education and the best possible working conditions and learning environment for students, faculty and staff. Some of the support we require comes from those who accredit their success as a technical professional to the exceptional level of education they received here; thereby giving back to their college a small measure of support to enhance the future for those science and technology students of today and tomorrow.

It is people like you who have played a major role in the succes of this initiative to date. Every single donation counts!! Please consider your choices and support the education of future technologists. I encourage you to fill out the enclosed Donor card. Please keep in mind that receipts will be issued for donations of $10 or more. My heartfelt gratitude and thanks to you for your undying support.

Very sincerly yours,

Mikhail Bruin, Dean of Student Services

513 - 2 Avro Place,
Erin Mills, ON   ,   M4D5Y7
May 12, 2009

Dr. Mikhail Bruin, Dean of Student Services
Division of Science and Technology
Waskasoo College
PO Box 1977
Forestville ON P6R 2T7

Dear Dean Bruin:

In today's world of business and industry, technical people have always been accused of poor English and not being able to write good letters and reports. An unfair criticism when considered generically but true when some individuals are assessed. I'm sorry, Mr. Dean, but you do fall in the latter category vis a vis your letter regarding the Communication for the future Fund (which by the way I supported last year as one of the contributors). My marked up copy of your letter is enclosed to illustrate my position of bad writing. If you are concerned about standards for technical grads please give a little more consideration to english and reports/letters in their curriculum.

In the education system these days more stress seems to be given to the facts you are conveying in your writing and less on communicating clearly and correctly. Perhaps in writing to friends on the Internet this approach might be 'acceptable.' However I think more is expected of instructors, staff <u>and Deans</u> at centres of higher learning. Maybe you should spend some of the fund money on someone who can thoroughly check the letters coming out of your office to insure that they are an <u>effective</u> communication. (Only 'Kidding!' but serious too.)

Please do not consider the previous comments except in the sense of constructive criticism both to yourself and to the staff member who wrote this letter for you. They are written a bit "tongue-in-cheek" and facetiously but the concern is still there.

Sincerely,

U.V. Ray
Waskasoo Alumnus '89

As you analyze this response to the dean's letter, ask yourself the following questions: How effective is this letter from U.V. Ray? Is he a better writer than the person who wrote the letter for the dean? How might his letter be made more effective? Do you think the dean can repair the ethos he has lost with Ray and with other alumni who did not directly express their concerns?

Case Study 2: Blogging with Philip

By Debora Rolfes and Jennifer MacLennan
Deb Rolfes is a Lecturer in Communication in the Ron and Jane Graham Centre for the Study of Communication in the College of Engineering, University of Saskatchewan. A

former technical writer and editor, Rolfes coordinates the Centre's Foundations of Professional Communication course and also teaches Advanced Professional Writing Techniques. In addition to her academic work, Rolfes serves as a Public Appointee to Council of the Association of Professional Engineers and Geoscientists of Saskatchewan.

Last fall Philip left home to attend college in a different province. It's been a great experience, but he's found himself missing his friends and family, especially when he's feeling stressed. One way he has come up with to stay in touch with everyone back home is to keep a blog. Nearly every day, Philip posts comments about his experiences as an engineering student. Most of his entries concern school and his struggles to keep on top of his assignments, but he also reports on what social life he manages to have. He thinks of his blog as a personal space where he can vent his frustrations among friends, as well as share the highs of his new life with the people who matter to him.

It is mid-term, and Philip is feeling the pressure of completing assignments and studying for exams, as well as trying to find a summer job. On Wednesday, for instance, he spent the whole day trying to solve a problem for Dr. Harding McAllister's class. He even skipped all his classes that day to spend time on the assignment, which had him completely baffled. After six frustrating hours of work, he finally asked a friend for help and discovered that he had been missing a handout that Dr. McAllister had distributed in class on a day that Philip had missed. The handout clarified the problem and gave suggestions about how to approach it. With it, Philip was finally able to complete the assignment just in time to get to old 'Hardline' McAllister's office before 5:00 p.m., when the professor would be leaving for the day.

However, although Phillip did manage to catch the professor in his office, McAllister refused to accept Philip's assignment, which had been due in class that morning. McAllister reminded Philip that he does not accept late assignments, as is clearly stated in the course syllabus. Philip tried to explain that it wasn't his fault because he had been missing the handout necessary to solve the problem, but Dr. McAllister refused to listen; he simply threw Philip's assignment—about eight hours' worth of work—into the garbage.

Angry and frustrated, Philip went straight to the college's computer lab and vented on his blog. His entry included the following material (the language has been cleaned up somewhat):

Being an engineering student sucks sometimes. I wasted the whole day doing this crappy assignment for him, when I could have been spending it on way more interesting stuff, and then the old buzzard turns around and dumps my work into the garbage, right in front of me. I felt like punching his smug bum-stubble face for making me miss all my classes for nothing. It wasn't my fault I didn't have the crappy handout I needed; if he didn't completely suck as a teacher, I'd have known how to do the freaking problem in the first place, and I wouldn't have been forced to miss class. Not that I wanted to go to his class—I never want to go to his class! He is as boring as it gets, and doesn't do anything to make this stuff interesting. In fact, unless there is a test, I am never going to go to this jerk's class again.

What really peeves me off more than the grade thing is how much crud you have to take when you're a student, massive BS from jerks who obviously are here only because they aren't good enough to get a job in the real world. No wonder old 'Hardline' is marooned here in this backwater: no real employer would keep him on the payroll for more than five minutes. If he weren't completely incompetent, the old prig would have a real job instead of being stuck here doing something he obviously hates and taking it out on poor students who are paying big bucks for their degrees. In my opinion, he's just a big waste of skin and he doesn't even deserve to be walking around on the same planet with the rest of us!

The stupid old buzzard shouldn't be allowed anywhere near a classroom or anywhere else. I or any other student shouldn't have to take this crud from somebody when it's our money paying his freaking salary. I sure wish this school had a no-jerks policy. Or, better yet, capital punishment for freaking shoddy teachers! If I ever get out of this place I'm going to sue this school and get that old buzzard fired.

By the following Monday, with exams over and assignments all caught up, Philip has pretty much forgotten about the McAllister incident. His attention is focused instead on the job interview he's going to in the afternoon.

At the interview, Philip's expectations are met: he's answered all the questions well, and he seems to have developed a great rapport with the two interviewers. So far, so good. Then one of the interviewers asks Philip how effectively he deals with conflict in the workplace. Philip is feeling pretty good at this point, so he gives a standard blah-blah answer about keeping lines of communication open and treating people with respect. Then the interviewer places on the table a printout of Philip's blog from the previous Wednesday, and asks him to explain how it exemplifies his approach to conflict.

Part A

Drawing on the principles of communication that you have learned in this course, analyze the event described above. Write your analysis in a short informal report addressed to your communication instructor. As you conduct your analysis of this case study, consider what Philip's blog posting communicates about his character, and consider, too, the potential fallout from posting such information on a public forum. (It might be useful to recall that some 77 per cent of employers now use Internet searches—including blogs and social network sites like Facebook—to conduct background checks on potential employees. You should also know that material posted to the web is pretty much online forever, even if you change your mind and delete it from your pages.)

Case Study 3: Bryan Wins a Scholarship

By Janelle Hutchinson and Jennifer MacLennan
Janelle Hutchinson is Assistant Registrar at the University of Saskatchewan, where she has also taught Foundations of Professional Communication for the Ron and Jane Graham Centre for the Study of Communication. With previous degrees in both microbiology and engineering, Hutchinson is currently completing a master's degree in communication.

Bryan White is a mechanical engineering major who has just started his third year of university. In many ways, he's pretty typical: he works hard, he parties hard when he can, and he's chronically short of cash. Take today, for instance: not only did he get to spend two hours stuck in line at the bookstore, but the bill for his books and supplies is enough to send him into a panic. At the moment, he's not sure how he's going to manage his rent and food for the rest of the term.

But for once, Bryan catches a break. When he arrives home from the bookstore, there's some good news waiting: a letter of congratulations from the Awards Office announcing that he's received the J.C. Hudson scholarship in the amount of $2,000. Bryan's too relieved and excited to read the details closely, but the letter contains some blah-blah about how Hudson has long been a supporter of the College of Engineering and of mechanical engineering students. Skimming the letter, Bryan makes the connection with the Hudson Lab and briefly wonders if it's the same Hudson; the letter suggests that if Bryan would like to write a thank you note, he can drop it off with the clerk in the Awards Office, and it will be mailed from there.

The next few weeks are a blur of assignments, mid-term exams, late nights, and the occasional pub-crawl. When the scholarship cheque arrives, Bryan is ecstatic to have the extra money in his pocket and even a little in the bank. He makes a mental note to get around to writing that darned acknowledgement letter, but he can't really think what he could possibly say to a gazillionaire. And anyway, he can't seriously believe it matters all that much. After all, $2,000 might be a lot to Bryan right now, but it's only a drop in the bucket to Hudson, who it turns out *is* the same Hudson as the Hudson Lab. Surely he has better things to do than sit around waiting for a letter from some kid who's still in school.

The days become shorter, the snow falls, and the temperature drops; end-of-term work piles up. Then all at once term is over and exams are looming, and Bryan's really looking forward to taking a break when they're done. On the last day of classes, however, he receives a message to call the Awards Office. When he calls, Bryan talks to an exasperated clerk who asks about his letter to Hudson. He feels a little guilty; he really should have written the thing. But the clerk's tone makes him defensive: doesn't she know that third-year mechanical engineering is the most difficult? Does she have any idea how busy he's been? Besides, Hudson gave him a scholarship, right? Doesn't he *want* Bryan to do well and stay focused on school? Not to mention the fact that no one said he *had* to write a letter. Plus, what on earth does he have to say to someone he's never even seen? It's not like there's anything personal here, is it?

Well, apparently it's personal to Hudson. It turns out he's been down their throats in the Awards Office because he never received a letter of thanks from the recipient of the scholarship. In fact, he's threatening to withdraw his support, and even wants to know if he can revoke Bryan's award. Although the rules prevent him from taking away Bryan's money, the clerk is still concerned about his potentially cancelling the scholarship for future students. Can Bryan *please* send an acknowledgement? Irritated, Bryan promises to write something immediately and drop it off at the Awards Office, in a sealed envelope. Counting the minutes that are being stolen from his study time, he hurries out to the drugstore, grabs the first thank you card he sees, and hastily writes inside: 'Dear Mr. Hudson, Thank you very much for the scholarship; the money will really help me out. Sincerely, Bryan White' and seals the envelope. The next morning Bryan ducks out from studying at the library to drop off the card at the Awards Office. What a relief, finally, to have that chore done! Now he can focus on studying for his exams.

In January, after a relaxing two weeks off, Bryan returns to university, only to receive another message from the Awards Office. Inexplicably, instead of satisfying Hudson, Bryan's card has inflamed the situation. The Awards clerk reminds Bryan that he will have to face Hudson at the Awards Presentation Evening in February, where donors and recipients meet for a formal presentation of the scholarships. She has no suggestions as to what he ought to do; she simply wants to alert him to Hudson's concerns.

After giving the matter a fair bit of thought, Bryan figures he has only three options, which are described below. The options for action, as Bryan sees them, are:

A. Apparently this Hudson guy is a bit of a crank, and Bryan figures anything he does will only make the man angrier. Proof of this is his reaction to Bryan's card. And hey, isn't it best to just let sleeping dogs lie? It's not like Hudson can take back the scholarship, so the best thing Bryan can do is to steer clear of the whole thing. He should stay away from the Awards Ceremony so he won't have to see the guy at all.

B. Bryan needs to write a letter to Hudson now, and tactfully set him straight. He can calmly explain exactly what he told the clerk in the Awards Office: that nobody told him he had to write a letter, that he's been too busy to get around to it anyway, and that his priorities are on his studies—that's how he won the scholarship in the first place, right? Although the old guy has been out of school for a lot of years and probably can't remember what it's like to be busy, he was an engineering student once too, so he should be able to understand what it's like when Bryan gently reminds him.

C. Bryan should do nothing until he meets Hudson at the Awards Ceremony in the spring; then he can explain the situation patiently in person. After all, it's not Bryan's fault that they pile on the work in third year or that nobody told him what to write. Hudson will surely have cooled off by then, and Bryan can approach him calmly and set him straight.

Part A

Choose any *one* of the three options listed above, and, drawing explicitly on the principles of communication discussed in this book, explain why it would *not* be in Bryan's best interest to act as the option describes.

As you compose your answer, be sure to consider any constraints present in the situation, and take into account the elements of rhetorical balance, relation, ethos, purpose, footing, the Nine Axioms, and the ethics of communication. No matter which option you choose, be sure to analyze the situation fully. Write your analysis in an informal report addressed to your communication instructor.

Part B

Drawing on the principles of communication covered in this book, fully analyze the situation, paying attention to relevant constraints, the elements of relation, communication ethics, rhetorical balance, ethos, and professionalism. You should also consider the potential face risks for everyone involved. On the basis of your analysis, propose a more appropriate course of action than the ones listed. Write your analysis in an informal report addressed to your own communication instructor.

Case Study 4: Sam Spade and University Ace Painters

By Jeanie Wills and Jennifer MacLennan

It's the end of August, and you are just finishing up your summer job with University Ace Painters. Painting houses is challenging, and there seems to have been a lot of turn-over in staff. In fact, apart from your manager, Sam Spade, you're now the longest-term employee in your unit—and you've been with U-Ace only since May. Sam is also a student, just like you, only he's slightly more experienced.

U-Ace's advertising emphasizes promptness and reliability as well as quality. As unit manager, Sam is responsible for signing contracts, arranging schedules, and assigning crews to get the work done on time. Unfortunately, he has been struggling for most of the summer to keep up with all the contracts he's signed, and he's seriously behind. To be fair, part of the problem with the schedule has been weather: it rained more than usual this summer, making outdoor prep work and painting difficult.

But more important than weather has been the fact that, for some reason, people keep quitting on Sam. He says it's because he's been stuck with a load of jerks, and lately this conviction has been coming through in his actions: you've seen him start to lose it over the past couple of weeks, snapping at the few employees he has left. Recently he's even started staying away from work—'taking time off', he calls it. Clients have been calling to find out what's happened to their painting jobs, and Sam has quit returning their calls, saying he's stressed enough and doesn't need their hassles. The last time you saw him, he told you he has no intention of ever working in the painting business again!

One client in particular, Norman Wells, has begun to pose a problem for Sam. Early in the summer, Sam signed a contract to paint the guy's house in June. Wells paid a 25 per cent deposit—$1,250. It rained in June, though, and the good weather that followed in July and August was spent on other jobs that Sam had booked. Next week is the first week of September, and even with your limited experience in the field you can tell that this job isn't going to get done this year: the weather is already deteriorating, and Sam's painting staff (all students) will be returning to school soon.

You know that Norman Wells has called Sam repeatedly over the summer to ask about his paint job. Initially, Sam handled these calls by saying 'We'll be starting next week.' Each week, though, something else came up, and somehow the job never got started. Finally, Sam just quit taking the guy's calls, since Wells is plainly irritated and has begun asking for his deposit to be returned. Sam can't return the money just now since his cash flow is tied up in a couple of big jobs; he won't have the money until those are finished and paid for. Sam tells you that Norman Wells just doesn't understand the nature of the painting business, that he's a pain in the neck, and that it's impossible to make him happy. Sam says he is tired of being harassed by this client, who refuses to acknowledge the challenges facing painters.

Finally, on the last Friday of August, Norman Wells calls so frequently that Sam is driven to answer the phone. After so many unsuccessful attempts to reach Sam, Wells is outraged. He cancels the job and demands his money back. Sam promises to return the deposit on Monday, when he is expecting payment for a job he has completed. However, on Monday the payment doesn't come through. Sam can't face talking to Norman Wells again, so he decides to just wait until the money comes in and then refund the deposit. By the end of the week, Sam finds out that Norman Wells has lodged a formal complaint against him with the District Manager of University Ace Painters. Without talking to Norman Wells, Sam writes a cheque for $1,250, sticks it in an envelope with no cover letter or note, and drops it in the mailbox at the client's house.

Below you will find three possible courses of action for Sam to take next. They are:

A. Once Norman Wells cancelled the job, the only exigence was to refund his deposit, which Sam has now done. Sam really has no further responsibility to the client.

Also, because he doesn't want to return to the painting company next year, he doesn't owe them an explanation either. In fact, the company is aware of the challenges Sam has faced all summer, so they probably don't need an explanation. There is no need to do anything more.

B. The most important thing now is for Sam to save his reputation with University Ace Painters; although he isn't going to work for them anymore, he might need a reference sometime. He should write to the District Manager explaining that the challenges of the summer—including the weather, the unreliable staff, and the client's harassment—were not his fault, and pointing out the unreasonableness of this client. After all, he had no intention of keeping Norman Wells' money, and Sam should make it clear how unfair it is that the client has lodged a formal complaint.

C. Before Sam approaches the District Manager of University Ace Painters, he should straighten out this whole thing with Norman Wells. Now that the guy has his money back and has likely calmed down, Sam should send him an e-mail pointing out how unfair it was for Wells to lodge the complaint in the first place, and asking him to write Sam a letter of apology, with a copy to the District Manager, excusing Sam from responsibility, since after all it wasn't Sam's fault the weather didn't cooperate or that all his employees were jerks. And anyway, he never had any intention of keeping the guy's money.

Part A

Choose any *one* of the three options outlined above, and, drawing explicitly on the principles of communication that you have learned in this course, explain why it would *not* be in Sam's best interest to act as the option describes. Write your analysis in an informal report addressed to your communication instructor.

As you compose your answer, be sure to consider any constraints present in the situation, and take into account the elements of rhetorical balance, relation, ethos, purpose, footing, the Nine Axioms, and the ethics of communication. No matter which option you choose, be sure to analyze the situation fully.

Part B

Drawing on the principles of communication covered in this book, fully analyze the situation, paying attention to relevant constraints, the elements of relation, communication ethics, rhetorical balance, ethos, and professionalism. You should also consider the potential face risks for everyone involved. On the basis of your analysis, propose a more appropriate course of action than the ones listed. Write your analysis in an informal report addressed to your own communication instructor.

Case Study 5: The Bricklin Error

You have an interest in automotive design, and in particular you are fascinated by the specifications of the only exclusively Canadian automobile of the last half-century, the famous Bricklin, a Delorian-style sports car produced in Saint John, New Brunswick, between 1974 and 1976.

You know, for example, that the Bricklin exceeded safety standards of its time, and featured unique gull-wing doors and a built-in roll cage, side roll bars, and shock absorption. During a recent round of class presentations in front of a combined audience of four communication classes, one of the speakers from another class section, Chris Dunbar, proposed organizing a group of engineering students to build a Bricklin replica. Discussion turned to the unique design features of this car, including the body, which Chris noted was constructed of colour-impregnated acrylic bonded to fibreglass.

You were positive that this statement was wrong, since you recently read that the body was actually constructed of carbon impregnated epoxy, which does not crack the way acrylic or fibreglass does. During the comment session, you confidently pointed out this error in front of the four class groups. Chris tried to defend his assertion, but you were so positive that you overrode his objections, pretty much discrediting a major portion of his research.

However, after the speech session ended, you visited <www.bricklin.org> (a really interesting site if you would like to learn more about this fascinating Canadian car). There you discovered that Chris was right and you were the one who was wrong. While it is true that many of the later restorations were made of epoxy, the original was constructed from acrylic bonded to fibreglass, just as Chris had said in his speech.

Your class will not meet again until next week, and the four groups won't be together again at all, but you feel that the speaker and the rest of the class should be notified of your error. Since the event occurred in front of the entire group of all four class sections, and since it clearly embarrassed Chris, it is only fair that the correction should also be public.

Part A

Drawing on the principles of communication covered in this book, fully analyze the situation, paying attention to relevant constraints, the elements of relation, communication ethics, rhetorical balance, ethos, and professionalism. You should also consider the potential face risks for everyone involved. On the basis of your analysis, propose a more appropriate course of action than the ones listed. Write your analysis in an informal report addressed to your own communication instructor.

Part B

Write an appropriate message to be distributed via e-mail to the class mailing list. Structure your answer in memo format and address it to Chris Dunbar. As you write your message, be sure to consider all of the issues of content and relation arising out of this event. Take special care to adopt a suitable tone and develop your ideas appropriately.

Case Study 6: Dean and Jerry Make a Great Team

By Debora Rolfes and Jennifer MacLennan

Jerry is just coming to the end of the heaviest term of his college program. Not only has he had a full load of technical classes, but he's also been taking a required research class that involves working with a partner to prepare and present a research report. Jerry is not so keen on writing or public speaking, so he's relieved to have been paired with Dean, the smartest student in his year. Dean has won all the awards, is always on the honour list, and has his pick of summer jobs. Jerry sees this as a chance to pull off a top mark in a class in which he initially expected to do poorly.

Nevertheless, Jerry has felt a bit of pressure to contribute his share to the research project. Since he isn't a particularly good writer or speaker, Jerry has taken on the task of researching and summarizing the information needed for the report; Dean will then do the bulk of the writing and will take the lead at the presentation. Though he wasn't crazy about the task to begin with, Jerry discovers plenty of interesting material in the library and online, and in the end he is quite proud of the package of notes he hands over to Dean: 80 pages neatly divided into themes, 60 pages covering research proving their main thesis, and 20 pages of research that challenges their conclusions.

Dean has turned Jerry's research into a really good 15-page report; certainly the instructor thought so, and lavished praise on the quality of the writing. (Nothing was said about the quality of the research.) The 10-minute presentation is next; Jerry and Dean plan to highlight the relevant issues and present the major arguments in support of their thesis. Dean, the confident speaker, will take the lead, and Jerry will contribute only up to his comfort level; both will take questions during the follow-up Q/A session.

The presentation goes well; Dean is excellent and even Jerry manages to get through it without throwing up. But in the Q/A session, two things happen that really burn him up. First, it's as though Jerry is completely invisible. Most of the questioners direct their questions to Dean, and one of the guest adjudicators even congratulates *him* on the quality of the research! Second, one of the judges asks whether there is any research to support the opposite point of view. Although they didn't draw from it in the presentation, Jerry, who did the research, knows there's plenty: in fact, he gave Dean 20 pages of notes documenting the opposite case. Imagine his surprise, then, when he hears Dean state that the team discovered no valid research supporting the opposite point of view and that all reputable sources support the conclusion put forward in the presentation. The adjudicator looks somewhat doubtful, but he doesn't say anything more.

Jerry isn't sure what he ought to do about this situation, but several options have occurred to him. They are:

A. Dean's just wrong on this score, and Jerry should jump in and set the record straight, right then and there. Anyway, this will let him deal publicly with the real issue, which is that he hasn't been getting fair credit for his contributions. He should grab the opportunity to demonstrate that he knows more than Dean does about the situation.

B. Jerry should just let it go. After all, the purpose of working in a team is to learn teamwork, and challenging Dean's answer will be a public admission that Jerry can't work well with his partner. After all, what does it matter whether Dean was wrong, as long as the presentation went well and they got a good grade? Jerry should be just be glad it's over and that he's got a better mark than he expected in this class.

C. This whole thing stinks. Jerry's done most of the work, but he's almost invisible as far as the instructor and the adjudicators are concerned. He's not a confident enough speaker to interrupt the proceedings now, but after the presentation is over he should have it out with Jerry about why he has been stealing the credit for all the work the team did.

D. The issue here is an ethical one. Jerry shouldn't bring it out into the open in front of the whole gathering, but he should go to the professor later and report Dean's unethical behaviour in taking credit for the whole report and in lying about the other research.

Part A

Choose any *one* of the three options described above, and, drawing explicitly on the principles of communication that you have learned in this course, write an informal report in which you explain why the option you have selected is *not* a good solution to the exigence facing Jerry. Be sure to identify that exigence and to assess the potential face risks associated with whichever option you select. Consider, too, any constraints present in the situation, and take into account the elements of rhetorical balance, relation, ethos, purpose, footing, and the ethics of communication. Address your report to your communication instructor.

Part B

Drawing on the principles of communication covered in this book, fully analyze the situation, paying attention to relevant constraints, the elements of relation, communication ethics, rhetorical balance, ethos, and professionalism. You should also consider the potential face risks for everyone involved. On the basis of your analysis, propose a more appropriate course of action than the ones listed. Write your analysis in an informal report addressed to your communication instructor.

Case Study 7: Carlos Shuts Down the Plant

By Debora Rolfes and Jennifer MacLennan

In early February, Carlos was very excited to receive an offer of summer employment with Testamek Engineering. He was thrilled to be able to get his name known at a company that offers one of the best internship programs in the industry. Although for now the position involves more manual labour than engineering tasks, the job is great for getting his foot in the door at Testamek, because his new supervisor, Kim Watson, is also the person in charge of the company's internship program. Carlos hopes to use this summer job to catch Watson's eye so that he can successfully apply for an internship after completing his next year of school. He is sure that an internship will lead to an offer of full-time employment once he graduates.

Carlos's job involves doing safety inspections and preventive maintenance at several Testamek plants around the province. Much of his work is done on weekends, when the plants are not running at full capacity so less productivity is lost if they need to be shut down for repairs. When he interviewed with the company in January, and again when he accepted the job offer in February, Carlos made clear to Kim Watson that he would need time off to attend his sister's wedding on the second weekend of August. Watson assured Carlos that, when the time came to arrange the August schedule, she would be certain to accommodate Carlos's request.

Now it is the middle of August, and Carlos has just returned from his sister's wedding. Because he made the request so long in advance and was given the go-ahead, he didn't bother to confirm the schedule before heading out of town for the wedding, as planned. When he walks in on Monday morning, however, he is surprised to find himself in a serious jam.

It turns out that Kim Watson never did formally approve his weekend off, and Carlos was scheduled to help with the equipment upgrade at the central plant. When Carlos did not show up for work, the plant manager called the district supervisor of Testamek to complain about the shortage of manpower, pointing out that the upgrade would take an extra day, and the plant would have to shut down on Monday. The district supervisor phoned Kim Watson, who rushed to fill Carlos's spot on the upgrade team, but by the time she could get there, they were so far behind schedule that the upgrade could not be completed until Monday. The shut-down has put everyone in a bad mood: the union is up in arms with head office, and the CEO has just chewed out the district supervisor, who in turn has demanded to know what kind of slack operation Kim Watson thinks she's running. Watson has just hung up the phone when Carlos appears in her office to ask what all the excitement is about. In response, he receives a stern lecture about reliability and responsibility.

Below are three possibilities for how Carlos could respond to Kim Watson:

A. It's too bad about the shut-down, but it's totally not Carlos's fault. The important thing is for Carlos not to lose his temper at being unjustly accused, and to give Kim Watson a chance to apologize for chewing him out. To put things right, and to save his own face, he needs to remind Watson of the facts: he requested the time off in good faith way back in February, and Watson approved it, so he was completely in the right to take the weekend off to go to the wedding.

B. It's too bad about the shut-down, but it's totally not Carlos's fault. Carlos needs to call the plant manager and the district supervisor to explain that the mistake was not his, but Kim Watson's. After all, it's not fair that the lost productivity should be blamed on him when he hasn't done anything wrong. The best way for Carlos to redeem himself as a responsible worker is for the higher-ups to know what really happened and not think of Carlos as a slacker.

C. It's too bad about the shut-down, but even though it's totally not Carlos's fault, he needs to suck it up and apologize to Kim Watson. After all, although Carlos isn't at fault, he still needs Watson on his side if he's going to get an internship next year, so buttering her up now is probably a good idea.

Part A

Choose any *one* of the three options described above, and, drawing explicitly on the principles of communication discussed in this book, write an informal report, addressed to your communication instructor, that explains why the option you have selected is *not* a good solution to the exigence facing Carlos. Be sure to identify that exigence and to assess the potential face risks associated with whichever option you select. Consider, too, any constraints present in the situation, and take into account the elements of rhetorical balance, relation, ethos, purpose, footing, and the ethics of communication.

Part B

Drawing on the principles of communication covered in this book, fully analyze the situation, paying attention to relevant constraints, the elements of relation, communication ethics, rhetorical balance, ethos, and professionalism. You should also consider the potential face risks for everyone involved. On the basis of your analysis, propose a course of action for Carlos that is more appropriate than the ones listed. Write your analysis in an informal report addressed to your communication instructor.

Part C

The mix-up with the weekend upgrade at Testamek's biggest plant has left Kim Watson's department with some public relations mending to do. She has decided it's best that Carlos write a letter to the district supervisor of Testamek to explain and apologize for the confusion that led to the unscheduled Monday shut down of the central plant.

Imagine you are Carlos. Write the letter that he should send to the district supervisor of Testamek. Make sure that the letter is correctly formatted and that it adheres to the guidelines provided for writing a letter of conciliation. Address the letter to Mr. Jamshed Ramtej, District Supervisor, South-Central Saskatchewan, Testamek Engineering, 1331 Centre Street, Saskatoon SK, S0K 1J1.

Case Study 8: Presentation Interruptus

After a busy term as group leader on your senior project, you and your team are scheduled to showcase your work in a formal presentation to an audience of faculty members, other students in your discipline, and professionals in the field. The evening is tightly scheduled, with six groups presenting, and each group has been allotted a maximum of twenty minutes—fifteen to deliver the presentation and an additional five minutes to answer questions. You have been told that you cannot under any circumstances exceed this time limit, and for the sake of the other presenters and the adjudicators your supervising professor has said he will be ruthless. Presentations are scheduled to begin at 5:30 p.m., a half hour after the last class for the day has finished. Your group, made up of Laura, Colin, Tess, and yourself, has been scheduled to go first.

Everyone on the team is well prepared and confident; you've been practising together, and are ready, with everything smoothly and precisely scheduled so as to fit into your allotted fifteen minutes. However, just as you have finished introducing the project and have stepped back to let Laura come forward with the second segment, a student you do not recognize enters the room. He doesn't take a seat, but instead heads straight for the front of the room where your group is presenting.

Before anyone can react, the guy walks right across the front of the room, passing in front Laura, who has been startled into silence. He seems not to realize or care what's going on, because without a word to anyone, he begins to rummage among some chairs and boxes that are stacked in the front corner. Laura, who has faltered, resumes speaking, but she is clearly having some difficulty collecting her thoughts. Puzzled by the disturbance and anxious about your group's presentation, you quietly approach the stranger and ask him to leave. He seems not to have heard you, so you touch him lightly on the arm to get his attention, and repeat your whispered request. However, instead of reacting with embarrassment, he snaps his arm roughly away from your touch and shouts, 'Get your hands off me! I just came to pick up my backpack!' He finishes this outburst by calling you an ugly name, then grabs up the pack and stomps out, slamming the door loudly.

Although this interruption has actually taken only two or three minutes, it is enough to throw your presentation off track. Laura picks up where she left off, and you all proceed as best you can to normalize the situation, but you've lost your momentum, and from then on nothing seems to go as planned. By the fifteen-minute mark, your presentation is not quite finished, but your professor stops you anyway and initiates the question period.

At this point it's not clear how your grade will be affected, but the incident has left you and your classmates feeling frustrated and angry because the well-polished talk you prepared has not materialized. When you corner your professor at the end of the evening, he says only that unexpected things sometimes happen, and what matters is how effectively and professionally you adapted to the situation.

Part A

Drawing on the principles of communication discussed in this book, analyze the event described above in order to answer the three questions that follow. Write your analysis in a short informal report addressed to your communication instructor.

A. What challenges of face and footing does this incident create for you, as group leader?
B. As an ethical communicator, and especially as leader of the project team, what are your primary communicative responsibilities in this situation? Why?
C. If the unknown student's behaviour can be understood as a kind of message, what is he communicating? To whom? How much thought did he give to the audience for his action?

Part B

This experience has sensitized you to the impact of something you've witnessed many times in the college: students who walk into a room where a class is in session in order to retrieve a forgotten item. In the past, you wouldn't have paid much attention, but now that you've experienced this yourself, you no longer regard such disruptions as harmless. In fact, on one or two occasions, you have sensed that the professor was just as distressed by the interruption to his class as your project team members were when their presentation was derailed. You even suspect that the casual acceptance of this kind of disruption contributed to the behaviour of the stranger who compromised your presentation.

You have been discussing this issue with your design group, and they feel that your new-found insight should be communicated to other students. As group leader, you have been elected to send a mass e-mail message to all of the students in your program. One of your readers will be the Dean, who will have to approve your message before it is circulated.

Write the message that you hope to distribute to your fellow students, bearing in mind the challenges of face and footing, and the constraints that these impose.

Case Study 9: Why Chris Should Use a Pencil

As the last assignment of the term for your communication class, you have been asked to collect and organize all the written work you've done over the course and hand it in to your instructor in a writing portfolio. This compendium is expected to contain all the original graded writing for the course, and it is supposed to be arranged in a way that will demonstrate not only your writing progress, but also attitude, work habits, and professionalism. This portfolio of your work will constitute 15 per cent of your final grade, as laid out on the course outline and as discussed in class.

As you work one evening in the computer lab, you encounter Christian Matthews, one of your classmates. You don't know him all that well, except that you've seen enough of him to have formed the opinion that he's arrogant and a bit of a hot-head. Right now he seems to be in a terrible flap over the writing portfolio assignment.

Though the portfolio requirement has been clear since the beginning of the course, Chris claims to have forgotten that the graded assignments would need to be re-submitted. When he shows you his collection of graded work, you quickly see what he's wound up about: on nearly every one of the assignments, he has written angry and often sarcastic responses to the professor's comments, in ink. Most of his remarks are of a tone and content—including profanities—that would be inappropriate for anyone else to see, let alone an instructor of professional communication. You're no prude, but it's a bit of a shock even to you to see some of this stuff written in black and white on a course assignment.

Not surprisingly, Chris dislikes the thought of the professor seeing his amended assignments. He argues that his responses to the professor were justified by her comments on his assignments, and he was just giving as good as he got. And anyway, those remarks are his own business, not hers. Now all he has to do is figure out a way to get himself off the hook. Unfortunately for him, Chris's options are limited, since failure to hand in a complete portfolio could result in a loss of 15 per cent of his final course mark. Chris's average in the course stands at 55 per cent, and he can't afford to throw away 15 per cent; he needs all the remaining grades that he can get.

Chris tells you he is toying with three possible courses of action, shown below.

A. The instructor is a professional and should be capable of remaining objective in her assessment of the assignments. Chris should assume that his communication professor will understand what happened, and hand in the entire portfolio as it stands, including the comments, without any further explanation.

B. Chris should cross out only the worst of the profanity, and leave the rest of his comments as they are. He should assume that his communication professor will understand what happened, and he should hand in the portfolio without any further explanation.

C. Seeing his comments might unfairly prejudice the professor against Chris. He should black out all of his comments so that they can't be seen and then hand in the portfolio with a brief note explaining that the blacked-out comments were simply notes to himself that were made after the graded assignment came back.

Part A

Choose any *one* of the three options described above, and, drawing explicitly on the principles of communication discussed in this book, write an informal report that explains why the option you have selected is *not* a good solution to the exigence facing Chris. Be sure to identify that exigence and to assess the potential face risks associated with whichever option you select. Consider, too, any constraints present in the situation, and take into account the elements of rhetorical balance, relation, ethos, purpose, footing, and the ethics of communication.

Part B

Drawing on the principles of communication covered in this book, fully analyze the situation facing Chris, paying attention to relevant constraints, the elements of relation, communication ethics, rhetorical balance, ethos, and professionalism. You should also consider the potential face risks for everyone involved. On the basis of your analysis, propose a course of action for Chris that is more appropriate than the ones listed. Write your analysis in an informal report addressed to your communication instructor.

Appendix B

How Texts Communicate: Some Suggestions for Reading Critically

Reading critically means more than simply passing your eyes over words on a page. Instead, like other forms of communication, reading is an active process that requires careful attention to both verbal and nonverbal elements, to both content and relation. Becoming a better reader will make you a better communicator in general, will improve your critical skills, and will actually, in the long run, save you time and confusion.

The texts you read—from technical reports to your textbooks to newspapers and magazines—are as various as the writers who produced them. They may be personal or impersonal, accessible or challenging, formal or informal. They may be informative, descriptive, narrative, or persuasive. But in spite of their differences, the words you read all share a common feature. No matter what their purpose, their intended audience, or their author, they are all the products of deliberate communicative choices made by a human being in order to bring about a desired result or achieve a desired goal. Reading carefully and thoughtfully means that you pay attention not only to the content of the document but also to the relationship it is building with its audience, to its assumptions about the situation and the reader, and to the attitude it displays toward the audience, the situation, the subject, and the writer herself.

Reading for pleasure and reading for work or study are really different activities. The stories we read for pleasure create their own narrative momentum, which doesn't require us to puzzle out the pattern of the writer's thinking or to remember details of an argument. They are typically organized chronologically, which is one of the easiest organizational patterns to follow and remember. The sorts of texts you read for school or work are rarely as accessible or pleasurable as novels or magazine articles, and are less likely to use the chronological pattern of organization. They are therefore typically more challenging to understand and to retain.

In this segment we are going to focus on the reading you do for professional purposes, learning three levels of skills to help master these difficult kinds of reading. First, you will learn some 'quick fixes' to help you read more critically, or analytically. These can be mastered immediately, and they will make your reading much more effective right away.

Advantages of Reading Actively

- To process large amounts of reading material more efficiently and quickly
- To provide an overview of content and promote greater involvement in the interaction
- To increase understanding

Second, we will consider a slightly more complex study-reading method that will help you to manage large amounts of information efficiently. It is designed to help you with the kinds of typical texts you encounter on the job: reports, instruction manuals, policy and procedures documentation, and so on. Finally, we will consider a set of more detailed questions designed to help you read more in-depth materials with greater care and attention. At times you may be asked not only to comment on the explicit content of a text, but also on its unexpressed agenda, its embedded purpose, and the ways in which it creates particular effects. As we know already, it is often the implicit, unspoken elements of a message that are the most influential and long-lasting. The in-depth questions are designed to guide you in uncovering what those meanings are and how they work.

Three Quick Fixes for Better Reading

How many times have you finished reading something for a class, only to find that you had no idea what you had just read? The time you put in reading the material was time wasted, since you understood very little and retained even less. If you wanted to retain the material, you had to re-read the entire text, and even then you might have found that your eyes tended to wander across the page without taking in much of what you were reading. You might also find your mind straying from the task, and realize that you'd just read several pages without taking in anything: your eyes moved across the page, but you weren't really paying attention. The problem is not necessarily with your ability to understand and remember; the problem is with your reading strategy.

Many readers mistakenly approach work-related texts as though they are novels: they simply start reading at the beginning and continue to the end, expecting to pick up the details on the way. While this is a fine strategy for pleasure reading, it is ineffective for other kinds of reading tasks. Here are three 'quick fixes' you can use immediately to improve both your understanding and your retention. They don't take much longer than a single reading, and they take far less than reading a text twice.

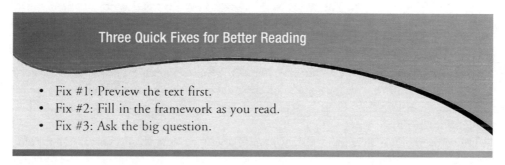

Three Quick Fixes for Better Reading

- Fix #1: Preview the text first.
- Fix #2: Fill in the framework as you read.
- Fix #3: Ask the big question.

Fix #1: Preview the text first

Before you ever read another document for school or work, take a few minutes to preview the whole thing first. Try to get a sense of its main purpose and the general shape of its argument. Read the summary or the introduction, and the conclusion. Make note of the headings and subheadings in the body of the text. If there are no headings or subheadings, scan the first and last sentence of major paragraphs or sections.

Taking a few moments to do this will actually save you time in the long run, because it will give you a clearer sense of what the text is doing and where it's going. It will be much easier to understand and remember what you're reading if you know what to expect before you start. Make it a habit *always* to take a few minutes to preview before you begin reading.

Fix #2: Fill in the framework as you read

Once you have previewed the chapter or report, you will have a clearer idea about the framework around which the arguments are organized, and about its main purpose. As a result, you can read more knowledgeably and with an expectation about what is going to be presented. Because you know what to expect, you can be more engaged and alert as you read, and you can link the material in the reading to the framework you've already identified with your preview. You will even be able to take quicker and more efficient notes, because you've inferred an outline structure for the chapter.

Use a pencil rather than a highlighting pen to mark important ideas, since with a pencil you can jot down a brief outline as you read. Look for the main points and quickly list them in the margin. You should make your comments right in the book if you can, since your brief comments and notes will be right alongside what you've read and you'll easily be able to find them later. Writing your brief notes in the margins will also mean that you can work efficiently no matter where you are reading: you don't need to be sitting at a desk or in front of your computer.

Fix #3: Answer the big question

Once you have previewed and then read the text, you are in a position to consider how it communicates on a relational, nonverbal level. One way to understand the relationship established or maintained in the text is to ask the big question: 'Who is saying what to whom, and for what purpose?'

This question is really three distinct questions: who is speaking, to whom is she speaking, and what does she want? There is no need, at the beginning, to answer these questions in detail, but you should think about what they can tell you about the dynamic that is created or maintained. For example, consider the e-mail letter of congratulations shown in Figure 5.2 (Chapter 5), from Randy Alexander to Peter Holowaczok. *Who is saying what to whom, and for what purpose?* The explicit dynamic appears to be a more senior employee offering congratulations to a junior employee for his achievement in becoming employee of the month, and offering some helpful suggestions for his work.

However, it's clear that the explicit dynamic doesn't tell the whole story. *Who is saying what to whom?* Judging by the tone, emphasis, and language in the message, the dynamic that is being created is one of hostility and jealousy. The writer seems both threatened by and jealous of the other man's success; although he doesn't say so directly, he seems to feel that his own deserving work has not been recognized.

However, instead of approaching those who could act on this problem, he chooses to vent his frustration and anger on a junior employee through condescending language, highhanded suggestions, and a sarcastic tone. Here, the nonverbal cues clearly contradict the verbal cues, making the analysis of the relational elements a little easier. What should Peter Holowaczok learn from this exchange? He should take care around Randy Alexander, who appears bitter and jealous, and who takes pot-shots at someone who is not in a position to defend himself.

Although it's unlikely that the relational elements of communication will always be as thinly veiled as they are in this example, there will always be some evidence in the text that communicates information about relation. Asking the big question of *Who is saying what to whom?* will help you to pay careful attention to this dynamic so that your own messages can respond effectively to the messages of others.

How the Pros Do It: Study-Reading by the SQ3R Method

During World War II, the American military developed an efficient reading method to assist recruits in quickly reading and mastering the large amounts of training material facing them. Known as 'SQ3R', it was made available to the public in Francis P. Robinson's book, *Effective Study* (1946: 29–35).

The SQ3R method is similar to the quick fixes we have just discussed, but it is somewhat more elaborate. It was designed primarily for reading textbook materials which are organized for teaching, and which use headings, bullets, checklists, chapter summaries, and other visual and organizational devices to aid the reader. In fact, a comparison of textbooks published before and after the study-reading method was popularized shows that textbook design has gradually evolved to accommodate some of the reader-friendly principles of SQ3R.

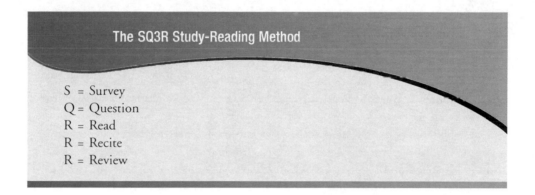

The SQ3R Study-Reading Method

S = Survey
Q = Question
R = Read
R = Recite
R = Review

The study-read method is a five-step process that enables you to read a text efficiently by making several quick passes through it rather than trying to read it all at once.

S=Survey

As in the preview step discussed earlier, the 'survey' step in SQ3R involves glancing over the headings in the chapter to identify the few main ideas that the chapter discusses. In your quick survey, you should also read the final summary paragraph if the chapter has one. This survey should not take more than a minute and will reveal the three to six central ideas in the chapter. The survey will help you organize the ideas as you read them later.

Q=Question

The second step involves formulating a question out of each of the headings. If, for example, the heading is 'Study-Reading by the SQ3R Method', your question might be 'What does "SQ3R" stand for?' Thinking about the main points in the text as questions will increase your active participation in what you are reading, and so increase your comprehension. Rephrasing the heading as a question will also make important points stand out, so they are easier to find. It doesn't take long to turn a heading into a question, but it does take conscious effort, and helps keep your attention as you read to find the answer.

R=Read

Now read the text as you normally would, from beginning to end. However, as you read, look for the answers to the questions you posed. Reading to find answers to your own questions will keep you actively attentive and involved and prevent the kind of wandering of attention that sometimes occurs with unfocused reading.

R=Recite

Stop when you have read the first headed section. Try to state the answer to your question out loud. Express your answer in your own words, and try to give an example. If you can do this, you will know you've actually learned what is in the section; if you can't, then take another look. You may want to jot down an outline of these main ideas as you go, but there is no need to rewrite the text. Brief notes should be enough. Continue this process until you have finished the entire reading.

R=Review

Once you have finished the reading, return to your brief notes to get an overview of the chapter's contents. You can check your memory by trying to recite the main ideas for each point once again.

The benefits of the SQ3R method are well known. It offers a way of processing large amounts of reading material fairly quickly and efficiently, and works well for reading technical material and reports as well as textbooks. The first few times you try it, it will take a little longer than your normal approach to reading, but once you have the hang of it you will find that it takes no longer than a single read-through, but with the added benefit of increased understanding and retention.

Detailed Questions for Close Critical Reading

In addition to reading a text or report to glean its content and general information, you will need to be able to read with a little more sensitivity to unspoken agendas, implications, and motives. The questions below are designed to help with the task of close critical reading in cases where what's going on in the communication interaction is not so immediately obvious, as is the case, for example, in Wayne C. Booth's essay 'The Rhetorical Stance', on page 44.

As you will recall from the Nine Axioms of Communication, what is left unsaid can be as important, or even more important, than what is explicitly stated. It is in the nonverbal elements of the message that the relationship between speaker and audience is framed. However, these can also be much more difficult to analyze accurately and fully.

The questions below provide a kind of framework for thinking about texts that you must understand more deeply. They will help you to figure out the relational dynamics of the document you are reading, but they will also provide you with a method for understanding how, in general, written communication influences its intended audiences. The questions have been clustered into categories for a 'levels of analysis' approach to reading.

Subject, purpose, and meaning

The first step in understanding the meaning of any written material is to be sure you have grasped its topic and purpose. Think not only about what the message actually says, but also about the way the tone and nonverbal qualities confirm or contradict the explicit content.

1. What is the topic of this work?
2. Define any special terms introduced or used in the reading.
3. Does this work have an explicit statement of purpose? If so, what is it? Where is it found?
4. Is there any distinction between its stated purpose and its actual purpose?
5. Is the audience being asked to undertake any specific action(s)? What are they?
6. What is the context or setting in which this message was created? How has the context shaped the message?
7. How is the selection organized? (That is, what pattern of organizations is employed?)
8. What evidence, or what kind of evidence, is provided to support the argument? Is anything significant left out?
9. Does the speaker misrepresent aspects of the problem?
10. Can you find examples of propaganda devices or fallacious reasoning?

The character of the speaker: Ethos

As you know, all communication creates an image of the writer or speaker and establishes (or undermines) that person's credibility, authority, and footing. The following questions are an aid to understanding how the speaker's presentation of self contributes to the meaning and purpose of the selection.

1. Does the speaker display sincerity, authority, and credibility? Pick out some examples.
2. What is the speaker's stance, or attitude, toward the audience? Does the speaker address you with appropriate respect?
3. Does the speaker have, or establish, an appropriate footing?
4. Does the speaker appear sincere? How does she gain authority or credibility?
5. Based on these elements, describe the character of the person who is speaking. How does she appear to see herself in this interaction?
6. What common ground does the speaker create between herself and the audience? In other words, what values does the speaker seem to share with her intended reader?
7. How personal or impersonal is this passage?
8. What is the tone of the selection?

Style and strategy

In a communication act, a strategy is any device or method that a communicator uses to influence an audience's attitudes, feelings, actions, or beliefs. Communication strategies may involve the kind of language that the speaker employs, the use of visuals and images to convey strong messages, or the way the message is actually structured and organized. Verbal strategies include such devices as specialized language or jargon, striking comparisons, humour, irony or sarcasm, and propaganda devices such as name-calling or bandwagon appeals. Structural strategies or devices may include organization patterns, repetition and parallel constructions, or even numbering of items. Visual elements include illustrations and diagrams, borders, special print features such as boldfacing or underlining, and even the use of white space.

In short, any method that can help a writer to sway an audience can be considered a communicative or rhetorical device.

1. Explain the meaning of the title. Why do you think the writer chose this particular title?
2. Does the passage employ any kind of specialized vocabulary or jargon? What effect does this kind of language have on the audience who will be reading the passage?
3. Does the writer attempt to sway your opinion using emotional arguments or appeals? Give an example.
4. What kind of evidence does the writer present to support the argument?
5. Does this selection employ humour? If so, what are the qualities that make it funny? How does humour help the writer to communicate her message?
6. What details does the author emphasize in this selection? What role do these play in making the passage effective? What are they meant to communicate?
7. Is this passage formal, informal, or casual writing? How can you tell? How suitable is its chosen style to the purpose and audience for which it was written?
8. Is the selection ironic? Is it satirical? Does it employ parody? How do you know? What is the effect of these devices?
9. Metaphors and similes are forms of figurative comparison that compare two things that are essentially unlike. Find some particularly effective metaphors or similes. How do they work? What is their effect on the intended audience?
10. A symbol is a thing that stands for some meaning, usually an abstraction, beyond itself: a national flag stands for patriotism, a red rose and a box of chocolates for romance, the green faces of Roughriders fans for enthusiastic support of their team. Does the writer employ any such symbols? If so, what are they, and what do they represent? Why do you think the author chose to use symbolism?

Structure

The structure of a message refers to the number and arrangement of its significant parts. A typical report, for example, employs the five standard parts familiar to you as 'SIDCRA'. However, what is most interesting from the point of view of message design is the internal structure of the discussion, which is where the choices of the writer become most evident and significant. Essentially, in analyzing the structure of a message, you are looking for the types of sections or divisions contained in the discussion, the number of these sections, and the order into which they are arranged. The arrangement of these parts can make a difference in how the reader experiences the meaning of the message.

1. Into how many parts is the discussion divided? Is this division significant?
2. Where is the main purpose expressed? How many reasons are given to support the arguments in the discussion?
3. In what order are the reasons presented? What effect does this ordering of parts have on the passage?

4. What kind of evidence does the author use to support his position? Is it convincing?

5. What device does the author use to open the selection? To close it?

6. Does the author use any unusual sentence or paragraph structure (for instance, inversion)? Why might this be?

7. What contribution to the meaning or impact of the passage, if any, is made by its physical layout (including paragraphing, numbering, headings, categories, illustrations, etc.)?

Speaker–audience relationship

In addition to providing some kind of content, all communication attempts to establish, or helps to maintain, a relationship between the speaker and the audience. Looking closely at the selection can help you to identify the kind of reader that the speaker or writer intends to address. These questions are meant to help you uncover this information.

1. Who are the intended readers of this passage? Are they general readers, or are they specialized? How can you tell?

2. Is any specific group excluded by this passage? Is this exclusion significant?

3. What is the speaker's attitude toward the audience? Are you part of the audience?

4. What assumptions does the writer make about the reader's needs, expectations, concerns, or prior experience?

5. What assumptions does the writer make about the audience's beliefs, fears, prejudices, or desires?

6. What attention is paid by the writer to the emotional impact of the discourse on the audience? In what direction does the writer attempt to move them emotionally?

7. How does the speaker appeal to the audience's self-interest?

8. Would you like to meet this speaker or writer in person? Why or why not?

9. What effect does the writer want the audience to experience?

These in-depth questions are intended to help you get the most out of your critical reading. They are a useful place to begin if you are asked to assess someone else's messages. If you can learn to think your way through any of your readings—whether for this class or another—using these terms, you will develop a critical habit of reading that will help you to understand much of the way everyday discourses influence and engage you. Such critical skills are helpful in every class, and in every situation in which people use language to influence each other.

Reading actively using one or more of these methods will improve both your immediate comprehension and your overall understanding of the communication process. Like any skill, critical reading takes practice to master, but it also gets easier and more efficient with practice. As reading attentively becomes a habit, you will find that it also takes much less time and effort, and that your awareness of what is being communicated, and of the dynamic that is operating in any interaction, becomes much keener. As with other communication skills, improving your reading skill will pay handsome dividends in your professional and personal interactions.

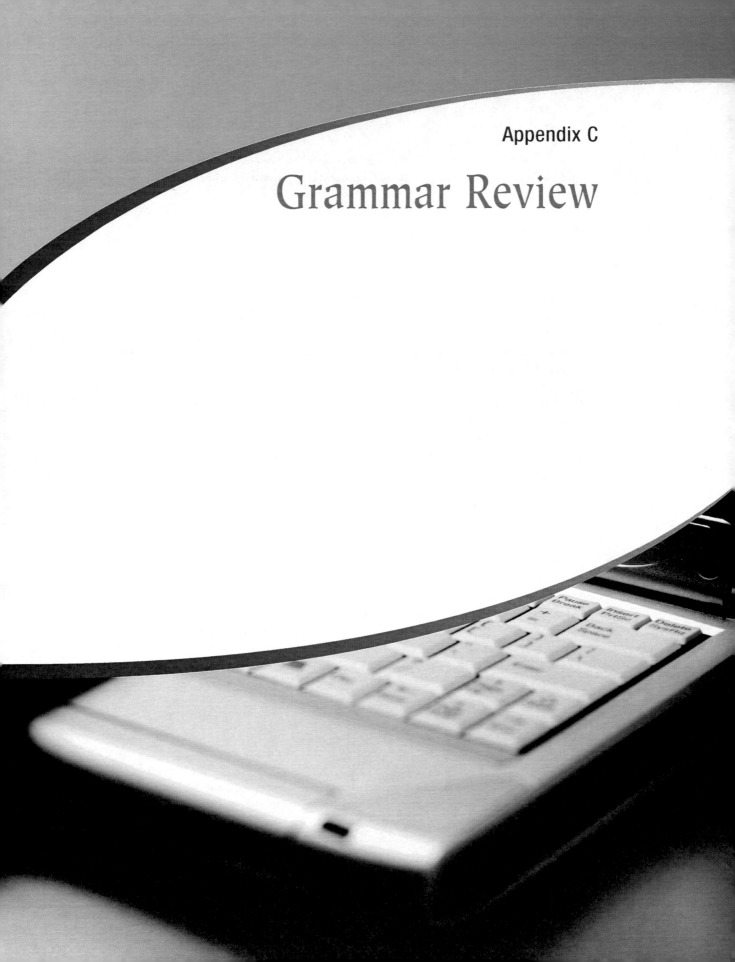

Grammar Review

Writing effectively means choosing your words carefully and putting them into an understandable order so that your reader receives the message clearly and without ambiguity. Part of this process involves using correct grammar. Incorrect grammar can undermine the clarity of your writing, and may sometimes create unintended meanings. In a professional situation this can mean embarrassment, a loss of credibility, and even a loss of revenue. It quite literally pays to give some attention to what you're really saying in your work.

As well, you will recall that the accuracy and command in your written work contribute to the way others judge your professionalism and competence. Poor grammar reflects badly on your professional abilities, making you appear negligent or unskilful, or both. Remember that even those who are weak in these areas themselves will notice someone else's mistakes, and they may be just as unforgiving—in some cases more so—than your professors.

As you know from Chapter 1, one of the most common complaints that colleges hear from employers, no matter what the field, is that graduates can't communicate clearly and accurately in writing. The most visible problem is a poor command of spelling and grammar, and most readers are able to spot these weaknesses in other people's writing. It pays to take care with your sentence structure and usage, and to proofread carefully.

This appendix is included to provide you with a handy guide to avoiding the most common grammar errors. If you need a more thorough review, your communication instructor will be able to recommend a more comprehensive book.

Common Sentence Errors

Though there are many ways to mangle the language, the following six errors in grammatical structure seem to occur with frequency.

- subject–verb agreement errors
- sentence fragments
- run-on sentences
- pronoun, tense, and person agreement errors
- modifier errors
- faulty parallelism

In order to understand these faults and correct them in your writing, it is important first to have a clear understanding of how sentences are built.

Word groups

Most of these common sentence errors arise from faulty sentence constructions. Sentences, as you likely know, are made up of a subject (the person or agent who acts) and a verb or verb cluster (the action that is performed, or the state of being expressed). Every sentence, no matter how complex or how long, must feature both of these essential elements.

Simple sentences typically contain only one verb, though more complex structures may be built by adding additional clauses and phrases to the basic structure. Consider the following simple sentences; subjects are marked with a single underline, verbs with a double underline:

The <u>dog</u> <u>lunged</u>.
<u>Tom</u> <u>screamed</u>.
The <u>car</u> <u>stopped</u>.
The <u>driver</u> <u>jumped</u> out.

These simple sentences are the sort that you first learned to read: a simple subject consisting of a single word, and a single verb. Unfortunately, you'll quickly realize that this basic structure is not sufficient to communicate complex ideas or nuance of thought. To communicate more sophisticated ideas, you need to be able to add information, to vary the structure of your sentences, and to elaborate or refine your statements with modifiers. Consider this revised and enlarged version:

The <u>dog</u> <u>lunged</u> at Tom, biting him viciously. As <u>Tom</u> <u>screamed</u> in pain, a passing <u>car</u> <u>screeched</u> to a stop. The <u>driver</u> <u>jumped</u> out and, after driving off the dog, <u>bundled</u> Tom into the back seat of his car and <u>sped</u> away. The whole <u>thing</u> <u>was</u> over in just seconds.

You can quickly see that the structures in this version are much more elaborate than the simple sentences above. In fact, the excerpt contains two simple sentences, each including modifying words and phrases, along with one complex sentence and one compound sentence.

Compound and complex sentences are made by adding additional subject–verb structures—clauses—to the initial simple sentence structure. You may also add phrases that help to explain your meaning. Let's take a closer look at these two structures—clauses and phrases—in order to understand how compound and complex sentences are created.

A **clause** is any group of words that contains a verb and its grammatical subject. Clauses are essential structures for building sentences, which by definition must contain at least one clause (that is, every sentence must feature a subject and a verb). Thus, the simple sentences featured in the example above are also single clauses.

There are two types of clauses. The first is known as an **independent clause**; this term signifies that the structure of the clause is grammatically complete and makes sense without the addition of further information. Independent clauses are important, because they are the fundamental units from which sentences are made.

The second type of clause is known as a **dependent clause**. These clauses are formed by adding a joining word called a subordinate conjunction, which changes the clause from a complete statement into a modifying structure that depends on another clause to make its meaning clear and complete.

In order to understand the relationship between independent and dependent clauses, let's return to the simple sentences from above. Each of the items in the first column is complete, but look at what happens when a subordinate conjunction is added:

The <u>dog</u> <u>lunged</u>.	Just as the <u>dog</u> <u>lunged</u>,
<u>Tom</u> <u>screamed</u>.	While <u>Tom</u> <u>screamed</u>,
The <u>driver</u> <u>jumped</u>.	When the <u>car</u> <u>stopped</u>,
The <u>driver</u> <u>jumped</u> out.	After the <u>driver</u> <u>jumped</u> out,

Each of the clauses on the right has been reduced to a lesser (or subordinate) role, and we wait for something more to complete the thought. The subordinate conjunctions 'just as', 'while', 'when', and 'after' change the meaning of these simple sentences, altering their independent clauses to dependent structures that make no sense on their own. In order to complete these thoughts and make them into sentences, however, we need to add another clause—this time an independent one. For example:

Just as the <u>dog</u> <u>lunged</u>, Tom began to run.
While <u>Tom</u> <u>screamed</u>, the dog sunk its teeth into his leg.
When the <u>car</u> <u>stopped</u>, the dog ran away.
After the <u>driver</u> <u>jumped</u> out, everything happened very quickly.

Remember that every sentence must have at least one independent clause. Sentences like these, which contain both independent and dependent (subordinate) clauses, are known as **complex sentences** because they are made up of two different types of clauses.

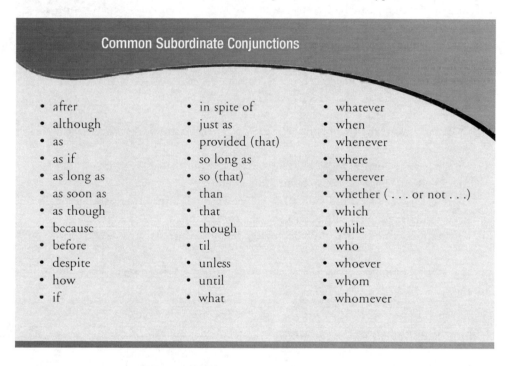

Common Subordinate Conjunctions

- after
- although
- as
- as if
- as long as
- as soon as
- as though
- because
- before
- despite
- how
- if

- in spite of
- just as
- provided (that)
- so long as
- so (that)
- than
- that
- though
- til
- unless
- until
- what

- whatever
- when
- whenever
- where
- wherever
- whether (. . . or not . . .)
- which
- while
- who
- whoever
- whom
- whomever

Like a complex sentence, a **compound sentence** also contains two or more clauses. However, instead of subordinating one idea to another as a complex sentence does, a compound sentence joins independent clauses together using one of six **coordinate conjunctions** (and, but, or, nor, yet, and so). In a compound sentence, the clauses are equally important to the meaning of the sentence.

A passing <u>motorist</u> <u>spotted</u> Tom, and <u>stopped</u> to help.
The <u>dog</u> <u>bit</u> Tom badly, but fortunately the <u>wound</u> <u>was</u> not life-threatening.
<u>They</u> <u>sent</u> Tom home from the hospital this morning, so <u>he</u> <u>must be doing</u> all right.

A **compound-complex sentence**, as you may have guessed, contains two or more independent clauses, plus one or more dependent clauses. The examples below are compound-complex structures. See if you can identify the independent and dependent clauses in each. (Hint: To help you identify the clauses, look for the subject–verb pairs and for any subordinate conjunctions.)

After I saw what happened to Tom, I became more fearful of dogs and made an effort to avoid them whenever I could.

Tom says that he still likes dogs in spite of what happened to him, and he is not going to allow this experience to make him afraid.

I think it just goes to show that you can never be too careful, and I will sure be on the lookout for vicious dogs in the future.

As you build your sentences by combining clauses, you can also use phrases that act as modifiers or even nouns. A phrase is a meaningful grouping of words that is neither a clause nor a sentence (that is, it contains no verb or no subject). A phrase is not an essential part of a sentence; it is used strictly to elaborate or modify. No matter how long it might be, a phrase cannot stand alone as a sentence because it is missing the subject–verb combination that makes a complete statement. The following are phrases:

- climbing up the hill
- across the street
- beside the store with the big sign out front
- over between the drive and the garage
- with my dad
- around the corner on Woodill Street, across from the candy store
- in Danny Morrison's shop behind the laundromat
- at the ball field behind Colby School, down the hill from the parking lot
- meeting my boyfriend's parents for the first time
- up in the attic behind the flue, beside the old lawn furniture

Because these groups of words lack a complete verb or a subject, they are phrases, even though some may be quite long.

Joining clauses to make sentences

As we have learned, independent clauses may be combined into longer sentences known as compound sentences. These are usually built of related independent clauses, joined in any of several ways. The following sample illustrates the different methods that can be used to build compound sentences:

Two related independent clauses:

Dave frequently dribbles. He plays basketball.

These may be joined by:

- using a coordinate conjunction (and, but, or, nor, yet, and so):
  ✓ Dave frequently dribbles, so he plays basketball. (compound sentence)

- using a subordinate conjunction (such as those listed above):
  - ✓ Because Dave frequently dribbles, he plays basketball. (complex sentence)
- using a semicolon:
  - ✓ Dave frequently dribbles; he plays basketball.

The following are common *incorrect* ways of joining two independent clauses.

- no joining method, simply running two clauses together:
  - ✗ Dave frequently dribbles he plays basketball.
- using a comma:
  - ✗ Dave frequently dribbles, he plays basketball.

Be sure to use only one of the correct methods at a time. It is, for example, also incorrect to use the semicolon *and* a conjunction to join two clauses:

✗ Because Dave frequently dribbles; he plays basketball.
✗ Dave frequently dribbles; and he plays basketball.

Six Common Sentence Errors

1. Subject–verb agreement

Subjects of sentences agree with their verbs in two ways. First, they agree in number. This means that singular subjects always take singular verbs, and plural subjects take plural verbs. Singularity of the verb is determined by its subject.

he walks	but	*they* walk
sings		sing
does		do
is		are

Notice that the 's' on the end of a verb does not make it plural; only nouns are made plural by the addition of an 's'. In fact, regular verbs are made *singular* by the addition of 's' to the end.

Second, subjects of sentences should agree with their verbs in what is known as 'person'. This word refers to the form of pronouns: first-person pronouns are those that refer to the speaker—that is, 'I' or 'we'. Second-person pronouns are used for direct address to another person—that is, 'you'. Third-person pronouns are used to speak of others who are not directly addressed by the speaker—'he', 'she', 'it', and 'they'. All nouns are third-person.

While regular verbs in English are consistent except for the third-person singular (which adds an 's'), irregular verbs change form depending on the 'person' of the pronoun subject. Luckily, there aren't many irregular verbs in English, and you will be familiar with most of them just from speaking the language. Listing the forms of the verb that go with each of these pronoun subjects is called 'conjugating' the verb. Here is the conjugation of our most commonly used irregular verb, the verb 'to be'.

	Singular forms	Plural forms
First	I **am**	we **are**
Second	you **are**	you **are**
Third	he, she, it, or one **is**	they **are**
	All nouns are third person.	

As you write, take care to match subjects with the appropriate verb forms, by person and number. This is easy enough to do when subject and verb occur together in the sentence, but when they are separated by phrases or other words it is more difficult. Fortunately, there are some easy-to-learn rules that can help:

a) Subjects compounded with 'and' always take plural verbs.

> Bob and Devon <u>were</u> with me when it happened.

b) Subjects compounded with 'either. . .or', 'neither. . .nor', and 'or' take verbs that agree with the subject closest to the verb.

> Neither the Kennedys nor Sheila <u>is</u> happy with the result.

> Neither Sheila nor the Kennedys <u>are</u> happy with the result.

c) Words ending in '-one', '-thing', and '-body' are always singular.

> Everybody <u>was</u> present at last night's meeting.

> Everything <u>is</u> all right.

d) Phrases such as 'together with', 'in addition to', 'along with', 'apart from', and 'as well as' are not part of the subject and do not influence the choice of verb.

> Joyce, along with her friends, <u>is</u> going to the movie.

e) Collective nouns may take singular or plural verbs, depending on their context. If the group, family, committee, audience, or class acts in unison, it is singular.

> The committee <u>has made</u> a decision.

If they act individually, the verb is plural.

> The committee <u>have argued</u> about this issue for months.

f) The word 'each' is always singular; 'both' is always plural.

> Each of these <u>is</u> perfect for my sister.

> Both of them <u>have</u> advantages.

2. Sentence fragments

A fragment is a part of a sentence that has been treated as a complete sentence. Remember that complete sentences always contain at least one independent clause. Do not punctuate phrases or dependent clauses as sentences.

✗ Running down the street and around the corner.
✗ The thing being that I don't like him.
✗ After I had finished the laundry and the cleaning.
✗ For example, scrubbing, polishing, and waxing.

To fix these, either:

- join them to an independent clause; or
- add whatever is missing.

In the case of the second example, the word 'being' is not a complete verb; therefore, this word group cannot be a sentence. Change the '-ing' form (known as the present participle) to the simple present 'is'.

✓ John was running down the street and around the corner.
✓ The thing is that I don't like him.
✓ After I had finished the laundry and the cleaning, I took a nap.
✓ I hate household chores, for example, scrubbing, polishing, and waxing.

3. Run-on sentences

This mistake is created by trying to cram too much information into a single sentence without correctly joining the elements that make up the structure of the sentence; to correct it, break the elements up in some way. The most common run-on sentences are created by putting two independent clauses together with only a comma.

✗ I slept in, I missed the bus.

This is incorrect. As is explained above, the only permissible ways to join clauses are with a coordinate conjunction, as in the first example sentence, below; with a subordinate conjunction, as in the second example; and with a semicolon, as in the third example.

✓ I slept in, so I missed the bus.
✓ Because I slept in, I missed the bus.
✓ I slept in; I missed the bus.

4. Pronoun, tense, and person agreement

Always strive for consistency in pronouns, person, and tense. Jumping from one to another person or tense is confusing; using ambiguous or inaccurate pronouns is likewise confusing.

✗ Ted asked the neighbour to move his car. (Whose car? Ted's or the neighbour's?)

✗ A person should mind their own business. ('A person' is only one; 'their' is plural. Pronouns should always agree with their antecedents in number [singular-plural] and gender [he-she-it].)

✗ His piece of cake was bigger than hers, which made her angry. ('Which' must refer to a single noun antecedent; a pronoun should not be used to refer to a whole idea.)

Always maintain consistent tense, unless you need to refer to a different time frame. Generally, there are three kinds of time you may refer to in writing: past, present, and future. We tend to write about events in the past or present, and the rule is the same for both tenses. If you're writing in the past tense, stay with the past tense unless the time references change. The same applies to writing in present tense, and future tense, too, if you happen to be using it.

✗ So he came up to me and says, 'Who do you think you are?' (This is incorrect due to the switch from past 'came' to present 'says' when the time referred to has not changed.)

Keep person (I, you, he or she, we, you, they) consistent. The most common problem with person agreement is moving from the first person 'I' to the second person 'you', as shown below; if you stop to think about the meaning of this sentence, it really doesn't make sense.

✗ My apartment faces a busy highway, so when I'm trying to sleep in, the noise of the traffic keeps you awake. (Why would the traffic keep you awake if I'm the one sleeping?)

The second common error in person agreement is switching from the use of third person 'one' or 'a person' to second person 'you'.

✗ One should always keep your eyes open. (In a sentence such as this one, you may use 'you' or 'one', but don't mix them in the same sentence.)

5. Modifier Problems

Modifiers are words or groups of words that describe, explain, intensify, or negate other words or groups of words. The two kinds are *adjectives*, which modify nouns or noun substitutes, and *adverbs*, which modify verbs, adjectives, or other adverbs. Modifier errors occur when the modifier is either misplaced or 'dangling'. The best rule for correcting both of these problems is to place the modifier as close as possible to the word or phrase it modifies; if that item is not in the sentence, rewrite the sentence so the meaning is clear.

Misplaced Modifiers

In the case of this error, the modifier is in the wrong position in the sentence. Put the modifier as close as possible to the thing modified.

✗ I only ate half my dinner. (I only ate it; I didn't dance with it or take it to a movie! Probably I intend the 'only' to modify the 'half'.)

✓ I ate only half my dinner.

✗ I almost earned fifty dollars this morning. (Unless I mean that I had a chance to earn this money, but instead earned nothing at all, I need to move the modifier 'almost' so that it modifies the amount of money I earned.)

✓ I earned almost fifty dollars this morning.

Dangling Modifiers

The modified element, though implied, is not actually given in the sentence. Rewrite the sentence so that the modified element is clear.

✗ Running alongside the river, a treasure chest lay in the bushes. (Since the treasure chest can't run, this sentence doesn't make sense. Who saw the treasure chest? Who was running?)

✓ Running alongside the river, Ted spotted a treasure chest lying in the bushes.

✗ After drawing a picture, I understood what she meant. (This sentence makes it sound as though I drew the picture myself, whereas it is more likely that the other person explained her meaning by drawing a picture.)

✓ After Nancy drew a picture, I understood what she meant.

6. Faulty parallelism

This error occurs when you are using lists or series of items. Whenever you are speaking of more than one item, place them all in the same grammatical form. Use nouns with nouns, adjectives with adjectives, '-ing' words with '-ing' words, clauses with clauses.

✗ Professionals include doctors and people who practise law.

✗ I like running, jumping, and to sing.

✗ She's pretty, but has ambition too.

Replace such faulty parallelism with corrected forms:

✓ Professionals include doctors and lawyers.

✓ Professionals include people who practise medicine and people who practise law.

✓ I like running, jumping, and singing.

✓ I like to run, jump, and sing.

✓ She's pretty, but ambitious too.

✓ She has beauty and ambition too.

This coverage of grammar is necessarily a brief overview. There are many more subtleties to good grammar than there is room to cover in this supplement. A good grammar handbook will give you more information, should you require it. Your communication teacher will be able to recommend one.

Assignments and Exercises

Section A: Sentence errors with answer key

The following sentences contain errors of the types explained above. See if you can correct them. The answer key follows.

1. I only lived in Ottawa for four months.
2. Doing his homework, the TV was distracting.
3. The thing being that I really enjoy their company.
4. Take me with you, I'll miss you too much if I stay here alone. In this scary place with no phone.
5. Give me a bite of your sandwich, I haven't had lunch.
6. Darlene's answer almost was right.
7. Charlene, but not the others, are going camping.
8. I nearly told you a hundred times! Don't call me!
9. A person should mind their own business.
10. One should always keep your eyes open.
11. Doing a test is better than explanations, you can see the rules in action.
12. I didn't want his sympathy, I sent him away forever.
13. If a mosquito bites your face, it should be squashed.
14. On the table was his hat and gloves, so I knew he was home.
15. I only mailed half my cards at Christmas.
16. In college I took English, History, and a course in people and society.
17. If I want to do a good job, you should never overlook details.
18. There was three people on the bus: a student, a mail carrier, and a man who worked on cars.
19. I love lasagna. Even though it's fattening.
20. I don't want to go to the party with him. The reason being that I had a lousy time when I dated him before.
21. Jeff looks familiar to me; because I have a friend who looks just like him.
22. There are lots of things you can do in winter. Skiing, skating, and hikes are only three of them.
23. Running up the stairs, someone tripped Lucy and she fell on her arm, breaking it in two places.
24. Where is Donna's dictionary, she'll be lost without it.
25. Neither Bill nor his friends is willing to help.
26. If the dog sleeps in your bed, it should be disinfected.
27. Being too large a sandwich, she declined to eat it.
28. It really made me laugh. The day she told us about Ted.
29. He is a kind person who has generosity too.
30. If a person is nervous, they should try to relax more.
31. Lola likes to wear soft sweaters, eat exotic food, and taking bubble baths.

32. My sister's boyfriend is stingy, sloppy, and doesn't have much ambition.
33. I noticed a crack in the window walking into the house.
34. Eating a hot dog, mustard dropped onto my shirt.
35. What do you think of this, Red Deer is the fourth largest city in Alberta.
36. When you're stuck. You can use your dictionary for help.
37. Hallowe'en is my least favourite holiday, I'm afraid of ghosts.
38. Although I like Christmas, since I love all the sparkle and magic.
39. I nearly earned a hundred dollars last week.
40. Jerry invited only Millie and me, I guess you can't come.

Answer key

1. I lived in Ottawa for <u>only</u> four months.
2. As <u>he</u> <u>did</u> his homework, the TV was distracting. *or* Doing his homework, <u>Ted</u> <u>found</u> the TV distracting.
3. The thing <u>is</u> that I really enjoy their company. *or* I really enjoy their company.
4. Take me with you<u>;</u> I'll miss you too much if I stay here alone in this scary place with no phone.
5. Give me a bite of your sandwich<u>.</u> I haven't had lunch.
6. Darlene's answer was <u>almost</u> right.
7. Charlene, but not the others, <u>is</u> going camping.
8. I told you <u>nearly</u> a hundred times! Don't call me!
9. A person should mind <u>her</u> <u>or</u> <u>his</u> own business. *or* <u>People</u> should mind their own business.
10. One should always keep <u>one's</u> eyes open. *or* <u>You</u> should always keep your eyes open.
11. Doing a test is better than explanations, <u>because</u> you can see the rules in action.
12. I didn't want his sympathy, <u>so</u> I sent him away forever.
13. <u>A</u> mosquito <u>that</u> bites your face should be squashed.
14. On the table <u>were</u> his hat and gloves, so I knew he was home.
15. I mailed <u>only</u> half my cards at Christmas.
16. In college I took English, History, and <u>Sociology</u>.
17. If I want to do a good job, <u>I</u> should never overlook details. *or* If <u>you</u> want to do a good job, you should never overlook details.
18. There <u>were</u> three people on the bus: a student, a mail carrier, and a <u>mechanic</u>.
19. I love lasagna<u>,</u> even though it's fattening.
20. I don't want to go to the party with him. I had a lousy time when I dated him before. *or* I don't want to go to the party with him<u>,</u> <u>because</u> I had a lousy time when I dated him before.
21. Jeff looks familiar to me because I have a friend who looks just like him.
22. There are lots of things you can do in winter. Skiing, skating, and <u>hiking</u> are only three of them.
23. Running up the stairs, <u>Lucy</u> <u>tripped</u> and fell on her arm, breaking it in two places.
24. Where is Donna's dictionary<u>?</u> <u>She'll</u> be lost without it.
25. Neither Bill nor his friends <u>are</u> willing to help.
26. <u>Your</u> <u>bed</u> should be disinfected if the dog sleeps in <u>it</u>.
27. <u>Because</u> <u>the</u> <u>sandwich</u> <u>was</u> <u>too</u> <u>large</u>, she declined to eat it.

28. It really made me laugh <u>t</u>he day she told us about Ted.
29. He is a kind <u>and generous</u> person.
30. If <u>people are</u> nervous, they should try to relax more. *or* <u>People who are</u> nervous should try to relax more.
31. Lola likes to wear soft sweaters, eat exotic food, and <u>take</u> bubble baths.
32. My sister's boyfriend is stingy, sloppy, and <u>unambitious</u>.
33. <u>Walking into the house,</u> I noticed a crack in the window.
34. <u>As I was</u> eating a hot dog, mustard dropped onto my shirt.
35. What do you think of this<u>?</u> Red Deer is the fourth largest city in Alberta.
36. When you're stuck<u>,</u> you can use your dictionary for help.
37. Hallowe'en is my least favourite holiday, <u>because</u> I'm afraid of ghosts.
38. I like Christmas, since I love all the sparkle and magic.
39. I earned <u>nearly</u> a hundred dollars last week.
40. Jerry invited only Millie and me, <u>so</u> I guess you can't come.

Section B: More sentence errors

The following sentences, like those in Section A, contain errors of the type discussed above.

1. He doesn't know what he's talking about. But that never stopped him before.
2. Can I borrow your calculator, I need to figure something out.
3. Looking over my shoulder, Tim was about a block behind me.
4. Allan is obsessive, and he also has compulsions.
5. I want to try that ride again. Even though I was really scared.
6. I forget, is it 'where no one has gone before', or 'where no man has gone before'.
7. He only wanted a sandwich.
8. I almost bought a hundred copies.
9. If you want to go. I will go with you.
10. Dave, along with his brothers, were in the room.
11. Here comes the doctor, I wonder what he will say.
12. My friend is tall, slender, and looks beautiful.
13. Laura is doing her project, it's on *This Hour Has 22 Minutes*.
14. There was a sandwich and a glass of beer on the counter.
15. Gwen went for an interview, she didn't get the job.
16. Can you believe it, Alex changed his name.
17. Standing on the corner, a car ran through a puddle and soaked me.
18. Qualified individuals need only apply.
19. An individual should protect their credit rating.
20. There was three big mistakes in his report, he didn't notice them.
21. I hate that commercial. The one where the dog talks.
22. My mom is a great baker, you should taste her pies.
23. Waiting in line, my briefcase got stolen.
24. Dave hates rap, he says it should be spelled with a 'c'.
25. Don't get upset, I was only joking.
26. I only finished half my dessert.
27. Devon dislikes him; because he is a jerk.
28. Cheryl is so rude, maybe it's because she is so unpopular.

29. There are lots of reasons for leaving that place: the people are surly, the weather is bad, and it's an ugly town.
30. If you knew her as well as I do, you would see what is wrong. That she is just running away from her problems.
31. I am going downtown tomorrow, I want to get a new CD.
32. In living common law, a child is considered illegitimate.
33. My first big crush occurred at the age of thirteen.
34. Upon entering the room, there is a large cupboard.
35. I couldn't believe the weather we had in October, it was just like July.
36. The lady on the corner by the bus stop, whose hat blew off in the wind yesterday.
37. Although I hate typing, if I wait for her to do it, and I'd never get it done.
38. Not all of these sentences contain mistakes, does this one?
39. When depressed or lonely, a dog is always beside you wagging his tail.
40. After studying all night, I only got 68 per cent on the exam.
41. Being a math major, the test was easy for Jane.
42. Bill swatted the wasp that stung him with a newspaper.
43. My friend said in May we will be taking a trip to Hawaii.
44. Clyde and Charlotte decided to have two kids on their wedding day.
45. We could see the football stadium driving across the bridge.
46. Garage doors can either be opened sideways or upwards.
47. Poker is a great game, it takes skill as well as luck.
48. How can you treat him that way? When he has always been fair to you.
49. When you get here on Friday night, you will get to see Barb. If she decides to show up.
50. When I went to the door, I saw that it was Norm, who else would it be at 2 a.m.?
51. The students no longer like the math teacher who failed the test.
52. One of my friends used to joke about working overseas, and nobody believed him. Until he did it.
53. After Christmas, the number of gift exchanges are no surprise to us.
54. Two-thirds of his car were covered by a white powder.
55. I only miss my friends, nothing else about living there.
56. We saw the injury, it was far worse than we expected.
57. Harold passed high school English, he can't read or write.
58. As I was watching TV last night, I see that the economy is in trouble.
59. Neither of those answers are correct.
60. My friend Norm knows more about music than me.
61. After criticizing both my work and my attitude, I was fired.
62. A large group of students are going on the field trip.
63. As a scientist, the only way a consumer can be injured by a microwave is if they trip over it.
64. The obituary column lists the names of those who have died recently for a nominal fee.
65. You go see what he wants, I'll wait here for you.
66. I'll be glad to help when you need me I'll be at my phone.
67. The combination of alcohol and tranquillizers are dangerous.
68. Everybody was excited, we were allowed to use the pool.
69. His style is clear, engaging, and a delight to read.
70. When caught, the weapon was still in the suspect's hand.

71. I count the cash, it came to $300.
72. I removed the rugs in order to clean the floor and for coolness in the summer.
73. The guard wouldn't permit Alfred and I to enter the building.
74. She borrowed an egg from a neighbour that was rotten and smelled bad when cracked.

Punctuation

orrect and accurate punctuation is essential to your written messages. Like road signs on a highway, punctuation marks help to direct the reader on the journey through your written work. As such, they provide a courtesy to your readers, because they help others to understand the meaning and intention of your message.

This review is designed to remind you of the basic uses of the most common punctuation marks. Though style guides differ somewhat, the following general rules should see you through most basic punctuation needs. The important thing is that you remember to follow a consistent style throughout your document. For more detailed information, consult a style manual.

Reviewing Common Punctuation Marks

There are three common forms of 'full stop' punctuation: the period, the question mark, and the exclamation point.

The Period (.)

1. Use a period to mark the end of a sentence.
2. Use a period following an abbreviation: etc., Dr., Sask.

Some common abbreviations (TV, DVD) don't require periods. Neither do the new two-letter provincial abbreviations used by the post office: NS, NB, PE, NF, QC, ON, MB, SK, AB, BC.

3. When an abbreviation falls at the end of the sentence, use only one period, omitting the abbreviation period.

> Since Jerry completed dentistry school, he loves to be called Dr.

The Question Mark (?)

1. Use a question mark only after a direct question.

> Where are you taking that box?

> Why did you bring him with you?

2. Never use a question mark for an indirect question.

> I wonder whether Shirley has a copy of this book.

> I asked him where he intended to take that box.

A question mark is end punctuation and should not be directly followed by a period, a comma, a semicolon, or a colon.

The Exclamation Point (!)

1. Use an exclamation point after an exclamatory word (interjection) or phrase:

   Wow!

   Hey!

   How about that!

2. Use an exclamation point for emphasis when a statement or question is meant to be read with force.

   What did you do that for!

   I just won the lottery!

In formal writing, and most business writing, you should avoid the exclamation point. Occasionally it is useful in sales letters, for emphasis, but too many exclamation points will create an overly loud or hysterical impression.

   You can win!

   Act now and save!

   No Down Payment! No Interest!

The Semicolon (;)

1. Use a semicolon to separate two independent clauses that are closely related in meaning.

   I am tired of Shawn; I really wish he would go away.

   I built my first model two years ago; now I'm hooked.

   I have a sinus infection; I went swimming without nose plugs.

2. Use a semicolon before conjunctive adverbs such as 'however', 'therefore', 'thus', and 'consequently' when they are used to join two related clauses.

   I don't want to deal with those people ever again; however, they are my relatives.

   Ernesto didn't prepare well enough for his presentation; consequently, he felt like a fool in front of the class.

3. Use a semicolon to separate items in a series, but only if the individual items in the series already contain commas.

> I have invited Madhu, my cousin; Nancy, my best friend; and Ian, Nancy's brother.

> I have to replace my DVD player, which is ten years old; my computer, which is five years old; and my television, which is practically an antique.

The Colon (:)

1. Use a colon to introduce a list on two occasions: when the list is vertical, or when the introductory clause is independent.

> Please bring the following supplies with you:
> > camera,
> > film,
> > flash attachment,
> > batteries, and
> > lenses.

> I can't believe how many things I have to do this week: prepare my presentation for Professional Communication; organize my project for Technical Design; finish packing for my vacation; and get my hair cut.

2. Use a colon after an independent clause if what follows (a word, phrase, or another independent clause) explains or enlarges upon the first one.

> Wait until you hear what he gave me: a machine for making rubber stamps.

> Vernon is the perfect place to stay away from: my in-laws live there.

3. Use a colon to introduce a formal quotation.

> In *Second Words*, Margaret Atwood says: 'A voice is a gift: it should be cherished and used, to utter fully human speech, if possible.'

If the quotation is lengthy (over three lines), begin it on a new line following the colon and indent it.

4. Use a colon after the salutation of a business letter.

> Dear Dr. Faried:

> Dear Ms. Bergen:

5. Use a colon between a title and a subtitle.

Inside Language: A Canadian Language Anthology

Interpersonal Communication for Canadians: An Interdisciplinary Approach

The Comma (,)

1. Use commas to separate items in a list.

   Betty, Elaine and Debbie are close friends.

   I can bring my cat, my dog, or my fish.

   The comma before the coordinate conjunction is optional; it may be used to avoid confusion.

   ✗ Be alert for inclement weather, falling rocks and wildlife. [Was the wildlife falling or only the rocks?]
   ✓ Be alert for inclement weather, falling rocks, and wildlife.

2. Use a comma following someone's name in a direct address to that person; do not use a comma when the name is the subject of the sentence.

   ✓ Bill, will you hand me that book on economics?
   ✗ Bill, handed me the book.

3. Use a comma after an introductory dependent clause.

   Because I was late, I missed the pizza.
   Whenever he participates, we have problems.
   If I want you for anything, I'll call.

4. Use a comma after a lengthy introductory phrase.

   After the best day of my life, I was exhausted.

   Before the graduation dance, Ely came down with the measles.

5. Use a comma before a coordinate conjunction (and, or, nor, but, yet, so) that joins two independent clauses.

   I went downtown, and Roxanne joined me.

   I went for the interview, but somebody else got the job.

   You can omit the comma if the two clauses have the same subject.

   I went for the interview and I got the job.

I went for the interview and got the job.

6. Use a comma after conjunctive adverbs such as 'however', 'therefore', 'thus', 'moreover', and 'consequently.'

I like him very much; moreover, I think he is an outstanding accountant.

7. Use commas to set apart phrases or clauses that interrupt a sentence between its subject and verb.

David, who has the office beside mine, has accepted a job with another firm.

Feral, the little rascal, didn't finish her homework.

8. Use a comma before a short, direct quotation.

Paul said, 'I'd like to nail that guy.'

Don't use a comma for indirect quotations.

Paul said that he'd like to nail that guy.

9. Use a comma to separate parts of an address, if they appear on the same line.

57 Campus Drive, Saskatoon, Saskatchewan

10. Use a comma to separate the day and month when identifying a date.

Saturday, November 13

The Apostrophe (')

1. Use an apostrophe to indicate possession in nouns, but not in pronouns.

Paul's book

David's minutes

Maureen's comments

whose book (NEVER who's book—that's who is)

its colour (NEVER it's colour—that's it is)

Singular nouns, as above, add an apostrophe and an 's'; plural nouns or others ending in 's' usually don't need an additional 's' added.

The Inghams' house

the students' grades

its colour (NEVER it's colour—that's it is)

However, when the possessive word is pronounced as though it had an additional syllable, you may wish to add the second 's'.

Chris's test results

Iris's new gloves

its colour (NEVER it's colour—that's it is)

For plural nouns not ending in 's' add apostrophe and 's'.

children's coats

criteria's validity

2. Use apostrophes in contractions.

can't	there's
won't	what's
they're	it's (it is)
wasn't	I've
he's	we're

Quotation Marks (" ")

1. Use quotation marks for indicating direct speech, but not indirect speech.

David asked, "Do you need a ride to the airport?"

David asked if I need a ride to the airport.

2. Quotation marks within quotation marks are usually indicated by single marks within double ones.

She said, "You know what Joseph Campbell says: 'Follow your bliss'."

3. Use quotation marks to indicate that a word is slang, an inappropriate usage, or someone else's wording, but be very careful not to overuse them in this way.

I don't think "intimacy" is quite the right word for this concept.

I should have realized the truth when he said he was "cool".

4. Use quotation marks for the titles of short works, such as poems, short stories, essays, articles, songs, or chapters in a book.

"The Rime of the Ancient Mariner"

"Home on the Range"

"Chapter Eight: The Job Application"

Enclose commas and periods within the quotation marks; semicolons and colons are placed outside the quotation marks. Other end punctuation (question marks and exclamation points) falls outside unless the original phrase was a question or exclamation.

Title Treatments

1. Italicize (or underline if you can't italicize) the titles of book-length works wherever they appear in your writing.

Hamlet

Lovable Soft Toys

Effective Business Communication

2. Place the titles of short works (essays, book chapters, poems, short stories, songs, recipes, or articles) into quotation marks.

"Chapter Eight: The Job Application"

"Introduction: Are You a Designer?"

"Stopping by Woods on a Snowy Evening"

3. Do not underline the titles of your own reports or essays, or place them in quotation marks, on the title page of your paper.

The Agony and the Exigence: A Rhetorical Analysis of Two Presentations

Innovations in Training:
A Proposal for Improving Our Report Writing Workshops

4. If your title contains the title of another work, you should treat the title of the other work appropriately, depending on whether it is a short or long work.

✓ Method or Madness? An Analysis of Motive in <u>Hamlet</u>

✓ Method or Madness? An Analysis of Motive in *Hamlet*
✓ Miles to Go Before I Sleep: Hypothermia in Frost's 'Stopping by Woods on a Snowy Evening'

This brief refresher is not intended to be a comprehensive guide to punctuation usage, but should provide enough detail for everyday usage. For a more comprehensive guide to punctuation conventions, you may wish to consult a good English handbook or manual of style, such as *The Chicago Manual of Style* or Strunk and White's *Elements of Style*. Your communication instructor will be able to recommend one.

Notes

Chapter 1

1. Including, for instance, a Senior Drilling Engineer, Ultra Deep Water, posted by SGF Global for an unidentified oil company in Houston, Texas (posting at http://www.oilcareers.com/content/job search/job_advert.asp?jobadid=28036); Senior Software Developer for First Quadrant (posting at http://www.firstquadrant.com/careers.html); Project Manager for Cardinal Health (posting at http://stlouis.craigslist.org/hea/204630640.html); Inventory Control Manager for Jabil Circuit (posting at http://www.jabil.com/careers/jobDescription.asp?id=2557); Senior Librarian for the Arizona Library (posting at http://www.lib.az.us/jobs/joblisting.cfm?jobID=489), and numerous others.
2. An exception is the University of Saskatchewan's College of Engineering, which offers its Engineering Communication Option, a specialization in communication that can be taken as an add-on to the engineering degree. It is the only program of its kind in Canada. See http://grahamcentre.usask.ca/ECO.html.
3. Known as the *Precepts*, it was composed in Egypt by Ptah-Hotep. See James McCroskey, 'A Rhetorical Tradition', *An Introduction to Rhetorical Communication*, 6e (New Jersey: Prentice Hall, 1993), 2.
4. An eighth category of 'Miscellaneous' traits was also generated (see Hein, 1998: 8).
5. For a thorough discussion of footing, see George L. Dillon, *Rhetoric as Social Imagination: Explorations in the Interpersonal Functions of Language* (Bloomington, Indiana: Indiana University Press, 1986).
6. For more on the importance of face in human interaction, see Erving Goffman, 'On Face Work' *Interaction Ritual* (Garden City, NY: Anchor Books, 1967), 5–23.

Chapter 2

1. Bitzer's essay, 'The Rhetorical Situation', appears on pp. 17–21 of Chapter 1.

Chapter 3

1. You can find samples online at http://www.cbc.ca/mercerreport/ or in one of Mercer's books: *Rick Mercer Report: The Book* (Toronto: Doubleday Canada, 2007) or *Streeters* (Toronto: Doubleday Canada, 1999).

Chapter 4

1. You can find the entire text of Aristotle's *Rhetoric* online at http://www2.iastate.edu/~honeyl/Rhetoric/index.html.
2 Such behaviour actually signals selfishness or narcissism, a disregard of others' well-being, a failure of socialization, and even, when carried to an extreme, possible psychopathology. On this latter point, see Paul Babiak and Robert Hare, *Snakes in Suits* (Toronto: HarperCollins, 2006); Sgt Matt Logan, 'The Psychopathic Offender: How Identifying the Traits Can Solve Cases', *Royal Canadian Mounted Police Gazette* 66 (2004), available at http://www.gazette.rcmp.gc.ca/article-en.html?&article_id=39. See also the classic work by Harvey Cleckley, *The Mask of Sanity*, 5th ed. (Augusta, GA: Emily Cleckley, 1988), available at http://www.cassiopaea.org/cass/sanity_1.PdF.
3. For a more extensive and very readable discussion of the root and nature of ethics, see Peter Singer, *Practical Ethics*, 2nd ed. (Cambridge, UK: Cambridge University Press, 1993).
4. Many of these can be found online at the Center for the Study of Ethics in the Professions at http://ethics.iit.edu/codes/.
5. Including, for example, those posted online by Queen's University (http://www.queensu.ca/secretariat/senate/policies/codecond.html), the University of Toronto (http://www.utoronto.ca/govcncl/pap/policies/studentc.html), Athabasca University (http://www.athabascau.ca/calendar/page11.html), and McMaster University (http://www.mcmaster.ca/univsec/policy/Student Code.pdf), to mention only a few.
6. Curiously, the Canadian Association of University Teachers shows no similar code on its website.
7. Such a policy was practised in much of Canada during the early twentieth century, and was still going on in some jurisdictions, notably Alberta, until the 1970s.

Chapter 9

1. The problem of identity and credential theft is widespread, according to several sources. A recent news report declared it the third most reported consumer crime in Canada; the same report noted that it is the number one consumer crime in the US. See CBC News, *The National.* Broadcast. Toronto: Canadian Broadcasting Corporation, 30 September 2001. See also Michael Gilbert, 'Identity Thieves'. Available from http://www.abanet.org/journal/oct98/10FIDENT.html (October 1998).

References

Abrahamson, D. 2005. 'The Facebook.com: Big Brother with a Smile', *Prisonplanet.com*, 9 June. Available at http://www.prisonplanet.com/articles/june2005/090605thefacebook.htm.

Ambert, A.M. 2007. 'The Rise in the Number of Children and Adolescents who Exhibit Problematic Behaviours: Multiple Causes', *Contemporary Family Trends*. Ottawa: Vanier Institute. Available at http://www.vifamily.ca/library/cft/behavior.pdf.

American Association of University Teachers. 1987. 'Code of Professional Ethics'. Available at http://ethics.iit.edu/codes/coe/amer.assoc.univ.prof.pro.ethics.1987.html.

American Library Association. 1939. 'History of the Code of Ethics—1939 Code of Ethics for Librarians'. Available at http://www.ala.org/Template.cfm?Section=coehistory&Template=/ContentManagement/ContentDisplay.cfm&ContentID=8875.

American Management Association. 2006. '2006 Workplace E-Mail, Instant Messaging & Blog Survey: Bosses Battle Risk by Firing E-Mail, IM & Blog Violators', 11 July. Available at http://www.amanet.org/press/amanews/2006/blogs_2006.htm.

American Society of Agronomy. n.d. 'Certified Crop Advisor Code of Ethics'. Available at https://www.agronomy.org/cca/coe.html.

Andrews, F.M., and S.B. Withey. 1976. *Social Indicators of Well-Being: Americans Perceptions of Life Quality*. New York: Plenum Press.

Argyle, M., J. Crossland, and M. Martin. 1989. 'Happiness as a Function of Personality and Social Encounters', in *Recent Advances in Social Psychology*, J.P. Forgas and J.M. Innes, eds. Netherlands: Elsevier.

Aristotle. 1954. *The Rhetoric*, Friedrich Solmsen, ed., W. Rhys Roberts, trans. New York: Random House/The Modern Library.

Barber, K., ed. 1998. *The Canadian Oxford Dictionary*, 1st ed. Toronto: Oxford University Press.

Barchilon, M. 1998. 'Writing for Engineering Fields', in *The Practice of Technical and Scientific Communication*, pp. 37–48. Stamford, CN: Ablex Publishing.

Barker, L., R. Edwards, C. Gaines, K. Gladney, and F. Holley. 1980. 'An Investigation of Proportional Time Spent in Various Communication Activities by College Students', *Journal of Applied Communication Research* 8: 101–9.

BBC News. 2005. 'Bullying Costs UK £1.3m a Year', *BBC News*, 26 October. Available at http://news.bbc.co.uk/1/hi/business/4379326.stm.

Beer, D., and D. McMurrey. 1997. 'Engineers and Writing', in *A Guide to Writing as an Engineer*, pp. 1–10. New York: John Wiley and Sons.

Berko, R., M. Brooks, and J.C. Spielvogel. 1995. *Pathways to Careers in Communication*. Annandale, VA: Speech Communication Association.

Bitzer, L. 1968. 'The Rhetorical Situation', *Philosophy and Rhetoric* 1 (Winter): 1–14.

Bixler, S., and Dugan, L.S. 2000. *5 Steps to Professional Presence: How to Project Confidence, Competence, and Credibility at Work*. Cincinnati, OH: Adams Media Corporation.

Blogscholar.com. 2007. 'Academia and the Dangers of Facebook', 14 June. Available at http://www.blogscholar.com/index.php?option=com_content&task=view&id=94&Itemid=2.

Booth, W.C. 1963. 'The Rhetorical Stance', *College Composition and Communication* 14 (3) Annual Meeting Los Angeles, 1963: Toward a New Rhetoric (October 1963): 139–45.

Brown, P., and S.J. Levinson. 1987. *Politeness: Some Universals in Language Use*. Cambridge: Cambridge University Press.

Buehler, M.A., and R. VanBuren. 1980. *The Levels of Edit*. Pasadena, CA: Jet Propulsion Laboratory California Institute of Technology. Available at http://www.io.com/~tcm/etwr2379/planners/levels_of_edit.pdf.

Buonopane, R.A. 1997. 'Engineeirng Education for the 21st Century', *Chemical Engineering Education* 31: 166–7.

Burgess, G., and H. Burgess. 1997. 'The Meaning of Civility'. University of Colorado Conflict Research Consortium. Available at http://www.colorado.edu/conflict/civility.htm.

Burton, R. 2008. 'An Engineer's Rhetorical Journey', in *Readings for Technical Communication*, Jennifer MacLennan, ed. Toronto: Oxford University Press Canada.

Cairney, R. 2003. 'What's so Stressful about Campus Life? Grades, Romance and Adjusting to Campus, Survey Says', *University of Alberta Folio*, 12 September. Available at http://www.ualberta.ca/~publicas/folio/41/01/03.html.

Canadian Council of Professional Engineers. n.d. 'Code of Ethics'. Available at http://ethics.iit.edu/codes/coe/can.council.pro.engineers.a.html.

Carnegie, D. 1955. *Public Speaking and Influencing Men in Business*. New York: Associated Press.

Casperson, D.M. 1999. *Power Etiquette: What You Don't Know Can Kill Your Career*. New York: AMACOM.

Centre for Suicide Prevention. 2000. 'Stress in the Workplace', *SEIC Alert #42* (October). Available at http://www.suicideinfo.ca/csp/assets/alert42.pdf.

CollegeRecruiter.com. 2006. 'NBC Interview', May. Available at http://www.collegerecruiter.com/weblog/archives/2006/05/nbc_interview.php.

Cortina, L.M., V.J. Magley, J.H. Williams, and R.D. Langhout. 2001. 'Incivility in the Workplace: Incidence and Impact', *Journal of Occupational Health Psychology* 6: 64–80.

Dale Carnegie & Associates. 1995. *The Leader in You*. New York: Pocket Books.

Dombrowski, P. 2000. *Ethics in Technical Communication*. Boston: Allyn & Bacon.

Durham, C.M. 2007. 'Promoting the Standards of Professionalism and Civility', *Utah Bar Journal*. Available at http://webster.utahbar.org/barjournal/2007/03/promoting_the_standards_of_pro.html.

Facebook.com. 2007. 'Terms of Use', 24 May [revised]. Available at http://www.facebook.com/terms.php.

Flemming, R.J., and G. Wacker. 1980. 'Communications Training in an Engineering College', in *Proceedings of the Canadian Conference on Engineering Education*, pp. 122–33. Ottawa, ON: Canadian Council of Professional Engineers.

Forni, P.M. 2002. *Choosing Civility*. Boston: St. Martin's Press.

Forni, P.M. 2003. *Choosing Civility: The Twenty-Five Rules of Considerate Conduct*. New York: St. Martin's Griffin.

Forni, P.M. n.d. The Other Side of Civility', *The Civility WebSite*. Available at http://web.jhu.edu/civility/ArticlesandPressReleases.html.

Freeman, C. n.d. 'Civility in the Workplace', *Mental Health Canada*. Available at http://www.mentalhealthcanada.com/article_detail.asp?lang=e&id=41.

Frye, N. 1963. *The Well Tempered Critic*. Bloomington, IN: Indiana University Press.

Gandhi, U. 2007. 'Youth Behaviour Getting Worse, Study Finds—Societal Shifts Such as Lack of Role Models to Blame for "Erosion of Civility", Author Says', *Globe and Mail*, 21 February. Available at http://www.fradical.com/Youth_behaviour_getting_worse.htm.

Glossop, R. 2002. 'Societal Influences'. Plenary Address at the Vanier Institute of the Family Fear and Loathing Symposium, 24 May.

Goffman, E. 1959. *The Presentation of Self in Everyday Life*. New York: Anchor Books.

Goffman, E. 1967. *Interaction Ritual*. Garden City NY: Anchor Books.

Goffman, E. 1967. 'On Face-Work', *Interaction Ritual: Essays on Face-to-Face Behaviour*. New York: Anchor Books.

Greene, J.O., and B.R. Burleson. 2003. *Handbook of Communication and Social Interaction Skills*. New York: Lawrence Erlbaum and Associates.

Halloran, S.M. 1982. 'Aristotle's Concept of Ethos, or if not His, Somebody Else's', *Rhetoric Review* 1 (September): 58–63.

Hart, R. 1997. *Modern Rhetorical Criticism*, 2nd ed. Boston: Allyn & Bacon.

Harvey, S., and L. Keashly. 2005. 'Emotional Abuse: How the Concept Sheds Light on the Understanding of Psychological Harassment (in Quebec)', *Pistes* 7 (November). Available at http://www.pistes.uqam.ca/v7n3/articles/v7n3a15en.htm.

Hawayaka, S.I., and A.R. Hayakawa. 1990. *Language in Thought and Action*, 5th ed. New York: Harcourt, Brace, Jovanovich.

Hein, L. 1998. 'Are We Competent?', *Professional Edge* 54 (February–March): 8–9.

Helmes, R., R.D. Chrisjohn, and R.D. Goffin. 1998. 'Confirmatory Factor Analysis of the Life Satisfaction Index', *Social Indicators Research* 45: 371–90.

Hoey, J. 2001. 'Employer Satisfaction with Alumni Professional Preparation', *North Carolina State University, University Planning and Analysis, 1997*. Available at http://www2.acs.ncsu.edu/UPA/survey/reports/employer/employ.htm. Last accessed 14 June 2001.

Holmvall, C.M., and L. Francis. 2007. 'How Rude: Incivility in the Workplace Hurts More than Just Feelings', *The Workplace Review* (November). Available at http://www.smu.ca/academic/sobey/workplacereview/Nov2007/HowRude.pdf.

Jackson Lewis, LLP. 2006. 'Can Workplace Policies Minimize Your Organization's Potential Risk from Employee Blogs?', 8 February. Available at http://www.jacksonlewis.com/legalupdates/article.cfm?aid=895.

Jacoby, N. 1999. 'Etiquette Crisis at Work: Employees Say They've Had Enough of Incivility, Bad Manners', *CNN Money*, 29 November. Available at http://money.cnn.com/1999/11/29/life/q_manners/.

Jarecke, G.W., and N.K. Plant. 2006. *Seeking Civility: Common Courtesy and the Common Law*. Boston: Northeastern University Press.

Johnson, L. 2006. 'Scott [Attorney] Warns of Facebook Dangers', *UTD Mercury*, 18 September. Available at http://media.www.utdmercury.com/media/storage/paper691/news/2006/09/18/Feature/Scott.Warns.Of.Facebook.Dangers-2279556.shtml.

Jones, B. 2004. 'Conversation "Dying" Even Though We Spend 25% of Our Lives Communicating', *British Gas News*, 20 May. Available at http://www.britishgasnews.co.uk/index.asp?PageID=19&Year=2004&NewsID=567.

Keashly, L., V. Trott, and L.M. MacLean. 1994. 'Abusive Behaviour in the Workplace: A Preliminary Investigation', *Violence and Victims* 9(4): 341–57.

Kilpatrick, W. 1992. *Why Johnny Can't Tell Right from Wrong: Moral Illiteracy and the Case for Character Education*. New York: Simon and Schuster.

Lasica, J.D. 1998a. 'The Net Has Forgotten How to Forget: The Digital Attic has Begun Collecting and Storing Scraps of Our Lives—Forever', *The American Journalism Review* (June). Available at http://www.jdlasica.com/articles/coljun98.html.

Lasica, J.D. 1998b. 'Digital Footsteps: If You've Ventured Onto the Net, Your Past May Follow You in Ways You'd Never Imagine', *Salon* (November). Available at http://www.jdlasica.com/articles/digital.html.

Lindseth, E.L. 1955. 'The Meaning and Importance of Communication', Lecture. Publication No. L56-21. Washington, DC: Industrial College of the Armed Forces, 14 September.

McAlister, J. 1984. 'Why Engineers Fail', *Machine Design*, 23 February: 47–9.

McCormick, D. 2007. 'Bullying in the Workplace', *Port Alberni Online*, 3 May. Available at http://www.alberni.ca/articles/articles/180/1/Bullying-in-the-Workplace/Page1.html.

MacIsaac, D., and L. McLean. 1998. 'Teaching Engineers How to Communicate Effectively', in *Proceedings of the Canadian Conference on Engineering Education*, pp. 289–96. Ottawa, ON: Canadian Council of Professional Engineers.

MacLennan, J. 2001. 'Banishing Speak and Spell: A New Approach to Teaching Communicatoin to Engineers'. Keynote address, Canadian Council on Engineering Education, August, Victoria, BC.

Millar, E. 2007. 'A New Use for Facebook', *Maclean's* 120 (1 October): 60.

Mitchell, C. 2003. *A Short Course in International Business Ethics*. Novato, CA: World Trade Press.

Mitrano, T. 2006. 'Thoughts on Facebook', *Cornell University Office of Information Technologies*, April. Available at http://www.cit.cornell.edu/policy/memos/facebook.html.

Montreal Gazette. 2007. 'A Sinister Synergy Threatens Civility', *Gazette*, 1 March. Available at http://www.canada.com/montrealgazette/news/editorial/story.html?id=6423acdd-78fb-46fa-8e4d-d7 d5ca75f21e.

Myers, D.G. 1999. 'Close Relationships and Quality of Life', in *Well-Being: The Foundations of Hedonic Psychology*, pp. 374–91, D. Kahneman, E. Diener, and N. Schwarz, eds. New York: Russell Sage Foundation.

Oatley, K. 1992. *Best Laid Schemes: The Psychology of Emotions*. Cambridge, UK: Cambridge University Press.

Olson, A. n.d. 'Authoring a Code of Ethics: Observations on Process and Organization', Illinois Institute of Technology Centre for the Study of Ethics in the Professions. Available at http://ethics.iit.edu/codes/Writing_A_Code.html.

Ornatowski, C. 2003. 'Between Efficiency and Politics: Rhetoric and Ethics in Technical Writing', in *Professional Writing and Rhetoric: Readings from the Field*, Tim Peeples, ed. New York: Longman.

Orwell, G. 1956. 'Politics and the English Language', in *The Orwell Reader*, Richard H. Rovere, ed. New York: Harcourt, Brace, and World.

Plotnik, A. 1996. *The Elements of Editing*. New York: Macmillan.

PMAC. n.d. 'Code of Ethics, The Purchasing Management Association of Canada'. Available at http://pmac.ca/about/ethics.asp.

Post, P. 2004. *Emily Post's Etiquette*, 17th ed. New York: HarperCollins.

Robinson, F.P. 1946. *Effective Study*. New York: Harper and Bros.

Rude, C. 1998. *Technical Editing*, 2nd ed. Boston: Allyn & Bacon.

Ruitenbeek, H.M. 1965. *The Individual and the Crowd: A Study of Identity in America*. New York: New American Library.

Scott, E. 2006. 'The Healthy Workplace: Creating a Culture of Civility, Respect and Mental Safety', *CrossCurrents: The Journal of Addiction and Mental Health* (22 December). Available at http://goliath.ecnext.com/coms2/gi_0199-6421094/The-healthy-workplace-creating-a.html.

Sewerin, C. 2004. 'What is a Licensed Professional?', *Engineering Dimensions* (Sept.–Oct.). Available at http://www.peo.on.ca/publications/DIMENSIONS/septoct2004/Webwatch.pdf.

Shannon, C., and W. Weaver. 1949. *The Mathematical Theory of Communication*. Urbana: University of Illinois Press.

Shaw, S. 1998. 'Understanding Bullying in the Workplace', *The UVic Ring*. Available at http://ring.uvic.ca/98mar20/Bullying.html.

Sommerville, M. 2002. 'Ethical Dilemmas in Medicine', McGill Faculty of Medicine Mini-Med Study Corner. Available at http://www.medicine.mcgill.ca/minimed/archive/Sommerville2002.htm.

Spanier, G.B. 2000. 'The Crisis of Civility: A Message from President Spanier', *Penn State Intercom*, 19 October. Available at http://www.psu.edu/ur/archives/intercom_2000/Oct19/civility.html.

Staples, K., and C. Ornatowski, eds. 1997. *Foundations for Teaching Technical Communication: Theory, Practice, and Program Design*. Stamford, CN: Ablex Publishing.

Trane, Inc. 2001. 'Sales Engineer Position advertisement'. Available at http://www.trane.com. Last accessed 15 May 2001.

Truss, L. 2005. *Talk to the Hand: The Utter Bloody Rudeness of the World Today, or Six Good Reasons to Stay Home and Bolt the Door*. New York: Gotham Books.

Urbanski, L. 2002. 'Workplace Bullying's High Cost: $180M in Lost Time, Productivity', *Orlando Business Journal*, 15 March. Available at http://orlando.bizjournals.com/orlando/stories/2002/03/18/focus1.html.

US Department of Labor. 1991. *What Work Requires of Schools: A SCANS Report for America 2000*.

Washington, DC: Secretary's Commission on Achieving Necessary Skills.

Valle, D. n.d. 'Non-cognitive Experiences, Mental Health, and Academic Progress', *Network: A Journal of Faculty Development*. Available at http://www.nyu.edu/frn/publications/millennial.student/network-journal/Articles/Mental-health-Valle.html.

Waite, A. 2006. 'Beware of Facebook Danger', *University of Maryland Diamondback*, 5 October. Available at http://media.www.diamondbackonline.com/media/storage/paper873/news/2006/05/10/Opinion/Beware.Of.Facebook.Danger-2325542.shtml.

Whitmore, J. 2005. *Business Class: Etiquette Essentials for Success at Work*. New York: St Martin's Press.

Index